FOR REFERENCE

Do Not Take From This Room

DAY BY DAY: THE SIXTIES

P.

DAY BY DAY: THE SIXTIES

Volume I
1960–1964

by **Thomas Parker**
and
Douglas Nelson

Facts On File Publications
460 Park Avenue South
New York, N.Y. 10016

12.289
R
909.82
Par
90.00/set

ROCK SPRINGS PUBLIC LIBRARY
Sweetwater County Branch
Rock Springs, Wyoming

DAY BY DAY: THE SIXTIES

Copyright © 1983 by Facts On File, Inc.

All rights reserved. No part of this book may be reproduced or utilized in any form or by any means, electronic or mechanical, including photocopying, recording or by any information storage and retrieval system, without permission in writing from the Publisher.

Library of Congress Cataloging in Publication Data

Parker, Thomas
  Day by day, the sixties.

  Includes index.
  1. History, Modern—1945-   —Chronology. I. Title.
D848.L4   1985   909.82′02′02   80-22432
ISBN 0-87196-384-1 Vol. 1
ISBN 0-87196-046-X Vol. 2
ISBN 0-87196-648-4 Vol. Set

Photographs courtesy of Wide World Photos

Printed in the United States of America

10 9 8 7 6 5 4 3 2 1

CONTENTS

EDITOR'S PREFACE

Day by Day: the 1960s is part of a decade-by-decade chronology of world events which begins with *Day by Day: the 1940s*. The series is designed to provide both quick reference to specific events and a broad overview of the years during and after World War II.

Most of the material in *Day by Day* is based on the Facts on File yearbooks, supplemented by major newspapers and scholarly reference works. The emphasis throughout is on events of public record, reported in the news media. The enormous number of events covered in this volume makes it impossible to treat any single one in great detail. Readers interested in more information are advised to consult one of the many reference works on the period.

Entries in *Day by Day* are grouped into 10 categories, designed to facilitate the location and comparison of events. In general, entries on each left-hand page involve international affairs, while right-hand pages deal mostly with U.S. domestic developments. Significant accidents and weather phenomena are placed in the region in which they occurred, since they often had important political, social and economic consequences for the inhabitants.

Accidents and weather reports in the U.S. are included in the Science and Technology column. Each year is preceded by a monthly summary of events to include developments which cannot be fixed to a single date.

One of the main objectives of *Day by Day* is to provide an immediate sense of the 1960s, a "feel" for what it was like to live during the decade. To this end, the terminology of the period is used whenever it represents common, polite usage. Thus, "Negro" appears in preference to "black." "Russia" is similarly used instead of "Soviet Union," consistent with common journalistic practice.

Day by Day: the 1960s includes an index designed to facilitate reference to specific events. For this reason, it is keyed to dates and columns rather than page numbers.

The editor would like to thank a number of people without whose help the volume would not have been possible. Cynthia Crippen handled the enormous job of indexing with patience and precision. Janet Scott served as a valuable intermediary between the computer and editor.

INTRODUCTION

Like any decade, the 1960s were a kaleidoscope of achievements and failures. On the international scene, decolonization, a relaxation of tensions in scattered areas and sporadic advances for democracy contrasted sharply with warfare, skirmishing and widespread unrest. While Venezuela established a stable democratic system, most of the rest of Latin America remained under authoritarian rule. In black Africa decolonization occurred fairly peacefully everywhere except in Angola and Mozambique (still ruled by Portugal). Yet a tragic civil war in Nigeria claimed an estimated toll of over a million lives. Political tensions did abate in Europe, as a true reconciliation took place between West Germany and France, coupled with the beginnings of political detente between West Germany and its Eastern European neighbors. In contrast, an established democracy was crushed in Greece, as was an emerging democracy in Czechoslovakia. The Arab-Israeli conflict erupted into open warfare in the Middle East in June 1967, when Israel defeated the armies of Egypt, Syria and Jordan. The decade ended with daily aerial duels and artillery exchanges between Israel and the other three combatants. Tensions also increased in Southeast Asia, which was shaken by a protracted land war in Indochina, civil war in Indonesia and domestic turmoil in Communist China. But not all developments in this region during the 1960s were negative: Thailand, Malaysia, Singapore, the Philippines and Indonesia overcame their border disputes and formed a regional association that made solid economic progress.

For the United States the sixties were years of triumph and tragedy. The contrasts seen in international affairs were more than matched by developments in American foreign policy and on the domestic front. This was perhaps one of the worst decades in terms of foreign policy in the nation's history: An inconclusive land war in South Vietnam dragged on for years with no end in sight. On the other hand, America scored a triumph with the first successful manned lunar expeditions. Domestic events included the assassinations of three American leaders: President John F. Kennedy, the Rev. Martin Luther King Jr. and Sen. Robert F. Kennedy. While violence against civil rights workers in the South and against ordinary urban citizens in the North became endemic, the decade nonetheless saw the end of segregation in the South and a decline in the level of racially motivated job discrimination throughout the country. As the decade passed, the involvement in Vietnam came to have increasing repercussions at home, with marches, protests and demonstrations adding to the existing domestic unrest. Yet the Vietnam experience brought one positive result, prodding Congress into taking a more assertive role in foreign affairs.

But the foregoing sketch of the 1960s only indicates their broad outlines. To capture and define the essence of the decade, we must consider in greater detail the ebb and flow of the events that shaped it—forming its particular texture of unrest and change. Let's begin with developments in the Western Hemisphere.

In Latin America the 1960s saw the consolidation of communism in Cuba. After a little more than a year in power, in February 1960, Cuban Premier Fidel Castro ordered the nationalization of all major Cuban-owned properties; five months later all foreign-owned properties were nationalized as well. These actions were followed by trade agreements with the Soviet Union and Communist China, which made possible Cuba's economic survival after the United States instituted a commercial boycott of all Cuban products on February 3, 1961. Castro also survived the April 17, 1961 Bay of Pigs invasion, launched by Cuban exiles who had the financial and military support of the United States. The invasion was crushed within three days, however, since the Cuban people failed to rise up against Castro.

The military victory over the U.S.-backed invaders left Castro in a stronger position than ever, and on December 2, 1961 he publicly proclaimed for the first time that he was a Marxist-Leninist. That declaration was followed by several years of attempted subversion of a number of Latin American governments, particularly those of Venezuela and Colombia. By 1964 every country in Latin America except Mexico had broken diplomatic relations with Cuba. But Castro failed to engineer the downfall of any of the governments he had targeted to be overthrown. His unsuccessful efforts ultimately culminated in the death of one of his closest revolutionary associates, Ernesto "Ché" Guevara, killed by Bolivian government troops on October 8, 1967 after his small Communist guerrilla band had been routed. By the end of the 1960s, the Communist system was firmly entrenched in Cuba, but Castro had failed to export his revolution to any other Latin American country.

In contrast to Cuba, democracy seemed to consolidate itself in Venezuela, where—on March 11, 1969—Rafael Caldera became the first popularly elected president to succeed another popularly elected president who had completed his term. This was not the case, however, in Brazil, where the armed forces seized power on April 2, 1964 in a bloodless coup against leftist President Joao Goulart. Brazilian military officers subsequently engineered several smooth transfers of power among themselves, and by the end of the sixties, they appeared firmly established as the country's rulers.

During the 1960s violent unrest broke out against the United States in Panama. On January 9, 1964 rioters protested the U.S. presence in the Canal Zone, but American President Lyndon B. Johnson refused to make any immediate concessions. His nationalistic policies were repeated when serious internal strife broke out between various political factions in the Dominican Republic. Johnson sent in U.S. troops in May 1965 to prevent a

Marxist faction from gaining power. After moderate military leaders took control of the situation, the approximately 30,000 American soldiers were withdrawn during 1966.

The new administration of President Richard M. Nixon acted with circumspection, however, in the face of a challenge to U.S. economic interests in Peru. The military, which had assumed power in 1968, began nationalizing U.S. property in January and February of 1969. The American government acquiesced to the more assertive Peruvian policies.

Turning to the northern part of the hemisphere, Canada saw the rise of a more assertive French-Canadian community in the 1960s. A separatist movement gained a certain following, which included French President Charles de Gaulle, who ended a July 24, 1967 speech in Montreal with the movement's slogan—"Long live a free Quebec." The new Canadian prime minister, Pierre Elliot Trudeau, who took power on April 20, 1968, promised to institute reforms but opposed complete independence for Quebec, his native province.

The sixties brought the decolonization of Africa. Independence came to all the French colonies and to Somalia, Zaire and Nigeria in 1960; to Tanganyika and Sierra Leone in 1961; to Uganda in 1962; to Kenya and Zanzibar in 1963; to Zambia and Malawi in 1964; to Gambia in 1965; to Botswana, the last remaining British colony, in 1966; and to Equatorial Guinea in 1968. By the end of the decade, only Angola and Mozambique were still controlled by a European colonial country (Portugal).

Relatively friendly relations with the West were established by most of the newly independent African countries—especially the former West African French colonies, which (with the exception of Guinea) retained their close economic ties with France. Similarly, the most important African countries in terms of wealth and population—Nigeria, Ethiopia and the Congo (Kinshasa)—also remained relatively friendly toward the West and welcomed foreign investment and technological aid. This was particularly true of the Congo (Kinshasa) where the Western powers helped to put down a rebellion in the copper-rich province of Katanga in 1960 with the help of United Nations troops and in 1966 with the help of U.S. transport planes. The most notable exception to the moderate, pro-Western orientation of the newly independent African states was Ghana, where President Kwame Nkrumah welcomed Soviet aid and technicians. Nkrumah, however, was overthrown by the army in 1966, and his socialist domestic experiment was ended.

Independence also came to Rhodesia (Zimbabwe) when its ruling white minority unilaterally cut that nation's ties with Great Britain on October 11, 1965. Despite the economic sanctions imposed by the Western powers, Rhodesia managed to hold its own economically, thanks to its South African connection.

In general, the newly independent African nations dealt successfully with their domestic ethnic divisions. The major exception was Nigeria, where the Ibos (one of the country's tribal groups) declared themselves independent in August 1967. The federal government launched a vigorous counterattack against the new state—known as Biafra—and fighting continued throughout 1968 and 1969. The most tragic aspect of the war was the starvation of hundreds of thousands of Biafrans due to the disruptive effects of the fighting, the area's isolation from the rest of the world and the federal government's lack of cooperation in its dealings with international relief organizations. Biafra was probably the greatest human tragedy of the 1960s.

In the Middle East the 1960s saw the independence of two countries: Kuwait and Algeria. Britain granted Kuwaiti independence peacefully on June 19, 1961 but declared that it would protect the new state from the territorial claims of Iraq. In contrast, the independence of Algeria was a bloody, drawn-out affair. During 1960 and 1961 urban guerrilla warfare sapped the will of the French to retain their North African colony, and the

French Algerians—sensing the inevitability of Arab independence—attempted to declare their independence from France in January 1960 and April 1961, only to be put down by the French army. France finally proclaimed Algerian independence on July 3, 1962. Almost all of the French living there chose to leave for the safety of Europe.

The 1960s also brought an end to Egyptian President Gamal Abdel Nasser's dream of Arab unity under his own leadership. His plans began to disintegrate on September 29, 1961, when Syria decided to terminate its three-year union with Egypt. When civil war broke out after an army coup overthrew the Yemeni monarchy on September 27, 1962, Nasser tried to recoup his lost prestige by sending in Egyptian troops to back the republican side. His hope was to bring down the moderate Saudi and Jordanian regimes, which backed the royalists. By 1963 over 30,000 Egyptian troops had been sent to Yemen, but a decisive victory eluded them right up until their departure in 1967.

Nasser's greatest setback, of course, was his defeat in the 1967 Arab-Israeli war. He precipitated the chain of events leading up to the war on May 18, by ordering the U.N. peacekeeping troops stationed in the Sinai Peninsula to withdraw from their positions immediately. When they had done so, Nasser tightened the vise still further by announcing a blockade to prevent Israeli ships from passing through the Strait of Tiran, the sea route by which Israel obtained its oil imports. After the United States failed to persuade Nasser to rescind his blockade, Israel launched an air attack against Egypt and Jordan in the early hours of June 5. It caught the entire Egyptian air force on the ground, destroying it within an hour. Having won control of the air, Israeli troops smashed into the Sinai and raced all the way to the Suez Canal. In tougher fighting, the Israelis drove Jordanian troops out of the Arab sector of Jerusalem and off the west bank of the Jordan River. Then on May 9 Israel attacked Syria's troops and drove them off the Golan Heights. The fighting ended on May 11, with Israel having gained a complete victory. There would be no more illusions about destroying the Jewish state by conventional military means, and Nasser's prestige was irrevocably damaged.

The year 1967 also marked another important event in the Middle East: British troops left Aden (later to be called South Yemen) and granted the country its independence after months of guerrilla warfare. By the end of the year, Aden had allied itself with the Soviet Union and had accepted Soviet military and technical aid. Similarly, the West lost another ally in 1969, when Libyan officers led by Mohammad Quaddafi overthrew the monarchy on September 1 and proclaimed on Islamic republic.

In Europe the 1960s were characterized by detente and increasing independence of Europe from both the United States and the Soviet Union. The decade began with a true reconiliation between France and West Germany and ended with the beginnings of reconciliation between West Germany and its Eastern European neighbors. In between, France challenged American influence in Western Europe, and the Eastern European countries tried, with varying degrees of success, to put a measure of distance between themselves and the Soviet Union.

The year 1960 saw the full flowering of West German-French rapprochement. Numerous trade agreements were signed, and German troops even returned to France for the first time since World War II as part of a training exercise. This new relationship culminated in the January 22, 1963 signing of a Franco-German treaty, which provided for annual consultations between the heads of state of both countries.

Several days later, on January 29, French President Charles de Gaulle began his offensive against American influence in Europe, when he vetoed Britain's application to join the Common Market on the grounds that London was too closely linked with Washington. On March 9, 1966 de Gaulle pushed his diplomatic offensive one step further, making the dramatic announcement that France would withdraw from the military organizations of NATO (the North Atlantic Treaty Organization) and that U.S. troops would have to leave French soil.

De Gaulle's highly nationalistic foreign policy was undercut, however, in May 1968, when all of Paris and most of the rest of France were crippled by student unrest and workers' strikes. The crisis began when university students in Paris stopped attending classes and began demonstrating in the streets. They were joined by striking workers. After several weeks of almost complete paralysis, the strikes and demonstrations began to fade, and in June, French moderates and conservatives crushed the left in parliamentary elections. Nevertheless, President de Gaulle's prestige was tarnished. In order to recoup he called for a national referendum on April 27, 1969, which he narrowly lost. The next day he resigned and declared his support of Georges Pompidou, who then went on to win the presidential election on June 15. Europe had thus lost its most original and most decisive statesman.

In a move similar to France's adoption of a more assertive stance toward the United States, several Eastern European countries also tried to assert their independence vis-a-vis the Soviet Union during the sixties. Albania began to publicly vilify Russia and forbid Soviet ships the use of its ports in 1960. This was followed by Rumania's refusal to subordinate itself to the overall economic plans of the Soviet bloc, discussed during the course of 1964. Much more serious and spontaneous unrest took place at the beginning of 1968 in Poland, where workers and students protested against both the domestic regime and the Soviet occupation.

The most vigorous anti-Soviet dissent took place in Czechoslovakia, where in 1968—under the leadership of Party Secretary Alexander Dubcek—the government adopted a liberalization program, which included the end of press censorship. During June and July tense negotiations took place between Czech and Soviet leaders in which the Czech government refused to abandon its reform program. Finally, on August 20, 1968, under cover of darkness, troops from the Soviet Union and four Eastern European nations invaded the fledgling democracy and occupied all the major Czechoslovak cities. During the following months Soviet agents and their Czech collaborators ground away at the reform movement, until during 1969 Dubcek, its leading liberal, was forced out of the party and into a position as a gardener, marking the end of Czechoslovakia's experiment in democracy.

Democracy had its ups and downs in other European countries as well. On May 27, 1960 Turkey's 10-year-old parliamentary government was overthrown when the army deposed Premier Adnan Menderes because of his frequent abuses of power. Menderes was executed on September 17, 1961, with the army remaining in power until new elections were held. Similarly, the Greek army intervened in a parliamentary crisis and overthrew the civilian government on April 21, 1967. Numerous arrests followed, and reports of political intimidation and even torture emanated from the birthplace of European democracy. In contrast, democracy made some headway in another European country on the periphery of the continent: Portugal. On September 27, 1968 the country's authoritarian President Antonio de Oliveira Salazar suffered a serious heart attack and was replaced by Premier Marcelo Caetano, who promised to slowly liberalize Portugal's political life. Opposition leaders then began to speak out for the first time in decades.

The decline in the intensity of Cold War tensions in Europe had its most immediate effect on West Germany. After West Germany had weathered the Berlin crisis of 1961, a domestic debate began about the pros and cons of accepting the territorial losses imposed upon it by the Soviet Union after World War II and whether East Germany might even be recognized as a separate state. As a result of the debate, West Germany broke a long-standing policy and resumed diplomatic relations with Yugoslavia, even though Yugoslavia had diplomatic relations with East Germany. West Germany's new course gained additional momentum when Social Democrat Willy Brandt was elected chancellor on October 21, 1969. Brandt had campaigned on a platform of accepting the territorial losses of World War II and possibly recognizing East Germany. His coming to power guaranteed that the political detente that had marked the 1960s in Europe would continue to develop.

The 1960s were marked in the Soviet Union by the overthrow of Premier Nikita Khrushchev on October 19, 1964. Khrushchev was subsequently criticized publicly for his "harebrained schemes" and placed under house arrest at his country home. At first no single leader emerged to dominate the Soviet political scene, but by 1968 it was apparent that Party Secretary Leonid Brezhnev had become the Kremlin's most powerful figure.

For Britain and the two republics of Ireland, the most important event of the sixties was the arrival of British troops in Northern Ireland on August 14, 1969. Repeated clashes between the republic's Catholic minority and its Protestant majority had preceded the decision to send in troops. As the clashes had intensified, the government of Northern Ireland no longer felt capable of controlling the situation and finally requested the help of British soldiers, who were (initially, at least) welcomed by both sides.

In Asia the 1960s were dominated by the war in Indochina, which dragged on for the entire decade. At first the fighting centered in Laos. The Communists had threatened to take power in that country during 1960 and 1961 but were prevented from doing so by government troops aided by U.S. military supplies and advisers. During 1962 the Communist offensive shifted to South Vietnam, and President John F. Kennedy decided to send in several thousand U.S. troops to support the inexperienced South Vietnamese army.

Attention focused in 1963 on the shaky South Vietnamese government itself. The regime was dominated by Roman Catholic refugees from North Vietnam, which did not sit well with the Buddhist majority in the South. Frequent demonstrations took place against President Ngo Dinh Diem, followed on November 1, 1963 by a bloody U.S.-backed coup in which the armed forces overthrew and killed Diem. His removal, however, did not solve the problem of the government's instability and unpopularity; a number of coups and counter-coups followed.

During 1964 attention shifted toward the two real protagonists of the war: the United States and North Vietnam. Hanoi increased its infiltration into the South and harassed U.S. shipping. Two of these attacks took place on August 2 and 4, when North Vietnamese torpedo boats attacked several American destroyers. Despite the insignificant damage that resulted, President Lyndon B. Johnson made the momentous decision to bomb North Vietnam for the first time. Moreover, he publicly committed his prestige to the war by justifying the attack on national television and asking Congress for a resolution supporting the bombing and any future action that might be needed to protect American forces. Finally, Johnson ordered more U.S. troops sent to the South, with America's commitment standing at 20,000 men by the end of 1964.

The phase of the war in which Americans served chiefly as advisers ended in 1965, with U.S. troops beginning to fight for the first time as independent units. By the end of the year, 185,000 U.S. soldiers were in the South, and of the 1,643 combat fatalities since 1961, 1,404 had occurred during 1965.

Attention shifted back to the domestic politics of South Vietnam in 1966. Antigovernment demonstrators tried to bring down the regime, gaining control of the northern provinces from about the middle of March to the middle of May, with the government regaining control of those provinces during the latter part of

May. In June the government promised to hold parliamentary elections later in the year. The elections, which took place on September 11, were considered a success, since 80 percent of the population voted despite widespread Viet Cong terrorism. For the first time South Vietnam seemed on its way toward establishing a stable government. An equally important feature of 1966 was the continued buildup of American forces, which reached a total of 380,000 troops.

During 1967 the fighting in South Vietnam continued to intensify, with savage combat raging around the U.S. marine base at Khesanh, in particular. The air war also escalated, and the North Vietnamese capital of Hanoi was attacked for the first time on May 19, as was the port of Haiphong on September 17. The South Vietnamese government also continued in 1967 to make progress toward creating stable institutions, including a more effective army and improved political processes. On September 3 Gen. Nguyen Van Thieu was elected the country's first president. U.S. troop strength had increased to 474,300 by the end of the year.

The largest Communist offensive of the war marked the start of 1968. It was launched on January 30 and penetrated every major South Vietnamese city, including Saigon. Communist forces captured several provincial capitals and held on to the northern city of Hue for three weeks. While militarily the offensive was a standoff, politically it was a defeat for the United States; and on March 31 President Johnson ordered a halt to the bombing of North Vietnam with the exception of its southernmost province. Moreover, Johnson's offer of public negotiations was accepted by the North Vietnamese, with the American and North Vietnamese delegations meeting for the first time on May 3 in Paris. On October 31 President Johnson announced that in return for a complete halt to the bombing of North Vietnam, the North had agreed to allow the South Vietnamese government and the Communist National Liberation Front to join the talks.

The year 1969 saw the start of the deescalation of the war. On June 8 President Richard M. Nixon announced the first withdrawal ever of American troops—25,000 of them—from South Vietnam. This was followed by a major speech Nixon made on July 25 in Guam, stating that in the future the security of Asia—including South Vietnam—would primarily be the responsibility of Asians. In keeping with this new policy, the president announced two more withdrawals of U.S. troops later in the year. The pullout of these three groups of soldiers signaled the beginning of the end of the American military involvement in Indochina.

The 1960s were also marked by three other important confrontations in Asia: between India and China, between India and Pakistan, and between Russia and China. The first—the India-China conflict—broke out on October 20, 1962, when after months of skirmishing, Communist Chinese forces overran Indian positions on both the eastern and western sectors of their disputed Himalayan frontier. The war ended after several days, with China having established its military superiority and enforced its border claims. In contrast to the decisive 1962 Chinese victory, the 1965 border war between India and Pakistan ended in a rough stalemate. Both sides conquered parts of their opponent's territory in the disputed province of Kashmir during the heavy tank battles of September, but neither side gained a decisive advantage. And in January 1966 an Indian-Pakistani peace agreement restored all captured territories. But the final Asian conflict of the decade—that between Russia and China—was clearly the most momentous. Periodic skirmishing finally escalated into major artillery duels on March 2, 1969, with both sides claiming Damansky (Chenpao) Island in the Ussuri River. Although inconclusive, the fighting did reveal the extent of the rivalry between the two major Communist powers.

Within China several important domestic events took place during the sixties. The Communist regime exploded its first atom bomb on October 16, 1964 (which perhaps had something to do with the downfall of Nikita Khrushchev three days later). In addition, intense political ferment, known as the Cultural Revolution, rocked the country during 1966–67. The unrest was spearheaded by militant youths, called Red Guards, who routinely ransacked homes, rounded up citizens and insulted foreigners. They began their campaign of intimidation in June 1966 with the encouragement of Chinese Communist leader Mao Tse-tung, who feared that he was losing control over the party and the government bureaucracy. But the movement soon got out of hand, and hundreds—probably thousands—of people lost their lives in near civil war conditions. The campaign culminated on August 22, 1967, when the Red Guards sacked the British chancery in Peking and roughed up its employees. After this incident, calls for an end to the unrest were issued with increasing frequency and were made by former Red Guard supporters, including Mao Tse-tung himself. As 1967 drew to a close, calm began to return to Communist China for the first time since the campaign of disruption had begun.

But the most serious civil strife to occur in Asia during the 1960s took place in Indonesia. The unrest was precipitated by an attempted coup on September 30, 1965 by the Indonesian Communist Party. The coup's leaders managed to murder most of the country's top military officers and arrest President Sukarno (who had been in poor health). But they did not reckon with the strong anti-Communist and anti-Chinese sentiments of the Indonesian population, the vast majority of whom were Islamic. Those army officers who survived the coup banned the Communist Party and led a movement in which hundreds of thousands of suspected Communists (many of them members of the country's Chinese minority) were either arrested or killed. By March 1966 the army was in firm control of the country, and President Sukarno was politically discredited, as were his former friendly policies toward Communist China. Indonesia then opened itself up to Western investment and adopted the capitalist economic model of the advanced industrial countries.

In contrast with Indochina, China and Indonesia, other developing Asian nations demonstrated noteworthy stability and economic growth. These included Malaysia, which gained its independence from Britain on September 16, 1963, and Singapore, which broke away from Malaysia on August 9, 1965. These two countries, together with Thailand, the Philippines and Indonesia, formed the Association of Southeast Asian Nations (ASEAN) on August 8, 1967. This new regional grouping sought close economic ties with the West and encouraged both domestic and international private enterprise. During the 1960s the nations in this group registered some of the most impressive economic growth rates in the developing world.

A final important Asian event of the 1960s took place on January 23, 1968, when North Korean patrol boats captured the U.S. intelligence ship *Pueblo* off the coast of North Korea. The North Koreans charged that the ship had been in their territorial waters; the Americans denied it. The charges and counter-charges dragged on for more than 10 months, until the crew was finally released on December 22, 1968.

The 1960s saw a marked improvement in the relations between the Soviet Union and the United States, as continuous confrontation gave way to a less abrasive relationship. The decade began on a somber note, however, when the Soviets shot down an American reconnaissance plane over their territory on May 1, 1960. Several weeks later at the Paris summit conference, Soviet Premier Nikita Khrushchev demanded a public apology from U.S. President Dwight Eisenhower. When Eisenhower refused, Khrushchev stormed out of the conference. The next summit meeting—on June 3–4, 1961—went only slightly better, with Khrushchev continually goading President John F. Kennedy about the recent Bay of Pigs debacle in Cuba and apparently concluding that the young president would not respond forcefully to aggressive Soviet political strategies. Thus, Khrushchev ordered the construction of the Berlin wall on August 13, 1961 and the resumption of Soviet above-ground nuclear testing that September 1.

Khrushchev's most audacious move, though, took place in October 1962, when he tried to clandestinely install offensive missiles in Cuba. The Kennedy administration learned of this on October 16; after a week of intense secret debate, it decided to forgo an aerial bombardment of the missile sites in favor of surrounding Cuba with a naval blockade to permit the inspection of all incoming Soviet bloc ships that could be transporting the missiles. The decision was announced by President Kennedy in a nationwide television address on October 22; four days later a Soviet-chartered freighter was stopped and searched. On October 28 Soviet Premier Khrushchev agreed to dismantle the missiles under United Nations supervision in return for an American pledge not to invade the Caribbean island.

The crisis had a sobering effect upon the Soviet Union. It soon reduced its harassment in Berlin and toned down its verbal criticism of the United States. The improved relations culminated in the signing on July 25, 1963 of a treaty banning the testing of nuclear weapons in the atmosphere, and soon thereafter a communications hot line was established between Washington and Moscow.

During the rest of the sixties, Soviet-American relations remained on a fairly even keel despite the tensions stemming from the Vietnam War. On June 23, 1967 President Lyndon B. Johnson and Soviet Premier Aleksei Kosygin met in Glassboro, New Jersey. During the conference Johnson and Defense Secretary Robert McNamara emphasized the need to begin negotiations on limiting defensive missile systems that would upset the strategic arms balance between the two countries. The Soviets were wary at first but were later receptive, and on October 25, 1969 both countries announced the beginning of the Strategic Arms Limitation talks (SALT). Thus, by the end of the sixties, the superpowers had established a relationship in which cooperation was sometimes possible in spite of their rivalry.

Within the United States during the 1960s, the most important domestic issues were the civil rights movement and the debate over the wisdom of American participation in the Vietnam War. The civil rights movement began with an attack on segregated public facilities in the South. On February 2, 1960 four black college students sat down quietly at a segregated lunch counter in Greensboro, North carolina and refused to leave when service was denied them. Within months similar sit-ins had taken place throughout the South and resulted, in most cases, in peaceful desegregation. Civil rights activists known as "freedom riders" focused on segregated facilities in interstate bus stations during 1961. In 1962 the principal crisis revolved around the integration of the University of Mississippi. After a black applicant, James Meredith, was denied admission, the U.S. Supreme Court ruled on September 10 that he had to be accepted. When state police prevented him from entering the university campus, President Kennedy sent in federal troops to enforce the court order and put down rioting white protesters.

In 1963—the 100th anniversary of Abraham Lincoln's Emancipation Proclamation—the civil rights movement burgeoned into a searing national issue. Hundreds of black adults and children took to the streets—and willingly went to jail—to demonstrate their opposition to discrimination. Violent confrontations centered on Birmingham, Alabama, where the Rev. Martin Luther King Jr. began a series of protest marches in April. City officials, led by Sheriff Eugene "Bull" Connor, tried to intimidate the demonstrators with police dogs and electric cattle prods. The spectacle of German shepherds attacking defenseless marchers was televised on national news broadcasts, causing an uproar in the North. In May an uneasy truce was shattered when the home of a black civil rights worker was bombed. This touched off the first large-scale rioting of the decade in Birmingham's black neighborhood.

The civil rights movement continued to gain momentum during 1963, however, when President Kennedy made a televised address to the nation on June 11 in which he said that racial discrimination could no longer be accepted: "The events in Birmingham and elsewhere have so increased the cries for equality that no city or state legislative body can prudently choose to ignore them." He then proposed legislation prohibiting discrimination in most public facilities and enabling the attorney general to fight school segregation and voting restrictions more vigorously. The high point of the year occurred on August 28, when 200,000 demonstrators, 80 percent of whom were black, gathered at the Lincoln Memorial to urge passage of the legislation. The most moving moment came during the closing speech by perhaps the finest American orator of the 1960s—Martin Luther King, Jr. In a vibrant voice, he said: "No, we are not satisfied until justice rolls down like water and righteousness like a mighty stream. . . . Go back to Mississippi, go back to Alabama, go back to South Carolina . . . knowing that somehow this situation can and will be changed."

The year 1964 was also marked by violent resistance to desegregation. In the deep South, judges refused to convict whites charged with bombing black homes, and white clergymen opposed to segregation were driven from their pulpits. At least 24 black churches were set on fire, and the burning crosses of the Ku Klux Klan often illuminated the night skies of Mississippi and Alabama. The violence was also aimed at the young southern blacks and northern whites who spearheaded voter registration drives. On June 24 three of them—James Chaney, Michael Schwerner and Andrew Goodman—were murdered in Mississippi. Despite such tragedies, the movement was making undeniable progress. The civil rights bill President Kennedy originally submitted was passed by Congress in June, and during the fall more southern schools were desegregated.

The following year, 1965, proved to be crucial for the civil rights movement and for race relations. For the first time, blacks in the North engaged in as much violence as whites in the South. The worst riot took place in Los Angeles during August. Like many such incidents, the unrest was sparked by the arrest of a black by a white policeman (in this case, for a speeding violation). For six days marauding bands of black youths pillaged stores and set fires, and gun battles with police left 43 dead. In the South the level of violence also remained high, with several civil rights workers having been murdered in Selma, Alabama. But segregation was on the defensive, and the passage of the 1965 Civil Rights Act empowered the federal government to dispatch examiners to register black voters in the face of local resistance.

Black civil rights militants who rejected Martin Luther King, Jr.'s doctrine of nonviolence, and who even questioned the very goal of integration, emerged during 1966. The militants, who preferred the term *black* as opposed to *Negro*, believed in the concept of "black power." The movement alienated many whites, since black power advocates such as Stokely Carmichael threatened violence if their demands were not quickly met. This was also the first year in which there was significantly more violence by blacks in the North than by whites in the South. Major riots took place in Chicago and Cleveland, and the disorders in northern cities seemed to be becoming a regular feature of the hot summer months. In contrast, violence in the South seemed to be on the decline. Several blacks won electoral races for the first time, and fewer white candidates made openly racist appeals.

During 1967 the worst urban violence in 20th-century America staggered the nation. Major riots took place in most northern cities, with Newark, New Jersey and Detroit particularly hard hit. The Newark riot broke out on July 12, when black youths began to loot stores and set fires. Both firemen and policemen were shot at, and after days of disorders the death toll stood at

26. Detroit was even worse. The unrest began there on July 23, when several liquor stores were looted. The police refrained from taking forceful measures, and within a few hours much of the downtown and black neighborhoods were aflame. Army troops were called in for the first time to put down the disorders. After five days Detroit began to return to normal. The death toll stood at 43: It was the worst race riot in 20th century America.

As in the South, however, positive trends could be discerned behind the daily headlines of violence. Two black mayors—Carl Stokes of Cleveland, Ohio and Richard Hatcher of Gary, Indiana—were elected in November as the black voter registration drives began to pay off.

The assassination of Martin Luther King, Jr. dominated 1968. The Georgia pastor had gone to Memphis, Tennessee to lead a march in support of striking sanitation workers. On April 3 he told a crowd of supporters: "Like anybody, I would like to live a long life. But I'm not concerned about that now. . . . I've seen the promised land. I may not get there with you, but I want you to know tonight that we, as a people, will get to the promised land." Less than 24 hours later, he was dead—a victim of assassin James Earl Ray. In 125 cities across the nation, disorders broke out, some lasting two or three days. Washington and Chicago were particularly hard hit. Overall, 55,000 troops were used to contain the violence, and 49 people died. In response to the assassination, Congress finally passed the administration's open-housing bill, which forbade discrimination in the sale and rental of about 80 percent of the nation's housing. And in June the U.S. Supreme Court ruled that all such discrimination was unconstitutional.

The year 1969 proved to be still another turning point for the civil rights movement. The number of urban disorders in the North declined for the first time since 1965, as blacks continued to make steady gains in central city governments. Having achieved significant progress in the areas of school and public accommodations desegregation as well as open-housing legislation, civil rights organizations decided to focus more on job discrimination. And on September 4 the National Association for the Advancement of Colored People announced plans for legal action aimed at halting work on federally financed construction projects until more black workers were hired.

In American domestic politics, the 1960s began with the presidential primaries. For the Republicans there was only one serious candidate, Vice President Richard M. Nixon; while the Democrats had two contenders—Sen. John F. Kennedy of Massachusetts and Sen. Hubert H. Humphrey of Minnesota. Kennedy won their first confrontation in April in the Wisconsin primary, but many attributed his victory to the large Catholic population in Milwaukee. In May, however, Kennedy again decisively defeated Humphrey in West Virginia, a state with a small Catholic population. Humphrey then withdrew from the race.

During the ensuing campaign between Kennedy and Nixon, no major policy differences emerged. A minor issue involved the defense of the Chinese off-shore islands of Quemoy and Matsu, which were held by the Nationalist Chinese. Nixon felt they should be defended against Communist Chinese attack, while Kennedy seemed more cautious. But the real issue was probably Kennedy's Catholicism, though he tried to defuse the question by emphasizing his belief that politics and religion shouldn't mix.

Kennedy won a narrow victory on November 8, 1960, thanks to a strong showing in the northern industrial states and in the South, where his vice presidential candidate, Sen. Lyndon B. Johnson of Texas, proved an asset. Perhaps the main reason for Kennedy's victory, however, was his ability to communicate a sense of vigor and assertiveness. He represented the coming of age of the generation that had fought and won World War II. It was a generation confident that most problems could be solved and that America should take the lead in solving them. And it was just this spirit that the young president captured in his January 20, 1961 inaugural address, when he pledged that the United States would "pay any price" to defend freedom around the world. Never had America felt more confident and more in control of its destiny.

But the romantic glow of the Kennedy era was short-lived: On November 22, 1963 the president was assassinated by Lee Harvey Oswald, who was in turn killed by Jack Ruby. The nation's confidence was shaken: It had lost a popular leader, and there were doubts about the facts of the assassination. Fortunately, Vice President Lyndon Johnson assumed power quickly, promising to pursue the policies of the slain president. In his first address to Congress, he declared: "No memorial oration or eulogy could more eloquently honor President Kennedy's memory than the earliest possible passage of the civil rights bill for which he fought so long."

The 1964 presidential campaign was dominated by the issues of civil rights and increasing street crime in the northern cities. Gov. George Wallace of Alabama, a staunch segregationist, entered a number of primaries and won more than 30 percent of the Democratic vote in Wisconsin, Indiana and Maryland. The Republican candidate, Sen. Barry Goldwater of Arizona, also stressed the crime problem and his opposition to the 1964 Civil Rights Act, which prohibited discrimination in most places of public accommodation. But Goldwater was widely regarded as an extremist—particularly in foreign affairs, where he advocated the bombing of North Vietnam. This led to a decisive victory for President Johnson and his vice presidential candidate, Hubert Humphrey, with the Democratic ticket winning all but five southern states and Arizona.

President Johnson began his new four-year term on a note of exuberant optimism: He believed that poverty could be eradicated in America and the Communists simultaneously defeated in Vietnam. In fact, his January 20, 1965 inaugural address expressed, for the last time, an almost evangelical vision of America:

The American covenant called on us to help show the way for the liberation of man, and that is our goal. . . . If American lives must end, and American treasure be spilled, in countries that we barely know, that is the price that change has demanded. . . . We believe that every man must someday be free.

But Americans ultimately proved unwilling to spill their "treasure" in along, inconclusive land war in South Vietnam. While President Johnson's decision in early 1965 to increase U.S. troop strength and shift Americans from an advisory role to a combat one was widely accepted, it was nonetheless questioned by some intellectuals and students. During 1966 these doubts increased and spread to many civil rights leaders and even to the general public. This emerging uneasiness was partly reflected in the strong comeback registered by the Republican Party in the congressional and gubernatorial races of November 1966.

Antiwar activity burgeoned during 1967, as it became apparent that no quick victory was in sight. Demonstrations occurred frequently in major cities; and on college campuses students protested the presence of military recruiters and representatives of the Dow Chemical Company, which manufactured napalm used in Vietnam. The biggest antiwar demonstration of the year took place in Washington, D.C. on October 21: Approximately 55,000 people gathered at the Lincoln Memorial. Many of them also marched across the Potomac River to the Pentagon, where they clashed with the Army troops guarding the building.

As the 1968 presidential campaign approached, however, opponents of the Vietnam War found a new channel for their frustrations in the candidacy of Sen. Eugene McCarthy of Minnesota, who announced on November 30, 1967 that he would run in several Democratic primaries. Initially, few took him seriously: At best it was thought that he was a stalking horse for Sen.

Robert F. Kennedy of New York, who had become one of the major critics of the Johnson administration's policies. But the complexion of the campaign changed totally after the successful Communist Tet offensive, launched on January 30, 1968, made the U.S. public realize that the war was not being won and that it could drag on indefinitely. As a result, McCarthy did surprisingly well in the March 12 New Hampshire primary, where he won 42 percent of the vote to Johnson's 48 percent. It was now apparent that the president was vulnerable, and on March 16 Sen. Robert Kennedy announced his candidacy for president.

Kennedy's announcement, plus the continuing decline of Johnson's popularity, led the president to state in a March 31 speech that he would neither seek nor accept the nomination of the Democratic Party for another presidential term. With Johnson out of the race, Vice President Hubert Humphrey felt free to declare his own candidacy on April 27. During May, Kennedy and McCarthy faced each other four times: Kennedy won in Indiana, the District of Columbia and Nebraska; while McCarthy took Oregon. The views of both candidates were similar, though Kennedy seemed to favor a slower withdrawal from Vietnam. Their personalities were the deciding factor, with Kennedy appealing strongly to working class and minority groups while McCarthy was popular with the middle class. On June 4 Kennedy won a key victory in California, and it appeared that he would go on to win the Democratic nomination. Then, shortly after midnight, as he was thanking his supporters, he was assassinated by an Arab immigrant, Sirhan Sirhan. This left the field wide open for Vice President Humphrey.

The national conventions of the two parties could hardly have been more dissimilar. The Republicans convened amid the opulence of Miami Beach, Florida, where it was a foregone conclusion that former Vice President Richard M. Nixon would win the nomination. The Democrats met in Chicago in a convention hall surrounded by barbed wire, antiwar demonstrators and the Chicago stockyards. The mood was nasty both inside and outside the hall. Chicago's Democratic Mayor Richard Daley manipulated the agenda in favor of the supporters of Vice President Humphrey and did not hesitate to cut off electric power to the microphones of speakers who were criticizing his tactics. Outside the convention hall a significant minority of the antiwar protesters felt that they had nothing to lose and were intent upon provoking a violent confrontation with the police. They persisted in throwing rocks and bottles and using obscene language until the police finally lost all self-control and went on an 18-minute clubbing spree on the night of August 28. That same evening the Democrats nominated Humphrey as their presidential candidate. Final casualty figures for the Chicago convention were reportedly as follows: 1,000 demonstrators treated for tear gas and injuries, 101 of them hospitalized; 122 police injured, 49 hospitalized. But the most serious casualty of all was the Democratic Party and its candidate, Hubert Humphrey.

During the first month of the campaign, everything seemed to favor Nixon. His crowds were large and orderly, while Humphrey's often included antiwar hecklers who drowned out his defensive and apologetic speeches. By mid-October, however, the Humphrey campaign had begun to gain momentum, and he steadily closed the gap in the opinion polls. What's more, a week before election day Sen. Eugene McCarthy said that Humphrey's position on the war had come close enough to his own to make it possible for him to support the vice president. Further help came on October 31, when President Johnson announced that he would be ordering a complete halt to the bombing of North Vietnam the following day in return for North Vietnam's agreement to enlarge the peace talks to include the South Vietnamese government and the Communist National Liberation Front. Despite this last-minute surge, Richard Nixon emerged the winner on November 5, with 43.4 percent of the vote to Humphrey's 42.7 percent and former Gov. George Wallace's 13.5 percent.

Nixon began his presidential term on January 20, 1969 with a call for a reduction in the stridency that had characterized the tone of much of the political debate in America since the escalation of the Vietnam War. In the spring, however, the outbreak of two major student revolts made it apparent that militant demands were still much in fashion. On April 9 about 300 students seized Harvard University's main administration building in protest against the school's association with defense industries. The militants managed to gain the sympathy of a larger group of relatively moderate students, and for about one week university classes were boycotted. Later in the same month black students at Cornell University seized an administrative building in order to force acceptance of their demands that disciplinary measures against several of their colleagues be dropped. Like the Harvard militants, they were successful in gaining the backing of a significant number of moderate students, and the charges were dropped. When the protesters emerged on April 20 from the Cornell building they had occupied, they were carrying rifles and shotguns—symbolic of the degree of violence that had become a part of student and civil rights protests.

The closing year of the decade also saw the growing assertiveness of Congress vis-a-vis the judicial and executive branches of government. Congress forced the resignation on May 14 of Supreme Court Justice Abe Fortas, accused of having accepted a $20,000 payment from the family foundation of financier Louis Wolfson, who was serving a one-year prison term for selling unregistered securities. Similarly, on November 21 the senate rejected President Nixon's nominee to succeed Fortas, Clement Haynesworth, because of his failure to withdraw from court cases in which his financial interests may have been involved.

Congress also asserted itself through a growing willingness to make its foreign policy views known. And for the first time since World War II, the Pentagon was put on the defensive, as an antimilitary bloc formed in the House and Senate. Congressional criticism of defense spending and cost overruns became more frequent, with calls being heard for cutbacks in the extensive network of U.S. bases abroad. More specifically, on June 25 the Senate passed a resolution calling on the executive branch to refrain from committing troops or financial resoures to foreign countries without the express approval of Congress. Similarly, the Senate just barely defeated two amendments that would have prohibited deployment of President Nixon's proposed Safeguard antiballistic missile system (the vote, on August 6, was 50 to 50).

During 1969 antiwar activity continued at a high level, despite President Nixon's three separate announcements of U.S. troop withdrawals totaling 110,000 men. A nationwide series of demonstrations took place on October 15; it included rallies, speeches, church and synagogue services, readings of the names of the Vietnam war dead, tolling of bells, candlelight marches, teach-in seminars, folk song concerts, vigils, wreath layings and door-to-door canvassing. The Nixon administration counterattacked on October 19, when Vice President Spiro Agnew said that such activities had been "encouraged by an effete corps of impudent snobs who characterize themselves as intellectuals." Undeterred, 250,000 protesters gathered in Washington, D.C. on November 15 for the largest demonstration of the year. They marched down Pennsylvania Avenue and attended a rally on the grounds of the Washington Monument. This was followed by a 40-hour March Against Death, in which approximately 46,000 people each carried the name of one U.S. soldier killed in Vietnam from Arlington National Cemetery to the grounds of the Capitol.

Despite the passions of the antiwar protesters, 1969 marked the beginning of the end of an era of rapid social change and political violence. It was the first year in which large-scale rioting decreased in northern cities, and it was the first year in which U.S. troops were withdrawn from Vietnam. Perhaps the change was best symbolized by the retirement of Chief Justice of the United States Earl Warren, a social activist, and the confirmation of Warren Burger as chief justice—the latter considered a moderate on civil rights and a critic of the Court's trend toward broadening the rights of criminal suspects. America was looking for stability after a decade of tumultuous change.

The 1960s were a vigorous decade in the arts. Two new writers—Gabriel Garcia Marquez and Alexander Solzhenitsyn—produced major works. Garcia Marquez, who was born in Colombia, described the mythical Latin American town of Macondo in his 1969 book *One Hundred Years of Solitude*. The town represented Latin America in a microcosm: local autonomy yielding to state authority, anticlericalism, party politics, the coming of the United Fruit Company and abortive revolutions. In addition to the often brutal historical world, Garcia Marquez evoked the delicate magic of a fairy-tale world:

A short time later, when the carpenter was taking measurements for the coffin, through the windows they saw a light rain of tiny yellow flowers falling. They fell on the town all through the night in a silent storm, and they covered the roofs and blocked the doors and smothered the animals who slept outside. So many flowers fell from the sky that in the morning the streets were carpeted with a compact cushion and they had to clear them away with shovels and rakes so that the funeral procession could pass by.

Russian writer Solzhenitsyn also described the brutality of history in *One Day in the Life of Ivan Denisovich* (1962), but in a much starker manner. The book covered a typical day of an inmate in a Stalinist prison camp in which life is reduced to its most primitive essentials:

The prisoners were at their coldest and hungriest when they checked in through the gates in the evening, and their bowl of hot and watery soup without any fat was like rain in a drought. They gulped it down. They cared more for this bowlful than freedom, or for their life in years gone by and years to come.

The cinema of the sixties was dominated by two Europeans—Federico Fellini of Italy and Ingmar Bergman of Sweden. Fellini produced two black-and-white films on the blase Italian upper class: *La Dolce Vita* (1961) and *8½* (1963). He then turned to color for the first time in *Juliet of the Spirits* (1965), in which the grotesque predominates.

In contrast to Fellini's Latin exuberance, Ingmar Bergman portrayed the somber and lonely world of northern Europe. *Winter Light* (1963) dealt with the collapse of the marriage of a Swedish pastor. *The Silence* (1964) depicted the jealous relationship of two sisters and a young child in a country where they could not speak the language and were totally isolated. Bergman's *Persona* (1967) consisted largely of an intense monologue by a nurse taking care of a former actress who refused to speak. In a similar vein, his *The Hour of the Wolf* (1968) related the story of a woman nursing her husband, who was slowly going insane. In *Shame* (1969) Bergman turned to a theme of greater social relevance: the devastating effects of war upon a young couple.

In architecture the Americans held sway. They led the attack on the "international style," which had been dominant since the 1930s. The principal spokesman for the revolt was U.S. architect Robert Venturi, who argued in his book *Contradictions and Complexity in Architecture* (1966) that the pristine and symmetrical lines of modern buildings should be enriched with more detail, variety and references to the past. Perhaps the best architect of the decade was the American Louis Khan, whose massive, cavernous buildings recalled the architecture of ancient Rome.

Two Americans also dominated the scene in painting: Mark Rothko and Richard Lindner. Rothko painted large, luminous color bands, which seemed to hover on the surfaces of his canvases. In contrast, Lindner was a representational artist. He excelled in garish potraits of New York men and women, his bright reds, yellows and greens catching the raucousness of the country's largest city.

In music the American George Crumb (a 1968 Pulitzer Prize winner) astounded listeners with his novel use of instruments—the cords of pianos were plucked; the strings of cellos were rubbed vertically—which produced an eerie, extraterrestrial sound.

The most important achievement in medicine during the decade of the 1960s was the first human heart transplant, performed by South African doctors on December 3, 1967. It was followed by hundreds of such operations, many involving transplants of other organs.

In space the sixties brought a series of dramatic achievements, crowned by the landing of the first men on the moon. This decade of manned space exploration began on April 12, 1961, when Soviet Maj. Yuri Gagarin became the first man to successfully orbit the Earth. The Soviet success challenged the Americans: On May 25, 1961 President John F. Kennedy called for a manned American expedition to the moon by the end of the decade. The U.S. program scored its first major success on February 20, 1962, when astronaut John Glenn orbited the Earth. Then the first U.S. lunar probe hit the moon on February 2, 1964. Other lunar probes, as well as manned Earth and lunar orbital missions, followed. The program culminated in July and November of 1969, when two teams of American astronauts landed on the moon and walked on its surface for several hours.

Taking all of these developments together, one can say that the 1960s saw the end of the bipolar world of the postwar era, in which the Soviet Union and, to a greater degree, the United States were predominant. In its place there emerged a truly global and pluralistic system—one in which each nation asserted itself politically. Within the United States, the decade also saw the end of the American public's unquestioning acceptance of authority, with widespread attacks on legally sanctioned racial segregation and pervasive patterns of discrimination as well as militant opposition to the increasingly unpopular war in Vietnam heralding a period of greater assertiveness and heightened political awareness.

YEARLY
SUMMARIES

	World Affairs	Europe	Africa & the Middle East	The Americas	Asia & the Pacific
1960	Nikita Khrushchev, Harold Macmillan, Dwight D. Eisenhower and Charles de Gaulle meet at a summit conference in Paris.	France conducts its first nuclear explosion. . . . Soviet Union shoots down a U.S. reconnaissance plane over central Asia. . . .Turkish armed forces overthrow Premier Adnan Menderes.	Nigeria, the Belgian Congo and most French-speaking African colonies become independent.	Cuba allies itself with the Soviet Union.	South Korean Pres. Syngman Rhee resigns after anti-government demonstrations break out . . . Communists capture the Laotian capital of Vientiane
1961	U.N. Secy. Gen. Dag Hammarskjold dies in a plane crash over Northern Rhodesia.	Britain sends troops to Kuwait to counter Iraqi annexation threats. . . . Turkish army executes former Premier Adnan Menderes. . . . Soviet Union constructs the Berlin Wall.	Kuwait becomes independent. . . . Syria withdraws from its union with Egypt.	Cuba repulses an invasion of anti-Castro exiles at the Bay of Pigs.	Laotian Communists capture the strategic central plain.
1962	OAS expels Cuba.	France agrees to grant Algerian independence.	Yemeni army officers overthrow the monarchy and proclaim a republic.	Soviet Union tries to install offensive nuclear weapons in Cuba.	Communist China overruns many Indian positions along their disputed Himalayan frontier.
1963	U.S. and the Soviet Union establish an emergency communications link between Moscow and Washington. . . . U.S. Britain and the Soviet Union sign a treaty prohibiting nuclear tests in the atmosphere.	France and Germany sign a major treaty calling for close cooperation. . . . France vetoes Britain's entry into the Common Market.	U.S. troops occupy Kolwezi, the last major secessionist stronghold in Katanga.	Venezuelan voters elect Raul Leoni as president despite wide-spread leftist terrorism.	South Vietnamese military leaders overthrow Pres. Ngo Dinh Diem.
1964	U.N. ends its four-year military operation in the Congo.	Soviet Communist party replaces Soviet leader Nikita Khrushchev with Aleksei Kosygin and Leonid Brezhnev.	Saudi ruling family dethrowns King Saud and replaces him with Prince Faisal.	Anti-U.S. riots leave 20 Panamanians and four U.S. soldiers dead in the Canal Zone. . . . Brazilian Army overthrows Pres. Joao Goulart and names Gen. Humberto Castelo Branco as president.	U.S. planes bomb North Vietnam after North Vietnamese patrol boats attack U.S. destroyers in international waters. . . .Communist China conducts its first nuclear test.
1965	U.N. calls on Britain to use force against Rhodesia.	Greek deputies topple the government as demonstrations take place throughout the country.	Col. Houari Boumedienne overthrows Algerian Pres. Ahmed Ben Bella. . . . Rhodesia declares its independence from Britain unilaterally.	14,000 U.S. troops land in the Dominican Republic after battles break out between rival political factions.	Fierce fighting takes place between India and Pakistan during several weeks. . . . Indonesian Army arrests thousands of Communists after a Communist coup attempt fails to topple Pres. Sukarno.
1966	U.N. unanimously votes for sanctions against Rhodesia.	French Pres. De Gaulle takes France out of NATO's military organization and tells US troops to leave French territory. . . .West German Parliament elects Kurt Georg Kiesinger as chancellor. . . .British P.M. Harold Wilson's Labor Party wins a landslide victory. . . . West Germany indicates that it wants to improve relations with East European countries.	Syrian radicals led by Maj. Gen. Salah Jedid take power in a bloody coup. . . . Ghanaian military leaders overthrow Pres. Kwame Nkrumah in a violent coup. . . . A military coup led by Moslem Hausas overthrows Nigerian Pres. Maj. Gen. Johnson Aguiyi Ironsi. . . .	A bloodless coup headed by Lt. Gen. Juan Carlos Ongania ousts Argentinian Pres. Arturo Illia. . . . Brazilian voters elect Artur Costa e Silva as president in an unopposed election.	An anti-government movement known as the Cultural Revolution begins in Communist China. . . . Indonesia and Malaysia sign an agreement ending their political confrontation. . . . Violent anti-government demonstrations led by militant Buddhists take place in South Vietnam.
1967	U.N. Relief Commissioner Laurence Michelmore says that at least 100,000 Arabs have left the Israeli occupied West Bank of the Jordan River.	A Greek military junta assumes power in a military coup. . . . Reports indicate that the Soviet Union is planning to shift 50,000 troops from Eastern Europe to the Soviet-Chinese border.	Israel defeats Egypt, Jordan and Syria in six days of fighting and occupies large portions of their territory. . . . Nigeria's eastern region secedes and declares its independence as the Republic of Biafra. . . . Soviet Union establishes a major presence in the newly independent country of South Yemen.	Bolivian Army crushes a guerrilla movement and kills its prominent communist leader Ernest Ché Guevara.	U.S. increases its bombing of North Vietnam and its troop strength South Vietnam to more than 400,000 men. . . . Communist China successfully tests its first hydrogen bomb. . . . Militant Communist Chinese Red Guards harass foreign diplomatic personnel as the Cultural Revolution continues.
1968	International refief organizations from the West fly in food and medicine to starving Biafrans despite harassment from the Nigerian federal government.	Soviet troops invade Czechoslovakia and crush its refrom movement. . . . Student and worker strikes bring French life to a virtual standstill for a month. . . . France explodes its first thermonuclear device. . . .	Nigerian civil war continues amid reports of wide-spread starvation in the breakaway province of Biafra. . . . Nine Persian Gulf states agree to federate after Britain says that it will withdraw from the area by 1971.	Pierre Elliott Trudeau becomes Canadian Prime Minister. . . .Violent clashes take place between students and federal troops in Mexico City, leaving scores dead.	Communist troops launch the heaviest offensive of the Vietnamese War and hold several major towns for several weeks. . . . North Korea captures the *U.S.S. Pueblo* and holds its crew for about ten months.
1969	International Monetary Fund votes to create special drawing rights to help foster world trade.	Soviet troops reportedly clash with Communist Chinese troops along their border. . . . French Pres. De Gaulle resigns. . . .French voters elect George Pompidou as president. . . . Willy Brandt becomes West Germany's fourth chancellor. . . .	Frequent air attacks and artillery barrages take place between Israel and its Arab neighbors. . . . Libyan military ousts the monarchy and proclaims a republic. . . . Golda Meir becomes Israel's prime minister after the death of P.M. Levi Eshkol.	A border war takes place between Honduras and El Salvador. . . .Venezuela's first peaceful transition of political power occurs when Rafael Rodriguez becomes the country's 43rd president.	Communist Chinese troops reportedly clash with Soviet forces along their border. . . . North Vietnamese leader Ho Chi Minh dies in Hanoi at 79. . . . Pakistani Pres. Mohammad Ayub Khan resigns from office after months of government unrest.
	A	**B**	**C**	**D**	**E**
	Includes developments that affect more than one world region, international organizations and important meetings of major world leaders.	*Includes all domestic and regional developments in Europe, including the Soviet Union, Turkey, Cyprus and Malta.*	*Includes all domestic and regional developments in Africa and the Middle East, including Iraq and Iran and excluding Cyprus, Turkey and Afghanistan.*	*Includes all domestic and regional developments in Latin America, the Caribbean and Canada.*	*Includes all domestic and regional developments in Asia and Pacific nations, extending from Afghanistan through all the Pacific Islands, except Hawaii.*

U.S. Politics & Social Issues	U.S. Foreign Policy & Defense	U.S. Economy & Environment	Science, Technology & Nature	Culture, Leisure & Life Style
Negro college students stage the first sit-in in a variety store in Greensboro, NC. . . . Sen. John Kennedy defeats V.P. Richard Nixon in the presidential election.	U.S. places restrictions on imports and exports from Cuba.	U.S. officials announce that the 1959 balance of payments deficit was a record $3.7 billion.	First U.S. nuclear submarine fires a nuclear missile.	Saint-John Perse wins the 1960 Nobel prize in literature.
Segregationist mobs attack Freedom Riders when they try to integrate Alabama bus stations.	Pres. Kennedy orders major increases in defense spending after an acrimonious summit meeting with Soviet Premier Nikita Khrushchev in Vienna.	U.S. announces the highest unemployment rate since 1941.	Soviet Maj. Yuri Gagarin becomes the first man to successfully orbit the earth. . . . Alan Shepard becomes the first U.S. astronaut to achieve suborbital flight. . . . U.S. and the Soviet Union resume underground nuclear testing.	Pope John calls for the convening of the Church's 21st ecumenical council for 1962.
U.S. marshals escort Negro student James Meredith as he integrates the University of Mississippi.	U.S. lifts its naval blockade of Cuba after the Soviet Union agrees to remove its offensive missiles.	U.S. reports the 1961 balance of payments deficit to be $2.4 billion.	U.S. and the Soviet Union resume nuclear tests in the atmosphere. . . .John Glenn becomes the first U.S. astronaut to orbit the earth.	Pope John opens the Vatican Council in Rome.
A major civil rights march takes place in Washington, D.C. . . . Lee Harvey Oswald assassinates Pres. John Kennedy in Dallas, Tex.	Pres. Lyndon Johnson promises to continue the foreign policy of former Pres. John Kennedy.	Pres. Kennedy submits a federal budget with the largest deficit in history, $10 billion.	National Science Foundation announces a joint U.S.-Soviet project to measure cosmic rays.	Pope John XXIII dies in Rome and is succeeded by Pope Paul VI.
U.S. Senate invokes cloture and passes a major civil rights bill. . . . Summer racial riots rock nine northern cities. . . . Pres. Johnson wins 44 states in a decisive victory over Republican candidate Barry Goldwater.	Congress gives its near unanimous approval for the U.S. bombing of North Vietnam.	U.S. indicts eight steel compaines for price-fixing.	Three Soviet cosmonauts make the world's first multi-seat spacecraft orbit.	Jean Paul Satre wins the 1964 Nobel Prize in Literature.
Pres. Johnson sends Congress a budget containing the biggest expansion of domestic welfare programs since the New Deal. . . .Large-scale rioting leaves 33 dead in the black neighborhoods of Los Angeles.	Pres. Johnson orders daily raids against North Vietnam and doubles the draft; Congress expresses its approval.	Federal Reserve Board defies Pres. Johnson and raises the discount rate to 4.5%.	Mariner 4 photos of Mars depict a desolate planet.	Swiss architect Le Corbusier dies at Cap Matin in France at 77.
Major riots break out among black youths in Los Angeles and other northern cities. . . . Certain Negro Civil rights activists criticize the goal of integration and call for "black power". . . . Republicans make moderate gains in Congressional and gubernatorial races.	Anti-war demonstrations take place in major U.S. cities. . . . Rev. Martin Luther King Jr. calls for a complete pull-out of U.S. troops from south Vietnam.	Labor Secy. William Willard Wirtz announces that unemployment figures are the lowest since 1953. . . . U.S. reports that 1966 is the most inflationary year since 1957.	First man-made object to touch another planet, Soviet satellite Venus 3, crashes into Venus.	Metroplitan Opera opens its first season in the new opera house at Lincoln Center in N.Y.C.
Worst riot in the 20th century breaks out in Detriot. . . . Negroes riot in other major U.S. cities. . . . Sen. Eugene McCarthy (D, Minn.) announces that he will enter five or six Democratic presidential primaries in 1968 in a drive to end the war in Vietnam.	Pres. Johnson meets with Soviet Premier Aleksei Kosygin in Glassboro, N.J. . . . Criticism and doubts about the Vietnamese War continue to grow.	U.S. Commerce Dept. reports that personal income has risen to record levels.	South African surgeons perform the world's first human heart transplant operaton on Louis Washkansky who survives for 18 days.	Two American Univ. professors announce that 700 pages of manuscripts and drawings by Leonardo da Vinci have been found in the Spanish Library in Madrid.
Richard Nixon defeats V.P. Hubert Humphrey in the presidential election. . . . Assassins kill Dr. Martin Luther King Jr. and Sen. Robert Kennedy. . . . Pres.-elect Nixon appoints Professor Henry Kissinger as his national security advisor.	Pres. Johnson announces that he will neither seek nor accept another presidential term. . . . North Vietnam and the U.S. begin public negotiations in Paris.	U.S. officials see no let-up in the continuing American balance-of-payments deficit.	U.S. launches Apollo 7, the spacecraft designed to carry the first Americans to the moon.	U.S. composer George Crumb wins the Pulitzer Prize for music. . . .Knopf publishes John Updike's *Couples* . . . . Lopert Pictures releases Ingmar Bergman's film *Hour of the Wolf* .
Warren Burger becomes the Chief Justice of the U.S. Supreme Court. . . . Supreme Court Justice Abe Fortas resigns because of financial improprieties. . . . Senate rejects Pres. Nixon's Supreme Court nominee Clement Haynsworth. . . .	Pres. Nixon announces three troop withdrawals from South Vietnam totalling 110,000 men. . . . U.S. and the USSR begin arms control talks. . . . U.S. eases curbs on trade with Communist China.	U.S. Federal Reserve announces a rise in its discount rate to six percent, the highest in 40 years.	Two teams of U.S. astronauts land on the moon and walk on its surface.	Vatican proposes closer ties with Jews, including possible joint prayer ceremonies. . . . Samuel Beckett wins the Nobel Prize in literature. . . . Knopf publishes John Cheever's *Bullet Park* .
F	G	H	I	J
Includes elections, federal-state relations, civil rights and liberties, crime, the judiciary, education, health care, poverty, urban affairs and population.	*Includes formation and debate of U.S. foreign and defense policies, veterans' affairs and defense spending. (Relations with specific foreign countries are usually found under the region concerned.)*	*Includes business, labor, agriculture, taxation, transportation, consumer affairs, monetary and fiscal policy, natural resources, and pollution.*	*Includes worldwide scientific, medical and technological developments, natural phenomena, U.S. weather, natural disasters, and accidents.*	*Includes the arts, religion, scholarship, communications media, sports, entertainment, fashions, fads and social life.*

Soviet Premier Nikita Khrushchev makes an angry speech at the U.N. Oct. 11 after the General Assembly defeats his motion to discuss disarmament.

Young negros stage a sit-down at a lunch counter in Greensboro, N.C.

After 11½ years on death row, Caryl Chessman is executed on May 2.

Presidential candidates John F. Kennedy and Richard M. Nixon hold a nationally televised campaign debate on October 7.

The royal wedding party is shown on the balcony of Buckingham Palace after the marriage of Princess Margaret to Antony Armstrong-Jones on May 6.

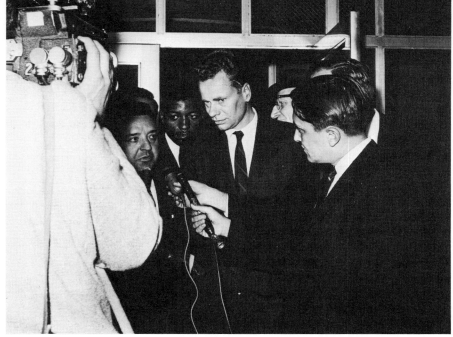

Charles Van Doren outside New York's Criminal Court, after his arraignment Oct. 15 on a perjury charge stemming from his role in fixed television quiz shows.

Simone Signoret and Charleton Heston pose with their Oscars after winning Academy Awards. Signoret won for *Room at the Top,* Heston for *Ben-Hur.*

Australian athlete Herb Elliott sets a new world record as he crosses the finish line to win the 1,500 meter run at the Rome Olympics.

Downed U-2 pilot Francis Gary Powers testifies at his espionage trial in Moscow's Hall of Columns.

French President Charles De Gaulle, British Prime Minister Harold Macmillan and American President Dwight Eisenhower leave the Elysee Palace May 17, following the collapse of the East-West summit Conference.

	World Affairs	Europe	Africa & the Middle East	The Americas	Asia & the Pacific
Jan.	U.S., British and Soviet delegations resume negotiations on a treaty to end nuclear testing.	Cyprus independence talks break up over the size of British military base to remain on the island.	French military officers in Algeria try to wrest political control from government authorities.	Dominican Republic ruler Rafael Trujillo says he has foiled a plot against him.	India and Pakistan announce agreement on the demarcation of their western border.
Feb.	OAS votes to investigate charges of human rights abuses in the Dominican Republic.	France conducts its first nuclear explosion.	French Army quells a revolt of dissident military officers in Algeria.	Cuba signs a major trade agreement with the Soviet Union.	Pakistani voters elect Gen. Mohammad Ayub Khan as president.
March	U.N. Law of the Sea Conference opens in Geneva.	French Pres. de Gaulle rejects the concept of an Algeria ruled only by Frenchmen.	South African police kill more than 50 protesting blacks at Sharpesville.	Venezuela institutes a major agrarian reform program.	Indonesian Pres. Sukarno suspends the Parliament.
April	U.N. calls on South Africa to change its apartheid policy.	Turkey proclaims martial law after student riots break out.	Mali and Senegal conclude independence negotiations with France.	Venezuela puts down a brief military revolt in western Venezuela.	South Korean Pres. Syngman Rhee resigns after violent anti-government demonstrations break out.
May	Summit conference breaks up after Pres. Eisenhower refuses to apologize to the Soviet Union for US reconnaissance flights over Soviet territory.	Soviet Union shoots down a U.S. reconnaissance plane over central Asia. . .Turkish armed forces overthrow Premier Menderes.	Israeli agents kidnap former Gestapo chief Adolf Eichmann in Argentina and smuggle him back to Israel.	Cuba resumes diplomatic relations with the Soviet Union.	Laotian Prince Tiao Somsanith forms a new cabinet.
June	International Commission of Jurists reports that Communist China is trying to destroy the Buddhist religion in Tibet.	France invites Algerian nationalists to begin cease-fire negotiations in France.	Former Belgian Congo (Leopoldville) becomes independent.	Cuba nationalizes a U.S.-owned petroleum refinery after it refuses to process Soviet oil.	Japan cancels Pres. Eisenhower's scheduled visit in the face of widespread anti-U.S. riots.
July	U.N. votes to send troops to the Congo in wake of breakdown in government authority.	France agrees to grant independence to Mauritania, Chad, the French Congo, the Central African Republic and Gabon.	Katanga province declares its independence from the Congo.	Cuba nationalizes the two remaining foreign owned oil refineries in Cuba.	Hayato Ikeda becomes Japanese premier.
Aug.	U.N. calls on Belgium to withdraw its troops from Katanga province in the Congo.	Cyprus becomes independent.	Dahomey becomes independent.	Joaquin Balaguer replaces Pres. Hector Trujillo in the Donimican Republic.	Communist Pathet Lao forces capture the Laotian capital of Vientiane.
Sept.	At the U.N. Soviet Premiur Nikita Khrushchev pounds his desk with his shoe and calls for the ouster of U.N. Secy. Gen. Dag M. Hammarskjold.	France agrees to evacuate its troops from Morocco by 1961.	Congolese Pres. Joseph Kasavubu and Premier Patrice Lumumba issue orders ousting one another.	Ecuador renounces its 1942 border treaty with Peru.	Laotian government declares a state of emergency as Communists push their offensive.
Oct.	U.N. Communist delegates heckle western delegates during debate on the Congo.	France agrees to train German military units on French soil.	Nigeria becomes independent.	Brazilian voters elect Janio da Silva Quadros president.	Laos agrees to accept a Soviet offer of financial aid.
Nov.	International Court of Justice rules that Nicaragua must transfer a piece of disputed border territory to Honduras.	France pledges to grant Algeria complete independence if its citizens vote for it.	Fighting breaks out between U.N. troops and the Congolese army.	Nicaragua repels a guerrilla invasion based in Costa Rica.	Pro-U.S. candidates win elections on the Ryukyu Islands.
Dec.	U.N. calls for the independence of all remaining colonies.	French Pres. de Gaulle's plea for an independent nuclear force becomes law despite disapproval of the French Senate.	Sixty-five die as large-scale rioting by European citizens breaks out in Algiers.	Leftist students surrender the Venezuelan Central University buildings to police.	Laotian Premier Souvanna Phouma flees Vientiane for Cambodia.

A	B	C	D	E
Includes developments that affect more than one world region, international organizations and important meetings of major world leaders.	Includes all domestic and regional developments in Europe, including the Soviet Union, Turkey, Cyprus and Malta.	Includes all domestic and regional developments in Africa and the Middle East, including Iraq and Iran and excluding Cyprus, Turkey and Afghanistan.	Includes all domestic and regional developments in Latin America, the Caribbean and Canada.	Includes all domestic and regional developments in Asia and Pacific nations, extending from Afghanistan through all the Pacific Islands, except Hawaii.

U.S. Politics & Social Issues	U.S. Foreign Policy & Defense	U.S. Economy & Environment	Science, Technology & Nature	Culture, Leisure & Life Style
U.S. Supreme Court rules that military trials for civilian military employees abroad are unconstitutional.	U.S. protests seizure of US property by the Cuban government.	Pres. Eisenhower predicts a budget surplus for fiscal year of more than $4 billion.	Soviet Union claims to have fired a rocket 8,000 miles into the Pacific Ocean.	Associated Press names world heavyweight champion Ingemar Johansson as male athlete of 1959.
Black college students stage the first sit-in in a variety store in Greensboro, N.C.	U.S. says it will cut off military aid to Cuba and the Dominican Republic on June 30, 1960.	Pres. Eisenhower vetos a bill providing funds for a water pollution control program.	Soviet Union claims firing a second multi-stage rocket into the central Pacific Ocean	Winter Olympic games open in Squaw Valley, Calif.
Police arrest hundreds of black protestors as sit-ins spread throughout the South.	Pres. Eisenhower confers with British P.M. Harold Wilson about upcoming negotiations on the suspension of nuclear tests.	U.S. officials announce that the 1959 balance of payments deficit was a record $3.7 billion.	U.S. launches Pioneer 5 into orbit around the sun.	Pope John XXIII names the Roman Catholic Church's first African cardinal.
Race riots break out in Biloxi, Miss. after blacks try to integrate the city's beaches.	U.S. says it has agreed to sell enriched uranium to France.	18th U.S. census begins.	U.S. launches its first weather satellite.	Franch actress Simone Signoret wins the best actress award for 1959.
Nashville, Tenn. lunch counters desegregate without incident.	U.S. announces that it plans to resume underground nuclear testing.	U.S. officials announce that the GNP has passed $1/2 trillion.	Soviet Union launches a satellite containing a model cabin for astronauts.	Princess Margaret Rose, sister of British Queen Elizabeth II, marries Antony Armstrong-Jones.
A U.S. court orders Dallas, Tex. to integrate its public schools.	U.S. Senate Foreign Relations Committee accuses the administration of mishandling the U-2 reconnaissance plane incident.	U.S. Federal Reserve Board authorizes a reduction in the discount rate from 4% to 3.5%.	U.S. launches an advanced weather satellite.	Floyd Patterson knocks out Ingemar Johansson to regain the world heavyweight boxing championship.
Democrats choose Sen. John Kennedy (Mass.) and Republicans choose V.P. Richard Nixon as their presidential nominees.	Pres. Eisenhower virtually halts Cuban sugar sales to the U.S.	U.S. reports a federal budget surplus of $1 billion for the year ending June 30, 1960.	U.S. reports the first firing of a nuclear missile from a submarine.	Pope John XXIII calls for an end to fighting in the Congo.
Senate rejects a medicare plan for the elderly by a 51-44 vote.	U.S. breaks diplomatic relations with the Dominican Republic.	SEC approves the registration of the National Stock Exchange, Inc.	Soviet Union says it has orbited a satellite containing two dogs.	Roman Catholic Church in Cuba voices its concern over the growth of communism there.
V.P. Nixon and Sen. John Kennedy face each other in the first televised presidential debate.	Pres. Eisenhower orders the Panamanian flag to be flown in the Canal Zone along with the U.S. flag.	U.S. restricts export sales to Cuba and the Dominican Republic.	U.S. announces the creation of an agency to coordinate all military and civilian space activities.	1960 Summer Olympics end in Rome with Soviet athletes in first place.
In their second debate, V.P. Nixon says the U.S. should defend the Chinese offshore islands of Quemoy and Matsu while Sen. Kennedy says it probably should not.	U.S. recalls its ambassador to Cuba.	U.S. Federal Reserve Board allows member banks to count cash on hand as part of their reserves.	U.S. says it will definitely resume underground nuclear testing.	Saint-John Perse wins the 1960 Nobel prize in literature.
Sen. John Kennedy wins the 1960 presidential elections.	U.S. launches its first nuclear missile submarine.	Pres. Eisenhower orders all U.S. agencies to cut their spending abroad in order to cut the balance of payments deficit.	U.S. professors Willard Libby and Donald Glaser win the 1960 Nobel prize in chemistry.	Mrs. John Kennedy gives birth to John Fitzgerald Kennedy, Jr.
Supreme Court rules that discrimination in interstate bus terminals is unconstitutional.	U.S. fails to get Canada to join in a trade embargo of Cuba.	U.S. officials report unemployment rate of 6.3%.	Eisenhower administration says that communications satellites should be developed by private industry.	Archbishop of Canterbury Geoffrey Fisher pays a historic call on Pope John in the Vatican.

F	G	H	I	J
Includes elections, federal-state relations, civil rights and liberties, crime, the judiciary, education, health care, poverty, urban affairs and population.	*Includes formation and debate of U.S. foreign and defense policies, veterans' affairs and defense spending. (Relations with specific foreign countries are usually found under the region concerned.)*	*Includes business, labor, agriculture, taxation, transportation, consumer affairs, monetary and fiscal policy, natural resources, and pollution.*	*Includes worldwide scientific, medical and technological developments, natural phenomena, U.S. weather, natural disasters, and accidents.*	*Includes the arts, religion, scholarship, communications media, sports, entertainment, fashions, fads and social life.*

	World Affairs	Europe	Africa & the Middle East	The Americas	Asia & the Pacific
Jan. 1	Soviet Premier Nikita S. Khrushchev reveals the USSR will probably reduce conventional troop levels even if its recent disarmament proposal fails to win Western acceptance, adding that missiles would make up for any future cuts in manpower. . . . A Soviet naval newspaper, *Soviet Fleet*, renews charges of a Dec. 31 South Korean attack upon an unarmed USSR hydrographic vessel, despite official South Korean denials. . . . Prof. Max Huber, International Court of Justice president, 1925-1927, International Red Cross president, 1928-1944, dies at 85 in Zurich.	Bank of France begins circulating new franc, equivalent to 100 old francs or nearly 20¢ (U.S.). The new currency realigns the franc with other European coins of similar valuation.	Premier Ahmadou Ahidjo formally proclaims Cameroon an independent state, ending 50 years of French-administered trusteeship.		Indonesia begins enforcement of a decree barring all resident aliens, principally Chinese from trading in rural areas and designated Indonesian cities.
Jan. 2	Cuban State Min. Raul Roa leaves for Middle and Far East to prepare for a mid-1960 conference of "third power bloc" nations, proposed originally by Maj. Ernesto Guevara, president of the National Bank of Cuba.	Eighty members of the newly-formed Direct Action Committee against Nuclear War are arrested while trying to halt traffic into an RAF Thor missile site near Harrington, England.		Cuban government seizes 57 of Cuba's largest trucking firms for allegedly conspiring to consolidate all Cuban trucking. . . . Paul Sauvé, Premier of Quebec Province since Sept. 1959, dies of a heart attack at 52.	
Jan. 3	In a recorded Moscow radio broadcast, Khrushchev pledges not to resume atomic tests unless Western powers do so first, and reaffirms Soviet readiness to conclude a test-ban agreement.		Iranian government claims sovereignty over ½ of the Shatt al Arab River dividing Iran and Iraq in an apparent renunciation of a 1937 agreement giving Iraq full control of the river. . . . An Israeli government directive officially defines a "Jew" (for religious registration purposes) as "a person born of a Jewish mother who does not belong to another religion or one who was converted (to Judaism) in accordance with Jewish law", overturning an earlier directive that allowed any Israeli to register as a Jew.		A Laotian army communique reports military commanders have assumed temporary control of the Laotian government pending the formation of a new cabinet to replace that of ousted Premier Phoui Sananikone.
Jan. 4	New Year's messages exchanged by Khrushchev and Eisenhower are made public: Soviet and U.S. hopes for disarmament and peace in 1960.	Cabinet ministers from the European "outer seven" nations (Austria, Britain, Denmark, Norway, Portugal, Sweden and Switzerland) conclude a convention establishing a European Free Trade Association similar in purpose to the six-nation European Economic Community (Common Market). . . . Sources in West Germany, Western Europe, Britain and the U.S. report a continuing flurry of anti-Jewish incidents in the wake of the December 25th desecration of a Cologne synagogue.	An International Red Cross Committee reports some improvements in French prison camps for Algerian rebels but charges that torture and brutality are still common. French newspapers carrying the report are banned from Algeria. . . . Liberian Pres. William V.S. Tubman begins a four-year term.		P.M. Nehru predicts early settlement of Indian-Pakistani disputes over eastern borders and the division of the Indus River waters, but sees no compromise on Kashmir until Pakistan withdraws its troops from disputed territory. . . . Nehru refuses comment on a New Delhi report that Chinese Communists recently had increased, from 40,000 to 48,000 square miles, the extent of Indian territory claimed by China.
Jan. 5		West German Chancellor Konrad Adenauer assures German Jewish leaders that "wire-pullers" behind recent anti-Semitic acts will be punished. . . . Spanish Civil Guards trap and kill Catalan anarchist Francisco Sabater, 47, believed to be the last of the guerilla leaders who continued to resist the Franco regime after the end of the Spanish Civil War in 1939.	British Prime Minister Harold Macmillan begins an 18,000-mile, good-will tour through British Africa.		

A	B	C	D	E
Includes developments that affect more than one world region, international organizations and important meetings of major world leaders.	*Includes all domestic and regional developments in Europe, including the Soviet Union, Turkey, Cyprus and Malta.*	*Includes all domestic and regional developments in Africa and the Middle East, including Iraq and Iran and excluding Cyprus, Turkey and Afghanistan.*	*Includes all domestic and regional developments in Latin America, the Caribbean and Canada.*	*Includes all domestic and regional developments in Asia and Pacific nations, extending from Afghanistan through all the Pacific Islands, except Hawaii.*

U.S. Politics & Social Issues	U.S. Foreign Policy & Defense	U.S. Economy & Environment	Science, Technology & Nature	Culture, Leisure & Life Style	
	Gen. David M. Shoup, 55, W.W. II Medal of Honor winner, is named U.S. Marine Corps commandant, succeeding retired Gen. Randloph McC(all) Pate.			Washington Univ. defeats Wisconsin, 44 to 8, in the Rose Bowl.	**Jan. 1**
Sen. John F. Kennedy (Mass.), 42, announces his candidacy for the Democratic Presidential nomination, making him the first serious Catholic contender for the office since Alfred E. Smith in 1928. Sen. Hubert Humphrey (Minn.) is the only other announced Democratic candidate to date. . . . Pres. Dwight D. Eisenhower proclaims May 1 as Law Day and calls for ceremonies demonstrating "devotion to the rule of law."		Dr. John H. Talbott, editor of the *Journal of the American Medical Association*, charges that government warnings on tainted cranberries have caused "undue" public alarm, adding that food laws are sometimes "too categorical" in banning the use of chemicals. . . . Eight striking members of the United Packinghouse Workers are fined $100 for violence against nonstrikers at Wilson & Co.'s Albert Lea, Minn. packing plant during December.	Dr. John H. Reynolds of the Univ. of California estimates the age of the solar system at 4,950,000 years based on the study of a meteorite that fell in North Dakota 41 years ago.	Federal Trade Commission issues complaints against seven record Companies and eight distributing firms charging them with payment of "payola" to disc jockeys for airing certain records. . . . Oscar Wilde's last and long-withheld manuscript, De Profundis, written in 1896, is made public at the British Museum. . . . Bobby Fischer, 16, of Brooklyn, retains U.S. chess championship in a tournament in New York.	**Jan. 2**
Richard E. Hickock, 28, confesses that he and Perry E. Smith, 31, murdered Herbert V. Clutter and his family in their rural Garden City, Kan. home.	A study by the Senate Government Operations Sub-Committee, headed by Henry M. Jackson (D., Wash.), concludes that Mao Tse-tung and other Communist party leaders have transformed Red China "from a prostrate colossus to a giant on the march in 10 short years."		American Airlines Boeing 707 sets new Los Angeles-New York Commercial speed record of three hrs., 52 min.		**Jan. 3**
Roy Wilkins tells the annual meeting of the NAACP that Democratic Senate Majority Leader Lyndon Johnson (Tex.) would gain little Negro or Northern support in a bid for the Democratic Presidential nomination. . . . Atlanta Board of Education, complying with U.S. District Court rulings, amends its school integration plan to speed handling of transfer applications and to prohibit barring a pupil from a school because of fear of "economic retaliation."	U.S. Air Force issues a training manual linking the Natl. Council of Churches to Communism and labelling the idea that Americans "have a right to know what's going on" as a "foolish remark." . . . *The Uncertain Trumpet* by former Army Chief of Staff Gen. Maxwell Taylor is published. The book warns U.S. military strength is declining below safe levels.	United Steelworkers of America and 11 major steel companies reach agreement on a new two-and-a-half year contract. The settlement, coming near the end of the 80-day Taft-Hartley injunction that halted a 116-day nationwide strike, provides for a 14¢ hourly wage increase over two years and increased medical, pension and unemployment benefits. . . . National Airlines DC-6B crashes near Bolivia, N.C. All 34 passengers and crewmen are killed.		Albert Camus, 46, Algerian-born French novelist ("The stranger", "The Fall"), playwright ("Caligula") and Nobel Prize winner (1957) is killed in auto accident near Villeneuve-Guyard, France.	**Jan. 4**
Special Advisory Committee on Child Welfare publishes a report urging Congress to authorize research into the causes of family instability. It recommends the federal government share the costs of child welfare services with the states. . . . Norris Brown, 96, U.S. Senator (R, Neb.) 1907-1913, who introduced the 16th Amendment (income tax) dies in Seattle.		U.S. Census estimates value of new construction in 1959 at $54.3 billion, a one-year record and 11% increase over 1958. . . . American Motors Corp. discloses that Pres. George Romney in effect denied himself a $100,000 bonus placing by a $225,000 ceiling on company salaries.	Sloan-Kettering Institute reports the first long-term control of cancer through treatment with several simultaneously administered drugs in a two-year old research project pioneered by the National Cancer Institute. . . . The New York Times reports budget restrictions and rising costs are delaying U.S. programs for manned space flight. The U.S. still hopes to put a man in space by 1961, but more advanced projects such as the two-man space lab may be delayed by at least a year.		**Jan. 5**

F	G	H	I	J
Includes elections, federal-state relations, civil rights and liberties, crime, the judiciary, education, health care, poverty, urban affairs and population.	*Includes formation and debate of U.S. foreign and defense policies, veterans' affairs and defense spending. (Relations with specific foreign countries are usually found under the region concerned.)*	*Includes business, labor, agriculture, taxation, transportation, consumer affairs, monetary and fiscal policy, natural resources, and pollution.*	*Includes worldwide scientific, medical and technological developments, natural phenomena, U.S. weather, natural disasters, and accidents.*	*Includes the arts, religion, scholarship, communications media, sports, entertainment, fashions, fads and social life.*

	World Affairs	Europe	Africa & the Middle East	The Americas	Asia & the Pacific
Jan. 6		West German cabinet approves a new law establishing punishment and fines for incitement against a religious or racial group following a week of anti-Semitic incidents. . . . Britain's Campaign for Nuclear Disarmament appeals to the U.S. to resume its moratorium on nuclear testing.		Cuban government expropriates 70,000 acres of farm land belonging to the U.S.-owned Manati Sugar Co.	Iraqi Premier Abdul Karim el Kassem's cabinet lifts five-year old ban on political parties, permitting the reestablishment of certain regulated, non-Western-oriented parties by government license.
Jan. 7	Soviet Union announces plans to test booster rockets over the central Pacific about 1100 miles southwest of Hawaii during late January and February.	West Berlin Parliament adopts a resolution condemning recent anti-Jewish acts and urging a ban on all neo-Nazi organizations.		Jorge Zayas, editor of the Havana newspaper *Avance*, editorializes against the Castro government's definition of freedom of the press, claiming that "in Cuba you can think like the leader or you can be labeled a counter-revolutionary."	Kou Abhay, 70, is appointed provisional premier of Laos by King Savang Vathana. The Kou cabinet, which is charged with returning Laos to civilian rule, is believed to represent a compromise between rival political factions headed by ex-Premier Phoui Sananikone and Brig. Gen. Phoumi Nosavan.
Jan. 8			Iraqi Premier Abdul Karim el-Kassem publicly appeals to the Syrian people to free themselves from the "despotic injustice" allegedly suffered under the Egyptian-dominated United Arab Republic.		
Jan. 9	Ex-Pres. Harry Truman labels Soviet intentions to use the central Pacific for rocket tests as "an act of provocation".		Egyptian Pres. Gamal Nasser formally inaugurates construction on the Soviet-funded Aswan High Dam Project on the Nile River.		
Jan. 10	Japanese Premier Nobusuke Kishi proposes that the U.S. look into Russia's Pacific test plans, adding that the tests might hamper Japanese fishing.	Pres. Tito of Yugoslavia decorates 109 Orthodox, Roman Catholic and Moslem priests for their "services to the state." It is the first time Yugoslav religious leaders have been officially honored since W.W.II. . . . Central Committee of the Soviet issues a formal directive instructing party propagandists to improve and intensify their explanation of Communist policies and goals in order to deepen the belief in the party's cause among ordinary Soviet citizens.	Chief Counsel of the American NAACP, Thurgood Marshall, arrives in Nairobi, Kenya to advise African representatives scheduled to attend a Kenya constitutional conference scheduled for Jan. 18 in London. . . . At a state dinner for visiting P.M. Macmillan, Ghana's P.M. Kwame Nkrumah urges Britain to join with Ghana in supporting the liberation of African states still under colonial control.	Dr. Harold L. Geisart of George Washington Univ. reports that Central America leads the world in rate of population growth, averaging an increase of one million persons annually. Geisart predicts a Central American population of 150 million by the year 2000.	North Vietnamese Pres. Ho Chi Minh welcomes the return of the first of some 70,000 North Vietnamese expatriates who had fled to Thailand during the French-Communist War in Indochina. . . . Indian Congress Party member Damodaram Sanjivayya is elected chief minister of Andhra State, becoming the first untouchable ever to achieve a state premiership.
Jan. 11	After a seven-year lapse, the USSR and U.S. resume negotiations over settlement of the Soviet lend-lease debt to the U.S.	West German Chancellor Konrad Adenauer tells the West Berlin Parliament that the "legal status of West Berlin must not be touched upon" at the upcoming summit negotiations with the Soviets. . . . Despite vigorous denunciations by government officials, anti-Semitic acts continue to spread in West Berlin, West Germany and other European countries. The West German Interior Ministry reports that 120 anti-Jewish incidents have occurred in West Germany alone since Dec. 25, 1959.		Cuban government formally rejects a U.S. note protesting the seizure of American-owned property in Cuba.	India and Pakistan announce an agreement for delineating the borders between India and West Pakistan and for preventing border clashes.

A	B	C	D	E
Includes developments that affect more than one world region, international organizations and important meetings of major world leaders.	*Includes all domestic and regional developments in Europe, including the Soviet Union, Turkey, Cyprus and Malta.*	*Includes all domestic and regional developments in Africa and the Middle East, including Iraq and Iran and excluding Cyprus, Turkey and Afghanistan.*	*Includes all domestic and regional developments in Latin America, the Caribbean and Canada.*	*Includes all domestic and regional developments in Asia and Pacific nations, extending from Afghanistan through all the Pacific Islands, except Hawaii.*

U.S. Politics & Social Issues	U.S. Foreign Policy & Defense	U.S. Economy & Environment	Science, Technology & Nature	Culture, Leisure & Life Style	
Eighty-sixth Congress convenes second session with Democrats controlling both houses for sixth straight year. . . . House Speaker Sam Rayburn (D, Tex.) urges support of discharge petition to force controversial civil rights bill from Rules Committee to the House floor. . . . U.S. District Court Judge Boyd Sloan issues order instructing Dobbs Houses, Inc. to end the discriminatory seating of Negroes at its Atlanta airport restaurant.	White House announces Pres. Eisenhower will leave Feb. 23 on a two-week good-will tour of Latin America with scheduled stops in Brazil, Argentina, Chile and Uruguay. . . . White House announces French Pres. Charles DeGaulle will travel to U.S. April 22 for three days of talks with Eisenhower. . . . Defense Secy. Thomas Gates Jr. is reported to have told the Joint Chiefs of Staff that he will break future deadlocks among the Joint Chiefs.	Controller Gen. Joseph Campbell reports to Congress serious abuses in soil bank program, including unwarranted annual payments in excess of $54 million. . . . Civil Aeronautics Board reports that 257 passengers and 37 crewmen were killed in U.S. airline crashes in 1959.		NCAA suspends Univ. of Oklahoma indefinitely for failure to disclose football-player recruiting fund records. . . . Broadway showman Billy Rose announces donation of his modern sculpture collection to Israel's new National Museum in Jerusalem. . . . Heavyweight boxing champion Ingemar Johansson of Sweden and Wimbledon tennis champion Maria Esther Bueno of Brazil are named the Outstanding Athletes of 1959 by the AP.	**Jan. 6**
Pres. Eisenhower, in his State of the Union message, asks Congress to consider seriously the Administration-sponsored voting rights bill and other recommendations of the Civil Rights Commission. . . . Rep. Richard M. Simpson (R, Pa.), ranking Republican member of the House Ways and Means Committee and long-time foe of federal spending, dies in Bethesda, Md. at the age of 59.	Noting in his State-of-the-Union address that recent Soviet behavior indicated a lessening of East-West tensions, Eisenhower declares "dependable agreements" must replace force in the settlement of international disputes.	In his State-of-the-Union address, Eisenhower forecasts a budget surplus of $200 million for fiscal 1960 and $4.2 billion for fiscal 1961. The surplus budgets are part of the Administration's program to counter rising inflation. . . . New violence is reported against nonstrikers in Albert Lea, Minn. after Gov. Orville Freeman (D) withdraws National Guard units maintaining order at the Wilson & Co. packing plant.	In his State-of-the-Union message, Pres. Eisenhower reports that expenditures for space exploration will be "practically doubled" in the next fiscal year.". . . . The bathysphere *Trieste*, with Lt. Donald Walsh and Jacques Piccard aboard, sets new world ocean-diving record of 24,000 feet in the Pacific Marianas Trench near Guam.	Sid Gillman, former coach of the Los Angeles Rams, is named head coach of the L.A. Chargers of the projected American Football League.	**Jan. 7**
Dr. George E. Haynes, 79, the first Negro to receive a Ph.D. from Columbia Univ. and the co-founder of the National Urban League (1910), dies in Brooklyn. . . . *The New York Times* reports that a recent TV film in which Sen. Wayne Morse (D, Ore.) attacks Presidential candidate John Kennedy (D, Mass.) as an enemy of labor has become widely circulated among labor organizations.				Gillette Razor Co. announces NBC has decided to drop the popular Gillette-sponsored *Friday Night Fights* this coming September. The NBC decision comes in the wake of recent disclosures of racketeer involvement in boxing and corruption in the TV industry.	**Jan. 8**
Ex-Gov. Jimmie H. Davis wins Louisiana's Democratic gubernatorial primary following a campaign in which he pledged to prevent the racial integration of the state's public schools. . . . Leaders of the American Protestant Episcopal Church endorse "morally-acceptable" forms of birth control in countries where population growth is threatening "the survival of old and young."		Teamsters Pres. James R. Hoffa confirms that ex-Sen. George H. Bender (R, O.) has resigned as Chairman of the union's Hoffa-appointed anti-crime "commission", becoming the third member to quit since 1959.		Ford Foundation reports that it contributed almost $120 million to educational and cultural projects during 1959. . . . French publisher Michel Gallimard, 42, dies in Paris of injuries suffered in the auto accident that killed Albert Camus.	**Jan. 9**
	U.S. Army Secy. Wilber M. Brucker, while visiting Taiwan, formally pledges that the U.S. will defend the Nationalist-held islands of Quemoy and Matsu from a Communist Chinese attack. . . . Senate Democratic whip Mike Mansfield (Mont.) urges State Secy. Herter to protest Russian plans to use the Pacific as a testing site, adding that the agreement for a spring summit meeting ought to be reconsidered if the Soviets fail to respond.	Sens. John Marshall Butler (R, Md.) and J. William Fulbright (D, Ark.) charge White House aides forced an inflationary settlement in the steel industry.		Delmore Schwartz, New York writer and critic, is named recipient of Yale Univ. Library's Bollinger Poetry Prize for his book *Summer Knowledge*. . . . Norman Podhoretz, 30, is named editor of the American Jewish Committee's magazine *Commentary*, succeeding the late Elliot Cohen.	**Jan. 10**
Gov. S. Ernest Vandiver tells the Georgia legislature that he will deny funds to any state school that desegregates. . . . U.S. District Judge J. Skelly Wright orders Washington Parish, La. officials to restore to the voting lists the names of 1377 Negroes removed because of technical challenges by members of the local Citizens Council.	Gen. Thomas D. White, Air Force Chief of Staff, and a number of Democratic Senators sharply criticize the Eisenhower Administration's decision to cut back development of the B-70, a long-range bomber designed to replace the B-52. . . . Thomas S. Gates, Jr. is nominated to be Defense Secretary by Pres. Eisenhower.	AFL-CIO Pres. George Meany publicly defends the labor record of Democratic presidential candidate John Kennedy, noting that Kennedy "worked tirelessly" to revise the controversial 1959 labor reform bill in the interest of American workers. . . . Commerce Secy. Frederick H. Mueller reports retail sales in the U.S. in 1959 increased 8% over 1958.		Tommy Manville, 65, asbestos heir, weds Christina Erdlen, 20, in New York (his 13th marriage and 11th wife).	**Jan. 11**

F	G	H	I	J
Includes elections, federal-state relations, civil rights and liberties, crime, the judiciary, education, health care, poverty, urban affairs and population.	*Includes formation and debate of U.S. foreign and defense policies, veterans' affairs and defense spending. (Relations with specific foreign countries are usually found under the region concerned.)*	*Includes business, labor, agriculture, taxation, transportation, consumer affairs, monetary and fiscal policy, natural resources, and pollution.*	*Includes worldwide scientific, medical and technological developments, natural phenomena, U.S. weather, natural disasters, and accidents.*	*Includes the arts, religion, scholarship, communications media, sports, entertainment, fashions, fads and social life.*

	World Affairs	Europe	Africa & the Middle East	The Americas	Asia & the Pacific
Jan. 12	Soviet, British and American delegates resume nuclear test-ban talks in Geneva, but observers see little chance for a quick settlement of the inspection and enforcement problems that have deadlocked the talks for 14 months.	East German CP Politburo reports the country's industrial production rose by nearly 12% during 1959.	The state of emergency imposed in Kenya during the Mau Mau uprisings of October 1952 is officially ended by Gov. Patrick Renison. The action abolishes almost all the martial law restrictions that had been placed on the African population.		Japanese Premier Kishi's cabinet announces the adoption of a liberalized trade program, easing import restrictions on goods from the U.S. and other foreign countries.
Jan. 13	A 13-nation Special Economic Committee consisting of the U.S., Canada and 11 West European nations completes meetings in Paris after agreeing on steps to improve Western economic cooperation and increase aid to underdeveloped nations.	USSR Ministry of Internal Affairs (MVD) is abolished by order of the Supreme Soviet Presidium. The police and internal security responsibilities of the MVD which have not already been taken over by the State Security Committee (KGB) will be given to the internal affairs ministries of the 15 Soviet republics. . . . French Finance Minister and leader of the conservative Independent Party, Antoine Pinay, resigns from Premier Michel Debré's cabinet after policy disagreements with Pres. Charles de Gaulle.	British Labor Party proposes a month-long boycott of all South African goods to protest that country's race policies. . . . Nigerian P.M. Abubaker Tafawa Balewa declares his country will not surrender its anticipated independence to the African Union proposed by Kwame Nkrumah of Ghana.		Indonesian Pres. Sukarno promulgates decrees giving himself the power to abolish opposition parties and to direct the political mobilization of the Indonesian people.
Jan. 14	Soviet Premier Khrushchev indicates that disarmament, a treaty with Germany, the formation of a free city in West Berlin, and a nuclear test ban are the major issues the Soviets wish to discuss with the Western leaders at the upcoming summit. . . . U.S., Canada and 18 member nations of the Organization for European Economic Cooperation agree in Paris to begin work on creating a new 20-nation Atlantic trade group.	Soviet Premier Khrushchev's annual address to the Supreme Soviet highlights economic progress made in 1959 including an 11% increase in industrial production and a 10% rise in the output of consumer goods. . . . British Board of Trade statistics released today indicate that exports for 1959 reached an all-time high of $9.3 billion. Import totals were estimated at just under $11.2 billion. . . . Premiers of West Germany's 10 states agree to support strong police and court action against anti-Jewish vandals.			N. Sanjeeva Reddy is inaugurated as President of India's Congress Party, succeeding Mrs. Indira Gandhi.
Jan. 15	U.S., USSR, and other countries reach preliminary agreements on a cooperative project for tracking space vehicles at an international Space Science Symposium in France.	USSR's Supreme Soviet unanimously approves Premier Khrushchev's proposal to reduce Soviet troop strength by 1.2 million men. The reduction is thought to be a result of a growing Soviet confidence in its nuclear and missile capabilities.			South Vietnamese Pres. Ngo Dinh Diem arrives in Taipei for 4 days of talks with Nationalist Chinese Pres. Chiang Kai-shek. . . . Indian P.M. Jawalharlal Nehru defends his country's continuing refusal to join in military alliances despite recent alleged Communist Chinese incursions into Indian territory, claiming that India's influence in the world depends on maintenance of its non-alignment policy.
Jan. 16		In a TV address to the West German people, Chancellor Adenauer calls upon them to give a "good thrashing" on the spot to any "lout" caught committing an anti-Semitic act. . . . Tass reports Soviet CP Presidium members Alexei Kirichenko and Nikolai Belyayev have both been reassigned to new party posts. Both transfers are believed to be demotions.	A formal request for Queen Elizabeth to grant Nigeria its independence as scheduled Oct. 1, 1960 is approved by the Nigerian Federal Parliament. The action comes in the midst of British P.M. Macmillan's official visit to Nigeria.		Tokyo police clash with thousands of leftist students protesting the Kishi cabinet's decision to sign a new mutual defense pact with the U.S. . . . The Japanese Finance Ministry announces exports rose 20.2% in 1959 to a new post-war peak of over $3.4 billion.
Jan. 17	American and Soviet officials announce Pres. Eisenhower will visit the USSR June 10 to 19. The trip is to return the visit of Premier Khrushchev, who toured the U.S. in September 1959.	Thousands of British Jews and non-Jews conduct a silent march past the West German embassy in London to protest the recent anti-Semitic outbreaks.	Jordan's King Hussein criticizes his fellow Arab leaders for failing to take a responsible approach to the Palestinian refugee problem.		India's ruling Congress Party concludes its 65th annual convention after endorsing the policy of non-alignment and pledging support for the African and Algerian nationalist movements. . . . Gen. Wei Li-Huang, 64, one of 13 deputy chairmen of Communist China's defense council, dies in Peking. A former Nationalist leader, he defected from Taiwan in 1955.

A	B	C	D	E
Includes developments that affect more than one world region, international organizations and important meetings of major world leaders.	Includes all domestic and regional developments in Europe, including the Soviet Union, Turkey, Cyprus and Malta.	Includes all domestic and regional developments in Africa and the Middle East, including Iraq and Iran and excluding Cyprus, Turkey and Afghanistan.	Includes all domestic and regional developments in Latin America, the Caribbean and Canada.	Includes all domestic and regional developments in Asia and Pacific nations, extending from Afghanistan through all the Pacific Islands, except Hawaii.

U.S. Politics & Social Issues	U.S. Foreign Policy & Defense	U.S. Economy & Environment	Science, Technology & Nature	Culture, Leisure & Life Style	
Senate Democratic Party liberals fail in a caucus vote to take away majority leader Lyndon B. Johnson's (Tex.) power of appointment over the party's policy committee. Liberals had accused Johnson of too often compromising with the Eisenhower Administration. . . . In the wake of several anti-Jewish incidents in American cities, Pres. Eisenhower informs the National Conference of Christians and Jews that the U.S. will not allow bigotry to "spread one inch.". . . . Atty. Gen. William P. Rogers appears personally to ask the Supreme Court to reverse a district court ruling that declared the voting portions of the 1957 Civil Rights Act unconstitutional.	Senate Foreign Relations Committee releases a report prepared by the Brookings Institute calling for the replacement of the State Department with a three-unit Foreign Affairs Department to handle (1) foreign political affairs, (2) foreign economic activities and (3) cultural affairs. The report also recommends the creation of a national security office in the White House.	FAA announces a $118 million program to increase air safety by upgrading air traffic control through improved radar equipment.	HEW Secy. Arthur S. Flemming announces the Public Health Service will begin publishing "raw data" on radiation levels March 1 and begin testing radiation levels in all 60 U.S. milkshed areas July 1. . . . General Electric Co. demonstrates a new thermoplastic tape capable of recording both visual images and sound simultaneously.	Princeton Univ. informs Asst. Prof. Otto Butz, 36, that he will be dropped from the faculty for his role in editing *The Unsilent Generation*, a book of essays that displeased faculty members because of passages dealing with drinking and sex. . . . Golfer Dow Finsterwald wins $5,500 first prize in the Los Angeles Open. . . . Nevil Shute, 60, English novelist (*On the Beach*) and inventor, dies in Australia.	Jan. 12
Pres. Eisenhower tells reporters a recent Civil Rights Commission proposal to authorize the President to appoint federal voting registrars for Southern states may be unconstitutional.		AFL-CIO adopts a legislative program calling for an increase in the minimum wage to $1.25 an hour, federal aid to depressed areas, equal rights for minorities, federal aid to education, tax reform and a low-cost housing program. . . . Pres. Eisenhower renews an appeal to Congress to lift the 4.5% ceiling on government bonds, claiming that the present limit hampers sound debt management.	Dr. Edward Weiss, pioneer in the field of psychosomatic medicine, dies of a heart attack in Philadelphia at the age of 64.		Jan. 13
Criticizing Pres. Eisenhower as a "weak" leader, Democratic hopeful Sen. John Kennedy promises to provide strong Presidential leadership in the tradition of Lincoln, Roosevelt, and Truman. . . . A special U.S. grand jury in Biloxi, Miss. reports it has insufficient evidence to warrant indictments against anyone in the April 1959 lynching of Mack Charles Parker.		Long-time labor leader John L. Lewis formally resigns as president of the United Mine Workers. Ex-UMW V.P. Thomas Kennedy succeeds Lewis and former Lewis aide W. (Tony) Boyle is named vice-president. . . . FAA official tells a Senate committee that N.Y. attorney Julian Andrew Frank might have exploded a bomb that caused the death of himself and 33 others in the crash of a National Airlines plane near Bolivia, N.C. Frank reportedly had previously insured his life for nearly $1 million.	Pres. Eisenhower indicates that greatly increased funding and effort will be spent during 1960 and 1961 for U.S. efforts to develop "super-booster" space rockets.	Pres. Eisenhower is considered the world's "outstanding personality" of the 1950s, according to a Gallup Poll survey conducted in the U.S. and 10 other Western countries.	Jan. 14
Three Queens (N.Y.) youths are arrested and charged with treason for allegedly forming a Nazi-type group and for conspiring to attack Jews in the neighboring Fresh Meadows area. The N.Y. state treason statute carries a mandatory death sentence.			Ski-equipped Air Force planes from Fairbanks, Alaska rescue the last of a team of American scientists trapped on a disintegrating ice floe near Point Barrow.		Jan. 15
At a Republican rally in Miami, V.P. Nixon disputes Kennedy's characterization of Eisenhower as a "weak" leader, claiming that Kennedy sees the Presidency "too much in terms of personality."	A report prepared for the Senate Foreign Relations Committee by the Harvard Center for International Affairs warns against basing American policy on the assumption that Soviet totalitarianism is about to erode under rising living conditions.	Anthony Provenzano, a Hoffa supporter currently facing bribery charges, is re-elected president of the Hoboken (N.J.) local of the International Teamsters, defeating an anti-Hoffa slate led by Thomas O'Hara.	American scientists bounce a radio signal off a huge aluminized balloon floating 250 miles in space, marking the first successful use of a man-made space reflector to maintain a continuous radio signal.		Jan. 16
				Frederick S. Pearson 2nd, 47, humorist and former managing editor of Country Life, dies in New York.	Jan. 17

F	G	H	I	J
Includes elections, federal-state relations, civil rights and liberties, crime, the judiciary, education, health care, poverty, urban affairs and population.	Includes formation and debate of U.S. foreign and defense policies, veterans' affairs and defense spending. (Relations with specific foreign countries are usually found under the region concerned.)	Includes business, labor, agriculture, taxation, transportation, consumer affairs, monetary and fiscal policy, natural resources, and pollution.	Includes worldwide scientific, medical and technological developments, natural phenomena, U.S. weather, natural disasters, and accidents.	Includes the arts, religion, scholarship, communications media, sports, entertainment, fashions, fads and social life.

	World Affairs	Europe	Africa & the Middle East	The Americas	Asia & the Pacific
Jan. 18	A strong condemnation of the recent anti-Semitic wave from Pope John XXIII is reported by Jewish leaders who visited the Vatican this week.	Opposition by Greek Cypriot leader Archbishop Makarios, to Britain's plan to retain sovereignty over military enclaves leads to the suspension of a London conference on the implementation of the 1959 Cyprus independence accords. The deadlock is expected to delay Cypriot independence, scheduled for Feb. 19, at least a month.	European and African residents of Southern Rhodesia clash at Salisbury airport while awaiting the arrival of visiting British P.M. Macmillan. The fighting begins when Europeans tear down African banners appealing to Britain to refuse Rhodesia dominion status and to keep its right to veto legislation affecting Africans. . . . European and African Kenyan leaders begin talks in London on the revision of Kenya's constitutional status. . . . French Pres. de Gaulle meets with Mali Federation leaders from Sudan and Senegal to discuss ground-rules for future negotiations over independence.	Over 100 persons are arrested in Venezuela in connection with an alleged plot to overthrow the Betancourt government. . . . Canadian P.M. John Diefenbaker calls for the amendment of the British North American Act (Canada's constitution) to broaden Canada's power to amend its constitution without the sanction of the British Parliament.	
Jan. 19	U.S. State Dept. responds negatively to a Soviet challenge to follow the USSR's example in reducing troop strength, contending that any genuine disarmament negotiation must await the 10-nation disarmament conference scheduled for Geneva on March 15. . . . U.S. and Japan conclude a new mutual security treaty that returns full sovereignty to Japan in defense matters and makes both countries equal partners in a defensive alliance designed to maintain security in the Far East. The pact supersedes a 1951 treaty that had given the U.S. primary responsibility for the defense of Japan.		French Pres. de Gaulle's liberal self-determination plan for Algeria is openly challenged by a meeting of Algiers region mayors. The criticism comes one day after Brig. Gen. Jacques Massu, Commander of the Algiers region, publicly hinted that the army might not accept de Gaulle's program. . . . The rebel Algerian Provisional Government announces in Tunis a reorganization of its ruling cabinet; Premier Ferhat Abbas is retained, but extremists, both Communist and pan-Arab, are replaced by moderates more inclined to negotiate with France. . . . Macmillan tells a Salisbury meeting that the Rhodesian federation will not be granted dominion status until both Europeans and Africans express support for full independence.		
Jan. 20		USSR launches the first of a series of controversial rocket test shots targeted for the central Pacific. Tass reports the missile fell within the designated impact area.	After meeting with de Gaulle, French Premier Michel Debré's cabinet reaffirms its intention to carry out a liberal policy toward Algeria, despite rightist opposition. . . . Round-table talks on the Congo's political future are convened in Brussels. . . . South African P.M. Hendrik Verwoerd announces he will submit legislation for a plebiscite on the transformation of the country into a republic.	Castro charges in an interview that U.S. Amb. Philip W. Bonsal and Spanish Amb. Juan Pablo de Lojendio conspired with Cuban counter-revolutionaries against his regime.	White House announces that Pres. Eisenhower will stop for talks in Japan on his way home from a visit to the Soviet Union scheduled for mid-June. . . . Soviet Pres. Kliment Y. Voroshilov arrives in New Delhi to begin an 18-day visit to India and Nepal.
Jan. 21		Soviet Central Statistical Board reports industrial production in the USSR increased by 11% in 1959; grain output, however, fell by almost 13%.	African residents of Northern Rhodesia protest alleged domination by white settlers and plans for federation with Southern Rhodesia during an official visit by British P.M. Macmillan.	U.S. Amb. Bonsal is recalled to Washington from Cuba for special consultations following a series of vehemently anti-American speeches by Premier Castro in which he charged the U.S. with encouraging counter-revolutionary elements in Cuba.	
Jan. 22			Gen. Massu is fired as commander of the Algiers region following his public criticism of official French policy toward Algeria.		New China news agency reports Communist Chinese industry and agriculture surpassed their 1959 production targets and fulfilled the output objectives of the 5-year plan.

A	B	C	D	E
Includes developments that affect more than one world region, international organizations and important meetings of major world leaders.	*Includes all domestic and regional developments in Europe, including the Soviet Union, Turkey, Cyprus and Malta.*	*Includes all domestic and regional developments in Africa and the Middle East, including Iraq and Iran and excluding Cyprus, Turkey and Afghanistan.*	*Includes all domestic and regional developments in Latin America, the Caribbean and Canada.*	*Includes all domestic and regional developments in Asia and Pacific nations, extending from Afghanistan through all the Pacific Islands, except Hawaii.*

ROCK SPRINGS PUBLIC LIBRARY
Sweetwater County Branch
Rock Springs, Wyoming

U.S. Politics & Social Issues	U.S. Foreign Policy & Defense	U.S. Economy & Environment	Science, Technology & Nature	Culture, Leisure & Life Style	
Sen. Hubert H. Humphrey (D, Minn.) opens his Wisconsin Presidential primary campaign with a TV speech endorsing a strong voting rights bill and criticizing the Eisenhower Administration for failure to support an adequate missile development program. . . . A report on education issued by the Democratic Advisory Council urges greater federal support of American education, because "in a world threatened by . . . the Soviet Union, education becomes a means for national survival."	Eisenhower Administration budget calls for a $50 million increase in defense spending to a peacetime record of $40.99 billion. Defense accounts for 54% of the total budget.	Pres. Eisenhower submits his fourth balanced budget since taking office. Expenditures for fiscal 1961 are estimated at just under $80 billion, a $2.5 billion increase over 1960. Revenues, however, are expected to reach $84 billion, leaving a surplus of $4.1 billion, the largest in 13 years. . . . Eisenhower tells Congress that the expected 1961 budget surplus should go for debt reduction and not a tax cut. . . . Fifty persons aboard a Capital Airlines jet-prop die when it crashes near Holdcroft, Va.	Requested appropriations for space programs and rocket development are doubled, to $600 million, in the Eisenhower Administration's 1961 budget.		Jan. 18
	Thomas S. Gates, Jr., Eisenhower nominee for Defense Secy. sparks a renewed controversy over the comparative military strength of the U.S. and USSR by testifying that earlier estimates of Soviet weapons development had been exaggerated and that there was no genuine "deterrent gap" in favor of the USSR. . . . Army Secy. William Brucker tells Washington newsmen that the U.S. did not "omit" the islands of Quemoy and Matsu from its pledge to defend the Nationalist regime on Taiwan from Communist Chinese aggression.	Brotherhood of Railroad Trainmen votes to eliminate race requirements for membership from the union's constitution at a convention in Cleveland.		Robert Montgomery, actor-producer and White House advisor on Presidential telecasts, testifies to the FCC that reports of quiz-show fixing and payola were widespread within the broadcasting industry long before the charges were made public.	Jan. 19
Park Forest, Ill. residents organize a protective association aimed at ostracizing the family of Asst. Prof. Charles Wilson, the only Negroes in the community.	Defense Secy. Gates tells a press conference the downward revision in the estimates of Soviet strength are based on improved intelligence calculations and not on partisan or budgetary considerations as some Democrats have charged.	In his Annual Economic Report, Eisenhower tells Congress the U.S. GNP climbed to an annual rate of $482 billion in the final quarter of 1959. . . . FBI agents arrest Robert Vernon Spears in Phoenix, Ariz. on a stolen card charge. He is suspected of bombing a National Airlines plane that crashed in the Gulf of Mexico on Nov. 16, 1959. Spears was listed as one of the dead in the crash.	Scientists at a Boston meeting of the American Meteorological Society estimate that test-caused nuclear fallout currently in the atmosphere will descend within two to three years. The estimate is a downward revision of earlier calculations.	Clarence George Wellington, ex-editor of the *Kansas City Star* and the man Ernest Hemingway said "taught me to write", dies of a heart attack at 69.	Jan. 20
Despite intense lobbying by supporters, a discharge petition to dislodge the civil rights bill from the Southern-dominated House Rules Committee still has only 176 of the needed 219 signatures. . . . Democratic leader Lyndon Johnson (Tex.) tells reporters that the Senate will act on a bill of its own if the House fails to adopt a civil rights measure by Feb. 15.	U.S. Secy. of State Herter tells the Senate Foreign Relations Committee that Red Chinese participation would be essential to any effective East-West disarmament agreement; he said such participation, however, would not imply U.S. recognition of Peking.				Jan. 21
Southern House members announce they will oppose promotion of Negro congressman Adam Clayton Powell (N.Y.) to the chairmanship of the House Labor and Education Comm. Powell, the second ranking Democrat on the Committee, is slated to succeed retiring chrmn. Graham A. Barden (D, N.C.). . . . Treason charges against three New York youths accused of organizing a Nazi-style party are reduced to disorderly conduct and conspiracy to commit assault.				Middleweight boxer Paul Pender, 29, wins a 15-round split decision over 38-year old Sugar Ray Robinson in Boston, Mass.	Jan. 22

F	G	H	I	J
Includes elections, federal-state relations, civil rights and liberties, crime, the judiciary, education, health care, poverty, urban affairs and population.	Includes formation and debate of U.S. foreign and defense policies, veterans' affairs and defense spending. (Relations with specific foreign countries are usually found under the region concerned.)	Includes business, labor, agriculture, taxation, transportation, consumer affairs, monetary and fiscal policy, natural resources, and pollution.	Includes worldwide scientific, medical and technological developments, natural phenomena, U.S. weather, natural disasters, and accidents.	Includes the arts, religion, scholarship, communications media, sports, entertainment, fashions, fads and social life.

	World Affairs	Europe	Africa & the Middle East	The Americas	Asia & the Pacific
Jan. 23			Rescue workers in Coalbrook, South Africa begin boring a 15-inch air and food tunnel in an effort to reach 440 miners trapped 500 feet below the earth's surface by a rockslide on Jan. 21.		
Jan. 24	Senate Subcommittee reports post-Stalin changes in Soviet policy can be traced in part to Premier Khrushchev's "gregarious, extroverted and garrulous personality."	Radio Moscow reports the death of Gen. Mikhail Sergeevich Malinin, Soviet deputy chief of staff and commander of the Russian troops who crushed the Hungarian revolt of 1956.	Angered by the dismissal of Massu, armed Algiers rightists attack local security forces in an open rebellion against de Gaulle's self-determination plan for Algeria. The fighting leaves 24 dead and over 100 wounded. A state of seige is declared in Algiers. . . . Nine Policemen are killed by rioting Africans in Durban, South Africa when they attempt to raid illegal liquor stills.		Ten thousand supporters greet Premier Kishi on his return to Tokyo after signing a new U.S.-Japan defense treaty in Washington. The welcome contrasts sharply with the leftist student riots that accompanied his departure.
Jan. 25		Ex.-Lt. Cmndr. Horst Ludwig confesses in a Karlsruhe, West Germany court that he has been an East German spy for three years. . . . Belgium cabinet decides to equip the Belgian air force with the U.S. Lockheed F-104G Starfighters instead of the French-designed Mirage III jets.	French troops and tanks seal off Algiers from the rest of Algeria. De Gaulle denounces the rebellion in a broadcast to Algeria and vows to uphold the republic. . . . Tunisian Pres. Habib Bourguiba calls upon France to withdraw its forces from the French naval and air base at Bizerte by Feb. 8. The demand comes amid growing North African opposition to French plans to test a nuclear bomb in the Sahara. . . . Colonial officials in the Belgian Congo announce nationalist leader Patrice Lumumba has been released from jail to attend a Brussels conference on the political future of the Congo.		Afghan Air Force is reported to have MiG jets in an effort to quell a local rebellion by Kandahar Province tribesmen against the pro-Soviet policies of Premier Mohammed Daoud's government.
Jan. 26	CIA Director Allen Dulles labels the current Soviet Pacific missile tests a bluff designed to convince the world of an illusory Soviet military superiority.		French Premier Michel Debré confers with army commanders in Algiers and transmits de Gaulle's order to put down the rightist uprising. . . . Debré and other cabinet members reportedly may resist de Gaulle's proposals for firm action against the rebels and their sympathizers. . . . Skirmishes between Israeli and UAR forces in the Israeli-Syrian demilitarized zone, the first since 1958, break out at the southern end of the Sea of Galilee following a dispute between local Arab farmers and Israeli police.	During conferences with Amb. Bonsal, Pres. Eisenhower tells newsmen that while Castro's anti-American attacks are wholly unfair, the U.S. will not become a party to any reprisals and will continue to respect Cuba's right to make internal reforms.	Twenty-seven South Vietnamese soldiers are killed in a terrorist attack on an army outpost 50 miles north of Saigon. . . . Thirty-one Koreans are trampled to death by a "stampede" of commuters rushing to catch a train in Seoul.
Jan. 27	Soviet negotiators at the U.S.-British-Soviet test-ban talks in Geneva reject in advance a reported Western proposal to bar all "detectable" nuclear tests, but to permit small underground atomic explosions. . . . U.S. breaks off recently resumed Lend-Lease debt negotiations with the USSR in the face of a Soviet demand that the talks be broadened to cover a general U.S.-USSR trade agreement.	The recent wave of anti-Semitism is reported declining throughout Europe, except in West Germany where the number of anti-Jewish acts since Christmas is said to have exceeded 400.	A firm timetable for granting the Belgian Congo unconditional independence by June 30 is proposed by Belgian officials and accepted by Congolese delegates at a political conference in Brussels.	Oswando Aranha, Brazilian foreign minister and President of the UN General Assembly 1947-1948, dies in Rio de Janeiro.	

A	B	C	D	E
Includes developments that affect more than one world region, international organizations and important meetings of major world leaders.	Includes all domestic and regional developments in Europe, including the Soviet Union, Turkey, Cyprus and Malta.	Includes all domestic and regional developments in Africa and the Middle East, including Iraq and Iran and excluding Cyprus, Turkey and Afghanistan.	Includes all domestic and regional developments in Latin America, the Caribbean and Canada.	Includes all domestic and regional developments in Asia and Pacific nations, extending from Afghanistan through all the Pacific Islands, except Hawaii.

U.S. Politics & Social Issues	U.S. Foreign Policy & Defense	U.S. Economy & Environment	Science, Technology & Nature	Culture, Leisure & Life Style	
	Senate Democratic leader Lyndon Johnson (Tex.) strongly challenges the recent Administration downgrading of Soviet strength estimates, adding that the "future of 175 million Americans" should not be staked on "the ability of some official to read Nikita Khrushchev's mind.". . . . Sens. Jacob Javits (R, N.Y.) and Wayne Morse (D, Ore.) make public a State Dept. directive instructing U.S. missions to use every feasible means to discourage racial or religious bias against American minorities by foreign powers. The action is believed to be aimed especially at Arab discrimination against American Jews.		The U.S. Navy bathysphere *Trieste* descends 37,800 feet to the floor of the Pacific Marianas Trench, 250 miles southwest of Guam, the deepest known point in the world's oceans, setting a new world diving record. . . . Dr. H. Percy Wilkins, British astronomer and moon researcher, dies in London.		Jan. 23
A. Philip Randolph, President of the Brotherhood of Sleeping Car Porters, announces plans for Negro marches at both political party conventions to demonstrate support for stronger civil rights planks. . . . Seventeen Chicago policemen from the Summerdale police district are suspended on charges of operating a burglary/bribery ring. The suspensions come one day after the resignation of Chicago police commissioner Timothy J. O'Connor.	Air Force Secy. Dudley C. Sharp denies there is any "overall deterrent gap."		Bassett Jones, 82, U.S. engineer who pioneered the high-speed passenger elevator, dies in New York.	Ashihoi Hino, Japanese novelist and winner of the Akutagama Prize (Japan's highest literary award), dies of a heart attack at 52. . . . Pro golfer Ken Venturi wins the Bing Crosby invitational tourney in Pebble Beach, Calif. . . . German auto racers, Walter Schock and Rolf Moll win the Warsaw to Monte Carlo Grand Prix.	Jan. 24
Senate passes a clean elections bill providing for ceilings on individual contributions and to total expenditures in Congressional and Presidential campaigns. . . . Pres. Eisenhower rejects N.Y. Gov. Rockefeller's proposal to transfer the 10% federal telephone tax to the states for the support of schools.	A Governor's Conference committee on civil defense, headed by Gov. Rockefeller (R, N.Y.) urges Pres. Eisenhower to support a national program for the construction of nuclear fall-out shelters.		Gavril Tiklov, Soviet founder of the sciences of astrobotomy and astrobiology, dies at 85.	Donald H. McGannon, President of Westinghouse Broadcasting Co. and Chairman of the Natl. Assn. of Broadcasters TV code committee, recommends the enactment of a law providing stiff penalties for offering or accepting payola bribes. . . . Endowment of a new Newhouse Communications Center at Syracuse Univ. by the Newhouse Foundation is announced. The foundation was established by publisher Samuel I. Newhouse, 64, and his wife.	Jan. 25
Atty. Gen. William P. Rogers outlines an Administration bill to protect Negro voting rights. The bill, which authorizes federal courts to appoint election referees, is offered as a substitute for a Civil Rights Commission proposal to appoint federal voting registrars. . . . Senate by voice vote approves a bill authorizing the distribution of up to $5 million to aid local and state governments in the development of programs to combat juvenile delinquency.	Pres. Eisenhower publicly defends the Defense Dept.'s revised method for estimating comparative Soviet and American military strength.			Los Angeles Rams general manager Alvin Rozelle, 33, is named commissioner of the National Football League, succeeding the late Bert Bell.	Jan. 26
	Sen. Stuart Symington (D, Mo.) joins a growing number of Democrats in criticizing the Administration for allegedly distorting Soviet military capacity in order to justify curtailment of the B-70 bomber program and for the failure to increase defense spending.				Jan. 27

F	G	H	I	J
Includes elections, federal-state relations, civil rights and liberties, crime, the judiciary, education, health care, poverty, urban affairs and population.	*Includes formation and debate of U.S. foreign and defense policies, veterans' affairs and defense spending. (Relations with specific foreign countries are usually found under the region concerned.)*	*Includes business, labor, agriculture, taxation, transportation, consumer affairs, monetary and fiscal policy, natural resources, and pollution.*	*Includes worldwide scientific, medical and technological developments, natural phenomena, U.S. weather, natural disasters, and accidents.*	*Includes the arts, religion, scholarship, communications media, sports, entertainment, fashions, fads and social life.*

	World Affairs	Europe	Africa & the Middle East	The Americas	Asia & the Pacific
Jan. 28	U.N. Subcommission on Discrimination and Protection of Minorities votes unanimously to condemn recent outbreaks of anti-Semitism and to call for a U.N. study of the incidents.	In a message to West German Chancellor Adenauer, Premier Khrushchev warns that unless the West shows some "understanding" of the Soviet proposal for a free city of West Berlin, the Soviet bloc will be forced to "negotiate" a unilateral settlement of all German border questions. . . . A continuing dispute over the extent of military enclaves to be retained by Britain leads to the indefinite suspension of London talks on the final terms for Cyprus' independence.	French Delegate Gen. Paul Delouvrier broadcasts an appeal for French soldiers, Moslems and insurgents to rally to de Gaulle to avert civil war. He attributes the disturbances to "a tragic misunderstanding." The French government disavows the speech. . . . French police begin rounding up and detaining right-wing French leaders sympathetic to the insurrection.	Premier Castro conspicuously omits any hostile reference to the U.S. during a Havana address commemorating the birth of Cuban patriot Jose Marti. The speech comes one day after Argentine Amb. Julio Amoeda reportedly told Castro that his extreme anti-U.S. stand was unpopular in Latin America. . . . Sources in the Dominican Republic report blanket arrests of up to 2000 persons in an apparently successful effort to foil a conspiracy against the government of Generalissimo Rafael Leonidas Trujillo Molina.	Burma and Communist China sign a 10-year non-aggression pact and agree on a settlement of a century-old boundary dispute in formal ceremonies in Peking.
Jan. 29	A delegation of Soviet republican premiers and provincial party chairmen arrive in New York to begin a 24-day tour of the U.S. The trip returns a similar visit to the USSR of American governors in 1959.		In a dramatic TV and radio address, French Pres. de Gaulle reaffirms his Algerian policies and calls upon Frenchmen everywhere "to reunite with France" and end the uprising. He concludes by advising the French army: "Your mission does not carry with it any equivocation or interpretation.". . . . The revolutionary Algerian Provisional Government instructs its Moslem supporters to stay out of the struggle between the de Gaulle government and the Algiers insurrectionists.		Japan rejects as unwarranted interference a Soviet note asking the Japanese Parliament not to ratify the recently negotiated U.S.-Japan mutual security pact. . . . Nepalese and Indian leaders jointly announce in New Delhi that Nepal's foreign trade, traditionally financed and controlled by India, will soon be transferred to Nepali control.
Jan. 30		Preaching at the Cologne synagogue where the recent wave of anti-Semitic desecrations began, Pres. Joachim Prinz of the American Jewish Congress calls upon Germany to face its past, adding that it is the "moral rebirth" of the entire German people that the world now awaits. . . . Ex-Lt. Cmndr. Horst Ludwig is convicted of treason in a West German court and is sentenced to 5 years in prison.	Three Independent French Cabinet members, including Finance Secy. Valery Giscard D'Estaing, announce they will take no further part in Independent Party deliberations in view of the group's failure to support fully de Gaulle's action against the Algiers insurrection.	Argentine Naval units begin a hunt for an unidentified "mystery" submarine detected in Golfo Nuevo. . . . CIA makes public a recent intelligence report describing Cuban Premier Castro as "not a Communist...(but) increasingly susceptible to Communist propaganda."	
Jan. 31			Apparently stirred by de Gaulle's nationally broadcast appeal for loyalty, the formerly hesitant French army begins to take decisive steps against the Algiers rebels. Reinforcements are brought into the city and rebel positions are surrounded.		
Feb. 1	After a second successful launching, the Soviet Union announces the end of its controversial rocket shots into the central Pacific.	Twelve million French workers stage a one-hour nationwide work stoppage to demonstrate labor support for de Gaulle in the current Algerian crisis.	Algiers right-wing rebels give up their armed resistance to de Gaulle's policies after learning that the French army would not effectively support their cause. . . . British Colonial Secy. Iain MacLeod proposes the creation of an independent Kenya with a parliamentary government that would assure leadership by the African majority at a London conference on Kenya's political future.		An Indian CP slate led by ex-Chief Min. E. M. S. Namboodiripad is defeated in Kerala State elections by a coalition made up of the Congress and People's Socialist Parties and the Moslem League. The vote comes in the wake of violent pre-election clashes that left four dead.
Feb. 2				Robert Cutler, ex-presidential assistant for national security, is named by Pres. Eisenhower as the new executive director of the Inter-American Development Bank.	William S. Morrison succeeds Sir William Slim as Australia's 14th governor general.

A	B	C	D	E
Includes developments that affect more than one world region, international organizations and important meetings of major world leaders.	Includes all domestic and regional developments in Europe, including the Soviet Union, Turkey, Cyprus and Malta.	Includes all domestic and regional developments in Africa and the Middle East, including Iraq and Iran and excluding Cyprus, Turkey and Afghanistan.	Includes all domestic and regional developments in Latin America, the Caribbean and Canada.	Includes all domestic and regional developments in Asia and Pacific nations, extending from Afghanistan through all the Pacific Islands, except Hawaii.

U.S. Politics & Social Issues	U.S. Foreign Policy & Defense	U.S. Economy & Environment	Science, Technology & Nature	Culture, Leisure & Life Style	
				San Francisco Giant centerfielder Willie Mays signs an $80,000 contract, joining St. Louis Cardinal first baseman Stan Musial as the highest-paid major league players.	Jan. 28
Rep. David M. Hall (D, N.C.) dies at the age of 41 after a 25-year fight against bone disease.		Association of American Railroads, over the protest of eastern commuter lines, votes not to support proposed federal aid to save financially weak commuter roads. . . . Farm organization leaders meet with White House aides to seek assurances that HEW Secy. Arthur Flemming will cause no further public "scares" over the use of agricultural chemicals. . . . National Safety Council reports U.S. traffic fatalities in 1959 totaled 37,800, an increase of 800 over 1958.		Dr. James Bossard, U.S. sociologist and leading authority on child development, dies in Philadelphia at 71.	Jan. 29
	The AEC in its annual report to Congress says that during 1959 emphasis continued on development programs "designed to ... increase the arsenal of nuclear weapons," especially smaller weapons for battleground and missile use. The report also notes that 37 nuclear subs and 3 atomic-powered surface vessels are in use or under construction.		Paul Codos, French aviation pioneer who set a number of long distance flight records in the late 1920s and 1930s, dies at the age of 63.	Boston U. high-jumper John Thomas, 18, sets a new world record in the Millrose games in New York with a leap of 7 feet, 1.5 inches. . . . Carol Heiss wins the U.S. women's singles figure skating championship in Seattle.	Jan. 30
Committee for Economic Development recommends that a larger share of the cost of U.S. public education be transferred to the states and away from local property taxes and urges accelerated consolidation of small school districts.		Amalgamated Lithographers Local 17, ending a two-month strike, signs a 2-year contract with major San Francisco printing firms providing for a wage increase and permitting workers to engage in secondary boycotts despite a court decision and the apparent prohibition against them in the Labor Reform Act of 1959.			Jan. 31
	Sen. Stuart Symington (D, Mo.) introduces a bill to modernize the U.S. defense establishment by placing all the uniformed services under a single chief of staff.	William Lewis is elected president of Teamsters Local 237 (N.Y.), becoming the first Negro to head an integrated Teamsters local.		Rod Laver, 22, and Margaret Smith, 17, win the men's and women's singles in Australian National Tennis Championships.	Feb. 1
Senate approves, 70 to 18, and sends to the House a proposed 23rd Amendment to the Constitution that would ban poll taxes as a requirement for voting in federal elections. . . . Ex-Univ. of Michigan mathematician Dr. H. C. Davis begins a six-month contempt of Congress sentence for his 1953 refusal to answer questions of a House Un-American Activities subcommittee concerning his political beliefs.	SAC commander Gen. Thomas S. Power recommends to a Senate Preparedness subcommittee that nuclear-armed SAC bombers be placed on constant airborne alert to protect U.S. retaliatory capability from a surprise Soviet attack. . . . House of Representatives adopts a resolution stating that the Panamanian flag should not be flown over Canal Zone territory without a special treaty.	Pres. William Presser of Teamsters Joint Council 41 in Cleveland is convicted in Washington of contempt of Congress for refusing to tell a Senate committee whether he destroyed subpoenaed records.			Feb. 2
F	G	H	I	J	
Includes elections, federal-state relations, civil rights and liberties, crime, the judiciary, education, health care, poverty, urban affairs and population.	Includes formation and debate of U.S. foreign and defense policies, veterans' affairs and defense spending. (Relations with specific foreign countries are usually found under the region concerned.)	Includes business, labor, agriculture, taxation, transportation, consumer affairs, monetary and fiscal policy, natural resources, and pollution.	Includes worldwide scientific, medical and technological developments, natural phenomena, U.S. weather, natural disasters, and accidents.	Includes the arts, religion, scholarship, communications media, sports, entertainment, fashions, fads and social life.	

	World Affairs	Europe	Africa & the Middle East	The Americas	Asia & the Pacific
Feb. 3		Hungary formally denies recent BBC allegations that over 50 participants in the 1956 revolt have been executed during the past six months.	Amidst the Algerian crisis, the French National Assembly grants de Gaulle power to rule by decree for a period of one year. Only Communists and some rightist deputies from Algeria oppose the measure. . . . British P.M. Harold Macmillan tells the South African legislature that Britain recognizes the growing "strength of African national consciousness" and can no longer support policies designed to ensure domination by white Europeans.		
Feb. 4	A renewed Soviet offer to reopen Lend-Lease debt talks as part of general discussions on a long-term U.S.-Soviet trade agreement is rejected by the U.S. State Dept.	The leaders of the eight Warsaw Pact nations, meeting in Moscow, warn that they are prepared to sign a separate East German peace treaty if Western powers reject Soviet proposals to make West Berlin a free city. . . . Official Soviet census report sets the total population of the USSR at 208,826,650.	Scattered fighting between Israel and UAR troops continues along the Syrian-Israeli border with each side reporting a few casualties. . . . Premier Sylvanus E. Olympio of Togoland labels as "insulting" recent proposals by Ghana P.M. Kwame Nkrumah that Togoland become a province of Ghana when it gains its independence in April.	Soviet Deputy Premier Anastas I. Mikoyan arrives in Cuba to open a Soviet trade exposition.	Premier Pham Van Dong reports that North Vietnam's collectivization program has reached 44% in agriculture, 60% in handicrafts and 45% in industry through the formation of joint state-private enterprises.
Feb. 5		U.S. State Dept. labels the Warsaw Pact declaration on West Berlin bellicose and inconsistent with repeated Soviet peace professions.	Minister Delegate Jacques Soustelle is dismissed from the French cabinet on de Gaulle's orders for his overt support of the rightist uprising in Algiers.		
Feb. 6		Arnold Strunk and Paul-Josef Schoenen, admitted pro-Nazis, are sentenced to prison terms of 14 and 10 months, respectively, for the Christmas day desecration of a Cologne synagogue—the act which began the recent wave of anti-Semitic incidents in Europe.			Ex-Premier U Nu's faction of the Anti-Fascist People's League wins an overwhelming victory in Burma's general elections, marking a return to civilian control after two years of military rule under Gen. New Win. . . . UPI correspondent in Canton, China, Bill Yim, is reported to have been sentenced to one year in prison for alleged "spy activities" against the Communist Chinese government.
Feb. 7			UAR rejects a U.N.-delivered Israeli offer for cease-fire talks to end the current skirmishing along the Syria-Israel border because of Israel's refusal to compromise its claim to the disputed demilitarized zone south of Galilee.		
Feb. 8	Soviet spokesmen charge American evidence on the extreme difficulty of detecting small-scale atomic tests is partial and distorted.	Yugoslavian courts sentence eight Roman Catholics to prison on charges of anti-state activities and conspiring to revive a separate Croatian state. Fourteen others were sentenced to jail Jan. 29. . . . Poland's Central Statistical Board reports industrial production rose 9% in 1959, while farm output fell 1.3%.	Tunisian Pres. Habib Bourguiba postpones his demand for a French withdrawal from its base at Bizerte in order to allow the de Gaulle government to concentrate on defeating the Algiers rightist uprising. . . . South African External Affairs Min. Eric H. Luow accuses British P.M. Macmillan of supporting the surrender of white South Africans to black domination "for the sake of Britain's foreign policy." . . . Arab League Council meets in Cairo to consider Israeli-Syrian tension and the Palestinian question.		Indonesian information department announces that newsprint purchases will be permitted only for those newspapers which support Pres. Sukarno's political program.

A	B	C	D	E
Includes developments that affect more than one world region, international organizations and important meetings of major world leaders.	Includes all domestic and regional developments in Europe, including the Soviet Union, Turkey, Cyprus and Malta.	Includes all domestic and regional developments in Africa and the Middle East, including Iraq and Iran and excluding Cyprus, Turkey and Afghanistan.	Includes all domestic and regional developments in Latin America, the Caribbean and Canada.	Includes all domestic and regional developments in Asia and Pacific nations, extending from Afghanistan through all the Pacific Islands, except Hawaii.

U.S. Politics & Social Issues	U.S. Foreign Policy & Defense	U.S. Economy & Environment	Science, Technology & Nature	Culture, Leisure & Life Style	
Pres. Eisenhower appoints Henry Merritt Wriston, 70, ex-president of Brown Univ., as chairman of the Commission on National Goals, a body charged with developing "a broad outline of national objectives and programs for the next decade or longer." Frank Pace Jr. is named commission vice chairman.	Pres. Eisenhower derides claims that the U.S. has to "catch up" with the USSR in missiles. "A deterrent has no added power, once it has become completely adequate," he says. He concedes the Russians will be ahead of the U.S. in space exploration for "some time." . . . Pres. Eisenhower tells a news conference "we should not deny our allies what the ...potential enemy already has," indicating an apparent willingness to share control of U.S. nuclear weapons. . . . Eighteen House Democrats introduce a resolution to resume the U.S. moratorium on nuclear testing which expired Dec. 31, 1959.	Labor Dept. reports union membership in the U.S. declined by 400,000 between 1956 and 1959 to a total of 18.1 million. . . . A Washington State Supreme Court upholds the 1957 larceny conviction of retired Teamsters Pres. Dave Beck. . . . IRS rules farmers must list soil bank benefits as income on their federal tax returns.			Feb. 3
Senate passes a Democratic-sponsored bill providing $1.83 billion in federal aid to public schools, despite a strong administration opposition.	Federation of American Scientists labels Pres. Eisenhower's implied proposal to share U.S. nuclear technology with allied nations as "catastrophic folly."			*Grant Moves South* by Bruce Catton is published.	Feb. 4
Sen. Stuart Symington (D, Mo.) tells a National Democratic Club luncheon that he would be "very seriously" interested in the party's presidential nomination, but currently has no firm plans to declare himself an official candidate.	Lt. Gen. Bernard A. Schriever, Air Force research command chief, tells the House Astronautics Committee that the administration has "committed" the U.S. to second place in the missile race.		A 25-billion electron-volt synchrotron, the largest in the world, is inaugurated in Meyrin, Switzerland by the 13-nation European Organization for Nuclear Research.		Feb. 5
V.P. Richard Nixon tells California newspaper publishers that foreign policy and national security will be the prime issues in the 1960 presidential campaign.	Prominent Democratic Senators, including J.W. Fulbright (Ark.) and John Kennedy (Mass.), applaud the recent White House decision to increase economic aid to Asian countries.		National Committee on Radiation Protection and Measurement (U.S.) reports human beings could absorb massive doses of radiation from nuclear blasts without suffering serious physical injury.	House Special Subcommittee on Legislative Oversight recommends legislation to make rigging TV quiz shows a crime, make networks as well as local stations subject to periodic FCC licensing and empower the FTC to seek court injunctions against "unfair or deceptive" business practices in broadcasting.	Feb. 6
			Dr. Igor Vasilevich Kurchatov, 57, the physicist who directed the Soviet programs that developed the atomic and hydrogen bombs, dies in Moscow of a heart ailment. . . . Dr. Karl Mabach, 80, German gasoline and diesel engine designer (for the *Graf Zeppelin* and other airships), dies in Friedrichshafen.	Boy Scouts of America begin week-long celebrations marking the organization's 50th anniversary. . . . Arnold Palmer wins $12,000 first prize in the Palm Springs Desert Classic golf tournament.	Feb. 7
Senate GOP Leader Everett M. Dirksen (Ill.) introduces the Administration's civil rights legislation "package" to authorize federal voting referees, establish penalties for using threats or force to obstruct court-ordered school desegregation, aid communities in integrating schools and authorize federal officers to enter bombing cases. . . . Sit-ins by Negro students to protest the "local custom" of refusing lunch-counter service to seated Negroes is reported to have spread from Greensboro (Feb. 1) to other major North Carolina cities.	Secy. of State Christian Herter tells a Washington news conference that the Warsaw declaration indicates a hardening of the Soviet position on Berlin, but not a time-bound ultimatum.			House Subcommittee on Legislative Oversight begins public hearings on the extent of payola bribes paid to disc jockeys by the recording industry. . . . NFL Commissioner Pete Roselle announces an agreement with AFL chief Joe Foss to prohibit either league from trying to lure players from the other.	Feb. 8

F	G	H	I	J
Includes elections, federal-state relations, civil rights and liberties, crime, the judiciary, education, health care, poverty, urban affairs and population.	Includes formation and debate of U.S. foreign and defense policies, veterans' affairs and defense spending. (Relations with specific foreign countries are usually found under the region concerned.)	Includes business, labor, agriculture, taxation, transportation, consumer affairs, monetary and fiscal policy, natural resources, and pollution.	Includes worldwide scientific, medical and technological developments, natural phenomena, U.S. weather, natural disasters, and accidents.	Includes the arts, religion, scholarship, communications media, sports, entertainment, fashions, fads and social life.

	World Affairs	Europe	Africa & the Middle East	The Americas	Asia & the Pacific
Feb. 9			French officials, under instructions from de Gaulle, complete a week-long crackdown on rightist leaders and organizations in Algiers. The crackdown is reported to be the first stage of a general reorganization of the military and civil administration in Algeria. . . . Iraqi political parties are legalized for the first time since the 1958 revolution. All must operate under government license.	Acting on charges brought by Venezuela, the OAS appoints a council to investigate the recent blanket political arrests in the Dominican Republic.	
Feb. 10		An Italian delegation, headed by Pres. Giovanni Gronchi, ends a stormy five-day state visit to the USSR during which the Italians publicly clashed with Premier Khrushchev over Berlin and over the relative merits of communism vs. Christian Democratic ideas. . . . Cardinal Alojzije Stepinac, Roman Catholic primate of Yugoslavia, who served a five-year prison term (1946-1951) for allegedly collaborating with the Nazis, dies in his native village of Krasic at age 61.	French officials begin implementation of the de Gaulle-ordered reformation of the Algerian administration, including dissolution of the Algerian home guard, suppression of the army's conservative Fifth Bureau, reorganization of the Algerian police and courts and the arrest of known rightist agitators. . . . Pres. Julius Nyerere of the Tanganyika African Union predicts full independence for Tanganyika within five years.	Military courts in Havana hand down prison sentences of three to 30 years to 104 Cubans charged with conspiring against the Castro government.	Soviet Premier Khrushchev arrives in New Delhi on the first leg of his goodwill tour to four southeast Asian neutralist nations—India, Burma, Indonesia, and Afghanistan.
Feb. 11	U.S. presents to the Geneva test-ban conference a draft treaty that would bar all controllable and detectable nuclear tests and would provide for a minimum of 40 on-site inspections. Soviet delegates immediately reject the offer as a "half-measure."	One hundred twenty-two persons are injured in rioting that accompanies a mass meeting of some 30,000 French farmers in Amiens to protest government agricultural policy and de Gaulle's suppression of Algiers rightists. It is the first major anti-government demonstration since the 1958 Algiers coup.	Jordanian Foreign Min. Musa Nasir, attending an Arab League conference in Cairo, reports that while the Arab states disagree over numerous political issues, they are "completely united" in declaring war against Israel should it carry out threats to divert Jordan River waters into the Negev Desert. . . . U.S. Embassy in Rabat announces the SAC base at Ben Slimane will be closed by the end of March and three U.S. squadrons withdrawn from Morocco by June. . . . The final death toll in the Coalbrook, South Africa mine disaster is set at 417.	Forty persons are sentenced to 30-year jail terms for conspiring to overthrow the government of Gen. Rafael Trujillo Molina in the Dominican Republic. The latest sentences bring the number of alleged conspirators recently sentenced to 30-year terms to at least 120.	In a speech to the Indian Parliament, Premier Khrushchev pledges Soviet support for the liberation of third world peoples and praises India's non-alignment doctrine.
Feb. 12		Hungarian CP Central Comm. orders a temporary halt to the collectivization of agriculture.	Two Israeli soldiers are killed and one wounded as sporadic fighting continues in the demilitarized zones along the Syrian-Israeli border.		Communist Chinese officials receive a letter from Indian P.M. Nehru inviting Chou En-lai to India for talks on the India-China border dispute. News of the letter provokes cries of "betrayal" from Indian Socialist Party leaders who favor stronger action against the Chinese incursions.
Feb. 13	France becomes the world's fourth nuclear power after the successful testing of a plutonium bomb in the Sahara Desert.	Pres. de Gaulle hails France's successful nuclear test as a major step in restoring French grandeur and influence in world affairs. . . . British Labor Party leader Hugh Gaitskell announces a shift away from the party's emphasis on near-total nationalization because of voter apprehension over the threat to private property.	Ghana P.M. Kwame Nkrumah publicly denounces the French A-test and orders a freeze on all French assets in Ghana "until... the effects on the population of Ghana of the present experiment" are known.	Cuban Premier Castro and Soviet Deputy Premier Anastas Mikoyan conclude a commercial-aid agreement in which the Soviets promise $100 million in low interest loans to Cuba over the next four years.	
Feb. 14	UAR calls upon Asian and African states to seek unified U.N. action to condemn the French test. . . . Soviet Premier Khrushchev, visiting India, tells New Delhi newsmen that he "regrets" the French test, but does not believe it will harm the projected East-West summit talks.				Afghanistan makes public a Soviet agreement to provide $22 million in financial and technical aid for the construction of a hydroelectric and irrigation dam on the Kabul River near Jalabad.

A	B	C	D	E
Includes developments that affect more than one world region, international organizations and important meetings of major world leaders.	Includes all domestic and regional developments in Europe, including the Soviet Union, Turkey, Cyprus and Malta.	Includes all domestic and regional developments in Africa and the Middle East, including Iraq and Iran and excluding Cyprus, Turkey and Afghanistan.	Includes all domestic and regional developments in Latin America, the Caribbean and Canada.	Includes all domestic and regional developments in Asia and Pacific nations, extending from Afghanistan through all the Pacific Islands, except Hawaii.

U.S. Politics & Social Issues	U.S. Foreign Policy & Defense	U.S. Economy & Environment	Science, Technology & Nature	Culture, Leisure & Life Style	
N. J. Supreme Court rules private builders cannot bar Negroes from buying homes on which FHA has agreed to provide mortgage loans. . . . A crude bomb rips a hole in the side of the home of Carlotta Walls, one of five black students enrolled at Little Rock (Ark.) Central High; it is reportedly the first direct attack upon any of the Negroes attending the Little Rock school. . . . Millionaire industrialist and brewer Adolph Coors 3rd is reported missing after police discovered his bloodstained truck abandoned near Morrison, Colo.		Pres. Eisenhower asks Congress to develop "a sensible and economically sound" agricultural program based on "realistic" price supports.			Feb. 9
Company spokesmen for Woolworth and S. H. Kress stores, targets of the current sit-in protests, say it is corporate policy to let store managers decide serving rules and not to interfere with "local customs."			Pres. Eisenhower makes his first visit to the Cape Canaveral space center.		Feb. 10
Pres. Eisenhower attacks the recently passed Senate bill providing $1.8 billion in federal aid to schools as improper federal interference in local affairs.	American Jewish Congress sharply criticizes the Agriculture and Commerce Depts. and the Navy for allegedly cooperating with an Arab boycott against ships trading with Israel.	A record 177-day copper strike against the Anaconda Co. in Montana ends following approval of a new two-and-a-half-year contract by members of the Mine, Mill and Smelters Workers Union.		In the wake of extensive hearings, the FCC proposes legislation to make broadcasting deception, such as quiz-show rigging and payola, punishable by up to one year in prison. . . . Popular late-night TV host Jack Paar dramatically walks off his program after announcing that he is quitting NBC because the network had cut out a joke from the previous pre-recorded show without notifying him.	Feb. 11
		White House announces Pres. Eisenhower has asked his Science Advisory Committee to give him a full report on the use of chemical additives in food.			Feb. 12
		Teamsters Pres. Jimmy Hoffa announces a new two-year pact with the Railway Express Agency providing for raises of up to 60¢ an hour.			Feb. 13
		AFL-CIO Exec. Council proposes a broad "anti-recession" program, including relaxed credit controls, expanded government construction, increased military spending, higher wages and tax reform.		Robert (Junior) Johnson, 28, of Ronda, N.C., wins the Daytona 500 stock car race in a 1959 Chevrolet.	Feb. 14

F	G	H	I	J
Includes elections, federal-state relations, civil rights and liberties, crime, the judiciary, education, health care, poverty, urban affairs and population.	Includes formation and debate of U.S. foreign and defense policies, veterans' affairs and defense spending. (Relations with specific foreign countries are usually found under the region concerned.)	Includes business, labor, agriculture, taxation, transportation, consumer affairs, monetary and fiscal policy, natural resources, and pollution.	Includes worldwide scientific, medical and technological developments, natural phenomena, U.S. weather, natural disasters, and accidents.	Includes the arts, religion, scholarship, communications media, sports, entertainment, fashions, fads and social life.

	World Affairs	Europe	Africa & the Middle East	The Americas	Asia & the Pacific
Feb. 15	In an address in Bhilai, India, Khrushchev charges that Western aid to underdeveloped nations is simply "a weapon of a new colonial policy."	Chancellor Adenauer warns that Western capitulation to Soviet demands for a free city of West Berlin might lead to the eventual loss of all West Germany.	Protesting France's Saharan nuclear test, Morocco announces formal nullification of the 1956 French-Moroccan diplomatic accord and recalls its ambassador to France. . . . British P.M. Macmillan, just returned from his African tour, predicts that Ghana and Nigeria will retain close ties with the Commonwealth.	OAS votes to ask its Peace Committee to investigate Venezuelan charges that the Dominican Republic is consistently violating human rights.	
Feb. 16	The Soviet delegation to the Geneva talks, responding to the American proposal of Feb. 11, reiterates its plan for a complete end to all tests, but adds for the first time a provision allowing a limited number of on-site inspections. The addition is considered a major concession. . . . France announces it will not seek participation in the current U.S.-USSR-British test ban talks in Geneva, adding that such a ban ought to be adopted only as part of a comprehensive agreement to eliminate existing nuclear stockpiles.	British Defense Ministry issues a White Paper calling for a record peace-time defense budget of $4.5 billion to pay for a planned shift from nuclear to mobile conventional forces.	UAR Pres. Gamal Nasser calls upon Iraqi Premier Abdul Karim el-Kassem to fulfill his pledges of cooperation against Israel by sending troops to the Syrian border.	U.S. Navy team arrives with special equipment to assist Argentina in the hunt for two unidentified submarines believed located off its Atlantic coast.	Soviet Premier Khrushchev arrives in Rangoon for a day-and-a-half visit to Burma.
Feb. 17		*Pravda* reports the Soviet CP and government is considering a plan to reorganize its armed forces into a territorial system of citizen reservists. . . . A West German White Paper reports over 600 anti-Jewish acts in West Germany since Christmas, but concludes that anti-Semitism is distinctly a minority sentiment among the German population as a whole. . . . Vatican readiness to reach a church-state accord with Yugoslavia is expressed by Pope John XXIII in a memorial mass for the late Cardinal Stepinac.			Field Marshal Mohammed Ayub Khan is sworn in as president of Pakistan.
Feb. 18	U.N. Secy. Gen. Dag Hammarskjold describes the situation in the Middle East as "deteriorating" and urges immediate action by the Security Council.		Red Cross predicts permanent paralysis for many of the almost 10,000 Moroccans who were poisoned last year by cooking oil contaminated with a high-phosphate engine lubricant.	A small plane crashes 100 miles east of Havana, Cuba, allegedly while trying to fire-bomb sugar cane fields. Castro later identifies the two crewmen as Americans.	Pres. Sukarno and hundreds of thousands of Indonesians welcome Soviet Premier Khrushchev on his arrival in Jakarta.
Feb. 19	Leaders of the Western delegations to the March disarmament conference conclude preliminary strategy talks in Washington without arriving at a common position.	U.S., Britain and France reject a Soviet maneuver to gain Western recognition of East Germany by refusing to accept Soviet travel passes marked valid for the "(East) German Democratic Republic." . . . Hans C. Hansen, premier of Denmark since 1955, succumbs to cancer at age 53.			

A	B	C	D	E
Includes developments that affect more than one world region, international organizations and important meetings of major world leaders.	Includes all domestic and regional developments in Europe, including the Soviet Union, Turkey, Cyprus and Malta.	Includes all domestic and regional developments in Africa and the Middle East, including Iraq and Iran and excluding Cyprus, Turkey and Afghanistan.	Includes all domestic and regional developments in Latin America, the Caribbean and Canada.	Includes all domestic and regional developments in Asia and Pacific nations, extending from Afghanistan through all the Pacific Islands, except Hawaii.

U.S. Politics & Social Issues	U.S. Foreign Policy & Defense	U.S. Economy & Environment	Science, Technology & Nature	Culture, Leisure & Life Style	
Senate Democratic leader Lyndon Johnson redeems a 1959 pledge to bring a civil rights bill to the Senate floor by introducing it as an amendment to a completely unrelated House-passed bill. The unusual procedure, necessitated by the Senate's failure to dislodge the original rights bill from the Southern-dominated Rules Committee, surprises and angers the bill's opponents. . . . Negro demonstrators leaving a Woolworth lunch counter in High Point, N.C. clash with a group of whites who had gathered outside the store. Forty-three Negro students were arrested during a similar protest in Raleigh two days earlier.		Pres. George Meany tells AFL-CIO convention that he has been unable to break a ban on Negro members by Local 26 of the Internat. Union of Electrical Workers, which controls electrical work on government projects in Washington, D.C.		Nat. Boxing Assn. withdraws its recognition of Archie Moore, 43, as light-heavyweight champion on the grounds that he has failed to meet the NBA requirements that the title be defended every six months.	**Feb. 15**
Peaceful sit-ins by Negro students protesting lunch-counter segregation have spread to at least 15 cities in five Southern states. . . . U.S. District Court in Baltimore rules that the refusal of a local restaurant to seat a Negro was a private, not public, matter and violated no laws. . . . Gallup Poll survey indicates 72% of Americans believe the provision of birth control information should be legal throughout the U.S.	Pres. Eisenhower asks Congress to approve a $4.2 billion foreign aid appropriation for fiscal 1961, a one billion dollar increase over 1960.	IRS Commissioner Dana Latham announces a crackdown against taxpayers who deliberately omit their interest and dividend income on their tax returns.		After an exchange of apologies, TV talk show host Jack Paar meets with NBC officials and agrees to return to his program March 7.	**Feb. 16**
Peace officers in Portsmouth, Va. use K-9 police dogs to break up a skirmish following a sit-in protest at a local variety store.	Pres. Eisenhower angrily denies recent charges that his administration has become complacent about defense and has misled the public about the extent of Soviet strength. . . . Pres. Eisenhower appoints a special nine-member committee to analyze and evaluate the U.S. overseas information and propaganda programs. . . . Eisenhower administration is reported to have ordered an intensified Defense Dept. study into unmanned seismic recorders capable of detecting underground nuclear tests.	Alexander Leonard Guterma is sentenced to nearly five years in prison and fined $160,000 for conspiring to defraud the government by not filing reports of stock deals with the SEC. Guterma was convicted by a New York federal jury Jan. 27.			**Feb. 17**
Republican members of the House Rules Committee, at the urging of Pres. Eisenhower, join with Northern Democrats in voting to release the long bottled-up civil rights bill. Debate is scheduled to begin March 10.	Secy. of State Herter outlines the West's goals for the March disarmament talks in Geneva: (1) a more stable military environment with less risk of war by miscalculation; (2) a reduction in arms; (3) strengthened international peace-keeping machinery, including provision for international inspections. . . . House Armed Services Committee agrees to a full investigation of U.S. military training manuals in the wake of public protest over a recent Air Force manual that asserted communist infiltration of the Nat. Council of Churches and explicitly denied the public's "right to know."			V.P. Richard Nixon opens the 1960 Winter Olympics in ceremonies at Squaw Valley, Calif.	**Feb. 18**
Francis E. Walter (D, Pa.), chrmn. of the House Committee on Un-American Activities, joins a number of conservative, fundamentalist church leaders in defending an Air Force manual that linked the Nat. Council of Churches with communism. . . . Convicted kidnapper Caryl Whittier Chessman receives a 60-day reprieve from California Gov. Edmund Brown just 10 hours before he was to die in the gas chamber. The stay comes amid an outpouring of appeals from opponents of capital punishment all over the world.	Senate Democratic leader Lyndon Johnson charges the administration has not told the public the truth about defense and the missile gap. . . . A U.S. Navy memorandum is given to Congress saying the Navy is withdrawing from its oil-cargo contracts cancellation clauses that seem to sanction the Arab boycott of vessels trading with Israel. . . . Congress begins consideration of a Feb. 18 administration request to appropriate $64 million as the initial U.S. contribution to the International Development Assn.	Members of the United Packinghouse Workers of America ratify a new two-year contract with Wilson and Co., ending a 16-week strike.		British Queen Elizabeth II gives birth to her third child and second son. The infant boy replaces Princess Anne, 9, as second in line for the throne.	**Feb. 19**
F	**G**	**H**	**I**	**J**	
Includes elections, federal-state relations, civil rights and liberties, crime, the judiciary, education, health care, poverty, urban affairs and population.	*Includes formation and debate of U.S. foreign and defense policies, veterans' affairs and defense spending. (Relations with specific foreign countries are usually found under the region concerned.)*	*Includes business, labor, agriculture, taxation, transportation, consumer affairs, monetary and fiscal policy, natural resources, and pollution.*	*Includes worldwide scientific, medical and technological developments, natural phenomena, U.S. weather, natural disasters, and accidents.*	*Includes the arts, religion, scholarship, communications media, sports, entertainment, fashions, fads and social life.*	

	World Affairs	Europe	Africa & the Middle East	The Americas	Asia & the Pacific
Feb. 20	Five Soviet republican premiers and seven provincial party chairmen end a two-week cross-country U.S. tour during which they confronted anti-communist Hungarian protesters and frequent questions about the sincerity of Soviet peace professions. . . . Premier Khrushchev, visiting Indonesia, details Soviet plans for the creation of a Friendship of Peoples University to enroll eventually 4,000 students from Asia, Africa and Latin America.	Sources in Madrid report Spanish police have arrested more than 100 persons in connection with the Feb. 18 bombing of the city hall. . . . Adone Zoli, 72, Italian premier 1957-1958, dies in Rome.	Brussels conference on the future of the Congo ends with agreement on a 16-point program for establishment of an independent Congo by June 30. . . . While on tour in Syria, UAR Pres. Nasser reiterates his pledge to lead a unified Arab effort to liberate Palestine.	Canadian External Affairs Secy. Howard C. Green says Canada will take a more "independent" approach on disarmament and other East-West problems. Green says Canada favors halting "nuclear tests of any kind" regardless of detection problems.	Sources in Manila report a shake-up of Philippine Pres. Carlos P. Garcia's cabinet in an effort to stem growing charges of government financial corruption. . . . Chinese National Assembly in Taipei unanimously rejects Pres. Chiang Kai-shek's pro forma offer to resign because of his failure to retake the Chinese mainland.
Feb. 21		Finance Min. Viggo Kampmann is appointed Danish premier to succeed the late Hans C. Hansen.	London conference on Kenya's political future ends after endorsing proposals for increased political participation by Africans. . . . Voters in Cameroon approve a constitutional referendum establishing a strong presidential system on the model of the French Fifth Republic.		
Feb. 22			UAR decrees marriage reforms ending the Moslem male's right to personal divorce without court decree and granting to wives divorce and alimony rights for specified abuses. Legal polygamy, with a limit of four wives, is retained.	Pres. Eisenhower leaves on his 14-day good-will tour to Brazil, Argentina, Chile and Uruguay.	Reacting to visiting Premier Khrushchev's repeated endorsement of communism as the solution to underdevelopment, Pres. Sukarno tells a Surabaya rally that Indonesia will remain neutralist and will find its own way to a just society. . . . A coalition cabinet is sworn in, ending direct rule by the central Indian government in Kerala State. Direct rule was imposed in 1959 when the central government dismissed a Communist cabinet.
Feb. 23				Brazilian Pres. Juscelino Kubitschek escorts visiting Pres. Eisenhower on a tour of Brazil's partially completed inland capital city of Brasilia.	
Feb. 24		Italian Premier Antonio Segni and his minority Christian Democratic cabinet resign after losing the parliamentary support of the conservative Liberal Party. . . . Officials in Bonn confirm reports of West German efforts to obtain logistic bases in Spain, but promise that no agreement will be concluded without NATO approval.			
Feb. 25	U.S. Amb.-to-the-U.N., Henry Cabot Lodge, returns from a two-week visit to the USSR during which he conferred with Premier Khrushchev.	French Armed Forces Ministry announces plans to form a special motorized nuclear division.	Israel formally protests to the U.N. Security Council an alleged Arab troop build-up along the Syrian-Israeli border and in the Sinai Peninsula.	Visiting Pres. Eisenhower promises Brazilian business and agricultural leaders in Sao Paulo that the U.S. "shall continue to support Brazilian development." The visit is marred by the collision of a U.S. Navy plane with a Brazilian airliner over Rio. The 61 dead include 19 members of the U.S. Navy band.	

A	B	C	D	E
Includes developments that affect more than one world region, international organizations and important meetings of major world leaders.	*Includes all domestic and regional developments in Europe, including the Soviet Union, Turkey, Cyprus and Malta.*	*Includes all domestic and regional developments in Africa and the Middle East, including Iraq and Iran and excluding Cyprus, Turkey and Afghanistan.*	*Includes all domestic and regional developments in Latin America, the Caribbean and Canada.*	*Includes all domestic and regional developments in Asia and Pacific nations, extending from Afghanistan through all the Pacific Islands, except Hawaii.*

U.S. Politics & Social Issues	U.S. Foreign Policy & Defense	U.S. Economy & Environment	Science, Technology & Nature	Culture, Leisure & Life Style	
		U.S. Census Bureau reports America's farm population declined 15.5% during the 1950s to a total of 21,172,000.	Dr. Marcel Schein, 57, Czech-born authority on cosmic rays and a participant in the development of the U.S. atomic bomb, dies in Chicago.	Sir Charles Leonard Woolley, 79, the British archeologist who uncovered the city of Ur in Iraq, dies in London.	**Feb. 20**
Sen. John L. McClellan (D, Ark.) receives the Freedom Foundation's George Washington Award for his "integrity and courage" in assailing communism and corruption.	In a radio-TV address, Pres. Eisenhower responds to growing criticism of his defense policies by asserting that the U.S. has "an indestructable force... ample for today and constantly developing to meet the needs of tomorrow." . . . N. Y. Gov. Nelson Rockefeller announces plans to build a $4 million fall-out and blast-proof shelter near Albany to serve as an alternate state government seat in the event of atomic war.		George W. Borg, 71, inventor and former chmn. of Borg-Warner, dies in Janesville, Wisc.		**Feb. 21**
Univ. of California criminologist, Orlando W. Wilson, is appointed Chicago police superintendent by Mayor Richard J. Daley. Wilson pledges to clean up Chicago's scandal-ridden police department.			Dr. Samuel Mitchell, astronomer who calculated the distance of over 1,000 stars, dies at 85 in Bloomington, Ind.		**Feb. 22**
Senate Democratic leader Lyndon Johnson announces he will call around-the-clock sessions beginning Feb. 29 to wear down an expected Southern filibuster against a vote on the civil rights bill. . . . Supreme Court unanimously overturns the conviction of two Arkansas Negro women who refused to reveal the names of NAACP members to Little Rock city officials on grounds that the city had no constitutional right to the information.	Prominent recent critic of defense policies, Sen Stuart Symington (D, Mo.), renews charges that the public is being misled on the extent of the ICBM "missile gap" between the U.S. and USSR. . . . U.S. Senate ratifies a UNESCO treaty abolishing trade and tariff barriers to the importation of educational and scientific materials for non-commercial use.	Eisenhower vetoes a water-pollution control bill that would have provided federal funds for the building of local sewage treatment plants. . . . Teamsters Pres. James Hoffa announces that he will seek a single nationwide contract for 400,000 long-distance and local truckers when the current regional contracts expire in the spring of 1961.		Franklin P. Adams, 78, famed newspaper columnist and author, dies in N.Y. . . . Ebbets Field, the former home of the Brooklyn Dodgers (1913-1957), is closed and demolition begins to clear the site for a housing project.	**Feb. 23**
The source of recently published charges against the Nat. Council of Churches is reported to be Rev. Carl McIntire, an "unfrocked" Presbyterian minister and long-time critic of the Council.	Air Force announces the first successful launching of the new Titan ICBM; the missile reportedly landed in the designated impact area 5,000 miles southwest of Cape Canaveral.	U.S. grand jury in St. Louis indicts six Teamsters officials for making illegal campaign contributions.			**Feb. 24**
Montgomery, Ala. police, led by club-carrying Sheriff Mac Butler, clear Negro demonstrators from the county courthouse lunchroom in the first of the recent sit-ins to be staged in the so-called "deep South." . . . Va. Gov. J. Lindsay Almond Jr. signs into law three anti-trespassing bills in a move to crack down on sit-in demonstrations.			HEW Secy. Arthur Flemming recommends reducing the maximum permissible level of radioactive strontium-90 in milk for human consumption.	Lillian Hellman's *Toys in the Attic* opens in N.Y. to favorable reviews.	**Feb. 25**

F	G	H	I	J
Includes elections, federal-state relations, civil rights and liberties, crime, the judiciary, education, health care, poverty, urban affairs and population.	*Includes formation and debate of U.S. foreign and defense policies, veterans' affairs and defense spending. (Relations with specific foreign countries are usually found under the region concerned.)*	*Includes business, labor, agriculture, taxation, transportation, consumer affairs, monetary and fiscal policy, natural resources, and pollution.*	*Includes worldwide scientific, medical and technological developments, natural phenomena, U.S. weather, natural disasters, and accidents.*	*Includes the arts, religion, scholarship, communications media, sports, entertainment, fashions, fads and social life.*

	World Affairs	Europe	Africa & the Middle East	The Americas	Asia & the Pacific
Feb. 26	Soviet test-ban negotiator Semyon K. Tsarapkin says that the USSR will join a joint U.S.-British-Soviet research program to improve nuclear test detection if it is preceded by an agreement to ban all atomic testing.	British Queen Elizabeth announces the engagement of her sister, Princess Margaret, 29, to a professional photographer and commoner, Antony Armstrong-Jones.		U.S. State Dept. announces military aid to Cuba and the Dominican Republic will not be continued after June 30. . . . Clashes between police and supporters of ousted dictator Juan Peron mark Pres. Eisenhower's arrival in Buenos Aires for talks with Argentine Pres. Arturo Frondizi.	Communist Chinese Premier Chou En-lai accepts P.M. Nehru's invitation to visit New Delhi for talks on the China-India border question.
Feb. 27	Pres. de Gaulle declares France would gladly renounce possession of nuclear weapons if the other atomic powers would do likewise.		French Armed Forces Ministry discloses over 13,000 French soldiers have been killed in Algeria during the past five years.		
Feb. 28		Male residents of Switzerland's Geneva Canton narrowly approve a referendum granting women the right to vote and hold public office. . . . Fights break out between Laborites and members of the neo-Fascist British Union Movement following a Labor Party rally in London in support of an anti-apartheid boycott of all South African goods.			Sukarno and Khrushchev sign an aid agreement providing $250 million in Soviet credits for Indonesia. A cultural exchange agreement is also signed.
Feb. 29		In a Jakarta speech Premier Khrushchev reiterates his warning that he is prepared to sign a separate East German peace treaty if the West rejects Soviet proposals on Berlin. . . . U.S., Britain and France are reported to have agreed to inform Soviet occupation authorities of their intent to resume military transport flights to Berlin at altitudes above the 10,000-foot ceiling demanded by the USSR.	Premier Ferhat Abbas of the rebel Algerian Provisional Government reaffirms rebel willingness to begin talks with France on the implementation of de Gaulle's self-determination program. . . . Arab League ends its Cairo conference without resolving UAR-Jordanian differences on the Palestine question.		U.S. makes public a note from the Dalai Lama of Tibet thanking the U.S. for its support of Tibetan autonomy during the 1959 U.N. debate on Tibet. . . . World Bank announces a program for more than $750 million in aid to India and Pakistan for development of the Indus River.
March 1		Soviet Embassy in East Berlin warns that Western attempts to exceed the 10,000 foot ceiling by Berlin-bound planes would be regarded as "a unilateral violation of East German air sovereignty."	An estimated 4,500 Moroccans die and 45,000 are left homeless as two earthquakes, a tidal wave and flash fire devastate the Atlantic coast resort city of Agadir. Survivors are being evacuated by joint U.S.-French-Moroccan rescue teams. . . . Pres. Sekou Toure proclaims Guinea's withdrawal from the franc zone and the creation of a domestic currency to replace the French colonial franc.	Visiting Pres. Eisenhower promises a joint session of the Chilean Congress continued U.S. support of the mutual defense concept of the 1947 Rio Defense Treaty.	The Kishi cabinet approves a Japanese-Soviet agreement for substantially increased trade. It simultaneously rejects Soviet protests over the new security treaty with the U.S. . . . Nationalist Chinese Defense Ministry reports the loss of a military motor junk in a clash with Communist Chinese gunboats north of the Matsu Islands.
March 2		Gen. Lauris Norstad, supreme NATO commander, announces a British-French-U.S. agreement to form an integrated nuclear-armed NATO task force.	Tunisian Pres. Habib Bourguiba, who met with Pres. Eisenhower in December 1959, claims that Eisenhower would support an immediate truce in Algeria as a first step to French-rebel negotiations.	Pres. Eisenhower tells a joint session of the Uruguayan Congress that the U.S. has no desire to "impose our concepts of political, cultural or economic life upon any nation."	Twelve Japanese are crushed to death by a crowd fighting for seats at a free Yokohama theater concert.
March 3			Denying suggestions that his self-determination policy was the product of military weakness, de Gaulle promises French army officers that "there will be no Dienbienphu" in Algeria. The statement draws praise from rightist leaders and angry denunciation from Algerian rebel partisans.		Soviet Premier Khrushchev, visiting Afghanistan, pledges continued Soviet aid and declares his support for Afghanistan in its territorial disputes with Pakistan and Iran. . . . North Vietnam protests alleged U.S. efforts to make Laos a virtual U.S. military base against North Vietnam.

A	B	C	D	E
Includes developments that affect more than one world region, international organizations and important meetings of major world leaders.	Includes all domestic and regional developments in Europe, including the Soviet Union, Turkey, Cyprus and Malta.	Includes all domestic and regional developments in Africa and the Middle East, including Iraq and Iran and excluding Cyprus, Turkey and Afghanistan.	Includes all domestic and regional developments in Latin America, the Caribbean and Canada.	Includes all domestic and regional developments in Asia and Pacific nations, extending from Afghanistan through all the Pacific Islands, except Hawaii.

U.S. Politics & Social Issues	U.S. Foreign Policy & Defense	U.S. Economy & Environment	Science, Technology & Nature	Culture, Leisure & Life Style	
Prominent Protestant leaders request a formal apology from Air Force Secy. Dudley Sharp and House Un-American Activities Committee chmn. Francis Walter for charges that the Nat. Council of Churches was communist-infiltrated.		Agriculture Dept. reports that net farm income dropped from $13.1 billion in 1958 to $11 billion in 1959. . . . A Senate Select Committee on Labor and Management Practices labels as "complete dishonesty" Teamsters Pres. James Hoffa's promise to clean up his union.	The first of three experimental, high-altitude X-15 rocket-planes is delivered to the Air Force by North American Aviation Co.		Feb. 26
Nashville police arrest 100 Negro and white students after fights broke out in two stores where the Negroes were conducting lunch-counter sit-ins.					Feb. 27
Independent Klansmen from 17 Southern states meet in Atlanta to form a single unified body called the Knights of the Ku Klux Klan, Inc.	American Jewish Congress renews charges that Jews are barred from State Dept. assignments in Pakistan and Air Force duties in Saudi Arabia.		Dr. Ezra Jacob Kraus, 74, horticulturist who discovered the basic carbohydrate-nitrogen growth rate principle in plants, dies in Corvallis, Ore.	USSR, with especially strong performances in speed skating and skiing, wins the unofficial team championship in the 1960 Winter Olympics. Sweden places second, the U.S. third.	Feb. 28
Eighteen Southern senators, led by Richard B. Russell (D, Ga.), begin filibuster aimed at forestalling Senate action on a pending civil rights bill. . . . Supreme Court upholds Negro registration and voting rights by overturning a U.S. dist. court decision that ruled the voting portions of the 1957 Civil Rights Act unconstitutional. . . . Gov. John Patterson (Ala.) warns that it may be impossible to prevent violence if Negroes "continue to provoke whites."	Adm. Robert L. Dennison is named commander of NATO naval forces and the U.S. Atlantic Fleet, succeeding retiring Adm. Jerauld Wright.	Pres. Eisenhower invokes the Railway Labor Act to block a threatened March 2 conductor's strike against the N.Y. Central.			Feb. 29
Black students at Tuskegee Institute begin a full-scale boycott of local white merchants to protest a 1957 Alabama state law that redrew Tuskegee city boundaries to exclude nearly all Negroes as residents and voters.		A Santa Fe passenger train en route to Chicago from San Francisco collides with an oil tank truck near Bakersfield, Calif. Fourteen persons are killed.		Robert Carson, 53, American skyscraper architect, dies in Los Angeles of a heart attack.	March 1
Fifty-seven Negroes are arrested by Nashville police after refusing to leave the lunch counters of the Greyhound and Trailways bus stations in the face of bomb threats. No bombs were found. . . . Willem Marie Louis Van Rie, 31, the radio operator of the Dutch liner *Utrecht*, accused of murdering divorcee Lynn Kauffman with whom he had an affair during a 44-day voyage from Singapore, is acquitted by a Boston jury.					March 2
Michigan Democratic Gov. G. Mennen Williams, the only six-term governor in American history, announces he will not seek re-election.		FAA announces it will provide $58 million to 314 U.S. airports to improve air travel safety.		Carol Heiss, 20, of N.Y. wins the women's world figure skating title in Vancouver, B.C. . . . American TV stars Lucille Ball and Desi Arnaz announce their separation and pending divorce in Hollywood.	March 3
F	G	H	I	J	
Includes elections, federal-state relations, civil rights and liberties, crime, the judiciary, education, health care, poverty, urban affairs and population.	Includes formation and debate of U.S. foreign and defense policies, veterans' affairs and defense spending. (Relations with specific foreign countries are usually found under the region concerned.)	Includes business, labor, agriculture, taxation, transportation, consumer affairs, monetary and fiscal policy, natural resources, and pollution.	Includes worldwide scientific, medical and technological developments, natural phenomena, U.S. weather, natural disasters, and accidents.	Includes the arts, religion, scholarship, communications media, sports, entertainment, fashions, fads and social life.	

	World Affairs	Europe	Africa & the Middle East	The Americas	Asia & the Pacific
March 4		The recent military base talks between West Germany and Spain, reminiscent to some of the Nazi-Franco alliance, reportedly have provoked mild criticism from Western powers and an angry condemnation from the USSR. . . . French government decrees new price supports for farm products to meet growing rural unrest.	Moroccan King Mohammed V announces that he will pledge his personal fortune as collateral for a loan to rebuild the earthquake-devastated city of Agadir. Estimates of the dead now run as high as 12,000.	A French freighter loaded with Cuban-bought ammunition and explosives blows up in Havana harbor, killing 75 to 100 persons.	
March 5		Premier Khrushchev returns to Moscow from his tour of Asian nations.	Guinea formally establishes diplomatic relations with East Germany. The announcement comes two days after Guinean Pres. Sekou Toure signed a $35 million Soviet loan agreement.	Cuban Premier Castro publicly suggests the explosion of the French munitions freighter was caused by U.S.-directed sabotage. . . . Venezuelan Pres. Romulo Betancourt signs an Agrarian Reform Act designed to help some 700,000 farmers acquire their own land.	Pres. Sukarno, by special decree, dissolves the Indonesian Parliament for allegedly obstructing his plans for "guided democracy."
March 6	Four starving Russian Navy men, adrift on the Pacific for 49 days in a disabled landing craft, are rescued by the U.S. carrier *Kearsage* .				India's Central Family Planning Board seeks $210 million budget increase for the government's birth control programs.
March 7	Five Western nations resume preliminary talks in Paris aimed at hammering out an agreed-upon disarmament plan to present to Soviet-bloc nations at the Geneva disarmament talks.	U.S. Min. Edward Page Jr. arrives in Sophia to restore U.S.-Bulgarian diplomatic relations broken since 1950.	Returned from a three-day inspection of Algeria, de Gaulle reiterates his hopes for the establishment of an "Algerian Algeria" closely linked to France. . . . UAR Pres. Nasser publicly accuses Jordan of surrendering to Western "imperialism" and failing to do its part in resisting Israeli "ambitions."	Canadian Defense Min. George Pearkes makes public U.S. plans to provide Canada with $72 million worth of Bomarc missiles and launching equipment.	Pakistan For. Min. Manzur Qadir challenges Afghanistan to agree to a referendum among the Pathan population of disputed Pushtunistan on which country they wish to join. . . . India announces tentative acceptance of a Soviet offer to cooperate in the building of a nuclear power station in India.
March 8			Portugal firmly denies widespread rumors of an Angolan nationalist uprising against Portuguese rule.		
March 9		U.S. Secy. of State Herter tells newsmen the West has no immediate plans to resume Soviet-opposed high-altitude flights from West Germany to Berlin, but retains the right to should such flights become an "operational necessity." . . . Foreign Trade Min. Nikolai S. Patolichev reports Soviet foreign trade has increased 62%, more than any other nation's, since 1955.			An Indonesian MiG-17 flown by an air force pilot strafes the Presidential Palace in Jakarta. No members of Sukarno's family are injured but 18 others are wounded. . . . P.M. Nehru denies reports that India has agreed to accept Soviet aid to build a nuclear power plant.
March 10		Czech ambassador to Britain announces a Czech veterans organization will seek murder indictments in West German courts against 37 Bonn government officials who reportedly served as Nazi judges in Czechoslovakia.	At a White House meeting, Israeli P.M. David Ben-Gurion urges Pres. Eisenhower to seek a summit agreement on the Middle East that would end continued Soviet build-up of UAR military strength.		
March 11		West German Bundestag approves indemnification treaties providing a total of $18 million to Norwegian and Danish victims of Nazi war crimes.			

A	B	C	D	E
Includes developments that affect more than one world region, international organizations and important meetings of major world leaders.	Includes all domestic and regional developments in Europe, including the Soviet Union, Turkey, Cyprus and Malta.	Includes all domestic and regional developments in Africa and the Middle East, including Iraq and Iran and excluding Cyprus, Turkey and Afghanistan.	Includes all domestic and regional developments in Latin America, the Caribbean and Canada.	Includes all domestic and regional developments in Asia and Pacific nations, extending from Afghanistan through all the Pacific Islands, except Hawaii.

U.S. Politics & Social Issues	U.S. Foreign Policy & Defense	U.S. Economy & Environment	Science, Technology & Nature	Culture, Leisure & Life Style	
N.Y. Gov. Nelson Rockefeller reiterates his decision not to be a vice-presidential candidate.				Leonard Warren, 49, a Metropolitan Opera baritone since 1938, dies of a stroke during a performance in N.Y. . . . . Oscar Robertson, Jerry West, Jerry Lucas, Darrall Imhoff, and Tony Jackson are named to the AP All-American basketball team.	March 4
				Natl. Boxing Assn. restores the light-heavyweight crown to Archie Moore after learning that the 43-year-old fighter is planning to defend his title against leading contenders.	March 5
Upholding New York state's right of eminent domain, the U.S. Supreme Court rules 6-3 that the Tuscarora Indians must sell part of their tribal lands for a Niagara River hydroelectric project. . . . Five hundred state and local police turn back about 800 Negro demonstrators attempting a protest march on the Alabama state capitol in Montgomery.			Roy Knabenshue, aviation pioneer and the Wright brothers' general manager, dies at 83.		March 6
A charge by Gov. Wesley Powell, Nixon's N.H. primary campaign chairman, that Kennedy is "soft on communism" is publicly repudiated by Nixon. . . . Four masked white youths in Houston, Tex. kidnap and torture a 27-year-old Negro man in retaliation against a sit-in demonstration by Texas Southern Univ. students.	In a TV report on his recent trip, Pres. Eisenhower claims that despite some misunderstandings U.S.-Latin American relations are at an all-time high.			Fourteen thousand members of the AFL-CIO Screen Actors Guild walk out at seven of Hollywood's eight big studios to support demands for residual payments to actors in movies sold to TV.	March 7
V.P. Nixon and Sen. John Kennedy (D, Mass.) roll up record votes in New Hampshire's presidential primary. Neither candidate faced serious opposition.	Israeli Prime Min. David Ben-Gurion arrives in Boston for an informal weeklong visit to the U.S.	*Parade* magazine publisher, Arthur H. Motley, is elected president of the U.S. Chamber of Commerce.			March 8
Richard L. Neuberger, U.S. Senator (D, Ore.) since 1954, dies in Portland of a brain hemorrhage at 47.	Herter tells newsmen that the U.S. has strongly protested Castro's "baseless" anti-American charges, but adds there is currently no plan to sever U.S.-Cuban relations.		By a vote of 398 to 10, the House approves the Administration's request for a $915 million NASA appropriation.	AFL Commissioner Joe Foss announces he has filed a deposition with the Justice Dept. accusing the NFL of franchising a club in Dallas in an illegal campaign to destroy the AFL.	March 9
A cloture motion to break the continuing Southern filibuster against the Senate civil rights bill fails by a vote of 53-42. . . . Industrialist Bernard Goldfine is indicted in Boston on charges of evading federal income taxes.	NATO commander Lauris Norstad assures a Joint Congressional Atomic Energy Committee that there are no plans to turn over U.S. nuclear weapons to the control of a proposed multi-nation NATO nuclear force.	A three-man arbitration board orders Wilson packing company to rehire 3,000 United Packinghouse Workers who had been replaced during a recently settled strike.		FCC Chrm. Charles Doerfer resigns under pressure after admitting to a House subcommittee that had accepted a vacation cruise on the yacht of George B. Storer, owner of 12 TV and radio stations. FCC member Frederick W. Ford will succeed Doerfer as chairman.	March 10
		Pres. Eisenhower asks Congress to authorize postal rate hikes, raising first class mail from 4¢ to 5¢ and air mail from 7¢ to 8¢. . . . Justice Dept. asks the Supreme Court to compel the E. I. du Pont Co. to dispose of its 63 million shares of GM stock.	NASA successfully launches a 94-pound radio-equipped satellite (Pioneer V) into orbit around the sun; it is only the third (one Soviet, two U.S.) man-made object to be projected into a solar orbit.	High-jumper John Thomas breaks his own world record with a jump of 7 feet 2.5 inches at the Chicago Relays.	March 11
F	G	H	I	J	
Includes elections, federal-state relations, civil rights and liberties, crime, the judiciary, education, health care, poverty, urban affairs and population.	*Includes formation and debate of U.S. foreign and defense policies, veterans' affairs and defense spending. (Relations with specific foreign countries are usually found under the region concerned.)*	*Includes business, labor, agriculture, taxation, transportation, consumer affairs, monetary and fiscal policy, natural resources, and pollution.*	*Includes worldwide scientific, medical and technological developments, natural phenomena, U.S. weather, natural disasters, and accidents.*	*Includes the arts, religion, scholarship, communications media, sports, entertainment, fashions, fads and social life.*	

	World Affairs	Europe	Africa & the Middle East	The Americas	Asia & the Pacific
March 12	Dr. Benjamin Alfonso Cohen, 63, Chilean diplomat and former U.N. official, dies in N.Y.	Premier Khrushchev, scheduled to visit France March 15, announces that he will postpone the trip till March 23 because of illness. . . . Soviet CP reports party membership at an all-time high of 8,017,000.	Responding to recent Egyptian attacks, Jordan's King Hussein declares that his nation would willingly join the UAR if the latter were genuinely "prepared to open a final battle with the common enemy, Israel."		Pres. Chiang Kai-shek is renominated by the dominant Kuomintang Party for a third term as Nationalist Chinese president, despite a constitutional limit of two terms. . . . Chinese newspapers reaching Hong Kong confirm an unsuccessful revolt against Communist rule occurred in Tsinghai Province on the China-Tibet border in 1958.
March 13		Soviet Amb.-to-West Germany Andrei A. Smirnov reportedly tells a meeting of West German leaders that the USSR would oppose German reunification until the Western sector demonstrated its "peace-loving" intentions by abolishing "monopoly capital" and freeing the working class. . . . British P.M. Macmillan concludes two days of private talks with French Pres. de Gaulle.			
March 14	Western delegations to the Geneva disarmament conference make public a joint proposal for the gradual reduction of conventional and nuclear armament under strict international controls. The three-stage Western plan, worked out in France March 7-10, provides for an International Disarmament Organization to supervise implementation of the agreement. . . . Israeli P.M. Ben-Gurion and West German Chancellor Adenauer, both visiting the U.S., meet informally to discuss recent anti-Semitic incidents in Germany. Report of the meeting draws criticism from Israeli leftists.	Soviet occupation authorities, responding to Western protests, rescind special travel passes with which they had sought to imply Western recognition of East Germany. . . . British Labor Party's vice chairman, Richard H.S. Crossman, resigns to protest the party leadership's support of a British nuclear deterrent.	Rebel Algerian Provisional Government charges bellicose statements made by de Gaulle after his recent visit to Algeria had "closed the door on negotiation and peace." . . . Israeli P.M. Ben-Gurion meets in N. Y. with U.N. Secy. Gen. Dag Hammarskjold to discuss Israel-UAR border clashes and use of the Suez Canal.	Flooding in Pernabuco, Brazil kills an estimated 100 persons.	
March 15	The 10-nation Geneva disarmament talks formally begin with the reading of goodwill messages from Pres. Eisenhower, Premier Khrushchev and U.N. Secy. Gen. Hammarskjold. . . . Soviet delegation at the opening session of the Geneva talks expresses its opposition to the rigid controls and protracted timetable in the Western delegates' proposed disarmament plan, and urges that consideration be given to a total and immediate disarmament pact.	Eisenhower promises West German Chancellor Adenauer that West Berlin's "freedom" would not be sacrificed to Soviet demands at the forthcoming summit talks.	An Algerian known only by the *nom de guerre* Boumedienne is named chief of staff of the rebel forces. . . . Ghana asks France to investigate an alleged plot to attack Ghana by groups in neighboring French-administered Togoland.	Argentine Pres. Arturo Frondizi declares a state of "internal war" in the wake of scattered terrorist attacks on government personnel and facilities.	South Korean Pres. Syngman Rhee, 84, is re-elected without opposition to a fourth consecutive four-year term.
March 16	Soviet Geneva delegation rejects a British proposal for a separate treaty banning nuclear weapons from outer space, arguing that the conference should seek a single comprehensive disarmament plan.	West German Chancellor Adenauer, visiting the U.S., calls for a plebiscite on the future of West Berlin as a means of providing Western summit negotiators with hard evidence of West Berlin's opposition to Soviet proposals for a "free city." . . . British Labor Party announces it has revised Clause Four of its charter (stating the party's commitment to nationalization) to include an explicit acknowledgment of the role of private enterprise.	A bill providing for Congolese general elections prior to the June 30 independence date is approved by the Belgian Parliament.		Philippine Pres. Carlos Garcia denies that his "Filipino First" economic policy threatens American or other foreign investment.
March 17			Algerian rebel sources report France ignored a mid-February rebel offer to begin Algerian ceasefire talks. France denies the receipt of any such offer.	Lt. Cmndr. Miguel Pons Goizueta, the Cuban naval attache in Washington, resigns, accusing the Cuban government of being "under the most absolute influence of international communism." The Cuban government later accuses him of absconding with $110,000.	

A	B	C	D	E
Includes developments that affect more than one world region, international organizations and important meetings of major world leaders.	Includes all domestic and regional developments in Europe, including the Soviet Union, Turkey, Cyprus and Malta.	Includes all domestic and regional developments in Africa and the Middle East, including Iraq and Iran and excluding Cyprus, Turkey and Afghanistan.	Includes all domestic and regional developments in Latin America, the Caribbean and Canada.	Includes all domestic and regional developments in Asia and Pacific nations, extending from Afghanistan through all the Pacific Islands, except Hawaii.

U.S. Politics & Social Issues	U.S. Foreign Policy & Defense	U.S. Economy & Environment	Science, Technology & Nature	Culture, Leisure & Life Style	
A mistrial is declared in the Los Angeles trial of Dr. R. Bernard Finch and his mistress, Carole Tregoff, for the murder of Finch's wife.					March 12
		Natl. Housing Conference recommends creation of a "Dept. of Housing and Urban Redevelopment" to consolidate all federal housing activities.		Philadelphia Warrior Wilt Chamberlain becomes first NBA player to win Rookie of the Year and the league's mvp award.	March 13
Spokesmen at the N.Y. headquarters of the Woolworth, Kresge, Kress and Grant chain stores say they will not integrate lunch counters until Southern public opinion changes. . . . Improper conduct charges against Manhattan Borough Pres. Hulan Jack, the highest elected Negro office-holder in the U.S., are dismissed by a N.Y. court for lack of evidence.		James Hoffa tells a rally of 9,000 Teamsters that he will wage an all-out fight against lawmakers who are allegedly trying to destroy the union. . . . Nine Internatl. Mine, Mill and Smelter Workers officials are convicted in Denver of falsely denying CP membership on NLRB affidavits.		The Sportsmanship Brotherhood Plaque is awarded to Jack Twyman for taking care of Maurice Stokes, his ex-Cincinnati Royals teammate striken with encephalitis in 1958.	March 14
Police in Orangeville, S.C. use fire hoses and tear gas to disperse about 1,000 Negroes protesting lunch-counter segregation; 350 of the demonstrators are arrested.	Thomas G. Lanphier Jr. resigns his vice presidency with General Dynamics Corp., maker of the Atlas ICBM, in order to continue his criticism of Eisenhower administration defense policies.	An FAA order goes into effect barring airline pilots older than 59 from making commercial flights. About 47 pilots are immediately affected. . . . Labor Dept. reports that February unemployment fell to 4.8%, lowest since October 1957.	W.R. Grace & Co. disclose that for nearly a year it has been producing a strong and versatile plastic film by bombarding polyethylene with an "atomic gun."		March 15
Pres. Eisenhower, at a White House press conference, endorses the presidential candidacy of V. P. Nixon. . . . San Antonio, Tex., among the first major Southern cities to integrate its public transportation, becomes the first to open variety store lunch counters to Negro customers. . . . Seventeen Negroes arrested during Atlanta's first sit-in demonstrations face criminal charges under Georgia's just-passed "anti-sit-in" laws.	Defense Secy. Thomas Gates tells the Senate Preparedness Subcommittee that the U.S.'s overall destructive nuclear power is "several times" greater than the USSR's.				March 16
Pres. Eisenhower asks Congress to liberalize U.S. immigration law by doubling the number of quota admissions and expanding allowances for refugees.	Pres. Eisenhower announces he will visit Portugal on his return from the Paris summit meeting in May.	All 63 persons aboard a Northwest Airlines Electra turboprop are killed when the plane explodes in mid-air over Indiana. . . . Pres. Eisenhower outlines to Congress plans for a joint business-government drive to reduce the U.S. balance of payments deficit through a major export drive.			March 17

F	G	H	I	J
Includes elections, federal-state relations, civil rights and liberties, crime, the judiciary, education, health care, poverty, urban affairs and population.	Includes formation and debate of U.S. foreign and defense policies, veterans' affairs and defense spending. (Relations with specific foreign countries are usually found under the region concerned.)	Includes business, labor, agriculture, taxation, transportation, consumer affairs, monetary and fiscal policy, natural resources, and pollution.	Includes worldwide scientific, medical and technological developments, natural phenomena, U.S. weather, natural disasters, and accidents.	Includes the arts, religion, scholarship, communications media, sports, entertainment, fashions, fads and social life.

	World Affairs	Europe	Africa & the Middle East	The Americas	Asia & the Pacific
March 18		A request for a special National Assembly session to deal with growing unrest among French farmers, signed by a majority of the Assembly deputies, is denied by Pres. de Gaulle. Critics label the action unconstitutional.	South Africa's militant Pan-Africanist Congress launches mass protests against the government's racial pass and apartheid policies. . . . Israeli P.M. Ben-Gurion, in Britain for talks with P.M. Macmillan, tells a London press conference that Israel intends to divert some Jordan River waters for irrigation purposes despite strong Arab opposition. . . . Pres. Nasser appoints seven new ministers to the UAR's Syrian regional cabinet, filling the vacancies created by the withdrawal of all Baath Party members from the government.	Dominican Republic refuses to permit an OAS investigation into Venezuelan charges that human rights are being violated in the Dominican Republic.	A Communist Chinese People's Court sentences Bishop James E. Walsh, 69, an American Maryknoll missionary, and 12 Chinese priests to long prison terms because of their "counter-revolutionary" refusal to sever ties with Vatican. . . . South Korean sources report that a proposal by Syngman Rhee for a military assault on North Korea has been rejected by Pres. Eisenhower.
March 19	Soviet test-ban negotiators in Geneva offer to accept a U.S.-proposed ban, limited to large, detectable tests, if the West will agree to a four-year voluntary moratorium on small underground blasts not covered by the formal agreement. U.S. State Dept. and the British Foreign Office announce they will give the Soviet offer serious study. . . . Pres. Eisenhower reportedly has assured Premier Khrushchev that the U.S. currently has no plans to share its nuclear weapons with its Western allies.			Bolivian government troops in La Paz crush a brief revolt by rightist elements in the national police force.	
March 20					
March 21	Soviet delegates to the three-nation test ban talks explain that their proposed four-year voluntary moratorium on small nuclear testing would allow completion of joint research on improving test detection, the results of which might clear the way for a more comprehensive and permanent test-ban.		Fifty-six Africans are killed and over 160 wounded as South African police open fire on a crowd of 20,000 persons protesting the government's racial pass system in Sharpeville, near Johannesburg.	A U.S. two-engine Piper Comanche is shot down near Matanzas, Cuba.	Nepal and Communist China agree to begin talks over long-standing border disputes. . . . Rightist Dudley S. Senanayake is sworn in as Ceylon's new prime minister following an overwhelming parliamentary victory by conservative and rightist parties. . . . Nationalist Chinese Assembly in Taipei overwhelmingly re-elects Chiang Kai-shek to his third six-year term as president.
March 22	France announces its opposition to the test-ban proposal being considered by the USSR, Britain and the U.S., claiming it benefits only those countries that have already completed advanced nuclear testing.	In London, 600 persons clash with police during an angry demonstration outside the South Africa House. . . . British Queen Elizabeth II chooses the name Andrew Albert Christian Edward for her second son, born Feb. 19.	South African opposition parties—Liberals, Progressives and the United Party—blame P.M. Henrik Verwoerd's apartheid race policies for yesterday's violence. . . . UAR's National Union political front opens a Cairo recruiting office for Arab volunteers wishing to join the Algerian rebels.		Through ambassadorial channels in Poland, the U.S. delivers a formal protest against the imprisonment of Bishop James Walsh by the Communist Chinese.
March 23	Soviet disarmament negotiators say that they too favor strict controls and inspection, but insist that discussion of specific control provisions must await agreement on a general disarmament plan.	Soviet Premier Khrushchev arrives in Paris for an 11-day state visit to France. Anti-Communist refugees have reportedly been rounded up and sent to Corsica for the duration of the visit. . . . Polish sources report conclusion of Roman Catholic Church-Polish government agreement in which the state pledges liberalization of anti-church restrictions in exchange for church support of public programs to improve labor discipline and respect for state property.	Moroccan sources report growing political strife between leftist supporters of Premier Abdullas Ibrahim and conservative elements backed by Crown Prince Moulay Hassan. Widespread arrests are reported.		

	A	B	C	D	E
	Includes developments that affect more than one world region, international organizations and important meetings of major world leaders.	Includes all domestic and regional developments in Europe, including the Soviet Union, Turkey, Cyprus and Malta.	Includes all domestic and regional developments in Africa and the Middle East, including Iraq and Iran and excluding Cyprus, Turkey and Afghanistan.	Includes all domestic and regional developments in Latin America, the Caribbean and Canada.	Includes all domestic and regional developments in Asia and Pacific nations, extending from Afghanistan through all the Pacific Islands, except Hawaii.

U.S. Politics & Social Issues	U.S. Foreign Policy & Defense	U.S. Economy & Environment	Science, Technology & Nature	Culture, Leisure & Life Style	
Eugene G. Smith, Little Rock police chief who rose to national prominence during the city's school integration crises in 1957 and 1959, kills his wife and commits suicide a few hours after his son's conviction on burglary charges.		Pres. Eisenhower averts a Pan American World Airways strike by creating a three-man emergency board to investigate a contract dispute involving the airline's 6,000 clerks.			March 18
				Ohio State defeats California, 75-55, to win the NCAA national basketball title. . . . Bill Nieder, 26, sets a world 16-lb. shotput record of 63 feet 10 inches.	March 19
The New York Times reports that demonstrations in sympathy with Southern Negro sit-in protests have occurred at over 20 Northern colleges. . . . V.P. Nixon says he supports the death penalty as a necessary deterrent to serious crime.		Commerce Dept. reports the U.S. balance of payments deficit rose to a record $3.702 billion in 1959.		Bradley wins the National Invitation Basketball Tournament in N.Y. by defeating Providence 88-72. . . . (Mary Agnes) Polly Thomson, 75, Scottish-born teacher and companion of Helen Keller, dies in Bridgeport, Conn.	March 20
		California water officials begin a campaign to win voter approval of a water development designed to channel northern California river water into arid regions in the southern part of the state. . . . Pres. Eisenhower indicates that he would favor congressional action to end federal regulation of producers of natural gas.			March 21
At a White House meeting, Pres. Eisenhower and GOP leaders turn down several proposals by HEW Secy. Arthur Flemming for federally funded voluntary health insurance for the aged, concluding that more study is needed before an appropriate bill can be given to Congress. . . . AP reports more than 1,000 Negroes have been arrested in connection with lunch-counter protests since the first sit-in in Greensboro, N.C., Feb. 1.	State Dept. spokesman Lincoln White says the U.S. deplores the "tragic loss of life resulting from the measures taken against the demonstrators in South Africa." . . . A new Air Force regulation allowing base commanders to transfer the time-honored service custom of "KP" duty from servicemen to hired civilians is disclosed.				March 22
			An effort to place an Explorer satellite into orbit fails when the third stage of its Juno II launching rocket misfires. It is the fourth U.S. satellite launch failure since Feb. 4.		March 23

F	G	H	I	J
Includes elections, federal-state relations, civil rights and liberties, crime, the judiciary, education, health care, poverty, urban affairs and population.	Includes formation and debate of U.S. foreign and defense policies, veterans' affairs and defense spending. (Relations with specific foreign countries are usually found under the region concerned.)	Includes business, labor, agriculture, taxation, transportation, consumer affairs, monetary and fiscal policy, natural resources, and pollution.	Includes worldwide scientific, medical and technological developments, natural phenomena, U.S. weather, natural disasters, and accidents.	Includes the arts, religion, scholarship, communications media, sports, entertainment, fashions, fads and social life.

	World Affairs	Europe	Africa & the Middle East	The Americas	Asia & the Pacific
March 24	Britain and the U.S. announce that P.M. Macmillan will meet with Eisenhower in Washington to discuss a Western reply to the Soviet A-ban proposal.	Khrushchev and Pres. de Gaulle begin formal discussions in Paris on the political future of Europe.			International Press Institute, meeting in Tokyo, expels Indonesia's IPI chapter because of that country's "suppression of the press."
March 25		Soviet Premier Khrushchev completes a series of Paris speeches in which he repeatedly warns against a rebirth of German militarism and appeals to France to join the USSR in resisting it. . . . Italian Christian Democrat Fernando Tambroni announces the formation of a minority cabinet to succeed that of out-going Premier Antonio Segni. The pro-Western Segni will be retained as foreign minister.		U.S. Amb.-to-Cuba Philip Bonsal, who returned to Havana March 20, delivers three diplomatic notes denying Cuban charges that U.S. is frustrating Cuban reforms.	
March 26	British P.M. Macmillan arrives in Washington to meet with Pres. Eisenhower to discuss a reply to the Soviet test-ban offer.		A temporary suspension of racial pass laws by the Verwoerd government fails to allay anger among African opponents of the general apartheid system. . . . France agrees to grant Madagascar independent status within the French Community. . . . U.S. Amb.-to-UAR G. Frederick Reinhardt signs an agreement to provide $47 million in U.S. development loans to the UAR's Egyptian region.	Havana's channel four TV station is placed under state control; it is the fifth of seven Havana stations to lose its private independent status. . . . Canadian Bureau of Statistics reports unemployment rose in February to 8.9% of the work force.	
March 27		British Labor head Hugh Gaitskell urges P.M. Macmillan to persuade the U.S. to accept the Soviet test ban offer.	Iraqi Premier Abdul Karim el-Kassem announces plans to train Palestinian Arabs for a war to restore their homeland. . . . UPI reports at least five persons have been killed in Bagdad in street fighting between Communists and Iraqi nationalists.	Despite a defeat in the popular vote, the Argentine government's Intransigent Radical Party retains enough incumbents to maintain a majority in the Chamber of Deputies.	Pres. Sukarno announces the appointment of 261 members to a new Indonesian Parliament that will help him implement his "guided democracy" program. Sukarno pledges free elections to replace the appointees before the end of 1962.
March 28	Italian disarmament delegates outline a Western proposal for a joint East-West International Disarmament Organization to supervise the implementation of a disarmament pact.	Twenty Glasgow firemen are killed when a burning warehouse filled with whiskey explodes. It is the worst toll of firemen in any single British fire.		*The New York Times* reports that some 300 Greek, Spanish and Yugoslav nationals had been invited in 1959 to the Dominican Republic on the promise of employment and then forced to train for a planned invasion of Cuba. Those who refused are allegedly in Dominican jails.	Indonesia Foreign Min. Subandrio warns Communist China that its criticism of Indonesia's treatment of Chinese aliens may cause further anti-Chinese "unrest."
March 29	In a joint communique issued after two days of meetings, Pres. Eisenhower and P.M. Macmillan announce they will accept the recent Soviet test-ban proposal if the USSR agrees in advance to strict control and inspection provisions and a shortened moratorium.	In a private meeting, Generalissimo Francisco Franco assures Don Juan de Bourbon, pretender to the Spanish crown, of his eventual ascendance to the throne.	South African Parliament votes to consider government proposals banning all African and Asian political organizations.	Chile and Argentina agree to submit border and navigation disputes to independent, third party arbitration.	An agreement providing for a 10% increase in Soviet-Chinese trade is signed in Peking.
March 30	Commenting on the two conferences being held in Geneva, Khrushchev says there appears to be "little common ground" on general disarmament, but that "prospects are good" for a U.S.-British-USSR test-ban pact. . . . Soviet disarmament negotiators indicate the USSR is prepared to discuss extension of its four-year time limit for the accomplishment of total world disarmament.	Rumania and the U.S. sign an agreement in Washington to settle $60 million in claims by U.S. citizens against Rumania for $24.5 million.	South Africa declares a state of national emergency in the face of widespread strikes and mass protests against the racial pass laws and other apartheid policies of P.M. Verwoerd's Nationalist Party regime. . . . Verwoerd denounces a U.N. Security Council decision to discuss South African racial strife as unwarranted domestic interference.		Communist-China estimates its 1959 GNP at $95 billion. A 23% increase is projected for fiscal 1960. . . . The Communist Chinese finance ministry presents the National People's Congress with a record budget of $28 billion; $2.3 billion of the total is earmarked for defense.

A	B	C	D	E
Includes developments that affect more than one world region, international organizations and important meetings of major world leaders.	Includes all domestic and regional developments in Europe, including the Soviet Union, Turkey, Cyprus and Malta.	Includes all domestic and regional developments in Africa and the Middle East, including Iraq and Iran and excluding Cyprus, Turkey and Afghanistan.	Includes all domestic and regional developments in Latin America, the Caribbean and Canada.	Includes all domestic and regional developments in Asia and Pacific nations, extending from Afghanistan through all the Pacific Islands, except Hawaii.

U.S. Politics & Social Issues	U.S. Foreign Policy & Defense	U.S. Economy & Environment	Science, Technology & Nature	Culture, Leisure & Life Style	
House passes (311 to 109) and sends to the Senate a civil rights bill that would authorize the appointment of federal referees in districts where voter discrimination is alleged. The bill also makes obstruction of school desegregation orders a federal crime. . . . Sen. Stuart Symington announces that he will actively seek the Democratic Party's presidential nomination.				Chinese Nationalists ban the export of pirated editions of foreign-language books. The action follows protests by American and other book publishers.	March 24
	State Secy. Herter tells Washington newsmen that while the U.S. acknowledges concessions in the Soviet test-ban offer, it has serious objections to the length of the proposed moratorium and to the vagueness of control and inspection provisions.	Bureau of Labor Statistics reports the consumer price index, after a two-month decline, climbed to a record level in February (125.6% of the 1947-1949 average).		A U.S. court of appeals in New York rules that D. H. Lawrence's *Lady Chatterley's Lover* is not obscene and cannot be barred from the mails. . . . Philadelphia Warrior star Wilt Chamberlain announces his resignation from the NBA, saying that his decision had "some connection" with racial problems.	March 25
Tenn. Gov. Buford Ellington charges that a March 25 state capitol sit-in demonstration, filmed by CBS news, was deliberately staged by the network. CBS Pres. Frank Stanton denies the charge. . . . Gadsden, Ala. police arrest Hubert Jackson, 16-year-old self-styled Nazi, for the March 25 bombing of a Jewish synagogue that left one worshipper critically wounded.			Dr. Emil H. Grubbe, 85, pioneer in X-ray therapy for cancer, whose early experiments made him a cancer victim in 1895, dies in Chicago of bronchial pneumonia caused by the spread of cancer to his lungs. He had undergone 93 operations since 1895 to remove tumors.	Dallas Long breaks his own world shot-put record with a throw of 64 feet 6.5 inches in Los Angeles.	March 26
A joint report of the White House Conference on Children and Youth, meeting in College Park, Md., urges greater federal involvement in solving child welfare and youth related problems. . . . A rash of cross-burnings and well attended rallies today and yesterday mark an apparent revival of Ku Klux Klan activities throughout the deep South.	A report of the U.S. Jewish Labor Committee charges Soviet-bloc nations with systematically suppressing Jewish cultural and religious life.				March 27
V.P. Nixon tells 7,000 Republicans at a Lincoln, Nebraska dinner that he intends to campaign on the issues and not on personalities. . . . Rep. Russell V. Mack (R, Wash.), 68, dies of a heart attack on the House floor.	Supreme Court upholds the 1957 espionage conviction of Col. Rudolf Abel by a 5-4 vote. Abel claimed evidence used against him had been seized illegally.		Medical authorities with the World Health Organization report cigarette smoking appears to be a "major causative factor" in the worldwide increase in the incidence of lung cancer.	Pope John XXIII installs seven new members of the College of Cardinals, including the first Negro to be elevated in modern times.	March 28
Richard Hickock and Perry Smith are sentenced to be hanged for the 1959 murder of the Herbert Clutter family in Garden City, Kan.	Rear Adm. John F. Davidson is named superintendent of the U.S. Naval Academy.			O'Keefe Center for the Performing Arts is dedicated in Toronto, Canada.	March 29
Pres. Eisenhower says at a Washington press conference that he opposes compulsory federal medical-care insurance for the aged, calling it "socialized medicine."		A Senate Committee on Unemployment Problems, headed by Sen. Eugene McCarthy (D, Minn.), says that federal policies must be designed to create more jobs for the U.S.'s growing population. . . . Agriculture Dept. reports cigarette production in 1959 reached a record 490 billion, a 4% increase over 1958.		*Clea* by Lawrence Durrell is published in New York.	March 30

F	G	H	I	J
Includes elections, federal-state relations, civil rights and liberties, crime, the judiciary, education, health care, poverty, urban affairs and population.	Includes formation and debate of U.S. foreign and defense policies, veterans' affairs and defense spending. (Relations with specific foreign countries are usually found under the region concerned.)	Includes business, labor, agriculture, taxation, transportation, consumer affairs, monetary and fiscal policy, natural resources, and pollution.	Includes worldwide scientific, medical and technological developments, natural phenomena, U.S. weather, natural disasters, and accidents.	Includes the arts, religion, scholarship, communications media, sports, entertainment, fashions, fads and social life.

	World Affairs	Europe	Africa & the Middle East	The Americas	Asia & the Pacific
March 31		A government White Paper reports that Britain's GNP rose $1.9 billion in 1959 to a total of $58.32 billion.	Over 300 African leaders are reportedly arrested under the South African emergency regulations.	Canadian Finance Min. Donald Flemming presents Parliament with $5.88 billion balanced budget for fiscal 1960-1961.	
April 1	Western negotiators reiterate their appeals for immediate negotiations to prevent the launching of nuclear weapons into orbit around the earth. Soviet delegates again reject the proposal. . . . Asked by French newsmen for his reaction to France's second successful nuclear test, Khrushchev says that it simply underscores the need for a test-ban accord. . . . U.N. Security Council votes 9-0 to urge South Africa to end apartheid and political repression. Britain and France abstain, saying that South African racial strife is an internal affair.	France conducts its second successful A-test in the Sahara. . . . NATO defense ministers, meeting in Paris, agree to help West Germany find foreign training and logistic bases within the NATO community.	Dr. Hastings K. Banda, head of the Nyasaland African National Congress, is released from prison after serving 14 months for his part in sponsoring 1959 racial protest demonstrations.	Generalissimo Rafael Trujillo resigns as leader of his long dominant Dominican Party, ostensibly to encourage the formation of opposition parties in the Dominican Republic.	Tuanku Abdul Rahman, 65, paramount ruler of Malaya since it gained independence in 1957, dies of a heart ailment in Kuala Lumpur.
April 2	Japan reports its Antarctic whaling fleets filled their 1960 legal kill quota of 5,216 blue whales. Combined with totals from other whaling countries, the 1960 kill numbers 14,676.	U.S. State Dept. rejects Premier Khrushchev's assertion at a Paris press conference that a Soviet-East German peace treaty would automatically void "all the rights of the occupying powers" in Berlin.			
April 3		Premier Khrushchev ends his French visit without reaching any agreement on the outstanding problems of disarmament, Germany, or European security.			King Norodom Suramarit, 64, of Cambodia, dies.
April 4		British Parliament receives a government budget calling for expenditures of $15.89 billion in fiscal 1961. . . . Speaking in Chicago, State Secy. Herter warns that failure to end the division of Germany will "inevitably" risk continued world peace.	An accord granting the Mali Federation (the republics of Senegal and Sudan) full independence within the French Community is signed in Paris.		Japan and South Korea announce plans to reopen talks April 15 on the resumption of diplomatic relations broken in 1959. . . . Both Nepal and Communist China claim exclusive sovereignty over Mt. Everest during border talks held in Katmandu, Nepal. . . . Pres. Eisenhower turns down a request from Philippine Pres. Carlos Garcia for a 200,000 ton increase in the Philippine sugar quota.
April 5	Western delegates formally reject Premier Khrushchev's plan for total disarmament because it lacks an inspection system.	Laborites and Liberals in Parliament criticize Britain's abstention on the April 1 U.N. Security Council resolution condemning South African race policies.	South African legislature passes a government bill outlawing the Pan-Africanist Congress, the African National Congress and all other non-white political organizations.		U Nu is sworn in to succeed Gen. Ne Win as premier of Burma.
April 6		Premier Khrushchev's recent warnings to French audiences about a rebirth of German militarism draws an angry repudiation from the West German foreign ministry.	South African Justice Min. Francois C. Erasmus announces the reinstatement of the temporarily suspended racial pass laws. Africans who burned their passes during recent protests will be issued new ones. . . . French Army announces the successful completion of an eight-month campaign against rebel forces in the Kabylia Mts. east of Algiers.	Columbian Pres. Alberto Lleras Camargo, visiting the U.S., tells a joint session of Congress that increased aid for economic development is urgently needed if order and democracy are to survive in Latin America. . . . Internat. Monetary Fund in Washington announces approval of $100 million in stand-by credits for Venezuela.	Indian Defense Min. Krishna Menon reports that Communist Chinese planes violated Indian-claimed air space along the disputed northeast border at least 43 times during February and March. . . . Chinese officials claim that commune system has been extended to the vast majority of Communist China's population.
April 7	Soviet disarmament negotiators formally announce their rejection of the West's three-stage disarmament plan. The statement comes one day after the Western nations rejected Khrushchev's total and immediate disarmament formula.	French Pres. de Gaulle, addressing the British Parliament during his first visit to England since W.W.II, urges the destruction of all existing nuclear weapons as an essential step to attaining world peace.	Strikes and demonstrations by Africans protesting South African race laws begin to ebb in the face of mass detentions and firm police measures. . . . Tunisian Pres. Bourguiba reveals a French offer to withdraw its troops from the Bizerte base by Oct. 31.	In a speech to the National Press Club, Colombian Pres. Camargo Lleras expresses concern over the American public's apparent acceptance of dictatorships in Latin America.	
	A	**B**	**C**	**D**	**E**
	Includes developments that affect more than one world region, international organizations and important meetings of major world leaders.	*Includes all domestic and regional developments in Europe, including the Soviet Union, Turkey, Cyprus and Malta.*	*Includes all domestic and regional developments in Africa and the Middle East, including Iraq and Iran and excluding Cyprus, Turkey and Afghanistan.*	*Includes all domestic and regional developments in Latin America, the Caribbean and Canada.*	*Includes all domestic and regional developments in Asia and Pacific nations, extending from Afghanistan through all the Pacific Islands, except Hawaii.*

U.S. Politics & Social Issues	U.S. Foreign Policy & Defense	U.S. Economy & Environment	Science, Technology & Nature	Culture, Leisure & Life Style	
Several thousand students at the all-Negro Southern University boycott classes to protest a Louisiana board of education order suspending 18 students arrested during sit-in demonstrations.				*The Best Man*, a play by Gore Vidal opens to favorable reviews in N.Y.	March 31
Three white GIs, stationed at Ft. Benning, Ga., are sentenced to 30 days in jail for violating Georgia's new anti-trespass law when they attempted to get service at a Negro grill in Columbus, Ga.			A TV-equipped weather satellite, Tiros I, is successfully launched into earth orbit from Cape Canaveral and is reportedly transmitting clear pictures of the earth's cloud cover. . . . U.S. State Dept. announces an agreement with Yugoslavia for cooperation in the development of peaceful uses of atomic energy.		April 1
		A special cabinet committee on economic affairs predicts "great expansion" in U.S. economic growth during the 1960's.		Ex-middleweight champ Sugar Ray Robinson, 39, scores a first round knockout over Tony Baldoni, 29, in a non-title bout in Baltimore. . . . Lt. Bill Neider sets a world shotput record of 65 ft. 7 inches in Austin, Texas.	April 2
			Dr. Harold R. Nelson, nuclear physicist who helped develop the A-bomb, dies at 55 in a boating accident. . . . British Agricultural Research Council reports that average levels of radioactive strontium-90 in British milk increased 40% in the first half of 1959.		April 3
A special grand jury is called in Marshall, Texas to probe "possible outside influences" lying behind the first Negro demonstrations in Marshall since Reconstruction.		Supreme Court upholds a minority union's right to urge consumer boycotts of a firm's products provided it does not prevent the pickup or delivery of goods. The decision reverses previous NLRB rulings.	Pres. Eisenhower declares April 12 as "Vaccination Day" to commemorate the 5th anniversary of the announcement of the Salk polio vaccine.	*Ben Hur* wins a record 11 Academy Awards, including an Oscar for best picture and the best actor award for its star, Charlton Heston.	April 4
Sen. John Kennedy easily defeats Sen. Hubert H. Humphrey in the Wis. Democratic presidential primary. Humphrey says the forthcoming W. Va. primary will provide a more "decisive" test of support.			The 1960 Atoms for Peace Prize is awarded to Dr. Walter Zinn and Dr. Alvin Weinberg, pioneers in the development of nuclear reactors.		April 5
				Gamble Benedict, 19, Remington typewriter heiress, marries Rumanian-born hairdresser Andre Porumbeanu, 35, after an elopement in defiance of her family. . . . *The New York Times* is selected as the best U.S. daily paper in a poll of U.S. editors.	April 6
Reputed mobster Johnny Dio is convicted of conspiracy and tax evasion.	House passes by voice vote a bill designed to keep retired military officers from taking jobs with defense firms and then pressuring the Pentagon to do business with their new firms.	FHA reports the average price of an FHA-mortgaged home in 1959 was $14,329.			April 7
F	**G**	**H**	**I**	**J**	
Includes elections, federal-state relations, civil rights and liberties, crime, the judiciary, education, health care, poverty, urban affairs and population.	*Includes formation and debate of U.S. foreign and defense policies, veterans' affairs and defense spending. (Relations with specific foreign countries are usually found under the region concerned.)*	*Includes business, labor, agriculture, taxation, transportation, consumer affairs, monetary and fiscal policy, natural resources, and pollution.*	*Includes worldwide scientific, medical and technological developments, natural phenomena, U.S. weather, natural disasters, and accidents.*	*Includes the arts, religion, scholarship, communications media, sports, entertainment, fashions, fads and social life.*	

	World Affairs	Europe	Africa & the Middle East	The Americas	Asia & the Pacific
April 8	Having rejected both the Soviet and Western draft proposals, the 10-nation disarmament conference in Geneva agrees to recess from April 29 to June 6.	British House of Commons votes unanimously to "deplore" South African racial policies. . . . The Netherlands agrees to a West German offer of $66 million in payments to Dutch victims of the Nazi occupation. . . . Duncan Sandys, British aviation minister is divorced in London from Diana Churchill for desertion.	South African police continue to take emergency actions against Africans despite the apparent collapse of the protests and strike against apartheid. At least 400 government critics have been arrested since March 30. The African National Congress and the Pan-Africanist Congress, the two leading African political organizations, are banned for a one-year period. . . . Secy Gen. Hammarskjold says yesterday's confiscation of a shipment of Israeli cement from a Greek freighter by UAR officials constitutes a violation of U.N. Charter principles.	In a letter replying to a list of questions submitted by Chilean student groups, Pres. Eisenhower charges that Cuba's leaders have "betrayed" the goals of their revolution and have deliberately tried to disrupt amicable U.S.-Cuba relations.	
April 9			South African P.M. Henrik Verwoerd is shot twice in an assassination attempt by a white opponent of apartheid. Verwoerd is expected to recover.		Indian Defense Min. Krishna Menon tells parliament that a 500,000-man territorial reserve force will be organized to defend India in the event of attack from Communist China.
April 10			An estimated 300 persons are reported killed in leftist terrorist attacks designed to disrupt Cameroon's first national elections. . . . Cameroon Premier Ahmadou Ahidjo's dominant Union Party wins 60 of 100 seats in the National Assembly. The formerly outlawed leftist Union of Cameroon Peoples wins 22 seats.		South Korea's opposition Democratic Party appeals in court for nullification of the March 15 presidential elections, claiming massive vote fraud.
April 11		Italian Premier Fernando Tambroni's 17-day old Christian Democratic cabinet resigns after half its members quit because of Tambroni's parliamentary reliance on Neo-Fascist support. Tambroni stays on as caretaker premier. . . . West Germany's All-German Affairs Ministry estimates that during 1959 50,000 West German residents moved to the Eastern Zone while 143,000 East Germans moved to the West.	South African Public Works Min. Paul Saur, who has temporarily assumed government leadership, tells parliament that Verwoerd's race policies will be continued. . . . Rebel Algerian Provisional Government says it will welcome volunteers from any nation in its fight against France.		An unofficial 19-nation Conference against Colonialism in Africa and Asia, meeting in New Delhi, calls for U.N. action against continued Communist Chinese "colonization" of Tibet.
April 12	Six Western nations, meeting in Washington to discuss a unified strategy for the May summit conference, agree on a tentative agenda to include: (1) disarmement and A-test ban; (2) Germany and Berlin; (3) other East-West problems.	West German Chancellor Adenauer, concerned about possible Western summit compromises on Berlin, criticizes West Berlin Mayor Willy Brandt for failing to hold a plebiscite that would demonstrate Berliner opposition to any change in the city's status.	French Premier Michel Debré, visiting Algeria warns France will partition Algeria if the majority of Moslems chose the "disatrous" course of complete independence from French rule. . . . South African government announces a program to increase white immigration greatly in order to reduce dependence on African labor.		
April 13	Western nations informally agree to propose reunification of Berlin as a first step toward reunifying Germany at the forthcoming East-West summit in Paris.	British government announces its decision to halt development of the Blue Streak ballistic missile, the major weapon in Britain's planned independent nuclear strike force.	South African sources report that many white employers are dismissing African workers and hiring Cape Coloreds (persons of mixed blood), who largely abstained from recent racial protests.		
April 14	Western delegations to the 10-nation disarmament talks offer to halt all further production of atomic weapons and to allow international inspection of Western A-bomb plants. The U.S. appeals to the USSR to agree to such a halt as a first step to general disarmament. . . . Soviet test-ban negotiators accept a U.S.-British proposal to begin talks looking toward the formation of a joint research program to improve nuclear test detection.	Jean Marin is re-elected as head of Agence France Presse despite government efforts to oust him and regain control over the French news agency.	U.N. Secy. Gen. Hammarskjold announces that a petition sponsored by African nations to have a General Assembly discussion on continued French A-tests in north Africa has failed to receive the necessary majority of signatures.		Sir Hisamuddin Alam Shah, sultan of Selangor, is elected to a five-year term as paramount ruler of Malaya.
	A	**B**	**C**	**D**	**E**
	Includes developments that affect more than one world region, international organizations and important meetings of major world leaders.	*Includes all domestic and regional developments in Europe, including the Soviet Union, Turkey, Cyprus and Malta.*	*Includes all domestic and regional developments in Africa and the Middle East, including Iraq and Iran and excluding Cyprus, Turkey and Afghanistan.*	*Includes all domestic and regional developments in Latin America, the Caribbean and Canada.*	*Includes all domestic and regional developments in Asia and Pacific nations, extending from Afghanistan through all the Pacific Islands, except Hawaii.*

U.S. Politics & Social Issues	U.S. Foreign Policy & Defense	U.S. Economy & Environment	Science, Technology & Nature	Culture, Leisure & Life Style	
Overcoming a Southern anti-civil rights filibuster for the first time, the Senate passes (71 to 18) a modified version of the House rights bill providing for federal voting referees in districts where racial discrimination has been proven in court.	V.P. Nixon tells a group of U.S. church leaders that the U.S. should provide birth control information to underdeveloped nations who seek it.			Pro tennis champ Pancho Gonzalez announces he will retire from competition May 1.	April 8
A *Southern School News* survey reveals that despite the 1954 Supreme Court desegregation order, 94% of the South's Negro students still attend segregated schools and that there has been no desegregation in Alabama, Georgia, Louisiana, Mississippi and South Carolina.			Researchers for the Sloan-Kettering Cancer Institute report the isolation of cancer-causing agents in tobacco tars and to a lesser extent in other chemicals present in cigarette smoke.	Move bit-player William Stanciu is mortally shot in the Hollywood apartment of Beverly Aadland, 17, "protege" of the late Errol Flynn. Aadland later says the shooting was accidental. . . . Boston defeats St. Louis in the seventh game of the NBA playoffs to win the series 4-3.	April 9
Ex-Pres. Herbert Hoover becomes a trustee of Americans for Constitutional Action, a group formed to help elect conservatives to Congress.				Arnold Palmer, 30, wins the prestigious Masters golf tournament in Augusta, Ga. . . . Women are ordained as pastors in Sweden's Evangelical Lutheran Church for the first time in the church's history.	April 10
Secy. Arthur Flemming announces that HEW will begin publication of a permanent list of so-called "diploma mills" institutions–that sell degrees without regard to academic achievement. . . . James Murphy, official Senate reporter since 1896, dies at 83.		Pres. Maurice Hutcheson of the AFL-CIO Carpenters Brotherhood is convicted of contempt of Congress for refusing to answer Senate committee questions about possible misuse of union funds.		Nat. Institute of Arts and Letters awards its Brunner Award for architecture to Louis Kahn of Philadelphia.	April 11
Otto Kerner wins the Illinois Democratic gubernatorial nomination in a three-man primary race.	White House announces Pres. Eisenhower will visit South Korea June 22 during his scheduled trip to Japan. . . . A U.S. Court of Appeals upholds a lower court decision dismissing a suit by 39 persons, including Nobel-winner Linus Pauling, that sought to halt U.S. nuclear tests on grounds that they endanger human health.	Labor Dept. reports unemployment jumped from 4.8% in February to 5.4% in March.			April 12
	Seafarers' International Union pickets and prevents the unloading of the UAR cargo ship *Cleopatra* as a protest against the Arab boycott of Israeli-trading vessels and against alleged mistreatment of U.S. seamen in Arab ports.		U.S. launches into earth orbit an experimental radio-signaling satellite, Transit-I, designed to aid in ocean navigation.		April 13
Tennessee Democrats select a 66-member delegation to the national convention, which, though officially uncommitted, is known to favor Texas Sen. Lyndon Johnson. . . . American Communications Association members, Bernard Silber and Frank Grumman, receive four-month prison sentences for refusing to answer House Un-American Activities Committee questions in 1957.	State Dept. announces Polaris missiles may be sold to Britain and other NATO countries for use on a coordinated NATO-wide basis.	Commerce Dept. reports average U.S. family income rose from $6,260 to $6,520 in 1959. The increase represents a 3% rise in "real income" (after adjustments for inflation).	Dr. William W. Christmas, 94, aviation pioneer and the third American to fly a plane, dies in New York.	Gallup Poll on U.S. religious beliefs reveals that 55% of Americans believe Christ will return to earth, 74% believe in an afterlife, and over 80% attended church at least once in 1959. . . . Montreal Canadiens win the National Hockey League's Stanley Cup for the fifth consecutive year, beating Toronto four games to none.	April 14
F	G	H	I	J	
Includes elections, federal-state relations, civil rights and liberties, crime, the judiciary, education, health care, poverty, urban affairs and population.	*Includes formation and debate of U.S. foreign and defense policies, veterans' affairs and defense spending. (Relations with specific foreign countries are usually found under the region concerned.)*	*Includes business, labor, agriculture, taxation, transportation, consumer affairs, monetary and fiscal policy, natural resources, and pollution.*	*Includes worldwide scientific, medical and technological developments, natural phenomena, U.S. weather, natural disasters, and accidents.*	*Includes the arts, religion, scholarship, communications media, sports, entertainment, fashions, fads and social life.*	

	World Affairs	Europe	Africa & the Middle East	The Americas	Asia & the Pacific
April 15	Representatives from 55 countries conclude a four-day Afro-Asian Solidarity Conference in Guinea after resolving to support the Algerian rebels and other developing nations' nationalist movements.	USSR Central Statistical Board reports Soviet industry has exceeded its production goals by 4% during the first quarter of 1960. . . . East Germany reports agriculture has been 100% collectivized, making it the only country besides the USSR to achieve complete farm collectivization. . . . Eric Peugeot, 4, grandson of the French auto manufacturers, is released unharmed by kidnappers after his father delivers an undisclosed ransom payment. The boy was abducted April 12.		Cuban troops are reported dispatched to the Sierra Maestra mountains to combat an insurgent force of about 200 anti-Castro rebels.	
April 16					Riots against alleged corruption in recent elections and against the continuing rule of Pres. Syngman Rhee are reported spreading throughout South Korea.
April 17		East German CP First Secy. Walter Ulbricht announces Soviet-bloc leaders are currently working on a plan to settle the Berlin question which they intend to present at the forthcoming summit talks. . . . West Berlin Mayor Brandt announces plans for a May 1 "Freedom Rally" to make sure world opinion does not overlook West Berlin's desire for continued freedom.			
April 18		Some 75,000 Britons gather in London to demand unilateral British nuclear disarmament and the closing of U.S. atomic bases in England. . . . Pres. Tito, in an address to Yugoslavia's Socialist Alliance Congress, attacks West Germany for following the same militarist course that "plunged mankind into the...catastrophe" of W.W.II.	An April 14 call by leaders of the banned African National Congress for a nationwide strike against South African racial policies goes largely unheeded by African workers. The failure is attributed to government warnings of severe penalties against strikers.	French Pres. Charles de Gaulle arrives in Ottawa to begin a 17-day visit to the Western Hemisphere. . . . Canada and the USSR conclude a three-year mutual trade pact providing for a substantial increase in Canadian-Soviet trade.	
April 19	The 10-nation Geneva disarmament talks resume after the Easter recess.			Cuban Premier Castro says in a CBS interview that there are parallels between America's anti-communism and that of Hitler and Mussolini. . . . Pres. Eisenhower approves a program aimed at improved U.S.-Panamanian relations through expanded employment opportunities for Panamanians in the Canal Zone.	At least 127 persons are killed and more than 700 wounded as South Korean police open fire on crowds of up to 100,000 people protesting election irregularities and police repression. . . . Pho Preung is approved by the Cambodian National Assembly to succeed the resigned Prince Norodom Sihanouk as premier.
April 20		In what is described as a "major statement of pre-summit policy," Undersecy. of State C. Douglas Dillon tells the AFL-CIO World Affairs Conference that under no circumstances would the U.S. agree to "slavery" for the West Berliners. Dillon adds the problem of Berlin can only be solved through German reunification. . . . Anglo-French Channel Tunnel Study Group issues a final report recommending the construction of a three-tube, cross-channel system of railway tunnels at an estimated cost of $275 million.			South Korean Pres. Rhee pledges to make every effort to redress the grievances underlying the country's current political unrest.

A	B	C	D	E
Includes developments that affect more than one world region, international organizations and important meetings of major world leaders.	Includes all domestic and regional developments in Europe, including the Soviet Union, Turkey, Cyprus and Malta.	Includes all domestic and regional developments in Africa and the Middle East, including Iraq and Iran and excluding Cyprus, Turkey and Afghanistan.	Includes all domestic and regional developments in Latin America, the Caribbean and Canada.	Includes all domestic and regional developments in Asia and Pacific nations, extending from Afghanistan through all the Pacific Islands, except Hawaii.

U.S. Politics & Social Issues	U.S. Foreign Policy & Defense	U.S. Economy & Environment	Science, Technology & Nature	Culture, Leisure & Life Style	
	The AEC announces the U.S. has agreed to provide France with a shipment of uranium-235 for research on an experimental nuclear submarine engine.				April 15
		Complying with the 1959 Labor and Management Reporting Act, major U.S. unions report their current assets to the Labor Dept.: UMW:$110 million; Teamsters:$38 million; UAW:$30 million.		The merger of Alfred A. Knopf Publishing Co. and Random House, Inc. is announced in New York; the two companies are to remain editorially separate.	April 16
A group of Southern Negro college students, meeting in Raleigh, N.C., announce the formation of a Student Non-violent Coordinating Committee to guide and support anti-segregation efforts. The Rev. Martin Luther King is named adviser to the new student group.				Charles Mohr, 22, Univ. of Wisconsin student, dies of a brain injury sustained April 9 while unsuccessfully defending his NCAA boxing title against Stu Bartell of San Jose State in Madison, Wis. . . . U.S. chess champ Bobby Fischer, 17, and Boris Spassky of Russia tie for first place in an international tournament at Mar del Plata, Argentina.	April 17
Sen. John Kennedy, campaigning in W. Va., says that if religion is a valid objection to his election as president, then "I shouldn't have served in the House,...the Senate, [or]...the U.S. Navy." . . . U.S. Fifth Circuit Court of Appeals in New Orleans upholds a lower court ruling that a Montgomery, Ala. ordinance barring Negroes from city parks is unconstitutional. The parks have been closed to all persons since the lower court decision.	Defense Dept. announces 5,500 men will be drafted in June, the lowest monthly call since the Korean War.	Commerce Dept. reports U.S. personal income rose to a record $393.5 billion in March. . . . Supreme Court rules 5-4 that railway unions have the right to strike for a voice in company decisions to eliminate jobs, even when such eliminations are approved by state regulatory bodies.	Dr. John Roderick Heller, 55, is elected president of Memorial Sloan-Kettering Cancer Center.	Pres. Eisenhower throws out the first ball, opening the 1960 baseball season in Washington.	April 18
The city of Montgomery, Ala. files a libel suit against The New York Times for allegedly false statements that appeared in an advertisement seeking to raise legal expense funds for the Rev. Martin Luther King. . . . A dynamite bomb destroys the home of Z. Alexander Looby, a Nashville city councilman and NAACP lawyer who recently defended 153 students arrested for sit-in activities. No one is injured.	In an unusual criticism of the Rhee regime, the U.S. Amb.-to-South Korea Walter P. McConaughy describes current South Korean unrest as a genuine public dissatisfaction with "repressive measures unsuited to a free democracy." . . . Pres. Eisenhower authorizes creation of a new State Dept. agency to deal with disarmament talks with the USSR. . . . U.S. Army displays a new radar system that reportedly can take detailed pictures of enemy territory from aircraft flying many miles away over friendly territory.			New York Drama Critics Circle chooses Lillian Hellman's Toys in the Attic as the best American play on Broadway in the 1959-1960 season. Fiorello! is named best musical.	April 19
Rep. Chester Bowles (Conn.) is named chairman of the 1960 Democratic convention platform committee.				Middleweight champ Gene Fullmer retains his title in a 15-round draw against Joey Giardello.	April 20

F	G	H	I	J
Includes elections, federal-state relations, civil rights and liberties, crime, the judiciary, education, health care, poverty, urban affairs and population.	Includes formation and debate of U.S. foreign and defense policies, veterans' affairs and defense spending. (Relations with specific foreign countries are usually found under the region concerned.)	Includes business, labor, agriculture, taxation, transportation, consumer affairs, monetary and fiscal policy, natural resources, and pollution.	Includes worldwide scientific, medical and technological developments, natural phenomena, U.S. weather, natural disasters, and accidents.	Includes the arts, religion, scholarship, communications media, sports, entertainment, fashions, fads and social life.

	World Affairs	Europe	Africa & the Middle East	The Americas	Asia & the Pacific
April 21	USSR Geneva delegation rejects a Western proposal to set up a mobile international inspection team as part of a military manpower reduction pact, claiming that such a unit would offer too great an opportunity for espionage.		Public Works Min. Paul Sauer, government leader since the wounding of Verwoerd, causes a split in South Africa's ruling Nationalist Party by urging the easing of pass and liquor regulations against Africans.	A minor revolt against the Venezuelan government of Pres. Romulo Betancourt collapses after a brief skirmish with government troops. About 200 persons are arrested in connection with the brief uprising.	South Korean cabinet resigns in the face of growing anti-government demonstrations. Protesters say the resignation is an insufficient substitute for fair elections.
April 22	Frederick Eaton, chief U.S. disarmament negotiator, accuses the USSR of "an obsessive emphasis on secrecy" in its refusal to accept Western proposals for inspection and controls of an arms agreement.	West Berlin sources report increased Communist police efforts to halt growing numbers of East Germans trying to flee to West Berlin. An estimated 11,000 East Germans have crossed into the Western sector since April 1.		Premier Castro reports that Cuban dollar reserves have risen to $142 million from a low of $77 million at the end of the Batista government.	
April 23	Pres. de Gaulle, visiting the U.S., tells the National Press Club that the problems of Berlin and Germany should be second to the question of nuclear and conventional disarmament at the forthcoming summit.	Soviet Deputy Premier Anastas Mikoyan labels U.S. policy on Berlin, as outlined in a recent speech by Under Secy. of State Douglas Dillon, as an incredible product of the Cold War.	French Pres. de Gaulle's program to restaff the Algerian military command with men loyal to his policies is virtually completed with appointment of Lt. Gen. Jean Crepin to succeed Gen. Maurice Challe as Algerian commander-in-chief.		Ceylon's parliament is dissolved after it votes no-confidence in P.M. Dudley S. Senanayake's government. New elections are announced for July. . . . Rev. Toyohiko Kagawa, 71, Japanese Christian convert credited with organizing 250 Japanese churches, dies in Tokyo.
April 24	Pres. Eisenhower and Pres. de Gaulle, after meeting at Camp David, issue a general statement indicating full agreement on "how we should proceed at the summit meeting."		Two major earthquakes in southern Iran kill an estimated 700 persons.		Nationalist Chinese Kuomintang party sweeps the local elections for the Formosa provincial assembly.
April 25		Jacques Soustelle, a leader in the May 1958 coup that returned de Gaulle to power and a founder of the Gaullist UNR party, is expelled from the UNR for his refusal to support de Gaulle's Algerian policy. . . . Premier Khrushchev reiterates his warning that the West would lose its right of access to Berlin should the Soviets be forced to sign a separate peace treaty with East Germany.		Cuba announces the nationalization of all foreign trade under the auspices of a newly-created Bank of Foreign Commerce.	Indian P.M. Nehru and Communist Chinese Premier Chou En-lai end a week of talks in New Delhi without reaching agreement on the China-India border dispute. . . . Amanullah, 68, ex-King of Afghanistan (1919-1929) and leader of the movement that ended British rule, is reported to have died in Zurich, Switzerland. He was forced to abdicate in 1929 by opponents of his program to abolish the slavery of women.
April 26	An 88-nation U.N. conference on the law of the sea ends its deliberations at Geneva after failing to resolve national differences on fishing rights and territorial waters.				An estimated 200,000 people join Socialist Party-sponsored demonstrations throughout Japan protesting the ratification of the new U.S.-Japan security treaty. . . . Pres. Rhee agrees to order new elections and to reform South Korea's governmental system in an effort to quell continuing political unrest.
April 27		Pres. Eisenhower rejects repeated Soviet contentions that a USSR-East German peace treaty would void Western occupation rights in Berlin. . . . At least 15 police are injured and 50 persons arrested in riots near Cracow, Poland, begun when authorities remove a cross from a new church. . . . Turkish Parliament grants near-dictatorial powers to a special commission investigating the opposition Republican People's Party.	An independent republic of Togo is officially proclaimed in Lome, capital of the former French-administered Togoland.		Syngman Rhee, South Korea's first and only president, resigns after promises of reform failed to stem spreading anti-government demonstrations. For. Min. Huh Chung will succeed Rhee pending new elections.

A	B	C	D	E
Includes developments that affect more than one world region, international organizations and important meetings of major world leaders.	Includes all domestic and regional developments in Europe, including the Soviet Union, Turkey, Cyprus and Malta.	Includes all domestic and regional developments in Africa and the Middle East, including Iraq and Iran and excluding Cyprus, Turkey and Afghanistan.	Includes all domestic and regional developments in Latin America, the Caribbean and Canada.	Includes all domestic and regional developments in Asia and Pacific nations, extending from Afghanistan through all the Pacific Islands, except Hawaii.

U.S. Politics & Social Issues	U.S. Foreign Policy & Defense	U.S. Economy & Environment	Science, Technology & Nature	Culture, Leisure & Life Style	
House passes, 288-95, the Senate version of the 1960 Civil Rights Act and sends it to the President. . . . Sen. Robert C. Byrd (D, W. Va.), an outspoken opponent of Kennedy's Presidential candidacy, is described in a *New York Herald Tribune* story as a former Ku Klux Klan organizer. . . . Baroness Kathleen Rothschild de Koenisgswarter, 46, is sentenced in Wilmington, Del. to three year's imprisonment (but released on bail) on charges of possessing $10 worth of marijuana.	House passes a bill to authorize $4,038,500,000 in foreign aid by a 243-130 vote and sends it to the Senate. . . . U.S. State Dept. urges the Seafarers' Union to halt its picket of a UAR cargo ship, saying that such private efforts to force "shifts in the policy of foreign governments" was "embarrassing" to the U.S. The request is rejected by SIU Pres. Paul Hall.	Labor Secy. James P. Mitchell says the administration supports an increase in the federal minimum wage from $1.00 to $1.10, but opposes as "extreme" the $1.25 figure backed by the AFL-CIO. . . . Nat. Assn. of Real Estate Bds. reports the average interest rate on new home mortgages is 6%. . . . Civil Aeronautics Board member Whitney Gilliland is named to succeed James Durfee as CAB chairman.		Plans for a June 20 re-match between world heavyweight champ Ingemar Johansson and Floyd Patterson are disclosed in New York.	April 21
The tax evasion trial of Rep. Adam Clayton Powell (D, N.Y.) ends in a mistrial in a U.S. district court in N.Y.		Pres. Eisenhower, acting under the Railway Labor Act, creates a three-man emergency board to investigate a dispute between major rail companies and non-operating railroad unions. The action postpones for 60 days a threatened May 4 strike.		Three U.S. Lutheran denominations merge at a Minneapolis meeting to form the 2.25-million member American Lutheran Church. . . . The organization of a new pro American Basketball League to start operation in the 1960-1961 season is announced in Chicago.	April 22
			Dr. Max Theodor Felix von Laue, 80, German physicist, winner of the 1914 Nobel physics prize for X-ray research and prominent anti-Nazi, dies of auto injuries in Berlin.	Dyrol Burleson of the Univ. of Oregon becomes the fastest American miler ever with a time of 3:58.6 at an Oregon-Stanford dual meet.	April 23
Capt. Angus Boatwright, of Key West, Fla., skipper of the cabin cruiser *Muriel III*, is shot to death by a one of three castaways he rescued from a small island in the Bahamas. The castaways are later captured by a Cuban gunboat.				Actress Hope Emerson, 62, dies in Hollywood of a liver ailment.	April 24
Fights between blacks and whites and spreading racial tension are reported in Biloxi, Miss. following an April 24 attempt by some 40 Negroes to use the city's "white-only" beaches. . . . Alabama Public Service Commissioner Ralph Smith charges NBC "staged and directed" anti-segregation demonstrations in Montgomery between Feb. 27 and March 7. NBC denies the charge.	Senate Foreign Relations Committee Chmn. J. William Fulbright (D, Ark.) condemns Seafarers' Union picketing of a UAR ship as a "coercive" effort to force American foreign policy in "special-interest directions."	Bureau of Labor Statistics reports that cost of living index rose to a record high again in March.			April 25
Sen. Kennedy wins write-in Democratic primary races in Pennsylvania and his native Massachusetts. . . . American Council of Churches (16 Protestant fundamentalist denominations) declares its formal opposition to the election of a Roman Catholic as President. . . . A clergymen's advisory committee to the Planned Parenthood Federation makes public its new birth control plan urging the dissemination of birth control information but designed to exempt anyone with ethical or religious objections. . . . Reputed Chicago crime boss Anthony Accardo is arrested on federal income tax charges.				The NCAA votes to end a 10-year agreement honoring AAU suspensions against NCAA and other college athletes.	April 26
	Pres. Eisenhower denies to newsmen widely circulated reports that the U.S. had urged South Korean Pres. Rhee's resignation, saying that the change in government had been effected by the South Korean people themselves. . . . Defense Secy. Thomas Gates orders the armed services to make sure that information in military manuals is relevant, accurate and in "good taste."		American Institute of Physics' Heinemann Prize for mathematical physics is awarded to Danish physicist Aage Bohr, 38, son of Niels Bohr, who won the 1922 Nobel physics prize.		April 27

F	G	H	I	J
Includes elections, federal-state relations, civil rights and liberties, crime, the judiciary, education, health care, poverty, urban affairs and population.	*Includes formation and debate of U.S. foreign and defense policies, veterans' affairs and defense spending. (Relations with specific foreign countries are usually found under the region concerned.)*	*Includes business, labor, agriculture, taxation, transportation, consumer affairs, monetary and fiscal policy, natural resources, and pollution.*	*Includes worldwide scientific, medical and technological developments, natural phenomena, U.S. weather, natural disasters, and accidents.*	*Includes the arts, religion, scholarship, communications media, sports, entertainment, fashions, fads and social life.*

	World Affairs	Europe	Africa & the Middle East	The Americas	Asia & the Pacific
April 28		British government announces curbs on consumer and bank credit in an effort to control rising inflation and a growing foreign trade deficit. . . . Soviet sources report that Rabbi Simkh Teper and three religious assistants have been convicted by a "comrades court" of holding "doubtful" political discussions.		Carlos Ibanez del Campo, dictatorial former Chilean president (1927-31, 1952-58), dies of cancer at 82.	New South Korean governmment under acting Pres. Huh Chung promises constitutional reforms, better use of U.S. aid money, and new elections within three months. . . . South Korea's vice-president-elect and long-time Liberal Party aide to Rhee, Lee Ki Poong, commits suicide after learning of Rhee's resignation. . . . Communist Chinese Premier Chou En-lai, in Nepal for border talks, concedes that the summit of Mt. Everest lies in Nepalese territory.
April 29	The deadlocked 10-nation Geneva disarmament conference recesses until June 7 after failing to agree on a communique summarizing the first 32 sessions.	Italian Premier Fernando Tambroni's Christian Democratic cabinet continues in power after Pres. Giovanni Gronchi refuses to accept Tambroni's April 9 resignation.		The creation of a five-nation Central American free trade area is announced in San Jose, Costa Rica.	Allen L. Pope, an American shot down while flying a rebel bomber against government targets in Indonesia, is sentenced to death by a Jakarta military court. . . . A friendly crowd, including even some of the rebellious students responsible for his overthrow, bids a cheerful farewell to retiring South Korean Pres. Rhee as he leaves the Presidential Palace in Seoul.
April 30		At least 3,000 Turkish students are arrested for participation in demonstrations protesting alleged political and civil repression by the regime of Premier Adnan Menderes. Ten students have been killed in clashes with police since the protests began April 28.	A CENTO Ministerial Council, meeting in Tehran, calls for summit efforts to halt Soviet propaganda campaigns against Pakistan and Iran. . . . Petroleum Information Bureau in London reports that Middle East oil production reached 63 million tons in January-March 1960, an increase of 8 million tons over the same period in 1959. . . . Arab dockworkers begin a boycott of U.S. shipping in retaliation against U.S. union picketing of the UAR cargo ship *Cleopatra* . UAR Pres. Nasser rebukes Eisenhower for being "slack" in his effort to end the picketing.	Paraguayan officials report that government troops have successfully turned back a rebel invasion from Argentina aimed at overthrowing the regime of Gen. Alfredo Stroessner.	Eighteen prominent South Vietnamese, led by ex-Economy Min. Tran Van Van, announce the formation of a Liberty and Progress Party to oppose the "dictatorial methods" of Pres. Ngo Dinh Diem.
May 1		An estimated 800,000 West Berliners attend a "freedom rally" to hear Mayor Willy Brandt proclaim the city's determination to avoid Communist rule.		In a three-and-a-half-hour May Day oration, Cuban Premier Castro accuses the U.S. State Dept. of "preparing an aggression against Cuba through Guatemala."	
May 2			Twelve people are killed in Baghdad rioting between Iraqi nationalists and Communists.		Acting South Korean Pres. Huh Chung denies that the U.S. pressured Rhee to resign, and says that State Dept.'s public criticism of repression had the positive effect of encouraging restraint in attempts to control demonstrations during the political crisis.
May 3	USSR test ban negotiators accept a Western proposal for joint underground nuclear detonations as part of an East-West scientific program to improve methods for detecting such tests. . . . Lenin Peace Prizes are awarded to Cyrus Eaton, U.S. industrialist, Pres. Sukarno of Indonesia, Laurent Casanova of France, and Aziz Sharif of Iraq.	Agreements granting West Germany air, supply and weapons-testing bases in France are signed in Bonn. . . . West German Refugee Min. Theodor Oberlaender resigns from the Adenauer cabinet in the face of growing demands for his dismissal as a former Nazi official.	Israeli foreign ministry reports Soviet rejection of an Israeli request for personal talks between P. M. David Ben-Gurion and Premier Khrushchev. . . . British Colonial Office announces that Sierra Leone will become independent April 27, 1961. . . . France protests to the U.N. the granting of attack bases to Algerian rebels by Tunisia. The protest comes in reply to Tunisian complaints against French assaults on rebel positions within Tunisia.		Ex-South Korean Home Min. Choi In Kyu is arrested on charges of having used his control of election machinery to insure a Liberal Party victory in the March 15 elections. . . . Student demonstrations are resumed in Seoul to protest alleged delays in carrying out reforms and new elections.

A	B	C	D	E
Includes developments that affect more than one world region, international organizations and important meetings of major world leaders.	Includes all domestic and regional developments in Europe, including the Soviet Union, Turkey, Cyprus and Malta.	Includes all domestic and regional developments in Africa and the Middle East, including Iraq and Iran and excluding Cyprus, Turkey and Afghanistan.	Includes all domestic and regional developments in Latin America, the Caribbean and Canada.	Includes all domestic and regional developments in Asia and Pacific nations, extending from Afghanistan through all the Pacific Islands, except Hawaii.

U.S. Politics & Social Issues	U.S. Foreign Policy & Defense	U.S. Economy & Environment	Science, Technology & Nature	Culture, Leisure & Life Style	
	Against the objections of the Administration and Foreign Relations Committee Chmn. Fulbright, the Senate adopts an amendment to the foreign aid bill opposing aid to the UAR unless it opens the Suez Canal to Israel.	An administration-opposed bill to channel $1 billion of federal home loan money into the housing industry is passed by the House and sent to the Senate.			April 28
The quadrennial general conference of the U.S. Methodist Church votes to abolish gradually its separate all-Negro Central Jurisdiction within the church's administrative hierarchy. . . . National Association of Evangelicals adopts a formal resolution expressing "doubt" over whether a Roman Catholic President "could fully resist the pressures of the ecclesiastical hierarchy."	State Dept. announces the lifting of the 1956 U.S. ban on travel to Hungary; passport restrictions, however, will continue for Albania, Communist China, North Korea and North Vietnam. . . . U.S. Navy confirms reports that a Soviet radar-loaded trawler was in the vicinity of the U.S. nuclear submarine *George Washington* during missile-firing tests.	*Wall Street Journal* reports first-quarter U.S. corporate earnings are up 6.6% over the same period in 1959.		Popular American TV disc jockey, Dick Clark, tells a special House subcommittee that he never knowingly accepted "payola" despite committee data indicating that he often played records from companies in which he had a financial interest.	April 29
		Harry Babcock, FTC director since 1957, dies in Washington.			April 30
				Dr. Charles Holden, British architect, designer of London skyscrapers and subway stations, dies at 84.	May 1
Convicted kidnapper and prison author, Caryl Chessman, 38, is executed in a San Quentin Prison gas chamber after having received eight stays of execution and worldwide attention from capital punishment opponents. . . . Thirteen prominent Protestant clergymen issue a statement condemning the presence of anti-Catholicism in the current presidential primary campaigns.	Pres. Eisenhower asks Congress not to reduce his $4.175 billion foreign aid request, contending that any cut would seriously weaken "efforts to resist communist expansion." . . . Senate approves Pres. Eisenhower's $4.125 million foreign aid request, but refuses to withdraw an administration-opposed amendment calling for an end to aid to the UAR.	Supreme Court rules that farmer cooperatives are not immune from antitrust action if they actually attempt to monopolize markets.		Columbia Univ. announces the 1959 Pulitzer Prize winners: fiction- Allen Drury for *Advise and Consent* ; biography- Samuel E. Morison for *John Paul Jones* ; poetry- William D. Snodgrass for *Heart's Needle* .	May 2
Sen. Kennedy captures Indiana's 34-vote convention delegation by defeating token opposition in the state's Democratic presidential primary. Hubert Humphrey meanwhile defeats Wayne Morse (D, Ore.) in the Washington, D. C. primary, assuring him of nine first ballot votes at the convention. . . . General Assembly of the Southern Presbyterian Church rejects a resolution opposing election of a Roman Catholic president.				A special House committee investigating broadcast ethics reports that a mail survey it conducted showed that record companies had paid over $200,000 in payola to 207 disc jockeys in 42 cities.	May 3

F	G	H	I	J
Includes elections, federal-state relations, civil rights and liberties, crime, the judiciary, education, health care, poverty, urban affairs and population.	*Includes formation and debate of U.S. foreign and defense policies, veterans' affairs and defense spending. (Relations with specific foreign countries are usually found under the region concerned.)*	*Includes business, labor, agriculture, taxation, transportation, consumer affairs, monetary and fiscal policy, natural resources, and pollution.*	*Includes worldwide scientific, medical and technological developments, natural phenomena, U.S. weather, natural disasters, and accidents.*	*Includes the arts, religion, scholarship, communications media, sports, entertainment, fashions, fads and social life.*

	World Affairs	Europe	Africa & the Middle East	The Americas	Asia & the Pacific
May 4		A NATO foreign ministers conference, meeting in Istanbul, reaffirms a hardening Western position that a Berlin solution can come only through German reunification.	R. M. Sobukwe, leader of the banned Pan Africanist Congress, is convicted by a Johannesburg court of planning the recent protests against South Africa's racial pass laws; he is sentenced to three years in jail.	U.S. grand jury charges that the downing of small plane carrying two Americans over Cuba had been staged by the fliers in complicity with the Castro government to embarrass the U.S.	Pres. Eisenhower and Indian Food Min. S. K. Patil sign a $1.2 billion Indian-U.S. grain purchase agreement.
May 5	The shooting down of an alleged U.S. spy plane over central Russia on May 1 is claimed by Premier Khrushchev in a dramatic speech to the Supreme Soviet. Spokesmen for NASA acknowledge that a U-2 weather research plane is missing, but firmly deny that it was on an espionage mission.	Soviet CP Central Committee announces a major shake-up of the leadership of the party and the Soviet government. Among the most significant changes is the promotion of State Planning Chmn. Alexei N. Kosygin to first deputy premier. . . . Premier Khrushchev outlines fiscal reforms aimed at revaluing the ruble to approximate equality with the U.S. dollar. . . . Turkish P.M. Adnan Menderes is jeered and jostled by a crowd of students shouting demands for political freedom as he walks to a political meeting.	A decision to grant Somaliland full independence by July 1 is announced in London by British Colonial Secy. Iain Macleod.		South Korean government presents a six-point plan to help stabilize the nation's economy.
May 6	U.S. State Dept. confirms that an off-course weather research plane may have been downed by the Soviets, but insists that there was "absolutely no—NO—deliberate attempt to violate Soviet airspace."	West German justice ministry announces it will not seek an extension of the 15-year statute of limitations on Nazi war crimes (except murder) scheduled to expire this year. . . . Princess Margaret of Britain weds commoner Antony Armstrong-Jones.		Jacques Mornard, who assassinated Leon Trotsky in 1940, is released from a Mexico City jail after serving a 20-year sentence.	
May 7	Reversing its previous stand, the U.S. State Dept. publicly admits that the downed U-2 plane had been sent over Soviet territory "to obtain information now concealed behind the Iron Curtain." The admission comes only hours after Khrushchev discloses that U-2 pilot Francis Gary Powers has been captured and has confessed his "intelligence mission."	Leonid I. Brezhnev, 54, Ukrainian CP official, is named by Premier Khrushchev to succeed the retiring Kliment Y. Voroshilov, 79, as chairman of the Presidium of the USSR's Supreme Soviet.	UAR Pres. Nasser charges that U.S. foreign policy is under the sway of "Zionist Jewish Israeli imperialism."	Cuba and the USSR announce that diplomatic relations, interrupted since 1952, will soon be resumed on the embassy level.	Several high South Korean officials in the toppled Rhee government are arrested on corruption charges.
May 8	Khrushchev warns that countries permitting the U.S. to use their territory for spy missions against the USSR are risking attack from Soviet missiles.	Turkey announces it had never given permission to an American plane to fly over the USSR and could not be blamed for such flights.		Dr. Roberto Francisco Chiari, leader of the opposition Liberal Party, is elected president of Panama, defeating former Pres. Ricardo Arias Espinosa, 100,152 to 86,192.	Conservative anti-Communist and centrist candidates overwhelm leftist opposition in general elections to the Laotian national assembly.
May 9	During a visit to the Moscow exhibit of U-2 wreckage and equipment, Premier Khrushchev tells newsmen that "if such aggressive actions continue, this might lead to war." . . . After conferring with Pres. Eisenhower, State Secy. Herter publicly defends U.S. aerial reconnaissance as a necessary precaution against the "danger of surprise attack" from the USSR and says that it will be continued.		Congolese soldiers and Leopoldville police clash in the midst of heightened state of tribal tensions.		

A	B	C	D	E
Includes developments that affect more than one world region, international organizations and important meetings of major world leaders.	Includes all domestic and regional developments in Europe, including the Soviet Union, Turkey, Cyprus and Malta.	Includes all domestic and regional developments in Africa and the Middle East, including Iraq and Iran and excluding Cyprus, Turkey and Afghanistan.	Includes all domestic and regional developments in Latin America, the Caribbean and Canada.	Includes all domestic and regional developments in Asia and Pacific nations, extending from Afghanistan through all the Pacific Islands, except Hawaii.

U.S. Politics & Social Issues	U.S. Foreign Policy & Defense	U.S. Economy & Environment	Science, Technology & Nature	Culture, Leisure & Life Style	
During an hour-long debate on W. Va. television, Democratic Presidential hopefuls Kennedy and Humphrey reveal little policy disagreement except on issue of raising personal income tax exemptions, which Humphrey favors and Kennedy opposes. . . . HEW Secy. Arthur Flemming outlines an administration bill for a federally subsidized, state-administered voluntary Medicare system to provide health insurance for persons over 65. . . . Matthew J. Connelly and T. Lamar Caudle, former Truman administration officials convicted of tax fraud, begin serving their two-year prison sentences after years of legal maneuvering.	Both Sen. Kennedy and Sen. Humphrey, during a W. Va. political debate, express opposition to U.N. membership for Communist China until it changes its "belligerent" foreign policy. . . . In a statement criticizing Castro's suppression of collective bargaining, the AFL-CIO charges that Cuba is becoming "an outpost" of Soviet subversion in Latin America.				**May 4**
Most Democrats, favoring a health care plan under Social Security, indicate they will oppose the administration's Medicare proposal. Opposition to the plan is also expressed by the AFL-CIO and the American Medical Association.				Sen. Estes Kefauver (D, Tenn.) introduces a bill to bar any baseball club from owning or controlling more than 100 players.	**May 5**
Pres. Eisenhower signs the 1960 Civil Rights Act.	Seafarers' Union ends its picket against a UAR cargo ship after the State Dept. promised to investigate union claims of seamen harassment in Arab ports.	Congress passes a banking reform act which provides for increased federal regulation of bank mergers.	At least 30 are dead as tornadoes rip through southeastern Oklahoma and Arkansas.	Detroit Red Wing Gordie Howe, 32, is named the NHL's most valuable player for 1960. . . . A Swiss climbing team headed by Max Eiselin scales the 26,795-ft. Dhaulagiri in the Himalayas; it was the highest unclimbed peak in the world.	**May 6**
V.P. Nixon warns that a Democratic-supported proposal for including health insurance among the current Social Security benefits would "open the door for socialized medicine." . . . Delegates supporting the presidential nomination of Lyndon Johnson win a near sweep of Texas' precinct conventions.	Pres. Eisenhower announces plans to resume underground nuclear testing as part of an expanded program to improve detection techniques.		Dr. Robert A. Cooke, 79, pioneer in allergy research, dies in New York.	Sunny Blue Farm's Venetian Way, ridden by Bill Hartack, wins the 1960 Kentucky Derby. . . . Chess Master Mikhail Tol, 23, of Soviet Latvia defeats world champion Mikhail Botvinnick in a two-month Moscow series. He is the youngest world champion in the 20th century.	**May 7**
	A report presented to the U.S. Joint Atomic Energy Committee hearings on detection asserts that nuclear detonations of up to 100 kilotons can be concealed by using "large-hole" muffling techniques.	A plan to end the half-century-old dispute between Arizona and California over division of the waters of the Colorado River is proposed by ex-U.S. Judge Simon Rifkind, a special master ordered by the Supreme Court to resolve the issue. Rifkind's plan is a victory for Arizona's demand for more of the water.			**May 8**
Invoking a provision of the just passed 1960 Civil Rights Act, the Justice Dept. asks to examine the voting registration records of four Southern counties with high Negro populations but no registered Negro voters. . . . Atlanta School Board, faced with a Georgia state law prohibiting integration, is granted a one-year delay in implementing court-ordered desegregation.	After a secret briefing on the U-2 incident, congressional leaders from both parties agree to avoid partisan criticism of U.S. intelligence activities. . . . Democrat Sen. Eugene McCarthy, however, calls for closer supervision of the CIA and its activities.	Teamsters ask U.S. Court of Appeals to halt further action of its board of monitors until the membership of the board is legally decided.	Food and Drug Administration approves for the first time the sale of an oral birth control pill.		**May 9**
F	**G**	**H**	**I**	**J**	
Includes elections, federal-state relations, civil rights and liberties, crime, the judiciary, education, health care, poverty, urban affairs and population.	*Includes formation and debate of U.S. foreign and defense policies, veterans' affairs and defense spending. (Relations with specific foreign countries are usually found under the region concerned.)*	*Includes business, labor, agriculture, taxation, transportation, consumer affairs, monetary and fiscal policy, natural resources, and pollution.*	*Includes worldwide scientific, medical and technological developments, natural phenomena, U.S. weather, natural disasters, and accidents.*	*Includes the arts, religion, scholarship, communications media, sports, entertainment, fashions, fads and social life.*	

	World Affairs	Europe	Africa & the Middle East	The Americas	Asia & the Pacific
May 10	USSR formally protests the U-2 mission as an aggressive act calculated to restore Cold War tensions and poison the pre-summit atmosphere. . . . U.S. State Dept. says the U.S. takes sole responsibility for its flights over the USSR and would defend its allies from any retaliatory attack from Soviet missiles.				
May 11		Intergovernmental Committee for European Migration reports it has resettled one million displaced persons since its formation in 1952. . . . French National Assembly approves a constitutional amendment permitting former French colonies in Africa to become independent and yet remain within the French Community. . . . French officials report 2,792 persons (mostly pro-French Moslems) have been killed in Algerian terrorist attacks carried out in France over the past four years.	South Africa announces the suspension of emergency regulations in selective districts where order has been restored.	The *Diaria de la Marina*, Cuba's oldest paper and critic of the Castro regime, is seized by a group representing the printshop workers of Havana. The seizure is condemned as plain "confiscation" by the Inter-American Press Association.	One-time international playboy and now Pakistan Amb.-to-U.N., Prince Aly Khan dies in an auto accident near Paris at the age of 48.
May 12	Replying to a formal Soviet protest note, the U.S. State Dept. says that the U-2 mission was authorized for "purely defensive purposes" and was in no way intended to prejudice the success of the summit.		Pres. Kenneth Kaunda of Northern Rhodesia's outlawed United National Independence Party calls for non-violent African protests against continued European domination of Northern Rhodesia.	Matthew Duke, an American pilot engaged in flying political refugees out of Cuba, is ambushed and killed by Cuban troops after landing to pick up passengers near Havana.	Soviet technicians report the discovery of substantial oil and natural gas deposits in northern Afghanistan.
May 13	Prime ministers of 10 British Commonwealth nations end 10 days of talks in London without taking any action on the issue of South African apartheid.	Norway announces extension of its territorial fishing waters from 4 to 12 miles.	An appeal by rightist leaders for an Algiers general strike to commemorate the May 13, 1957 Algiers uprising that returned de Gaulle to power is ignored by all but a few hundred high school students. . . . Fighting between Babuba and Lubia tribesmen is reported spreading in the Belgian Congo.	Premier Castro tells a TV audience that a government patrol boat chased a U.S. sub out of Cuban territorial waters May 6. The U.S. Navy denies any violation of Cuban waters.	Communist China protests what it describes as forcible Indonesian attempts to "obstruct" the repatriation of Chinese aliens in Indonesia.
May 14	Premier Khrushchev arrives in Paris pledging to make the summit conference "a success" despite what he described as recent Western efforts to "revive the Cold War."	West German Chancellor Adenauer meets with French Pres. de Gaulle on the eve of the Paris summit to make a final appeal against any unilateral Western concessions to Soviet demands on Germany or Berlin.	Jomo Kenyatta, exiled former leader of the Mau Mau terrorist campaign, is elected president of a proposed Kenya African National Union by representatives of 80 African political groups, meeting in Nairobi. . . . Reports from the Congo say 13 Congolese have been killed in the past three days in political clashes in Elizabethville, capital of Katanga Province. . . . Lebanese Premier Rashid Karami resigns to permit the formation of a caretaker cabinet pending new parliamentary elections.		
May 15	During a brief pre-summit meeting with de Gaulle and Macmillan, Khrushchev re-emphasizes his anger over the U-2, but indicates his willingness to go ahead with the summit negotiations.	Turkish P.M. Adnan Menderes promises supporters he will not resign despite growing anti-government demonstrations.			
May 16	Paris summit meeting adjourns abruptly only hours after it began when Premier Khrushchev demands a full apology from Pres. Eisenhower over the U-2 incident as a condition for continuing the meeting. Eisenhower issues a statement dismissing Khrushchev's demand as "unacceptable" and pointing out that the Soviets had already been assured of the suspension of further U-2 missions.		Justice Min. Francois C. Erasmus reports 1,900 Africans have been arrested for political and other offenses under South Africa's recent emergency regulations.	Cuban Agrarian Reform Institute announces the complete expropriation of 271,410 acres of land owned by the United Fruit Co.	

A	B	C	D	E
Includes developments that affect more than one world region, international organizations and important meetings of major world leaders.	Includes all domestic and regional developments in Europe, including the Soviet Union, Turkey, Cyprus and Malta.	Includes all domestic and regional developments in Africa and the Middle East, including Iraq and Iran and excluding Cyprus, Turkey and Afghanistan.	Includes all domestic and regional developments in Latin America, the Caribbean and Canada.	Includes all domestic and regional developments in Asia and Pacific nations, extending from Afghanistan through all the Pacific Islands, except Hawaii.

U.S. Politics & Social Issues	U.S. Foreign Policy & Defense	U.S. Economy & Environment	Science, Technology & Nature	Culture, Leisure & Life Style	
Humphrey withdraws as a presidential candidate following his loss today to Kennedy in the W. Va. Democratic primary. . . . Kennedy, running unopposed, wins the Nebraska Democratic presidential primary, assuring himself at least 10 of the state's 16 first-ballot votes. . . . The lunch counters of six major Nashville, Tenn. department stores are peacefully desegregated after four weeks of negotiations between merchants and Negro leaders.	Democratic Senate leader Lyndon Johnson says that Congress considers U.S. intelligence activities necessary and supports their continuation.	Ex-Stereotypers Union negotiator Levi S. McDonald is convicted in Portland, Ore. of master-minding the bombing of Portland newspaper delivery trucks in January. He is later sentenced to a 10-year prison term.	The nuclear submarine *U.S.S. Triton* completes the first known undersea circumnavigation of the world. . . . A new method of tenderizing meat—by pre-slaughter injections of papain, a protein-affecting enzyme from the papaya plant—is announced in Chicago by Swift & Co.		May 10
Republican National Committee names Chicago industrialist Charles H. Percy chairman of the GOP platform committee at the national convention.	In a Washington news conference Eisenhower defends U.S. espionage missions as a "distasteful necessity" since "no one wants another Pearl Harbor."	National Fire Protection Association reports that there were 410 major U.S. fires in 1959 with a record $356 million in damage. . . . John D. Rockefeller Jr., 86, millionaire philanthropist and father of N.Y. Gov. Nelson Rockefeller, dies in Tucson, Ariz.	The world's longest passenger liner, the *S.S. France*, is launched at St. Nazaire, France.		May 11
Office of Vital Statistics reports the U.S. birth rate fell .8% during 1959.		Lockheed Aircraft Corp. reports that two *Electra* airliner crashes in 1959 and 1960 have been traced to high speed oscillation that caused the wings to shear off. Design modifications are expected to cost $25 million.			May 12
Ex-Pres. Truman announces his support of Sen. Stuart Symington (Mo.) for the Democratic presidential nomination.	Maj. Gen. William C. Westmoreland, 46, is nominated by Pres. Eisenhower to become the 45th superintendent of the U.S. Military Academy at West Point.	Pres. Eisenhower vetoes a federal aid bill to provide $250 million to areas with chronic unemployment, calling the measure wasteful and unnecessary.			May 13
	Navy launches the atomic-powered submarine *Abraham Lincoln*, the fourth U.S. Polaris-armed vessel.	Pres. Eisenhower signs into law a bill authorizing a $251,476,000 AEC construction program during fiscal 1961. . . . A special Presidential committee urges the creation of a permanent U.S. government panel to propose rules on the use and control of chemical food additives.			May 14
		A Tax Foundation study indicates that the average American family last year paid about 25% of its total income in federal, state and local taxes.	USSR launches a 10,000-pound satellite space ship bearing a dummy space man in what is regarded as an important preliminary step toward manned space flight.	Don Cardwell, 24, in his first start with the Chicago Cubs, pitches a no-hitter against the St. Louis Cardinals.	May 15
Former Democratic presidential candidate Adlai Stevenson urges adoption of a law requiring TV networks to provide major Presidential candidates free time for "a great TV debate." The national networks and Republican Party leaders oppose the proposal. . . . U.S. District Court Judge J. Skelly Wright orders New Orleans public schools to begin desegregation by September 1960.	Pres. Eisenhower signs a $4.086 billion foreign aid authorization bill. The measure includes two controversial provisions allowing the President to withhold aid from the UAR and Cuba.			Alain Resnais' film *Hiroshima, Mon Amour* opens in New York.	May 16

F	G	H	I	J
Includes elections, federal-state relations, civil rights and liberties, crime, the judiciary, education, health care, poverty, urban affairs and population.	*Includes formation and debate of U.S. foreign and defense policies, veterans' affairs and defense spending. (Relations with specific foreign countries are usually found under the region concerned.)*	*Includes business, labor, agriculture, taxation, transportation, consumer affairs, monetary and fiscal policy, natural resources, and pollution.*	*Includes worldwide scientific, medical and technological developments, natural phenomena, U.S. weather, natural disasters, and accidents.*	*Includes the arts, religion, scholarship, communications media, sports, entertainment, fashions, fads and social life.*

	World Affairs	Europe	Africa & the Middle East	The Americas	Asia & the Pacific
May 17	Macmillan and de Gaulle unsuccessfully attempt to persuade Khrushchev to withdraw his demand for a U-2 apology and return to the summit talks. Macmillan tells newsmen there is little hope for saving the conference.		Congo sources report that *de facto* authority in the Stanleyville areas has passed from Belgian officials to African nationalists, particularly Patrice E. Lumumba, leader of the Congolese National Movement.	In a letter published in Cuba's two remaining independent newspapers, *El Crisol* and *Informacion*, the Archbishop of Santiago urges Cuban Catholics not to cooperate with communism.	Pakistani Pres. Ayub Khan tells a Karachi press conference that his government has strongly protested alleged U.S. use of Peshawar airfield for spy flights over the USSR.
May 18	In a tumultuous two-and-a-half hour post-summit press conference, Soviet Premier Khrushchev angrily denounces the U.S. for carrying out "aggressive" spy missions and for sabotaging the summit conference. He also warns that the USSR intends to sign an East German peace treaty that will end Western occupation rights in Berlin.				
May 19	The 15-member NATO Permanent Council expresses "complete solidarity" with the Western Big Three leaders in the wake of the Paris summit failure.		British Colonial Secy. Ian Macleod and P.M. Sir Abubaker Tafawa Balewa reach "complete agreement" in London on procedures for granting Nigeria independence by Oct. 1.		International Commission of Jurists, a non-governmental organization recognized by the U.N., charges Communist China with genocide in its occupation of Tibet.
May 20	Returning home from Paris, Pres. Eisenhower tells a welcoming crowd of 200,000 that "it is quite clear that [the Soviets]...wanted no talks whatsoever...." . . . Addressing an East Berlin rally on his return from Paris, Khrushchev pledges not to alter the "existing situation" in Germany and Berlin until a new summit meeting is held.	Praising Eisenhower's "wisdom and courage" during the summit crisis, British P.M. Macmillan tells Parliament that "the Soviet attitude in Paris" was hard to understand. . . . West German Bundesrat (upper House) approves a record federal budget for 1961 of $9.972 billion (45% for defense).	King Mohammed V of Morocco dismisses the leftist cabinet of Premier Abdallah Ibrahim to form a moderate "government of national union around the throne" with himself as premier.		Massive Japanese leftist demonstrations to protest the Japanese-U.S. mutual defense pact begin. . . . South Korean Army chief of staff, Song Yo Chan, resigns in the face of charges from high officers that he tampered with the military vote in recent national elections.
May 21		One thousand cadets from the Turkish War College march through Ankara in support of student protests against the Menderes government.			
May 22		Under the current martial law provisions, the Turkish government of Premier Menderes announces the closing of all colleges and universities and the tightening of censorship on the press and private mail.	Congolese National Movement, headed by Patrice Lumumba, emerges as the strongest Congolese political group in elections for the Congo's first Chamber of Representatives.		
May 23	U.N. Security Council convenes to hear Soviet charges of U.S. aggression by its U-2 flight. . . . P. M. David Ben-Gurion informs the Israeli Knesset of the capture of S.S. Gen. Adolf Eichmann, alleged planner of the Nazi program for exterminating the Jews.	British Labor Party leader Hugh Gaitskell denounces as "the basest hypocrisy" current suggestions that Britain should carry out unilateral nuclear disarmament, eject the U.S. from British bases and then depend on the U.S.'s nuclear deterrent for defense from Soviet attack.			Yen Hsi-shan, 67, former Nationalist China premier (1949-1950), dies in Taipei.
	A	**B**	**C**	**D**	**E**
	Includes developments that affect more than one world region, international organizations and important meetings of major world leaders.	*Includes all domestic and regional developments in Europe, including the Soviet Union, Turkey, Cyprus and Malta.*	*Includes all domestic and regional developments in Africa and the Middle East, including Iraq and Iran and excluding Cyprus, Turkey and Afghanistan.*	*Includes all domestic and regional developments in Latin America, the Caribbean and Canada.*	*Includes all domestic and regional developments in Asia and Pacific nations, extending from Afghanistan through all the Pacific Islands, except Hawaii.*

U.S. Politics & Social Issues	U.S. Foreign Policy & Defense	U.S. Economy & Environment	Science, Technology & Nature	Culture, Leisure & Life Style	
Sen. Kennedy defeats Sen. Wayne Morse (D, Ore.), 200,252 to 49,225, in Maryland's Democratic primary. . . . The Rev. Martin Luther King praises the non-violent discipline of recent anti-segregation protests in a speech to 1,500 Negro college students who gathered in Atlanta to commemorate the sixth anniversary of the Supreme Court school integration decision. . . . An all-white Little Rock, Ark. jury convicts Herbert Monts, a Negro, of bombing the home of Carlotta Walls, one of five Negro students at Little Rock Central H.S.				Vatican newspaper *L'Osservatore Romano* asserts editorially that the church has "the right and the duty to intervene" in politics and that it expects "dutiful discipline" from Roman Catholic citizens. . . . NBA approves the transfer of the Minneapolis Laker franchise to Los Angeles.	May 17
		Rep. William Widnall (R, N.J.) introduces an administration bill to provide $180 million in federal aid to economically depressed regions. The bill is designed as a substitute for the $251 million Democratic bill vetoed by the President. . . . Commerce Dept. reports the value of U.S. goods licensed for export to Soviet bloc countries reached a post-war record of $35.4 million in the first quarter of 1960.			May 18
	Former Democratic presidential candidate Adlai Stevenson repeats his earlier charges that administration "blunders" in the handling of the U-2 incident gave Khrushchev an excuse to wreck the summit.	Federal grand jury in Philadelphia returns three indictments charging eight electrical equipment manufacturers and six persons with rigging price bids since 1958 in the sale of about $50 million worth of electrical goods to U.S. agencies and others.	Prof. Adolf Butenandt, 57, succeeds Dr. Otto Hahn, 81, as president of the Max Planck Society for the Promotion of Sciences.	Alan Freed, 38, the disc jockey who reputedly coined the term "rock'n'roll," is arrested in New York on charges of accepting payola bribes from record companies.	May 19
John Kennedy outpolls native son Sen. Wayne Morse, 111,076 to 70,995, in Oregon's Democratic presidential primary. . . . Southern Baptist Convention, meeting in Miami, adopts a resolution warning against the election of a Roman Catholic ("inescapably bound...by the demands of his church") to political office.	Thirty-eight Democratic representatives send to the White House a statement expressing concern over "the damage to our prestige" caused by the U-2 incident and urge a full congressional inquiry into the matter. . . . Air Force fires a 110-ton Atlas ICBM a record 9,000 miles down the South Atlantic missile range to a target area in the Indian Ocean. . . . GAO charges the Air Force with extreme "laxity" in its financial and technical supervision of the $2 billion-a-year ICBM program.	Prof. Edwin Emil Witte, economist and a principal author of the Federal Social Security Act of 1935, dies at 73 in Madison, Wis.		*La Dolce Vita* by Italian director Federico Fellini wins the top award at the Cannes Film Festival.	May 20
Sen. Wayne Morse (D, Ore.) quits the Democratic Presidential race, saying he will support Kennedy.			British science magazine *Nature* reports the discovery by Columbia Univ. researchers of two different shapes of human sperm—round-headed and oval-headed; the two shapes appear to be sex determinants, with round heads producing boy babies and oval heads producing girls. . . . Prof. Jean Thibaud, 59, French physicist whose experiments in the 1930s verified Einstein's theory that matter is converted into radiation, dies in Lyon, France.	Bally Ache, with Bob Ussery up, wins the Preakness in Baltimore. . . . Univ. of Illinois wins its third straight Big 10 outdoor track and field championship.	May 21
	Democratic Party Advisory Council charges that the handling of the U-2 affair was indicative of a general "collapse" in the administration's foreign policy.	Commerce Dept. reports that the U.S. federal debt rose 4.5% during 1959 to a record total of $243.2 billion.			May 22
		Pres. Eisenhower postpones a threatened midwest rail strike for 60 days by appointing an emergency board to investigate wage and working conditions disputes between the Switchmen's Union of North America and 16 railroads.	Georges Claude, 89, French inventor of neon light, who served a four-year term for collaborating with the Nazis during W.W.II, dies in Paris.	American Unitarians and Universalists vote to merge into a single Unitarian Universalist Association effective May 1961.	May 23

F	G	H	I	J
Includes elections, federal-state relations, civil rights and liberties, crime, the judiciary, education, health care, poverty, urban affairs and population.	Includes formation and debate of U.S. foreign and defense policies, veterans' affairs and defense spending. (Relations with specific foreign countries are usually found under the region concerned.)	Includes business, labor, agriculture, taxation, transportation, consumer affairs, monetary and fiscal policy, natural resources, and pollution.	Includes worldwide scientific, medical and technological developments, natural phenomena, U.S. weather, natural disasters, and accidents.	Includes the arts, religion, scholarship, communications media, sports, entertainment, fashions, fads and social life.

	World Affairs	Europe	Africa & the Middle East	The Americas	Asia & the Pacific
May 24		In a speech to the Bundestag, West German Chancellor Adenauer says that the summit failure confirms his view that East-West negotiations can do little to solve the problems of Germany and Berlin.	Egyptian Pres. Nasser decrees the nationalization of four leading Cairo newspapers, ostensibly to protect them from foreign influence.		Dr. Ida S. Scudder, American-born founder of the Vellore India Medical Mission, who had practiced medicine in India since 1900, dies in Kokaikanal at age 90.
May 25	In a nationwide TV address on the summit collapse, Pres. Eisenhower asserts that Khrushchev's apology demands were "obviously" unacceptable and aimed at ruining the conference. . . . Eisenhower explains that the U.S. initially denied the U-2 spy flight "to protect the pilot" and his mission.				SEATO military advisers meet in Washington to discuss recently renewed Communist Chinese shelling of the Nationalist-held islands of Quemoy and Matsu.
May 26	U.N. Security Council votes 7-2 to reject a Soviet resolution condemning the U.S. as an aggressor for the U-2 flights over the USSR.		King Hussein tells Western newsmen that "free and fair" elections will be held in Jordan by October if the country "remains calm." . . . Israeli government reports the downing of a UAR MiG jet in a dog fight over the Negev desert. The UAR denies the report.		An estimated two million Japanese join nationwide protest demonstrations against Pres. Eisenhower's proposed visit.
May 27	In response to May 13 notes from the USSR charging complicity in U.S. espionage missions, the governments of Pakistan, Turkey and Norway each disclaim any responsibility for U.S. U-2 flights and protest Soviet threats of retaliatory attacks. . . . Concluding its debate on the U-2 incident, the U.N. Security Council adopts a resolution urging renewed efforts to achieve international agreements on disarmament and a nuclear test ban. . . . U.S.-Britain-USSR test ban talks resume in Geneva after a 2-week recess.	A military junta, headed by Lt. Gen. Cemal Gursel, seizes power in Turkey after bloodlessly overthrowing the regime of Premier Adnan Menderes. Gursel announces the lifting of political and press restrictions and promises free elections as soon as possible.	Israeli P.M. Ben-Gurion tells newsmen that Adolf Eichmann had been arrested under a 1950 law allowing Israeli courts jurisdiction over Nazi war crimes and would be tried publicly to inform "world public opinion" of the truth of Nazi persecution. . . . Ousted Moroccan Premier Abdulla Ibrahim says that his National Union party will fight the new royal regime as an attempt to establish a "Fascist dictatorship."		
May 28		Italian foreign ministry categorically denies a recent Khrushchev claim that U.S. U-2s had used Italian air bases.			U.S. Pacific commander Adm. Harry D. Felt reports to SEATO military advisers that while the situation in South Vietnam is "worsening," he has confidence in the 150,000 man South Vietnamese army. . . . A tropical storm strikes the Philippines, killing at least 166 persons and leaving some areas of Manila under at least 15 feet of water.
May 29		More than 100 persons are arrested in Zielona Gora, Poland when 5,000 persons clash with police over the seizure of a church-operated building.		Earthquakes and mudslides continue to devastate central and southern Chile. The number of dead and missing is estimated at more than 5,700.	Ex-Korean Pres. Rhee and his wife leave Seoul for Hawaii for what is described as an indefinite period of "rest and recuperation."
May 30	Soviet Marshal Rodion Malinovsky says at a Kremlin meeting that he has ordered Soviet rocket forces to strike "at any base from which a plane might fly to violate the territory of the Soviet Union."		Moderate candidates backing de Gaulle's self-determination policy win an overwhelming victory in general council elections in Algeria's 13 departments. Many urban Moslems and some European rightists boycott the elections.		South Korean National Assembly adopts a new state security law ending government powers to suppress newspapers and other political activity.

A	B	C	D	E
Includes developments that affect more than one world region, international organizations and important meetings of major world leaders.	Includes all domestic and regional developments in Europe, including the Soviet Union, Turkey, Cyprus and Malta.	Includes all domestic and regional developments in Africa and the Middle East, including Iraq and Iran and excluding Cyprus, Turkey and Afghanistan.	Includes all domestic and regional developments in Latin America, the Caribbean and Canada.	Includes all domestic and regional developments in Asia and Pacific nations, extending from Afghanistan through all the Pacific Islands, except Hawaii.

U.S. Politics & Social Issues	U.S. Foreign Policy & Defense	U.S. Economy & Environment	Science, Technology & Nature	Culture, Leisure & Life Style	
Sen. Frank Church (Ida.) is chosen to be the keynote speaker at the Democratic national convention.	Air Force launches a 5,000-pound Midas II satellite designed to give the U.S. an early warning against surprise missile attack.	A Special House Subcommittee on Legislative Oversight completes two weeks of hearings into the operations of the Federal Power Commission which focused on allegations of an unethical relationship between commissioners and gas company representatives.	Deadly earthquakes and huge mountain slides that rocked Chile May 21-22 trigger Pacific tidal waves that bring death and massive flooding to Hawaii and Japan.		May 24
		Bureau of Labor Statistics reports that the U.S. cost of living index rose to a record high in April.		FCC announces 28 of 72 record companies accused of making payola payments have agreed in writing to cease the practice. . . . Robert F. Kennedy, 34, father of seven, brother of Sen. John Kennedy and ex-counsel to the Senate Committee on Labor-Management Practices, is named Father of the Year by the National Father's Day Committee.	May 25
The House passes a $1.3 billion school aid bill which includes a special amendment barring funds to districts that resist desegregation orders. The amendment is believed to assure defeat for the bill in the Senate.	State Secy. Herter tells the House Foreign Affairs Committee that the summit crisis has not seriously affected progress at the Geneva nuclear test-ban talks. . . . Former U.S. Amb.-to-USSR George F. Kennan recommends closer State Dept. supervision of national security affairs to assure "better coordination of military policy with national policy than we have had in recent years." . . . Senate votes not to ratify an international accord that would give the World Court jurisdiction over sea disputes.	Congress sends the President a bill providing for a two-year Public Health Service study of the effects of motor vehicle pollution on health.			May 26
A Negro American Labor Council, headed by A. Philip Randolph, is formed in Detroit to combat racial discrimination in U.S. labor unions. . . . Jess Lanier, mayor of Bessemer, Ala., files a $500,000 libel suit against The New York Times for allegedly false statements that appeared in an April 18 article on Birmingham area racial conditions.	Senate Foreign Relations Committee begins hearings into the U-2 affair and the collapse of the summit talks.			James Montgomery Flagg, magazine illustrator best known for his recruiting poster depicting Uncle Sam saying "I want you", dies in New York at 83. . . . Benny (Kid) Paret of Cuba becomes the world welterweight champ, defeating Don Jordan of Los Angeles in a 15-round decision.	May 27
			Lt. Col. Boris M. Adrianov, flying a Soviet turbo-jet, sets a world jet speed record of 1297.8 mph.		May 28
		National Education Association reports that New York leads all states in school expenditures with a figure of $559 per pupil.		Jim Beatty runs a 3.58 mile in the Caifornia Relays, the fastest ever run by an American.	May 29
Alabama Gov. John Patterson files libel suits against The New York Times and five Negro leaders because of statements in an ad seeking funds for the legal defense of Martin Luther King on perjury charges.				Pope John XXIII announces preparations for the Roman Catholic Church's first ecumenical council since 1869. . . . Boris L. Pasternak, Russian poet, novelist and Nobel Prize winning author of the controversial Dr. Zhivago, dies of lung cancer at age 70 in Moscow. . . . Jim Rathmann, 31, driving a Ken-Paul Special, wins the 44th Indianapolis 500 motor race.	May 30
F	G	H	I	J	
Includes elections, federal-state relations, civil rights and liberties, crime, the judiciary, education, health care, poverty, urban affairs and population.	Includes formation and debate of U.S. foreign and defense policies, veterans' affairs and defense spending. (Relations with specific foreign countries are usually found under the region concerned.)	Includes business, labor, agriculture, taxation, transportation, consumer affairs, monetary and fiscal policy, natural resources, and pollution.	Includes worldwide scientific, medical and technological developments, natural phenomena, U.S. weather, natural disasters, and accidents.	Includes the arts, religion, scholarship, communications media, sports, entertainment, fashions, fads and social life.	

	World Affairs	Europe	Africa & the Middle East	The Americas	Asia & the Pacific
May 31	In a major post-summit address to the nation, French Pres. de Gaulle calls for renewed efforts to achieve a world "detente" based on gradual disarmament and increased East-West cooperation. Toward that end, de Gaulle promises to build a strong France within a revived and independent European community.	Walther Funk, 69, Hitler's minister of economics, 1937-1945, dies in Dusseldorf, West Germany.	In his first public appearance since he was wounded April 9, P.M. Henrik Verwoerd tells a South African Independence Day rally that the nation's white population must and would remain "the guardian of the black man."	In the wake of a renewed outbreak of Communist and Peronist attacks, Pres. Arturo Frondizi asks the Argentine congress to enact a new law making terrorism punishable by death.	Prince Tiao Somsanith, an opponent of negotiations with Laos' Communist-led rebels, becomes Laotian premier, succeeding the caretaker government of Kou Abhay.
June 1		Turkish ruling junta announces the arrest of 403 parliamentary supporters of ousted Premier Menderes.	Congo leader Patrice Lumumba says certain Belgian colonial officials are trying to prevent him from assuming national leadership once the Congo becomes independent.	Dr. Teodoro Picado, 60, Costa Rican president (1944-48), dies in Managua, Nicaragua where he had lived since the overthrow of his government.	Most of the 138 Liberal Party deputies in the South Korean National Assembly resign from the party, leaving the former opposition Democratic Party as the strongest Assembly group.
June 2	USSR makes public a revised disarmament proposal that includes many of the control and inspection provisions demanded by the West. The plan, reportedly prepared for presentation at the abortive summit, calls for: (1) The creation of an international control organization; (2) supervision of disarmament measures by aerial and ground inspection; (3) gradual destruction of nuclear weapons and delivery systems.	P.M. Macmillan tells a Conservative Party rally that Britain will not be swayed by Soviet threats from its policy of close cooperation with the U.S. . . . Paula Wolf, 64, sister of Adolf Hitler, dies in Berchtesgaden, Germany.			Representatives of the SEATO pact, meeting in Washington, warn of stepped-up Communist subversion in southeast Asia following the collapse of the summit.
June 3	At a Kremlin press conference, Khrushchev describes the Eisenhower presidency as "a time of trouble" for the U.S. and the world. The remark follows a number of recent public outbursts in which Khrushchev has derided Eisenhower as weak, incompetent and dangerous.	In a Moscow press conference crowded with personal attacks on Western leaders, Soviet Premier Khrushchev says that West German Chancellor Adenauer "should long have been straightjacketed and put into a lunatic asylum." . . . Finnish Premier Veino Sukselainen fails to create a five-party coalition to assure parliamentary approval of Finnish membership in the European Free Trade Association. . . . Turkey's ruling junta accuses former officials of the ousted Menderes regime of deliberately killing peaceful students during recent anti-Menderes demonstrations.	Four former West African French colonies—Ivory Coast, Dahomey, Voltaic and Niger Republics—announce that they will seek full independence within the French Community.	Moscow sources report that Soviet Premier Khrushchev has accepted an invitation to visit Cuba in the near future.	
June 4	Pres. Eisenhower says Khrushchev's personal insults against Western leaders have actually "brought the West closer together than...ever." State Secy. Herter dismisses the attacks as Khrushchev's attempt to "divest himself of all responsibility...for the destruction of the Paris summit."			In a diplomatic note delivered in Havana the U.S. State Dept. charges the Cuban government with conducting an "official campaign of slander" against the U.S. The note specifically denies charges of U.S. hostility toward Cuba as well as recent Cuban claims that expropriated American property owners had been fully reimbursed. . . . Canadian P.M. John Diefenbaker, visiting the U.S., describes Canadian-U.S. ties as "a model relationship" for the world.	
June 5		*The New York Times* reports the West German Social Democratic Party has abandoned its old demand for negotiations with the USSR on German reunification and is prepared to support a bipartisan West German foreign policy along the lines set down by Adenauer.		Victor Paz Estenssoro of the Nationalist Revolutionary Movement is elected president of Bolivia, defeating two leftist challengers.	A Cambodian plebiscite reveals virtually unanimous support for the policies of Prince and ex-Premier Norodom Sihanouk.

A	B	C	D	E
Includes developments that affect more than one world region, international organizations and important meetings of major world leaders.	Includes all domestic and regional developments in Europe, including the Soviet Union, Turkey, Cyprus and Malta.	Includes all domestic and regional developments in Africa and the Middle East, including Iraq and Iran and excluding Cyprus, Turkey and Afghanistan.	Includes all domestic and regional developments in Latin America, the Caribbean and Canada.	Includes all domestic and regional developments in Asia and Pacific nations, extending from Afghanistan through all the Pacific Islands, except Hawaii.

U.S. Politics & Social Issues	U.S. Foreign Policy & Defense	U.S. Economy & Environment	Science, Technology & Nature	Culture, Leisure & Life Style	
Defying an AFL-CIO ban on candidate endorsements, the Textile Workers Union announces its unqualified support for Sen. Kennedy.		Supreme Court rules old treaty provisions give Florida and Texas ownership rights over the oil deposits and other undersea resources for a distance of 10.5 miles off their Gulf shores.	A study by the Joint Commission on Mental Health reports one out of every four Americans seek professional help for emotional disturbance at some time in their lives.		May 31
Reporters Don Oberdorfer and Walter Pincus begin publishing a series of investigative articles exposing gross expense account abuses by U.S. congressmen.	NASA Dir. Hugh L. Dryden explains to the Senate Foreign Relations Committee that the false U-2 "cover story" initially put out by his agency was provided by the CIA.			National Council of Churches releases a report assailing the "pathological preoccupation with sex and violence" in current films and TV.	June 1
	A statement from Soviet Premier Khrushchev asking U.S. Democrats to speak out against the Eisenhower administration's foreign policy provokes a strongly worded defense of bipartisanship from Senate Democratic leader Lyndon Johnson. Johnson says "Americans—Republican or Democrat—will stand united against...efforts to divide the country.". . . Defense Secy. Gates tells the Senate Foreign Relations Committee the U-2 spy flights gave the U.S. "vital information" on USSR war potential. He also asserts that a Soviet decision to attack bases from which U.S. reconnaissance missions were flown would mean general war.	Despite a plea for restraint from Labor Secy. James P. Mitchell, the AFL-CIO Amalgamated Clothing Workers vote to use boycotts and strikes against import garment competition from Japan and other low-wage countries. . . . Federal Reserve Board authorizes member banks to cut the rediscount rate from 4% to 3½%.		A contract dispute between the AFL-CIO Actors' Equity Union and New York theatres leads to a complete shut-down of legitimate Broadway productions for the first time since 1919.	June 2
House Ways and Means Committee approves $325 million-a-year federal medical assistance bill for the elderly poor. The bill, supported by the administration, replaces a more expensive and extensive Democratic proposal to provide health insurance to all Social Security recipients.				Jockey Johnny Longden, 53, announces he will retire from racing July 25.	June 3
U.S. District Court Judge T. W. Davidson orders the Dallas (Tex.) school board to begin implementation of its voluntary integration plan no later than September 1961.					June 4
		Members of the International Longshoremen's Association and Great Lakes area pier employers agree to a new three-year contract, ending a 20-day strike that had halted commerce through the St. Lawrence Seaway.			June 5

F	G	H	I	J
Includes elections, federal-state relations, civil rights and liberties, crime, the judiciary, education, health care, poverty, urban affairs and population.	Includes formation and debate of U.S. foreign and defense policies, veterans' affairs and defense spending. (Relations with specific foreign countries are usually found under the region concerned.)	Includes business, labor, agriculture, taxation, transportation, consumer affairs, monetary and fiscal policy, natural resources, and pollution.	Includes worldwide scientific, medical and technological developments, natural phenomena, U.S. weather, natural disasters, and accidents.	Includes the arts, religion, scholarship, communications media, sports, entertainment, fashions, fads and social life.

	World Affairs	Europe	Africa & the Middle East	The Americas	Asia & the Pacific
June 6	Israel makes public a note to Argentina expressing regret for any violation of Argentine law that may have attended the capture of ex-S.S. Gen. Adolf Eichmann. The note claimed that Eichmann voluntarily agreed to be brought to Israel for trial.	In ceremonies commemorating the 16th anniversary of D-Day, French Foreign Min. Maurice Couve de Murville says that post-war events have transformed West Germany from the "peril that she...so cruelly represented" to a cornerstone of Western freedom.		Jose Maria Velasco Ibarra, a political independent, is reelected to his fourth term as president of Ecuador.	
June 7	U.S. informs the USSR it will give "careful and serious study" to the new Soviet disarmament plan.		Twenty-five African tribesmen and five African policemen are reported killed in clashes in the remote Pondoland area of South Africa.	Bolivia announces that the U.S. has agreed to extend $2.7 million in industrial credit to the state-owned Bolivian oil monopoly. The U.S. loan, the first to any nationalized oil monopoly, comes shortly after the publication of a similar offer from the USSR. . . . Peruvian Pres. Manuel Prado Ugarteche appoints five new ministers to his reorganized ruling cabinet.	White House announces Pres. Eisenhower will make his scheduled goodwill trip to Japan despite increasingly violent anti-American demonstrations there.
June 8	Argentina formally protests the Israeli capture of Adolf Eichmann as a violation of Argentine and international law and demands his return to Argentina pending legal application for extradition to Israel.			OAS charges the Dominican Republic with gross violations of basic political rights in its treatment of opponents of the Trujillo regime.	
June 9				An OAS report documenting violations of human rights in the Dominican Republic is denounced by Dominican Foreign Min. Porfirio Herrera Baez as part of a conspiracy against his country.	Demonstrations by Japanese leftists against the impending visit of Pres. Eisenhower continue to grow in number and violence. . . . Typhoon Mary batters Hong Kong with 135 mph winds, leaving scores dead and at least 20,000 homeless.
June 10	White House Press Secretary James Hagerty is mobbed by 6,000 anti-American demonstrators following his arrival in Tokyo to make final arrangements for Pres. Eisenhower's scheduled visit to Japan. . . . In a personal letter to Argentine Pres. Arturo Frondizi, Israeli Premier Ben-Gurion admits that the Israeli captors of Eichmann violated Argentine law, but appeals for understanding and acceptance of the "imperative moral force" that precipitated their actions.	Nearly one million French civil servants strike for 24 hours to protest the inadequacy of a 5% pay increase.		In a TV speech, Premier Castro asserts that U.S. Secy. of State Herter has conferred with Nicaraguan exiles about launching an invasion against Cuba from Nicaragua.	
June 11	Thirteen nations sign an extension of the Internat. Coffee Agreement, but four members of the current agreement refuse to sign immediately because of disputes over quotas.				
June 12	Pres. Eisenhower begins his two-week goodwill tour of the Far East, flying from Washington to a stopover in Alaska.	The ruling Turkish military junta makes public a provisional constitution granting full legislative powers to an army-dominated National Union Committee presided over by Gen. Cemal Gursel.			
June 13		West German Economics Min. Ludwig Erhard, Adenauer's heir-apparent as leader of the Christian Democratic Union, tells newsmen that his personal differences with Adenauer have been resolved and that the CDU would enter the 1961 elections as a unified party.	Belgian Congo Resident Min. Walter van der Meersch asks Patrice Lumumba to explore the possibility of forming the Congo's first ruling parliamentary cabinet.	A bloodless one-day revolt by about 400 anti-Peronist soldiers in San Luis collapses when others in the Argentine Army refuse to join the rebellion.	Prince Norodom Sihanouk, ex-king and premier of Cambodia, agrees to become Cambodian chief of state again.
	A	B	C	D	E
	Includes developments that affect more than one world region, international organizations and important meetings of major world leaders.	Includes all domestic and regional developments in Europe, including the Soviet Union, Turkey, Cyprus and Malta.	Includes all domestic and regional developments in Africa and the Middle East, including Iraq and Iran and excluding Cyprus, Turkey and Afghanistan.	Includes all domestic and regional developments in Latin America, the Caribbean and Canada.	Includes all domestic and regional developments in Asia and Pacific nations, extending from Afghanistan through all the Pacific Islands, except Hawaii.

U.S. Politics & Social Issues	U.S. Foreign Policy & Defense	U.S. Economy & Environment	Science, Technology & Nature	Culture, Leisure & Life Style	
Justice Dept. reports it has asked to examine the voting registration records of 12 Southern counties where systematic racial discrimination has been alleged.	U.S. and British defense officials announce a U.S. agreement to sell Skybolt air launched missiles to Britain when they become available in 1964-1965. . . . Ex-Pres. Truman tells a Chicago news conference that his administration rejected proposals for aerial spy flights because "espionage is a dirty deal. I didn't want to be part of it."	International Association of Machinists strikes the Convair Division of the General Dynamics Corp., causing work stoppages at Cape Canaveral and three other AF missile-launching bases. . . . U.S. Treasury, employing a new debt management technique, offers to exchange 2½% bonds maturing in 1961 for new 3¾% bonds maturing in 1964.	American Heart Association reports mounting evidence showing "a statistical association" between heavy cigarette smoking and heart disease. . . . Freeport Sulphur Co. announces the start of operations at the world's first offshore sulphur mine in the Gulf of Mexico.	Dr. Frank Spaulding, 93, U.S. educator and founder of the Yale Univ. Graduate School, dies in La Jolla, Calif.	June 6
In the first suit filed under the new 1960 Civil Rights Act, the Justice Dept. charges Bienville Parish, La. voting registrars with systematic racial discrimination. . . . Vanderbilt Univ. accepts the resignation of 12 divinity school faculty members who quit to protest the university's expulsion of a Negro student for participating in sit-in demonstrations.	A nuclear-armed Bomarc anti-aircraft missile catches fire in its launching shelter near McGuire AF Base, causing a minor leakage of radioactive material but no injuries.	UAW and IAM members strike United Aircraft Corp. plants in Connecticut. Some 20,000 workers are reportedly on strike.			June 7
	Secy. of State Herter tells a Univ. of Pittsburgh graduating class that "hermit nations" like the USSR are "a danger to our world community."	House sends to the Senate a bill extending high wartime corporate tax rates through fiscal 1961.	Encyclopedia Britannica Films announces it will begin marketing recently developed "self-instruction machines" to be used in high school language and math courses.		June 8
Rep. Walter Judd (R, Minn.) is named keynote speaker for the GOP national convention.		Pennsylvania units of the AFL and CIO merge after five years of disputes are ended by the personal intervention of AFL-CIO Pres. George Meany. N.J. remains the only state in which the AFL and CIO remain separate. . . . Senate passes and sends to the House a bill to reduce federal wheat surpluses by requiring a 20% reduction in wheat acreage.		ABC TV announces the signing of a five-year contract to televise games of the new American Football League.	June 9
				Paul Pender retains N.Y. and Mass. recognition as middleweight champ by winning a 15-round split decision over Sugar Ray Robinson in Brookline, Mass.	June 10
		Comptroller General's office reports there has been a costly duplication of effort between NASA and the AF in the development of the Atlas rocket series.		Celtic Ash, ridden by Bill Hartack, wins the Belmont Stakes.	June 11
				Broadway theater productions re-open following a June 9 settlement of a contract dispute between actors and the League of New York Theaters.	June 12
Vanderbilt Univ. announces it will allow James M. Lawson Jr., expelled for leading sit-in demonstrations, to obtain his degree after all.	State Dept. makes public a report indicating that Soviet-bloc countries employ an estimated 300,000 persons in 27 espionage and national security organizations throughout the world.	Labor Dept. reports unemployment fell .1% in May to a seasonally adjusted rate of 4.9%.		A Rome court announces the annulment of Ingrid Bergman's Mexican proxy marriage to Roberto Rossellini on the grounds that she was still legally married to her former husband at the time of the marriage.	June 13
F	G	H	I	J	
Includes elections, federal-state relations, civil rights and liberties, crime, the judiciary, education, health care, poverty, urban affairs and population.	Includes formation and debate of U.S. foreign and defense policies, veterans' affairs and defense spending. (Relations with specific foreign countries are usually found under the region concerned.)	Includes business, labor, agriculture, taxation, transportation, consumer affairs, monetary and fiscal policy, natural resources, and pollution.	Includes worldwide scientific, medical and technological developments, natural phenomena, U.S. weather, natural disasters, and accidents.	Includes the arts, religion, scholarship, communications media, sports, entertainment, fashions, fads and social life.	

	World Affairs	Europe	Africa & the Middle East	The Americas	Asia & the Pacific
June 14	Israeli For. Min. Golda Meir rejects Latin American suggestions that Eichmann be transferred to the Argentine Embassy in Tel Aviv pending an International Court decision on jurisdiction over his case.	Ana Pauker, 66, Rumanian foreign minister purged in 1952, is reported dead.	In a TV address, French Pres. de Gaulle appeals directly to the leaders of the Algerian rebellion to come to Paris for open negotiations on "an honorable end to the fighting." . . . U.N. Trusteeship Council reports that Belgium has agreed to hold general elections in the Ruanda-Urundi trust territory as a prelude to discussions of Ruanda-Urundi independence by the General Assembly in 1961.		One million cheering Filipinos welcome President Eisenhower in the largest reception ever given a foreign visitor. . . . Heavy fighting between Tibetans and Communist Chinese is reported from New Delhi.
June 15	Western delegates to the Geneva disarmament talks launch a sweeping criticism of the recently revised Soviet disarmament proposal despite the fairly positive reaction first accorded the plan one week earlier. Chief U.S. delegate Frederick Eaton claims that the Soviet proposal to liquidate foreign bases would "unbalance" the military situation in Europe.		A Kenya government White Paper announces the gradual elimination of all racial land barriers in the British colony.	Three anti-Castro Cubans are shot by a firing squad in Santiago; they are the first to be executed under a 1959 decree making counter-revolutionary actions punishable by death.	Massive rioting outside the Japanese Diet climaxes three weeks of growing student unrest against the new Japanese-American security pact; 870 persons are injured and one killed in the fighting between police and students. . . . Following an enthusiastic reception in Manila, visiting Pres. Eisenhower publicly reiterates the American position that an attack on the Philippines would be viewed as an attack on the U.S. . . . South Korean National Assembly approves a sweeping revision of the nation's constitution, replacing the presidential system with a cabinet form of government modeled on Britain's.
June 16			The formation of a Front for a French Algeria, including all Moslem and European groups favoring full Algerian integration within France, is announced in Algiers by V.P. Bachaga Boualem of the National Assembly. . . . The state of emergency imposed in Nyasaland in March 1959 is ended.	Cuban government expels two U.S. embassy aides for allegedly "conspiring with counter-revolutionaries."	At the request of Premier Nobusuke Kishi, Pres. Eisenhower agrees to postpone his scheduled trip to Japan. . . . Japanese Premier Kishi blames cancellation of Pres. Eisenhower's goodwill visit on the actions of Communist-led rioters. He adds that he has no intention to resign or dissolve the Diet.
June 17				David Torino, Argentine newspaper publisher who was frequently jailed in the 1940's for his opposition to the Peron regime, dies in Salta, Argentina.	
June 18				U.S. State Dept. expels two Cuban consular officials in retaliation for Cuba's June 16 expulsion of two U.S. embassy attaches accused of counter-revolutionary activity. . . . Dr. Joao Carlos Muniz, 67, Brazilian U.N. delegate (1946), Security Council president (1950), and one of the founders of the International Atomic Energy Agency, dies in Teresopolis, Brazil.	A Taipei rally of 300,000 cheer visiting Pres. Eisenhower's promise of continued U.S. recognition of Nationalist China as "the only rightful representative of China."
June 19		USSR creates an All-Russian Economic Council to supervise and coordinate the 70 regional economic councils established in 1957 to decentralize the Soviet economy.			Despite several weeks of violent protests by leftist students, the Japanese Diet ratifies the U.S.-Japan mutual security pact. . . . Scattered demonstrations protesting the U.S. refusal to return Okinawa to Japanese rule mark Pres. Eisenhower's brief stop-over on the island en route to South Korea. . . . Communist Chinese end a massive three-day bombardment of the Nationalist-held Quemoy Islands, undertaken to demonstrate their open "contempt" for Eisenhower's visit to Formosa.

A	B	C	D	E
Includes developments that affect more than one world region, international organizations and important meetings of major world leaders.	Includes all domestic and regional developments in Europe, including the Soviet Union, Turkey, Cyprus and Malta.	Includes all domestic and regional developments in Africa and the Middle East, including Iraq and Iran and excluding Cyprus, Turkey and Afghanistan.	Includes all domestic and regional developments in Latin America, the Caribbean and Canada.	Includes all domestic and regional developments in Asia and Pacific nations, extending from Afghanistan through all the Pacific Islands, except Hawaii.

U.S. Politics & Social Issues	U.S. Foreign Policy & Defense	U.S. Economy & Environment	Science, Technology & Nature	Culture, Leisure & Life Style	
House Un-American Activities Chmn. Francis Walter says that recent newspaper stories critical of committee members' expense account practices "played into the communists' hands by smearing the committee."		Allis-Chalmers Co. pleads guilty to antitrust violations in the sale of heavy electrical equipment. Twelve other companies facing similar charges plead innocent.		Ex-middleweight champ Jake La Motta tells a Senate Anti-Monopoly Subcommittee that he "threw" a 1947 light-heavyweight fight against Billy Fox in exchange for a promoters' agreement to get him a bout with then middleweight champ Marcel Cerdan. . . . Univ. of Illinois dismisses assistant biology professor Leo F. Koch, 44, for publicly condoning premarital sexual intercourse for adult college students.	June 14
Senate passes a bill to repeal the National Defense Education Act requirement that students seeking government loans be required to sign affidavits denying they are subversives.	Senate Foreign Relations Committee unanimously recommends ratification of the U.S.-Japanese defense treaty by the full Senate.		The development of a super-strength, heat-resistant aluminum oxide fiber, suitable for use in space vehicles, is reported by representatives of Horizons, Inc.		June 15
Supporters of John Kennedy claim he has 710½ of the 761 votes needed to be nominated on the first ballot at the Democratic national convention. . . . Congress approves, pending ratification by the states, a Constitutional amendment granting District of Columbia citizens the right to vote for the president and vice president. . . . Preliminary Census Bureau figures show that U.S. population grew to 179.5 million in 1960, an increase of over 18 million since 1950.				Alfred Hitchcock's film thriller *Psycho* is released in New York.	June 16
		Sporadic pilot walkouts against FAA rulings that third pilots must occasionally give up their seats to flight efficiency inspectors, which began June 10, continue to disrupt U.S. airline schedules.		Red Sox star Ted Williams hits his 500th career home run in a game against the Cleveland Indians. . . . American Football League files an antitrust suit in Washington, charging the NFL with trying to monopolize professional football by preventing AFL teams from obtaining playing facilities.	June 17
Republican presidential hopeful Nixon tells a Houston, Tex. rally that the next president must exercise "moral leadership" in the battle against racial discrimination. . . . The quadrennial meeting of the Methodist Church's all-white Northeastern Jurisdiction votes to invite 572 northeastern Negro Methodist churches to join its membership.				Arnold Palmer wins the U.S. Open golf championship in Denver. . . . Kansas Univ. wins the NCAA national track and field championships in Berkeley, Calif.	June 18
Rep. Douglas H. Elliott, 39, (R, Pa.) who was elected in April to fill the unexpired term of Richard Simpson, takes his own life near Chambersburg, Pa.	Undersecy. of State C. Douglas Dillon tells reporters that the cancellation of Pres. Eisenhower's trip to Japan should not cause the American public to "panic."	Commerce Dept. reports that the median annual income for all persons employed in the U.S. rose to a record $2,606 in 1959.		Former Indy 500 winner Jimmy Bryan, 33, dies of injuries suffered in a crash at the start of a 100-mile championship race in Langhorne, Pa.	June 19

F	G	H	I	J
Includes elections, federal-state relations, civil rights and liberties, crime, the judiciary, education, health care, poverty, urban affairs and population.	*Includes formation and debate of U.S. foreign and defense policies, veterans' affairs and defense spending. (Relations with specific foreign countries are usually found under the region concerned.)*	*Includes business, labor, agriculture, taxation, transportation, consumer affairs, monetary and fiscal policy, natural resources, and pollution.*	*Includes worldwide scientific, medical and technological developments, natural phenomena, U.S. weather, natural disasters, and accidents.*	*Includes the arts, religion, scholarship, communications media, sports, entertainment, fashions, fads and social life.*

	World Affairs	Europe	Africa & the Middle East	The Americas	Asia & the Pacific

June 20

Africa & the Middle East: de Gaulle's offer of negotiations for settlement of the Algerian rebellion on the basis of his self-determination plan is formally accepted by the Algerian Provisional Government. . . . A number of French political leaders, headed by Jacques Soustelle and ex-Premier Georges Bidault, agree to form a unified political movement to oppose de Gaulle's Algerian policies.

Asia & the Pacific: Pres. Eisenhower reaffirms the U.S. commitment to the defense of South Korea in a speech before the National Assembly in Seoul.

June 21

World Affairs: In a major address to the Rumanian CP Congress on the eve of a 12-nation Communist-bloc summit, Premier Khrushchev declares that war with the capitalist countries is not inevitable and urges a flexible interpretation of Marxist-Leninist theory. The speech is seen as part of a growing ideological rift between the Soviets and the Chinese over relations with the West.

Africa & the Middle East: Patrice Lumumba replaces Joseph Kasavubu as premier-designate of the Congo after Lumumba's Congolese National Movement succeeds in mustering a majority in the newly-elected Congolese parliament. Kasavubu is expected to be elected president of the House of Representatives, the second-highest post in the new nation.

June 22

Asia & the Pacific: Hours after the ratification of the new U.S.-Japanese treaty, Premier Kishi announces he will resign as soon as the "situation is stable." . . . A three-week old heat wave in northern India is reported to have killed almost 400 people.

June 23

World Affairs: U.N. Security Council approves, 8-0, a resolution calling upon Israel to make "appropriate reparation" for the violation of Argentine sovereignty committed in the transfer of Adolf Eichmann from Argentina to Israel.

June 24

Africa & the Middle East: Representatives attending the second conference of independent African states in Addis Ababa resolve to support economic and diplomatic sanctions against South Africa.

The Americas: Venezuelan Pres. Romulo Betancourt is slightly wounded in an assassination attempt. Venezuelan authorities report the arrest of the principal plotters.

June 25

Europe: Rumanian CP Congress ends after re-electing Gheorghe Gheorghiu-Dej as a party first secretary.

Asia & the Pacific: Indonesia's new parliament, appointed by Pres. Sukarno to consult with him in the implementation of his plans for "guided democracy", is inaugurated in Jakarta.

June 26

A	B	C	D	E
Includes developments that affect more than one world region, international organizations and important meetings of major world leaders.	Includes all domestic and regional developments in Europe, including the Soviet Union, Turkey, Cyprus and Malta.	Includes all domestic and regional developments in Africa and the Middle East, including Iraq and Iran and excluding Cyprus, Turkey and Afghanistan.	Includes all domestic and regional developments in Latin America, the Caribbean and Canada.	Includes all domestic and regional developments in Asia and Pacific nations, extending from Afghanistan through all the Pacific Islands, except Hawaii.

U.S. Politics & Social Issues	U.S. Foreign Policy & Defense	U.S. Economy & Environment	Science, Technology & Nature	Culture, Leisure & Life Style	
Overturning two lower court decisions, the Supreme Court rules that the Civil Rights Commission may subpoena voting registrars without disclosing the names of persons charging voting irregularities.		In a speech to N.D. Republicans, V.P. Nixon outlines his farm policy, including a plan for U.N. distribution of U.S. food surpluses to needy nations.		Floyd Patterson recaptures the world heavyweight championship by knocking out Ingemar Johansson in the fifth round of their title bout in New York. Patterson is the first man in modern boxing history to regain the heavyweight crown. . . . National Academy of Television Arts & Sciences awards Emmys to *Playhouse 90* for the best dramatic series, to the *Huntley-Brinkley Report* for the best news show and to *The Untouchables* for best actor (Robert Stack), best scenic design, best cinematography and best camera work.	June 20
	Secy. of State Herter admits to a Senate Appropriations Committee that his office had initially misjudged the intensity of the Japanese riots which explains why the President's trip was not cancelled sooner.	House rejects an administration-backed Senate bill to cut wheat acreage by 20%, but leave price supports at the current 75% of parity.		West German sprinter Armin Hary breaks the world record for the 100 meters with a time of 10 seconds flat.	June 21
New York Mayor Robert Wagner bans a proposed American Nazi Party rally in the city's Union Square on the grounds that the group's purpose is to incite violence.	Senate ratifies the U.S.-Japan security treaty by a vote of 90 to 2. The pact becomes effective immediately.				June 22
Former Wis. Democratic Party Chmn. James Doyle announces a nationwide movement to draft Adlai E. Stevenson for the Democratic presidential nomination. Stevenson has said he would not seek the nomination.	American foreign policy officials complete work on a new disarmament plan to be presented at the Geneva talks as a substitute for the revised plan offered by the USSR June 7. The new plan stresses strictly supervised measures against surprise attacks and a rigid timetable for destruction of nuclear delivery systems.				June 23
		Bureau of Labor Statistics reports that the cost of living rose to another record high in May.			June 24
NAACP's annual convention adopts a resolution pledging its resources and full support to the current sit-in campaigns.	Senate Foreign Relations Committee makes public its report on the U-2 incident which criticizes the administration for mishandling the affair and thereby contributing to the failure of the summit.		German-born astronomer Walter Baade, 67, author of radically new hypotheses on the universe's age and size, dies in Goettingen, Germany.	John Thomas of Boston Univ. sets a new outdoor high jump record with a leap of 7 ft. 2 in.	June 25
Supporters of John Kennedy and Richard Nixon launch intensive efforts to round up gubernatorial political backing as the annual Governors' Conference opens in Glacier National Park, Mont. Nelson Rockefeller is among four Republican governors who have refused to promise support for Nixon's candidacy. . . . A conference of university educators in New York labels current college admission tests undemocratic and unfair to racial minorities. . . . Henrik Shipstead, 79, former GOP Senator from Minnesota and isolationist, dies in Alexandria, Minn.	Dismissing Senate criticism of the handling of the U-2 incident, Sen. Barry Goldwater (R, Ariz.) says the U-2 mission and the breakdown of the summit were "one of the great victories we have achieved over communism since the second World War."		National Science Foundation announces plans to establish a National Center of Atmospheric Research to stimulate and coordinate study of weather.	Oliver Gendebien and Paul Frere of Belgium, driving a Ferrari, win the 24-hour Le Mans grand prix of auto racing.	June 26

F	G	H	I	J
Includes elections, federal-state relations, civil rights and liberties, crime, the judiciary, education, health care, poverty, urban affairs and population.	*Includes formation and debate of U.S. foreign and defense policies, veterans' affairs and defense spending. (Relations with specific foreign countries are usually found under the region concerned.)*	*Includes business, labor, agriculture, taxation, transportation, consumer affairs, monetary and fiscal policy, natural resources, and pollution.*	*Includes worldwide scientific, medical and technological developments, natural phenomena, U.S. weather, natural disasters, and accidents.*	*Includes the arts, religion, scholarship, communications media, sports, entertainment, fashions, fads and social life.*

	World Affairs	**Europe**	**Africa & the Middle East**	**The Americas**	**Asia & the Pacific**
June 27	Delegates from the Communist-bloc nations walk out of the Geneva disarmament talks to protest the Western nations' decision to submit a counter-proposal rather than continue negotiation on the Soviet plan for total disarmament. Khrushchev blames the suspension on the bad faith of the U.S. and urges that the disarmament question be submitted to the U.N. General Assembly. . . . The leaders of 12 ruling Communist parties, meeting in Bucharest, Rumania, issue a declaration reaffirming their unified support of Khrushchev's peaceful co-existence thesis.	Harry Pollitt, long-time leader in the British Communist Party, dies at the age of 69.		U.S. State Dept. files a memo with the OAS Peace Commission accusing Cuba of continuing a deliberate policy of slander and distortion against the U.S.	Acting South Korean Pres. Huh Chung orders elections for a new National Assembly to begin July 29. . . . Typhoon Olive strikes the northern Philippines, leaving 104 dead, 500 missing and 60,000 homeless.
June 28			South African officials announce the relaxation of emergency measures imposed during black uprisings in the spring.		Diplomatic communiques between Communist China and Nepal indicate heavy fighting between Chinese troops and Tibetan guerillas. . . . A Nepalese officer is killed and 10 to 17 of his soldiers are captured by Communist Chinese troops in northeastern Nepal near the Tibetan border.
June 29	Communist Chinese publicly reject Khrushchev's thesis on the non-inevitability of war voiced at the recent Communist summit, labelling it "modern revisionism" based on an undue fear of nuclear war.	In a note to the USSR, British P.M. Macmillan criticizes the Soviet walkout from the arms talks as "incomprehensible" and indicative of bad faith.	After four days of talks, emissaries of the Algerian Provisional Government and French representatives fail to agree on the conditions for a full-scale discussion of a cease-fire.	Cuban government seizes the Texas Company petroleum refinery in Santiago after the company refused a government order to refine Soviet-purchased oil.	
June 30	U.N. Secy. Gen. Hammarskjold urges the Western nations to "let the dust settle" before trying to reopen East-West disarmament negotiations through the U.N.	Soviet Premier Khrushchev arrives in Vienna for a nine-day state visit to Austria. . . . West Germany's Social Democratic Party announces it will abandon its neutralist position on foreign policy and give whole-hearted support to the NATO alliance as the only hope for eventual German reunification.	Belgian King Baudouin I proclaims an independent Republic of Congo in Leopoldville ceremonies attended by Congo Pres. Joseph Kasavubu and Premier Patrice Lumumba.		A study prepared by the CIA, State and Defense Depts. reports that Communist Chinese industrial production is growing at an annual rate of 23% with relatively little Soviet assistance.
July 1		Cyprus and Great Britain announce agreement on final terms for Cypriot independence to be granted in mid-August. A total of 99 square miles of the island will be retained by Britain for military bases.	Ghana is proclaimed an independent republic within the British Commonwealth in ceremonies which also include the inauguration of Kwame Nkrumah as the republic's first president. . . . Republic of Somalia is formed by a merger of the former British Somaliland with the former Italian-administered U.N. trust territory of Somalia.	Cuban government completes takeover of all privately-owned oil processing facilities with the announcement that Esso and Shell properties will be transferred to the Cuban Petroleum Institute. Britain and the U.S. later deliver formal protests.	Japan rejects as "slanderous" continuing Soviet protests against the new U.S.-Japanese treaty.
July 2	In separate notes, Britain, France and the U.S. deny Khrushchev's charge that the West caused the breakdown of disarmament talks and call upon the USSR to return to the Geneva meeting. . . . U.S. Defense Dept. says that if a missing RB-47 reconnaissance plane has strayed over Soviet territory it was not deliberate.	Ex-Pres. Vincent Auriol, 75, announces his resignation from the French constitutional council in protest against de Gaulle's alleged effort to assume arbitrary and personal rule in France.	South African P.M. Verwoerd tells a political rally that Britain and other Western nations are sacrificing South Africa to gain favor with new black nations.		
July 3	Khrushchev tells newsmen that he thinks that new high-level East-West talks are unlikely until after the American elections.		Lebanon completes voting for a new 99-member parliament in what has proved the most peaceful election in its history.		Communist Chinese Premier Chou En-lai formally apologizes to Nepal for a June 29 Chinese attack on Nepalese border troops, explaining that they were thought to be Tibetan guerrillas.
July 4			A statement issued by the Algerian Provisional Government in Tunis attributes the collapse of preliminary cease-fire talks to a French "refusal to negotiate." . . . Israel announces the completion of its first nuclear reactor at the Nahal Sorek research center.		
	A	**B**	**C**	**D**	**E**
	Includes developments that affect more than one world region, international organizations and important meetings of major world leaders.	*Includes all domestic and regional developments in Europe, including the Soviet Union, Turkey, Cyprus and Malta.*	*Includes all domestic and regional developments in Africa and the Middle East, including Iraq and Iran and excluding Cyprus, Turkey and Afghanistan.*	*Includes all domestic and regional developments in Latin America, the Caribbean and Canada.*	*Includes all domestic and regional developments in Asia and Pacific nations, extending from Afghanistan through all the Pacific Islands, except Hawaii.*

U.S. Politics & Social Issues	U.S. Foreign Policy & Defense	U.S. Economy & Environment	Science, Technology & Nature	Culture, Leisure & Life Style	
	In a national TV address, Pres. Eisenhower reports the general success of the administration's Asian policy and of his recent Far East tour despite the cancellation of his visit to Japan.				June 27
In what is seen as a repudiation of the policies of Agriculture Secy. Ezra Taft Benson, N.D. rural voters give Democratic Rep. Quentin Burdick a victory in a special senatorial election over Republican Gov. John E. Davis.	Sen. J. William Fulbright charges in a Senate speech that U.S. "prestige and influence" has "reached a new low" as a result of the U-2 incident.			House passes a bill to outlaw payola and quiz-show rigging, providing for large fines and jail terms up to one year.	June 28
The nation's governors at their annual conference call upon Congress to enact an old-age health plan based on Social Security payments by a 30 to 13 vote.		A federal grand jury in Philadelphia returns indictments against 21 companies and 15 individuals for conspiracy to fix prices in the sale of heavy electrical equipment.		Middleweight champion Gene Fullmer successfully defends his title by scoring a TKO over Carmen Basilio in the 12th round of a championship bout in Salt Lake City.	June 29
New York Post joins the St. Louis Post-Dispatch in endorsing Adlai Stevenson for the Democratic presidential nomination.	Congress passes and sends to Pres. Eisenhower a $40 billion military appropriations bill, $661 million more than the administration had requested.	House defeats a Democratic bill to increase the minimum wage to $1.25 an hour and extend coverage to 3.5 million more workers. . . . Pres. Eisenhower signs a compromise bill extending wartime corporate and excise tax rates for another fiscal year.			June 30
Congress easily overrides Pres. Eisenhower's veto of a bill to provide a 7.5% pay increase to federal employees. . . . National Education Association adopts a compromise resolution on integration after rejecting a specific pledge to support the Supreme Ct. desegregation decision.			The first artificial synthesis of chlorophyll is announced independently by scientists in West Germany and at Harvard Univ. . . . Both houses of Congress pass a compromise bill providing the full $915 million requested by the administration for NASA.	CBS news discloses evidence which allegedly indicates that long-missing U.S. aviator Amelia Earhart was executed by Japanese soldiers on the island of Saipan in 1937. . . . Australian Neale Fraser wins the men's singles tennis championship at Wimbledon, England.	July 1
Ex-Pres. Harry Truman, in an apparent protest against the probable nomination of John Kennedy, tells a nationwide TV audience that he will not attend the Democratic National Convention.		FTC reports a record 157 antitrust complaints were filed in fiscal 1960.		John Thomas's high jump of 7 ft. 3¾ in. yesterday and Don Bragg's pole vault of 15 ft. 9½ in. today set new world marks at a U.S. Olympic qualifying meet in Palo Alto, Calif. . . . Maria Esther Bueno, 20, of Brazil, wins the women's singles tennis championship at Wimbledon.	July 2
Congress begins a six-week recess for the national political conventions.	House and Senate approve a conference committee bill granting Pres. Eisenhower the authority, as he has requested, to make discretionary cuts in Cuba's sugar import quota.		Dr. Alberto Carlo Blanc, 53, French-born paleontologist and leading authority on prehistoric man, dies in Rome.		July 3
		A record 442 Americans die in auto accidents over the July 4th weekend.		Mickey Wright wins the Ladies' Professional Golf Association Championship in French Lick, Ind.	July 4

F	G	H	I	J
Includes elections, federal-state relations, civil rights and liberties, crime, the judiciary, education, health care, poverty, urban affairs and population.	Includes formation and debate of U.S. foreign and defense policies, veterans' affairs and defense spending. (Relations with specific foreign countries are usually found under the region concerned.)	Includes business, labor, agriculture, taxation, transportation, consumer affairs, monetary and fiscal policy, natural resources, and pollution.	Includes worldwide scientific, medical and technological developments, natural phenomena, U.S. weather, natural disasters, and accidents.	Includes the arts, religion, scholarship, communications media, sports, entertainment, fashions, fads and social life.

	World Affairs	Europe	Africa & the Middle East	The Americas	Asia & the Pacific
July 5				Cuban Amb.-designate-to-U.S. José Miro Cardona resigns his post, citing irreconcilable "ideological differences" between himself and Cuban policy-makers.	
July 6		Aneurin Bevin, 62, deputy leader of the British Labor Party since 1955 and long-time spokesman for the party's left wing, dies of cancer in Chesham, England.	Tribal warfare, civil strife and violent army mutinies against remaining Belgian officers mar the Congo Republic's first week of independence. Scores are reported killed and hundreds wounded as the fighting spreads from Leopoldville to surrounding provinces. . . . French Pres. de Gaulle, on tour in Normandy, tells newsmen the movement toward peace in Algeria would continue despite the recent failure of preliminary cease-fire talks.		
July 7		USSR conducts rocket-firing tests in the southwest Pacific for the second time this year. . . . Czech CP conference unanimously approves a new national constitution to serve as a basis for the advent of "pure communism."			
July 8	Soviet Premier Khrushchev attacks U.S. "aggression", West German militarism, and Austrian neutralism during a 10-day state visit to Austria.		Belgians and other Europeans begin fleeing the Congo in the face of increasing attacks on whites by mutinous Congolese soldiers.		Former officials of the Rhee government, on trial in Seoul, confess to extensive rigging of the March 15 South Korean elections.
July 9		Eleven persons are reported killed in scattered Communist-led riots protesting Italian Premier Fernando Tambroni's reliance on neo-Fascist votes to keep his minority Christian Democratic cabinet in power. . . . Khrushchev announces that Soviet production goals for the first half of 1960 were surpassed by 4%.		Pres. Eisenhower asserts the U.S. will uphold its traditional policy of preventing foreign "interference" in Latin America. The statement comes in response to a Khrushchev warning that the USSR would support the Castro regime "with rockets" against any U.S. intervention in Cuba.	
July 10	Congo Republic appeals to the U.N. for military assistance in controlling the disorders plaguing the newly independent nation.		Eight hundred Belgian troops are flown to Katanga Province at the request of provincial Premier Moise Tshombe in an attempt to restore order to strife-torn Elizabethville. The intervention is lauded by Congo Pres. Joseph Kasavubu and condemned by Premier Patrice Lumumba.		
July 11	USSR discloses the July 1 downing of an American RB-47 reconnaissance jet engaged in what the Soviets describe as a spy mission over its territorial waters in the Barents Sea. Two of the six crewmen are reported rescued and awaiting trial as spies. . . . Cuban Foreign Min. Raul Roa asks the U.N. Security Council to consider alleged U.S. aggression against Cuba. . . . Norway, accused by the USSR of complicity in the RB-47 mission, publicly denies any connection with the incident.		In a statement condemning the "communist" tactics of the Lumumba government, Tshombe proclaims the "total independence" of Katanga Province from the Congo Republic. Tshombe pledges close ties between Katanga and Belgium.		

A	B	C	D	E
Includes developments that affect more than one world region, international organizations and important meetings of major world leaders.	Includes all domestic and regional developments in Europe, including the Soviet Union, Turkey, Cyprus and Malta.	Includes all domestic and regional developments in Africa and the Middle East, including Iraq and Iran and excluding Cyprus, Turkey and Afghanistan.	Includes all domestic and regional developments in Latin America, the Caribbean and Canada.	Includes all domestic and regional developments in Asia and Pacific nations, extending from Afghanistan through all the Pacific Islands, except Hawaii.

U.S. Politics & Social Issues	U.S. Foreign Policy & Defense	U.S. Economy & Environment	Science, Technology & Nature	Culture, Leisure & Life Style	
Promising to be a "working president," Senate Majority Leader Lyndon B. Johnson (Tex.) announces his candidacy for the Democratic presidential nomination.					July 5
	Pres. Eisenhower, employing recently passed congressional authorization, orders a 20% cut in Cuba's sugar export quota to the U.S. The move is in retaliation against Castro's continuing anti-U.S. policies. . . . In his first press conference since the summit collapse, Pres. Eisenhower says he remains ready and willing to conduct international discussions of East-West differences.			The Subterraneans, a film based on Jack Kerouac's novel about the beat generation, opens in N.Y., starring Leslie Caron and George Peppard.	July 6
		Dr. Hugh Bennett, 79, U.S. Soil Conservation Service chief (1933-1952), whose methods were copied worldwide, dies in Burlington, N. C.	Scientists at Hughes Aircraft Co. announce the first known amplification of light through a device called a "laser" (light amplification by stimulated emission of radiation). According to the developers, laser beams may eventually be used in astronomical telescopes, as a form of light radar, and as a germ killer.	Dr. Barbara Moore, a Russian-born British physician, completes a 3,387-mile walk across the U.S. from San Francisco to New York.	July 7
	Pentagon confirms that delays in construction set back the operational date of Atlas ICBM launching sites as much as five months.				July 8
Following five months of Negro demonstrations, a special mayor's committee in Charlotte, N.C. announces desegregation of the city's downtown lunch counters. Charlotte is the 11th Southern city to adopt a general desegregation policy this year. . . . UPI reports that Mississippi's State Sovereignty Commission voted to provide $20,000 in tax dollars to the segregationist Citizens Council for a radio-TV series.				Rafer Johnson, 24, scores 8,683 points to set a new world decathlon record at the National AAU decathlon championship in Eugene, Ore. . . . Australian golfer Ken Nagle wins the British Open at St. Andrews, Scotland, defeating Arnold Palmer by one stroke.	July 9
After being received with mixed cheers and boos, John Kennedy tells an NAACP-sponsored civil rights rally that he approved of recent Southern sit-in demonstrations.		Commerce Dept. reports U.S. consumer spending in 1959 reached a record $313.8 billion, a 6.9% increase over 1958.			July 10
Sen. Frank Church (Idaho) opens the Democratic National Convention in Los Angeles with a keynote assault on the "false prosperity" and declining U.S. prestige brought about by eight years of Republican leadership.	Pres. Eisenhower outlines to newsmen a proposal for a cooperative hemispheric effort to advance the social, economic and political welfare of Latin American peoples.		RCA announces the development of a thermionic energy converter capable of producing electricity directly from heat.	Harper Lee's To Kill A Mockingbird is published. . . . Bill Hartack wins his 2,500th race, riding Missus Beau to victory at Monmouth Park, N.J.	July 11

F	G	H	I	J
Includes elections, federal-state relations, civil rights and liberties, crime, the judiciary, education, health care, poverty, urban affairs and population.	Includes formation and debate of U.S. foreign and defense policies, veterans' affairs and defense spending. (Relations with specific foreign countries are usually found under the region concerned.)	Includes business, labor, agriculture, taxation, transportation, consumer affairs, monetary and fiscal policy, natural resources, and pollution.	Includes worldwide scientific, medical and technological developments, natural phenomena, U.S. weather, natural disasters, and accidents.	Includes the arts, religion, scholarship, communications media, sports, entertainment, fashions, fads and social life.

	World Affairs	Europe	Africa & the Middle East	The Americas	Asia & the Pacific
July 12	U.S. rejects the Soviet version of the RB-47 incident, insisting instead the plane was outside Soviet airspace on a legitimate electro-magnetic research flight as part of a program long known to the Soviet government. The statement condemns the attack on the craft as cynical and reckless and demands the immediate release of the two surviving crewmen.	Laborites in Great Britain, where the downed RB-47 was based, ask P.M. Macmillan to undertake a formal review of British base agreements with the U.S.	Despite opposition from Pres. Kasavubu and Premier Lumumba, Belgian troops continue to undertake military action against Congolese forces alleged to be endangering the safety of resident Europeans.	Referring to recent Soviet-American exchanges over Cuba, Premier Khrushchev tells a Kremlin news conference that "the Monroe Doctrine has outlived its time."	A large percentage of India's two million civil servants go on strike for higher wages despite government threats of prosecution.
July 13	Hammarskjold calls a special session of the U.N. Security Council at the request of the Congo government to consider UN action against Belgian troops deployed to protect whites from Congolese attacks. . . . Soviets ask the U.N. Security Council to convene to debate the RB-47 incident. . . . USSR delivers a memo to the U.S. protesting the frequent low-altitude "buzzing" of Soviet vessels in international waters by American planes.	National Executive Committee of Britain's Labor Party votes to abandon its recent campaign to soften the party's stand on the nationalization of industry.			Indonesian sources report 10,000 resident Chinese have left for Communist China under the 1959 Chinese-Indonesian repatriation agreement.
July 14	U.N. Security Council authorizes Secy. Gen. Hammarskjold to send U.N. troops to the Congo Republic to restore order and end the fighting between Congolese and intervening Belgian forces.	U.S. is reported to have agreed to British requests for advance notification of any further reconnaissance flights from British bases that the USSR might regard as provocative.	Israeli Justice Ministry discloses that Adolf Eichmann has chosen Robert Servatius, Cologne lawyer who defended executed Nazi leader Fritz Sauckel, as his defense attorney.		
July 15	Khrushchev announces the USSR intends to accede to a request from Premier Lumumba for military support if Belgian troops are not immediately withdrawn from the Congo.		In a speech to the Congolese parliament, Premier Lumumba demands an immediate end to Belgian intervention which he says is aimed at overthrowing the Congo's independence. . . . Independence has, as of today, been granted to 11 of the 12 African member-states of the French Community in agreements signed or ratified in Paris since June 10.	Clement Barbot, alleged chief of the Haitian secret police, is arrested for plotting to overthrow Pres. Francois Duvalier.	KISHI, Nobusuke Nobusuke Kishi resigns as Japanese premier after his government failed to control leftist demonstrations against Pres. Eisenhower's cancelled trip to Japan and the new U.S.-Japan security treaty. . . . Ho Chi Minh and Pham Van Dong are unanimously reelected as president and premier of North Vietnam by the National Assembly.
July 16		Field Marshal Albert Kesselring, commander of German forces in Italy during W.W. II, dies at age 74.			Reports reaching New Delhi indicate that Chinese troops have cleared the Shekar region of Tibetan resistance after four weeks of fighting. . . . A strike by Indian civil servants ends.
July 17	Austria formally requests U.N. General Assembly action on the "problem of the Austrian minority in Italy."		Tshombe calls upon all Congolese provinces to join with Katanga in an anti-Lumumba, anti-Communist federation. . . . The inauguration of patrols by the recently arrived U.N. security force is said to have reduced tensions in the strife-torn Congo Republic.		
July 18			Premier Lumumba's request for Soviet troop intervention in the Congo is repudiated by the Congolese Senate. . . . U.N. Secy. Gen. Hammarskjold discloses that Belgian troops have agreed to a U.N. order to limit further military action in the Congo.	OAS votes to consider "threats" to continental solidarity and regional defense posed by the current dispute between Cuba and the U.S. . . . Guatemalan officials report that government troops have repulsed a rebel attack on a military base in the northern province of Alta Verapaz.	Hayato Ikeda, 60, who succeeded Kishi as leader of the Liberal Democratic Party on July 14, is approved by the Diet as the new Japanese premier.
July 19	U.N. Security Council votes to refer a Cuban complaint against alleged U.S. "economic aggression" to the OAS. The vote follows a bitter debate in which U.S. Amb. Henry Cabot Lodge Jr. and Soviet Amb. Arkady Sobolev exchanged warnings against intervening in Cuban affairs.			Guatemalan Pres. Miguel Ydigoras Fuentes decrees a 30-day "state of emergency" following a rebel invasion in the northern provinces and a terrorist bombing of a movie theatre in Guatemala City.	
	A	**B**	**C**	**D**	**E**
	Includes developments that affect more than one world region, international organizations and important meetings of major world leaders.	Includes all domestic and regional developments in Europe, including the Soviet Union, Turkey, Cyprus and Malta.	Includes all domestic and regional developments in Africa and the Middle East, including Iraq and Iran and excluding Cyprus, Turkey and Afghanistan.	Includes all domestic and regional developments in Latin America, the Caribbean and Canada.	Includes all domestic and regional developments in Asia and Pacific nations, extending from Afghanistan through all the Pacific Islands, except Hawaii.

U.S. Politics & Social Issues	U.S. Foreign Policy & Defense	U.S. Economy & Environment	Science, Technology & Nature	Culture, Leisure & Life Style	
Democratic convention adopts the strongest civil rights plank in the party's history, pledging to support Negro voting rights, to accelerate school desegregation and to prevent race discrimination in employment. . . . Micahel Fekecs, 24, a former Hungarian freedom fighter, is captured in Union, N.J. after a six-hour gun battle with police. He was sought for six murders, including those of two policemen.	State Dept. issues a statement declaring that no U.S. troops will be sent to the Congo, not even as part of a possible U.N. contingent.	Labor Dept. reports that unemployment climbed to 5.5% in June as a record number of young people entered the job market.			July 12
Despite strong Southern backing for Lyndon Johnson and a last minute emotional demonstration on behalf of Adlai Stevenson, John F. Kennedy wins the Democratic presidential nomination on the convention's first ballot by a vote of 806 to 409 for Johnson, his nearest rival. Kennedy needed 761 votes to win.	German-born U.S. rocket expert Wernher von Braun asserts the U.S. leads the Soviets in the ICBM missile race by virtue of the technical superiority of the American weapons.			National League wins both ends of major league baseball's two-game all-star series: 5-3 in Kansas City July 11 and 6-0 in New York today.	July 13
Lyndon B. Johnson, Kennedy's choice as his running mate, wins the Democratic vice presidential nomination by acclamation of the national convention.	U.S. Agriculture and State Depts., in a move to compensate for reduced sugar imports from Cuba, authorize six other nations to increase their 1960 sugar export quotas.		Duc Maurice de Broglie, 85, French physicist noted for his pioneering research into radioactivity, dies in Paris.		July 14
In accepting his party's nomination, Democratic candidate Kennedy calls for "more sacrifice" to conquer the "New Frontier" and attacks the Republicans as "the party of the past."		Directors of the Great Northern and Northern Pacific Railways vote to merge, forming the largest rail system in the U.S.	Sir Ernest Rock Carling, British pioneer in the use of radium treatments for cancer, dies at 83 in London.	Hazel Wheeler of Three Rivers, Mich. files a $9 million libel suit charging that Robert Traver's novel *Anatomy of a Murder* is identifiably based on events in her life. . . . Lawrence Tibbett, 63, operatic baritone, dies in N.Y. after brain surgery.	July 15
Sen. Henry M. Jackson (Wash.), 48, is elected chairman of the Democratic National Committee, succeeding Paul M. Butler.				American novelist John P. Marquand, 66, originator of the *Mr. Moto* detective series and author of the Pulitzer Prize-winning *The Late George Apley*, dies in Kent's Island, Mass.	July 16
			Dr. Aaron Gorelik, Egyptian-born heart surgeon noted for the development of an operation to increase the heart's blood supply, dies of a stroke at age 58 in New York.		July 17
Pres. Eisenhower announces that Democratic candidates Kennedy and Johnson will be briefed on current secret national security matters.	Air Force announces that the U.S. bomber-oriented air defense system will be revised to provide a greater protection against enemy missile attacks.		August Thyssen Co. announces the establishment in Cologne of a multi-million-mark Fritz Thyssen Foundation for the advancement of science.	National League club owners tentatively approve expansion of the league to 10 teams.	July 18
U.S. Court of Appeals in Philadelphia orders the total integration of Delaware public schools by the fall of 1961.	Gen. Charles D. Palmer, deputy commander of the U.S. European Command, dedicates Europe's largest U.S. military cemetery near St. Avold, France. The land, where 10,489 W.W. II soldiers are buried, was donated by the French government.	Commerce Dept. reports corporate cash dividends during the first half of 1960 rose 6.5% over the same period in 1959.		FTC is reported to have charged 12 more record distributors with giving "payola" to disc jockeys since July 5.	July 19

F	G	H	I	J
Includes elections, federal-state relations, civil rights and liberties, crime, the judiciary, education, health care, poverty, urban affairs and population.	*Includes formation and debate of U.S. foreign and defense policies, veterans' affairs and defense spending. (Relations with specific foreign countries are usually found under the region concerned.)*	*Includes business, labor, agriculture, taxation, transportation, consumer affairs, monetary and fiscal policy, natural resources, and pollution.*	*Includes worldwide scientific, medical and technological developments, natural phenomena, U.S. weather, natural disasters, and accidents.*	*Includes the arts, religion, scholarship, communications media, sports, entertainment, fashions, fads and social life.*

	World Affairs	Europe	Africa & the Middle East	The Americas	Asia & the Pacific
July 20	In a Security Council debate, Belgian Foreign Min. Pierre Wigny defends his nation's intervention in the Congo and promises withdrawal as soon as the U.N. forces restore order.		A crowd of 20,000 Africans is dispersed by Rhodesian police near Salisbury when it attempts to protest the arrests of 360 Africans during demonstrations at Bulawayo. . . . Lebanese Pres. Fouad Chebab names ex-Premier Saeb Salem to succeed the caretaker Premier Ahmed Dauouk.		
July 21			First National Assembly of the UAR, made up of 400 Egyptian and 200 Syrian delegates, convenes in Cairo.		Mrs. Sirimavo Bandaranaike succeeds Dudley S. Senanayake as Ceylon's prime minister, becoming the first woman to hold the prime ministry of a modern state.
July 22	U.N. Security Council calls upon Belgium to withdraw its forces from the Congo and urges all other nations to refrain from intervention there. The appeal is expected to temper Soviet threats to intervene. . . . U.S. calls for the reconvening of the 82-nation U.N. disarmament commission to continue discussion of arms reduction in light of the breakdown of the 10-nation talks in Geneva.			Guatemalan demonstrators opposed to the recently imposed state of national emergency clash violently with local police units.	
July 23				Cuban economic officials report they have used their recently acquired Soviet industrial credits to buy 32 factories from Eastern European countries. . . . Communist China signs a five-year agreement to buy a half million tons of Cuban sugar annually at world market prices.	
July 24		Marshal Andrei A. Grechko, Soviet deputy defense minister, is named to succeed Marshal Ivan S. Konev as supreme commander of Warsaw Pact forces.	Premier Lumumba arrives in New York to seek greater U.N. support for Belgian troop withdrawal and possible U.S. economic aid for the strife-torn Congo.		
July 25	Replying to Soviet charges of espionage, U.S. Amb.-to-U.N. Henry Cabot Lodge asserts the attack on the RB-47 occurred far outside Soviet territorial waters.		Tshombe publicly warns the entry of U.N. troops into Katanga will be forcibly resisted.		
July 26	USSR vetoes a U.S.-sponsored U.N. Security Council resolution calling for an impartial investigation into the RB-47 incident. The Council had previously rejected a Soviet-proposed condemnation of U.S. spy flights.	Ex-Premier Amintore Fanfani forms Italy's 22d post-war cabinet, replacing fellow Christian Democrat Fernando Tambroni, whose cabinet resigned rather than continuing to depend on neo-Fascist parliamentary support.	Twelve Africans are reported killed in Southern Rhodesia during riots protesting the government's arrest of key African nationalist leaders.		
July 27	U.S., British, and Soviet delegates to the Geneva test-ban talks agree in principle to bar atmospheric tests as well as all underground detonations registering over 4.75 on the Richter Scale.	British P.M. Macmillan names Sir Alexander Douglas-Home as new foreign secretary, replacing Selwyn Lloyd. M.P. Edward Heath will speak in the Commons for Home, who sits in the House of Lords.	Hammarskjold confers with the Belgian cabinet and demands a speedy withdrawal of all Belgian troops from the Congo.		Mrs. Bandaranaike, Ceylon's new prime minister, denies reports that she intends to move her country in a "Marxist" direction.
July 28		A Laborite motion to censure British P.M. Macmillan for naming Sir Alexander Douglas-Home as foreign secretary fails by a vote of 332-220.	Arab League declares a boycott against Iran for its continuing de facto recognition of Israel.	Andres Cova Salas, 43, Cuban-born leader of Fidel Castro's 26th of July Movement in Venezuela, is killed by police after he refused them entry into his Caracas home.	

A	B	C	D	E
Includes developments that affect more than one world region, international organizations and important meetings of major world leaders.	Includes all domestic and regional developments in Europe, including the Soviet Union, Turkey, Cyprus and Malta.	Includes all domestic and regional developments in Africa and the Middle East, including Iraq and Iran and excluding Cyprus, Turkey and Afghanistan.	Includes all domestic and regional developments in Latin America, the Caribbean and Canada.	Includes all domestic and regional developments in Asia and Pacific nations, extending from Afghanistan through all the Pacific Islands, except Hawaii.

U.S. Politics & Social Issues	U.S. Foreign Policy & Defense	U.S. Economy & Environment	Science, Technology & Nature	Culture, Leisure & Life Style	
	Navy successfully launches two Polaris missiles from a nuclear-powered submarine on its first attempts from a submerged vessel.	Pres. Eisenhower announces the achievement of a $1-billion budget surplus during fiscal 1960. The surplus reflects a $1.6 billion cut in the cost of farm price supports.			July 20
Salvador (Cape Man) Agron, 16, and Luis Antonio (Umbrella Man) Hernandez, 18, are convicted in N.Y. of the murders of two 16-year-old youths in a playground in 1959.				Francis Chichester, 59, defeats four rivals to win the trans-Atlantic solo race in his sloop *Gypsy Moth III* in the record time of 40 days.	July 21
		Bureau of Labor Statistics reports the U.S. cost of living reached a record high in June for the fourth consecutive month.		Racer Jack Brabham of Australia, driving a Cooper-Climax, wins the British Grand Prix in Silverstone, England.	July 22
Rockefeller and Nixon meet secretly in N.Y. and agree on the essential elements in the GOP election platform.				Betsy Rawls wins the U.S. Women's Open golf tournament for the 4th time.	July 23
			The New York Times reports a million-fold light amplifier capable of detecting a single photon has been developed by scientists at the Imperial College in London.	Jay Hebert wins the PGA in Akron, Ohio.	July 24
Rep. Walter Judd (Minn.) opens the Republican National Convention in Chicago with a keynote speech praising the administration's achievement of "prosperity without war."		Treasury announces plans for reducing the $289-billion federal debt by $600 million with surplus funds from the 1960 budget.			July 25
Nelson Rockefeller publicly eliminates himself from consideration as either a GOP presidential or vice presidential candidate. . . . Segregationist Gov. Orval E. Faubus outpolls four opponents in Ark.'s Democratic gubernatorial primary. . . . Greenville, S.C. imposes curfew following a week of sit-in related violence.	In a convention speech defending his administration, Pres. Eisenhower angrily denies Democratic charges of a weakened U.S. military capacity.				July 26
By a near unanimous vote, Republican convention delegates name V. P. Richard Nixon as the party's presidential nominee. A party platform, including a pledge to continue school desegregation, was adopted earlier over some Southern opposition.	GOP convention approves a platform plank endorsing Eisenhower's foreign policy record and urging continued efforts toward a negotiated settlement of outstanding East-West differences.	Federal Reserve Board cuts the legal margin required for stock purchases from 90% to 70%. . . . A passenger helicopter crashes in a Chicago suburb, killing all 13 persons aboard, in the first U.S. crash of a scheduled commercial helicopter.			July 27
Republican convention unanimously acclaims Amb.-to-U.N. Henry Cabot Lodge as the GOP vice presidential nominee. . . . Calling the Democratic policies "disastrous", GOP candidate Nixon accepts his nomination with a promise to "build" on the Eisenhower achievements and to bring "the greatest progress in civil rights since...Lincoln."			NASA announces that the advanced manned space project which will succeed the current Mercury program will be named Project Apollo and will be aimed at putting a man on the moon by 1970.		July 28

F	G	H	I	J
Includes elections, federal-state relations, civil rights and liberties, crime, the judiciary, education, health care, poverty, urban affairs and population.	Includes formation and debate of U.S. foreign and defense policies, veterans' affairs and defense spending. (Relations with specific foreign countries are usually found under the region concerned.)	Includes business, labor, agriculture, taxation, transportation, consumer affairs, monetary and fiscal policy, natural resources, and pollution.	Includes worldwide scientific, medical and technological developments, natural phenomena, U.S. weather, natural disasters, and accidents.	Includes the arts, religion, scholarship, communications media, sports, entertainment, fashions, fads and social life.

	World Affairs	Europe	Africa & the Middle East	The Americas	Asia & the Pacific
July 29	Padillo Nervo, president of the U.N. Disarmament Commission, begins polling the 82 member-nations to see if a majority will agree to a U.S. request for reconvening the Commission.	The USSR, in notes to Britain, France and the U.S., formally protests West German plans to establish a radio network headquarters in West Berlin.			Democratic Party wins majorities in both houses of South Korea's new bicameral legislature; members of ex-Pres. Rhee's Liberal Party, ousted after the fraudulent March elections, win only a handful of seats.
July 30		Abderrahmane Laklifi, a Moslem terrorist convicted of a 1958 attack on a Lyons, France police station, is executed in Lyons despite last minute clemency appeals from Soviet Premier Khrushchev and Moroccan King Mohammed V.			Chairman Liu Ming-yi of the All China Federation of Trade, a leading Communist Chinese trade official, is granted admission into Japan to attend the annual congress of the leftist Sohyo trade union federation.
July 31	Congo leader Lumumba tells newsmen that he intends to ask the U.N. Security Council to designate special observers to supervise the withdrawal of Belgian troops from the Congo.		Algerian rebel terrorists kill 13 European bathers at Caroubier Beach near Chenoua.		Typhoon Shirley strikes Taiwan killing 104 and leaving 55,000 homeless.
Aug. 1	Opposing the U.S. suggestion for a reconvening of the disarmament commission, the USSR proposes that Khrushchev, Eisenhower and other heads of state meet in the 1960 U.N. General Assembly session for a public discussion of world disarmament. Amb. Lodge labels the Soviet proposal as "a frivolous maneuver."		In a letter to the U.N. Security Council, Congolese Premier Lumumba charges Belgium with ignoring U.N. calls for troop withdrawals and illegally supporting the secession of Katanga Province.		Premier Chou En-lai, speaking at a reception in Peking, denies Red China has abandoned "peaceful co-existence" and calls for a "peace pact" with the U.S. in Asia. State Dept. spokesman Lincoln White dismisses the statement as a "propaganda gesture." . . . Malaya ends its 12-year-old emergency regulations against Communist guerrillas. Only some 600 guerrillas are believed still active. . . . Pakistan officially transfers its capital from Karachi to Rawalpindi.
Aug. 2			U.N. Secy. Gen. Hammarskjold reports that U.N. contingents have replaced Belgian forces in all Congolese provinces except secessionist Katanga.	Inter-American Peace Committee of OAS hears Cuban charges of U.S. "economic aggression" and counter-revolutionary activity against the Castro regime. . . . A trade agreement between Cuba and East Germany is announced in East Berlin.	
Aug. 3		USSR Geology Ministry announces the discovery of high grade iron ore deposits in the Kursk region totaling an estimated 30 billion tons.	Israel and Argentina issue joint statements declaring the Eichmann capture "incident" closed.	Joaquin Balaguer is sworn in as titular president of the Dominican Republic, but real power is expected to remain in the hands of Generalissimo Rafael Trujillo.	
Aug. 4			Representatives of Britain and both white and African factions in Nyasaland agree on a new constitution that will provide for eventual self-government by the African majority.		An agreement on formation of a Nagaland state within India is announced in New Delhi.
Aug. 5	In a letter to British P.M. Macmillan, Soviet Premier Khrushchev expresses a willingness to attend a new East-West summit following the U.S. presidential elections.		Hammarskjold announces he will seek specific U.N. authorization to send U.N. troops into Katanga. The announcement comes a few hours after Katanga officials refused to allow an advance group of U.N. civilians to land at Elizabethville.	Paraguayan military authorities report a 200-man guerrilla force has been wiped out after a month of fighting along Paraguay's border with Argentina.	
	A	**B**	**C**	**D**	**E**
	Includes developments that affect more than one world region, international organizations and important meetings of major world leaders.	Includes all domestic and regional developments in Europe, including the Soviet Union, Turkey, Cyprus and Malta.	Includes all domestic and regional developments in Africa and the Middle East, including Iraq and Iran and excluding Cyprus, Turkey and Afghanistan.	Includes all domestic and regional developments in Latin America, the Caribbean and Canada.	Includes all domestic and regional developments in Asia and Pacific nations, extending from Afghanistan through all the Pacific Islands, except Hawaii.

U.S. Politics & Social Issues	U.S. Foreign Policy & Defense	U.S. Economy & Environment	Science, Technology & Nature	Culture, Leisure & Life Style	
Sen. Thruston B. Morton (Ky.) is unanimously reelected as GOP National Committee chairman. . . . A state court in New Orleans upholds a Louisiana law barring schools from obeying federal desegregation orders without prior permission from the state legislature. . . . Robert P. Bass, 86, former New Hampshire governor and chairman of the Brookings Institute, dies.			Dr. André Danjon, the director of the Paris Observatory, reports that the day has been lengthened $1/10$ of a second because of three solar eruptions in July 1959 which slowed the earth's rotation.	FCC rejects proposals for radio and TV censorship on the grounds that media expression is protected by the First Amendment. . . . Dr. Clyde Kluckhohn, 55, Harvard professor and pioneer in modern cultural anthropology, dies in Santa Fe, N.M.	July 29
U.S. Office of Education awards Georgetown Univ. an NDEA grant to develop methods for teaching African languages to English-speaking students.		Indiana & Michigan Electric Co. begins operation of the world's largest single generating unit (475,000 kw.) near Terre Haute, Ind.			July 30
Richard Nixon joins John Kennedy in accepting a network offer of free prime time for a series of face-to-face TV debates on the campaign issues. . . . Black Muslim leader Elijah Mohammed, at a New York rally of 4,000 followers, calls for the creation of a separate American Negro state in the U.S. or Africa. . . . Ford Foundation announces the awarding of $2.3 million to 14 U.S. universities to improve the preparation of college teachers by strengthening the quality of master's degree programs.			A 30 ft. shift in the location of the North Pole over the past 60 years is reported by Dr. William Markowitz at an international geophysics conference in Helsinki, Finland.	Big 10 Conference places the Indiana University football program on one-year probation for alleged recruiting violations.	July 31
In a prepared statement Democratic presidential candidate Kennedy attacks V.P. Nixon's views on farm policy as unprincipled, inconsistent and "disastrous."		American Meat Institute reports that the net income of the U.S. meat packing industry rose from $82 million in 1958 to $135 million in 1959, the highest mark since 1947.			Aug. 1
		Commerce Dept. reports productivity in the U.S. steel industry increased 12% in 1959.	A federal jury in Miami supports a plaintiff's contention that 30 years of smoking Lucky Strike cigarettes caused the lung cancer death of Edwin Green, but refuses to award damages on the grounds that the dangers of cigarettes were not sufficiently known at the time Green contracted cancer.	American and National League officials vote to expand each league from 8 to 10 teams by 1962. . . . Bob Gutowski, 25, world pole-vault record holder (15 ft. $8^1/4$ in.), dies in an auto near Las Pulgas, Calif.	Aug. 2
V.P. Nixon opens his presidential campaign with a speaking tour in Hawaii during which he praises its model of racial harmony.		Federal mediators help work out a three-year agreement that ends a month-old strike by the Railroad Trainmen against the Long Island Rail Road.		*The Last Temptation of Christ* by Nikos Kazantzakis is published in translation in N.Y.	Aug. 3
	Washington sources report Polaris missile submarines, scheduled to operate in the western Pacific by 1962, will be based in Guam instead of Japan to avoid more protests over U.S. military presence in Japan.		Defense Dept. and NASA agree to a $1 million settlement for infringing on patented rocket inventions of the late Dr. Robert Goddard, missile pioneer who died in 1945. . . . NASA test pilot Joseph Walker sets a world air speed record of 2,196 mph. in the experimental X-15 rocket plane.	Cincinnati second baseman Billy Martin fractures Chicago Cub pitcher Jim Brewer's jaw during a mid-game brawl.	Aug. 4
	Defense Dept. confirms that two National Security Agency employees, Bernon F. Mitchell and William H. Martin, disappeared June 24 and apparently defected to the USSR.	Agriculture Dept. reports 66% of the $58.7 billion dollars spent for U.S. food products in 1959 went to marketing costs rather than to the farmer; this represents the highest marketing percentage since 1933.		Detroit manager Jimmy Dykes is traded to Cleveland for manager Joe Gordon in what is thought to be the first manager trade in major league baseball history.	Aug. 5

F	G	H	I	J
Includes elections, federal-state relations, civil rights and liberties, crime, the judiciary, education, health care, poverty, urban affairs and population.	*Includes formation and debate of U.S. foreign and defense policies, veterans' affairs and defense spending. (Relations with specific foreign countries are usually found under the region concerned.)*	*Includes business, labor, agriculture, taxation, transportation, consumer affairs, monetary and fiscal policy, natural resources, and pollution.*	*Includes worldwide scientific, medical and technological developments, natural phenomena, U.S. weather, natural disasters, and accidents.*	*Includes the arts, religion, scholarship, communications media, sports, entertainment, fashions, fads and social life.*

	World Affairs	Europe	Africa & the Middle East	The Americas	Asia & the Pacific
Aug. 6		A 26-member Greek Cypriote Communal Chamber and a 30-member Turkish Cypriote Communal Chamber are chosen in separate elections by the two ethnic communities.		Victor Paz Estenssoro is sworn in as president of Bolivia.	In a message read during ceremonies commemorating the 15th anniversary of the bombing of Hiroshima, Japanese Premier Hayato Ikeda appeals to the world to renounce the production and use of nuclear weapons.
Aug. 7		Figures released by Soviet Deputy Premier Aleksei Kosygin estimate total USSR economic wealth—the value of all resources and equipment—at $240 billion.	The Congo's Abako Party, headed by Pres. Joseph Kasavubu, calls for the replacement of the centralized Lumumba regime with a confederation of autonomous provincial states.	In a memo to the OAS Peace Committee, the U.S. State Dept. asserts that Cuba's "open league with the Soviet Union" poses the "gravest danger" to the hemisphere.	An investigating committee of the International Commission of Jurists publishes a report in Geneva documenting charges that Communist China committed genocide in its occupation of Tibet.
Aug. 8	U.S. formally rejects Soviet protests over its plans to equip NATO nations, including West Germany, with Polaris missiles, claiming the U.S. has every right to provide its allies with whatever is "necessary to ensure their security."	Tass reports the Soviet government plans to build over 100,000 retail stores throughout the USSR during 1961.		OAS council, meeting in Washington, votes to conduct an emergency foreign ministers' meeting in Costa Rica Aug. 16 to discuss Caribbean tensions and the threat of foreign subversion. . . . U.S. Amb.-to-Cuba Philip Bonsal delivers a note to the Castro government charging it with harassing and detaining U.S. newsmen.	
Aug. 9	U.N. member-nations, over Soviet opposition, vote to reconvene the U.N. Disarmament Commission Aug. 16.		Security Council orders U.N. forces into secessionist Katanga Province to replace Belgian troops maintained there in defiance of a U.N. demand for their removal. . . . Returning from his mission to N.Y., Lumumba calls up Congolese troops and threatens an all-out invasion of Katanga.	David Alfaro Siqueiros, mural painter and secretary general of the Mexican CP, is arrested for allegedly organizing a student riot in Mexico City today.	Rebellious Laotian army units seize power in Vientiane and force the resignation of Premier Tiao Samsonith in an effort to end the warfare between government forces and the pro-Communist Pathet Lao guerrillas.
Aug. 10			Katanga Premier Tshombe wires Hammarskjold that U.N. forces will be accepted in Katanga on the condition that no effort be made to restore the province to the control of the central Congo government of Lumumba.		
Aug. 11		Pres. de Gaulle, Chancellor Adenauer and P.M. Macmillan conclude a series of meetings aimed at finding mechanisms to give political direction to NATO and to avoid destructive competition between the Common Market and the Outer Seven. . . . British Trawlers Federation orders British fishermen to remain outside Iceland's 12-mile limit despite the expiration of a three-month truce in the British-Icelandic fishing "war".		At a Havana labor rally Premier Castro accuses the Roman Catholic Church in Cuba of "systematic provocations" against the government.	
Aug. 12			U.N. Secy. Gen. Hammarskjold personally leads a 240-man advance guard of the U.N. Force into the Congo's Katanga Province to implement the Security Council order for the withdrawal of Belgian troops.		Posun Yun, 62, a leader of the "Old Guard" Democrats, is elected to a five-year term as South Korean president by a joint session of the Legislature. He succeeds Rhee and interim president Huh Chung.

A	B	C	D	E
Includes developments that affect more than one world region, international organizations and important meetings of major world leaders.	*Includes all domestic and regional developments in Europe, including the Soviet Union, Turkey, Cyprus and Malta.*	*Includes all domestic and regional developments in Africa and the Middle East, including Iraq and Iran and excluding Cyprus, Turkey and Afghanistan.*	*Includes all domestic and regional developments in Latin America, the Caribbean and Canada.*	*Includes all domestic and regional developments in Asia and Pacific nations, extending from Afghanistan through all the Pacific Islands, except Hawaii.*

U.S. Politics & Social Issues	U.S. Foreign Policy & Defense	U.S. Economy & Environment	Science, Technology & Nature	Culture, Leisure & Life Style	
				Bangu of Brazil defeats Kilmarnock of Scotland 2-0 in New York to win the American Challenge Cup in the International Soccer League's first title playoff. . . . Patrice Jacob's Hail to Reason, Bob Ussery up, wins the $136,000 Sapling at Monmouth Park.	Aug. 6
Sen. Hugh Scott (R, Pa.) attacks Kennedy for seeking to "buy" votes through the Kennedy Foundation by paying the air fare of African students to the U.S. after the State Dept., according to Kennedy, refused to do so.		Commerce Dept. reports the U.S. balance of payments deficit declined 25% in the first half of 1960 compared to the same period in 1959.		Luis Angel Firpo, 65, the Argentine boxer defeated by Jack Dempsey in 1923 for the heavyweight title, dies in Buenos Aires.	Aug. 7
Eisenhower sends a special message to the reconvening Congress requesting quick action on foreign aid, civil rights and other priority bills sponsored by the administration.					Aug. 8
A Negro family of six swims undisturbed at previously all-white public beach in Miami Beach, Fla. . . . Alaskans vote against moving the state capital from Juneau in a statewide referendum. . . . Senate tables Eisenhower's civil rights bill the same day it is introduced after Democrats contend there is insufficient time to debate the bill before the election adjournment.	U.S. Secy. of State Herter, criticizing the lack of progress in the Geneva test-ban talks, warns that the U.S. might be forced to resume underground testing. . . . A proposed reorganization of the Army to achieve "100% vehicular mobility, ground or air," is disclosed in Washington at the annual meeting of the Association of the U.S. Army.	White House releases a Budget Bureau report which warns the enactment of Democratic-sponsored spending bills now before Congress would wipe out the $4-billion surplus estimated in Pres. Eisenhower's 1961 budget.			Aug. 9
Pres. Eisenhower denies to newsmen rumors that he and Nixon disagree over defense plans and spending. . . . Officials of national variety store chains inform the Justice Dept. that their lunch counters have been desegregated in at least 69 Southern cities.	U.S. Senate ratifies an international accord establishing Antarctica as a peaceful scientific preserve.		Dr. Oswald Veblen, 80, internationally-noted geometrician, dies in Brooklin, Me.	Wilt Chamberlain, who resigned from the NBA in March, rejoins the Philadelphia Warriors under a three-year contract, which will make him the highest paid professional athlete. . . . Frank Lloyd, 73, Scottish-born film director and winner of 1935 Academy Award for *Mutiny on the Bounty* dies in Santa Monica, Calif.	Aug. 10
Overturning a state court decision, Federal Judge Frank M. Johnson rules that Montgomery Co., Ala. voting registrars must surrender voting records to the scrutiny of the Justice Dept.		A United Air Lines-Capital Airlines merger agreement is filed with the CAB.	A U.S. helicopter retrieves an instrument capsule from the Discoverer XIII satellite after it landed in the Pacific Ocean, marking the first known recovery of a payload from space.		Aug. 11
Tuscarora Indians agree to accept $850,000 from the N.Y. State Power Authority for the use of land near Niagara Falls for a reservoir. . . . The coffin of George Nash, Winnebago Indian and W.W.I veteran, is removed from a grave beside that of his wife in a Troy, Mich. cemetery because of the cemetery's "Caucasian only" restriction. The family declines an offer of burial in the Arlington National Cemetery.		Federal Reserve Board cuts the discount rate from 3.5% to 3%.	Echo I, a 100-ft. balloon designed to aid worldwide communications by reflecting radio and TV waves, is successfully launched into earth orbit from Cape Canaveral.	Jack Nicklaus and Deane Beman give the U.S. a team victory in the Americas Cup amateur golf championship for the fifth straight year.	Aug. 12

F	G	H	I	J
Includes elections, federal-state relations, civil rights and liberties, crime, the judiciary, education, health care, poverty, urban affairs and population.	*Includes formation and debate of U.S. foreign and defense policies, veterans' affairs and defense spending. (Relations with specific foreign countries are usually found under the region concerned.)*	*Includes business, labor, agriculture, taxation, transportation, consumer affairs, monetary and fiscal policy, natural resources, and pollution.*	*Includes worldwide scientific, medical and technological developments, natural phenomena, U.S. weather, natural disasters, and accidents.*	*Includes the arts, religion, scholarship, communications media, sports, entertainment, fashions, fads and social life.*

	World Affairs	Europe	Africa & the Middle East	The Americas	Asia & the Pacific
Aug. 13	Soviet newspaper *Pravda* charges U.N. Secy. Gen. Hammarskjold with playing a "disgraceful role" by refusing to help the Congo government restore order in Katanga Province. . . . International Law Association, meeting in Hamburg, West Germany, resolves that no nation has the right to make sovereignty claims in space.			Cuba again rejects U.S. protests over the seizure of American-owned property by the Castro government.	
Aug. 14	Yugoslav Communist Party newspaper *Borba* reports that many Soviet technicians and advisers working in Communist China are being withdrawn.		Belgian command announces the formal end of the Belgian military presence in Katanga.		North Korean Premier Kim Il Sung proposes a temporary federation between North and South Korea as a first step to peaceful reunification.
Aug. 15	French Pres. de Gaulle appeals to Soviet Premier Khrushchev for a resumption of the 10-nation disarmament talks rather than transferring the discussions to the General Assembly.		Secy. Gen. Hammarskjold calls for an emergency Security Council meeting to discuss threats by Congo Premier Lumumba to invade Katanga and to expel white U.N. troops unless the U.N. agrees to help suppress Katanga's secession.		Laotian Prince Souvanna Phouma announces the formation of a neutralist cabinet pledged to seeking peace between the government and Pathet Lao rebels.
Aug. 16	Reconvened U.N. Disarmament Commission hears a U.S. proposal for a rapid and substantial reductions in U.S. and Soviet nuclear weapons arsenals. Soviet Deputy For. Min. Vasily Kuznetsov rejects the U.S. plan as impractical.	East and West Germany sign a trade agreement in Berlin which contains assurances of continued freedom of traffic between West Berlin and West Germany. It is the first long-term agreement between the two German governments. . . . Former British crown colony of Cyprus is formally proclaimed an independent republic in ceremonies at Nicosia presided over by Pres.-elect Archbishop Makarios.	Lumumba renews demands that white U.N. troops be replaced by Asian-African observers as a condition for continued U.N. operations in the Congo.	A staff report presented at the opening session of the OAS Foreign Ministers' Conference in San Jose, Costa Rica charges that Caribbean tensions have been heightened by USSR's desire to intervene in inter-American affairs. . . . Troops led by Castro reportedly crush an anti-government uprising of naval officers at a base near Casa Blanca.	
Aug. 17	U-2 pilot Francis Gary Powers pleads guilty to espionage at the opening session of his public trial in Moscow.			Haitian National Assembly grants Pres. Francois Duvalier power to rule by decree for six months to cope with the country's current economic crisis.	Pres. Sukarno breaks diplomatic relations with the Netherlands on the 15th anniversary of Indonesian independence.
Aug. 18	The 82-nation U.N. Disarmament Commission urges the earliest possible resumption of big-power negotiations on disarmament.			U.S. Secy. of State Herter proposes an OAS committee be formed to supervise free elections in the Dominican Republic during a speech to the OAS Foreign Ministers' Conference in San Jose, Costa Rica.	
Aug. 19	Soviet Supreme Court sentences U-2 pilot Francis Gary Powers to 10 years "deprivation of freedom" following a two-day trial marked by prosecution attacks on U.S. espionage activities. Pres. Eisenhower expresses regret at the severity of the sentence.	West German Bundeswehr issues a public memorandum declaring that an adequate defense for West Germany requires universal conscription, continued membership in NATO, and the acquisition of nuclear arms.		Nicaraguan government announces a ban on political discussions on radio news programs.	Ex-Vice Pres. John Chang, leader of the "new faction" Democratic Party, is elected South Korean premier.
Aug. 20	U.N. Secy. Gen. Hammarskjold announces that Indian Rajeshwar Dayal will succeed Ralph Bunche as his personal representative in the Congo. The change is seen as an effort to restore harmony among the constituent units in the U.N. Force amidst the turbulent Congo situation.		Congo Premier Lumumba charges that white U.N. troops hope to substitute U.N. colonialism for Belgian colonialism. . . . Premier Mamadou Dia announces that Senegal has seceded from its partnership with Sudan in the Mali Federation following a dispute between the two nations over the leadership of the federation.	OAS foreign ministers vote unanimously to sever diplomatic relations with the Dominican Republic for its alleged "aggression" against Venezuela by aiding a plot to overthrow the government of Pres. Romulo Betancourt.	
	A	**B**	**C**	**D**	**E**
	Includes developments that affect more than one world region, international organizations and important meetings of major world leaders.	*Includes all domestic and regional developments in Europe, including the Soviet Union, Turkey, Cyprus and Malta.*	*Includes all domestic and regional developments in Africa and the Middle East, including Iraq and Iran and excluding Cyprus, Turkey and Afghanistan.*	*Includes all domestic and regional developments in Latin America, the Caribbean and Canada.*	*Includes all domestic and regional developments in Asia and Pacific nations, extending from Afghanistan through all the Pacific Islands, except Hawaii.*

U.S. Politics & Social Issues	U.S. Foreign Policy & Defense	U.S. Economy & Environment	Science, Technology & Nature	Culture, Leisure & Life Style	
Nixon, campaigning in Portland, Me., tells reporters that he has differed with Eisenhower administration on "several" matters, one of them being agricultural policy. . . . Senate Finance Committee approves an administration-sponsored bill to provide federal support to state programs of medical assistance to needy aged persons.			U.S. Geological Survey completes a year-long photo-geologic study of the moon designed to provide data for selecting possible future landing sites on the moon.	Royal Native, Bill Hartack up, wins the Matron's Handicap at Arlington Park.	Aug. 13
A federal judge orders the integration of the first grade of the Houston school system, the largest segregated school district in the U.S.	Democratic National Committee Chmn. Sen. Henry M. Jackson (Wash.) says if the U.S. delays much longer in resuming nuclear testing, it may fall behind the Soviets in atomic weapon improvement.			Australian racer Jack Brabham wins his second consecutive world drivers' championship by finishing first in the Portugal Grand Prix.	Aug. 14
	Pres. Eisenhower nominates Army Gen. Lyman L. Lemnitzer to be chairman of the Joint Chiefs of Staff, succeeding the retiring Gen. Nathan Twining.	AEC asserts that proposed nuclear explosions 35 miles from the Eskimo village of Point Hope, Alaska will do no harm to the community.	Dr. Charles Edward Kennet Mees, 78, a pioneer in photographic research and a former Eastman-Kodak executive, dies in Honolulu.		Aug. 15
		Air Transport Association reports the aviation industry has spent $50 million in research to muffle jet engine noise over the last five years. . . . TVA sources report the cost of electric power in the TVA area runs about 60% less than the national average.	Parachutist AF Capt. Joseph Kittinger, Jr, conducting tests for the U.S. space program, sets two world records when he ascends in a balloon to a record 102,800 ft., then jumps setting a free-fall mark of 85,300 ft. before opening his chute.		Aug. 16
Acting under a new state law, La. Gov. Jimmie H. Davis announces he has taken over administration of the state school system to prevent implementation of court-ordered desegregation. Davis promises to go to jail before yielding. . . . Assailing the administration's bill for medical assistance to the elderly as "unsatisfactory," Sen. Kennedy introduces legislation, similar to that passed in the House, that would provide medical care for the aged under Social Security.	Defense Secy. Thomas S. Gates announces formation of a central planning group to assign nuclear weapons to specific targets in case of war.	Commerce Dept. reports the U.S. GNP climbed to the record annual rate of $505 billion during the second quarter of 1960.			Aug. 17
	Pres. Eisenhower names Gen. George H. Decker new Army chief of staff.	Senate passes Sen. John Kennedy's bill to raise the federal minimum wage to $1.25 and extend its coverage to four million additional workers.		Lew Burdette of the Milwaukee Braves pitches a 1-0 no-hit victory over the Philadelphia Phillies.	Aug. 18
	White House announces that James J. Wadsworth will be named U.N. ambassador to replace Henry Cabot Lodge who is quitting to campaign as the GOP vice-presidential candidate. . . . U.S. government sources disclose the adoption of a new policy forbidding foreign countries to purchase Cuban sugar with U.S. loans.	U.S. railroads and 11 unions representing 500,000 non-operating employees end their 15-month wage dispute by agreeing in Chicago to a 2% increase in wages and other benefits.	An instrument capsule parachuting back to earth from the Discoverer XIV satellite is snatched in mid-air by an AF C-119 plane in a successful recovery experiment conducted 200 miles south of Hawaii.		Aug. 19
			USSR reports a satellite launched Aug. 19 carrying two dogs has been safely returned to earth with its occupants apparently unharmed; it is the first time live animals have been retrieved from orbit.		Aug. 20

F	G	H	I	J
Includes elections, federal-state relations, civil rights and liberties, crime, the judiciary, education, health care, poverty, urban affairs and population.	Includes formation and debate of U.S. foreign and defense policies, veterans' affairs and defense spending. (Relations with specific foreign countries are usually found under the region concerned.)	Includes business, labor, agriculture, taxation, transportation, consumer affairs, monetary and fiscal policy, natural resources, and pollution.	Includes worldwide scientific, medical and technological developments, natural phenomena, U.S. weather, natural disasters, and accidents.	Includes the arts, religion, scholarship, communications media, sports, entertainment, fashions, fads and social life.

	World Affairs	Europe	Africa & the Middle East	The Americas	Asia & the Pacific
Aug. 21	USSR renews its request for a U.N. General Assembly debate on the question of U.S. espionage arising out of the U-2 and RB-47 incidents.				Right-wing loyalist forces in Laos call off a planned attack on the neutralist regime in Vientiane to allow for negotiations between loyalist leader Phoumi Nosavan and Premier Souvanna Phouma.
Aug. 22	U.N. Security Council, in emergency session, endorses Secy. Gen. Hammarskjold's use of the U.N. Force in the Congo and his refusal to grant demands from Premier Lumumba for help in suppressing secession in Katanga. During the debate, the USSR backed Lumumba's criticism of the U.N. . . . U.S.-British-Soviet test-ban talks adjourn for a one month recess.	USSR is reported to have expelled a number of U.S. students, tourists and embassy personnel accused of spying. The expulsions coincide with the public trial of Francis Gary Powers.	Lumumba withdraws his threat to oust U.N. troops from the Congo and replace them with forces from friendly African and Asian nations. . . . Algerian Provisional Government proposes a U.N.-controlled referendum to settle Algeria's future.	In a document submitted to the OAS Foreign Ministers' Conference, the U.S. charges Cuban agents with trying "to spread the communist revolution throughout Latin America."	
Aug. 23	Addressing a farewell luncheon, U.S. Amb-to-U.N. Lodge says that Pres. Eisenhower is considering attending the General Assembly debate on disarmament.		Aly Maher Pasha, 77, premier of Egypt four times between 1936 and 1952, dies in Geneva.	Colombian For. Min. Julio César Turbay Ayala appeals to Cuba in a speech to the OAS to disavow Soviet support in its dispute with the U.S.	Newly elected South Korean Premier John Chang announces the formation of a coalition cabinet made up of "Old Guard" and "New Faction" Democrats.
Aug. 24		East German sources report the arrest of 147 members of an alleged U.S. espionage ring. . . . West Berlin Mayor Willy Brandt is nominated as leader of the Social Democratic Party's 1961 campaign against Chancellor Adenauer.	Congolese government troops are sent into Kasai Province by Premier Lumumba to put down the secessionist movement that has spread to that region.		
Aug. 25			Forces in Katanga Province are reportedly preparing defenses against a possible attack from the regular Congolese troops of the central Lumumba government.	At a meeting of the OAS foreign ministers, Cuban Foreign Min. Raul Roa says Cuba is determined to maintain its close relationship with the USSR.	Floods along the Mahanadi River and its tributaries in India take 65 lives and leave 1.5 million people homeless.
Aug. 26		USSR orders the expulsion of George P. Winters, economic attaché at the U.S. Embassy in Moscow, on charges of attempted espionage. . . . Turkish Pres. Cemal Gursel begins appointing a new cabinet, following the dismissal yesterday of 10 ministers by order of the National Union Committee.		U.S. severs diplomatic relations with the Dominican Republic in compliance with the OAS foreign ministers' resolution of Aug. 20. . . . American-owned meat-packing factories are seized by units of the Cuban militia.	Indian Parliament's lower house approves a $21-billion, five-year plan designed to expand India's mixed state-private economy.
Aug. 27		Reports indicate 250,000 East Germans, including city dwellers, students, CP officials and diplomats, have been forced to aid in the harvest at collective farms during August.	An agreement to provide the UAR with long-term Soviet credits to finance the second stage of the Aswan High Dam project is signed in Moscow. . . . Congo forces loyal to Lumumba retake Kasai Province from secessionist forces who had earlier proclaimed the independent republic of "Mining State" there. . . . Congolese troops attack and injure three white U.N. soldiers and eight U.S. airmen stationed at U.N. headquarters in Stanleyville.		
Aug. 28			Congo Premier Lumumba demands that the U.N. Force be removed from his country just as soon as the last Belgian soldier is withdrawn. . . . In an effort to calm growing anti-white anger, Lumumba tells his supporters: "never hate Europeans, but exploitation."	At its final session the OAS Foreign Ministers' Conference adopts a "Declaration of San Jose" condemning communist intervention in the affairs of Latin America. The Cuban delegation walks out during the vote.	
	A	B	C	D	E
	Includes developments that affect more than one world region, international organizations and important meetings of major world leaders.	Includes all domestic and regional developments in Europe, including the Soviet Union, Turkey, Cyprus and Malta.	Includes all domestic and regional developments in Africa and the Middle East, including Iraq and Iran and excluding Cyprus, Turkey and Afghanistan.	Includes all domestic and regional developments in Latin America, the Caribbean and Canada.	Includes all domestic and regional developments in Asia and Pacific nations, extending from Afghanistan through all the Pacific Islands, except Hawaii.

U.S. Politics & Social Issues	U.S. Foreign Policy & Defense	U.S. Economy & Environment	Science, Technology & Nature	Culture, Leisure & Life Style	
Sen. Hugh Scott (R, Pa.) charges in a TV interview that large amounts of Kennedy Foundation and Kennedy family money are being spent in an effort to "buy" the presidential election.	Dr. Edward Teller, a leader in the development of the U.S. hydrogen bomb, publicly urges the resumption of U.S. nuclear tests to perfect smaller, cheaper and more flexible atomic weapons.		Dr. David B. Steinman, 73, designer of over 400 bridges including Straits of Mackinac Bridge, dies in N.Y.	British historian Sir Lewis B. Namier, 72, dies in London.	Aug. 21
		Association of American Railroads reports the net income of U.S. railroads fell 20% during the first half of 1960 compared to the same period in 1959. . . . American Merchant Marine Institute reports that the U.S. cargo and passenger fleet totaled 668 vessels (267,537 tons) as of July 1.		Chicago Cubs pitcher Jim Brewer files a $1-million suit against Cincinnati second baseman Billy Martin because of injuries suffered in a fight during an Aug. 4 game in Chicago.	Aug. 22
Senate passes the administration's contributory, federally assisted Medicare plan for the aged after voting down a Social Security-based program backed by Sen. Kennedy and Democratic liberals.	Pres. Eisenhower asks Congress for authority to cut the Dominican Republic's sugar export quota to the U.S. in the event the OAS votes economic sanctions against the Dominican Republic.	Leading U.S. banks cut their prime interest rates from 5% to 4.5%.		Oscar Hammerstein 2d, librettist, lyricist and producer, whose credits include *Oklahoma*, *South Pacific*, and *The Sound of Music* (all with composer Richard Rodgers), dies of cancer at age 65. . . . Avery Brundage, 72, is unanimously reelected president of the International Olympic Committee.	Aug. 23
Pres. Eisenhower signs into law a bill suspending the radio-TV "equal time" requirement for major-party presidential and vice-presidential candidates during the 1960 campaign.			U.S. Surgeon General gives approval to the use of a new live-virus, oral polio vaccine developed by Dr. Albert Sabin. The decision follows an extensive inquiry into the drug's safety.		Aug. 24
				Italian Pres. Giovanni Gronchi formally opens the 17th Summer Olympic Games in Rome.	Aug. 25
General Board of the AFL-CIO formally endorses the Democratic ticket of John Kennedy and Lyndon Johnson.	American Legion National Commander Martin McKneally denounces Francis Gary Powers as "a weak American" who "served his country badly" during his Moscow trial.	NLRB rules that the Kohler Co. of Kohler, Wis. used unfair labor practices in prolonging a UAW strike that began in 1954 and orders the company to rehire any of the strikers who apply for reinstatement. The NLRB simultaneously cites the UAW for illegal picketing that led to violence. . . . Bureau of Labor Statistics estimates a family of four needs an annual income of $6,000 to maintain an adequate standard of living.		One Danish cyclist dies and two are hospitalized from sunstroke suffered during the 100-km. race at the Rome Olympic games. All three riders took a blood circulation stimulant before the race.	Aug. 26
Nixon informs a convention of the Zionist Organizations of America that, if elected, he will assign Henry Cabot Lodge to work toward an overall settlement of Middle East disputes.	AEC discloses the U.S. has detonated 169 nuclear devices since August 1945.				Aug. 27
National Catholic Conference for Interracial Justice calls for an end to segregation in public accommodations, housing and Catholic parishes.	Ignoring a last minute administration appeal to restore cuts, Congress passes a compromise foreign aid appropriation of $3.7 billion, $500 million less than Eisenhower requested.				Aug. 28

F	G	H	I	J
Includes elections, federal-state relations, civil rights and liberties, crime, the judiciary, education, health care, poverty, urban affairs and population.	*Includes formation and debate of U.S. foreign and defense policies, veterans' affairs and defense spending. (Relations with specific foreign countries are usually found under the region concerned.)*	*Includes business, labor, agriculture, taxation, transportation, consumer affairs, monetary and fiscal policy, natural resources, and pollution.*	*Includes worldwide scientific, medical and technological developments, natural phenomena, U.S. weather, natural disasters, and accidents.*	*Includes the arts, religion, scholarship, communications media, sports, entertainment, fashions, fads and social life.*

	World Affairs	Europe	Africa & the Middle East	The Americas	Asia & the Pacific
Aug. 29	Ralph Bunche, recently relieved of his post as U.N. Rep.-to-Congo, tells newsmen that the Congo's "turbulent atmosphere" will severely "test the U.N.'s capacity to muster international cooperation."		Jordanian Premier Hazza Majali is killed in the explosion of a bomb placed in his office by an unknown assassin. King Hussein names Bahjat al-Talhouni to succeed the slain premier. . . . Iranian Premier Manouchehr Eghbal resigns amid popular discontent over allegedly fraudulent elections which retained his National Party in power.	Cuba signs a cultural exchange agreement with North Korea.	Laotian King Savang Vathana officially installs Prince Souvanna Phouma as neutralist premier of Laos, averting a threatened civil war between royal loyalists and the rebel army units that ousted former Premier Samsonith.
Aug. 30	Soviet Premier Khrushchev tells Western newsmen that Kennedy appears smarter than Nixon, but that neither candidate offers much hope of improving relations between the U.S. and the USSR.			Castro condemns the Declaration of San Jose as an imperialistic U.S. maneuver and says Cuba will continue to rely on Soviet "rocket support." . . . Paraguayan government announces that the state of emergency imposed during rebel attacks from across the Argentine border will be continued for at least 90 days.	Prince Souvanna Phouma offers Laotian cabinet posts to Brig. Gen. Phoumi Nosavan and four other conservative anti-communists in an effort to avert civil war between his own neutralist supporters and the royal troops led by Phoumi.
Aug. 31		East Germany imposes a five-day curb on travel from West Germany to Berlin in an attempt to curtail scheduled Berlin meetings of associations of former war prisoners. The action is denounced by the Western powers.	Delegates from 13 nations end a three-day "Conference of Independent African States" in Leopoldville. The meetings, called by Lumumba, were designed in part to demonstrate African support for Lumumba's government. . . . State of emergency imposed in many parts of South Africa during racial unrest in March is ended by Justice Min. Francois C. Erasmus.	Supporters of Dominican dictator Rafael Trujillo sack the headquarters of the two major opposition parties and nearly lynch an opposition leader.	
Sept. 1	Soviet government announces that Khrushchev will head the USSR's delegation to the 15th U.N. General Assembly opening on Sept. 20.	Division within France over Algeria is reportedly deepening. Over 100 leftist intellectuals, including Jean-Paul Sartre, issue a manifesto denouncing the French army's "Nazi" tactics against Algeria's "legitimate" war for independence.	France and Morocco announce the conclusion of an agreement for the withdrawal of all French ground troops from Moroccan military bases by March 1961. . . . Julius K. Nyerere is appointed chief minister of Tanganyika by the British governor. Nyerere's party won 70 of 71 seats in elections completed today for the colony's first elected council.	In his inaugural address as president of Ecuador, José Maria Velasco Ibarra renounces the 1942 border treaty with Peru.	Sir Hisamuddin Alam Shah, paramount ruler of Malaya since April and first Malayan sultan to make a pilgrimage to Mecca (1952), dies at age 62.
Sept. 2		Political criticism relating to the Congo collapse forces Belgian P.M. Gaston Eyskens to form a new coalition cabinet.	USSR is reported to have delivered several aircraft to the Lumumba regime for use in transporting Congolese troops loyal to the premier.	Premier Castro announces that Cuba will become the first Latin American nation to recognize Communist China.	
Sept. 3		Soviet Premier Khrushchev, visiting Finland, urges Denmark and Norway to sever ties with NATO and emulate the neutralism of Finland. . . . Yugoslavia issues a statement warning that proposed further efforts to re-arm West Germany would obstruct settlement of outstanding European problems.		Nationalist China breaks diplomatic relations with Cuba in the wake of Castro's public pledge to recognize Red China.	Neutralist Laotian government of Souvanna Phouma is reportedly dropping all outstanding treason charges against certain leaders of the pro-communist Pathet Lao. . . . Severe flooding in India's Punjab state leaves at least 55 dead.
Sept. 4		Polish CP First Secy. Wladislaw Gomulka warns that strict sanctions will be taken against private farmers who persist in obstructing the state's program of agricultural collectivization.			

A	B	C	D	E
Includes developments that affect more than one world region, international organizations and important meetings of major world leaders.	*Includes all domestic and regional developments in Europe, including the Soviet Union, Turkey, Cyprus and Malta.*	*Includes all domestic and regional developments in Africa and the Middle East, including Iraq and Iran and excluding Cyprus, Turkey and Afghanistan.*	*Includes all domestic and regional developments in Latin America, the Caribbean and Canada.*	*Includes all domestic and regional developments in Asia and Pacific nations, extending from Afghanistan through all the Pacific Islands, except Hawaii.*

U.S. Politics & Social Issues	U.S. Foreign Policy & Defense	U.S. Economy & Environment	Science, Technology & Nature	Culture, Leisure & Life Style	
Congress gives final approval to an administration-sponsored compromise medical assistance bill for the elderly poor. Sen. Barry Goldwater (Ariz.) was the lone Republican senator opposing the measure.	Pres. Eisenhower appeals to lawyers attending the annual meeting of the American Bar Association to support the repeal of the "Connally Reservation" which gives the U.S. the right to remove "domestic" cases from the jurisdiction of the World Court.	Agriculture Dept. reports the average U.S. farmer produces enough to feed 24 persons; the figure represents a 100% increase in farm productivity since 1930.			Aug. 29
Negro lunch-counter "sit-ins" spark three days of racial strife in Jacksonville, Fla. Fifty persons are reported injured and over 100 black and white youths arrested. . . . N.Y. Supreme Court rules the state is not required to grant American Nazi Party leader George Lincoln Rockwell a speaking permit on the grounds that the First Amendment does not protect the right to speech if violence is the inevitable result.		A new minimum wage measure dies as congressional conferees fail to reconcile the $1.25 bill passed by the Senate with the $1.15 bill passed by the House.		Congress passes a broadcast disclosure bill designed to end payola and quiz show rigging.	Aug. 30
Congress passes a stop-gap housing bill extending current programs after it became clear that the House would not pass the new omnibus housing measure adopted in the Senate. . . . Twenty-eight black students enroll in eight previously all-white Knoxville, Tenn. schools without incident.	State Dept. discloses that Dr. Maurice H. Halperin, former wartime head of the OSS's Latin American Division, is in Moscow, ostensibly engaged in research for the Soviet Academy of Sciences. Halperin later rejects suggestions that he is advising the Soviets on Latin American affairs. . . . Senate passes and sends to the House a bill to create a Freedom Academy for the study and teaching of "cold war tactics" by U.S. government officials.	Congress votes to raise price supports on Grade B milk over administration opposition.	Dr. G. Canby Robinson, 81, medical educator and pioneer researcher in psychosomatic medicine, dies in Greenport, N.Y.		Aug. 31
Supreme Court unanimously turns down requests for delays in implementing school desegregation orders in three cases brought by Houston, Tex., New Orleans, La. and the state of Delaware. . . . Dr. Francis E. Townsend, 93, founder of an old-age pension plan that gained wide public support in the mid-1930s as a solution to the depression, dies in Los Angeles.	Congress fails to give Pres. Eisenhower the requested power to cut Dominican Republic sugar quotas as House and Senate conferees find it impossible to agree on a compromise measure. The debate on the question in both houses revealed some strong opposition to any U.S. sanctions against the Trujillo regime.	*Congressional Quarterly* reports that 86th Congress' second session appropriated $73,634,335,992, just under the sum requested by Pres. Eisenhower. . . . A strike by maintenance workers forces a shut-down of the Pennsylvania Railroad, the nation's biggest rail carrier, for the first time in its 114-year history.		U.S. divers Gary Tobian and Bob Webster win Olympic gold medals in the springboard and platform competition.	Sept. 1
	Fifteen U.S. soldiers are killed and 26 wounded when a shell fired during a training exercise in West Germany hits three tents. . . . U.S. Commerce Dept. prohibits the shipment to Cuba and the Dominican Republic of any motor vehicle or parts that could be used for military purposes.	The formal filing of the NLRB's rulings in the controversial Kohler Co. dispute marks the official end of the six-year strike against the company.			Sept. 2
				U.S. Olympic gold medal winners in the swimming events are: Mike Troy, 200-meter butterfly (Sept. 2); Bill Mulliken, 200-meter breaststroke (Aug. 31); Lynn Burke, 100-meter backstroke (Sept. 3); Carolyn Schuler, 100-meter butterfly (Aug. 30).	Sept. 3
		In his final Labor Day address, Pres. Eisenhower lauds the U.S. system for creating better living standards, better working conditions and greater security than any society in history. . . . A month-long UAW strike against United Aircraft Co. plants in Conn. collapses as picket lines fail to dissuade employees from returning to their jobs.	Dr. Frederick Wellman, 90, ex-medical missionary to Portuguese West Africa, researcher into tropical diseases, and painter, dies in Chapel Hill, N.C.	U.S. boxer Cassius Clay wins the Olympic gold medal in the light-heavyweight division; Wilbert McClure and Eddie Crook are U.S. gold medal winners in the light-middleweight and middleweight classes.	Sept. 4

F	G	H	I	J
Includes elections, federal-state relations, civil rights and liberties, crime, the judiciary, education, health care, poverty, urban affairs and population.	*Includes formation and debate of U.S. foreign and defense policies, veterans' affairs and defense spending. (Relations with specific foreign countries are usually found under the region concerned.)*	*Includes business, labor, agriculture, taxation, transportation, consumer affairs, monetary and fiscal policy, natural resources, and pollution.*	*Includes worldwide scientific, medical and technological developments, natural phenomena, U.S. weather, natural disasters, and accidents.*	*Includes the arts, religion, scholarship, communications media, sports, entertainment, fashions, fads and social life.*

	World Affairs	Europe	Africa & the Middle East	The Americas	Asia & the Pacific
Sept. 5	U.N. study reveals that mining and manufacturing production in the non-communist world has more than doubled in the last 20 years.	In a note to Britain, the USSR protests alleged NATO plans to equip West Germany with Polaris missiles capable of carrying nuclear warheads. . . . In a Paris address, French Pres. de Gaulle renews proposals for a reorganization and decentralization of NATO to reduce American domination and to preserve the "national character" of member states.	French Pres. de Gaulle rejects Algerian rebel proposals for a U.N. referendum to decide Algeria's political future, claiming that the matter is beyond "the competence of the U.N."	A Latin American economic aid conference opens in Bogota with a plea from Colombian Pres. Alberto Lleras for a coordinated, effective aid system.	Laos' pro-communist Pathet Lao rebels announce they will not negotiate with Souvanna Phouma's neutralist government until it agrees to exclude all rightists from the cabinet.
Sept. 6	Bernon F. Mitchell, 31, and William H. Martin, 29, U.S. National Security Agency employees missing since June 24, appear at a Moscow news conference to confirm that they defected to the USSR in response to allegedly immoral U.S. espionage activities.		Jordan's King Hussein tells Western newsmen that UAR Pres. Nasser had advance personal knowledge of the conspiracy behind the assassination of Premier Majali. . . . U.N. Force closes Congo airports in an effort to prevent the use of Soviet planes to transport Congolese troops against secessionists in the provinces. . . . An attempt by Congo Pres. Kasavubu to oust the regime of Premier Lumumba fails when Leopoldville police and soldiers demonstrate their continuing support for Lumumba.	U.S. Undersecy. of State C. Douglas Dillon tells the Bogota aid conference that $500 million appropriated by Congress was only the "first step" in the U.S. effort to develop a broad social development program for Latin America. . . . Argentina reports a favorable balance of trade during 1959 for the first time in recent years. . . . El Salvador reports it has crushed a "widespread communist plot" to overthrow the government.	
Sept. 7	Secy. Gen. Hammarskjold requests a special Security Council meeting to clarify his mandate in the Congo and to express U.N. opposition to the Soviet provision of planes to the Lumumba government. . . . Pres. Eisenhower declares the U.S. is taking a "most serious view" of the USSR's supplying aircraft to the Lumumba government.	Wilhelm Pieck, 84, Communist president of East Germany since 1949, dies in East Berlin.	U.N. Force closes Congo airports and suspends broadcasts over Leopoldville radio in an effort to forestall open fighting between Kasavubu and Lumumba partisans.	Venezuela petitions for the extradition of former president Marcos Perez Jimenez in a U.S. court in Miami. . . . Cuban representatives to the Bogota economic aid conference blast U.S. social development proposals as an effort to buy off revolutionary fervor throughout Latin America.	
Sept. 8	In a note delivered directly to Khrushchev, the U.S. requests the immediate release of the two flyers captured when the Soviets shot down their RB-47 plane over the Barents Sea.	East Germany announces that West German citizens wishing to enter East Berlin will henceforth be required to apply for a special travel permit. The rule does not apply to West Berliners.			
Sept. 9		The annual meeting of the British Trades Union Congress calls for unilateral British nuclear disarmament but continued British participation in the nuclear-armed NATO alliance.	Lumumba announces that he has assumed Kasavubu's functions as chief of state and has taken personal command of the Congolese army. . . . In his report to the Security Council, Hammarskjold says that attacks by Congolese troops on Baluba tribesmen in Kasai Province amount to attempted genocide. . . . Belgium announces the complete withdrawal of its troops from the Congo.	U.N. Security Council rejects without a vote a Soviet proposal that it endorse the OAS foreign ministers' decision to impose sanctions against the Dominican Republic.	At least 40 persons are dead in India's Assam State following riots by Assamese-speaking dissidents protesting the use of Bengali as the state's official language.
Sept. 10	A U.S. memo delivered to the Soviet U.N. mission says that for security reasons Premier Khrushchev will be restricted to Manhattan during his visit to the U.N. General Assembly.		U.N. command reports the Congolese army has agreed to a U.N.-supervised cease-fire in its campaign against secessionist forces in Kasai and Katanga Provinces. . . . Hundreds are reported killed in fighting between Congolese troops and Baluba tribal warriors in secessionist Kasai Province.	Venezuelan constitutional guarantees, suspended since the attempt on Pres. Romulo Betancourt's life in June, are officially restored.	Pro-Western Laotian anti-Communists, led by Brig. Gen. Phoumi Nosavan, form a revolutionary committee aimed at overthrowing the newly installed neutralist cabinet of Souvanna Phouma. Gen. Phoumi had earlier indicated he would accept an offer to join the Souvanna Phouma cabinet.
Sept. 11		Western Allied powers protest East Germany's new travel restrictions as a violation of the four-power agreements on Berlin.	The break-up of the Mali Federation of Senegal and Sudan is made final with the recognition by France of Senegal's independence.	The economic aid conference in Bogota adopts a U.S.-proposed social development program aimed at improving rural life, land use, housing, educational opportunities, public health and industrial investment throughout Latin America.	
	A	**B**	**C**	**D**	**E**
	Includes developments that affect more than one world region, international organizations and important meetings of major world leaders.	*Includes all domestic and regional developments in Europe, including the Soviet Union, Turkey, Cyprus and Malta.*	*Includes all domestic and regional developments in Africa and the Middle East, including Iraq and Iran and excluding Cyprus, Turkey and Afghanistan.*	*Includes all domestic and regional developments in Latin America, the Caribbean and Canada.*	*Includes all domestic and regional developments in Asia and Pacific nations, extending from Afghanistan through all the Pacific Islands, except Hawaii.*

U.S. Politics & Social Issues	U.S. Foreign Policy & Defense	U.S. Economy & Environment	Science, Technology & Nature	Culture, Leisure & Life Style	
Earl Kemp Long, 65, three-time governor of Louisiana and recently nominated as a Democratic candidate for Congress, dies of a heart attack in Alexandria, La.	Robert Marx, 71, founder and first national commander of the Disabled American Veterans, dies in Charlevoix, Mich.	Labor Dept. reports real income for U.S. factory workers has increased 40% since 1947.			Sept. 5
Harrison E. Salisbury, reporter with *The New York Times*, is indicted in Bessemer, Ala. on 42 counts of criminal libel for an article on local race relations published in April. . . . 12 Negro students attend the first day of classes at Little Rock (Ark.) Central High School without incident.	In a speech before the Industrial College of the Armed Forces, Pres. Eisenhower asserts that the maintenance of a strong military deterrent will remain the top U.S. priority as long as potential aggressors seek world conquest. . . . House Un-American Activities Committee chairman Francis Walters (D, Pa.) announces plans to investigate personnel and security policies of the National Security Agency and other federal agencies following the defection of two NSA employees.	AEC reduces the maximum permissible radiation dosage for workers in nuclear plants from 15 roentgens a year to five. . . . U.S. traffic deaths over the Labor Day weekend number 415.	Hurricane Donna strikes Puerto Rico killing over 100 persons.		Sept. 6
A group of 150 Protestant churchmen, headed by the Rev. Norman Vincent Peale, issues a statement in Washington questioning the independence from Church influence of a Roman Catholic President.	Pres. Eisenhower says the defection of two U.S. code experts to the USSR proves the need for a review and tightening of security checks.	U.S. Treasury reports federal gold reserves dropped below $19 billion for the first time since May 1940. In a position paper issued in Washington, Nixon proposes heavy government support of scientific research to put the U.S. permanently ahead of the Soviets in science.		U.S. Olympic gold medal winners in track and field events are: Wilma Rudolph, 100 (Sept. 2) and 200-meters (Sept. 3); Rafer Johnson, decathlon (Sept. 6); Glenn Davis, 400-meter hurdles (Sept. 2); Otis Davis, 400-meters (Sept. 6); Ralph Boston, broad jump (Sept. 2); Don Bragg, pole vault (Sept. 7); Bill Nieder, shot put (Sept. 6); Al Oerter, discus (Sept. 7). . . . French director André Cayette's *Crossing of the Rhine* wins the highest award at the Venice Film Festival.	Sept. 7
Sen. Lyndon Johnson formally launches his vice presidential campaign with a Boston speech in which he identifies the decline of U.S. prestige as the "overriding issue" of the election. . . . In a speech before the National Urban League, N.Y. Gov. Nelson Rockefeller praises the sit-in campaign as an "inspiring example" to the nation.			Pres. Eisenhower praises U.S. space achievements in a speech dedicating NASA's George C. Marshall Space Flight Center in Huntsville, Ala.		Sept. 8
Nixon returns to the campaign trail after a 10-day hospitalization for a knee infection.	State Dept. announces the creation of a U.S. Disarmament Administration to advise the President on disarmament policy.	Labor Dept. attributes the 5.9% unemployment rate for August to a continuing slump in auto and steel production.		Swedish opera star Jussi Bjoerling, 49, dies in Sweden.	Sept. 9
Rep. Edith Nourse Rogers (R, Mass.), who has served in Congress since 1925, longer than any other Congresswoman, dies in Boston at age 79.	Sen. James Eastland (D, Miss.), chairman of the Senate Internal Security Subcommittee, publicly charges that low-level State Dept. planners, working with members of the press, "handed Cuba to Castro...in the same way China was handed to the Communists." State Secy. Herter denounces the allegation.	Teamsters Pres. James Hoffa announces completion of negotiations for a new two-year contract with 1,500 eastern firms employing over 50,000 long-haul truckers.		Nancy Anne Fleming, 18, of Michigan, is chosen Miss America for 1960.	Sept. 10
				USSR wins the Summer Olympic Games in Rome with 43 gold medals and 807½ pts.; U.S. finishes second with 34 gold medals and 564½ pts.	Sept. 11

F	G	H	I	J
Includes elections, federal-state relations, civil rights and liberties, crime, the judiciary, education, health care, poverty, urban affairs and population.	*Includes formation and debate of U.S. foreign and defense policies, veterans' affairs and defense spending. (Relations with specific foreign countries are usually found under the region concerned.)*	*Includes business, labor, agriculture, taxation, transportation, consumer affairs, monetary and fiscal policy, natural resources, and pollution.*	*Includes worldwide scientific, medical and technological developments, natural phenomena, U.S. weather, natural disasters, and accidents.*	*Includes the arts, religion, scholarship, communications media, sports, entertainment, fashions, fads and social life.*

	World Affairs	Europe	Africa & the Middle East	The Americas	Asia & the Pacific
Sept. 12	Secy. Gen. Hammarskjold, in his annual report to members of the U.N., opposes formation of a standing U.N. military force as "unnecessary and impractical."	First Secy. Walter Ulbricht of the East German Communist Party is named chairman of a new Council of State created by parliament to supersede the East German presidency.	Three African states participating in the U.N. Force (UAR, Ghana and Guinea) threaten to withdraw troops unless the U.N. returns control of the Congo airports to the Congolese. . . . Premier Lumumba is detained for three hours by Congolese troops acting on orders from Pres. Kasavubu and then released.	Lt. Exio de Jesus Saldivia, right-wing officer of the Venezuelan National Guard, is arrested after unsuccessfully appealing to the people of Caracas to join him in a revolt against the government of Pres. Betancourt.	Japanese Foreign Min. Zentaro Kosaka arrives in Washington and personally delivers a formal apology for the cancellation of Pres. Eisenhower's June visit to Japan. . . . Laotian troops under the command of the neutralist Souvanna Phouma cabinet are reportedly engaged in battles against both the pro-Communist forces of the Pathet Lao and the anti-Communist rebels led by Gen. Phoumi.
Sept. 13	USSR protests U.S. travel restrictions on Khrushchev's U.N. visit as "an unfriendly act" designed to interfere with the work of the Soviet delegation.		U.N. Force reopens Congo airfields to "peaceful traffic." . . . Congolese parliament votes Lumumba "special powers" to resist efforts by Kasavubu and other dissidents to overthrow his regime. . . . Guinean Pres. Sékou Touré and Communist Chinese Premier Chou En-lai sign an agreement providing a $25 million Chinese loan for Guinean economic development.		Communist Chinese Foreign Ministry says that a recent series of ambassadorial contacts with the U.S. in Warsaw proved fruitless because of a U.S. refusal to negotiate "fundamental issues." . . . Indonesian Pres. Sukarno orders a complete suspension of political party activity until Nov. 30.
Sept. 14	In an unprecedented personal attack on the Secretary General, the Soviet U.N. delegation charges Hammarskjold with misusing his power in the Congo for the benefit of Western "colonialists." . . . U.N. Security Council votes not to seat either the pro-Lumumba or anti-Lumumba delegations sent to represent the Congo. . . . White House announces that Pres. Eisenhower will address the U.N. General Assembly on Sept. 22.	The *New York Times* reports a high-level shake-up in the leadership of Albania's Communist Party.	Congolese military units, led by Col. Joseph Mobutu, place Lumumba under house arrest and assume temporary direction of the strife-torn Congo government. Mobutu says the action was necessitated by the chaos resulting from the continuing power struggle between Lumumba and Kasavubu.	U.S. Congressmen, attending Mexico's 150th independence anniversary celebrations, boycott ceremonies in protest against an earlier pro-Castro speech by Chamber of Deputies Pres. Emilio Sanchez Piedras.	
Sept. 15				International Court of Justice in The Hague begins hearings into the longstanding border dispute between Honduras and Nicaragua. . . . Several persons are reported killed in riots in El Salvador protesting the state of siege proclaimed Sept. 5. . . . Cubana Airlines' N.Y. assets and one of its planes are seized under a N.Y. court order because of the airline's unpaid bills.	
Sept. 16			The ruling army regime of Col. Mobutu orders Soviet diplomats and embassy personnel to leave the Congo within 48 hours.		
Sept. 17	USSR vetoes a Tunisian-sponsored U.N. Security Council resolution backing Hammarskjold's role in the Congo. The U.S. immediately requests an emergency General Assembly meeting to deal with the crisis of confidence caused by the Soviet veto.			Acting on a State Dept. recommendation, Pres. Eisenhower orders the Panamanian flag flown alongside the U.S. flag in the Canal Zone. . . . Cuban authorities in Havana charge seven Americans, including two U.S. Embassy aides, with alleged espionage activities. . . . Cuba nationalizes three U.S.-owned banks in Havana.	Communist China formally rejects Indian charges that Chinese aircraft have repeatedly violated Indian airspace.
Sept. 18		Candidates of Swedish Premier Tage Erlander's Social Democratic Party score an overwhelming victory over Conservatives who campaigned for the repeal of Sweden's comprehensive social welfare system.	Col. Mobutu orders the withdrawal of all Congolese forces from secessionist Katanga and Kasai Provinces.	Cuba temporarily restricts U.S. Amb. Philip Bonsal to the immediate vicinity of the U.S. Embassy in retaliation against travel restrictions imposed upon Communist heads of state attending the U.N. General Assembly in New York.	

A	B	C	D	E
Includes developments that affect more than one world region, international organizations and important meetings of major world leaders.	Includes all domestic and regional developments in Europe, including the Soviet Union, Turkey, Cyprus and Malta.	Includes all domestic and regional developments in Africa and the Middle East, including Iraq and Iran and excluding Cyprus, Turkey and Afghanistan.	Includes all domestic and regional developments in Latin America, the Caribbean and Canada.	Includes all domestic and regional developments in Asia and Pacific nations, extending from Afghanistan through all the Pacific Islands, except Hawaii.

U.S. Politics & Social Issues	U.S. Foreign Policy & Defense	U.S. Economy & Environment	Science, Technology & Nature	Culture, Leisure & Life Style	
Sen. Kennedy, denying charges that his Catholicism makes him politically beholden to the Vatican, pledges to make all official decisions as president "without regard to outside religious pressures or dictates."		An agreement on disputed work rules ends a 12-day strike by maintenance workers' unions against the Pennsylvania Railroad.			Sept. 12
Nixon tells newsmen Kennedy's disavowal of religious influence "should be accepted without questioning" and the whole matter dropped from the campaign. . . . Thomas C. Hennings Jr., liberal Democratic senator from Mo. since 1950 and leading civil rights advocate, dies in Washington at age 57. . . . Justice Dept. files suit under the 1957 Civil Rights Act seeking to restrain 27 persons and two banks from using economic pressure to dissuade Haywood County, Tenn. Negroes from registering to vote.			Hurricane Donna, described as the most destructive in U.S. Weather Bureau history, kills 30 and leaves thousands homeless as it sweeps along the Atlantic coast from Florida to Canada.		Sept. 13
		Kohler Co., complying with an NLRB ruling, announces that it has offered to rehire about 1,400 employees who participated in the UAW's six-year strike against the company.	Sir Arthur P. M. Fleming, 79, British electrical engineer whose early research led to the development of radar, dies on the Isle of Wight, England.		Sept. 14
		NLRB announces that most of New York's 20,000 taxi drivers have voted not to be represented by the Teamsters Union.		Hockey's greatest scorer, Maurice (Rocket) Richard, 39, of the Montreal Canadiens, announces his retirement.	Sept. 15
FBI reports that major crimes in the U.S. numbered a record 1.5 million in 1959, a 1% increase over 1958 and 70% increase since 1950. . . . Six Negroes are arrested in New Orleans for demonstrating against alleged job discrimination by store-owners in a downtown shopping center.	In a TV campaign speech, Kennedy explains that his criticism of U.S. foreign policy should not be misinterpreted as an attempt to "divide" the country. . . . Chmn. Francis Walters of the House Un-American Activities Committee says homosexuality may have been involved in the case of two former National Security Agency employees who defected to the USSR, adding that "sexual perversion is quite a problem in the NSA."	Brotherhood of Railroad Trainmen end a crippling two-week strike against three of U.S. Steel Corp.'s subsidiary railroads after signing a new wage and benefit contract.		Milwaukee Braves pitcher Warren Spahn, 39, throws a 4-0 no-hit victory over Philadelphia. . . . Amos Alonzo Stagg, 98, announces his retirement as the advisory coach of the Stockton College football team.	Sept. 16
	ABC, CBS, and NBC agree to a State Dept. request not to give Premier Khrushchev special TV time during his visit to the U.N.		AP reports that nearly 44.5 million persons were using fluoridated drinking water as of Aug. 2.	Neale Fraser wins the men's singles tennis title at Forest Hills, N.Y. . . . Deane Beman wins the U.S. Amateur Golf Championship in St. Louis.	Sept. 17
					Sept. 18

F	G	H	I	J
Includes elections, federal-state relations, civil rights and liberties, crime, the judiciary, education, health care, poverty, urban affairs and population.	*Includes formation and debate of U.S. foreign and defense policies, veterans' affairs and defense spending. (Relations with specific foreign countries are usually found under the region concerned.)*	*Includes business, labor, agriculture, taxation, transportation, consumer affairs, monetary and fiscal policy, natural resources, and pollution.*	*Includes worldwide scientific, medical and technological developments, natural phenomena, U.S. weather, natural disasters, and accidents.*	*Includes the arts, religion, scholarship, communications media, sports, entertainment, fashions, fads and social life.*

	World Affairs	Europe	Africa & the Middle East	The Americas	Asia & the Pacific
Sept. 19	Khrushchev, Castro and other world leaders arrive in New York under a heavy blanket of police and FBI security.	Floods caused by torrential Alpine rains leave 36 dead in Italy.			Indian P.M. Nehru and Pakistani Pres. Ayub Khan sign an agreement in Karachi ending a 13-year dispute over division of Indus River waters.
Sept. 20	U.N. General Assembly, in emergency session, votes 70-0 (Soviet-bloc abstaining) to approve an African-Asian resolution supporting Hammarskjold's action in the Congo. . . . The regular meeting of the General Assembly opens by voting U.N. admission for Cyprus and 13 newly-independent African states.	NATO begins the largest air-land-sea maneuvers in its history.	Mobutu installs a 15-member non-political "High Commission" to rule the Congo pending settlement of political strife between Kasavubu and Lumumba.	Premier Castro, in New York for the General Assembly session, moves his delegation from their designated downtown accommodations to "a humble hotel" in Harlem where he is visited by Premier Khrushchev.	Laotian government of Souvanna Phouma orders the expulsion of the Thai ambassador in retaliation for Thailand's alleged support of Souvanna Phouma's right-wing opponents.
Sept. 21	An official government statement indicates that France will play a very limited role in the current U.N. General Assembly session. The action is believed to reflect French opposition to any U.N. involvement in the Algerian question.		Secy. Gen. Hammarskjold warns Katanga leader Tshombe that U.N. troops will use force to prevent the continuation of attacks by Katanga troops on the Baluba tribesmen living in the province.		
Sept. 22	In his address before the General Assembly, Pres. Eisenhower urges the following: praise for Hammarskjold's action in the Congo; U.N. support for emerging African nations; peaceful uses of space; increased food and economic aid to poor countries; resumption of 10-nation Geneva disarmament talks; and speedy conclusion of a nuclear test ban. . . . In his address to the U.N., Yugoslav Pres. Tito declares his opposition to the rearming of West Germany and to France's policy in Algeria. . . . Japanese For. Min. Zentaro Kosaka recommends to the U.N. General Assembly enlargement of the Security Council to assure representation of newly admitted Asian and African states.	West German Finance Min. Franz Etzel presents the Bundestag with a record $10.7 billion budget for 1961, including $2.7 billion earmarked for defense.	Teheran sources report the USSR has offered Iran economic aid in exchange for an Iranian promise to prevent the U.S. from using its bases there for an attack on the USSR. . . . Sudan Republic withdraws from the French Community and renames itself the Republic of Mali. The action is seen as protest against France's alleged involvement in the break-up of the Mali Federation of Senegal and Sudan.	Cuban sources report the USSR has promised to buy all the sugar that would normally have gone to the U.S.	
Sept. 23	Secy. of State Herter denounces Khrushchev's call to revise the U.N. charter and force Hammarskjold out as "a real declaration of war against the structure, the personnel and the location" of the U.N.	The Treasury reports Britain suffered a $25-million trade deficit during the second quarter of 1960 which compares with $123 million surplus during the same period in 1959.	Ghanian Pres. Kwame Nkrumah criticizes the U.N. Force's failure to support the legitimate Congo government in his speech to the General Assembly.		After four days of talks Indian P.M. Nehru and Pakistani Pres. Ayub Khan issue a statement promising "cooperative relations," but containing no mention of the continuing Kashmir dispute.
Sept. 24	Premier Khrushchev's two-and-a-half hour address to the General Assembly includes the following: condemnation of U.S. spy flights and "aggression"; criticism of Hammarskjold's pro-Western abuse of power in the Congo; praise for the Cuban revolution; proposals for total disarmament; and a plan to replace the office of U.N. Secretary General with a three-man executive.			Enrique Pérez Serantes, archbishop of Santiago, charges in a pastoral letter that Cuba's Communists are trying to destroy all Catholic influence in the country. . . . Cuba formally recognizes Communist China and North Korea.	
Sept. 25	Premier Khrushchev tells reporters that rejection of the USSR proposal to replace Hammarskjold with a three-man executive would intensify Cold War tensions.				

A	B	C	D	E
Includes developments that affect more than one world region, international organizations and important meetings of major world leaders.	Includes all domestic and regional developments in Europe, including the Soviet Union, Turkey, Cyprus and Malta.	Includes all domestic and regional developments in Africa and the Middle East, including Iraq and Iran and excluding Cyprus, Turkey and Afghanistan.	Includes all domestic and regional developments in Latin America, the Caribbean and Canada.	Includes all domestic and regional developments in Asia and Pacific nations, extending from Afghanistan through all the Pacific Islands, except Hawaii.

U.S. Politics & Social Issues	U.S. Foreign Policy & Defense	U.S. Economy & Environment	Science, Technology & Nature	Culture, Leisure & Life Style	
Democrats from 9 states meeting with Sen. Kennedy in Charleston, W. Va. agree that unemployment should be a central issue in the presidential campaign.	A plane carrying U.S. military personnel and their families crashes on Guam killing 78 of the 94 persons aboard.	New York Stock Exchange prices fall over 15 points on the Dow-Jones index in the sharpest one-day drop since 1955. . . . Kennedy, addressing the United Steelworkers Convention, states his opposition to USW Pres. David J. McDonald's proposal for a 32-hour work week.			Sept. 19
Kennedy tells a Washington audience that he will take quick action during "the first 90 days" of his administration to rebuild free-world military strength against Communist threats in Cuba, southeast Asia and elsewhere.		Teamsters Pres. James Hoffa orders a preliminary study into the possibility of organizing farm laborers in 12 Midwestern states.	Dr. Ernest William Goodpasture, 73, pathologist who developed a method for the mass production of vaccines (1931), dies in Nashville, Tenn.	*The Hostage*, a play by Brendan Behan, opens in N.Y.	Sept. 20
Eight Negro parents are arrested in New Rochelle, N.Y. for a sit-in demonstration against de facto segregation in one of the city's all-white elementary schools.	Nixon charges that Kennedy's "disparaging" criticism of U.S. foreign policy and defense is harming American unity and the U.S. position vis-a-vis the USSR. Kennedy denies the charge, claiming that he is simply telling the truth.		U.S. Air Force completes its first successful test of the "Scout" rocket, a missile being developed to provide a fairly inexpensive and reliable means of launching satellites.		Sept. 21
	U.S. hospital ship *Hope* leaves San Francisco for a seven-month medical mission to Indonesia.				Sept. 22
Kennedy and Nixon outline their respective farm policies with Kennedy stressing supply management and Nixon emphasizing expanded marketing.		United Steelworkers of America end a four-day convention marked by sharp confrontations between supporters and opponents of USW Pres. David McDonald. . . . Bureau of Labor Statistics reports that for the first time since January the U.S. cost of living did not increase in August.	Soviet cancer researchers visiting the Sloan-Kettering Center tell American scientists that they have isolated a specific antigen present in stomach cancer.	Three runners break the four-minute mile in Dublin, Ireland meet: Herb Eliot of Australia (3.57), Terry Sullivan of Rhodesia (3.59.8) and Gordon Pirie of Britain (3.59.9).	Sept. 23
	The first atomic-powered aircraft carrier, the *U.S.S. Enterprise*, described by the Navy as the largest ship ever built, is launched in Newport News, Va.	Sen. James E. Murray (D, Mont.) charges that a Nixon-supported plan to give federally owned lands to Western states would lead to the biggest "land grab" in U.S. history.			Sept. 24
Kennedy declares he "strongly favors" federal school aid to pay teacher salaries. Nixon is opposed.			The fifth US attempt to put a satellite into orbit around the moon fails when the second stage of the Atlas-Able launch rocket misfires.	New York Yankees and the Pittsburgh Pirates clinch the American and National League pennants. . . . Emily Post, 86, newspaper columnist and leading U.S. authority on etiquette, dies in New York. . . . Boston Red Sox star Ted Williams says he is quitting as an active player at the end of the 1960 season.	Sept. 25
F	G	H	I	J	
Includes elections, federal-state relations, civil rights and liberties, crime, the judiciary, education, health care, poverty, urban affairs and population.	Includes formation and debate of U.S. foreign and defense policies, veterans' affairs and defense spending. (Relations with specific foreign countries are usually found under the region concerned.)	Includes business, labor, agriculture, taxation, transportation, consumer affairs, monetary and fiscal policy, natural resources, and pollution.	Includes worldwide scientific, medical and technological developments, natural phenomena, U.S. weather, natural disasters, and accidents.	Includes the arts, religion, scholarship, communications media, sports, entertainment, fashions, fads and social life.	

	World Affairs	Europe	Africa & the Middle East	The Americas	Asia & the Pacific
Sept. 26	Secy. Gen. Hammarskjold, addressing the U.N. General Assembly, defends his conduct in the Congo against Soviet charges of bias. An enraged Khrushchev pounds his desk as Hammarskjold concludes. . . . In his speech to the U.N., Castro praises Soviet friendship for small nations and charges the U.S. with economic and military "aggression" against the Cuban revolution.	A six-week wildcat seamen's strike that crippled British shipping ends when wildcatters vote to return to work.	Special U.N. Rep.-to-The Congo Rajeshwar Dayal reports that the republic faces disease, chaos and disintegration unless its political leaders quickly end their factional strife. . . . U.N. Force in the Congo now numbers 16,382 troops from 27 nations.		
Sept. 27	U.S. proposes to the resumed Geneva test-ban conference a 27-month moratorium on small underground tests during which the U.S., Britain and USSR could complete joint research on detection methods. The Soviets reject the proposed moratorium as too brief and renew their demand for a four to five year ban.		UAR Pres. Nasser tells the General Assembly that the U.N. has disregarded its responsibility to protect the rights of the Palestinians.		Pres. Sukarno orders the closing of eight Indonesian newspapers, including *Nusuntara*, the only remaining anti-Communist daily.
Sept. 28		NATO Permanent Council votes to integrate all West European air defense forces into a single NATO command. The vote comes after two years of French opposition that is ended with a compromise giving France exclusive control over part of its air force.		Venezuela protests a U.S. decision to buy 321,857 tons of Dominican sugar on the grounds that it violates the Aug. 20 OAS resolution to impose sanctions against the Dominican Republic. . . . Argentine police begin a crackdown on communist organizations and activities.	
Sept. 29	In a General Assembly address frequently interrupted by outbursts from Khrushchev, British P.M. Macmillan praises Hammarskjold and the U.N. Congo operation.	The Turkish Democratic Party, founded by ousted Premier Adnan Menderes in 1945, is officially dissolved by an Ankara civil court.	Pres. Kasavubu gives formal approval to the assumption of power in the Congo by the interim High Commission under Col. Mobutu. . . . Israeli Foreign Ministry makes public a list of 23 prominent former Nazis it claims are now working for the UAR.	U.S. State Dept. urges the return of all "non-essential" U.S. citizens living in Cuba because of increasing police harassment of Americans.	Cambodian Premier Sihanouk, in his U.N. address, calls for an East-West agreement to protect the neutrality of Cambodia and Laos and keep them from becoming involved in the rivalry between North and South Vietnam.
Sept. 30	A proposal for a new summit between Eisenhower and Khrushchev to discuss current international tensions is presented to the General Assembly by five neutralist leaders (Nehru, Nasser, Tito, Sukarno, and Nkrumah).	West Germany announces that it will not consider renewal of its trade agreement with East Germany unless restrictions on West German access to East Berlin are lifted.			
Oct. 1			Former British colony of Nigeria becomes an independent nation in Lagos ceremonies presided over by P.M.-elect Alhaji Abubakar Tafawa Balewa.	In his inaugural address, new Panamanian Pres. Roberto F. Chiari praises the U.S. decision to increase aid for Latin American development.	Premiers U Nu and Chou En-lai sign an agreement in Peking ending Burmese-Chinese border disputes.
Oct. 2	Pres. Eisenhower turns down the neutralist call for a new summit, saying he sees nothing in the current Soviet attitude that would promise any results from such a meeting.			Janio da Silva Quadros, candidate of the minority Christian Democratic Party, wins Brazil's presidential election.	In a radio speech, neutralist Laotian Premier Souvanna Phouma says he will not allow a Communist victory in Laos because it is incompatible with the country's Buddhist religion and culture.
Oct. 3	Premier Khrushchev says he would be willing to meet with Eisenhower only if the U.S. apologized in advance for the U-2 and RB-47 incidents. . . . Hammarskjold rejects Khrushchev's demand that he quit his U.N. post.		King Hussein tells the General Assembly that Jordan has been the target of continuing subversion and abuse from the UAR.		

A	B	C	D	E
Includes developments that affect more than one world region, international organizations and important meetings of major world leaders.	Includes all domestic and regional developments in Europe, including the Soviet Union, Turkey, Cyprus and Malta.	Includes all domestic and regional developments in Africa and the Middle East, including Iraq and Iran and excluding Cyprus, Turkey and Afghanistan.	Includes all domestic and regional developments in Latin America, the Caribbean and Canada.	Includes all domestic and regional developments in Asia and Pacific nations, extending from Afghanistan through all the Pacific Islands, except Hawaii.

U.S. Politics & Social Issues	U.S. Foreign Policy & Defense	U.S. Economy & Environment	Science, Technology & Nature	Culture, Leisure & Life Style	
In the first of four scheduled TV debates, Nixon asserts the Democratic domestic program will involve excessive federal spending and federal control. Kennedy defends his program as necessary to counter the recessionary economic downturn caused by outdated GOP fiscal policies.		Terence McShane is sworn in in Washington by a U.S. judge as chairman of the board of monitors to oversee the operations of the Teamsters Union. An appeals court later rules McShane cannot serve until it studies an appeal by Teamsters' Pres. Hoffa.			Sept. 26
Federal Civil Rights Commission begins hearings in New Orleans to investigate complaints of voter discrimination in 17 Louisiana parishes.		Commerce Clearing House reports that per capita state taxes rose to a record $101 during fiscal 1960.		Estelle Sylvia Pankhurst, 79, British suffragist, champion of women's social and sexual rights and more recently fighter for Ethiopian independence, dies in Addis Ababa.	Sept. 27
	Seventeen U.S. Jewish organizations call for greater U.S. and world pressure against alleged Soviet repression of the Russian Jewish community.	New York Stock Exchange expels Anton Homsey of DuPont, Homsey and Co. for "fraudulent acts"; it is the first such action in 22 years.		The film *Sunrise at Campobello*, starring Ralph Bellamy as FDR, is released in N.Y.	Sept. 28
Pres. Eisenhower tells a GOP dinner that Nixon's contribution to high level foreign policy over the last eight years has given him the experience to be a great leader. . . . N.Y. State Commission Against Discrimination announces plans to investigate charges of tenant-selection discrimination against the N. Y. City Housing Authority.	Kennedy labels recent administration foreign policy efforts as a record of failure, citing the summit collapse, communist advances in Cuba and Africa, and the lack of a test-ban or disarmament agreements as examples.		Scientists at the Sloan-Kettering Institute report the first clear evidence linking a virus to forms of human cancer other than leukemia.	*Irma La Douce*, a musical about a French prostitute, opens to favorable reviews in N.Y.	Sept. 29
			International Atomic Energy Agency, meeting in Vienna, adopts a U.S. proposal governing the distribution of nuclear materials despite strong Soviet-bloc opposition.	Vance Packard's analysis of obsolescence in the U.S. market economy, *The Wastemakers*, is published in New York.	Sept. 30
				Roi Ottley, 54, American Negro journalist and author of books on black history and culture, dies in Chicago.	Oct. 1
In a campaign position paper, Nixon outlines a program for extensive federal support of medical research and doctor education.		Seventy thousand members of the International Union of Electrical Workers strike the General Electric Co. over GE's refusal to keep an automatic cost-of-living clause in a new contract.		AP reports major league baseball attendance during the 1960 season totalled a record 19,910,610.	Oct. 2
"Stand-ins" to protest discrimination in voter registration are organized by SCLC leader Rev. Martin Luther King. . . . U.S. narcotics agents in New York seize 110 pounds of heroin, described as the largest drug seizure in U.S. history. Four persons are arrested including the Guatemalan ambassador to Belgium.	AEC Chmn. John McCone, noting the failure to reach agreement in Geneva, says the U.S. will soon resume nuclear testing in connection with its detection research program.	Labor Dept. seeks court invalidation of elections of officials in the National Maritime Union in the first major legal test of the Landrum-Griffin Act. NMU officials are accused of various forms of illegal electioneering. . . . Commerce Dept. reports U.S. personal incomes rose to a record annual rate of $408.4 billion in September.	Sources in Communist China report that over half of the nation's farmlands have been damaged by severe storms and floods during 1960.	Chicago Cubs slugger Ernie Banks ends the season with 41 home runs, tops in the major leagues.	Oct. 3

F	G	H	I	J
Includes elections, federal-state relations, civil rights and liberties, crime, the judiciary, education, health care, poverty, urban affairs and population.	Includes formation and debate of U.S. foreign and defense policies, veterans' affairs and defense spending. (Relations with specific foreign countries are usually found under the region concerned.)	Includes business, labor, agriculture, taxation, transportation, consumer affairs, monetary and fiscal policy, natural resources, and pollution.	Includes worldwide scientific, medical and technological developments, natural phenomena, U.S. weather, natural disasters, and accidents.	Includes the arts, religion, scholarship, communications media, sports, entertainment, fashions, fads and social life.

	World Affairs	Europe	Africa & the Middle East	The Americas	Asia & the Pacific
Oct. 4	British P.M. Macmillan concludes a series of private talks with Khrushchev that centered on Berlin and a possible summit in early 1961.	East German Pres. Walter Ulbricht calls for new negotiations to assure Western access to Berlin and East German "sovereignty."			U.S. presents Japan with a $600,000 grant for the construction of medical facilities in Hiroshima and Nagasaki.
Oct. 5		British Labor Party conference passes a resolution urging unilateral abandonment of atomic weapons. Party leader Hugh Gaitskell says he will "fight, fight and fight" to reverse the call for the "suicidal path of unilateral disarmament."	Nationalist Party proposals to transform South Africa from a constitutional monarchy loyal to the British crown into an independent republic are approved by a slight margin in a nationwide whites-only referendum.		In a speech frequently interrupted by Khrushchev, Philippine representative Francisco Delgado charges that the history of Western colonialism was less oppressive than continuing Soviet colonialism in eastern Europe.
Oct. 6	Neutralist leaders withdraw their resolution urging an Eisenhower-Khrushchev summit after the West indicates its opposition to face-to-face meetings between the two leaders.	Repressive press laws enacted under the Menderes government are repealed by Turkey's ruling military committee.		Cuban Armed Forces Ministry reports that a counter-revolutionary force from the U.S., including three U.S. citizens, has landed in Oriente Province.	
Oct. 7	Khrushchev says he has been assured by P.M. Macmillan that a Big four summit will be held soon after Eisenhower's successor takes office. . . . Nigeria becomes the 99th member of the U.N.	Pres. de Gaulle declares that France will insist on a final veto over the use of nuclear weapons as a condition of French participation in a joint NATO atomic force. . . . British Board of Trade announces plans for a 30% increase in British-Soviet trade during fiscal 1961.	USSR discloses it has given de facto recognition to the rebel Algerian Provisional Government.		Sources in Kabul report fighting has broken out between Afghan and Pakistani troops in the Baijur region of the Afghan-Pakistan border. . . . Typhoon Kit strikes the Philippine Islands leaving at least 50 people dead or missing.
Oct. 8	General Assembly votes 42 to 34 (22 abstentions) not to discuss the admission of Communist China to the U.N. The vote is the closest since the issue first came up in 1951.	West German Chancellor Adenauer rejects de Gaulle's proposed reorganization of NATO into a loosely coordinated alliance of national armies as unworkable in time of crisis.	Seven Africans are killed and more than 100 Africans and whites wounded when police machine gun rioters near Salisbury, Southern Rhodesia.		Taipei magazine publisher Lei Chen is convicted of sedition for his press criticism and active political opposition to Nationalist China's ruling Kuomintang Party.
Oct. 9	In a two-hour interview on an independent station in Newark, N.J., Premier Khrushchev declares that the USSR will "never start a war, so you can sleep in peace."		Ghana Pres. Kwame Nkrumah publicly denies widespread reports that his government is considering nationalization of all foreign enterprises.		Nepali Foreign Ministry announces that Nepal and Communist China have reached agreement on procedures for surveying and demarcating disputed boundary territory.
Oct. 10		Warsaw Pact members issue a public declaration calling upon all W.W. II Allies to prevent the arming of West Germany with nuclear weapons.	Israeli Foreign Min. Golda Meir, in her speech to the General Assembly, challenges UAR Pres. Nasser to accept face-to-face negotiations with Israeli P.M. David Ben-Gurion on a Mideast non-aggression pact.	Guatemalan U.N. delegate Luis Coronado Lira charges in the General Assembly that Cuban agents are organizing an "invasion" against his country.	At least 5,000 persons are killed by a cyclone and tidal wave that struck the Bay of Bengal coastal area in East Pakistan.
Oct. 11	General Assembly votes down a Soviet proposal that disarmament be debated immediately by the full General Assembly. Khrushchev tells newsmen that the defeat brings the world "closer to war."		A British government commission recommends that the member states of the Central African Federation (Northern and Southern Rhodesia and Nyasaland) be given greater autonomy as part of general program to increase African political representation. Federation P.M. Roy Welensky condemns the recommendation as extreme, while African nationalists denounce it as insufficient. . . . U.N. command in the Congo refuses to permit the arrest of Lumumba by troops loyal to Mobutu.	Canadian P.M. John Diefenbaker dismisses Defense Min. George Pearkes in the face of political criticism that Canada's defenses have become over-dependent on the U.S. . . . Gen. Rodolfo Larcher resigns as Argentine secretary of war in a dispute with military leaders.	Negotiations are reportedly underway in Laos to end the three-way civil strife among Souvanna Phouma neutralists, Nosavan rightists and Pathet Lao Communists.
	A	**B**	**C**	**D**	**E**
	Includes developments that affect more than one world region, international organizations and important meetings of major world leaders.	*Includes all domestic and regional developments in Europe, including the Soviet Union, Turkey, Cyprus and Malta.*	*Includes all domestic and regional developments in Africa and the Middle East, including Iraq and Iran and excluding Cyprus, Turkey and Afghanistan.*	*Includes all domestic and regional developments in Latin America, the Caribbean and Canada.*	*Includes all domestic and regional developments in Asia and Pacific nations, extending from Afghanistan through all the Pacific Islands, except Hawaii.*

U.S. Politics & Social Issues	U.S. Foreign Policy & Defense	U.S. Economy & Environment	Science, Technology & Nature	Culture, Leisure & Life Style	
	Kennedy tells reporters that Eisenhower used "good judgment" in declining a neutralist proposal to meet Khrushchev.	An Eastern Airlines Electra en route from Boston to Atlanta crashes in Boston Harbor killing 61. . . . Budget Bureau estimates the fiscal 1961 budget surplus, originally estimated at over $4 billion, will be closer to $1 billion because of a sagging economy and reduced tax revenues. . . . Thirty-six top executives of the Chrysler Corp. are cleared by a lawyer-accountant team hired by Chrysler to investigate charges of conflict of interest and mishandling of funds.	A 500-pound Courier communications relay satellite is placed in earth orbit from Cape Canaveral. . . .		Oct. 4
				Jean Anouilh's play *Becket*, starring Sir Laurence Olivier, opens in New York. . . . New York's Casey Stengel, 70, sets a major league record by appearing as a manager in his 10th world series.	Oct. 5
	Joseph N. Welch, 69, Boston attorney who acted as Army counsel during the 1954 Army-McCarthy hearings, dies in Cape Cod, Mass.	A special National Academy of Sciences committee, established at the request of HEW, reports that there is no evidence for charges that the Food and Drug Administration had disregarded public safety in its decisions on the safety of new drugs.			Oct. 6
In their second TV debate, Nixon and Kennedy disagree sharply over whether the U.S. should fight to defend the Nationalist-held islands of Quemoy and Matsu off the China coast if attacked. Nixon favors defending them as a matter of "principle", while Kennedy opposes doing so on strategic and military grounds.	During his TV debate with Nixon, Kennedy suggests that Pres. Eisenhower should have tried to save the May summit by expressing "regret" to Khrushchev over the U-2 incident. . . . George Meany and other labor leaders meet with Defense Secy. Thomas Gates and pledge "full cooperation" to eliminate delays in the missile base program.	Labor Dept. reports 42 of the nation's 150 major industrial centers have an unemployment rate exceeding 6%.		NBA announces the granting of new team franchises to Chicago and Pittsburgh.	Oct. 7
				Arnold Palmer is named "golfer of the year" in a PGA poll.	Oct. 8
	The 18th American Assembly, meeting in New York, issues a report urging the reorganization and up-grading of the U.S. foreign service.	FAA reports over 70,000 civilian airplanes are now registered in the U.S.		Howard Glenn, 24, guard for the AFL's N.Y. Titans, dies of injuries suffered in a game against the Houston Oilers.	Oct. 9
Ex-Pres. Truman is quoted as telling a Texas audience that if they voted for Nixon "you ought to go to hell." Truman later denies the remark. Told of GOP demands for an apology, he says, "Tell 'em to go to hell." . . . *Christian Science Monitor* reports 768 of 2,834 school districts in 17 Southern states have begun desegregation.	Air Force's Winter Study Group makes public a plan to develop a system of back-up command centers capable of surviving an initial nuclear assault. . . . Senate Foreign Relations Committee Chmn. J. William Fulbright (D, Ark.) tells reporters the trend of General Assembly voting on Communist China indicates that it will ultimately be seated.				Oct. 10
In an Albuquerque speech, Nixon declares he will never hand "to the communists one inch of free territory." . . . Dr. Linus Pauling, U.S. Nobel Prize winner, refuses for the second time to give a Senate Internal Security subcommittee the names of scientists who helped him circulate an international petition calling for a nuclear weapons ban.	Air Force fails in its first attempt to place a reconnaissance satellite into earth orbit due to a malfunction in the last stage of the launch rocket.				Oct. 11

F	G	H	I	J
Includes elections, federal-state relations, civil rights and liberties, crime, the judiciary, education, health care, poverty, urban affairs and population.	Includes formation and debate of U.S. foreign and defense policies, veterans' affairs and defense spending. (Relations with specific foreign countries are usually found under the region concerned.)	Includes business, labor, agriculture, taxation, transportation, consumer affairs, monetary and fiscal policy, natural resources, and pollution.	Includes worldwide scientific, medical and technological developments, natural phenomena, U.S. weather, natural disasters, and accidents.	Includes the arts, religion, scholarship, communications media, sports, entertainment, fashions, fads and social life.

	World Affairs	Europe	Africa & the Middle East	The Americas	Asia & the Pacific
Oct. 12	Premier Khrushchev pounds his desk with his shoe in anger over a speech by Philippine delegate Lorenzo Sumulong condemning Soviet colonialism in East Europe. The incident comes in the midst of a debate on a Soviet resolution against colonialism which was finally suspended when U.N. General Assembly Pres. Frederick Boland (Ireland) broke his gavel trying to restore order.	East German Foreign Trade Ministry announces a partial embargo on Soviet bloc exports to West Germany in retaliation against the Adenauer government's threat not to renew a trade agreement with East Germany. . . . West Germany classifies as a state secret the reported discovery by a Frankfurt chemical firm of an inexpensive process for the production of fissionable uranium-235 from non-fissionable uranium-238.		Peruvian Chamber of Deputies endorses Pres. Pedro Beltran's plan to nationalize U.S.-owned oil properties in Peru.	Chmn. Inejiro Asanuma, 61, of Japan's Socialist Party and a leading opponent of the recent U.S.-Japanese security treaty, is stabbed to death by a 17-year old nationalist fanatic. . . . Castro Alejandro, military leader of the pro-Communist Huk Balahap rebels, is captured by Philippine police near Manila. . . . Indonesia issues a press decree banning all but "constructive" criticism of Pres. Sukarno's policies and programs.
Oct. 13	At his farewell appearance before the U.N. session, Khrushchev threatens a Soviet boycott of future disarmament talks unless they are limited to his proposals for total world disarmament.	USSR's Central Statistical Board reports Soviet industrial production rose 10% during the first nine months of 1960.	Sources in Portuguese Angola report 30 people have been killed and hundreds wounded in clashes between Portuguese troops and pro-independence demonstrators.	A U.S. citizen and 12 Cuban exiles are executed by Cuban authorities for their part in an Oct. 5 invasion aimed at overthrowing the Castro regime. Two other Americans are executed Oct. 16.	Typhoon Lola, the second major storm to hit the Philippines in a week, leaves 41 dead.
Oct. 14		The trials of ex-Turkish Premier Menderes and 526 former members of his regime on charges ranging from embezzlement to high treason begin before a special court on Yassi Ada island.		U.S. submits to the U.N. a detailed "fact sheet" refuting the anti-U.S. charges leveled by Cuban Premier Castro in his Sept. 26 U.N. address.	
Oct. 15		P.M. Macmillan tells a Conservative Party conference that he favors a renewed effort to hold a four-power summit meeting, particularly on the problems of Germany and Berlin.			Former Portuguese enclaves of Dadra and Nagar Aveli, north of Bombay, are officially transfered to Indian control.
Oct. 16			Congo leader Mobutu meets with Katanga chief Tshombe and they reportedly agree on the future of Katanga as an autonomous unit within the Congo Republic.		
Oct. 17	In its final session, the General Assembly unanimously adopts an Indian peace resolution calling upon all nations "to refrain from actions likely to aggravate international tensions."	The New York Times reports Yugoslav bishops have asked the government for a full restoration of Roman Catholic rights and properties.	French Roman Catholic cardinals and archbishops issue a statement in Paris deploring excesses committed by both sides in the continuing Algerian warfare. . . . Egyptian authorities report Suez Canal operations during 1959 yielded a profit of over $47 million, 16-and-a-half times the amount paid in royalties to Egypt in the last year before the canal was nationalized (1955).		U.S. resumes aid to Laos after a 10-day suspension ostensibly imposed to review the program in light of the confused fighting between neutralists, rightists and pro-Communists.
Oct. 18	A U.N. bulletin reports that trade in the non-Communist world rose to record levels during the first half of 1960.				Capt. Kong Le, the leader of the military coup that placed neutralist Souvanna Phouma in power, is placed under technical arrest for failing to heed Souvanna's order for a ceasefire in the fighting against rightist rebels.
Oct. 19		Ex-cabinet Min. Jacques Soustelle and other French rightists announce the creation of a National Regroupment movement to press for firm suppression of the Algerian revolution.	Agreements for the independence of Mauritania from France by late November are signed in Paris; it is the last of the 12 autonomous French Community states to be granted full independence.	Riots break out in Caracas, Venezuela following the arrest of three pro-Castro leftist leaders.	U.S. Development Loan Fund agrees to extend $25 million in credits to help India meet the capital requirements of its second five-year plan.
	A	**B**	**C**	**D**	**E**
	Includes developments that affect more than one world region, international organizations and important meetings of major world leaders.	*Includes all domestic and regional developments in Europe, including the Soviet Union, Turkey, Cyprus and Malta.*	*Includes all domestic and regional developments in Africa and the Middle East, including Iraq and Iran and excluding Cyprus, Turkey and Afghanistan.*	*Includes all domestic and regional developments in Latin America, the Caribbean and Canada.*	*Includes all domestic and regional developments in Asia and Pacific nations, extending from Afghanistan through all the Pacific Islands, except Hawaii.*

U.S. Politics & Social Issues	U.S. Foreign Policy & Defense	U.S. Economy & Environment	Science, Technology & Nature	Culture, Leisure & Life Style	
Speaking in Harlem, Lodge promises there will be a Negro in Nixon's cabinet if he is elected. Nixon later says he will appoint the best men regardless of race.	U.S. Secy. of State Herter is reportedly studying plans for a NATO air and submarine nuclear force under direct NATO command.				Oct. 12
A reiteration of their differences over Quemoy and Matsu dominates the third TV debate between Kennedy and Nixon. . . . A Nixon campaign source discloses that Pres. Eisenhower has agreed to serve as a roving goodwill ambassador in the Nixon administration, should Nixon win the election.	Ex-Pres. Truman charges that the Eisenhower-Nixon position on Cuba amounts to a surrender of the Monroe Doctrine.			Bill Mazeroski's home run in the bottom of the ninth gives Pittsburgh a 10-9 victory over the New York Yankees in the seventh and deciding game of the world series. . . . A federal jury acquits Thurman A. Whiteside of charges of conspiring with ex-FCC Commissioner Richard A. Mack to award a Miami TV station to a National Airlines subsidiary.	Oct. 13
Pres. Eisenhower turns 70, becoming the oldest man in American history to serve as President.				The 2.5-million member United Lutheran Church votes to merge with three other Lutheran bodies, which have a combined membership of 700,000.	Oct. 14
White House Press Secy. James Hagerty tells reporters that contrary to Democratic insinuations Nixon and Pres. Eisenhower are in full agreement on the Quemoy and Matsu question.					Oct. 15
		Commerce Secy. Frederick Mueller approves Toledo, O. as the site of the first foreign trade zone on the Great Lakes end of the St. Lawrence Seaway.		Abe Saperstein is elected commissioner of the newly-formed American Basketball Association.	Oct. 16
National chain stores report that lunch counters in 150 stores in 112 Southern towns have been integrated.	In a Detroit speech, Pres. Eisenhower calls upon other free nations to cooperate more actively in a worldwide program of mutual aid to stem the communist tide. . . . Lt. Gen. Arthur Trudeau tells a Philadelphia conference of U.S. engineers that the USSR can produce a missile almost 30% faster than the U.S.			The National League grants franchises to New York and Houston. The American League is to grant franchises to Los Angeles and Minneapolis-St. Paul Oct. 26 in the first major league baseball expansion in several decades. . . . The Rise and Fall of the Third Reich, a history of Nazi Germany by William L. Shirer, is published in N.Y. . . . Fourteen TV quiz winners, including Charles Van Doren, are arrested on charges of perjury for falsely testifying that they had not been given quiz answers in advance.	Oct. 17
Kennedy tells the annual convention of the American Legion the central issue of the day is the erosion of U.S. military power and influence after eight years of budget-cutting GOP leadership. . . . Pres. Eisenhower labels charges by Kennedy and other Democrats of a declining U.S. prestige as the thought of "fear-mongering people who like to peddle gloom." . . . Lodge again tells reporters that "there will be a qualified Negro in the cabinet" if Nixon is elected.	In a bridge dedication speech in Red Wing, Minn., Pres. Eisenhower calls upon Americans to give steadfast support to the U.N.	Representatives at the Appalachian Governors' Conference in Lexington, Ky. agree to work together to try to ease the region's chronic unemployment. . . . Pacific dock owners agree to provide a $5 million a year fund to the International Longshoremen's Union in exchange for union approval to mechanize and modernize dock operations. . . . Agriculture Dept. lifts all acreage restrictions on sugar beets for 1961.	Researchers at Indiana Univ. report the observation of hereditary changes in paramecia in which genes were not involved.	Casey Stengel, manager of the New York Yankees since 1949, is dismissed by the club owners after they refused his demand for sole authority over player policy. . . . Paul Richards of the Baltimore Orioles is named the American League's "manager of the year." Pittsburgh manager Danny Murtaugh won similar honors in the National League. . . . Never on Sunday, a Greek film directed by Jules Dassin and starring Melina Mercouri, is released in N.Y.	Oct. 18
		Dress industry employers and International Ladies Garment Workers Union agree on a program of payments into a fund for benefits to garment workers laid off because of business failures.			Oct. 19

F	G	H	I	J
Includes elections, federal-state relations, civil rights and liberties, crime, the judiciary, education, health care, poverty, urban affairs and population.	Includes formation and debate of U.S. foreign and defense policies, veterans' affairs and defense spending. (Relations with specific foreign countries are usually found under the region concerned.)	Includes business, labor, agriculture, taxation, transportation, consumer affairs, monetary and fiscal policy, natural resources, and pollution.	Includes worldwide scientific, medical and technological developments, natural phenomena, U.S. weather, natural disasters, and accidents.	Includes the arts, religion, scholarship, communications media, sports, entertainment, fashions, fads and social life.

	World Affairs	Europe	Africa & the Middle East	The Americas	Asia & the Pacific
Oct. 20	Premier Khrushchev, reporting to Moscow newsmen on his U.N. visit, says that the General Assembly's debate of his resolution against colonialism was a Soviet policy triumph. Khrushchev also reveals that the USSR has developed nuclear subs capable of launching missiles. . . . A recent heavy demand pushes the price of gold on the London market to a peak of $40.60.			U.S. State Dept. announces an immediate embargo on U.S. exports to Cuba; Amb. Philip Bonsal is recalled to Washington.	
Oct. 21	Soviet-bloc delegations make clear their refusal to contribute to the cost of U.N. operations in the Congo.	Britain launches its first nuclear submarine, the 3,500-ton *Dreadnought*.	Pres. de Gaulle appeals for French national unity on Algeria, where "peace is at the door."		
Oct. 22		Khrushchev tells a delegation of Cuban journalists visiting Moscow that Soviet per capita production will be "much greater" than U.S. by 1980.	The second Arab Petroleum Congress, meeting in Beirut, resolves to seek greater control over the price-setting and related policies of foreign-owned oil companies operating in Arab states.		
Oct. 23			Algerian Provisional Premier Ferhat Abbas says that rebel leaders, despairing of a negotiated settlement or of Western aid, are "finding the support we need among the communists."	Puerto Rico's three Roman Catholic bishops order the island's Catholics not to vote for Gov. Luiz Munoz Marin's Popular Democratic Party Nov. 8. They assail the party's stand on birth control and common law marriage. . . . *The New York Times* reports Dominican Republic exiles are meeting in Venezuela to organize a drive to oust the Trujillo regime.	
Oct. 24		West Berlin receives a special message from Pres. Eisenhower reaffirming continued American support of the city's freedom.	Drunken and unruly Congolese troops are reported terrorizing the African quarter of Leopoldville.	Pres. Eisenhower stops for a brief goodwill meeting with Mexican Pres. Adolfo Lopez Mateos in Ciudad Acuna on the Mexican-U.S. border.	Japanese Premier Hayato Ikeda's Liberal-Democratic Party votes to hold national elections Nov. 20 to provide a tension-resolving referendum on the new U.S.-Japanese security treaty.
Oct. 25	Cuban Foreign Min. Raul Roa tells the U.N. General Assembly that the U.S. is preparing a "massive invasion" of Cuba. The U.S. delegation dismisses the charges as a "reckless" attempt to create a "false crisis."	French National Assembly approves the authorization of $1.2 billion over the next three years for the development of an independent French nuclear strike force. . . . P.M. Macmillan reports to Parliament on the achievement of a "satisfactory" agreement with the U.S. concerning prior consultation over missions undertaken by U.S. planes based in Britain. . . . An agreement for training West German army and air force units at French bases is signed and made public in Paris.	A Cairo court convicts six foreigners and 11 Egyptians on charges of spying for Israel.	Cuba nationalizes 166 U.S.-owned enterprises, valued at $250 million, in retaliation against the U.S. embargo on exports to Cuba.	
Oct. 26		The three Western allies warn the USSR that they would hold it fully responsible for the consequences of any attempt to restrict the use of air corridors linking Berlin with West Germany.	Belgium rejects a note from Sec. Gen. Hammarskjold protesting the reported return of many former Belgian colonial officials to Katanga and calling their presence a cause of continuing tension. . . . Mutinies, riots and disorder among the Congolese army troops in Leopoldville endanger the interim High Commission government of Col. Mobutu. At U.N. request, Mobutu orders the army confined to barracks in an effort to restore discipline.	A six-man junta in El Salvador overthrows the government of Pres. José Maria Lemus in a bloodless coup. Lemus flees to Costa Rica.	Gen. Toshizo Nishio, 78, commander of the Japanese armed forces in China during W.W. II, dies in Tokyo.

A	B	C	D	E
Includes developments that affect more than one world region, international organizations and important meetings of major world leaders.	Includes all domestic and regional developments in Europe, including the Soviet Union, Turkey, Cyprus and Malta.	Includes all domestic and regional developments in Africa and the Middle East, including Iraq and Iran and excluding Cyprus, Turkey and Afghanistan.	Includes all domestic and regional developments in Latin America, the Caribbean and Canada.	Includes all domestic and regional developments in Asia and Pacific nations, extending from Afghanistan through all the Pacific Islands, except Hawaii.

U.S. Politics & Social Issues	U.S. Foreign Policy & Defense	U.S. Economy & Environment	Science, Technology & Nature	Culture, Leisure & Life Style	
Sen. J. William Fulbright (D, Ark.) accuses the State Dept. and the White House of trying to help Nixon by suppressing a U.S. Information Agency survey documenting a decline in U.S. world prestige.	Kennedy issues a four-point program for dealing with the Cuban situation which includes a pledge to support anti-Castro forces in exile. . . . Army, Navy, Air Force and Marine Corps agree to work together on the development of a transport plane that can take off and land vertically.	President's Council of Economic Advisers reports the annual rate of the U.S. GNP declined slightly during the third quarter of this year. . . . Of the major labor unions endorsing presidential candidates, all are backing Kennedy except for Hawaii's International Longshoremen's Union which announced for Nixon.	Sir MacFarlane Burnet, of Melbourne Univ., and Peter B. Medawar, professor of zoology at London Univ., win the Nobel Prize for medicine for their research in immunological tolerance; their work has been viewed as a step toward the transplantation of human organs.		Oct. 20
During their fourth TV debate, Nixon counters Kennedy's charge of inaction toward Cuba by claiming that Kennedy's own proposal to encourage anti-Castro exiles amounts to an illegal intervention in Cuban affairs. A renewal of differences over Quemoy and Matsu and U.S. prestige levels dominates the rest of the debate.		Treasury Dept. publicly denies European rumors that the U.S. is considering devaluation of the dollar.	American Telephone and Telegraph Co. discloses plans to launch an earth satellite for use in a trans-Atlantic telephone-TV communications system.		Oct. 21
Nixon charges that Kennedy's proposal to support an anti-Castro revolution in Cuba is "the most...reckless...ever made...by a presidential candidate."		International Union of Electrical Workers ends a three-week strike against General Electric after agreeing to accept GE's insistence on cancellation of the cost-of-living escalator clause.	American Heart Association presents the Albert Lasker Awards to Dr. Karl Link, Dr. Irving Wright and Dr. Edgar Allen for their work on anticoagulants for heart disease.	Artists Marc Chagall and Oskar Kokoschka are awarded the $15,000 Erasmus Prize for 1960.	Oct. 22
Kennedy denies he has advocated intervention in Cuba, claiming that he only proposed giving the strongest possible moral support to the forces of freedom.				British racer Stirling Moss, driving a Lotus Monte Carlo, wins the Pacific Grand Prix in Monterey, Calif.	Oct. 23
	Justice Dept. turns down a request for parole from Harry Gold, imprisoned former Soviet agent involved in the Rosenberg spy case.			National Council of Churches reports that U.S. church membership in 1959 rose to a record 112 million, including 65.5 million Protestants, 41 million Roman Catholics, and 5.5 million Jews.	Oct. 24
Rev. Martin Luther King, one of 80 persons arrested during mass sit-in demonstrations in Atlanta Oct. 22, is sentenced to four months in prison for violating an earlier probated traffic sentence.	Adlai Stevenson tells a Bethesda, Md. audience that the main effect of the administration's embargo on Cuba will be to drive Castro "further into the Soviet orbit."		Harry Ferguson, Irish-born inventor and automotive pioneer who won a $350 million settlement from Henry Ford Sr. after accusing him of infringing on his farm tractor patents, dies in England at 75.	National Boxing Assn. withdraws its recognition of Archie Moore as world lightheavyweight champion for the second time this year because of his failure to defend his title.	Oct. 25
Two N.Y. youths who founded a Nazi-like party are acquitted of charges of conspiring to assault Jews.				French-born poet Alexis Leger St. Leger, 73, wins the Nobel Prize for literature. A pioneer of modern poetry, he writes under the pen name of St. John Perse.	Oct. 26

F	G	H	I	J
Includes elections, federal-state relations, civil rights and liberties, crime, the judiciary, education, health care, poverty, urban affairs and population.	Includes formation and debate of U.S. foreign and defense policies, veterans' affairs and defense spending. (Relations with specific foreign countries are usually found under the region concerned.)	Includes business, labor, agriculture, taxation, transportation, consumer affairs, monetary and fiscal policy, natural resources, and pollution.	Includes worldwide scientific, medical and technological developments, natural phenomena, U.S. weather, natural disasters, and accidents.	Includes the arts, religion, scholarship, communications media, sports, entertainment, fashions, fads and social life.

	World Affairs	Europe	Africa & the Middle East	The Americas	Asia & the Pacific
Oct. 27	U.N. General Assembly unanimously adopts an amended version of the "food for peace" program proposed by Pres. Eisenhower in his Sept. 22 address to the U.N. . . . FBI arrests Igor Melekh, a Soviet citizen and chief of the U.N.'s Russian language section, on charges of espionage. Soviet delegation to the U.N. condemns the arrest as harassment designed to prevent Russians from getting high U.N. posts.	Austria and Italy announce resumption of negotiations on their dispute over the German-language Bolzano area of northern Italy.			A Japanese-North Korean agreement for the voluntary repatriation of Koreans from Japan to North Korea is officially extended for one year. About 40,000 Koreans have already taken advantage of the treaty. Laotian Premier Souvanna Phouma announces he has accepted "in principle" a Soviet offer of aid to his neutralist regime.
Oct. 28	For the 17th time since 1901, the Nobel Peace Prize Committee decides that no prize will be given in 1960.			U.S. State Dept. in a note to the OAS charges Soviet bloc nations with supplying Cuba "thousands of tons" of weapons to further the spread of revolution in Latin America. . . . U.S. transfers to Panama part of the U.S.-owned Panama Railroad.	
Oct. 29	Sec. Gen. Hammarskjold names a 15-nation Asian-African conciliation team to go to the Congo and seek a political agreement among Lumumba, Kasavubu, Mobutu and other rival leaders.	*The New York Times* reports that three prominent leaders of the 1956 Hungarian revolt are being retried by a Budapest military court in an alleged attempt to change their sentences from life imprisonment to death. . . . West German government announces that Alfred Frenzel, a Socialist deputy in the Bundestag, has been arrested on charges of spying for Czechoslovakia.	Col. Mobutu tells newsmen that as long as he is in power the Soviets will never be allowed to regain their former influence in Congolese affairs.	In a Tass interview, Premier Khrushchev renews his promise to aid Cuba with Soviet rockets in the event it is attacked by the U.S.	
Oct. 30				Thousands of Cuban militiamen are placed on special alert to prepare for an "imminent U.S. invasion."	
Oct. 31			A seven-member cabinet committee is appointed to study secret material on the forced resignation of Israeli Secy. Gen. Pinhas Lavon in 1955 as defense minister as the result of false testimony and charges by a group in the Defense Ministry. . . . A male heir is born to Shah Mohammed Rezi Pahlevi of Iran.	Cuban government announces a ban on the emigration of technically-skilled persons.	Over 4,000 persons die in the second tidal wave to hit the Bay of Bengal region of East Pakistan this month. The earlier wave, on Oct. 10, killed almost 6,000. . . . Nepalese troops arrest persons believed to be responsible for recent provincial uprisings.
Nov. 1	General Assembly votes 45-29 to reject a Soviet-supported Cuban request for an immediate Assembly debate of alleged U.S. aggression against Cuba.	P.M. Macmillan announces that Britain has agreed to the basing of U.S. nuclear-powered Polaris submarines at Holy Loch, Scotland.	French military sources report that an estimated 172,000 people have died in Algerian fighting since 1954, including 145,000 rebels, 13,000 French soldiers and 14,000 Moslem and European civilians.	Pres. Eisenhower declares the U.S. will take "whatever steps" are necessary to maintain its treaty-guaranteed rights at the Guantanamo naval base in Cuba.	
Nov. 2			Emperor Haile Selassie opens Parliament with a speech praising both U.S. and Soviet aid to Ethiopia.	U.S. Navy announces it has placed clearly marked land mines around its Guantanamo (Cuba) naval base to defend against a possible attack. Cuban Pres. Osvaldo Dorticos Torrado claims Cuba will "never commit the stupidity" of assaulting the base.	South Korean House of Representatives votes to request South Korean admission to the U.N. . . . A Thai agreement to establish relations with the USSR is disclosed in Bangkok. . . . Otoya Yamaguchi, 17, assassin of Japanese Socialist leader Inejiro Asanuma, hangs himself in a Tokyo prison.

A	B	C	D	E
Includes developments that affect more than one world region, international organizations and important meetings of major world leaders.	*Includes all domestic and regional developments in Europe, including the Soviet Union, Turkey, Cyprus and Malta.*	*Includes all domestic and regional developments in Africa and the Middle East, including Iraq and Iran and excluding Cyprus, Turkey and Afghanistan.*	*Includes all domestic and regional developments in Latin America, the Caribbean and Canada.*	*Includes all domestic and regional developments in Asia and Pacific nations, extending from Afghanistan through all the Pacific Islands, except Hawaii.*

U.S. Politics & Social Issues	U.S. Foreign Policy & Defense	U.S. Economy & Environment	Science, Technology & Nature	Culture, Leisure & Life Style	
Rev. Martin Luther King is released on bond from Ga. state prison after serving five days of a four-month sentence for violation of a probated traffic court sentence. The release comes one day after Sen. Kennedy telephoned Mrs. King promising to intervene on her husband's behalf. . . . Nixon issues a campaign statement pledging to visit every Eastern European nation with "the message of freedom" if elected President. . . . *The New York Times* endorses Kennedy for President.	A Joint Congressional Economic sub-committee reports that a consolidation and reform of procurement procedures by the separate branches of the armed forces could save the government $2 billion plus annually.				Oct. 27
Pres. Eisenhower steps up his political activity on behalf of the GOP ticket in a series of speeches stressing Nixon's "experience and maturity" for national leadership.		Terence McShane is ousted as chairman of the Teamsters' monitors when an appeals court rules the union can veto the appointment of a chairman. . . . Pres. Maurice Hutcheson and two other officials of the AFL-CIO Brotherhood of Carpenters are convicted in Indianapolis of bribery involving quick-profit land deals. Hutcheson is later sentenced to a two-to-12-year prison term.		Thomas Edison, Henry David Thoreau and composer Edward MacDowell are enshrined in NYU's Hall of Fame for Great Americans.	Oct. 28
					Oct. 29
Responding to GOP criticism, Kennedy pledges to pursue sound fiscal policies and not to devalue the dollar.		Kennedy says that if elected he will work to remove artificial barriers to U.S. foreign trade as a way of improving the U.S. payments balance.			Oct. 30
	Defense Dept. orders more rapid development of the B-70 supersonic bomber. The acceleration was made possible by Congress' authorization of $190 million more than the administration had requested for the B-70. . . . A House subcommittee asks the White House for documents concerning audits and reports of possible malfeasance in aid programs for Latin America.	Sewell Lee Avery, 86, former Montgomery Ward chairman who was bodily removed from his Chicago offices after refusing to comply with a 1944 War Labor Board order extending an unexpired CIO contract, dies in Chicago.		Dutch painter Karel Appel receives the 1960 Guggenheim International Art Award for his abstract painting *Woman with Ostrich*.	Oct. 31
		A last minute contract agreement on wage hikes averts a threatened newspaper strike against all New York dailies. . . . ICC agrees to guarantee a $4.5-million Chase Manhattan Bank loan to the New Haven Railroad.			Nov. 1
Pres. Eisenhower campaigns vigorously for the Nixon-Lodge ticket in N.Y.C. and its suburbs. . . . Montgomery, Ala. voter registrars rule Martin Luther King ineligible to cast an absentee ballot in the Nov. 8 election because of an unpaid poll tax.	In a TV address Kennedy proposes that U.S. aid missions to underdeveloped countries be supplemented by a volunteer "peace corps" of young Americans who would provide technical assistance and act as goodwill ambassadors.	Labor Dept. reports the 1950s witnessed "steady improvement in the social and economic status of Negroes." The figures, however, show that in certain economic areas Negro gains fell short of comparable advances made by the white population.	Dr. Ralph Falk, 77, who contributed to the development of the first medically acceptable intravenous feeding solutions, dies in Chicago.	A London jury rules that D.H. Lawrence's *Lady Chatterley's Lover* is not obscene in the first major test of Britain's new obscene publications law. . . . Conductor Dimitri Mitropoulos, 64, dies of a heart attack in Milan while rehearsing at La Scala. . . . John Updike's novel *Rabbit, Run* is published in New York.	Nov. 2

F	G	H	I	J
Includes elections, federal-state relations, civil rights and liberties, crime, the judiciary, education, health care, poverty, urban affairs and population.	*Includes formation and debate of U.S. foreign and defense policies, veterans' affairs and defense spending. (Relations with specific foreign countries are usually found under the region concerned.)*	*Includes business, labor, agriculture, taxation, transportation, consumer affairs, monetary and fiscal policy, natural resources, and pollution.*	*Includes worldwide scientific, medical and technological developments, natural phenomena, U.S. weather, natural disasters, and accidents.*	*Includes the arts, religion, scholarship, communications media, sports, entertainment, fashions, fads and social life.*

	World Affairs	Europe	Africa & the Middle East	The Americas	Asia & the Pacific
Nov. 3	In a report to the General Assembly, U.N. Rep.-to-Congo Rajeshwar Dayal warns of deteriorating conditions due to the inability of the Mobutu regime to restore authority and to the growing intervention by returning Belgian colonial officials. He concludes that restoration of Pres. Kasavubu and the Lumumba-controlled Congo parliament may offer the only hope for restoring order.	Hugh Gaitskell retains leadership of Britain's Parliamentary Labor Party by defeating Harold Wilson in a poll of Laborite MPs. Wilson had offered himself as a compromise candidate between leftists favoring unilateral British nuclear disarmament and the more conservative Laborites led by Gaitskell. . . . Leftists in the British Labor Party sharply criticize the government's decision to permit the basing of U.S. Polaris submarines at Holy Loch, Scotland.		State Dept. announces the U.S. plans to give $10 million in grants and credits to the new Central American Bank for Economic Integration. . . . Ambassadors to Cuba from Brazil, Argentina, Canada, Mexico, France, and the UAR unite in an "action committee" to try to end the Cuban government's practice of ignoring their formal protests.	India's Maharashtra State begins a program of compensation payments ($4.20) to all males submitting to sterilization through vasectomy.
Nov. 4	U.N. delegations from Belgium and the U.S. deny Dayal's charges that Belgian actions were hindering solution of the Congo crisis. . . . Igor Melekh, a Soviet U.N. employee arrested for alleged espionage, is released from a New York prison on $50,000 bail.		French Pres. de Gaulle, in a nationwide TV address, pledges to respect the formation of an independent Algerian republic if a proper election shows that a majority of Algerian Moslems desire it. He adds that preparations for such an election must await the achievement of a secure ceasefire.		
Nov. 5			*Pravda* reports a deterioration in Soviet-Iraqi relations which it attributes to increasing anti-Communist influence in the Iraqi government.		
Nov. 6		Erich Raeder, 84, German navy commander during W.W. II and Nuremberg war criminal, dies in Kiel.		Cuban exiles announce in New York the formation of a Revolutionary Movement of the People to overthrow the Castro regime.	
Nov. 7	Congo Pres. Kasavubu arrives in New York to appeal personally for U.N. recognition of the anti-Lumumba delegation which he and Col. Mobutu have selected to represent the Congo in the General Assembly.	Returns from local elections in Italy reveal that centrist candidates outpolled leftists in provincial races, but that leftists scored majorities in the municipalities.	French rightists in Algeria and France denounce de Gaulle's latest Algerian declaration as a virtual endorsement of the rebel drive for complete independence. . . . Britain announces Zanzibar will be granted self-government under its elected Legislative Council in January 1961.	Argentine workers go out in a 24-hour general strike to protest Pres. Arturo Frondizi's veto of a bill raising severance pay. . . . A 24-hour general strike disrupts Chile as workers protest a 10% wage hike as inadequate.	
Nov. 8		British P.M. Macmillan declares there is an understanding that the U.S. will not use nuclear weapons without "the fullest consultations with her allies."	Eight Irish members of the U.N. Force in the Congo are killed by Baluba tribesmen while on patrol in northern Katanga.	Gov. Luis Munoz Marin is re-elected governor of Puerto Rico by a landslide despite the opposition of Roman Catholic bishops. . . . A strike by about 500,000 federal transportation workers closes most of Brazil's ports and railroads. . . . Following talks with British and West Indian officials the U.S. agrees to give up its military bases in the West Indies.	South Vietnam charges North Vietnam with beginning a direct invasion from bases in Laos.
Nov. 9	Khrushchev telegrams congratulations to Pres.-elect Kennedy and expresses hope for an improvement in Soviet-American relations as "in Franklin Roosevelt's time."	A Madrid court orders 10 prominent Spaniards to face trial on charges of publicly criticizing the Franco regime and of attempting to form an opposition political organization.			

A	B	C	D	E
Includes developments that affect more than one world region, international organizations and important meetings of major world leaders.	Includes all domestic and regional developments in Europe, including the Soviet Union, Turkey, Cyprus and Malta.	Includes all domestic and regional developments in Africa and the Middle East, including Iraq and Iran and excluding Cyprus, Turkey and Afghanistan.	Includes all domestic and regional developments in Latin America, the Caribbean and Canada.	Includes all domestic and regional developments in Asia and Pacific nations, extending from Afghanistan through all the Pacific Islands, except Hawaii.

U.S. Politics & Social Issues	U.S. Foreign Policy & Defense	U.S. Economy & Environment	Science, Technology & Nature	Culture, Leisure & Life Style	
	In an open letter to both presidential candidates ex-AEC commissioner Thomas Murray warns that the Soviets may have developed an enormously powerful neutron bomb. He adds the U.S. will not be able to make a comparable weapon until the moratorium on nuclear testing is lifted.	Labor Dept. reports there were fewer strikes during the first nine months of 1960 than in any similar period since W.W. II.	Ex-U.S. Atomic Energy Commission Prof. Willard F. Libby wins the Nobel Prize in chemistry for his invention of a device to determine the age of objects by measuring their radioactivity. . . . An Explorer VIII satellite, carrying instruments to survey the ionosphere, is successfully launched from Cape Canaveral.	Pittsburgh Pirates pitcher Vernon Law wins the Cy Young Award for 1960.	**Nov. 3**
Lyndon Johnson is booed and jostled by a Dallas crowd angry over his support of the party's civil rights plank.			Dr. Frederic H. Coensegen of the Lawrence Radiation Laboratory announces a controlled thermonuclear reaction has been achieved at the Livermore, Calif. laboratory. . . . Sir Harold Spencer Jones, 70, British astronomer who headed a 12-year project to determine precisely the sun's distance from the earth (calculated at 93,005,000 miles in 1942), dies in London.		**Nov. 4**
Editor and Publisher magazine reports that 731 U.S. daily papers have endorsed Nixon, while 208 have backed Kennedy. Despite the lead, Nixon's support is lowest ever given to a GOP candidate in the 24 years of the *E&P* poll.	Air Force reports that in light of recent successful tests the first Minuteman ICBM missile squadron will be operational by July 1962, one year ahead of schedule.	A federal court orders five major rail companies to pay compensation to a Kansas City trucking firm which the court says they conspired to put out of business.		Silent film comedian Mack Sennett dies in Woodland Hills, Calif.	**Nov. 5**
Louisiana legislature passes a package of 28 bills aimed at blocking federally ordered public school desegregation. The measures include a bill voiding federal orders considered unconstitutional and another authorizing the legislature's take-over of the New Orleans School Board which has indicated a readiness to begin integration.	A U.S. Army study suggests that the U.S. may fall below the USSR in military might because of "a gap in cold war outlays in favor of the USSR."				**Nov. 6**
On election eve, the Gallup and Princeton Research Service polls indicate that Kennedy will win by a 1% to 3% margin. The final Roper Associates poll, however, shows Nixon with a slight lead. . . . The second murder trial of Dr. R. Bernard Finch and his mistress Carole Tregoff ends with another hung jury in Los Angeles.				USSR wins the Olympic chess tourney in Leipzig, East Germany; U.S. places second.	**Nov. 7**
By a narrow margin, Kennedy defeats Nixon to become the 35th President of the U.S. Kennedy, 43, is the youngest man and first Roman Catholic to win the nation's highest office. Sen. Lyndon Baines Johnson, 52, of Texas is elected Vice President. . . . Democrats retain firm control of Congress, although Republicans make small gains in both houses. Final returns show the Senate with 64 Democrats, 36 Republicans and the House with 260 Democrats, 177 Republicans. Democrats also capture 15 of the 27 contested gubernatorial races.				Norma Gladys Cappagli, 21, of Argentina wins the Miss World Beauty Contest in London.	**Nov. 8**
With late returns confirming Kennedy's narrow victory, Nixon formally concedes defeat at 9:45 A.M. (Pacific time) in a congratulatory telegram to Kennedy. . . . Conservative Republican Barry Goldwater (Ariz.) attributes the GOP defeat to Nixon's stance as a "me-too candidate"; Goldwater adds: "I want to figure in 1964."		A two-day strike by 4,600 New York teachers, the first in the city's history, ends as teachers accept a school board offer to drop suspension orders against those who return to work. . . . Robert McNamara, 44, is appointed president of Ford Motor Co., succeeding Henry Ford II.	Dr. Emery Rovenstine, 65, leading international anesthesiologist, dies in New York.		**Nov. 9**
F	G	H	I	J	
Includes elections, federal-state relations, civil rights and liberties, crime, the judiciary, education, health care, poverty, urban affairs and population.	*Includes formation and debate of U.S. foreign and defense policies, veterans' affairs and defense spending. (Relations with specific foreign countries are usually found under the region concerned.)*	*Includes business, labor, agriculture, taxation, transportation, consumer affairs, monetary and fiscal policy, natural resources, and pollution.*	*Includes worldwide scientific, medical and technological developments, natural phenomena, U.S. weather, natural disasters, and accidents.*	*Includes the arts, religion, scholarship, communications media, sports, entertainment, fashions, fads and social life.*	

	World Affairs	Europe	Africa & the Middle East	The Americas	Asia & the Pacific
Nov. 10	Communist party leaders from 81 nations gather in Moscow for a world Communist congress.	West German Chancellor Adenauer urges Pres.-elect Kennedy and Premier Khrushchev to clarify their current views on world problems before an attempt is made to set up a Big Four summit meeting.	*New York Herald Tribune* reports French Pres. de Gaulle has informed the Debré cabinet that he will order preliminary action designed to bring about the creation of an "Algerian Republic" in which the major posts will be held by Moslems. Some opposition within the cabinet is expected.		A group of South Vietnamese paratroopers launch an attempted coup against the government of Ngo Dinh Diem; fighting is reported near the presidential palace.
Nov. 11			Paris newspaper *Le Monde* reports French troops in various parts of Algeria are making preliminary contacts with local rebel leaders in an attempt to negotiate informal truce agreements.	A 200-300 man Nicaraguan rebel force invades Nicaragua from Costa Rica, capturing three towns in Carazo Province. . . . U.S. State Dept. charges Cuba with discrimination by national origin in the execution of three Americans charged with participating in an Oct. 5 invasion of Oriente Province. . . . Brazilian transport workers end their strike after a promise of a pay raise.	Laotian military commanders in the royal capital of Luang Prubang publicly renounce their allegiance to Prince Souvanna's neutralist Vientiane government and proclaim their support for Gen. Phoumi's anti-Communist Savannakhet committee.
Nov. 12		Khrushchev renews his call for talks among all "interested nations" on a W.W. II peace treaty with East and West Germany.	AP reports Congolese troops loyal to pro-Lumumba leader Antoine Gizenga have gained virtual control over the city of Stanleyville in Oriental Province.		South Vietnamese troops loyal to Pres. Ngo Dinh Diem crush an attempted Saigon coup against his regime by dissident paratroop units.
Nov. 13	*The New York Times* reports that a group of prominent Americans and Russians, some of them close to Kennedy and Khrushchev, have met in private talks at Dartmouth College.	Turkish Pres. Cemal Gursel announces that he is replacing the military-dominated National Union Committee with a new civilian body as a step toward the return of democratic rule.		U.S. Commerce Dept. reports that the Cuban government has seized nearly $1 billion worth of U.S.-owned property since the Castro regime came to power.	Conservative pro-U.S. candidates win an overwhelming victory in local elections for the Okinawa legislature over leftists who favor an immediate U.S. withdrawal from the island.
Nov. 14	Belgian Foreign Min. Pierre Wigny denounces U.N. operations in the Congo as a "failure" and warns that Belgium may quit the U.N. if Hammarskjold persists in his "stupid" demand for the withdrawal of all Belgian nationals from the Congo.		France announces that several nearly pacified areas of Algeria have been set aside as truce zones to demonstrate the conditions envisaged by Pres. de Gaulle after the achievement of an Algerian ceasefire.	Costa Rican authorities claim that Cuban-marked planes have been sighted dropping supplies to Nicaraguan rebels encamped along the Nicaragua-Costa Rica border.	
Nov. 15		USSR announces a 10% upward revaluation of the ruble. . . . Premier Viggo Kampmann's Social Democratic Party increases its parliamentary strength in Denmark's general elections but still lacks an absolute majority.	Morocco announces it has accepted an offer of military aid from the USSR.		
Nov. 16	U.N. Secy. Gen. Hammarskjold temporarily postpones sending the 15-nation political conciliation group to the Congo in the face of Congolese Pres. Kasavubu's public opposition to the proposed mission.		French cabinet discloses that Pres. de Gaulle is planning to hold a national referendum on a bill for the interim reorganization of the Algerian administration pending the achievement of self-determination. . . . Israeli Premier David Ben-Gurion denies that the resignation of Pinhas Lavon was engineered by a clique within the defense ministry.	Pres. Eisenhower orders U.S. Navy warships to patrol the Caribbean waters off Guatemala and Nicaragua in an effort to prevent a suspected Communist-led invasion of the two countries from Cuba. According to the U.S. State Dept., Guatemala and Nicaragua formally requested the protection. . . . Guatemalan troops crush a three-day revolt by leftist army officers.	Laotian Premier Souvanna Phouma protests the continuation of U.S. military aid to rightist army units in revolt against his neutralist cabinet.
Nov. 17		Khrushchev formally opens the USSR's new Friendship University for foreign students.			Laos' neutralist cabinet announces plans to establish relations with Communist China and North Vietnam.

A	B	C	D	E
Includes developments that affect more than one world region, international organizations and important meetings of major world leaders.	*Includes all domestic and regional developments in Europe, including the Soviet Union, Turkey, Cyprus and Malta.*	*Includes all domestic and regional developments in Africa and the Middle East, including Iraq and Iran and excluding Cyprus, Turkey and Afghanistan.*	*Includes all domestic and regional developments in Latin America, the Caribbean and Canada.*	*Includes all domestic and regional developments in Asia and Pacific nations, extending from Afghanistan through all the Pacific Islands, except Hawaii.*

U.S. Politics & Social Issues	U.S. Foreign Policy & Defense	U.S. Economy & Environment	Science, Technology & Nature	Culture, Leisure & Life Style	
Kennedy accepts an invitation to meet with Pres. Eisenhower to make all necessary arrangements for an "orderly transfer of executive responsibility." . . . U.S. District Judge J. Skelly Wright issues restraining orders nullifying Louisiana's just passed anti-integration laws, including a measure which gave control of New Orleans schools to a committee of the state legislature.	Pres.-elect Kennedy tells reporters that he intends to retain Allen Dulles as CIA director and J. Edgar Hoover as FBI chief.			Dr. Isadore Freed, 60, Russian-born composer, pianist and founder of the Philadelphia Chamber Orchestra, dies of a heart attack in Oceanside, New York.	Nov. 10
N.C. Gov. Luther Hodges commutes the 15-day jail sentences of six Negroes convicted of trespassing in 1956 on a "white only" city-owned Greensboro golf course on the condition they pay $7,000 in accumulated court costs.	In a British TV interview, Kennedy adviser Chester Bowles urges a "two-China policy" for the U.S. The statement brings immediate GOP attacks. Bowles's office says the interview was taped before the election.	A six-week bus strike in Miami, Fla. ends when drivers agree to a new wage pact.			Nov. 11
					Nov. 12
A second special session of the La. legislature convenes at Gov. Jimmie Davis's request to discuss the school integration crisis again; within hours the legislature passes measures reasserting its control over New Orleans schools and closing all La. schools Nov. 14, the date scheduled for court-ordered integration.	Associate Supreme Court Justice William O. Douglas urges the admission of Communist China to the U.N. in the hope that U.N. membership would help curb China's "outlaw" policies.			Negro entertainer Sammy Davis Jr., 34, marries Swedish actress May Britt, 24.	Nov. 13
Despite persistent obstruction by state officials, U.S. marshals enforce La.'s first court-ordered integration by escorting four Negro students past angry white crowds into two New Orleans schools. . . . Supreme Court rules a 1957 Alabama law resetting the boundaries of Tuskegee is unconstitutional if Negro voters were effectively eliminated by the change. . . . HEW begins hearings on a 1960 La. law prohibiting relief payments to families headed by an unmarried parent; about 95% of the affected families are black.	Asst. Defense Secy. Frank Berry warns that doctors will have to be drafted into the army unless there is an immediate increase in the number of physicians who volunteer.	A seven-year cartel suit against Standard Oil of New Jersey and Gulf Oil Corp. ends with both firms agreeing to refrain from price-fixing and market control practices.		André Malraux's *Metamorphosis of the Gods* is published in N.Y. in a translation by Stuart Gilbert. . . . *The Virgin Spring*, a Swedish film directed by Ingmar Bergman, is released in New York.	Nov. 14
Census Bureau reports U.S. population stood at 179,323,175 as of April 1. Population shifts will require changing the representation from 25 states in the U.S. House. California will gain eight seats.	*U.S.S. George Washington* becomes the first atomic submarine to put to sea armed with nuclear missiles.	Pres. Eisenhower announces the establishment of a permanent Committee on Migratory Labor to advise the President.			Nov. 15
Final vote tallies show Kennedy with an electoral vote total of 300 to Nixon's 223.	Convicted atomic-secret spy David Greenglass is released on parole after serving almost nine-and-a-half years of a 15-year sentence.	Pres. Eisenhower orders all federal agencies to cut overseas expenses wherever possible in an effort to slow the outflow of U.S. gold caused by a growing balance of payments deficit; he specifically orders a 60% reduction in the number of civilian and military dependents living abroad.		Clark Gable, celebrated Hollywood film star and winner of an Academy Award for his role in *It Happened One Night* (1934), dies of a heart attack at 59.	Nov. 16
New Orleans suffers the worse riots since local schools were integrated as nearly 200 are arrested. . . . Univ. of Tennessee trustees vote to admit Negro undergraduates for the first time.				Dick Groat of the Pittsburgh Pirates is named the National League's Most Valuable Player for 1960.	Nov. 17

F	G	H	I	J
Includes elections, federal-state relations, civil rights and liberties, crime, the judiciary, education, health care, poverty, urban affairs and population.	Includes formation and debate of U.S. foreign and defense policies, veterans' affairs and defense spending. (Relations with specific foreign countries are usually found under the region concerned.)	Includes business, labor, agriculture, taxation, transportation, consumer affairs, monetary and fiscal policy, natural resources, and pollution.	Includes worldwide scientific, medical and technological developments, natural phenomena, U.S. weather, natural disasters, and accidents.	Includes the arts, religion, scholarship, communications media, sports, entertainment, fashions, fads and social life.

	World Affairs	Europe	Africa & the Middle East	The Americas	Asia & the Pacific
Nov. 18		Paul Faure, 82, French Socialist leader who was barred from postwar politics because of alleged collaboration with the Nazis, dies in Paris. . . . British National Service Ministry announces the end of military conscription, in effect since June 1939.		International Court of Justice in The Hague awards Honduras sovereignty over 300 square miles of disputed border land claimed by Nicaragua. . . . Cuban Foreign Min. Raul Roa denounces U.S. naval patrols in the Caribbean as an act of aggression. . . . U.S. State Dept. claims Soviet weaponry and mass conscription have increased Cuba's armed forces 10-fold over the past year, making it "far larger than any other army in Latin America."	
Nov. 19	Soviet Rep.-to-U.N. Valerian Zorin charges that the U.S. and Belgium have used the U.N. to install Col. Mobutu's "pro-Fascist band" as rulers of the Congo. . . . Semi-annual session of the General Agreement on Tariffs and Trade ends in Geneva after approving plans to deal with the disruption of markets caused by sudden waves of cheap imports.		Algerian Provisional Government condemns de Gaulle's plans to reorganize the Algerian administration as simply another maneuver to postpone genuine self-determination.	Diplomatic sources in Havana report that the USSR has urged the Castro regime to ease its attacks upon the U.S., especially its threat to use Soviet rockets. . . . The U.S. protests to the Cuban Foreign Ministry the near fatal shooting of a U.S. Embassy clerk in Havana by a Cuban army officer.	
Nov. 20			UAR census figures show Egypt with a population of just over 26 million.		Prince Souvanna Phouma concludes a preliminary agreement with Pathet Lao leaders to end Laos' six-year civil war through the formation of a coalition government made up of neutralists, Communists and rightists. . . . In an election which is being interpreted as a popular endorsement of the recent U.S.-Japan defense treaty, Premier Hayato Ikeda's Liberal-Democratic Party scores a major victory over the opposition Socialist Party.
Nov. 21	Secy. Gen. Hammarskjold reports that the U.N. treasury has been virtually emptied by Congo operation and that the U.N. Force would have to be withdrawn in late December if $20 million in new funds is not raised quickly. . . . USSR expels Irving McDonald, asst. air attaché at the U.S. Embassy in Moscow, for "intelligence activities."	Vice Pres.-elect Lyndon Johnson visits the NATO parliamentary conference in Paris to give personal assurances of continued U.S. support for NATO defense goals under the forthcoming Democratic administration.	Two Tunisian U.N. soldiers are killed in the first direct fighting between the U.N. Force and Congolese regulars. The incident occurred when U.N. troops attempted to prevent Congolese soldiers from arresting Nathaniel Welbeck, Ghana's official representative to the Congo.		Netherlands Interior Ministry claims that a small band of well-armed Indonesian infiltrators have landed on the coast of Netherlands New Guinea. . . . P.M. Nehru tells Parliament India will not hesitate to shoot down Communist Chinese aircraft violating Indian airspace.
Nov. 22	U.S. delegation to the Geneva test-ban talks rejects as "absurdly low" a Soviet offer to permit three on-site inspections annually in the USSR.		U.N. General Assembly votes 53 to 24 (Soviet-bloc and some African nations opposing) to seat the Congolese delegation representing Kasavubu and Mobutu rather than the rival delegation sent by Lumumba.		
Nov. 23				A strike by Haitian university students prompts the imposition of martial law and a government decree banning all student organizations.	
Nov. 24		USSR agrees to Finnish participation in the European Free Trade Association on the condition that Finland maintains most-favored-nation status for Soviet trade.	Pres. Kasavubu leaves New York for the Congo without agreeing to Secy. Gen. Hammarskjold's plan to send a U.N. political conciliation mission to the strife-torn Congo.	Archbishop Francois Poirer, Roman Catholic primate of Haiti, is expelled by the government for allegedly contributing to recent student unrest.	Sikh extremists, demonstrating for a Punjabi-speaking state, stone police guarding the Indian Parliament, injuring almost 100 of the guards.

A	B	C	D	E
Includes developments that affect more than one world region, international organizations and important meetings of major world leaders.	Includes all domestic and regional developments in Europe, including the Soviet Union, Turkey, Cyprus and Malta.	Includes all domestic and regional developments in Africa and the Middle East, including Iraq and Iran and excluding Cyprus, Turkey and Afghanistan.	Includes all domestic and regional developments in Latin America, the Caribbean and Canada.	Includes all domestic and regional developments in Asia and Pacific nations, extending from Afghanistan through all the Pacific Islands, except Hawaii.

U.S. Politics & Social Issues	U.S. Foreign Policy & Defense	U.S. Economy & Environment	Science, Technology & Nature	Culture, Leisure & Life Style	
A federal court orders New Orleans schools to continue integrated classes pending the court's review of a school board petition seeking suspension of the integration order. Almost no white students are attending the two integrated schools and racial tensions in the city are reportedly high. . . . Reputed Chicago crime boss Anthony Accardo is sentenced to six years in prison for tax evasion.	U.S. State Dept. statement expresses concern over the apparent increase in Communist influence in the Laotian government.	Chrysler Corp. announces the discontinuation of its DeSoto line, which has been on the market since 1928.			Nov. 18
	Sen. Stuart Symington (D, Mo.), considered a prospective Defense Secy., discloses that he has told Kennedy he would rather remain in the Senate than take a cabinet appointment.		President's Science Advisory Committee publishes a report urging greatly increased federal support for basic research and graduate education in science.	The annual meeting of U.S. Roman Catholic bishops concludes with a resolution deploring "the decline of personal responsibility" and "sense of individual obligation" in American life.	Nov. 19
	In reply to a message from Pres. Sékou Touré of Guinea, Pres. Eisenhower denies allegations that the U.S. is opposed to freedom for the Congo and other African states.	Striking Los Angeles bus and streetcar mechanics, whose pickets were honored by railway unions, vote to end a four-day walkout which had affected commuter transportation throughout southern California.	*The New York Times* reports Soviet scientists have concluded that a small comet collided with the earth on the night of June 30, 1908, explaining the lack of darkness over wide areas that night. The phenomenon had given rise to many fantastic hypotheses, including several theories of extra-terrestrial visitation.	Novelist Norman Mailer is arrested in New York on charges of stabbing his wife in their Manhattan apartment. . . . Meredith Wilson's play *The Unsinkable Molly Brown* opens in New York to mixed reviews.	Nov. 20
					Nov. 21
School Supt. James Redmond announces there are no funds to pay New Orleans teachers because of a legislative freeze on state aid to the district.	U.S. Navy's most powerful atomic submarine, the 410-foot *Ethan Allen*, is launched at Groton, Conn.				Nov. 22
Louisiana House of Representatives unanimously passes a resolution accusing Pres. Eisenhower of "making common cause with the communist conspiracy" by permitting the court-ordered desegregation of New Orleans schools. . . . U.S. Communist Party announces the expulsion of Alexander Bittleman, long-time party theoretician, for "revisionist" views.			Tiros II, a 280-pound weather satellite equipped to photograph the earth's cloud cover, is successfully launched from Cape Canaveral. NASA says the cloud pictures will be made available to meteorologists throughout the world.	Frank Howard, 24, of the Los Angeles Dodgers is named National League "Rookie of the Year." Baltimore Orioles shortstop Ron Hansen, 22, won rookie honors in the American League.	Nov. 23
	Vice Pres.-elect Johnson, visiting the Paris NATO conference, tells newsmen that the administration's current efforts to reduce the cost of maintaining U.S. military presence in Europe "do not necessarily reflect the policies Sen. Kennedy may follow."				Nov. 24

F	G	H	I	J
Includes elections, federal-state relations, civil rights and liberties, crime, the judiciary, education, health care, poverty, urban affairs and population.	*Includes formation and debate of U.S. foreign and defense policies, veterans' affairs and defense spending. (Relations with specific foreign countries are usually found under the region concerned.)*	*Includes business, labor, agriculture, taxation, transportation, consumer affairs, monetary and fiscal policy, natural resources, and pollution.*	*Includes worldwide scientific, medical and technological developments, natural phenomena, U.S. weather, natural disasters, and accidents.*	*Includes the arts, religion, scholarship, communications media, sports, entertainment, fashions, fads and social life.*

	World Affairs	Europe	Africa & the Middle East	The Americas	Asia & the Pacific
Nov. 25		West Berlin Mayor Willy Brandt opens his campaign as the Social Democratic Party's Chancellor-designate nominee with a dramatic TV address in which he confirms rumors that he was an illegitimate child and that he assumed his present name after fleeing Germany in 1933.		AP reports the USSR has begun to dump large quantities of Cuban sugar on the world market at well below the usual world market price.	
Nov. 26		Annual conference of NATO parliamentarians approves U.S. proposals to establish joint U.S.-NATO control over nuclear weapons assigned to European defense tasks. The proposals are aimed at reducing European fears of unilateral American military action and especially at discouraging French plans to create an independent nuclear striking force. . . . Vienna talks between Austrian and Yugoslav officials end with settlement of W.W. II claims against Austria. Austria will reportedly grant Yugoslavia $10 million in credits.			P.M. Walter Nash's Labor Party is defeated by the free enterprise National Party in national elections for New Zealand's 80-seat House of Representatives.
Nov. 27			In a note to the U.N., Ghana Pres. Nkrumah charges the U.S., Britain and France with aiding Belgium in attempts "to regain control over the Congo." . . . Col. Mobutu and Pres. Kasavubu meet with Katanga chief Tshombe and other secessionist leaders in an effort to work out a program to restore coordinated political authority throughout the Congo.		
Nov. 28	A U.S. court in New York rules that Igor Melekh, a Soviet U.N. employee accused of spying, is not protected by diplomatic immunity.	Pres. Tito announces that a new Yugoslavian Constitution, scheduled for adoption in 1962, will reduce unnecessary state interference in economic production. . . . Derek Jan de Geer, 89, ex-Netherlands premier convicted of collaboration with the Nazis in 1947, dies in The Hague.	Premier Lumumba narrowly escapes a detachment of Congolese troops attempting to arrest him on orders from Col. Mobutu. The Mobutu government charges U.N. complicity in Lumumba's flight from Leopoldville. . . . France grants full independence to the Republic of Mauritania. Morocco, which has long claimed sovereignty over Mauritanian territory, proclaims a day of national mourning to protest France's recognition of the new nation's independence.	Venezuelan Pres. Romulo Betancourt suspends constitutional civil liberties following four days of violent anti-government demonstrations.	Supreme People's Court of Communist China pardons and releases 50 major "war criminals" who had been closely associated with the old Nationalist regime.
Nov. 29	In a proposal to the General Assembly Budgetary Committee the U.S. offers to pay half the cost of U.N. Congo operations during 1960.			A total of eight persons are reported to have been killed in recent riots in Caracas, Venezuela.	
Nov. 30	Sources in Moscow report that the just concluded world congress of Communist leaders spent much of its time debating the conflicting ideological positions presented by Soviet Premier Khrushchev and Chinese Pres. Liu Shao-chi. . . . In what are reputed to be personal memoirs published in *Life* magazine, Adolf Eichmann says he feels no regret for his part in the Nazi extermination of the Jews.		South Africa decrees a state of emergency in the Pondoland African reserve after days of rioting by Africans opposed to the tribal authorities appointed by the government.	Argentine troops crush a one-day revolt of pro-Peronists in Santa Fe and Salta Provinces. . . . Venezuelan delegation to the OAS charges the Dominican Republic with supplying arms to Venezuelan exiles for an eventual invasion.	Communist China and Cuba conclude an economic cooperation agreement in which China promises to provide long term loans and to buy one million tons of Cuban sugar.
Dec. 1		French news sources report that 2,998 persons, mostly Moslems, have been killed in Algerian-related terrorist attacks within France since January 1956.	Congo Premier Lumumba is arrested by Congolese troops loyal to Col. Mobutu and Pres. Kasavubu on charges of inciting rebellion. . . . UAR nationalizes all Belgian assets in Egypt in retaliation for alleged Belgian influence in the decision to expel UAR diplomats from the Congo Republic.	U.S. formally recognizes El Salvador's new six-man ruling junta.	Over 2,500 church-operated schools, mostly Roman Catholic, are transferred to the control of the Ceylonese government.

A	B	C	D	E
Includes developments that affect more than one world region, international organizations and important meetings of major world leaders.	*Includes all domestic and regional developments in Europe, including the Soviet Union, Turkey, Cyprus and Malta.*	*Includes all domestic and regional developments in Africa and the Middle East, including Iraq and Iran and excluding Cyprus, Turkey and Afghanistan.*	*Includes all domestic and regional developments in Latin America, the Caribbean and Canada.*	*Includes all domestic and regional developments in Asia and Pacific nations, extending from Afghanistan through all the Pacific Islands, except Hawaii.*

U.S. Politics & Social Issues	U.S. Foreign Policy & Defense	U.S. Economy & Environment	Science, Technology & Nature	Culture, Leisure & Life Style	
Sit-ins aimed at lunch-counter segregation resume peacefully in Atlanta after a one-month "truce" period. . . . Mrs. John F. Kennedy gives birth to a son, John Fitzgerald Kennedy Jr., at Georgetown Hospital in Washington.	On Pres. Eisenhower's order, Secy. of State Christian Herter refuses a House committee request for data on U.S. aid programs to South America.		American Dental Association reports that voters turned down proposals to fluoridate water supplies in 29 of 34 communities that voted on the issue in the Nov. 8 elections.	CBS radio's last and oldest soap opera, *Ma Perkins*, goes off the air after 28 years and 7,200 installments. The end of the radio "soaps" is attributed to competition from TV and local radio disc jockey programs.	Nov. 25
John E. Rankin, Miss. congressman from 1921 to 1953, co-author of the TVA bill, and outspoken white supremacist, dies at age 78 in Tupelo, Miss.	Treasury Secy. Robert Anderson returns from a week of talks in Europe where he unsuccessfully sought British, French and West German financial help in paying the cost of maintaining U.S. troops in West Germany. The talks are part of an administration campaign to reverse the U.S.' growing balance of payments deficit.				Nov. 26
New Deal brain-truster Donald Richberg, 79, co-author of the National Industrial Recovery Act and NRA general counsel (1933-35), dies in Charlottesville, Va.	The final report of Pres. Eisenhower's Commission on National Goals calls for a substantial increase during the 1960s in U.S. foreign aid to underdeveloped countries and increased military aid to anti-communist nations in Southeast Asia.	President's Commission on National Goals identifies urban regeneration and an unemployment rate below 4% as major economic goals of the 1960s.	The final report of the Commission on National Goals urges greater emphasis on basic scientific research in the 1960s, including those areas that will increase American military capability.		Nov. 27
U.S. Court of Appeals overturns the convictions of 20 defendants in the Apalachin crime conspiracy trial, ruling there is no proof a crime took place or was planned at the 1957 meeting.		Labor Secy. James Mitchell intervenes to end a jurisdictional dispute between NASA and two AFL-CIO unions which had halted construction on Cape Canaveral launch facilities since Nov. 18. . . . U.S. traffic deaths over the Thanksgiving weekend number 442.		American-born Negro novelist Richard Wright, 52, dies in Paris of a heart attack. . . . A UPI poll names Minnesota the nation's number one major college football team.	Nov. 28
Gov. Nelson Rockefeller tells an Albany, N.Y. news conference that Nixon will remain a vital force in GOP affairs, but not necessarily the party's chief leader.	Sen. J. William Fulbright (D, Ark.), thought to be Kennedy's choice for Secy. of State tells reporters he "will not be a candidate" for the post. . . . Dr. Robert Soblen, brother of convicted Soviet spy Jack Soble, is arrested by the FBI on two counts of espionage.			Heisman Trophy goes to Navy halfback Joe Bellino as the outstanding college football player of 1960.	Nov. 29
A three-judge federal court reaffirms the New Orleans public school desegregation plan and voids three Louisiana laws designed to thwart integration. Meanwhile, mobs of angry white women revile and shove white parents accompanying their children to schools despite a boycott. . . . Five Negroes are served in Atlanta's YWCA cafeteria, marking the first desegregation of a public cafeteria in the city since the sit-in campaign began.	Ex.-Secy. of State Dean Acheson tells a meeting of Kansas City lawyers that the U.S. should recognize Chiang Kai-shek as the head of a self-contained Formosan state and not the leader of China, "which he is not."		U.S. Public Health Service reports that the U.S. death rate has dropped to 9.4 per 1,000 persons, 1% lower than in 1959.	The five-bishop Roman Catholic Episcopal Committee urges U.S. Catholics to join a national "protest" against the "alarming departure" from decency and morality by the Hollywood film industry.	Nov. 30
Pres.-elect Kennedy announces that he intends to name Gov. Abraham Ribicoff (D, Conn.) as Secy. of HEW. . . . Alabama Atty. Gen. MacDonald Gallion refuses for the third time to comply with U.S. Atty. Gen William Roger's order to open Sumter County voter registration records to federal inspection.	Defense Secy. Thomas Gates orders an end to the purchase of "foreign items" for resale in military base stores overseas as part of an administration program to lessen the U.S. gold drain. . . . Pres.-elect Kennedy's Washington office announces that Michigan Gov. G. Mennen Williams (D.) will be named Assistant Secy. of State for African Affairs.	Auto industry sources report that the number of U.S. autos rose from 36 million to over 57 million during the 1950s.	Univ. of Pittsburgh announces that a team of its scientists have synthesized a substance identical to ACTH, a hormone which stimulates the production of cortisone.	Exiled Rumanian writer Vintila Horia rejects the Goncourt Prize for literature after French Communists charge he wrote pro-Fascist articles for Rumanian newspapers during W.W. II. . . . Detroit Red Wings forward Gordie Howe breaks the all-time NHL scoring record with his 1,093 goal in a game against Boston.	Dec. 1
F	G	H	I	J	
Includes elections, federal-state relations, civil rights and liberties, crime, the judiciary, education, health care, poverty, urban affairs and population.	*Includes formation and debate of U.S. foreign and defense policies, veterans' affairs and defense spending. (Relations with specific foreign countries are usually found under the region concerned.)*	*Includes business, labor, agriculture, taxation, transportation, consumer affairs, monetary and fiscal policy, natural resources, and pollution.*	*Includes worldwide scientific, medical and technological developments, natural phenomena, U.S. weather, natural disasters, and accidents.*	*Includes the arts, religion, scholarship, communications media, sports, entertainment, fashions, fads and social life.*	

	World Affairs	Europe	Africa & the Middle East	The Americas	Asia & the Pacific
Dec. 2		U.N. special committee on Hungary, headed by Leslie Munro of New Zealand, reports that Soviet troops are continuing to occupy Hungary in violation of the principle of self-determination.		Leftist students at the Central Univ. in Caracas, Venezuela surrender to police, ending several days of anti-government riots in which 15 persons were killed. . . . A threatened strike by Canadian railway workers is prevented when Parliament passes emergency legislation barring a strike until May 1961.	
Dec. 3		Hungarian officials report a 40% increase in industrial production under the three-year Soviet-aided reconstruction plan inaugurated in the wake of the 1956 Hungarian revolt.			
Dec. 4	USSR vetoes a Security Council measure admitting Mauritania to the U.N. after the Council rejected a Soviet proposal to take up simultaneously the question of U.N. admission for Outer Mongolia.		Pro-Lumumba forces, headed by Bernard Salumu, assume power in Stanleyville, capital of Oriental Province, and demand the immediate release of the arrested premier.		
Dec. 5	U.S., British and Soviet delegates to the 273d session of the Geneva test-ban conference agree to recess their talks until Feb. 7, 1961. . . . France walks out as the U.N. General Assembly begins discussion of the Algerian question.	Five rightists, released on bail to await trial in Paris for their role in the January Algiers uprising, fail to appear in court and are reported to have fled France.	U.N. Rep.-to-Congo Rajeshwar Dayal reports that Lumumba has suffered "serious injuries" from a beating inflicted by Congolese soldiers after his capture. . . . In a series of public statements, the USSR calls for the immediate release of Lumumba and the restoration of the pro-Lumumba Congolese parliament. . . . South Africa seizes the passport of Alan Paton, president of the multi-racial Liberal Party, upon his return from a trip to the U.S. where he lectured against apartheid.		Preliminary talks aimed at gaining rightist participation in the proposed coalition Laotian government break down; renewed fighting is expected between Souvanna's neutralist forces and rightist rebels centered in Savannakhet.
Dec. 6	A manifesto issued in Moscow by the leaders of 81 national Communist parties proclaims the unity of all Communists in the continuing struggle against capitalism. The manifesto reaffirms Soviet leadership of world communism and endorses Khrushchev's peaceful co-existence doctrine, but its overall tone is much more strident than the 1957 Moscow peace declaration, a fact believed to reflect the growing ideological influence of the Communist Chinese.	De Gaulle's proposal for an independent French nuclear strike force receives final approval by the Senate and Assembly. . . . East and West Germany begin trade talks in Berlin.	Col. Mobutu turns down a U.N. request for a Red Cross inquiry into the treatment of Lumumba by his captors. U.S. and other nations appeal for humane treatment and "due process" toward the ex-premier.	Argentine government outlaws the pro-Peronist Social Justice Party for its alleged involvement in the Nov. 30 anti-government uprising.	
Dec. 7			Lumumba supporters now controlling Oriental Province announce they will begin executing resident Europeans unless Lumumba is freed within 48 hours. . . . South African P.M. Verwoerd announces plans to extend apartheid to the nation's 1.5 million coloreds (persons of mixed blood).	White House announces Pres. Eisenhower has recalled U.S. Navy ships that were sent to Guatemala and Nicaragua to guard against a possible Communist-led invasion.	In an official government statement, the USSR denounces the U.S. as responsible for the continuing division of Korea and calls for an immediate U.S. withdrawal as a first step toward reunification. . . . Pope John XXIII announces the establishment of a Roman Catholic Church hierarchy in both North and South Vietnam.

A	B	C	D	E
Includes developments that affect more than one world region, international organizations and important meetings of major world leaders.	*Includes all domestic and regional developments in Europe, including the Soviet Union, Turkey, Cyprus and Malta.*	*Includes all domestic and regional developments in Africa and the Middle East, including Iraq and Iran and excluding Cyprus, Turkey and Afghanistan.*	*Includes all domestic and regional developments in Latin America, the Caribbean and Canada.*	*Includes all domestic and regional developments in Asia and Pacific nations, extending from Afghanistan through all the Pacific Islands, except Hawaii.*

U.S. Politics & Social Issues	U.S. Foreign Policy & Defense	U.S. Economy & Environment	Science, Technology & Nature	Culture, Leisure & Life Style	
Congressional hearings into the operations of the New York Port Authority end after hearing charges of corruption and incompetence.	Eisenhower authorizes the spending of $2 million for the relief and resettlement of 30,000-40,000 anti-Castro Cuban refugees in Florida and Louisiana.	Agriculture Dept. reports U.S. farm exports exceeded $1 billion during the third quarter of 1960.	A Soviet space satellite launched Dec. 1 and carrying two dogs veers off course and burns as Soviet scientists attempt to bring it back to earth by radio signal.	The Most Rev. Geoffrey Fisher, archbishop of Canterbury, visits Pope John XXIII in the Vatican, marking the first meeting between Anglican and Roman Catholic church heads since the founding of the Church of England in 1534.	Dec. 2
	Pres.-elect Kennedy says Gov. Luther H. Hodges (D, N. C.) will be his nominee for Commerce Secy.			*Camelot*, a musical comedy based on a T.H. White novel, opens on Broadway starring Richard Burton and Julie Andrews.	Dec. 3
	Kennedy appoints a 10-member committee, headed by Sen. Paul Douglas (D, Ill.), to draft a program of federal aid to areas of chronic unemployment.		A Scout missile, developed by NASA as a relatively inexpensive satellite-launching rocket, fails to fire properly in its first test launch.	The Rev. Dr. Eugene Carson Blake of the United Presbyterian Church in the U.S. proposes the merger of the Presbyterian, Methodist and Episcopalian churches and the Church of Christ into a single Protestant body.	Dec. 4
Supreme Court rules, 7-2, that segregation in bus terminal restaurant facilities violates the Interstate Commerce Act. . . . The Southern Education Reporting Service reports that 6.3% of all Southern Negro students are now attending integrated classes, a .3% increase over 1959. There are still no integrated classes in Alabama, Georgia, Mississippi or South Carolina; token integration is reported in Louisiana, North Carolina, Florida and Virginia.	A six-member civilian committee, headed by Sen. Stuart Symington (D, Mo.), presents Pres.-elect Kennedy with a detailed proposal for reorganizing the Defense Dept. which includes a plan to require the Secy. of Defense to report to Congress on long-term military needs and goals prior to submitting the defense budget. . . . U.S. State Dept. announces it will contribute its part to reducing the U.S. balance of payments deficit by gradually phasing out foreign aid procurement in 18 countries.				Dec. 5
Twenty-three white pupils brave a jeering crowd and enter New Orleans' integrated William Frantz School. A complete white boycott remains in effect at McDonough No. 19, the city's other integrated school. . . . Pres. Eisenhower and cabinet members confer with Pres.-elect Kennedy to work out a smooth transfer of responsibilities to the new administration. . . . After two mistrials, a New York jury finds Manhattan Borough Pres. Hulan Jack guilty on two counts of conflict-of-interest violations.	In response to pressure from the House Subcommittee on Government Secrecy, the Defense Dept., with the reluctant consent of the Secy. of State, makes public replica photos and descriptive data about the A-bombs dropped on Hiroshima and Nagasaki in August 1945.	Treasury Dept. reports that the official 1960 budget surplus totaled $1,224,047,421.			Dec. 6
A back-to-school movement by white pupils to New Orleans' integrated William Frantz school is reportedly weakening in the face of intensifying threats and vandalism against families of the returning students. . . . New Orleans School Supt. James Redmond reports that a legislative freeze on all funds to the city's two integrated schools threatens their imminent closing. . . . Office of Education reports that college and university enrollment increased in 1960 for the ninth consecutive year to a record total of 3,610,007 (including 1,339,367 women).	Navy releases a previously confidential salvage report indicating that three U.S. sailors had lived over two weeks in an air pocket in the battleship *West Virginia* after it had been sunk in the 1941 attack on Pearl Harbor.	Pres.-elect Kennedy announces that he has selected Rep. Steward Udall (D, Ariz.) to be Interior Secy. . . . A federal grand jury in Orlando, Fla. indicts Teamster Pres. James Hoffa on 12 counts of mail fraud involving the alleged misuse of $500,000 of union funds in the operation of the Sun Valley (Fla.) land company.	Prof. Walter Noddack, 67, German scientist who with his wife discovered the elements rhenium and masurium (1925), dies in Bamburg. . . . Hughes Aircraft Co. announces that it is offering for sale to private companies a 32-pound earth satellite for use in relaying telephone and TV signals.		Dec. 7

F	G	H	I	J
Includes elections, federal-state relations, civil rights and liberties, crime, the judiciary, education, health care, poverty, urban affairs and population.	Includes formation and debate of U.S. foreign and defense policies, veterans' affairs and defense spending. (Relations with specific foreign countries are usually found under the region concerned.)	Includes business, labor, agriculture, taxation, transportation, consumer affairs, monetary and fiscal policy, natural resources, and pollution.	Includes worldwide scientific, medical and technological developments, natural phenomena, U.S. weather, natural disasters, and accidents.	Includes the arts, religion, scholarship, communications media, sports, entertainment, fashions, fads and social life.

	World Affairs	Europe	Africa & the Middle East	The Americas	Asia & the Pacific
Dec. 8			Soviet Rep.-to-U.N. Valerian Zorin publicly accuses Hammarskjold of helping "hired assassins" bring down the legitimate Lumumba regime in the Congo.	West Indies Federation agrees to allow the U.S. to retain its lend-lease naval base at Chaguaramas, Trinidad until 1977.	
Dec. 9		Agreements establishing a Rumanian-U.S. cultural exchange program are signed in Washington.	French Pres. de Gaulle arrives in Tlemcen in eastern Algeria to begin a six-day tour to present personally his plan for a national referendum on Algeria's future. De Gaulle intends to avoid major cities where hostile European demonstrations are feared. . . . U.N. Congo command orders Ethiopian U.N. troops into Stanleyville to protect Europeans from threatened reprisals by Lumumba supporters.	About 1,000 members of the Cuban Electrical Workers Union demonstrate in Havana against communist efforts to take over the union. . . . Student demonstrators supporting Ecuador in its boundary dispute with Peru stone the U.S. and Peruvian embassies in Quito.	Laotian Premier Souvanna Phouma flees to Cambodia following the collapse of his neutralist regime in the face of an imminent assault on the capital by troops of Gen. Phoumi Nosavan's rightist Savannakhet Committee.
Dec. 10	Communist Chinese Pres. Liu Shao-chi returns from the world communist congress in Moscow amid an intense propaganda campaign stressing Sino-Soviet friendship and unity.		Pres. de Gaulle tells French military officers in Blida, Algeria that it is "useless" to pretend that Algeria is "a province of France like our Lorraine." . . . Violence erupts in Algiers as pro-de Gaulle Moslems clash with anti-de Gaulle European rightists. . . . At least 100 Baluba tribesmen are reported to have been killed in recent attacks upon U.N. troops and Katanga police in northern Katanga Province.	Cuban National Bank Pres. Ernesto Guevara, during a Moscow visit, says that Cuba "wholeheartedly supports" the Dec. 6 manifesto of the world communist congress. . . . A Cuban firing squad in Manicaragua executes six convicted counter-revolutionaries, raising to 582 the total number of persons executed since Castro took power in January 1959.	
Dec. 11	U.S. State Dept. reports that Soviet-bloc aid to underdeveloped countries rose from $978 million in 1958 to $1.349 billion in the first 10 months of 1960. . . . A Soviet statement issued through Tass states that the USSR will hold Britain directly responsible for any incident involving U.S. Polaris submarines based at Holy Loch, Scotland.				Leftist members of the collapsed neutralist government join with pro-Communist Laotian army leaders to form a new government in Vientiane following the flight of Souvanna Phouma.
Dec. 12		Soviet-West German trade talks break down over German insistence that an agreement be drawn up including West Berlin.	Six of the 18 nations that initially contributed troops to the U.N. Force are reported to have ordered their contingents withdrawn from the Congo.	Leaflets urging Cubans to overthrow the Castro regime are air-dropped over Havana and other major Cuban cities by a Miami-based exile group calling itself the Democratic Revolutionary Front.	The new leftist cabinet in Laos, headed by Quinim Polsena, reportedly receives an offer of military assistance from the USSR.
Dec. 13		USSR denounces the U.S. proposal to make NATO an independent nuclear power as a "monstrous scheme" intended to breed "military conflicts in the heart of Europe." . . . House of Commons rejects a Laborite motion to censure the Macmillan government for failing to demand greater control over U.S. nuclear weapons based in Britain.	A new Congolese government is proclaimed in Stanleyville by Antoine Gizenga, deputy premier in the former Lumumba government and an alleged pro-Communist. Gizenga appeals for U.N. recognition as the lawful leader of the Congo.		In a note to the U.S., the USSR charges the U.S. with intervening in Laos to support the rightist rebels under Phoumi Nosavan. . . . U.S. formally denies Soviet charges that it has aided rightist rebel forces in Laos.

A	B	C	D	E
Includes developments that affect more than one world region, international organizations and important meetings of major world leaders.	Includes all domestic and regional developments in Europe, including the Soviet Union, Turkey, Cyprus and Malta.	Includes all domestic and regional developments in Africa and the Middle East, including Iraq and Iran and excluding Cyprus, Turkey and Afghanistan.	Includes all domestic and regional developments in Latin America, the Caribbean and Canada.	Includes all domestic and regional developments in Asia and Pacific nations, extending from Afghanistan through all the Pacific Islands, except Hawaii.

U.S. Politics & Social Issues	U.S. Foreign Policy & Defense	U.S. Economy & Environment	Science, Technology & Nature	Culture, Leisure & Life Style	
Kennedy tells a Washington press conference that he will ask Congress to create a cabinet-level Urban Affairs Dept.	Adlai Stevenson tells reporters that he has accepted an offer from Pres.-elect Kennedy to serve as U.S. ambassador-to-the-United Nations, adding that Kennedy had promised him a significant role in the formation of American foreign policy. . . . In a speech to the National Association of Manufacturers, Sen. Barry Goldwater (R, Ariz.) suggests the U.S. could best reduce its balance of payments deficit by ending all foreign economic aid, adding that the U.S. has been trying to "buy the love of the world" when "we should be demanding [respect]."	After hearing a report from the Joint Economic Committee, Pres. Eisenhower describes the U.S. economy as "quite solid" despite disturbing increases in unemployment. . . . The second threatened strike against N.Y. newspapers in six weeks is canceled following the last-minute acceptance of a new two-year contract by the 3,000-member Newspaper Deliverers' Union. . . . Twenty-nine U.S. electrical equipment manufacturers plead guilty to federal price-fixing and antitrust charges.	General Electric Co. successfully sent 710,000 volts of electrical energy over a half-mile transmission, exceeding a six-year-old Soviet short-line high-voltage record.		Dec. 8
U.S. marshals begin a daily escort of white children to and from New Orleans' integrated Frantz school to protect them from jeering segregationist crowds.					Dec. 9
A Gallup Poll analysis of the Nov. 8 presidential election indicates that Roman Catholics "shifted sharply to the Democratic Party in 1960," while the party split among Protestants remained about the same as in 1956.			Frank Trenholm Coffyn, the last of the original Wright Brothers exhibition team and inventor of several aviation devices, dies at 82 in Palo Alto, Calif.	Benny (Kid) Paret retains his world welterweight championship by scoring a unanimous 15-round decision over Frederico Thompson of Argentina.	Dec. 10
Sen. Mike Mansfield (D, Mont.) asks Northern liberal Democrats to postpone a fight on the Senate filibuster lest it disrupt party unity and thus endanger Pres.-elect Kennedy's legislative program. . . . Thousands of Negroes march on the business district of Atlanta to show support for the continuing sit-in campaign against lunch-counter segregation.			Carnegie Institute reports the discovery of a cluster of possibly colliding galaxies by scientists at the Mount Palomar Observatory in California. The galaxies are believed to be the most distant objects yet observed.	Seventeen spectators are killed in three separate sports car crashes at the conclusion of the Argentine Grand Prix in Buenos Aires. Two of the drivers involved are arrested for negligence.	Dec. 11
Fourteen unpledged Presidential electors from Mississippi and Alabama issue a statement calling upon other Southern electors to join with them in casting their electoral college ballots for Sen. Harry F. Byrd (D, Va.) in an effort to keep Kennedy from becoming President. . . . Supreme Court upholds lower court rulings which found Louisiana's anti-integration laws unconstitutional. . . . Supreme Court, by a 5-4 vote, overturns an Arkansas law requiring teachers to disclose all their organizational memberships during the preceding five years on the grounds that it violates the right of free association.	Dean Rusk, president of the Rockefeller Foundation, is announced as Pres.-elect Kennedy's choice for Secy. of State.	Labor Dept. reports that November unemployment amounted to 6.3%, the largest for November since the U.S. began issuing monthly estimates in 1940. . . . New York Supreme Court upholds a state law prohibiting strikes by public employees. . . . Commerce Dept. reports U.S.-owned overseas enterprises produce over $35-billion worth of goods annually and employ more than three million workers.			Dec. 12
Pres. Eisenhower, speaking informally to industrial leaders visiting the White House, says that Sen. Kennedy's telephone intervention in connection with the Georgia jailing of Martin Luther King played a major role in swinging the Negro vote to the Democrats.	Kennedy announces that Robert McNamara, Ford Motor Co. president, will be named Secy. of Defense.			An Italian team defeats the favored U.S. in a semifinal round of the Davis Cup tennis tournament, marking the first time in 24 years the U.S. failed to make the finals.	Dec. 13

F	G	H	I	J
Includes elections, federal-state relations, civil rights and liberties, crime, the judiciary, education, health care, poverty, urban affairs and population.	*Includes formation and debate of U.S. foreign and defense policies, veterans' affairs and defense spending. (Relations with specific foreign countries are usually found under the region concerned.)*	*Includes business, labor, agriculture, taxation, transportation, consumer affairs, monetary and fiscal policy, natural resources, and pollution.*	*Includes worldwide scientific, medical and technological developments, natural phenomena, U.S. weather, natural disasters, and accidents.*	*Includes the arts, religion, scholarship, communications media, sports, entertainment, fashions, fads and social life.*

	World Affairs	Europe	Africa & the Middle East	The Americas	Asia & the Pacific
Dec. 14	U.N. General Assembly votes 89-0 (U.S. abstaining) to support independence for all colonial countries and peoples. . . . USSR vetoes a Western-sponsored U.N. Security Council resolution granting Secy. Gen Hammarskjold increased powers to meet the Congo crisis created by the arrest of Lumumba. The USSR had originally requested the session on Dec. 7 to consider a Soviet resolution demanding Lumumba's release.	The ruling National Unity Committee in Turkey announces the formation of an appointed bicameral legislature charged with drafting democratic constitutional and electoral reforms by May 1961. . . . A charter creating a new international economic organization—to be known as the Organization for Economic Cooperation and Development—is signed in Paris by Canada, U.S. and 18 European nations. The new body will replace the 18-member Organization for European Economic Cooperation.	Four days of rioting touched off by de Gaulle's visit to Algeria leaves 124 dead and hundreds injured. De Gaulle cuts short his scheduled tour and returns to France.	Anti-Castro leaders of the Cuban Electrical Workers Union seek asylum in several Latin American embassies on the eve of a Havana rally called to "purify" their union. . . . Canadian unemployment in November rose to 6.6%, the highest November figure since W.W. II.	
Dec. 15		Belgian King Baudouin, 30, marries Dona Fabiola de Mora y Aragon, 32, of Spain in a Brussels ceremony. . . . French cabinet approves a crackdown on rightist opposition to de Gaulle's Algerian policies.	Mobutu government in Leopoldville charges the USSR with supplying arms to Gizenga's pro-Lumumba forces in Stanleyville.		King Mahendra Bir Bikram Shah Deva assumes personal rule of Nepal after suspending Parliament and arresting Premier B.P. Koirala on charges of causing internal strife "under the guise" of democratic reform.
Dec. 16	General Assembly once again takes up consideration of the Congo crisis after the USSR vetoes a Security Council resolution authorizing a continuation of current U.N. Congo operations.	U.S. presents the NATO Council with an offer to provide five Polaris-bearing nuclear submarines as an initial contribution toward the creation of a NATO nuclear strike force. The U.S. would retain control over deployment of the warheads. Britain, France and West Germany voice support for the plan. . . . British Overseas Migration Board reports that during 1959 177,499 persons immigrated to Britain, the largest group coming from the West Indies.	Algerian Provisional Premier Ferhat Abbas denounces de Gaulle's referendum plan as a "sinister masquerade" and urges Algerian Moslems to oppose it.	Pres. Eisenhower announces the extension of the U.S. ban on Cuban sugar purchases through March 1961.	Right-wing anti-Communist rebels led by Gen. Phoumi Nosavan take control of the Laotian capital, Vientiane, after defeating leftist defenders under the command of Capt. Kong Le.
Dec. 17			Loyal Ethiopian troops crush a three-day rebellion against Emperor Haile Selassie by members of the Imperial Guard. Leaders of the unsuccessful coup, which occurred while Selassie was in Brazil, claimed that the Emperor is an obstacle to modernization and social justice. . . . The South African 1960 census shows the nation's population comprised of nearly 11 million Africans, three million Europeans, 1.5 million mixed bloods and one half million Asians.		A U.S. note delivered to the Soviet Embassy in Washington charges the USSR and its "partner" North Vietnam with instigating the "fratricidal war in Laos."
Dec. 18			A conference in London to review Rhodesia and Nyasaland Federation's Constitution ends without producing any agreement between African and European delegates on the Federation's future.		A new Laotian government is proclaimed in Vientiane by Prince Boun Oum, leader of the right-wing Savannakhet Committee.
Dec. 19	U.N. General Assembly votes 63-8 (U.S. abstaining) to affirm the U.N.'s responsibility to help bring about Algeria's independence. The adoption of the general measure follows the defeat of an African-Asian resolution calling for a U.N.-supervised referendum in Algeria on the country's political future.			Cuban National Bank Pres. Ernesto Guevara signs a declaration in Moscow expressing Cuban support for Khrushchev's foreign policy, especially his backing of "national liberation" movements in Latin America. A $168-million Cuban-Soviet trade deal is also signed. . . . International Longshoremen's Association announces in New York that its members will refuse to work on ships bearing cargo to or from Cuba.	
Dec. 20	A four-day General Assembly debate on the Congo crisis caused by the arrest of Lumumba ends without any agreement on what action the U.N. should take. Hammarskjold says he will continue current policies until otherwise directed. . . . The U.N. General Assembly approves, without opposition, a resolution calling upon nuclear and non-nuclear nations to work against the further spread of atomic capability.	British P.M. Macmillan tells Parliament that he will raise the matter of a new East-West summit in his first contacts with the incoming Kennedy administration. . . . Soviet Finance Ministry presents a record peacetime 1961 budget of $86 billion to the Supreme Soviet.	In a TV address broadcast in France and Algeria, de Gaulle asks Algerian rebels to accept new peace talks and he appeals to the French people for support of his Algerian policies in the forthcoming national referendum.	Canadian Finance Ministry proposes increased taxes on profits accruing to aliens, primarily U.S. citizens, from business and investments in Canada. . . . White House discloses that the number of Cuban refugees fleeing to the U.S. has risen to well over 1,000 a week.	
	A	**B**	**C**	**D**	**E**
	Includes developments that affect more than one world region, international organizations and important meetings of major world leaders.	*Includes all domestic and regional developments in Europe, including the Soviet Union, Turkey, Cyprus and Malta.*	*Includes all domestic and regional developments in Africa and the Middle East, including Iraq and Iran and excluding Cyprus, Turkey and Afghanistan.*	*Includes all domestic and regional developments in Latin America, the Caribbean and Canada.*	*Includes all domestic and regional developments in Asia and Pacific nations, extending from Afghanistan through all the Pacific Islands, except Hawaii.*

U.S. Politics & Social Issues	U.S. Foreign Policy & Defense	U.S. Economy & Environment	Science, Technology & Nature	Culture, Leisure & Life Style	
A special election board, made up of four Republicans and one Democrat, certifies Kennedy's victory in the disputed Illinois election, ending GOP hopes that a recount might give Nixon a majority in the Electoral College. . . . Justice Dept. asks in federal court for a permanent injunction to restrain 82 white businessmen and landowners from using economic pressure to keep Fayette County, Tenn. Negroes from voting; it was the third use of the 1957 Civil Rights Act in Tennessee this year.					Dec. 14
Richard Paul Pavlick, 73, a former mental patient, is arrested in West Palm Beach, Fla. on charges of planning a suicidal assassination attempt on the life of Pres.-elect Kennedy.	Pres.-elect Kennedy announces that Rep. George McGovern (D, S.D.) will serve as administrator of the "food-for-peace" program.	Kennedy tells reporters in Washington that he has chosen N.Y. labor lawyer Arthur Goldberg to be Labor Secy. and Minn. Gov. Orville Freeman to be Secy. of Agriculture.	U.S. fails in its sixth effort to put a satellite into moon orbit when an Atlas-Able rocket explodes shortly after lift-off from Cape Canaveral.	*Exodus*, the Otto Preminger film based on the novel by Leon Uris, is released in New York.	Dec. 15
Pres.-elect Kennedy names his younger brother, Robert F. Kennedy, to be Attorney General.	Secy. of State Herter tells the NATO Council in Paris that the U.S. payments deficit may force a reshaping of U.S. overseas military commitments.	A United Air Lines DC-8 collides with a TWA Super-Constellation over New York Harbor killing all 134 persons aboard both planes. . . . C. Douglas Dillon, a Republican and Undersec. of State in the Eisenhower administration, is named by Kennedy as his choice for Secy. of the Treasury.			Dec. 16
Kennedy completes his cabinet appointments with the naming of J. Edward Day as Postmaster General. . . . Ellen Steinberg, a St. Louis heiress, offers the fund-frozen New Orleans school board $500,000 to help keep integrated schools open.	A U.S. Air Force plane crashes in Munich, West Germany, killing all 20 persons aboard and 30 on the ground.			*Editor and Publisher* magazine reports that only 50 of the nation's 130 major cities have two or more competitively owned daily newspapers.	Dec. 17
	AEC Commissioner, John McCone says on NBC's *Meet the Press* program that he believes the USSR is secretly continuing nuclear tests despite its professed moratorium.	Joint Economic Committee reports that government subsidy programs have increased from $1.9 billion in 1951 to $7.46 billion in 1960; farm subsidies, the largest single group, have grown from $900 million to over $3.5 billion.			Dec. 18
Members of the Electoral College formally elect John Kennedy 35th President by a vote of 300 to 219 for Nixon. Fourteen unpledged electors from Mississippi and Alabama cast their votes for Sen. Harry Byrd of Virginia. . . . Supreme Court upholds a 1956 Narcotics Control Act that requires witnesses to testify when promised immunity from prosecution.	A fire sweeps the U.S. aircraft carrier *Constellation*, under construction in the Brooklyn Navy Yard, killing 49 workmen and causing $75 million in damages.		After a series of failures, the U.S. successfully completes an unmanned test launch of a Project Mercury capsule, the type NASA hopes to use soon to put a man in orbit.		Dec. 19
	State Dept. cancels a policy prohibiting U.S. government scientists from attending international meetings also attended by scientists from Communist China.	Pres. Eisenhower authorizes Commerce Secy. Frederick Mueller to begin planning for the U.S. exhibit at the 1964-1965 New York World's Fair.	Carrier Corp. announces it has begun operation of a 15,000-gallon-a-day pilot plant at Wrightsville Beach, N.C. to convert sea water to fresh water by freezing.	*Tunes of Glory*, a British film starring Alec Guinness, is released in N.Y. . . . Insurance executive Charles O. Finley's purchase of controlling interest in the Kansas City Athletics baseball team is approved by AL club owners.	Dec. 20

F	G	H	I	J
Includes elections, federal-state relations, civil rights and liberties, crime, the judiciary, education, health care, poverty, urban affairs and population.	*Includes formation and debate of U.S. foreign and defense policies, veterans' affairs and defense spending. (Relations with specific foreign countries are usually found under the region concerned.)*	*Includes business, labor, agriculture, taxation, transportation, consumer affairs, monetary and fiscal policy, natural resources, and pollution.*	*Includes worldwide scientific, medical and technological developments, natural phenomena, U.S. weather, natural disasters, and accidents.*	*Includes the arts, religion, scholarship, communications media, sports, entertainment, fashions, fads and social life.*

	World Affairs	Europe	Africa & the Middle East	The Americas	Asia & the Pacific
Dec. 21	Hammarskjold names Maj. Gen. Sean McKeown of Ireland to replace Swedish Maj. Gen. Carl Carlsson von Horn as commander of the U.N. Force in the Congo.		Saudi Arabian King Saud forces the resignation as premier of his brother, Crown Prince Faisal, following differences between the two men over the 1961 budget and the extent of power exercised by Faisal. . . . Israeli government denies reports circulating in the U.S. that it has begun work on developing an atomic bomb.	In a statement to the OAS Council, Cuba charges the U.S. with luring Cuban refugees to the U.S. . . . Venezuelan government troops quickly quell a brief uprising of right-wing Navy officers. . . . Paraguayan troops rout a 70-man rebel invasion force from Argentina after they tried to capture a military base three miles from Asuncion.	
Dec. 22			U.N. civilian operations officers report that more U.N. food supplies are needed in the Congo to prevent starvation among refugees from tribal warfare.	Cuban Anti-Communist Front, a U.S.-based exile group, announces plans to establish a Radio Free Cuba "dedicated to the overthrow of Fidel Castro."	USSR and North Vietnam sign an aid accord in Moscow providing $47 million in Soviet loans to North Vietnamese industrial projects.
Dec. 23	Foreign Min. Andrei Gromyko tells the Supreme Soviet that the USSR looks forward to an improvement in relations with the U.S. after Pres.-elect Kennedy takes office.		UAR Pres. Gamal Nasser says that an Israeli attempt to build nuclear weapons would result in war with the Arab states.	Informacion, Cuba's only remaining non-government-owned newspaper, suspends publication for lack of advertising.	A Soviet note delivered to Britain suggests that the two nations, co-chairmen of the 1954 Geneva Conference on Indochina, reconvene the conference to deal with the current crisis in Laos.
Dec. 24			Pres. Kwame Nkrumah of Ghana, Mali Pres. Modibo Keita, and Guinea Pres. Sékou Touré announce plans for an African political union and for the creation of a common economic and monetary policy.		
Dec. 25		A Belgian austerity program imposed by the Eyskens cabinet to meet the economic problems caused by the loss of the Congo leads to a nationwide wave of Socialist-led protest strikes; transportation, production and usual Christmas season activities are disrupted.			
Dec. 26	British scientist and author Sir Charles P. Snow warns a meeting of the American Academy for the Advancement of Science that the worldwide proliferation of nuclear weapons is near and the likelihood of their eventual use is growing all the time.	French Independent Party leaders join with Radicals and Communists in urging a defeat of de Gaulle's Algerian policies in the forthcoming national referendum. The Gaullist UNR and the Socialists have announced they will support de Gaulle's position. . . . Tito proclaims Yugoslav support for the USSR on most issues in its conflict with the West. . . . Soviet government announces that many of its seven-year production targets have been increased due to unexpected gains in industrial output.	A joint session of the Ethiopian Legislature unanimously reaffirms loyalty to Emperor Haile Selassie.	Cuban National Bank Pres. Ernesto Guevara, just returned from a three-month tour of communist nations, announces that the USSR has promised extensive aid to Cuba's industrial development.	Cambodian Prince Sihanouk returns from a three-month world tour that ended with a goodwill visit to Communist China.
Dec. 27	France explodes its third atomic device at its nuclear test site in southwestern Algeria. The test is immediately denounced by the USSR, Japan, East Germany, and Morocco. A U.S. statement says it remains opposed to "the proliferation of atomic capabilities."	Yugoslav Finance Min. Nikola Mincev announces the start of a Western-aided fiscal reform program designed to stimulate Yugoslav trade with the West.	In a speech to the 25th Zionist Convention, Israeli Premier David Ben-Gurion declares that every religious Jew who fails to emigrate to Israel "daily violates the precepts of Judaism."		Experts attending an American Association for the Advancement of Science symposium on Communist Chinese science conclude that basic and theoretical research in China remains of minor significance.

A	B	C	D	E
Includes developments that affect more than one world region, international organizations and important meetings of major world leaders.	*Includes all domestic and regional developments in Europe, including the Soviet Union, Turkey, Cyprus and Malta.*	*Includes all domestic and regional developments in Africa and the Middle East, including Iraq and Iran and excluding Cyprus, Turkey and Afghanistan.*	*Includes all domestic and regional developments in Latin America, the Caribbean and Canada.*	*Includes all domestic and regional developments in Asia and Pacific nations, extending from Afghanistan through all the Pacific Islands, except Hawaii.*

U.S. Politics & Social Issues	U.S. Foreign Policy & Defense	U.S. Economy & Environment	Science, Technology & Nature	Culture, Leisure & Life Style	
A federal court in New Orleans disallows the Louisiana Legislature's attempt to thwart integration by withholding state funds and overturns a state law abolishing the New Orleans school board. . . . House Legislative Oversight Subcommittee releases a staff report which accuses the Civil Aeronautics Board, the Federal Power Commission and the ICC of inefficiency, laxity toward the public welfare, and conflict of interest violations. . . . The Subcommittee also clears Thomas G. Corcoran of any improper activity in representing clients before the FPC.	Commerce Dept. reports that net U.S. foreign aid outlays dropped from $4.6 billion in 1959 to $4.1 billion in fiscal 1960.	The U.S. tanker *Pine Ridge* breaks in half in stormy seas off Cape Hatteras. Eight crewmen are lost.	NASA announces it has chosen Space Technology Laboratories Inc. to develop and build a standardized satellite which can be used for a variety of space science missions.		Dec. 21
FBI Dir. J. Edgar Hoover reports to the Attorney General that the U.S. Communist Party is still the nation's largest subversive group.	Commerce Dept. reports the U.S. balance of payments deficit rose to $1.152 billion in the third quarter of 1960, a 35% increase over the second quarter.	Pres. Eisenhower names Labor Secy. James Mitchell to head an inquiry into "featherbedding" disputes between rail unions and railroads.			Dec. 22
	Pres. Eisenhower instructs State Secy. Herter to ignore Controller Gen. Joseph Campbell's order to cut off funds for the State Dept.'s Inspector General's Office for withholding from Congress information on U.S. aid to South America. Eisenhower had authorized withholding the data on Nov. 25.	Kennedy announces he will appoint Univ. of Minnesota economics professor Walter Heller as chairman of the Council of Economic Advisers.			Dec. 23
U.S. Prisons Dir. James Bennett reports that the federal prison population has increased for the 11th consecutive year to a record total of 23,160.				Pres. Eisenhower and Eleanor Roosevelt head a Gallup Poll as the man and woman "most admired" by Americans. It is the ninth consecutive year that Eisenhower has led the list and the 12th for Mrs. Roosevelt.	Dec. 24
					Dec. 25
James Landis presents Pres.-elect Kennedy with a report severely criticizing federal regulatory agencies and urging wide-ranging reforms including better planning, higher standards of ethical conduct, and greater administrative independence.			Giuseppe Mario Bellanca, 74, Italian airplane designer who built the first plane to make a non-stop trans-Pacific flight (October 1931), dies in New York.	Philadelphia Eagles defeat the Green Bay Packers, 17-13, to win the NFL championship.	Dec. 26
The U.S. Fourth Circuit Court of Appeals in Richmond, Va. upholds the legal right of restaurant operators to select customers on the basis of race. . . . A Kennedy aide indicates that the major TV networks have agreed to live broadcasts of some Kennedy news conferences.	Kennedy designates Texas lawyer John B. Connally Jr. to be Secy. of the Navy.	*Oil and Gas Journal* reports U.S. oil production fell from 7,043,000 barrels a day in 1959 to 7,019,000 in 1960. Worldwide oil production increased 7% in the same period. . . . National Safety Council reports that 488 persons died in auto accidents over the Christmas weekend.			Dec. 27

F	G	H	I	J
Includes elections, federal-state relations, civil rights and liberties, crime, the judiciary, education, health care, poverty, urban affairs and population.	*Includes formation and debate of U.S. foreign and defense policies, veterans' affairs and defense spending. (Relations with specific foreign countries are usually found under the region concerned.)*	*Includes business, labor, agriculture, taxation, transportation, consumer affairs, monetary and fiscal policy, natural resources, and pollution.*	*Includes worldwide scientific, medical and technological developments, natural phenomena, U.S. weather, natural disasters, and accidents.*	*Includes the arts, religion, scholarship, communications media, sports, entertainment, fashions, fads and social life.*

	World Affairs	Europe	Africa & the Middle East	The Americas	Asia & the Pacific
Dec. 28		*The New York Times* reports the U.S., West Germany, Italy, Belgium and the Netherlands have signed a $1.5 billion NATO agreement for production of the F-104G Starfighter. . . . Marshal Alphonse-Pierre Juin, 72, France's highest ranking soldier, publishes an open letter denouncing de Gaulle's policies for Algeria.	Israeli Premier Ben-Gurion is reported to have threatened his resignation unless his cabinet reversed its approval of a report supporting ex-Defense Min. Lavon's charges that army officers had conspired to force his resignation in 1955.	Nearly 90% of Uruguay's unions respond to a Communist labor group call for a 24-hour general strike to protest government economic policies.	Sen. Mike Mansfield (D, Mont.) charges that the U.S. expenditure of $300 million in aid to Laos over the past eight years constituted a "gross over-commitment."
Dec. 29		West Germany agrees on a renewal of trade accords with East Germany in exchange for an assurance that restrictions on West German entry into East Berlin will be eased.	A Jordanian court sentences 11 men to death, seven of them in absentia, for complicity in the Aug. 29 assassination of Premier Hazza Majali. Two of the men convicted in absentia were described as members of the UAR's intelligence service.		Burmese officials deny Nationalist Chinese charges that they had given Communist China permission to move troops across northern Burma.
Dec. 30				Peru breaks diplomatic relations with Cuba, charging the Castro government with aiding pro-Communist rebels in Peru. . . . Thirteen persons are killed when troops fire on rioters in Chilpancingo, Mexico.	The new Laotian government for Boun Oum appeals to the U.N. for aid against what it said was an invasion by troops from North Vietnam.
Dec. 31	Cuban Foreign Min. Raul Roa asks the U.N. Security Council for an emergency meeting to investigate his charges of an imminent U.S. "military aggression" against Cuba.	A new three-year Soviet-West German trade agreement is signed in Bonn without the written assurances concerning the freedom of Berlin originally demanded by the West Germans.	In a major speech broadcast in France and Algeria, Pres. de Gaulle appeals to voters for "an immense approval" of his Algerian reform plans in the referendum to be held Jan. 6. . . . U.N. Force closes Stanleyville airport to all incoming flights after it learned that Soviet transports were flying in supplies to the city's pro-Lumumba rebels.		U.S. issues a declaration saying that it "would take the most serious view" of any intervention in Laos by North Vietnam or Communist China. . . . Leftist Laotian forces under Kong Le are reportedly moving north for an attack on the old royal capital of Luang Prabang.

A	B	C	D	E
Includes developments that affect more than one world region, international organizations and important meetings of major world leaders.	*Includes all domestic and regional developments in Europe, including the Soviet Union, Turkey, Cyprus and Malta.*	*Includes all domestic and regional developments in Africa and the Middle East, including Iraq and Iran and excluding Cyprus, Turkey and Afghanistan.*	*Includes all domestic and regional developments in Latin America, the Caribbean and Canada.*	*Includes all domestic and regional developments in Asia and Pacific nations, extending from Afghanistan through all the Pacific Islands, except Hawaii.*

U.S. Politics & Social Issues	U.S. Foreign Policy & Defense	U.S. Economy & Environment	Science, Technology & Nature	Culture, Leisure & Life Style	
Final official returns from the 1960 presidential election show Kennedy with 34,221,531 votes (49.7%) to Nixon's 34,108,778 (49.6%), a margin of 113,057. Minor party candidates received less than 1% of the total. . . . Kennedy names Harvard Law Prof. Archibald Cox as Solicitor General.		Agriculture Dept. reports the average American consumed 1,488 pounds of food in 1960.	Dr. James Van Allen, discoverer of the earth's radiation belts, tells an American Association for the Advancement of Science symposium that the outermost Van Allen belt disintegrated and reformed during mid-November for as yet unknown reasons. The discovery was made from data supplied by the Explorer VII satellite.	Australia defeats Italy to retain the prestigious Davis Cup tennis title.	Dec. 28
		NLRB reports receiving a record number of unfair labor practices complaints during 1960.	Dr. Frederick Russell, 90, developer of the first successful typhoid vaccine, dies in Louisville, Ky.	Deborah Kerr (*The Sundowners*) and Burt Lancaster (*Elmer Gantry*) win the New York Film Critics' Awards for best performances in 1960.	Dec. 29
Two U.S. courts issue restraining orders to prevent 700 Negro sharecroppers from being evicted for having registered to vote.		Bureau of Labor Statistics estimates that 3,300 strikes, involving 1,400,000 U.S. workers, began in 1960; it is the lowest total since 1947.			Dec. 30
Kennedy names Robert Weaver, national chairman of the NAACP, to become the administrator of the U.S. Housing and Home Finance Agency; it is the highest federal administrative post ever assumed by a Negro.	BUNDY, McGeorge Kennedy designates Harvard dean McGeorge Bundy to serve as special presidential adviser on national security matters.			Olympic decathlon champion Rafer Johnson wins the 1960 AAU Sullivan Award as the year's outstanding athlete.	Dec. 31

F	G	H	I	J
Includes elections, federal-state relations, civil rights and liberties, crime, the judiciary, education, health care, poverty, urban affairs and population.	*Includes formation and debate of U.S. foreign and defense policies, veterans' affairs and defense spending. (Relations with specific foreign countries are usually found under the region concerned.)*	*Includes business, labor, agriculture, taxation, transportation, consumer affairs, monetary and fiscal policy, natural resources, and pollution.*	*Includes worldwide scientific, medical and technological developments, natural phenomena, U.S. weather, natural disasters, and accidents.*	*Includes the arts, religion, scholarship, communications media, sports, entertainment, fashions, fads and social life.*

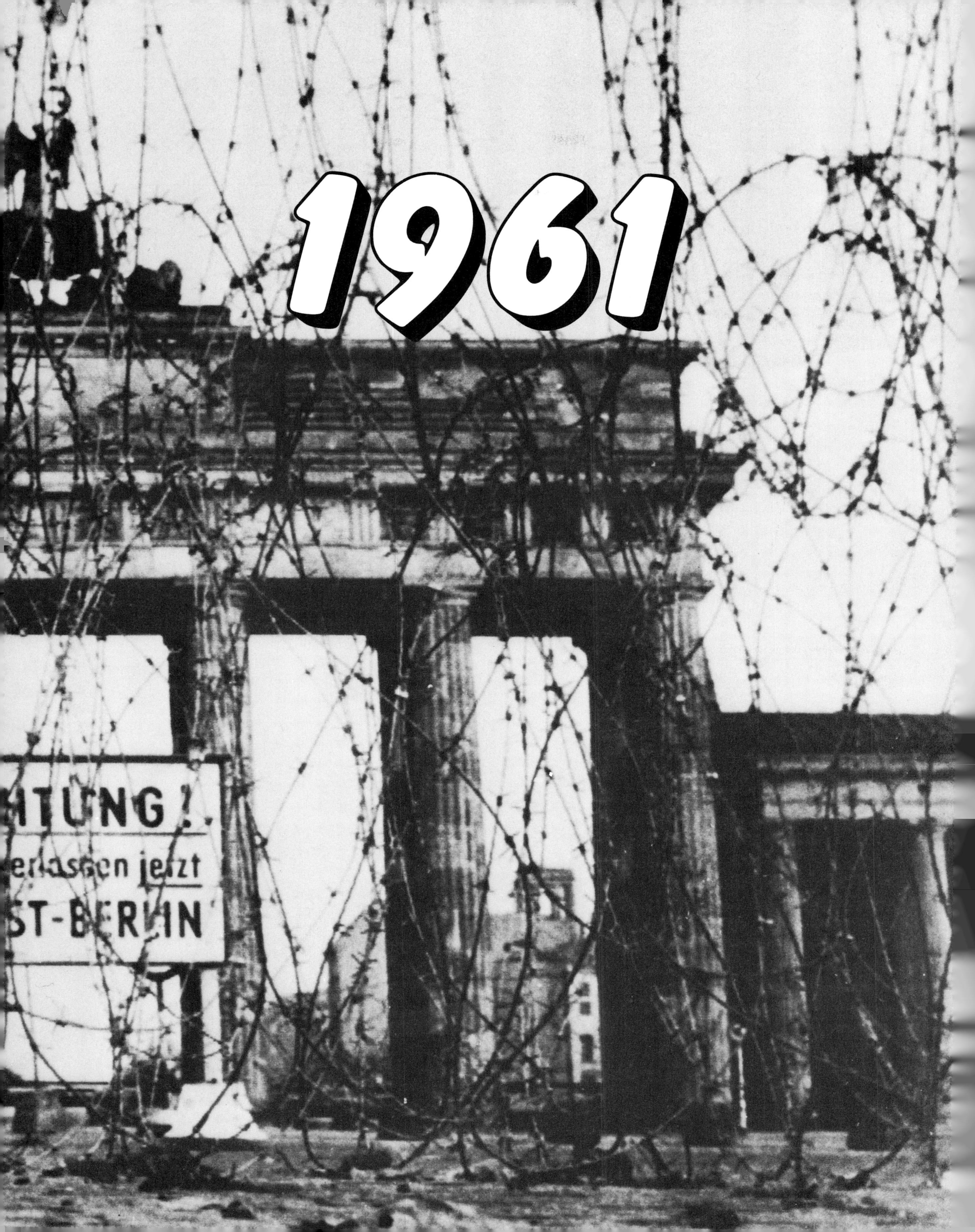
1961

President John F. Kennedy delivers his inaugural address Jan. 20. Seated in the front row are Vice President Lyndon Johnson, former Vice President Richard Nixon and former President Harry Truman.

Soviet Cosmonaut Major Yuri Gagarin and Russian Premier Nikita Khrushchev during a welcome for Gagarin at Moscow Airport Apr. 14. Gagarin, the first man in space, made one orbit around the earth.

Alan B. Shepard, Jr., America's first man in space, is lifted out of his space craft following his sub-orbital flight on May 5.

Fidel Castro at the front during the Bay of Pigs invasion in April.

A barbed wire barrier blocks the border separating East and West Berlin. The East Germans closed the border on Aug 13 and began erecting a concrete wall two days later.

Dancer Rudolf Nureyev defects from the Soviet Union in June.

Soviet Premier Nikita Khrushchev welcomes President Kennedy to the Russian Embassy in Vienna during their June summit conference.

Former Gestapo officer Adolf Eichmann testifies in his own defense at his trial in Jerusalem.

Sweden's Ingemar Johansson hits the canvas after Floyd Patterson's knockout punch, ending their heavyweight championship fight in Miami Beach.

Freedom Rider Jim Zwerg after he was beaten May 20 at the bus station in Montgomery, Alabama.

	World Affairs	Europe	Africa & the Middle East	The Americas	Asia & the Pacific
Jan.	OAS votes for limited sanctions against the Dominican Republic.	French voters endorse Algerian self-determination.	Israeli Premier David Ben-Gurion resigns.	Venezuela adopts a new constitution providing for a strong central government.	Laotian Comminists capture the strategic central plain.
Feb.	U.N. Secy. Gen. Dag Hammarskjold refuses to comply with Soviet demands that he resign.	Belgian King Baudouin dissolves Parliament and calls for new elections.	Deposed Congolese Premier Patrice Lumumba is murdered by unknown assailants.	Canadians debate whether or not to accept U.S. nuclear weapons on their territory.	Australia makes a major wheat sale to Communist China.
March	U.N. troops withdraw from the Congolese port of Matadi.	France limits the political powers of the French police in Algeria.	Algerian nationalists agree to resume negotiations with France.	Brazil establishes diplomatic relations with three East European countries.	Communist forces continue their successful offensive in central Laos.
April	U.N. calls on Belgium to withdraw its troops from the Congo.	French Pres. de Gaulle assumes near dictatorial powers after army dissidents' revolt in Algeria.	French army puts down dissident army units after they capture Algiers.	Cuba repulses an invasion of anti-Castro exiles at the Bay of Pigs.	Laos says that U.S. soldiers will work as advisers to the Laotian army.
May	An international conference on Laos deadlocks after the Soviets insist that the Communists be seated as equals of the official government.	France announces a 30-day cease-fire in Algeria.	Tanganyika becomes independent.	Assassins murder Dominican Republic dictator Rafael Trujillo.	South Korea bans hundreds of newspapers.
June	Antarctica 1959 treaty comes into force.	France breaks off peace talks with Algerian nationalists.	Kuwait becomes independent.	U.S. abandons efforts to exchange U.S. tractors for Cuban invasion prisoners.	South Korean military curbs all political freedoms.
July	U.N. defeats a resolution calling for the withdrawal of British troops from newly independent Kuwait.	Britain sends troops to Kuwait to counter Iraqi annexation threats.	Tunisian and French troops clash at the French base at Bizerte.	Cuban Premier Castro says there will be only one political party allowed in Cuba.	Gen. Park Chung Hi becomes chairman of South Korea's military junta.
Aug.	U.N. calls on France to withdraw from its naval base in Tunisia.	Soviet Union closes all crossings between East and West Berlin. . .Soviet Union announces the resumption of all nuclear tests.	British authorities release Kenyan nationalist Jomo Kenyatta from prison.	Brazilian Pres. Janio da Silva Quadros resigns following charges that he was moving towards the Soviet Union.	India annexes the Portugese enclaves of Dadra and Nagar Aveli.
Sept.	U.N. Secy. Gen. Dag Hammarskjold dies in a plane crash over Northern Rhodesia.	Soviet Union resumes nuclear testing. . .Turkish army executes former Premier Adnan Menderes. . .France agrees to withdraw from its naval base in Tunisia.	Syria withdraws from its political union with Egypt.	Joao Goulart Becomes president of Brazil.	Afghanistan breaks diplomatic relations with Pakistan.
Oct.	U.N. troops and secessionist Katangese rebels agree to a truce.	U.S. and Soviet tanks face each other at the major crossing between East and West Berlin.	Congolese government troops enter Katanga province.	Latin American nations begin receiving US aid under the Alliance for Progress program.	Prince Souvanna Phouma becomes premier of a new Laotian government.
Nov.	Soviet Union vetos the admission of Kuwait to the UN.	East Germans begin constructing a wall between East and West Berlin.	Mutinous Congolese soldiers attack Europeans.	Venezuela breaks off diplomatic relations with Cuba because of alleged subversion.	Malaysia and Singapore agree to form a federation.
Dec.	U.N. troops fight their way into Elizabethville against Katangese rebels.	Allied foreign ministers disagree on a unified plan for negotiating with the Soviet Union on Berlin.	Egypt says all foreign-owned land will be nationalized.	Colombia breaks off diplomatic relations with Cuba.	Indian troops annex the Portugese colony of Goa.

A	B	C	D	E
Includes developments that affect more than one world region, international organizations and important meetings of major world leaders.	Includes all domestic and regional developments in Europe, including the Soviet Union, Turkey, Cyprus and Malta.	Includes all domestic and regional developments in Africa and the Middle East, including Iraq and Iran and excluding Cyprus, Turkey and Afghanistan.	Includes all domestic and regional developments in Latin America, the Caribbean and Canada.	Includes all domestic and regional developments in Asia and Pacific nations, extending from Afghanistan through all the Pacific Islands, except Hawaii.

U.S. Politics & Social Issues	U.S. Foreign Policy & Defense	U.S. Economy & Environment	Science, Technology & Nature	Culture, Leisure & Life Style
Georgia repeals school segregation laws.	John Kennedy becomes the 35th president of the US.	Pres. Eisenhower submits a surplus federal budget for the fiscal year ending on June 30, 1962.	British physicist Sir John Cockcroft wins the 1961 Atoms for Peace award.	Anglican officials nominate Arthur Ramsey to succeed Geoffrey Fisher as the archbishop of Canterbury.
Pres. Kennedy calls for increased benefits for the aged.	Pres. Kennedy calls for better U.S. Soviet relations.	Justice Dept. says it will prosecute electrical appliance companies for price-fixing.	U.S. test-fires the Minuteman missile for the first time.	National Council of Churches approves the use of artificial methods for birth control.
Pres. Kennedy warns against any discrimination in federal hiring practices.	Pres. Kennedy calls for a Peace Corps of volunteer Americans working in the developing world.	U.S. unemployment rate is the highest since 1941.	Soviet Union orbits a spacecraft carrying a dog.	Floyd Patterson defeats Ingemar Johansson to retain the heavyweight championship.
Supreme Court rules that restaurants on publicly owned property cannot refuse to serve Negroes.	U.S. removes Gen. Edwin Walker because of attempted indoctrination of his troops with the views of the rightist John Birch Society.	U.S. sues General Motors for monopolizing the diesel-electric locomotive industry.	Soviet Maj. Yuri Gagarin becomes the first man to successfully orbit the earth.	Elizabeth Taylor wins the best actress award of 1960.
Segregationist mobs attack Freedom Riders when they try to integrate Alabama bus stations.	State Secy. Dean Rusk says the U.S. will assign five Polaris missile submarines to NATO.	Pres. Kennedy blocks a nationwide railroad strike for 60 days.	Alan Shepard becomes the first U.S. astronaut to achieve suborbital flight.	Harper Lee's *To Kill a Mockingbird* wins the 1961 Pulitzer Prize for literature.
Supreme Court forbids the use of illegally seized evidence in state criminal trials.	Acrimony dominates the meeting of Pres. Kennedy and Soviet Premier Khrushchev in Vienna.	Senate rejects Pres. Kennedy's plan to reorganize the SEC.	American Medical Association endorses the oral polio vaccine developed by Albert Sabin.	Arthur Ramsey becomes the 100th Archbishop of Canterbury.
Senate passes six bills dealing with price-fixing.	Pres. Kennedy calls for major increases in defense spending.	New York, New Haven and Hartford Railroad declares bankruptcy.	Capt. Virgil Grissom completes the second U.S. suborbital flight.	Pope John calls for more aid for the developing countries.
House defeats a school construction bill.	Pres. Kennedy orders 1,500 men to West Berlin.	U.S. Commerce Dept. calls for subsidies for railroads.	U.S. test launches a moon orbit satellite around the earth.	Guinea expels Bishop Gerard de Millville for criticizing the nationalization of all schools.
U.S. forbids discrimination in interstate bus travel.	U.S. sends four fighter plane squadrons to Europe.	Pres. Kennedy asks steel companies not to increase prices.	U.S. resumes underground nuclear testing.	Cuba deports over 100 Catholic priests.
Pres. Kennedy calls on Southern governors to ease the way for integration.	Pres. Kennedy calls for an extensive fallout shelter program.	AFL-CIO votes against re-admitting the Teamsters Union.	George von Bekesy wins the 1961 Nobel Prize in medicine for his work on hearing.	Ivo Andrei of Yugoslavia wins the 1961 Nobel Prize in literature.
Pres. Kennedy names a panel to study youth unemployment.	U.S. resumes negotiations with the Soviet Union on a nuclear test ban treaty.	Pres. Kennedy signs the Delaware River development project.	Melvin Calvin wins the 1961 Nobel Prize in chemistry.	New York's Metropolitan Museum buys Rembrandt's *Aristotle Contemplating the Bust of Homer* .
Supreme Court reverses the convictions of 16 Negro students convicted of participating in sit-ins.	Pres. Kennedy makes a good-will tour of Latin America.	AFL-CIO calls for higher wages and shorter working hours.	U.S. announces that a manned orbital flight will be made during 1962.	Pope John calls for the convening of the Church's 21st ecumenical council during 1962.

F	G	H	I	J
Includes elections, federal-state relations, civil rights and liberties, crime, the judiciary, education, health care, poverty, urban affairs and population.	*Includes formation and debate of U.S. foreign and defense policies, veterans' affairs and defense spending. (Relations with specific foreign countries are usually found under the region concerned.)*	*Includes business, labor, agriculture, taxation, transportation, consumer affairs, monetary and fiscal policy, natural resources, and pollution.*	*Includes worldwide scientific, medical and technological developments, natural phenomena, U.S. weather, natural disasters, and accidents.*	*Includes the arts, religion, scholarship, communications media, sports, entertainment, fashions, fads and social life.*

	World Affairs	Europe	Africa & the Middle East	The Americas	Asia & the Pacific
Jan. 1	In a New Year's address, Soviet Premier Nikita Khrushchev offers to make a fresh start at improving East-West relations by forgetting the tensions caused by the U-2 incident in his dealings with the incoming U.S. administration of Pres.-elect John F. Kennedy.		Troops of the central Congolese government of Col. Joseph Mobutu and Pres. Joseph Kasavubu, temporarily based in the Belgian-administered U.N. trust territory of Ruanda-Urundi, launch an attack on rebel forces loyal to imprisoned ex-Congo Premier Patrice Lumumba in adjacent Kivu Province.		The newly established right-wing Laotian government of Prince Boun Oum reports that Communist-supported rebels have stepped-up their military counter-offensive and have captured the strategically important Plaines de Jarres in central Laos. The government also claims that six North Vietnamese battalions have "invaded" Laos to support the Communist insurgents.
Jan. 2	In a formal protest note U.N. Secy. Gen. Dag Hammarskjold criticizes Belgium for permitting Congolese troops to use Ruanda-Urundi as a base for military actions.	Soviet citizens begin exchanging old rubles for the new revalued ones at a rate of 10 to one; the complete retirement of the old currency is expected to take three months.	Britian's Commonwealth Relations Office announces that a new Bechuanaland constitution, to become effective in 1961, will provide for an elected Legislative Council made up of equal numbers of Africans and Europeans.	Claiming that most American Embassy employees are spies, Cuban Premier Fidel Castro orders the U.S. to reduce its Havana embassy staff to 11 persons within 48 hours.	Pres. Eisenhower orders U.S. military forces in the Pacific to an "increased state of readiness" following a briefing on the current Laos situation. . . . British Foreign Secy. Alexander Douglas-Home publicly urges the reconvening of the International Control Commission for Laos, originally created by the 1954 Geneva Conference on Indochina.
Jan. 3			Congo sources report that the U.N. Force has arranged a truce in the fighting along the Ruanda-Urundi border.	Citing Castro's demand for an Embassy staff reduction as but the last in a long series of provocations, Pres. Dwight Eisenhower announces the complete severing of U.S. diplomatic relations with Cuba.	The U.S. State Dept. charges that the USSR and North Vietnam have been directly supplying Communist rebels in Laos since mid-December. . . . Pres. Sukarno makes public a land reform decree designed to give five acres of land to each family of Indonesia's landless rural population of 42 million.
Jan. 4		Socialist-led work stoppages and demonstrations called to protest Belgian Premier Gaston Eyskens' proposed economic austerity program continue to cripple Belgium's economy. Clashes between police and demonstrators are increasing daily. . . . A group of 16 retired French generals issue a declaration urging French voters to defeat Pres. de Gaulle's proposals for Algerian self-determination in the special Jan. 6 referendum.	Pro-Lumumba demonstrators demanding the release of the former premier greet U.N. Secy. Gen. Hammarskjold as he arrives in Leopoldville for talks with Congo leaders.	The USSR and Communist China denounce the U.S. decision to break relations with Cuba as part of a continuing campaign to overthrow the legitimate Castro government. . . . The OAS Council, meeting in Washington, votes to impose limited economic sanctions against the Dominican Republic for its alleged violation of basic human rights. The action conforms to a recommendation made by the OAS foreign ministers' conference in August 1960.	Reports from foreign military experts in Laos suggest that the government's official claim of a large North Vietnamese invasion is probably exaggerated. . . . Sir Syed Putra is installed for a five-year term as Malaya's third elected paramount ruler.
Jan. 5		Belgian Premier Eyskens' Social Christian-Liberal coalition cabinet resumes negotiations with Socialist Party Pres. Leo Collard and other leftist leaders in an effort to end the continuing strikes and disorders.	Nigeria breaks diplomatic relations with France in protest against France's third nuclear test explosion Dec. 27, 1960 in southwest Algeria. . . . Israeli Premier David Ben-Gurion hints that he will resign if a special government inquiry exonerates ex-Defense Min. Pinhas Lavon from responsibility for an undisclosed military mishap in 1955 that led to Lavon's dismissal. Lavon has charged that he was wrongly blamed for the incident by a government clique that included Ben-Gurion and Gen. Moshe Dayan, then Israeli chief of staff.	In an official statement, the Cuban government places responsibility for the break in U.S.-Cuban relations on America's consistently "aggressive and unfriendly" policies toward the Castro government. . . . The U.N. Security Council rejects without a vote Cuban charges that the U.S. is planning an "immediate invasion" of Cuba.	King Mahendra Bir Bikram Shah Deva declares Nepal's first attempt at democracy a "failure" and says he will try to improve the nation's political ability through a program of "guided democracy" under his personal rule.
Jan. 6		French Pres. de Gaulle goes on national TV to make a final appeal for voter support of his Algerian policies in the upcoming referendum. He calls for a "majority proportionate to the issue.". . . Sixty-five persons are injured in clashes between police and anti-government rioters in Liege, Belgium after demonstrators wrecked a railway station, a bank and a local newspaper.		Cuban National Bank Pres. Ernesto Guevara tells a Cuban TV audience that communist countries have pledged enough economic assistance to compensate for the loss of the U.S. sugar market. . . . Although most Latin American governments expressed support for the U.S. break with Cuba, the governments of Ecuador, Chile, Argentina, Venezuela, Brazil, and Bolivia refused to make any official comment.	
	A	**B**	**C**	**D**	**E**
	Includes developments that affect more than one world region, international organizations and important meetings of major world leaders.	*Includes all domestic and regional developments in Europe, including the Soviet Union, Turkey, Cyprus and Malta.*	*Includes all domestic and regional developments in Africa and the Middle East, including Iraq and Iran and excluding Cyprus, Turkey and Afghanistan.*	*Includes all domestic and regional developments in Latin America, the Caribbean and Canada.*	*Includes all domestic and regional developments in Asia and Pacific nations, extending from Afghanistan through all the Pacific Islands, except Hawaii.*

U.S. Politics & Social Issues	U.S. Foreign Policy & Defense	U.S. Economy & Environment	Science, Technology & Nature	Culture, Leisure & Life Style	
	Sen. Mike Mansfield (D, Mont.) proposes that the U.S. substantially reduce its troop levels in Europe on the condition that the USSR make a reciprocal cut in its Eastern European forces. Mansfield says the plan would help the U.S. gold drain without materially affecting the military balance in Europe.	Pres.-elect John Kennedy releases a special economic report recommending increased unemployment compensation, an expanded surplus food distribution plan, and a multi-faceted federal program to stimulate the economic development of depressed regions. Kennedy calls the plan his "most important domestic priority.". . . The Standard and Poor's index of 500 stocks closes the year at 57.78, two points below the mark of Dec. 31, 1959.		The Houston Oilers of the new American Football League defeat the Los Angeles Chargers in the AFL's first championship game.	**Jan. 1**
	Kennedy announces that John J. McCloy will serve as his principal disarmament adviser and negotiator.	The U.S. Justice Dept. reports that during 1960 it filed a record 90 new criminal and civil anti-trust cases (of which more than 30 were successfully terminated).		The Univ. of Washington beats the Univ. of Minnesota, 17-7, in the annual Rose Bowl classic. . . . Bobby Fischer, 17, clinches his fourth consecutive U.S. chess championship in New York by drawing with Hungarian grandmaster Pal Benko.	**Jan. 2**
Party caucuses name leaders for the new 87th Congress. Senate Democrats choose Mike Mansfield (Mont.) to replace Lyndon Johnson as majority leader and Hubert Humphrey (Minn.) as whip; Senate Republicans re-elect Everett Dirksen (Ill.) and Thomas Kuchel (Calif.) as top minority leaders. In the House, Democratic Rep. Sam Rayburn (Tex.) wins his ninth term as Speaker. . . . Rep. John W. McCormack (D, Mass.) and Rep. Charles A. Halleck (R, Ind.) are re-elected as leaders of their respective parties on the House floor.	Pres.-elect Kennedy's State Secy.-designate Dean Rusk says the Kennedy administration does not wish to commit itself on the Eisenhower decision to break relations with Cuba until it has all the facts.	Three technicians are killed in an explosion of an atomic reactor at the National Reactor Testing Station in Idaho Falls, Ida. AEC Commissioner John McCone says the resultant escape of radioactivity was "largely confined" to the test building.			**Jan. 3**
Pres. Eisenhower accepts the resignation of State Undersecy. C. Douglas Dillon and wishes him well in his future post as Treasury Secretary in the Kennedy Administration. Disclosure of the comment comes amidst reports that Eisenhower was disappointed by Dillon's decision to join the Kennedy cabinet.	White House Press Secy. James Hagerty tells newsmen that the severance of U.S.-Cuban diplomatic relations will have no effect on the status of the U.S. Guantanamo naval base.	N.Y. Stock Exchange prices advance a total of $5 billion, the best daily gain since Nov. 15, 1957. The Dow Jones average climbs over 11 points.			**Jan. 4**
Conservative Republican Sen. Barry Goldwater (Ariz.) tells a *New York Herald Tribune* interviewer that the 1964 GOP presidential contest will probably involve "Nelson Rockefeller, Dick Nixon and myself."		Pres.-elect Kennedy's special task force on the economy, headed by MIT professor Paul Samuelson, urges the adoption for fiscal 1962 of a $3-$5 billion program to combat the current economic slump and prevent a possibly serious recession. . . . The N.Y. Federal Reserve Bank reports that the net outflow of gold from the U.S. Treasury increased from $1.078 billion in 1959 to $1.689 billion in 1960.	The New Jersey Health Dept. discloses that 14 persons in the Camden area have died of serum hepatitis after receiving sedative inoculations from Dr. Albert Weiner, an osteopath specializing in psychotherapy.		**Jan. 5**
Kennedy makes public a wide-ranging, four year, $10 billion program of federal aid to U.S. public schools. . . . A U.S. district court in Macon, Ga. orders the University of Georgia to discontinue barring the admission of qualified Negro applicants. The court also prohibits Ga. Gov. S. Ernest Vandiver from withholding state funds to the university.	Sen. J. William Fulbright (D, Ark.) tells reporters that State Secy. Herter provided a rather gloomy review of the current world situation in his appearance before a closed session of the Senate Foreign Relations Committee.				**Jan. 6**

F	G	H	I	J
Includes elections, federal-state relations, civil rights and liberties, crime, the judiciary, education, health care, poverty, urban affairs and population.	Includes formation and debate of U.S. foreign and defense policies, veterans' affairs and defense spending. (Relations with specific foreign countries are usually found under the region concerned.)	Includes business, labor, agriculture, taxation, transportation, consumer affairs, monetary and fiscal policy, natural resources, and pollution.	Includes worldwide scientific, medical and technological developments, natural phenomena, U.S. weather, natural disasters, and accidents.	Includes the arts, religion, scholarship, communications media, sports, entertainment, fashions, fads and social life.

	World Affairs	Europe	Africa & the Middle East	The Americas	Asia & the Pacific
Jan. 7		Responding to recent disclosures that U.S. nuclear weapons are being stored in Holland, the USSR formally warns the Netherlands that the use of its territory as a U.S. nuclear base would bring the "terrible risk" of retaliation in the event of atomic war.	King Mohammed V of Morocco, Pres. Gamal Nasser of the UAR, Pres. Kwame Nkrumah of Ghana, Pres. Sekou Toure of Guinea, Pres. Modibo Keita of Mali, and Premier Ferhat Abbas of the Algerian Provisional Government conclude a four-day African summit in Casablanca. The talks produced criticism of the U.N.'s Congo operation, pledges of support for the Algerian rebellion and a demand for an end to colonialism.	Cuba continues to make much-publicized military preparations against a U.S. "invasion" which Premier Castro claims will come before the end of Eisenhower's term on Jan. 20. Thousands of suspected "counter-revolutionaries" are reportedly being arrested by Cuban army authorities.	In a statement warning of the serious implications for all of Southeast Asia should Laos fall to the Communists, the U.S. State Dept. calls upon all free world countries to support Laos "through whatever measures seem most promising."
Jan. 8		De Gaulle's proposed Algerian self-determination program wins approval from over 72% of the voters participating in the special referendum carried out in France, Algeria and all overseas French territories. The turnout was generally high, although many Moslems, in apparent compliance with rebel instructions, boycotted the voting. . . . Scotland Yard announces the arrest of five persons on charges of seeking British submarine detection secrets for the USSR.	A World Zionist Congress, meeting in Jerusalem, appeals for the emigration to Israel of Jews living in other countries, especially those in Algeria, Tunisia and Morocco.		Two North Vietnamese prisoners and a quantity of Communist Chinese arms are displayed to newsmen in Vientiane to support Laotian government claims of a Communist "invasion.". . . Indian P.M. Jawaharlal Nehru declares his support for Punjabi as the dominant language of Punjab State in a gesture designed to end fasts and demonstrations by Punjabi-speaking Sikh religious leaders.
Jan. 9	The U.N. Security Council is called into special session to hear Soviet charges of continuing Belgian intervention in the internal affairs of the Congo.	De Gaulle supporters in France hail the Algerian referendum as proof of popular support for de Gaulle's policies. French rightists, however, lament the outcome as a virtual "abandonment" of Algeria to the rebels. . . . Socialist leaders in the Belgian Parliament appeal for serious political negotiations to end the continuing wave of disorders; Premier Gaston Eyskens replies that he is prepared to compromise.	Pro-Lumumba forces led by Antoine Gizenga are reportedly moving from their strongholds in Oriental and Kivu Provinces into northern Katanga where they are being joined by local Baluba tribesmen opposed to the separatist regime of Katanga Pres. Moise Tshombe.	The semi-official Cuban newspaper *Revolucion* charges that the U.S. is militarily reinforcing its naval base at Guantanamo.	Communist Chinese Premier Chou En-lai signs an agreement in Rangoon to provide Burma with an $85 million interest-free loan over the next six years.
Jan. 10		The Belgian Socialist Party publicly disavows the violence and sabotage that have attended the Socialist-sponsored general strike against the government's proposed economic policies.		*The New York Times* reports that foreign military experts, mostly from the U.S., are training guerrilla forces near an American-owned commercial air field in Guatemala. Guatemalan Pres. Miguel Fuentes claims the men are being trained to defend against a Cuban invasion, but his political foes insist they are being prepared for an attack on Cuba. . . . Canadian Defense Minister Douglass Harkness denies reports that U.S. nuclear weapons have been or will be based in Canada.	An emergency meeting of SEATO, called to discuss U.S. charges of Communist intervention in Laos, ends without adopting any specific proposals. . . . Sinhalese replaces English as the official language of Ceylon, despite reports that a majority of the nation's 200,000 civil servants cannot work in the language.
Jan. 11		In his first statement since the Algerian referendum, French Pres. de Gaulle lauds the "positive and massive" support given his policies.	U.N. headquarters in Leopoldville announces that it is dispatching a 600-man force to Katanga in an effort to prevent fighting between Katangan troops and the invading pro-Lumumba forces. . . . UAR Deputy Foreign Min. Zulficar Sabry issues a statement warning that the UAR will resist any efforts by U.S. Pres.-elect Kennedy to fulfill his "campaign promises" to help Israeli Zionism.		

A	B	C	D	E
Includes developments that affect more than one world region, international organizations and important meetings of major world leaders.	Includes all domestic and regional developments in Europe, including the Soviet Union, Turkey, Cyprus and Malta.	Includes all domestic and regional developments in Africa and the Middle East, including Iraq and Iran and excluding Cyprus, Turkey and Afghanistan.	Includes all domestic and regional developments in Latin America, the Caribbean and Canada.	Includes all domestic and regional developments in Asia and Pacific nations, extending from Afghanistan through all the Pacific Islands, except Hawaii.

U.S. Politics & Social Issues	U.S. Foreign Policy & Defense	U.S. Economy & Environment	Science, Technology & Nature	Culture, Leisure & Life Style	
	Pres. Eisenhower thanks Defense Secy. Thomas Gates for helping to maintain a U.S. "military power, second to none, with the greatest striking power in our history." The statement came in a letter accepting Gates' resignation.	Kennedy announces the designation of Willard Wirtz, law associate of Adlai Stevenson, as Labor Undersecretary.		U.S. race tracks report that over 32 million people bet a record $2.4 billion on thoroughbred horse races during 1960.	**Jan. 7**
	Pres.-elect Kennedy releases a draft report outlining plans for a "peace corps" of young, highly-trained American volunteers to provide technical assistance to people in underdeveloped nations. Kennedy first suggested the idea during his presidential campaign.			Yale Univ. Library's Bollingen Poetry Prize is awarded to Stanford professor Yvor Winters for his *Collected Poems*.	**Jan. 8**
		The Census Bureau estimates that U.S. exports rose from a total of $16.3 billion in 1959 to $19.4 billion in 1960, while imports fell from $15.2 to $14.9 during the same period.		Various ceremonies throughout the nation, including a re-enactment of the bombardment of Fort Sumter supply ships, mark the beginning of a five-year centennial celebration of the American Civil War.	**Jan. 9**
The Univ. of Georgia, faced with a federal court order, admits two Negro students; the event marks the first desegregation in Georgia's public education system.	A proposal to improve the U.S. cultural exchange programs by providing aid to foreign educational institutions is presented to Pres.-elect Kennedy by a special task force headed by Univ. of Michigan Prof. James Davis.			Samuel Dashiell Hammett, 66, detective writer whose novels included *The Maltese Falcon* (1930) and *The Thin Man* (1932), dies in New York. Hammett's books were banned from U.S. overseas libraries in the early 1950's following his conviction in 1951 for refusing to give information about leftist organizations to which he belonged. Pres. Eisenhower ordered the books restored in 1953.	**Jan. 10**
The Senate votes down two proposals that would have significantly weakened the filibuster strategy. Opponents to the reform proposals included Southern conservatives and some Democratic liberals who did not want to endanger Kennedy's legislative program by a bitter floor fight. . . . Conservative Republicans begin circulating a "manifesto" of new direction for the GOP which calls for tough regulation of labor unions, a limit on social welfare programs, and "a hard anti-communist line" abroad and at home. American Medical Association Pres. E. Vincent Askey claims that a plan to tie an aged health care program to Social Security, recommended by Pres.-elect Kennedy's special task force on health care, would result in massive governmeNuclear Testing inference and poorer medical care.	A special Presidential Committee on Information Activities Abroad recommends a progressive expansion and improvement in U.S. propaganda efforts. . . . Kennedy names Iowa lawyer George Ball as State Undersecy. for Economic Affairs. . . . A "manifesto" currently being circulated among conservative Republicans recommends that U.S. policy toward non-communist countries be based more "on their friendship for the U.S. and their willingness to resist communism, than on the ideological character of their governments."	During his confirmation hearing before the Senate Finance Committee, Treasury Secy.-designate Douglas Dillon says he believes there will be a budget deficit in fiscal 1962.	Pres.-elect Kennedy releases a special task force report calling for a thorough re-assessment of the U.S. space program. The report identified the development of powerful booster rockets capable of lifting heavy payloads into space as a priority goal and it criticized the "exaggerated emphasis" given the Mercury program since it is "very unlikely that we shall be first in placing a man into orbit.". . . NASA scientists in charge of the Mercury program estimate that the cost of putting a man in orbit will be almost twice the original estimate.		**Jan. 11**

F	G	H	I	J
Includes elections, federal-state relations, civil rights and liberties, crime, the judiciary, education, health care, poverty, urban affairs and population.	Includes formation and debate of U.S. foreign and defense policies, veterans' affairs and defense spending. (Relations with specific foreign countries are usually found under the region concerned.)	Includes business, labor, agriculture, taxation, transportation, consumer affairs, monetary and fiscal policy, natural resources, and pollution.	Includes worldwide scientific, medical and technological developments, natural phenomena, U.S. weather, natural disasters, and accidents.	Includes the arts, religion, scholarship, communications media, sports, entertainment, fashions, fads and social life.

	World Affairs	Europe	Africa & the Middle East	The Americas	Asia & the Pacific
Jan. 12	Soviet Deputy Foreign Min. Valerian Zorin, addressing the U.N. Security Council, accuses Belgium of directly assisting in the Congolese army's Ruanda-Urundi-based attack on Kivu Province and demands that Belgium be removed from the administration of the Ruanda-Urundi trust territory.	The Hamburg (Germany) Health Dept. rules that six doctors who participated in the "eugenic" murder of 56 children during W.W. II can continue to practice medicine.	The Katanga government announces that it has rejected a U.N. truce plan and has ordered its airforce to attack pro-Lumumba forces located in the northern part of the province. . . . Belgium, in a note to U.N. Secy. Gen. Hammarskjold, explains that it allowed Congolese troops to move across Ruanda-Urundi because local Belgian officials did not want to risk an incident by attempting to disarm the soldiers.	Uruguay expels the Cuban ambassador and a Soviet Embassy aide for allegedly participating in recent pro-Castro demonstrations and disorders in Montevideo. . . . The Vatican announces the excommunication of all Roman Catholic Haitian government officials connected with the Jan. 10 expulsion of Bishop Remy Augustin.	The U.S. State Department confirms that the U.S. has recently provided Laos with four armed T-6 training planes for use in fighting the leftist rebels. . . . Burma announces that its troops have begun an offensive against refugee Chinese Nationalist troops near the borders of Thailand and Laos. Burma says that Nationalist China has been supplying the refugee troops with arms by airdrop from Formosa.
Jan. 13	Deputy U.S. Rep.-to-U.N. James Barco tells the Security Council that the Soviet accusations against Belgium are a "total distortion" designed to hide the fact that "rebel elements" with foreign support are the real cause of the current Congo crisis.	In a speech to a plenary meeting of the Soviet CP Central Committee, Premier Nikita Khrushchev angrily denounces Soviet agricultural officials for distorting farm production statistics and for failing to meet the current seven-year plan production goals. . . . Belgian Premier Eyskens' controversial austerity bill, calling for increased taxes and reduced government spending, passes the Chamber of Deputies by a 115-90 vote and is sent to the Senate.	The Justice Ministry of the UAR publishes draft legislation providing for increased recognition of women's rights. The proposals include a measure ending the legality of divorce by simple oral declaration of the husband.	Cuban Pres. Osvaldo Dorticas Torrado tells a Havana rally that Cuba will "claim" the U.S. naval base at Guantanamo "in proper time.". . . The New York Times reports that an estimated 15,000 Cubans are being held as political prisoners by the Castro government.	
Jan. 14	The U.N. Security Council refuses to adopt a Soviet resolution condemning Belgian "aggression" in the Congo.	Socialist leaders from Belgium's Walloon district, center of the resistance to the government's austerity plan, appeal to King Baudouin for the reorganization of Belgium into a federation that would assure Walloonian autonomy.		A Cuban military court sentences Robert Gentile, an American, to 30 years in prison for his role in an organization which allegedly planned to assassinate "prominent government figures."	Laotian rebel forces continue to win significant battles in their counter-offensive against troops of the ruling Boum Oum government.
Jan. 15			Israeli Pres. Itzhak Ben-Zvi meets with Premier Ben-Gurion and other political leaders in an effort to end the continuing controversy surrounding the 1955 Lavon affair.	A 10,000-15,000-man Cuban army force is reported to have begun a drive against an estimated 1,000 anti-Castro rebels located in the Escambray Mountains of Las Villas Province.	
Jan. 16				The State Dept. announces a ban on travel to Cuba except by special government authorization. . . . Cuban government sources report the defeat of two rebel forces in the Escambray Mountains of Las Villas Province.	The USSR formally protests the U.S.'s provision of planes to Laos's Boum Oum government as a violation of the 1954 Geneva Agreement on Indochina.
Jan. 17	In a farewell news conference, U.S. Amb.-to-U.N. James Wadsworth says that he believes the USSR would live up to any agreement that it may make on nuclear testing and disarmament. He also says there is no evidence to support recent charges that the Russians are conducting clandestine atomic tests.			Canada and the U.S. reach agreement on the development of water power and storage facilities along the Columbia River.	Laotian sources report that government troops have re-taken Vang Vieng, a strategically important rebel supply center north of Vientiane. . . . Communist China and the Soviet Union send separate messages to exiled former Laotian Premier Souvanna Phouma reaffirming their recognition of his neutralist cabinet as the legitimate government of Laos.

A	B	C	D	E
Includes developments that affect more than one world region, international organizations and important meetings of major world leaders.	Includes all domestic and regional developments in Europe, including the Soviet Union, Turkey, Cyprus and Malta.	Includes all domestic and regional developments in Africa and the Middle East, including Iraq and Iran and excluding Cyprus, Turkey and Afghanistan.	Includes all domestic and regional developments in Latin America, the Caribbean and Canada.	Includes all domestic and regional developments in Asia and Pacific nations, extending from Afghanistan through all the Pacific Islands, except Hawaii.

U.S. Politics & Social Issues	U.S. Foreign Policy & Defense	U.S. Economy & Environment	Science, Technology & Nature	Culture, Leisure & Life Style	
The University of Georgia suspends its two Negro students following an on-campus riot by several hundred anti-integrationist whites. The University cited the "personal safety" of the Negroes as the reason for their dismissal. . . . In his last State of the Union speech, Pres. Eisenhower lists reduced unemployment, improved balance of payments, fiscally sound economic growth, and upgraded health and education programs as America's chief domestic goals in the years ahead.	In his final State of the Union message Pres. Eisenhower reviews the foreign and domestic accomplishments of his eight-year administration and outlines the major unsolved problems that still lie ahead. Eisenhower says that communism still poses a grave threat and an immediate danger in Berlin, Laos, Cuba and Africa.		The first launching in the joint Italian-U.S. space program takes place with the firing of a two-stage Italian-made rocket from Sardinia in the Mediterranean to a height of 105 miles.	Chicago Cubs president Phil K. Wrigley announces that, starting with the 1961 season, a staff of eight coaches will run the team instead of a single manager.	Jan. 12
U.S. District Judge William Bootle in Macon, Ga. orders Univ. of Georgia officials to reinstate the two suspended Negro students. . . . A three-judge federal court in New Orleans issues an order voiding a resolution adopted Jan. 12 by the La. Legislature to declare New Orleans School Supt. James Redmond a "usurper in office."		Auto industry statistics show that U.S. passenger car sales in 1960 climbed to a record 6,147,600, an increase of 650,000 over 1959.	The AP reports that an Italian scientific team, headed by Daniele Petrucci, has claimed to have repeatedly achieved human fertilization in a test tube and to have kept an embryo alive for 29 days. The experiments, which are aimed at revealing chromosomal behavior in sex determination, are criticized as "immoral" in the Vatican's semi-official *L'Observatore Romano*.		Jan. 13
The Univ. of Georgia expels 13 white students for their part in the Jan. 11 anti-Negro riot.	Kennedy designates West Virginia Univ. Pres. Elvis Stahr to be Secretary of the Army. Ga. Gov. S. Ernest Vandiver had earlier declined the post.	In a further move to halt the U.S. gold drain, Pres. Eisenhower orders all U.S. citizens and businesses to stop buying or holding gold overseas.	Japan's Science and Technology Agency discloses that it plans to use a U.S. Scout rocket to launch its first operational satellite sometime in 1963.	The National Institute of Arts and Letters' Gold Medal for Sculpture is awarded to William Zorach, 74, of New York.	Jan. 14
A Civil Rights Commission report on school discrimination recommends that federal funds be withheld from colleges and universities that practice racial discrimination.	Delegates to a second Conference to Plan a Strategy for Peace, meeting at Columbia Univ., assert that world stability would be enhanced by the admission of Communist China to the U.N.		An Atlantic storm collapses a U.S. Air Force radar tower 105 miles off the New Jersey coast, killing all 28 men stationed there.	Dr. Joachim Prinz, president of the American Jewish Congress, calls for the dissolution of the U.S. Zionist movement in favor of a more general movement to encourage close ties between free world Jews and those living in Israel.	Jan. 15
The Univ. of Georgia's two Negro students return to classes without incident.	Pres. Eisenhower's budget for fiscal 1962 calls for a slight increase over 1961 in defense outlays and a slight decrease in foreign aid spending.	Pres. Eisenhower presents Congress with his proposed budget for fiscal 1962. The budget, which many expect will be altered by the incoming Kennedy administration, calls for expenditures of $80.9 billion and receipts of $82.3 billion, making it the fifth balanced budget submitted during the eight-year Eisenhower presidency.	Eisenhower's 1962 budget calls for a 20% increase in spending for space exploration. The President's budget message, however, suggests that the current Mercury program may be the last U.S. manned space flight project unless further testing shows "valid scientific reasons" for developing additional programs.	N.Y. Yankees outfielder Mickey Mantle signs a 1961 contract for $75,000, making him the highest paid player in the American League.	Jan. 16
New York Republican Sens. Jacob Javits and Kenneth Keating introduce into the Senate a seven-part civil rights proposal that includes provisions to end the poll tax, to make lynching a federal crime, and to provide federal aid to school districts attempting to desegregate. . . . Francis Cardinal Spellman, archbishop of New York, denounces Kennedy's education task force for leaving parochial schools out of its proposals for school aid. . . . A Gallup poll reveals that 20% of Americans think Pres. Eisenhower will be remembered as a "great President", 45% as "good", 25% as "fair" and 7% as "poor".	Pres. Eisenhower, in a nationally-televised "farewell address", warns that the developing "conjunction of an immense military establishment and a large arms industry" in a single "military-industrial complex" may lead to a "disastrous rise of misplaced power" if it is allowed to gain an "unwarranted influence" in national affairs.	A special task force report on natural resources, submitted to Pres. Elect Kennedy, concludes that "atomic power, developed and financed by the people, should be made available from federal nuclear plants as soon as production costs can be materially reduced."	Britain and France announce plans to hold an international conference in February to look into the possibility of establishing a cooperative, multi-national program for space exploration.	The Most Rev. Dr. Geoffrey Fisher, 73, announces that he will retire as Archbishop of Canterbury and Church of England primate. . . . The U.S. Methodist Church reports that its membership increased 11% over the past decade.	Jan. 17

F	G	H	I	J
Includes elections, federal-state relations, civil rights and liberties, crime, the judiciary, education, health care, poverty, urban affairs and population.	Includes formation and debate of U.S. foreign and defense policies, veterans' affairs and defense spending. (Relations with specific foreign countries are usually found under the region concerned.)	Includes business, labor, agriculture, taxation, transportation, consumer affairs, monetary and fiscal policy, natural resources, and pollution.	Includes worldwide scientific, medical and technological developments, natural phenomena, U.S. weather, natural disasters, and accidents.	Includes the arts, religion, scholarship, communications media, sports, entertainment, fashions, fads and social life.

	World Affairs	Europe	Africa & the Middle East	The Americas	Asia & the Pacific
Jan. 18	The USSR makes public a Jan. 6 policy speech by Premier Khrushchev in which he pledged full and unreserved communist support for "national liberation" wars such as those in Algeria and Cuba. Khrushchev, however, reiterated the Soviet desire to avoid a general nuclear war as well as "local wars" of the Indochina variety that could lead to world conflict.	The Central Committee of the Soviet CP formally approves a Khrushchev-proposed sweeping reorganization of the administration of Soviet agriculture. The action comes in the wake of charges by Khrushchev that Soviet farm administrators had lied in claiming to have achieved farm goals set by the seven-year plan. . . . Except in the Socialist union strongholds of Liege and Charleroi, the strikes against Belgium's proposed austerity program are rapidly waning.	The central Congo government and the government of Katanga announce that imprisoned ex-Premier Lumumba has been transferred from a prison near Leopoldville to a facility in Jadotville in Katanga. Fears that the growing pro-Lumumba demonstrations in Leopoldville might have led to the freeing of the ex-Premier are believed to be behind the move. . . . The Algerian Provisional Government and France exchange public messages indicating that both sides are prepared to reopen negotiations toward a settlement of the Algerian rebellion.	Cuba begins demobilization of civilian militia forces who were called on alert to prepare for a "Yankee invasion." Castro says the completion of the Eisenhower administration has ended the threat of an attack. . . . The Canadian Bureau of Statistics reports that unemployment had risen by mid-December, 1960 to 8.2% of the work force.	
Jan. 19			The U.N. Congo Force Command says it did not act to prevent the transfer of Lumumba because it regarded the matter as an "internal affair" beyond its jurisdiction.	Complying with OAS sanctions the U.S. Commerce Dept. orders a ban on shipment of petroleum products and machine parts to the Dominican Republic.	Ex-Laotian Premier Souvanna Phouma, in exile in Cambodia, blames the U.S.'s intransigent insistence on pro-Western policies for the collapse of his neutralist government and the current Laotian civil war. . . . Foreign ministers from South Vietnam, South Korea, Nationalist China and the Philippines meet in Manilla to declare a common front against communist expansion in Asia.
Jan. 20		Ex-Yugoslav V.P. Milovan Djilas is released on parole after serving a four-year prison sentence for his public opposition to Tito's policies during the Hungarian revolt in 1956.	U.N. headquarters in Leopoldville confirms reports that pro-Lumumba forces controlling Oriental and Kivu Provinces have arrested and beat Europeans in retaliation for Lumumba's transfer to Katanga.	In a portion of his inaugural address directed to Latin America, Kennedy offers a "new alliance for progress" to assist "free governments in casting off the chains of poverty." . . . Premier Castro tells a Havana rally that Cuba is ready to "begin anew" diplomatic relations with the U.S., if the U.S. is willing to improve its attitude toward Cuba.	The Central Committee of the Chinese CP, headed by Chmn. Mao Tse-tung, orders the immediate curtailment of the five-year plan for a "great leap" forward in industry in favor of an intensified program to stimulate seriously lagging farm production.
Jan. 21	In the first exchange of messages between the USSR and the incoming Kennedy administration, both Khrushchev and Kennedy express a desire for a fresh attempt at solving East-West problems. . . . The Central Committee of the Chinese Communist Party issues a declaration in Peking affirming the Soviet view on the non-inevitability of a major war. The statement also labels the U.S. as the "main enemy of the whole world."	Walloonian Socialist union leaders vote to end their 33-day strike against the Belgian government's austerity program.			A proposal for ending the Laotian civil war by reactivating the International Control Commission for Laos is presented to the USSR by British Amb. Sir Frank Roberts. The new Kennedy administration is reportedly in favor of the British proposal. . . . Laotian sources report that government troops have been halted in their efforts to dislodge leftist rebel forces from their strongholds in the Plaine des Jarres.
Jan. 22	Moscow sources report that Khrushchev has informed U.S. Amb.-to-USSR Llewellyn Thompson of his readiness for a face-to-face meeting with Pres. Kennedy.	A group of Portuguese and Spanish exiles, with the complicity of crew members, capture the Portuguese cruise ship *Santa Maria* in the Caribbean Sea. The seizure is reportedly the first step in a plan for the eventual overthrow of the dictatorial regime of Portuguese Premier Antonio Salazar.	Yugoslavia appeals to the U.N. to take Lumumba and all other Congolese political prisoners under its "direct protection." . . . An emergency meeting of the non-governmental Afro-Asian Solidarity Council, meeting in Cairo, calls upon the UAR, Guinea, Indonesia, and Morocco to make their U.N. Congo Force contingents available to the pro-Lumumba forces controlling Oriental Province.		The U.S. provides the Laotian army with two more armed training planes; two of the four planes originally provided have been lost in attacks on rebel positions.
Jan. 23	The International Atomic Energy Agency's (IAEA) Board of Governors adopts a U.S.-proposed (and Soviet-opposed) plan providing for the inspection of IAEA-aided nuclear facilities to insure that no IAEA nuclear materials are diverted to military uses.	Citing international laws governing piracy, the U.S. and Britain announce they will help Portugal hunt for the captured Portuguese cruiser *Santa Maria* .	U.N. Force officials warn the pro-Lumumba regime in Oriental Province that they will not tolerate the arbitrary arrest and punishment of law-abiding Europeans.	Venezuelan Pres. Romulo Betancourt and the national Congress jointly promulgate a new constitution providing for a strong central government headed by a nonsucceeding president elected every five years. The new Venezuelan constitution replaces the one decreed by the Perez Jiménez regime in 1953.	Pres. Ayub Khan returns to Pakistan after a 10-day visit to Europe during which he received a $35 million loan, a pledge from West Germany and $10 million credit agreement from Yugoslavia.

A	B	C	D	E
Includes developments that affect more than one world region, international organizations and important meetings of major world leaders.	*Includes all domestic and regional developments in Europe, including the Soviet Union, Turkey, Cyprus and Malta.*	*Includes all domestic and regional developments in Africa and the Middle East, including Iraq and Iran and excluding Cyprus, Turkey and Afghanistan.*	*Includes all domestic and regional developments in Latin America, the Caribbean and Canada.*	*Includes all domestic and regional developments in Asia and Pacific nations, extending from Afghanistan through all the Pacific Islands, except Hawaii.*

U.S. Politics & Social Issues	U.S. Foreign Policy & Defense	U.S. Economy & Environment	Science, Technology & Nature	Culture, Leisure & Life Style	
The Census Bureau reports that U.S. enrollments in schools and colleges rose from 30 million at the end of 1950 to over 46 million at the end of 1960.	Pres. Eisenhower tells a farewell news conference that his greatest disappointment in office has been the inability to achieve a sure basis for world peace.	Pres. Eisenhower's eighth Economic Report to Congress predicts "a period of sound economic growth" despite the current slump in GNP rate. . . . In reply to a question at his final news conference, Pres. Eisenhower says he does not "go in very much" for the theory that increasing federal spending a few billion dollars will significantly stimulate the economy.	Dr. Thomas A. Dooley 3d, physician noted for his medical missionary work in Southeast Asia since 1954 and the founder of Medico Inc., an international voluntary health organization, dies of cancer in New York at the age of 34.	Former quarterback Norm Van Brocklin, 34, signs a three-year contract as head coach of the Minnesota Vikings, the NFL's newest expansion franchise.	Jan. 18
The Office of Education reports that rising school enrollments have raised the U.S. classroom shortage from 135,000 during 1959-1960 to over 142,000 in 1960-1961.	MIT economics professor Walt Rostow is named by Kennedy as Deputy Assistant to the President for National Security Affairs.	Pres.-elect Kennedy meets with AFL-CIO Pres. George Meany in an effort to allay labor resentment over Defense Secy.-designate Robert McNamara's refusal to appoint AFL-CIO V.P. Joseph Keenan as Assistant Defense Secretary for Manpower.			Jan. 19
John F. Kennedy and Lyndon B. Johnson are sworn in as President and Vice President. In his inaugural address, Kennedy pledges a dedicated defense of human freedom and concludes with an appeal to Americans to "ask not what your country can do for you--ask what you can do for your country."	A promise that the U.S. will "pay any price, bear any burden" to defend the free world marks the foreign policy keynote of Pres. Kennedy's inaugural address.				Jan. 20
Pres. Kennedy, in his first Executive Order, directs that the surplus food distributed to needy families be immediately increased by 100%. . . . Pres. Kennedy's 10 cabinet nominations are formally confirmed by the Senate without significant opposition. Confirmation hearings on the nominees were held prior to the inauguration.			The European Organization for Nuclear Research announces that two years of experiments have shown that the *mu meson* (muon) is not a particle of the atom's nucleus, but is a heavy electron weighing about 207 times the regular electron.		Jan. 21
		The Commerce Dept. reports that U.S. consumers spent a record $328.2 billion (about $1,820 per capita) for goods and services in 1960; the figure represents a 5% increase over 1959.		Three Americans set world indoor track records in a Los Angeles meet: Wilma Rudolph (women's 60-yd. dash, 6.9 seconds); Ralph Boston (broadjump, 25 feet, 10 inches); and Parry O'Brien (shotput, 63 feet 1 1/2 inches).	Jan. 22
In a 5-4 vote the Supreme Court upholds a Chicago ordinance barring public showing of motion pictures without prior approval of city censors. Chief Justice Earl Warren speaking for the minority, says the ruling threatens eventual censorship on all forms of communication.	Secy. of State Dean Rusk issues a statement indicating that the new administration will rely on traditional diplomatic contacts rather than public meetings of government heads in its initial approach to East-West problems.	The Marquardt Corp. of Los Angeles announces that it has designed a commercial nuclear generating plant that would cost little more to build than a comparable steam plant. . . . A two-week strike of N.Y. ferryboat crewmen, which forced 100,000 commuters to find alternate methods of getting to work, ends when both sides accept Labor Secy. Arthur Goldberg's proposal to submit the strike issues to the President's commission on railway work-rules disputes.	The Conference Board of the Mathematical Sciences reports a serious U.S. shortage of trained mathematicians for teaching, research and industry.		Jan. 23

F	G	H	I	J
Includes elections, federal-state relations, civil rights and liberties, crime, the judiciary, education, health care, poverty, urban affairs and population.	*Includes formation and debate of U.S. foreign and defense policies, veterans' affairs and defense spending. (Relations with specific foreign countries are usually found under the region concerned.)*	*Includes business, labor, agriculture, taxation, transportation, consumer affairs, monetary and fiscal policy, natural resources, and pollution.*	*Includes worldwide scientific, medical and technological developments, natural phenomena, U.S. weather, natural disasters, and accidents.*	*Includes the arts, religion, scholarship, communications media, sports, entertainment, fashions, fads and social life.*

	World Affairs	Europe	Africa & the Middle East	The Americas	Asia & the Pacific
Jan. 24	British P.M. Harold Macmillan tells Parliament that he no longer considers an East-West summit meeting an urgent necessity in the light of current world conditions.	West Germany announces that it has agreed to begin talks with Poland on the resumption of diplomatic relations.	The rebel Algerian Provisional Government issues a statement re-emphasizing its demand that France provide political guarantees of a genuine Algerian self-determination as a condition of any cease-fire agreement. . . . U.N. Secy. Gen. Hammarskjold discloses that he has unsuccessfully urged Pres. Joseph Kasavubu to return Lumumba to Leopoldville and permit him to participate in planned talks on the Congo's political crisis.	Cuban sources report that at least 10 persons have been executed for counter-revolutionary activity during the past week.	
Jan. 25	The Soviet Union and the U.S. simultaneously announce that the USSR has agreed to free the two surviving crewmen of a U.S. Air Force RB-47 jet shot down July 1, 1960 over the Barents Sea off northern Russia.	The Central Statistical Board reports that Soviet industrial production has increased 22.1% during the first two years of the current seven-year plan.	Kennedy announces at his first presidential press conference that he has ordered an emergency airlift of food and medical supplies to famine-stricken areas of the Congo.	El Salvador's ruling military junta, in power since the overthrow of the José Lemus regime in Oct., 1960, is replaced by another military junta claiming to be "anti-communist and constitutional."	Kennedy tells reporters in Washington that the U.S. will work to help create an "independent, peaceful and uncommitted" Laos which is "not dominated by either side."
Jan. 26	U.N. Secy Gen. Hammarskjold says that the declared intentions of Yugoslavia, Indonesia, Guinea, Morocco and the UAR to withdraw their contingents from the U.N. Congo Force threatens to cripple further U.N. operations in the Congo.	*The New York Times* reports that statistics released by the Soviet Central Statistical Board Jan. 25 indicate that per capita income in the USSR averaged $980 in 1960. The 1960 estimate of U.S. per capita income was $2,300.	Great Britain and the UAR re-establish full diplomatic relations for the first time since ties were broken in the aftermath of the 1956 Suez crisis.		The Laotian government publicly admits that its charges of an invasion by North Vietnamese and other foreign communist forces were false and were made in a bid for domestic and foreign support. . . . The Boun Oum government also says that it is prepared to grant Prince Souvanna Phouma safe conduct to Laos for talks with King Savang Vathana on his possible inclusion in a new coalition cabinet.
Jan. 27	Capt. John R. McKone and Capt. Freeman Olmstead, the released RB-47 fliers, arrive at Andrews Air Force Base (Md.) where At his first U.N. news conference, U.S. Amb. Adlai Stevenson says that Pres. Kennedy would probably be willing to meet informally with Khrushchev should the Soviet Premier come to New York to attend the resumed General Assembly session Mar. 7. . . .	The Portuguese exiles in command of the captured cruiser *Santa Maria* announce the formation of an "Independent Junta of Liberation" to rally forces against the Salazar regime in Portugal.	The government of Katanga publicly denies rumors that it is creating a Belgian-led mercenary "foreign legion."		Laotian sources report that despite the continuing Soviet airlift of supplies to rebel positions, government troops are beginning to succeed in their counterattacks against rebel forces except in the Plaines des Jarres region.
Jan. 28		Discussions begun Jan. 27 in Milan between Italy and Austria on their dispute over the German-language Bolzano area of northern Italy end in deadlock after Italy rejects an Austrian proposal for complete Bolzano autonomy.	Congo Pres. Kasavubu informs U.N. Secy. Gen. Hammarskjold that his government will seek foreign military aid unless the U.N. Force is immediately ordered to suppress the pro-Lumumba revolt.		

A	B	C	D	E
Includes developments that affect more than one world region, international organizations and important meetings of major world leaders.	Includes all domestic and regional developments in Europe, including the Soviet Union, Turkey, Cyprus and Malta.	Includes all domestic and regional developments in Africa and the Middle East, including Iraq and Iran and excluding Cyprus, Turkey and Afghanistan.	Includes all domestic and regional developments in Latin America, the Caribbean and Canada.	Includes all domestic and regional developments in Asia and Pacific nations, extending from Afghanistan through all the Pacific Islands, except Hawaii.

U.S. Politics & Social Issues	U.S. Foreign Policy & Defense	U.S. Economy & Environment	Science, Technology & Nature	Culture, Leisure & Life Style	
A U.S. District Court in New York orders the New Rochelle School Board (N.Y.) to develop a school desegregation plan for the 1961-1962 academic year. The order follows the Court's ruling that despite the presence of a few white students the school board had purposely maintained the Lincoln School as a racially segregated school for Negroes.	In an informal chat with newsmen former Pres. Eisenhower says that recent Soviet peace professions cannot be judged sincere until they are accompanied by deeds. . . . Plans for a vastly increased global food-for-peace program oriented to the U.S. foreign policy are presented to Pres. Kennedy by a special task force headed by Murray Lincoln, president of CARE.		Dr. Francesco Giordani, 64, atomic scientist ex-president of the Italian National Committee for Nuclear Research, dies in Naples.	Alfred Gilbert, 76, toy manufacturer, inventor of the erector set, and ex-Olympic athlete (he established a world pole-vault record of 12 ft., 7 in. in 1908), dies in Boston.	**Jan. 24**
Pres. Kennedy holds the first regular presidential news conference ever to be telecast "live.". . . White House Press Secy. Pierre Salinger tells a National Press Club meeting that in the past too much security information had been made public.	In remarks accompanying his announcement of the release of the RB-47 crewmen, Pres. Kennedy says that U.S. flights over Soviet territory have been suspended since May, 1960 and remain so. . . . Pres. Kennedy indicates little interest in suggestions that the U.S. offer Communist China food to help alleviate reported famine conditions, saying that there is "no indication" that China would respond favorably to U.S. aid.	Teamster Pres. James Hoffa appears again before the Senate Permanent Investigating Subcommittee under Sen. John McClellan (D, Ark.) which has resumed its inquiry into possible Teamster Union misconduct. Hoffa denies charges that he permitted corruption in N.Y. Teamster Local 239.			**Jan. 25**
	The Ford Foundation announces that it will extend over $8 million in grants to four U.S. universities for the expansion of international relations and Asian study programs.	A Washington conference of 450 farm group leaders ends without achieving any consensus on how to solve U.S. farm problems. they are greeted by their families and Pres. Kennedy. . . .			**Jan. 26**
The two-month white student boycott of New Orleans' integrated McDonough No. 19 school is broken by Gregory Thompson, the nine-year old son of a Walgreen drug store clerk. Federal marshals escorted Thompson to class past a jeering crowd of white women.		The Bureau of Labor Statistics reports that the U.S. cost of living index rose 1.5% during 1960. . . . The Labor Dept. reports that average hourly wages for U.S. factory workers rose from $2.27 in December 1959 to $2.32 in December 1960.			**Jan. 27**
	The State Dept. announces plans for sending 150 U.S. teachers to Africa in a pilot project of Pres. Kennedy's proposed Peace Corps program. . . . Noted radio and TV commentator Edward R. Murrow is named by Pres. Kennedy as director of the U.S. Information Agency.		A program said to call for the launching of more than 500 space rockets in five years--20 of them in 1961--is approved by France's new Commission for Spatial and Scientific Research.	Valeri Brumel, 18, of the USSR breaks the world indoor high jump record by leaping 7 ft. 4.5 in. at a meet in Leningrad. . . . Bradley Lord, 21, of Boston wins the men's senior title in the U.S. national figure-skating championships in Colorado Springs.	**Jan. 28**

F	G	H	I	J
Includes elections, federal-state relations, civil rights and liberties, crime, the judiciary, education, health care, poverty, urban affairs and population.	Includes formation and debate of U.S. foreign and defense policies, veterans' affairs and defense spending. (Relations with specific foreign countries are usually found under the region concerned.)	Includes business, labor, agriculture, taxation, transportation, consumer affairs, monetary and fiscal policy, natural resources, and pollution.	Includes worldwide scientific, medical and technological developments, natural phenomena, U.S. weather, natural disasters, and accidents.	Includes the arts, religion, scholarship, communications media, sports, entertainment, fashions, fads and social life.

	World Affairs	Europe	Africa & the Middle East	The Americas	Asia & the Pacific

Jan. 29

World Affairs: —

Europe: British P.M. Macmillan and French Pres. de Gaulle meet outside Paris to discuss Europe's threatened economic division and its long-term relationship to the U.S.

Africa & the Middle East: Troops commanded by the Gizenga regime in Oriental and Kivu Provinces and by other pro-Lumumba groups are reportedly consolidating their position in northern Katanga and advancing into the northern sectors of Equator and Kasai Provinces. Forces loyal to the central government of Kasavubu and Mobutu meanwhile are reported to be launching a counterattack on Oriental Province.

The Americas: Sources in the Dominican Republic report that local Roman Catholic bishops have appealed to Generalissimo Rafael Trujillo for help in ending what they called the government's unwarranted interference in religious affairs. . . . The Cuban government is reportedly seeking a large number of citizen volunteers to work in the cane fields in an effort to meet the government's goal of producing six million tons of sugar from the current crop.

Jan. 30

Africa & the Middle East: Hammarskjold tells Congo Pres. Kasavubu that his demand for U.N. action against the pro-Lumumba rebels will be conveyed to the Security Council, but that the current U.N. Force mandate prevents it from intervening in internal political struggles. . . . The U.S. State Dept. says that 30 American missionaries are among the whites being detained by pro-Lumumba forces in Oriental and Kivu Provinces.

Asia & the Pacific: Premier Hayato Ikeda, in a major policy speech, tells the Diet that "Japan welcomes any improvement of relations, particularly expansion of trade" with Red China.

Jan. 31

Africa & the Middle East: David Ben-Gurion resigns as premier of Israel in opposition to a Dec. 25, 1960 cabinet decision absolving ex-Defense Min. Pinhas Lavon of blame for an undisclosed security mishap for which he had been forced to resign, in 1955.

The Americas: In his inaugural address as Brazil's new president, Jânio da Silva Quadros promises to seek "democratic" solutions to Brazil's "terrible financial situation."

Feb. 1

World Affairs: U.N. Secy. Gen. Dag Hammarskjold appeals to the Security Council for increased powers to meet the Congo situation, but urges it to turn down Kasavubu's request for U.N. intervention against the pro-Lumumba factions.

A	B	C	D	E
Includes developments that affect more than one world region, international organizations and important meetings of major world leaders.	*Includes all domestic and regional developments in Europe, including the Soviet Union, Turkey, Cyprus and Malta.*	*Includes all domestic and regional developments in Africa and the Middle East, including Iraq and Iran and excluding Cyprus, Turkey and Afghanistan.*	*Includes all domestic and regional developments in Latin America, the Caribbean and Canada.*	*Includes all domestic and regional developments in Asia and Pacific nations, extending from Afghanistan through all the Pacific Islands, except Hawaii.*

U.S. Politics & Social Issues	U.S. Foreign Policy & Defense	U.S. Economy & Environment	Science, Technology & Nature	Culture, Leisure & Life Style	

Jan. 29

Jan. 30

In his first State of the Union message, Kennedy cites urban renewal, improved health care programs, a strengthened educational system, and a new housing program under a new housing and urban affairs department as the major social goals of his administration. Kennedy also briefly observes that race discrimination continues to disturb "the national conscience.". . . At the urging of Gov. S. Ernest Vandiver, the Georgia legislature repeals a series of recently passed laws aimed at blocking public school desegregation.

In his State of the Union address to Congress, Pres. Kennedy says that America's domestic problems pale "when placed beside those which confront us around the world." Kennedy's foreign policy recommendations include: continued vigilance against the "ambitions" of the USSR and China; increased aid to Latin America as part of a new "alliance for progress;" a better informed U.S. approach to disarmament; the establishment of a Peace Corps; and continued support for the U.N. . . . In its annual report to Congress, the Atomic Energy Commission warns that continued U.S. observance of a voluntary nuclear test moratorium will further slow progress on weapons development while the USSR might be making significant advances through clandestine tests.

In his State of the Union message, Kennedy tells Congress he will submit a broad range of programs to reverse the current "recession," including measures to improve unemployment compensation, to stimulate housing and construction, to encourage increased capital investment, and to promote economic growth in chronically depressed regions. . . . As for fiscal policy, Kennedy pledges a "sound dollar" and a balanced budget based on anticipated revenues from a recovered economy.

In his State of the Union message, Kennedy urges international cooperation in the exploration of space, saying that such scientific endeavors should be removed "from the bitter and wasteful competition of the Cold War". . . . The U.S. Atomic Bomb Casualty Commission reports that there are still 230,000 people suffering physical effects, ranging from burns to cancer, from the 1945 bombing of Hiroshima and Nagasaki.

Jan. 31

In what is regarded as a major victory for liberal pro-Kennedy forces, the House votes 217 to 212 to increase the membership of the conservative-dominated House Rules Committee from 12 to 15. The new appointments are expected to bring an end to the committee's practice of blocking liberal legislation from reaching the floor. . . . Pres. Kennedy names Harvard history professor Arthur M. Schlesinger Jr as presidential special assistant and speech writer.

The State Dept. announces the appointment of Adolf Berle, 66, as chairman of a special task force to coordinate U.S. policy toward Latin America. . . . The Air Force successfully launches into earth orbit an experimental reconnaissance satellite dubbed the Samos II. The U.S. hopes to have a network of operational Samos-type satellites in orbit by 1963 to replace the U-2 reconnaissance planes.

A special task force on farm problems, headed by J. Norman Efferson, reports to Pres. Kennedy that overproduction of grains is "becoming unmanageable" and recommends a greatly expanded land retirement program.

A U.S. Marine helicopter recovers a Project Mercury capsule bearing an apparently unharmed 37 and-a-half pound chimpanzee following a successful test launch from Cape Canaveral to a height of 155 miles.

The Pittsburgh Pirates are selected as the "athletic team of the year" in an AP poll of sportswriters and broadcasters.

Feb. 1

The family of Gregory Thompson, the only white student to break the boycott at McDonough No. 19 school, is reportedly moving from New Orleans. John Thompson, the boy's father, had earlier told reporters that he had been instructed not to report at his job at a local Walgreen store.

Military officials describe the first test-firing of a solid fuel three-stage Minuteman ICBM as a complete success. The missile landed on target 4,500 miles down-range from its launch site at Cape Canaveral. . . . At his second news conference Pres. Kennedy defends a White House decision to alter a speech by Adm. Arleigh Burke, chief of naval operations, which (in its original draft) had been highly critical of the USSR.

Pres. Kennedy discloses at a Washington news conference a series of executive orders designed to combat the current economic slump. They include: an immediate reduction in maximum interest on federally-insured home loans; the acceleration of federal public works projects in high unemployment areas; and the creation by the Agriculture Dept. of a pilot food stamp program for needy families.

Dr. Robert Glover, pioneer in the development of open heart surgery and specialist in the correction of damaged heart valves, succumbs to cancer at the age of 47.

The New York Times, the *St. Louis Post-Dispatch*, and the *Christian Science Monitor* are chosen the best three U.S. newspapers in a nationwide poll of publishers.

F	G	H	I	J
Includes elections, federal-state relations, civil rights and liberties, crime, the judiciary, education, health care, poverty, urban affairs and population.	Includes formation and debate of U.S. foreign and defense policies, veterans' affairs and defense spending. (Relations with specific foreign countries are usually found under the region concerned.)	Includes business, labor, agriculture, taxation, transportation, consumer affairs, monetary and fiscal policy, natural resources, and pollution.	Includes worldwide scientific, medical and technological developments, natural phenomena, U.S. weather, natural disasters, and accidents.	Includes the arts, religion, scholarship, communications media, sports, entertainment, fashions, fads and social life.

	World Affairs	Europe	Africa & the Middle East	The Americas	Asia & the Pacific
Feb. 2		Responding to U.S. appeals for assistance in meeting its balance of payments problem, West Germany offers to pay the U.S. nearly $1 billion, part of which is to be used as prepayment of its outstanding post-war economic aid debt and part is to be used as a credit for future military purchases from the U.S.			Hanoi radio reports that an interim Pathet Lao government has been established in rebel-held regions of Laos pending the return from Cambodian exile of Prince Souvanna Phouma. . . . Communist Chinese Foreign Min. Chen Yi tells a Peking rally that China is prepared to help restore the "lawful" Souvanna government to power on request.
Feb. 3		Following negotiations with U.S. and British officials, the Portuguese exiles commanding the captured cruiser *Santa Maria* agree to surrender the vessel in Recife, Brazil. Incoming Brazilian Pres. Quadros promised political asylum to the exiles.		*The New York Times* reports that the Cuban government is building a huge 120-kilowatt radio station to broadcast revolutionary propaganda to other Latin American countries. . . . Premier Castro orders the dismissal of 120 judges as part of his campaign to remove "disloyal" officials. . . . The Inter-American Development Bank makes its first loan: a $3.9 million credit to Peru for Arequipa's water and sewage systems.	
Feb. 4	The USSR agrees to delay resumption of the U.S.-British-Soviet test-ban talks in Geneva to allow the U.S. to complete the preparation of new proposals. The talks are now scheduled to begin again Mar. 21.			The Cuban government nationalizes the Yateras Water Co. aqueduct that supplies water to the U.S. naval base at Guantanamo, but makes no effort to cut off water to the base.	
Feb. 5		The Polish government announces that a resumption of diplomatic relations with West Germany could come only after a West German "renunciation" of claims to the former German Oder-Neisse frontier taken over by Poland in 1945. The announcement comes amidst reports of secret West German-Polish talks on restoring some kind of diplomatic ties.		A joint Canadian-American Committee denies reports that Canada is attempting to take advantage of the U.S.'s anti-Castro embargoes by increasing trade with Cuba. . . . Cuban Pres. Osvaldo Dorticos Torrado tells a Havana rally that Roman Catholic school teachers who describe the Castro regime as communist are engaged "in criminal work against the revolution."	
Feb. 6	In his first official press conference, U.S. State Secy. Dean Rusk says that the release of the RB-47 fliers does not mean that serious Soviet-U.S. differences "have suddenly disappeared."	Speaking of Berlin State Secy. Dean Rusk says the new Kennedy administration will retain the traditional American position on "the security and the safety of the people of that city.". . . Three leaders of Portugal's opposition Liberal Party call upon the government to "return fundamental liberties" to the Portuguese people.	State Secy. Dean Rusk tells reporters that U.S. will try to help formulate a strengthened U.N. plan capable of giving Congolese leaders an opportunity "to work out their own constitutional and political arrangements."	State Secy. Rusk says the U.S. must work to point Latin American governments "in the direction of social and economic reform" in order to prevent a repetition of "the tragedy exemplified by. . . Cuba."	State Secy. Rusk says an independent, uncommitted and stable Laos is the goal of current U.S. policy toward that strife-torn nation. Rusk also reaffirms a continuing U.S. commitment to Nationalist China. . . . The Australian Wheat Board confirms that it has recently negotiated the sale of over one million tons of wheat to Communist China.

A	B	C	D	E
Includes developments that affect more than one world region, international organizations and important meetings of major world leaders.	Includes all domestic and regional developments in Europe, including the Soviet Union, Turkey, Cyprus and Malta.	Includes all domestic and regional developments in Africa and the Middle East, including Iraq and Iran and excluding Cyprus, Turkey and Afghanistan.	Includes all domestic and regional developments in Latin America, the Caribbean and Canada.	Includes all domestic and regional developments in Asia and Pacific nations, extending from Afghanistan through all the Pacific Islands, except Hawaii.

U.S. Politics & Social Issues	U.S. Foreign Policy & Defense	U.S. Economy & Environment	Science, Technology & Nature	Culture, Leisure & Life Style	
	Pres. Kennedy designates David Bruce as U.S. Ambassador-to-Britain.	Pres. Kennedy sends Congress an outlined economic program designed "to restore momentum" to the U.S. economy. The proposals include: extension of benefits to unemployed persons who have exhausted their regular benefits; prompt enactment of an area redevelopment bill; a two-stage increase in the minimum wage to $1.25; and a wide range of increased benefits under Social Security.	Delegates from 12 Western European nations end three days of discussions in Strasbourg, France on Anglo-French proposals for international cooperation in satellite projects.	Novelist Norman Mailer pleads innocent to assault charges stemming from the Nov. 20 stabbing of his wife, Adele, who refused to sign a complaint.	Feb. 2
Acting on recommendations from HEW Secy. Abraham Ribicoff, Pres. Kennedy orders the creation of a $4 million program to aid Cuban refugees living in the U.S.		Rep. Elmer Holland (D, Pa.) makes public a special report that indicates that 25% of all U.S. office and clerical jobs have been eliminated by electronic office machines in the past five years and that automation will eliminate four million more such jobs in the next five years.	NASA officials report that the chimpanzee Ham endured without apparent injury a gravity pull of 18 "G's" during his test ride in a Project Mercury capsule Jan. 31.		Feb. 3
			The USSR announces the successful launching by "an improved multi-stage rocket" of a 14,000 pound Sputnik V satellite, the largest ever placed in earth orbit.		Feb. 4
	V.P. Lyndon Johnson, addressing a B'nai Zion meeting in New York, says that the U.S. hopes for an end to the costly arms race among the nations of the Middle East.	West German Defense Min. Franz Josef Strauss tells reporters that West Germany is not very enthusiastic over British proposals for a cooperative European satellite-launching program.			Feb. 5
	Secy. of State Dean Rusk holds his first official press conference to outline the foreign policy views of the new administration. Rusk says he will keep the press as well informed as possible, but adds that in the past "premature publicity" has sometimes frustrated U.S. foreign policy efforts. . . . Pres. Kennedy informs Congress that he is rescinding the current limitation on military dependents abroad since it is not an effective way of reducing the deficit and it hurts "morale and recruitment in the armed forces."	In a special message to Congress on the balance of payments problem, Kennedy rejects "protectionism," reduced aid to developing countries, and limitations on military dependents as solutions to the growing U.S. deficit. Instead he proposes a multi-faceted program aimed at increasing the level of U.S. industrial and farm exports. . . . Twenty-nine major manufacturing firms and 44 of their officials, convicted of price-fixing in the sale of electrical equipment, are fined a total of $1,924,500 by U.S. District Judge J. Cullen Ganey in Philadelphia.			Feb. 6

F	G	H	I	J
Includes elections, federal-state relations, civil rights and liberties, crime, the judiciary, education, health care, poverty, urban affairs and population.	Includes formation and debate of U.S. foreign and defense policies, veterans' affairs and defense spending. (Relations with specific foreign countries are usually found under the region concerned.)	Includes business, labor, agriculture, taxation, transportation, consumer affairs, monetary and fiscal policy, natural resources, and pollution.	Includes worldwide scientific, medical and technological developments, natural phenomena, U.S. weather, natural disasters, and accidents.	Includes the arts, religion, scholarship, communications media, sports, entertainment, fashions, fads and social life.

	World Affairs	Europe	Africa & the Middle East	The Americas	Asia & the Pacific
Feb. 7		The evidence against five persons accused of delivering British submarine secrets to the USSR is outlined by government prosecutors at a pre-trial hearing in London.	Anti-government riots in Portuguese Angola leave 27 dead and scores wounded following three days of street fighting with police. The riots and demonstrations are said to have been planned to coincide with the capture of the cruiser *Santa Maria* by anti-Salazar forces.		
Feb. 8		Pres. Kennedy tells a Washington news conference that the question of the U.S. offer to supply nuclear weapons for a NATO atomic strike force remains under study and that no firm agreement has been reached. . . . The Portuguese government permits Lisbon and Oporto newspapers to publish the text of a statement by three Liberal Party opposition leaders criticizing the Salazar regime's repression of fundamental political liberties.			An agreement to provide South Korea with continued U.S. economic and technical assistance is signed in Seoul by U.S. Amb. Walter McConnaughy and South Korean Foreign Min. Il Hyung Chung.
Feb. 9	A February 8 speech urging Communist China's admission to the U.N. by the Earl of Home, British foreign Secretary, prompts a State Dept. declaration reaffirming U.S. opposition to a seat for Red China.	A French jet fighter, on patrol off the Mediterranean coast of Algeria to guard against air supply of rebel forces, fires twice across the path of a USSR Ilyushin 18 prop-jet plane carrying Soviet Pres. Leonid Brezhnev enroute to a state visit to Guinea. . . . U.S. administration officials make clear that they regard West Germany's Feb. 2 offer of $1 billion in prepayments as an insufficient response to the need for a greater European role in carrying the West's defense and foreign aid burdens, currently borne by the deficit-plagued U.S.		Cubana Airlines says it is suspending its Havana-Miami service because Miami Airport authorities have refused to provide "guarantees" against hostile demonstrations at the field. . . . Members of the U.S. Congress, headed by Senate Majority Leader Mike Mansfield, conclude three days of talks with their Mexican counterparts in Guadalajara, Mexico.	Indian Amb.-to-U.S. M.C. Chagla tells a Washington news conference that India favors the creation of a neutral Laos governed by a coalition of all currently conflicting groups as a way of discouraging what he calls "Chinese expansionism."
Feb. 10		French officials express "sincere regrets" over the firing on a plane carrying Soviet Pres. Leonid Brezhnev.	The Katanga government announces that ex-Congo Premier Lumumba escaped Feb. 9 from the isolated farm prison near Mutshatsha where he had been held since his transfer from a Leopoldville prison in January; his whereabouts are reportedly unknown. . . . U.N. Secy. Gen. Hammarskjold orders an investigation into the alleged escape of ex-Congo Premier Lumumba. The order comes after Hammarskjold received a message from nine Asian-African nations voicing fears that the reported escape "may be a camouflage. . .in preparation for announcing the death of Mr. Lumumba."	An estimated 40,000 Cuban government troops are reported to have surrounded an unknown number of anti-Castro rebels in the Escambray Mountains; both sides are said to be suffering heavy casualties. . . . A pact providing for U.S. retention of military bases in the West Indies Federation in exchange for continued economic aid is signed in Port of Spain, Trinidad.	
Feb. 11		In a note to the French government, Soviet Foreign Min. Andrei Gromyko demands punishment of those responsible for the "attack" on Pres. Brezhnev's plane. France promises a full inquiry into the incident. . . . The heads of state of the six European Economic Community nations conclude two days of talks in Paris on French proposals for increased political and economic coordination. A second EEC summit is scheduled for mid-May.	The discovery of an abandoned and wrecked police car, said to have been used by Lumumba in his escape, is reported by Katanga officials near Kasaji, on a road leading to pro-Lumumba strongholds in northern Katanga. . . . Morocco announces that it will accept a Soviet offer of unconditional economic and industrial aid extended by Soviet Pres. Brezhnev during his state visit Feb. 9-10.	Cuban Premier Castro asserts in a TV address that U.S. encouragemeNuclear Testing of counter-revolution in Cuba gives him the right to promote revolution throughout Latin America.	

A	B	C	D	E
Includes developments that affect more than one world region, international organizations and important meetings of major world leaders.	*Includes all domestic and regional developments in Europe, including the Soviet Union, Turkey, Cyprus and Malta.*	*Includes all domestic and regional developments in Africa and the Middle East, including Iraq and Iran and excluding Cyprus, Turkey and Afghanistan.*	*Includes all domestic and regional developments in Latin America, the Caribbean and Canada.*	*Includes all domestic and regional developments in Asia and Pacific nations, extending from Afghanistan through all the Pacific Islands, except Hawaii.*

U.S. Politics & Social Issues	U.S. Foreign Policy & Defense	U.S. Economy & Environment	Science, Technology & Nature	Culture, Leisure & Life Style	
	The White House announces that at least 20 career ambassadors, including Amb.-to-USSR Llewellyn Thompson Jr., will be retained in their posts.	Kennedy sends Congress a proposed bill to raise the minimum wage from $1 to $1.25 an hour over a three-year period and to extend the coverage to an additional 4,300,000 workers. . . . The National Safety Council reports that 38,200 persons were killed in U.S. auto accidents during 1960.			**Feb. 7**
Commenting on the school integration controversy in New Orleans, Kennedy tells a Washington news conference that the administration is "carefully considering" various actions to speed implementation of "the court decision."	Pres. Kennedy tells a Washington news conference that the Defense Dept. is currently conducting a review of U.S. defenses to determine if an actual "missile gap" favoring the USSR does exist and, if so, to what extent. . . . Former Amb.-to-USSR George F. Kennan is designated by Pres. Kennedy to be U.S. Ambassador-to-Yugoslavia.				**Feb. 8**
The Senate confirms by voice vote the nomination of Robert C. Weaver as administrator of the Housing and Home Finance Agency--the highest federal post ever held by a Negro. . . . the Bureau of Indian Affairs; Crow is the first person of Indian descent to head the Bureau since 1871.	Senate Republicans, led by GOP leader Everett Dirksen, charge the Kennedy administration with soft-pedalling the "missile-gap" issue after having unfairly belabored it during the presidential campaign. . . . Pres. Kennedy's "food-for-peace" program director, George McGovern, discloses that the U.S. plans to make available to Latin American countries feed grain and other surplus foods to encourage them to launch land reform programs.	Labor Dept. Manpower Chief Seymour Wolfbein tells reporters that the U.S. unemployment situation is "the worst since early World War II." The remark follows the release of a Labor Dept. report indicating that over one half the nation's 150 major industrial areas have a "substantial and persistent" labor surplus. . . . Picket line violence breaks out in a growing dispute between U.S. labor groups and Imperial Valley, California growers over the use of contract Mexican laborers (braceros).	*The New York Times* reports that calculations based on data from the U.S. satellites Vanguard I and II reveal the shape of the earth as a slightly irregular ellipsoid.	Henry Lewis, 28, conducts the Los Angeles Philharmonic in Los Angeles, becoming the first Negro ever to conduct a major U.S. symphony orchestra at its home auditorium. . . . New York Giants football star Frank Gifford, 31, announces his retirement to become a sportscaster with WCBS Radio in New York.	**Feb. 9**
An increasing number of sit-in demonstrators, arrested under various state and local trespass laws are reportedly refusing to pay fines and instead are accepting jail sentences. The action, which is becoming known as the "jail-in" movement, dates from the Feb. 6 jailing of 13 protesters in Rock Hill, S.C. . . . Kennedy asks Congress to authorize nine new U.S. circuit court and 50 new U.S. district court judgeships to help relieve the "serious congestion" of the federal courts.		Labor Secy. Goldberg, touring economically depressed areas in the Midwest, tells reporters "we are in a full-fledged recession. I think it's time to say this in no uncertain terms."	Prof. Leonid Sedov, chairman of the Astronautics Committee of the Soviet Academy of Sciences denies rumors that Sputnik V, launched Feb. 4, carried a human passenger. . . . A special committee of the U.N. World Meteorological Organization reports that there is an urgent need for an agreement on the international distribution of data obtained from future weather satellites.		**Feb. 10**
	The Senate Internal Security Subcommittee releases earlier testimony from ex-U.S. Amb.-to-Brazil (1946-1947) William Pawley, indicating that he headed a secret CIA-aided mission to Cuba in 1958 aimed at blocking Fidel Castro's rise to power.				**Feb. 11**

F	G	H	I	J
Includes elections, federal-state relations, civil rights and liberties, crime, the judiciary, education, health care, poverty, urban affairs and population.	*Includes formation and debate of U.S. foreign and defense policies, veterans' affairs and defense spending. (Relations with specific foreign countries are usually found under the region concerned.)*	*Includes business, labor, agriculture, taxation, transportation, consumer affairs, monetary and fiscal policy, natural resources, and pollution.*	*Includes worldwide scientific, medical and technological developments, natural phenomena, U.S. weather, natural disasters, and accidents.*	*Includes the arts, religion, scholarship, communications media, sports, entertainment, fashions, fads and social life.*

	World Affairs	Europe	Africa & the Middle East	The Americas	Asia & the Pacific
Feb. 12	U.S. and British newspapers report that Western governments have come into possession of documents indicating that the Chinese-Soviet ideological and political differences, which emerged at the Nov. 1960 Communist Congress, were far more severe and fundamental than previously believed in the West.		Katanga officials announce they will not cooperate in a U.N. investigation of the Lumumba escape, claiming that the matter is an "internal" affair.		
Feb. 13		Britain, France and the U.S. formally protest East Germany's refusal to permit West German leaders of the Evangelical Church to attend an All-German Church Synod service in East Berlin. . . . West German Chancellor Konrad Adenauer authorizes the reopening of talks with the U.S. on how West Germany can help meet the West's payments deficit and foreign aid problems.	The government of Katanga announces that ex-Premier Lumumba was killed Feb. 12 by unnamed Katanga tribesmen at an unidentified location somewhere near Kasaji. The body was identified and buried on the spot and Katanga authorities say they will resist further inquiry into the matter. . . . slaying provokes demonstrations and official denunciations in communist-bloc, African and Asian countries, where the murder was blamed on the U.N. and Western powers, particularly Belgium.		
Feb. 14	In an official declaration the USSR withdraws its recognition of Sec. Gen. Hammarskjold and demands his immediate dismissal as U.N. chief, citing his alleged "complicity" with Belgium in the murder of Lumumba as grounds. Just prior to the declaration, the USSR announced it would join with the UAR in formally recognizing the pro-Lumumba regime of Antoine Gizenga as the legitimate Congo government.	The British-led European Free Trade Association (EFTA) announces an agreement to accelerate tariff reductions among member states, an action that would bring internal EFTA tariffs closer to the levels fixed by the European Economic Community (EEC) and facilitate negotiations between the rival economic blocs.		Cuban Premier Castro charges the U.S. with giving "direct military support" to anti-government rebels in the Escambray Mountains.	In a report to Parliament on the 1960 India-China border negotiations, the Indian Foreign Ministry accuses Communist China of continuing to illegally occupy 12,000 miles of Indian territory.
Feb. 15	In an address to the Security Council Hammarskjold firmly declines Soviet demands for his resignation, claiming that he did all his mandate would allow to protect Lumumba and that his stepping down now would only weaken the U.N. . . . In a cable to Pres. Kennedy, Premier Khrushchev urges a renewed effort by both countries to achieve a U.S.-Soviet agreement on disarmament.	In a message to the NATO Permanent Council in Paris, Pres. Kennedy reaffirms the U.S. commitment to NATO defenses, but calls upon its European partners to take on a larger share of the West's aid responsibilities to the world's new nations.	The U.N. Conciliation Commission on the Congo reports reaching agreement on a preliminary Congolese peace plan based on a gradual broadening of the central government to include a coalition of conflicting groups. The plan also recommends changes in the Congo Constitution aimed at introducing a federal system of government. . . . East Germany, Yugoslavia and Ghana follow the USSR and UAR in recognizing the Gizenga regime as the legitimate government of the Congo.		Communist Chinese Premier Chou En-lai says that China would not oppose the reactivation of the International Control Commission for Laos if it were preceded by a new 14-nation conference on Laos. . . . Indian P.M. Nehru, in a speech to Parliament, asserts that "any aggress against Bhutan (an Indian protectorate) will be regarded as agression against India." The declaration is interpreted as a warning to Communist China (Nationalist), Republic of which has claimed 300 sq. miles of Bhutanese territory.
Feb. 16			Israeli Pres. Izhak Ben-Zvi asks David Ben-Gurion to try to form a new government to replace the six-party coalition cabinet that fell after Ben-Gurion's Jan. 31 resignation over the controversial Lavon affair.	Nicaragua appeals to the OAS' Inter-American Peace Commission to prevent Honduras from forcibly evicting Nicaraguans from disputed border territory awarded to Honduras by the International Court of Justice in Nov., 1960. Nicaragua claims it needs more time to complete an orderly withdrawal.	

A	B	C	D	E
Includes developments that affect more than one world region, international organizations and important meetings of major world leaders.	Includes all domestic and regional developments in Europe, including the Soviet Union, Turkey, Cyprus and Malta.	Includes all domestic and regional developments in Africa and the Middle East, including Iraq and Iran and excluding Cyprus, Turkey and Afghanistan.	Includes all domestic and regional developments in Latin America, the Caribbean and Canada.	Includes all domestic and regional developments in Asia and Pacific nations, extending from Afghanistan through all the Pacific Islands, except Hawaii.

U.S. Politics & Social Issues	U.S. Foreign Policy & Defense	U.S. Economy & Environment	Science, Technology & Nature	Culture, Leisure & Life Style	
			A large earth-orbiting satellite, launched earlier in the day, is successfully used by Soviet scientists as a platform to launch a second probe toward Venus; it is the first attempt ever made to use a satellite as a launching site for a space probe.		Feb. 12
Kennedy submits to Congress a bill to finance health care for the elderly through increased Social Security taxes.	Pres. Kennedy names Lt. Gen. James Gavin as Ambassador-to-France.	Kennedy tells a meeting of the National Industrial Conference Board that his administration will work for a "full-fledged alliance" with U.S. business to help increase production and cut unemployment. . . . Labor Secy. Arthur Goldberg announces the creation of a special office to study unemployment problems resulting from automation.		Arnold Palmer defeats Doug Sanders in an 18-hole playoff to win the Phoenix Open golf tournament.	Feb. 13
The N.Y. Appellate Division, overturning a state Supreme Court decision, rules that New York City cannot legally deny U.S. Nazi Party leader George Lincoln Rockwell a permit to speak simply because it suspects his address will incite violence.	During appearances before the Senate Foreign Relations Committee, State Undersecy. George Ball and Treasury Secy. Douglas Dillon urge ratification of the Organization for Economic Cooperation and Development (OECD), saying that the failure of the U.S. to join would ruin the organization.	Interior Secy. Stewart Udall announces a six-month moratorium in the sale of unreserved public domain lands as part of an effort to halt "unethical" practices by certain land "promoters."	Pres. Kennedy cables congratulations to Premier Khrushchev on the USSR's successful launch of a Venus probe from an earth-orbiting launch satellite.		Feb. 14
		Saying that "we have been in a recession for some months," Pres. Kennedy urges Congress to take quick action on his proposed economic measures.	In a cable replying to a congratulatory message from Pres. Kennedy on the USSR's launching of a Venus space probe, Premier Khrushchev expresses approval of Kennedy's inaugural speech appeal for joint Soviet-U.S. efforts to conquer outer space and disease.	Eighteen members of the U.S. ice figure-skating team, bound for a championship meet in Prague, are among the 72 persons killed in the crash of a Sabena Airlines Boeing 707 near the Brussels International Airport.	Feb. 15
Pres. Kennedy appoints Ramsey Clark, 33, son of Supreme Court Justice Tom C. Clark, as an Assistant Attorney General.	Defense Dept. scientists tell the House Science and Astronautics Committee that the chances of developing a completely secure nationwide anti-missile defense system are small.	The administration presents Congress with an "emergency" farm bill providing federal cash payments to farmers who reduce corn and feed-grain acreage. . . . Senate and House GOP leaders, Everett Dirksen (Ill.) and Charles Halleck (Ind.), blame the continuing economic slump on inaction by the Democratic-controlled Congress and on the Kennedy administration's "habit" of "talking the country into a depression" by exaggerating the low state of the economy.		Clarence (Dazzy) Vance, 69, Brooklyn Dodger pitcher (1922-35) and member of baseball's Hall of Fame, dies in Homasassa Springs, Fla.	Feb. 16

F	G	H	I	J
Includes elections, federal-state relations, civil rights and liberties, crime, the judiciary, education, health care, poverty, urban affairs and population.	*Includes formation and debate of U.S. foreign and defense policies, veterans' affairs and defense spending. (Relations with specific foreign countries are usually found under the region concerned.)*	*Includes business, labor, agriculture, taxation, transportation, consumer affairs, monetary and fiscal policy, natural resources, and pollution.*	*Includes worldwide scientific, medical and technological developments, natural phenomena, U.S. weather, natural disasters, and accidents.*	*Includes the arts, religion, scholarship, communications media, sports, entertainment, fashions, fads and social life.*

	World Affairs	Europe	Africa & the Middle East	The Americas	Asia & the Pacific
Feb. 17		Following talks with the U.S., West Germany announces it has agreed to begin an ongoing $1 billion-a-year foreign aid program in order to assume a share of the West's aid burden and help ease the current U.S. foreign payments deficit. . . . The National Federation of the French Press and the Confederation of the French Press publish a joint protest against recent French government seizures of newspapers, particularly in Algeria.		Ex-Mexican Pres. Lazaro Cardenas publicly accuses the Mexican press of imposing a virtual "blackout" on coverage of the leftist-sponsored Latin-American Conference for National Sovereignty, Economic Emancipation and Peace, scheduled for Mexico City Mar. 5.	Burma charges that Nationalist Chinese guerrillas, active in the China-Burma-Thailand border area, are being supplied with U.S. weapons.
Feb. 18		More than 2,000 British demonstrators, including philosopher Bertrand Russell, march on the Defense Ministry to protest the presence of U.S. Polaris submarines in Britain and to support demands for general nuclear disarmament.	In a letter to Hammarskjold, Pres. Kwame Nkrumah of Ghana proposes that a new all-African U.N. Force be sent to the Congo and be given full power to restore law and order there.	Students enrolled in Roman Catholic and other private schools circulate leaflets in Havana expressing opposition to the government's plan to send high school students into the interior to teach literacy to the Cuban peasants; they charge that the program amounts to a "plan of totalitarian indoctrination."	
Feb. 19					In a declaration issued in Vientiane, King Savang Vathana proclaims the neutrality of Laos and calls upon all foreign powers to respect it. The royal statement also confirms the Boun Oum regime as the legal government of Laos.
Feb. 20		Belgian King Baudouin I dissolves Parliament and schedules new national elections for Mar. 26. The action follows the resignation of seven Liberal Party members from Premier Gaston Eyskens' Social Christian Party-dominated coalition cabinet. . . . The USSR announces the creation of a new All-Union Agricultural Machine Agency to encourage lagging farm production.		*The New York Times* reports that the U.S. economic embargo of Cuba has seriously impaired the operations of many industries, particularly those formerly owned by U.S. firms, by causing a shortage of essential spare parts. . . . Venezuelan officials report that government forces have quelled a Caracas revolt and arrested more than 100 soldiers and civilians, including ex-military attaché in the Dominican Republic Col. Edito Contreras, the alleged leader of the uprising.	The British Foreign Office joins the U.S. State Dept. in expressing its full support for the Laotian neutrality declaration issued Feb. 19.
Feb. 21	The U.N. Security Council votes 9-0 (USSR abstaining) to authorize U.N. troops to use military force to prevent a full-scale Congolese civil war in the wake of ex-Premier Lumumba's murder. The resolution also calls for (a) depoliticization of the Congo army, (b) removal of all Belgian military and political personnel, (c) the reconvening of the Congo Parliament, and (d) an inquiry into Lumumba's death. . . . The adoption of the Security Council's Congo resolution comes after the 8-1 rejection of a Soviet draft resolution demanding dissolution of the U.N. Congo Force and dismissal of Secy. Gen Hammarskjold.	In a meeting with retiring NATO Secy. Gen. Paul-Henri Spaak, Pres. Kennedy pledges U.S. cooperation in efforts to expand NATO coordination in the economic and political fields. . . . A second Soviet news agency (in addition to Tass) is established in Moscow under the name Novosti (News).	Pres. Tshombe of Katanga orders a general mobilization of his forces to prevent U.N. troops from attempting to carry out the Security Council's recent Congo Resolution. . . . A program of constitutional reforms for Northern Rhodesia, prepared by Britain's Macmillan government, appears to have little support in Northern Rhodesia.	Bolivian Pres. Victor Paz Estenssoro declares a nationwide state of siege to thwart what the government described as a revolutionary plot by the Communist Party and the Authentic National Revolutionary Movement.	Prince Souphanouvong, leader of the Pathet Lao, denounces King Savang Vathana's Laotian neutrality declaration in a statement broadcast by Hanoi radio. . . . Over 10,000 persons stage an unruly demonstration before the U.S. Embassy in Rangoon, Burma to protest alleged shipments of U.S.-made arms to Nationalist Chinese guerrillas in northern Burma.
Feb. 22	In messages to Indian P.M. Nehru and the heads of 66 other nations, Soviet Premier Khrushchev proposes the creation of an all-African international force (to replace U.N. Congo mission) with full power to restore order under the "legitimate" Gizenga government. Khrushchev also reiterates his call for replacing Secy. Gen. Hammarskjold with a three-member U.N. executive.		Joseph Ileo, premier of the newly reorganized central Congo government of Pres. Kasavubu, warns that his government will oppose, by force if necessary, implementation of the Security Council's Congo resolution, specifically its order for depoliticization of the army. . . . Israeli Atty. Gen. Gideon Hausner presents a Jerusalem court with a 15-count indictment against Adolf Eichmann, accusing him of calculated actions leading to the deaths of "millions of Jews."		Prince Souvanna Phouma arrives in a rebel-held area of the Plaines des Jarres where he is recognized as the titular head of a recently formed provisional Laotian cabinet. It is Souvanna's first visit to Laos since fleeing to Cambodia after the ousting of his neutralist government in December 1960 by forces of the current Boun Oum regime.

A	B	C	D	E
Includes developments that affect more than one world region, international organizations and important meetings of major world leaders.	*Includes all domestic and regional developments in Europe, including the Soviet Union, Turkey, Cyprus and Malta.*	*Includes all domestic and regional developments in Africa and the Middle East, including Iraq and Iran and excluding Cyprus, Turkey and Afghanistan.*	*Includes all domestic and regional developments in Latin America, the Caribbean and Canada.*	*Includes all domestic and regional developments in Asia and Pacific nations, extending from Afghanistan through all the Pacific Islands, except Hawaii.*

U.S. Politics & Social Issues	U.S. Foreign Policy & Defense	U.S. Economy & Environment	Science, Technology & Nature	Culture, Leisure & Life Style	
	The administration asks Congress to amend the U.S. Sugar Act to empower the President to deny the Dominican Republic any portion of the sugar quota formerly assigned to Cuba.				Feb. 17
		Citing the State's estimated 8% unemployment rate, Conn. Gov. John Dempsey (D) declares an "unemployment emergency" and orders, under a stand-by law, that the maximum duration of unemployment compensation benefits be extended from 26 to 36 weeks.	A U.S. Thor-Agena-B rocket is launched into polar orbit and then refired during its second revolution around the earth. The test was designed to perfect a system "of satellite stabilization and control in orbit."	Jimmy Bostwick, 24, an amateur, wins the U.S. Open tennis championship for the second consecutive year.	Feb. 18
The three Roman Catholic bishops of Georgia and South Carolina announce that parochial schools in the two states will be desegregated no later than the public schools.	In a CBS-TV interview U.S. Amb.-to-U.N. Adlai Stevenson says that, in his opinion, the two worst problems facing the world today are the spread of nuclear weapons and the "growing gap" between rich and poor nations.	The Commerce Dept. reports that U.S. GNP rose from $482.1 billion in 1959 to a record $503.2 billion in 1960; the annual rate of GNP, however, declined sharply during the second half of 1960 from levels reached early in the year.		Hank van der Grift of the Netherlands wins the world speed-skating title in Goteborg, Sweden.	Feb. 19
Kennedy sends Congress a special education message proposing a five-year $5.6 billion program of federal aid to education aimed at achieving "a new standard of excellence" in U.S. schools. . . . The Supreme Court upholds a Connecticut law that permits localities to supply buses to non-profit private (including parochial) schools. . . . Lousiana Gov. Jimmie Davis signs eight segregation bills passed by the Legislature Feb. 19 to block public school desegregation.	The Agriculture Dept. reports that the U.S. government gave needy Americans and foreigners over 1.7 billion pounds of food during the last half of 1960 (about 75% distributed outside the U.S.).	Kennedy sends Congress a bill to provide $400 million in grants and loans for communities and unemployed workers in economically depressed areas. . . . Americans interviewed in a recent Gallup poll estimate that a family of four needs a minimum of $84 a week to "get along" in 1961.			Feb. 20
At a White House meeting, Kennedy presents Democratic Congressional leaders with a list of 16 measures he considers "must" legislation; they include: extension of unemployment benefits; including the elderly heath care plan; minimum-wage hike; aid to distressed areas; increased federal aid to schools, colleges, and community health programs.	Pres. Kennedy includes ratification of the Organization for Economic Cooperation and Development among 16 bills which he deems as "must" legislation.	According to Commerce Dept. figures, world steel production rose from 321 million ingot tons in 1959 to a record 355 million tons in 1960. The U.S. remains the leading producer with 28% of the world total; Russia ranks second with about 20%.	A Project Mercury capsule successfully completes a "dry run" test launch, during which it was subjected to the worst conditions it could be expected to meet in any future manned flights.		Feb. 21
			NASA announces that it has narrowed down the candidates for the first U.S. manned space flight to three astronauts; they are: Marine Lt. Col. John Glenn, 39; Air Force Capt. Virgil Grissom, 35; and Navy Cmndr. Alan Shepard. . . . France reports the recovery intact of a space capsule bearing a live rat after it had been launched to an altitude of 90 miles above the western Sahara by means of a French Veronique rocket.	Dominick James La Rocca, 71, jazz performer and composer famed as the creator of the first Dixieland jazz band, dies in New Orleans.	Feb. 22

F	G	H	I	J
Includes elections, federal-state relations, civil rights and liberties, crime, the judiciary, education, health care, poverty, urban affairs and population.	Includes formation and debate of U.S. foreign and defense policies, veterans' affairs and defense spending. (Relations with specific foreign countries are usually found under the region concerned.)	Includes business, labor, agriculture, taxation, transportation, consumer affairs, monetary and fiscal policy, natural resources, and pollution.	Includes worldwide scientific, medical and technological developments, natural phenomena, U.S. weather, natural disasters, and accidents.	Includes the arts, religion, scholarship, communications media, sports, entertainment, fashions, fads and social life.

	World Affairs	Europe	Africa & the Middle East	The Americas	Asia & the Pacific
Feb. 23		West German sources report that Premier Khrushchev, in a Feb. 17 note to Chancellor Adenauer, has withdrawn Soviet concessions made at Geneva in 1959 and has renewed his earlier demand that any solution of the Berlin problem provide for the ultimate transformation of Berlin into a demilitarized "free city.". . . West German Chancellor Adenauer completes two days of talks with British P.M. Macmillan on ways of ending the threatened economic division of Europe between the six-nation EEC and the seven-member EFTA.	The U.N. Congo Command reports that 14 political prisoners held by the Gizenga regime in Stanleyville have been executed in apparent retaliation for the killing Feb. 19 of six pro-Lumumbist prisoners by the South Kasai regime under Albert Kalonji.	Roman Catholic bishops disclose in a published letter that they have rejected Pres. Joaquin Balaguer's request that they award Generalissimo Rafael Trujillo the title of "Benefactor of the Roman Catholic Church of the Dominican Republic."	Indonesian army officials report that 1960 casualties in the drive against anti-government rebels totaled 4,828 rebels killed and 7,034 captured; government casualties numbered 643 killed and 236 wounded.
Feb. 24		The Soviet CP journal *Kommunist* publishes an outline of a new party constitution intended to make a "scientific principle" of peaceful co-existence and to prepare the way for the maturation of pure communism in the USSR. The document, sanctioned by Khrushchev, is slated for consideration at the CP Congress in October.	Congolese soldiers loyal to the Lumumbist regime of Antoine Gizenga gain control of Luluabourg, capital of Kasai Province, in what is reported to be the first stage of a major offensive against the Kasavubu government.	The U.S. State Dept. issues a policy statement saying that the U.S.-CUBAN differences cannot be settled until the Castro regime restores the Cuban people's right to "freely choose their own destiny.". . . Cuba announces the establishment of a Ministry of Industry, headed by Ernesto (Ché) Guevara, to oversee and coordinate industrial production and expansion. The new ministry is part of a general government reorganization aimed at providing more efficient control of the Cuban economy.	
Feb. 25	U.S. Amb.-to-U.N. Stevenson tells a New York news conference that Khrushchev's Feb. 22 demand for an end to U.N. activities in the Congo was motivated by resentment over the U.N.'s effectiveness in preventing Soviet dominance in central Africa.		The central Congolese government demands that the U.N. Force act immediately to halt the Lumumbist advances into new areas of the Congo. . . . Belgium breaks diplomatic relations with the UAR in protest against the UAR's failure to prevent the sacking of the Belgian Embassy in Cairo by demonstrators angry over the murder of ex-Congo leader Lumumba.		Cambodia and Burma turn down an American-backed appeal from King Savang Vathana to participate with Malaya in a commission to help restore peace to Laos and ensure Laotian neutrality.
Feb. 26			Diplomatic sources report that over 20 communist-bloc and neutralist countries have recognized the Gizenga faction as the legitimate Congo government. . . . King Mohammed V of Morocco, 51, dies of heart failure while undergoing minor surgery. His son, Crown Prince Moulay Hassan, 31, is immediately proclaimed as King Hassan II.	Cuban authorities claim that government troops have defeated the anti-government resistance forces centered in the Escambray Mountains.	
Feb. 27		Edward Heath, Britain's Lord Privy Seal, presents Common Market representatives with proposals for coordinating tariffs on non-farm imports by Britain and the EEC. The plan is regarded as a major step toward ending the regional tariff barriers created by the rival EFTA and EEC trade blocs. . . . Britain and Iceland announce in London an agreement ending their long-standing fishing rights dispute.	Hammarskjold warns Congo Pres. Kasavubu that he is fully prepared to back with force the U.N. Security Council's order to halt unrest in the Congo. . . . Following a private conference near Paris, Tunisian Pres. Habib Bourguiba and French Pres. De Gaulle issue a joint statement expressing confidence in the possibility of a speedy settlement of the Algerian rebellion. The meeting is considered a major step toward the resumption of direct French-rebel peace negotiations.	Cuban security police foil an attempt by three youths to assassinate Cuban National Bank Pres. Ernesto(Ché) Guevara.	
Feb. 28	U.N. Secy. Gen. Hammarskjold discloses that he has requested 22 African nations to contribute 6,000 new troops to the U.N. Force in the Congo.	NATO officials announce a new four-year agreement to redistribute the annual cost of maintaining NATO installations. The new pact reduces the deficit-troubled U.S. share from 36.9% to 30.8% of the total cost. . . . British P.M. Macmillan, responding to Labor and Liberal Party demands, announces the formation of a Royal Commission to investigate possible monopolistic practices in the ownership and operation of British newspapers and periodicals.	The three major anti-Lumumbist groups--the central Congo government, and the secessionist regimes of Katanga and South Kasai Provinces--sign an agreement in Elizabethville to establish a common front against the "danger of U.N. trusteeship, communist tyranny and a Korean-style war" in the Congo. . . . David Ben-Gurion informs Israeli Pres. Ben-Zvi that he has been unable to form a government and that his Mapai Party will propose new Parliamentary elections.		Indian Finance Min. Morarji Desai presents Parliament with a $594 million defense budget for fiscal 1961-1962; the figure represents about 28% of the total Indian budget.
	A	B	C	D	E
	Includes developments that affect more than one world region, international organizations and important meetings of major world leaders.	*Includes all domestic and regional developments in Europe, including the Soviet Union, Turkey, Cyprus and Malta.*	*Includes all domestic and regional developments in Africa and the Middle East, including Iraq and Iran and excluding Cyprus, Turkey and Afghanistan.*	*Includes all domestic and regional developments in Latin America, the Caribbean and Canada.*	*Includes all domestic and regional developments in Asia and Pacific nations, extending from Afghanistan through all the Pacific Islands, except Hawaii.*

U.S. Politics & Social Issues	U.S. Foreign Policy & Defense	U.S. Economy & Environment	Science, Technology & Nature	Culture, Leisure & Life Style	
Senate GOP leader Everett Dirksen pledges to "unfurl" a civil rights bill in the Senate soon since "nothing has been advanced" by the Kennedy administration. . . . The general board of the National Council of Churches, meeting in Syracuse, N.Y., adopts a resolution approving artificial birth control methods as a moral means of responsible family planning.	The White House announces that Pres. Kennedy has rejected a suggestion by Rep. Thomas Lane (D, Mass.) that the U.S. offer to help alleviate Communist China's predicted food shortage in exchange for the release of Americans held in China. The White House announces that administration officials have helped work out an agreement on the representational dispute that has led to the most paralyzing airline strike in commercial aviation history. Pilots for six of the seven affected airlines are reportedly returning to work.		In his natural resources message to Congress, Pres. Kennedy pledges that when the know-how of economic desalinization is achieved, "it will be made available to every nation."		Feb. 23
Kennedy submits to Congress draft bills to expand community health facilities and to provide scholarships to talented students for training as doctors and dentists.		The major U.S. auto manufacturers announce plans to install seat belt hardware as standard front-seat equipment on all 1962 models.			Feb. 24
In a telegrammed message to a Civil Rights Commission conference on education, Pres. Kennedy praises those educators, parents and students who have been on the "front lines" in the fight for school desegregation.					Feb. 25
Former Pres. Eisenhower denies that he described the Kennedy administration as "too much left of center." The remark was earlier attributed to Eisenhower by Sen. Karl Mundt (R, S.D.) in a speech to his constituents.			The American Cancer Society reports that the cancer-cure rate is increasing about 1% a year. . . . The New York Times quotes a NASA study as saying that the U.S. space program has now surpassed the Soviet effort "in its breadth of interest, originality of concept and volume of research."	Marvin Panch, driving a 1960 Pontiac, wins the Daytona 500 stock car race in the record of 149.6 mph.	Feb. 26
Kennedy sends Congress a draft bill for a three-year $2.3 billion program of federal aid to primary and secondary schools to be used at the states' discretion for either construction or teachers' salaries.	Pres. Kennedy names Harvard Prof. Henry Kissinger, 37, as a part-time consultant on national security affairs.				Feb. 27
The AFL-CIO Executive Council approves a resolution urging an end to segregated locals, but rejects AFL-CIO V.P. A. Philip Randolph's proposal to set a six-month deadline for compliance.	Secy. of State Dean Rusk rejects as "highly inaccurate" a Feb. 27 Washington Evening Star report that he had recommended sharp restrictions on the role of nuclear weapons in the U.S. international defense policy. He says he favors strengthening the free world's conventional defense forces while maintaining its nuclear deterrent.	Pres. Kennedy submits to Congress a plan to meet the growing costs of completing the interstate super-highway system by raising taxes on trucks and cancelling a scheduled reduction in gasoline tax. . . . The AFL-CIO Executive Council, at its annual meeting, adopts anti-recession recommendations including proposals for an immediate withholding tax cut, a greatly expanded public housing program, and reduction of oil and gas depletion allowances.			Feb. 28

F	G	H	I	J
Includes elections, federal-state relations, civil rights and liberties, crime, the judiciary, education, health care, poverty, urban affairs and population.	Includes formation and debate of U.S. foreign and defense policies, veterans' affairs and defense spending. (Relations with specific foreign countries are usually found under the region concerned.)	Includes business, labor, agriculture, taxation, transportation, consumer affairs, monetary and fiscal policy, natural resources, and pollution.	Includes worldwide scientific, medical and technological developments, natural phenomena, U.S. weather, natural disasters, and accidents.	Includes the arts, religion, scholarship, communications media, sports, entertainment, fashions, fads and social life.

	World Affairs	Europe	Africa & the Middle East	The Americas	Asia & the Pacific
March 1		The French cabinet makes public a formal decree restricting the police and political powers of the French army in Algeria and returning certain of these functions to civilian control.	Congolese troops under the Kasavubu regime kill 44 civilians in Luluabourg in an apparently random retaliation for pro-Lumumbist demonstrations against the central Congo government. The Congolese soldiers had just reoccupied the city following the unexplained withdrawal of forces commanded by the Stanleyville regime of Antoine Gizenga.	The leftwing People's United Party wins all 18 seats in British Honduras' newly-expanded Legislative Assembly. The elections were the first held under a new constitution designed to give British Honduras eventual self-government within the Commonwealth. . . . Eduardo Victor Haedo, head of Uruguay's nine-man ruling Executive Council is formally inaugurated as president in ceremonies in Mercedes. In his inaugural address, Haedo praises the U.S. and denounces "interference" in Latin America "by outside forces."	Ceylonese government troops are airlifted to the Tamil-speaking northern provinces to quell the Tamil Federal Party's spreading non-violent campaign (satyagraha) against the government's Jan. 20 decision to make Sinhalese the country's only official language. . . . Indonesian Pres. Sukarno orders the dissolution of six groups for opposing government policy.
March 2	In a report to the General Assembly, Secy. General Hammarskjold estimates that $135 million will be needed to sustain U.N. operations in the Congo throughout 1961.	According to Tass dispatches at least six high-level regional agricultural officials have been ousted as part of the current Soviet campaign to reform and reorganize farm production in the USSR. . . . Thoutousands of Italian students join in anti-Austrian demonstrations throughout Italy touched off by the continuing Italian-Austrian dispute over the Bolzano region of northern Italy.	*The New York Times* reports that the Katanga government of Pres. Tshombe currently controls more financial resources than the central Congo government or any other of the Congolese factions. . . . French troops complete the evacuation of all their military bases in Morocco under the terms of a 1960 French-Moroccan agreement. . . . The Algerian Provisional Government announces its readiness to resume direct peace negotiations with France.		Thailand warns it will take "forcible action" to remove any Chinese Nationalist guerrillas found operating in Thai territory.
March 3	In their first news conference since returning to the U.S., the two surviving crewmen of the downed RB-47 say their plane was at least 50 nautical miles from the Russian land mass when fired upon by a Soviet fighter plane.		The U.N. Congo Command warns Katanga that U.N. troops will remain in the Province until all Belgians are withdrawn in conformity with Security Council resolutions. . . . Responding to appeals from Hammarskjold, India announces preparations to send a 3000-man combat unit to bolster the dwindling U.N. Force in the Congo. Tunisia and Liberia also promise additional manpower.		*The New York Times* publishes a Mar. 1 dispatch from northern Laos indicating that massive shipments of Soviet arms accompanied by North Vietnamese military advisers are on the way to the Pathet Lao rebels. . . . The U.S. State Dept. charges that reports of Soviet aid to the Pathet Lao proves that the USSR is trying to obstruct peace in Laos in order to ensure communist control of rebel-held areas.
March 4		West Germany, in an effort to halt domestic inflation and ease pressure on the U.S. dollar, announces an immediate 4.75% upward revaluation of the mark.	Sudanese U.N. troops withdraw from two U.N. Congo installations following two days of fighting with Congolese troops under the command of the Kasavubu government. U.N. officials protest the fighting and demand that the surrendered posts be returned to U.N. control.	Adolph Berle, head of a special U.S. task force on Latin American policy, completes two days of talks with Brazilian Pres. Janio Quadros, during which Quadros reportedly voiced opposition to a plan for an inter-American meeting to consider measures against an alleged communist build-up in Cuba. . . . Argentine Foreign Min. Diogenes Taboada cables Cuban and U.S. officials proposing that Argentina mediate the continuing dispute between the two countries.	
March 5		Greek sources report the formation of a new centrist party, the Democratic Center Agrarian Liberal Union, under the leadership of ex-Premier George Papandreou.		The coalition government of Pres. Jorge Allesandri Rodriguez retains control of both houses of the Chilean legislature in nationwide congressional elections.	The Nationalist Chinese government announces that it will remove to Formosa all Chinese guerrillas in the Burma-China-Thailand border area who are "responsive to the offer of being evacuated."
March 6	A meeting between U.S. Amb.-to-U.N. Stevenson and Soviet Foreign Min. Gromyko, aimed at shortening the reconvened General Assembly session by dropping certain Cold War issues from the agenda, ends without agreement.	The Netherlands, following the lead of its trading partner West Germany, effects an immediate 4.75% upward revaluation of the Dutch guilder. Swiss officials say the Swiss franc will remain unchanged.			

A	B	C	D	E
Includes developments that affect more than one world region, international organizations and important meetings of major world leaders.	Includes all domestic and regional developments in Europe, including the Soviet Union, Turkey, Cyprus and Malta.	Includes all domestic and regional developments in Africa and the Middle East, including Iraq and Iran and excluding Cyprus, Turkey and Afghanistan.	Includes all domestic and regional developments in Latin America, the Caribbean and Canada.	Includes all domestic and regional developments in Asia and Pacific nations, extending from Afghanistan through all the Pacific Islands, except Hawaii.

U.S. Politics & Social Issues	U.S. Foreign Policy & Defense	U.S. Economy & Environment	Science, Technology & Nature	Culture, Leisure & Life Style	
The Roman Catholic hierarchy in the U.S.--including all five American cardinals--decides at a Washington meeting to oppose the administration's federal aid to education bill unless it is amended to include assistance to parochial schools. At about the same time Pres. Kennedy reiterates to reporters his view that "the Constitution clearly prohibits aid to . . . the parochial school."	Kennedy signs an executive order establishing "on a temporary pilot basis" a Peace Corps of trained Americans to provide technical assistance to foreign nations. The pilot project will be in effect until Congress authorizes the creation of a permanent Peace Corps. . . . Pres. Kennedy affirms at his news conference that his administration is "anxious to . . . see conventional forces strengthened, not only in Western Europe, but throughout the world."	The House passes and sends to the Senate the administration-backed bill to extend unemployment compensation to workers who have exhausted their benefits under state unemployment programs; it is the first major administration anti-recession measure to pass in either house.		The 1961 All-American collegiate basketball team, as picked in an AP and UPI poll of sports writers and broadcasters, is announced in New York: Jerry Lucas (Ohio State), Tom Stith (St. Bonaventure), Terry Dischinger (Purdue), Roger Kaiser (Georgia), and Chet Walker (Bradley).	March 1
The U.S. 8th Circuit Court of Appeals orders the Little Rock, Ark. school board to take "affirmative action", in more than a "token fashion," toward public school desegregation.	*The New York Times* reports that Pres. Kennedy has received a greater public response on the creation of a Peace Corps than on any other issue since taking office.	*The Wall Street Journal* reports that 1960 corporate profits fell from $12 billion in 1959 to $11.7 billion in 1960. . . . Pres. Kennedy orders a speed-up in the $270 million postoffice construction program in an effort to help stimulate an economic recovery.	In hearings before the Senate Space Committee NASA officials outline a 10-year program of lunar space probes to end with the landing of a manned vehicle on the moon by 1971.	Artist Pablo Picasso, 79, marries Jacqueline Roque, 33, his model, in Valauris, France (second for both).	March 2
	Presidential aide Arthur M. Schlesinger Jr., just returned from a Latin American tour, reports to Pres. Kennedy that Castro is losing popularity in Latin America because he has come to be regarded as a "symbol of communist penetration."	Labor Secy. Arthur Goldberg discloses at a House Banking subcommittee hearing that the unemployment rate in the construction trades has reached 22%.	Pravda discloses that Soviet scientists lost radio contact with the Venus I interplanetary probe on Feb. 27.	Soviet highjumper Valeri Brumel, 18, sets a new indoor, board take-off record of seven ft. three-and-a-half in. at the annual Knights of Columbus meet in New York.	March 3
The National Urban League releases a 50-city survey showing the unemployment of Negroes to be two to three times the national average.	Kennedy names his brother-in-law, R. Sargent Shriver, 45, as director of the newly formed Peace Corps.	Labor Secy. Goldberg orders the withdrawal of 2,800 braceros from southern California fields in an effort to ease tension between growers and U.S. farm labor organizers.		Gene Fullmer, 29, scores a 15-round decision over Sugar Ray Robinson, 41, in Las Vegas to retain the middleweight title.	March 4
				Henry Canby, 82, American literary scholar and critic, founder and first editor of the *Saturday Review of Literature* (1924), dies in Ossining, N.Y.	March 5
Pres. Kennedy orders the creation of a Committee on Equal Employment Opportunity to help eliminate racial discrimination in the employment practices of the federal government. . . . Evidence obtained by use of a device that physically encroached on a defendant's house is ruled inadmissible by a unanimous decision of the Supreme Court.	Peace Corps Director R. Sargent Shriver tells reporters that Corps volunteers will probably receive draft deferments but not exemption from military service.	Dr. Walter Heller, chmn. of the President's Council of Economic Advisers, tells a Joint Congressional Economic Committee hearing that a gradual upturn in the sagging economy should begin within the next few months.		Cardinal Marcello Mimmi, 78, a cardinal-bishop since 1953 and one of the candidates to succeed Pope Pius XII in 1958, dies in Rome.	March 6

F	G	H	I	J
Includes elections, federal-state relations, civil rights and liberties, crime, the judiciary, education, health care, poverty, urban affairs and population.	*Includes formation and debate of U.S. foreign and defense policies, veterans' affairs and defense spending. (Relations with specific foreign countries are usually found under the region concerned.)*	*Includes business, labor, agriculture, taxation, transportation, consumer affairs, monetary and fiscal policy, natural resources, and pollution.*	*Includes worldwide scientific, medical and technological developments, natural phenomena, U.S. weather, natural disasters, and accidents.*	*Includes the arts, religion, scholarship, communications media, sports, entertainment, fashions, fads and social life.*

	World Affairs	Europe	Africa & the Middle East	The Americas	Asia & the Pacific
March 7	Ghana Pres. Nkrumah opens the reconvened 15th regular session of the U.N. General Assembly with an address calling for the creation of an all-African-Asian U.N. Force to oversee a solution to the Congo crisis.				Govind Ballabh Pant, 73, Indian Home Minister since 1955 and deputy leader of the Congress Party since 1958, dies in New Delhi.
March 8	British P.M. Macmillan opens the 10th postwar conference of Commonwealth prime ministers in London. . . . Pres. Kennedy tells a news conference that his administrations's first efforts to negotiate an improvement in U.S.-Chinese relations have been stymied by Communist Chinese demands that any agreement be preceded by a U.S. disavowal of support for Nationalist China.	The U.S. nuclear submarine *Patrick Henry*, armed with 16 Polaris missiles, arrives at its base in Holy Loch, Scotland where it will be stationed under the terms of a 1960 U.S.-British base agreement. Scattered pacifist demonstrations preceded the ship's arrival.	Central Congo Pres. Kasavubu, Katanga chief Tshombe, and Albert Kalonji of South Kasai Province arrive with other anti-leftist provincial leaders in the Malagasy Republic for a conference on the political future of the Congo. Antoine Gizenga, leader of the leftist Stanleyville regime, declines to attend.	Speeches and resolutions critical of U.S. policy in the Western Hemisphere mark the climax of a four-day, leftist-sponsored Latin American Conference for National Sovereignty held in Mexico City. . . . Cuba formally rejects an Argentine offer to mediate U.S.-Cuban differences claiming that recent American actions have shown that the U.S. is unprepared for serious negotiations.	
March 9			In a cable to Secy. Gen. Hammarskjold, the delegates to the Congo political conference, meeting in the Malagasy Republic, ask that all U.N. action in the Congo be suspended pending the results of their talks. . . . An offer by the Central Congo government to return two U.N. installations in exchange for a measure of Congolese control over future U.N. operations is rejected by Hammarskjold.		The exiled Dalai Lama of Tibet issues an appeal from his home in India asking the U.N. General Assembly "to help restore the independence of (Communist Chinese-occupied) Tibet."
March 10				*The New York Herald Tribune* reports that representatives of anti-Castro groups in the U.S. have secretly organized a provisional Cuban government dedicated to the overthrow of the Castro regime. José Miró Cardona, premier during the early days of Castro's rule, is said to have been named provisional president.	Gen. Phoumi Nosavan, representing Laos' rightist Boun Oum cabinet, completes two days of talks with exiled neutralist Prince Souvanna Phouma in the Cambodian capital of Pnom Penh. The two men issue a statement calling for a policy of strict Laotian neutrality, the cessation of foreign interference, and the inauguration of Souvanna-supervised negotiations between rival Laotian factions. . . . Indonesia asks Britain to cease representing Dutch interests in Indonesia thereby breaking the last remaining tie with the Netherlands.
March 11		The Estonian SSR Supreme Court convicts and sentences to death three Estonians on charges of participating in the mass murder of 125,000 Russians, Germans, Jews and others at the Nazi concentration camp at Jagala, Estonia during World War II.		Two Cuban army officers, including U.S.-born Maj. William Morgan, 32, are executed by a Cuban military firing squad after being convicted of supplying arms to anti-Castro rebels in the Escambray Mountains during the fall of 1960.	Reports from Teheran, Iran say that at least eight persons have been killed and 20 injured in connection with anti-government riots growing out of the elections to the Majlis which began Jan. 10.

A	B	C	D	E
Includes developments that affect more than one world region, international organizations and important meetings of major world leaders.	Includes all domestic and regional developments in Europe, including the Soviet Union, Turkey, Cyprus and Malta.	Includes all domestic and regional developments in Africa and the Middle East, including Iraq and Iran and excluding Cyprus, Turkey and Afghanistan.	Includes all domestic and regional developments in Latin America, the Caribbean and Canada.	Includes all domestic and regional developments in Asia and Pacific nations, extending from Afghanistan through all the Pacific Islands, except Hawaii.

U.S. Politics & Social Issues	U.S. Foreign Policy & Defense	U.S. Economy & Environment	Science, Technology & Nature	Culture, Leisure & Life Style	
The Atlanta Chamber of Commerce announces that local businessmen have agreed to a gradual desegregation of lunch counters and other facilities (on a timetable similar to that adopted by the Atlanta public schools) in exchange for a pledge from Negro leaders to end immediately the sit-in demonstrations against segregated stores. . . . A Georgia Court of Appeals revokes Martin Luther King's one-year prison sentence for a traffic violation on grounds that the traffic conviction did not constitute a probation violation as the lower court had ruled.	In a letter to congressional leaders, Pres. Kennedy proposes that Congress amend the Battle Act to permit U.S. economic aid to communist nations of Eastern Europe.	Labor Secy. Goldberg reports that the U.S. unemployment rate rose from 6.6% in January to a seasonally adjusted rate of 6.8% in February, the highest level since July 1941. . . . Treasury Secy. Douglas Dillon tells the Joint Congressional Economic Committee that despite expectations of an economic recovery beginning in April the recession had already forced the administration to revise upward its estimate of budgetary deficits for fiscal 1961 and 1962.			March 7
At his regular press conference, Kennedy calls upon Congress not to let the parochial school controversy kill the administration's aid-to-public-education bill. . . . In a Senate speech Sen. Milton Young (R, N.D.) expresses concern over "spreading influence" of the ultraconservative John Birch Society. Young cites Society founder Robert Welch's published charge that Dwight Eisenhower was a communist agent as evidence of the group's extremism.	Defense Secy. Robert McNamara issues a directive giving the Air Force primary responsibility for militarily-related space development programs and projects. The Army and Navy will retain the right to "conduct preliminary research to develop new ways of using space technology."	Labor Secy. Arthur Goldberg, testifying before the Senate Finance Committee on behalf of the jobless benefit extension bill, says that unemployment will continue to be a serious problem even if the economy makes a predicted upturn in April.			March 8
Senate Democratic Majority leader Mike Mansfield proposes a separate bill on authorizing federal loans to private schools as a way of freeing the administration's school-aid bill from the growing parochial school controversy. . . . Kennedy sends Congress an omnibus housing message containing various proposals aimed at (a) providing decent housing for all Americans; (b) ensuring the sound development of rapidly expanding urban areas; and (c) stimulating the U.S. construction industry. If enacted, the proposals would cost the federal government roughly $3 billion over the next five years.	Kennedy names Dr. Harold Brown, 33, chief U.S. scientist at the Geneva testban talks (1958-1959), to be the Defense Dept.'s director of research and engineering.	The Washington Post Co. announces the acquisition of a 59% interest in *Newsweek* magazine, the second largest U.S. news periodical.	In an experiment aimed at improving life support equipment, Soviet scientists launch into orbit and successfully recover a 10,000-pound spacecraft carrying a dog and other small animals.		March 9
Clarence Mitchell of the NAACP tells the Senate Education Subcommittee that aid-to-education grants should contain strong "anti-segregation safeguards." . . . The House passes and sends to the Senate an administration-backed bill (HR4884) to authorize $305 million in federal money for an aid program for needy children of unemployed parents.		A joint congressional conference committee begins work on resolving differences in two emergency feed grain control bills passed by the House and Senate. The major difference is the Senate version's elimination of a controversial House provision designed to encourage farmer participation in acreage reductions by enabling the government to sell its surplus grain at any price not less than 17% below support levels.			March 10
Seventeen interdepartmental committees, including 16 established during the Eisenhower years, are ordered abolished by Pres. Kennedy as part of a program to "clarify and pinpoint executive responsibility."		The N.Y. Port Authority, in a report to N.Y. Gov. Nelson Rockefeller and N.J. Gov. Robert Meyner, recommends the building of a $355 million World Trade Center in lower Manhattan.	*The Journal of the American Medical Association* publishes a report indicating that the number of strains of disease-causing staph germs resistant to commonly used antibiotics is increasing. The study cites excessive or indiscriminate use as a possible factor.		March 11

F	G	H	I	J
Includes elections, federal-state relations, civil rights and liberties, crime, the judiciary, education, health care, poverty, urban affairs and population.	Includes formation and debate of U.S. foreign and defense policies, veterans' affairs and defense spending. (Relations with specific foreign countries are usually found under the region concerned.)	Includes business, labor, agriculture, taxation, transportation, consumer affairs, monetary and fiscal policy, natural resources, and pollution.	Includes worldwide scientific, medical and technological developments, natural phenomena, U.S. weather, natural disasters, and accidents.	Includes the arts, religion, scholarship, communications media, sports, entertainment, fashions, fads and social life.

	World Affairs	Europe	Africa & the Middle East	The Americas	Asia & the Pacific
March 12			Following five days of talks, anti-leftist Congolese leaders announce agreement on the formation of a new confederation of Congo states loosely governed by a president and Council which will replace the current central government. Kasavubu is named president of the new confederation. . . . Leaders at the Congo political conference also demand curtailment of U.N. Congo activities on the grounds that intervention is no longer needed "since reunion has been achieved between (Congo) authorities."	Roman Catholic Bishop Thomas Reilly of San Juan issues a statement charging the regime of Generalissimo Trujillo with "acts of intimidation and persecution" against the Roman Catholic Church of the Dominican Republic.	The New York Times reports that Indonesian Pres. Sukarno has sent Mrs. Poedjoboentord Supeni, his "roving ambassador", to visit Afro-Asian nations and seek support for the convening of a second Bandung Conference to ease international tensions.
March 13	Commonwealth prime ministers, meeting in London, approve the admission of Cyprus as the 12th Commonwealth member state. . . . Canadian P.M. John Diefenbaker opens the Commonwealth Conference debate on South Africa's application for renewed membership (as a republic) by denouncing the Verwoerd government's apartheid policies.	West Berlin Mayor Willy Brandt, visiting the U.S., comes away from a meeting with Pres. Kennedy expressing full confidence that the new administration would maintain the uncompromising support given to West Berlin by the U.S. in the past.		At a White House reception for 250 Latin American diplomats Pres. Kennedy outlines a 10-year, 10-point "Alliance for Progress" program aimed at improving the material well-being of hemispheric peoples without sacrificing political liberty. Highlights of the proposal include: intensified social planning to ensure that the benefits of economic growth are widely shared; increased U.S. financial, technical, and scientific aid to Latin America; and greater hemispheric economic integration.	The Boun Oum cabinet publicly endorses the statement of principles on a Laotian peace settlement issued Mar. 10 by Gen. Phoumi Nosavan and Prince Souvanna Phouma.
March 14	Macmillan presents the Commonwealth conference with a compromise proposal on South Africa which accepts its application for renewed membership, but censures its racial policies.		In a note to Hammarskjold, Belgium charges that the U.N. Force in the Congo is failing to provide protection to white residents.	The New York Times reports that a daily newspaper, the Tribuna Liberal, founded Jan. 20 in Asuncion, Paraguay, has become the nation's first newspaper to openly criticize Pres. Alfredo Stroessner since he took power seven years ago. . . . Castro tells a Havana University audience that Cuba will form a free provisional government of Puerto Rico if anti-Castro forces go ahead with a reported plan to create a provisional Cuban government in the U.S.	
March 15	Addressing the Commonwealth conference, P.M. Henrik Verwoerd announces that South Africa is withdrawing its application for renewed membership because of the "vindictive" interference in its internal affairs by other member states.		A Security Council resolution calling for a U.N. investigation into the disorders in Portuguese Angola fails to gain a needed majority as six nations abstain. The U.S. and USSR were among the minority voting for the resolution.	The Cuban government orders all citizens and foreign residents to surrender all their foreign securities and currency to the Cuban National Bank by April 3. The money and stocks are to be exchanged for Cuban pesos.	Pres. Kennedy, meeting with Washington newsmen, reiterates U.S. support for the Boun Oum government and blames the failure to achieve a truly neutral Laos on "a small minority backed by personnel and supplies from outside."
March 16	The U.N. General Assembly votes 74-0 to censure South Africa for its continued administration of the former German colony of South West Africa in defiance of repeated U.N. demands that the territory be made a U.N. trusteeship.	The British Labor Party expels five leftwing MP's from the Parliamentary Labor Party for opposing the defense policies of party leader Hugh Gaitskell.	Africans opposed to Portuguese rule are reported to have killed more than 150 Portuguese in riots in northern Angola. . . . Leaders of South Africa's English-speaking white community issue statements condemning Verwoerd's decision to quit the Commonwealth as a betrayal of the nation's best interests. . . . Congo Pres. Joseph Kasavubu formally protests the arrival of additional Indian troops sent to bolster the U.N. Congo Force.	Haiti University students, on strike to protest the jailing of student demonstrators since Nov. 22, 1960, begin returning to classes.	The New York Times reports that Viet Cong guerrillas in South Vietnam have been killing an average of 500 pro-government villagers a month. The Times estimates the total Viet Cong force at about 9,000 men.
March 17	The Commonwealth prime minister's conference ends in London with the issuance of a final communique urging total world disarmament and the speedy achievement of a test-ban agreement. . . . A U.S.-Soviet agreement providing for the exchange of teachers and scholars in the fields of law, history and literature is signed in Moscow. . . . The U.N. Human Rights Commission ends its 17th session after approving studies into the rights of arrested persons.	The West German Bundestag (lower house) approves a record $12 billion federal budget for 1961.	The Petroleum Information Bureau reports in London that Middle East oil production rose 14.4% in 1960 to a record 264 million metric tons, about one quarter of the total world production.		U.S. State Dept. spokesmen say that additional American military advisers have been assigned to training missions with the Laotian army. . . . The Nationalist Chinese government begins to airlift an estimated 5,000 Nationalist guerrillas out of Thailand. Guerrilla forces are still reported active in Burma.

A	B	C	D	E
Includes developments that affect more than one world region, international organizations and important meetings of major world leaders.	Includes all domestic and regional developments in Europe, including the Soviet Union, Turkey, Cyprus and Malta.	Includes all domestic and regional developments in Africa and the Middle East, including Iraq and Iran and excluding Cyprus, Turkey and Afghanistan.	Includes all domestic and regional developments in Latin America, the Caribbean and Canada.	Includes all domestic and regional developments in Asia and Pacific nations, extending from Afghanistan through all the Pacific Islands, except Hawaii.

U.S. Politics & Social Issues	U.S. Foreign Policy & Defense	U.S. Economy & Environment	Science, Technology & Nature	Culture, Leisure & Life Style	
					March 12
Cardinal Francis Spellman, Roman Catholic archbishop of New York, issues a statement reiterating his opposition to any federal school aid bill that excludes parochial schools. . . . During a meeting with Pres. Kennedy, Eleanor Roosevelt expresses concern over the small number of women appointed to government posts and leaves a three-page list of women qualified for top-level jobs. The AP reports that only nine women are among 240 Kennedy appointees so far.			Dr. Luis Alvarez, 49, of the Univ. of California, is named recipient of the 1961 Albert Einstein Award ($5,000) for his contributions to physical theory and his part in developing the ground-control-approach blind-landing system for planes during the 1940's.	Floyd Patterson, 26, retains the world heavyweight championship by knocking out former champ Ingemar Johansson, 28, of Sweden during the sixth round of their title bout in Miami Beach, Fla.	**March 13**
A preliminary report of the U.S. Census Bureau reveals that Washington D.C. is the only major American city in which a majority of the population is Negro (53.9%). . . . Atlanta has the second highest Negro percentage with 38.3%. . . . Msgr. Frederick Hochwalt, director of the Education Department of the National Catholic Welfare Conference, tells the Senate Education Subcommittee that loans to parochial schools should be part of the aid-to-education bill.	In a special message Kennedy calls upon Congress to appropriate immediately the $500 million earmarked for the Inter-American Fund for Social Progress, noting that unless the U.S. fulfills its promise of aid, Latin Americans may "turn to communism or other forms of tyranny.". . . Pres. Kennedy designates Edwin Reischauer, 50, director of the Harvard-Yenching Institute, to be ambassador to Japan.	The Justice Dept. and the TVA file a joint civil antitrust suit against General Electric, Allis-Chalmers, I-T-E Circuit Breaker Co. and Westinghouse Electric Corp. to recover more than $12 million in damages for alleged overcharges on 1951-1960 purchases of $25 million worth of large circuit breakers. . . . The CAB awards to Delta and National Airlines the last unassigned U.S. coast-to-coast air routes (from southern Florida to California).	In a public speech Premier Khrushchev predicts that the USSR will put a man in space in the near future.	The National Book Awards for the best books of 1960 are presented in New York to the following: William Shirer, non-fiction (*The Rise and Fall of the Third Reich*); Conrad Richter, fiction (*The Waters of Kronos*); and Randall Jarrell, poetry (*The Woman at the Washington Zoo*). . . . A modern English prose translation of the New Testament, the New English Bible, is published in London by the Oxford and Cambridge Univ. Presses.	**March 14**
	Harvard economics professor John Kenneth Galbraith, 52, is named by Kennedy as ambassador to India.	The Senate passes and sends to the House a bill (S1) to provide $394 million in Treasury-financed loans and grants to economically-depressed regions.			**March 15**
	By a wide margin the Senate ratifies a treaty providing for U.S. membership in the Organization for Economic Cooperation and Development; the U.S. is the first of the 20 signatories to ratify the pact.	In his farm message to Congress, Kennedy proposes as a solution to the problems of agricultural supply and marketing the establishment of national farmer advisory committees for every commodity for which a new supply adjustment program is planned. . . . A slightly altered emergency unemployment compensation bill (HR4806) is passed by the Senate, 84-4, and sent to a House-Senate conference.	The discovery of wax in an old meteorite fragment is reported at the New York Academy of Sciences by Drs. Bartholomew Nagy and Douglas Hennesy of Fordham Univ. and Warren Meinschein of the Esso Research Co. The three scientists contend that the organic-like wax suggests that life exists elsewhere in the universe.		**March 16**
Ex-Vice Pres. Richard Nixon writes the *Los Angeles Times* to endorse the newspaper's editorial stand against the John Birch Society.		The Commerce Dept. reports that U.S. personal incomes dropped from an annual rate of $406.6 billion in January to $405.9 billion in February.		The National Institute of Arts and Letters names Ieoh Ming Pei, Chinese-born New York architect, as recipient of its Brunner Award for architecture. . . . The New York District Attorney's office discloses the arrest of two N.Y. gamblers for bribing Univ. of Connecticut and Seton Hall Univ. basketball players to fix games in favor of bettors.	**March 17**

F	G	H	I	J
Includes elections, federal-state relations, civil rights and liberties, crime, the judiciary, education, health care, poverty, urban affairs and population.	Includes formation and debate of U.S. foreign and defense policies, veterans' affairs and defense spending. (Relations with specific foreign countries are usually found under the region concerned.)	Includes business, labor, agriculture, taxation, transportation, consumer affairs, monetary and fiscal policy, natural resources, and pollution.	Includes worldwide scientific, medical and technological developments, natural phenomena, U.S. weather, natural disasters, and accidents.	Includes the arts, religion, scholarship, communications media, sports, entertainment, fashions, fads and social life.

	World Affairs	Europe	Africa & the Middle East	The Americas	Asia & the Pacific
March 18	At a Washington meeting U.S. State Secy. Dean Rusk reportedly informs Soviet Foreign Min. Gromyko that the U.S. is prepared to back the Boun Oum government if the USSR continues to frustrate efforts to neutralize Laos by aiding the Pathet Lao. Gromyko is said to have insisted that the USSR was simply supporting the legal Laotian government, that of Prince Souvanna Phouma.	Polish CP First Secy. Wladislaw Gomulka charges in a speech to a Warsaw audience that Polish Roman Catholic clerics "belong" more "to the Vatican" than to Poland.	Sources in Leopoldville report that the Gizenga government has rejected the creation of a Congolese confederation under Kasavubu.		Laotian sources report that the Pathet Lao-led rebel advance is continuing to gain momentum and that rebel forces are now within 22 miles of the royal capital of Luang Prabang.
March 19	U.N. sources report that Hammarskjold has extended the term of Rajeshwar Dayal, his personal representative in the Congo, despite repeated demands for his dismissal from the central Congolese government.	West Berlin Mayor Willy Brandt tells a group of U.S. Jewish leaders in New York that his country has completely broken with its anti-Semitic past. . . . In a Lenten church service in Warsaw, Cardinal Stefan Wyszynski, Roman Catholic primate of Poland, accuses the government of engaging in "a program of atheization" designed "to free our youth from God."	Macmillan tells Parliament that P.M. Verwoerd had made continued South African membership in the Commonwealth impossible by his continued adherence to racial ideas "abhorrent to the ideals with which mankind is struggling in this century."		
March 20		By a fairly close vote, delegates to the Italian Socialist Party's national congress continue the party's policy of limited cooperation with the ruling Christian Democratic Party and its opposition to the Communist Party.	Pres. Kasavubu tells reporters that the U.N. mission to the Congo has failed and all U.N. troops should be immediately withdrawn. . . . Thousands of South African supporters of the Nationalist government cheer P.M. Verwoerd upon his arrival in Johannesburg after attending the Commonwealth conference in London.	Cuban government forces capture an American and four Cubans as they attempt to land from a motor launch near Cabanas Bay on the north coast of Pinar del Rio Province.	Laotian Information Min. Bouavan Norasing makes public proposals that the Pathet Lao-led rebels set up provisional governments to rule the areas they currently control and then cooperate in founding a coalition central government with the Boun Oum regime.
March 21	The U.S.-British-Soviet test-ban talks, recessed since Dec. 5, 1960, resume in Geneva with the presentation of a revised Western proposal containing several concessions to Soviet demands made before the recess.	The Rumanian Grand National Assembly approves a major reorganization of the governmental structure to improve administrative efficiency. The plan calls for the creation of a powerful 13-man State Council to replace the current ruling Presidium.	The U.N.'s Congo Conciliation Committee reports that a six-week inquiry into the Congo situation has shown that the country is "on the verge of catastrophe" from civil war, famine and the threat of foreign intervention.		The Boun Oum cabinet announces it is prepared to resume peace negotiations with exiled Laotian former-Premier Prince Souvanna Phouma. . . . Washington sources report that the Kennedy administration has ordered an immediate increase in military aid to the Boun Oum government to offset the effect of communist arms now being sent to the advancing Laotian rebel forces.
March 22		A London jury convicts and sentences (from 15 to 25 years) five persons accused of spying on Britain's Underwater Detection Establishment in Portland.	In a Stanleyville interview with a *New York Herald Tribune* reporter, Antoine Gizenga denies that he is pro-communist but insists that he is the legitimate successor (as Congo premier) to the late Patrice Lumumba.	*The New York Times* reports that two rival anti-Castro groups in the U.S.--the Democratic Revolutionary Front and the Revolutionary Movement of the People-- have agreed to recognize ex-Cuban Premier José Miró Cardona as president of a "Revolutionary Council" dedicated to Castro's overthrow.	
March 23	British Amb.-to-USSR Sir Frank Roberts presents the Soviet government with an Anglo-U.S. proposal which urges the USSR to join in appealing to both the Laotian government and the Pathet Lao rebels for an immediate cease-fire and which recommends the convening of a new international conference on Laos following the achievement of peace.	The USSR announces that it is ending prior censorship of news dispatches sent out of the Soviet Union by foreign correspondents.	The Central Congo government is reportedly preparing to dispatch a negotiating team to Stanleyville for talks with Gizenga regime.		In a prepared statement to a televised news conference, Pres. Kennedy declares that the U.S. will not tolerate the "loss" of Laos to the advancing rebel forces of the pro-communist Pathet Lao movement, adding that "if the communists. . . move in and dominate this country, it would endanger the. . .peace of all of southeast Asia."

A	B	C	D	E
Includes developments that affect more than one world region, international organizations and important meetings of major world leaders.	Includes all domestic and regional developments in Europe, including the Soviet Union, Turkey, Cyprus and Malta.	Includes all domestic and regional developments in Africa and the Middle East, including Iraq and Iran and excluding Cyprus, Turkey and Afghanistan.	Includes all domestic and regional developments in Latin America, the Caribbean and Canada.	Includes all domestic and regional developments in Asia and Pacific nations, extending from Afghanistan through all the Pacific Islands, except Hawaii.

U.S. Politics & Social Issues	U.S. Foreign Policy & Defense	U.S. Economy & Environment	Science, Technology & Nature	Culture, Leisure & Life Style	
					March 18
The Protestant Episcopal Church formally urges its members to work for the abolition of capital punishment in the U.S.		The FTC accuses four drug manufacturers of making false advertising claims about the speed with which their products relieve pain.	At least 266 people are reported dead in the wake of tornadoes that swept across East Pakistan.		**March 19**
In hearings before House and Senate Education Subcommittees and in public statements, spokesmen for major Protestant and Jewish groups declare their opposition to any bill extending federal aid to parochial schools. . . . The Supreme Court upholds a series of rulings by the New Orleans federal district court rejecting state moves to block the desegregation of New Orleans public schools.	The *Congressional Quarterly* reports that the 100 biggest U.S. defense contractors received contract awards totaling $15.4 billion between July 1959 and June 1960.				**March 20**
	The House passes and sends to the Senate a bill to extend until 1963 the current Sugar Act under which the President can halt sugar imports from Cuba and bar extra sugar imports from the Dominican Republic.	Pres. Kennedy warns his Advisory Committee on Labor-Management Policy that it is "quite possible" that the U.S. will continue to have an unemployment rate of 6-7% even with an economic recovery in the summer.		By a vote 67-13 the Senate passes and sends to the House a bill authorizing $1 million in grants to each state over five years to buy equipment for educational TV broadcasts.	**March 21**
Rep. L. Mendel Rivers (D, S.C.), in a House speech, defends the John Birch Society which has become the object of growing criticism and controversy within the Congress.	Kennedy sends to Congress a message outlining an enlarged and integrated U.S. foreign aid program aimed at making the 1960's a "decade of development" for the world's poorer nations.	A conference committee-drafted compromise version of the emergency feed grains bill is passed by both houses and signed by Pres. Kennedy. . . . The N.Y. Federal Reserve Bank reports that the U.S. Treasury's gold stocks have risen for two consecutive weeks for the first time since January-February 1958.			**March 22**
Ralph Chaplin, 73, militant U.S. labor leader, who was jailed under the Espionage Act for his activities in the Industrial Workers of the World (1918-1923), composer of labor songs ("Solidarity Forever," 1915) and author, dies in Tacoma, Washington.	Kennedy signs the convention for U.S. membership in the Organization for Economic Cooperation and Development. The *Theodore Roosevelt*, the Navy's fourth Polaris submarine, launches three Polaris missiles, two unsuccessfully, in underwater tests 200 miles south of Cape Canaveral.			Kennedy appoints Oklahoma football coach Bud Wilkinson to act as special consultant for the development of a national youth fitness program.	**March 23**

F	G	H	I	J
Includes elections, federal-state relations, civil rights and liberties, crime, the judiciary, education, health care, poverty, urban affairs and population.	Includes formation and debate of U.S. foreign and defense policies, veterans' affairs and defense spending. (Relations with specific foreign countries are usually found under the region concerned.)	Includes business, labor, agriculture, taxation, transportation, consumer affairs, monetary and fiscal policy, natural resources, and pollution.	Includes worldwide scientific, medical and technological developments, natural phenomena, U.S. weather, natural disasters, and accidents.	Includes the arts, religion, scholarship, communications media, sports, entertainment, fashions, fads and social life.

	World Affairs	Europe	Africa & the Middle East	The Americas	Asia & the Pacific
March 24	Espionage charges against Igor Melekh, Russian U.N. employee, are dismissed by U.S. District Judge Edwin Robson in Chicago at the request of Atty. Gen. Robert Kennedy and the State Dept. State Dept. spokesmen explain the decision as part of a move to improve protection of U.S. citizens in the USSR.				Ex-Laotian Premier Souvanna Phouma, on a world tour, tells reporters in Paris that the West's proposals for establishing a truly neutral Laos are "the most reasonable solution" yet offered for ending Laotian strife. . . . Laotian sources report that 16 U.S. transport helicopters are currently being readied for use by the Laotian army.
March 25	Delegates from 73 nations, meeting in New York, vote to adopt a Single Convention on Narcotic Drugs to replace nine existing international conventions on drug traffic control. Burma and seven Soviet-bloc nations abstain.				About 10,000 South Koreans join in public demonstrations against government-proposed bills to repress communist political activity.
March 26		Air India announces plans for direct weekly flights between Prague, Czechoslovakia and New York, beginning May 1, the first regular commercial flights between eastern Europe and the U.S.	The Roman Catholic-dominated Democratic Party wins 43 seats in Uganda's 82-seat Legislature as more than 1,200,000 Ugandans vote in the first country-wide election in the British protectorate's history.		British P.M. Macmillan and Pres. Kennedy meet in Key West, Fla. for urgent talks on the Laos crisis. The two leaders issue a joint statement expressing their common desire for the achievement of a "truly neutral" Laos and their hope for a positive Soviet contribution to that goal.
March 27		Over 20,000 rock-throwing Portuguese demonstrate outside the U.S. Embassy in Lisbon to protest U.S. support for a U.N. investigation into the Angola situation. . . . Belgian Premier Gaston Eyskens resigns after returns from the Mar. 26 parliamentary elections showed a loss of support for his Christian Social party.	Imam Ahmed, ruler of Yemen, is shot and seriously wounded by an unknown assassin while on an inspection tour of the Red Sea port city of Hodeida.		The Indian Home Ministry announces that an official census completed in February estimates the country's population at 438 million, a 21.5% increase over the last 10 years and about 8 million more than had been projected. . . . The U.S. State Dept. reports that an Air Force C-47 with eight men aboard, missing since March 23, was shot down by Pathet Lao ground fire while making a survey of rebel positions in the Plaine des Jarres.
March 28	*The New York Times* reports that Soviet-bloc countries, France, and 19 Latin American nations have refused to pay their share of the assessed costs of the 1960 and 1961 U.N. Congo operations.	Albania's Enver Hoxha is the only Warsaw Pact head of state not to appear at the Pact's annual political conference in Moscow.	The Israeli Knesset (Parliament) votes unanimously to hold new elections Aug. 15.		
March 29		Polish sources report the issuance of a Communist Party memorandum calling for government moderation toward the Polish Roman Catholic Church.	Twenty-eight anti-apartheid South Africans are acquitted of charges of conspiring to overthrow the government by a three-judge panel in Pretoria.		Member states of SEATO, meeting in Bangkok, Thailand, agree to take joint "appropriate" action in Laos should the civil war there threaten the country's independence and neutrality. U.S. administration officials are reported to have wanted a more explicit warning of military intervention by SEATO.
March 30	The U.S. delegation to the U.N. informs the General Assembly that U.S. is prepared to pledge a "sizeable" contribution above its assessment to help defray the cost of the U.N. Congo operations.				

A	B	C	D	E
Includes developments that affect more than one world region, international organizations and important meetings of major world leaders.	Includes all domestic and regional developments in Europe, including the Soviet Union, Turkey, Cyprus and Malta.	Includes all domestic and regional developments in Africa and the Middle East, including Iraq and Iran and excluding Cyprus, Turkey and Afghanistan.	Includes all domestic and regional developments in Latin America, the Caribbean and Canada.	Includes all domestic and regional developments in Asia and Pacific nations, extending from Afghanistan through all the Pacific Islands, except Hawaii.

U.S. Politics & Social Issues	U.S. Foreign Policy & Defense	U.S. Economy & Environment	Science, Technology & Nature	Culture, Leisure & Life Style	
In what is regarded as a major legislative set-back for the administration, the House rejects, 186-185, a compromise version of the Kennedy-backed minimum wage bill (HR3935) and instead passes a more limited measure (HR5560) sponsored by a coalition of Republicans and Southern Democrats.	Sen. Barry Goldwater joins with other Republican congressional leaders in voicing strong support for Kennedy's tough stand on Laos.	In a message to Congress, Pres. Kennedy proposes that expenditures for non-military items in the fiscal 1962 budget be increased by $2.332 billion, leaving a total budget of $83.187 billion. The message concedes that this will result in a deficit of at least $1.754 billion, but adds that earlier hopes raised by the Eisenhower administration for a surplus in 1962 were, from the beginning, based on unrealistic revenue estimates. . . . Pres. Kennedy signs the jobless-aid-extension bill; it is the administration's first major anti-recession measure to become law.		Providence (R.I.) College wins the annual National Invitation (basketball) Tournament in New York with a 62-59 finals victory over St. Louis Univ.	**March 24**
The National Civil War Centennial Commission announces that the meeting place of its fourth national assembly, to be held in Charleston, S.C. Apr. 11, has been shifted to the Charleston Naval Station to avoid segregated hotels. The decision follows pressure from several state delegations and from Pres. Kennedy, an ex-officio Commission member.			The National Academy of Sciences announces that Dr. Martin Schwarzschild, Princeton astronomy professor, has been chosen winner of the Henry Draper Medal for his work in stellar evolution. A 10,000 pound satellite carrying a female dog is launched into orbit by Soviet scientists and then returned to earth by radio command with its passenger apparently unharmed. It is the third known Soviet test flight involving a dog.	Cincinnati beats Ohio State, 70-65, to win the NCAA national basketball championship.	**March 25**
The American Civil Liberties Union declares its opposition to federal aid to parochial schools on grounds that it violates the constitutional separation of church and state.				Jack Nicklaus of Ohio State Univ. wins the Western Amateur Golf Tournament in New Orleans.	**March 26**
			Dr. W.D. Armstrong, physiological chemistry professor at the Univ. of Minnesota Medical School, tells a Joint Congressional Atomic Subcommittee that experiments with radioactive fluorides indicate that fluoridation of water supplies poses no danger to human health.		**March 27**
The administration sends congressional leaders a Justice Dept.-prepared legal memo supporting Pres. Kennedy's view that direct federal aid to parochial schools is unconstitutional.	Pres. Kennedy asks Congress to increase fiscal 1962 defense appropriations $1.954 billion to a total of $43.794 billion. The additional funds are to be used to speed up the Polaris submarine and Minuteman ICBM programs and to increase U.S. ability to respond with conventional weapons to limited aggression.	The Budget Bureau issues newly revised estimates of expenditures and revenues for fiscal 1961 and 1962 which project a probable deficit of $2.169 billion for 1961 and $2.826 billion for 1962.	Scientists at a Moscow press conference confirm that an orbital trip rather than a ballistic flight is being planned for the first Soviet attempt to put a man in space. The scientists also inform reporters that the animals so far recovered from orbital flight appear healthy, although "some highly refined changes in cell structure" have been observed.	Powell Crosley Jr., 74, industrialist, radio manufacturer, developer of the pioneering radio station WLW (1921), and since 1936 principal owner of the Cincinnati Reds baseball team, dies in Cincinnati.	**March 28**
The 23d Amendment, granting District of Columbia citizens the right to vote in presidential elections, is enacted after Kansas becomes the 34th state to ratify the measure. . . . A Gallup poll indicates that 57% of all persons interviewed opposed federal aid to parochial schools but that 66% of Catholics favored such aid.		The House passes and returns to the Senate an amended bill (S1) to provide $394 million in loans and grants to economically depressed areas. The House version substitutes financing by direct congressional appropriations for the Senate's proposal to have Treasury financing. . . . General Electric Co. announces that 15 GE officials sentenced for antitrust violations have resigned from the firm.			**March 29**
Sens. Thomas Dodd (D, Conn.) and Thomas Kuchel (R, Calif.), in Senate speeches, urge a full-scale investigation into the John Birch Society.	Kennedy announces his selections for a 33-member National Advisory Council for the Peace Corps, including Vice Pres. Johnson, Supreme Court Justice William O. Douglas and Eleanor Roosevelt.		NASA civilian test pilot Joseph Walker sets a manned-flight altitude record of 32 miles during a test of the experimental X-15 rocket plane.		**March 30**
F	G	H	I	J	
Includes elections, federal-state relations, civil rights and liberties, crime, the judiciary, education, health care, poverty, urban affairs and population.	*Includes formation and debate of U.S. foreign and defense policies, veterans' affairs and defense spending. (Relations with specific foreign countries are usually found under the region concerned.)*	*Includes business, labor, agriculture, taxation, transportation, consumer affairs, monetary and fiscal policy, natural resources, and pollution.*	*Includes worldwide scientific, medical and technological developments, natural phenomena, U.S. weather, natural disasters, and accidents.*	*Includes the arts, religion, scholarship, communications media, sports, entertainment, fashions, fads and social life.*	

	World Affairs	Europe	Africa & the Middle East	The Americas	Asia & the Pacific
March 31	The Warsaw Pact's Political Consultative Committee, which met in Moscow March 27-28, issues a communique reaffirming the members' conviction that a NATO-supported West Germany represented the single greatest danger to world peace. . . . The White House says that the Secret Service is conducting "a routine investigation" of a rumored plot by pro-Castro Cubans to kidnap the President's daughter, Caroline, during the Kennedy family's Easter vacation in Palm Beach, Fla.		Gen. Mengestu Newaye, convicted leader of the unsuccessful Dec. 14-17, 1960 revolt against Haile Selassie, is hanged in Addis Ababa, Ethiopia. . . . The Katanga government announces that a mixed force of Katanga troops and white mercenaries have retaken rebel held positions in the northern part of the province.		
April 1	The USSR, replying to an Anglo-American note of March 23, informs Britain that it is prepared to issue a joint appeal for a cease-fire in Laos and to join with other nations in an international conference on Laos. Pres. Kennedy issues a statement welcoming the Soviet response.		Katanga Pres. Moise Tshombe denounces a U.N. decision to send a detachment of newly arrived Indian troops to northern Katanga to prevent further fighting there; he calls the order an "act of war" and threatens to resist with force.	Acting under the just-signed Sugar Act extension law, the U.S. Agriculture Dept. withdraws from the Dominican Republic its share of the 1961 sugar quota formerly assigned to Cuba.	An Indonesian-Communist Chinese friendship and cultural agreement is signed in Jakarta.
April 2			The New York Times reports that Pres. Tshombe's Katanga forces number 5,000-7,000 men and are considered the only Congolese soldiers still disciplined and combat-ready. According to the Times, Katanga also has a supporting mercenary army of 3,000-4,000 whites, mostly from Rhodesia and South Africa.		Communist Chinese Foreign Min. Chen Yi tells a Jakarta news conference that his government will send troops to the Laotian regime of Souvanna Phouma if they are needed to resist intervention by SEATO nations.
April 3	The U.N. General Assembly 51-10 approves a three-week extension of Secy. Gen. Hammarskjold's authority to pay for U.N. military operations in the Congo.	London police break up a sit-down demonstration in front of the U.S. Embassy by some 30,000 followers of the Campaign for Nuclear Disarmament protesting the basing of U.S. Polaris submarines in Britain.	Vice Pres. Lyndon Johnson is among delegates from 71 countries attending ceremonies marking Senegal's first full year of independence.	A State Dept. report closely supervised by Pres. Kennedy charges that Cuba has become a "Soviet satellite" and a "danger to the authentic and autonomous revolution of the Americas. . ."	The British Foreign Office describes the recent Soviet response to the West's Laotian proposals as "favorable," but cautions that the mechanics of a cease-fire and the timing of an international conference still need to be worked out.
April 4	Chief Soviet test-ban negotiator Semyon Tsarapkin expresses approval at some recently offered Western concessions, but says that a formal reply must await a thorough study of the proposal by Soviet scientists.	British P.M. Macmillan arrives in Washington to begin a series of talks with Pres. Kennedy aimed at increasing policy coordination among the Western allies.	Mobs of crudely armed Katangans attack Swedish U.N. troops guarding the Elizabethville airport after Pres. Tshombe publicly urged a popular uprising to drive the U.N. from Katanga.		Laotian Deputy Premier Phoumi Nosavan says the Boun Oum government is ready to meet with "any Laotian leader" to discuss a cease-fire and formation of a coalition government.
April 5	Secy. Gen. Hammarskjold presents the General Assembly with a "standing offer of resignation" which it may accept whenever it believes the USSR is justified in demanding his dismissal for misconduct of the U.N. Congo operations. . . . Soviet charges of U.S. aggression in connection with the U-2 and RB-47 incidents are formally withdrawn from the General Assembly Political Committee in what Rep.-to-U.N. Valerian Zorin calls a gesture of good will toward the Kennedy administration.			Cuban Foreign Min. Raul Roa charges in a New York interview that the U.S. is actively supporting preparations for a Cuban invasion by a counter-revolutionary force of "mercenaries" and "adventurers.". . . José Miró Cardona, president of the provisional anti-Castro Cuban National Revolutionary Council, meets with Adolph Berle, coordinator of U.S. Latin American policy to explain the objectives of his organization.	Fighting between forces of the Boun Oum government and Pathet Lao rebels continues despite growing signs of an East-West consensus on a Laotian truce.
April 6					In a statement broadcast via Peking radio, Prince Souphanouvong, leader of the Pathet Lao movement, declares his readiness to open negotiations on a Laotian cease-fire. . . . Washington sources report that the policy talks between British P.M. Macmillan and Pres. Kennedy have produced agreement on the desirability of a broad coalition government in Laos and on the need for Western support of the guerrilla-harassed regime of South Vietnamese Pres. Ngo Dinh Diem.

A	B	C	D	E
Includes developments that affect more than one world region, international organizations and important meetings of major world leaders.	Includes all domestic and regional developments in Europe, including the Soviet Union, Turkey, Cyprus and Malta.	Includes all domestic and regional developments in Africa and the Middle East, including Iraq and Iran and excluding Cyprus, Turkey and Afghanistan.	Includes all domestic and regional developments in Latin America, the Caribbean and Canada.	Includes all domestic and regional developments in Asia and Pacific nations, extending from Afghanistan through all the Pacific Islands, except Hawaii.

U.S. Politics & Social Issues	U.S. Foreign Policy & Defense	U.S. Economy & Environment	Science, Technology & Nature	Culture, Leisure & Life Style	
California Republican Congressmen Edgar Hiestand and John Rousselot acknowledge to newsmen their membership in the John Birch Society and reaffirm their support for the group's patriotic and anti-communist principles.	A National Student Association-sponsored Conference on Youth Service Abroad endorses Pres. Kennedy's Peace Corps plan, but urges that the corps not be used as a cold war tool. . . . Pres. Kennedy signs a compromise bill extending the Sugar Act until June 1962.				March 31
	A New York City "peace march", which attracted an estimated 3,500 persons, ends with a rally at the U.N. plaza. Earlier in the day the march passed 31 Quakers conducting a "silent witness" for peace outside an Armed Forces Recruiting booth in Times Square.	The Commerce Dept. reports that personal income in the U.S. increased in March for the first time in five months.			April 1
				Australian Jan Andrew, 17, swims the 100-meter butterfly in world record time of 1 min. 8.9 secs. in a Tokyo meet.	April 2
			Plans for a joint British-U.S.-French program to test communications satellites are announced in Washington.		April 3
	Amb.-to-Iceland Tyler Thompson is named director general of the U.S. Foreign Service.	The Securities and Exchange Commission makes public proposed new rules governing the advertising practices of the 1,800 investment advisers licensed by the SEC.			April 4
Sen. Barry Goldwater (R, Ariz.) says that despite "some very unfortunate" statements by its founder, the John Birch Society has attracted many prominent and intelligent citizens and should not be blindly criticized.		The Small Business Administration announces the lowering of interest rates to 4% on loans to businesses in 285 labor-surplus areas.			April 5
		Atty. Gen. Robert Kennedy tells a Washington news conference that recent price-rigging cases indicate a need for a code of ethics among U.S. management groups.	The League of Red Cross Societies in Geneva announces that it has sent 20,000 doses of vaccine to Ethiopia in an effort to stem a yellow fever epidemic which has already claimed several thousand lives. . . . The Atoms for Peace Award of a gold medallion and $75,000 is presented to British physicist Sir John Cockcroft for his contributions to the growth of international cooperation in nuclear science.		April 6

F	G	H	I	J
Includes elections, federal-state relations, civil rights and liberties, crime, the judiciary, education, health care, poverty, urban affairs and population.	Includes formation and debate of U.S. foreign and defense policies, veterans' affairs and defense spending. (Relations with specific foreign countries are usually found under the region concerned.)	Includes business, labor, agriculture, taxation, transportation, consumer affairs, monetary and fiscal policy, natural resources, and pollution.	Includes worldwide scientific, medical and technological developments, natural phenomena, U.S. weather, natural disasters, and accidents.	Includes the arts, religion, scholarship, communications media, sports, entertainment, fashions, fads and social life.

	World Affairs	Europe	Africa & the Middle East	The Americas	Asia & the Pacific
April 7	Hammarskjold reports to the General Assembly that only $17 million had so far been contributed to an envisioned $100 million U.N. economic assistance fund for the Congo.	P.M. Macmillan, in the U.S. for talks with Pres. Kennedy, tells an MIT audience that Europe and America must settle problems causing "unease in NATO" in order to achieve an urgently needed "unity of purpose" among the Western allies.		Haitian Pres. Francois Duvalier issues a decree abolishing the nation's bicameral legislature and calling for its replacement by a single Assembly after the next elections.	
April 8		Following four days of talks, Pres. Kennedy and P.M. Macmillan issue a joint statement indicating a "very high level of agreement" on the following issues: the need for renewed efforts to ensure the strength, cohesion and adaptability of the NATO alliance; the need to correct the Western payments imbalance and increase aid to underdeveloped nations; and the importance of improved East-West ties.	Officials in Yemen disclose that five Yemenis have been sentenced to death for participating in the March 27 plot to assassinate Yemen leader Imam Ahmed. . . . Pres. Nkrumah issues a decree requiring Ghanian public officials to sever foreign and domestic business relations or face removal from office. Nkrumah also announces increased restrictions on the activities of independent political organizations.	José Miró Cardona, leader of Cuban exiles in the U.S., issues a statement in New York calling upon the Cuban people to take up arms against the Castro government.	
April 9	The USSR makes public a Soviet-Chinese aid agreement for 1961. The pact provides for very limited Soviet food and credit assistance to China despite the reported near famine conditions there, and it is regarded by many Western observers as a sign of a further deterioration in Sino-Soviet relations.	Zog I (Ahmed Bey Zogu), 65, deposed king of Albania (1928-1939), dies in Suresnes, France of a liver ailment.	AP reports that Kasai Province leader Albert Kalonji has proclaimed himself "king" of the Baluba peoples.		
April 10		The U.S. State Dept., responding to an apparent hardening of the Soviet position on Berlin, issues a statement declaring that the Kennedy administration considers the U.S. "no longer bound" by concessions it made at the 1959 Geneva conference on Germany. . . . Pres. Kennedy, in a speech to the NATO Military Committee in Washington, emphasizes the need to strengthen NATO's conventional military capability. The speech is regarded as part of a policy drift away from U.S. support for a large nuclear deterrent under joint NATO control.	In a nationally televised speech, West German Chancellor Adenauer welcomes the forthcoming trial of Adolph Eichmann in Israel as an opportunity that "justice may be done."	Pres. Miguel Ydigoras Fuentes of Guatemala tells a *New York Times* reporter that guerrillas being trained by foreigners in his country would not be used to invade Cuba unless Cuba first attacked Guatemala. . . . *The New York Times* reports that the anti-Castro National Revolutionary Council has decided to invade Cuba with small diversionary guerrilla units, rather than with one massive force.	South Vietnamese Pres. Ngo Dinh Diem is re-elected to a fifth term in nationwide balloting, receiving 85% of the vote, according to official returns.
April 11	French Pres. de Gaulle announces at a Paris news conference that France does "not wish to participate either by her men or her money in any present or possible enterprises" of the United Nations. The French U.N. delegation has been boycotting many recent U.N. activities.	An Ansbach, West German court sentences Karl Chmielewski, ex-SS officer at the Mauthausen concentration camp, to life imprisonment for his role in the torture death of 282 camp inmates.	The trial of Adolph Eichmann, Nazi German director of the Gestapo's Bureau for Jewish Affairs, begins before a three-judge panel in Jerusalem with the reading of a 15-count indictment charging Eichmann with leading responsibility for the murder of millions of Jews. . . . The U.N. Security Council adopts a resolution calling upon Israel to refrain from displaying heavy military equipment in Jerusalem during its forthcoming Independence Day celebrations.	U.S. Treasury Secy. Douglas Dillon tells the annual meeting of the Inter-American Bank board in Rio de Janeiro that the U.S. hopes to increase the flow of public and private capital to Latin America as part of its Alliance-for-Progress program.	
April 12		West German Chancellor Adenauer meets with Pres. Kennedy in Washington. A joint communique, issued after their talks, includes the following points:(1) a reaffirmation of past pledges to "preserve the freedom of. . .West Berlin" pending. . .the restoration of Berlin as the capital of a reunified country; (2) a promise of continued support for NATO; (3) an agreement to seek new ways of solving the payments imbalance problem.	Replying to an opening jurisdictional challenge from Robert Servatius, Eichmann's defense attorney, Israeli prosecutor Gideon Hausner defends Israel's moral and legal right to try and judge Eichmann.	Pres. Kennedy tells newsmen that the U.S. would make no direct military attempt to overthrow Castro nor would it support attempts by Cuban exiles to mount an offensive from the U.S.	Pres. Kennedy tells Washington reporters that the rumor of a recent sharp increase in Soviet military aid to the Laotian Pathet Lao forces is unfounded.

A	B	C	D	E
Includes developments that affect more than one world region, international organizations and important meetings of major world leaders.	Includes all domestic and regional developments in Europe, including the Soviet Union, Turkey, Cyprus and Malta.	Includes all domestic and regional developments in Africa and the Middle East, including Iraq and Iran and excluding Cyprus, Turkey and Afghanistan.	Includes all domestic and regional developments in Latin America, the Caribbean and Canada.	Includes all domestic and regional developments in Asia and Pacific nations, extending from Afghanistan through all the Pacific Islands, except Hawaii.

U.S. Politics & Social Issues	U.S. Foreign Policy & Defense	U.S. Economy & Environment	Science, Technology & Nature	Culture, Leisure & Life Style	
The NAACP files a complaint with the President's Equal Job Opportunity Committee charging that Lockheed Aircraft Corp.'s $1 billion contract with the Defense Dept. violates Pres. Kennedy's recent executive order barring discrimination by government contractors.			Researchers at the Roswell Park Memorial Institute in Buffalo, N.Y. report the first known cases in which tumors in humans were induced by injections of a virus. The injections were given to five volunteers already suffering from terminal cancer.		April 7
The Republican National Committee makes public a study of the 1960 presidential election which shows that the expected Republican defeat in the big cities was coupled with an unexpected GOP loss in many big city suburbs. . . . Pres. Kennedy signs a bill (S153) reviving presidential authority to reorganize the Executive branch.			Dr. Sergio de Carvalho of the Rand Development Corp. Cancer Research Laboratory reports the discovery of a specific abnormality in the ribonucleic acid (RNA) of all cancerous cells.		April 8
			The discovery of cancer-inhibiting (as well as cancer-causing) substances in cigarette smoke is reported by researchers at the Sloan-Kettering Cancer Institute.		April 9
		The Dow-Jones industrial average of stock prices climbs 8.38 points to a record 692.06. The previous high was 685.47 on Jan. 5, 1960.		Gary Player of South Africa outplays Arnold Palmer to win the Masters championship at the Augusta National Golf Club.	April 10
Pres. Kennedy informs his Equal Job Opportunity Committee that his executive order barring job discrimination by government contractors was not intended "to make. . .a harsh. . .mandate for those sincerely and honestly seeking compliance."		The Justice Dept. files six more damage suits against 11 electrical supply firms for allegedly overcharging government agencies for various electrical equipment between 1956 and 1960.	The Soviet Council of Ministers announces the formation of a State Committee for Coordinating Scientific Research charged with the task of narrowing the gap between theoretical research and production.	The National Institute of Arts and Letters' Rosenthal Award for an outstanding American novel goes to John Knowles, 35, author of *A Separate Peace* . . . . The Boston Celtics capture the National Basketball Association championship by defeating St. Louis four games to one in the NBA finals.	April 11
	Pres. Kennedy announces the formation of a special advisory panel, headed by Eugene Black, to help in the planned reorganization of U.S. foreign aid programs.	A federal grand jury in New York indicts the General Motors Corp. on charges of using unfair practices in an effort to monopolize the manufacture and sale of railroad locomotives.	The USSR puts the first man into space. Yuri Gagarin, 27-year old Soviet Air Force pilot, is launched, completes a single orbit and returns safely to earth. Khrushchev hails flight as a Soviet triumph. Kennedy cables his congratulations and admits to Washington reporters that the U.S. is behind in manned space projects. . . . The AEC announces that a new heavier-than-uranium element--Element 103--has been discovered and produced through nuclear means at the Lawrence Radiation Laboratory in Berkeley, Calif.		April 12
F	G	H	I	J	
Includes elections, federal-state relations, civil rights and liberties, crime, the judiciary, education, health care, poverty, urban affairs and population.	Includes formation and debate of U.S. foreign and defense policies, veterans' affairs and defense spending. (Relations with specific foreign countries are usually found under the region concerned.)	Includes business, labor, agriculture, taxation, transportation, consumer affairs, monetary and fiscal policy, natural resources, and pollution.	Includes worldwide scientific, medical and technological developments, natural phenomena, U.S. weather, natural disasters, and accidents.	Includes the arts, religion, scholarship, communications media, sports, entertainment, fashions, fads and social life.	

	World Affairs	Europe	Africa & the Middle East	The Americas	Asia & the Pacific
April 13	The U.N. General Assembly votes 95-1 (Portugal opposed, Spain and South Africa absent) to condemn South Africa's apartheid racial policies as "repugnant to human dignity" and to urge all states to work within the Charter to bring about their abandonment.		Portugal begins sending reinforcements to northern Angola where an anti-government uprising is reported spreading.		
April 14				Pres. Kennedy, in a speech before the OAS Council in Washington, proposes a summer meeting of the Inter-American Economic and Social Council to discuss means of implementing his Latin American Alliance for Progress program.	Indonesian radio announces that all contingents of the rebel forces in the northern Celebes have agreed to end their anti-government insurrection. . . . The Pathet Lao advance resumes in central Laos following a three-day undeclared truce during the Buddhist New Year holiday.
April 15			In a report submitted to Hammarskjold, the U.N. command in the Congo charges the Katanga government with carrying out a military recruiting program in Europe with the complicity of Belgian officials. . . . The U.N. General Assembly adopts a resolution renewing its demand for an immediate withdrawal of all Belgian military and political personnel from Katanga and other Congo provinces.	Three Cuban air bases are bombed by Cuban-piloted, U.S.-made B-26 bombers. Cuban Foreign Min. Raul Roa charges in the U.N. that the air attacks are a "prologue to the large-scale invasion" of Cuba being planned by the U.S.	Indonesian Pres. Sukarno signs a decree permitting the existence of only eight designated political parties and reserving to himself the authority to abolish those should they ever oppose the government's "left progressive ideology."
April 16		*Pravda* reports the dismissal of several high Tadzhikstan Republic leaders on charges of "gross political errors," including mismanagement of collective farms and nepotism.			The USSR transmits to Britain an undisclosed "clarification" of its terms for seeking a Laotian peace settlement. The message reportedly accepts the terms outlined by the West March 23, but leaves unspecified the target date for establishing a cease-fire.
April 17	A "Second Congress of Vienna" concludes six weeks of discussions in Vienna on U.N. International Law Commission proposals for the revision of traditional diplomatic usages and immunities. The delegates adopt a draft code for consideration by other nations.	West German Chancellor Adenauer, visiting the U.S., tells a *New York Times* reporter that West Germany would not oppose the Kennedy administration's apparent desire to continue U.S. control over NATO's nuclear deterrent, if clear guarantees were given that the weapons would be used if needed for Europe's defense.	Adolph Eichmann pleads "not guilty" to the 15-count indictment charging him with responsibility for the murder of six million Jews. Earlier in the day the three-judge Israeli tribunal turned down a defense motion to disqualify itself on grounds of prejudice. . . . Pres. Kasavubu signs a U.N. agreement to cooperate in the implementation of the provisions of the Security Council's Feb. 21 Congo resolution.	An anti-Castro rebel invasion force lands at dawn on the beaches of the Bahia de Cochinos (Bay of Pigs) in Cuba's southern Las Villas Province. Government troops resist the landing and heavy casualties are reported on both sides. . . . U.S. Amb.-to-U.N. Stevenson labels as "totally false" charges by Cuban Foreign Min. Raul Roa that today's invasion of Cuba was financed and planned by the U.S. State Dept. and CIA.	U.S. State Secy. Rusk tells reporters that while the Apr. 16 Soviet "clarification" note on Laos contained "constructive elements," it was unacceptably vague on "the key point of the timing of the cease-fire. . .and verification."
April 18	The U.S. and Britain present the Soviet negotiators at Geneva with a revised draft of a proposed test-ban agreement. Controversial provisions in the draft include a demand for at least 20 annual on-site inspections of suspected treaty violations and a proposal that the control commission be headed by a single administrator. . . . The U.S. informs the U.N. that it is prepared to pay one half the costs incurred by the U.N. Congo Force until the General Assembly reconvenes in September.			Heavy fighting is reported from the Cuban Bay of Pigs area as the rebels try to break out of their beachhead, now encircled by counter-attacking government forces. . . . Soviet Premier Khrushchev cables Pres. Kennedy demanding a halt to what he calls U.S.-sponsored "aggression" against Cuba and warning that the USSR will "render (Cuba) . . .all necessary assistance in beating back the armed attack." Kennedy denies the charge and cautions against any Soviet interference in Latin America.	Ex-Laotian Premier Souvanna Phouma, in Moscow for talks with Soviet leaders, cancels a planned meeting with Pres. Kennedy after learning that Kennedy would only see him as a private citizen and not as a Laotian official.

A	B	C	D	E
Includes developments that affect more than one world region, international organizations and important meetings of major world leaders.	Includes all domestic and regional developments in Europe, including the Soviet Union, Turkey, Cyprus and Malta.	Includes all domestic and regional developments in Africa and the Middle East, including Iraq and Iran and excluding Cyprus, Turkey and Afghanistan.	Includes all domestic and regional developments in Latin America, the Caribbean and Canada.	Includes all domestic and regional developments in Asia and Pacific nations, extending from Afghanistan through all the Pacific Islands, except Hawaii.

U.S. Politics & Social Issues	U.S. Foreign Policy & Defense	U.S. Economy & Environment	Science, Technology & Nature	Culture, Leisure & Life Style	
A three-year-old tax fraud indictment against Rep. Adam Clayton Powell Jr. (D, N.Y.) is dismissed in New York after U.S. prosecutors concede their inability to gain a conviction.	*Overseas Weekly*, a private newspaper for U.S. servicemen stationed in Europe, claims that Maj. Gen. Edwin Walker, commander of the Army's 24th Division in Germany, has organized a rightwing propaganda campaign to instruct his troops in "a positive approach toward the defeat of open communist subversion of the American way of life."	Kennedy sends Congress a special message proposing various legislative and administrative steps to increase the efficiency, effectiveness and accountability of the Federal Power Commission and other U.S. regulatory agencies.	*The New York Herald Tribune* says that, according to "Red Chinese sources," the USSR has put at least two men in orbit within the past year but that both died in flight.		April 13
		Postmaster General J. Edward Day asks Congress to authorize an increase in postal rates (first class mail would go to 5¢ per ounce) to help offset the Post Office's estimated $840 million deficit in 1962.	Soviet cosmonaut Yuri Gagarin is awarded the USSR's highest honor-- the title of Hero of the Soviet Union with the Order of Lenin and the Gold Star.		April 14
A Dade County, Fla. Circuit Court upholds the constitutionality of a state law requiring daily recitation of the Lord's Prayer and Bible-readings in the public schools.		United Auto Workers Pres. Walter Reuther reveals in an article in the UAW newspaper, *Solidarity*, that the UAW plans to demand annual salaries instead of hourly wages in future negotiations with the "Big three" auto makers.	In a carefully controlled Moscow news conference, cosmonaut Yuri Gagarin says that special space ships designed for flights to the moon are being built in the USSR. He says he would like to be the first man to make a lunar flight.		April 15
About 125 delegates from 18 rightwing political groups, meeting in Chicago, issue a "declaration of conservative principles" on which they plan to found a third national party. The principles include opposition to the U.N., suspension of nuclear test-ban talks and non-recognition of communist governments.			Reported discrepancies in official Soviet descriptions of Maj. Yuri Gagarin's orbital flight lead to doubt in some Western circles about the precise nature and even the actuality of the mission.	Winners of the 15th annual Antoinette Perry (Tony) Awards for "distinguished achievement" in the New York theatre are: best play Jean Anouilh's *Becket* ; best musical Michael Stewart's *Bye Bye Birdie* ; best musical performance Richard Burton in *Camelot* . . . . The Chicago Blackhawks defeat the Detroit Red Wings, four games to two, to win their first Stanley Cup hockey championship in 23 years.	April 16
The Supreme Court rules in a Wilmington, Delaware case that a privately-operated restaurant leasing space from a state agency cannot refuse to serve Negroes.	The Army announces that Maj. Gen. Edwin A. Walker, commander of the 24th Division in Germany, has been relieved of command pending an investigation into charges that he has used his position to indoctrinate his troops with John Birch Society views.	Kennedy sends Congress a farm bill containing most of the proposals outlined in his Mar. 16 special farm message. . . . The House passes and sends to the Senate a bill (HR6100) to provide operating subsidies to U.S. passenger ships. . . . The Supreme Court, in a series of decisions, overturns four previous NLRB rulings which had prohibited unions from using certain contract mechanisms designed to ensure the hiring of only union members.		The Motion Picture Academy names "Oscar" winners for best film achievements of 1960: best movie *The Apartment* ; best performance by an actor Burt Lancaster (*Elmer Gantry*); best actress Elizabeth Taylor (*Butterfield 18*).	April 17
Kennedy submits to Congress a bill to create a cabinet-level Urban Affairs and Housing Dept.		Complying with a personal request from Pres. Kennedy, the Amalgamated Clothing Workers agrees to cancel its scheduled May 1 boycott of Japanese textiles imported for making men's clothing.		The Vatican's Sacred Congregation of Rites rules that Saint Philomena, "The Martyred Virgin," has been venerated in error and will be stricken from the roll of Catholic saints. . . . The Texaco *Huntley-Brinkley Report* receives the 1960 George Foster Peabody Award for achievement in TV news. CBS Pres. Frank Stanton is awarded the special Peabody award for his role in televising the *Great Debates* of the 1960 Presidential campaign.	April 18

F	G	H	I	J
Includes elections, federal-state relations, civil rights and liberties, crime, the judiciary, education, health care, poverty, urban affairs and population.	Includes formation and debate of U.S. foreign and defense policies, veterans' affairs and defense spending. (Relations with specific foreign countries are usually found under the region concerned.)	Includes business, labor, agriculture, taxation, transportation, consumer affairs, monetary and fiscal policy, natural resources, and pollution.	Includes worldwide scientific, medical and technological developments, natural phenomena, U.S. weather, natural disasters, and accidents.	Includes the arts, religion, scholarship, communications media, sports, entertainment, fashions, fads and social life.

	World Affairs	Europe	Africa & the Middle East	The Americas	Asia & the Pacific
April 19	The U.N. General Assembly votes 48-18 (33 abstentions including the U.S. and USSR) to ask the Security Council to reconsider applications for U.N. admission from Mauritania and Outer Mongolia. . . . Soviet chief delegate Semyon Tsarapkin rejects the West's April 18 test-ban proposal, citing the number of inspections and proposed structure of the control commission as unacceptable.	Walter Lippmann reports that Khrushchev told him, in an exclusive interview, that the USSR could not accept an indefinite prolongation of the status quo in Germany because of the probability that West Germany would soon be given nuclear weapons. . . . Greek sources report that 60 Albanian officials have been executed and thousands imprisoned in a purge directed by CP First Secy. Enver Hoxha against opponents of his Stalinist policies and his anti-Soviet alliance with the Communist Chinese.	Greek Premier Constantine Caramanlis, visiting the U.S., tells the National Press Club that Greece needs continued American aid "to prove that totalitarianism is not indispensable for the development of a small country."	The U.S.-based Cuban National Revolutionary Council, which directed the Apr. 17 Bay of Pigs landing, reports that a "major portion" of the rebel force has broken out of the beachhead and joined other anti-Castro guerillas in the Escambray Mountains. Havana radio, however, reports that the rebels remained trapped on the beach.	The Laotian government announces that the U.S. has agreed to form a 300-man Military Assistance Advisory Group to advise Laotian troops in combat.
April 20		A special Turkish court on Yassiada Island convicts deposed Premier Adnan Menderes on charges of violating the Turkish Constitution.	Israel displays tanks and other weapons in an Independence Day parade through Jerusalem in defiance of U.N. opposition to the presence of military weapons in the city. . . . The U.N. General Assembly approves, 73-2, a resolution calling on Portugal to observe its U.N. Charter obligation to maintain human rights and freedom in Angola.	A Cuban communique signed by Premier Castro announces that government soldiers have completely defeated the rebel force at the Las Villas beachhead. . . . In a speech to newspaper editors in Washington, Pres. Kennedy says that, despite the apparent failure of the current anti-Castro invasion, the U.S. remains ready to take whatever action is needed to prevent outside communist penetration in Latin America, especially when it threatens U.S. security.	
April 21	A resolution to continue U.N. aid for Arab refugees of the 1947-1948 Arab-Israeli war is passed by the General Assembly on a vote of 37 to 17 (38 abstentions).		For the third day, the Israeli tribunal trying Adolph Eichmann hears tape recorded statements made by Eichmann during an extended pre-trial interrogation. In them, Eichmann insists that he "obeyed orders blindly," but never had the rank or authority to affect the actual fate of Jews under his supervision.	The Cuban National Revolutionary Council issues a communique admitting that the anti-Castro landing did not achieve its objectives. Council Pres. José Miró Cardona denies widespread reports that the CIA actively assisted in the planning and execution of the landing. . . . Havana newspapers report that over 14,000 persons suspected of anti-Castro activity have been arrested since the rebel landing on Apr. 17.	
April 22	The 15th session of the U.N. General Assembly formally adjourns after authorizing Secy. Gen. Hammarskjold to spend up to $10 million monthly on Congo operations until the question of continued financing is settled at the next regular Assembly session. Soviet-bloc nations opposed the authorization.	A rightwing military coup d'etat, headed by former Algerian commander Gen. Maurice Challe and aimed at defeating de Gaulle's Algerian policies, is launched in Algeria with the support of the First Parachute Regiment of the French Foreign Legion.		In a message to Pres. Kennedy, Khrushchev reiterates his denunciation of U.S. involvement in the Cuban attack and warns that continued U.S. support for the Cuban exiles "could lead to a new global war." Khrushchev also denies earlier U.S. charges that the Soviets were establishing bases in Cuba.	Pathet Lao forces drive government troops from the provincial capital of Vang Vieng. Four U.S. military advisers assigned to the Laotian army are reported missing.
April 23	Anti-American demonstrations linked to the Cuban situation continue in several Latin American and European capitals.	Pres. de Gaulle, amidst reports of growing Algerian support for the rightist rebels, goes on national television to announce that he has assumed extraordinary powers to crush the revolt. Major French trade unions and all but rightist political groups declare their allegiance to de Gaulle in the emergency.			
April 24		Algerian coup leader Maurice Challe tells an Algiers rally that insurgents are prepared to fight on to preserve "French Algeria." In France precautions against a feared invasion by the insurgents are relaxed. . . . A Mosbach, West German court sentences ex-SS Sgt. Franz Mueller to life in prison on charges of shooting to death at least 50 Jews at the Cracow, Poland labor camp.	Almost all major Congolese leaders, except Antoine Gizenga, premier of the dissident leftist regime based in Stanleyville, meet in Coquilhatville, Equator Province, for a conference called by Congo Pres. Kasavubu to discuss the country's political future.	White House Press Secy. Pierre Salinger issues a statement saying that Pres. Kennedy accepts full responsibility for the U.S. part in the abortive Cuban invasion. . . . Honduras breaks diplomatic relations with Cuba. Over 2,000 pro-Castro Hondurans gather to protest the decision.	Britain and the USSR, acting as co-chairmen of the 1954 Geneva Conference on Indochina, issue a joint appeal for a cease-fire between the Laotian government of Boun Oum and the Pathet Lao forces to be supervised by the Indian-Polish-Canadian International Control Commission for Laos. The joint statement also sets May 12 as the date for a new 14-nation conference on Laos.

A	B	C	D	E
Includes developments that affect more than one world region, international organizations and important meetings of major world leaders.	Includes all domestic and regional developments in Europe, including the Soviet Union, Turkey, Cyprus and Malta.	Includes all domestic and regional developments in Africa and the Middle East, including Iraq and Iran and excluding Cyprus, Turkey and Afghanistan.	Includes all domestic and regional developments in Latin America, the Caribbean and Canada.	Includes all domestic and regional developments in Asia and Pacific nations, extending from Afghanistan through all the Pacific Islands, except Hawaii.

U.S. Politics & Social Issues	U.S. Foreign Policy & Defense	U.S. Economy & Environment	Science, Technology & Nature	Culture, Leisure & Life Style	
				The 1960 Marjory Peabody Waite Award for integrity in the arts is given to Providence, R.I. novelist Edward McSorley.	April 19
The House passes, 400-14, and sends to the Senate a slightly modified administration bill to raise and liberalize Social Security benefits, including a provision permitting men to retire on Social Security at age 62.		A coalition of Democratic and liberal Republican senators succeeds in passing the administration's bill to raise the minimum wage to $1.25 over the next two years and extend the program to four million new workers. A more limited hike to $1.15 has already passed in the House.			April 20
	Pres. Kennedy announces to newsmen that 28 geologists, surveyors and engineers will be sent to Tanganyika in September to help build roads as the first overseas Peace Corps project.		A French TV correspondent asserts that the USSR sent Serge Ilyushin, son of the Soviet plane designer, into orbit four or five days before the Gagarin flight, but that Ilyushin had returned to earth unconscious and seriously injured.	Grigori Chukhrai and Vanentin Yoshov, authors of the Soviet film *Ballad of a Soldier* are among 26 recipients of the Lenin Prize for 1961.	April 21
In an election authorized under a new state law, white residents of St. Helena Parish, La. vote overwhelmingly to close their public schools rather than integrate them. The vote makes local students eligible for a new program of state grants to pay private school tuition costs.	Pres. Kennedy appoints retired Gen. Maxwell Taylor to head an investigation into the CIA's role in the Cuban landing and in U.S. military operations in general.		The UPI reports that usually reliable Moscow sources deny reports of a pre-Gagarin orbital flight by Serge Ilyushin.	A bill to permit New York City to build an $18 million baseball stadium in Flushing Meadows for use by New York's new National League franchise is signed by Gov. Rockefeller.	April 22
	Interior Secy. Stewart Udall charges in a TV interview that the Kennedy administration inherited the plans and preparations for the unsuccessful Cuban invasion from Pres. Eisenhower.	The Commerce Dept. reports that per capita income in the U.S. rose from $2,159 in 1959 to a record $2,242 in 1960.			April 23
		United Auto Workers Pres. Walter Reuther and other industrial union leaders meet with AFL-CIO Pres. George Meany to discuss growing membership drive friction between industrial and craft unions within the Federation. . . . Kennedy presents Congress with a $375 million federal program to modernize "antiquated" U.S. airports for use by jet aircraft.		Jay Hebert defeats Ken Venturi in a playoff to win the $40,000 Houston Open golf tournament.	April 24

F	G	H	I	J
Includes elections, federal-state relations, civil rights and liberties, crime, the judiciary, education, health care, poverty, urban affairs and population.	Includes formation and debate of U.S. foreign and defense policies, veterans' affairs and defense spending. (Relations with specific foreign countries are usually found under the region concerned.)	Includes business, labor, agriculture, taxation, transportation, consumer affairs, monetary and fiscal policy, natural resources, and pollution.	Includes worldwide scientific, medical and technological developments, natural phenomena, U.S. weather, natural disasters, and accidents.	Includes the arts, religion, scholarship, communications media, sports, entertainment, fashions, fads and social life.

	World Affairs	Europe	Africa & the Middle East	The Americas	Asia & the Pacific
April 25	Secy. Gen. Hammarskjold makes public a letter from U.S. Amb.-to-U.N. Stevenson proposing the creation of a U.N. Peace Corps similar to the program begun by the U.S.	Reports from pro-government French forces moving into Algiers indicate that many garrisons, earlier thought to be under rebel control, have remained loyal. . . . Social Christian Party Pres. Theo Lefevre is sworn in as premier of a new Belgian cabinet made up of 11 Social Christians and nine Socialists. . . . France detonates its fourth nuclear device near Reggan, in the Sahara Desert.	Katanga Pres. Tshombe, attending the Congo conference in Coquilhatville, accuses Pres. Kasavubu of betraying the Congolese people by agreeing to cooperate in the implementation of the U.N.'s Feb. 21 resolution. Tshombe is also known to oppose a reported Kasavubu proposal to reduce the autonomy of member states in the newly declared Congo confederation.	Peruvian Pres Manuel Prado y Ugarteche cables Castro urging him to "suspend. . .the executions" of political prisoners.	The British-Soviet truce proposal is accepted in principle by both sides in the Laotian fighting but no date is set for the cease-fire. The Pathet Lao are reportedly continuing their advance against government positions. . . . Indonesian Pres. Sukarno confers in Washington with Pres. Kennedy. The two leaders issue a joint communique warning against "imperialism in all its manifestations" and pledging support for a neutral Laos.
April 26		In a message to de Gaulle, coup leader Gen. Challe announces his surrender and offers to place himself "at the disposition of justice." The coup collapsed when it became clear that 80% of the French forces in Algeria were resisting rebel appeals for support.	Troops of the central Congolese government arrest Pres. Tshombe after he and his delegation walked out of the Coquilhatville political conference.	The OAS Inter-American Defense Board approves by a 12-1 vote (Cuba opposing) a U.S. proposal to bar Cuba from attending the board's secret sessions "as long as there exists the present evident alliance of Cuba with the Soviet-bloc."	The U.S. begins a new airlift of arms to Laotian government troops following reports of an intensified Pathet Lao offensive around Luang Prabang. . . . Anti-government disobedience in the Tamil-speaking regions of Ceylon continues. Premier Sirimavo Bandaranaike charges that the Tamil Federal Party, sponsor of the opposition, is using the language issue to disguise its plan to create a separate Tamil state.
April 27			The central Congo government agrees to return two captured posts to the U.N. . . . The British West African colony of Sierra Leone becomes an independent country.	Cuban Pres. Osvaldo Dorticos announces that despite U.S. backing of the recent anti-Castro invasion, Cuba remains willing to negotiate its differences with the U.S. with a view toward re-establishing diplomatic "and even friendly relations.". . . *The New York Times* reports that the nearly 1,000 men lost or captured in the ill-fated Bay of Pigs invasion constituted almost the entire military component of the anti-Castro Cuban National Revolutionary Council.	
April 28		Various European sources report that the purge against allegedly pro-Russian opponents of Albanian CP First Secy. Enver Hoxha is continuing.	The cabinet of arrested Katanga Pres. Tshombe issues a statement warning the central Congo government of a "general civil war" if Tshombe is not released soon. . . . AP reports from South Africa that 1,000 whites and thousands of Africans have been killed in northern Angola since the mid-March outbreak against Portuguese rule began.	A spokesman for the U.S. State Dept. rejects yesterday's peace-talk bid from Cuban Pres. Dorticos, saying that "communism in this hemisphere is not negotiable.". . . Argentine Pres. Arturo Frondizi announces that he is forming a new cabinet in response to rightist pressure from within his own Radical Intransigent Party.	The Indian-Canadian-Polish International Control Commission, meeting in New Delhi, issues a communique expressing "complete agreement" on the need for a speedy solution of matters delaying a Laotian cease-fire.
April 29		The French government announces the disbanding of all the military units that took part in the Algiers coup attempt. . . . A massive sit-down demonstration in London's Whitehall section by supporters of the Campaign for Nuclear Disarmament leads to the arrest of 826 participants.	Presidents Kwame Nkrumah of Ghana, Sekou Toure of Guinea, and Modibo Keita of Mali sign a charter to merge their countries into a single Union of African States.		
April 30		The USSR awards a 1960 Lenin Peace Prize to Cuban Premier Fidel Castro. Guinean Pres. Sekou Toure is among the other recipients.	The delegates remaining at the Congo's Coquithatville conference authorize Pres. Kasavubu to take whatever steps necessary to reorganize the Congo army, including disarming the separatist army of Katanga.	Cuban Industry Min. Ernesto (Ché) Guevara, in a TV address, praises the Cuban revolution as "the first socialist revolution in America. . ." The U.S. State Dept., through the Swiss Embassy, advises the estimated 600-1,000 American citizens still in Cuba to leave "in the near future."	
May 1		The U.S. issues firm denials of French newspaper reports that the CIA had aided the Algiers military uprising.		In a three-and-a-half-hour May Day address, Castro proclaims Cuba a Socialist country and declares it will no longer hold formal elections, but instead depend directly on the people's will as expressed in mass rallies. Castro also warns that the U.S.'s "aggressive policy" toward Cuba is "putting New York in danger of becoming another Hiroshima."	

A	B	C	D	E
Includes developments that affect more than one world region, international organizations and important meetings of major world leaders.	*Includes all domestic and regional developments in Europe, including the Soviet Union, Turkey, Cyprus and Malta.*	*Includes all domestic and regional developments in Africa and the Middle East, including Iraq and Iran and excluding Cyprus, Turkey and Afghanistan.*	*Includes all domestic and regional developments in Latin America, the Caribbean and Canada.*	*Includes all domestic and regional developments in Asia and Pacific nations, extending from Afghanistan through all the Pacific Islands, except Hawaii.*

U.S. Politics & Social Issues	U.S. Foreign Policy & Defense	U.S. Economy & Environment	Science, Technology & Nature	Culture, Leisure & Life Style	
The National Educational Association predicts a 135,000-teacher shortage for the 1961-1962 school year.	The House passes and sends to the Senate a bill to provide the $500 million requested by the administration for its Alliance for Progress program. The House bill also authorizes $100 million for reconstruction programs in earthquake-devastated Chile.	The Senate Antitrust Subcommittee, headed by Sen. Estes Kefauver (D, Tenn.), completes a week of hearings into price-fixing charges against leading suppliers of electrical equipment.	A NASA attempt to place a Mercury capsule carrying a robot pilot in orbit fails when the Atlas booster veers off course shortly after launch.	The Commerce Dept. estimates that U.S. coffee consumption totals about 400 million cups per day, or 16 pounds per capita annually.	April 25
The Justice Dept. begins action to force the reopening of public schools in Prince Edward County, Va. after state and local officials closed them to avoid court-ordered desgregation.		The Bureau of Labor Statistics reports that the spendable income of the average American factory worker rose to $80.89 a week in March, a 67¢ increase over February.		The American Academy of Arts and Letters selects actor Frederic March as the winner of its medal for good diction on the stage.	April 26
Kennedy sends to Congress a message urging the adoption of a proposed tightening of conflict-of-interest laws and outlining intended executive actions to ensure a high level of ethical conduct on the part of federal employees.	After outlining the grave international dangers facing the U.S., Pres Kennedy tells an audience of newspaper publishers that American newsmen need to exercise greater "self-restraint" in handling information related to national security.	The United Auto Workers convention in Detroit endorses a proposal by UAW Pres. Walter Reuther for a law that would authorize a reduction of the 40-hour week without loss of pay during periods of high unemployment.	The U.S. launches into orbit a 95-pound satellite (Explorer XI), equipped with special telescopic instruments to determine the direction and source of high energy gamma rays in space.	An application by the Russian Orthodox Church to join the World Council of Churches is made public at Council headquarters in Geneva.	April 27
The Justice Dept. files suit in Shreveport, La. to force an end to allegedly discriminatory practices in the registration of Negro voters in East Carroll Parish. None of the parish's 4,183 eligible Negro voters is currently registered.	James Hagerty, ABC vice president for news and ex-Eisenhower press secretary, cables the White House to inform Kennedy that ABC will "do its best" to follow his recommendations on the management of national security news.	A new federal grand jury in Philadelphia will hear fresh evidence of conspiracy and price-rigging in the electrical equipment industry. Sen. Estes Kefauver (D, Tenn.), chairman of the Senate Judiciary Subcommittee currently investigating the electical suppliers, had suggested that a new jury was needed to inquire into possible perjury charges.		Warren Spahn, 40, of the Milwaukee Braves, pitches a 1-0 no-hitter against the San Francisco Giants in Milwaukee. It is Spahn's second no-hitter and 290th major league win.	April 28
The Ford Foundation announces the granting of funds totaling almost $7.5 million to help solve America's urban and poverty-related problems.					April 29
	Senate Foreign Relations Committee Chmn. J. William Fulbright tells a TV panel that he opposes any plan to send U.S. troops to Laos because the "terrain and conditions" there would make effective military action very difficult.				April 30
	Ex-Pres. Eisenhower tells reporters that he is against a "witch-hunting investigation" into the ill-fated Cuban invasion and instead hopes the country will concentrate on the continuing task of preventing "a communist stronghold" in the Western Hemisphere.	Pres. Kennedy signs a compromise bill to provide $394 million worth of Treasury-financed federal aid to economically depressed regions. The Labor Dept. reports that 20 major industrial areas and 90 smaller communities currently qualify for assistance under the provisions of the law. . . . The First National City Bank reports that first-quarter corporate earnings in 1961 were down 22% from one year ago.	A Camden, N.J. jury indicts Dr. Albert Weiner on 15 counts of manslaughter on charges of giving sedative inoculations that caused the death of 15 persons from serum hepatitis.	Columbia Univ. announces the winners of the 1961 Pulitzer Prizes; they include: fiction-Harper Lee (*To Kill a Mockingbird*); biography-David Donald (*Charles Sumner and the Coming of the Civil War*); poetry-Phyllis McGinley (*Times Three*).	May 1
F	G	H	I	J	
Includes elections, federal-state relations, civil rights and liberties, crime, the judiciary, education, health care, poverty, urban affairs and population.	*Includes formation and debate of U.S. foreign and defense policies, veterans' affairs and defense spending. (Relations with specific foreign countries are usually found under the region concerned.)*	*Includes business, labor, agriculture, taxation, transportation, consumer affairs, monetary and fiscal policy, natural resources, and pollution.*	*Includes worldwide scientific, medical and technological developments, natural phenomena, U.S. weather, natural disasters, and accidents.*	*Includes the arts, religion, scholarship, communications media, sports, entertainment, fashions, fads and social life.*	

	World Affairs	Europe	Africa & the Middle East	The Americas	Asia & the Pacific
May 2			In a statement issued in Elizabethville, the Katanga cabinet renews its demand for the release of Tshombe and declares that his government is now prepared to cooperate fully with the U.N. . . . Moroccan King Hassan II announces the formation of a new rightwing coalition cabinet; Hassan retains his post as premier.	U.S. State Dept. spokesman Lincoln White tells newsmen that Castro's May Day speech proclaiming socialism in Cuba proves that his regime belongs to the communist-bloc. . . . Cuban government sources report that the number of rebels captured since the April 17 landing has reached 1,122. . . . Argentina, Uruguay, Mexico, Peru, Brazil and Chile ratify a Feb. 18 agreement creating a six-nation free trade zone in Latin America.	
May 3		Portuguese Premier Antonio Salazar announces a cabinet reorganization aimed at coping with the rebellion in Angola. It is the second major cabinet shift in the last month. . . . British Foreign Office aide George Blake is sentenced to 42 years in prison after he pleaded guilty to charges of spying for the Soviet Union.		Brazilian Pres. Jañio Quadros cables Cuban Pres. Dorticos a Brazilian offer to help mediate U.S.-CUBAN differences. . . . High school students in Costa Rica launch a three-day strike to dramatize their demand for a break in diplomatic relations with Cuba.	Government and Pathet Lao officials agree on a general truce and fighting is ordered halted on all Laotian fronts.
May 4			Tunisian Pres. Habib Bourguiba, on a state visit to the U.S., praises the U.S. commitment to self-determination during the recent U.N. discussions of the Angola crisis.	U.S. Amb.-to-U.N. Stevenson leaves on an 18-day tour of 10 Latin American nations to discuss Pres. Kennedy's Alliance for Progress program.	
May 5			Portugal sends 3,400 more troops to Angola, raising the number of government forces there to over 15,000. . . . Shah Mohammed Riza Pahlevi appoints Dr. Ali Amini as premier of Iran to replace Jafar Sharif-Imami who resigned in the face of growing student demonstrations against the government.	Pres. Kennedy tells a Washington news conference that the U.S. is not now training nor planning to train a Cuban exile force for another attempt to overthrow Castro.	
May 6	Soviet Premier Khrushchev tells reporters that full-scale disarmament talks between the USSR and the U.S. will be resumed "in a short time." Kennedy administration spokesmen view the statement as premature and emphasize that the U.S. has agreed only to begin discussing terms and conditions for the possible resumption of substantive talks.	The Presidium of the Supreme Soviet adds embezzlement, counterfeiting, and violence committed in places of confinement to the list of capital crimes punishable by death.	Katanga Interior Min. Godefroid Munongo, who has apparently assumed government leadership since the arrest of Tshombe, warns that his regime will "fight to the last man" before surrendering to Pres. Kasavubu's plan for a highly centralized Congo state.	The Cuban National Bank issues a decree prohibiting the ownership of foreign capital by Cubans.	After two days of preliminary cease-fire talks, military representatives of the Boun Oum government and Pathet Lao forces are reported deadlocked on the question of a permanent site for negotiations on formal armistice machinery to maintain the current cease-fire.
May 7				*The New York Times* reports that greatly increased steel production, a doubling of electrical power, and self-sufficiency in textiles are among the goals in Cuban Industry Minister Guevara's five-year plan for Cuban industry.	Laotian sources report sporadic fighting despite the truce declaration of May 3.
May 8		Secy. of State Dean Rusk, addressing the annual spring meeting of the NATO Council in Oslo, renews the U.S.'s offer to provide NATO with a fleet of five Polaris submarines. Rusk, however, omits any reference to the Eisenhower administration's plan for joint NATO control over the nuclear fleet. . . . In a nationwide address, de Gaulle thanks the French people for their support in the suppression of the Algerian coup. He promises that he will continue to work for a negotiated cease-fire with the Moslem Algerian rebels.			The three-nation International Control Commission for Laos arrives in Vientiane to begin verification and supervision of the cease-fire declared May 3 by the Laotian government and Pathet Lao rebels. . . . A report issued by the National Science Foundation (U.S.) estimates that school enrollment in Communist China now totals 97 million students, an increase of over 60 million since 1949.

A	B	C	D	E
Includes developments that affect more than one world region, international organizations and important meetings of major world leaders.	*Includes all domestic and regional developments in Europe, including the Soviet Union, Turkey, Cyprus and Malta.*	*Includes all domestic and regional developments in Africa and the Middle East, including Iraq and Iran and excluding Cyprus, Turkey and Afghanistan.*	*Includes all domestic and regional developments in Latin America, the Caribbean and Canada.*	*Includes all domestic and regional developments in Asia and Pacific nations, extending from Afghanistan through all the Pacific Islands, except Hawaii.*

U.S. Politics & Social Issues	U.S. Foreign Policy & Defense	U.S. Economy & Environment	Science, Technology & Nature	Culture, Leisure & Life Style	
A bill to provide $3.298 billion over three years in federal aid to public schools is approved by a Senate Labor and Public Welfare subcommittee, 8-1, with Sen. Barry Goldwater as the lone opponent. . . . Morris Udall, 38, is elected to the Arizona second congressional district seat vacated by his brother, Interior Secy. Stewart Udall.	In testimony before separate Senate committees, State Secy. Rusk and CIA Director Allen Dulles assert that the CIA acted in the Cuban landing incident with the approval and supervision of the administration. Some Congressmen had expressed concern over whether the CIA had involved the U.S. in the affair on its own initiative.	Interior Secy. Stewart Udall announces the rejection of 15 identical bids submitted to the Reclamation Bureau for the sale of $1,250,000 worth of electrical equipment. Udall says that when suppliers use the same price lists, "competitive bidding becomes a farce." . . . Kennedy announces that he will ask Congress for federal aid to industries, including textiles, which are "seriously. . .threatened" by increased imports.	Bad weather forces cancellation of the first U.S. attempt at a manned sub-orbital space flight.		May 2
	For the third time in a week, Pres. Kennedy meets with the National Security Council to discuss possible U.S. moves in the face of the worsening Laotian military situation and the apparent refusal of the Communist rebels to accept an immediate cease-fire.	The House passes and sends to the Senate a bill (HR6441) to expand the federal water pollution control program and transfer it from the Surgeon General's office to HEW.			May 3
Two chartered Freedom Buses, carrying black and white members of CORE (Congress of Racial Equality), leave Washington for Birmingham, Ala. to test the desegregation of bus terminal facilities throughout the South.	Following a meeting with Pres. Kennedy on Indochina, Senate Foreign Relations Chmn. Fulbright tells reporters he would support sending U.S. combat troops to South Vietnam if needed. Fulbright says that South Vietnam, unlike Laos, has shown a genuine determination to resist communism.	The House passes by voice vote and sends to the Senate a bill (HR6713) to provide $11 billion in additional funds to finance a $37 billion interstate highway system scheduled for completion in 1972.	U.S. Navy scientist Victor Prather drowns in an ocean recovery mishap after he and another Navy officer set a manned balloon altitude record of 21.5 miles.		May 4
Pres. Kennedy issues an executive order prohibiting heads and assistant heads of executive departments and agencies from accepting any outside employment for pay.	The President's Board of Consultants on Foreign Intelligence Activities is reactivated by Pres. Kennedy. MIT Corp. head James Killian is named chairman.		Navy Cmndr. Alan Shepard Jr., 37, becomes the first U.S. astronaut as he rides a 2,300-pound Project Mercury capsule dubbed "Freedom 7" to an altitude of 115 miles in a 15-minute suborbital flight that ends with a safe splash-down in the Atlantic 302 miles from Cape Canaveral.	The official Catholic Directory for 1961 is issued in New York. It indicates that the number of U.S. Roman Catholics rose from 40.8 million in Jan., 1960 to 42.1 million at the beginning of 1961 (23.5% of the total U.S. population). Enrollment in Roman Catholic schools is listed at over 5.6 million.	May 5
Atty. Gen. Robert Kennedy, addressing Law Day exercises at the Univ. of Georgia Law School, pledges strict enforcement of civil right statutes and court decisions. He adds that the Univ. of Georgia's recent graduation of two Negro students will help in the U.S. struggle against world communism. . . . Former Vice Pres. Nixon, appearing on a Chicago TV program, blames his loss in the 1960 election on Pres. Eisenhower's failure to appear in Chicago and on the high unemployment jump in Oct., 1960.	The State Dept. announces the establishment of the Special Operations Center, a new advisory group to aid in handling U.S. world crises. Two teams, one for Cuba and one for South Vietnam, have so far been assigned to the new center. . . . Pres. Kennedy creates a special Food for Peace Council to provide policy advice to Food for Peace Director George McGovern.		Premier Khrushchev cables Pres. Kennedy his congratulations on the "U.S.'s latest achievement in man's conquest of space."	Jack Price's Carry Back, Johnny Sellers up, wins the 87th running of the Kentucky Derby.	May 6
				Sam Snead wins golf's Tournament of Champions in Las Vegas.	May 7
Sen. Joseph S. Clark (D, Pa.) and Rep. Emanuel Celler (D, N.Y.) introduce in the Senate and House six identical bills designed to fulfill the civil rights plank of the 1960 Democratic platform.		Pres. Kennedy signs a compromise bill (HR4884) to provide $200 million for emergency aid to needy children of unemployed parents. . . . The American Association of Fund-Raising reports that private donations to charity rose in the U.S. from $6.1 billion in 1959 to $6.5 billion in 1960.	Pres. Kennedy, at a White House ceremony, presents astronaut Alan Shepard with NASA's Distinguished Service Medal. In his remarks Kennedy contrasts the open news coverage of Shepard's flight with the secrecy surrounding the Soviet space program.	The Metropolitan Baseball Club Inc., owner of New York's new National League franchise, announces that its team will be called the Mets.	May 8

F	G	H	I	J
Includes elections, federal-state relations, civil rights and liberties, crime, the judiciary, education, health care, poverty, urban affairs and population.	*Includes formation and debate of U.S. foreign and defense policies, veterans' affairs and defense spending. (Relations with specific foreign countries are usually found under the region concerned.)*	*Includes business, labor, agriculture, taxation, transportation, consumer affairs, monetary and fiscal policy, natural resources, and pollution.*	*Includes worldwide scientific, medical and technological developments, natural phenomena, U.S. weather, natural disasters, and accidents.*	*Includes the arts, religion, scholarship, communications media, sports, entertainment, fashions, fads and social life.*

	World Affairs	Europe	Africa & the Middle East	The Americas	Asia & the Pacific
May 9		Delegates to the NATO Council meeting in Oslo agree to support the establishment of temporary committees to coordinate the policies of NATO member states toward specific problems or areas. The plan is regarded as a compromise with French Pres. de Gaulle's proposal for formal and continuous political consultations.	The central Congo government formally charges Katanga Pres. Tshombe, imprisoned since Apr. 26, with "treason" against the Congolese state. . . . Shah Mohammed Pahlevi dissolves the Iranian Parliament and empowers Premier Ali Amini to rule by decree pending new elections.	The U.S. State Dept. reports that more than 300 U.S. citizens registered with the Swiss Embassy in Havana for repatriation to the U.S. have not yet received Cuban permits to leave the country.	
May 10		Delegates to the NATO Council meeting issue a final communique containing a U.S.-backed resolution calling for a general extension of NATO's world role. The message says that NATO states must assume new responsibilities because "the menace which drew them together is now not only military but also has world-political, economic, scientific and psychological aspects."	The Algerian Provisional Government and France issue a joint communique in Tunis announcing that formal talks on conditions for an Algerian cease-fire will begin in France May 20. De Gaulle's recently demonstrated control over Algerian rightists is regarded as a major factor in the rebel decision to agree to talks.	In a policy statement on the anti-Castro landings in Cuba, Brazilian Pres. Jañio da Silva Quadros declares that Brazil would never recognize a new Cuban government brought to power by direct or indirect foreign intervention. . . . The Cuban National Revolutionary Council announces in New York that it is preparing "new plans" to overthrow Castro in the near future.	A Colombo court convicts and sentences to death Talduwe Somorama Thero, a Buddhist monk, for the Sept. 25, 1959 assassination of Ceylonese Premier Solomon Bandaranaike.
May 11			Iranian Premier Ali Amini announces a 15-point program to counter official corruption and to save the country from financial bankruptcy. The program includes: land reforms, import restrictions, export incentives, expansion of farm industries, and a crackdown on corrupt office-holders.		The Australian Wheat Board announces that Australia has agreed to sell Communist China 750,000 tons of wheat.
May 12		Three political opponents of the Salazar regime are arrested after holding a May 11 news conference in Lisbon to announce a program of democratic reforms for Portugal.	A *New York Times* correspondent reports that Portuguese troops have captured 71 Ghanians fighting with the Angola rebels, thereby lending support to Portuguese suspicions of official Ghanian support for the uprising.		At a Saigon reception, visiting U.S. Vice Pres. Johnson calls South Vietnamese Pres. Diem "the Churchill of today." . . . The three-nation International Control Commission for Laos officially confirms that a cease-fire has been achieved.
May 13		Turkish Pres. Cemal Gursel discloses that 140 persons have been arrested since May 9 on charges of plotting to overthrow the government.	Congo Pres. Kasavubu challenges the leaders of the dissident Gizenga regime to agree to a reconvening of the Congolese Parliament as a first step in the formation of a unified coalition government for the Congo.	At least four persons are killed in street fighting between followers and opponents of ex-Peruvian Pres. Manuel Odria. Odria plans to run in the next presidential elections.	Representatives of Laos' three warring factions sign an agreement in Namone formally accepting the cease-fire imposed in Laos May 3. . . . Pres. Diem and Vice Pres. Johnson issue a joint communique in Saigon announcing a $40 million increase in U.S. military and economic aid to South Vietnam. . . . Hong Kong dispatches report that recent Peking radio broadcasts describe China as suffering massive food shortages.
May 14		West German Defense Min. Franz-Josef Strauss, in a press interview, indicates his government's displeasure with the Kennedy administration's apparent decision not to back creation of a joint NATO nuclear deterrent force.		Wayne Morse (D, Ore.), chairman of a Senate subcommittee investigating the Apr. 17 Bay of Pigs landing, says he has heard no evidence to confirm that Soviet MiGs were used to repel the invaders or even "that there was a single Russian MiG in Cuba."	

A	B	C	D	E
Includes developments that affect more than one world region, international organizations and important meetings of major world leaders.	Includes all domestic and regional developments in Europe, including the Soviet Union, Turkey, Cyprus and Malta.	Includes all domestic and regional developments in Africa and the Middle East, including Iraq and Iran and excluding Cyprus, Turkey and Afghanistan.	Includes all domestic and regional developments in Latin America, the Caribbean and Canada.	Includes all domestic and regional developments in Asia and Pacific nations, extending from Afghanistan through all the Pacific Islands, except Hawaii.

U.S. Politics & Social Issues	U.S. Foreign Policy & Defense	U.S. Economy & Environment	Science, Technology & Nature	Culture, Leisure & Life Style	
White House Press Secy. Pierre Salinger tells newsmen that the Clark-Celler civil rights bills are "not administration-backed." . . . Former Vice Pres. Nixon tells the Detroit Press Club that Pres. Kennedy's proposal for press restraint on security matters involved a "profound misunderstanding" of free press's role and could become a "cloak for errors, misjudgments and other failings of government."	A bill to provide $600 million for aid to Latin America is passed by the Senate and sent to a conference committee where slight differences with the previously passed House version are to be worked out. The bill's supporters said the money would be used to help bring about significant social and economic reforms in the recipient countries.	The House and Senate approve and send to the President a conference committee bill to raise the minimum wage to $1.25 and extend its coverage to 3.6 million additional workers. The conference bill, which was almost identical to the Senate's version, drew opposition from conservatives in the House who had earlier succeeded in passing a more limited measure.	DuPont Corp. announces the development of a new chemical, Baymal, whose heat-resistant, water-repellent, hardening, and bonding characteristics promise a wide variety of possible uses.	In a speech to the National Association of Broadcasters Convention, FCC Chmn. Newton Minow denounces American TV programming as "a vast wasteland" of "game shows, violence,. . .formula comedies,. . .more violence,. . .(and) most of all, boredom." He warns that license renewals will no longer be automatically granted and that the FCC will conduct public hearings on all renewal applications.	May 9
NAACP Executive Secy. Roy Wilkins labels the Kennedy administration's refusal to support the Clark-Celler bills as "mistaken and regrettable." . . . Two Freedom Riders, a Negro and a white, are arrested in Winnsboro, S.C. after they entered a segregated restaurant together.			American Telephone and Telegraph Co., one of the companies seeking NASA assistance in the development of a communications satellite system, says it will have a launch-ready satellite built by early 1962.	The first five British authors to be honored as Companions of Literature by the Royal Society of Literature are the following: Sir Winston Churchill, Somerset Maugham, E.M. Forster, G.M. Trevelyan and John Masefield. The honor is to be limited to no more than 10 living British authors.	May 10
Kennedy sends Congress a proposed bill to provide federal assistance to local and state agencies involved in the fight against juvenile delinquency.	Vice Pres. Johnson arrives in Saigon on a "fact-finding mission" to help the administration determine the extent and nature of U.S. aid needed by South Vietnam. . . . The Senate passes, 43-36, a bill (S1215) to amend the Battle Act to give the President authority to extend aid to Soviet satellite countries in eastern Europe.	The House passes and sends to the Senate a bill to extend until Dec. 31, 1963 the program of importing Mexican farm laborers (braceros).		Pope John XXIII canonizes Bertilla Boscardin (1888-1922) as a Roman Catholic saint. . . . The merger of the American Unitarian Association and the Universalist Church of America is completed at a joint convention in Boston.	May 11
			The U.S. Air Force announces the establishment of a regular "space research pilot course" to provide a trained pool of highly skilled aerospace pilots for the U.S.'s expanding space program.	Mikhail Botvinnik, 49, of Leningrad, regains the world chess championship after defeating Mikhail Tal, 24, of Soviet Latvia, by 13 points to 8 in a two-month series in Moscow. . . . Auto racer Tony Bettenhausen, 44, is killed as a car he was test driving for the Indianapolis 500 race crashes into a steel fence at the speedway.	May 12
			The National Institute of Dental Research in Bethesda, Md. releases a study supporting the theory that tooth decay may be a transmissible disease caused by bacteria.	Frank James (Gary) Cooper, 60, longtime American film star and winner of two Academy Awards (for *Sergeant York* in 1941 and *High Noon* in 1953), dies in Hollywood of cancer.	May 13
The second of two CORE Freedom Buses is fire-bombed and destroyed by a white crowd near Anniston, Ala. The passengers escaped the burning bus without serious injuries. Earlier in the day Anniston whites beat up riders on the first Freedom Bus, causing at least one injury requiring hospitalization.	Americans for Democratic Action adopt a resolution urging U.S. recognition of and a U.N. seat for Red China at their annual convention in Washington.			In an address to Italian labor groups, Pope John XXIII calls for a worldwide effort against poverty in underdeveloped nations.	May 14

F	G	H	I	J
Includes elections, federal-state relations, civil rights and liberties, crime, the judiciary, education, health care, poverty, urban affairs and population.	Includes formation and debate of U.S. foreign and defense policies, veterans' affairs and defense spending. (Relations with specific foreign countries are usually found under the region concerned.)	Includes business, labor, agriculture, taxation, transportation, consumer affairs, monetary and fiscal policy, natural resources, and pollution.	Includes worldwide scientific, medical and technological developments, natural phenomena, U.S. weather, natural disasters, and accidents.	Includes the arts, religion, scholarship, communications media, sports, entertainment, fashions, fads and social life.

	World Affairs	Europe	Africa & the Middle East	The Americas	Asia & the Pacific
May 15	The Soviet delegation at the Geneva test-ban talks warns that the USSR will be forced to resume atomic testing if the U.S. and Britain do not take steps to end France's nuclear tests. The Western delegates reject the warning as "ridiculous."	British P.M. Macmillan names a special committee to study the country's security system in the wake of a recent series of espionage convictions.	All U.N. personnel are ordered withdrawn from the Congo's South Kasai Province after more than 50 U.N. troops had been killed in tribally-related attacks on their garrison at Port-Francqui. The U.N. says it can do nothing to end the "endemic" tribal warfare in the area.	Delgates from 21 American states conclude a 10-day meeting in Chile of the U.N. Economic Commission for Latin America after agreeing on the need for greater hemispheric economic integration, increased foreign aid, and strong internal development programs. . . . The first of 100,000 volunteer teachers leave Havana for the Cuban interior, marking the start of a national campaign to end illiteracy among the peasants.	
May 16	The 14-nation international conference on Laos, co-chaired by Britain and the USSR, is formally convened in Geneva. Communist Chinese Foreign Min. Chen Yi opens the debate with a sweeping attack on the U.S. role in Laos and Southeast Asia. Cambodian Prince Norodom Sihanouk follows with an appeal to contending Laotian leaders to work together toward the creation of a coalition government.		Sources in Iran report that hundreds of local officials, army officers, and judges have been either dismissed or arrested since Premier Ali Amini announced his May 11 campaign against electoral and financial corruption.		A mixed force of South Korean military units, headed by army chief of staff Lt. Gen. Chang Do Young, seizes control of Seoul and deposes the reform government of Premier John Chang. The coup leaders proclaim an interim military government dedicated to anti-communism, competence and South Korean reconstruction.
May 17	In speeches to the Laos conference in Geneva, U.S. State Secy. Rusk and Soviet Foreign Min. Gromyko indicate general agreement on the goal of a neutral Laos and the need to end foreign troop intervention. The two, however, differ sharply over truce controls, with the U.S. demanding a strong, independent control commission and the USSR insisting that the commission be subject to a veto by the great powers.			Cuban Premier Castro, in a televised speech, offers to exchange the 1,214 rebels captured in the Apr. 17 invasion for 500 U.S.-built heavy tractors. . . . Pres. Kennedy ends a two-day visit to Canada during which he called for increased U.S.-Canadian efforts to strengthen NATO and to aid underdeveloped nations in Latin America and elsewhere.	Agreement in principle to a plan for the formation of a coalition Laotian government, representative of all warring factions, is reached at talks in Namone. . . . Deposed South Korean Premier John Chang comes out of hiding to express public support for the military junta's assumption of power.
May 18					
May 19	The U.S. and the USSR announce that Pres. Kennedy and Premier Khrushchev will hold a personal meeting (not a formal "summit") in Vienna June 3-4. The meeting, to follow Pres. Kennedy's planned May 31 trip to Paris, will be the first private contact between the two world leaders.				Prince Boun Oum of the royal Laotian government, Prince Souphanouvong of the Pathet Lao and Prince Souvanna Phouma of the deposed neutralist regime begin talks in Zurich on the possible formation of peaceful coalition government in Laos. The meeting comes amidst a deepening deadlock in the 14-nation conference on Laos being held in Geneva.
May 20		A meeting between French Pres. de Gaulle and West German Chancellor Adenauer in Bonn is reported to have produced complete agreement on the West's continuing obligation to defend the freedom of West Berlin. French-West German differences over the structure of NATO and Europe's political future, however, are reportedly left unresolved by the brief talks.	Representatives of France and of the Moslem rebel Algerian Provisional Government meet in Evian-les-Bains, France to begin formal negotiations toward settling the seven-year Algerian rebellion. France declares a unilateral 30-day Algerian truce as a demonstration of goodwill toward the talks.	Castro's offer of a prisoner-tractor exchange is accepted by a private U.S. committee, headed by Eleanor Roosevelt, Walter Reuther and Dr. Milton Eisenhower. The State Dept. says it will not bar the group's efforts.	Lt. Gen. Chang Do Young, leader of the military junta that seized power May 16 in South Korea, becomes the chief minister in a new cabinet named by the junta to replace the deposed government of Prime Minister Chang.
May 21			French bombardment of Algerian rebel positions along the Moroccan border, which began May 19, is reportedly continuing despite France's unilateral cease-fire proclamation of May 20.		Over 100 accused gangsters are paraded through the streets of Seoul under police guard in what the ruling junta describes as a demonstration of its intention to end organized crime in South Korea.

A	B	C	D	E
Includes developments that affect more than one world region, international organizations and important meetings of major world leaders.	*Includes all domestic and regional developments in Europe, including the Soviet Union, Turkey, Cyprus and Malta.*	*Includes all domestic and regional developments in Africa and the Middle East, including Iraq and Iran and excluding Cyprus, Turkey and Afghanistan.*	*Includes all domestic and regional developments in Latin America, the Caribbean and Canada.*	*Includes all domestic and regional developments in Asia and Pacific nations, extending from Afghanistan through all the Pacific Islands, except Hawaii.*

U.S. Politics & Social Issues	U.S. Foreign Policy & Defense	U.S. Economy & Environment	Science, Technology & Nature	Culture, Leisure & Life Style	
A group of 30-40 white youths attack and severely beat Negro and white Freedom Bus riders in Birmingham, Ala. CBS correspondent Howard K. Smith reports that the attack occurred "under Police Commissioner Eugene Connors' window," but officers did not appear until 10 minutes later. . . . The Justice Dept. discloses that Atty. Gen. Kennedy has telephoned Alabama officials asking for police protection for the Freedom Riders. Gov. John Patterson issues a statement saying he will not "guarantee their safe passage."	The May issue of the Army journal, *Military Review*, reports that U.S. military leaders have located and mapped what they believe to be at least 37 Soviet missile-launching sites in the USSR.	The SEC announces plans for a full investigation of the rules and practices of the American Stock Exchange; it is the first SEC probe into a major exchange since 1938 when Richard Whitney was ousted as the N.Y. Stock Exchange president on embezzlement charges.	*The New York Times* reports that the U.S. plans to fire three similarly instrumented space probes in late 1961 as part of the first U.S. attempt to hit the moon.		May 15
Rep. George Huddleston Jr. (D, Ala.) tells newsmen that the Freedom Riders got "just what they asked for" in "trespassing upon the South and its well established...customs."	Richard Gibson, acting secretary of the New York-based, pro-Castro Fair Play for Cuba Committee, tells a Senate Internal Security Subcommittee investigating the possibility of Cuban government support for the group, that the committee kept no financial or membership records. Gibson denies any Fair Play Committee connection with the U.S. Communist Party.		Charles Pfizer and Co., Inc. announces in New York the development of a synthetic antibiotic (Terramycin) effective against many bacteria.	Rod Serling, writer of the *Twilight Zone* series, *Perry Mason* star Raymond Burr, and the Huntley-Brinkley news team are among the winners of the National Academy of Television Arts' Emmy Awards for the 1960-1961 TV season.	May 16
	The U.S. House approves, 401-2, a resolution calling on the OAS to impose sanctions against Cuba and to exclude its delegates from the Inter-American Defense Board.	The Dow-Jones industrial stock price average climbs to a record high 705.52. . . . The Commerce Dept. reports that the GNP rate in the first quarter of 1961 fell to $499.8 billion, $3.7 billion below the final quarter of 1960.			May 17
				Spanish director Luis Bunuel's film *Viridiana* is a Gold Palm Grand Prix winner at the Cannes (France) Film Festival.	May 18
Pres. Kennedy signs into law a bill (S912) creating 10 new circuit judgeships and 63 new district judgeships.	Sen. Albert Gore (D, Tenn.) calls for the replacement of the entire Joint Chiefs of Staff for their poor advice in the illfated Bay of Pigs invasion.	Kennedy sends Congress a bill to increase the Labor Dept.'s power to act against mismanagement of union pension funds.	Soviet space and aerodynamics expert Prof. Mstislav Keldysh is unanimously elected president of the Soviet Academy of Sciences.	Jockey Willie Shoemaker, aboard Guaranteeya in the third race at Hollywood Park, Inglewood, Calif., wins his 4,000th career race. Shoemaker, 29, is the fourth winningest jockey in horse race history.	May 19
Violence erupts in Montgomery, Ala. as mobs attack Negro and white Freedom Riders who entered the city by bus from Birmingham to test segregation barriers in interstate terminals. Ten Freedom Riders, four newsmen and five Negro bystanders are injured. Following a statement expressing "deepest concern" from Pres. Kennedy, Atty. Gen. Robert Kennedy announces that 350-400 U.S. Marshals will be sent to Montgomery to help state and local officials preserve order.		The Commerce Department reports that average U.S. family income rose to $6,900 in 1960, an increase of $300 over 1959. The figures indicate that over 13% of U.S. families earn less than $2,000.		Kentucky Derby winner, Carry Back, with Johnny Sellers up, wins the Pimlico Futurity in Baltimore.	May 20
A crowd of over 1,000 Montgomery, Ala. whites gather in an apparent design to attack 1,500 Negroes attending a mass church meeting to hear Dr. Martin Luther King. Gov. John Patterson declares martial law in Montgomery, calls out National Guard troops and requests assistance from the special detachment of U.S. Marshals in a successful effort to prevent violence.		Commerce Secy. Luther Hodges reports that U.S. exports to the USSR and its European satellite countries rose from $89 million in 1959 to a 13-year high of $193 million in 1960. Almost 75% of the exports went to Poland.		John Kelley, 30, wins the national AAU marathon (26 mile race) in Yonkers, N.Y. for the sixth consecutive year.	May 21

F	G	H	I	J
Includes elections, federal-state relations, civil rights and liberties, crime, the judiciary, education, health care, poverty, urban affairs and population.	Includes formation and debate of U.S. foreign and defense policies, veterans' affairs and defense spending. (Relations with specific foreign countries are usually found under the region concerned.)	Includes business, labor, agriculture, taxation, transportation, consumer affairs, monetary and fiscal policy, natural resources, and pollution.	Includes worldwide scientific, medical and technological developments, natural phenomena, U.S. weather, natural disasters, and accidents.	Includes the arts, religion, scholarship, communications media, sports, entertainment, fashions, fads and social life.

	World Affairs	Europe	Africa & the Middle East	The Americas	Asia & the Pacific
May 22	An eight-nation committee formed to study reorganization of the U.N. Secretariat is reportedly deadlocked on conflicting proposals for curtailing the powers of the Secretary General through a division of his executive responsibilities. The proposals are aimed at finding a compromise between the present U.N. structure and Soviet demands for a three-man executive.	The Turkish Constituent Assembly approves a three-month extension of martial law in Ankara and Istanbul.	A statement issued by the Moroccan Information Agency warns that a French effort to force an Algerian settlement based on the country's "Balkanization" could lead to "general war" in North Africa.	A 10-man committee of captured Cuban rebels, sent by Castro to negotiate the prisoner-tractor exchange, meets in Washington with Eleanor Roosevelt and other members of the Tractors for Freedom Committee.	The U.S. State Dept. issues a statement expressing offical regret that the South Korean junta "found it necessary to suspend temporarily the democratic and constitutional processes. . .of Korea." . . . Fighting between Pakistani troops and a mixed force of Afghan tribesmen and government regulars is reported in the Khyber Pass near Peshawar, Pakistan. The outbreak stems from an alleged May 19 Afgan attack on Pakistani border posts.
May 23		Soviet-West German negotiations on cultural exchanges are broken off in Bonn after the Soviet delegation insisted that West Berliners be excluded from the proposed exchanges.	Belkacem Krim, chief Algerian rebel representative at the Evian talks, tells reporters that the Algerian Provisional Government will not accept a French self-determination plan which reserves to France the right to partition Algeria and to maintain control over oil-rich Sahara. Self-determination, he adds, will have to apply to the "entire national territory."		An intensification of Viet Cong military activity is reported to have begun in northern South Vietnam near Hué.
May 24	The governing council of the U.N. Special Fund votes to grant Cuba $3 million for agricultural research despite vigorous U.S. opposition.		Portuguese officials announce that a May 12 report that 71 Ghanians had been captured while fighting for the Angolan rebels has proven to be untrue.		Maj. Gen. Dang Van Minh is named commander-in-chief of South Vietnam's newly reorganized army.
May 25	Rajeshwar Dayal, Hammarskjold's personal representative in the Congo, resigns in the face of growing opposition from the central Congo government which has accused him of partiality toward the dissident Gizenga forces.		Israeli Premier Ben-Gurion, on a North American tour, tells a Montreal press conference that a "great powers" agreement upholding the independence and integrity of all Middle East nations would greatly help to reduce tensions in the region.		
May 26		Moscow sources report that eight Soviet submarines have been recalled from Valona Albania, the USSR's only port on the Mediterranean. The departure of the ships is said to be linked to Albania's support of Communist Chinese criticism of Khrushchev's leadership.	Louis Joxe, representing France at the Evian talks, tells reporters that France does not wish to partition Algeria, but will retain the right to do so should the outcome of Algerian self-determination endanger the security and interests of the European population there.		The Soviet delegation at the Laos conference refuses a British request that the conference discuss a reply to a May 24 appeal from the three-nation International Control Commission for further instructions on how it should attempt to enforce the Laos truce.
May 27		A new Turkish Constitution providing for a bicameral parliamentary-type government is approved unanimously by the ruling National Union Committee, headed by Gen. Cemal Gursel.			The U.S. charges at the Geneva conference that increasingly frequent Pathet Lao truce violations are being encouraged by the USSR's refusal to support plans to make truce supervision effective.

A	B	C	D	E
Includes developments that affect more than one world region, international organizations and important meetings of major world leaders.	*Includes all domestic and regional developments in Europe, including the Soviet Union, Turkey, Cyprus and Malta.*	*Includes all domestic and regional developments in Africa and the Middle East, including Iraq and Iran and excluding Cyprus, Turkey and Afghanistan.*	*Includes all domestic and regional developments in Latin America, the Caribbean and Canada.*	*Includes all domestic and regional developments in Asia and Pacific nations, extending from Afghanistan through all the Pacific Islands, except Hawaii.*

U.S. Politics & Social Issues	U.S. Foreign Policy & Defense	U.S. Economy & Environment	Science, Technology & Nature	Culture, Leisure & Life Style	
FBI agents arrest four Anniston, Ala. whites in connection with the May 14 fire-bombing of a Freedom Bus. . . . The Supreme Court rules that Louisiana cannot use two old state laws to compel the NAACP to disclose the names of its members and the organizational affiliations of its officers. . . . The Senate, currently debating the administration's school aid bill, votes to reject an amendment that would bar aid to segregated schools.	Pres. Kennedy nominates Gen. Curtis LeMay to succeed retiring Gen. Thomas White as Air Force chief of staff.	The Supreme Court rules that E.I. du-Pont de Nemours and Co. must divest itself of its 63 million shares of General Motors stock within 10 years.		The General Assembly of the United Presbyterian Church (U.S.), meeting in convention in Buffalo, N.Y., calls upon the Protestant Episcopal Church to join in a study of a proposed merger of Presbyterians, Episcopalians, Methodists and United Church of Christ members into a single Protestant body.	**May 22**
Martin Luther King tells a Montgomery news conference that the Freedom Rides will continue. Gov. Patterson denounces King as a "menace to the city" of Montgomery.					**May 23**
Two Freedom Buses, under National Guard escort, travel from Montgomery, Alabama to Jackson, Mississippi. Almost immediately upon their arrival, all the passengers are arrested for violating segregation ordinances in the heavily-guarded Jackson bus terminal. . . . Atty. Gen. Kennedy appeals to the Freedom Riders for a "cooling off" period in light of the "very difficult" situation in Alabama and Mississippi.	Pres. Kennedy, explaining that the U.S. cannot be a party to official negotiations with Castro, publicly urges American citizens to contribute to the private Tractors for Freedom fund. Sen. Goldwater attacks the appeal as "lending prestige of the government to this surrender to blackmail."		The FCC announces in Washington that it has decided to limit ownership of the first commercial communications satellite to phone and telegraph companies providing worldwide service. The companies involved will build the satellite and then reimburse NASA for the cost of putting it in orbit.		**May 24**
CORE national director James Farmer sends a message from his Jackson, Miss. jail cell calling upon supporters to extend the Freedom Ride movement to railroad and airline terminals. . . . By a vote of 49-34, the Senate passes and sends to the House the administration's aid-to-education bill (S1021).	Kennedy asks Congress to authorize an additional $535 million for foreign military and economic aid contingency funds so that the U.S. can better meet sudden world crises. He also requests a $2.4 million increase in the U.S. Information Agency budget to expand radio propaganda efforts in Latin America and Southeast Asia.	In his special appearance before Congress, Pres. Kennedy declares that economic recovery "is under way" but that a manpower training program is needed to find a complete solution to the continuing problem of unemployment.	In his so-called second State of the Union address, Kennedy calls for "a major national commitment" to achieve the goal "before this decade is out, of landing a man on the moon and returning him safely to earth."		**May 25**
The Southern Christian Leadership Conference, the Student Non-Violent Coordinating Committee, the Nashville Christian Leadership Council and CORE announce the establishment in Atlanta of a Freedom Ride Coordinating Committee.	Kennedy sends Congress a proposed bill calling for an Act for International Development (AID) to consolidate the major U.S. foreign economic aid programs (excepting Peace Corps and Food for Peace). . . . GOP leaders Sen. Everett Dirksen and Rep. Charles Halleck, issue a joint statement sharply criticizing the Tractors-for-Prisoners exchange and Pres. Kennedy's public endorsement of it. The Commerce Dept. reports that new housing starts in the U.S. rose to 118,700 in April, marking the fourth consecutive monthly increase. . . . Spokesmen for labor, the missile industry and construction contractors agree to a no-strike, no-lockout pledge covering U.S. missile and space bases.		U.S. space expert Dr. Werner von Braun reports that a radical breakthrough in engine design of the Saturn rocket may permit a significant acceleration of the U.S. space program. Von Braun predicts that a planned C-3 version of the Saturn, capable of putting men in lunar orbit, may be operational by the late 1960's.		**May 26**
Montgomery police arrest six white youths in connection with the May 25 gunshot wounding of Rev. Solomon Saay, a Negro minister prominent in the recent anti-segregation campaign. . . . In a special election for the Senate seat vacated by V.P. Johnson, John Tower beats Democrat William Blakeley to become the first Republican Senator from Texas since Reconstruction.	An amended bill (HR6518) to provide $600 million in Alliance for Progress aid to Latin America, which passed the Senate May 25, 41-26, is signed into law by Pres. Kennedy. . . . Ex-V.P. Richard Nixon tells newsmen that President Kennedy's support of the tractor-prisoner exchange with Cuba will "encourage every tinhorn dictator . . . to try to take advantage of America."	The Federal Highway Administration reports that motor vehicle registration in the U.S. rose to a record 73,895,274 in 1960.	Scientists for Union Carbide Nuclear Co. in Oak Ridge, Tenn. report in the *Journal of the American Medical Association* that low-level nuclear radiation in small doses is harmless to humans and may even increase life expectancy.	Villanova wins the team title at the IC4A outdoor track meet in New York.	**May 27**
F	**G**	**H**	**I**	**J**	
Includes elections, federal-state relations, civil rights and liberties, crime, the judiciary, education, health care, poverty, urban affairs and population.	*Includes formation and debate of U.S. foreign and defense policies, veterans' affairs and defense spending. (Relations with specific foreign countries are usually found under the region concerned.)*	*Includes business, labor, agriculture, taxation, transportation, consumer affairs, monetary and fiscal policy, natural resources, and pollution.*	*Includes worldwide scientific, medical and technological developments, natural phenomena, U.S. weather, natural disasters, and accidents.*	*Includes the arts, religion, scholarship, communications media, sports, entertainment, fashions, fads and social life.*	

	World Affairs	Europe	Africa & the Middle East	The Americas	Asia & the Pacific
May 28				Brazil announces the signing of agreements providing for $1.65 billion worth of trade between Brazil and communist nations of eastern Europe.	The South Korean junta orders the arrest of several prominent businessmen and civilian officials on charges of amassing illegal fortunes. The junta also outlaws 834 of South Korea's 916 newspapers and news agencies on charges of corrupt activities.
May 29	The U.S. and British delegations to the Geneva talks offer to reduce their demand for a minimum of 20 annual on-site inspections down to 12.				
May 30		Speaking at a reception in honor of the newly opened British Trade Fair in Moscow, Khrushchev declares that Soviet leaders now "consider our heavy industry built" and will no longer "give it priority."	UAR breaks diplomatic relations with South Africa in protest against its apartheid policies.	Rafael Leonidas Trujillo Molina, 69, dictator of the Dominican Republic since 1930, is shot to death by assassins in Ciudad Trujillo.	
May 31	Chief Soviet test-ban delegate Semyon Tsarapkin says that the West's recently reduced inspection quota is still "artificially high" and unacceptable.	Pres. Kennedy, arriving for talks in France, is warmly greeted by Pres. de Gaulle and by crowds of Parisians estimated to number one million or more. Following their first meeting, the two leaders are reported to have reached complete agreement on the need to meet with force any Soviet threat to West Berlin. . . . Former generals Maurice Challe, considered the leader of the April Algiers uprising, and Andre Zeller, a prominent co-conspirator, are convicted and sentenced to 15 years imprisonment by a French military tribunal in Paris.	South Africa officially becomes a republic; South Africa's last ties to the British Commonwealth are simultaneously dissolved.	Sources in the Dominican Republic report that Trujillo was killed by gun fire from a car carrying 7 persons. The assassins were allegedly led by Gen. Juan Tomas Diaz.	
June 1			British troop reinforcements from Kenya are sent to the British protectorate of Zanzibar to help prevent feared ethnic violence during forthcoming legislative elections.	Lt. Gen. Rafael Trujillo, Jr., son of the assassinated dictator Rafael Leonidas Trujillo, is elevated to the newly created post of chief of staff of the Dominican Republic's armed forces.	
June 2		Former Soviet Premier Vyacheslav Molotov, now the Soviet representative to the International Atomic Energy Agency, is among the dignitaries greeting Premier Khrushchev upon his arrival in Vienna. The two men, who have not met since Molotov launched his unsuccessful challenge to Khrushchev's leadership in 1957, are reported to have shook hands with visible embarrassment.	Algerian rebel spokesmen at the Evian talks reject as unacceptable an alleged French demand that the Sahara be excluded from any Algerian self-determination plan.		The World Bank and a six-nation Western consortium agree in Washington to lend India $2.25 billion over two years to help launch that nation's third five-year economic plan.
June 3	Pres. Kennedy and Premier Khrushchev meet in Vienna for two days of personal discussion on world problems. It is the first major East-West confrontation since the abortive summit of May, 1960.	Generalissimo Francisco Franco denounces Western-style democracy and capitalism in a speech opening the new Spanish Cortos (Parliament) in Madrid.		The OAS's Inter-American Peace Committee agrees to a Mexican request that it send observers to the Mexican state of Chiapas to investigate Guatemalan charges that Cuban troops are being trained there for an assault on Guatemala. Guatemala opposes the mission.	

A	B	C	D	E
Includes developments that affect more than one world region, international organizations and important meetings of major world leaders.	Includes all domestic and regional developments in Europe, including the Soviet Union, Turkey, Cyprus and Malta.	Includes all domestic and regional developments in Africa and the Middle East, including Iraq and Iran and excluding Cyprus, Turkey and Afghanistan.	Includes all domestic and regional developments in Latin America, the Caribbean and Canada.	Includes all domestic and regional developments in Asia and Pacific nations, extending from Afghanistan through all the Pacific Islands, except Hawaii.

U.S. Politics & Social Issues	U.S. Foreign Policy & Defense	U.S. Economy & Environment	Science, Technology & Nature	Culture, Leisure & Life Style	
					May 28
Atty. Gen. Robert Kennedy asks the ICC to issue strict regulations requiring the desegregation of interstate transportation and terminal facilities. . . . In four decisions the U.S. Supreme Court upholds the constitutionality of state "blue laws" prohibiting the conduct of certain types of business on Sunday. The Court majority contends that a state's power to provide a respite from labor cannot be equated with state promotion of a religion in violation of the First Amendment.	Sen. Hubert Humphrey, in a Senate speech, backs acceptance of Castro's prisoner-tractor offer, saying that it "demonstrates strength--not weakness-- when (the U.S.) takes action to save human lives."	Kennedy submits to Congress a draft bill to provide subsistence payments to unemployed workers who enroll in job retraining programs.	Dr. Arnold Gesell, 80, a leading authority on child development and founder of the Child Development Clinic at Yale University (1911), dies in New Haven, Conn.		May 29
The Southern Regional Council, composed of Negroes and whites, warns that the civil rights movement will be taken over by "extremists" if the South fails to respond to legitimate demands for change.			The Gallup Poll releases a survey indicating that only 33% of Americans favor spending the estimated $40 billion it will cost to put a man on the moon.	A.J. Foyt, driving a Bowes Seal Fast Special, wins the Indianapolis 500 with a record average speed of 130.131 mph.	May 30
Maverick Democrat Samuel Yorty, running without regular party support, defeats Republican incumbent Norris Paulson to become mayor of Los Angeles.	Kennedy sends Congress a bill establishing the Peace Corps on a permanent basis and authorizing it to spend up to $40 million in fiscal 1962.				May 31
				The *Journal of the American Medical Association* reports that researchers at the National Institutes of Health have identified the respiratory syncytial (RS) virus as a major cause of severe respiratory illness in infants and of the common cold in adults.	June 1
U.S. Judge Frank Johnson Jr. in Montgomery, Ala. issues a restraining order to halt interstate travel in Alabama "for the purpose of testing segregation laws." Johnson, at the same time, issues an injunction barring the Montgomery Police from withholding full protection from interstate travelers. . . . Rep. William E. Miller (R, N.Y.) is elected to succeed Sen. Thruston Morton (R, Ky.) as chairman of the Republican National Committee.				George Kauffman, 71, playwright, director and winner of two Pulitzer Prizes for drama, dies in New York.	June 2
			Dr. Hans A. Berthe, Cornell University physics professor, receives the AEC's Enrico Fermi Award of $50,000 for his "contributions to nuclear and theoretical physics. . .and to the security of the U.S."	José Rigores of Cuba, ex-Pan American boxing champion, dies in New York from a brain injury suffered in a six-round featherweight bout with Anselmo Castillo of Puerto Rico.	June 3

F	G	H	I	J
Includes elections, federal-state relations, civil rights and liberties, crime, the judiciary, education, health care, poverty, urban affairs and population.	*Includes formation and debate of U.S. foreign and defense policies, veterans' affairs and defense spending. (Relations with specific foreign countries are usually found under the region concerned.)*	*Includes business, labor, agriculture, taxation, transportation, consumer affairs, monetary and fiscal policy, natural resources, and pollution.*	*Includes worldwide scientific, medical and technological developments, natural phenomena, U.S. weather, natural disasters, and accidents.*	*Includes the arts, religion, scholarship, communications media, sports, entertainment, fashions, fads and social life.*

	World Affairs	Europe	Africa & the Middle East	The Americas	Asia & the Pacific
June 4	A joint affirmation of support for a neutral Laos is the only area of concrete agreement cited in an official communique summarizing Pres. Kennedy and Premier Khrushchev's two days of talks in Vienna.		The Congo Republic (Leopoldville) renounces all treaties with Portuguese Angola to protest "the massacres and tortures of the defenseless" in Angola.		
June 5		Pres. Kennedy stops in London on his return home from Vienna to brief P.M. Macmillan on his talks with Khrushchev.		The Dominican Republic government announces that of the seven persons said to have shot Trujillo, three, including Gen. Diaz, have been killed, three captured, and one is still at large. Over 60 other persons are reported to have been arrested for questioning concerning the assassination plot. . . . The OAS agrees to a June 2 U.S. request that it send a fact-finding team to the Dominican Republic to investigate charges of police terror there since Trujillo's assassination.	
June 6	In a TV address to the nation, Pres. Kennedy reports that he and Soviet Premier Khrushchev gave frank expression to their widely differing views on Germany, disarmament, nuclear testing, and the political future of underdeveloped nations during their Vienna meeting. While admitting that "no spectacular progress" was made, Kennedy says that "at least the chances of a dangerous misjudgment on either side should now be less."	U.S. Deputy Defense Secy. Roswell Gilpatric says at a Washington news conference that U.S. forces serving with NATO would use their nuclear weapons if Western Europe were in danger of being conquered by conventional Soviet forces.	Dissident Congo leader Antoine Gizenga informs Secy. Gen. Hammarskjold that he is willing to support the reconvening of the Congo Parliament provided that the U.N. provides protection to the attending delegates. . . . Newspapers in the UAR report growing official displeasure there over continuing Soviet press criticism of the UAR's restrictions on domestic communist political activity.		South Korea's ruling junta-cabinet assumes full dictatorial powers and renames itself the Supreme Council for National Reconstruction. The action marks the virtual abolition of the republican form of government established by South Korea's 1948 constitution.
June 7			Israeli author Yeheil Dinur collapses while testifying about conditions at the Auschwitz concentration camp. Dinur is among the last of 113 prosecution witnesses to testify to crimes and atrocities that allegedly took place under the auspicies of Adolph Eichmann.	Bolivia declares a national state of siege to cope with an alleged pro-Castro, communist plot to overthrow the government of Pres. Victor Paz Estenssoro. . . . Cuba nationalizes all remaining private and parochial schools as part of a general program to establish nationwide free public education.	Averell Harriman, chief U.S. representative at the Laos conference, charges that the Pathet Lao have launched a full offensive against government troops in "blatant violation" of the cease-fire. Later in the day, the U.S. announces that Harriman will not take part in further conference meetings until the USSR accepts measures for enforcing the cease-fire. . . . Japanese Premier Hayato Ikeda's Liberal-Democratic cabinet withdraws an anti-demonstration bill which had provoked widespread criticism from Socialists and other leftist groups.
June 8		The USSR protests to the Western allies what it calls provocative plans to hold a meeting of the West German Bundesrat (upper house) in Berlin June 16.		An OAS fact-finding commission begins an on-site inquiry into charges of political repression in the Dominican Republic following the assassination of Generalissimo Trujillo.	Pakistani Finance Min. Mohammed Shoaib describes as inadequate a $320 million economic aid pledge from the World Bank and a six-nation Western consortium. Pakistan had requested over $900 million. . . . The South Korean junta bars university students and professors from engaging in any political activities on their campuses.
June 9	The Yugoslav news agency Tanyug reports that a "little summit" meeting of leaders of uncommitted nations will be held in Belgrade beginning Sept. 1.	West German Bundesrat Pres. Franz Meyers says that a planned June 16 Berlin session had been cancelled well before the Soviets protested.	The U.N. Security Council by a 9-0 vote approves a resolution calling upon Portugal to halt "repressive measures" in Angola and to cooperate with a U.N. investigation of conditions there. . . . The Evian talks on Algeria are reported to have reached an impasse over the questions of possible partition and control of the Sahara.	U.S. Amb. Stevenson, on a 10-nation Latin American tour, tells an official luncheon in Montevideo, Uruguay that Pres. Kennedy regards "economic development" as the "most imperative" objective in Latin America.	

A	B	C	D	E
Includes developments that affect more than one world region, international organizations and important meetings of major world leaders.	Includes all domestic and regional developments in Europe, including the Soviet Union, Turkey, Cyprus and Malta.	Includes all domestic and regional developments in Africa and the Middle East, including Iraq and Iran and excluding Cyprus, Turkey and Afghanistan.	Includes all domestic and regional developments in Latin America, the Caribbean and Canada.	Includes all domestic and regional developments in Asia and Pacific nations, extending from Afghanistan through all the Pacific Islands, except Hawaii.

U.S. Politics & Social Issues	U.S. Foreign Policy & Defense	U.S. Economy & Environment	Science, Technology & Nature	Culture, Leisure & Life Style	
				Emile Griffith retains the world welterweight title by scoring a technical knockout against Gaspar Ortega of Mexico in Los Angeles.	June 4
The Supreme Court, by 5-4 decisions, upholds federal laws requiring "communist-action" groups to register with the Justice Dept. (1950 McCarran Act) and making it illegal to belong to a party which advocates the violent overthrow of the government (1940 Smith Act).		The House passes and sends to the Senate a bill (HR10) to grant tax deferrals (on up to $2,500 of income) to self-employed persons for the building of retirement funds.	A $14 million launching site for the new Saturn rocket series, the biggest U.S. launch facility built so far, is completed at Cape Canaveral by the Army Corps of Engineers and formally turned over to NASA.	Jacob Sher's Sherluck, a 65-1 long shot, wins the $148,000 Belmont Stakes. Kentucky Derby winner Carry Back, the prerace favorite, finishes seventh.	June 5
	Pres. Kennedy tells congressional leaders that the U.S. will not attempt to break off the Geneva test talks despite the apparent lack of progress.	Sony Corp., a Tokyo-based manufacturer of electronic equipment, offers $3.5 million worth of its common stock for sale on the U.S. market, marking the first public sale in the U.S. of a Japanese firm's common stock.	NASA medical experts report to newsmen that Alan Shepard suffered no ill effects from his May 5 suborbital space flight. . . . The Chicago Heart Association announces that it has developed a practical mass screening program for finding heart defects in school children.		June 6
Three Negroes are arrested for seeking to use segregated dining facilities at the Jackson (Ala.) Municipal Airport following their arrival on a Freedom Flight from St. Louis. Their arrest brings to 29 the total number of persons charged with segregation-related violations in Jackson since June 2.	Peace Corps director R. Sargent Shriver urges U.S. business and labor to provide unpenalized two-yr. leaves of absence for Corps volunteers.	Kennedy sends Congress a bill to provide an estimated $100 million a year for a youth job training and placement program.			June 7
White House Press Secy. Pierre Salinger discloses that Pres. Kennedy has been in almost constant pain since straining his back during a tree planting ceremony in Canada May 16.			The American Health Insurance Institute reports that although the life expectancy of U.S. women is six years longer than for men, women suffer a greater number of acute health conditions.		June 8
	In a Washington speech delivered during his state visit to the U.S., Pres. Fulbert Youlou of the Congo Republic (Brazzaville) advises Americans not to assume always that "what is good for the richest country on earth is good for the poorest continent."	The Area Redevelopment Administration announces the first 114 areas eligible to receive U.S. economic aid under the recently enacted area redevelopment bill. . . . The Commerce Dept. reports that the total value of "new construction put in place" rose in May for the third consecutive month.	A molecular, impulse-block hypothesis to explain the effect of certain anesthetic gases on the brain is described by Dr. Linus Pauling at the Third World Conference of Psychiatry in Montreal.		June 9

F	G	H	I	J
Includes elections, federal-state relations, civil rights and liberties, crime, the judiciary, education, health care, poverty, urban affairs and population.	Includes formation and debate of U.S. foreign and defense policies, veterans' affairs and defense spending. (Relations with specific foreign countries are usually found under the region concerned.)	Includes business, labor, agriculture, taxation, transportation, consumer affairs, monetary and fiscal policy, natural resources, and pollution.	Includes worldwide scientific, medical and technological developments, natural phenomena, U.S. weather, natural disasters, and accidents.	Includes the arts, religion, scholarship, communications media, sports, entertainment, fashions, fads and social life.

	World Affairs	Europe	Africa & the Middle East	The Americas	Asia & the Pacific
June 10		The USSR makes public a detailed memorandum on Germany calling for the signing of a final World War II peace treaty with both German states and the transformation of West Berlin into a demilitarized free city within East Germany. The memo reiterates Soviet intentions to sign a separate East German treaty should the West reject its proposals.		Brazilian troops are sent to Recife to help quell student demonstrations caused by a June 7 University of Recife decision to prohibit a campus address by Celia Guevara, mother of Cuban Industry Min. Ché Guevara.	An agreement by Japan to repay the U.S. $490 million in debts incurred during the U.S. occupation over the next 15 years is signed in Tokyo. Soviet Premier Khrushchev promises visiting Pres. Sukarno full support in Indonesia's dispute with the Netherlands over control of New Guinea.
June 11	Tass publishes a policy memorandum outlining Soviet terms for an agreement on a nuclear test-ban and disarmament. The document restates Russian insistence on: (a) a three-member executive to supervise a test-ban treaty; (b) a maximum of three on-site inspections annually to check against test-ban violations; (c) agreement to the goal of general disarmament prior to the creation of control and inspection machinery.	West German Chancellor Adenauer, referring to the June 10 Soviet memo on Germany, tells a Hanover rally "We will never accept these Russian demands." West Berlin Mayor Willy Brandt links the Soviet terms to the "disastrous Munich agreement of 1938.". . . Violent anti-government demonstrations by French farmers protesting falling food prices are reportedly spreading in Brittany and other parts of France. The disturbances began June 4.	At least 64 persons are dead and more than 1,000 have been arrested in 10 days of violent election-related clashes between Africans and Arabs on the island of Zanzibar, a British protectorate.		
June 12	Chief Soviet test-ban negotiator Semyon Tsarapkin tells the Western delegates at the Geneva talks that the USSR regards its June 11 memorandum as the only acceptable basis for continued negotiations. Britain and the U.S. denounce the statement as an attempt to "dictate" to the conference.				The Communist Chinese delegation at the Laos conference charges that U.S., French and British proposals for strengthening international supervision of the Laos truce are merely pretexts for Western intervention. . . . Premier Chou En-lai, at a Peking reception for North Vietnamese Premier Pham Van Dong, charges that the U.S. is "preparing to embark on a war adventure in South Vietnam."
June 13		British P.M. Macmillan announces in Parliament the formation of a three-man commission to consult with Commonwealth nation leaders concerning a possible British application to join the European Economic Community (Common Market). . . . Pres. Kennedy exchanges views on Europe's political and defense problems with visiting Italian Premier Amintore Fanfani.	France breaks off the Evian talks on Algeria saying that a suspension is needed to find new ways of breaking the current deadlock.	Four U.S. farm machinery experts arrive in Havana for negotiations on Premier Castro's offer to exchange 1,214 captured rebels for 500 U.S. tractors. . . . U.S. Amb.-to-U.N. Adlai Stevenson tells reporters following talks with Paraguayan leaders that Pres. Alfredo Stroessner had assured him "free and fair" elections would soon be held in Paraguay.	
June 14	Arthur Dean, chief U.S. delegate at the Geneva test-ban talks, accuses the Soviets of failing to make any effort to match the concessions offered by the West when the talks reconvened March 21.	The New York Times reports that the Western powers have been consulting on a reply to the USSR's German memorandum that might open the way to resumed negotiations. . . . Italian police reinforcements are sent to the northern province of Bolzano to deal with a current wave of bombings and violence on the part of German-speaking elements demanding greater local autonomy.		A Dominican Republic government spokesman reports that three prominent Dominican exiles, including Juan Bosch, have been invited to return home and to establish opposition newspapers. . . . In a revision of his original offer, Cuban Premier Castro demands that the U.S. provide 1,000 farm tractors, instead of 500, in exchange for the captured Bay of Pigs invaders.	
June 15	In a report to the Russian people on his Vienna meeting with Kennedy, Premier Khrushchev renews his ultimatum that the German problem must be settled "this year." He also reiterates the USSR's willingness to accept any Western proposals on control and inspection, if the West will "accept our proposals on universal and complete disarmament."	East German CP First Secy. Walter Ulbricht warns that if an East German-Soviet peace treaty is signed, the Western powers will have to negotiate agreements with East Germany on the continuation of free access to Berlin.	Despite the deadlock in the Evian talks and reports that fighting in Algeria has continued, France announces that its proclaimed Algerian cease-fire will be extended "indefinitely."	Augusto Guillermo Arango, chairman of the OAS fact-finding committee that just completed a weeklong inquiry in the Dominican Republic, tells reporters he "could not find any unrest" there.	
	A	**B**	**C**	**D**	**E**
	Includes developments that affect more than one world region, international organizations and important meetings of major world leaders.	*Includes all domestic and regional developments in Europe, including the Soviet Union, Turkey, Cyprus and Malta.*	*Includes all domestic and regional developments in Africa and the Middle East, including Iraq and Iran and excluding Cyprus, Turkey and Afghanistan.*	*Includes all domestic and regional developments in Latin America, the Caribbean and Canada.*	*Includes all domestic and regional developments in Asia and Pacific nations, extending from Afghanistan through all the Pacific Islands, except Hawaii.*

U.S. Politics & Social Issues	U.S. Foreign Policy & Defense	U.S. Economy & Environment	Science, Technology & Nature	Culture, Leisure & Life Style	
		An AEC investigating board reports that the AEC and its contractor, Combustion Engineering Inc., shared responsibility for the Jan. 3 accidental explosion at an SL-1 nuclear reactor in Idaho Falls, Ida.	A Dublin University research team claims to have confirmed the existence of cancer-produced coagulative fibrin in the tissues of diseased persons that enables the cancer to spread. . . . Konstantin Rudnev is named chairman of the USSR's new State Committee for the Coordination of Scientific Research, a post from which he will direct the Soviet space and rocket programs.	Archie Moore scores a 15-round decision over Italian Giulio Rinaldi to retain the world light-heavyweight championship recognized by New York, California, Massachusetts, Europe and the British Commonwealth.	June 10
	Rep. William Miller (R, N.Y.), GOP national chairman, charges that the Apr. 17 Cuban invasion failed because Kennedy ignored an Eisenhower administration-prepared plan to give the Cuban exile invaders air support.		An Iranian earthquake destroys the village of Dehkuyek, leaving at least 50 dead.	Phil Hill of Santa Monica, Calif. and Oliver Gendebien of Belgium, driving a Ferrari, win the 24-hour Le Mans auto race.	June 11
The Senate passes, 65-25, and sends to the House a slightly modified version of the administration's $6.19 billion omnibus housing bill (S1922). . . . Newsmen in Palm Beach, Fla. report that Pres. Kennedy, who is vacationing there, has walked with crutches for the past several days in an effort to relieve a severe back strain.	Former Pres. Eisenhower tells reporters he approved a program to train Cuban exiles, but never authorized a specific invasion plan nor did he promise air support. . . . Army Secy. Elvis Stahr announces that former 24th Army Division commander Maj. Gen. Edwin Walker has been given an oral "admonishment" as a result of an investigation into charges that he engaged in controversial rightwing political activities "contrary" to military customs.	The Supreme Court rules that the AEC is not required to make a definitive safety finding for a nuclear power reactor prior to its construction.			June 12
	The Kennedy administration launches a series of high-level policy meetings to discuss military and political measures by which the U.S. can demonstrate its determination to defend its position in Berlin against mounting Soviet pressures. . . . Irvin Scarbeck, a second Secretary of the U.S. Embassy in Warsaw, is arrested in Washington on charges of transmitting classified documents to the Polish government. Scarbeck is the first U.S. Foreign Service officer ever to be formally charged with espionage.	Kennedy sends Congress a draft bill to modernize the federal-state unemployment system by providing both "recession-only" and regular unemployment benefits.			June 13
Pres. Kennedy orders the emergency distribution of surplus food to Fayette and Haywood County (Tenn.) Negroes who have suffered "severe hardship" from alleged economic reprisals for their participation in a voter registration drive.	Rep. Chet Holifield (D, Calif.), chairman of the Joint Congressional Committee on Atomic Energy, declares that he and a majority of his committee feel the time has come for a resumption of U.S. nuclear testing. . . . A proposal that the entire city of Berlin be made an internationally guaranteed free city is offered in a Senate speech by Senate majority leader Mike Mansfield. The plan, which Mansfield outlined, ("on my own responsibility") as "a new way" to a solution of the Berlin problem, draws criticism from Senate GOP leaders and administration spokesmen.				June 14
Pres. Kennedy's planned reorganization of the FCC is vetoed in the House by a 323-77 vote. Opponents of the plan charged it gave the FCC chairman excessive power. (Presidential reoganization plans are subject to congressional veto.)	Pres. Kennedy awards the Collier Trophy to Adm. William Raborn for his contributions to the Polaris project.	The Senate passes and sends to joint conference a modified administration bill (HR6713) to authorize $11.56 billion to complete the interstate highway system by 1972.			June 15

F	G	H	I	J
Includes elections, federal-state relations, civil rights and liberties, crime, the judiciary, education, health care, poverty, urban affairs and population.	*Includes formation and debate of U.S. foreign and defense policies, veterans' affairs and defense spending. (Relations with specific foreign countries are usually found under the region concerned.)*	*Includes business, labor, agriculture, taxation, transportation, consumer affairs, monetary and fiscal policy, natural resources, and pollution.*	*Includes worldwide scientific, medical and technological developments, natural phenomena, U.S. weather, natural disasters, and accidents.*	*Includes the arts, religion, scholarship, communications media, sports, entertainment, fashions, fads and social life.*

	World Affairs	Europe	Africa & the Middle East	The Americas	Asia & the Pacific
June 16				A special OAS committee on the Dominican Republic recommends that current OAS sanctions against that nation be continued until it can be determined whether any genuine change in its allegedly repressive political policies will come in the wake of Generalissimo Trujillo's death. . . . *The New York Times* publishes an interview with Premier Castro in which he predicts that Cuba will become a fully socialized country within five years.	South Vietnam and the U.S. reach agreement on a program for the direct training and combat supervision of Vietnamese troops by U.S. advisers. . . . A Western proposal to provide the International Control Commission for Laos with six aircraft and communications equipment for truce supervision is rejected by Soviet Foreign Min. Gromyko.
June 17	In a formal note delivered to the USSR, the U.S. warns that it will not continue indefinitely its voluntary suspension of nuclear testing in the absence of progress at the Geneva test-ban talks. The note cites Russian demands for a three-man executive to administer the test control machinery and a limited number of inspections as obstacles to an agreement.	French Premier Michel Debré announces a government program of short-term price supports and long-term regional economic development projects in an effort to ease continuing anti-government demonstrations by French farmers.		Britain announces that the West Indies Federation will become independent May 31, 1962 if the federation members accept the proposals of a constitutional conference held in London May 31-June 16. . . . Leftist student demonstrations in Lima mark U.S. Amb. Stevenson's discussions with Peruvian leaders on hemispheric economic and social problems.	The Laotian government of Boun Oum claims that Pathet Lao forces have captured 19 government positions since the cease-fire went into effect.
June 18					
June 19	U.S.-Soviet preliminary talks on the date, site and composition of a new round of disarmament negotiations begin in Washington.	The Central Committee of the Soviet Communist Party appoves in principle a proposed revision of party rules designed to increase "inner-party democracy. . .and self-criticism." . . . Twelve prominent Hungarian Roman Catholics are sentenced to jail terms ranging from two-and-a-half to 12 years by a Budapest court for alleged "crimes against the state." . . . A bomb planted in the Paris office of the Tunis weekly *Afrique Action* injures six. It is the latest in a series of rightist terrorist actions that have accompanied the French negotiations with the Algerian rebels at Evian.	After two weeks of U.N.-assisted negotiations, delegations representing the Gizenga and Kasavubu regimes announce their agreement on plans to reconvene the Congo Parliament. . . . Britain signs an agreement ending its 62-year protectorate over oil-rich Kuwait and pledging to help defend the new nation's independence.	The Tractors for Freedom Committee rejects Castro's revised demand for 1,000 U.S. tractors and gives him until June 23 to act on the original agreement to exchange the captured rebels for 500 tractors.	
June 20	Chief U.S. test-ban negotiator Arthur Dean is recalled to Washington in what is regarded as an expression of the U.S. belief that the Geneva talks are hopelessly deadlocked.		Adolph Eichmann, taking the witness stand in his own behalf, reiterates his claim that he acted only on the orders of "my superiors." . . . The Algerian Provisional Government calls upon France to resume negotiations on an Algerian settlement by June 28.	Canadian Finance Min. Donald Fleming presents Parliament with a $6.4 billion budget, including a deliberate $650 million deficit designed to stimulate Canada's underemployed economy.	South Vietnamese sources report it has launched a major counter-offensive against Viet Cong guerillas in the Mekong Delta area south of Saigon.
June 21	An eight-man U.N. committee charged with studying possible reforms of the U.N.'s executive structure reports that it has been unable to reach agreement on any of the proposals advanced by the USSR and other states for fundamental structural changes--particularly the demand for replacing the Secretary General with a three-man executive. . . . Replying to the U.S. June 17 note, Soviet Premier Khrushchev says that the USSR will resume nuclear testing should the U.S. do so.	In a Kremlin speech, Khrushchev again cites the end of this year as a deadline for concluding a German peace and ending the Western occupation of Berlin.			
June 22		U.S. State Secy. Rusk says that recent Soviet ultimatums on West Germany and Berlin have seriously heightened world tensions.	Katanga Pres. Moise Tshombe, imprisoned by the Congolese central government since April 26, is released after publicly pledging to support the reconvening of the Congo Parliament.		The establishment of a Joint Japan-U.S. Committee on Trade and Economic Affairs is announced following talks between Pres. Kennedy and visiting Japanese Premier Hayato Ikeda.
	A	**B**	**C**	**D**	**E**
	Includes developments that affect more than one world region, international organizations and important meetings of major world leaders.	*Includes all domestic and regional developments in Europe, including the Soviet Union, Turkey, Cyprus and Malta.*	*Includes all domestic and regional developments in Africa and the Middle East, including Iraq and Iran and excluding Cyprus, Turkey and Afghanistan.*	*Includes all domestic and regional developments in Latin America, the Caribbean and Canada.*	*Includes all domestic and regional developments in Asia and Pacific nations, extending from Afghanistan through all the Pacific Islands, except Hawaii.*

U.S. Politics & Social Issues	U.S. Foreign Policy & Defense	U.S. Economy & Environment	Science, Technology & Nature	Culture, Leisure & Life Style	
Thirteen Freedom Riders are arrested in two Florida cities as the anti-segregation movement spreads further into the South.	In a Washington speech Kennedy asks for broad support of his foreign aid program, claiming that the aid is essential if the U.S. is to successfully counter "communist-controlled" movements in underdeveloped countries. . . . Pres. Kennedy names ex-State Secy. Dean Acheson to head a policy task force charged with mapping out possible U.S. responses to threatened Soviet moves concerning Berlin.			Rudolf Nureyev, 23, star of the Kirov Opera ballet group of Leningrad, leaves his touring troupe in Paris and asks for French political asylum.	June 16
				Gene Littler wins the U.S. Open golf tournament in Birmingham, Mich. . . . Southern California wins the team title at the National Collegiate Athletic track and field championships in Philadelphia.	June 17
Bernard Brous and Dale Jensen are arrested for blowing up three AT&T communications towers in Utah and Nevada. The two tell newsmen they committed the sabotage in the name of the American Republican Army, a rightwing group of unknown membership which they say plans to seize power in the U.S.			The Air Force recovers a 300-pound instrument capsule which had been ejected on radio command from the orbiting Discoverer XXV satellite (launched June 16). It is the fifth U.S. capsule retrieved from orbit.	Soviet high jumper Valeri Brumel, 19, sets a new world outdoor record of 7 ft. 3 1/8 in. in a Moscow meet. . . . Phil Hill, driving a Cooper, wins the Belgian Grand Prix at Francorchamps.	June 18
In a 5-4 decision, the Supreme Court rules "that all evidence obtained by searches and seizures in violation of the Constitution is, by that same authority, inadmissible in a state court." . . . The Supreme Court invalidates a provision of the Maryland Constitution requiring state officeholders to declare a "belief in the existence of God." . . . The U.S. Supreme Court refuses to review a Connecticut Supreme Court ruling upholding a state law which prohibits physicians to recommend the use of birth control devices.		The AFL-CIO Communications Workers of America are reported to have signed a two-year contract with American Cable and Radio Corp. which guarantees the reassignment of any employee whose job is eliminated by automation. . . . The Supreme Court rules that a 1951 Railway Labor Act amendment does not allow use of a union-shop employee's dues for political purposes over the employee's objection.			June 19
	In a speech to the National Press Club, Treasury Secy. Douglas Dillon predicts that the U.S. economy may "well be in the midst of an economic boom" by "this time next year."				June 20
Overton Brooks (D, La.), chairman of the House Space Committee, announces that the National Science Foundation has agreed to revoke a grant awarded to Edward Yellin, a Univ. of Illinois graduate student, who had been convicted of contempt for his 1958 refusal to answer House Un-American Activities Committee questions about communist activity.		An experimental $1.25 million salt water purification plant designed to provide drinking water for the 14,000 residents of Freeport, Tex. is officially put into operation. It is the first of five scheduled U.S. pilot plants. . . . Senate Republicans and conservative Democrats muster enough votes to veto Pres. Kennedy's proposed reorganization of the SEC. Opponents charged that the plan failed to specify limits in the delegation of rule-making authority.		The Most Rev. Dr. Arthur Michael Ramsey is confirmed as the 100th archbishop of Canterbury and primate of all England. Dr. Geoffrey Francis Fisher, archbishop of Canterbury since 1945, retired May 31.	June 21
	A joint conference bill (S1852) authorizing $12.571 billion for procurement of aircraft, missiles and ships in fiscal 1962, which passed the House and Senate June 12, is signed by Pres. Kennedy.	The Senate passes by voice vote and sends to joint conference a bill (HR6441) to authorize $440 million in grants to states to help communities build sewage treatment facilities.			June 22

F	G	H	I	J
Includes elections, federal-state relations, civil rights and liberties, crime, the judiciary, education, health care, poverty, urban affairs and population.	*Includes formation and debate of U.S. foreign and defense policies, veterans' affairs and defense spending. (Relations with specific foreign countries are usually found under the region concerned.)*	*Includes business, labor, agriculture, taxation, transportation, consumer affairs, monetary and fiscal policy, natural resources, and pollution.*	*Includes worldwide scientific, medical and technological developments, natural phenomena, U.S. weather, natural disasters, and accidents.*	*Includes the arts, religion, scholarship, communications media, sports, entertainment, fashions, fads and social life.*

	World Affairs	Europe	Africa & the Middle East	The Americas	Asia & the Pacific
June 23		Road blocks, building seizures and other disturbances by French farmers protesting falling prices continue despite a nationally broadcast appeal for cooperation with the government from Premier Debré.		Castro officially rejects the Tractors for Freedom Committee's final offer to exchange 500 U.S. tractors for captured rebels, saying that it is inadequate compensation for the damage caused by the U.S.-encouraged invasion. . . . Upon his return from Latin America, Adlai Stevenson tells reporters that political and economic conditions are continuing to deteriorate there despite a growing official recognition of the need for reform. He also reports that the U.S.'s role in the Bay of Pigs invasion was generally disapproved in South America.	In a New York speech, visiting Japanese Premier Ikeda expresses concern over the "protectionist tendencies" shown recently by some U.S. labor unions.
June 24			Tshombe returns to Elizabethville where he is given an emotional welcome by thousands of Katangan supporters.		South Korean Foreign Min. Kim Hong Il tells a Seoul news conference that South Korea's ruling junta would seek reunification through peaceful means and would not resort to ex-Pres. Syngman Rhee's threat to use force.
June 25		Premier Khrushchev, in a speech broadcast from Soviet Kazakhstan, predicts that the USSR will overtake the U.S. in overall economic production by 1970. . . . Two days of resumed Italian-Austrian talks over the disputed German-speaking Bolzano district in northern Italy again end in a deadlock over differing proposals to provide some measure of regional autonomy. Both nations charge the other with responsibility for the recent violence in Bolzano.	Citing historical ties dating back to the Ottoman Empire, Iraq claims sovereignty over the former British protectorate of Kuwait.		
June 26		Lt. Col. Jean Brechignac, a supporter of the April Algiers uprising, is convicted and sentenced to two years imprisonment, bringing to eight the total number of French military officers jailed for their part in the unsuccessful rebellion.	Sheik Sir Abdullah al-Salim al-Shabah of Kuwait dismisses Iraqi claims of sovereignty and warns that Kuwait will fight to defend its independence. Britain announces it will assist Kuwait in resisting foreign interference.	Venezuelan troops quell a four-and-a-half hour military rebellion in Barcelona, 150 miles east of Caracas.	
June 27		French sources report that 17 departments between the Belgian border and the Mediterranean have been hit by farmer protests.	French Pres. de Gaulle tells newsmen that he remains determined to find a settlement of the Algerian problem before the end of 1961. . . . Saudi Arabia and the UAR issue statements expressing opposition to Iraq's claim over Kuwait.	Florida newspapers report that a mixed group of Americans and Cuban exiles, numbering less than 100, are planning and training near Miami for another Cuban landing.	
June 28		In his third major policy statement on Germany since the Vienna talks, Khrushchev asserts that a German peace treaty would pose no threat to Western interests in or access to a demilitarized West Berlin. Kennedy tells newsmen that U.S. will resist all Soviet efforts to make the German partition permanent or to deprive West Berlin of the protection afforded by Western occupation. . . . Representatives of the seven European Free Trade Association states conclude two days of meetings in London on the possibility of EFTA membership in the rival European Economic Community.	Pres. de Gaulle tells a Verdun audience that France would partition Algeria only as a "last resort" should the pro-French and Moslem populations find it impossible to live together in peace. . . . In a speech to the Katangan Assembly, Pres. Tshombe repudiates his June 22 promise to participate in the reconvening of the Congolese Parliament. Instead he pledges to do everything necessary to defend "an independent Katanga."	Anti-Castro students attack a pro-Castro audience at the Buenos Aires University law school shortly after the start of a speech by Mrs. Celia Guevara, mother of Cuban Industry Min. Ernesto (Ché) Guevara.	

A	B	C	D	E
Includes developments that affect more than one world region, international organizations and important meetings of major world leaders.	*Includes all domestic and regional developments in Europe, including the Soviet Union, Turkey, Cyprus and Malta.*	*Includes all domestic and regional developments in Africa and the Middle East, including Iraq and Iran and excluding Cyprus, Turkey and Afghanistan.*	*Includes all domestic and regional developments in Latin America, the Caribbean and Canada.*	*Includes all domestic and regional developments in Asia and Pacific nations, extending from Afghanistan through all the Pacific Islands, except Hawaii.*

U.S. Politics & Social Issues	U.S. Foreign Policy & Defense	U.S. Economy & Environment	Science, Technology & Nature	Culture, Leisure & Life Style	
		The Commerce Dept. reports that wage and salary payments rose in May for the third consecutive month.	U.S. Air Force Maj. Robert White flies the experimental X-15 rocket plane at a speed of 3,690 mph., a new world record for winged planes.		June 23
Pres. Kennedy is reportedly recovering his full health after a lengthy bout with back strain and a recent viral infection.			The White House announces that Pres. Kennedy has asked the National Space Council to present recommendations for "bringing into optimum use at the earliest practicable time operational communications satellites."	Frank Budd, 21, of Villanova, runs the 100-yd. dash in world record time of 9.2 sec. at AAU national championships in New York.	June 24
Eleven Negroes and nine whites are arrested in the Jackson, Miss. train terminal after refusing to leave a segregated waitng room.					June 25
The Justice Dept., at the request of the CAB and FAA, files suit in the U.S. district court in New Orleans to end segregation in terminal facilities at New Orlean's new, federally-funded Moisant International Airport. . . . A suit to end segregated facilities at the Mobile, Ala. airport is filed in Mobile by the NAACP on behalf of three Negro army reservists. . . . The Senate passes, 90-0, and sends to conference the administration's Social Security liberalization bill (HR6027).	Pres. Kennedy recalls retired Gen. Maxwell Taylor to active service to act as Presidential Military Representative for foreign and military policy. Taylor is known as a proponent of increasing the U.S.'s conventional military capability and of reducing the policy reliance on massive nuclear retaliation.	Pres. Kennedy names a fact-finding commission under an emergency provision of the Taft-Hartley Act in an attempt to end an 11-day old strike by five maritime unions which has idled about one quarter of the entire U.S. merchant fleet. . . . Kennedy sends Congress a draft bill to accelerate the U.S. salt-water purification research program.			June 26
AFL-CIO Executive Council member A. Philip Randolph charges that the council has not made a serious effort to end "Jim Crow unionism.". . . U.S. Judge T. Whitfield Davidson orders the Dallas school board to begin integration according to a previously approved grade-a-year plan beginning with the first grade.	Vice Pres. Johnson tells the U.S. Governors Conference in Hawaii that the administration is "not ready to run away from Berlin under Russian threats.". . . The Institute of International Education reports that the number of foreign students studying, teaching or training in the U.S. totaled a record 69,683 in 1960.	Chmn. Estes Kefauver (D, Tenn.) of the Senate Judiciary, Anti-trust and Monopoly Subcommittee issues a report describing U.S. prescription drug prices as "unreasonable" when compared to industry costs and the prices charged for the same U.S. drugs sold abroad.		Rev. Dr. Franklin Clark Fry, president of the Lutheran World Federation, tells a Federation conference in Warsaw that Pope John XXIII's ecumenical efforts have led to a "greater friendliness among the Christian churches than existed before."	June 27
Congress passes and sends to the President a compromise version of an administration-backed omnibus housing bill (S1922).	Pres. Kennedy announces that he has ordered a scientific inquiry to determine if evidence exists that the Soviets have been conducting secret atomic tests in violation of the voluntary moratorium established in 1958. . . . A GOP-sponsored resolution opposing the admission of Red China to the U.N. (SCon. Res. 34) passes the Senate 76-0. The action comes amidst a growing Republican concern over officially denied rumors that the administration has been considering a possible two-Chinas U.N. membership policy.	In a message to the quarterly meeting of the AFL-CIO Executive Council, Pres. Kennedy declares that the U.S. has "emerged from the recession." A spokesman for the Executive Council, however, disputes the President's economic optimism, saying that "real recovery is nowhere in sight.". . . . Pres. Kennedy, responding to Khrushchev's recent boasts of Soviet economic supremacy by 1970, tells reporters that the USSR will not surpass the U.S. economically "at any time in the 20th century."			June 28

F	G	H	I	J
Includes elections, federal-state relations, civil rights and liberties, crime, the judiciary, education, health care, poverty, urban affairs and population.	Includes formation and debate of U.S. foreign and defense policies, veterans' affairs and defense spending. (Relations with specific foreign countries are usually found under the region concerned.)	Includes business, labor, agriculture, taxation, transportation, consumer affairs, monetary and fiscal policy, natural resources, and pollution.	Includes worldwide scientific, medical and technological developments, natural phenomena, U.S. weather, natural disasters, and accidents.	Includes the arts, religion, scholarship, communications media, sports, entertainment, fashions, fads and social life.

	World Affairs	Europe	Africa & the Middle East	The Americas	Asia & the Pacific
June 29		Pres. Kennedy meets with the National Security Council to review a report prepared by ex-State Secy. Acheson on policy alternatives for meeting Soviet pressures in Berlin.	The USSR ousts an Israeli embassy official for allegedly distributing anti-Soviet Zionist propaganda in Moscow.	Pro-Communist Venezuelan demonstrators protest a visit to Maracaibo by U.S. Amb.-to-Venezuela Teodoro Moscoso. It is the second major anti-American demonstration in Venezuela this month.	
June 30	U.S.-Soviet differences over the scope of preliminary talks aimed at clearing the way for a resumption of full-scale disarmament negotiations lead to a suspension of the preliminary talks. The USSR wished to discuss a general outline of the proposals to be considered at the resumed meetings, while the U.S. insisted on confining the preparatory talks to purely formal issues. . . . U.N. sources report that Portugal has refused to permit a five-nation U.N. subcommittee to investigate conditions in Angola.	In a speech to the National Assembly, Portuguese Premier Antonio Salazar accuses the U.S. of serving communist subversion in Africa by voting with the USSR on U.N. resolutions condemning Portuguese rule in Angola.		A spokesman for the disbanded Tractors for Freedom Committee says the group has no intention of attempting to re-open negotiations with Cuban Premier Castro on a prisoner exchange.	
July 1		The U.S. Dept. of Agriculture reports that Yugoslavia has purchased $33 million worth of U.S. farm products under the Food for Peace program.	An advance force of 600 British commandos and a squadron of RAF jet fighters arrive in Kuwait in response to a June 30 request for British military assistance from Sheik Abdullah. . . . Holden Roberto, a leader of the uprising in Angola, charges in a Leopoldville news conference that Portuguese troops have killed 25,000 civilians in their attempt to crush the Angolan revolt.		
July 2	Moscow diplomatic sources report that no high ranking Soviet officials were present at Peking celebrations marking the 40th anniversary of the Chinese Communist Party. The report is seen as further evidence of a deepening rift in Sino-Soviet relations.		The U.N. Security Council convenes at Britain's request to discuss the Kuwait-Iraqi crisis. Iraqi Rep.-to-U.N. Adnan Pachachi, with backing from the Soviet delegation, denounces the dispatch of British troops to Kuwait. Britain, with support from France, defends the action as a legitimate fulfillment of a treaty obligation with an independent nation.		General of the Army Douglas MacArthur, 81, arriving for what he calls a "sentimental journey" in the Philippines, tells a huge welcoming crowd at the Manila airport: "I have returned."
July 3	In a report to the U.N., Secy. Gen. Hammarskjold proposes that the Secretariat's professional staff be reorganized to more accurately represent the geographic composition of the U.N.'s entire membership. The reform plan specifically rejects Soviet demands for a political redistribution of all U.N. Secretariat posts so as to give parity to the Western, Soviet and neutralist blocs.	The EFTA states inaugurate a 10% tariff reduction on each others' industrial goods as part of a gradual plan to form a free trade community among the member nations.		Incomplete returns from yesterday's Mexican House of Deputies elections indicate a sweep of all 178 seats by the government's Revolutionary Institutional Party (PRI). A passenger aboard a Cubana Pak Air Line plane in flight between Varadero Beach and Havana forces the pilot at gunpoint to fly to Miami. Thirteen of the 16 passengers ask for asylum in the U.S.	Lt. Gen. Chang Do Young resigns as chairman of South Korea's ruling Supreme Council for National Reconstruction to allow the junta's vice-chairman Gen. Pak Chung Hi to hold the top post. Pak is now regarded as the chief figure behind the May 16 military revolution. . . . The 14-nation Geneva conference on Laos remains deadlocked over Western demands that the International Control Commission be strengthened before any other issues are taken up.
July 4	Pres. Kennedy and Premier Khrushchev exchange American Independence Day messages expressing both nations' desire to work for a solution to pressing international disputes.		Iraqi infantry forces and tank units are said to be massing near the Kuwait border, but no fighting has yet been reported. . . . The Katangan Assembly votes to prohibit Katanga deputies and Senators from attending any future meeting of the Congo Parliament.		South Korea's ruling military junta issues a 30-page statement accusing former Premier John M. Chang and 11 associates of aiding South Korean communists while in office.

A	B	C	D	E
Includes developments that affect more than one world region, international organizations and important meetings of major world leaders.	Includes all domestic and regional developments in Europe, including the Soviet Union, Turkey, Cyprus and Malta.	Includes all domestic and regional developments in Africa and the Middle East, including Iraq and Iran and excluding Cyprus, Turkey and Afghanistan.	Includes all domestic and regional developments in Latin America, the Caribbean and Canada.	Includes all domestic and regional developments in Asia and Pacific nations, extending from Afghanistan through all the Pacific Islands, except Hawaii.

U.S. Politics & Social Issues	U.S. Foreign Policy & Defense	U.S. Economy & Environment	Science, Technology & Nature	Culture, Leisure & Life Style	
An amended joint conference bill (HR6027) to liberalize Social Security benefits for an estimated 4.4 million persons and to permit men to retire at 62 passes both houses of Congress and is sent to the President.	In a Senate speech J. William Fulbright warns against compromising the U.S.'s basically sound foreign policy by over-commitment to "peripheral struggles." "Cuba, Laos, the Soviet cosmonaut" are not, he argues, "a threat to our national security. . .by reacting to them injudiciously, we disfigure our national style and undermine our policies."	The Labor Dept. reports that the number of major U.S. industrial areas with more than 6% unemployment declined from a record high of 101 in March and April to 96 in May and to 88 in June. . . . Kennedy signs into law a bill (S610) creating a U.S. Travel Service in the Commerce Dept. to promote foreign tourism in America. . . . Kennedy signs a joint conference bill (HR 6713) authorizing funds for the completion of the U.S. Interstate Highway Program.	Three satellites--one of them equipped with a newly developed atomic power source--are successfully launched into orbit from Cape Canaveral in the first triple launch ever attempted.		June 29
A resolution endorsing the 1954 Supreme Court decision on school desegregation is adopted by the National Education Association at the close of its annual convention in Atlantic City, N.J.		Pres. Kennedy signs a bill extending the 52% tax rate on corporate income. He also signs an administration bill (HR7677) to increase the ceiling on the national debt by $5 billion to a $298 billion total for fiscal 1962. . . . Trans World Airlines, Inc. files a civil antitrust suit in New York against Howard Hughes, 55, and his personal corporation, Hughes Tool Co., charging them with acquiring and using controling interest in TWA "for their own purposes" and contrary to the best interests of the airline.	The U.S. Navy reports that a nuclear-powered Transit IV-A navigational satellite launched yesterday with two others is "working perfectly."		June 30
				Mickey Wright 26, wins the U.S. Women's Open golf tournament in Springfield, N.J. for $1,800.	July 1
	Pres. Kennedy is reported to have asked the FBI to investigate an alleged Pentagon leak which led to the publication in the July 3 issue of *Newsweek* of the Joint Chiefs of Staff's recommendations on Berlin policies. . . . Sens. Bourke Hickenlooper (R, Ia.) and Henry Jackson (D, Wash.) add their support to growing congressional pressures for a resumption of U.S. atomic tests.	At a news conference on the eve of the Brotherhood of Teamsters convention in Miami, Teamster Pres. Hoffa accuses the Justice and Labor Depts. and Atty. Gen. Robert Kennedy of conducting a "vendetta" against the U.S. labor movement.		Nobel Prize-winning novelist Ernest Hemingway, 61, dies in Ketchum, Ida. of a self-inflicted gun wound in the head.	July 2
Minnesota Gov. Elmer Anderson orders the state's Human Rights Commission to investigate the treatment of six Minnesotan Freedom Riders imprisoned in Jackson, Miss.		Acting on the recommendation of the recently appointed Presidential fact-finding commission, the Justice Dept. seeks and obtains a temporary Taft-Hartley law injunction to the 18-day strike of five U.S. maritime unions.			July 3
				La Notte, an Italian film written and directed by Michelangelo Antonioni, wins a Golden Bear (top prize) at the Berlin film festival.	July 4

F	G	H	I	J
Includes elections, federal-state relations, civil rights and liberties, crime, the judiciary, education, health care, poverty, urban affairs and population.	*Includes formation and debate of U.S. foreign and defense policies, veterans' affairs and defense spending. (Relations with specific foreign countries are usually found under the region concerned.)*	*Includes business, labor, agriculture, taxation, transportation, consumer affairs, monetary and fiscal policy, natural resources, and pollution.*	*Includes worldwide scientific, medical and technological developments, natural phenomena, U.S. weather, natural disasters, and accidents.*	*Includes the arts, religion, scholarship, communications media, sports, entertainment, fashions, fads and social life.*

	World Affairs	Europe	Africa & the Middle East	The Americas	Asia & the Pacific
July 5	In a formal reply to the U.S. test-ban note of June 17, the USSR charges that American complaints about the lack of progress in the Geneva talks are simply a pretext for justifying a resumption of U.S. atomic testing.	Queen Elizabeth names former British Prime Minister Sir Anthony Eden the Earl of Avon.	Pres. Joseph Kasavubu announces that the Congolese Parliament will be reconvened in mid-July. *The New York Times* reports that Congolese army commander, Gen. Joseph Mobutu, had opposed the decision to reconvene. . . . Nearly 100 Algerian Moslems are dead and several hundred wounded following five days of strikes, riots and demonstrations in protest against an alleged French plan to partition Algeria into Moslem and French sectors.		
July 6		CP First Secy. Walter Ulbricht tells the East German Volkskammer (lower house) that a Soviet-East German peace treaty which would end Allied rights in West Berlin is "on history's calender for 1961."	British military spokesmen report that they doubt Iraqi troops will be ordered to attack Kuwait in the face of the more than 4,000 British troops now stationed there. . . . Eichmann concludes 12 days of defense testimony with the claim "I have never killed anyone."		
July 7	The USSR casts its 95th veto in the U.N. Security Council to preveNuclear Testing adoption of a British resolution calling for international recognition of Kuwait's independence and territorial integrity.	Turkish Pres. Cemal Gursel announces that national elections will be held in October.	In a personal message to Pres. de Gaulle, Tunisian Pres. Habib Bourguiba demands that France agree to negotiations on the withdrawal of French forces from Bizerte, the last French-held base on Tunisian territory. . . . Iraqi Premier Abdul Kassem tells newsmen in Baghdad that Iraq never had any intention of using force to press its claims over Kuwait.	The first anti-government demonstrations to be permitted in the Dominican Republic in 31 years erupt into street violence. Sources in Ciudad Trujillo report one dead, six injured and 20 arrested.	
July 8		Soviet Premier Khrushchev announces that the USSR has suspended planned troop reductions and has authorized a 25% increase in defense spending for 1961. Khrushchev describes the moves as unavoidable in the face of a Western military build-up amidst the deepening East-West crisis over the future of Germany and Berlin.		Dominican Pres. Joaquin Balaguer orders an investigation into possible communist or pro-Castro influence behind the disturbances that followed yesterday's rally of opposition groups.	*The New York Times* reports that Outer Mongolia has accepted an American offer to establish diplomatic relations with the U.S. The U.S. originally proposed the diplomatic ties to determine if Outer Mongolia was genuinely independent and qualified for U.N. membership.
July 9	Chinese Foreign Min. Chen Yi, in a Peking address, denies reports of a growing ideological rift between Communist China and the USSR and reaffirms China's support for the 1957 Moscow Declaration on peaceful co-existence.	An agreement to grant Greece associate member status in the European Economic Community is signed in Athens.	(Jay David) Whittaker Chambers, 60, confessed ex-communist spy whose public testimony before the House Un-American Activities Committee in 1948 led to the imprisonment (1951-1954) of ex-State Dept. official Alger Hiss for perjury, dies of a heart attack in Westminster, Md.	*The New York Times* reports that Argentina had a $27.5 million unfavorable balance of trade during the first quarter of 1961.	
July 10					

A	B	C	D	E
Includes developments that affect more than one world region, international organizations and important meetings of major world leaders.	Includes all domestic and regional developments in Europe, including the Soviet Union, Turkey, Cyprus and Malta.	Includes all domestic and regional developments in Africa and the Middle East, including Iraq and Iran and excluding Cyprus, Turkey and Afghanistan.	Includes all domestic and regional developments in Latin America, the Caribbean and Canada.	Includes all domestic and regional developments in Asia and Pacific nations, extending from Afghanistan through all the Pacific Islands, except Hawaii.

U.S. Politics & Social Issues	U.S. Foreign Policy & Defense	U.S. Economy & Environment	Science, Technology & Nature	Culture, Leisure & Life Style	
	General Douglas MacArthur, on a visit to the Philippines, tells an informal gathering of Filipino Congressmen that the U.S. during the Korean War could have destroyed Communist China's war-making ability "for generations to come."		Israeli scientists launch a 600-pound, multi-stage rocket to an altitude of 50 miles. Israel says the rocket was designed to carry out meteorological experiments in the stratosphere and ionosphere.		July 5
The Justice Dept. files suit in U.S. district court in Mississippi to ban discrimination against prospective Negro voters in Clarke and Forrest counties. Only 25 of the over 10,000 eligible Negro voters in the two counties are registered.	*The New York Herald Tribune* reports that the FBI investigation of Pentagon leaks had been ordered not to find the leak but to emphasize the credibility of the July 3 *Newsweek* story that the U.S. was studying major military moves to deal with the Berlin crisis.	Representatives of the American Medical Association and the U.S. Chamber of Commerce appear before the Senate Antitrust and Monopoly Subcommittee to voice their opposition to a proposed bill by subcommittee chairman Estes Kefauver that would bar excessive prescription drug prices. . . . The National Safety Council reports that a record 509 Americans lost their lives in auto accidents over the 4th of July weekend.	Flooding in the Honshu district of Japan leaves 265 people dead, over 1,200 injured and 87 missing.		July 6
The N.Y. Court of Appeals rules that public schools violate no constitutional prohibition when they use a non-sectarian prayer recommended by the Board of Regents.	Adolf Berle Jr., who is believed to have played an important role in the planning of the unsuccessful Bay of Pigs landing, announces his retirement as chairman of Pres. Kennedy's task force on Latin America.	The Teamsters convention in Miami Beach ends, after the 2,200 delegates overwhelmingly re-elected James Hoffa to a second five-year term as union president. The delegates also vote (a) to raise Hoffa's salary from $50,000 to $75,000; (b) to more than double the percentage of union dues sent from the locals to the national union; and (c) to authorize Hoffa to organize workers in any industry.		Australian Rod Laver defeats American Chuck McKinley in straight sets to win the men's singles championship of the All-England tennis tourney at Wimbledon. . . . New Zealander Murray Halberg, 28, runs the two-mile in world record time 8 min. 30 sec. at an international meet in Jyvaeskylae, Finland.	July 7
				Angela Mortimer, of England, wins the women's singles title at Wimbledon. . . . Mary Stewart, 15, of Vancouver, B.C. swims the women's 110-meter butterfly in world record time of 1 min. 10 sec. at an international AAU meet in Tacoma, Wash.	July 8
Another week of arrests arising out of segregation tests in Jackson, Miss. brings to 216 the total number of Negro and white Freedom Riders who have been arrested in that city since May 24. . . . The annual report of the NAACP indicates that Negro political activity increased 95% in 1960 in those areas where the organization sponsored voter registration drives.					July 9
	U.S. Defense Secy. Robert McNamara discloses that Pres. Kennedy has ordered a general review of U.S. military strength and planned defense expenditures in light of the continuing Berlin crisis and Khrushchev's July 8 announcement of increased Soviet defense spending. . . . The Defense Dept. issues a directive instructing armed forces commanders to refrain from conducting political indoctrination programs among their troops.	An 80-day injunction against continuance of the U.S. maritime strike is issued by U.S. Judge Sylvester Ryan in New York. The injunction, issued under a national "health and safety" provision of the Taft-Hartley Act extends the temporary injunction ordered earlier by Ryan.		The U.S. film, *The Defiant Ones*, wins the Prague Film Festival Award for the best movie aimed at "better relations between people."	July 10

F	G	H	I	J
Includes elections, federal-state relations, civil rights and liberties, crime, the judiciary, education, health care, poverty, urban affairs and population.	*Includes formation and debate of U.S. foreign and defense policies, veterans' affairs and defense spending. (Relations with specific foreign countries are usually found under the region concerned.)*	*Includes business, labor, agriculture, taxation, transportation, consumer affairs, monetary and fiscal policy, natural resources, and pollution.*	*Includes worldwide scientific, medical and technological developments, natural phenomena, U.S. weather, natural disasters, and accidents.*	*Includes the arts, religion, scholarship, communications media, sports, entertainment, fashions, fads and social life.*

	World Affairs	Europe	Africa & the Middle East	The Americas	Asia & the Pacific
July 11	In a Moscow speech, Premier Khrushchev denounces the U.N.'s resistance to Soviet proposals for a tripartite U.N. executive and warns that the USSR would use force to prevent enforcement of a decision by the U.N. as presently constituted if it were detrimental to Soviet security.	The special Paris military tribunal condemns to death in absentia eight generals and colonels who took a leading part in the April Algiers coup attempt.			A treaty renewing Communist China's pledge to assist North Korea against any future armed attack is signed in Peking. The USSR signed a similar mutual defense pact with North Korea on July 6.
July 12		West Germany formally rejects a Feb. 17 Soviet proposal for direct Soviet-West German negotiations on a World War II peace treaty, adding that West Germany would never accept a settlement that denied the eventual reunification of the German people. . . . French Pres. de Gaulle tells a nationwide TV audience that there is "no chance" that the West will capitulate to Soviet demands on a German settlement.			Pakistani Pres. Ayub Khan, in an address to a joint session of Congress during his state visit to the U.S., couples an appeal for expanded American aid to his country with a somber warning that "unless Pakistan is able to meet the economic needs of its people, in another 15 or 20 years we shall be overtaken by communism."
July 13		Soviet Foreign Min. Gromyko and Yugoslav Foreign Min. Koca Popovic sign a joint communique in Moscow pledging to continue efforts toward improving Soviet-Yugoslav relations.		U.S. Amb.-to-U.N. Adlai Stevenson tells the House Foreign Affairs Committee that most Latin American leaders would oppose any unilateral U.S. action against Cuba--such as a blocade or use of force--without prior OAS sanction. . . . James Coyne resigns as governor of the Bank of Canada in the midst of a political controversy growing out of his outspoken opposition to Canadian Finance Min. Donald Fleming's policies of currency expansion and deficit spending.	Pakistani Pres. Ayub Khan tells a National Press Club audience in Washington that American arms aid to India would put a "tremendous strain" on U.S.-Pakistani relations.
July 14	U.S. State Secy. Rusk issues a Kennedy-approved statement declaring that the U.S. would use its Security Council veto to block adoption of Soviet proposals for a three-man U.N. executive.	Canada and India follow Australia and New Zealand in expressing concern over possible harm to the economic wellbeing of the Commonwealth nations should Britain join the European Economic Community. . . . By a 3-2 margin, Turkish voters approve a new national parliamentary constitution in a nationwide referendum.			
July 15	Britain and the U.S., in a note to Secy. Gen. Hammarskjold, formally request that the deadlocked test-ban question be brought before the next session of the General Assembly scheduled to begin Sept. 19.	Soviet cosmonaut Yuri Gagarin ends a five-day goodwill visit to Great Britain.			
July 16			The French government formally rejects a July 7 Tunisian demand to begin talks on the withdrawal of French troops from their base at Bizerte. The statement asserts that an atmosphere of Tunisian "threats" precludes French participation in negotiations at this time.		

A	B	C	D	E
Includes developments that affect more than one world region, international organizations and important meetings of major world leaders.	Includes all domestic and regional developments in Europe, including the Soviet Union, Turkey, Cyprus and Malta.	Includes all domestic and regional developments in Africa and the Middle East, including Iraq and Iran and excluding Cyprus, Turkey and Afghanistan.	Includes all domestic and regional developments in Latin America, the Caribbean and Canada.	Includes all domestic and regional developments in Asia and Pacific nations, extending from Afghanistan through all the Pacific Islands, except Hawaii.

U.S. Politics & Social Issues	U.S. Foreign Policy & Defense	U.S. Economy & Environment	Science, Technology & Nature	Culture, Leisure & Life Style	
Maryland Gov. J. Millard Tawes publicly apologizes for four recent incidents in which African diplomats were denied service in segregated Maryland restaurants.	Deputy Defense Secy. Roswell Gilpatric reveals to a Washington news conference that the current general defense review includes a study of possible mobilization of National Guard and Army Reserve units.			The National League All-Stars score a 5-4 victory over the American League in the first game of this year's two-game All-Star series. . . . Terry Downes of London wins New York, Massachusetts and Europe recognition as world middleweight champion by scoring a ninth round TKO over title defender Paul Pender of Massachusetts.	July 11
About 1,000 delegates to the annual NAACP convention in Philadelphia take a Freedom Train ride to Washington where a special delegation meets with Pres. Kennedy. The NAACP leaders praise the President for his executive action in civil rights but express dismay over his failure to give clear support to new rights legislation.	Commenting on Pakistani Pres. Ayub Khan's speech to Congress in which he linked poverty with the triumph of communism, GOP Sen. Hugh Scott says that Khan was "the best witness. . . yet heard at the Capitol" for passage of the administration's foreign aid program.		Tiros III, a 285-pound weather satellite equipped to photograph the birth and development of hurricanes, is successfully launched into orbit by NASA scientists at Cape Canaveral.		July 12
NAACP chief counsel Thurgood Marshall, in a speech to the group's annual convention, calls for an integration campaign against "every segregated facility."	The Defense Dept. announces that 1,300 copies of its new orientation film, *The Challenge of Ideas*, are being distributed to the armed forces to replace two unsanctioned but frequently used indoctrination films produced by conservative political groups.	A 12-count mail fraud indictment against Teamster Pres. James Hoffa is dismissed by U.S., Judge Joseph Lieb in Orlando, Fla. because of technical defects in the indictment process. The charges involved alleged misuse of union pension funds. . . . *The Wall Street Journal* reports that Western European investment in U.S. plants and other facilities now totals an estimated $3.5 billion, up over $500 million since January 1959.			July 13
Kennedy sends Congress a proposed Washington home rule bill that would permit D.C. citizens to elect a mayor, a seven-member legislative council, and a non-voting delegate to the House of Representatives.		Seven brokerage firms and 26 officers are indicted by a New York federal grand jury on charges of conspiring to defraud the public in the sale of United Dye and Chemical Corp. stock.		A plea for worldwide aid to underdeveloped countries is stressed by Pope John XXIII in a 25,000 word papal encyclical outlining the Roman Catholic Church's social views and responsibilities. The letter also reaffirms the Church's opposition to birth control practices.	July 14
Amidst growing national attention, the city of Newburgh, N.Y. adopts a controversial code governing the distribution of welfare funds. The new rules require able-bodied male relief recipients to work on city jobs and they prohibit payments to persons who quit jobs and to unwed mothers who continue to have illegitimate children.			*The New York Times* reports that Rutgers Univ. scientists have patented a new antibiotic called candicidin which is said to be effective against highly resistant yeast-like fungi in humans and plants.	Arnold Palmer wins the British Open golf tournament in Birkdale, England.	July 15
The 52d annual NAACP convention concludes in Philadelphia after delegates adopted resolutions endorsing the sit-in and freedom ride movements and condemning the John Birch Society and other organizations (including black nationalist groups like the Black Muslims) for advocating racial separation.				Valeri Brummel of the USSR highjumps 7 ft. 4 in. and Ralph Boston of the U.S. broadjumps 27 ft. 1 3/4 in. to set new world records at a U.S.- Soviet track meet in Moscow. . . . Jacques Anquetil, 27, of France, wins the 22-day, 2,750-mile Tour de France bicycle race which finished in Paris. . . . The Annociade Museum of Modern Art in St. Tropez, France reports the theft of 57 modern paintings valued at about $2 million.	July 16

F	G	H	I	J
Includes elections, federal-state relations, civil rights and liberties, crime, the judiciary, education, health care, poverty, urban affairs and population.	*Includes formation and debate of U.S. foreign and defense policies, veterans' affairs and defense spending. (Relations with specific foreign countries are usually found under the region concerned.)*	*Includes business, labor, agriculture, taxation, transportation, consumer affairs, monetary and fiscal policy, natural resources, and pollution.*	*Includes worldwide scientific, medical and technological developments, natural phenomena, U.S. weather, natural disasters, and accidents.*	*Includes the arts, religion, scholarship, communications media, sports, entertainment, fashions, fads and social life.*

	World Affairs	Europe	Africa & the Middle East	The Americas	Asia & the Pacific
July 17	U.S. and Soviet envoys open a second round of preliminary talks in Moscow on proposals for a resumption this summer of full-scale East-West disarmament talks.	In parallel notes, Britain, France and the U.S. inform the USSR that Premier Khrushchev's proposals for settlement of the Berlin and German questions are wholly unacceptable to the West and could not be the basis for serious negotiations on these problems.	Pres. Habib Bourguiba, addressing the Tunisian National Assembly, says he will give France 24 hours to begin negotiations on French troop withdrawals from Bizerte and on Tunisian claims to a French-occupied border region of the Sahara. In the event of a French refusal, Bourguiba says he will order the Bizerte base surrounded and the Tunisian flag raised over the disputed Saharan territory.		
July 18		The leaders of the six EEC nations reach an agreement in Bonn on the establishment of a system of regular political consultation and cooperation.	France rejects the Tunisian ultimatum on negotiations and warns that French forces will take "necessary" measures to protect the Bizerte installation and to prevent a Tunisian incursion into the Sahara.		The Japanese cabinet approves a five-year, $3.3 billion plan to expand the nation's armed forces.
July 19			Shots fired at a French helicopter landing at Bizerte by Tunisian forces under orders to surround the French base quickly escalate into heavy fighting. . . . Britain begins withdrawing the emergency troops which were sent to the former British protectorate of Kuwait during its crisis with neighboring Iraq. . . . U.N. sources in Kasai and Kivu Provinces report that hundreds and perhaps thousands of persons have been killed during several months of tribal warfare.	Mexican Pres. Adolfo Lopez Mateos announces that he has ordered the compensated expropriation of 266,760 U.S.-owned acres on the Tehuantepec Isthmus in Oaxaca state; it is the first Mexican expropriation of U.S. property since 1958.	
July 20		Berlin sources report a marked increase in the number of East German refugees fleeing to West Berlin to seek asylum in West Germany. The increased exodus is attributed to fears that the current Berlin dispute may lead to an interruption in access to the West.	French troops, supported by tanks and aircraft, break the Tunisian blockade and drive into the residential sections of Bizerte. A French demand for the city's surrender is rebuffed by its Tunisian defenders. Pres. Bourguiba announces the severing of diplomatic relations with France. . . . Representatives of France and of the rebel Algerian Provisional Government meet in Lugrin, France to resume negotiations on conditions for a negotiated end to the Algerian rebellion.		
July 21			The withdrawal of British troops from Kuwait is temporarily suspended in the face of renewed Iraqi threats against the former British protectorate.	Economy Min. Roberto Aleman announces that industrial development credits totaling $154.5 million from the U.S. and $50 million from the International Bank have been pledged to Argentina.	
July 22	The U.N. Security Council, which convened yesterday to discuss the French-Tunisian crisis, votes 10-0 to call on both sides to immediately cease fighting and return their forces to the positions they occupied before the shooting began.		France and Tunisia inform the Security Council that a cease-fire has been achieved in Bizerte. French troops, however, are reported to be remaining in the advanced positions within the city which they occupied during the fighting.	A U.S. plan to subsidize an increased number of daily commercial flights from Cuba to the U.S. and to pay the airfare of all those wishing to leave is thwarted by a Cuban Transport Ministry order limiting Cuba-U.S. flights to no more than two a day.	

A	B	C	D	E
Includes developments that affect more than one world region, international organizations and important meetings of major world leaders.	Includes all domestic and regional developments in Europe, including the Soviet Union, Turkey, Cyprus and Malta.	Includes all domestic and regional developments in Africa and the Middle East, including Iraq and Iran and excluding Cyprus, Turkey and Afghanistan.	Includes all domestic and regional developments in Latin America, the Caribbean and Canada.	Includes all domestic and regional developments in Asia and Pacific nations, extending from Afghanistan through all the Pacific Islands, except Hawaii.

U.S. Politics & Social Issues	U.S. Foreign Policy & Defense	U.S. Economy & Environment	Science, Technology & Nature	Culture, Leisure & Life Style	
				The U.S. wins the men's team title, 124-111, at the U.S.-Soviet track meet in Moscow. The USSR won the women's competition, 68-39. . . . Tyrus (Ty) Cobb, the first major league player elected to baseball's Hall of Fame and considered by many to have been the game's greatest star, dies of cancer at 74.	July 17
Sen. Barry Goldwater tells reporters he would "like to see every city in the country" adopt Newburgh, N.Y.'s rigid welfare rules. N.Y. Gov. Nelson Rockefeller is opposed to the Newburgh plan. . . . A bill to create a Child Care Institute in the Public Health Service for expanded research into child health problems is presented to Congress by Pres. Kennedy.		The Commerce Dept. reports that total U.S. personal incomes rose to a record seasonally-adjusted rate of $416.7 billion in June up #13.5 billion from the recession "low" in February.			July 18
In a special appeal at his regular news conference, Pres. Kennedy urges the strengthening of "all programs which contribute to the physical fitness of our youth," adding that many foreign youths have "moved ahead" of American youth in fitness.	The AEC denies reports that it has been ordered to prepare for a resumption of nuclear tests. . . . Kennedy denies rumors that he has sought the resignation or transfer of Undersecy. of State Chester Bowles for his outspoken views on foreign policy.				July 19
	Responsibility for "a greatly accelerated civil defense effort, including a nationwide fall-out shelter program," is transferred from the Office of Civil and Defense Mobilization to the Defense Dept. by executive order of Pres. Kennedy.	Pres. Kennedy signs a compromise bill (HR6441) expanding the U.S. water pollution control program and increasing aid to communities for the construction of sewage treatment plants. . . . The House votes 231-179 to veto the administration's reorganization plan for the National Labor Relations Board.			July 20
			U.S. Air Force Capt. Virgil (Gus) Grissom rides a Mercury capsule called Liberty Bell 7 to an altitude of 118 miles and then "splashes down" in the Atlantic after a 16-min. suborbital flight. A premature automatic hatch opening upon splash-down forces Grissom to dive from the craft which sinks despite a helicopter recovery effort. Grissom is rescued uninjured.		July 21
	A ceremonial phone call from Canadian P.M. John Diefenbaker in White Horse, Yukon Territory to Pres. Kennedy in Hyannisport, Mass. marks the completion of a new trans-Canada microwave telecommunications network linking the U.S. with Alaska.		The Federation Aeronautique Internationale in Paris announces official recognition of world records achieved by Soviet Maj. Yuri Gagarin in his orbital flight Apr. 12 and by U.S. Cmndr. Alan Shepard in his suborbital flight May 5. . . . The National Geographic Society reports that Zinjanthropus boisei, a primitive toolmaking race of man of whom fossil remnants were found in Tanganyika in 1959, probably lived over 1.75 million years ago, much earlier than had been previously thought.		July 22

F	G	H	I	J
Includes elections, federal-state relations, civil rights and liberties, crime, the judiciary, education, health care, poverty, urban affairs and population.	Includes formation and debate of U.S. foreign and defense policies, veterans' affairs and defense spending. (Relations with specific foreign countries are usually found under the region concerned.)	Includes business, labor, agriculture, taxation, transportation, consumer affairs, monetary and fiscal policy, natural resources, and pollution.	Includes worldwide scientific, medical and technological developments, natural phenomena, U.S. weather, natural disasters, and accidents.	Includes the arts, religion, scholarship, communications media, sports, entertainment, fashions, fads and social life.

	World Affairs	Europe	Africa & the Middle East	The Americas	Asia & the Pacific
July 23	The Soviet armed forces newspaper *Krasnava Zvezda* charges that the U.S. launchings of the Midas III and Tiros III satellites into orbits over Soviet territory constitute acts of espionage and aggression.		Reports from Paris and Tunis estimate that 670 Tunisian soldiers and civilians and 30 French troops were killed in the three-and-a-half days of fighting at Bizerte. Estimates of the wounded run over 1000.		
July 24		U.S. Defense Secy. McNamara concludes three days of meetings with NATO officials during which he urged a general strengthening of Western defenses in the face of the continuing Berlin tensions.	With members of Ben Gurion's Mapai Party abstaining, the Israeli Knesset (Parliament) votes 54-0 to uphold a cabinet decision exonerating ex-Defense Min. Pinhas Lavon.	In a published report on his recent Latin American tour, Adlai Stevenson declares that Latin American governments can successfully resist communism only by working to eliminate the poverty and insecurity which encourages its spread.	
July 25			U.N. Secy. Gen Hammarskjold conducts a two-day, Tunisian-requested, on-the-spot inspection of the situation at Bizerte. . . . A U.N. subcommittee commissioned to investigate conditions in Angola reports to the U.N. that it has been barred admission to the territory by Portugal.	Brazilian Pres. Janio Quadros announces plans to resume diplomatic relations with the USSR broken since 1947. . . . Six Soviet-built MiG jet fighters participate in a military air show over Havana. It is the first public display of the MiGs by the Cuban air force.	
July 26				Premier Castro announces that all Cuban political, military, labor and other revolutionary organizations will be integrated into a single "United Party of Cuba's Socialist Revolution.". . . Although Cuban officials released the passengers and crew of the hijacked Eastern Air Lines Electra, Premier Castro says that the plane will not be returned unless the U.S. agrees to return all seized Cuban planes flown to the U.S.	
July 27		Berlin sources report an increase in East German army and police surveillance of highway traffic to Berlin in an apparent effort to discourage the increased flow of East German refugees bound for West Berlin. . . . The British House of Commons, over heavy Labor and Liberal opposition, votes to approve a new series of austerity measures proposed by P.M. Macmillan's Conservative government.	The Congolese Parliament formally reconvenes under U.N. protection outside of Leopoldville. The pro-Gizenga faction, which includes almost half of the more than 200 delegates in attendance, unexpectedly captured a number of key Parliamentary posts during preliminary elections held July 25. No Katanga representatives are present despite repeated appeals to Tshombe for his cooperation. . . . Declarations of support and aid for Tunisia from other Arab states continue to be reported throughout the Middle East.		
July 28		A special British election court rules that Anthony Wedgewood-Benn is legally a peer and thus ineligible to take his recently won seat in the House of Commons.	A second U.N. Security Council meeting devoted to the Bizerte crisis hears a report from Secy. Gen. Hammarskjold confirming Tunisian charges that French forces have failed to comply with the terms of the Security Council's cease-fire resolution. . . . The resumed French-Algerian rebel talks being held in Lugrin are suspended after the two parties became hopelessly deadlocked over claims to the Sahara and its oil and mineral resources.		
July 29			A two-day Security Council debate on the Bizerte crisis ends without agreement.	Two members of the 10-man team of Cuban captives who had come to the U.S. to negotiate the abortive tractors-for-prisoners exchange announce in Miami that they are renouncing their pledge to return to Cuba.	

A	B	C	D	E
Includes developments that affect more than one world region, international organizations and important meetings of major world leaders.	*Includes all domestic and regional developments in Europe, including the Soviet Union, Turkey, Cyprus and Malta.*	*Includes all domestic and regional developments in Africa and the Middle East, including Iraq and Iran and excluding Cyprus, Turkey and Afghanistan.*	*Includes all domestic and regional developments in Latin America, the Caribbean and Canada.*	*Includes all domestic and regional developments in Asia and Pacific nations, extending from Afghanistan through all the Pacific Islands, except Hawaii.*

U.S. Politics & Social Issues	U.S. Foreign Policy & Defense	U.S. Economy & Environment	Science, Technology & Nature	Culture, Leisure & Life Style	
				The Japanese film *The Island* and the Soviet movie *The Clear Sky* win Grand Prize honors at the Moscow Film Festival. . . . Bernard Bartzen, of Dallas, Tex., wins the U.S. national clay courts tennis title in Chicago.	July 23
FBI director J. Edgar Hoover reports that the U.S. crime rate in 1960 increased an "astounding" 14% over 1959 and was up 98% from 1950. . . . An Eastern Air Lines Electra, enroute from Miami to Tampa, is hijacked by an armed passenger and forced to fly to Havana, Cuba.		The Agriculture Dept. reports that U.S. stocks of wheat, corn and sorghum stood at all-time record levels at the start of the 1961 marketing season (late June).			July 24
	Pres. Kennedy appears on national TV to outline a long-term program to increase the manpower, weaponry and combat readiness of the U.S. armed forces. Kennedy says the build-up is necessary to assure fulfillment of U.S. commitments in Germany and elsewhere. Public and congressional reaction to the President's speech is reportedly favorable.				July 25
The Justice Dept., at the request of the CAB and FAA, files suit in Montgomery to end racial segregation at Montgomery's Dannelly Field airport. . . . Negroes dine at 36 previously segregated restaurants in Dallas, Tex. as the first step in a citywide citizens' plan to prepare the community for this fall's scheduled school desegregation. . . . The White House issues a Civil Service Commission-drafted ethics code for federal employees designed to prohibit any activity that might raise even "a reasonable question" concerning a conflict of public duties and private interests.	Pres. Kennedy sends Congress a draft resolution authorizing him to call up the Ready Reserve, extend armed forces enlistments and increase the monthly draft calls. . . . Defense Secy. McNamara says that the additional civil defense funds requested by the President will be used to make fall-out shelters available to one-fourth of the U.S. population "in the near future."				July 26
GOP spokesmen couple expressions of support for Kennedy's expanded defense requests with demands for reduced spending on domestic programs.		After reducing the powers of the proposed farmer advisory committees, the Senate passes the administration's omnibus farm bill (S1643) and sends it to joint conference where differences with the House version (HR8230) are to be reconciled.			July 27
The U.S. Public Health Service estimates that illegitimate births increased from 180,000 in 1958 to 221,000 in 1959. The figure represents about 5.2% of 4,295,000 live births recorded in the U.S. in 1959. . . . The Senate passes and sends to the House six anti-racket bills requested by Atty. Gen. Robert Kennedy.	The Senate, without opposition, passes a resolution (SJ Res. 120) and a bill (S2311) authorizing the President to call up as many as 250,000 reservists and to buy $958.6 million worth of military equipment to deal with the deepening Berlin crisis.	American Medical Association's House of Delegates adopts a resolution permitting to consult or teach with osteopaths who follow accepted medical tenets.	The discovery by Soviet astronomers of an unprecedentedly large cluster of white dwarf stars in the Lyra constellation is reported by the news agency Tass. . . . The American Medical Association's House of Delegates, meeting in New York, adopts a resolution recommending massive use of the Sabin live-virus polio vaccine. The proposal was opposed by Dr. Jonas Salk, who asserted the superior safety and practicality of his killed-virus Salk vaccine over the Sabin oral type.	Ten modern paintings, including works by Picasso and Miro and valued at more than $400,000 are stolen from the Pittsburgh home of retired steel executive G. David Thompson.	July 28
	A special Vietnam task force presents Pres. Kennedy with a report urging expanded U.S. aid to enable South Vietnam to increase its armed forces by 15% and to begin a resettlement program for residents of indefensible villages.				July 29

F	G	H	I	J
Includes elections, federal-state relations, civil rights and liberties, crime, the judiciary, education, health care, poverty, urban affairs and population.	Includes formation and debate of U.S. foreign and defense policies, veterans' affairs and defense spending. (Relations with specific foreign countries are usually found under the region concerned.)	Includes business, labor, agriculture, taxation, transportation, consumer affairs, monetary and fiscal policy, natural resources, and pollution.	Includes worldwide scientific, medical and technological developments, natural phenomena, U.S. weather, natural disasters, and accidents.	Includes the arts, religion, scholarship, communications media, sports, entertainment, fashions, fads and social life.

	World Affairs	Europe	Africa & the Middle East	The Americas	Asia & the Pacific
July 30	Washington sources report that Soviet Premier Khrushchev outlined his current views on the Berlin and German questions during two days of meetings July 26-27 with John J. McCloy, Pres. Kennedy's adviser on disarmament.	A new Khrushchev-approved program for the Soviet Union CP is published by the Moscow newspaper *Pravda* . The program, which outlines policy goals over the next 20 years, is designed to upgrade and further communize economic life in the USSR and to promote the triumph of world socialism within an international context of "peaceful co-existence."	The millionth immigrant since the founding of the Israeli state arrives in Tel Aviv.		
July 31		P.M. Macmillan announces to Parliament that he will seek formal negotiations on the terms and conditions for British membership in the EEC. Macmillan's speech is followed by announcements from the six other EFTA states that they too will seek some kind of association with the EEC.	Congo Pres. Kasavubu meets in Brazzaville with Tshombe, but fails to win his approval for Katangan participation in the reconvened session of the Congo Parliament.		
Aug. 1		Premier Khrushchev tells a Kremlin reception that the USSR has sufficient military force to repel any foreign attack. The assertion comes amidst reports of a U.S. military build-up in connection with the current Berlin tensions. . . . The East German Health Ministry announces that it has asked the government to consider measures to restrict travel between East and West Germany in view of an alleged West German polio epidemic.	Tunisian Pres. Habib Bourguiba dispatches leading officials to the U.S., USSR and other states to seek support in Tunisia's conflict with France over the Bizerte naval base. . . . Dahomey forces forcibly seize the 172-year old Portuguese enclave of Ajuda, located on the Gulf of Guinea about 37 miles from Porto-Novo.		Nationalist Chinese V.P. Gen. Chen Cheng, on a 10-day state visit to the U.S., ends a second day of talks with Pres. Kennedy during which he received a promise of continued U.S. opposition to U.N. admission for Communist China. Chen is reported to have rebuffed a Kennedy suggestion that Nationalist China withdraw its plan to veto U.N. admission for Outer Mongolia.
Aug. 2		Moscow sources report that Premier Khrushchev told visiting Italian Premier Amintore Fanfani that the current crisis over Berlin would lead to renewed negotiations and not to war.	The reconvened Congo Parliament unanimously confirms Pres. Joseph Kasavubu's appointment of Cyrille Adoula as the nation's new premier. Adoula, a former Kasavubu supporter whose leftist views made him acceptable to the Gizenga faction, immediately announces the formation of a national unity cabinet including Antoine Gizenga as first vice premier.	The Cuban government orders the integration of Cuban craft unions into "vertical" industrial unions as part of a general "socialist" reorganization of the nation's labor system.	
Aug. 3		The British House of Commons votes 313-5 to endorse the government's decision to seek negotiations on British membership in the EEC.	Congo Premier Adoula, in his inaugural address, declares that his government will reintegrate Katanga into the Congo.		A rise in the life-expectancy of the average Indian from 32 years in 1941 to 47.5 in 1961 is cited by P.M. Nehru as "one measure of the success" of state economic planning.
Aug. 4		Soviet notes containing a request for Western participation in a conference on a World War II peace treaty with Germany and on a settlement of post-war frontiers in Europe are delivered to Britain, France and the U.S. A similar note delivered to West Germany warns that that nation would not survive a war over the Berlin question for "even a few hours.". . . The East Berlin Governing Council institutes a number of special fiscal and economic policies designed to discourage East Berliners from holding or seeking jobs in the city's Western sectors.	U.N. Secy Gen. Hammarskjold officially recognizes the Adoula cabinet as the only legitimate Congo government.	The New Democratic Party, an amalgam of the Canadian Labor Congress, the Socialist farmers' Cooperative Commonwealth Federation, and other smaller dissident groups, is formed at a founding convention in Ottawa.	Nationalist Chinese V.P. Chen Yi tells reporters at the U.N. that rumors that Communist China is on the verge of developing a nuclear bomb are "sheer nonsense."

A	B	C	D	E
Includes developments that affect more than one world region, international organizations and important meetings of major world leaders.	Includes all domestic and regional developments in Europe, including the Soviet Union, Turkey, Cyprus and Malta.	Includes all domestic and regional developments in Africa and the Middle East, including Iraq and Iran and excluding Cyprus, Turkey and Afghanistan.	Includes all domestic and regional developments in Latin America, the Caribbean and Canada.	Includes all domestic and regional developments in Asia and Pacific nations, extending from Afghanistan through all the Pacific Islands, except Hawaii.

U.S. Politics & Social Issues	U.S. Foreign Policy & Defense	U.S. Economy & Environment	Science, Technology & Nature	Culture, Leisure & Life Style	
The U.S. Public Health Service names a special commission to study the sharp increase in the number of reported syphilis cases in the U.S. Over 19,000 new cases were reported in fiscal 1961, up 50% from the previous year.				Jerry Barber defeats Don January in a play-off to win the PGA tournament in Chicago.	July 30
		The U.S. Treasury reports that the federal debt rose to a record $293,172,794,984 on July 26. . . . The Small Business Administration reports that it approved a record 3,068 business loans totaling $154 million during the first half of 1960.		The second game of this year's two-game major league baseball All-Star series ends in a rain-stopped 1-1 tie.	July 31
	An "advisory" notice to prepare for active duty is sent to 64 National Guard and seven Air Force Reserve units by the Defense Dept.	The Dow-Jones industrial stock price average finishes the day at a record 713.94, surpassing the previous high of 705.96 set May 19. . . . The First National City Bank reports that profits of selected corporations during the second quarter of 1961 rose 19% above the first quarter but remained slightly below the earnings for the same period in 1960.			Aug. 1
	In a joint communique issued at the conclusion of meetings with Nationalist Chinese V.P. Gen. Chen Cheng, Pres. Kennedy pledges that South Vietnam "shall not be lost to the communists for lack of any (American) support."				Aug. 2
The Justice Dept. files suits under provisions of the Civil Rights Acts of 1957 and 1960 seeking federal injunctions against racial discrimination in voter registration in Montgomery County, Ala. and Walthall and Jefferson Davis counties in Mississippi. . . . FBI agents overpower and arrest the captors of a Continental Airlines 707 during a refueling stop in El Paso, Tex., foiling the hijackers' plan to force the pilot to fly to Cuba.					Aug. 3
Robert Welch Jr., head of the John Birch Society, announces a cash contest for the best college student essay on the grounds for impeaching Chief Justice Earl Warren.		Pres. Kennedy signs a bill (HR6345) providing $756 million in fiscal 1962 appropriations for the Interior Dept. and related agencies.			Aug. 4

F	G	H	I	J
Includes elections, federal-state relations, civil rights and liberties, crime, the judiciary, education, health care, poverty, urban affairs and population.	Includes formation and debate of U.S. foreign and defense policies, veterans' affairs and defense spending. (Relations with specific foreign countries are usually found under the region concerned.)	Includes business, labor, agriculture, taxation, transportation, consumer affairs, monetary and fiscal policy, natural resources, and pollution.	Includes worldwide scientific, medical and technological developments, natural phenomena, U.S. weather, natural disasters, and accidents.	Includes the arts, religion, scholarship, communications media, sports, entertainment, fashions, fads and social life.

	World Affairs	Europe	Africa & the Middle East	The Americas	Asia & the Pacific
Aug. 5		The heads of the eight Warsaw Pact states conclude a three-day conference in Moscow after issuing an official communique declaring their joint determination to sign an East German peace treaty before the year's end.	Leaders of the Gizenga regime formally announce the voluntary dissolution of their separate Stanleyville government and affirm the full authority of the new Congolese cabinet of Premier Cyrille Adoula.	In a message read to the Inter-American Economic and Social Conference in Uruguay, Pres. Kennedy promises more than $1 billion in U.S. aid during the first year of his Alliance for Progress program. . . . A new Bolivian constitution increasing the power and authority of the president is formally inaugurated. The new government compact also separates church and state and abolishes capital punishment.	
Aug. 6		Western foreign ministers, meeting in Paris to coordinate a response to Soviet demands on Berlin, agree to affirm their willingness to negotiate, but not to do so under the threat of a separate USSR-East German peace treaty. . . . Moscow sources report that Khrushchev has warned visiting Premier Fanfani that Italy and Britain would be destroyed by Soviet missiles should the West force a war over Berlin.			
Aug. 7		In a nationwide TV speech in reply to Pres. Kennedy's July 25 address on Berlin, Premier Khrushchev couples an appeal for Western participation in a German peace treaty with a renewed threat to sign a separate Soviet-East German pact that would terminate Western occupation rights in Berlin. He also warns that Soviet troops may be moved westward to meet a NATO build-up.		U.S. Treasury Secy. Dillon tells the Inter-American Economic and Social Conference that Latin American states may receive as much as $20 billion from the U.S. and other Western sources over the next 10 years if they achieve the necessary domestic reforms.	In a speech to Parliament, Nehru outlines India's third five-year plan, which will cost an estimated $24 billion and extend through 1966. Major goals are food grain self-sufficiency, expanded steel production, improved educational and health services, and a 15% rise in per capita income.
Aug. 8		The NATO Permanent Council announces in Paris that it will begin intensified consultations with member states on appropriate responses to the deepening Berlin crisis. . . . Britain withdraws $1.5 billion from the International Monetary Fund in order to cover its growing international debt and bolster the pound sterling.		Cuban Industry Min. Ernesto (Ché) Guevara tells the Inter-American Economic Conference that Cuba would support the U.S. Alliance for Progress if it were sincerely aimed at increasing social justice rather than imperialist exploitation.	
Aug. 9				A Pan American DC-8, enroute from Mexico City to Guatemala, is seized by an armed French Algerian passenger and forced to fly to Cuba. Cuban officials agree to release the plane and passengers, except the hijacker, for a return flight to the U.S.	
Aug. 10	Pres. Kennedy announces that chief U.S. test-ban negotiator Arthur Dean will be sent back to Geneva Aug. 24 in what appears to be a final U.S. effort to achieve a test agreement. Kennedy cites the Soviet demand for a three-member control administration as the chief obstacle to agreement and hints that a Soviet failure to compromise will force a resumption of U.S. testing.	Great Britain makes formal application to join the European Economic Community. The application is a necessary preliminary to the opening of negotiations on the special conditions posed by Britain for its membership in the six-nation EEC.	U.N. Secy. Gen. Hammarskjold announces that a special session of the General Assembly will be called Aug. 21 to discuss the French-Tunisian dispute over the status of the French naval base at Bizerte. The action comes after the Security Council had twice failed to find a solution to the problem.		
Aug. 11		For the second time in recent days Soviet Premier Khrushchev publicly warns that hundreds of millions might die if war comes over the Berlin crisis.	France announces that it is relaxing its unilateral Algerian cease-fire order to allow French forces to respond more freely to an alleged increase in rebel attacks.		The U.S. State Dept. announces that it is suspending plans to establish diplomatic relations with Outer Mongolia.

A	B	C	D	E
Includes developments that affect more than one world region, international organizations and important meetings of major world leaders.	Includes all domestic and regional developments in Europe, including the Soviet Union, Turkey, Cyprus and Malta.	Includes all domestic and regional developments in Africa and the Middle East, including Iraq and Iran and excluding Cyprus, Turkey and Afghanistan.	Includes all domestic and regional developments in Latin America, the Caribbean and Canada.	Includes all domestic and regional developments in Asia and Pacific nations, extending from Afghanistan through all the Pacific Islands, except Hawaii.

U.S. Politics & Social Issues	U.S. Foreign Policy & Defense	U.S. Economy & Environment	Science, Technology & Nature	Culture, Leisure & Life Style	
			Soviet cosmonaut Yuri Gagarin concludes a 10-day goodwill tour to Cuba and Brazil.	Gene Fullmer retains the National Boxing Association middleweight championship by scoring a 15-round decision over Florentine Fernandez, of Cuba, in Ogden, Utah.	Aug. 5
			The USSR announces the successful launching of its second manned orbital space mission. The pilot of the 10,430 pound Vostok II spacecraft is Maj. Gherman Stepanovich Titov.	Dukla of Czechoslovakia wins the International Soccer League's American Challenge Cup.	Aug. 6
	Dr. Robert Soblen, who was convicted July 13 on two counts of wartime espionage for the Soviet Union, is sentenced to life in prison by U.S. Judge William Herlands.	A bill (S857) establishing a 26,000-acre Cape Cod National Seashore Area is signed by Pres. Kennedy.	Soviet cosmonaut Gherman Stepanovich Titov ends a 25-hour space flight with a safe landing after completing 17 orbits around the earth. . . . Psychologist Henry F. Garrett, writing in a University of Chicago Press publication, challenges the widespread conviction that all races have potentially equal ability, suggesting that the equality doctrine may prove to be the "scientific hoax of the century."	Dr. Frank Daniel Buchman, 83, founder of an international spiritual reconstruction movement in Oxford, England now known as the Moral Re-Armament Movement (1921), dies of a heart attack in Freudenstadt, Germany.	Aug. 7
Charles Boineau is elected to the South Carolina General Assembly in a special election, becoming the first Republican to win a seat in the statehouse since Reconstruction.	The Navy's *Ethan Allen*, the longest and most powerful Polaris submarine, is commissioned in Groton, Conn. Eight pacifists are arrested for their unsuccessful effort to disrupt the commissioning.	A compromise version of the administration's feed grain bill (S1643) is signed by Pres. Kennedy.	Prof. Trofim D. Lysenko, 63, is reported to have been elected president of the Soviet Academy of Agricultural Sciences.		Aug. 8
Cook County (Chicago) Court Judge James B. Parsons is appointed by Kennedy to be U.S. judge for the Northern Illinois District, making him the first Negro to hold a federal district judgeship in the continental U.S.					Aug. 9
Pres. Kennedy announces at a Washington press conference that he has approved a plan by which V.P. Johnson would assume Presidential responsibilities should he himself ever become unable to fulfill them.	A compromise bill (HR7851) appropriating $46.66 billion to the Defense Dept. is passed by both houses of Congress without any opposing votes. The appropriation is $266 million higher than the President's total 1962 defense budget requests. . . . Roger Hilsman Jr., director of the State Dept.'s intelligence and research section, proposes that the U.S. become more deeply involved in preparations for anti-guerrilla warfare as the best means of preventing further communist expansion.				Aug. 10
The Wisconsin legislature, despite pressure from a 12-day sit-in, rejects three bills designed to combat racial discrimination in housing and employment.		A bill (S1815) creating a special Assistant Labor Secretary post to deal with the problems of American working women is signed by Pres. Kennedy. . . . A bill (HR6611) designed to improve the U.S. payments balance by reducing the amount of duty free goods allowed to returning U.S. travelers (from $500 to $100) is signed by Pres. Kennedy.		Milwaukee Braves pitcher Warren Spahn, 40, scores his 300th major league win in a 2-1 triumph over the Chicago Cubs.	Aug. 11
F	G	H	I	J	
Includes elections, federal-state relations, civil rights and liberties, crime, the judiciary, education, health care, poverty, urban affairs and population.	Includes formation and debate of U.S. foreign and defense policies, veterans' affairs and defense spending. (Relations with specific foreign countries are usually found under the region concerned.)	Includes business, labor, agriculture, taxation, transportation, consumer affairs, monetary and fiscal policy, natural resources, and pollution.	Includes worldwide scientific, medical and technological developments, natural phenomena, U.S. weather, natural disasters, and accidents.	Includes the arts, religion, scholarship, communications media, sports, entertainment, fashions, fads and social life.	

	World Affairs	Europe	Africa & the Middle East	The Americas	Asia & the Pacific
Aug. 12		Warsaw Pact nations call upon East Germany to institute border "controls" in Berlin in order to prevent alleged espionage and subversive activities against Warsaw Pact states.		A one-day bloodless revolt led by Argentine air force officers collapses after it fails to arouse a popular uprising against the government. . . . Cuba agrees to return an Eastern Air Lines Electra hijacked to Havana July 24 in exchange for the release by the U.S. of a captured Cuban gunboat taken to Key West, Fla. July 29. The agreement was negotiated through the Swiss Embassy in Havana.	South Korean junta chief Pak Chung Hi announces that national elections to restore full civilian rule will be held in May 1963.
Aug. 13	The U.N.'s Statistical Office estimates that world population has reached approximately three billion and is growing at a rate of 46 to 55 million, or 1.7%, a year.	The border between the Soviet and Western sectors of Berlin is ordered closed to all East Germans by the East German government. Police erect a temporary barbed-wire barrier. . . . The order, which does not apply to Western travel into East Berlin, is to remain in force until "the conclusion of a German peace treaty." . . . Pres. Kennedy denounces the border action as a "violation of the four-power status of Berlin."			
Aug. 14		Telephone, telegraph and postal communications between East Berlin and the West are cut off. . . . Over 5,000 West Berliners stage a march to demand retaliation against the border closing.	The three-judge Israeli tribunal, after hearing final arguments, adjourns to deliberate its decision in the Eichmann case.	The captain and a portion of the crew of a sugar-laden Cuban freighter bound for an undisclosed communist port take control of the vessel and sail to Norfolk, Va. where they request political asylum.	Soviet Deputy Premier Anastas Mikoyan arrives in Japan for an eight-day state visit, the first by a high-ranking Russian official in over 70 years. . . . South Korea's ruling junta grants amnesty to 5,600 prisoners and reduces the sentences of 9,300 others in a move aimed at inspiring public confidence in the new regime.
Aug. 15		East German workmen begin building a concrete wall along the length of the 25-mile East-West Berlin border to replace the barbed-wire barrier erected Aug. 13-14. . . . East Germany announces that all West Berlin vehicles will henceforth require special permits to enter East Berlin. . . . West German Chancellor Adenauer proposes that the West might impose economic sanctions against the Soviet bloc in retaliation for the Berlin border closing.	David Ben-Gurion's Mapai Party wins 42 of 120 Knesset seats in Israel's fifth general elections. Despite a loss of five seats, the Mapai remains the strongest party in the Knesset.		Master Tara Singh, 76, a spiritual-political leader of India's six-and-a-half million Sikhs, begins a fast "unto death" in an effort to persuade P.M. Nehru to agree to the creation of a separate Punjabi-language state.
Aug. 16		An Aug. 15 note from the U.S. Britain and France officially protesting the Berlin border closings as a violation of four-power agreements is formally rejected by the Soviet commandant in East Berlin. . . . West Berlin Mayor Willy Brandt tells a crowd of 250,000 gathered outside city hall that he expects "not merely words but political action" from the West in the face of the border actions.			Japanese Premier Hayato Ikeda meets with visiting Soviet Deputy Premier Anastas Mikoyan and receives a warning that Japan would risk Soviet attack in the event of an East-West war because of the presence of U.S. military bases there.
Aug. 17		The U.S., Britain and France send identical notes to the Kremlin blaming the USSR for the Berlin border closing and demanding that the Soviets "put an end to these illegal measures." . . . French Pres. de Gaulle orders an undisclosed number of ground and air units shifted from Algeria to France because of the Berlin crisis. . . . East Germany's Free German Youth organization calls upon its two million members to volunteer for the armed services in view of the continuing Berlin crisis.		The U.S. and 19 other American nations attending the Inter-American Economic Conference in Punta del Este, Uruguay sign the Alliance for Progress Charter and a special declaration pledging to work for democratic social and economic reforms; Cuba abstains.	Indian Pres. Rajendra Prasad, ignoring Portuguese protests, signs a constitutional amendment incorporating into India the former Portuguese enclaves of Dadra and Nagar Aveli, north of Bombay. . . . Pres. Sukarno announces a general amnesty for members of rebel forces throughout Indonesia if they "surrender unconditionally" by Oct. 5.

A	B	C	D	E
Includes developments that affect more than one world region, international organizations and important meetings of major world leaders.	Includes all domestic and regional developments in Europe, including the Soviet Union, Turkey, Cyprus and Malta.	Includes all domestic and regional developments in Africa and the Middle East, including Iraq and Iran and excluding Cyprus, Turkey and Afghanistan.	Includes all domestic and regional developments in Latin America, the Caribbean and Canada.	Includes all domestic and regional developments in Asia and Pacific nations, extending from Afghanistan through all the Pacific Islands, except Hawaii.

U.S. Politics & Social Issues	U.S. Foreign Policy & Defense	U.S. Economy & Environment	Science, Technology & Nature	Culture, Leisure & Life Style	
A U.S. Census Bureau report, based on 1960 figures, shows that 31,469,488 Americans live in a "supermetropolis" stretching for nearly 500 miles from Lawrence-Haverhill, Mass. to Washington, D.C.	*The New York Times* reports that the U.S. is abandoning its efforts to persuade the industrial nations of Europe and Asia to pledge 1% of their gross national product for aid to less developed nations. The plan had been widely criticized as an overly rigid formula.				Aug. 12
A Gallup Poll indicates 85% of Americans favor welfare restrictions such as those adopted by Newburgh, N.Y.				Eight paintings by Paul Cezanne are stolen from a special exhibition of the artisit's works in Aix-en-Provence, France.	Aug. 13
	Pres. Kennedy asks Congress for $73 million for stockpiling food and medical supplies as part of the nation's expanded civil defense program.				Aug. 14
	Senate GOP leader Dirksen and House Republican leader Charles Halleck tell newsmen they have strong evidence suggesting that the USSR has violated its professed nuclear test moratorium and, in view of that, urge an immediate resumption of U.S. tests.		An 83-pound satellite dubbed Explorer XII, equipped to gather data on electrons and protons in space, is launched into orbit from Cape Canaveral.		Aug. 15
Martin Luther King announces the launching of a Negro "stand-in" movement to protest discrimination in voter registration. King says the movement will aim at doubling the number of Southern Negro voters within two years.	The Army announces that 84,000 enlisted men scheduled for release in early 1962 will be retained on active duty for up to four additional months. The Navy and Air Force announced similar extension plans earlier in the week.	The Commerce Dept. reports that personal incomes in the U.S. rose to a record annual rate of $419 billion in July, up $1.9 billion over June.	Dr. Mikhail A. Klochko, a leading Soviet scientist and winner of the Stalin Prize in chemistry, asks and receives political asylum in Canada where he is attending an international conference. Dissatisfaction with Soviet restrictions on scientific freedom is reportedly the reason for Klochko's defection.		Aug. 16
	Four Teamster locals in Cincinnati vote to leave the International Brotherhood of Teamsters. Reportedly a number of other locals throughout the country are considering similar action. . . . The Labor Dept. reports that production per man-hour in the U.S. increased by about 2.5% in 1960. The increase in agricultural productivity was 6%.		The U.S. Public Health Service announces that it has licensed the manufacture of one variety of Sabin oral vaccine which is effective against Type I polio virus. Licenses for the Sabin vaccines effective against Type II and III viruses are still pending.		Aug. 17

F	G	H	I	J
Includes elections, federal-state relations, civil rights and liberties, crime, the judiciary, education, health care, poverty, urban affairs and population.	*Includes formation and debate of U.S. foreign and defense policies, veterans' affairs and defense spending. (Relations with specific foreign countries are usually found under the region concerned.)*	*Includes business, labor, agriculture, taxation, transportation, consumer affairs, monetary and fiscal policy, natural resources, and pollution.*	*Includes worldwide scientific, medical and technological developments, natural phenomena, U.S. weather, natural disasters, and accidents.*	*Includes the arts, religion, scholarship, communications media, sports, entertainment, fashions, fads and social life.*

	World Affairs	Europe	Africa & the Middle East	The Americas	Asia & the Pacific
Aug. 18		The USSR flatly rejects yesterday's Western protests over the Berlin border closings, saying that it had no control over East Germany's "sovereign" right to "defend its interests.". . . Pres. Kennedy orders that the U.S. forces stationed in West Berlin be immediately increased from 5,000 to 6,500.	Antoine Gizenga publicly confirms his personal support of the Adoula government. The statement comes in the wake of a trip to Stanleyville by Premier Adoula during which he pledged to pursue the late Patrice Lumumba's goal of a unified and neutral Congo.	Argentine Pres. Arturo Frondizi discloses in a TV speech that he had recently met secretly with Argentine-born Cuban Industry Min. Ernesto (Ché) Guevara to inform him that Argentina would continue to combat communist subversion in the hemisphere.	Hong Kong sources report that a cholera epidemic in Red China may have taken as many as 30,000 lives so far. Some reports suggest that the epidemic is being blamed on U.S. germ warfare by Communist officials.
Aug. 19		U.S. V.P. Johnson arrives in West Berlin to assure personally West German leaders of full U.S. support in the crisis caused by the Communist closing of Berlin borders.	In the wake of the announcement that Antoine Gizenga has agreed to end his dissident Stanleyville regime, central Congo Premier Cyrille Adoula declares that his efforts will now be turned toward ending the secession of Katanga.		
Aug. 20		West Berlin Mayor Willy Brandt says that V.P. Johnson's visit "erased any doubts among the people" about U.S. support for the city's freedom.			
Aug. 21		The U.S. State Dept. abruptly cancels plans to sign a commercial airlines route agreement with the USSR "in view of the international (Berlin) situation.". . . Forty-six whites are arrested and at least 20 persons are injured during race riots in which several thousand whites attacked the homes of Asian, Arab and Negro residents of Middlesbrough, London's slum district.	Kenyan African nationalist Jomo Kenyatta, 71, is granted full liberty after serving nine years in confinement for his role in the 1953 Mau Mau uprising. Most Kenyan leaders expect that Kenyatta will serve as chief of state after the nation gains its independence.	Dr. Cheddi Berret Jagan's leftist People's Progressive Party wins a controling majority in nationwide elections for British Guiana's Legislative Council.	
Aug. 22		The East German Interior Ministry announces that West Berliners seeking entry into East Berlin will be confined to four designated crossing points and will be required to purchases special permits from the East German travel agency. . . . A Yiddish bimonthly literary review called *Soviet Homeland* appears in Moscow. It is the first such publication since Stalin ordered the abolition of all Yiddish-language institutions in 1948.			
Aug. 23		The USSR charges the three Western powers with abusing their air access rights to Berlin by flying West German leaders and "spies" to West Berlin for "provocations" against East Germany "and other socialist countries."		Chilean Pres. Jorge Alesandri orders military control imposed on five provinces beset by copper, steel and railroad strikes.	
Aug. 24		Pres. Kennedy, responding to yesterday's Soviet protest concerning Western flights into Berlin, issues a statement saying that any interference with free access to West Berlin would be viewed as an aggressive act against the U.S.	South African P.M. Henrik Verwoerd replaces Justice Min. Francois Erasmus and other department heads in a move to bring more rightwingers into his government.	The U.S. right to retain its naval base at Guantanamo, Cuba is challenged by Cuba's chief U.N. delegate during a speech to the General Assembly's special session on the Bizerte crisis. U.S. Amb. Stevenson dismisses the Cuban contention as "a new doctrine of international. . . lawlessness.". . . Several persons are dead following a week of political violence between pro- and anti-government groups in the Dominican Republic.	Dr. Inkongliba Ao, head of the new Indian state of Nagaland, is killed by a fanatical nationalist opposed to Nagaland's incorporation into India.

A	B	C	D	E
Includes developments that affect more than one world region, international organizations and important meetings of major world leaders.	Includes all domestic and regional developments in Europe, including the Soviet Union, Turkey, Cyprus and Malta.	Includes all domestic and regional developments in Africa and the Middle East, including Iraq and Iran and excluding Cyprus, Turkey and Afghanistan.	Includes all domestic and regional developments in Latin America, the Caribbean and Canada.	Includes all domestic and regional developments in Asia and Pacific nations, extending from Afghanistan through all the Pacific Islands, except Hawaii.

U.S. Politics & Social Issues	U.S. Foreign Policy & Defense	U.S. Economy & Environment	Science, Technology & Nature	Culture, Leisure & Life Style	
Judge Learned Hand, 89, member of the second U.S. circuit Court of Appeals, 1924-1951 and celebrated legal scholar, dies in New York.	Rival, curtailed versions of the administration's foreign aid bill are passed by the Senate and House and sent to joint conference. The House version omits a principal feature of the administration's foreign aid plan--the authority to borrow from the Treasury to finance long-term development loans.	The Commerce Dept. reports that U.S. GNP rose from an annual rate of $500.8 billion (in current dollars) during 1961's first quarter to a record rate of $516.1 billion during the second quarter.	A bill to provide $1.67 billion in appropriations for the National Aeronautics and Space Administration is signed by Pres. Kennedy.		Aug. 18
				Composer Aaron Copland, 60, receives the Edward MacDowell Medal for his contributions to American music.	Aug. 19
		The Commerce Dept. reports that per capita income in the U.S. rose to a record average of $2,223 in 1960, up $63 from 1959. . . . The Commerce Dept. reports that U.S. exports to Soviet bloc nations in 1960 totaled $193.5 million and consisted largely of agricultural products; U.S. imports from the Soviet bloc countries amounted to $83.8 million.		U.S. Army Lt. Jay Silvester surpasses his own world discus record with a throw of 199 ft. 2.5 in. at an international military meet in Brussels.	Aug. 20
U.S. District Judge Ben Dawkins in Shreveport, La. orders the reinstatement of about 570 Negroes who had been purged from the Bienville Parish voting rolls in 1956.					Aug. 21
Appeal hearings for 189 Freedom Riders, convicted of breach-of-the-peace violations in Jackson, Miss. police court, begin before Hinds County Judge Russel Moore.		UAW Pres. Walter Reuther describes as "woefully inadequate" the latest contract offers from the Big Three auto makers. Negotiations for a new contract began June 30. . . . Kennedy signs a compromise appropriation bill (HR5954) providing $4.368 billion for the U.S. Post Office, about $55 million less than the administration requested.		The *Wall Street Journal* reports that Japan and India rank first and second in the production of feature-length motion pictures.	Aug. 22
		The Senate passes, 60-31, and sends to the House a Kennedy-proposed bill (S1991) to create a $655 million four-year job retraining program.	Ranger I, a 650-pound satellite launched to test components of later Rangers aimed at the moon, fails to achieve a planned secondary orbit.	Goya's portrait of the Duke of Wellington, valued at nearly $400,000, is stolen from the National Gallery in London. It is the last in a recent rash of art thefts that have swept through Europe and the U.S.	Aug. 23
The conviction of Henry Thomas, the first of 189 Jackson, Miss. Freedom Riders to appeal breach-of-peace judgments, is upheld by the Hinds County court. . . . U.S. Judge Oren Lewis in Richmond, Va. bars Prince Edward County (Va.) officials from using public funds to operate segregated private schools while the county's public schools are closed. The ruling comes in response to a suit filed by the NAACP.			NASA announces plans for a $60 million expansion of the Cape Canaveral base to accommodate launch facilities for the Apollo moon program.		Aug. 24

F	G	H	I	J
Includes elections, federal-state relations, civil rights and liberties, crime, the judiciary, education, health care, poverty, urban affairs and population.	Includes formation and debate of U.S. foreign and defense policies, veterans' affairs and defense spending. (Relations with specific foreign countries are usually found under the region concerned.)	Includes business, labor, agriculture, taxation, transportation, consumer affairs, monetary and fiscal policy, natural resources, and pollution.	Includes worldwide scientific, medical and technological developments, natural phenomena, U.S. weather, natural disasters, and accidents.	Includes the arts, religion, scholarship, communications media, sports, entertainment, fashions, fads and social life.

	World Affairs	Europe	Africa & the Middle East	The Americas	Asia & the Pacific
Aug. 25		CP First Secy. Walter Ulbricht tells an East Berlin rally that East Germany would make no immediate effort to control Western air traffic into Berlin, but would leave the matter in Soviet hands until the signing of a German peace treaty.	The U.N. General Assembly, in special session on the Bizerte crisis, votes 66-0 (30 abstentions) to uphold Tunisia's position in its dispute with France. The U.S. decision to abstain draws criticism from several Afro-Asian delegations. . . . The U.N. Congo Force begins reinforcing its 3,000-man garrison in Katanga in what is openly described as a preparatory step toward forcing the disarmament of Katanga's army and the expulsion of its roughly 500 white mercenary officers.	Jañio da Silva Quadros resigns as Brazilian President, saying that conservative opposition, at home and abroad, to his domestic reforms and to his policy of closer relations with communist nations, has made his continuation in office impossible.	
Aug. 26		France, Britain and the U.S. file identical protests with the USSR over recent East German restrictions governing West Berliner, West German and Allied entry into East Berlin. . . . British P.M. Macmillan tells reporters that while the Berlin situation is indeed serious, "nobody is going to fight about it."	Katanga Pres. Tshombe tells newsmen in Elizabethville that "we are ready to die" rather than to submit to negotiations with the central Congo government under a U.N. threat of force.	Cuban and Soviet leaders charge that the U.S. forced the resignation of Brazilian Pres. Jañio da Silva Quadros because of his refusal to support America's anti-communist policies. The U.S. State Dept. rejects the accusations. . . . Official acknowledgment of food shortages and industrial production difficulties marks the opening of a three-day "criticism" meeting of Cuba's National Production Congress.	The Burmese Parliament approves a constitutional amendment making Buddhism the country's state religion.
Aug. 27		Italian Premier Amintore Fanfani issues a statement asserting that the Berlin border closings might have been averted had Western powers agreed to his early August appeals to participate in immediate negotiations with the Soviets.	Ferhat Abbas is ousted as the premier of the rebel Algerian Provisional Government and replaced by Benyoussef Ben Khedda. The shift is expected to lead to a more militant, less compromising posture on the part of the Algerian rebels.	Dr. Cheddi Jagan, leader of British Guiana's ruling People's Progressive Party, calls upon Britain to grant his nation immediate independence. . . . The U.S. Senate Internal Security Sub-committee reports that Cuban propaganda to "subvert the American Negro against his own government" has met no success.	
Aug. 28			Portuguese Overseas Provinces Min. Adriano Moreira announces the granting of Portuguese citizenship and full political rights to 10 million previously disenfranchised Africans in the territories of Angola, Mozambique and Portuguese Guinea.		Indian P.M. Nehru, in a speech to Parliament, declares his support for full and continued Western access to Berlin. An Aug. 23 speech by Nehru, in which he implied recognition of a Soviet right to control Berlin access, had drawn sharp criticism in the U.S. . . . Pres. Sukarno decrees that the Indonesia government will henceforth receive 60% of the profits of foreign oil companies instead of the previous 50%.
Aug. 29		The USSR discloses that its plan for a long-term military manpower demobilization, announced in 1960, has been suspended in light of increasing world tensions. . . . West German Pres. Heinrich Luebke makes an unannounced flight in a U.S. military plane to West Berlin in deliberate defiance of Soviet opposition to the use of Berlin air corridors by West German officials.	The U.N. Congo Force in Katanga issues an ultimatum demanding that all white mercenaries surrender for deportation within 24 hours.	Brazilian sources report the emergence of a serious government crisis caused by an apparent division among military leaders over whether to permit Brazil's leftist V.P. Joao B. Goulart to succeed resigned Pres. Quadros.	
Aug. 30		Pres. Kennedy announces that retired Gen. Lucius Clay will be sent to West Berlin Sept. 15 "as his personal representative" with ambassadorial rank. He also says that the U.S. hopes for a peaceful settlement of the Berlin crisis, but is not prepared to negotiate on current Russian demands for a "free city." . . . West German Chancellor Adenauer publicly retracts an Aug. 29 election speech in which he claimed that recent Soviet actions in Berlin had been designed to help the Social Democratic Party of Willy Brandt.	French Pres. de Gaulle tells reporters that the change in Algerian rebel leadership will not affect his plans for a speedy "self-determination" of Algeria's future.		

A	B	C	D	E
Includes developments that affect more than one world region, international organizations and important meetings of major world leaders.	Includes all domestic and regional developments in Europe, including the Soviet Union, Turkey, Cyprus and Malta.	Includes all domestic and regional developments in Africa and the Middle East, including Iraq and Iran and excluding Cyprus, Turkey and Afghanistan.	Includes all domestic and regional developments in Latin America, the Caribbean and Canada.	Includes all domestic and regional developments in Asia and Pacific nations, extending from Afghanistan through all the Pacific Islands, except Hawaii.

U.S. Politics & Social Issues	U.S. Foreign Policy & Defense	U.S. Economy & Environment	Science, Technology & Nature	Culture, Leisure & Life Style	
	Defense Secy. Robert McNamara announces that 46,500 Army, 23,600 Air Force and 6,400 Navy reservists are being ordered to active duty because of the Berlin crisis. . . . An administration bill (S2000) making the Peace Corps a permanent agency and authorizing $40 million for the Corps in fiscal 1962 passes the Senate by voice vote.	The Senate passes and sends to the President a bill authorizing the SEC to investigate the rules governing major U.S. stock exchanges.	Explorer XIII, a 127-pound satellite designed to study micrometeoroids, is successfully launched from Wallops Island, Va.		Aug. 25
		Negotiators for the UAW and the American Motors Corp. announce agreement on a profit-sharing plan for AMC employees. . . . Teamster Pres. Hoffa flies to Cincinnati to take personal charge of an advertising campaign aimed at quashing further defections of local unions from the International Brotherhood.			Aug. 26
					Aug. 27
	The Peace Corps' first overseas contingents are honored by Pres. Kennedy with a White House reception on the eve of their departure for Tanganyika and Ghana.	A threatened cancellation of the N.Y. Metropolitan Opera's 1961-1962 season is revoked after representatives of the AFL-CIO Federation of Musicians agreed to submit their wage dispute with management to the binding arbitration of Labor Secy. Arthur Goldberg.	The Gordon Research Conference on Cancer, meeting in New London, N.H., hears evidence from California Institute of Technology researchers indicating that virus-produced cancer cells do not themselves contain the virus.		Aug. 28
					Aug. 29
The Senate approves a rider to a House bill that would extend the life of the Civil Rights Commission for two years. . . . Representatives of 25 African U.N. delegations issue a statement deploring "recurrent and serious" incidents of racial bias suffered by African diplomats in the U.S.		The ICC proposes a program of federal subsidies to U.S. railroads "to ameliorate the railroad passenger deficit problem."		Harold Johnson of Philadelphia retains his light-heavyweight boxing title by scoring a 15-round decision over Eddie Cotton of Seattle in Seattle.	Aug. 30

F	G	H	I	J
Includes elections, federal-state relations, civil rights and liberties, crime, the judiciary, education, health care, poverty, urban affairs and population.	Includes formation and debate of U.S. foreign and defense policies, veterans' affairs and defense spending. (Relations with specific foreign countries are usually found under the region concerned.)	Includes business, labor, agriculture, taxation, transportation, consumer affairs, monetary and fiscal policy, natural resources, and pollution.	Includes worldwide scientific, medical and technological developments, natural phenomena, U.S. weather, natural disasters, and accidents.	Includes the arts, religion, scholarship, communications media, sports, entertainment, fashions, fads and social life.

	World Affairs	Europe	Africa & the Middle East	The Americas	Asia & the Pacific
Aug. 31	The USSR announces that it has decided to resume atomic testing because of what it calls "war threats" from the West. The decision is immediately denounced in the West. Red China applauds the Soviet action as necessary to "the defense of world peace."		Spain evacuates its last remaining military bases in Morocco.	The U.S. Congress, as part of a general foreign aid act, authorizes a total U.S.-Cuba trade embargo.	
Sept. 1	The U.S. announces that the USSR has detonated a "substantial" atmospheric nuclear device in Siberia.		The U.N. Congo command severs relations with the Katanga government.	Latin American sources report that the Cuban government has agreed to grant safe passage out of Cuba to more than 800 persons who have been living in asylum in foreign embassies in Havana. . . . *The New York Times* reports that hundreds of Cuban exiles in the U.S. have returned to Cuba during the last few months.	The 14-nation Geneva conference on Laos reconvenes briefly and then adjourns until Sept. 26. Efforts to break the conference's deadlock are reportedly continuing in private, informal talks among the conference's chief delegations. . . . India discloses the purchase of 12 MiG-19 jet fighters from the USSR. Officials say the planes were acquired to match 12 U.S. F-104's recently bought by Pakistan.
Sept. 2	Most of the delegations to the 25-nation conference of non-aligned states, which began in Belgrade Sept. 1, express shock and regret over the Soviet resumption of atomic testing.	The USSR delivers notes to the Western Allies insisting they had never been granted unlimited civil use of air corridors to Berlin. . . . Khrushchev sends a note to Italian Premier Fanfani saying he would welcome Western proposals on the time and place for high-level talks on Berlin and other East-West problems.		The Brazilian congress approves a constitutional amendment greatly curbing the power of the presidency in an effort to quiet rightist objections to the presidential succession of V.P. Joao Goulart. Ex-Pres. Quadros resigned Aug. 25. . . . Ex-Cuban Pres. Carlos Prio Socarras, overthrown by Batista in 1952, announces in Miami plans to form an anti-Castro Cuban government-in-exile.	
Sept. 3	Pres. Kennedy and P.M. Macmillan jointly propose to Premier Khrushchev that their three nations agree immediately "not to conduct nuclear tests which take place in the atmosphere and produce radioactive fallout."		Gizenga arrives in Leopoldville to assume his post as first vice premier in the Congo's new coalition cabinet.		
Sept. 4	The U.S. Atomic Energy Commission announces that it has confirmed a second Soviet nuclear test in the atmosphere.	The Trades Union Congress, British labor's governing body, expels the 240,000-member Electrical Trades Union for refusing to purge communists from its leadership. . . . French police order unemployed Moslems living in France to return to Algeria. Many of these persons are suspected of extorting money from working Moslems to fund the Algerian rebellion.	Benyoussef Ben Khedda, the new chief of the Algerian Provisional Government, says that the rebels will continue to fight to sustain their claim to the Sahara.		Japan formally protests the Soviet resumption of nuclear tests as "an attempt to attain political objectives by creating fear."
Sept. 5	The USSR's third nuclear test since its Aug. 31 decision to end the voluntary moratorium is reported by the U.S. AEC. . . . Pres. Kennedy orders the resumption of underground, non-fallout-producing nuclear tests by the U.S. . . . The conference of unaligned nations meeting in Belgrade votes to appeal directly to Pres. Kennedy and Premier Khrushchev for an immediate end to "their war preparations."	An attempt to assassinate French Pres. de Gaulle fails as a home-made bomb rolled under his car misfires. A rightist opponent of de Gaulle's Algerian policy is arrested.	French Pres. de Gaulle tells a Paris news conference that France had "never contested" the principle of Tunisian sovereignty over Bizerte, but that it could not immediately withdraw its forces from the base in view of the current world tensions. . . . De Gaulle also says that France might be willing to grant sovereignty over the Sahara to an independent Algeria provided that it could protect the safety and economic interests of the French community in the Saharan region.	Dr. Cheddi Jagan is sworn in as premier of British Guiana.	

A	B	C	D	E
Includes developments that affect more than one world region, international organizations and important meetings of major world leaders.	Includes all domestic and regional developments in Europe, including the Soviet Union, Turkey, Cyprus and Malta.	Includes all domestic and regional developments in Africa and the Middle East, including Iraq and Iran and excluding Cyprus, Turkey and Afghanistan.	Includes all domestic and regional developments in Latin America, the Caribbean and Canada.	Includes all domestic and regional developments in Asia and Pacific nations, extending from Afghanistan through all the Pacific Islands, except Hawaii.

U.S. Politics & Social Issues	U.S. Foreign Policy & Defense	U.S. Economy & Environment	Science, Technology & Nature	Culture, Leisure & Life Style	
A last-ditch administration effort to get a school aid bill enacted in the current congressional session fails as the House votes, 242-170, to reject consideration of a school construction aid measure. Conservative opposition to federal control and the unresolved controversy over aid to private schools are credited with the defeat. . . . House majority leader John McCormack (Mass.) is elected Acting Speaker to replace Speaker Sam Rayburn who is at home in Texas recuperating from a lumbago attack.	A compromise version of the administration's controversial foreign aid bill passes the House, 260-132, and the Senate, 69-24. The bill requires annual congressional appropriations for long-term development loans and thus denies the administration its requested authority to borrow directly from the Treasury.			Valeri Brumel of the USSR breaks his own world high-jump record with a leap of 7 ft. 4 1/2 in. at an international meet in Sofia, Bulgaria.	Aug. 31
William Z. Foster, 80, three-time presidential candidate of the U.S. Communist Party and honorary Party chairman since 1957, dies in Moscow where he was being treated for a heart ailment.		A TWA Constellation crashes into a field in Hinsdale, Ill. near Chicago killing all 78 persons aboard. It is the fourth worst air disaster in U.S. history.		Eero Saarinen, Finnish-born U.S. modern architect, dies in Ann Arbor, Mich. at age 51.	Sept. 1
			Nobel Prize-winning U.S. scientist, Dr. Linus Pauling, cables Premier Khrushchev on behalf of "11,000 scientists in 50 countries" asking for an end to the new nuclear tests.		Sept. 2
		Pres. Kennedy hails the new minimum wage law which went into effect Sept. 2 as "one of the most important domestic accomplishments" of his administration.			Sept. 3
	Kennedy signs the compromise $4.25 billion foreign aid act (S1983).		Dr. Francis E. Knock of Chicago's Presbyterian-St. Luke's Hospital reports that many sulfydryl-inhibitor compounds, found in normal body cells, can be used to enhance the cancer-killing effect of radiation treatment.	Nelson Stacy, driving a 1961 Ford, wins the Southern 500 mile stock car race at Darlington, S.C.	Sept. 4
Pres. Kennedy signs a bill (S2268) making airplane hijacking a federal crime punishable by imprisonment or death.		The AP reports that 384 persons died in automobile accidents over the Labor Day weekend. . . . Kennedy signs into law an emergency bill (HR8922) adding $20 million to the Small Business Administration's authority to make regular business loans.			Sept. 5

F	G	H	I	J
Includes elections, federal-state relations, civil rights and liberties, crime, the judiciary, education, health care, poverty, urban affairs and population.	Includes formation and debate of U.S. foreign and defense policies, veterans' affairs and defense spending. (Relations with specific foreign countries are usually found under the region concerned.)	Includes business, labor, agriculture, taxation, transportation, consumer affairs, monetary and fiscal policy, natural resources, and pollution.	Includes worldwide scientific, medical and technological developments, natural phenomena, U.S. weather, natural disasters, and accidents.	Includes the arts, religion, scholarship, communications media, sports, entertainment, fashions, fads and social life.

	World Affairs	Europe	Africa & the Middle East	The Americas	Asia & the Pacific
Sept. 6	An appeal for "peaceful co-existence" and strong denunciation of colonialism, including U.S. interference in Cuba, is issued as part of a 27-point declaration adopted by the 25-nation conference of unaligned states in Belgrade, Yugoslavia. . . . According to an AEC statement, the USSR explodes another nuclear device in the atmosphere.			Castro announces that Cuban doctors, engineers and technicians who have fled to the U.S. will lose their citizenship and will be barred from ever returning to Cuba.	The International Control Commission for Laos, in a report to the 14-nation Geneva conference, warns that the truce "may deteriorate rapidly" if rapid progress is not made toward a permanent settlement. . . . Afghanistan severs diplomatic relations with Pakistan following an escalation of a long-standing dispute over a border region occupied by Pathan tribesmen.
Sept. 7	Soviet Premier Khrushchev says in a *New York Times* interview that he is willing to meet personally with Pres. Kennedy to seek solutions of the "major international issues now causing concern." He also warns that the USSR has developed superior nuclear weapons and would be forced to use them should a full East-West war break out.	The U.S. determination to defend its Berlin position with nuclear weapons if necessary is stressed by Asst. Defense Secy. Paul Nitze in a speech to the Washington convention of the U.S. Army Association.	For the second day in a row Katangans in Elizabethville, angered by the continuing U.N. military build-up, launch mob attacks against U.N. personnel.	V.P. Joao Goulart is inaugurated as president of Brazil. Goulart names Dr. Tancredo de Almeida Neves as premier under Brazil's new parliamentary constitution which divides executive authority between the president and a premier. . . . In a *New York Times* interview, Khrushchev asserts that "as far as we know, Castro is not a. . .communist. . . . He is just a revolutionary and patriot."	
Sept. 8		The U.S., Britain and France deliver parallel notes to the USSR, rejecting the Soviets' Sept. 2 assertion that Western air rights to Berlin were limited. They add that any interference in traffic to Berlin will constitute an "aggressive action." . . . The Polish Education Ministry makes public an Aug. 19 edict placing severe restrictions on the teaching of Roman Catholicism to Polish children.	Tunisian Pres. Habib Bourguiba announces that he is suspending his demand for an immediate French withdrawal from Bizerte until the end of "the present world crisis."		
Sept. 9	In a message to Pres. Kennedy and P.M. Macmillan, Premier Khrushchev rejects their recent proposals for an immediate atmospheric test-ban, saying that such an agreement should be part of a general disarmament pact.	A general build-up of Soviet bloc armed forces in the face of the Berlin crisis is approved at a meeting of Warsaw Pact defense ministers in Warsaw. . . . The Defense Dept. announces that 40,000 Army troops are being sent to Europe to bring U.S., NATO, and Seventh Army forces there to "full combat strength." . . . Terrorist violence and bombings by supporters of autonomy for the German-speaking population of South Tyrol erupt in several Italian cities. About 50 persons, mostly Austrian and German students, are arrested.		Brazil's newly appointed cabinet issues a communique approving continuation of ex-Pres. Quadros' foreign policy of improving Brazilian relations with communist nations and Cuba.	
Sept. 10		Berlin sources report a continuing series of escape efforts by East Berliners. Several attempts to leap from upper story apartment windows across the border wall into West Berlin have been observed.	In the latest of a recent series of conciliatory moves, France and Tunisia exchange prisoners taken during the July fighting over Bizerte. . . . Some 4,000 Arab League troops are airlifted to Kuwait to replace the withdrawing British forces.	The largest public demonstration ever held against the Castro regime erupts in Havana as 4,000 Roman Catholics march to protest government cancellation of a church festival procession. One person is killed and seven are wounded.	
Sept. 11		A proposal for the internationalization of West Berlin under strict U.N. supervision is publicly advanced by Canadian P.M. Diefenbaker. . . . The USSR formally rejects the Aug. 26 Western protests of restrictions on access to East Berlin, saying that East Germany, "known to be an independent sovereign state," has every right to regulate its borders.	Pres. Tshombe announces his rejection of a "final" U.N. request that negotiations begin with the central Congo government on ending Katanga's secession.		

A	B	C	D	E
Includes developments that affect more than one world region, international organizations and important meetings of major world leaders.	Includes all domestic and regional developments in Europe, including the Soviet Union, Turkey, Cyprus and Malta.	Includes all domestic and regional developments in Africa and the Middle East, including Iraq and Iran and excluding Cyprus, Turkey and Afghanistan.	Includes all domestic and regional developments in Latin America, the Caribbean and Canada.	Includes all domestic and regional developments in Asia and Pacific nations, extending from Afghanistan through all the Pacific Islands, except Hawaii.

U.S. Politics & Social Issues	U.S. Foreign Policy & Defense	U.S. Economy & Environment	Science, Technology & Nature	Culture, Leisure & Life Style	
Pres. Kennedy issues a statement congratulating Little Rock, Ark., Dallas, Tex. and communities in four other Southern states for achieving the desegregation of formerly all-white schools without incident.	Army Secy. Elvis Stahr Jr. discloses at the annual U.S. Army Association convention an Army-proposed aid plan to help under-developed countries form special military units to combat internal terrorist forces. . . . Stahr also says that the current bolstering of U.S. military manpower will allow American forces in Europe to "be brought to full strength."	Appealing to a concern for the "national interest," Pres. Kennedy writes to the heads of the 12 largest U.S. steel makers and asks them to forego a steel-price increase in the near future. . . . The Senate passes and sends to the House a bill (S174) setting aside 6,773,080 acres of land in 44 national parks as part of a National Wilderness Preservation System.	Kennedy signs a bill authorizing increased U.S. contributions of nuclear material to world organizations for peaceful research purposes.		Sept. 6
Mayor Robert Wagner, running as an independent reform candidate, defeats regular Democratic (Tammany Hall) candidate Arthur Levitt in New York City's Democratic mayoral primary. . . . Four more schools are desegregated in New Orleans as the city begins its second year of integrated education. Although no disturbances were reported, the white student boycott which began last year appears to be spreading to the newly integrated schools.					Sept. 7
U.S. Judge G. Harrold Carswell approves the Escambia County (Fla.) school board's gradual desegregation plan and orders it begun in the fall of 1962.			A study reported in the Journal of the American Medical Association reveals a high statistical correlation between heavy cigarette smoking and coronary heart disease.		Sept. 8
The federal Civil Rights Commission issues a report urging legislation to end all racially discriminatory voting qualifications and to require that voting districts be "substantially equal" in population.	The 14,200-ton guided-missile cruiser Long Beach, the Navy's first nuclear surface vessel, is commissioned at the Boston Naval Shipyard.	The White House releases a special aviation task force report which urges greater emphasis on the promotion of low-fare U.S. air passenger transport.		Maria Beale Fletcher, 19, of Asheville, N.C. is crowned "Miss America" at the annual beauty pageant in Atlantic City, N.J.	Sept. 9
				Phil Hill, of Santa Monica, Calif., wins the Italian Grand Prix at Monza to clinch the 1961 world drivers' championship. Hill's team-mate, Count Wolfgang von Trip, and 11 spectators are killed during the race when von Trip's Ferrari skid off the track. . . . Roy Emerson defeats fellow Australian Rod Laver in straight sets to win the men's national tennis championship at Forest Hills (N.Y.C.). Darlene Hard of Long Beach, Calif. wins the women's title.	Sept. 10
	Former Pres. Eisenhower tells reporters that there was "absolutely no planning for an invasion" of Cuba during his administration. An unnamed source close to the White House calls Eisenhower's denial inaccurate.	UAW members go on strike at 92 of General Motors Corp.'s 129 U.S. plants after union and GM negotiators fail to resolve a working conditions dispute before the strike deadline. Contract talks are continuing. . . . N.Y. Gov. Rockefeller appears before an ICC hearing in Washington to urge a broad, coordinated federal effort to solve the current "railroad crisis." . . . The Senate passes and sends to joint conference a bill (HR 2010) to extend the Mexican farm labor program for two years.	Hurricane Carla, described as the fiercest hurricane in 61 years, strikes the U.S. gulf coast forcing 500,000 Texas coastal residents to evacuate their homes. Related tornadoes and flooding are blamed for the deaths of 39 persons in Texas, Mississippi, Louisiana and Missouri.		Sept. 11
F	G	H	I	J	
Includes elections, federal-state relations, civil rights and liberties, crime, the judiciary, education, health care, poverty, urban affairs and population.	Includes formation and debate of U.S. foreign and defense policies, veterans' affairs and defense spending. (Relations with specific foreign countries are usually found under the region concerned.)	Includes business, labor, agriculture, taxation, transportation, consumer affairs, monetary and fiscal policy, natural resources, and pollution.	Includes worldwide scientific, medical and technological developments, natural phenomena, U.S. weather, natural disasters, and accidents.	Includes the arts, religion, scholarship, communications media, sports, entertainment, fashions, fads and social life.	

	World Affairs	Europe	Africa & the Middle East	The Americas	Asia & the Pacific
Sept. 12		Socialist, conservative, and about half of the 206 Gaullist deputies boycott the National Assembly to protest French Pres. de Gaulle's retention of emergency rule-by-decree powers. . . . British philosopher and nuclear arms opponent, Bertrand Russell, 89, is sentenced to seven days in jail for refusing a court order to call off a sit-down demonstration scheduled for Sept. 16 at the U.S. Polaris base at Holy Loch.	French Premier Debré rules as out of order a Socialist-sponsored National Assembly motion to censure de Gaulle for his apparent willingness to consider an independent Algeria, including the Sahara, with no formal ties to France.	The Cuban Interior Ministry issues a statement accusing the Roman Catholic Church of plotting to overthrow the Castro regime. . . . An anti-government riot in Ciudad Trujillo leaves two dead and at least 40 wounded. The violence is observed by an OAS committee sent to the Dominican Republic to investigate political conditions.	
Sept. 13		Kennedy tells Indonesian Pres. Sukarno and Mali Pres. Modibo Keita, who are visiting Washington on behalf of the Belgrade neutralist conference, that he has little hope for fruitful Berlin negotiations with the USSR at the present time.	U.N. Congo forces launch an armed attack upon Katangan army positions in an attempt to force a reintegration of the secessionist Katanga regime into the Congo Republic--an objective which months of negotiations have failed to achieve. The action is taken under the authority of the Feb. 21, 1961 U.N. resolution calling for the preservation of a unified Congo state.		
Sept. 14			Fighting between U.N. and Katanga forces is reported continuing in Elizabethville, Stanleyville and Jadotville. Pres. Moise Tshombe calls upon Katangans to fight "to the last bullet."	Airplane tickets held by more than 15,000 U.S.-bound Cubans are cancelled as the Cuban government announces a virtual prohibition on emigration. . . . Thousands of Ciudad Trujillo residents defy a Dominican government ban to attend the funeral of Dr. Victor Estrella Liz, one of two persons killed in yesterday's anti-government riot.	
Sept. 15	Pres. Kennedy announces that U.S. today ended its three-year atomic test moratorium with the underground detonation of a low-yield nuclear device in Nevada. Kennedy says the action was forced by the Soviet decision to persist in their current series of atmoshpheric tests, which now number 10.	A meeting of Western foreign ministers on the Berlin crisis concludes in Washington after the participants issued a communique blaming the Soviet Union's actions in Berlin for the current heightening of world tension. . . . Ex-Turkish Premier Adnan Menderes is convicted on charges of violating the Turkish Constitution during his 10 years in office and sentenced to death.	Katangan troops, led by white officers, mount a counter-offensive against U.N. positions in Elizabethville and Jadotville. Sources in Elizabethville estimate that casualties on both sides may run into the hundreds.		Indonesian sources report mass surrenders by rebel troops under Pres. Sukarno's general amnesty program announced Aug. 17.
Sept. 16	The U.S. detonates its second low-yield nuclear device in as many days.	East German authorities begin work to further enlarge and reinforce the 25-mile Berlin Wall in an effort to stop the continuing trickle of refugees attempting to run, swim or batter their way into West Berlin.	U.N. reinforcements are sent to Katanga, but Katangan troops, officered by Belgians, prevent a detachment from relieving the surrounded U.N. garrison in Jadotville. . . . Major U.N. powers express reservations over the U.N. Congo Force's decision to employ direct force against Katanga.		
Sept. 17		Early returns from today's West German elections indicate that Chancellor Adenauer's Christian Democratic Union has lost its absolute majority control of the Bundestag (lower house). The vote shows the Christian Democrats with 241 seats (a loss of 40) out of a total 494; the Social Democrats, led by Brandt, won 190 (a gain of 22) and the Free Democrats took 66. . . . Former Turkish Premier Menderes, convicted by a special tribunal of capital political crimes, is executed by hanging.	The Iraqi government announces the suppression of a separatist revolt by Kurdish tribesmen in northern Iraq.	The Cuban government orders the immediate deportation (to Spain) of 136 Roman Catholic priests, roughly half of all the clergy still in Cuba, for alleged anti-state activity.	

A	B	C	D	E
Includes developments that affect more than one world region, international organizations and important meetings of major world leaders.	Includes all domestic and regional developments in Europe, including the Soviet Union, Turkey, Cyprus and Malta.	Includes all domestic and regional developments in Africa and the Middle East, including Iraq and Iran and excluding Cyprus, Turkey and Afghanistan.	Includes all domestic and regional developments in Latin America, the Caribbean and Canada.	Includes all domestic and regional developments in Asia and Pacific nations, extending from Afghanistan through all the Pacific Islands, except Hawaii.

U.S. Politics & Social Issues	U.S. Foreign Policy & Defense	U.S. Economy & Environment	Science, Technology & Nature	Culture, Leisure & Life Style	
The Senate passes and sends to the President a House-approved bill (HR9000) to extend for two years the federal school aid provisions of the 1958 National Defense Education Act. The two-year extension dashes administration hopes for a reconsideration of its recently defeated federal aid plan during the next session of Congress.	The State Dept's protocol chief, Angier Biddle Duke, meets with representatives of 30 states to discuss ways to assure that traveling African diplomats would encounter no racial bias in their use of public accommodations. Mississippi, Alabama and South Carolina refused to send representatives to the meeting.				Sept. 12
The State Dept. publicly asks the Maryland legislature to pass a bill banning racial segregation in public facilities. The appeal stresses the need to avoid future humiliations of African ambassadors "by private reataurant owners."			An unmanned Project Mercury capsule carrying a robot astronaut is successfully recovered after making a single orbit around the earth. NASA officials say that despite minor malfunctions a man could have survived the flight.		Sept. 13
					Sept. 14
			The National Cancer Institute launches a two-year experiment under which 6,000 cancer patients will be treated with every anti-cancer drug that has shown promise.		Sept. 15
Ex-Pres. Eisenhower, returning to partisan political activity, attacks the Kennedy administration's "lavish" domestic programs and its "indecision" in foreign policy.				Jack Nicklaus of Columbus, Ohio wins the U.S. amateur golf championship at Pebble Beach, Calif.	Sept. 16
			Typhoon Nancy strikes the coast of central Japan leaving 185 dead and 137,000 homeless.		Sept. 17

F	G	H	I	J
Includes elections, federal-state relations, civil rights and liberties, crime, the judiciary, education, health care, poverty, urban affairs and population.	*Includes formation and debate of U.S. foreign and defense policies, veterans' affairs and defense spending. (Relations with specific foreign countries are usually found under the region concerned.)*	*Includes business, labor, agriculture, taxation, transportation, consumer affairs, monetary and fiscal policy, natural resources, and pollution.*	*Includes worldwide scientific, medical and technological developments, natural phenomena, U.S. weather, natural disasters, and accidents.*	*Includes the arts, religion, scholarship, communications media, sports, entertainment, fashions, fads and social life.*

	World Affairs	Europe	Africa & the Middle East	The Americas	Asia & the Pacific
Sept. 18	U.N. Secy. Gen. Dag Hammarskjold is killed in the crash of a U.N. airliner near Ndolo, Northern Rhodesia where he was flying to meet with Pres. Tshombe in an attempt to negotiate an end to the fighting between U.N. and Katangan forces. The reason for the crash is unknown; an investigation is planned. . . . Statements of tribute to the late Secretary General are issued by nations throughout the world. The USSR is among the few nations refraining from public comment.		The 158-man Irish U.N. garrison at Jadotville surrenders to Katangan forces.		
Sept. 19	The 16th regular session of the U.N. General Assembly opens in New York amidst an atmosphere of crisis caused by the death of Secy. Gen. Dag Hammarskjold. . . . Soviet Foreign Min. Andrei Gromyko tells reporters at the U.N. in New York that the USSR will not agree to the designation of an acting secretary general and instead will demand General Assembly action on its plan for a three-member U.N. executive.		The cease-fire negotiations with Pres. Tshombe, that were to have been held by Hammarskjold, open in Ndola, Northern Rhodesia with Mahmoud Khiari of Tunisia representing the U.N.	Jamaicans, in an island-wide referendum, vote to leave the 10-member West Indies Federation when they become independent in 1962.	
Sept. 20	The U.S. and the USSR present the General Assembly with a list of agreed upon principles and goals to govern a resumption of East-West disarmament talks. The joint declaration does not deal with specific issues of implementation which still divide the two countries.	East German police begin evacuating houses bordering on West Berlin in order to prevent refugees from continuing to escape by jumping from windows into the Western sector.	The U.N. reports that 20 U.N. soldiers have been killed, 63 wounded and 186 captured in the fighting against Katanga that began Sept. 13. Katanga losses are believed greater. . . . Premier Cyrille Adoula of the central Congolese government warns that the Congo will "spare no effort" to end Katanga's secession.	Pope John XXIII formally protests Cuba's Sept. 17 deportation to Spain of 136 Roman Catholic priests.	Malaya and Singapore announce formal plans to merge the two territories into a "Greater Malayasia Union" by June 1963.
Sept. 21	The General Assembly's Steering Committee votes to include debate on a nuclear test-ban and on U.N. membership for Red China as part of its recommended agenda for the Assembly's 16th regular session. It was the first time that Western nations made no effort to block inclusion of the Chinese issue.	French Pres. de Gaulle says the West would be risking "disaster" if it agreed to hasty negotiations with the Soviets on Germany.	A cease-fire, worked out between Katangan Pres. Tshombe and U.N. civil operations chief Mahmoud Khiari on Sept. 20, is put into effect throughout Katanga.		
Sept. 22	In remarks to foreign correspondents in N.Y., U.S. State Secy. Dean Rusk calls for immediate General Assembly action to find an acting successor to Hammarskjold. . . . The U.S. Atomic Energy Commission continues its practice of reporting all Soviet atomic tests, today announcing the 15th explosion of the current series. . . . Cambodian Prince Sihanouk, Japanese Foreign Min. Zentaro Kosaka and Iranian Foreign Min. Hossein Ghods Nakhai each express opposition to the Soviet "troika" proposal in their speeches to the U.N. General Assembly.		Israeli Arab anger over the government's close supervision of their activities erupts into three days of mass demonstrations and riots. . . . Pres. Nkrumah names himself as commander-in-chief of Ghana's armed forces.	Dominican Republic Pres. Joaquin Balaguer invites opposition leaders to participate with him in the formation of a coalition government.	
Sept. 23		Gen. Lucius Clay, Pres. Kennedy's personal representative to West Berlin, issues a statement declaring that there has been no change in the U.S. position on Germany. The announcement is intended to reassure West German leaders who were upset over Gen. Clay's Sept. 22 remark that eventual recognition of East Germany may be inevitable.			

A	B	C	D	E
Includes developments that affect more than one world region, international organizations and important meetings of major world leaders.	Includes all domestic and regional developments in Europe, including the Soviet Union, Turkey, Cyprus and Malta.	Includes all domestic and regional developments in Africa and the Middle East, including Iraq and Iran and excluding Cyprus, Turkey and Afghanistan.	Includes all domestic and regional developments in Latin America, the Caribbean and Canada.	Includes all domestic and regional developments in Asia and Pacific nations, extending from Afghanistan through all the Pacific Islands, except Hawaii.

U.S. Politics & Social Issues	U.S. Foreign Policy & Defense	U.S. Economy & Environment	Science, Technology & Nature	Culture, Leisure & Life Style	
A suit accusing the Chicago Board of Education of altering school district lines to maintain a segregated pattern is filed in U.S. district court in Chicago on behalf of the parents of 32 Negro school children. . . . Georgia Tech, by admitting three Negro students, becomes the first Georgia college to voluntarily desegregate.					Sept. 18
The Senate votes 43-37 to reject a rules change that would weaken the filibuster device. . . . Atty. Gen. Robert Kennedy resigns from Washington's fashionable Metropolitan Club because of the club's continuing policy of discrimination against Negroes.	The Defense Dept. announces that an additional 73,000 men from two Army National Guard divisions will be called to active duty effective Oct. 15.	Commerce Secy. Luther Hodges reports that the U.S. GNP rose from a record annual rate of $516.1 billion in 1961's second quarter to an annual rate of $526 billion in the third quarter.	NASA announces that it has selected Houston, Texas as the site for a $60 million research and command center for the Project Apollo moon program.		Sept. 19
	At the request of Chmn. Strom Thurmond (D, S.C.), the Senate Armed Services Committee votes to study alleged Defense Dept. policies relating to the suppression of anti-communist views by military personnel. The action comes in the wake of a revived controversy over the reprimand given Maj. Gen. Edwin Walker for conducting a rightwing indoctrination program among his troops.	The UAW's General Motors Council approves the new three-year contract with GM but authorizes continuation of strikes at certain GM plants where local disputes remain unsettled. . . . A compromise version of an administration bill (HR8102) extending the Federal Aviation Act and authorizing $225 million for a three-year program of airport modernization is signed by Pres. Kennedy.		The N.Y. Yankees beat Baltimore, 4-2, to clinch their 26th American League pennant. During the game, the 154th of the season, Roger Maris hit his 59th homer, one short of Babe Ruth's 154-game season record. . . . The U.S. defeats Mexico, three sets to two, to win the American-zone finals of the Davis Cup tennis tournament.	Sept. 20
Pres. Kennedy signs legislation extending the life of the Civil Rights Commission until Nov. 30, 1963.	Sen. Margaret Chase Smith (R, Me.) charges that the Kennedy administration's strategic emphasis on limited war and conventional forces appears to be an open admission that the U.S. is unwilling to use atomic weapons and thus weakens America's "nuclear credibility."				Sept. 21
At the request of Atty. Gen. Kennedy, the ICC issues rules prohibiting racial discrimination in interstate buses and bus facilities. The rules are to be effective Nov. 1. . . . Ivan Allen, a moderate on segregation, defeats avowed segregationist Lester Maddox in Atlanta's Democratic mayoral primary.		The White House releases letters from seven U.S. steel companies written in reply to Kennedy's Sept. 6 appeal for a temporary price freeze. Most were critical of the President's intervention. . . . Pres. Kennedy signs a bill (HR7916) authorizing $75 million for a five-year salt water conversion program.		Newton Minow, chairman of the U.S. FCC, urges American TV networks to produce high quality children's programs in place of the current "dull, gray and insipid" ones. . . . Antonio Abertando of Argentina becomes the first man to make a non-stop, round-trip of the English Channel; the feat took over 43 hours.	Sept. 22
Kennedy nominates Thurgood Marshall, chief counsel for the NAACP since 1938, to be a judge on the U.S. Second Circuit Court of Appeals.	Replying to criticism from Sen. Margaret Chase Smith, Defense Secy. Robert McNamara asserts that the administration has worked to strengthen the U.S. nuclear deterrent and would not hesitate to employ atomic weapons if necessary.				Sept. 23

F	G	H	I	J
Includes elections, federal-state relations, civil rights and liberties, crime, the judiciary, education, health care, poverty, urban affairs and population.	Includes formation and debate of U.S. foreign and defense policies, veterans' affairs and defense spending. (Relations with specific foreign countries are usually found under the region concerned.)	Includes business, labor, agriculture, taxation, transportation, consumer affairs, monetary and fiscal policy, natural resources, and pollution.	Includes worldwide scientific, medical and technological developments, natural phenomena, U.S. weather, natural disasters, and accidents.	Includes the arts, religion, scholarship, communications media, sports, entertainment, fashions, fads and social life.

	World Affairs	Europe	Africa & the Middle East	The Americas	Asia & the Pacific
Sept. 24				The Cuban Interior Ministry announces the arrest of 12 persons on charges of plotting to assassinate Premier Castro with technical support from the U.S. CIA.	
Sept. 25	In an address to the U.N. General Assembly, Pres. Kennedy praises the work of the late Dag Hammarskjold and reiterates U.S. opposition to renewed Soviet demands for a three-man U.N. executive. Kennedy also outlines a five-part U.S. proposal to end the production, testing, transfer and stockpiling of nuclear weapons. . . . Soviet Foreign Min. Gromyko rejects Pres. Kennedy's nuclear test ban proposals, saying that they should be part of a complete and general disarmament pact.	Kennedy tells the U.N. General Assembly that the West is ready to defend its obligations in West Berlin "by whatever means are forced upon it.". . . Ex-French Premier Pierre Mendes-France charges that de Gaulle's personal domination of the government is creating a "political void" which could increase the risk of civil strife.		Military leaders from Honduras, Nicaragua, Panama, Guatemala and Costa Rica end a three-day meeting in Guatemala City after approving a call for a joint Central American military program to combat communist infiltration.	Pres. Kennedy, in his address to the U.N., warns that should guerrilla action prove "successful in Laos and South Vietnam, the gates will be open" to communist subversion throughout Asia.
Sept. 26	Indian P.M. Nehru, who has been recommended in Western circles as a possible successor to Hammarskjold as U.N. Secretary General, tells newsmen in New Delhi that he could not consider the post.				Dutch Foreign Min. Joseph Luns tells the General Assembly that his government is unwilling to transfer control of Netherlands New Guinea to the U.N. . . . The U.S. State Dept. issues a statement condemning the alleged continuation of Russian supplies to the Pathet Lao forces in Laos.
Sept. 27	The USSR presents the General Assembly with an eight-point proposal designed to reduce world tensions and clear the way for a general disarmament accord. The plan calls for a freezing of military budgets, abolition of foreign bases, and the signing of a NATO-Warsaw Pact non-aggression treaty. . . . Acting on a Security Council recommendation, the General Assembly admits Sierra Leone as the 100th U.N. member state.		Algiers sources report an intensifying campaign of demonstrations and terrorism by European rightists opposed to de Gaulle's increasingly liberal views on Algeria.	Argentine Pres. Arturo Frondizi praises the U.S. Alliance for Progress program in his speech to the U.N. General Assembly.	
Sept. 28	Britain and the U.S. submit to the U.N. General Assembly a resolution calling for U.N. support of a treaty to ban atmospheric nuclear tests.		Syrian army officers lead a successful one-day revolt against Egyptian domination of the Syrian region of the UAR, ending the four-year union of Syria and Egypt. UAR Pres. Nasser called off Egyptian resistance to the uprising a few hours after it began.		
Sept. 29	The late U.N. Secy. Gen. Hammarskjold is buried in Uppsala, Sweden in the first state funeral accorded a Swedish commoner since 1900.		Syria's revolutionary command installs Dr. Mahmoun al-Kuzbari, a conservative law professor, as the head of a new all-civilian cabinet. . . . UAR Pres. Nasser explains to a Cairo crowd that he suspended resistance against the Syrian revolt "so that no Arab blood would be shed."	The Brazilian Chamber of Deputies approves a liberal domestic economic and social reform program submitted by Premier Tancredo Neves and based largely on the policies of ex-Pres. Quadros.	

A	B	C	D	E
Includes developments that affect more than one world region, international organizations and important meetings of major world leaders.	Includes all domestic and regional developments in Europe, including the Soviet Union, Turkey, Cyprus and Malta.	Includes all domestic and regional developments in Africa and the Middle East, including Iraq and Iran and excluding Cyprus, Turkey and Afghanistan.	Includes all domestic and regional developments in Latin America, the Caribbean and Canada.	Includes all domestic and regional developments in Asia and Pacific nations, extending from Afghanistan through all the Pacific Islands, except Hawaii.

U.S. Politics & Social Issues	U.S. Foreign Policy & Defense	U.S. Economy & Environment	Science, Technology & Nature	Culture, Leisure & Life Style	
The Civil Rights Commission, noting that only 44 school districts have initiated desegregation in the last two years, issues a 12-point program to speed public school integration. The plan includes measures to suspend U.S. education aid to states that delay implementing desegregation measures.	Sumner Welles, 68, a high-level U.S. State Dept. official 1933-1943 and a developer of the "good neighbor policy" toward Latin America, dies in Bernardsville, N.J.			Heads of 12 major Eastern Orthodox Churches gather for a week-long conference in Rhodes, Greece. It is the first such conference since 1787. . . . The USSR wins the world weight-lifting championships in Vienna, Austria.	Sept. 24
Pres. Kennedy appeals to Maryland civic leaders to voluntarily desegregate restaurants and public services in order to prevent any further instances of discrimination against African diplomats.			In his speech to the General Assembly, Kennedy recommends that the U.N. Charter be extended to outer space to assure that national space programs remain confined to peaceful purposes.		Sept. 25
	A compromise bill (HR9033) appropriating $4.123 billion in fiscal 1962 for foreign aid, almost $861 million less than the administration requested, is passed by the House and Senate and sent to the President. . . . Sen. Barry Goldwater (R, Ariz.), at a New York news conference, praises Pres. Kennedy's U.N. address, but adds "I have no faith in disarmament; there is always one s.o.b. in the world who won't go along with it."	A bill (HR8302) to appropriate almost $952 million in fiscal 1962 for construction at U.S. military bases is signed by Pres. Kennedy.		Yankee outfielder Roger Maris hits his 60th home run of the season.	Sept. 26
Ex-V.P. Nixon announces at a Los Angeles news conference that he will not be a candidate for President in 1964, but will run for governor in California in 1962. . . . The first session of the 87th Congress ends after the Senate reluctantly passed a House supplemental appropriations bill. The $1.126 billion measure generated resentment in the Senate because the House had deleted the agreed upon Treasury financing provision of the bill and then adjourned, leaving the Senate with no choice but to accept the House version or reject the bill entirely.	Pres. Kennedy announces his nomination of ex-AEC Chmn. John McCone to succeed the retiring Allen Dulles as director of the CIA.			The Cincinnati Reds beat the Chicago Cubs, 6-3, to clinch their first National League pennant since 1940. . . . Hilda Doolittle (H.D.), 75, U.S.-born Imagist poet, author of the verse tragedy *Hippolytus*, dies in Zurich of a heart attack.	Sept. 27
Many previously segregated restaurants and other public facilities in Atlanta are integrated without incident in accordance with a citizens' plan adopted last March. . . . Ex-California Gov. Goodwin Knight, embroiled in a GOP primary race with Richard Nixon for the Califorian gubernatorial nomination, charges that a Nixon campaign aid attempted to "buy" him out of the race with a promise of a state office appointment once Nixon was elected.					Sept. 28
The Southern Regional Council reports that the Negro sit-in movement, which began in Feb. 1960, has led to at least some desegregation in 108 cities in 20 states. The movement, however, has had no reported effect on practices in Alabama, Louisiana, Mississippi or South Carolina.			The National Cancer Institute receives for use in its comprehensive chemotherapy experiment a sample of the controversial anti-cancer drug Krebiozen. The value of Krebiozen has been the subject of academic and judicial dispute for several years.	The Protestant Episcopal Church's House of Bishops concludes its 60th triennial conference after issuing a pastoral letter urging continued efforts toward the reunion of all Christendom. The Bishops voted earlier in the conference to study United Presbyterian proposals for a merger of major U.S. Protestant churches. . . . Ex-N.Y. Yankee manager Casey Stengel, 71, signs a one-year contract to manage the National League's expansion N.Y. Mets.	Sept. 29
F	G	H	I	J	
Includes elections, federal-state relations, civil rights and liberties, crime, the judiciary, education, health care, poverty, urban affairs and population.	*Includes formation and debate of U.S. foreign and defense policies, veterans' affairs and defense spending. (Relations with specific foreign countries are usually found under the region concerned.)*	*Includes business, labor, agriculture, taxation, transportation, consumer affairs, monetary and fiscal policy, natural resources, and pollution.*	*Includes worldwide scientific, medical and technological developments, natural phenomena, U.S. weather, natural disasters, and accidents.*	*Includes the arts, religion, scholarship, communications media, sports, entertainment, fashions, fads and social life.*	

	World Affairs	Europe	Africa & the Middle East	The Americas	Asia & the Pacific
Sept. 30		For the third time in 10 days U.S. State Secy. Rusk meets in New York with Soviet Foreign Min. Gromyko to discuss terms of a possible resumption of East-West negotiations on Berlin. No break-throughs have yet been reported. . . . French Pres. de Gaulle formally relin-quishes the special decree powers he had assumed during the April Algiers coup attempt.	Syria's interim revolutionary government orders the immediate expulsion of all Egyptians, military and civilian. . . . More than 2,000 Africans have been arrested in Northern Rhodesia during six weeks of anti-government rioting which began as a protest against British-spon-sored constitutional reforms which Afri-can leaders claim will do nothing to increase their influence in the white-dominated government. . . . Ghana Pres. Kwame Nkrumah reorganizes his cabinet to insure the government's com-mitment to "socialist ideals."	The National Civic Union, the major opposition group in the Dominican Re-public, presents a list of conditions that would have to be met before it accepted Pres. Joaquin Balaguer's Sept. 22 offer to join a coalition regime. Among the terms is a demand that Dominican armed forces chief Rafael Trujillo Jr. and his family be deported.	
Oct. 1			UAR Pres. Gamal Nasser breaks rela-tions with Jordan and Turkey after both nations recognized the revolutionary government in Syria. . . . The former British-administered U.N. trust territory of Southern Cameroon, which gained formal independence Sept 30, merges with the Cameroon Republic to form the Federal Republic of Cameroon.		Sikh spiritual-political leader Tara Singh ends a 47-day political fast after P.M. Nehru agrees to investigate charges of Hindu religious and social discrimination against India's Sikh population.
Oct. 2			Syria's new premier, Mahmoun al-Kuz-bari, tells reporters that his government will pursue a policy of neutrality and nonalignment in world affairs. . . . A fruitful renewal of French-Algerian rebel peace talks in the near future is predict-ed by de Gaulle in a nationwide TV address.		South Vietnamese Pres. Ngo Dinh Diem declares that Viet Cong activity against the government has grown from a gueril-la campaign to a "real war" during the last six months.
Oct. 3	About 30 pacifists from the U.S. and eight other countries arrive in Moscow where they win permission to argue their case for unilateral disarmament and an end to nuclear tests. The group, which began a world peace march in San Francisco last December finds that many Muscovites were unaware of the USSR's decision to resume atomic tests.	The French National Assembly con-venes amidst indications that center and left parties are considering formation of a non-communist anti-Gaullist opposi-tion bloc.	The Ghanian government announces that 48 political opponents of Pres. Nkrumah have been prosecuted for crimes "against the constitution." . . . France withdraws its troops back to the confines of its military installations from the advanced positions which it had occupied in the city of Bizerte during the fighting with Tunisian troops July 20-21.		The U.S. Military Advisory Group in South Vietnam is currently reported to number 685 men. . . . The AP reports that recent speeches and editorials in Communist China confirm earlier indica-tions of a severe set-back in agricultural and industrial production.
Oct. 4				Cuban Pres. Osvaldo Dorticos an-nounces in Moscow that communist nations have agreed to buy at least 4,860,000 tons of Cuban sugar annually over the next four years.	The Ceylonese goverment releases from detention 15 parliamentary dele-gates of the dissident Tamil Federal Party to allow them to participate in legislative elections.
Oct. 5		*The New York Times* reports that the U.S. has quietly urged West Germany to pursue direct discussions with East Ger-many on the meaning of Soviet and East German promises of guaranteed access to West Berlin. . . . The British Labor Party wraps up its annual conference after adopting resolutions condemning the Communist closing of the Berlin border and the basing of U.S. Polaris submarines in Britain.	Nasser announces in a Cairo radio broadcast that he has given up all claims to Syria as part of the UAR. . . . British Commonwealth Secy. Duncan Sandys concludes two days of talks with Pres. Kwame Nkrumah over recent Ghanian newspaper charges that Britain was obstructing U.N. operations in the Con-go.	The British Colonial Office announces that Jamaica will be granted full inde-pendence in early 1962.	A Nepal-Communist China boundary treaty, which locates the peak of Mount Everest precisely on the border, is signed in Peking.

A	B	C	D	E
Includes developments that affect more than one world region, international or-ganizations and important meetings of major world leaders.	*Includes all domestic and regional de-velopments in Europe, including the Soviet Union, Turkey, Cyprus and Malta.*	*Includes all domestic and regional de-velopments in Africa and the Middle East, including Iraq and Iran and exclud-ing Cyprus, Turkey and Afghanistan.*	*Includes all domestic and regional de-velopments in Latin America, the Carib-bean and Canada.*	*Includes all domestic and regional de-velopments in Asia and Pacific nations, extending from Afghanistan through all the Pacific Islands, except Hawaii.*

U.S. Politics & Social Issues	U.S. Foreign Policy & Defense	U.S. Economy & Environment	Science, Technology & Nature	Culture, Leisure & Life Style	
	Senate Foreign Relations Committee Chmn. J. William Fulbright tells reporters in London that he would support U.S. moves to explore the meaning of Soviet offers to guarantee full access to a "free city" of West Berlin.	A bill (HR9076) appropriating $1.3 billion for public works and $2.6 billion for the AEC in fiscal 1962 is signed into law by Pres. Kennedy.		Benny Paret, of Cuba, regains the world welterweight championship by outpointing title holder Emile Griffith in a 15-round New York bout.	Sept. 30
Americans for Democratic Action charge that the legislative record of the first session of the 87th Congress reveals an "astonishing indifference to real national needs."					Oct. 1
			Researchers at the National Cancer Institute (Bethesda, Md.) report the discovery of a cancer growth-inhibiting agent in the blood of normal persons unafflicted by the disease. . . . A technique to reduce a heart patient's body temperature to 15 degrees centigrade, at which his heart could be stopped for up to 55 minutes during an operation, is reported by the British medical journal *The Practitioner*.		Oct. 2
A bill (S2393) extending for two years the National Defense Education Act and continuing aid to schools in federally "impacted" areas is signed by Pres. Kennedy with "extreme reluctance."		The Labor Dept. reports that the seasonally adjusted unemployment rate was 6.8% in September, the 10th straight month in which the jobless rate has hovered between 6.6% and 6.9%. . . . Nearly 120,000 UAW members strike the Ford Motor Co. as union and company negotiators fail to resolve outstanding non-economic issues before the midnight strike deadline. It is the UAW's first company-wide strike against Ford in its 20-year relationship with the company.		British Queen Elizabeth names Anthony Armstrong-Jones, husband of Princess Margaret, as the Earl of Snowdon.	Oct. 3
Kennedy appoints a bipartisan commission to seek ways of reforming presidential campaign financing so as to avoid an "undesirable" dependence on the large contributions of special interests. . . . The *Congressional Quarterly* reports that the 87th Congress approved during its first session 172 of Pres. Kennedy's record 355 legislative requests. . . . Kennedy signs into law an anti-crime bill (HR468) extending the Fugitive Felon Act to cover any felony.	Kennedy signs a congressional resolution authorizing the U.S. to train French military personnel in the use of atomic weapons.	The *Congressional Quarterly* reports that the first session of the 87th Congress appropriated a peacetime record $84,265,217,636 for fiscal 1962.	In a paper delivered to the annual congress of the International Astronautical Federation in Washington, Soviet scientists reveal that cosmonaut, Gherman Titov suffered considerable "sea sickness" during his orbital mission Aug. 6-7.	Mikhail Tal of Soviet Latvia defeats U.S. champion Bobby Fischer, 14 1/2 to 13 1/2, to win the international chess masters tournament in Bled, Yugoslavia.	Oct. 4
The Civil Rights Commission urges presidential and congressional action to ban racial discrimination in federally-aided housing. The Commission also recommends that all U.S. supervised home financing institutions be prohibited from racial bias in the extension of credit. . . . Pres. Kennedy signs into law an administration bill (HR4998) providing increased federal aid for community health services.			A U.S. Air Force plan to girdle the earth with a belt of copper "needles" for communications purposes wins Pres. Kennedy's endorsement despite scientists' complaints that the project will "befoul space" and obstruct astronomical observation.		Oct. 5
F	**G**	**H**	**I**	**J**	
Includes elections, federal-state relations, civil rights and liberties, crime, the judiciary, education, health care, poverty, urban affairs and population.	*Includes formation and debate of U.S. foreign and defense policies, veterans' affairs and defense spending. (Relations with specific foreign countries are usually found under the region concerned.)*	*Includes business, labor, agriculture, taxation, transportation, consumer affairs, monetary and fiscal policy, natural resources, and pollution.*	*Includes worldwide scientific, medical and technological developments, natural phenomena, U.S. weather, natural disasters, and accidents.*	*Includes the arts, religion, scholarship, communications media, sports, entertainment, fashions, fads and social life.*	

	World Affairs	Europe	Africa & the Middle East	The Americas	Asia & the Pacific
Oct. 6		Pres. Kennedy and Soviet Foreign Min. Andrei Gromyko hold a two-hour conference at the White House in an effort to find an acceptable basis for negotiations on Berlin and Germany. Little substantive progress is reported.	A conference to draft a new constitution for the soon-to-be-independent Kenya ends in deadlock after Kenya's two major political parties refused to agree on terms for forming a coalition regime. Kenyan nationalist Jomo Kenyatta has warned that he will found a third party if the two groups persist in quarreling.		The U.S. is reported to have briefed SEATO military advisers, meeting in Bankok, on a plan for possible U.S. intervention in South Vietnam. . . . Afghan King Mahammad Zahir accepts an offer of U.S. mediation in the border dispute between Afghanistan and Pakistan.
Oct. 7		France announces that its current series of atmospheric nuclear tests (four in all) has been completed.			South Korea's ruling junta announces the arrest of members of a special government commission appointed to investigate business corruption. The officials are charged with accepting bribes.
Oct. 8		West Berlin Mayor Willy Brandt ends a three-day visit to the U.S. during which he received renewed assurance of American readiness to defend his city's liberty.			Leaders of Laos' three contending political factions agree to accept neutralist Prince Souvanna Phouma as the premier of a new coalition government. Serious disagreement, however, remains over the question of how to distribute cabinet posts.
Oct. 9			The British Colonial Office announces that Uganda will be granted its independence Oct. 9, 1962. . . . Israeli Foreign Min. Golda Meir proposes in a U.N. speech that the Arab states join Israel in a Middle East "pilot" disarmament project to parallel big power efforts for world disarmament.		
Oct. 10	The U.S. detonates its third underground nuclear device since suspending its voluntary test moratorium. The USSR is reported to have conducted 19 tests in the current series, including a 10-megaton atmospheric blast Oct. 8.	Thousands of Soviet, Polish and Czech troops are reported entering EAstronautics Germany to take part in the largest joint military maneuvers in the history of the Warsaw Pact.	The governor of Portuguese Angola announces that the African rebellion against Portuguese rule has been suppressed. . . . Ghana announces that it is sending 400 cadets to the USSR for military officers' training.		
Oct. 11	The General Assembly, in an unprecedented action, interrupts its scheduled debate and votes to censure a speech delivered earlier in the day by South African Foreign Min. Eric Louw. In his address, Louw had asserted that apartheid enabled South Africa to achieve greater stability and social progress than any other African country.	Sean Lemass is re-elected as Irish premier even though his ruling Fianna Fail Party lost its Dail Eireann (Parliament) majority in the Oct. 4 general elections.	Israeli Premier David Ben-Gurion reaffirms his government's oppostion to any plan for repatriation of Arab refugees to Israel.	Colombian Pres. Alberto Lleras declares a nationwide state of siege after the government reported crushing a revolt of rightwing army troops from a Bogota barracks.	Pres. Kennedy announces that he is sending Gen. Maxwell Taylor to Saigon to discuss how the U.S. can better assist South Vietnam against the Viet Cong. Kennedy says a decision on American troop commitments will await Taylor's report. . . . Reuters news agency reports that Communist Chinese Foreign Min. Chen Yi would support U.S. initiatives for Chinese-U.S. contacts on the foreign ministers level.
Oct. 12		Soviet Premier Khrushchev, in a letter to British Labor Party leaders, proposes a mutual NATO-Warsaw Pact withdrawal from their borderline positions in central Europe as a first step toward a general European "disengagement."	Tunisian Pres. Habib Bourguiba warns that there will be another "battle of Bizerte" if France persists in postponing negotiations on its evacuation of the base there.		
Oct. 13	Following two weeks of negotiations with Western delegations, Soviet Rep.-to-U.N. Valerian Zorin announces that the USSR is prepared to accept a single acting U.N. secretary general.		Syria resumes its separate seat in the U.N. Syrian independence from the UAR has been recognized by the USSR and several other nations. . . . Ahmed, Imam of Yemen, abdicates his rule in favor of his son, Premier Saifal Islam al Badr. . . . The International Commission of Jurists in Geneva issues a report accusing French troops of atrocities against Tunisian soldiers and civilians during the July fighting in Bizerte.	Premier Cheddi Jagan of British Guiana says in a New York speech that his government is "solidly dedicated to the creation of a socialist economic system."	Red China and Burma sign a supplementary border pact to be added to their October 1960 boundary treaty.
	A	**B**	**C**	**D**	**E**
	Includes developments that affect more than one world region, international organizations and important meetings of major world leaders.	*Includes all domestic and regional developments in Europe, including the Soviet Union, Turkey, Cyprus and Malta.*	*Includes all domestic and regional developments in Africa and the Middle East, including Iraq and Iran and excluding Cyprus, Turkey and Afghanistan.*	*Includes all domestic and regional developments in Latin America, the Caribbean and Canada.*	*Includes all domestic and regional developments in Asia and Pacific nations, extending from Afghanistan through all the Pacific Islands, except Hawaii.*

U.S. Politics & Social Issues	U.S. Foreign Policy & Defense	U.S. Economy & Environment	Science, Technology & Nature	Culture, Leisure & Life Style	
	Kennedy tells a presidential press luncheon that "any prudent family" should build a fall-out shelter as protection against thermonuclear attack.	George Roxburgh, business agent of Detroit Teamsters Local 299, is indicted by a federal grand jury on charges of accepting illegal payments from employers. Three other Teamster local officials were indicted on similar charges in September. The Brookings Institute reports that national committees spent over $25			Oct. 6
The Brookings Institute reports that national committees spent over $25 million on the national level during the 1960 Presidential campaign.	Washington sources report that the administration has decided to send troops to communist-threatened areas of Southeast Asia if they are necessary to their successful defense.	The Commerce Dept. reports that American consumers are now spending 40% of their expendable income on services, an increase of 5% since 1953.	Harvard Dr. Frederick Stare, in a speech to the first National Congress on Medical Quackery, sharply criticizes what he describes as the fraudulent health claims for "natural" or "organically" grown foods.		Oct. 7
The AFL-CIO Actors' Equity Association announces that its members will refuse to perform in segregated theaters after June 1, 1962.				N.Y. Yankee pitcher Whitey Ford, 32, sets a World Series record by pitching 32 consecutive scoreless innings of series play before retiring in the sixth inning of the fourth game against Cincinnati because of a toe injury.	Oct. 8
			The U.S. Public Health Service licenses the manufacture of a second Sabin live-virus oral vaccine to provide immunity against Type II polio virus.	The N.Y. Yankees shut-out Cincinnati, 7-0, to win the 1961 World Series, four games to one.	Oct. 9
The NAACP files job discrimination complaints against eight large government contractors with the President's Committee on Equal Employment Opportunity.		The AFL-CIO Executive Council votes 24-3 against re-admitting the Teamsters. AFL-CIO Pres. Meany charges that the Teamsters are more corruption-plagued "than ever."	Dr. James Van Allen charges that the U.S. space program is lagging because of a shortage of competent scientists within the NASA program.	The N.Y. Mets and Houston Colts, scheduled to begin National League play in 1962, purchase 22 and 23 players, respectively, from a player pool made available by the eight other National League clubs.	Oct. 10
The AFL-CIO Executive Council censures its only Negro member, A. Philip Randolph, for dividing "organized labor and the Negro community" by publicly accusing the AFL-CIO of bias.	The Defense Dept. discloses that 10,000 more U.S. air and ground troops, mostly from eight Air National Guard squadrons, will be sent to Europe beginning Nov. 1.	Teamster Pres. James Hoffa is reindicted by a U.S. grand jury in Orlando, Fla. on fraud charges involving the alleged misuse of union funds. The original indictment was dismissed July 12 on technical grounds.	U.S.A.F. Maj. Robert White pilots the experimental X-15 rocket-plane to a new winged aircraft altitude record of 215,000 ft.--more than 40 miles.	Chico (Leonard) Marx, 70, oldest member of the Marx Brothers comedy team, dies of a heart ailment in Hollywood, Calif.	Oct. 11
Ex-Pres. Eisenhower says in an NBC-TV interview that "creating an atmosphere of serenity and mutual confidence" was his greatest accomplishment as president.				A new national weekly newspaper called *World* goes on sale in about 100 U.S. cities.	Oct. 12
The Civil Rights Commission issues a report urging federal action against segregated unions and racially-discriminating employers involved in government contract work.	The State and Defense Depts. disclose the sale of 130 obsolescent U.S. Saberjets to Yugoslavia under an agreement worked out by the Eisenhower administration. The sale draws criticism from conservatives in both parties.				Oct. 13

F	G	H	I	J
Includes elections, federal-state relations, civil rights and liberties, crime, the judiciary, education, health care, poverty, urban affairs and population.	Includes formation and debate of U.S. foreign and defense policies, veterans' affairs and defense spending. (Relations with specific foreign countries are usually found under the region concerned.)	Includes business, labor, agriculture, taxation, transportation, consumer affairs, monetary and fiscal policy, natural resources, and pollution.	Includes worldwide scientific, medical and technological developments, natural phenomena, U.S. weather, natural disasters, and accidents.	Includes the arts, religion, scholarship, communications media, sports, entertainment, fashions, fads and social life.

	World Affairs	Europe	Africa & the Middle East	The Americas	Asia & the Pacific
Oct. 14	U.N. Food & Agriculture Organization reports that retail food costs are rising in almost every nation of the world and especially in underdeveloped countries.				North Vietnam protests to the International Control Commission for Vietnam that Gen. Maxwell Taylor's visit to Saigon is a prelude to U.S. military intervention in violation of the Geneva armistice. . . . A U.S. agreement to sell Pakistan $621 million worth of farm products over the next four years is signed in Karachi.
Oct. 15	U.S. Amb.-to-U.N. Adlai Stevenson says in an ABC news interview that Burmese Amb.-to-U.N. U Thant, 53, is being seriously considered for the post of acting U.N. secretary general and that he appears acceptable to the USSR.	European diplomatic sources report a growing rift among the Western allies over the question of Berlin negotiations with the Soviets. France and West Germany are reportedly unhappy with U.S. participation in exploratory talks on possible full-scale negotiations over Germany, believing that the West's position is non-negotiable.			
Oct. 16		Finnish Pres. Urho Kekkonen ends a two-day visit to Washington during which he stressed his government's commitment to strict neutrality in East-West affairs. . . . France's State Planning Commission makes public a four-year economic and social progress program aimed at achieving a 24% increase in industrial production and a 23% increase in private consumption.			
Oct. 17	In a six-and-a-half hour address to the opening session of the 23d Soviet CP Congress, Khrushchev announces that the USSR will "probably" end its current series of nuclear tests Oct. 30 with the detonation of a 50-megaton super bomb, by far the largest ever tested. The Soviet Premier also renewed his demand for a three-member U.N. executive.	In his lengthy speech to the CP Congress, Khrushchev offers to withdraw his year-end deadline for a German peace treaty if the West demonstrates a willingness to negotiate an overall German agreement. . . . Khrushchev also denounces the Stalinist errors and personality cult deviations of the Albanian Communist regime under Gen. Enver Hoxha. Visiting Communist Chinese Premier Chou En-lai ostentatiously refrains from applauding these remarks, further confirming reports of an Albanian-Chinese doctrinal alliance in opposition to Khrushchev.			
Oct. 18		State Secy. Rusk says that the U.S. welcomes Khrushchev's apparent offer to relax Soviet pressure on Berlin, but adds that the U.S. still regards Soviet terms for a German settlement as an unacceptable basis for negotiation. . . . The 22nd Soviet CP adopts a Khrushchev-approved 20-year party program and a new set of rules aimed at promoting internal party democracy. . . . An estimated 30,000 Moslems march in Paris to protest police curfew regulations barring them from the streets after 8:30 p.m.		A student protest at Santo Domingo University over the appointment of a "too pro-Trujillo" rector erupts into serious rioting between Ciudad Trujillo police and rock-throwing students.	A state of national emergency, empowering Pres. Diem to suspend the Constitution, is ratified by the South Vietnamese National Assembly in the wake of stepped-up Viet Cong attacks.
Oct. 19	Communist Chinese Premier Chou En-lai, in an address to the Soviet Party Congress, says that a "public denunciation" of ideological differences (a reference to Khrushchev's Oct. 17 attack on Albania) "does not contribute to the cohesion of the socialist camp.". . . Nationalist China, bowing to pressure from Afro-Asian states and the U.S. is reported to have decided not to use its Security Council veto to block U.N. admission for Outer Mongolia.	France and the U.S. announce the reactivation of four former American bases in France as part of the West's Berlin-related military build-up.		Over 200 Bolivian oppositionists are arrested in a government crack-down on an alleged polt to overthrow Pres. Victor Paz Estenssoro.	
	A	**B**	**C**	**D**	**E**
	Includes developments that affect more than one world region, international organizations and important meetings of major world leaders.	*Includes all domestic and regional developments in Europe, including the Soviet Union, Turkey, Cyprus and Malta.*	*Includes all domestic and regional developments in Africa and the Middle East, including Iraq and Iran and excluding Cyprus, Turkey and Afghanistan.*	*Includes all domestic and regional developments in Latin America, the Caribbean and Canada.*	*Includes all domestic and regional developments in Asia and Pacific nations, extending from Afghanistan through all the Pacific Islands, except Hawaii.*

U.S. Politics & Social Issues	U.S. Foreign Policy & Defense	U.S. Economy & Environment	Science, Technology & Nature	Culture, Leisure & Life Style	
					Oct. 14
	Nigerian university students stage an anti-U.S. protest following the public disclosure of a postcard written by a Peace Corps member which described Nigerian living conditions as primitive and squalid. The offending corpsman apologizes to students and Nigerian officials for "her senseless letter."	The 12-day strike against the Ford Motor Co. ends following ratification of a new three-year agreement worked out by Ford and UAW negotiators Oct. 12.			**Oct. 15**
Martin Luther King meets with Pres. Kennedy to urge stronger administration action against segregation. . . . Atty. Gen. Kennedy announces that the Illinois Central, the Southern and the Louisville & Nashville railroads have agreed to desegregate their terminal facilities.		Robert Weaver, head of the Housing and Home Finance Agency, announces the establishment of a U.S. Office of Transportation.		Italy eliminates the U.S. in the interzonal finals of the Davis Cup tennis tournament held in Rome.	**Oct. 16**
				The Ford Foundation announces grants totaling $1,470,000 for five new visual arts programs in the U.S.	**Oct. 17**
		The Commerce Dept. reports that total U.S. personal incomes rose to an annual rate of $420.2 billion in September, up about $800 million from the August rate.			**Oct. 18**
			The Caroline Institute in Stockholm awards the Nobel Prize in Medicine to Hungarianborn Dr. Georg von Bekesy for his research into the physical mechanisms of hearing.	Rabbi Joachim Prinz, president of the American Jewish Congress, says that the efforts of Pope John XXIII and of Protestant leaders to eliminate anti-Semitism has marked a new departure in Christian-Jewish relations.	**Oct. 19**

F	G	H	I	J
Includes elections, federal-state relations, civil rights and liberties, crime, the judiciary, education, health care, poverty, urban affairs and population.	Includes formation and debate of U.S. foreign and defense policies, veterans' affairs and defense spending. (Relations with specific foreign countries are usually found under the region concerned.)	Includes business, labor, agriculture, taxation, transportation, consumer affairs, monetary and fiscal policy, natural resources, and pollution.	Includes worldwide scientific, medical and technological developments, natural phenomena, U.S. weather, natural disasters, and accidents.	Includes the arts, religion, scholarship, communications media, sports, entertainment, fashions, fads and social life.

	World Affairs	Europe	Africa & the Middle East	The Americas	Asia & the Pacific
Oct. 20		An estimated 15,000 Algerian Moslems have been detained by Paris police in connection with four days of Moslem protests against security regulations.			
Oct. 21		Tension growing out of defiant U.S. challenges to recently intensified East German border identification checks climaxes with the bringing of Soviet and U.S. tanks face-to-face across the Berlin boundary. Pres. Kennedy had earlier ordered a suspension of the U.S. challenges and the tanks were shortly withdrawn.	Serious fighting between Bahutu and Watusi tribesmen is reported in the Belgian-administered trust territory of Ruanda.	The Bolivian government declares a state of siege amidst growing unrest over the rising cost of gasoline and transportation.	
Oct. 22	Armed U.S. military police enter East Berlin to ensure the right of passage of an American official who was denied entry into the Soviet sector by East German authorities. Identification checks on Western officials seeking entry into East Berlin intensified Oct. 15.				
Oct. 23	The 1961 Nobel Peace Prize is awarded in Oslo, Norway to late U.N. Secy. Gen. Dag Hammarskjold. The 1960 Peace Prize, withheld the previous year, is awarded to Albert John Luthuli, a Zulu chief and political leader in the African campaign against South Africa's apartheid policies. . . . Soviet scientists detonate a 30-megaton nuclear bomb, the largest man-made explosion in history.	Turkey's four major political parties agree to form a coalition civil government to replace the military junta after final returns showed that no party had won a majority in the parliamentary elections held Oct. 15.			
Oct. 24	World leaders express shock and dismay over yesterday's test of a high-yield 30-megaton bomb by the USSR. Student protests are staged in several European capitals.	West German Chancellor Konrad Adenauer, in a letter to Pres. Kennedy, expresses his firm opposition to any Western concessions on Berlin and the German problem. De Gaulle conveyed similar hard-line views to Kennedy in an Oct. 23 letter. . . . Malta is granted internal self-rule under a new British-approved constitution.	Algerian rebel Premier Benyoussef Ben Khedda calls upon France to open negotiations "on the means and the date of. . .independence as well as on a cease-fire."	Visiting British Guiana Premier Cheddi Jagan tells the National Press Club in Washington that his advocacy of socialism is not incompatible with the U.S. goal of maintaining" a democratic way of life."	In a complaint to the International Control Commission, South Vietnam formally charges North Vietnam with aggression aimed at overthrowing the Diem regime.
Oct. 25		Speakers at the Soviet CP Congress uniformly reiterate the major themes expressed in Premier Khrushchev's opening address of Oct. 17: a reaffirmation of the de-Stalinization program and renewed denunciation of the pro-Stalinist "anti-party plot of 1957.". . . Shooting and violence along the Berlin Wall are becoming a daily occurrence as East German border guards make every effort to foil the continuing escape trys by East German refugees.	Rashid Karame succeeds the resigned Saeb Salaam as Lebanese premier.	Anti-government rioting and demonstrations which began a week ago in Ciudad Trujillo are reported to have spread to several Dominican Republic cities.	
Oct. 26	The General Assembly orders a U.N. investigation into the causes of the Northern Rhodesian plane crash that killed Secy. Gen. Hammarskjold and 15 U.N. aides.	A joint session of the Turkish Assembly and Senate elects Gen. Cemal Gursel president of the second Turkish Republic.			In a personal message to Pres. Diem on the sixth anniversary of South Vietnam's independence, Pres. Kennedy reaffirms U.S. determination to help in resisting communist aggression.

A	B	C	D	E
Includes developments that affect more than one world region, international organizations and important meetings of major world leaders.	Includes all domestic and regional developments in Europe, including the Soviet Union, Turkey, Cyprus and Malta.	Includes all domestic and regional developments in Africa and the Middle East, including Iraq and Iran and excluding Cyprus, Turkey and Afghanistan.	Includes all domestic and regional developments in Latin America, the Caribbean and Canada.	Includes all domestic and regional developments in Asia and Pacific nations, extending from Afghanistan through all the Pacific Islands, except Hawaii.

U.S. Politics & Social Issues	U.S. Foreign Policy & Defense	U.S. Economy & Environment	Science, Technology & Nature	Culture, Leisure & Life Style	
			A report providing additional evidence that heavy smoking increases the risk of coronary heart disease is released by Dr. Joseph Doyle of the Albany (N.Y.) Medical Center College. . . . Dr. J. Gordon Barrow of Atlanta makes public a study showing that Trappist monks living on a low fat diet have a low rate of heart attacks, while Benedictine monks with high fat diets similar to that of most Americans have a high rate.		Oct. 20
	Deputy Defense Secy. Roswell Gilpatric declares that the U.S. nuclear force is so "lethal" that any enemy aggression "would be an act of self-destruction." The statement comes in the wake of GOP criticism that the administration has wrongly downplayed the nation's nuclear deterrent.		Some 350 million tiny copper wires are released into orbit by a Midas IV satellite as part of a U.S. military communications experiment known as Project West Ford. Announcement of the planned experiment had been met with protests from astronomers in the USSR and elsewhere.		Oct. 21
			A new method of brain surgery, which does not require the interruption of normal heart, liver and respiratory functions, is announced by doctors at the Stanford Univ. School of Medicine. The American Assembly, meeting in Harriman, N.Y., adopts a resolution warning the administration against "excessive" political and scientific emphasis on the race to put a man on the moon.		Oct. 22
		Teamster Pres. James Hoffa files a $1 million libel suit against AFL-CIO Pres. George Meany for his recent charges of corruption in the Teamster union.			Oct. 23
U.S. Judge Hobart Grooms rules as unconstitutional a Birmingham, Ala. ordinance requiring segregation of public recreation facilities.		Ex-Pres. Eisenhower, in a speech to a N.Y. GOP mayoral election rally, charges that the administration's economic policy will someday lead to "a controlled economy."			Oct. 24
					Oct. 25
		Following a budget meeting with the cabinet, Pres. Kennedy issues a statement saying that he intends to propose a balanced budget for fiscal 1963.		The Nobel Prize in Literature is awarded to Yugoslav writer, Dr. Ivo Andrie.	Oct. 26

F	G	H	I	J
Includes elections, federal-state relations, civil rights and liberties, crime, the judiciary, education, health care, poverty, urban affairs and population.	*Includes formation and debate of U.S. foreign and defense policies, veterans' affairs and defense spending. (Relations with specific foreign countries are usually found under the region concerned.)*	*Includes business, labor, agriculture, taxation, transportation, consumer affairs, monetary and fiscal policy, natural resources, and pollution.*	*Includes worldwide scientific, medical and technological developments, natural phenomena, U.S. weather, natural disasters, and accidents.*	*Includes the arts, religion, scholarship, communications media, sports, entertainment, fashions, fads and social life.*

	World Affairs	Europe	Africa & the Middle East	The Americas	Asia & the Pacific
Oct. 27	The U.N. General Assembly, by a vote of 87-11, adopts a resolution asking the USSR to cancel its announced plan to test a 50-megaton nuclear device. . . . The General Assembly, acting on Security Council recommendations, votes to admit Outer Mongolia and Mauritania as the U.N.'s 102d and 103d members.	In his concluding address to the CP Congress, Khrushchev says that a memorial should be erected in Moscow "to commemorate the comrades who became victims of arbitrary rule" under Stalin.			
Oct. 28	The U.N. General Assembly votes to establish a worldwide system of fallout monitoring stations.		Two Katanga jets bomb central government troops on the Katanga-Kasai border in apparent violation of the Katanga-U.N. truce accord signed Sept. 20.		
Oct. 29					
Oct. 30	A nuclear explosion with a force greatly exceeding the planned 50 megatons (estimates range from 62-90 megatons) is detonated by Soviet scientists in the USSR's Arctic proving grounds. . . . Ireland, Ghana and Venezuela are elected to fill three of the four vacant seats on the Security Council.	The anti-Stalinist thrust of the 22d Soviet CP Congress climaxes with the unanimous adoption of a resolution ordering the removal of Stalin's body from the Red Square mausoleum where it lay in state alongside that of Lenin. . . . A study published by the Twentieth Century Fund predicts that economic production in 18 Western European nations will continue to grow from its present historical high to an estimated combined GNP of $342 billion by 1970.	Troops of the central Congolese government launch an invasion into Katanga Province after receiving orders from Premier Cyrille Adoula "to liquidate the Katanga secession." Heavy Katangan resistance is reported. . . . Rightwing terrorism and demonstrations in opposition to de Gaulle's goal of a negotiated Algerian peace settlement is reported to have continued throughout October in almost all Algerian cities.		
Oct. 31	Soviet scientists set off two moderate yield nuclear devices, overturning earlier reports that yesterday's huge blast would be the last in the current Soviet series.	The Soviet CP concludes its 22nd Congress after approving a resolution calling on Albanian leaders to "renounce their erroneous views and to return to the road of unity."			
Nov. 1			Three French soldiers and 83 Algerian Moslems are dead in the wake of riots and demonstrations throughout Algeria marking the seventh anniversary of the Algerian nationalist rebellion.	In a letter to the OAS, the U.S. charges Cuba with a deliberate campaign to "overthrow and subvert the constitutional governments" of the Western Hemisphere.	The 14-nation Geneva conference reconvenes in formal session to approve a privately negotiated 12-point program providing for an end to foreign military involvement in Laos and for increased support for the Control Commission. China warns that the agreement will be meaningless if the U.S. sends troops to South Vietnam.
Nov. 2	Pres. Kennedy announces that he has ordered preparations for a resumption of U.S. nuclear tests in the atmosphere should they become necessary to ensure continued U.S. nuclear weapons superiority over the USSR.	Hugh Gaitskell is re-elected leader of the British Parliamentary Labor Party, defeating leftwing opponent Anthony Greenwood by a 2-1 margin.	Israel's nine-month old caretaker cabinet is dissolved as the Knesset votes to approve a new three-party coalition government under Premier Ben-Gurion.		The International Control Commission for Laos reports to the 14-nation Geneva conference that civil war is likely to resume unless a coalition Laotian government is formed soon.
Nov. 3	Burmese Amb.-to-U.N. U Thant is unanimously elected as acting U.N. secretary general, ending an East-West dispute that had left the U.N. leaderless since Hammarskjold's death Sept. 18. Thant immediately names Ralph Bunche of the U.S. and Georgi Arkadyev of the USSR as his principal advisers on "important questions."		A U.N. Congo command report on the renewed Congo-Katanga fighting in effect endorses the central Congo government's invasion by asserting that the Oct. 28 Katanga bombing incident had voided the U.N.-Katanga truce accord.	Cuba issues a decree limiting the right of foreign embassies to grant political asylum to anti-Castro Cubans. . . . *The New York Times* reports that the El Salvadorian government has decided to permit five opposition parties to participate in congressional elections scheduled for Dec. 17.	

A	B	C	D	E
Includes developments that affect more than one world region, international organizations and important meetings of major world leaders.	*Includes all domestic and regional developments in Europe, including the Soviet Union, Turkey, Cyprus and Malta.*	*Includes all domestic and regional developments in Africa and the Middle East, including Iraq and Iran and excluding Cyprus, Turkey and Afghanistan.*	*Includes all domestic and regional developments in Latin America, the Caribbean and Canada.*	*Includes all domestic and regional developments in Asia and Pacific nations, extending from Afghanistan through all the Pacific Islands, except Hawaii.*

U.S. Politics & Social Issues	U.S. Foreign Policy & Defense	U.S. Economy & Environment	Science, Technology & Nature	Culture, Leisure & Life Style	
	Defense Secy. McNamara announces that the administration has decided to end production of B-52 strategic bombers in 1961 and to suspend a scheduled acceleration in the production of the supersonic B-70 bomber. McNamara says the success of the current U.S. military build-up allowed the cut backs. . . . Irvin C. Scarbeck, a former foreign service officer in the U.S. Embassy in Warsaw, is convicted of passing embassy secrets to agents of the Polish government.	Pres. Kennedy announces two government-subsidized risk insurance programs to help U.S. exporters compete with foreign companies for overseas credit sales.	The U.S.'s new Saturn rocket system is successfully test-launched for the first time. . . . The Monsanto Chemical Co. reports that its researchers have arrested the aging process in baby chicks and mice by altering the amino acid balance in their diets. Inquiry into possible applications of the discovery for humans is being planned.		Oct. 27
					Oct. 28
		Budget Director David Bell estimates fiscal 1962 expenditures at $88,985 billion and revenues at $82.1 billion, leaving a deficit of $6.885 billion.			Oct. 29
In a series of reports sponsored by the Council for Basic Education, seven reading specialists charge that the "whole-word" method of reading instruction, used in U.S. schools for the last 30 years, is measurably less effective than the older "phonic method."		A contract guaranteeing employees a job or wages for life is agreed to by representatives of the Southern Pacific Railroad and the AFL-CIO Order of Railroad Telegraphers after almost three-and-a-half years of negotiation. . . . The Labor Dept. reports that the number of major U.S. industrial areas with unemployment exceeding 6% fell from 88 in July to 68 in October.			Oct. 30
Leon Bearden is sentenced to life in prison in El Paso, Tex. for the Aug. 3 hijacking of a Continental Airlines plane.	Congressional leaders of both parties call for a resumption of U.S. atmospheric tests after learning that the USSR had failed to halt its testing after the 50-megaton blast on Oct. 30.	Dissident Teamster locals in the Cincinnati area vote overwhelmingly in an NLRB election to quit the Teamsters and affiliate with AFL-CIO locals.	Hurricane Hattie strikes British Honduras killing 314 persons and devastating the capital city of Belize.		Oct. 31
Local authorities in Jackson, Miss., Shreveport, La., McComb, Miss. and Montgomery, Ala. defy new ICC regualtions barring segregation in interstate bus facilities.		State Undersecy. George Ball calls for a downward revision of U.S. tariffs in order to "dampen inflationary forces" and to maintain America's close trading relationship with Europe's Common Market nations.			Nov. 1
		Chrysler and the UAW reach agreement on a new three-year pact. . . . Members of the Japanese and U.S. cabinets meet in Hakone, Japan to discuss the two nations' common economic and trade problems.	The Nobel Prize in Chemistry is awarded to Univ. of California Prof. Melvin Calvin for his study of plant photosynthesis. The Physics Prize is jointly awarded to Stanford Univ. Prof. Robert Hofstadter (for research into nuclear structure) and Rudolf Moessbauer, of West Germany, (for relativity theory-related study of gamma rays).	James Thurber, 66, American humorist, cartoonist, and long-time contributor to the *New Yorker* magazine, dies in New York of pneumonia.	Nov. 2
CORE director James Farmer announces that 1,400 Freedom Riders will participate Nov. 11 in a test of segregation policies at restaurants along U.S. Route 40 in Maryland. Route 40 was chosen because of a number of recent racial incidents in that area involving African diplomats.	Gen. Maxwell Taylor, just returned from a three-week mission to South Vietnam and Thailand, reports his findings to Pres. Kennedy. Though unpublished, the report is said to urge U.S. pressure for a reorganization of the South Vietnamese government.		Representatives of eight European nations and Australia agree in London to a plan for the joint development and construction of peaceful satellite launchers.		Nov. 3
F	G	H	I	J	
Includes elections, federal-state relations, civil rights and liberties, crime, the judiciary, education, health care, poverty, urban affairs and population.	Includes formation and debate of U.S. foreign and defense policies, veterans' affairs and defense spending. (Relations with specific foreign countries are usually found under the region concerned.)	Includes business, labor, agriculture, taxation, transportation, consumer affairs, monetary and fiscal policy, natural resources, and pollution.	Includes worldwide scientific, medical and technological developments, natural phenomena, U.S. weather, natural disasters, and accidents.	Includes the arts, religion, scholarship, communications media, sports, entertainment, fashions, fads and social life.	

	World Affairs	Europe	Africa & the Middle East	The Americas	Asia & the Pacific
Nov. 4	Soviet scientists continue to detonate nuclear devices on an almost daily basis. The U.S. AEC has reported 31 Soviet tests since Sept. 1.	Final returns from the Oct. 29 Greek general elections give a clear victory to ex-Premier Constantine Caramanlis's National Radical Union. Opposition Liberal leader George Papandreou attributes the National Radical win to "fraud and bribing."	The central Congolese government announces that its invasion of Katanga has been repulsed and that the army is in full retreat.	Demonstrations against the allegedly inflationary policies of Pres. Jose Velasco Ibarra, which began Oct. 18, are reportedly intensifying and spreading throughout Ecuador.	
Nov. 5			Congo Vice Premier Antoine Gizenga, in Stanleyville ostensibly on personal business, defies a Premier Cyrille Adoula ultimatum to return to Leopoldville. The defiance is interpreted as a sign that Gizenga has resumed his opposition to the central government.		Indian P.M. Nehru arrives in New York to begin a 10-day state visit to the U.S. The visit comes amidst growing U.S. criticism of an allegedly pro-Soviet tone to India's professed neutrality.
Nov. 6	The U.N. General Assembly, over opposition from Western and Soviet blocs, votes to adopt an Indian resolution calling for immediate resumption of the voluntary moratorium on all nuclear tests.	In a speech marking the 20th anniversary of the Albanian CP, First Secy. Enver Hoxha denounces Khrushchev's peaceful co-existence doctrine as Marxist deviation and charges him with personal responsibility for the Soviet-Albanian rift. . . . The New York Times reports that most NATO members have expressed alarm over the U.S.'s show of force to back its defiance of new East German identification checks on civilian entry into East Berlin.			Indian P.M. Nehru begins four days of scheduled talks with U.S. Pres. Kennedy on world problems and the situation in Southeast Asia.
Nov. 7	Premier Khrushchev tells Kremlin reporters that the USSR will continue its nuclear test series indefinitely if the U.S. resumes atmospheric tests.	Sources close to Soviet Premier Khrushchev report that he has decided to avoid for the time being any Berlin actions which might deepen tensions there.		Jose Velasco Ibarra resigns as Ecuadorian president after the army withdraws support in the face of growing anti-government protests against his economic policies. . . . The Cuban government reports that the underground anti-Castro Revolutionary Popular Movement has been suppressed and most of its leaders arrested.	Livingston Merchant, U.S. diplomat sent by Pres. Kennedy to help mediate the current Pakistan-Afghanistan border dispute, announces in Karachi that his intervention has not led to any progress in the controversy.
Nov. 8	The Central Committee of the Chinese CP issues a clearly anti-Soviet statement congratulating the Albanian CP on its 20th anniversary and its tradition of "correct" leadership.		Nigerian U.N. troops restore order to Luluabourg after three days of attacks upon whites by marauding central Congolese soldiers enraged over the rout of their Katanga invasion.	Leftist Ecuador V.P. Carlos Arosemena Monroy is permitted to assume the presidency despite a brief army attempt to elevate a more conservative replacement for resigned Pres. Velasco.	
Nov. 9		Western news sources report that Premier Khrushchev has outlined a new and possibly more acceptable set of terms for a Berlin settlement in Moscow talks with Bonn Amb.-to-USSR Hans Kroll. The proposal is said to assure Western occupation rights without requiring formal recognition of EAstronautics Germany or Western commitment to a German peace treaty.		Ecuador's new Pres. Julio Arosemena Monroy says in his inaugural address that he will maintain close diplomatic relations with Cuba.	Indian P.M. Nehru tells a National Press Club lucheon in Washington that increased U.S. support to South Vietnam would only bring an identical response from the communists. The strengthening of the International Control Commission in Vietnam he says is "the only policy that could succeed there."
Nov. 10		The U.S. State Dept. confirms that it has received from Bonn Amb. Hans Kroll reports of a new Soviet Berlin offer, but as yet has received no official proposal from the USSR.			

A	B	C	D	E
Includes developments that affect more than one world region, international organizations and important meetings of major world leaders.	Includes all domestic and regional developments in Europe, including the Soviet Union, Turkey, Cyprus and Malta.	Includes all domestic and regional developments in Africa and the Middle East, including Iraq and Iran and excluding Cyprus, Turkey and Afghanistan.	Includes all domestic and regional developments in Latin America, the Caribbean and Canada.	Includes all domestic and regional developments in Asia and Pacific nations, extending from Afghanistan through all the Pacific Islands, except Hawaii.

U.S. Politics & Social Issues	U.S. Foreign Policy & Defense	U.S. Economy & Environment	Science, Technology & Nature	Culture, Leisure & Life Style	
The Gallup Co. releases a poll indicating that, in a choice between Rockefeller and Goldwater, 51% of rank and file Republicans favor Rockefeller while 33% favor Goldwater. An Oct. 27 poll of the delegates to the 1960 GOP convention, however, showed Goldwater favored over Rockefeller almost three to one.	The Army announces that it has accepted the resignation of Maj. Gen. Edwin Walker. Walker, who had been officially rebuked for rightwing indoctrination activities, said he could no longer serve under "little men" who "punish loyal service."				Nov. 4
					Nov. 5
	A fire breaks out on the newly commissioned carrier *Constellation*, killing four and injuring nine others.		A four-hour cyclone rips through Athens, Greece leaving 44 persons dead and 4,000 homes destroyed.		Nov. 6
Democratic N.Y. City Mayor Robert Wagner is re-elected to a third term. . . . Democrat Richard Hughes is elected as New Jersey's first Roman Catholic governor in an upset victory over ex-Labor Secy. James Mitchell.					Nov. 7
James Farmer, executive director of CORE, cancels a planned Nov. 11 Freedom Ride on Route 40 in Maryland after 35 restaurants along their route announced they would desegregate by Nov. 22.	Pres. Kennedy announces that former Pres. Eisenhower has agreed to serve as chairman of a new international "people-to-people" goodwill organization. . . . Kennedy discloses at his regular news conference that he will seek additional funds for defense next year.			Whitey Ford of the N.Y. Yankees wins the 1961 Cy Young Award as the major league's best pitcher.	Nov. 8
	Irvin Scarbeck is sentenced to 30 years in prison for passing U.S. diplomatic secrets to Polish government agents.		U.S.A.F. Maj. Robert White test flies the X-15 rocket plane at a new world record speed of 4,093 mph.	The Professional Golf Association at its annual convention in Hollywood, Fla. votes to eliminate from its constitution a provision restricting membership to "Caucasians' only. . . . A drought-related fire in Hollywood Hills, Calif. destroys 447 homes in the exclusive Bel Air-Brentwood suburbs, including those of ex-V.P. Nixon and a number of Hollywood movie personalities.	Nov. 9
	Pres. Kennedy appoints a commission to study the statistical methods and validity of U.S. employment-unemployment figures.		An orbit-bound E-model Atlas rocket, carrying a small monkey, is destroyed by radio signal after it veered off course following lift-off from Cape Canaveral.		Nov. 10

F	G	H	I	J
Includes elections, federal-state relations, civil rights and liberties, crime, the judiciary, education, health care, poverty, urban affairs and population.	*Includes formation and debate of U.S. foreign and defense policies, veterans' affairs and defense spending. (Relations with specific foreign countries are usually found under the region concerned.)*	*Includes business, labor, agriculture, taxation, transportation, consumer affairs, monetary and fiscal policy, natural resources, and pollution.*	*Includes worldwide scientific, medical and technological developments, natural phenomena, U.S. weather, natural disasters, and accidents.*	*Includes the arts, religion, scholarship, communications media, sports, entertainment, fashions, fads and social life.*

	World Affairs	Europe	Africa & the Middle East	The Americas	Asia & the Pacific
Nov. 11		The Russian city of Stalingrad is officially renamed Volgograd. A general "de-Stalinization" of place names is occurring throughout the Soviet-bloc. . . . Soviet newspapers confirm reports that several prominent Jewish leaders in Leningrad have been convicted and jailed for anti-Soviet crimes. . . . Candidates of Premier Antonio Salazar's National Union Party are re-elected without opposition to the Portuguese National Assembly.		Venezuela becomes the 10th nation in the Americas to sever diplomatic relations with Cuba. The government cites repeated Cuban insults against "the social order and institutions of Venezuela" as the reason for the break.	
Nov. 12		Moscow sources report that ex-Foreign Min. Vyacheslav Molotov, ex-Premier Georgi Malenkov, and ex-Pres. Kliment Voroshilov have been expelled from the Soviet CP for their role in the 1957 "anti-party plot" and their complicity in Stalin era "crimes."			Gen. Chung Hee Park, chairman of South Korea's Supreme Council for National Reconstruction, stops in Japan enroute to a state visit in the U.S. for talks with Premier Hayato Ikeda. Their meeting is officially described as a useful step toward resumption of normal relations between the two countries.
Nov. 13	Parallel notes delivered to the USSR, Britain and the U.S. propose reconvening the suspended three-nation test-ban talks in Geneva on or before Nov. 28. There have been no reported nuclear tests by either side since Nov. 4.	The West German government announces that Amb. Hans Kroll's talks with Khrushchev were "unauthorized" and that Kroll had been ordered back to Bonn to explain his actions. . . . Finnish Pres. Urho Kekkonen, responding to overt Soviet pressure, orders Finland's 1962 Parliamentary elections to be moved up to Feb. 4.			
Nov. 14		A new West German coalition cabinet, made up of Christian Democrats and Free Democrats, is sworn-in in the Bundestag. The Free Democrats agree to join the government only after Adenauer agrees to the dismissal of Foreign Min. Heinrich von Brentano and to a hard-line position against any Western concessions on Berlin. . . . West German press sources report there have been 268 "incidents" involving refugees trying to escape over the Berlin Wall since Aug. 13; at least eight persons have been killed and 69 wounded in the incidents.	A special U.N. investigating committee issues a report concluding that the late Patrice Lumumba of the Congo was probably murdered on explicit orders from the Katanga Provincial government.		Philippine V.P. Diosdado Masapagal, candidate of the Liberal Party, wins the Philippine presidential election, defeating current Pres. Carlos Garcia by a 4-3 margin. . . . South Korean leader Chung Hee Park concludes a meeting in Washington with Pres. Kennedy after receiving reassurances of continued U.S. military and economic support.
Nov. 15			U.N. officials report a wave of mutinies among Congolese army units stationed in Kivu and northern Katanga Provinces. The mutineers are believed to be sympathetic to Vice Premier Gizenga and his Stanleyville followers who apparently have withdrawn support from the central Congo government.	Two brothers of the late Generalissimo Rafael Trujillo return to the Dominican Republic after a brief exile, giving rise to rumors that a Trujillo-family coup attempt is imminent.	
Nov. 16			Katanga Pres. Tshombe denounces as "completely false" a U.N. report blaming him for the death of Patrice Lumumba. . . . The U.N. Congo Command announces that 13 Italian members of the U.N. Force, imprisoned by mutinous Congolese troops, were killed and dismembered by their captors on Nov. 11.	The Panamanian National Assembly unanimously adopts a resolution asking for negotiations with the U.S. on a new treaty to give Panama greater control over the canal.	

A	B	C	D	E
Includes developments that affect more than one world region, international organizations and important meetings of major world leaders.	Includes all domestic and regional developments in Europe, including the Soviet Union, Turkey, Cyprus and Malta.	Includes all domestic and regional developments in Africa and the Middle East, including Iraq and Iran and excluding Cyprus, Turkey and Afghanistan.	Includes all domestic and regional developments in Latin America, the Caribbean and Canada.	Includes all domestic and regional developments in Asia and Pacific nations, extending from Afghanistan through all the Pacific Islands, except Hawaii.

U.S. Politics & Social Issues	U.S. Foreign Policy & Defense	U.S. Economy & Environment	Science, Technology & Nature	Culture, Leisure & Life Style	
AFL-CIO Pres. Meany urges passage of a federal fair employment practices act to combat job discrimination against Negroes. AFL-CIO V.P. A. Philip Randolph calls the statement "belated, but significant." . . . Thirty-three persons are arrested following a day of protests against segregated restaurants in Baltimore and Annapolis, Md.	In a Veterans Day address, Pres. Kennedy asserts that a readiness to fight in defense of freedom is the "only way to maintain the peace."				Nov. 11
					Nov. 12
The U.S. Supreme Court overturns the conviction of Charles Hamilton on the ground that his court-appointed attorney did not appear at his arraignment. . . . The Court also upholds a lower court decision granting American Nazi leader George Lincoln Rockwell the right to obtain a permit to speak in a N.Y. City park.		The Commerce Dept. reports that the U.S. balance of payments deficit rose from $475 million in the second quarter of 1961 to $800 million in the third quarter. . . . The Dow-Jones stock average reaches a new record high of 728.43.		Norman Mailer receives a suspended sentence on a third degree assault conviction stemming from the Nov. 20, 1960 stabbing of his wife. . . . Cellist Pablo Casals, 84, performs at a White House recital after acceding to a personal request from Pres. Kennedy. Casals, a Spanish exile, had previously refused to perform in the U.S. because of its support of the Franco regime. . . . Davey Moore retains the world featherweight championship by winning a 15-round decision over Kazuo Takayama in Tokyo, Japan.	Nov. 13
		Labor Secy. Arthur Goldberg, at a White House regional conference in Cleveland, reiterates recent administration proposals for a reduction in the level of U.S. tariffs.			Nov. 14
		Kennedy appoints a special committee to study "the vital national problem" of high unemployment among out-of-school youth.	A Discoverer XXXV satellite, equipped to gather data on the effect of a space environment on human tissue, is launched into orbit from Vandenberg AF Base and then returned to a Pacific recovery area where it is successfully retrieved.	Rev. Arthur Lichtenberger, presiding bishop of the U.S. Protestant Episcopal Church, confers at the Vatican with Pope John XXIII, marking the first meeting between heads of the two churches.	Nov. 15
Rep. Sam Rayburn (D, Tex.), Speaker of the U.S. House of Representatives since 1940 (for all but two terms), dies of lung cancer in Bonham, Tex. at age 79. . . . Kennedy begins a three-day political tour of the Far Western states.		A California Appeals judge rules that unions cannot discipline members for engaging in political activities opposed by union leaders.			Nov. 16

F	G	H	I	J
Includes elections, federal-state relations, civil rights and liberties, crime, the judiciary, education, health care, poverty, urban affairs and population.	Includes formation and debate of U.S. foreign and defense policies, veterans' affairs and defense spending. (Relations with specific foreign countries are usually found under the region concerned.)	Includes business, labor, agriculture, taxation, transportation, consumer affairs, monetary and fiscal policy, natural resources, and pollution.	Includes worldwide scientific, medical and technological developments, natural phenomena, U.S. weather, natural disasters, and accidents.	Includes the arts, religion, scholarship, communications media, sports, entertainment, fashions, fads and social life.

	World Affairs	Europe	Africa & the Middle East	The Americas	Asia & the Pacific
Nov. 17		State Secy. Dean Rusk tells newsmen that removal of the Berlin Wall would be a goal of any future East-West negotiations on Germany, but not a precondition for such talks. The latter position had been suggested Nov. 16 by West German Chancellor Adenauer. . . . *The New York Times* reports that the new German proposals described by West German Amb.-to-USSR Hans Kroll had been discussed by Khrushchev, but not actually offered.			
Nov. 18				A published note from U.S. Secy. of State Dean Rusk to the U.S. consulate in Ciudad Trujillo conveys strong American opposition against a return to power by the Trujillo family and hints at possible U.S. action to prevent it.	
Nov. 19	Indian P.M. Nehru, Yugoslav Pres. Tito and UAR Pres. Nasser meet in Cairo for a one-day conference on the world problems facing neutralist nations.	East German soldiers and workmen begin a further fortification of the Berlin Wall by constructing anti-tank barriers near the major crossing points. . . . West German Chancellor Adenauer arrives in the U.S. for talks with Pres Kennedy amidst reports of a growing rift in Western policy thinking on Berlin.		Dominican Pres. Joaquin Balaguer declares a national state of emergency and announces that he has taken personal command of the armed forces. About the same time, U.S. warships arrive at the Dominican coast to dramatize U.S. support for Balaguer against a threatened Trujillo family coup.	
Nov. 20		Over 40,000 persons attend a West Berlin student protest marking the 100th day since the start of the Berlin Wall. . . . West German Amb.-to-USSR Hans Kroll returns to Moscow after being absolved of charges that he took an "unauthorized" diplomatic initiative.	Five Algerian rebel leaders imprisoned in France and 4,000 other Algerian prisoners end a 19-day hunger strike after French authorities agree to accord them treatment as political prisoners rather than criminals. Settlement of the prisoners' demands, which were supported by a Nov. 15 U.N. General Assembly resolution, is seen as a key step to clearing the way for renewed French-Algerian peace talks. . . . Mamoun Kuzbari, premier of Syria since it broke from the UAR Sept. 28, resigns, turning over rule to a caretaker cabinet until the Dec. 1 national elections.	The Trujillo brothers and Rafael Trujillo Jr. leave the Dominican Republic, ending fears of an imminent Trujillo family coup attempt. Juan Bosch, leader of the opposition Revolutionary Democratic Party, lauds the U.S. for its role in blocking the return of a Trujillo dictatorship. . . . An agreement by the U.S.'s new Agency for International Development to lend Brazil $50 million is announced in Washington.	
Nov. 21	The USSR announces its acceptance of the Nov. 13 Anglo-U.S. proposal for a resumption of the Geneva test-ban negotiations. . . . The Institute for Strategic Studies in London reports that the West continues to lead the Soviet bloc in every vital index of military strength.			Thousands of Ciudad Trujillo residents turn out to welcome anti-Trujillo oppositionists upon their return to the Dominican Republic after years in exile. . . . Cuba calls upon the U.N. Security Council and the OAS to hold emergency sessions on what it describes as U.S. "aggression" in the Dominican Republic.	
Nov. 22		After three days of conferences, Adenauer and Kennedy issue a joint statement expressing their complete agreement on the proper Western diplomatic and military responses to Soviet pressures on Berlin.			

A	B	C	D	E
Includes developments that affect more than one world region, international organizations and important meetings of major world leaders.	*Includes all domestic and regional developments in Europe, including the Soviet Union, Turkey, Cyprus and Malta.*	*Includes all domestic and regional developments in Africa and the Middle East, including Iraq and Iran and excluding Cyprus, Turkey and Afghanistan.*	*Includes all domestic and regional developments in Latin America, the Caribbean and Canada.*	*Includes all domestic and regional developments in Asia and Pacific nations, extending from Afghanistan through all the Pacific Islands, except Hawaii.*

U.S. Politics & Social Issues	U.S. Foreign Policy & Defense	U.S. Economy & Environment	Science, Technology & Nature	Culture, Leisure & Life Style	
In its 1961 final report the Civil Rights Commission charges that police brutality remains "a serious and continuing" national problem, especially as it affects Negroes. The Commission calls for congressional and judicial action to protect the rights of arrested persons. . . . N.Y. Gov. Nelson Rockefeller and his wife, Mary Todhunter Rockefeller, announce they will seek a divorce. A Rockefeller aide says the Governor's plan to seek re-election in 1962 will not be affected.					Nov. 17
Sen. Barry Goldwater, in Atlanta to attend a Southern GOP strategy conference, tells newsmen that while he believes the Supreme Court desegregation decision was morally right, he opposes federal enforcement of integration orders over state opposition. . . . In a political speech to a Democratic fund-raising dinner in Los Angeles, Pres. Kennedy lashes out at rightwing extremists who, he says, "find treason in our finest churches, in our highest court and even in the treatment of our water" in their search for "a convenient scapegoat."	Peace Corps director R. Sargent Shriver reports that the Corps currently has 742 volunteers working overseas or in training.		For the second consecutive time NASA scientists fail in an attempt to fire a Ranger satellite-vehicle from a primary earth orbit into a secondary orbit which would bring it near the moon. Officials say the set-backs will delay an attempt, originally scheduled for January 1962, to land Ranger III on the lunar surface.		Nov. 18
Sen. Barry Goldwater tells an NBC-TV *Meet the Press* panel that he is more concerned about "extremists to the left than. . . extremists to the right" because some of the former are "in government" while the latter are not.				The World Council of Churches, representing 175 Protestant and Orthodox bodies in 50 countries, opens its third general assembly in New Delhi, India. Offical observers from the Roman Catholic Church are in attendance for the first time. . . . Michael Rockefeller, 23, youngest son of N.Y. Gov. and Mrs. Nelson Rockefeller, is reported missing at sea in a small native boat off the southwest coast of Netherlands New Guinea.	Nov. 19
The Supreme Court upholds a Florida law which exempts women from jury duty unless they explicitly volunteer.				The Goncourt Prize is awarded in Paris to Jean Cau for his novel *La Pitie de Dieu*.	Nov. 20
	The Defense Dept., acting on a "lead received from the House Un-American Activities Committee," requests and receives the resignation of S. Wesley Reynolds, security director of the National Security Agency.				Nov. 21
			For the first time in the history of the U.S. space program, newsmen are kept in the dark about a "mystery" satellite launched earlier in the day from Point Arguello, Calif.	Frank Robinson of Cincinnati wins the National League's most valuable player award. MVP honors in the American League went to Yankee outfielder Roger Maris.	Nov. 22

F	G	H	I	J
Includes elections, federal-state relations, civil rights and liberties, crime, the judiciary, education, health care, poverty, urban affairs and population.	Includes formation and debate of U.S. foreign and defense policies, veterans' affairs and defense spending. (Relations with specific foreign countries are usually found under the region concerned.)	Includes business, labor, agriculture, taxation, transportation, consumer affairs, monetary and fiscal policy, natural resources, and pollution.	Includes worldwide scientific, medical and technological developments, natural phenomena, U.S. weather, natural disasters, and accidents.	Includes the arts, religion, scholarship, communications media, sports, entertainment, fashions, fads and social life.

	World Affairs	Europe	Africa & the Middle East	The Americas	Asia & the Pacific
Nov. 23				The Brazilian cabinet announces the resumption of diplomatic relations with the USSR. . . . Cuban Foreign Min. Raul Roa announces the revocation of a Nov. 3 government order prohibiting foreign embassies from granting asylum to anti-Castro Cubans. . . . Ciudad Trujillo is restored to its original name of Santo Domingo by a unanimous vote of the Dominican Congress.	
Nov. 24			The U.N. Security Council votes 9-0 to authorize the U.N. Congo Force to resist further Katangan military action against the authority of the central Congo government. The USSR vetoes a U.S.-sponsored amendment which would also have allowed U.N. action to suppress pro-Gizenga mutineers in the Congo army.	U.S. officials announce that Navy warships will remain along the Dominican Republic coast until the political situation stabilizes. The U.S. presence is denounced by Cuba as an act of aggression at an emergency Security Council meeting. The charge is denied by the regular Dominican delegate and by a temporary delegate representing the oppositionist National Civic Union.	
Nov. 25		During preliminary talks in Brussels on the terms of British entry into the Common Market, EEC members stress that the Commonwealth states would have the status of "outsider" nations should Britain join.	Pres. Tshombe warns that U.N. efforts to suppress his secessionist regime would be resisted "even if the whole Katanga population--black and white--has to die."		
Nov. 26		First Secy. Walter Ulbricht tells East German newsmen that the Berlin Wall will remain until West Germany quits NATO and dismisses its "Hitler generals." He also says that formal Western recognition of East Germany's statehood must be part of any German settlement. . . . In a TV address to the Finnish people, Pres. Urho Kekkonen suggests that Soviet anxieties and pressures concerning Finland's neutrality might best be eased by the retirement from politics of prominent anti-communists.	The UAR announces the arrest of nine Frenchmen in Cairo on charges of plotting to assassinate Pres. Nasser.		
Nov. 27	The U.N. General Assembly votes 97-0 to create a special committee to examine member states' adherence to the U.N.'s 1960 declaration for the abolition of colonialism.				
Nov. 28	The three-power nuclear test-ban talks reconvene in Geneva. A Soviet draft proposal for an immediate and total test-ban without international supervision is promptly rejected by the U.S. as "completely, totally, absolutely. . . unacceptable.". . . The text of a two-hour interview with Pres. Kennedy, in which he blames current world tensions on Soviet efforts to advance world communism by force and subversion, is published in full in the Soviet government newspaper *Izvestia* .		Two high-level U.N. civilian officials in Elizabethville are attacked and beaten by Katangan soldiers. . . . A special U.N. investigating committee issues a report condemning Portuguese rule in Angola and urging "drastic reforms" to meet the "genuine grievances" of the African majority.	A deadlock in negotiations between Dominican Pres. Joaquin Balaguer and the opposition National Civic Union on the formation of a reformist coalition government prompts opposition leaders to call for a general strike aimed at forcing Balaguer's ouster. Initial reports indicate wide support for the strike.	Indian P.M. Nehru tells Parliament that the government is building the army's military strength to a point where it can take effective action to recover territory occupied by the foreign powers.
Nov. 29		In statements to his regular Washington news conference, Kennedy stresses the U.S.'s earnest desire for negotiations with the USSR on a mutually acceptable resolution of Berlin differences.		Cuban Pres. Osvaldo Dorticos proclaims a new "revolutionary justice" law permitting the immediate execution of invaders and saboteurs.	

A	B	C	D	E
Includes developments that affect more than one world region, international organizations and important meetings of major world leaders.	Includes all domestic and regional developments in Europe, including the Soviet Union, Turkey, Cyprus and Malta.	Includes all domestic and regional developments in Africa and the Middle East, including Iraq and Iran and excluding Cyprus, Turkey and Afghanistan.	Includes all domestic and regional developments in Latin America, the Caribbean and Canada.	Includes all domestic and regional developments in Asia and Pacific nations, extending from Afghanistan through all the Pacific Islands, except Hawaii.

U.S. Politics & Social Issues	U.S. Foreign Policy & Defense	U.S. Economy & Environment	Science, Technology & Nature	Culture, Leisure & Life Style	
Former Pres. Eisenhower, in a nationally televised interview, deplores the recent "rise of extremists" in the U.S., adding that the country needs honest patriotism, not "super-patriots."					Nov. 23
AFL-CIO Political Education Committee reports that executives of 328 of the nation's largest corporations contributed in 1960 a total of $1,163,310 to Republican candidates and $57,963 to Democratic candidates.		The Labor Dept. reports that U.S. union membership declined from 17,117,000 (or 23.8% of the labor force) in 1959 to 17,049,000 (or 23.3% of the labor force) in 1960.			Nov. 24
	The biggest, fastest and most powerful warship ever built--the 85,000-ton, nuclear-powered aircraft carrier, U.S.S. Enterprise --is commissioned at Newport News, Va.			Bob Cousy of the Boston Celtics becomes the second player in NBA history to score more than 15,000 points.	Nov. 25
(Henry) Styles Bridges, 63, U.S. Senator from New Hampshire since 1937 and a principal GOP leader since 1952, dies in Concord, N.H. of complications arising from a heart condition.	Chester Bowles is relieved of his post as State Undersecretary and named by Pres. Kennedy as a special adviser on African, Asian and Latin American affairs.	The Joint Congressional Foreign Economic Policy Subcommittee issues the last of a series of reports which more or less support the Kennedy administration's recommendations on trade and tariff revisions.		Don Carter, for the fourth year out of the last five, wins the world invitational bowling tournament held in Chicago.	Nov. 26
		The Commerce Dept. reports that personal incomes rose to a record annual rate of $425 billion in October, up $4 billion from September. Housing starts also climbed to a record annual rate.		Oregon State runner Dale Story wins the individual title and Oregon State the team title at the national collegiate cross-country championship in East Lansing, Mich.	Nov. 27
	Pentagon sources report that the administration has decided to seek congressional authority to increase regular Army strength from 14 to 16 combat divisions.	Sen. Barry Goldwater tells a Minneapolis news conference that he opposes recent administration proposals for lower tariffs, saying: "We have to protect our basic industries."	NASA announces that Marine Lt. Col John Glenn has been selected for the first Project Mercury orbital flight.		Nov. 28
		Pres. Cornelius Haggerty of the AFL-CIO Building and Construction Trades Department publicly charges Walter Reuther, head of the AFL-CIO Industrial Union Department, with trying to "kidnap" the jurisdiction of craft unions. It is but the latest charge in a growing dispute between the craft and industrial sectors within the AFL-CIO.	A chimpanzee named Enos makes two orbits around the earth in a U.S. Project Mercury capsule and then is safely recovered from an Atlantic splash-down area south of Bermuda. A malfunction in the attitude-control rockets forced cancellation of a planned third orbit.		Nov. 29

F	G	H	I	J
Includes elections, federal-state relations, civil rights and liberties, crime, the judiciary, education, health care, poverty, urban affairs and population.	Includes formation and debate of U.S. foreign and defense policies, veterans' affairs and defense spending. (Relations with specific foreign countries are usually found under the region concerned.)	Includes business, labor, agriculture, taxation, transportation, consumer affairs, monetary and fiscal policy, natural resources, and pollution.	Includes worldwide scientific, medical and technological developments, natural phenomena, U.S. weather, natural disasters, and accidents.	Includes the arts, religion, scholarship, communications media, sports, entertainment, fashions, fads and social life.

	World Affairs	Europe	Africa & the Middle East	The Americas	Asia & the Pacific
Nov. 30	The USSR vetoes Kuwait's application for U.N. membership on the ground that it remains a virtual British colony.			Negotiations to end one-party rule in the Dominican Republic are broken off by representatives of the National Civic Union and the Balaguer government. The opposition-called general strike continues in force.	
Dec. 1	Acting U.N. Secy. Gen. U Thant tells newsmen that the Congo situation is "the important problem" facing the U.N.		Rightwing candidates win control of the Syrian Parliament in national elections.		
Dec. 2			Katangan soldiers kidnap 14 U.N. officials from their Elizabethville homes.	In a nationwide TV address, Cuban Premier Castro proclaims "I am a Marxist-Leninist and will be one until the day I die." He also plans for the formation of a single revolutionary party to create and administer "the dictatorship of the proletariat."	
Dec. 3	The Soviet newspaper *Izvestia* publishes an unsigned article rebutting the world views expressed by Pres. Kennedy in his Nov. 25 *Izvestia* interview. Kennedy's charge that the USSR wishes to impose communism on the world is dismissed as a "cock and bull story."		Citing recent Katanga attacks on U.N. personnel and positions, Acting Secy. Gen. Thant orders the U.N. Congo Force "to act vigorously to re-establish law and order in Katanga."	Dominican oppositionists charge that the U.S. has transformed its laudable peacekeeping interest in Dominican affairs into a partisan support for the allegedly unpopular Balaguer regime. The State Dept. denies the charge.	
Dec. 4	The U.N. General Assembly adopts two resolutions urging international action against the spread of nuclear weapons.			Santo Domingo police and pro-Balaguer crowds launch a terrorist campaign to break the anti-government general strike. Homes and businesses belonging to opposition leaders are attacked and looted. . . . Kennedy announces extension of the ban on sugar imports from Cuba through June 1962.	The 14 nations at the Geneva conference on Laos have reportedly accepted a joint British-USSR proposal on strengthening the effectiveness and authority of the International Control Commission. The agreement is considered a major breakthrough toward a comprehensive accord on Laos.
Dec. 5		The Israeli Knesset makes public an appeal to the USSR to permit Soviet Jews to freely emigrate to Israel.	A U.N. Force assault upon Katangan fortifications erected in Elizabethville in violation of the U.N.-Katanga truce accord immediately escalates into full-scale warfare. Fighting is said to be spreading throughout the province.		
Dec. 6		The Supreme Soviet approves a record fiscal 1962 state budget, which provides for a 44% increase in defense spending over 1961.	Heavy fighting between U.N. and Katangan troops is reported continuing. The Katanga cabinet announces that it considers itself at war with the U.N.		
Dec. 7			Pres. Tshombe bitterly denounces the U.S. for its political and material support of the current U.N. operations against Katanga. Earlier in the day U.S. Air Force transports began flying U.N. reinforcements and supplies into Katanga, marking the first direct American involvement in the Congo fighting.		Indian P.M. Nehru tells Parliament that Portugal's incompetent and provocative administration of its coastal enclaves has become "intolerable."
Dec. 8	In a series of public statements, France and Britain make clear their opposition to the U.N.'s forcible suppression of secessionist Katanga.	The Supreme Soviet approves the creation of centralized agencies to administer the USSR's fuel, mining and metal industries. The same industries had been decentralized in 1957.			

A	B	C	D	E
Includes developments that affect more than one world region, international organizations and important meetings of major world leaders.	*Includes all domestic and regional developments in Europe, including the Soviet Union, Turkey, Cyprus and Malta.*	*Includes all domestic and regional developments in Africa and the Middle East, including Iraq and Iran and excluding Cyprus, Turkey and Afghanistan.*	*Includes all domestic and regional developments in Latin America, the Caribbean and Canada.*	*Includes all domestic and regional developments in Asia and Pacific nations, extending from Afghanistan through all the Pacific Islands, except Hawaii.*

U.S. Politics & Social Issues	U.S. Foreign Policy & Defense	U.S. Economy & Environment	Science, Technology & Nature	Culture, Leisure & Life Style	
Twelve U.S. defense contractors file anti-bias pledges with the President's Equal Employment Opportunity Committee.					Nov. 30
A federal grand jury in Washington indicts the American Communist Party on charges of failing to register as a communist-action organization.		An increase in the interest rate banks are allowed to pay depositors--from 3% to 3 1/2%--is announced by the Federal Reserve Board.			Dec. 1
For the third straight day white crowds harass and assault Freedom Riders upon their arrival at a Greyhound bus terminal in McComb, Miss. The disturbances stem from local white resentment over a Nov. 21 federal court order requiring McComb authorities to comply with an ICC regulation barring segregation in inter-state bus terminals.					Dec. 2
				The World Council of Churches, meeting in its third general assembly, condemns anti-Semitism as "a sin against God and man."	Dec. 3
The Institute of International Education releases a survey showing that 77% of the African students in American colleges personally have encountered some form of racial bias while in the U.S.	Army Secy. Elvis Stahr calls a news conference to deny reports that he has received a "landslide of complaints" concerning the handling of the reservists and National Guardsmen called up in the Berlin crisis.			Floyd Patterson retains his world heavyweight title by knocking out Tom McNeeley in the fourth round of their title bout in Toronto, Canada.	Dec. 4
				Alabama is picked as the nation's best major college football team in 1961 by both the UPI's coaches' poll and the AP's sportswriters' poll. . . . In a speech before a National Football Foundation dinner in New York, Pres. Kennedy calls America an "underexercised" nation and urges mass support for youth fitness programs.	Dec. 5
		In a speech to a Washington meeting of the National Association of Manufacturers, Pres. Kennedy appeals for business cooperation in the administration's drive for a new U.S. trade and tariff policy.	NASA discloses that it has abandoned hope of putting a U.S. astronaut into orbit before the end of 1961.		Dec. 6
		The Labor Dept. reports the November unemployment rate as 6.1%; it is the first time the figure has dropped below 6.6% in nearly a year.	NASA announces that it is starting a new $500 million program to develop a two-man rendezvous vehicle capable of meeting a second vehicle in space.		Dec. 7
	State Secy. Dean Rusk discloses that the U.S. is consulting with its allies on the provision of joint technical defense support for South Vietnam.				Dec. 8

F	G	H	I	J
Includes elections, federal-state relations, civil rights and liberties, crime, the judiciary, education, health care, poverty, urban affairs and population.	Includes formation and debate of U.S. foreign and defense policies, veterans' affairs and defense spending. (Relations with specific foreign countries are usually found under the region concerned.)	Includes business, labor, agriculture, taxation, transportation, consumer affairs, monetary and fiscal policy, natural resources, and pollution.	Includes worldwide scientific, medical and technological developments, natural phenomena, U.S. weather, natural disasters, and accidents.	Includes the arts, religion, scholarship, communications media, sports, entertainment, fashions, fads and social life.

	World Affairs	Europe	Africa & the Middle East	The Americas	Asia & the Pacific
Dec. 9		France's opposition to negotiations on Berlin is made clear by Pres. de Gaulle during a five-hour Paris meeting with West German Chancellor Konrad Adenauer. . . . British police arrest 850 of 6,500 persons demonstrating against nuclear arms at three U.S. air bases in England. The 850 protesters face jail sentences up to three months.	Acting Secy. General Thant charges private Belgian firms with financing the Katangan resistance to the U.N. . . . The British-administered U.N. trust territory of Tanganyika becomes an independent country within the British Commonwealth.	The oppositionist National Civic Union calls off its two-week-old general strike on the basis of reports that Dominican Pres. Balaguer is prepared to step down in favor of an interim ruling coalition council. . . . Colombia severs diplomatic relations with Cuba in the wake of Castro's Dec. 8 speech denouncing Colombia and Panama as "accomplices of imperialism."	
Dec. 10		The Albanian ATA news agency reports that the USSR has recalled the staff of its Tirana embassy and has ordered the closing of the Albanian embassy in Moscow.	U.N. Congo Force commander-in-chief Sean McKeown blames Katanga's continuing resistance on mercenary "white extremists" who, he says, control Tshombe's army.	Dominican Pres. Balaguer firmly denies rumors that he intends to resign as the nation's chief executive. Following the statement, the National Civic Union announces suspension of further political negotiations with the government.	Nepalese King Mahendra Bir Bikram Shah Deva restores the civil rights he had suspended Dec. 15, 1960. The royal ban on political parties remains in force.
Dec. 11	The U.S. AEC estimates that the recent series of Soviet atmospheric tests have increased the radioactive fallout in the world environment by about 50%.		The three-judge Israeli tribunal finds Adolph Eichmann guilty on each of the 15 counts of war crimes, genocide, and Nazi membership charged in the indictment against him. The tribunal upholds Eichmann's right of appeal to the Israeli Supreme Court.		A U.S. aircraft carrier arrives in Saigon with 33 U.S. Army helicopters and 400 air and ground crewmen to operate them. The arrival marks the first overt indication of direct U.S. involvement in South Vietnam's war against the Viet Cong. . . . Japanese police arrest 13 persons on charges of conspiring in an ultra-nationalist rightwing plot to assassinate Premier Hayato Ikeda.
Dec. 12		State Secy. Rusk, British Foreign Secy. Lord Home, and West German Foreign Min. Gerhard Schroeder confer in Paris with French Foreign Min. Maurice Couve de Murville, but fail to win his support for a unified Western proposal for East-West negotiations on Berlin.			
Dec. 13		French Foreign Min. Couve de Murville tells a NATO Ministerial Council meeting that France regards military preparedness as the only appropriate Western response to current Soviet pressures on Berlin.	Heavy fighting between Katangan and U.N. troops is reportedly continuing in Elizabethville and other parts of the province with neither side gaining a decisive advantage.		
Dec. 14	The admission of Tanganyika brings U.N. membership to 104.	Premier Khrushchev warns that Soviet farm officials will be ousted from the Communist Party unless dramatic improvements are made in lagging farm production. . . . The Swiss Parliament elects Defense Min. Paul Chaudet as president for 1962.		Panama breaks diplomatic relations with Cuba. Castro had said Dec. 8 that he no longer valued ties with Panama's "government of traitors."	
Dec. 15	The General Assembly votes 48 to 37 (19 abstentions) to reject a Soviet proposal calling for Communist China's admission to the U.N. and the expulsion of Nationalist China. Britain, Denmark, Sweden and many unaligned states join the Soviet bloc in voting for the resolution.	The 15-member NATO Ministerial Council votes in Paris to back a coordinated Western effort to probe the possibility of full-scale East-West negotiations on the Berlin problem. . . . Austria, Sweden and Switzerland propose negotiations on their relationship to and possible association with the European Economic Community.	The U.N. Congo Force launches a major drive to force Katangans out of their strongholds in downtown Elizabethville. Battle reports suggest that Katangan resistance is beginning to weaken. . . . Adolph Eichmann is sentenced to death by hanging.		

A	B	C	D	E
Includes developments that affect more than one world region, international organizations and important meetings of major world leaders.	Includes all domestic and regional developments in Europe, including the Soviet Union, Turkey, Cyprus and Malta.	Includes all domestic and regional developments in Africa and the Middle East, including Iraq and Iran and excluding Cyprus, Turkey and Afghanistan.	Includes all domestic and regional developments in Latin America, the Caribbean and Canada.	Includes all domestic and regional developments in Asia and Pacific nations, extending from Afghanistan through all the Pacific Islands, except Hawaii.

U.S. Politics & Social Issues	U.S. Foreign Policy & Defense	U.S. Economy & Environment	Science, Technology & Nature	Culture, Leisure & Life Style	
		The President's panel on mental retardation recommends enactment of state laws to require PKU tests at birth in an attempt to combat mental retardation through early detection.			Dec. 9
			The U.S. conducts its first atoms-for-peace nuclear test under the AEC Project Plowshare program. An apparent miscalculation of the force of the blast leads to an unexpected discharge of highly radioactive steam into the atmosphere.	Final major league statistics show Pittsburgh's Roberto Clemente as the league's leading hitter with a .351 average.	Dec. 10
The Supreme Court unanimously overturns the breach-of-peace convictions of 16 persons arrested during a Baton Rouge, La. sit-in demonstration. The Court contended that their passive protest did not legally constitute a "public disturbance." . . . HEW Secy. Abraham Ribicoff orders a revision of the federal welfare program to eradicate abuses and to promote re-employment of recipients. Ribicoff says the reforms were in no way influenced by the controversial welfare rules adopted by Newburgh, N.Y.		The AFL-CIO convention unanimously backs a resolution barring the re-entry of the Teamsters into the AFL-CIO. . . . The delegates also approve the administration's proposals for a revision of U.S. trade and tariff policies. Pres. Kennedy had personally appealed for such support in a speech to the convention's opening session, Dec. 7.			Dec. 11
The AFL-CIO convention in Miami adopts a rather vague civil rights resolution which supports extension of union membership benefits to all American workers. The convention had earlier voted not to take up consideration of an Executive Council censure against A. Philip Randolph.			NASA administrator James Webb announces that the U.S.'s manned orbital flight series will begin in January 1962 and continue with a flight about every 60 days.		Dec. 12
		The AFL-CIO convention adjourns after approving a plan for settling intrafederation jurisdictional disputes between the craft and industrial departments. . . . The Health Insurance Institute reports that over 47 million Americans suffered accidental injuries in the year ending June 30, 1961.		Mrs Anna Mary Robertson (Grandma) Moses, American "primitive" painter, who took up painting at 78, dies in Hoosick, N.Y. at age 101.	Dec. 13
U.S. Atty. Macon Weaver files suit in Birmingham, Ala. to bar the city from continuing to enforce segregation ordinances in a bus terminal subject to the ICC's desegregation rule. . . . The National Catholic Welfare Conference releases a policy study asserting that federal aid to private church schools is both practical and constitutionally valid. . . . Kennedy establishes a President's Commission on the Status of Women, headed by Eleanor Roosevelt, to study ways of eliminating sex discrimination in the U.S.	Deputy Defense Secy. Roswell Gilpatric announces that the administration will ask Congress to appropriate $700 million to assist in the construction of community fall-out shelters.				Dec. 14
			NASA reports that data obtained from Explorer XII indicates that the radiation in the outermost Van Allen belt is too weak to be a "hazard to manned space flight." . . . NASA contracts with the Boeing Co. for the development and construction of a 2,500-ton Super-Saturn rocket for use in the Project Apollo moon program.		Dec. 15

F	G	H	I	J
Includes elections, federal-state relations, civil rights and liberties, crime, the judiciary, education, health care, poverty, urban affairs and population.	Includes formation and debate of U.S. foreign and defense policies, veterans' affairs and defense spending. (Relations with specific foreign countries are usually found under the region concerned.)	Includes business, labor, agriculture, taxation, transportation, consumer affairs, monetary and fiscal policy, natural resources, and pollution.	Includes worldwide scientific, medical and technological developments, natural phenomena, U.S. weather, natural disasters, and accidents.	Includes the arts, religion, scholarship, communications media, sports, entertainment, fashions, fads and social life.

	World Affairs	Europe	Africa & the Middle East	The Americas	Asia & the Pacific
Dec. 16				Pres. Kennedy arrives in Caracas for a brief state visit to Venezuela. The day's activities are highlighted by a visit to an Alliance-for-Progress-sponsored housing project and a brief address by Mrs. John F. Kennedy delivered in Spanish.	
Dec. 17	A proposed five-year coffee agreement among the world's coffee producing and coffee consuming nations is made public in Washington.			Over 500,000 Colombians cheer Pres. Kennedy's arrival in Bogota for a one-day state visit. At a dinner in his honor, Kennedy pledges redoubled U.S. efforts to help bring a "new day" in living standards of average Latin Americans.	
Dec. 18	The Federation of Rhodesia and Nyasaland informs the U.N. that its investigation into the death of Secy. Gen. Hammarskjold has failed to uncover any positive causes of the accident. . . . A resolution establishing a U.N. World Food Program for the distribution of food surpluses to food deficient peoples is passed by the General Assembly 89-0.		Acting Secy Gen. U Thant offers Katanga a cease-fire on the condition that Pres. Moise Tshombe agrees to immediate negotiations with central Congolese Premier Cyrille Adoula. The Katanga cabinet announces acceptance of the U.N. offer; fighting in Elizabethville ends. . . . The New York Times reports that Algerian rebels are training Angolan rebels in guerrilla warfare at bases in Tunisia.		Defense Min. V.K. Krishna Menon announces that Indian army troops have launched an invasion of the Portuguese coastal enclaves of Goa, Damao and Diu. Krishna Menon cites a complete breakdown in the administration of the enclaves as the reason for the attack.
Dec. 19	U.S. and Britain release a joint report to the U.N. Disarmament Commission in which they accuse the USSR of obstructing the reconvened Geneva test-ban talks. . . . The USSR casts its 99th U.N. Security Council veto to prevent adoption of a Western resolution calling for a cease-fire in the Indian attack upon three Portuguese enclaves. . . . The General Assembly votes unanimously to proclaim the 1960s as the U.N. Development Decade.		Katanga Pres. Tshombe flies to the U.N.-controlled Kitona air base to begin talks with Premier Adoula.	An agreement to form a coalition governing council, with Dominican Pres. Balaguer as temporary chairman, is reached in talks between the National Civic Union and representatives of the Balaguer regime.	Goa, Damao and Diu fall to Indian invaders after nominal Portuguese resistance. . . . Indonesian Pres. Sukarno announces that his army is making final preparations for the liberation of West Irian (Netherlands New Guinea) "from the shackles of Dutch colonialism."
Dec. 20	The General Assembly votes 58-13 (24 abstentions) to authorize U Thant to issue up to $200 million worth of U.N. bonds to cover the organization's current and anticipated deficit. . . . The General Assembly votes unanimously to approve a joint U.S.-USSR resolution creating an 18-nation Disarmament Committee to renew negotiations toward an "agreement on general and complete disarmament under effective international control."	The General Assembly votes 49-17 (32 abstentions) to deplore the USSR's "continued disregard" of U.N. resolutions concerning "the situation in Hungary."	The General Assembly votes 62-0 (38 abstentions) to call upon France and the Algerian Provisional Government to resume negotiations "with a view to implementing the right of the Algerian people to self-determination and independence respecting the unity and territorial integrity of Algeria."		A resolution demanding a "cessation of practices which deprive the Tibetan peoples of their fundamental human rights" is passed by the U.N. General Assembly over strong Soviet opposition.
Dec. 21	The General Assembly recesses its 16th regular session until Jan. 15, 1962.		Katanga agrees to accept the full authority of the central Congo government in an accord worked out by Pres. Tshombe and Premier Adoula at the Kitona air base.		Soviet Premier Khrushchev cables P.M. Nehru hailing India's seizure of Portuguese enclaves as "fully lawful and justified." The action had been criticized by the U.S. as a possible violation of the U.N. Charter. . . . The Canadian Agriculture Ministry announces the signing of a new contract to ship Communist China an additional $71 million worth of wheat and barley. . . . Five former aides to ex-South Korean Pres. Rhee are executed by hanging in Seoul.
Dec. 22	In separate statements, both U.S. Amb.-to-UN Stevenson and Soviet Deputy Foreign Min. Valerian Zorin praise the accomplishments of the just recessed General Assembly session.	Following a two-day meeting in Bermuda, Pres. Kennedy and British P.M. Macmillan reaffirm their intention to pursue preliminary talks toward new negotiations with the USSR over Berlin.	The Katanga cabinet announces that the Kitona accord "imposed" on Tshombe will not be binding unless ratified by the Katanga Parliament. . . . Premier David Ben-Gurion's participation in a nine-day Buddhist-style meditation retreat at the conclusion of his state visit to Burma provokes criticism from Israeli religious leaders.		

A	B	C	D	E
Includes developments that affect more than one world region, international organizations and important meetings of major world leaders.	Includes all domestic and regional developments in Europe, including the Soviet Union, Turkey, Cyprus and Malta.	Includes all domestic and regional developments in Africa and the Middle East, including Iraq and Iran and excluding Cyprus, Turkey and Afghanistan.	Includes all domestic and regional developments in Latin America, the Caribbean and Canada.	Includes all domestic and regional developments in Asia and Pacific nations, extending from Afghanistan through all the Pacific Islands, except Hawaii.

U.S. Politics & Social Issues	U.S. Foreign Policy & Defense	U.S. Economy & Environment	Science, Technology & Nature	Culture, Leisure & Life Style	
Over 700 Negroes, including Martin Luther King, have been arrested in Albany, Ga. during five days of demonstrations against the city's continuing enforcement of bus terminal segregation ordinances in contravention of the ICC's desegregation rules.	State Undersecy. George Ball confirms that the U.S. has agreed to lend Ghana $133 million for construction of a Volta River hydroelectric project. The question of aid to Ghana has been the subject of considerable political controversy in the U.S. because of the allegedly leftist orientation of the Nkrumah government.				Dec. 16
					Dec. 17
Negro leaders call off further protests in Albany, Ga. after city officials agree to comply with the ICC's bus terminal desegregation ruling and to hear other Negro desegregation demands at a public meeting early next year.				The AP names track star Wilma Rudolph as female athlete of the year for the second consecutive year.	Dec. 18
Joseph P. Kennedy, father of the President, suffers a severe stroke in Palm Beach, Fla.	Ex-V.P. Nixon joins with conservatives in both parties in criticizing the Kennedy administration's support of U.N. military action against Katanga. Nixon says that the defeat of anti-communist Katanga could hasten a communist takeover of the Congo.	Commerce Secy. Luther Hodges reports that personal incomes rose $3.8 billion in November to a record annual rate of $429 billion. . . . The Interior Dept. announces plans for a West Coast power grid that would feed electric power from the Pacific Northwest to the San Francisco and Los Angeles areas via a 1,000-mile transmission line.	Scientists of the National Institutes of Health report they have made a significant breakthrough in unraveling the "genetic code," a chemical system by which nature controls reproduction, heredity and protein formation.		Dec. 19
Navy Secy. John B. Connally resigns to become a Texas gubernatorial candidate.			A resolution barring "national appropriation" of celestial bodies and calling for international cooperation in the exploration and use of space is adopted unanimously by the U.N. General Assembly. . . . An earthquake strikes central Colombia, leaving at least 20 persons dead. . . . NASA test pilot Neil Armstrong, 31, successfully tests a new automated control system for a specially equipped X-15 rocket plane.	Moss Hart, 57, Pulitzer Prize-winning playwright and Tony award winning director, dies in Palm Springs, Calif. of a heart attack.	Dec. 20
	The Army announces that a Nike-Zeus antimissile missile test-fired from the White Sands, N.M. range successfully intercepted an in-flight rocket for the first time.			Pope John XXIII, in a Christmas message, calls upon world leaders to "shun all thought of force."	Dec. 21
The U.S. Communist Party announces that Negro civil rights leader and historian, W.E.B. DuBois, 93, has joined the party.					Dec. 22

F	G	H	I	J
Includes elections, federal-state relations, civil rights and liberties, crime, the judiciary, education, health care, poverty, urban affairs and population.	Includes formation and debate of U.S. foreign and defense policies, veterans' affairs and defense spending. (Relations with specific foreign countries are usually found under the region concerned.)	Includes business, labor, agriculture, taxation, transportation, consumer affairs, monetary and fiscal policy, natural resources, and pollution.	Includes worldwide scientific, medical and technological developments, natural phenomena, U.S. weather, natural disasters, and accidents.	Includes the arts, religion, scholarship, communications media, sports, entertainment, fashions, fads and social life.

	World Affairs	Europe	Africa & the Middle East	The Americas	Asia & the Pacific
Dec. 23		The Bonn Ministry for German Affairs reports that 10,000 East Germans have managed to escape to West Germany since the building of the Berlin Wall began Aug. 13.			
Dec. 24			Premier Adoula demands that Katanga act quickly to implement the Kitona agreement by sending representatives to the Congolese Parliament. . . . The U.N. announces that it has accepted a central government offer of 1,000 Congolese troops to reinforce the U.N. Force. . . . Pres. Nasser announces that the UAR will nationalize all foreign-owned farm lands for the benefit of peasants.	Argentine Pres. Arturo Frondizi confers with Pres. Kennedy in Palm Beach, Fla. on OAS policy toward Cuba.	
Dec. 25					
Dec. 26			Yemen's ties with the UAR federation are formally dissolved, leaving Egypt as the sole remaining UAR state. . . . The New York Times reports that the UAR has ordered all French nationals to leave the country on the expiration of their resident permits.		
Dec. 27			British naval reinforcements are sent to the Persian Gulf in response to revived fears of a possible Iraqi attack upon Kuwait.		
Dec. 28			Six deputies from Katanga arrive in Leopoldville and take their seats in the Congolese National Parliament. Katanga Pres. Tshombe insists that the action does not constitute full acceptance of the Kitona accord which still has not been ratified by the Katangan legislature.		
Dec. 29			Pres. de Gaulle announces that two French divisions and "a number of air formations" will be withdrawn from Algeria beginning in January.	The Dominican national Legislature approves a constitutional amendment establishing a seven-member Council of State to govern the country until February 1963. . . . The Dominican Party--the main political support of the former Trujillo regime--formally announces its dissolution.	
Dec. 30			Albert Kalonji, self-proclaimed king of an independent South Kasai state, is arrested by Congolese police in Leopoldville. His "kingdom" had been declared dissolved by the Congo Parliament Dec. 16.		The Indian Foreign Ministry reports that 22 Indian and 17 Portuguese troops were killed in the fighting over the Portuguese enclaves. . . . Diosdado Macapagal is inaugurated as the new president of the Philippines.
Dec. 31			Lebanese troops crush a rightwing army coup in Beirut aimed at overthrowing Pres. Fuad Chehab's government.		

A	B	C	D	E
Includes developments that affect more than one world region, international organizations and important meetings of major world leaders.	*Includes all domestic and regional developments in Europe, including the Soviet Union, Turkey, Cyprus and Malta.*	*Includes all domestic and regional developments in Africa and the Middle East, including Iraq and Iran and excluding Cyprus, Turkey and Afghanistan.*	*Includes all domestic and regional developments in Latin America, the Caribbean and Canada.*	*Includes all domestic and regional developments in Asia and Pacific nations, extending from Afghanistan through all the Pacific Islands, except Hawaii.*

U.S. Politics & Social Issues	U.S. Foreign Policy & Defense	U.S. Economy & Environment	Science, Technology & Nature	Culture, Leisure & Life Style	
					Dec. 23
				The Houston Oilers defeat the San Diego Chargers to win the American Football League championship.	**Dec. 24**
	The Commerce Dept. reports that U.S. foreign aid expenditures in fiscal 1961 totaled $5.2 billion, the highest in seven years.			Pope John XXIII announces in a papal bull that the 21st Ecumenical Council of the Roman Catholic Church will be held during 1962 at the Vatican.	**Dec. 25**
	A group of scientists attending the annual meeting of the American Association for the Advancement of Science in Denver issue a statement asserting that any fall-out shelter program, except an inconceivably large one, would be virtually ineffective in protecting the nation from nuclear attack.			For the 13th time in the last 14 years Eleanor Roosevelt is named the woman "most admired" by Americans, according to an annual Gallup Poll survey.	**Dec. 26**
The Census Bureau reports that a record 1,457,000 Negroes left the South for the North and West during the decade of the 1950's. . . . Following a recent examination, Pres. Kennedy is reported in excellent health and almost fully recovered from the back strain suffered this summer.		The Commerce Dept. estimates that the value of new construction put in place in 1961 totaled a record $57.5 billion, up 3% from 1960.			**Dec. 27**
The Justice Dept. files suit in New Orleans in an effort to invalidate an allegedly discriminatory Louisiana law requiring prospective voters to pass a state constitutional interpretation test. . . . Edith Bolling Wilson, widow of ex-Pres. Woodrow Wilson, dies in Washington at age 89.	Asst. State Secy. Harlan Cleveland discloses to newsmen that the Kennedy administration plans to seek congressional authorization for the U.S. purchase of up to half of the planned $200 million U.N. bond issue.	The Commerce Clearing House reports that the states paid a total of $3.5 billion in unemployment compensation benefits during the year ending Aug. 31, over $1 million more than during the previous 12 months. . . . The Department of Agriculture estimates that U.S. cigarette consumption in 1961 increased 4% over 1960.		A Gallup Poll survey shows Pres. Kennedy as the man "most admired" by Americans in 1961; Eisenhower is named second and Richard Nixon eighth.	**Dec. 28**
Alabama Circuit Court Judge Walter Jones issues a permanent injunction barring the NAACP from intrastate activities in Alabama. A temporary injunction has been in effect since 1956.					**Dec. 29**
	The Defense Dept. publishes a free 48-page civil defense pamphlet entitled "Fall-out Protection, What to Know and Do About Nuclear Attack."				**Dec. 30**
		The U.S. Bureau of Mines reports that natural gas output in 1961 totaled 13.4 trillion cubic feet, up 5% from 1960.	NASA announces plans to fire two satellite probes past Venus sometime in August 1962.	The Green Bay Packers defeat the New York Giants, 37-0, to win the National Football League championship.	**Dec. 31**

F	G	H	I	J
Includes elections, federal-state relations, civil rights and liberties, crime, the judiciary, education, health care, poverty, urban affairs and population.	Includes formation and debate of U.S. foreign and defense policies, veterans' affairs and defense spending. (Relations with specific foreign countries are usually found under the region concerned.)	Includes business, labor, agriculture, taxation, transportation, consumer affairs, monetary and fiscal policy, natural resources, and pollution.	Includes worldwide scientific, medical and technological developments, natural phenomena, U.S. weather, natural disasters, and accidents.	Includes the arts, religion, scholarship, communications media, sports, entertainment, fashions, fads and social life.

1962

The new and the old Coventry cathedrals. The original church was destroyed during World War II. The new building is shown for the first time without its scaffolding on Feb. 28.

After his space flight, astronaut John Glenn smiles and waves on board the aircraft carrier Randolph on Feb. 21.

Gen. Chung Hee Park becomes president of South Korea March 24.

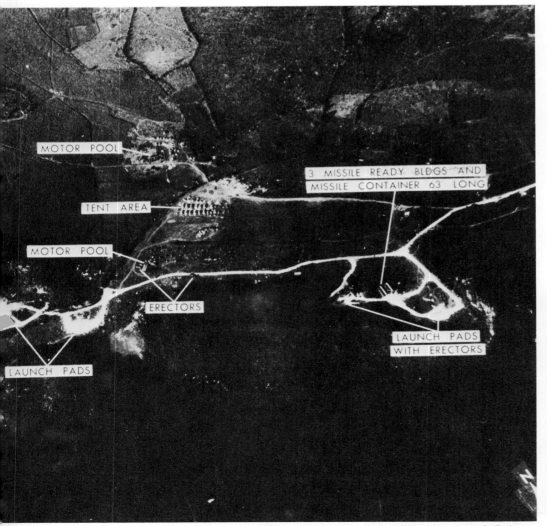

An aerial reconnaissance photo released by the U.S. Defense Department shows a Soviet missile complex in Cuba.

After serving as acting secretary general of the United Nations, U Thant is elected to a regular term on Nov. 30.

Pope John XXIII presides over the opening ceremony of the final session of the Second Ecumenical Council.

Elizabeth Taylor and Richard Burton relax on the set of *Cleopatra* during the filming near Rome.

Soviet scientist Lev Landau (right) receives the Nobel Prize for physics in a hospital in Moscow Dec. 10, while recuperating from a serious accident.

Rod Laver plays his winning match at Wimbledon against Martin Mulligan.

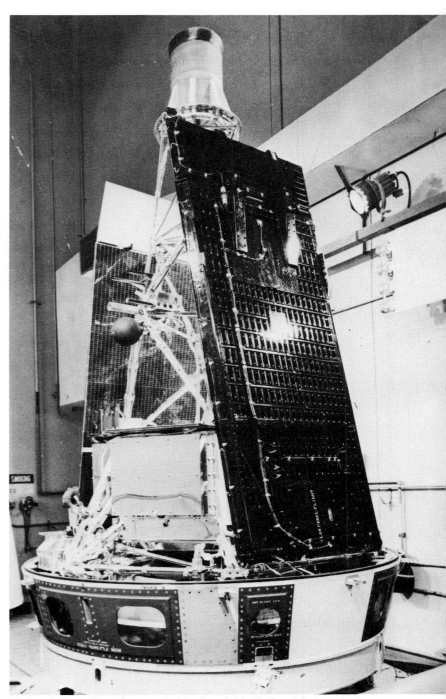

Mariner II sits at Cape Canaveral with wings folded before it is launched on Aug. 27. The spacecraft passes the planet Venus on Dec. 14.

	World Affairs	Europe	Africa & the Middle East	The Americas	Asia & the Pacific
Jan.	OAS expels Cuba.	U.S. and Soviet tanks withdraw from their confrontation along the Berlin Wall.	Morocco creates a free trade zone at Tangiers.	Rafael Bonelly becomes Dominican president after a military coup.	Holland damages two Indonesian torpedo boats.
Feb.	U.N. votes funding for a commission to investigate minority rule in Southern Rhodesia.	France and Algerian nationalists agree on a cease-fire accord.	Israel devalues the Israeli pound.	Argentina breaks diplomatic relations with Cuba.	Dissident pilots bomb the presidential palace of South Vietnamese Pres. Ngo Dinh Diem in Saigon.
March	Seventeen-nation disarmament conference opens in Geneva.	Italian Parliament approves a new center-left cabinet.	Syrian army assumes full governmental powers in Syria.	Argentine armed forces depose Pres. Arturo Frondizi in a bloodless coup.	Indian Parliament formally incorpoartes Goa into India.
April	U.N. condemns both Syria and Israel for combat raids.	French voters approve a peace settlement with Algerian nationalists by a heavy majority.	Kenya and Britain agree to terms for Kenyan internal self-government.	Ecuador breaks off diplomatic relations with Cuba.	India charges Communist China with sending troops into a disputed border area.
May	France and seven French-speaking West African countries agree to an African monetary union.	Spain declares a state of emergency in three of its northern provinces after strikes erupt.	Israel executes Gestapo chief Adolf Eichmann.	Venezuela bans the Venezuelan Communist Party.	Communist troops complete the occupation of northwest Laos.
June	Seventeen-nation disarmament conference recesses for one month.	Common Market approves tariff increases on U.S. goods.	Five major Arab states agree on a common market.	Venezuela crushes a military revolt at Puerto Cabello.	Rival political factions agree on a coalition government in Laos.
July	Fourteen-nation Laotian conference resumes in Geneva.	France formally grants independence to Algeria.	Supporters of Algerian leaders Ben Bella and Ben Khedda clash.	Peruvian armed forces oust Pres. Manuel Prado.	Communist China accuses India of border incursions.
Aug.	U.N. forces bar all air traffic over Katanga.	Soviet Union resumes nuclear test in the atmosphere.	Observers say that Algerian nationalist Ben Bella has seized most power in Algeria.	Jamaica becomes an independent country.	India agrees to manufacture Soviet engines for supersonic aircraft in India.
Sept.	U.N. estimates that world population is increasing at a 1.8% annual rate.	French Pres. de Gaulle proposes close cooperation between the armies of France and Germany.	Yemeni army officers overthrow the monarchy and proclaim a republic.	Argentine armed forces take political control in Buenos Aires.	Observers say that the new Laotian coalition government is unstable.
Oct.	U.N. votes 56-42 against the admission of Communist China.	Soviet Premier Nikita Khrushchev agrees to dismantle all offensive missiles in Cuba.	Uganda becomes an independent country.	Soviet Union tries to install offensive weapons in Cuba.	Communist China overruns many Indian positions along their disputed Himalayan frontier.
Nov.	U.N. votes 67-16 to request members to impose economic sanctions against South Africa.	Supporters of French Pres. de Gaulle win control of the National Assembly.	Saudi Arabia breaks diplomatic relations with Egypt.	Cuba rejects any form of international inspection of missiles on its territory.	Communist China orders a cease-fire after pushing back Indian troops.
Dec.	U.N. forces capture Elizabethville, capital of the separatist province of Katanga.	Soviet Union criticizes Communist China's attack on India.	Senegal puts down an attempted army coup.	Dominican voters elect Juan Bosch as president.	British troops crush a rebellion in the protectorate of Brunei.

A	B	C	D	E
Includes developments that affect more than one world region, international organizations and important meetings of major world leaders.	Includes all domestic and regional developments in Europe, including the Soviet Union, Turkey, Cyprus and Malta.	Includes all domestic and regional developments in Africa and the Middle East, including Iraq and Iran and excluding Cyprus, Turkey and Afghanistan.	Includes all domestic and regional developments in Latin America, the Caribbean and Canada.	Includes all domestic and regional developments in Asia and Pacific nations, extending from Afghanistan through all the Pacific Islands, except Hawaii.

U.S. Politics & Social Issues	U.S. Foreign Policy & Defense	U.S. Economy & Environment	Science, Technology & Nature	Culture, Leisure & Life Style
House defeats a bill for an urban affairs department.	U.S. calls for reduced tariffs between America and Europe.	U.S. orders the American Stock Exchange to end financial abuses.	U.S. moon rocket Ranger Three veers off course.	Peter Snell runs the mile in the record time of 3 minutes 54.4 seconds.
Pres. Kennedy asks for authority to increase federal spending in times of recession.	U.S. orders a ban on all trading with Cuba.	U.S. reports the 1961 balance of payments deficit to be $2.4 billion.	Col. John Glenn orbits the earth three times.	Pope John announces the creation of 10 new cardinals.
US Senate votes to ban the poll tax.	U.S. confirms that American pilots are flying combat-training missions with South Vietnamese pilots.	Pres. Kennedy appoints an emergency labor board to prevent a threatened railroad strike.	U.S. Titan 1 rocket covers more than 5,000 miles.	New Orleans Archbishop Joseph Rummel orders all Catholic schools to integrate in his diocese.
U.S. orders racial integration in military reserve units exclusive of the national guard.	U.S. and Soviet authorities resume normal contacts in Berlin.	Major U.S. steel companies rescind steel price increases under heavy government pressure.	U.S. resumes nuclear tests in the atmosphere.	New Orleans Bishop Rummel excommunicates three segregationists.
A U.S. court in Atlanta Ga. orders the redistricting of the state legislature.	U.S. sends additional troops to Thailand.	AFL-CIO George Meany calls for 35-hour work week.	American Medical Association denounces the Medicare plan for the elderly.	Edwin O'Connor's *The Edge of Sadness* wins the 1962 Pulitzer Prize for literature.
Supreme Court rules that prayer reading in public schools is unconstitutional.	U.S. begins the construction of fall-out shelters.	Pres. Kennedy calls for a reduction in personal and corporate income taxes.	U.S. fails to detonate a missile-borne nuclear device over the Johnston Island proving-ground.	Catholic Archbishop Paul Hallinan ends all segregation in Atlanta, Ga. Catholic schools.
Senate rejects Pres. Kennedy's Medicare program.	U.S. halts economic aid to Peru in wake of a military coup.	U.S. reports a budget deficit of $6 billion for the fiscal year ending June 30, 1962.	U.S. detonates its first hydrogen bomb underground in the U.S.	Pope Paul calls for peace in the Congo.
Congress approves an amendment to ban the poll tax.	U.S. supports a Soviet proposal that nuclear testing be terminated by Jan. 1, 1963.	A court grants railraod unions a temporary injunction against a management proposal to change work rules drastically.	U.S. launches spacecraft Mariner 11 towards Venus.	Archbishop of Canterbury Ramsey calls for peace in the Congo.
U.S. marshals escort Negro student James Meredith as he registers at the University of Mississippi.	Pres. Kennedy asks for authority to call up 150,000 reservists in case of an emergency.	AFL-CIO Pres. George Meany calls for a higher minimum wage.	U.S. officials say that they can put a man on the moon by the end of the decade.	U.S. retains the America's Cup when the Weatherly defeats Australia's Gretel.
Negro student James Meredith begins classes at the University of Mississippi.	U.S. announces that it will inspect all Soviet ships going to Cuba for offensive missiles.	Congress gives Pres. Kennedy authority to reduce tariffs.	U.S. astronaut Walter Schirra orbits the earth six times.	Pope John opens the Vatican Council in Rome.
U.S. prohibits discrimination in housing built or purchased with federal funds.	U.S. lifts the naval blockade of Cuba after the Soviet Union removes its offensive missiles.	Average purchasing power in the U.S. rises between 20% and 40% in the last decade.	Soviet physicist Lev Davidovich Landau wins the 1962 Nobel Prize in physics.	Pope John calls for peace in the Congo as civil war continues.
U.S. sues Miss. Gov. Ross Barnett with obstruction of justice in connections with the integration of the University of Mississippi.	Pres. Kennedy confers with British P.M. Harold Macmillain about differences over the proposed U.S. abandonment of the Skybolt missile.	International Longshoremen go on strike along the East Coast.	U.S. spacecraft Mariner 11 sends back information about Venus.	Leonardo da Vinci's *Mona Lisa* leaves Paris for an exhibition in Washington.

F	G	H	I	J
Includes elections, federal-state relations, civil rights and liberties, crime, the judiciary, education, health care, poverty, urban affairs and population.	Includes formation and debate of U.S. foreign and defense policies, veterans' affairs and defense spending. (Relations with specific foreign countries are usually found under the region concerned.)	Includes business, labor, agriculture, taxation, transportation, consumer affairs, monetary and fiscal policy, natural resources, and pollution.	Includes worldwide scientific, medical and technological developments, natural phenomena, U.S. weather, natural disasters, and accidents.	Includes the arts, religion, scholarship, communications media, sports, entertainment, fashions, fads and social life.

	World Affairs	Europe	Africa & the Middle East	The Americas	Asia & the Pacific
Jan. 1	In an exchange of New Year's messages, Pres. John Kennedy and Soviet Premier Nikita Khrushchev pledge to seek better relations and a firmer foundation for world peace.	Diego Martinez Barrio, 78, founder of the Spanish Republican Union (left-liberal) party in 1933 and Spanish premier for one day in 1936, dies in Paris. Barrio had been president of the Spanish Republic in Exile since 1945. . . . Portuguese soldiers defeat a band of 40 leftist rebels who attacked an army installation in Beja, 85 miles south of Lisbon.	Katangan Pres. Moise Tshombe charges that 13,000 troops of the central Congo government have crossed into northern Katanga and are advancing on Kongolo.	The Dominican Republic's governing Council of State is sworn in.	The New Zealand-administered U.N. trust territory of Western Samoa becomes an independent nation.
Jan. 2		The West's effort to determine Soviet terms for negotiations on the Berlin question is begun by U.S. Amb.-to-USSR Llewellyn Thompson during a two-hour Moscow meeting with Foreign Min. Andrei Gromyko. . . . West Berlin officials announce that 207,026 East Germans fled to West Berlin and West Germany during 1961, the majority of them before the building of the Berlin Wall in August.		Cuban Premier Fidel Castro tells a Havana rally of more than 500,000 persons, "We are Marxist-Leninists and we do not repent it.". . . A Dec. 31, 1961 claim by Guatemalan Pres. Miguel Ydigoras Fuentes that the U.S. had agreed to encourage Britain to "return" British Honduras to Guatemalan control in exchange for having allowed the training of anti-Castro Cubans in Guatemala is flatly denied by the U.S. State Dept.	Netherlands Premier Jan Eduard de Quay discloses that his government has dropped its demand that Indonesia accept the principle of self-determination for the Papuans of Netherlands New Guinea as a condition for negotiations over the disputed territory.
Jan. 3	U.S. and USSR are reported to have reached agreement to resume East-West disarmament talks under the auspices of the 17-nation U.N. Disarmament Committee. The talks, tentatively scheduled for Geneva March 14, would be the first full-scale disarmament negotiations since the collapse of the 10-nation arms conference in Geneva in 1960.	Portuguese Premier Antonio Salazar, in a speech to the National Assembly, says that Portugal will quit the U.N. because of its failure to block India's seizure of the Portuguese enclaves of Goa, Damao and Diu.		The U.S. State Dept. releases the text of a formal complaint to the OAS charging that Cuba has become "a bridgehead of Sino-Soviet imperialism and a base for communist subversion" within the Western Hemisphere. . . . The Vatican discloses that Cuban Premier Fidel Castro has been automatically ex-communicated from the Roman Catholic Church for ordering the imprisonment and deportation of Catholic bishops.	An Indonesian government spokesman, responding to recent Dutch concessions, says that Indonesia will drop its claim of sovereignty over New Guinea if the Netherlands will agree to Indonesian "administration" of the disputed territory pending a final settlement.
Jan. 4		Edward Heath, Britain's chief negotiator on entry into the European Economic Community, concludes two days of talks in Ottawa with Canadian P.M. John Diefenbaker during which he pledged that Britain would safeguard "the essential trade interests of Canada and the other Commonwealth nations."	Underground leaders of Algeria's extreme rightwing Secret Army Organization (OAS) issue an open call for general insurrection against French Pres. de Gaulle's efforts to negotiate an end to the Moslem rebellion. . . . Pres. Moise Tshombe urges the Katanga Assembly not to ratify two key provisions of the Kitona unity accord which he negotiated with central Congolese Premier Cyrille Adoula, Dec. 20, 1961. The two points opposed by Tshombe are acceptance of the Congo's Fundamental Law (constitution) and expulsion of all mercenaries from Katangan armed forces.	The OAS Council, meeting in Washington, votes, 20-0 (Cuba abstaining), to lift its diplomatic and economic sanctions against the Dominican Republic. The action rests on the expectation that the newly formed Dominican Council of State will avoid the repressive measures that led to the OAS's break with the toppled Trujillo regime.	In a speech to the annual convention of India's Congress Party, party Pres. Neelam Samjeeva Reddy warns that India is prepared to take whatever steps are necessary to recover border territory occupied by the Communist Chinese as well as disputed Kashmir territory held by Pakistan. . . . South Vietnam and the U.S. announce plans for a jointly sponsored reform program aimed at improving the living standards of the South Vietnamese population.
Jan. 5				Britain informs Guatemala that it is willing to "discuss informally" Guatemala's claims to British Honduras in order to ease tensions and clarify misunderstandings.	The 14-nation Geneva conference on Laos, resumed after a three week recess, votes to urge the leaders of the three Laotian factions to form a coalition government and to send a unified delegation to participate in the final work of the conference.
Jan. 6				U.S., Haiti and Guatemala resume diplomatic relations with the Dominican Republic.	

A	B	C	D	E
Includes developments that affect more than one world region, international organizations and important meetings of major world leaders.	Includes all domestic and regional developments in Europe, including the Soviet Union, Turkey, Cyprus and Malta.	Includes all domestic and regional developments in Africa and the Middle East, including Iraq and Iran and excluding Cyprus, Turkey and Afghanistan.	Includes all domestic and regional developments in Latin America, the Caribbean and Canada.	Includes all domestic and regional developments in Asia and Pacific nations, extending from Afghanistan through all the Pacific Islands, except Hawaii.

U.S. Politics & Social Issues	U.S. Foreign Policy & Defense	U.S. Economy & Environment	Science, Technology & Nature	Culture, Leisure & Life Style	
		Labor Dept. reports that an average wage increase of 7 1/2¢ an hour was provided in 1961 by union contracts covering about 5,700,000 workers. . . . About 6,500 UAW workers strike the Studebaker-Packard Corp. auto plant in South Bend, Ind.	The January issue of the *Bulletin of the Atomic Scientists* outlines a proposal by Dr. A. V. Topchiev, vice-president of the Soviet Academy of Sciences, for broad East-West cooperation in scientific research into peaceful uses of thermonuclear energy and other scientific problems.	Minnesota beats UCLA, 21-3, in the Rose Bowl game in Pasadena, Calif.	Jan. 1
NAACP Executive Secy. Roy Wilkins, speaking at the organization's annual meeting, praises Pres. Kennedy's "personal role" in civil rights, but expresses disappointment over his failure to issue a "long-promised" executive order barring segregation in federally aided housing. . . . Office of Education reports that the U.S. classroom shortage is less serious this year than last, but that there are still 1,694,000 more pupils than can be properly accommodated.		Agriculture Secy. Orville Freeman reports that U.S. farm income increased 9% during 1961 and that the government reduced its reserve stocks of feed grain for the first time since 1952.	U.S. atomic scientist Dr. Edward Teller outlines plans to pump water into an underground cavern created by the Dec. 10 atoms-for-peace nuclear test to ascertain whether the detonation's residual heat could be tapped for steam power.	Astronaut Virgil (Gus) Grissom, 35, presidential adviser Theodore Sorensen, 33, and FCC Chairman Newton Minow are included in the U.S. Junior Chamber of Commerce's list of 1961's "outstanding young men.". . . Wilma Rudolf Ward is named the winner of the AAU's 1961 Sullivan Memorial Trophy as the year's outstanding amateur athlete.	Jan. 2
A Mississippi court convicts five Negroes of conspiring to harm public trade by participating in a boycott of white-owned stores in Clarksdale, Miss.	Pres. Kennedy orders a permanent increase in regular Army strength from 14 to 16 divisions.				Jan. 3
The Mississippi House of Representatives adopts a resolution aimed at barring Negroes from sitting in the gallery by permitting entry only to persons with signed cards from legislature members.	U.S. Navy announces that the recently developed Sikorsky HSS2 has set a world helicopter speed record of 199.01 mph.			Begum Liaquat Ali Khan, Pakistani ambassador to Italy, is awarded the first International Gimbel Award for her role in the emancipation of Pakistani women.	Jan. 4
Census Dept. reports that the U.S. Negro population in 1960 was 18,871,831, approximately 10.5 of the total 179,323,175 population.	Defense Dept. announces that it has achieved its "strength objectives" arising from the Berlin crisis and will begin cutting monthly draft calls in February.	SEC investigators charge the American Stock Exchange with "manifold and prolonged abuses by specialists and floor traders and other instances of misconduct."			Jan. 5
Pres. Kennedy, speaking at a Democratic fund raising dinner in Columbus, Ohio, singles out medical care for the aged as one of his priority bills for the new session of Congress.	Pres. Kennedy tells a Democratic dinner in Columbus, Ohio that 1961 was a "year of achievement" in foreign policy. He cites the U.S. defense of the U.N.'s "integrity" after Hammarskjold's death, the launching of the Alliance for Progress, and the checking of Soviet influence in Africa as major accomplishments.			The Ford Foundation discloses that it spent $161 million on cultural and educational programs in 1961, $5 million less than in 1960. . . . Larry Evans wins the U.S. chess championship in New York.	Jan. 6

F	G	H	I	J
Includes elections, federal-state relations, civil rights and liberties, crime, the judiciary, education, health care, poverty, urban affairs and population.	Includes formation and debate of U.S. foreign and defense policies, veterans' affairs and defense spending. (Relations with specific foreign countries are usually found under the region concerned.)	Includes business, labor, agriculture, taxation, transportation, consumer affairs, monetary and fiscal policy, natural resources, and pollution.	Includes worldwide scientific, medical and technological developments, natural phenomena, U.S. weather, natural disasters, and accidents.	Includes the arts, religion, scholarship, communications media, sports, entertainment, fashions, fads and social life.

	World Affairs	Europe	Africa & the Middle East	The Americas	Asia & the Pacific
Jan. 7					Indonesian Pres. Sukarno, riding in a motorcade in Macassar in the Southern Celebes, escapes an assassination attempt as a grenade explodes several hundred yards behind his car; three bystanders are killed. . . . Nepalese sources report a growing resistance movement against King Mahendra Bir Bikra Shah Deva.
Jan. 8	The International Monetary Fund announces that the U.S., Japan and seven Western European countries have approved an accord for the allocation of up to $6 billion if one of their number should require emergency aid for currency stabilization.		The Congolese national parliament orders absent Deputy Premier Antoine Gizenga to return to Leopoldville from his Stanleyville stronghold and face charges of leading a secession movement against the central government. The resolution was presented and supported by members of Gizenga's own African Solidarity Party.	El Salvador's constituent assembly elects Supreme Court magistrate Eusebio Rodolfo Cordon to head a provisional government to replace the Civil-Military Directorate which has ruled the country since it seized power in a Jan. 25, 1961 coup.	Indonesian Pres. Sukarno attributes yesterday's attempt on his life to the work of Dutch "agents."
Jan. 9		West Germany makes public a Dec. 27, 1961 Soviet memo urging West Germany to quit NATO and enter direct negotiations with the USSR on German reunification.	Northern Rhodesia, complying with U.N. requests for cooperation, expels 27 Europeans believed to be enroute to Katanga to serve as mercenaries. . . . Israeli Knesset (Parliament) approves a directive permitting a limited program of cultural contacts with West Germany. The order, however, prohibits the establishment in Israel of branches of West German firms, organizations or cultural institutions.		Indonesian Foreign Min. Subandrio says that Pres. Sukarno has set a deadline of seven to 10 days on diplomatic efforts to resolve the dispute with the Netherlands over New Guinea.
Jan. 10			Sture Linner, Swedish head of U.N. operations in the Congo, issues a report charging that mercenaries had been the principal leaders of Katanga troops in their December 1961 offensive against the U.N. Force, and that hired troops are continuing to filter into Katanga.	AP reports that the USSR and Cuba have agreed to a $700 million trade pact for 1962, a $150 million increase over the 1961 agreement.	Lt. Gen. Chang Do Young, ex-titular head of South Korea's ruling junta, is sentenced to death in Seoul on charges of having tried to block the junta's rise to power during the May 16, 1961 coup.
Jan. 11	The U.N. Special Fund's governing council votes to approve a program of $42.8 million worth of aid to projects in 38 less-developed countries during 1962.				
Jan. 12		U.S. Amb.-to-USSR Llewellyn Thompson meets with Soviet Foreign Min. Gromyko in Moscow for the second of their conferences aimed at exploring the possibility for full-scale East-West negotiations over Berlin.			

A	B	C	D	E
Includes developments that affect more than one world region, international organizations and important meetings of major world leaders.	*Includes all domestic and regional developments in Europe, including the Soviet Union, Turkey, Cyprus and Malta.*	*Includes all domestic and regional developments in Africa and the Middle East, including Iraq and Iran and excluding Cyprus, Turkey and Afghanistan.*	*Includes all domestic and regional developments in Latin America, the Caribbean and Canada.*	*Includes all domestic and regional developments in Asia and Pacific nations, extending from Afghanistan through all the Pacific Islands, except Hawaii.*

U.S. Politics & Social Issues	U.S. Foreign Policy & Defense	U.S. Economy & Environment	Science, Technology & Nature	Culture, Leisure & Life Style	
		National Fire Protection Association estimates that U.S. fires in 1961 caused 11,700 deaths, 300 more than in 1960. . . . The AFL-CIO's Maritime Trades Department establishes an International Division as a rival to the Maritime Section of the International Transport Workers Federation.		Yale University Library awards its annual Bollingen Poetry Prize to John Wheelock, for *The Garden and Other Poems*, and to Richard Eberhart, for his life work.	Jan. 7
	In a letter released to newsmen, Army Secy. Elvis Stahr admits that there had been some difficulties during the recent Berlin-related military build-up arising from the fact that many reservists were not aware of their obligation to serve if called. . . . Defense Secy. Robert McNamara and State Secy. Dean Rusk brief congressional leaders on the administration's proposed $51 billion defense budget and on the current state of U.S. foreign policy.			Archbishop Theoklitos, primate of the Orthodox Church of Greece, dies in Athens. . . . National Football League reports a record 3,986,159 spectators attended regular season NFL games during 1961. . . . Pete Rozelle is re-elected to a five-year term as NFL commissioner.	Jan. 8
The House Democratic caucus unanimously elects Rep. Carl Albert (Okla.) to succeed Rep. John McCormack as Democratic Majority Leader.	The ninth in the U.S. series of underground nuclear tests resumed in 1961 is carried out at the AEC's Nevada proving grounds.	Democratic congressional leaders, attending a White House breakfast with Pres. Kennedy, are told that the national debt limit of $298 billion will have to be raised because the debt already exceeds $296.5 billion.		Two Los Angeles Hearst newspapers, the *Examiner* and the *Herald-Express*, merge to form the new *Los Angeles Herald-Examiner*. Another Los Angeles daily, the *Mirror*, ended publication Jan. 5.	Jan. 9
The second session of the 87th Congress convenes with Democrats holding a 64-36 majority in the Senate and 258-174 majority in the House. Rep. John W. McCormack (D, Mass.) is elected House Speaker to succeed the late Sam Rayburn. . . . Several prominent administration figures resign from the private Cosmos Club of Washington after the club rejected the application of Asst. State Secy. Carl Rowan, a Negro. . . . Federal Prisons Director James Bennett reports that the number of federal prisoners has increased for the 12th consecutive year; the present prison population stands at 23,791.		Ford Motor Co. announces plans for a two-for-one stock split pending approval by the stockholders.	An avalanche devastates Peru's Huaylas Valley, destroying 16 villages and killing more than 3,000 persons.		Jan. 10
In his State of the Union message, Pres. Kennedy singles out Social Security-financed medical care for the aged and legislative action to protect voting rights as among the most important business facing the current session of Congress.	A commitment to maintain a ready U.S. conventional warfare capacity, a pledge to continue U.S. aid to neutralist countries and a call for federal support of fallout shelter construction programs highlight the defense and foreign policy sections of Pres. Kennedy's State of the Union address. . . . Sen. Barry Goldwater announces that he has become a sponsoring member of the American Committee for Aid to Katanga Freedom Fighters, a private group opposed to U.S. and U.N. policies in the Congo.	In his State of the Union message, Kennedy stresses the need for reformed tariff and trade policies to ensure continued free and active trade between the U.S. and the Common Market as well as other traditional American trading partners. Kennedy also asks Congress to provide stand-by authority to cut personal income taxes in times of economic emergency.		In a speech to the National Press Club, FCC Chmn. Newton Minow says that more TV stations--probably using ultrahigh-frequency (UHF)--are needed to give U.S. viewers an adequate choice of programs.	Jan. 11
		A proposed merger of the nation's two largest rail systems, the Pennsylvania Railroad and the New York Central Railroad, to form the Pennsylvania N.Y. Central Transportation Co. is approved by directors of both roads.			Jan. 12

F	G	H	I	J
Includes elections, federal-state relations, civil rights and liberties, crime, the judiciary, education, health care, poverty, urban affairs and population.	*Includes formation and debate of U.S. foreign and defense policies, veterans' affairs and defense spending. (Relations with specific foreign countries are usually found under the region concerned.)*	*Includes business, labor, agriculture, taxation, transportation, consumer affairs, monetary and fiscal policy, natural resources, and pollution.*	*Includes worldwide scientific, medical and technological developments, natural phenomena, U.S. weather, natural disasters, and accidents.*	*Includes the arts, religion, scholarship, communications media, sports, entertainment, fashions, fads and social life.*

	World Affairs	Europe	Africa & the Middle East	The Americas	Asia & the Pacific
Jan. 13					
Jan. 14		The European Economic Community announces that member states have agreed to begin implementation of the "second stage" of their long-term plan for general economic integration. The "second stage," to be completed by 1966, calls for an additional 10% reduction in industrial goods tariffs among member states and the creation of a common tariff on imports from non-EEC states.	Dissident Congo leader Antoine Gizenga is taken into custody by central Congolese and U.N. troops after 300 of his followers launched an unsuccessful attempt to drive central Congolese army units out of Stanleyville. . . . A new, moderate African labor organization, the African Trade Union Confederation, is established at a meeting in Dakar, Senegal to rival the leftwing All-African Trade Union Federation founded last year in Casablanca, Morocco.	British Colonial Office invites British Guiana officials to attend a London conference in May to discuss a date for granting full independence to the British colony.	
Jan. 15	U.N. General Assembly reconvenes its 16th session to take up the two major items remaining from its 1961 agenda: the Angolan rebellion against Portuguese rule and the future of the Belgian-administered trust territory of Ruanda-Urundi.		French government warns Algerian Europeans that it will impose emergency measures restricting civil liberties if the current wave of rightwing terrorism is not ended immediately. The rebel Algerian Provisional Government announced Jan. 10 that it would begin taking direct action against the local European terrorist groups. . . . Shah Mohammed Riza Pahlevi signs an Iranian land reform bill providing for the government purchase of large estates and their resale to peasants.		
Jan. 16	U.S. and Britain inform the USSR that they are prepared to accept its demand that the question of a nuclear test-ban be referred to the planned Geneva conference on general disarmament.	The six EEC countries and the U.S. announce in Brussels an agreement for reciprocal tariff reductions designed to promote mutual trade in manufactured goods and to safeguard the duty-free status of most U.S. agricultural exports to Common Market countries. . . . Uhro Kekkonen is re-elected president of Finland, outpolling rival Communist, Opposition Social Democrat, and conservative party candidates.		A seven-man junta, reportedly headed by Maj. Gen. Rafael Rodriguez Echavarria and including former Trujillo aides, overthrows the Dominican Republic's recently created coalition Council of State. Opposition leaders in the National Civic Union denounce the coup as a prelude to military dictatorship.	The Netherlands navy reports that it sank two Indonesian torpedo boats Jan. 15 after they allegedly entered Dutch territorial waters off the southeastern coast of Netherlands New Guinea.
Jan. 17		Twelve Soviet tanks, stationed along the eastern side of the Berlin Wall since October 1961, are withdrawn to their regular base in East Germany. The U.S. withdrew a similar tank force from the western side Jan. 15.	Algerian sources report that more than 300 Moslems and Europeans have been killed as a result of intensified rightist terror attacks which began in early January.	U.S. State Dept. issues a statement expressing displeasure over the military coup in the Dominican Republic and hinting at possible economic and political action against the new government. . . . Guatemalan Foreign Ministry announces acceptance of a British offer of "informal" discussions on Guatemalan claims to British Honduras.	
Jan. 18		Valery Giscard d'Estaing, 35, is named the new French minister of finance, replacing the retiring Wilfred Baumgartner.		The Dominican Council of State, ousted by a military junta Jan. 16, is restored to power in a bloodless counter-coup. The restored Council is headed by National Civic Union member Dr. Rafael Filberto Bonnelly. Bonnelly succeeds ex-Pres. Joaquin Balaguer who resigned after being implicated in the junta's attempt to topple the Council. . . . OAS Inter-American Peace Committee accuses Cuba of conducting "subversive activities" against other American states and of violating the principles of the inter-American system by its virtual alliance with the Soviet-bloc.	Hanoi, North Vietnam radio announces that a provisional revolutionary government has been formed in the Viet Cong-held regions of South Vietnam under the name of the Vietnam People's Revolutionary Party.
	A	**B**	**C**	**D**	**E**
	Includes developments that affect more than one world region, international organizations and important meetings of major world leaders.	Includes all domestic and regional developments in Europe, including the Soviet Union, Turkey, Cyprus and Malta.	Includes all domestic and regional developments in Africa and the Middle East, including Iraq and Iran and excluding Cyprus, Turkey and Afghanistan.	Includes all domestic and regional developments in Latin America, the Caribbean and Canada.	Includes all domestic and regional developments in Asia and Pacific nations, extending from Afghanistan through all the Pacific Islands, except Hawaii.

U.S. Politics & Social Issues	U.S. Foreign Policy & Defense	U.S. Economy & Environment	Science, Technology & Nature	Culture, Leisure & Life Style	
The University of Virginia's Bureau of Public Administration issues a study indicating that rural voters are vastly over-represented (compared to big-city voters) in most state legislatures.	Sens. Philip Hart (D, Mich.) and Maurine Neuberger (D, Ore.), who completed a 15-nation African tour in October 1961, issue a report criticizing U.S. aid to the Rhodesias, Ethiopia, Liberia, Ghana, and Guinea on the grounds that those nations did not measure up to the minimum standards of free societies.			National Collegiate Athletic Association votes to create new federations to govern track and field, basketball and gymnastics. The new groups are expected to be used as weapons in the NCAA's dispute with the Amateur Athletic Association over the control of U.S. amateur sports. . . . Television comedian Ernie Kovacs, 42, dies in an auto accident in Los Angeles.	Jan. 13
American Civil Liberties Union, in its annual report, warns that U.S. rights are being threatened by the "governmentalization and militarization . . .of broad stretches of our life."	National Science Foundation publishes a report asserting that the superiority of the Soviet educational system for producing engineers and scientists constitutes a "major threat in the long-run struggle between democracy and totalitarianism."			The West defeats the East, 31-30, in the NFL's Pro-Bowl All-Star game in Los Angeles.	Jan. 14
	Pres. Kennedy tells a Washington news conference that "our failure to get an agreement on cessation of nuclear testing" was the "most disappointing event" of his first year in office. . . . About 1,700 women, mostly from New York, participate in a peace demonstration in front of the White House to protest nuclear testing.				Jan. 15
U.S. Judge H. Hobart Grooms in Birmingham, Ala. sentences five men to a year on probation for their part in the 1961 fire-bombing of a Freedom Bus. . . . Rep. Martha Griffiths (D, Mich.) becomes the first woman named to the powerful House Ways and Means Committee. . . . Ex-California Gov. Goodwin Knight withdraws from his GOP gubernatorial primary race with Richard Nixon because of ill health. Knight has been suffering infectious hepatitis since late November.	Defense Secy. McNamara describes the military situation in South Vietnam as encouraging after concluding two days of briefings on the subject in Hawaii with Gen. Lyman Lemnitzer, Joint Chiefs of Staff chairman, and Adm. Harry Felt, U.S. Pacific commander. . . . Pres. Kennedy sends Congress a reorganization plan providing for a revamping of the Army's central command.		Chmn. George Miller (D, Calif.) of the House Science and Astronautics Committee asserts that the social, economic and defense benefits of the manned U.S. moon program will more than outweigh its cost.		Jan. 16
In an appearance before the House Special Labor Subcommittee, Asst. State Secy. G. Mennen Williams urges support for a proposed equal employment opportunity bill, saying that racial bias in the U.S. hurts America's image in Africa.		Democratic members of the Joint Foreign Economic Policy Subcommittee issue a report warning of possible "disastrous consequences" if the administration's trade and tariff reform plan is not enacted. The report comes amidst a growing administration campaign to generate public and political support for its trade proposals.			Jan. 17
The administration's proposed fiscal 1963 budget estimates health, welfare and labor program expenditures at $5.348 billion, an increase of $145 million over fiscal 1962 and $667 billion over 1961. The figure represents about 6% of the total budget.	Pres. Kennedy's proposed fiscal 1963 budget calls for $54.744 billion of defense-related spending; this compares with $45.994 billion spent in 1961 and $52.644 billion estimated for 1962. . . . In an appearance before the Senate Foreign Relations Subcommittee on African Affairs, State Secy. Rusk defends U.S. support of U.N. operations in the Congo as the best way of preventing Soviet exploitation of the troubled Congolese situation.	Pres. Kennedy submits to Congress a balanced budget for fiscal 1963, calling for a peacetime record expenditure level of $92.537 billion and estimated revenues of $93 billion. Kennedy says that space and defense account for most of the increase over 1962 spending, which is now estimated at $89.1 billion. . . . The 9,000-member New York local of the AFL-CIO International Brotherhood of Electrical Workers ends a week-long strike after winning agreement to a contract establishing a 25-hour work week with a guaranteed five hours overtime.	The administration's proposed fiscal 1963 budget estimates total U.S. space expenditures at $3.787 billion, more than twice the amount planned for 1962 and over four times that spent in 1961.		Jan. 18
F	G	H	I	J	
Includes elections, federal-state relations, civil rights and liberties, crime, the judiciary, education, health care, poverty, urban affairs and population.	*Includes formation and debate of U.S. foreign and defense policies, veterans' affairs and defense spending. (Relations with specific foreign countries are usually found under the region concerned.)*	*Includes business, labor, agriculture, taxation, transportation, consumer affairs, monetary and fiscal policy, natural resources, and pollution.*	*Includes worldwide scientific, medical and technological developments, natural phenomena, U.S. weather, natural disasters, and accidents.*	*Includes the arts, religion, scholarship, communications media, sports, entertainment, fashions, fads and social life.*	

	World Affairs	Europe	Africa & the Middle East	The Americas	Asia & the Pacific
Jan. 19	Pres. Kennedy flies to New York to confer with Acting U.N. Secy Gen. U Thant on outstanding world problems; it is the first private meeting between the two leaders.	Sweden's military chiefs issue a report asserting that the acquistion of nuclear weapons is "essential if Sweden is to be able to repel an enemy attack."	U.N. sources report that 19 Roman Catholic missionaries have been killed and others captured by mutinous Congolese soldiers in northern Katanga. The soldiers are described as a pro-Gizenga band who have broken away from the main body of the central Congolese army.	Canadian Immigration Ministry announces the abolition of all racially and religiously based immigration rules.	Premier Boun Oum of the rightist Laotian government, Souvanna Phouma of the rebel neutralist faction, and Prince Souphanouvong of the pro-Communist Pathet Lao movement announce agreement in Geneva on the formation and make-up of a coalition Laotian government. The agreement reportedly came after Boun Oum, under U.S. pressure, acquiesced to the appointment of neutralists to head the defense and interior ministries in the new government.
Jan. 20			Antoine Gizenga is returned to Leopoldville and placed under U.N.-supervised house arrest. The Congolese Parliament stripped Gizenga of his post as first deputy premier on Jan. 15.	Rafael Bonnelly, head of the Dominican Republic's governing Council of State, describes his government as "left of center" but not extremist.	Indonesian sources disclose that Pres. Sukarno has accepted a Jan. 17 appeal from U.N. Acting Secy. Gen. U Thant for talks with Dutch officals on a peaceful settlement of the dispute over Netherlands New Guinea. Dutch Premier Jan Eduard de Quay announced his willingness to participate Jan. 18.
Jan. 21		Despite official rejections recent Soviet offers for direct negotiations with West Germany are reportedly attracting some consideration from Bonn political leaders. News reports also indicate that East German leaders are unhappy with the current Soviet direct talks strategy.		Twenty armed Guatemalans raid a British Honduran border town and raise the Guatemalan flag in place of the British Union Jack.	
Jan. 22	U.N. headquarters in New York announces that member states have been formally asked to subscribe to a planned $200 million U.N. bond issue.	USSR's Central Statistical Board reports that industrial production rose 9.2% in 1961, exceeding industrial production goals.	French government imposes a modified form of martial law on major Algerian cities in an effort to halt the continuing terrorist campaign against de Gaulle's policies by the rightist Secret Army Organization.	An OAS foreign ministers conference to consider alleged Cuban threats to hemispheric security opens in Punta del Este, Uruguay. A U.S.-prepared proposal for diplomatic and economic sanctions against Cuba is reportedly disfavored by several South American delegations who are expected to press for a more moderate response. . . . Pres. Kennedy announces the granting of a $25 million emergency credit to help the Dominican Republic meet an "urgent" balance of payments problem.	
Jan. 23		Mrs Leon Trotsky (Natalia Ivanova Sedova), 79, widow of the assassinated Russian revolutionist, dies in Corbeil, France.	South African P.M. Henrik Verwoerd announces that local home rule will be granted by mid-1963 to two million Negroes living in the Transkei African Reserve. The plan is part of Verwoerd's long-term policy of "separate development" of the white and black races in South Africa. . . . Iranian student demonstrations, which began Jan. 21 over academic issues, appear to be evolving into a nationwide anti-government protest.		
Jan. 24	British P.M. Harold Macmillan publicly confirms that he and Pres. Kennedy agreed at their December 1961 Bermuda meeting to resume nuclear tests in the atmosphere if the USSR was found to have "a significant advance" in weapons technology during its recent tests. . . . U.N. sources confirm that the USSR has asked U Thant to assign 80 more of the Secretariat's 1,300 professional posts to Soviet citizens and to promote 20 Russians now serving in U.N. posts.	The East German Volkskammer approves a military conscription law, the first in East Germany since World War II.			

A	B	C	D	E
Includes developments that affect more than one world region, international organizations and important meetings of major world leaders.	*Includes all domestic and regional developments in Europe, including the Soviet Union, Turkey, Cyprus and Malta.*	*Includes all domestic and regional developments in Africa and the Middle East, including Iraq and Iran and excluding Cyprus, Turkey and Afghanistan.*	*Includes all domestic and regional developments in Latin America, the Caribbean and Canada.*	*Includes all domestic and regional developments in Asia and Pacific nations, extending from Afghanistan through all the Pacific Islands, except Hawaii.*

U.S. Politics & Social Issues	U.S. Foreign Policy & Defense	U.S. Economy & Environment	Science, Technology & Nature	Culture, Leisure & Life Style	
	CIA Dir. John McCone reportedly tells the Joint Congressional Atomic Energy Committee that the USSR made substantial weapons progress during its recent nuclear test series, especially in the field of the anti-missile missile. The testimony is expected to intensify demands for a resumption of Western atmospheric nuclear tests.		NASA reports that data gathered from the Explorer 12 satellite indicates that the earth is girdled by a single thick Van Allen belt rather than two thinner belts as previously thought. NASA scientists say that Van Allen belt radiation may constitute a grave danger to space travel.	Charles Van Doren and nine other TV quiz show winners, charged in 1960 with falsely testifying that they had never been given advance questions and answers on the defunct shows *21* and *Tic Tac Dough*, are given suspended sentences in New York by a Special Sessions Court.	Jan. 19
					Jan. 20
The Gallup Poll releases a survey showing that 77% of Americans interviewed approve Kennedy's performance as President, while 11% disapprove.		The Licensed Beverage Industries, Inc. issues a study estimating that one out of every seven gallons of liquor consumed in the U.S. is produced illicitly.			Jan. 21
		Pres. Kennedy, in his first economic report to Congress, says the "economy has regained its momentum" and that with proper policies the U.S. can look forward to accelerated growth and reduced unemployment in 1962 and 1963. . . . American Stock Exchange Pres. Joseph Reilly resigns amidst SEC charges of misconduct in the administration of the Amex. . . . Atty. Gen. Robert Kennedy reports that the Justice Dept. filed 60 antitrust cases in 1961, compared with a record 90 cases in 1960.		Bob Feller, 43, ex-Cleveland Indian pitcher (1936-1956), and Jackie Robinson, ex-Brooklyn Dodger infielder (1947-1956) are named to major league baseball's Hall of Fame. Robinson is the first Negro to be inducted into the Hall of Fame. . . . Doug Ford wins the $50,000 Bing Crosby golf tournament at Pebble Beach, Calif.	Jan. 22
		Directors of American Airlines and Eastern Air Lines approve a merger of their lines into what would be the world's largest system. Final approval awaits action by the CAB and the firms' stockholders.	U.S. Weather Bureau discloses that the Tiros III satellite, launched July 12, 1961 with hurricane-hunting as its prime mission, detected more than 50 tropical storms during 1961.		Jan. 23
A coalition of Republicans and Southern Democrats on the House Rules Committee succeeds in killing the administration's bill to create a cabinet-level urban affairs department. Kennedy tells newsmen he will reintroduce the proposal in the form of an executive reorganization plan.		The House passes and sends to the Senate an administration bill (HR7927) to increase U.S. postal rates. Under the proposed rates, first class mail would be raised from 4¢ to 5¢, airmail from 7¢ to 8¢.	A U.S. Navy-directed attempt to launch five satellites into orbit with a single booster fails at Cape Canaveral because of a malfunction of the rocket's second stage.	A hearing on TV violence and its possible effect on juvenile behavior is held by the Senate Juvenile Delinquency Subcommittee.	Jan. 24

F	G	H	I	J
Includes elections, federal-state relations, civil rights and liberties, crime, the judiciary, education, health care, poverty, urban affairs and population.	Includes formation and debate of U.S. foreign and defense policies, veterans' affairs and defense spending. (Relations with specific foreign countries are usually found under the region concerned.)	Includes business, labor, agriculture, taxation, transportation, consumer affairs, monetary and fiscal policy, natural resources, and pollution.	Includes worldwide scientific, medical and technological developments, natural phenomena, U.S. weather, natural disasters, and accidents.	Includes the arts, religion, scholarship, communications media, sports, entertainment, fashions, fads and social life.

	World Affairs	Europe	Africa & the Middle East	The Americas	Asia & the Pacific
Jan. 25				Pres. Miguel Ydigoras Fuentes declares a modified form of martial law in Guatemala after an unsuccessful Jan. 24 attempt on his life which he attributes to communist plotters.	Forces of the rebel pro-Communist Pathet Lao movement are reported to have attacked Nam Tha, a key Laotian provincial center 95 miles northwest of Luang Prubang.
Jan. 26		*The New York Times* reports that French Pres. de Gaulle has warned Algerian rebels to agree to a truce quickly to thwart the rightist opponents of any French-rebel accord. . . . U.N. Congo operations chief, Sture Linner, says that Katanga appears to be attempting to comply with U.N. demands for the dismissal of mercenaries. . . . Tunisian Pres. Habib Bourguiba announces he has accepted a French proposal to resume negotiations July 1 on the withdrawal of French forces from their naval base at Bizerte.			The World Bank and a six-nation consortium announce an agreement to give Pakistan a $945 million credit to finance the first two years of a five-year development plan.
Jan. 27			Ex-Amb.-to-Iraq Wasfi al-Tall is named as new Jordanian premier, succeeding the resigned Bahjat Abdul Khadr Talhouni.		
Jan. 28			Iranian Premier Ali Amini tells newsmen that his government holds the USSR responsible for inciting the anti-government student riots in Teheran Jan. 21-23.		
Jan. 29	The U.S.-British-Soviet Geneva test-ban talks adjourn in failure after the USSR refused to accept its own repeated proposals that the test question be transferred to the forthcoming Geneva disarmament talks.			U.S. Commerce Dept. announces the lifting of all trade restrictions against the Dominican Republic.	
Jan. 30	Pres. Kennedy confers at the White House with Aleksei I. Adzhubei, editor of *Izvestia* and son-in-law of Soviet Premier Khrushchev, in one of a renewed series of contacts between U.S. and Soviet officials.		U.N. General Assembly, by a vote of 99-2, calls upon Portugal to end its repression of the Angolan rebellion against colonial rule and take necessary steps to prepare the African colony for independence. The Assembly earlier rejected a Soviet proposal for U.N. sanctions against Portugal. . . . U.N. Security Council refuses to place on its agenda a Soviet request for renewed debate on the U.N.'s failure to have mercenaries promptly removed from Katanga.	Cuban Pres. Osvaldo Dorticos Torrado tells the OAS foreign ministers' conference in Punta del Este that the exclusion of his country from OAS's affairs would mean the end of the OAS as a genuine regional organization.	

A	B	C	D	E
Includes developments that affect more than one world region, international organizations and important meetings of major world leaders.	Includes all domestic and regional developments in Europe, including the Soviet Union, Turkey, Cyprus and Malta.	Includes all domestic and regional developments in Africa and the Middle East, including Iraq and Iran and excluding Cyprus, Turkey and Afghanistan.	Includes all domestic and regional developments in Latin America, the Caribbean and Canada.	Includes all domestic and regional developments in Asia and Pacific nations, extending from Afghanistan through all the Pacific Islands, except Hawaii.

U.S. Politics & Social Issues	U.S. Foreign Policy & Defense	U.S. Economy & Environment	Science, Technology & Nature	Culture, Leisure & Life Style	
The Kennedy administration's first civil rights bill--a measure designed to safeguard the voting rights of Negroes and Puerto Ricans--is introduced in the Senate by majority leader Mike Mansfield. The bill would make a sixth grade education the only literacy test allowed to be used in determining voter qualification. . . . Montana Gov. Donald Nutter, 45, dies in a plane crash near Wolf Creek, Mont.		Pres. Kennedy sends Congress a draft trade expansion bill (HR9900) containing his proposals for a liberalized tariff policy.	Dr. Mina Reese, dean of graduate studies at the City University of New York, is named recipient of the Mathematical Association of America's first Award for Distinguished Service to Mathematics.	Eric Carlsson and Gunnar Haggbom, of Sweden, driving a Saab, win the 2,400-mile Oslo to Monte Carlo Rally. . . . Archbishop Iakavos, elected as primate of the Orthodox Church of Greece on Jan. 13, abdicates in the face of public clamor arising from charges that he was guilty of "unmentionable acts."	Jan. 25
Congressional Quarterly releases a study showing that predominantly suburban congressional districts are, on the average, 34.2% under-represented in Congress; urban districts are described as 5.7% under-represented and rural districts as 10.7% over-represented. . . . (Salvatore) Charles (Lucky) Luciano, 65, Sicilian-born ex-"king" of U.S. narcotics and prostitution rackets, who was deported to Sicily in 1946, dies of a heart attack in Naples, Italy.		Bureau of Labor Statistics reports that the U.S. cost-of-living index rose .5% in 1961, the lowest annual increase since 1955. Over the same period, the spendable income of the average American factory worker climbed a record 7%. . . . The U.S. Court of Appeals in Washington upholds an NLRB finding that the Kohler Co. had engaged in unfair labor practices during its eight-year dispute with the United Auto Workers.	*Journal of the American Medical Association* reports new evidence indicating that tuberculosis is "primarily an airborne infection" and that the tubercle bacillus can survive and cause an epidemic long after an infected person has left an area.	Orson Welles' *Citizen Kane* (U.S. 1941) is named the best film ever produced in a British Film Institute poll of 70 critics in 11 countries.	Jan. 26
	A Special Senate Armed Services Subcommittee concludes five days of hearings on the continuing controversy over administration supervision of the political speeches and activities of military leaders. The witnesses, who included ex-Pres. Eisenhower and top U.S. generals, generally agreed on the need for some high-level civilian control, but opposed petty interference.		The first U.S. attempt to put an astronaut in earth orbit is cancelled with only 20 minutes remaining in the count-down (because of bad weather). The mission, originally scheduled for Dec. 20, 1961, has been plagued by numerous delays.	New Zealand distance runner Peter Snell, 22, establishes a new world mile record of three minutes 54.4 seconds on a grass track in Cooks Gardens, Wanganui, New Zealand. . . . John Uelses, of the U.S. Marine Corps., sets a world indoor pole vault record of 15 ft. 10 1/4 in. at a Washington, D.C. meet.	Jan. 27
	Sen. Strom Thurmond (D, S.C.), a member of the Senate subcommittee investigating charges that the administration is "muzzling" anti-communist military officers, tells newsmen that "our State Department policy planners have sold our leaders on the idea that we do not want to win the cold war."		A Ranger III satellite, launched Jan. 26 from Cape Canaveral for a hard landing on the moon, misses its target by over 22,000 miles and heads out into a solar orbit. The satellite had gone off course shortly after launch when it achieved a speed in excess to that expected.	Edd Roush, 69, star major league outfielder (1913-1931), and Bill McKechnie, 74, who managed three different National League teams to pennants, are elected to the Baseball Hall of Fame.	Jan. 28
		The Center for the Study of Democratic Institutions publishes a report by Donald Michael on the vast economic and cultural implications of "cibernation," a term coined by Michael to describe the complex situations resulting from automation and the use of computers.		Fritz Kreisler, 86, Vienna-born violinist, composer of more than 200 published works, dies in New York of old age.	Jan. 29
A reorganization plan to create a cabinet-level Department of Urban Affairs is submitted to Congress by Pres. Kennedy. The plan will become effective in 60 days unless disapproved by a majority vote of either house. . . . Kennedy's previous statements that he intends to appoint Robert Weaver, a Negro, to head the new department, if established, draw bitter criticism from Republicans who charge him with attempting to exploit an unrelated racial issue.	Kennedy asks Congress to authorize the U.S. purchase of up to half of the U.N.'s special $200 million bond issue. A number of prominent congressional conservatives indicate they will oppose the request.				Jan. 30

F	G	H	I	J
Includes elections, federal-state relations, civil rights and liberties, crime, the judiciary, education, health care, poverty, urban affairs and population.	*Includes formation and debate of U.S. foreign and defense policies, veterans' affairs and defense spending. (Relations with specific foreign countries are usually found under the region concerned.)*	*Includes business, labor, agriculture, taxation, transportation, consumer affairs, monetary and fiscal policy, natural resources, and pollution.*	*Includes worldwide scientific, medical and technological developments, natural phenomena, U.S. weather, natural disasters, and accidents.*	*Includes the arts, religion, scholarship, communications media, sports, entertainment, fashions, fads and social life.*

	World Affairs	Europe	Africa & the Middle East	The Americas	Asia & the Pacific
Jan. 31		Eighteen Portuguese dissidents are wounded by police during a mass anti-government demonstration in Oporto.	Leaders from 19 African nations conclude a week-long conference in Lagos, Nigeria after tentatively agreeing to a draft charter for a loose confederation in the economic, cultural and political fields. The conference, which was boycotted by the "Casablanca group" (UAR, Morocco, Guinea, Mali, and Ghana), is believed to have hardened the division between left-leaning and moderate African nations.	OAS foreign ministers vote to exclude Cuba "from participation in the inter-American system" on the grounds that Marxism-Leninism is incompatible with the objectives of the OAS. The measure, a compromise which did not deprive Cuba of its OAS membership, received 14 votes; Cuba opposed, and Argentina, Brazil, Chile, Ecuador, and Mexico abstained.	
Feb. 1		U.S. Amb.-to-USSR Llewellyn Thompson meets with Soviet Foreign Min. Gromyko in his third attempt to "probe" Soviet terms for talks on Berlin. Little progress toward an agreement on full-scale negotiations is reported. . . . Italy files espionage charges against a Bulgarian Air Force pilot who crash-landed his MiG-17 jet Jan. 20 in southern Italy while on an alleged spy flight.	*The New York Times* reports that 220 Europeans and 335 Moslems were killed in Algeria during January as the result of rightwing terrorism.		U.N. Security Council votes to postpone discussion of Pakistani charges that India is preparing a military attack on Kashmir until after the current Indian general elections are concluded.
Feb. 2	U.S. AEC announces that it detected an underground Soviet nuclear test earlier in the day.	Italian Premier Amintore Fanfani's moderate Christian Democratic cabinet resigns after Christian Democratic Party leaders decided to try to organize a more left-leaning government with support from Italian Socialists.	Congo Premier Cyrille Adoula appears before the U.N. General Assembly to appeal for increased U.N. military assistance to suppress the Katangan secession.	In a nationally televised report, State Secy. Dean Rusk tells the American people that the OAS's recent action at Punta del Este proves that "Cuba stands alone in the Americas."	Rightist Laotian Premier Boun Oum cancels final talks on the formation of a coalition government in protest against a continuing Pathet Lao assault on Nam Tha, a provincial capital near Laos's border with Communist China.
Feb. 3				Pres. Kennedy orders an almost total embargo on U.S.-Cuban trade in order "to promote national and hemispheric security. . .by isolating Cuba.". . . Argentine sources report a serious political rift between Pres. Frondizi and the nation's military leaders over Argentina's abstention in the Jan. 31 OAS vote to exclude Cuba from hemispheric affairs. The military has reportedly pressured for a tougher stand against Cuba.	
Feb. 4		Portuguese Amb.-to-U.N. Vasco Viera Garin warns that the U.S. may lose its air bases in the Azores if it continues to back anti-Portuguese actions in the U.N.		Cuban Premier Castro denounces the Feb. 3 announcement of a U.S.-Cuban embargo as "another economic aggression" against his government. . . . National Liberation Party candidate Francisco Jose Orlich Bolmarcich is elected to a four-year term as president of Costa Rica.	South Vietnamese troops, accompanied by U.S. Air Force helicopters and crews, recapture the rebel-held village of Hung My. One of the helicopters was shot down, but the American crew was rescued.
Feb. 5	British P.M. Macmillan publicly denounces the "flood" of "irresponsible" anti-colonial resolutions being presented to the U.N. General Assembly, claiming that they could contribute to world chaos.	French Pres. de Gaulle, in a nationwide TV speech, reiterates France's intention to build a national nuclear striking force and to resist inroads on French sovereignty by NATO or other supranational political institutions currently being proposed by EEC members. . . . Pres. Uhro Kekkonen's ruling Agrarian Party replaces the Communists as the largest party in the Finnish Parliament.	In a speech broadcast in France and Algeria, de Gaulle reaffirms his determination to settle the Algerian rebellion and to suppress the rightist terror campaign against his policies. The address prompts praise from Algerian rebel leaders and defiant demonstrations from Algerian rightists. . . . U.N. officials in New York disclose that Katanga Pres. Moise Tshombe has agreed to the jointly supervised removal of white mercenaries from Katanga.		

A	B	C	D	E
Includes developments that affect more than one world region, international organizations and important meetings of major world leaders.	Includes all domestic and regional developments in Europe, including the Soviet Union, Turkey, Cyprus and Malta.	Includes all domestic and regional developments in Africa and the Middle East, including Iraq and Iran and excluding Cyprus, Turkey and Afghanistan.	Includes all domestic and regional developments in Latin America, the Caribbean and Canada.	Includes all domestic and regional developments in Asia and Pacific nations, extending from Afghanistan through all the Pacific Islands, except Hawaii.

U.S. Politics & Social Issues	U.S. Foreign Policy & Defense	U.S. Economy & Environment	Science, Technology & Nature	Culture, Leisure & Life Style	
	The Senate, by a 71-12 vote, confirms ex-AEC Chmn. John McCone as director of the CIA. . . . Lt. Cmndr. Samuel Gravely assumes command of the destroyer escort *U.S.S. Falgout*, becoming the first Negro to command a U.S. warship.	Kennedy sends Congress a farm bill (HR10010) aimed at increasing farm income, lowering the cost of U.S. farm programs, and reducing agricultural surpluses.	In a report to Congress, Kennedy praises the U.S. space program as a potential source of economic and military as well as scientific benefits.		Jan. 31
Kennedy sends Congress a special welfare message outlining proposals for the development of long-range public assistance programs which place "more stress on services instead of relief." A bill incorporating the President's proposals (HR10032) is introduced in the House by Wilbur Mills (D. Ark.). . . . Atty. Gen. Kennedy sends Congress a draft bill barring private wiretapping, but authorizing the Justice Dept. to use wiretaps, without court order, in espionage, treason and subversion cases.	Atty. Gen. Robert Kennedy embarks on a month-long semi-official goodwill tour around the world.	Health Insurance Institute reports that health and medical care expenditures by Americans rose from $3 billion in 1940 to $19.6 billion in 1960. The Institute estimates that almost 6% of the average U.S. personal expenditure dollar in 1960 went for medical care. . . . Census Bureau reports that U.S. exports in 1961 totaled a record $20.874 billion, 2% above the 1960 level.			Feb. 1
About 13,600 people are reported to have attended a three-day anti-communism school conducted in Oakland, Calif. by the Christian Anti-Communist Crusade. The group also sponsored a simultaneous "anti-communist leadership school" in Tulsa, Okla. . . . Ex-Major Gen. Edwin Walker, who resigned from the Army following a controversy over his alleged rightwing orientation of troops, files as a Democratic candidate for governor of Texas.		Commerce Dept. reports U.S. gross national product rose from a $504.4 billion total in 1960 to $521.3 billion in 1961.		Pope John XXIII proclaims Oct. 11 as the opening date of the 21st Ecumenical Council of the Roman Catholic Church. . . . German-born U.S. Marine Cpl. John Uelses, 24, becomes the first pole-vaulter to reach 16 ft.; Uelses unofficially cleared 16 ft. 1/4 in. at the Millrose games in New York.	Feb. 2
				Peter Snell, 22, of New Zealand, sets a new world outdoor half-mile record of 1 minute 45.1 seconds in Christchurch, New Zealand.	Feb. 3
	The New York Times reports that a major dispute has developed within the Kennedy administration over the advisability of resuming U.S. nuclear tests in the atmosphere.			Swiss Alpine guides Hilti von Allmen and Walter Etter become the first men to scale the northern face of the 14,700 foot Matterhorn peak in winter. . . . *The National Observer*, a weekly national newspaper published in Washington by Dow Jones & Co., begins publication.	Feb. 4
A threat of immediate suspensions ends a two-week sit-in demonstration by University of Chicago students against the administration's alleged tolerance of segregation in off-campus housing.			Dr. Herbert Kauffman of the University of Florida reports at a Gustav Stern Foundation symposium on viruses in New York that blinding eye infections caused by the virus herpes simplex have been effectively treated with the drug IDU (originally developed for cancer treatment).	Winners of the Helms Athletic Foundation's designations as the world's outstanding amateur athletes of 1961 are: broad jumper Ralph Boston (U.S.), high jumper Valeri Brumel (USSR), swimmers Tsuyoshi Yamanaka (Japan) and Dawn Fraser (Australia), sprinter Abdul Amu (Nigeria) and basketball player Wlamir Marques (Brazil). . . . A series of world disasters, predicted by Indian astrologers for the period between Feb. 3-5, fail to materialize.	Feb. 5

F	G	H	I	J
Includes elections, federal-state relations, civil rights and liberties, crime, the judiciary, education, health care, poverty, urban affairs and population.	*Includes formation and debate of U.S. foreign and defense policies, veterans' affairs and defense spending. (Relations with specific foreign countries are usually found under the region concerned.)*	*Includes business, labor, agriculture, taxation, transportation, consumer affairs, monetary and fiscal policy, natural resources, and pollution.*	*Includes worldwide scientific, medical and technological developments, natural phenomena, U.S. weather, natural disasters, and accidents.*	*Includes the arts, religion, scholarship, communications media, sports, entertainment, fashions, fads and social life.*

	World Affairs	Europe	Africa & the Middle East	The Americas	Asia & the Pacific
Feb. 6					
Feb. 7				Brazilian Foreign Min. San Thiago Dantas defends his delegation's decision to abstain from voting on the OAS's Jan. 31 anti-Cuban resolution as the best course for preserving hemispheric peace.	
Feb. 8	In a joint statement, Britain and the U.S. call upon the USSR to agree to a meeting of their three foreign ministers prior to the Geneva disarmament convention for a final discussion of the nuclear test question. The statement also discloses that Britain has made available to the U.S. its atmospheric nuclear testing site on Christmas Island in the Pacific.	P.M. Macmillan informs Parliament that Britain will test a low-yield nuclear weapon underground at the U.S. Nevada proving grounds within a few weeks. . . . An estimated 20,000 Parisians defy a French government ban and participate in angry demonstrations against the continuing wave of rightwing terrorist attacks. Eight persons are killed in clashes with police.	*The New York Herald Tribune* reports that 694 persons have been killed and 1,164 wounded in Algerian rightist violence since Jan. 1.	Argentina severs diplomatic relations with Cuba. The decision for the break is attributed to direct military pressure on the Frondizi government.	*The New York Times* reports that the U.S. currently has nearly 5,000 military personnel in South Vietnam, many of whom are engaged in quasi-combat ground and air support missions. The 1954 Geneva armistice limits South Vietnam to 685 foreign military advisers.
Feb. 9	A Rhodesian Federal inquiry commission issues a detailed report attributing the late Dag Hammarskjold's fatal plane crash in Northern Rhodesia to pilot error. . . . French Foreign Ministry discloses that it has informed the U.S. and Britain that "the French government has adopted a position of extreme reserve with regard to the Geneva (disarmament) meeting."	Britain, France and the U.S. formally reject Soviet demands that portions of the three air corridors to West Berlin be set aside for use by Russian aircraft on military maneuvers.	The Pan-African Freedom Movement ends a week-long conference in Addis Ababa after adopting resolutions denouncing South Africa, Portugal and Katanga Pres. Moise Tshombe. . . . Israel implements a 40% devaluation of the Israeli pound.	An agreement providing for the independence of Jamaica on Aug. 6 is signed in London.	A Pentagon spokesman discloses that the U.S. is forming a new Military Assistance Command (MAC) in Vietnam, headed by Gen. Paul Harkins. He adds that the new command is a demonstration of the U.S.'s belief that "this is a war we can't afford to lose.". . . U.S. Atty. Gen. Robert Kennedy holds an informal debate with leftist students in Kyoto, Japan during the Japanese leg of his world goodwill tour.
Feb. 10	U-2 pilot Francis Gary Powers and convicted Soviet spy Rudolf Abel are released from their prison terms and secretly exchanged at the border between West Berlin and East Germany. The exchange was reportedly negotiated by Brooklyn lawyer James Donovan, who had defended Abel during his 1957 espionage trial.	The Western commandants in Berlin protest the application to Berlin of East Germany's new military conscription law.			
Feb. 11	In a message delivered to the U.S. and Britain, Soviet Premier Khrushchev proposes that the forthcoming 17-nation Geneva disarmament conference be personally opened "by the heads of government" represented at the conference.			Cuban exile leader José Miro Cardona announces in Miami the organization of a pan-hemispheric anti-Castro alliance, which Cardona claims has the support of many prominent Latin American political leaders. . . . The Cuban Health Ministry announces the rationing of drugs and medicines because of shortages attributed to the U.S. embargo.	

A	B	C	D	E
Includes developments that affect more than one world region, international organizations and important meetings of major world leaders.	Includes all domestic and regional developments in Europe, including the Soviet Union, Turkey, Cyprus and Malta.	Includes all domestic and regional developments in Africa and the Middle East, including Iraq and Iran and excluding Cyprus, Turkey and Afghanistan.	Includes all domestic and regional developments in Latin America, the Caribbean and Canada.	Includes all domestic and regional developments in Asia and Pacific nations, extending from Afghanistan through all the Pacific Islands, except Hawaii.

U.S. Politics & Social Issues	U.S. Foreign Policy & Defense	U.S. Economy & Environment	Science, Technology & Nature	Culture, Leisure & Life Style	
A five-year $5.7 billion school aid program, including many of the proposals rejected by Congress last year, is resubmitted to Congress via a special message from Pres. Kennedy. . . . Dining facilities in 29 Memphis stores peacefully desegregate in accordance with a plan worked out by Negro and business leaders.				Warner Bros. Pictures, Inc. purchases the movie rights to the musical *My Fair Lady* from CBS for a record $5.5 million.	**Feb. 6**
Agreements with the President's Committee on Equal Employment Opportunities to eliminate hiring discrimination against Negroes are signed by 31 leading defense contractors. . . . Francis Cardinal Spellman, Roman Catholic archbishop of New York, tells a meeting of the Archdiocesan Teachers Institute that enactment of Pres. Kennedy's aid-to-public-education program would mean "the eventual end of our parochial schools."	Pres. Kennedy, at a Washington news conference, says that his decision on a possible resumption of atmospheric nuclear testing will depend on whether such tests prove essential for maintaining an effective atomic deterrent and for assuring U.S. superiority in anti-missile weaponry.	Both houses of Congress pass and send to conference slightly varying versions of an administration bill to strengthen the reporting provisions of the 1958 Welfare and Pension Plans Disclosure Act.	Kennedy asks Congress to charter a privately-owned, but federally-supervised, "communications satellite corporation" to own and operate a world communications satellite system.		**Feb. 7**
	An inquiry into military speech censorship, which was launched Jan. 31 by the Senate Preparedness Subcommittee, becomes embroiled in controversy as Pres. Kennedy invokes executive privilege to bar disclosure of which administration officials had censored specific speeches.	Agreement on a new three-year contract ends a 38-day United Auto Workers strike against the Studebaker-Packard Corp. plant in South Bend, Indiana.	Tiros IV, a 285-pound U.S. weather satellite equipped to photograph the earth's cloud cover and snow and ice distribution, is launched from Cape Canaveral.		**Feb. 8**
	In a letter to the *Washington Post*, William C. Foster, director of U.S. Arms Control and Disarmament Agency, warns that recent Soviet nuclear tests may have given the USSR "a superiority in the anti-missile and other strategic areas.". . . A draft bill to authorize $450 million for an incentive program to provide fall-out shelters for 20 million people by mid-1963 is presented to Congress by Defense Secy. Robert McNamara.			N.Y. State Boxing Commission strips Archie Moore of his world light-heavyweight title for refusing to fight two top challengers recognized by the commission.	**Feb. 9**
George Romney, president of American Motors Corp. since 1954, announces his candidacy for the Republican nomination for governor of Michigan. The announcement heightens speculation about Romney as a possible "dark horse" GOP presidential candidate in 1964. . . . An executive memo establishing new conflict-of-interest standards for federal advisers and consultants is issued by Pres. Kennedy.				Jim Beatty, 27, of Los Angeles, sets a new world indoor mile record of 3 min. 58.9 seconds at a Los Angeles meet. It is the first sub-four minute indoor mile ever recorded. Peter Snell of New Zealand sets a 1,000-yard indoor record of two min. six seconds in the same meet.	**Feb. 10**
The NAACP issues a list of 23 non-Southern communities that allegedly maintain some form of school segregation; Philadelphia, Cleveland, Chicago and Detroit are among the cities cited.				Charles McKinley wins the U.S. indoor men's tennis title in New York.	**Feb. 11**

F	G	H	I	J
Includes elections, federal-state relations, civil rights and liberties, crime, the judiciary, education, health care, poverty, urban affairs and population.	Includes formation and debate of U.S. foreign and defense policies, veterans' affairs and defense spending. (Relations with specific foreign countries are usually found under the region concerned.)	Includes business, labor, agriculture, taxation, transportation, consumer affairs, monetary and fiscal policy, natural resources, and pollution.	Includes worldwide scientific, medical and technological developments, natural phenomena, U.S. weather, natural disasters, and accidents.	Includes the arts, religion, scholarship, communications media, sports, entertainment, fashions, fads and social life.

	World Affairs	Europe	Africa & the Middle East	The Americas	Asia & the Pacific
Feb. 12				About 50,000 workers go on strike in Georgetown, capital of British Guiana, to protest Premier Cheddi Jagan's proposed budget and his general socialist orientation.	
Feb. 13	Pres. Kennedy, in a note to Premier Khrushchev, rejects the latter's Feb. 11 proposal for a quasi-summit meeting at the opening of the Geneva disarmament talks. Kennedy, however, adds that he would be willing to participate at the conference "when it appears that such participation could positively effect the chances of success."	Over 500,000 Parisians join a public funeral procession held for the victims of the Feb. 8 anti-terrorist demonstrations. It is said to be the largest public expression of leftist sentiment in Paris since the 1944 liberation.			Canadian news sources report that Communist China has purchased nearly $20 million worth of Canadian grain scheduled for delivery this summer.
Feb. 14		Soviet MiG jet fighters begin harassing Western planes in the Berlin air corridors after the West again refused repeated Soviet requests to use the air lanes.		Carlos Rafael Rodriguez, editor of the Cuban communist newspaper *Hoy*, replaces Fidel Castro as head of the National Institute of Agrarian Reform, a post from which Castro had once derived much of his political authority.	
Feb. 15			Empress Wolzero Menen, wife of Ethiopian Emperor Haile Selassie I and reformer who helped outlaw child marriages and harems, dies at 71 in Addis Ababa.	The U.N. General Assembly's Political Committee votes 50-11 (39 abstentions) to reject a Czech-Rumanian resolution urging the U.S. to cease interfering in Cuba's internal affairs. The action concludes a week-long debate of Cuban charges against the U.S. . . . Uruguay's governing Executive National Council votes to retain diplomatic relations with Cuba.	U.S. Amb.-to-South Vietnam Frederick Nolting tells a South Vietnamese audience in Saigon that the U.S. supports the Diem government as "the only hope for success against the Viet Cong," despite growing criticism of Diem's failure to carry out promised reforms.
Feb. 16				More than 500 British troops are flown to British Guiana, at the request of Premier Jagan, to help suppress a violent anti-government general strike in Georgetown.	
Feb. 17					
Feb. 18			Two French Air Force jets, piloted by reserve airmen sympathetic to the Secret Army Organization, conduct an unauthorized attack on an Algerian rebel base near Oujda, Morocco, killing five persons and wounding 30 others.		

A	B	C	D	E
Includes developments that affect more than one world region, international organizations and important meetings of major world leaders.	Includes all domestic and regional developments in Europe, including the Soviet Union, Turkey, Cyprus and Malta.	Includes all domestic and regional developments in Africa and the Middle East, including Iraq and Iran and excluding Cyprus, Turkey and Afghanistan.	Includes all domestic and regional developments in Latin America, the Caribbean and Canada.	Includes all domestic and regional developments in Asia and Pacific nations, extending from Afghanistan through all the Pacific Islands, except Hawaii.

U.S. Politics & Social Issues	U.S. Foreign Policy & Defense	U.S. Economy & Environment	Science, Technology & Nature	Culture, Leisure & Life Style	
Sen. Jacob Javits (R, N.Y.) says in a Lincoln Day speech in New York that the Republican Party must either reject ultra-conservatism or face "permanent minority status as a result of negativism.". . . Pres. Kennedy informs his Commission on the Status of Women that he will back a drive to prevent "discrimination by law or implication" against working women.			Torrential rains in Southern California cause flooding, mudslides and at least 20 deaths.		Feb. 12
A three-judge federal court in Augusta, Ga. rules that state and city ordinances requiring segregated seating on buses are unconstitutional.	Republican National Committee charges that the Kennedy administration has been "less than candid" about the nature and extent of U.S. military involvement in South Vietnam. . . . Pres. Kennedy tells newsmen that information concerning Francis Powers' U-2 mission, his capture and imprisonment will be made available to Congress and the press after Powers completes secret interrogation by the CIA.	Commerce Dept. reports that U.S. corporate profits rose from $45.1 billion in 1960 to $46.2 billion in 1961. . . . Howard Hughes and the Hughes Tool Co. file a $366 million antitrust suit against Trans World Airlines, charging that the company had been illegally wrested from Hughes' control. TWA had filed an anti-trust suit against Hughes in June, 1961, charging him with improper influence over TWA plane purchases.		Ch. Elfinbrook Simon, West Highland white terrier owned by Mrs. Florence Worcester, is chosen best-in-show at the Westminster Kennel Club Show in New York.	Feb. 13
	Pres. Kennedy reiterates at a Washington news conference that he has sent no U.S. combat troops ("in the generally understood sense of the word") to South Vietnam. He adds that he has been as "frank" as security conditions allow about the nature of American involvement in Vietnam. . . . The New York Herald Tribune reports that Dr. Hans Bethe, former member of the President's Science Advisory Committee, may face a reprimand for a security regulations violation arising from a speech in which he claimed that an effective anti-missile defense system was virtually unattainable.			Mrs. John F. Kennedy hosts a one-hour nationally-televised tour of the White House. . . . Metropolitan Chrysostomos, 81, is elected primate of the Orthodox Church of Greece, succeeding Archbishop Iakovos, who abdicated Jan. 25.	Feb. 14
Sen. Hugh Scott announces that he will run for the Pennsylvania Republican gubernatorial nomination in order to prevent the nomination of announced candidate Robert Woodside.	Ex-V.P. Richard Nixon announces his full support of the Kennedy administration's troop commitments in South Vietnam, adding "I only hope (Kennedy) will step up the build-up and under no circumstances curtail it because of possible criticism."			Aloisius Joseph Cardinal Muench, 72, only U.S. member of the Vatican Curia, dies in Rome.	Feb. 15
	Nearly 2800 college students participate in the second straight day of Washington, D.C. demonstrations against any resumption of U.S. nuclear tests in the atmosphere.			Gary Gubner, 19, an NYU sophomore, breaks his own world indoor shot-put record with a put of 64 ft. 11 3/4 in. at the N.Y. Athletic Club games.	Feb. 16
	Defense Secy. McNamara, speaking at a meeting of the American Bar Foundation in Chicago, says that administration military planning aims at creating effective responses to any kind of warfare--from local guerilla activity to nuclear attack. The address is considered a major statement of the U.S.'s intention to resist communist-inspired guerrilla movements like that in South Vietnam. . . . Pres. Kennedy instructs U.S. agencies to develop detailed plans for post-nuclear attack rehabilitation.		A 115-mph wind storm lashes the North Sea coast of Germany, smashing sea dikes and causing massive flooding in the port city of Hamburg. At least 343 persons are killed.		Feb. 17
				Italy wins the world bridge championship in New York for the fifth time in the last six years.	Feb. 18

F	G	H	I	J
Includes elections, federal-state relations, civil rights and liberties, crime, the judiciary, education, health care, poverty, urban affairs and population.	Includes formation and debate of U.S. foreign and defense policies, veterans' affairs and defense spending. (Relations with specific foreign countries are usually found under the region concerned.)	Includes business, labor, agriculture, taxation, transportation, consumer affairs, monetary and fiscal policy, natural resources, and pollution.	Includes worldwide scientific, medical and technological developments, natural phenomena, U.S. weather, natural disasters, and accidents.	Includes the arts, religion, scholarship, communications media, sports, entertainment, fashions, fads and social life.

	World Affairs	Europe	Africa & the Middle East	The Americas	Asia & the Pacific
Feb. 19	French Pres. de Gaulle calls for a conference of the world's four nuclear powers on an agreement to destroy and ban all means of delivery of nuclear weapons. The plan is not expected to win the approval of any of the other nuclear powers.	The rightwing Nationalist Party, headed by Dr. George Berg Olivier, defeats the leftwing Labor Party in general elections for Malta's new self-rule legislature.	French sources report that an agreement has been reached on an Algerian cease-fire and on creation of a provisional executive to administer the country pending a referendum on Algerian independence. The accord is the result of eight days of intense French-rebel negotiations at a secret site in France.	The anti-government general strike in Georgetown, British Guiana, is called off after Premier Jagan met with dissident leaders of the Guiana Trades Union Congress.	U.S. Atty. Gen. Robert Kennedy, during a world tour stop in Bangkok, Thailand, publicly reaffirms U.S. pledges to aid Thailand against either external aggression or internal subversion.
Feb. 20		West German Chancellor Adenauer suggests that the informal Berlin talks between U.S. Amb.-to-USSR Thompson and Soviet Foreign Min. Gromyko be temporarily suspended in view of their lack of progress. . . . A $4.819 billion defense budget, designed to provide Britain with a smaller, more mobile armed force dependent on nuclear weapons, is presented to Parliament.	The Israeli Knesset, by a close margin, votes to maintain military rule over the majority of Israeli Arabs. . . . Reports from Algeria indicate that the Secret Army Organization's terrorist campaign is continuing.	The U.S. requests that Cuba be added to the list of communist countries with whom NATO members are barred from trading strategic goods.	
Feb. 21		Italian Premier-designate Amintore Fanfani announces the formation of a center-left Christian Democratic cabinet dependent on Parliamentary support from Pietro Nenni's leftwing Socialist Party.		The Dominican Republic's governing Council of State decrees a state of emergency because of activities by alleged political agitators "of the extreme left and extreme right."	
Feb. 22	USSR agrees to accept a previously-rejected Western proposal for discussion of a nuclear test-ban at the forthcoming Geneva disarmament conference, but only on the condition that the talks be confined to Soviet plans for a self-policed ban. The U.S. immediately rejects the conditions.	Full-scale British-Common Market negotiations are resumed in Brussels. Britain asks the EEC Council to consider giving it a four-year exemption from Common Market farm policies to enable the Commonwealth to adjust to the new trade and price patterns. . . . Turkish troops suppress a bloodless army cadet uprising in Ankara aimed at overthrowing the regime of Pres. Cemal Gursel and Premier Ismet Inonu.			
Feb. 23	The 16th regular session of the U.N. General Assembly adjourns after voting to investigate political conditions in Southern Rhodesia and adopting a resolution on the freeing of Ruanda-Urundi from Belgian-administered U.N. trusteeship.	*Pravda* reports the completion of a reorganization of the Soviet economy into 17 separately-administered economic regions.			
Feb. 24					Communist Chinese Foreign Ministry broadcasts a statement warning that China will take "appropriate measures" to counter U.S. intervention in South Vietnam.
Feb. 25	Pres. Kennedy again rejects a renewed request from Soviet Premier Khrushchev for a summit-level meeting at the opening of the Geneva disarmament conference in March.			*The New York Times* reports that the Cuban government has organized a special three-man committee to direct a national effort to meet the current food shortage crisis.	
	A	**B**	**C**	**D**	**E**
	Includes developments that affect more than one world region, international organizations and important meetings of major world leaders.	*Includes all domestic and regional developments in Europe, including the Soviet Union, Turkey, Cyprus and Malta.*	*Includes all domestic and regional developments in Africa and the Middle East, including Iraq and Iran and excluding Cyprus, Turkey and Afghanistan.*	*Includes all domestic and regional developments in Latin America, the Caribbean and Canada.*	*Includes all domestic and regional developments in Asia and Pacific nations, extending from Afghanistan through all the Pacific Islands, except Hawaii.*

U.S. Politics & Social Issues	U.S. Foreign Policy & Defense	U.S. Economy & Environment	Science, Technology & Nature	Culture, Leisure & Life Style	
Supreme Court upholds a lower court ruling that a 1961 Louisiana law permitting the closing of public schools faced with federal integration orders is unconstitutional.		Commerce Dept. reports that the U.S. balance of payments deficit dropped from an average $3.5 billion annually in 1958-1960 to $2.4 billion in 1961. The reduction was due to an increase in U.S. exports and a slight decline in imports. . . . Dun & Bradstreet reports 1,447 U.S. businesses failed in January, the highest January failure total since 1939. . . . The National Safety Council reports 38,000 Americans lost their lives in traffic accidents in 1961.	Dr. George Nicholas Papanicolaou, 78, Greek-born medical researcher and developer of the Pap smear test for uterine cancer dies in Miami, Fla.	Dale Wright and Michael Mok, reporters for the *New York World Telegram & Sun* share the Heywood Broun Award for journalism of the American Newspaper Guild.	Feb. 19
American Association of School Administrators, meeting in Atlantic City, N.J., calls for enactment of a federal public school aid program 10 times larger than the administration's current request. HEW Secy. Abraham Ribicoff calls the proposal "unrealistic.". . . Kennedy sends Congress a draft bill to increase top government salaries to levels competitive with those of private industry.		The House passes and sends to the Senate a bill (HR10050) to raise the temporary ceiling on the national debt from $298 billion to $300 billion. . . . Treasury Dept. sends Congress a draft bill authorizing the replacement of silver certificates with $1 bills backed by gold.	Marine Lt. Col. John Hershel Glenn Jr., 40, circles the earth three times in a Project Mercury space capsule and comes down safely in the Atlantic, becoming the first American and third man to complete an orbital flight.		Feb. 20
Republicans and conservative Democrats in the House muster enough votes to veto Pres. Kennedy's reorganization plan to create a cabinet-level Dept. of Urban Affairs and Housing. Opponents of the plan say it would lead to federal encroachment on state authority.	Rep. John V. Lindsay (R, N.Y.), reflecting a general Republican skepticism over Atty. Gen. Robert Kennedy's current world tour, asks in a House speech "whether this kind of Madison Avenue approach is the stuff of which foreign policy is made."		Soviet Premier Khrushchev, in a message to Pres. Kennedy congratulating the U.S. on John Glenn's orbital flight, suggests that the U.S. and USSR pool "their efforts--scientific, technical and material--to explore outer space." Kennedy "welcomes" the proposal. . . . Representatives of 12 West European nations agree to cooperate in the establishment of a European Space Research Organization to carry out an extensive joint satellite program.		Feb. 21
					Feb. 22
The Roman Catholic magazine *The Commonweal* editorially criticizes recent attacks by Catholic leaders on the administration's aid-to-public-schools bill as exaggerated and misleading, adding that they will serve only to help defeat a needed program.	U.S. Army announces it is tripling the permanent strength of the Strategic Army Corps, a mobile alert force designed for use in "brushfire wars."	Labor Secy. Arthur Goldberg, in a speech to Chicago's Executive Club, says the federal government needs to take a more active role in collective bargaining to assure protection of the public and national interest.	*Time* magazine reports that thalidomide, a sedative drug marketed in Europe since 1957, has been found responsible for hundreds and perhaps thousands of severe birth deformities. The drug had been tested but not marketed in the U.S. . . . Pres. Kennedy flies to Cape Canaveral to present John Glenn with NASA's Distinguished Service Medal.	American Institute of Architects' 1962 Gold Medal is awarded posthumously to Eero Saarinen, Finnish-born U.S. architect. . . . Willie Brown of Houston, Tex. wins the North-South Negro golf tournament in Miami, Fla. Jackie Robinson and Althea Gibson win the men's and women's amateur titles.	Feb. 23
Gary, Indiana Mayor George Chacharis and several other local Indiana officials plead "not guilty" to federal income tax evasion charges.		Claiming that the U.S. economy is in the midst of the poorest recession recovery of the post-war era, the AFL-CIO Executive Council urges the administration to adopt "a more aggressive program" against unemployment.		Cleveland Browns fullback Jimmie Brown wins the 1961 NFL rushing title (1,408 yards) for the fifth consecutive season.	Feb. 24
				The Reading Reform Foundation, a non-profit organization headquartered in N.Y., announces "a nationwide campaign" to replace the current "look-say" method of teaching reading with the older phonic method. . . . Helmut Recknagel of East Germany wins his second consecutive world ski jumping title at the Nordic ski championships in Zakopane, Poland.	Feb. 25

F	G	H	I	J
Includes elections, federal-state relations, civil rights and liberties, crime, the judiciary, education, health care, poverty, urban affairs and population.	Includes formation and debate of U.S. foreign and defense policies, veterans' affairs and defense spending. (Relations with specific foreign countries are usually found under the region concerned.)	Includes business, labor, agriculture, taxation, transportation, consumer affairs, monetary and fiscal policy, natural resources, and pollution.	Includes worldwide scientific, medical and technological developments, natural phenomena, U.S. weather, natural disasters, and accidents.	Includes the arts, religion, scholarship, communications media, sports, entertainment, fashions, fads and social life.

	World Affairs	Europe	Africa & the Middle East	The Americas	Asia & the Pacific
Feb. 26		Albanian Premier Mehmet Shehu, in a nationwide radio address, calls upon his countrymen to "be ready to fight" against "diabolical" Khrushchev-inspired plots "against our party and our people.". . . The outlawed Irish Republican Army announces that it is abandoning its five-year campaign of violence against the partition of Ireland. The IRA campaign is said to have cost $14 million in property damage and at least 15 lives in the last five years.			P.M. Nehru's Congress Party wins an overwhelming victory in general elections for India's lower house of Parliament.
Feb. 27		The Presidium of the Supreme Soviet adds bribery, rape and attacks upon police to the list of criminal offenses punishable by death. . . . British House of Commons approves a bill, which the government describes as "necessary but distasteful," to curb immigration from Commonwealth nations, particularly by West Indian Negroes and Asians.	Israeli Finance Ministry presents the Knesset with a record $786 million budget for fiscal 1962.	U.N. Security Council refuses to include in its agenda Cuban charges that the anti-Castro resolutions adopted Jan. 31 by the OAS constitute a violation of the U.N. Charter.	The South Vietnamese presidential palace in Saigon is bombed by two dissident South Vietnamese Air Force officers flying U.S. AD-6 fighter-bombers. Pres. Diem and his influential brother, Ngo Dinh Nhu, escape injury. Pres. Kennedy cables Diem, praising his "calm" in the face of this "vicious act."
Feb. 28		Soviet Premier Khrushchev rejects French Pres. de Gaulle's proposal for a four-power summit on nuclear disarmament.	A constitutional revision giving Africans an opportunity to win a majority in Northern Rhodesia's Legislative Council is announced by the British Colonial Office. The new provisions are denounced by P.M. Roy Welensky and other white leaders of the Rhodesia-Nyasaland Federation.		
March 1	A small British underground nuclear device is detonated at the U.S. AEC proving grounds in Nevada; it is the first British atomic test since 1958.		Benedicto Kiwanuka is sworn in as Uganda's first prime minister to head a transitional self-rule government until the British protectorate gains its full independence in October.	Faustino Harrison is inaugurated president of Uruguay, succeeding Eduardo Victor Haedo.	Pakistan adopts a new constitution providing for a greatly strengthened presidential form of government. . . . U.S. State Secy. Dean Rusk tells a Washington news conference that he attaches little hope to reported Soviet-bloc proposals for peace talks on Vietnam, adding that if the Communists really want peace all they have to do is stop encouraging the Viet Cong.
March 2	A U.S. decision to resume nuclear tests in the atmosphere by mid-April is announced by Pres. Kennedy in a nationwide TV address. Kennedy explains that the tests could be cancelled if the USSR were to agree to an internationally-supervised test ban during the March disarmament talks in Geneva.	Italian Premier Fanfani tells Parliament that his proposed center-left government would continue support of NATO and European economic integration.			Gen. Ne Win retakes power in Burma in a bloodless army coup against P.M. U Nu's regime. The coup is attributed to Burmese military resentment over Nu's toleration of local autonomy movements and his support of legislation making Buddhism the state religion.
March 3	Most Western European nations express approval of U.S. plans to resume atmospheric nuclear testing; India and Japan protest the decision.	George Berg Olivier is sworn in as Malta's first prime minister under a new constitution granting the British colony self-rule.			The leaders of yesterday's coup in Burma issue a statement pledging to continue the nation's policy of "positive neutrality."
	A	**B**	**C**	**D**	**E**
	Includes developments that affect more than one world region, international organizations and important meetings of major world leaders.	*Includes all domestic and regional developments in Europe, including the Soviet Union, Turkey, Cyprus and Malta.*	*Includes all domestic and regional developments in Africa and the Middle East, including Iraq and Iran and excluding Cyprus, Turkey and Afghanistan.*	*Includes all domestic and regional developments in Latin America, the Caribbean and Canada.*	*Includes all domestic and regional developments in Asia and Pacific nations, extending from Afghanistan through all the Pacific Islands, except Hawaii.*

U.S. Politics & Social Issues	U.S. Foreign Policy & Defense	U.S. Economy & Environment	Science, Technology & Nature	Culture, Leisure & Life Style	
Supreme Court reaffirms its earlier decisions prohibiting statutory segregation of "interstate and intrastate transportation facilities."	Kennedy asks Congress to authorize $63 million in fiscal 1963 to support a significantly expanded Peace Corps. In a message accompanying the request, Kennedy praises the Corps' "early successes."	AFL-CIO Pres. George Meany tells newsmen that Labor Secy. Goldberg's Feb. 23 call for greater federal involvement in labor bargaining amounts to an infringement on the rights of a free people and free society.		The Educational Research Council of Greater Cleveland announces the development of a new mathematics teaching method based on "how and why things happen in mathematics rather than on traditional memorization of rules."	Feb. 26
In a special health message to Congress, Kennedy renews his request for a Social Security-financed health insurance for the aged. . . . Sen. Hugh Scott (R, Pa.) withdraws from the race for the Pennsylvania GOP gubernatorial nomination in favor of the candidacy of Rep. William E. Scranton. Scott had entered the race to block the nomination of Robert Woodside.	Air Force chief Gen. Curtis LeMay tells the Senate Defense Appropriations Subcommittee that the administration's budget for the B-70 bomber and Minuteman ICBM programs is inadequate.	James T. Bidwell, chairman of the N.Y. Stock Exchange's board of governors, resigns after being indicted by a federal grand jury on charges of income tax evasion (in 1956-1957).	In an appearance before the House Science and Astronautics Committee, U.S. astronaut John Glenn says that the USSR will continue to lead in space achievements for some time but that the U.S. will be first in the race to the moon. Glenn also cautions against possible risks in the manned space program: "There will be failures. There will be sacrifices."		Feb. 27
	House Armed Services Committee unanimously approves a bill (HR9751) authorizing over $13 billion for the procurement of aircraft, missiles and naval vessels in fiscal 1963. The bill includes $491 million, not requested by the administration, for use in the development and production of the controversial B-70 bomber. . . . Atty. Gen. Kennedy, back from a month-long world tour, tells reporters that he found a "tremendous reservoir of goodwill toward" the U.S., despite widespread misunderstandings of the U.S. social system.	Presidential Railroad Commission submits a report to Pres. Kennedy recommending a broad revision of work rules and labor practices designed to promote cost efficient operation of U.S. railroads. The report, which upheld management's right to implement labor-saving technology, failed to win the support of labor representatives on the Commission. . . . House passes and sends to conference a somewhat restricted version of the administration's job retraining bill (HR8399).	U.S. astronauts John Glenn, Alan Shepard and Virgil Grissom, in a joint appearance before the Senate Aeronautical and Space Sciences Committee, stress the benefits of manned space flight over unmanned space probes. . . . A Peruvian mudslide caused by torrential rains buries the Andean village of Conchucos, killing an estimated 60 people.	National Council of Churches (U.S.) votes to accept an invitation from the Russian Orthodox Church for an exchange of visits by church leaders of the two nations.	Feb. 28
National Catholic Welfare Conference publishes an 80-page pamphlet criticizing the disunifying excesses of extreme anti-communist groups.		U.S. District Judge Walter LaBuy issues a final judgment ordering E.I. du Pont de Nemours & Co. to divest itself of 63 million shares of General Motors stock within 34 months. . . . Kennedy sends Congress a conservation message calling for a user-fee financed Land Fund for the purchase of new national recreation areas. . . . An American Airlines jet enroute from New York to Los Angeles crashes shortly after take-off from Idlewild Airport, killing all 95 persons aboard. It is the worst single-plane disaster in U.S. civil aviation history.			March 1
		National Industrial Conference Board reports that incomes of U.S. families climbed from a median of $4,000 in 1947 to $5,600 in 1960.		Wilt Chamberlain of the Philadelphia Warriors scores an NBA record 100 points in a 169-147 Philadelphia win over the N.Y. Knickerbockers.	March 2
Incumbent New Orleans Mayor Victor Schiro, supported by pro-segregationists, defeats State Sen. Adrian Duplantier, a moderate on racial matters, in the city's Democratic mayoral primary.	Pres. Kennedy's decision to resume atmospheric tests is reportedly favored by Congressional leaders and virtually all high administration officials and advisors, except for U.N. Amb. Adlai Stevenson.	Labor Secy. Goldberg criticizes strikes by public school teachers as "inadmissible" in a speech to the annual convention of United Federation of Teachers. . . . Pres. Kennedy orders an emergency investigation to avert a threatened strike by 600,000 nonoperating employees against U.S. Class 1 railroads.			March 3

F	G	H	I	J
Includes elections, federal-state relations, civil rights and liberties, crime, the judiciary, education, health care, poverty, urban affairs and population.	*Includes formation and debate of U.S. foreign and defense policies, veterans' affairs and defense spending. (Relations with specific foreign countries are usually found under the region concerned.)*	*Includes business, labor, agriculture, taxation, transportation, consumer affairs, monetary and fiscal policy, natural resources, and pollution.*	*Includes worldwide scientific, medical and technological developments, natural phenomena, U.S. weather, natural disasters, and accidents.*	*Includes the arts, religion, scholarship, communications media, sports, entertainment, fashions, fads and social life.*

	World Affairs	Europe	Africa & the Middle East	The Americas	Asia & the Pacific
March 4	Soviet Premier Khrushchev denounces Kennedy's decision to resume atmospheric tests as "atomic blackmail."			Opposition leaders in British Guiana publish an open letter calling on Premier Cheddi Jagan to publicly disclaim any intention to pattern his government "after that of communist Cuba."	
March 5	France announces it intends to boycott the forthcoming 17-nation Geneva disarmament talks, saying that the conference "offers no hope of solutions."	In an address to a plenary meeting of the Soviet Communist Party Central Committee, Premier Khrushchev charges that farm mismanagement is responsible for a nearly across-the-board failure of Soviet agriculture to meet its annual and seven-year production goals. . . . Britain applies for membership in the European Atomic Energy Community (Euratom).			
March 6					Burma's new military junta, headed by Gen. Ne Win, abolishes official observance of the Buddhist sabbath.
March 7	Hong Kong sources report that Communist Chinese attacks on Khrushchev's "peaceful co-existence" doctrine were renewed in a recent edition of the Chinese CP theoretical journal *Hung Chi*			Ex-Pres. Jañio da Silva Quadros, in quasi-exile since his abrupt Aug. 25, 1961 resignation, returns to Brazil, telling supporters he has come to "fight for the republic about which we dream."	
March 8		Sources in the USSR report that Vyacheslav Molotov, 71, ex-Soviet foreign minister and recently the target of anti-Stalinist attacks by Khrushchev, has disappeared from public view since early February. . . . Turkish Parliament approves a law forbidding public criticism of the May 1960 revolution.		U.S. and the Dominican Republic sign an agreement providing for U.S. assistance in a reorganization of the Dominican Republic's armed forces "under a constitutional and democratic government."	
March 9		The Central Committee of the Soviet CP, meeting in Moscow, approves a Khrushchev-backed plan for reorganizing Russian agriculture by returning farm management to more direct CP control.		Official sources in Cuba announce the formation of a 25-member governing directorate apparently intended to provide Cuba with collective leadership. Castro is a member, but holds no special title. . . . University students in Guatemala City go on strike to protest alleged fraud in the December 1961 Guatemalan congressional elections.	U.S. State Dept. confirms news reports that American pilots have been flying combat-training missions with South Vietnamese airmen over Viet Cong-held positions.
March 10	A three-year agreement to stabilize world wheat and flour prices is reached in Geneva by 48 wheat exporting and importing countries. The USSR participates in the accord for the first time.		Roy Welensky resigns as prime minister of the Rhodesia-Nyasaland Federation in order to call new elections. Welensky says he will seek a popular mandate to take all necessary steps to block possible secessions by prospective African legislative majorities in Nyasaland and Northern Rhodesia.	British Foreign Office discloses that Britain and Haiti have recalled their ambassadors because of a dispute arising from British charges that foreign businessmen in Haiti were subject to extortion by semi-official groups.	
March 11			A new round of secret French-rebel negotiations on an Algerian truce are reported to have begun at an unknown site in France.		The Netherlands, complying with a request from Acting Secy. Gen. U Thant, releases 52 Indonesians captured in a Jan. 15 Dutch-Indonesian naval clash off the coast of Netherlands New Guinea.
	A	B	C	D	E
	Includes developments that affect more than one world region, international organizations and important meetings of major world leaders.	*Includes all domestic and regional developments in Europe, including the Soviet Union, Turkey, Cyprus and Malta.*	*Includes all domestic and regional developments in Africa and the Middle East, including Iraq and Iran and excluding Cyprus, Turkey and Afghanistan.*	*Includes all domestic and regional developments in Latin America, the Caribbean and Canada.*	*Includes all domestic and regional developments in Asia and Pacific nations, extending from Afghanistan through all the Pacific Islands, except Hawaii.*

U.S. Politics & Social Issues	U.S. Foreign Policy & Defense	U.S. Economy & Environment	Science, Technology & Nature	Culture, Leisure & Life Style	
The California GOP Assembly endorses Richard Nixon as its gubernatorial candidate. The Assembly also adopts, after a bitter debate, a Nixon-sponsored resolution condemning the John Birch Society.	Defense Dept. reports that the current series of U.S. underground tests has confirmed that the problem of detection is fully as difficult as had been claimed by U.S. negotiators at the Geneva disarmament talks.			USSR wins the world biathlon championship in Haemenlinna, Finland.	March 4
		U.S. Supreme Court rules that property owners near airports deserve "just compensation" because of the noise, vibration and fear caused by low-flying aircraft.			March 5
Pennsylvania State Judge Robert Woodside withdraws as a candidate for the GOP gubernatorial nomination after Republican county chairmen endorse William Scranton.	Francis Gary Powers appears at a public hearing of the Senate Armed Services Committee and recounts the details of his May 1, 1960 U-2 flight, crash and subsequent imprisonment. The testimony was preceded by the release of a CIA report which completely exonerated Powers of any misconduct during his mission.				March 6
Over 18,000 attend a rally of political conservatives sponsored by the Young Americans for Freedom at Madison Square Garden. Sen. Barry Goldwater tells the group that conservatism is "the wave of the future.". . . The House passes and sends to joint conference an administration-backed bill (HR132) authorizing a $25 million matching grant program to help states develop educational TV facilities.		Labor Dept. reports the seasonally adjusted unemployment rate dropped below 6% in January (to 5.8%) for the first time in 16 months. February unemployment is estimated at 5.6%.	A report on "Health and Smoking" by the British Royal College of Physicians concludes unequivocally that "cigarette smoking is a cause of lung cancer.". . . NASA successfully orbits the first of a planned series of solar observatory satellites designed to study sunspot activity, solar flares, and other solar phenomena.		March 7
The General Council of the United Presbyterian Church issues a statement denouncing those "Americans who would substitute militant anti-communism for the Gospel of Jesus Christ."		Joint Congressional Economic Committee, in its annual report on the President's Economic Message, gives general endorsement to the administration's tariff liberalization program, but urges that steps be taken to assure comparable cuts in Common Market tariffs and a greater sharing of the West's foreign aid burdens.			March 8
	Pres. Kennedy, at a news conference, defends continued U.S. aid to Brazil despite the recent uncompensated expropriation of a U.S.-owned telephone system by the governor of Rio Grande do Sul province.	Nine of the U.S.'s largest oil companies announce plans for the joint construction of a 1,600 mile, $350 billion pipeline to carry 25 million gallons of refined oil products from Houston, Texas to New York City daily.			March 9
			A landslide caused by heavy rains kills 23 persons in Pensilvania, Colombia.	National Basketball Association announces the members of its player-picked all-star team: Elgin Baylor and Jerry West (L.A.), Bob Pettit (St. Louis), Oscar Robertson (Cincinnati), and Bill Russell (Boston).	March 10
					March 11

F	G	H	I	J
Includes elections, federal-state relations, civil rights and liberties, crime, the judiciary, education, health care, poverty, urban affairs and population.	Includes formation and debate of U.S. foreign and defense policies, veterans' affairs and defense spending. (Relations with specific foreign countries are usually found under the region concerned.)	Includes business, labor, agriculture, taxation, transportation, consumer affairs, monetary and fiscal policy, natural resources, and pollution.	Includes worldwide scientific, medical and technological developments, natural phenomena, U.S. weather, natural disasters, and accidents.	Includes the arts, religion, scholarship, communications media, sports, entertainment, fashions, fads and social life.

	World Affairs	Europe	Africa & the Middle East	The Americas	Asia & the Pacific
March 12				Cuban Premier Castro announces in a TV broadcast that certain basic foods will be added to the list of items already rationed on a nationwide basis. Castro blames the shotages on the U.S. "blockade."	
March 13	U.S. State Secy. Rusk, Soviet Foreign Min. Gromyko, and British Foreign Secy. Lord Home meet in Geneva for discussions of a nuclear test-ban accord and other international problems while awaiting the start of the full-scale disarmament talks Mar. 14.	The Yugoslav parliament approves a bill granting amnesty to most of the government's political opponents.		U.S. State Dept. denies that Cuban food and medical shortages are the result of the U.S. trade embargo. . . . Union leaders, provincial insurgents, and opposition political groups join Guatemala City students in growing anti-government protests and demonstrations. Several persons have been wounded in clashes with police. . . . Pres. Kennedy, at a White House reception for Latin American ambassadors, urges wealthy and powerful Latin Americans to support the social reform goals of the Alliance for Progress program.	*The New York Times* reports that opposition leaders in South Vietnam have appealed to U.S. Amb. Frederick Nolting to intercede on behalf of a liberalization of Pres. Diem's government, contending that Diem's suppression of civil and political rights has alienated the bulk of the South Vietnamese population.
March 14					The Indian Parliament unanimously approves a constitutional amendment incorporating the former Portuguese enclaves of Goa, Diu, and Damao into the Indian Union.
March 15	The U.S. and the USSR present their basic disarmament proposals at the first working session of the 17-nation Geneva disarmament conference. The proposals are described as substantially the same as the disarmament plans presented to the U.N. by Premier Khrushchev in Sept. 1960 and by Kennedy in Sept. 1961. The Soviet plan envisages an immediate and total disbanding of armed forces; the U.S. proposal calls for staged reductions under strict international controls.		Creation of a unified Arab military force and a pan-Arab economic council is proposed by Iraqi Premier Abdul Karim Kassim and new Syrian Pres. Nazem el Kodsi following two days of talks in Rutba, Iraq.	Ex-Brazilian Pres. Jañio da Silva Quadros says in a nationally televised address that he resigned last Aug. 24 to prevent rightwing and communist opponents of his economic reforms from undermining Brazil's constitutional government.	Defense Secy. McNamara confirms at a Washington press conference that American personnel serving in South Vietnam have occasionally been directly involved in combat with Viet Cong guerillas. He stresses, however, that the U.S. forces are there for training and not combat.
March 16		In an impromptu Kremlin speech, Khrushchev declares that the USSR has developed an extra-long-range "global" missile capable of hitting the U.S. without crossing its arctic circle detection lines.	Mecca radio announces that Saudi Arabian Crown Prince Faisal, a brother of King Saud, has been promoted to deputy premier and foreign minister.	The Guatemalan army takes control of Guatemala City in an effort to suppress violent student-led demonstrations aimed at the ouster of Pres. Miguel Ydigoras Fuentes.	P.M. Nehru tells Parliament that he has informed Communist China that India would agree to negotiations on their border dispute only after the Chinese troops are withdrawn from contested territory.
March 17		Rumania announces completion of its farm collectivization program.	Israeli armed forces launch a pre-dawn attack on Syrian territory near the eastern shore of the Sea of Galilee. An Israeli communique says the air and ground raid is in retaliation against recent Syrian attacks on Israeli police boats on the Sea of Galilee.		Soviet Foreign Ministry issues a statement charging the U.S. with waging an "undeclared war" against South Vietnam's "national liberation movement" headed by the Viet Cong. . . . South Korea's ruling junta denies ex-Pres. Syngman Rhee's Mar. 16 request for permission to return to South Korea. In his appeal, Rhee expressed regret over his "errors" while in office.

A	B	C	D	E
Includes developments that affect more than one world region, international organizations and important meetings of major world leaders.	*Includes all domestic and regional developments in Europe, including the Soviet Union, Turkey, Cyprus and Malta.*	*Includes all domestic and regional developments in Africa and the Middle East, including Iraq and Iran and excluding Cyprus, Turkey and Afghanistan.*	*Includes all domestic and regional developments in Latin America, the Caribbean and Canada.*	*Includes all domestic and regional developments in Asia and Pacific nations, extending from Afghanistan through all the Pacific Islands, except Hawaii.*

U.S. Politics & Social Issues	U.S. Foreign Policy & Defense	U.S. Economy & Environment	Science, Technology & Nature	Culture, Leisure & Life Style	
		In letters to the House and Senate, Kennedy renews his plea for congressional action on his 1961 proposals for reforming the federal-state unemployment compensation system.	British Ministries of Health and Education launch a drive to inform the public about the dangers of cigarette smoking and its connection to lung cancer and other illnesses. . . . Dr. John Mallams, radiation therapist at Baylor University, reports that hydrogen peroxide injected into arteries supplying blood to tumor areas makes X-ray therapy more effective in treating localized cancers.	Polls by the AP and UPI pick Ohio State as the national collegiate basketball champion for the second straight year.	March 12
	Pres. Kennedy asks Congress to appropriate $4,878,500,000 for foreign aid in fiscal 1963; $1.5 billion of the total is earmarked for miliary aid.	Pres. Kennedy signs into law a bill (HR10050) establishing a new temporary debt ceiling of $300 billion. . . . Kennedy asks Congress to authorize $25 million in fiscal 1962 for preparation of the U.S.'s "Challenge to Greatness" exhibit at the 1964-1965 N.Y. World's Fair.	Dr. John Hatter, director of the Sloan-Kettering Cancer Center, says at an American Cancer Society seminar that about one-third of the new cancer cases diagnosed each year are being cured by existing techniques. This compares with a one-quarter cure rate 15 years ago.	Jerry Lucas of Ohio State is named to the AP and UPI All-American basketball teams for the third straight year.	March 13
Pres. Kennedy's youngest brother, Edward M. Kennedy, 30, announces his candidacy for the Democratic nomination for the U.S. Senate from Massachusetts.		Kennedy sends Congress a special message outlining a broad program of legislative and executive actions to protect consumers from unsafe products and misleading advertising. . . . The Commerce Dept. reports that U.S. disposable personal income rose from $351.8 billion in 1960 to $364.9 billion in 1961.	A rain-caused landslide in the Andes Mountains north of Oroyo, Peru kills 41 persons.		March 14
U.S. Communist Party leaders Gus Hall and Benjamin Davis are indicted in Washington on charges of failing to register the party as a communist-action organization in compliance with the Subversive Activities Control Act of 1950. The party itself had been indicted on similar charges in 1961.	Dr. Arthur H. Compton, 69, Nobel Prize-winning physicist (1927) and key figure in the W.W. II development of the atomic bomb, dies in Berkeley, Calif.	Kennedy signs a compromise bill (S1991) establishing a $435 million, three-year program to retrain unemployed workers. He describes it as "perhaps the most significant legislation in the area of employment since the historic Employment Act of 1946."	Discovery of an elusive anti-particle in the atom's nucleus, the anti-XI minus, is announced in the *Physical Review Letters*, the journal of the American Physical Society. . . . *Journal of the American Medical Association* reports the successful testing of a new vaccine designed to provide immunity against measles. . . . NASA announces that Air Force Maj. Donald (Deke) Slayton 38, the astronaut scheduled for the U.S. second orbital flight, has been withdrawn from the mission in light of the discovery of a slight, intermittent flutter in his heart rate.		March 15
N.Y. Gov. Nelson Rockefeller is divorced in Reno, Nevada by the former Mary Todhunter Clark.			The USSR orbits the first in a new series of earth satellites; the series is reportedly directed at gathering additional data for manned space flight and for improved "space vehicle construction."		March 16
			The White House makes public a March 7 letter from Kennedy to Khrushchev proposing joint U.S.-USSR cooperation in a variety of aerospace fields including a joint weather satellite system, a mutual satellite tracking service and cooperative research in the field of space medicine.		March 17

F	G	H	I	J
Includes elections, federal-state relations, civil rights and liberties, crime, the judiciary, education, health care, poverty, urban affairs and population.	Includes formation and debate of U.S. foreign and defense policies, veterans' affairs and defense spending. (Relations with specific foreign countries are usually found under the region concerned.)	Includes business, labor, agriculture, taxation, transportation, consumer affairs, monetary and fiscal policy, natural resources, and pollution.	Includes worldwide scientific, medical and technological developments, natural phenomena, U.S. weather, natural disasters, and accidents.	Includes the arts, religion, scholarship, communications media, sports, entertainment, fashions, fads and social life.

	World Affairs	Europe	Africa & the Middle East	The Americas	Asia & the Pacific
March 18		French Pres. de Gaulle appears on national television to appeal for popular support and approval of the French-Algerian peace agreement announced earlier in the day. De Gaulle says a national referendum on his Algerian policies will be held in France in early April.	France and the Algerian Provisional Government jointly announce the signing of a formal truce ending the over seven-year Moslem rebellion against French rule in Algeria. The agreement, worked out during week-long negotiations at Evian-les-Bains, includes provisions insuring a speedy Algerian self-determination referendum and full sovereignty for an independent, Moslem-governed Algerian state, expected to result from the referendum. . . . Algerian rebel Vice Premier Mohammed Ben Bella and four other prominent rebel leaders, imprisoned by the French since 1956, are freed following the truce announcement.		
March 19	Neutral delegates to the Geneva disarmament conference are reportedly pressing the U.S. and the USSR for a compromise that will clear the way for an agreement banning nuclear tests.		Dispatches from Algeria report that the cease-fire agreement announced yesterday by French and rebel representatives has been effectively imposed on all fronts. . . . The Secret Army Organization, Algeria's European terrorist underground, declares open warfare on the de Gaulle government and on the French-rebel peace accord.	Argentine military leaders pressure Pres. Frondizi into nullifying yesterday's congressional elections because of the unexpected victories scored by 44 Peronist candidates. Frondizi had earlier lifted the ban on Peronist candidates despite opposition from the military. . . . U.S. State Dept. denies recent Cuban charges that the Guantanamo naval base is being prepared as a beachhead for an eventual armed attack on Cuba.	
March 20	U.S., USSR, and Britain announce they will resume their three-power Geneva test-ban talks immediately in an effort to reach a preliminary agreement which could then be presented to the 17-nation disarmament conference.		Syria requests a meeting of the U.N. Security Council to consider its charges of Israeli aggression in connection with the March 17 raid on Syrian positions near the Sea of Galilee.	Argentine Pres. Frondizi confers with military leaders in an effort to quell growing pressure for his ouster. Frondizi agrees to a military demand that Peronist political activity be outlawed for two years. . . . In a formal protest to the OAS, Guatemala charges Cuba with supporting the recent political upheavals against the Ydigoras regime.	Indonesian and Dutch representatives open preliminary talks to settle the Netherlands New Guinea dispute at an undisclosed location outside Washington, D.C. The arrangements for the talks were reportedly made by the U.S. in cooperation with Acting U.N. Secy. Gen U Thant.
March 21			An expected terrorist campaign against French security forces in Algeria by the rightist Secret Army Organization begins in Oran with a sniper attack on military police in the central city. Attacks are also reported in Algiers and Mostaganem.		
March 22					
March 23			The Secret Army Organization "war" against a French-rebel Algerian peace is intensifying. At least 15 French soldiers have been killed and 75 wounded in two days of clashes with rightists in Algiers. De Gaulle orders the army "to crush without pity the armed insurrection."	The U.N. Security Council rejects a Cuban resolution asking that the OAS decision to exclude Cuba from the inter-American system be suspended on the ground that it is illegal. . . . Premier Fidel Castro is named first secretary of the Cuban Integrated Revolutionary Organization's (ORI) 25-member governing directorate.	

A	B	C	D	E
Includes developments that affect more than one world region, international organizations and important meetings of major world leaders.	Includes all domestic and regional developments in Europe, including the Soviet Union, Turkey, Cyprus and Malta.	Includes all domestic and regional developments in Africa and the Middle East, including Iraq and Iran and excluding Cyprus, Turkey and Afghanistan.	Includes all domestic and regional developments in Latin America, the Caribbean and Canada.	Includes all domestic and regional developments in Asia and Pacific nations, extending from Afghanistan through all the Pacific Islands, except Hawaii.

U.S. Politics & Social Issues	U.S. Foreign Policy & Defense	U.S. Economy & Environment	Science, Technology & Nature	Culture, Leisure & Life Style	
					March 18
U.S. District Judge H. Hobart Grooms in Birmingham, Ala. dismisses seven libel suits filed by Birmingham officials against *The New York Times* in connection with the *Times's* May 1960 articles on Birmingham-area race relations.					March 19
Atty. Gen. Kennedy sends Congress a draft civil rights bill aimed at curbing police brutality.	In a speech to the National Press Club, Sen. Henry Jackson says the U.S., in seeking its foreign policy goals, should rely less on the U.N. and more on NATO.	Pres. Kennedy signs into law a bill (HR8723) strengthening the enforcement provisions of the 1958 Welfare and Pension Plans Disclosure Act.	Soviet Premier Khrushchev, in a letter to Pres. Kennedy, accepts Kennedy's March 7 proposal for U.S.-USSR cooperation in space and says that he has instructed Soviet representatives to meet with U.S. counterparts for a discussion of possible joint projects.	National Institute of Arts and Letters' annual gold medals for general achievement are awarded to Nobel Prize-winning novelist William Faulkner and American historian Samuel Eliot Morison.	March 20
	The House unanimously passes and sends to the Senate a bill (HR9751) authorizing over $13 million in fiscal 1963 for procurement of aircraft, missiles and naval vessels. . . . Pres. Kennedy, commenting on Sen. Henry Jackson's recent criticism of the U.S. role in the U.N., says that American people strongly support the U.N. "because we believe it serves the interests of the United States." Kennedy adds that he sees no contradiction between strong support for NATO and for the U.N.				March 21
			British anthropologist Louis B. Leakey announces in Washington his 1961 discovery in Kenya of the remains of a man-like creature--apparently an ancestor of man--that lived an estimated 14 million years ago.		March 22
	Pres. Kennedy, in a speech at the University of California at Berkeley, proclaims that "the currents of history are carrying the world away. . .from communism and toward independence and freedom."				March 23

F	G	H	I	J
Includes elections, federal-state relations, civil rights and liberties, crime, the judiciary, education, health care, poverty, urban affairs and population.	Includes formation and debate of U.S. foreign and defense policies, veterans' affairs and defense spending. (Relations with specific foreign countries are usually found under the region concerned.)	Includes business, labor, agriculture, taxation, transportation, consumer affairs, monetary and fiscal policy, natural resources, and pollution.	Includes worldwide scientific, medical and technological developments, natural phenomena, U.S. weather, natural disasters, and accidents.	Includes the arts, religion, scholarship, communications media, sports, entertainment, fashions, fads and social life.

	World Affairs	Europe	Africa & the Middle East	The Americas	Asia & the Pacific
March 24					
March 25		The French government recalls its ambassador to the USSR in protest against the USSR's March 19 recognition of the rebel Algerian Provisional Government.	Recently freed Algerian rebel Vice Premier Mohammed Ben Bella, considered by many the symbolic leader of the Algerian revolution, tells a crowd of 2,000 rebel troops in Oujda, Morocco that the Algerian war will not be truly over until an independent Moslem government is installed on Algerian soil.	Argentine navy commanders, Frondizi's most adamant opponents, urge him to voluntarily resign as "the best patriotic solution" to the current political crisis.	
March 26		French Pres. de Gaulle appears on national television to open his campaign for a massive popular endorsement of the French-Moslem truce agreement in a nationwide referendum scheduled for April 8.	At least 50 European civilians are killed and 150 wounded in Algiers in the most serious fighting between European rightists and French troops since the Secret Army Organization began its guerrilla campaign a week ago.		Indonesian Pres. Sukarno recalls his delegation from the secret Dutch-Indonesian talks on New Guinea being held somewhere near Washington, D.C. No progress in the talks has yet been reported.
March 27		The private talks among the foreign ministers of Britain, the USSR and the U.S., being held in Geneva in conjunction with the 17-nation disarmament conference, conclude without concrete progress being reported. The meetings, originally planned as a discussion of nuclear test-ban proposals, were devoted largely to the Berlin problem.	French officials announce in Paris the final organization of a 12-man Provisional Executive to rule Algeria under recently-named interim High Commissioner Christian Fouchet. The Executive, made up of nine Algerian Moslems and three Algerian Europeans, is charged with preparing and conducting the Algerian self-determination referendum.	Havana radio reports that Communist leader Anibal Escalante, once regarded as the chief theoretician of the Cuban revolution, has been dismissed from the ruling directorate of Cuba's Integrated Revolutionary Organizations. Castro recently accused Escalante of abusing his public trust for personal ends.	
March 28	The 17-nation Geneva conference on disarmament is reportedly making little progress because of the continuing refusal of the U.S. and Soviet delegations to consider any but their own disarmament proposals as a basis for conference discussion.	*The New York Times*, citing West German sources, estimates that 5,000 persons have escaped from East Berlin since the building of the wall in August 1961. . . . A British government white paper reports that the nation's balance of payments deficit declined to $173.6 million in 1961, a significant improvement over the $882 million deficit recorded in 1960.	The Syrian army seizes control of the government in a bloodless coup. Army spokesmen say the new government will restore "constructive and just socialism" and renew friendly relations with "dear Egypt and sister Iraq.". . . The Secret Army Organization circulates leaflets in Algeria announcing that it has abandoned mass attacks and civilian street demonstrations in favor of concentrated guerrilla attacks on the French army. The group's terrorist campaign is reported continuing at a high level despite stepped-up French counter-measures.	Argentine Pres. Arturo Frondizi is ousted by a bloodless military coup and placed under arrest.	
March 29	Kennedy tells reporters in Washington that the U.S.-British-Soviet efforts to achieve a nuclear test-ban have apparently reached a final impasse in wake of the USSR's refusal to entertain any proposals for international verification.	Stefan Cardinal Wyszynski, Roman Catholic primate of Poland, is reported to have requested a parliamentary investigation of the Polish government's alleged anti-Roman Catholic Church policies.		Argentine troops use tear gas to break up demonstrations in Buenos Aires in support of arrested Pres. Frondizi.	

A	B	C	D	E
Includes developments that affect more than one world region, international organizations and important meetings of major world leaders.	Includes all domestic and regional developments in Europe, including the Soviet Union, Turkey, Cyprus and Malta.	Includes all domestic and regional developments in Africa and the Middle East, including Iraq and Iran and excluding Cyprus, Turkey and Afghanistan.	Includes all domestic and regional developments in Latin America, the Caribbean and Canada.	Includes all domestic and regional developments in Asia and Pacific nations, extending from Afghanistan through all the Pacific Islands, except Hawaii.

U.S. Politics & Social Issues	U.S. Foreign Policy & Defense	U.S. Economy & Environment	Science, Technology & Nature	Culture, Leisure & Life Style	
			National Academy of Sciences awards its annual John J. Carty Medal to Dr. Charles Townes for his pioneering development of the maser-microwave amplification by stimulated emission of radiation.	For the second straight year, the University of Cincinnati defeats Ohio State in the finals of the NCAA basketball championship. . . . Dayton University wins the National Invitational Basketball Tournament in New York with a 73-67 finals win over St. John's University. . . . Bill Russell of the Boston Celtics is named the NBA's most valuable player for the second straight year.	**March 24**
The Southern Regional Council issues a report in Atlanta praising the Kennedy administration's civil rights actions as "comparable" in importance to the 1954 school desegregation decision by the Supreme Court.					**March 25**
In what may prove a far-reaching decision, the Supreme Court rules, 6-2, that federal courts have the right and duty to try cases involving the districting and distribution of state legislative seats. The ruling, handed down in a Tennessee case, overturns the 1946 landmark case of Colegrove v. Green.					**March 26**
The Senate approves and sends to the House a constitutional amendment abolishing the poll tax as a requirement for voting in federal elections. The resolution (SJ Res. 29), which passed 77-16, was criticized not only by Southern Democrats, but also by northern civil rights supporters who favored a remedy through regular legislation rather than constitutional amendment. . . . Archbishop Joseph Francis Rummel orders an end to segregation in all Roman Catholic schools in the New Orleans archdiocese.	Kennedy administration officials conduct a series of press briefings to clarify current U.S. policy on the use of nuclear weapons. The briefings stress that U.S. defense strategy is geared primarily toward maintaining a devastating "second strike" capability sufficient to destroy and thus deter any nuclear aggressor against the U.S. . . . Officials, however, concede that the U.S. would not rule out first use of nuclear weapons in certain special situations, such as in the face of an overwhelming Soviet conventional assault on Europe.	SEC estimates that in 1961 American individuals saved a total of $16.9 billion, equalling a record set in 1958.	U.S. and Soviet representatives meet at the U.S.'s U.N. mission in the first of a series of projected talks on space cooperation. . . . U.S. Public Health Service licenses the manufacture of Type III Sabin live-virus oral vaccine designed to protect against Type III polio virus. The full range of Sabin oral vaccines is now licensed in the U.S.	Painter Charles Sheeler, 79, is named winner of the American Academy of Arts and Letters' 1962 Award of Merit Medal.	**March 27**
A Physicians Committee for Health Care for the Aged is formed in Washington to rally support for the administration's Social Security-financed aged health care plan.					**March 28**
Pres. Kennedy, at his news conference, endorses the Supreme Court's March 26 state-districting decision, saying that "the right. . .to have each vote count equally. . .is basic to the successful operation of a democracy.". . . *Six Crises* by Richard Nixon, a book analyzing some of the major international problems faced in the Eisenhower years, is published in New York.		The House, by a narrow party-line vote, passes and sends to the Senate a bill (HR10650) embodying the administration's tax revision proposals as first suggested by Kennedy in 1961.			**March 29**

F	G	H	I	J
Includes elections, federal-state relations, civil rights and liberties, crime, the judiciary, education, health care, poverty, urban affairs and population.	*Includes formation and debate of U.S. foreign and defense policies, veterans' affairs and defense spending. (Relations with specific foreign countries are usually found under the region concerned.)*	*Includes business, labor, agriculture, taxation, transportation, consumer affairs, monetary and fiscal policy, natural resources, and pollution.*	*Includes worldwide scientific, medical and technological developments, natural phenomena, U.S. weather, natural disasters, and accidents.*	*Includes the arts, religion, scholarship, communications media, sports, entertainment, fashions, fads and social life.*

	World Affairs	Europe	Africa & the Middle East	The Americas	Asia & the Pacific
March 30		Pres. Kennedy accepts the credentials of Anatoly F. Dobrynin as Soviet amb.-to-the-U.S. Dobrynin succeeds Mikhail Menshikov, who left the U.S. Jan. 4.		Dr. José Maria Guido, 51, formally assumes the presidency of Argentina, succeeding ousted Pres. Arturo Frondizi.	The Indonesian Foreign Ministry discloses that Pres. Kennedy has personally appealed to Pres. Sukarno for a resumption of the suspended secret Dutch-Indonesian talks on New Guinea. . . . Dutch military officials report recent battles with small bands of Indonesian troops attempting to land in remote regions of disputed Netherlands New Guinea.
March 31			Pro-Nasser army officers in northern Syria launch a counter-revolt against the armed forces high command, which took control of the government in a March 28 coup.	Venezuela, in an action signifying its refusal to recognize the new Guido regime in Argentina, closes its embassy in Buenos Aires.	
April 1		Swiss voters reject by a two to one margin a proposed constitutional amendment that would have barred the country from ever manufacturing, procuring, storing or using nuclear weapons.			
April 2			The Casablanca bloc of nations (UAR, Morocco, Ghana, Guinea, Mali and the Algerian Provisional Government) announce an agreement to form an African Common Market."		
April 3			The revolt of pro-Nasser army officers against Syria's new ruling junta ends after junta leaders agreed to insurgents' demands for clemency toward recently deposed Syrian Pres. Nazem el Kodsi and for a popular referendum on whether Syria should rejoin the UAR.	Ecuador breaks diplomatic relations with Cuba, Poland and Czechoslovakia.	
April 4	U.S. Defense Dept. announces that a rectangular area 600 by 800 nautical miles centered on Christmas Island in the Pacific will be closed to shipping and air traffic April 15 in preparation for U.S. nuclear tests.			Peronist leaders in Buenos Aires warn that there will be a "fight to the last consequences" if Peronist candidates who won in the March 18 Argentine provincial elections are barred from taking office.	

A	B	C	D	E
Includes developments that affect more than one world region, international organizations and important meetings of major world leaders.	Includes all domestic and regional developments in Europe, including the Soviet Union, Turkey, Cyprus and Malta.	Includes all domestic and regional developments in Africa and the Middle East, including Iraq and Iran and excluding Cyprus, Turkey and Afghanistan.	Includes all domestic and regional developments in Latin America, the Caribbean and Canada.	Includes all domestic and regional developments in Asia and Pacific nations, extending from Afghanistan through all the Pacific Islands, except Hawaii.

U.S. Politics & Social Issues	U.S. Foreign Policy & Defense	U.S. Economy & Environment	Science, Technology & Nature	Culture, Leisure & Life Style	
Pres. Kennedy designates Deputy Atty. Gen. Byron Raymond ("Whizzer") White, 44, to replace Supreme Court Justice Charles Evans Whittaker, 61, whose retirement from the Court (for health reasons) was announced yesterday. . . . HEW Secy. Ribicoff tells a House Education subcommittee that as of Sept. 1963 segregated schools will be considered "unsuitable" for children living on federal bases.					March 30
		AFL-CIO United Steelworkers of America and 11 of the nation's leading steel companies announce agreement on a new two-year contract providing for additional fringe benefits but no immediate general wage increase. Pres. Kennedy, who followed the negotiations closely, praises the "obviously non-inflationary" agreement.			March 31
	A Strategic Air Command spokesman confirms March 31 Washington news stories that SAC bombers had been alerted for a possible retaliatory attack on the USSR in late 1961 because of a malfunction in SAC communications. . . . Sen. Hubert Humphrey (D, Minn.), appearing on a ABC-TV program, says that recent suggestions that U.S. foreign policy has been transferred from normal channels to the U.N. are false and irresponsible. Humphrey's comments come amidst a growing public debate among congressional leaders and administration officials over U.S. policy toward the U.N.				April 1
Asst. Atty. Gen. Nicholas Katzenbach is appointed by Pres. Kennedy to succeed Byron White as Deputy Atty Gen.					April 2
U.S. District Judge J. Skelly Wright upholds a suit by 102 Negroes claiming that New Orleans' 1960 school desegregation plan has not proceeded with "all deliberate speed." Wright orders the schools to accept Negroes in the first six grades beginning with the fall term.		Sen. Philip Hart (D, Mich.) urges enactment of tougher laws against the deceptive labeling and packaging of basic grocery items. Hart's recommendation comes at the end of hearings into the matter by the Senate Antitrust and Monopoly Subcommittee.		Ex-world welterweight champion Benny (Kid) Paret, 25, dies in New York of injuries received March 24 when he lost a title bout by TKO to Emile Griffith in Madison Square Garden. . . . Eddie Arcaro, 46, the greatest money-winning jockey in horse racing history, announces his retirement after 31 years. . . . FCC Chmn. Newton Minow sharply criticizes radio and TV programming at the annual convention of the National Association of Broadcasters and warns that new federal rules may be required to curb excessive commercials on radio.	April 3
	Ex-Maj. Gen. Edwin Walker, testifying before the Special Senate Preparedness Investigating Subcommittee, charges that several high-ranking government officials are part of a "hidden control apparatus" aimed at bending U.S. policy to the will of the international communist conspiracy. . . . The Army announces tentative plans for an approximately 10% manpower reduction in the Army Reserve and National Guard. . . . Sen. John Tower (R. Tex.), in a Senate speech, charges that the U.N. has become a liability to the U.S.				April 4

F	G	H	I	J
Includes elections, federal-state relations, civil rights and liberties, crime, the judiciary, education, health care, poverty, urban affairs and population.	Includes formation and debate of U.S. foreign and defense policies, veterans' affairs and defense spending. (Relations with specific foreign countries are usually found under the region concerned.)	Includes business, labor, agriculture, taxation, transportation, consumer affairs, monetary and fiscal policy, natural resources, and pollution.	Includes worldwide scientific, medical and technological developments, natural phenomena, U.S. weather, natural disasters, and accidents.	Includes the arts, religion, scholarship, communications media, sports, entertainment, fashions, fads and social life.

	World Affairs	Europe	Africa & the Middle East	The Americas	Asia & the Pacific
April 5	The 17-nation Geneva disarmament conference meets informally as a committee of the whole to study measures for reducing world tensions as a prelude to disarmament. The Soviet delegation cites the West's anti-communist "war propaganda" as a major cause of current tensions.	The Soviet Academy of Agricultural Sciences accepts the resignation (for "health reasons") of its president, Prof. Trofim D. Lysenko. . . . A special task force committee appointed in May, 1961 to investigate the British security system, reports that communists in civil service unions and the activities of Soviet-bloc agents together pose a serious threat to Britain's security. The committee urges tightened procedures in the hiring and placement of civil service personnel.	The formation of an Angolan rebel government-in-exile is announced in Leopoldville, Congo Republic.		
April 6	Soviet Premier Khrushchev, referring to U.S. nuclear test preparations in the Pacific, indicates that a resumption of Western nuclear tests in the atmosphere will be followed by a similar move by the USSR.	West German sources report that the almost daily Soviet harassment of Western flights in the Berlin air corridors, which began Feb. 14, ended March 30 without explanation. Some observers attribute the suspension of Soviet activity to a general easing of East-West tensions over Berlin.			
April 7			The UAR discloses that 1961 espionage and conspiracy charges against four French citizens are being dropped in appreciation of the March 18 French-Algerian rebel truce agreement.	A military court in Havana sentences 1,179 prisoners, captured in the 1961 Bay of Pigs invasion, to 30 years in prison for treason. The Cuban government offers to suspend the sentences and free the men in exchange for a $62 million "indemnity." . . . The New York Times reports that Ecuador's unexpected April 3 decision to break relations with Cuba was the result of direct pressure by the military high command on the left-oriented civilian regime of Pres. Julio Arosemena Monroy.	
April 8		French voters, in a national referendum, overwhelmingly record their approval of Pres. de Gaulle's peace agreement with the Algerian rebels.			
April 9		Chancellor of the Exchequer Selwyn Lloyd presents Parliament with a fiscal 1963 budget estimating British government expenditures at just over $17.8 billion.	U.N. Security Council indirectly censures Israel for its March 16-17 raid on Syrian territory by voting 10-0 to reaffirm a 1956 Council resolution that had condemned similar Israeli reprisal attacks against Syria.	Brazilian Pres. Joao Goulart concludes a week-long visit to the U.S. during which he conferred twice with Pres. Kennedy, addressed a joint session of Congress, and appeared before the U.N.	
April 10	Pres. Kennedy and P.M. Macmillan address a joint appeal to Premier Khrushchev asking for serious Soviet consideration of an internationally supervised nuclear test-ban. Administration officials characterize the appeal as the West's final effort to win an acceptable ban before ordering the resumption of atmospheric tests.	Lord Privy Seal Edward Heath publicly states Britain's readiness to join with EEC members in negotiations on the formation of supranational European political institutions. British participation is favored by most EEC nations, but opposed by France.	The Secret Army Organization continues its campaign of violence against French army personnel and Moslem civilians despite newspaper reports of a growing reaction in Algeria's European community against the group's terrorist methods. . . . The Israeli Knesset overwhelmingly approves a resolution rejecting U.N. criticism of its recent reprisal raids against Syria. The resolution asserts that such retaliatory attacks are part of Israel's "unchallengeable" right to self-defense.	Officials of a Miami-based Cuban Families Committee arrive in Havana to negotiate the ransoming of sentenced Bay of Pigs prisoners with the Cuban government. . . . The Labor Party defeats the People's National Party in nationwide balloting to elect a new government for Jamaica when it becomes independent August 6.	

A	B	C	D	E
Includes developments that affect more than one world region, international organizations and important meetings of major world leaders.	Includes all domestic and regional developments in Europe, including the Soviet Union, Turkey, Cyprus and Malta.	Includes all domestic and regional developments in Africa and the Middle East, including Iraq and Iran and excluding Cyprus, Turkey and Afghanistan.	Includes all domestic and regional developments in Latin America, the Caribbean and Canada.	Includes all domestic and regional developments in Asia and Pacific nations, extending from Afghanistan through all the Pacific Islands, except Hawaii.

U.S. Politics & Social Issues	U.S. Foreign Policy & Defense	U.S. Economy & Environment	Science, Technology & Nature	Culture, Leisure & Life Style	
Herbert Hill of the NAACP charges that the administration's campaign to extract fair employment pledges from top defense contractors has so far "resulted in more publicity than progress."	The Senate, by a 70-22 vote, passes and sends to the House a compromise bill (S2768) authorizing the President to lend the U.N. up to $100 million. Although not explicitly stated in the bill, it is generally understood that the authorization would be used to buy half of the U.N.'s recently approved $200 million bond issue.	Texas financier Billie Sol Estes and three associates are indicted by a federal grand jury in El Paso, Tex. on several counts of fraud and conspiracy in connection with the alleged sale to U.S. financial firms of mortgages on non-existent farm equipment. . . . In a special message to Congress, Kennedy outlines a "far-reaching" revision of federal transportation policies, including a proposal for a three-year, $500 million program to revitalize and expand urban mass transportation systems.			April 5
Kennedy presents Congress with draft legislation to give the people of the Virgin Islands greater self-government.			USSR successfully orbits an unmanned earth satellite, Cosmos 2, designed to gather data on cosmic rays and the earth's radiation belts.		April 6
The U.S. Urban Renewal Administration orders all federally-aided urban renewal projects to comply with local and state anti-discrimination laws in "the sale, lease or occupancy of the property."				Paul Pender wins New York, Massachusetts, and European recognition as the world middleweight champion by scoring 15-round decision over champion Terry Downes of Great Britain in Boston.	April 7
				Juan Belmonte, 69, one of Spain's most famous matadors, commits suicide following a period of ill health.	April 8
	Defense Secy. McNamara tells the Senate Foreign Relations Committee that the U.S. commitment in South Vietnam is intended to assure that the government does "not want for equipment and training to cope with communist aggression."			The film adaptation of the Broadway musical *West Side Story* is named the best film of 1961 at the annual award ceremonies of the Motion Picture Academy. Sophia Loren is named "best actress" for her role in *Two Women* ; Maximillian Schell is awarded "best actor" for his performance in *Judgment at Nuremburg* . . . . Arnold Palmer wins his third Masters championship at the Augusta (Ga.) National Golf Club by defeating Gary Player and Dow Finsterwald in a 18-hole playoff.	April 9
		A steel price increase of approximately $6 per ton is announced by the U.S. Steel Corp. . . . Ford Motor Co. announces that because of "market conditions" it has dropped plans to build small, low-priced economy car in 1962. . . . Kennedy sends Congress a request to revive for one year the emergency program providing for a temporary expansion in the federal-state unemployment compensation program.		Tennessee Williams' *The Night of the Iguana* and Robert Bolt's *A Man for All Seasons* are chosen by the N.Y. Drama Critics Circle as the best American play and best foreign play to be produced on Broadway during the 1961-1962 season. . . . A two-sided Pablo Picasso painting (*Death of A Harlequin, Woman Sitting in A Garden*) is sold in London for $224,000-the largest sum ever paid for a painting by a living artist.	April 10

F	G	H	I	J
Includes elections, federal-state relations, civil rights and liberties, crime, the judiciary, education, health care, poverty, urban affairs and population.	*Includes formation and debate of U.S. foreign and defense policies, veterans' affairs and defense spending. (Relations with specific foreign countries are usually found under the region concerned.)*	*Includes business, labor, agriculture, taxation, transportation, consumer affairs, monetary and fiscal policy, natural resources, and pollution.*	*Includes worldwide scientific, medical and technological developments, natural phenomena, U.S. weather, natural disasters, and accidents.*	*Includes the arts, religion, scholarship, communications media, sports, entertainment, fashions, fads and social life.*

	World Affairs	Europe	Africa & the Middle East	The Americas	Asia & the Pacific
April 11		Pres. Kennedy tells reporters that Gen. Lucius Clay will soon end his mission as special presidential representative in West Berlin. West German newspapers criticize the withdrawal decision as evidence of a softening U.S. position on Berlin. . . . A serious rift is reportedly developing in relations between France and the French-protected principality of Monaco. The dispute is attributed to Prince Ranier III's resistance to French demands that Monaco end the tax-free privileges of its 20,000 residents.			
April 12	Western representatives at the 17-nation Geneva disarmament conference once again reject a renewed Soviet proposal for an unpoliced nuclear test moratorium.	Ex-Premier Georges Bidault announces in letters to the French press that he has gone underground to assume leadership of the Secret Army Organization's Council of Resistance.			
April 13	The April 10th appeal by Pres. Kennedy and P.M. Macmillan for an agreement on banning nuclear tests before the West resumes atmospheric testing is rejected by Soviet Premier Khrushchev.		Nazem el-Kodsi, deposed in the March 28 military coup, is reinstated as Syria's president by the same military leaders who overthrew him. . . . Ex-Gen. Edmond Jouhaud, a recently captured leader of the Secret Army Organization, is condemned to death by a Paris military tribunal after a three-day trial for insurrection.	A U.S.-Brazilian agreement to commit $276 million in Alliance for Progress funds for economic and social development in Brazil's poverty-stricken northeast is signed in Washington.	
April 14		A serious dispute is reportedly developing among Western powers over alleged U.S. support for a compromise proposal on Berlin. The compromise is said to involve de facto Western acknowledgment of East German sovereignty in exchange for firm guarantees of access to West Berlin. West Germany and France oppose such concessions. . . . Georges Jean Raymond Pompidou, 50, a close associate of Pres. de Gaulle, is named to succeed Michel Debré as French premier.		Sixty sick and wounded prisoners captured in the 1961 Cuban invasion are released and flown to Miami after representatives of a Miami-based Cuban Families Committee pledged to pay the Cuban government a $2.5 million "indemnity."	
April 15				Guatemalan Pres. Miguel Ydigoras Fuentes pledges in a nationwide TV address to remain in office to fight the "forces of Castro communism" which he claims are behind the growing demands for his ouster.	
April 16	The eight neutral delegations at the Geneva disarmament conference submit a joint appeal for a nuclear test-ban agreement subject to international supervision by a scientific commission drawn from nonaligned nations. The U.S. and Britain say they will study the plan.	Contacts on a possible interim accord to reduce tensions in Berlin are renewed in Washington between State Secy. Rusk and the new Soviet Amb.-to-U.S. Anatoly Dobrynin. The talks are reportedly being undertaken in a new atmosphere of compromise afforded by the apparent abandonment of Soviet demands for a final German settlement and by an increased flexibility in Western policy.		Bolivia severs diplomatic relations with Chile in a dispute over use of the waters of the Lauca River, which flows in both countries.	Communist China's National People's Congress concludes a three-week session in Peking, marking its first formal meeting since 1960. The Congress is reported to have approved a 10-point economic plan aimed primarily at increasing China's agricultural output. . . . Britain rejects a Soviet proposal for joint measures against growing American involvement in South Vietnam.

A	B	C	D	E
Includes developments that affect more than one world region, international organizations and important meetings of major world leaders.	Includes all domestic and regional developments in Europe, including the Soviet Union, Turkey, Cyprus and Malta.	Includes all domestic and regional developments in Africa and the Middle East, including Iraq and Iran and excluding Cyprus, Turkey and Afghanistan.	Includes all domestic and regional developments in Latin America, the Caribbean and Canada.	Includes all domestic and regional developments in Asia and Pacific nations, extending from Afghanistan through all the Pacific Islands, except Hawaii.

U.S. Politics & Social Issues	U.S. Foreign Policy & Defense	U.S. Economy & Environment	Science, Technology & Nature	Culture, Leisure & Life Style	
The Senate confirms the nomination of Byron White as an Associate Justice of the U.S. Supreme Court.	Pres. Kennedy announces at his Washington news conference that reservists called up in the Berlin crisis will be released in August barring any unforeseen changes in the international situation.	Five major American steel companies join U.S. Steel Corp. in announcing an across-the-board price increase. In an opening statement to a Washington news conference, Pres. Kennedy angrily denounces the price hikes as "a wholly unjustifiable and irresponsible defiance of the public interest."			April 11
The Senate Constitutional Rights Subcommittee ends two weeks of hearings on bills (S2750, S480 and S2979) designed to bar racially discriminatory literacy tests for voting. Subcommittee Chmn. Sam Ervin (D, N.C.) and other Southern Democrats oppose the measures as an infringement on states' rights. NAACP Executive Secy. Roy Wilkins charges that the bills are only "token" fulfillments of the administration's civil rights pledges.			NASA announces a $2 million scholarship program to increase graduate training in space science.		April 12
		Census Bureau reports that the median value of U.S. homes, according to owner estimates, is about $12,000.			April 13
		Price increases announced by U.S. Steel Corp. and by seven other steel firms are rescinded by all eight companies. The reversal is attributed to heavy pressure from the Kennedy administration and to the April 13 decision of Inland Steel Co. not to follow the general price rise.			April 14
American Jewish Congress, meeting in annual convention in New York, adopts a resolution opposing required Bible reading in U.S. public schools.			American Cancer Society reports that the number of cancer patients cured by treatment has risen from 160,000 in 1936 to 1,100,000 in 1961.		April 15
Roman Catholic Archbishop Joseph Francis Rummel, 85, of New Orleans excommunicates three Louisiana segregationists who publicly attacked his orders for the desegregation of archdiocesan schools. . . . William E. Morris, an employee of the Farm Credit Administration, is dismissed by the Agriculture Dept. for refusing to answer questions about his possible relationship with indicted Texas financier Billie Sol Estes. Morris is the second Agriculture Dept. employee to be publicly linked with the Estes scandal.		The American Association of Fund-Raising Council, Inc. reports that Americans contributed $8.7 billion to philanthropic causes in 1961, a $500 million increase over 1960.	Richardson-Merrell, Inc. (N.Y.) announces the withdrawal from the market of MER-29 (triparanol), an anti-cholesterol heart drug, because of the "possibility of an unacceptable incidence of side effects."		April 16

F	G	H	I	J
Includes elections, federal-state relations, civil rights and liberties, crime, the judiciary, education, health care, poverty, urban affairs and population.	Includes formation and debate of U.S. foreign and defense policies, veterans' affairs and defense spending. (Relations with specific foreign countries are usually found under the region concerned.)	Includes business, labor, agriculture, taxation, transportation, consumer affairs, monetary and fiscal policy, natural resources, and pollution.	Includes worldwide scientific, medical and technological developments, natural phenomena, U.S. weather, natural disasters, and accidents.	Includes the arts, religion, scholarship, communications media, sports, entertainment, fashions, fads and social life.

	World Affairs	Europe	Africa & the Middle East	The Americas	Asia & the Pacific
April 17					
April 18	A comprehensive draft treaty for general disarmament is presented to the 17-nation Geneva conference by the U.S. delegation. The plan specifies staged reductions in conventional arms, nuclear weapons, manpower and foreign military bases and outlines measures for verification and for avoiding accidental wars. . . . U.N. Economic & Social Council approves the creation of a three-year experimental World Food Program to supply $100 million worth of surplus food to needy nations.	Pres. Kennedy tells newsmen that an agreement with the Soviets to reduce tensions in Berlin is of vital importance to the U.S. and the West.			
April 19			Delegates from Ruanda and Urundi reject a U.N. proposal that the two Belgian-administered U.N. trust territories be merged into a single nation upon receiving their independence July 1.		The Burmese government makes public a decree severely restricting the cultural and educational activities of American and other foreign private agencies in Burma.
April 20	Valerian Zorin, chief of the Soviet delegation to the Geneva disarmament conference, tells newsmen that "there will be no negotiations" on a nuclear test ban if the U.S. goes ahead with its plans for a Pacific test series. . . . A new Soviet-Communist China trade agreement for 1962 is signed in Peking. The accord is linked by Western observers to recent indications of a relaxation in Sino-Soviet ideological tensions.	Athens police fight a five-hour battle to quell an anti-government demonstration held to protest alleged fraud in the October 1961 Greek elections. The demonstration was sponsored by George Papandreou's opposition Center Union party.	Ex-Gen. Raoul Salan, leader of the extreme rightist Secret Army Organization, is captured in Algiers and flown to Paris to face trial for insurrection against the French state. Salan is already under death sentence for his role in the April 1961 Algiers coup attempt.		
April 21		Yugoslav Foreign Min. Koca Popovic and visiting Soviet Foreign Min. Andrei Gromyko issue a joint communique in Belgrade confirming the two nations' "similarity of views on basic international questions" and pledging increased Soviet-Yugoslav cooperation in the future. . . . The New York Times reports from Bonn that West German officials remain opposed to any Berlin compromise that would involve de facto recognition of East Germany.			
April 22			The Secret Army Organization's campaign of terror against the French-Moslem peace agreement continues despite capture of its top leaders. According to the New York Herald Tribune, 3,858 persons have been killed in Secret Army attacks since Jan. 1.	Representatives of Britain, British Honduras and Guatemala issue a joint communique calling for the creation of a three-nation committee to "promote mutual economic and social development between Guatemala and British Honduras." The statement comes at the end of a five-day conference held in Puerto Rico to discuss ways of easing tensions resulting from Guatemala's claim to British Honduras.	
April 23		U.S. State Secy. Rusk and Soviet Amb.-to-U.S. Dobrynin reach agreement on a plan to elevate East-West discussions of Berlin into substantive negotiations. The new phase in the talks is scheduled to begin in mid-May.	UPI sources report heavy fighting between Iraqi soldiers and insurgent Kurdish tribesmen in northern Iraq. The rebels are reportedly demanding creation of an autonomous "Kurdistan" within Iraq.		New Delhi sources report that India has informed Communist China that it will not renew its 1954 trade agreement with the Peking government until the Chinese withdraw from disputed Indian border areas.

A	B	C	D	E
Includes developments that affect more than one world region, international organizations and important meetings of major world leaders.	Includes all domestic and regional developments in Europe, including the Soviet Union, Turkey, Cyprus and Malta.	Includes all domestic and regional developments in Africa and the Middle East, including Iraq and Iran and excluding Cyprus, Turkey and Afghanistan.	Includes all domestic and regional developments in Latin America, the Caribbean and Canada.	Includes all domestic and regional developments in Asia and Pacific nations, extending from Afghanistan through all the Pacific Islands, except Hawaii.

U.S. Politics & Social Issues	U.S. Foreign Policy & Defense	U.S. Economy & Environment	Science, Technology & Nature	Culture, Leisure & Life Style	
The President's Committee on Equal Employment Opportunity bars two firms from getting federal contracts on the ground that they persistently discriminate against minorities in employment. The two companies are Comet Rice Mills Inc. and Danly Machine Specialties.	U.S. Air Force Capt. Joseph Kauffman is convicted by court-martial in Weisbaden, West Germany of having passed military secrets to East German Communists.			Urich Franzen is named the 1962 recipient of the National Institute of Arts and Letters' Brunner Memorial Prize in Architecture.	April 17
Food for Peace director George McGovern announces that he will be a Democratic candidate for the South Dakota Senate seat currently held by Republican Sen. Francis Case. . . . The President's Commission on Campaign Costs releases a report recommending that individual political contributions up to $10 be tax deductible in order to encourage greater "political participation." The report also proposes a lifting of the current ceiling on individual contributions.	The House unanimously passes and sends to the Senate a bill (HR11289) to appropriate $47,839,491,000 for the Defense Dept. for fiscal 1963. The bill does not include appropriations for military construction, civil defense or foreign military aid.	In a reference to the recent steel price controversy, Pres. Kennedy tells reporters that he wants to "make it clear that this administration harbors no ill-will against. . .any industry, any corporation or segment of the American economy."	Dr. Jeremiah Stamler, in a paper delivered to a Symposium on Coronary Heart Disease in Philadelphia, reports that treatment with female sex hormones has been effective in improving the recovery rate among male heart attack victims.	Boston Celtics win their fourth straight National Basketball Association championship by defeating the Los Angeles Lakers, four games to three, in the final play-offs.	April 18
GOP congressional leaders issue a statement denouncing the Kennedy administration's behavior in the recent steel price controversy as "punitive, heavy-handed and frightening."	Major Arch Roberts is temporarily suspended from active duty by the Army a few hours after he accused Los Angeles Mayor Samuel Yorty of having a "communist background" in a speech to the annual meeting of the Daughters of the American Revolution. Roberts was formerly a psychological warfare expert under ex-Major Gen. Edwin Walker.	Commerce Dept. reports that the U.S. GNP rose from a seasonally adjusted annual rate of $542.2 billion in the final quarter of 1961 to a rate of $549 billion in the first quarter of 1962.		Enio Oksanen, of Helsinki Finland, wins the annual Boston (Mass.) Marathon. . . . An 11-day FCC inquiry into radio and TV broadcasting concludes in Chicago after hearing testimony from 120 witnesses. FCC examiner Robert E. Lee tells reporters that the hearings revealed that local programming needs are not being met by the national networks.	April 19
NAACP accuses nine West Coast cities of maintaining segregated public schooling. The group has leveled similar charges at 23 other cities in the Midwest and Northeast.					April 20
Census Bureau estimates present U.S. population at 186 million.	U.S. State Dept. study on worldwide Communist Party strength and activities estimates that membership has grown to about 40 million with the greatest increases coming in China and Cuba.			Carlos Ortiz wins the world lightweight boxing championship by scoring a 15-round decision over title holder Joe Brown in Las Vegas.	April 21
				Toronto Maple Leafs win the National Hockey League's Stanley Cup by defeating Chicago in the final play-offs, four games to two.	April 22
			NASA scientists report an almost total malfunction in the telemetry system of a Ranger 4 space probe launched earlier in the day for a planned hard-landing on the moon. Tracking data however indicates that the Ranger is still on course.		April 23
F	**G**	**H**	**I**	**J**	
Includes elections, federal-state relations, civil rights and liberties, crime, the judiciary, education, health care, poverty, urban affairs and population.	Includes formation and debate of U.S. foreign and defense policies, veterans' affairs and defense spending. (Relations with specific foreign countries are usually found under the region concerned.)	Includes business, labor, agriculture, taxation, transportation, consumer affairs, monetary and fiscal policy, natural resources, and pollution.	Includes worldwide scientific, medical and technological developments, natural phenomena, U.S. weather, natural disasters, and accidents.	Includes the arts, religion, scholarship, communications media, sports, entertainment, fashions, fads and social life.	

	World Affairs	Europe	Africa & the Middle East	The Americas	Asia & the Pacific
April 24	A Presidential order to resume U.S. nuclear testing in the atmosphere is announced by the Atomic Energy Commission.	The Supreme Soviet renames Nikita Khrushchev as premier after he formally relinquished his post at the end of his four-year term. Leonid Brezhnev is re-elected chairman of the 33-man Soviet Presidium.		Argentine Pres. José Maria Guido issues a decree cancelling the March 18 provincial election victories of Peronist candidates. Certain powerful military factions are reported to have wanted Guido to go further and outlaw all Peronist political activity.	
April 25	The U.S. tests a low-to-intermediate yield nuclear device in the atmosphere above Christmas Island in the central Pacific. The test, the U.S.'s first in the atmosphere since 1958, is sharply criticized by neutralist and third world leaders as well as by scattered pacifist groups in the West. . . . The Soviet delegation at the Geneva conference rejects as "utterly unacceptable" the draft disarmament treaty presented to the conference by the U.S. April 18.			Argentine Pres. Guido nullifies the results of the March 18 Chamber of Deputies elections in which Peronist candidates won 47 of 85 contested seats. Guido had previously annulled Peronist victories in provincial elections.	
April 26	The Soviet government announces that it will remain at the Geneva convention and continue discussion of a nuclear test-ban despite the U.S.'s resumption of atmospheric tests.	British P.M. Macmillan, in the U.S. for talks with Pres. Kennedy, tells a New York audience that the West should patiently continue negotiations with the USSR in the hope that Soviet leaders will eventually be ready to live in peace with other nations.			
April 27	The U.S. detonates a second atmospheric nuclear device in its test zone near Christmas Island.	Premier Georges Pompidou's new French cabinet is confirmed in office by a National Assembly vote of 259 to 128, with 119 abstentions. The unexpectedly weak majority is attributed to growing parliamentary resentment at Pres. de Gaulle's reported plans to transform France further toward a presidential republic.	P.M. Roy Welensky's United Federal Party wins almost every seat in general elections to the Rhodesia-Nyasaland Federation's federal assembly. The elections, called by Welensky to gain a popular mandate for preventing future efforts to break up the federation, were boycotted by all African parties.		
April 28	For the second day 2,000-3,000 Japanese students march through Tokyo streets to protest the U.S.'s current nuclear test series in the central Pacific.				
April 29	After three days of talks in Washington, Pres. Kennedy and P.M. Macmillan issue a joint communique expressing their determination to pursue negotiations with the USSR on Berlin, nuclear tests and disarmament and to meet at the summit level should it prove helpful.	The Irish government announces a general amnesty for all 29 IRA members now serving prison terms for terrorist acts.		Lt. Col. Julio Adalberto Rivera, running unopposed as a candidate of the National Conciliation Party, is elected president of El Salvador in nationwide balloting. Opposition parties boycotted the election.	
April 30			Milton Obote becomes Prime Minister of Uganda after his Peoples Party outpolled ex-Premier Benedicto Kiwanuka's Democratic Party in April 25 elections for the National Assembly. . . . A U.N. task force issues a report claiming that Britain's failure to give Africans in Southern Rhodesia equal political rights might eventually lead "to serious conflict and violence."		

A	B	C	D	E
Includes developments that affect more than one world region, international organizations and important meetings of major world leaders.	Includes all domestic and regional developments in Europe, including the Soviet Union, Turkey, Cyprus and Malta.	Includes all domestic and regional developments in Africa and the Middle East, including Iraq and Iran and excluding Cyprus, Turkey and Afghanistan.	Includes all domestic and regional developments in Latin America, the Caribbean and Canada.	Includes all domestic and regional developments in Asia and Pacific nations, extending from Afghanistan through all the Pacific Islands, except Hawaii.

U.S. Politics & Social Issues	U.S. Foreign Policy & Defense	U.S. Economy & Environment	Science, Technology & Nature	Culture, Leisure & Life Style	
An Administration civil rights bill (S2750) to limit use of literacy tests for voting is introduced to the Senate by majority leader Mike Mansfield (D., Mont.). Southern Democrats launch an immediate filibuster. . . . Labor Dept. announces that it will henceforth withhold approval of apprentice training programs that bar Negro applicants.		Commerce Secy. Luther Hodges tells newsmen that administration intervention in wage-price decisions will always be limited to those basic industries where poor decisions could adversely affect the national interest.	TV pictures are transmitted successfully by satellite relay for the first time as a signal from MIT's Lincoln laboratory in California is bounced off the Echo I and is received at the Millstone Hill laboratory in Westford, Mass.		April 24
					April 25
	For the second time this month the Air Force launches a secret satellite from Point Arguello, Calif.	A federal grand jury in New York indicts the U.S. Steel Corp., Bethlehem Steel Co. and two other firms on charges of conspiracy to fix prices in the sale of steel to the military between 1948 and 1961. U.S. Atty. Robert Morgenthau says the indictment is unrelated to the current steel price controversy.	The U.S. lunar probe Ranger 4, launched April 23, smashes into the dark side of the moon, becoming the second man-made (and first U.S.) object known to have landed on the lunar surface. U.S. scientists say the mission provided valuable engineering data despite a nearly complete malfunction of the Ranger's telemetry system. . . . The first international orbiting satellite, a 132-pound package of British scientific experiments in a U.S.-built casing, is launched from Cape Canaveral.		April 26
A member of the Black Muslims is killed and eight policemen are injured in a riot in front of the Muslim headquarters in Los Angeles. Muslim leader Malcolm X accuses the Los Angeles police of "Gestapo" tactics.	Army Secy. Elvis Stahr announces that Maj. Arch Roberts has been relieved from active duty because of "improper statements" he made in an uncleared April 19 speech to the Daughters of the American Revolution.	The Conference on Economic Progress (a Washington study group) releases a report on poverty in the U.S. claiming that more than 77 million Americans lived at substandard economic levels in 1960.			April 27
A three-judge federal court in Atlanta rules that a new Georgia county-unit primary election system is unconstitutional. The ruling comes in a suit filed under the recent Supreme Court reapportionment decision.	A bill (HR10700) authorizing almost $64 million in fiscal 1963 for an expanded Peace Corps program is signed by Pres. Kennedy. . . . Kennedy also signs an amended bill (HR9751) authorizing a $12.9 billion procurement program in fiscal 1963 for aircraft, missiles and naval vessels. The bill includes a controversial $488 million unrequested appropriation for the development of the B-70 bomber.		The Health and Labor Ministry of the Niger Republic reports that more than 10,000 persons have been stricken in a spinal meningitis epidemic and that at least 1,000 have died.	Marine Lt. Dave Tork sets a world outdoor pole-vault record of 16 ft 2 in. in Walnut, California. . . . Ipswich Town defeats Alston Villa, 2-0, to win the English soccer championship in London.	April 28
	U.S. Defense Dept. announces plans to detonate three H-bombs at varying altitudes ranging from 30 to 500 miles to test the effect of such explosions on radio communications and military electronics systems.		Researchers attending a special American Academy of Neurology Symposium in New York report the development of an apparently successful anti-migraine headache drug known as Methysergide, a synthetic derivative of lycergic acid. . . . Soviet cosmonaut Gherman Titov begins a 12-day tour of the U.S.		April 29
		Responding to business criticism over his role in the recent steel-price controversy, Pres. Kennedy tells the annual meeting of the U.S. Chamber of Commerce that his administration has no desire to set prices or wages, which he describes as "quite properly . . . private decisions."		Artist Pablo Picasso and Ghana Pres. Kwame Nkrumah are among the recipients of the USSR's Lenin Peace Prize for 1961.	April 30

F	G	H	I	J
Includes elections, federal-state relations, civil rights and liberties, crime, the judiciary, education, health care, poverty, urban affairs and population.	Includes formation and debate of U.S. foreign and defense policies, veterans' affairs and defense spending. (Relations with specific foreign countries are usually found under the region concerned.)	Includes business, labor, agriculture, taxation, transportation, consumer affairs, monetary and fiscal policy, natural resources, and pollution.	Includes worldwide scientific, medical and technological developments, natural phenomena, U.S. weather, natural disasters, and accidents.	Includes the arts, religion, scholarship, communications media, sports, entertainment, fashions, fads and social life.

	World Affairs	**Europe**	**Africa & the Middle East**	**The Americas**	**Asia & the Pacific**
May 1	Addressing the USSR's traditional May Day rally in Moscow, Soviet Defense Min. Rodion Malinovsky charges the U.S. with preparing for a preventive nuclear war against the USSR.	Three persons are killed and an estimated 100 injured in clashes between Portuguese police and anti-government May Day demonstrators in Lisbon and Oporto.		Argentine federal police announce the closing of all Peronist party centers by order of the interior ministry.	
May 2	A U.S. nuclear device in the "low megaton range" is exploded in the air above Christmas Island. The test, the third in the current U.S. series, is the first to exceed one megaton.		A Secret Army Organization bomb explodes in the Algiers port area, killing at least 62 Moslem longshoremen.		
May 3				Argentine Pres. José Guido appoints Jose Cantilo as defense minister to replace Ernesto Lanusse.	Dispatches from Laos indicate that Pathet Lao troops have launched a major offensive against royal Laotian government positions in northern Laos. . . . Chinese-Pakistani plans to negotiate a demarcation of the boundary between China and part of Kashmir controlled by Pakistan are announced in Dacca.
May 4			Algerian sources report that the Secret Army Organization has launched a series of premeditated attacks on Moslem civilians in an apparent effort to provoke Moslem retaliation against Algeria's European community.	Loyal Venezuelan troops crush a two-day revolt of marines and military policemen in Carupano, a naval base 250 miles east of Caracas.	Dutch military sources report that their forces have killed and captured several members of a small Indonesian invading force that had been air-dropped into northwest New Guinea on April 27. . . . *The New York Times* reports that at least 1,000 Moslems have been killed in six weeks of communal clashes with Hindus in the Malda district of West Bengal, India.
May 5		U.S. announces that it is transferring five nuclear-powered submarines and their complement of 80 Polaris missiles to NATO. The nuclear warheads designed for use on missiles will remain under the exclusive control of the U.S. President. . . . Gen. Francisco Franco orders a state of emergency in three of Spain's northern provinces, where thousands of coal miners and industrial workers have gone on strike demanding higher wages.	Ghana Pres. Kwame Nkrumah declares a "general amnesty" for all Ghanian political exiles and urges them to return to useful lives in their homeland.		
May 6		NATO Council of Ministers, meeting in Athens, issues a statement approving the continuation of the U.S.'s exploratory talks with the USSR on possible terms for settling the Berlin problem. . . . Italian Parliament's Electoral Assembly elects Foreign Min. Antonio Segni, a Christian Democrat and ex-premier, as president of the Italian Republic.		Guillermo Leon Valencia, candidate of the ruling Liberal-Conservative Coalition Party, is elected president of Colombia in nation-wide balloting.	Royal Laotian troops in northern Laos are reportedly retreating toward the Thai border in the face of a continuing offensive by Pathet Lao rebels.

A	B	C	D	E
Includes developments that affect more than one world region, international organizations and important meetings of major world leaders.	*Includes all domestic and regional developments in Europe, including the Soviet Union, Turkey, Cyprus and Malta.*	*Includes all domestic and regional developments in Africa and the Middle East, including Iraq and Iran and excluding Cyprus, Turkey and Afghanistan.*	*Includes all domestic and regional developments in Latin America, the Caribbean and Canada.*	*Includes all domestic and regional developments in Asia and Pacific nations, extending from Afghanistan through all the Pacific Islands, except Hawaii.*

U.S. Politics & Social Issues	U.S. Foreign Policy & Defense	U.S. Economy & Environment	Science, Technology & Nature	Culture, Leisure & Life Style	
Ex-Circuit Judge George C. Wallace and Alabama State Sen. Ryan deGraffenried lead seven other Democratic candidates in a primary race for the Alabama gubernatorial nomination. The two will meet in a run-off election later this year.		President's Advisory Committee on Labor-Management Policy issues a report urging revision of the Taft-Hartley Act to permit the President, without court orders, to bar a strike for 80 days in national emergencies. . . . A compromise bill (S205) authorizing a five-year, $32 million program of matching grants for expansion of educational TV facilities is signed by Pres. Kennedy. . . . Commerce Dept. releases revised statistics indicating that U.S. personal incomes rose from $400.002 billion in 1960 to a record $414.362 billion in 1961.	A group of British astronomers express concern that the U.S.'s announced plans to detonate a nuclear device at an altitude of 500 miles may do irreparable damage to the inner Van Allen radiation belt currently the subject of intensive scientific study. . . . Dr. William Luyten of the University of Minnesota announces his discovery of the smallest known star. The star, a white dwarf known as LP 327-186 and located in the constellation Taurus, is about 1,000 miles in diameter.	Ex-Pres. Eisenhower, speaking at the dedication of the Eisenhower Library, deplores what he considers a moral and aesthetic decline in American entertainment and arts. Eisenhower adds that while he does not object to the current dance craze, the "twist", he believes it represents "some kind of change" from the minuet.	May 1
Sen. James Eastland (D, Miss.) charges in a Senate speech that Chief Justice Earl Warren "decides for the communists" whenever the Supreme Court faces a decision between communism and U.S. security. . . . Nine Mississippi laws requiring segregated travel accommodations for whites and Negroes are ruled unconstitutional by U.S. District Judge Sidney Mize in Biloxi.	White House announces that Army Secy. Elvis J. Stahr Jr. will resign effective June 30 to become president of Indiana University.				May 2
House and Senate GOP leaders call for a full-scale congressional probe of the Agriculture Dept. in relation to the case of indicted financier Billie Sol Estes. Senate minority leader Everett Dirksen says the Estes case typifies the corruption "that has attached itself to billions of handouts from the Agriculture Dept."		House passes and sends to the Senate a bill (HR 11040) to charter a government-supervised private corporation to own and operate a satellite communications system.			May 3
		Pres. Kennedy, appearing at a ceremonial opening of a new New Orleans wharf, renews his appeal for quick congressional action on his trade and tariff reform proposals.		The official Catholic Directory for 1962 estimates that there are over 32.8 million Roman Catholics in the U.S. This represents an increase of 12.5 million members since 1952.	May 4
Ex-Maj. Gen. Edwin Walker finishes last in a six-man race for the Texas Democratic gubernatorial nomination.				George Pope Jr.'s Decidedly, Billy Hartack up, wins the Kentucky Derby in the record time of two minutes .4 seconds.	May 5
	U.S. detonates a nuclear-armed Polaris missile launched from a submarine near the Christmas Island testing area in the central Pacific. The test is the fifth in the U.S.'s current Pacific series and the first ever of a nuclear warhead launched from a submarine.			Martin de Porres, a 17th Century Dominican friar of Spanish and African ancestry, is proclaimed a Roman Catholic saint by Pope John XXIII.	May 6

F	G	H	I	J
Includes elections, federal-state relations, civil rights and liberties, crime, the judiciary, education, health care, poverty, urban affairs and population.	*Includes formation and debate of U.S. foreign and defense policies, veterans' affairs and defense spending. (Relations with specific foreign countries are usually found under the region concerned.)*	*Includes business, labor, agriculture, taxation, transportation, consumer affairs, monetary and fiscal policy, natural resources, and pollution.*	*Includes worldwide scientific, medical and technological developments, natural phenomena, U.S. weather, natural disasters, and accidents.*	*Includes the arts, religion, scholarship, communications media, sports, entertainment, fashions, fads and social life.*

	World Affairs	Europe	Africa & the Middle East	The Americas	Asia & the Pacific
May 7		West German Chancellor Konrad Adenauer publicly confirms his government's opposition to the current U.S.-Soviet diplomatic contacts on Berlin and to a U.S. proposal for establishing an international Berlin access authority that would include East Germany.			Indonesian Foreign Min. Subandrio announces in Moscow that the USSR has agreed to provide Indonesia with additional military supplies sufficient "to take care of the West Irian (Netherlands New Guinea) problem.". . . In separate public statements, the U.S. State Dept. and the British Foreign Office protest the recent Pathet Lao offensive as a violation of the Laotian truce accord and urge the USSR to intercede with the rebels to restore the cease-fire.
May 8	French government confirms that it conducted an underground nuclear test May 1 at its proving grounds in the Sahara Desert.				
May 9		West German sources report that Chancellor Adenauer has joined with French Pres. de Gaulle in opposing full British participation in the European Economic Community.	French officials report that the government's crack-down on Secret Army Organization terrorism is making progress in rural areas of Algeria, but that the problem in the major cities remains extremely serious.		U.S. Defense Secy. Robert McNamara arrives in Saigon for talks reportedly aimed at reducing friction between South Vietnamese and U.S. officials and at encouraging Pres. Diem's regime to a more effective prosecution of the war.
May 10		British Laborites and Liberals make sweeping gains at the expense of the Conservative Party in Borough Council elections held throughout England and Wales. . . . Norweigian Premier Einar Gerhardsen, currently visiting the U.S., tells reporters that he hopes that Norway, Britain and Denmark will be accepted as members of the European Economic Community.		Cuban Premier Castro says that his government is considering returning "improperly" nationalized farms to their original peasant owners in an effort to alleviate serious national food shortages.	
May 11	The U.S. delegation at the Geneva talks rejects a Soviet draft disarmament proposal calling for the liquidation within 18 months of all foreign military bases. The U.S. claims that the provision would "prejudice the Western military position at a time when disarmament was only in the first stage."				Pathet Lao troops are reported to have driven all government forces from northern Laos. Many of the government troops are said to have crossed into Thailand in an effort to escape the rebel advance. . . . V.P. Sarvepalli Radhakrishnan is elected president of India by the national electoral college.
May 12	Extensive discussions on ways to facilitate "information exchanges" between U.S. and the USSR are held in Moscow between Soviet Premier Khrushchev and visiting U.S. presidential Press Secy. Pierre Salinger.				Pres. Kennedy orders the U.S. Seventh Fleet to sail into the Gulf of Siam, off Thailand, in an apparent move to demonstrate U.S. concern over the deteriorating situation in Laos. . . . Indian P.M. Nehru, in an appearance before Parliament, denies The New York Times report that as many as 1,000 Moslems had been killed in communal fighting in West Bengal. Nehru claims that only 13 persons died in clashes.
May 13					Prince Boun Oum of the royal Laotian government is reported to have informed the leaders of Laos' two other contending factions that his government is prepared to reopen coalition negotiations. The Boun Oum regime reportedly has been under intense U.S. pressure to resume the talks since late 1961.

A	B	C	D	E
Includes developments that affect more than one world region, international organizations and important meetings of major world leaders.	Includes all domestic and regional developments in Europe, including the Soviet Union, Turkey, Cyprus and Malta.	Includes all domestic and regional developments in Africa and the Middle East, including Iraq and Iran and excluding Cyprus, Turkey and Afghanistan.	Includes all domestic and regional developments in Latin America, the Caribbean and Canada.	Includes all domestic and regional developments in Asia and Pacific nations, extending from Afghanistan through all the Pacific Islands, except Hawaii.

U.S. Politics & Social Issues	U.S. Foreign Policy & Defense	U.S. Economy & Environment	Science, Technology & Nature	Culture, Leisure & Life Style	
	"A Declaration of Republican Principle," issued on behalf of GOP congressional members charges that the Kennedy administration lacks the "will to meet effectively the assault of international communism on freedom." The statement specifically denounces the administration's Cuban and Laotian policies, its over-dependence on the U.N., its neglect of Europe, and excessive attention being given to underdeveloped nations.			Theodore White's *The Making of the President 1960* is named as the winner of the 1962 Pulitzer Prize for general non-fiction.	**May 7**
Public Health Service reports that a record 4,282,000 babies were born in the U.S. in 1961—25,000 more than in 1960.	National Council of Churches announces that it will discontinue its program of distributing U.S. surplus food to families on Formosa because of alleged inequities in the Nationalist Chinese government's food distribution system.	In a speech to the United Auto Workers convention in Atlantic City, Pres. Kennedy appeals to U.S. labor groups to seek responsible wage settlements keyed to productivity, adding that wages cannot rise faster than productivity "without defeating their own purpose through inflation.". . . Pres. Kennedy submits to Congress draft legislation for stand-by authority to make temporary income-tax cuts to combat recessions.			**May 8**
Pres. Kennedy, at his Washington press conference, denies reports that V.P. Johnson might be dropped from the Democratic ticket in 1964. He adds that Johnson has proved "invaluable" and "will be on the ticket if he chooses to run."					**May 9**
Southern School News (Nashville, Tenn.) reports that 7.6% of the Negro pupils in Southern schools attended integrated classes in 1962. The figure represents a .7% increase over 1961.	Ex-Pres. Eisenhower, at a Washington news conference, expresses general approval of the Kennedy administration's foreign policy, including its decision to expand the U.S. role in Vietnam.	House Agriculture Committee votes 18-17 to approve a bill (HR 11222) embodying the main features of the administration's farm program. Observers regard the close vote as a sign that the bill will face serious political opposition on the House floor. . . . N.Y. Federal Reserve Bank reports that the Treasury Dept.'s monetary gold stock dropped May 9 to a record low of $16,465 billion.	MIT engineers successfully bounce a laser beam off the lunar surface, marking the first time man-made light has been flashed to another celestial body.		**May 10**
Asst. Labor Secy. Jerry Holleman resigns after admitting that he had taken $1,000 from indicted Texas financial operator Billie Sol Estes.	AEC announces the successful testing of an underwater low-yield nuclear device somewhere in the eastern Pacific. The underwater test, presumably of an anti-submarine weapon, is the ninth in the U.S.'s current Pacific series.				**May 11**
			Journal of the Canadian Medical Association reports on successful transplants of aortic and mitral heart valves from dead men to persons critically ill with heart disease.		**May 12**
		New York City officials report that radioactive contamination of the city's air increased by 650% during 1961.		John Kelley wins the national AAU marathon in Yonkers, N.Y. for the seventh straight year.	**May 13**

F	G	H	I	J
Includes elections, federal-state relations, civil rights and liberties, crime, the judiciary, education, health care, poverty, urban affairs and population.	Includes formation and debate of U.S. foreign and defense policies, veterans' affairs and defense spending. (Relations with specific foreign countries are usually found under the region concerned.)	Includes business, labor, agriculture, taxation, transportation, consumer affairs, monetary and fiscal policy, natural resources, and pollution.	Includes worldwide scientific, medical and technological developments, natural phenomena, U.S. weather, natural disasters, and accidents.	Includes the arts, religion, scholarship, communications media, sports, entertainment, fashions, fads and social life.

	World Affairs	Europe	Africa & the Middle East	The Americas	Asia & the Pacific
May 14	U.S. presents the Geneva disarmament conference with a proposal to bar extension of East-West arms race into outer space.	Ex-Yugoslav Vice Pres. Milovan Djilas is convicted by a Belgrade court of revealing official state secrets in his book, *Conversations With Stalin*, scheduled to be published in the U.S. in late May.	Moslem gunners, riding in cars, shoot down 17 Europeans in the first act of Moslem counter-terrorism reported since the March 18 Algerian cease-fire agreement.		An Indonesian man is immediately arrested after shooting at Pres. Sukarno during a religious ceremony in Jakarta. Sukarno escaped uninjured. . . . Philippine Pres. Diosdado Macapagal announces that he has indefinitely postponed a scheduled June visit to the U.S. because of Congress' refusal to pass a bill (HR 8617) authorizing a $73 million payment to the Philippines for damages incurred there during W.W. II.
May 15	U.S. delegation at Geneva announces acceptance of Swedish proposals for the elimination of chemical, biological, and bacteriological weapons in the first stage of a disarmament plan.	Responding to recent West German criticism of U.S.-Soviet contacts over Berlin, Pres. Kennedy asserts that the heavy burden in Berlin borne by the U.S. gives it "some rights to at least explore the possibilities of finding a better solution than we now have.". . . Pres. de Gaulle, at a Paris news conference, reaffirms France's determination to become a nuclear military power, explaining that such a development is essential to reducing European dependence on the U.S.	A resolution of no confidence in the government of Premier David Ben-Gurion fails in the Israeli Knesset by a vote of 55-47. The resolution charged that the government's fiscal and monetary policies had failed to stabilize the economy.	The Brazilian government announces a food emergency in the drought-stricken nine-state area of northeast Brazil.	White House announces that Pres. Kennedy has ordered 5,000 U.S. troops to Thailand. The statement describes the move as a response to a Pathet Lao military build-up near the Thai-Laotian border. . . . Communist China, in a statement broadcast by Peking radio, warns that it will not "remain indifferent to America's threat of intervention in Laos."
May 16	Soviet Premier Khrushchev, on a visit to Bulgaria, tells reporters that the USSR is preparing a new series of nuclear tests in response to the U.S.'s current Pacific series. . . . Soviet delegation to Geneva says it will oppose proposals for the demilitarization of space unless they are tied to Western acceptance of Soviet proposals for a total liquidation of foreign bases and nuclear weapons delivery systems.	Five cabinet ministers—all members of the Roman Catholic Popular Republican Movement (MRP)—resign from the French cabinet to protest de Gaulle's European policies. The resigning ministers favor a supranational European political union and not the consultative federation of sovereign nation-states outlined by de Gaulle in his May 15 nationwide address.	The 17-nation U.N. Special Committee on Colonialism urges the General Assembly to back African demands for the creation of an independent Northern Rhodesia under a majority-rule constitution.		International Control Commission for Laos reports that Pathet Lao leaders have pledged to refrain from further military action in northwest Laos pending the planned resumption of talks on the formation of a coalition government.
May 17		Pres. Kennedy criticizes French Pres. de Gaulle's recent call for greater European independence through the development of its own nuclear deterrent. . . . Rumanian CP announces that it will welcome membership applications from former rank-and-file members of now defunct bourgeois and peasant parties.			Hong Kong authorities begin construction of a barbed-wire barrier on the border with Communist China in a renewed effort to prevent illegal immigration across the frontier. An estimated 50,000 refugees from famine-stricken regions in China are said to have entered Hong Kong since May 1; 40,000 of them have been returned to China.
May 18			Algerian sources report that a large number of Europeans, perhaps as many as 20,000, have left Algeria for France since the March 18 peace agreement. The exodus is reportedly continuing despite a Secret Army Organization threat to execute any European leaving Algeria without its permission.		Soviet Premier Khrushchev, in comments to Western newsmen, warns that the U.S.'s dispatch of troops to Southeast Asia could lead to a new "Korean"-type conflict involving other nations.
May 19	Soviet Premier Khrushchev, addressing a rally in Sofia, Bulgaria, warns that the U.S. would "receive the most crushing reply" from Soviet rockets should it dare launch a first-strike nuclear attack.	Paris police arrest five Secret Army Organization members who were reportedly preparing a plot to assassinate French Pres. de Gaulle.			An intensification of military activity between Dutch forces and bands of Indonesian paratroopers is reported in Netherlands New Guinea.
May 20				Pres. José Maria Guido issues decrees dissolving the Argentine Congress and temporarily abolishing all political parties. The actions are seen as part of the Argentine government's current campaign against a revival of Peronist political power.	

A	B	C	D	E
Includes developments that affect more than one world region, international organizations and important meetings of major world leaders.	Includes all domestic and regional developments in Europe, including the Soviet Union, Turkey, Cyprus and Malta.	Includes all domestic and regional developments in Africa and the Middle East, including Iraq and Iran and excluding Cyprus, Turkey and Afghanistan.	Includes all domestic and regional developments in Latin America, the Caribbean and Canada.	Includes all domestic and regional developments in Asia and Pacific nations, extending from Afghanistan through all the Pacific Islands, except Hawaii.

U.S. Politics & Social Issues	U.S. Foreign Policy & Defense	U.S. Economy & Environment	Science, Technology & Nature	Culture, Leisure & Life Style	
Senate puts aside consideration of an administration-backed voting rights bill (S2750) after a second unsuccessful cloture motion failed to break a three-week old Southern filibuster against the measure.		Supreme Court upholds the 1957 conviction of ex-Teamster's Pres. Dave Beck on charges of embezzling union funds.	The Planned Parenthood Federation reports that more than 1,000,000 women are currently using oral contraceptive pills in the U.S., Puerto Rico, Britain and South Africa.		May 14
Republican Sen. John Tower (Tex.), in a telegram to Pres. Kennedy, calls for the resignation of Agriculture Secy. Orville Freeman in light of revelations that at least three Agriculture Dept. employees accepted favors from Billie Sol Estes. . . . Kennedy sends Congress a request for a five-year, $50 million program of grants to improve services to older citizens. Kennedy also announces creation of a President's Council on Aging.					May 15
					May 16
Pres. Kennedy tells reporters that his administration is pursuing a full scale investigation of the Billie Sol Estes case. Plans for congressional probes into the Estes affair are announced in both the House and Senate.	In remarks to Washington newsmen, Pres. Kennedy says that he ordered the build-up of U.S. forces in Southeast Asia primarily to hasten a "diplomatic solution" to the Laotian civil war.	Pres. Kennedy tells a national conference on foreign trade policy in Washington that the well-being of "this great Atlantic community" depends on continued expansion of U.S. foreign trade. Kennedy couples the assertion with an appeal for passage of his full Trade Expansion Act.	A minor malfunction in the Project Mercury capsule's attitude-control system forces NASA to postpone the U.S.'s second attempt to put a man in orbit.	Ingemar Johansson wins the European heavyweight boxing championship in Goteborg, Sweden by knocking out Dick Richardson of Wales in the eighth round of their title bout.	May 17
U.S. Court of Appeals in New York reverses the 1961 contempt conviction of folksinger Pete Seeger for his 1955 refusal to answer questions about communism before the House Un-American Activities Committee.		Teamsters Pres. James Hoffa is indicted by federal grand jury in Nashville, Tenn. on charges of accepting illegal payments from Commercial Carriers Inc., a Detroit-based auto transport company. . . . U.S. Treasury Secy. Douglas Dillon, addressing the American Bankers Association's international monetary conference in Rome, urges European financial leaders to reform their "outmoded capital markets" in order to better meet their needs for domestic capital.		U.S. shotputter Dallas Long sets a new world record of 65 ft. 10 1/2 in. at the Coliseum Relays in Los Angeles.	May 18
Pres. Kennedy asserts that his administration stands for "a policy of constructive action on every major issue" in an address before 12,000 persons attending a Democratic fundraising rally in New York's Madison Square Garden.				Stan Musial, of the St. Louis Cardinals gets his 3,431st hit, setting a new National League record. . . . Donald Ross's Greek Money, John Rotz up, wins the 86th running of the Preakness in Baltimore.	May 19
Pres. Kennedy, in a nationally televised address before 20,000 senior citizens in Madison Square Garden, urges open public support of the administration's aged health care plan as embodied in the King-Anderson bill. The Madison Square Garden gathering was one of 33 similar pro-health care rallys held across the country.					May 20

F	G	H	I	J
Includes elections, federal-state relations, civil rights and liberties, crime, the judiciary, education, health care, poverty, urban affairs and population.	Includes formation and debate of U.S. foreign and defense policies, veterans' affairs and defense spending. (Relations with specific foreign countries are usually found under the region concerned.)	Includes business, labor, agriculture, taxation, transportation, consumer affairs, monetary and fiscal policy, natural resources, and pollution.	Includes worldwide scientific, medical and technological developments, natural phenomena, U.S. weather, natural disasters, and accidents.	Includes the arts, religion, scholarship, communications media, sports, entertainment, fashions, fads and social life.

	World Affairs	Europe	Africa & the Middle East	The Americas	Asia & the Pacific
May 21			Pres. Nasser presents the UAR National Congress with a "National Charter of Socialist Principles", a constitutional document aimed at increasing the role of farmers and workers in Egyptian political and economic life.		The Netherlands, in a note to U.N. Actg. Secy. Gen. U Thant, asks that U.N. observers be sent to Netherlands New Guinea to prevent further Indonesian "aggression" there. . . . Hong Kong residents, sympathetic to the illegal Chinese emigres being forced to return to China, clash with police detachments stationed along the Chinese border.
May 22			Katanga Pres. Tshombe returns to Leopoldville to resume negotiations with Premier Adoula on peacefully reintegrating separatist Katanga into the Congo.	Sixty-seven dissident Argentine deputies hold a meeting in the Congress building in defiance of Pres. Guido's May 20 decree dissolving the Legislature.	
May 23		Four members of the conservative Independent Party, including Finance Min. Valery Giscard d'Estaing, resign their French cabinet posts to protest de Gaulle's continuing opposition to the creation of a truly supranational European political unity. . . . West Berlin police fire more than 100 rounds into the Eastern sector to protect an East German youth attempting to swim to West Berlin under communist gunfire.	A military court in Paris convicts and sentences to life imprisonment ex-Gen. Raoul Salan for his role in leading the Secret Army Organization's terror campaign against the French-Moslem peace settlement. French Pres. de Gaulle is reportedly angered by the court's failure to impose the death sentence.	Brazilian cabinet approves a decree setting forth the procedures for nationalization of foreign-owned utility companies.	Actg. U.N. Secy. Gen. U Thant rejects a May 18 Dutch request for U.N. intervention in New Guinea, explaining that such intervention might "imply that I was taking sides in the controversy."
May 24	U.N. Educational, Scientific & Cultural Organization (UNESCO) estimates that 44% of the world's population is illiterate and that in at least 20 countries the illiteracy rate exceeds 95%.	Thousands of Spanish coal miners and industrial workers begin returning to their jobs after the government announced measures to facilitate their quest for higher wages.		Representatives of eight West Indian territories agree in London to form in 1964 a new West Indies Federation within the British Commonwealth. Jamaica will not be a member of the new federation. . . . OAS urges Chile and Bolivia to work toward a peaceful settlement of their dispute over the waters of the Lauca River.	The New York Times quotes Hong Kong officials as saying that hunger, not politics, was the chief motivation behind the recent flood of Chinese emigrants seeking entry into Hong Kong.
May 25	U.S. and the USSR announce to the Geneva conference a compromise agreement on a joint six-point Declaration Against War Propaganda which condemns all "appeals for war" and all "statements that war is necessary or inevitable."				Prince Souvanna Phouma, leader of Laos' neutralist faction, arrives in Laos from France to reopen talks on forming a coalition government. . . . Hong Kong officials report that the entry of illegal Chinese immigrants has "markedly diminished" in the past few days and that the situation on the border is returning to normal. Of the estimated 70,000 Chinese who streamed into Hong Kong during the past month, over 55,000 have already been returned to China.
May 26					Laotian sources report that Pathet Lao troops, allegedly supported by North Vietnamese regulars, have resumed their offensive against troops of the rightist Laotian government with heavy attacks in southern as well as northwestern Laos. . . . A six-point U.S. peace plan for settling the Dutch-Indonesian dispute over New Guinea is made public in Washington. The plan calls for the gradual transfer to Indonesia of the administration of New Guinea.
May 27		Gen. Francisco Franco, in a Madrid speech, blames communists, liberals and "lay organizations of the (Spanish Roman Catholic) church" for inspiring the nationwide strikes that have been in progress since April.			

A	B	C	D	E
Includes developments that affect more than one world region, international organizations and important meetings of major world leaders.	Includes all domestic and regional developments in Europe, including the Soviet Union, Turkey, Cyprus and Malta.	Includes all domestic and regional developments in Africa and the Middle East, including Iraq and Iran and excluding Cyprus, Turkey and Afghanistan.	Includes all domestic and regional developments in Latin America, the Caribbean and Canada.	Includes all domestic and regional developments in Asia and Pacific nations, extending from Afghanistan through all the Pacific Islands, except Hawaii.

U.S. Politics & Social Issues	U.S. Foreign Policy & Defense	U.S. Economy & Environment	Science, Technology & Nature	Culture, Leisure & Life Style	
American Medical Association sponsors a one-hour nationally televised program to rebut Pres. Kennedy's May 21 speech urging support for his aged health care plan. AMA spokesmen say the plan would lower the quality of hospital services and intrude on the normal doctor-patient relationship.	Pres. Kennedy nominates Defense Dept. general counsel Cyrus R. Vance to be Army Secretary.		Herbert Ratner, preventive medicine professor at Loyola University, asserts in a report released by the Center for the Study of Democratic Institutions that the U.S. may be the "unhealthiest" country in the world. Ratner cites mass treatment and over-medication, both exemplified by the Salk vaccine, as chief reasons for the low level of American medical care.	A U.S. district court in Baltimore acquits the National Football League of all antitrust charges brought against it by the American Football League.	**May 21**
		Agriculture Dept. announces that it will begin transferring about $50 million worth of grain from storage facilities controlled by indicted Texas financier Billie Sol Estes. . . . Commerce Dept. reports that the total debt of U.S. individuals, business and government climbed to a record $937 billion at the end of 1961.		The General Assembly of the United Presbyterian Church, meeting in Denver endorses a sex education program designed to communicate "concepts of responsible sexuality" within a "Christian context."	**May 22**
At his regular news conference, Pres. Kennedy criticizes the American Medical Association's continuing opposition to his medical-care-for-the aged bill.	Pres. Kennedy announces that increased numbers of Chinese refugees living in Hong Kong will be permitted to emigrate to the U.S. under a special emergency provision of the 1952 McCarran-Walter Immigration Act. The policy will not apply to those illegal Chinese refugees who have recently come to Hong Kong.			*The Exterminating Angel*, directed by Luis Bunuel, is named best film of the year at the Cannes (France) Film Festival. . . . National Basketball Association's board of governors approves the transfer of the Philadelphia Warriors' franchise to San Francisco.	**May 23**
		A speech by Pittsburgh Steel Company Pres. Allison Maxwell Jr., angrily denouncing Pres. Kennedy's high pressure tactics in the recent steel price controversy, draws a standing ovation from the 1,000 delegates attending a general meeting of the American Iron & Steel Institute.	Lt. Cmndr. Scott Carpenter, riding a Project Mercury capsule known as Aurora VII, returns safely to earth after completing a three-orbit flight. The successful mission was climaxed by a dramatic 39-minute search for Carpenter's spacecraft after he overshot his intended splash-down area by 250 miles.		**May 24**
House passes and sends to the Senate a bill (HR 11677) to require companies doing interstate business to pay equal wages to men and women doing equal work in the same plant. . . . A three-judge federal court in Atlanta rules that both houses of the Georgia legislature are unconstitutionally imbalanced in favor of rural areas. The court says it will "take such action as is necessary" if the situation is not remedied before 1963.	Senate Permanent Investigations Subcommittee concludes eight weeks of hearings into charges of excessive profits made by defense contractors involved in the missile procurement program. . . . Defense Dept. reports that three Soviet ships, equipped with intelligence-gathering devices, have been cruising in international waters near the U.S.'s Christmas Island testing area since early May.	The Senate, by a 42-38 vote, passes and sends to the House an amended farm bill, (S 3225) embodying the administration program for strict controls on wheat and feed-grain production. . . . AFL-CIO Pres. George Meany endorses proposals for a national 35-hour work week in a speech to the biennial convention of the Amalgamated Clothing Workers of America. The administration is firmly opposed to the 35-hour plan.	In a speech at the Seattle World's Fair, U.S. State Secy. Dean Rusk calls for the immediate institution of international supervision over space activities to keep space from becoming a military battleground.		**May 25**
The newly-merged Unitarian Universalist Association holds its first annual meeting in Washington. Delegates adopt a resolution urging members to boycott all organizations practicing racial discrimination.					**May 26**
	U.S. continues its current tests of a wide variety of nuclear devices. Fourteen atmospheric tests have so far been conducted in the central Pacific and 34 underground blasts have been detonated at the Nevada proving grounds.		U.S. Astronaut Scott Carpenter, appearing at a Cape Canaveral press conference, offers a theory to explain the glowing particles which both he and John Glenn observed during their orbital flights. Carpenter speculates that they were bits of frost which formed on the outside of the capsule.		**May 27**

F	G	H	I	J
Includes elections, federal-state relations, civil rights and liberties, crime, the judiciary, education, health care, poverty, urban affairs and population.	*Includes formation and debate of U.S. foreign and defense policies, veterans' affairs and defense spending. (Relations with specific foreign countries are usually found under the region concerned.)*	*Includes business, labor, agriculture, taxation, transportation, consumer affairs, monetary and fiscal policy, natural resources, and pollution.*	*Includes worldwide scientific, medical and technological developments, natural phenomena, U.S. weather, natural disasters, and accidents.*	*Includes the arts, religion, scholarship, communications media, sports, entertainment, fashions, fads and social life.*

	World Affairs	Europe	Africa & the Middle East	The Americas	Asia & the Pacific
May 28			The South African House of Assembly approves an anti-subversion bill vastly increasing the government's police powers.		Kennedy Administration officials confirm that the U.S. has rebuked Laotian leaders, and particularly right wing militant Gen. Phoumi Nosavan for their failure to heed American political and military advice. Laotian government spokesmen charged May 25 that the U.S. had demanded Gen. Phoumi's ouster.
May 29	Soviet delegation at Geneva announces its rejection of a previously accepted declaration against war propaganda after the West refused to accept Soviet amendments requiring participating states to enact legislation making war propaganda a criminal offense.	British and EEC negotiators, meeting in Brussels, announce tentative agreement on the tariffs to be applied to imports of manufactured goods from Commonwealth nations. No progress is reported on the controversial issue of commonwealth farm exports.	Israeli Supreme Court, ruling on an appeal, refuses to set aside the 1961 conviction and death sentence meted out to Adolf Eichmann by a special Jerusalem tribunal.		
May 30		In a Moscow address, Soviet Premier Khrushchev denounces the European Economic Community as a new form of "colonialism" harmful to the interests of underdeveloped nations. . . . U.S. State Secy. Rusk and Soviet Amb.-to-U.S. Anatoly Dobrynin hold their fourth preliminary meeting on possible negotiations over Berlin.		Brazilian Chamber of the Deputies defeats a rightist motion censuring the Foreign Ministry for not pursuing a strong anti-communist foreign policy.	
May 31		Gen. Ismet Inonu resigns as premier of Turkey in protest against growing demands for the granting of amnesties to imprisoned leaders of the late Premier Adnan Menderes' government.	Adolf Eichmann is executed by hanging in Israel for his role in Nazi Germany's mass murder of Jews during W.W. II. To the very end Eichmann denied legal or moral responsibility for the atrocities.		In a formal protest note to Peking, India charges that the proposed Kashmir border talks between China and Pakistan are part of China's "aggressive designs" against India.
June 1		Rumania signs a trade and political agreement with the U.S. . . . The USSR announces a 25% increase in the price of meat and dairy products as part of a new program to provide funds for lagging farm output.	Algerian sources report an abrupt halt in the Secret Army Organization's terrorist campaign in Algiers. The suspension is viewed as a sign that negotiations have begun between the terrorist group and the Algerian Provisional Executive.		
June 2		P.M. Macmillan flies to Paris for two days of private talks with Pres. de Gaulle on France's growing resistance to British membership in the EEC.	Iraq orders the recall of U.S. Amb. John Jernegan in protest against U.S. recognition of Kuwait.	Premier Woodrow Lloyd of Canada's Saskatchewan Province announces that a public-financed medical-care program will be implemented on schedule despite a threat from the province's doctors not to cooperate.	
June 3	Soviet government issues a statement declaring that the USSR will be forced to respond with appropriate measures if the U.S. carries out its planned high-altitude nuclear tests. Statement says the tests confirm that the U.S. is preparing for a first-strike nuclear war.		Thousands of Europeans continue to leave Algeria for France despite an apparent suspension of terrorist violence.	About 3,000 Venezuelan government troops crush a three-day uprising by 500 marines at the Venezuelan naval headquarters in Puerto Cabello. Pres. Romulo Betancourt blames the rebellion on communist and other leftist groups.	
June 4	A U.S. Thor missile bearing a thermonuclear warhead designed for a high-altitude detonation over the central Pacific is destroyed in mid-flight following a malfunction in the missile's electronic tracking system. The undetonated warhead falls into the Pacific, where, according to the AEC, it will cause no hazard to human life.		The South African government announces plans for a new immigration program designed to vastly increase the annual number of white settlers coming to South Africa. . . . The halt in Secret Army Organization terrorism in Algeria is reportedly continuing. The terrorists are said to be seeking negotiations on stronger guarantees for Algeria's Europeans after self-determination.	Peronist leaders in Buenos Aires announce plans to form a National Republican Front made up of non-Peronist opposition groups as well as Peronists. . . . Two U.S. Alliance for Progress agreements to provide aid for Brazil's poverty-stricken northeast are signed in Recife.	

A	B	C	D	E
Includes developments that affect more than one world region, international organizations and important meetings of major world leaders.	Includes all domestic and regional developments in Europe, including the Soviet Union, Turkey, Cyprus and Malta.	Includes all domestic and regional developments in Africa and the Middle East, including Iraq and Iran and excluding Cyprus, Turkey and Afghanistan.	Includes all domestic and regional developments in Latin America, the Caribbean and Canada.	Includes all domestic and regional developments in Asia and Pacific nations, extending from Afghanistan through all the Pacific Islands, except Hawaii.

U.S. Politics & Social Issues	U.S. Foreign Policy & Defense	U.S. Economy & Environment	Science, Technology & Nature	Culture, Leisure & Life Style	
House Inter-Governmental Relations Subcommittee begins hearings into possible irregularities in Agriculture Dept.'s leasing of grain storage warehouses from Texas financier Billie Sol Estes.		Prices on the N.Y. Stock Exchange suffer the sharpest decline since the "Black Tuesday" market crash of October 28, 1929. The Dow Jones industrial average drops 34.95 points, closing the day at 576.93. . . . The Senate passes and sends to the House a bill (S2965) to authorize a modified version of the administration's anti-recession public works spending program.	USSR announces the successful launching of Cosmos V, the fifth in its current series of earth satellite shots.		May 28
George Wallace, an outspoken segregationist, wins an easy victory in a Democratic primary run-off for the Alabama gubernatorial nomination.		Stock prices on the N.Y. Exchange rally, recovering almost 60% of yesterdays dramatic losses. Over 14,750,000 shares are traded, the second largest one-day total on record. The Dow Jones average closes at 603.96, up 27.03 points.		John (Buck) O'Neil is signed as a coach by the Chicago Cubs, becoming the first Negro coach in major league history.	May 29
Ex-V.P. Richard Nixon joins other GOP leaders in blaming the recent stockmarket fluctuations on the administration's "hostile climate toward business."				For the second time in his career, Rodger Ward wins the Indianapolis 500 auto race. Ward's previous victory came in 1959.	May 30
	A group of Harvard physicians publish a series of articles claiming that no civil defense-type nuclear survival program is feasible.	U.S. Chamber of Commerce announces that it has created at the President's request a committee to advise the government on the U.S.'s gold outflow problem.			May 31
	Sen. Stuart Symington (D, Mo.) asserts that losses resulting from mismanagement in the stockpiling of military materials have been "far greater than any I have seen in the Billie Sol Estes case."	U.S. Federal Radiation Council predicts that nuclear test fallout may lead to a moderate increase in the incidence of leukemia and bone cancer.			June 1
Conservative Democrat John Connally defeats liberal candidate Don Yarborough in a close run-off election for the Texas Democratic gubernatorial nomination.	White House sources announce the formation of a citizens' Chinese Refugee Relief Organization to assist in the resettlement of Chinese refugees coming to the U.S. from Hong Kong under the administration's emergency refugee program.			New Zealand track star Peter Snell is named by Queen Elizabeth II as a Member of the British Empire. Snell is among more than 2,000 persons cited in the Queen's birthday honors list.	June 2
				A New York-bound Air France jetliner, chartered by members of the Atlanta (Ga.) Art Association, crashes shortly after take-off from Paris' Orly International Air Field, killing 130 of the 132 passengers aboard. The crash, the worst single-plane disaster in aviation history, takes the lives of some of Atlanta's most prominent cultural leaders. . . . Bruce McLaren, driving a Couper Climax, wins the 195-mile Monte Carlo Grand Prix auto race.	June 3
Supreme Court overturns the convictions of six Negro Freedom Riders who had been arrested in Shreveport, La. in late 1961 on breach-of-peace charges. The court rules that there was insufficient "evidence of violence" to warrant the charges.					June 4

F	G	H	I	J
Includes elections, federal-state relations, civil rights and liberties, crime, the judiciary, education, health care, poverty, urban affairs and population.	Includes formation and debate of U.S. foreign and defense policies, veterans' affairs and defense spending. (Relations with specific foreign countries are usually found under the region concerned.)	Includes business, labor, agriculture, taxation, transportation, consumer affairs, monetary and fiscal policy, natural resources, and pollution.	Includes worldwide scientific, medical and technological developments, natural phenomena, U.S. weather, natural disasters, and accidents.	Includes the arts, religion, scholarship, communications media, sports, entertainment, fashions, fads and social life.

	World Affairs	Europe	Africa & the Middle East	The Americas	Asia & the Pacific
June 5			Condemned former Secret Army Organization leader Edmond Jouhaud issues an appeal from his death cell in Paris calling upon Algeria's Europeans to halt their battle against the French-Moslem peace agreement and to accept an independent Algeria as a reality.	An Argentine federal district judge rules that Pres. Guido's April 25 degree nullifying the March 18 congressional elections is unconstitutional. The government is expected to appeal.	
June 6			New Syrian Premier Bashir al-Azmah proposes a restoration of Syria's union with the UAR under a new federal constitution guaranteeing the Damascus government greater sovereignty and autonomy.		Damodaram Sangivayva is elected president of India's Congress Party, becoming the first Untouchable to hold a principal party post. . . . Seoul police block an anti-American march by 1,500 Korea University students angry over the alleged beating by two U.S. Army officers of a Korean civilian. The students are demanding a new U.S.-Korean agreement to permit the trial of U.S. military personnel by South Korean courts.
June 7		In protest notes to the U.S., Britain and France, the USSR blames the West for increasing the Berlin tensions by allowing West Berlin police to fire on East German frontier guards in an effort to abet recent escape attempts.	Dozens of public buildings in major Algerian cities are destroyed by bombs, marking an apparent resumption of Secret Army Organization terrorism. Despite the renewed violence, Algerian sources report that Secret Army Organization talks with the Algerian Provisional Executive and with Moslem rebel leaders are continuing.		
June 8	The eight neutral delegations to the Geneva disarmament conference call upon the U.S., Britain, and the USSR to renew their attempt to reach an agreement on the banning of nuclear weapons tests.	Harold Wilson, Laborite spokesman on foreign affairs, says that Britain's commitment to Commonwealth nations should not be sacrificed simply to win British membership in the Common Market. . . . French Pres. de Gaulle predicts in a television speech that the self-determination referendum to be carried out in Algeria July 1 will at last settle the Algerian problem and leave France free to strengthen its own state institutions and internal stability.			Pakistani Pres. Mohammed Ayub Khan announces the lifting of martial law, in force since his seizure of power in October 1958. . . . The government-controlled Saigon press reports that the Diem regime has taken steps to postpone the constitutionally-required National Assembly elections scheduled for August.
June 9		Gen. Francisco Franco and his cabinet suspend for two years the freedom of movement provisions of the Spanish constitution. The action is aimed at barring known oppositionists from residing in big cities and in strike centers.	Nigerian Foreign Min. Jaja Wachuku charges that the Ghanaian embassy in Lagos has been used as a "center of subversion" against the Nigerian government.		
June 10					

A	B	C	D	E
Includes developments that affect more than one world region, international organizations and important meetings of major world leaders.	Includes all domestic and regional developments in Europe, including the Soviet Union, Turkey, Cyprus and Malta.	Includes all domestic and regional developments in Africa and the Middle East, including Iraq and Iran and excluding Cyprus, Turkey and Afghanistan.	Includes all domestic and regional developments in Latin America, the Caribbean and Canada.	Includes all domestic and regional developments in Asia and Pacific nations, extending from Afghanistan through all the Pacific Islands, except Hawaii.

U.S. Politics & Social Issues	U.S. Foreign Policy & Defense	U.S. Economy & Environment	Science, Technology & Nature	Culture, Leisure & Life Style	
Ex-V.P. Richard Nixon wins the California Republican gubernatorial nomination in an easy primary victory over ultraconservative candidate Joseph Shell. . . . Wisconsin Supreme Court declares as unconstitutional the 1961 state law permitting parochial school students to ride public school buses.		Negotiators for the nation's leading railroad companies and for 11 rail unions announce in Chicago that they have agreed to accept the wage increase guidelines recommended by a presidential fact-finding board May 3. Both sides had previously criticized the board's recommendations. . . . Floyd Harmon, treasurer of Teamsters Local 614 in Pontiac, Mich., is indicted on charges of embezzling union funds. During the last four months over 30 officials of Teamsters locals have been indicted for illegal union-related activities.			June 5
Florida Supreme Court upholds a state law requiring daily Bible readings in Florida public schools.	Pres. Kennedy tells the graduating class of the U.S. Military Academy at West Point that current military responsibilities require a greater versatility than ever before because the "basic problems facing the world today are not susceptible to a final military solution."			Raymond Guest's Larkspur, Neville Sellwood up, wins the 183rd Epsom (England) Derby. . . . The Southern Baptist Convention, meeting in San Francisco, reaffirms its opposition to the dissemination of views that "undermine the faith in the historical accuracy and doctrinal integrity of the Bible."	June 6
"A Declaration of Republican Principle and Policy," severely critical of the Kennedy administration's domestic and foreign policies, is issued by Rep. Melvin Laird (R, Wis.), chairman of the Joint Senate-House Committee on Republican Principles.	Senate passes and sends to the House the administration's $4.662 billion foreign aid authorization bill. The measure restricts aid to communist countries of surplus agricultural products and authorizes suspension of aid to any country which expropriates U.S. property.	Pres. Kennedy announces at his news conference that he will ask Congress to enact across-the-board cuts in personal and corporate income taxes in 1963. He says the move is needed to bolster the economy's recovery from the 1961 recession. . . . A "Declaration of Republican Principle and Policy," issued by congressional Republicans, charges that the Kennedy administration has shown little concern for protecting America's "free competitive economy."	U.S. Surgeon Gen. Luther Terry announces that a Public Health Service advisory committee will begin a full-scale study of the effects of smoking on health and make appropriate recommendations for government action.	George Dawson, of Glen Ellyn, Illinois wins the 58th U.S. Seniors' Golf Association championship at Rye, N.Y.	June 7
Dismissed Asst. Agriculture Secy. James Ralph, testifying at the House Inter-Governmental Relations Subcommittee's probe into the Estes case, says that he contributed $400 (received as a gift from Estes) to various Democratic political campaign funds.			Dr. Jerome Wiesner is appointed by Pres. Kennedy to head the newly-created U.S. Office of Science and Technology.	U.S. distance-runner Jim Beatty sets a new world record for the two-mile run of eight minutes 29.8 seconds in a meet in Los Angeles.	June 8
Delegates at the Massachusetts Democratic state convention endorse Edward M. Kennedy, 30, youngest brother of the President, as their candidate for the Senate.	AEC announces the successful testing of an intermediate-range nuclear device dropped from a plane above the U.S. proving grounds at Christmas Island in the Central Pacific. The test is the 16th in the U.S.'s current Pacific series.	Agriculture Dept. reports that U.S. exports of corn and other feed-grains are up 16% over a year ago.		The 94th running of the Belmont Stakes is won by Jaipur, ridden by Willie Shoemaker and owned by George Widener.	June 9
Most Rev. Paul Hallinan, Roman Catholic Archbishop of Atlanta, announces that the archdiocese's 23 schools will be desegregated beginning in September. . . . A two-month Negro boycott against the *Philadelphia Bulletin* ends after Negro leaders announced that the paper had met their demands to end employment discrimination.				Igor Ter-Ovanesyan of the USSR sets a world broadjump record of 27 ft. three in. at a meet in Yerevan, Soviet Armenia.	June 10

F	G	H	I	J
Includes elections, federal-state relations, civil rights and liberties, crime, the judiciary, education, health care, poverty, urban affairs and population.	*Includes formation and debate of U.S. foreign and defense policies, veterans' affairs and defense spending. (Relations with specific foreign countries are usually found under the region concerned.)*	*Includes business, labor, agriculture, taxation, transportation, consumer affairs, monetary and fiscal policy, natural resources, and pollution.*	*Includes worldwide scientific, medical and technological developments, natural phenomena, U.S. weather, natural disasters, and accidents.*	*Includes the arts, religion, scholarship, communications media, sports, entertainment, fashions, fads and social life.*

	World Affairs	Europe	Africa & the Middle East	The Americas	Asia & the Pacific
June 11		West Berlin sources report that a total of 54 persons made successful escapes from East Berlin during the June 9-10 weekend. The escape attempts again provoked an exchange of gunfire between West Berlin and East German border guards.			An agreement on a coalition government ending the civil war in Laos is announced by the leaders of the country's three rival political factions. The accord provides for a 19-member cabinet headed by neutralist premier-designate Souvanna Phouma. Important government decisions will require unanimous agreement by a "troika" composed of Souvanna, Pathet-Lao chief Souphanouvong and rightist Gen. Phoumi Nosavan.
June 12			Katanga Pres. Tshombe and central Congo Premier Adoula break off negotiations after a month of meetings failed to produce an agreement on Congo reunification. . . . David K. Jawara is sworn in as Gambia's first prime minister. Jawara says his government plans to keep the former British West African dependency in the British Commonwealth.		
June 13	In a note to Pres. Kennedy, Soviet Premier Khrushchev expresses the USSR's satisfaction over the Laotian peace agreement, saying that it bodes well for future East-West efforts to reduce world tensions. Kennedy expresses similar sentiments in his reply.	Nearly 300 members of France's four leading center parties walk out of the National Assembly to demonstrate their dissatisfaction with de Gaulle's continuing opposition to proposals for the development of a formal European political community.	The Moslem rebel Algerian Provisional Government announces that it has rejected Secret Army Organization proposals for granting Algeria's Europeans guarantees beyond those contained in the March 18 French-Moslem peace accord.	Panamanian Pres. Roberto Chiari, on an official visit to the U.S., wins an agreement from Pres. Kennedy for the prompt initiation of high-level talks on "points of dissatisfaction" regarding the current Panama Canal Treaty.	
June 14	The 17-nation Geneva disarmament conference, in session for three months, begins a one-month recess after failing to break an apparently insurmountable East-West deadlock on disarmament proposals.				
June 15		East Berlin authorities begin construction of military-type fortifications along the Berlin Wall in response to the growing number of escape attempts, shootings and explosions that have occurred there.			
June 16		British Labor Party leader Hugh Gaitskell calls for immediate general elections, saying that recent by-elections indicate the Conservative government has "utterly lost the confidence of the country."		Cuban armed forces stage a military parade of troops and tanks in Cardenas about 70 miles east of Havana, in response to unspecified "counter-revolutionary provocations."	South Korean Premier Song Yo Chan and his cabinet resign in protest against the financial policies of the ruling military junta. Junta chairman Gen. Chung Hee Park is expected to replace Song as premier.
June 17		West German Chancellor Adenauer and West Berlin Mayor Willy Brandt, in speeches to a West Berlin rally of over 150,000 persons, call upon the USSR to accept a German settlement which would allow the German people to decide their own political future.	The Secret Army Organization proclaims a halt in its Algerian terrorist campaign after clandestine negotiations with Moslem nationalists produced an agreement on amnesty for past Secret Army terrorist acts.		Actg. U.N. Secy. Gen. U Thant informs Indonesian Pres. Sukarno that the Netherlands has accepted a proposed U.S. plan for settling the Dutch-Indonesian dispute over West New Guinea. . . . British Commonwealth Secy. Duncan Sandys meets with Indian P.M. Nehru to express British concern over a Soviet offer to sell India supersonic fighter-planes.
June 18			Leaders of the Oran division of the Secret Army Organization reject the Secret Army Moslem truce announced yesterday in Algiers and promise to continue "the fight." The truce is also denounced by militant elements in the rebel Algerian Provisional Government.	Canada's ruling Conservative Party fails to attain a working majority in the House of Commons following nationwide elections. The Conservatives, however, still have a 118-97 plurality over the Liberals, the next largest party.	

A	B	C	D	E
Includes developments that affect more than one world region, international organizations and important meetings of major world leaders.	Includes all domestic and regional developments in Europe, including the Soviet Union, Turkey, Cyprus and Malta.	Includes all domestic and regional developments in Africa and the Middle East, including Iraq and Iran and excluding Cyprus, Turkey and Afghanistan.	Includes all domestic and regional developments in Latin America, the Caribbean and Canada.	Includes all domestic and regional developments in Asia and Pacific nations, extending from Afghanistan through all the Pacific Islands, except Hawaii.

U.S. Politics & Social Issues	U.S. Foreign Policy & Defense	U.S. Economy & Environment	Science, Technology & Nature	Culture, Leisure & Life Style	
		Pres. Kennedy, speaking at Yale University graduation exercises, criticizes the outmoded economic myths being circulated to discredit his policies.			June 11
Three convicts are reported missing from Alcatraz Prison in San Francisco Bay after they apparently used kitchen spoons to dig through their four-inch cell-block walls. If the three men survived the 1.5 mile swim to the mainland, they will be the first successful escapees from Alcatraz in its 28-year history.		Labor Dept. reports that the seasonally adjusted unemployment rate declined from 5.5% in March and April to 5.4% in May.			June 12
		Treasury Secy. Douglas Dillon attributes the recent stock price decline to a recognition by the "investing public. . .that prices were too high."			June 13
		Prices on the sagging N.Y. Stock Exchange again drop sharply, forcing the Dow Jones Industrial average to a yearly low of 563.	An agreement creating a European Space Research Organization is signed in Paris by representatives of 10 Western European nations. The organization plans to sponsor joint satellite-launching missions by 1967.	World Council of Churches announces that five USSR churches have applied for membership.	June 14
Justice Dept. files suit in U.S. district court in Mobile, Ala. to bar Choctaw County voter-registration officials from discriminating against Negroes. It is the 28th voting suit brought by the Justice Department under the Civil Rights Acts of 1957 and 1960.					June 15
Delegates to the Massachusetts Republican state convention endorse Edward Brooke, a Negro, as their nominee for state attorney general.					June 16
				Jack Nicklaus, 22, defeats Arnold Palmer in an 18-hole play-off to win the 62d U.S. Open golf championship in Oakmont, Pa. . . . Brazil defeats Czechoslovakia, 3-1, to retain the World Soccer Cup in Santiago, Chile.	June 17
	Air Force launches a satellite of undisclosed mission from Vandenberg Air Force base in California. It is the third secret satellite launched by the Air Force since May 15.	Supreme Court rules that federal courts have no power to bar a strike called in violation of a labor contract's no-strike pledge.	NASA scientists successfully orbit Tiros V, a 286-pound meteorological satellite designed to gather data on the origin and development of hurricanes and other tropical storms.		June 18

F	G	H	I	J
Includes elections, federal-state relations, civil rights and liberties, crime, the judiciary, education, health care, poverty, urban affairs and population.	Includes formation and debate of U.S. foreign and defense policies, veterans' affairs and defense spending. (Relations with specific foreign countries are usually found under the region concerned.)	Includes business, labor, agriculture, taxation, transportation, consumer affairs, monetary and fiscal policy, natural resources, and pollution.	Includes worldwide scientific, medical and technological developments, natural phenomena, U.S. weather, natural disasters, and accidents.	Includes the arts, religion, scholarship, communications media, sports, entertainment, fashions, fads and social life.

	World Affairs	Europe	Africa & the Middle East	The Americas	Asia & the Pacific
June 19		Soviet Premier Khrushchev, speaking to railway workers during a visit to Bucharest, Rumania, renews past threats to sign a separate peace treaty with East Germany if the West refuses to participate in a general German peace settlement. Observers regard the speech as a confirmation that recent Berlin border incidents have rekindled major East-West tensions over Germany. . . . U.S. State Secy. Rusk arrives in Paris on a scheduled 10-day European trip devoted to the military and political problems facing the NATO alliance.	Rightwing terrorist attacks against Moslems are launched in Oran, Bone and other Algerian cities in defiance of the Secret Army truce pledge proclaimed June 17 in Algiers.	Argentine sources report a widespread outbreak of anti-Jewish acts dating from the May 31 execution of Adolf Eichmann in Israel.	India makes public a June 6 protest note accusing the Communist Chinese of "daily intruding into Indian territory" and constructing new military bases in Indian-claimed sectors of Kashmir. . . . Thailand announces that it will boycott all meetings of SEATO in retaliation for alleged U.S. favoritism toward Cambodia in a recent Thai-Cambodian border dispute.
June 20		West Berlin police begin building a system of trenches, barricades, and earthworks along the Berlin Wall, matching similar fortifications begun earlier in the week by East German authorities. . . . Following two days of talks in Paris, State Secy. Rusk flies to West Berlin to demonstrate America's continuing commitment to the city's freedom. Rusk says the Berlin Wall "will be broken eventually."	International Commission of Jurists denounces South Africa's proposed anti-subversion bill as the "culmination of a determined and ruthless attempt to enforce the doctrine of apartheid."	Following a series of Mexico City conferences, Pres. Kennedy and Pres. Adolfo Lopez Mateos issue a joint communique declaring that "a new era of understanding and friendship" has been reached between Mexico and the U.S.	The New York Times reports a massive build-up of Communist troops in Fukien Province opposite the Chinese Nationalist-held islands of Quemoy and Matsu.
June 21					
June 22			Imprisoned Secret Army Organization leader Raoul Salan publicly appeals to his former comrads to halt their terror campaign and accept the June 17 Algiers truce accord.		Laos' new coalition government, headed by Prince Souvanna Phouma is formally installed in ceremonies at Vientiane. In his inaugural address Premier Souvanna Phouma pledges to direct the government toward a policy of strict neutrality. . . . USSR casts its 100th U.N. veto to block implementation of a Security Counsel resolution urging Indian-Pakistani negotiations over disputed Kashmir.
June 23		Bonn sources report that West Germany has agreed to support continuation of U.S.-Soviet contacts over Berlin in exchange for a U.S. pledge not to renew its proposals for international Berlin access authority. The agreement was reportedly reached in talks between West German leaders and U.S. State Secy. Rusk.	Syrian Premier Bashir al-Azmah withdraws his June 6 proposal for a restoration of Syria's union with the UAR, explaining that his earlier suggestion may not have had the full support of Syrian public opinion.		Communist Chinese officials publicly acknowledge the current military build-up in South China. They describe the action as a response to preparations for a U.S.-sponsored invasion of the China mainland from Formosa.
June 24					Dutch military sources report that small bands of Indonesian invaders are continuing to land in Netherlands New Guinea.
June 25		U.S., Britain and France call on the USSR to join in four-power talks aimed at ending the current wave of violence along the Berlin Wall.	Algerian sources report that the collapse of the June 18 Secret Army truce pledge and the renewal of violence has accelerated the near-panic exodus of Algeria's Europeans. Nearly 300,000 of the 1,000,000-member European community have left the country in the last three months.		

A	B	C	D	E
Includes developments that affect more than one world region, international organizations and important meetings of major world leaders.	Includes all domestic and regional developments in Europe, including the Soviet Union, Turkey, Cyprus and Malta.	Includes all domestic and regional developments in Africa and the Middle East, including Iraq and Iran and excluding Cyprus, Turkey and Afghanistan.	Includes all domestic and regional developments in Latin America, the Caribbean and Canada.	Includes all domestic and regional developments in Asia and Pacific nations, extending from Afghanistan through all the Pacific Islands, except Hawaii.

U.S. Politics & Social Issues	U.S. Foreign Policy & Defense	U.S. Economy & Environment	Science, Technology & Nature	Culture, Leisure & Life Style	
A three-judge federal court in Oklahoma City overturns Oklahoma's legislative apportionment laws, ruling that they unconstitutionally discriminate against urban residents. . . . NAACP files suit in U.S. district court in Atlanta to end alleged segregation in patient-care and medical training at tax-supported city hospitals.	U.S. scientists fail in their second attempt to detonate a missile-borne nuclear device over the Johnston Island proving grounds in the central Pacific. An unspecified malfunction in the missile system forced destruction of the nuclear device prior to detonation.	Commissioner of Labor Statistics Ewan Clague is reported to have told an Atlantic City, N.J. audience that recent economic trends indicate a possible recession in 1963. . . . A bill (HR 10788) extending the President's authority to regulate imports of textiles and agricultural products is signed by Pres. Kennedy.			June 19
		Commerce Dept. reports that the deficit in the U.S. balance of payments dropped from an annual rate of $5.6 billion last quarter of 1961 to a $1.9 billion rate in the first quarter of 1962.			June 20
The administration's farm bill (HR 11222) to provide permanent supply-management controls for wheat and other feed-grains is defeated in the House by a vote of 215-205. White House Press Secy. Pierre Salinger terms the unexpected defeat a "staggering setback."		A West coast seamen's strike that had been halted in April by a Taft-Hartley injunction is settled nine days before the injunction's expiration date. Kennedy administration representatives played a prominent role in the final negotiations.			June 21
A three-judge U.S. court in Nashville, Tenn. rules that the reapportionment of Tennessee's two legislative houses must be based "on numbers of qualified voters without regard to any other factor."	In a political speech attacking the Kennedy administration, ex-Pres. Eisenhower unexpectedly criticizes the current heavy military expenditures generally favored by both Republican and Democratic leaders.	Ex-Pres. Eisenhower denounces the Kennedy administration for undermining "confidence" in the nation's economy through its excessive spending, deficit budgeting and hostility to the business and professional community.	In a presentation to the annual meeting of the American Medical Association, researchers from the Naval Medical Research Institute (Bethesda, Md.) describe the successful testing of a chemical "pacemaker," a capsule containing thyroid hormone that successfully stimulated natural electrical activity in a dog's heart.	St. Louis Cardinal veteran Stan Musial, 41, breaks the late Ty Cobb's major league record of 5,863 career total bases.	June 22
	Pres. Kennedy appoints a special advisory committee to study ways to combat racial discrimination in the armed forces.			Harold Johnson of Philadelphia retains the world light-heavyweight championship by scoring a 15-round decision over Gustav Scholz of West Germany.	June 23
				Phil Hill of the U.S. and Oliver Gendebien of Belgium win the 24-hour Le Mans (France) endurance race for the third time.	June 24
Supreme Court rules 6 to 1 that the use of an official prayer in New York state public schools is an unconstitutional violation of the First Amendment's clause forbidding the "establishment of religion.". . . Fifth Circuit Court in New Orleans issues an injunction to compel the all-white University of Mississippi to admit Negro applicant James Meredith. The court ruled that Meredith had been denied entry "solely because he was a Negro."	Washington sources report that the Kennedy administration has reluctantly approved Defense Dept. requests for the test detonation of two small nuclear devices in the atmosphere at the AEC's Nevada proving grounds. If carried out, they will mark the first atmospheric test conducted on the U.S. mainland since the resumption of U.S. nuclear testing.	Senate Permanent Investigation Subcommittee, in a report on hearings conducted in 1961, accuses Teamsters' Pres. James Hoffa of a "defiant indifference" to corruption and dishonesty in the management of Teamsters locals. Hoffa denounces the report as a "lie."			June 25

F	G	H	I	J
Includes elections, federal-state relations, civil rights and liberties, crime, the judiciary, education, health care, poverty, urban affairs and population.	Includes formation and debate of U.S. foreign and defense policies, veterans' affairs and defense spending. (Relations with specific foreign countries are usually found under the region concerned.)	Includes business, labor, agriculture, taxation, transportation, consumer affairs, monetary and fiscal policy, natural resources, and pollution.	Includes worldwide scientific, medical and technological developments, natural phenomena, U.S. weather, natural disasters, and accidents.	Includes the arts, religion, scholarship, communications media, sports, entertainment, fashions, fads and social life.

	World Affairs	Europe	Africa & the Middle East	The Americas	Asia & the Pacific
June 26				A private committee of prominent U.S. citizens is formed in New York to raise the $62 million demanded by the Cuban government as a ransom for the 1,178 prisoners captured in the 1961 Bay of Pigs invasion.	British North Borneo is formally claimed by the Philippines in a public statement by Pres. Diosdado Macapagal. The British Foreign Office rejects the claim.
June 27		Pres. Kennedy tells a Washington news conference that the U.S. cannot maintain large troop commitments in Europe indefinitely, but denies that there are any imminent plans for a troop-level reduction.			Pres. Kennedy issues a statement warning that the U.S. is prepared to respond to any Communist Chinese action against the islands of Quemoy and Matsu which appears to threaten Formosa.
June 28	U.N. General Assembly's 16th session, the longest in its history, ends after delegates voted to approve the independence of Ruanda-Urundi as two separate nations.	U.S. State Secy. Rusk meets with Portuguese Premier Antonio Salazar in Lisbon to discuss Portuguese objections to U.S. policy regarding Goa and Angola.			
June 29			Algerian sources report that the waning terrorist campaign conducted by extremist elements in the Secret Army Organization has apparently come to an end. No attacks have been reported since June 27. . . . An agreement to grant Uganda independence on October 9, 1962 is announced by British colonial officials in London.	Peruvian election officials announce that none of the three principal presidential candidates in the June 10 balloting received the one-third of the votes required for election. Choice of a president will be left to the new Congress scheduled to convene July 28.	
June 30					
July 1		Tariffs on industrial and other non-farm trade among the six EEC members are reduced 10%, bringing tariff levels down to 50% of what they were when the cuts began in 1959.	Five million Moslems and several thousand Europeans cast their ballots in a special nationwide referendum on whether Algeria shall become an independent nation; an overwhelmingly affirmative vote is expected.	Over 850 of Saskatchewan's 900 doctors go on strike to protest the institution of a provincial compulsory medical-care plan modeled after the British National Health Service. . . . Cuban military spokesmen charge that U.S. Navy aircraft carried out at least nine "spy flights" over Cuba during the last week of June. . . . Lt. Col. Julio Adalberto Rivera is inaugurated as president of El Salvador.	U.S. begins recalling some of the 1,800 marines sent to Thailand at the height of the recent Laotian crisis. . . . Japan's ruling Liberal-Democratic Party retains control of Parliament in nationwide elections.

A	B	C	D	E
Includes developments that affect more than one world region, international organizations and important meetings of major world leaders.	Includes all domestic and regional developments in Europe, including the Soviet Union, Turkey, Cyprus and Malta.	Includes all domestic and regional developments in Africa and the Middle East, including Iraq and Iran and excluding Cyprus, Turkey and Afghanistan.	Includes all domestic and regional developments in Latin America, the Caribbean and Canada.	Includes all domestic and regional developments in Asia and Pacific nations, extending from Afghanistan through all the Pacific Islands, except Hawaii.

U.S. Politics & Social Issues	U.S. Foreign Policy & Defense	U.S. Economy & Environment	Science, Technology & Nature	Culture, Leisure & Life Style	
Yesterday's Supreme Court decision against school prayer is denounced in Congress and bills to amend the Constitution to permit such prayers are introduced in both houses. Rep. Emanuel Celler (D,N.Y.) is as yet the only congressman to publicly defend the court's decision.			Dr. Irving Cooper reports at the American Medical Association meeting in Chicago that he has achieved success in a new bloodless brain surgery technique used on victims of Parkinson's Disease.		June 26
Pres. Kennedy tells a Washington news conference that the Supreme Court's June 25 school prayer decision should be welcomed as a reminder of the need for more prayer in American homes and greater church participation. Former Presidents Eisenhower and Hoover earlier issued statements critical of the ruling. . . . Senate Permanent Investigations Subcommittee headed by Sen. John McClellan (D, Ark.) begins hearings into the grain storage and cotton allotment dealings of indicted Texas financier Billie Sol Estes.	Pres. Kennedy, responding to ex-Pres. Eisenhower's recent defense spending criticism, says that current defense expenditures are necessitated by the fact that "we live in a very dangerous world."	Census Bureau reports that U.S. outlays for new construction reached record levels for the fourth consecutive month.	American Medical Association's House of Delegates meeting in Chicago, refuses to issue a statement on the effects of smoking on human health.		June 27
A N.Y. Supreme Court jury votes a $3.5 million libel award to John Henry Faulk, radio and TV performer who charged he had been blacklisted from the entire broadcast industry since 1957 because an Aware, Inc. bulletin had libelously characterized him as pro-communist. . . . About 8,000 New Yorkers attend an anti-communist rally in Madison Square Garden sponsored by the Christian Anti-Communism Crusade.	Administration's Migration and Refugee Assistance Act of 1962 is signed by Pres. Kennedy. The measure liberalizes admission quotas for foreign refugees and authorizes aid to Cuban refugees living in the U.S. . . . Convicted spy Dr. Robert Soblen, who fled the U.S. on June 23 to escape a life sentence, is arrested in Tel Aviv by Israeli police.	House, by a 298-125 vote, passes and sends to the Senate the administration's Trade Expansion Act of 1962 (HR 11970). . . . Five major U.S. aluminum companys sign a two-year contract with the AFL-CIO United Steelworkers of America providing for improved fringe benefits but no wage increase.			June 28
Twenty-one Democratic and five Republican Senators introduce an administration-supported compromise medical-care program which would provide elderly persons with insurance coverage for hospital costs, but not doctor bills.		U.S. Chamber of Commerce advocates an immediate cut in corporate and personal income tax rates to stimulate a full economic recovery. AFL-CIO Pres. George Meany had earlier endorsed a tax cut aimed especially at lower and middle income brackets. . . . Station WHCT-T.V. (Channel 18) in Hartford, Conn. begins pay-T.V. broadcasting as part of a three-year trial project.			June 29
				Vatican formally censures *The Phenomenon of Man* a book by the late French Jesuit paleontologist Father Pierre Teilhard de Chardin in which he sought to reconcile Catholic dogma with scientific discoveries relating to human evolution. . . . Los Angeles Dodger pitcher Sandy Koufax throws a 5-0 no-hit victory over the New York Mets.	June 30
	Convicted U.S. spy Dr. Robert Soblen is hospitalized in London after attempting to commit suicide while being flown from Israel to the U.S. where he is scheduled to begin a life sentence. . . . Pres. Kennedy signs a bill (S 3161) extending the Export Control Act of 1949 which authorizies the President to bar any exports considered detrimental to U.S. security.	Pres. Kennedy signs into law a bill (HR 11990) raising the temporary federal debt ceiling from $300 billion to $380 billion.	The Children's Bureau of HEW begins a mass infant screening program employing a new test to detect phyenylketonuria, a congential metabolic disorder leading to mental retardation. . . . *Physical Review Letters* reports the discovery by researchers at Brookhaven National Laboratory of two slightly differing kinds of neutrino—a nuclear particle with no mass or electrical charge.	Al Oerter sets a world discus record of 204 ft. 10 1/2 in. in a U.S. - Poland dual meet in Chicago.	July 1

F	G	H	I	J
Includes elections, federal-state relations, civil rights and liberties, crime, the judiciary, education, health care, poverty, urban affairs and population.	Includes formation and debate of U.S. foreign and defense policies, veterans' affairs and defense spending. (Relations with specific foreign countries are usually found under the region concerned.)	Includes business, labor, agriculture, taxation, transportation, consumer affairs, monetary and fiscal policy, natural resources, and pollution.	Includes worldwide scientific, medical and technological developments, natural phenomena, U.S. weather, natural disasters, and accidents.	Includes the arts, religion, scholarship, communications media, sports, entertainment, fashions, fads and social life.

	World Affairs	Europe	Africa & the Middle East	The Americas	Asia & the Pacific
July 2		Chancellor Adenauer arrives in Paris to begin the first major tour of France by a German head of state since World War II. The trip is viewed as a demonstration of the growing French-West German agreement on the creation of a new federated European unity.			The 13-nation Geneva conference on Laos reconvenes in an effort to seek a final accord on the independence and neutrality of Laos' new coalition government. . . . Soviet Premier Khrushchev pledges that the USSR will aid Communist China in repelling an attack that he says is being prepared by the Nationalist Chinese with the support of "aggressive" circles in the U.S.
July 3			Algeria's Electoral Control Commission reports that final official returns from the July 1 self-determination referendum show 5,975,581 votes in favor of independence, 16,534 against. Following the announcement French Pres. de Gaulle issues a proclamation recognizing the full independence of Algeria after 132 years of French rule. . . . De Gaulle also authorizes the transfer of sovereignty to the Algerian Provisional Executive pending the formation of a permanent Algerian government.		
July 4		In a radio TV address Pres. Kennedy proclaims America's readiness to join a newly united Europe in building a "concrete Atlantic partnership" of "full equality."	Algerian sources report that independence has intensified an internal political struggle between moderate elements headed by Algerian Provisional Government Premier Ben-Youssef Ben Khedda and leftist militants led by Mohammed Ben Bella. . . . Israeli and Jordanian soldiers briefly exchange gunfire across the Jerusalem border; at least five persons are killed.		
July 5			Mass celebrations hailing Algeria's independence are abruptly halted in Oran after fierce fighting erupts between Moslems and Europeans. Over 70 Moslems and more than 20 Europeans are reported killed in the clashes.		
July 6				Food shortages allegedly caused by the Brazilian government's anti-inflation programs provoke riots in Rio de Janeiro. At least 10 persons have been killed in the disorders.	Talduwe Thero, a Buddhist monk turned Christian, is executed in Ceylon for the September 1959 assassination of Premier Solomon Bandaranaike.
July 7				Cuban government discloses plans to reduce Havanna University Medical School's course from six years to five in an effort to meet the island's critical doctor shortage.	Seventeen persons are killed as Burmese troops fire on a crowd of 2,000 Rangoon University students demonstrating against a new dormitory curfew.
July 8					Communist China formally protests an alleged July 6 intrusion by Indian troops into disputed territory along India's border with the Sinkiang region of China. India dismisses the protest as a cover for alleged Chinese advances.

A	B	C	D	E
Includes developments that affect more than one world region, international organizations and important meetings of major world leaders.	Includes all domestic and regional developments in Europe, including the Soviet Union, Turkey, Cyprus and Malta.	Includes all domestic and regional developments in Africa and the Middle East, including Iraq and Iran and excluding Cyprus, Turkey and Afghanistan.	Includes all domestic and regional developments in Latin America, the Caribbean and Canada.	Includes all domestic and regional developments in Asia and Pacific nations, extending from Afghanistan through all the Pacific Islands, except Hawaii.

U.S. Politics & Social Issues	U.S. Foreign Policy & Defense	U.S. Economy & Environment	Science, Technology & Nature	Culture, Leisure & Life Style	
		Wall Street Journal reports that the U.S. cost of living has increased 13% over the last 10 years, the lowest decade increase of any major Western industrial country.			July 2
					July 3
The nation's governors end a four-day annual conference in Hershey, Pa. after failing to agree on resolutions concerning civil rights or the administration's aged-medical-care proposals.				British yachtsman Francis Chichester, piloting the Gypsy Moth III, sets a 33-day record for a trans-Atlantic solo voyage.	July 4
Pres. Kennedy tells Washington reporters that he cannot understand the American Medical Association's continuing opposition to a new compromise medical-care program which would not directly affect the doctor-patient relationship.	Pres. Kennedy names Asst. State Secy. Foy Kohler to succeed. Llewellyn Thompson as amb.-to-the-USSR. Thompson is to become an adviser on Soviet affairs to the State Dept.	Pres. Kennedy tells reporters that the administration's plans for a tax cut next year may be moved up sooner if economic trends appear to warrant faster action.		Pope John XXIII issues an encyclical expressing hope that the forthcoming ecumenical council, to open in Rome October 11, will contribute to the reunification of all Christians within the Roman Catholic Church.	July 5
	The first hydrogen device ever tested in the continental U.S. is detonated underground at the AEC's Nevada proving grounds.	The 813,000-member National Education Association concludes a week-long convention in Denver after adopting a resolution favoring "professional negotiations" rather than collective bargaining to settle disputes with school boards.		Rod Laver defeats Martin Mulligan to win the men's singles finals of the All-England tennis tourney in Wimbledon. . . . American novelist William Faulkner, 64, recipient of the 1949 Nobel Prize for literature, dies of a heart attack in Oxford, Mississippi. . . . Japan wins the men's team title in the world gymnastics championships held in Prague, Czechoslovakia.	July 6
	AEC announces the detonation of a low-yield nuclear device in the atmosphere above its Nevada proving grounds. It is the first atmospheric test to be carried out in the U.S. since October 1958. . . . Defense Dept. reports that the Project Vela underground detection research program has begun to yield significant improvements in the U.S.'s test-detection capability.	Defense Secy. McNamara informs Pres. Kennedy in a published memo that newly instituted reforms in department management and in military procurement procedures would save $15 billion over the next five years.	A Soviet E-166 sets a world jet-speed record of 1,652 mph in a test near Moscow.	Karen Susman, of Chula Vista, Calif. wins the women's singles title at Wimbledon.	July 7
HEW Secy. Abraham Ribicoff announces plans for a major government-sponsored study of the impact of T.V. on child behavior.				Pres. Kennedy describes as "shocking" a June 21 report of his Council on Youth Fitness indicating that almost half of American children cannot reach satisfactory levels on a basic physical fitness test.	July 8

F	G	H	I	J
Includes elections, federal-state relations, civil rights and liberties, crime, the judiciary, education, health care, poverty, urban affairs and population.	*Includes formation and debate of U.S. foreign and defense policies, veterans' affairs and defense spending. (Relations with specific foreign countries are usually found under the region concerned.)*	*Includes business, labor, agriculture, taxation, transportation, consumer affairs, monetary and fiscal policy, natural resources, and pollution.*	*Includes worldwide scientific, medical and technological developments, natural phenomena, U.S. weather, natural disasters, and accidents.*	*Includes the arts, religion, scholarship, communications media, sports, entertainment, fashions, fads and social life.*

	World Affairs	Europe	Africa & the Middle East	The Americas	Asia & the Pacific
July 9	U.S. successfully tests a missile-borne thermonuclear device at an altitude of 200 miles over its testing range in the central Pacific. The detonation produces spectacular visual displays visible for thousands of miles.	Almost 7,500 of the 40,000 U.S. reserve troops sent to Germany at the peak of the 1961 Berlin crisis are returned to the U.S.			The 14 nations attending the Geneva conference on Laos reach preliminary agreement on a Laotian neutrality declaration. The accord bars Laotian participation in any political and military alliances and prohibits use of Laotian territory by foreign armed forces.
July 10	Soviet Premier Khrushchev denounces the U.S.'s high altitude nuclear tests as a "challenge to mankind" which may have "very dangerous consequences for the conditions of man's life."	A proposal by Soviet Premier Khrushchev that the Western allies agree to the replacement of their occupation forces in West Berlin with U.N.-supervised troops drawn from smaller NATO and Warsaw Pact states is immediately rejected by the U.S. State Department. . . . West German Chancellor Adenauer tells reporters that his recent French visit had cemented the two countries' common front against "the spread of communism in Europe."	Representatives of Premier Ben Khedda's Algerian Provisional Government meet in Rabat, Morocco with dissident leader Mohammed Ben Bella in an unsuccessful effort to reach a political reconciliation between moderate and extremist factions of the Moslem nationalist movement.	Brazilian Chamber of Deputies confirms Social Democrat Francisco Brochado da Rocha as premier of Brazil.	Indian health officials say that nearly 450 persons have died in a two-week cholera epidemic in Calcutta. . . . Japanese Justice Ministry estimates membership in the Japanese CP at 90,000, up 10% from 1961. . . . Kim Hyun Chul is appointed premier of South Korea replacing junta chairman Gen. Chung Hee Park, who had temporarily assumed the post following the resignation of Song Yo Chan on June 16.
July 11		West Germany announces the "compulsory retirement" of Chief Prosecutor Wolfgang Fraenkel following a parliamentary investigation into his role as a member of the Nazi prosecutor's office during W.W. II.	Mohammed Ben Bella returns to Algeria to take personal command of the dissident forces opposed to the Ben Khedda government.		
July 12	U.S. State Secy. Rusk tells Washington reporters that recently achieved improvements in nuclear test-detection techniques may help reduce U.S.-Soviet differences on a test-ban treaty. . . . U.S. AEC announces that the series of 26 nuclear tests begun April 25 in the vicinity of Christmas Island has ended. No mention is made of the high-altitude nuclear tests underway at Johnston Island.	USSR issues a statement renewing its threat to sign a separate East German peace treaty if the West refuses Soviet demands for a withdrawal of occupation forces from West Berlin.			
July 13	Soviet Premier Khrushchev says the USSR may be forced to start another series of nuclear tests unless the U.S. quickly agrees to Soviet disarmament and atomic-ban proposals.	British P.M. Macmillan announces a major revision of his cabinet following a series of Conservative defeats in recent by-elections.		Official sources in Moscow report that Cuba's trade with the USSR totalled 529 million rubles in 1961, almost three times greater than the total trade in 1960.	France formally relinquishes control over four small Indian coastal enclaves in accordance with a 1956 French-Indian agreement.
July 14	Pres. Kennedy appeals for sincere Soviet cooperation in the forthcoming resumption of Geneva disarmament talks scheduled for July 16.				
July 15		Sir Barnett Janner, a leader of Britain's Jewish community, charges that a recent Soviet crack-down on "economic crimes" displayed a "distinct anti-Jewish bias." Janner cites the disproportionately large number of Jews among those sentenced to death for such crimes as embezzlement, currency speculation, and black-marketing.			
July 16	The New York Times publishes a study showing that only 18 of the U.N.'s 104 member states have fully paid their assessments for the U.N. forces in the Congo and the Middle East. The USSR tops the list of debtor states with arrears totaling $56 million.			Peruvian military leaders demand that the government cancel the results of the indecisive June 10 presidential elections. The cabinet of Pres. Manuel Prado y Ugarteche resigns after rejecting the demand.	
	A	B	C	D	E
	Includes developments that affect more than one world region, international organizations and important meetings of major world leaders.	Includes all domestic and regional developments in Europe, including the Soviet Union, Turkey, Cyprus and Malta.	Includes all domestic and regional developments in Africa and the Middle East, including Iraq and Iran and excluding Cyprus, Turkey and Afghanistan.	Includes all domestic and regional developments in Latin America, the Caribbean and Canada.	Includes all domestic and regional developments in Asia and Pacific nations, extending from Afghanistan through all the Pacific Islands, except Hawaii.

U.S. Politics & Social Issues	U.S. Foreign Policy & Defense	U.S. Economy & Environment	Science, Technology & Nature	Culture, Leisure & Life Style	
		Federal Reserve Board cuts the margin required for stock purchases from 70% to 50%.			July 9
			The world's first privately-owned earth satellite, a Telstar sphere built by the American Telephone & Telegraph Co., successfully relays TV pictures from the U.S. to Europe. The satellite was launched earlier in the day by NASA from Cape Canaveral.	World Council of Churches announces the receipt of an invitation to send observers to the October ecumenical council of the Roman Catholic Church. . . . National League defeats the American League to win the first game of major league baseball's two-game All-Star series. . . . Thirty-five French impressionist paintings, valued at nearly $1,000,000, are stolen from the O'Hana Art Gallery in London in the largest art theft in British history.	July 10
		Pres. Kennedy announces an immediate revision of federal tax depreciation schedules aimed at reducing business taxes by up to $1.5 billion in the coming year. . . . Pres. Kennedy signs a bill (HR 8031) giving the FCC authority to require TV manufacturers to equip sets to receive 70 ultra-high-frequency (UHF) channels.	A seven-minute TV program featuring prominent French entertainers is transmitted from France to the U.S. via the new Telstar satellite.	Scuba-diver Fred Baldasare of Calif. becomes the first person to swim the English Channel underwater.	July 11
FBI Director J. Edgar Hoover estimates that a record 1,926,090 major crimes were committed in the U.S. in 1961, up 3% over 1960. Seventy-one policemen were killed during the year, according to Hoover's report. . . . HEW Secy. Abraham Ribicoff resigns to become a Democratic candidate for the Senate from Connecticut.	House passes the administration's $4.688 billion foreign aid authorization bill (HR 11921) for fiscal 1963 after rejecting amendments that would have prohibited any aid to communist nations.				July 12
				Arnold Palmer shoots a record 276 to win his second straight British Open golf championship in Troon, Scotland. . . . Emile Griffith retains the world-welterweight championship in a 15-round decision over Ralph Dupas in Las Vegas.	July 13
Pres. Kennedy nominates Cleveland Mayor Anthony Celebrezze to succeed Abraham Ribicoff as HEW Secretary.		Pres. Kennedy signs a bill (HR 12154) revising the provisions of the Sugar Act and extending them through 1966.		Argentine model Norma Beatriz Nolan, 24, is named Miss Universe of 1962.	July 14
				Jacques Anquetil, of France, wins the 22-day Tour de France bicycle race for the second straight year.	July 15
					July 16

F	G	H	I	J
Includes elections, federal-state relations, civil rights and liberties, crime, the judiciary, education, health care, poverty, urban affairs and population.	Includes formation and debate of U.S. foreign and defense policies, veterans' affairs and defense spending. (Relations with specific foreign countries are usually found under the region concerned.)	Includes business, labor, agriculture, taxation, transportation, consumer affairs, monetary and fiscal policy, natural resources, and pollution.	Includes worldwide scientific, medical and technological developments, natural phenomena, U.S. weather, natural disasters, and accidents.	Includes the arts, religion, scholarship, communications media, sports, entertainment, fashions, fads and social life.

	World Affairs	Europe	Africa & the Middle East	The Americas	Asia & the Pacific
July 17	Arthur Lall, India's chief delegate to the Geneva disarmament conference, accuses the U.S. and the USSR of ignoring neutralist proposals for a nuclear test-ban, adding that he has become "skeptical" about the great powers' professed desire for a test accord. . . . A coroner's investigation in Northern Rhodesia rules that the September 18, 1961 death of U.N. Secy. Gen. Dag Hammarskjold was accidental.		An Israeli official reports that Israel and Jordan have decided to set up a joint committee to seek ways of preventing further clashes along the Jerusalem border.		
July 18		Soviet news agency *Tass* reports the appointment of Veniamin Dymshits, a Jew, as a deputy premier. Dymshits is the first Jew to hold a leading Soviet government position since the ouster of Deputy Premier Lazar Kaganovich in 1957.	A mob of nearly 10,000 Katangan women attack Indian U.N. troops stationed in Elizabethville.	A military junta overthrows the Peruvian government in a bloodless coup. The junta immediately voids the June 10 presidential election results and promises new elections in June 1963. The U.S. and several other American states sever relations with Peru in protest against the coup.	
July 19	Chief U.S. delegate Arthur Dean urges the Geneva disarmament conference to begin immediate work on measures to curtail the threat of war "by accident . . . or failure of communications."	East Germany closes its entire Baltic coast to all unauthorized persons in an effort to curb the growing number of sea-escapes to West Germany.	Assadollah Alam is appointed premier of Iran, succeeding Dr. Ali Amini. Amini resigned July 17 after failing to reduce Iran's $70 million budget deficit.	U.S. State Dept. announces an immediate suspension of economic and military aid to Peru. The action comes after Pres. Kennedy denounced the recent military coup in Peru as a "serious setback" to self-determination in the Americas.	
July 20	International Court of Justice at The Hague rules that all U.N. member states are legally obligated to share financial support of the U.N. peace forces in the Congo and the Middle East.	*New York Herald Tribune* reports that 11,200 East Germans have escaped to the West since the building of the Berlin Wall in August 1961.	France and Tunisia restore diplomatic relations broken since the July 20, 1961 clash over the French-held Bizerte naval base.		
July 21		Dispatches from the *Tass* news agency indicate that the USSR has successfully tested its first Polaris-type missiles from submerged submarines. . . . French Pres. de Gaulle is reportedly angry over Pres. Kennedy's failure to consult him on the appointment of Gen. Lyman Lemnitzer to replace Gen. Lauris Norstad as Supreme Allied (NATO) Commander.	UAR successfully launches four single-stage rockets at a test-site 50 miles northeast of Cairo. The rockets, reputedly built with the aid of 250 secretly-hired West German rocket experts, are said to have a range of 370 miles.		Dutch and Indonesian negotiators, meeting in the U.S., are reported to have agreed on a plan giving Indonesia administrative control over Netherlands New Guinea by May 1, 1963. . . . Indian and Communist Chinese troops clash briefly at two points in the Ladakh area on the Kashmir-China border.
July 22	USSR announces that it has been forced to order a resumption of nuclear testing as a result of the U.S.'s continued tests.	U.S. State Secy. Rusk meets with Soviet Foreign Min. Gromyko in Geneva in a continuing effort to find a basis of negotiation for a Berlin settlement. No progress is reported.	Mohammed Ben Bella and his supporters issue a declaration in Tlemcen, Algeria proclaiming themselves as the legitimate political leaders of the Moslem nationalist movement.		

A	B	C	D	E
Includes developments that affect more than one world region, international organizations and important meetings of major world leaders.	Includes all domestic and regional developments in Europe, including the Soviet Union, Turkey, Cyprus and Malta.	Includes all domestic and regional developments in Africa and the Middle East, including Iraq and Iran and excluding Cyprus, Turkey and Afghanistan.	Includes all domestic and regional developments in Latin America, the Caribbean and Canada.	Includes all domestic and regional developments in Asia and Pacific nations, extending from Afghanistan through all the Pacific Islands, except Hawaii.

U.S. Politics & Social Issues	U.S. Foreign Policy & Defense	U.S. Economy & Environment	Science, Technology & Nature	Culture, Leisure & Life Style	
A compromise version of the administration's medical-care-for-the-aged program is killed by a 52-48 Senate vote to table the measure for the remainder of the current session.	A tactical nuclear weapon, presumably the "Davy Crockett" nuclear mortar shell, is tested in the atmosphere under simulated battle conditions at the AEC's Nevada proving grounds.	Federal Reserve Board Chmn. William McChesney Martin tells a House committee that despite "a lot of pessimism" the U.S. is not in a recession.	Maj. Robert White pilots the U.S. X-15 rocket plane to an altitude of slightly more than 59.6 miles, marking the first time a winged vehicle had gone above 50 miles and thus achieved space flight.		July 17
	Defense Dept. announces the cancellation of a Navy project to build the world's largest moveable radio telescope in Sugar Grove, W. Va. The decision is attributed to unexpectedly high costs and to advances in satellite technology.	A Consumers Advisory Council is appointed by Pres. Kennedy to watch over consumers' interests.	French-born engineer Eugene Houtery, 70, inventor of the catalytic cracking process for producing gasoline, dies in Philadelphia, Pa.		July 18
		Treasury Dept. reports that the fiscal 1962 U.S. government deficit totalled $6.3 billion, second only to 1959's record peacetime deficit of $12.4 billion. . . . A farm bill (HR 12391), introduced as a substitute for the administration's previously defeated bill (HR 11222), is passed by the House and then sent to the Senate. The new bill extends current temporary wheat and feed-grains programs for another year.			July 19
	White House announces that Gen. Lyman Lemnitzer will succeed retiring Gen. Lauris Norstad as Supreme Allied (NATO) Commander and as commander-in-chief of U.S. forces in Europe. Gen. Maxwell Taylor will succeed Lemnitzer as chairman of the Joint Chiefs of Staff.	President's Council of Economic Advisers estimates that the U.S. GNP rose during the second quarter to an annual rate of $552 billion, up $7 billion from the first quarter but below the Council's January prediction.	Earthquakes in central and western Colombia kill 40 and injure more than 300.	The American League beats the National League, 9-4, to earn a split in this years two-game All-Star series.	July 20
A three-judge federal court in Montgomery orders the immediate reapportionment of the Alabama legislature under a temporary court-drafted plan. The decision marks the first reapportionment by a federal court since the March Supreme Court ruling that federal courts had jurisdiction in such cases.	Rep. Robert Kastenmeier (D, Wis.) charges in a letter to Pres. Kennedy that U.S. servicemen in Vietnam have condoned torture of Viet Cong prisoners. He asks action to halt the practice.	A threatened aerospace strike by AFL-CIO Machinists and the UAW is averted as both unions agree to comply with Pres. Kennedy's request not to strike for 60 days.		British social historian G.M. Trevelyan dies in Cambridge at the age of 86. . . . Scottish auto racer Jim Clark wins the British Grand Prix at Aintree, England.	July 21
Federal Bureau of Prisons reports that 42 persons were executed in the U.S. in 1961.		Swedish economist Dr. Gunnar Myrdal, in a *New York Times* interview, asserts that the U.S. will have to employ deficit spending and a tax cut if it is to cope with the current "stagnation crisis" in its economy.	The U.S.'s first attempt to send a space probe toward Venus fails as the Atlas-Agena-B booster bearing the Mariner I craft veers off-course shortly after launch. . . . Soviet Public Health Min. Sergei Kurashov tells over 5,000 delegates attending an International Congress on Cancer, in Moscow, that the "medical world" should be the loudest voice against radioactive fall-out. Gary Player wins the 44th Professional Golfers Association tournament in Newtown Square, Pa. . . . Valeri Brumel of the USSR sets a world high jump record of 7 ft. 5 in. as a U.S. men's team defeats a Soviet team in the fourth U.S.-Soviet track and field competition held in Palo Alto, Calif. The USSR won the women's team title.		July 22

F	G	H	I	J
Includes elections, federal-state relations, civil rights and liberties, crime, the judiciary, education, health care, poverty, urban affairs and population.	Includes formation and debate of U.S. foreign and defense policies, veterans' affairs and defense spending. (Relations with specific foreign countries are usually found under the region concerned.)	Includes business, labor, agriculture, taxation, transportation, consumer affairs, monetary and fiscal policy, natural resources, and pollution.	Includes worldwide scientific, medical and technological developments, natural phenomena, U.S. weather, natural disasters, and accidents.	Includes the arts, religion, scholarship, communications media, sports, entertainment, fashions, fads and social life.

	World Affairs	**Europe**	**Africa & the Middle East**	**The Americas**	**Asia & the Pacific**
July 23	Moscow sources report that the USSR favors the establishment of direct phone communications between the Kremlin and the White House. . . . Pres. Kennedy, speaking at his regular news conference, warns that the announced resumption of Soviet nuclear tests may force the U.S. to prepare a new series of its own.	Pres. Kennedy tells reporters that he doubts whether the Rusk-Gromyko conversations have contributed significantly toward a Berlin agreement. . . . In a speech to Yugoslavia's CP Central Committee, Pres. Tito says that his government has adopted an excessively liberal attitude toward Yugoslav writers and artists.		Doctors in Saskatchewan, Canada end their 23-day strike against a new provincial medical plan after the government agrees to call a special session of the Legislature to amend the program.	Representatives of the 14 delegations to the Geneva conference on Laos sign a joint protocol guaranteeing the freedom and neutrality of Laos and calling for the rapid withdrawal of all foreign military forces.
July 24	Indian Defense Min. V. K. Krishna Menon urges an immediate East-West agreement to prohibit the spread of nuclear armaments or of the techniques necessary for their development.			Argentine Pres. José Maria Guido issues a decree banning Peronists and Communists from running candidates in presidential and congressional elections. . . . Peru's recently installed military junta issues a decree conferring upon itself all constitutional executive and legislative powers.	
July 25			Fighting breaks out in the Algerian cities of Bone and Constantine between extremist supporters of Mohammed Ben Bella and moderates loyal to Premier Ben Khedda.		
July 26	World Jewish population totals 12.5 million according to estimates in the 1962 *American Jewish Yearbook*. Over 40% of all Jews live in the U.S., with the USSR and Israel having the next largest concentrations.				
July 27		East German State Planning Commission publicly admits that the nation's economy has failed to meet its production goals for foodstuffs, machinery, power and building materials during the first half of 1962.			
July 28		Sweden and Austria, both EFTA members, file applications for associate membership in the EEC.			
July 29		Soviet-sponsored eighth World Festival of Youths for Peace begins in Helsinki amidst angry demonstrations by Finnish anti-communists.	Ghana Pres. Nkrumah calls upon fellow Convention Peoples Party members to "crush" critics of the government's new austerity budget.	Ex-Pres. Manuel Prado y Ugarteche leaves Peru for France after being released by the military junta which deposed him in mid-July. . . . Three prisoners captured in the 1961 Cuban invasion arrive in Miami after friends and family paid $1,750,000 in ransom to the Cuban government.	

A	B	C	D	E
Includes developments that affect more than one world region, international organizations and important meetings of major world leaders.	*Includes all domestic and regional developments in Europe, including the Soviet Union, Turkey, Cyprus and Malta.*	*Includes all domestic and regional developments in Africa and the Middle East, including Iraq and Iran and excluding Cyprus, Turkey and Afghanistan.*	*Includes all domestic and regional developments in Latin America, the Caribbean and Canada.*	*Includes all domestic and regional developments in Asia and Pacific nations, extending from Afghanistan through all the Pacific Islands, except Hawaii.*

U.S. Politics & Social Issues	U.S. Foreign Policy & Defense	U.S. Economy & Environment	Science, Technology & Nature	Culture, Leisure & Life Style	
Pres. Kennedy says at his regular news conference that a Republican victory in the November Congressional elections would mean continued inaction on major administration programs.	Defense Secy. McNamara arrives in Hawaii for two days of strategy talks on South Vietnam. He tells reporters that a victory over the Viet Cong may "take years rather than months," but with U.S. help it can be achieved.				July 23
Pres. Kennedy issues an order to all federal agencies barring discrimination against women in appointments and promotions. . . .					July 24
The administration's welfare reform bill (HR 10606), designed to strengthen the rehabilitative over the strictly relief aspects of the welfare system, is signed by Pres. Kennedy. . . . Pres. Kennedy endorses Puerto Rican Gov. Luis Munoz Marin's plan for a plebiscite in which Puerto Ricans can express their preference for either statehood, independence or a permanent commonwealth association with the U.S.	A *New York Times* article by Homer Bigart asserts that, despite U.S. aid, a South Vietnamese victory over the Viet Cong remains "remote" because of Pres. Diem's failure to win popular support. It is one of several recent articles that appear to question the administration's official optimism regarding the South Vietnamese military situation.			The Soviet government is reported to have decided to permit (for the first time) publication of the late Boris Pasternak's novel *Doctor Zhivago* .	July 25
U.S. District Judge Marion Beatty rules that the apportionment of both houses of the Kansas legislature is unconstitutional. During the past two months state and federal courts have intervened on apportionment questions in all of the following states: Alabama, Florida, Georgia, Kansas, Maryland, Michigan, Oklahoma, Rhode Island, Vermont, and Wisconsin. . . . A U.S. district court in Richmond orders the reopening in September of all Prince Edward County (Va.) public schools "without regard to race."	U.S. fails for the third time in four attempts to conduct a high-altitude test of a missile-borne nuclear device. The failure occurred when the Thor carrier-rocket burst into flames on the Johnston Island launching pad shortly before take-off.	A group of liberal Senators launch a filibuster against a House-passed bill (HR 111040) to charter a private corporation to operate a satellite communications system. The opponents of the bill favor government ownership of the satellite network.	U.S. Public Health Service announces that researchers at the National Institute of Neurological Diseases & Blindness have isolated the virus responsible for German Measles (rubella).		July 26
Senate Judiciary Committee holds hearings on a constitutional amendment offered by Sen. James Eastland (D, Miss.) to permit prayer in public schools.					July 27
		General Electric Co. agrees to pay the federal government a record $7.4 million in damages for settlement of the first of more than 1,600 bid-rigging charges filed against it.	Soviet scientists successfully launch Cosmos VII, a satellite reportedly designed to study radiation, meteorites, and cloud formations.		July 28
					July 29

F	G	H	I	J
Includes elections, federal-state relations, civil rights and liberties, crime, the judiciary, education, health care, poverty, urban affairs and population.	Includes formation and debate of U.S. foreign and defense policies, veterans' affairs and defense spending. (Relations with specific foreign countries are usually found under the region concerned.)	Includes business, labor, agriculture, taxation, transportation, consumer affairs, monetary and fiscal policy, natural resources, and pollution.	Includes worldwide scientific, medical and technological developments, natural phenomena, U.S. weather, natural disasters, and accidents.	Includes the arts, religion, scholarship, communications media, sports, entertainment, fashions, fads and social life.

	World Affairs	Europe	Africa & the Middle East	The Americas	Asia & the Pacific
July 30		U.S. Army helicopters fly over East Berlin in an apparent effort to demonstrate Western air rights over the Soviet occupation sector. The action follows a renewal of alleged harassment by Soviet planes in the Berlin air corridors.			
July 31					British and Malayan negotiators agree in London on the formation of a Federation of Malaysia comprised of Malaya, Singapore, and the three British Southeast Asian protectorates of Brunei, Sarawak, and North Borneo.
Aug. 1	Pres. Kennedy announces that the U.S. is now prepared to accept previously rejected proposals for nationally-manned control posts to monitor an international nuclear test-ban agreement.		An assassin's bomb hurled at a car carrying Ghana Pres. Kwame Nkrumah kills four bystanders and injures 56; Nkrumah escapes unhurt.	Pres. Kennedy tells reporters that the U.S. is withholding recognition of Peru's military junta pending assurances that the new government intends to hold impartial elections. . . . Peronist-dominated labor groups call a two-day general strike to protest the Argentine government's failure to control inflation.	The U.S. House, under strong administration pressure passes a previously defeated bill (HR 11721) to authorize $73 million for Philippine war-damage claims.
Aug. 2		British news sources report that nearly 200 persons have been arrested during the past 10 days because of violence resulting from four fascist demonstrations.	Negotiators for Algeria's rival political factions announce that the moderate Ben Khedda regime has agreed to submit to the authority of a Political Bureau to be named by militant rebel leader Mohammed Ben Bella.		
Aug. 3	Archbishop of Canterbury Dr. Arthur Ramsey, just returned from a Soviet tour, says the Russian Church is thriving despite "intense anti-God propaganda."		Huge crowds turn out to welcome Mohammed Ben Bella as he returns to Algiers for the first time since his 1956 capture by the French.		A team of 30 Australian jungle war experts arrives in South Vietnam to join the U.S. training and advisory units there.
Aug. 4					
Aug. 5	Japanese, Swedish and U.S. scientists report monitoring the explosion of a powerful thermonuclear device in the atmosphere above the USSR's Arctic testing site. The detonation is believed to be the first in a series of new Soviet nuclear tests.	EEC negotiations with Britain on its possible entry into the Common Market are temporarily suspended after participants fail to find a satisfactory tariff formula for dealing with Commonwealth nations farm exports.			
Aug. 6	The U.S.'s recent offer to accept a test-ban agreement policed by nationally-manned detection systems is rejected by the Soviet delegation to the 17-nation Geneva disarmament conference.	East Germany announces quasi-rationing of meat and meat products, lending support to reports that East Germany's food shortage has reached serious dimensions.		Jamaica is proclaimed an independent nation within the British Commonwealth.	Indian P.M. Nehru discloses that Communist China has accepted an Indian offer to resume negotiations over disputed border regions.
	A	**B**	**C**	**D**	**E**
	Includes developments that affect more than one world region, international organizations and important meetings of major world leaders.	Includes all domestic and regional developments in Europe, including the Soviet Union, Turkey, Cyprus and Malta.	Includes all domestic and regional developments in Africa and the Middle East, including Iraq and Iran and excluding Cyprus, Turkey and Afghanistan.	Includes all domestic and regional developments in Latin America, the Caribbean and Canada.	Includes all domestic and regional developments in Asia and Pacific nations, extending from Afghanistan through all the Pacific Islands, except Hawaii.

U.S. Politics & Social Issues	U.S. Foreign Policy & Defense	U.S. Economy & Environment	Science, Technology & Nature	Culture, Leisure & Life Style	
					July 30
Arkansas Democrats renominate Orval Faubus for a fifth term as governor.					**July 31**
	Pres. Kennedy signs into law a fiscal 1963 foreign aid authorization bill (S2996) totaling $4.572 billion, $300,000 less than the administration originally requested. . . . The House cuts the administration's civil defense budget from the $695 million requested to $75 million.	Pres. Kennedy, appearing at his regular news conference, calls for tougher federal drug legislation, citing the tragic thalidomide cases as an example of the need to provide stronger consumer protection.			**Aug. 1**
Ex-N.Y. Supreme Court Justice James Keogh is sentenced to two years in prison on charges of attempting to "fix" a federal court sentence.					**Aug. 2**
	Pres. Kennedy writes congressional leaders asking them to restore fully the administration's requested appropriation for fall-out shelter construction and civil defense.		FDA announces in Washington plans to investigate a possible relationship between the oral contraceptive Enovid and thrombophlebitis, a serious blood vessel-clogging disease.	The NFL-champion Green Bay Packers defeat the College All Stars, 40-20, in Chicago.	**Aug. 3**
	The *U.S.S. James Monroe*, the nation's 12th Polaris missile submarine, is launched at Newport News, Va.				**Aug. 4**
The Saturday Evening Post publishes an article by ex-Pres. Eisenhower attacking the administration for excessive spending and for seeking to centralize power in the federal government.	Air Force launches into polar orbit a secret satellite; it is believed to be the third in a series of military reconnaissance satellite launches which began July 18.			Movie star Marilyn Monroe, 36, is found dead of an overdose of sleeping pills in her Los Angeles home. . . . America of Rio de Janeiro defeats Belenenses of Portugal to win the International Soccer League championship in New York.	**Aug. 5**
U.S. Fifth Circuit Court of Appeals orders implementation of a court-drafted plan to accelerate the desegregation of New Orleans' public school system.		Labor Dept. reports that the number of major U.S. industrial areas suffering substantial unemployment (over 6%) fell in July to 48, the lowest total in two years.		Mexico defeats the U.S. in the American Zone Davis Cup tennis semi-finals in Mexico City.	**Aug. 6**

F	G	H	I	J
Includes elections, federal-state relations, civil rights and liberties, crime, the judiciary, education, health care, poverty, urban affairs and population.	Includes formation and debate of U.S. foreign and defense policies, veterans' affairs and defense spending. (Relations with specific foreign countries are usually found under the region concerned.)	Includes business, labor, agriculture, taxation, transportation, consumer affairs, monetary and fiscal policy, natural resources, and pollution.	Includes worldwide scientific, medical and technological developments, natural phenomena, U.S. weather, natural disasters, and accidents.	Includes the arts, religion, scholarship, communications media, sports, entertainment, fashions, fads and social life.

	World Affairs	Europe	Africa & the Middle East	The Americas	Asia & the Pacific
Aug. 7			A seven-member Political Bureau named by Ben Bella formally assumes power in Algeria, in effect supplanting the Algerian Provisional Government of Premier Ben Khedda. . . . Congolese news sources report that rival Angola rebel groups have agreed to form a temporary common front to fight Portuguese rule.	Conservative Party leader Guillermo Leon Valencia succeeds Liberal Alberto Lleras Camargo as president of Colombia.	
Aug. 8	U.S. AEC reports monitoring another Soviet nuclear test detonated earlier in the day somewhere over central Siberia.				
Aug. 9					
Aug. 10	Western scientists report monitoring another Soviet nuclear test, the third in the recently resumed series.		The U.N.'s 17-nation committee on the abolition of colonialism urges enactment of strong U.N. sanctions against Portugal if it does not quickly free its African colony of Mozambique.	An OAS resolution calling for an immediate conference on anti-democratic coups in the Western Hemisphere fails to gain the necessary two-thirds vote required for passage. . . . Brazilian Premier Francisco Brochado da Rocha asks Congress for permission to rule by decree to cope with Brazil's deepening economic problems. . . . Canadian Finance Ministry reports a record peacetime budget deficit of $791,021,950 for the 1961-1962 fiscal year ending March 31.	
Aug. 11				A possible clash between loyal and rebellious Argentine army factions is averted as Pres. Guido agrees to rebel demands to name a strong anti-Peronist as war secretary and army commander.	
Aug. 12					
Aug. 13		Unruly crowds of Berliners harass and threaten East German border guards as they gathered to mark the first anniversary of the Berlin Wall.			

A	B	C	D	E
Includes developments that affect more than one world region, international organizations and important meetings of major world leaders.	Includes all domestic and regional developments in Europe, including the Soviet Union, Turkey, Cyprus and Malta.	Includes all domestic and regional developments in Africa and the Middle East, including Iraq and Iran and excluding Cyprus, Turkey and Afghanistan.	Includes all domestic and regional developments in Latin America, the Caribbean and Canada.	Includes all domestic and regional developments in Asia and Pacific nations, extending from Afghanistan through all the Pacific Islands, except Hawaii.

U.S. Politics & Social Issues	U.S. Foreign Policy & Defense	U.S. Economy & Environment	Science, Technology & Nature	Culture, Leisure & Life Style	
Atty. Gen. Robert Kennedy, speaking to a Democratic conference in Seattle, defends F.B.I. Director Hoover from recent charges that he has been promoting anti-communist hysteria.		Administration economic adviser Walter Heller tells the Joint Economic Committee that the disappointing recovery from the 1961 recession is due almost entirely to poor "investment in plant, equipment and inventories.". . . RCA Chmn. David Sarnoff issues a statement urging the compulsory merger of all U.S. international communications concerns into a single private company exempt from antitrust legislation.			Aug. 7
Elizabeth Duncan is executed in the San Quentin Prison gas chamber for her role in the November 1958 murder of her pregnant daughter-in-law.	Senate GOP leader Everett Dirksen, N.Y. Gov. Nelson Rockefeller and several congressional Republicans criticize the Kennedy administration's revision of U.S. test-ban policy as an unwarranted concession to the USSR.				Aug. 8
	The State Dept. issues a statement denying recent Republican charges that the administration's revised position on a test-ban treaty involved a risk to U.S. security.	Public Health Service reports that life expectancy in the U.S. rose in 1961 to a record 70.2 years, while the infant death rate fell to a record low of 25.3 per 1,000.	Typhoon "Patsy" strikes the central Philippines, leaving 23 dead and 133 missing.	German-born Swiss novelist and poet Hermann Hesse, 85, winner of the 1946 Nobel Prize for literature, dies of a heart attack in Montagnola, Switzerland.	Aug. 9
The NLRB announces that it will nullify results of bargaining elections in which racial propaganda has been injected into the campaign.	Ex-Pres. Herbert Hoover, 88, speaking at the dedication of his Presidential Library in West Branch, Ia., says that the "communist-influenced" U.N. should be replaced by a world "council of free nations.". . . Pres. Kennedy signs a compromise fiscal 1963 defense appropriations bill (HR 11289) totaling $48,136,247,000—$285 million less than the administration requested.	Commerce Dept. reports that the U.S. balance of payments deficit dropped from an annual rate of $1.9 billion during the first quarter to a $1 billion rate in the second quarter.	Soviet Ministry of Health announces the development of an early pregnancy abortion machine capable of removing a fetus by vacuum in a nearly painless one-minute operation.		Aug. 10
A Gallup Poll indicates that 79% of all Americans interviewed approve of religious observances in public schools.	Charles Bohlen is named by Pres. Kennedy to succeed Lt. Gen. James Gavin as U.S. ambassador to France.	GOP Congressional leaders issue a statement criticizing the Kennedy administration for the "sub-par" recovery of the economy over the past year.	Soviet cosmonaut Andrian Nikolayev is launched into orbit aboard his spaceship, Vostok III, from an undisclosed site in the USSR.		Aug. 11
			A second Soviet spacecraft, Vostok IV, piloted by Pavel Popovich, is placed in a nearly identical orbit with the Vostok III craft launched yesterday. The twin ships are reportedly in visual and radio contact.	Arnold Palmer wins the American Golf Classic in Akron, Ohio for $9,000 to set a one year tournament money-winning record of $80,198.	Aug. 12
	State Secy. Rusk, addressing the annual convention of the VFW, denies rightwing charges that the Kennedy administration is following a "no-win foreign policy."	Pres. Kennedy signs a bill (HR 10786) establishing a standard 40-hour work-week on all federal or federally-aided projects. . . . The AFL-CIO Executive Council approves plans for a campaign to attain a national 35-hour work-week with no reduction in pay. The Council also backs an immediate cut in personal income taxes. . . . Commerce Dept. reports the U.S. GNP rose to a record annual rate of $552 billion in the quarter ending June 30.			Aug. 13

F	G	H	I	J
Includes elections, federal-state relations, civil rights and liberties, crime, the judiciary, education, health care, poverty, urban affairs and population.	Includes formation and debate of U.S. foreign and defense policies, veterans' affairs and defense spending. (Relations with specific foreign countries are usually found under the region concerned.)	Includes business, labor, agriculture, taxation, transportation, consumer affairs, monetary and fiscal policy, natural resources, and pollution.	Includes worldwide scientific, medical and technological developments, natural phenomena, U.S. weather, natural disasters, and accidents.	Includes the arts, religion, scholarship, communications media, sports, entertainment, fashions, fads and social life.

	World Affairs	Europe	Africa & the Middle East	The Americas	Asia & the Pacific
Aug. 14		West and East German border guards exchange fire over the Berlin Wall, causing the death of at least one East German patrolman. Violence along the Wall has become an almost daily occurrence.			
Aug. 15	Italy joins the eight neutral delegations of the Geneva disarmament conference in calling for an immediate ban on above-ground and underwater nuclear tests.				A formal agreement turning the administration of Netherlands New Guinea over to Indonesia is signed by Dutch and Indonesian representatives at U.N. headquarters in New York.
Aug. 16		Soviet officials expel U.S. journalist Whitman Bassow, head of *Newsweek's* Moscow bureau, for allegedly writing "crudely slanderous dispatches" about the USSR. An agreement to merge the British colony of Aden with the adjoining British-controlled Federation of South Arabia is announced in London. . . . The Arab League votes to admit Algeria.			Deposed South Korean Premier John Chang is arrested in Seoul on charges of conspiring to assassinate South Korea's junta leaders and regain power.
Aug. 17		An angry and frustrated crowd of West Berliners look on as an East German youth slowly bleeds to death after being shot down and left unattended by East Berlin border guards.	Algerian sources report a series of crises arising from the refusal of certain nationalist military units to recognize the authority of the civilian Political Bureau headed by Ben Bella.	U.S. State Dept. announces formal recognition of the new Peruvian military junta and resumption of U.S. economic aid to Peru.	South Vietnamese political dissidents announce in Tokyo the formation of a non-communist National Council of the Vietnamese Revolution dedicated to the removal of Pres. Ngo Dinh Diem.
Aug. 18		West Berlin mobs numbering up to 10,000 persons, angered by yesterday's slaying of an East German escapee, stone buses carrying Soviet personnel on official business in West Berlin.		Cuba's National Agrarian Reform Institute announces that the nation's cooperative farms will be transformed into government-operated collectives in an effort to increase agricultural production.	
Aug. 19		Serious labor unrest erupts once again in northwest Spain as coal miners seek to add a shorter work-week to their recently won demand for higher wages.			
Aug. 20	U.S. and Soviet delegates to the Geneva conference agree to an Indian request to make one more private effort to resolve the test-ban problem.	West Germany announces that East Germans who participate in the shooting of refugees will be listed as criminals and will be subject to the "severest punishment prescribed by law."	Actg. U.N. Secy. Gen. U Thant presents the Security Council with a U.N.-drafted plan for settling the still unresolved dispute between the central Congolese government and secessionist Katanga. The plan calls for the completion of a new Congolese constitution which would include specific arrangements for the division of tax revenues between the central and provincial governments.	The Argentine government of Pres. José Guido, under pressure from the nation's military leaders, continues its crackdown against Peronist and communist political activities.	Prince Norodom Sihanouk, Cambodian chief of state, proposes that the 14 nations who attended the Geneva conference on Laos be reconvened to settle Cambodia's border disputes with Thailand and South Vietnam.

A	B	C	D	E
Includes developments that affect more than one world region, international organizations and important meetings of major world leaders.	*Includes all domestic and regional developments in Europe, including the Soviet Union, Turkey, Cyprus and Malta.*	*Includes all domestic and regional developments in Africa and the Middle East, including Iraq and Iran and excluding Cyprus, Turkey and Afghanistan.*	*Includes all domestic and regional developments in Latin America, the Caribbean and Canada.*	*Includes all domestic and regional developments in Asia and Pacific nations, extending from Afghanistan through all the Pacific Islands, except Hawaii.*

U.S. Politics & Social Issues	U.S. Foreign Policy & Defense	U.S. Economy & Environment	Science, Technology & Nature	Culture, Leisure & Life Style	
A filibuster by liberal Senators against the administration's communications satellite bill (HR 11040) is successfully broken by a vote to impose cloture. The action marks the first successful use of the cloture device since 1927. . . . Six men and a woman rob a U.S. mail truck of $1,551,277 in Plymouth, Mass; it is the largest cash robbery in U.S. history.		Pres. Kennedy signs a compromise bill (HR 10409) appropriating $5.33 billion for the Labor Dept., HEW, and related agencies.	Pres. Kennedy signs a bill (HR11737) authorizing $3.74 billion in fiscal 1963 for NASA, about $43 million less than he originally requested. . . . Italian and French workers complete a 7.2 mile tunnel through the Alps' Mont Blanc--connecting Chamonix, France and Courmayer, Italy. Scheduled for traffic in 1964, it will be the world's longest highway tunnel and the first all-weather route through the Alps.		Aug. 14
			The USSR's twin orbiting cosmonauts are returned safely to earth after completeing 64 and 48 orbits respectively.		Aug. 15
	A report in *Flight International* magazine (London) asserts that the U.S. Air Force has secretly launched at least 20 military reconnaissance satellites since Nov. 22, 1961.				Aug. 16
	House Armed Services subcommittee accuses the Defense Dept. of failing to provide a well-prepared and adequate armed reserve force. . . . A four-and-one-half-month Senate Armed Forces subcommittee investigation into stockpiling is suspended abruptly after a dramatic clash between Chmn. Stuart Symington (D. Mo.) and ex-Treasury Secy. George Humphrey. Humphrey appeared before the committee to face charges that he reaped excessive profits on stockpiling contracts as an officer of the M.A. Hanna Co.	Pres. Kennedy awards FDA medical officer Dr. Frances Kelsey a gold medal for distinguished federal service for her role in preventing the U.S. marketing of the birth-defect-causing drug Thalidomide.		A Los Angeles County coroner's report labels the death of Marilyn Monroe as a "probable suicide."	Aug. 17
About 500 persons in Englewood, N.J. attend a rally to protest segregation in the city's schools. Many Negro leaders boycotted the meeting because its organizers had extended an invitation to controversial Black Muslim leader, Malcolm X.	The U.S. Navy's 13th Polaris-firing submarine, the *Alexander Hamilton* is launched at Groton, Conn.	Pres. Kennedy ends a two-day Western states tour in which he stressed need for a national program to conserve natural resources.	Floodwaters from the Hacha River inundate the Colombian mountain town of Florencia, killing at least 135 persons.	American miler Jim Beatty sets a new U.S. mile record of three minutes 56.5 seconds at a meet in London. . . . Emile Griffith retains the world welterweight championship by winning a split decision over Dennis Moyer in Tacoma, Wash.	Aug. 18
				Homero Blancas, playing the Premier course in Longview, Tex., shoots a 55—the lowest competitive golf round ever registered in the U.S.	Aug. 19
About 80 integrationists from Cairo, Ill. meet with Gov. Otto Kerner (D.) to demand greater police protection for civil rights activists. Six Negroes were beaten by a white crowd Aug. 17 as they tried to integrate a Cairo skating rink.		Treasury Dept. announces that the U.S. national debt has passed $300 billion for the first time.			Aug. 20

F	G	H	I	J
Includes elections, federal-state relations, civil rights and liberties, crime, the judiciary, education, health care, poverty, urban affairs and population.	Includes formation and debate of U.S. foreign and defense policies, veterans' affairs and defense spending. (Relations with specific foreign countries are usually found under the region concerned.)	Includes business, labor, agriculture, taxation, transportation, consumer affairs, monetary and fiscal policy, natural resources, and pollution.	Includes worldwide scientific, medical and technological developments, natural phenomena, U.S. weather, natural disasters, and accidents.	Includes the arts, religion, scholarship, communications media, sports, entertainment, fashions, fads and social life.

	World Affairs	Europe	Africa & the Middle East	The Americas	Asia & the Pacific
Aug. 21		The three Western Commandants jointly announce they will station an allied ambulance near the Berlin Wall "to give medical assistance to any future refugee victim of communist bullets on the East Berlin side of the wall.". . . State Secy. Rusk meets with Soviet Amb. Dobrynin in Washington to renew U.S. requests for a four-power meeting to discuss recent Berlin Wall incidents.			
Aug. 22	Representatives to the 17-nation Geneva disarmament talks vote to recess their meetings from Sept. 8 to Nov. 12 in an apparent admission of their inability to bridge Soviet-Western differences over either a test-ban agreement or an arms control pact.	USSR announces that it is formally abolishing the office of Soviet commandant in East Berlin as a preliminary step toward concluding a German peace treaty. The U.S. State Dept. denounces the action as a Soviet effort to abdicate its responsibility for communist violence along the Berlin Wall. . . . French Pres. de Gaulle escapes an assassination attempt by gunmen presumed to be members of the Secret Army Organization.		Pres. Kennedy says at a news conference in Washington that Cuba is receiving "large quantities" of Soviet military equipment and increased numbers of Russian technicians.	
Aug. 23		U.S., Britain and France issue a joint communique declaring that the USSR's decision to abolish its Berlin commandant's post will have no effect on "either allied rights or Soviet responsibilities in Berlin."			
Aug. 24				Two small gunboats, manned by a group of Miami-based Cuban exiles, launch a brief off-shore attack on the Havana suburb of Miramar and then return to Florida. Cuba blames the attack on the U.S.	
Aug. 25	Swedish scientists report monitoring the sixth and seventh nuclear tests in the current Soviet series.				
Aug. 26					
Aug. 27	A Soviet plan for an uninspected cessation of atmospheric nuclear tests by Jan. 1, 1963 and for a simultaneous unpoliced moratorium on all underground tests is presented to the Geneva conference. . . . Britain and the U.S. announce that they are prepared to accept a limited nuclear test-ban treaty excluding underground tests, which would not require the on-site inspection provisions long opposed by the USSR.	U.S., Britain and France again appeal for Soviet participation in a four-power meeting to discuss ways of halting the growing violence along the Berlin Wall.			
Aug. 28	Soviet officials at the Geneva disarmament conference reject yesterday's U.S.-British proposal for a limited test-ban treaty, claiming that it would encourage continued underground testing. The Soviets reiterate their opposition to any ban requiring on-site inspections.	In a TV interview West German Chancellor Adenauer expresses his opposition to full British participation in future European political talks. The statement draws sharp criticism in Britain and within West German political circles.	UAR walks out of an Arab League conference to protest a planned debate of charges of UAR interference in Syrian affairs. . . . Agreements fixing the terms for future French aid to Algeria and for joint exploitation of the Sahara's mineral wealth are signed in Paris.		

A	B	C	D	E
Includes developments that affect more than one world region, international organizations and important meetings of major world leaders.	Includes all domestic and regional developments in Europe, including the Soviet Union, Turkey, Cyprus and Malta.	Includes all domestic and regional developments in Africa and the Middle East, including Iraq and Iran and excluding Cyprus, Turkey and Afghanistan.	Includes all domestic and regional developments in Latin America, the Caribbean and Canada.	Includes all domestic and regional developments in Asia and Pacific nations, extending from Afghanistan through all the Pacific Islands, except Hawaii.

U.S. Politics & Social Issues	U.S. Foreign Policy & Defense	U.S. Economy & Environment	Science, Technology & Nature	Culture, Leisure & Life Style	
			The pilots of the recent Soviet twin orbit mission, Andrian Nikolayev and Pavel Popovich, tell reporters in Moscow that their spacecrafts had never been closer than three miles. The statement contradicts rumors in the West that the two ships had "docked" in space. . . . At least 17 persons are reported killed in two earthquakes that rocked southern Italy.	Jim Beatty, at a Helsinki, Finland meet, breaks his own August 18 mile-record with a new time of three minutes and 56.3 seconds.	Aug. 21
	Pres. Kennedy discloses at his news conference that two U.S. nuclear-powered submarines have made "an historic rendezvous" under the polar icecap and then surfaced together near the North Pole.	A compromise farm bill containing at least some provisions of the administration's originally proposed farm program passes the Senate and is returned to the House. . . . Atty. Gen. Kennedy reports that identical bidding in government contracts occurs in only about 1% of all cases.			Aug. 22
		Minnesota officials urge state farmers to feed dairy cattle hay and dry grain rather than pasture in an effort to reduce the level of fall-out-caused radioactive substances in milk. . . . The Senate unanimously passes and sends to the House an administration-backed bill (S 1552) curbing harmful and ineffectual drugs. The strong support for the measure is attributed in part to recent disclosures linking the drug Thalidomide to serious birth defects.	*Christian Science Monitor* reports that data from satellite-borne radiotelescopes, orbiting above the ionosphere, have led to significant astronomical discoveries.		Aug. 23
			U.S. AEC announces cancellation of plans to use an underground nuclear device to excavate a harbor near Cape Thompson in northwest Alaska. The decision is unofficially attributed to protests from Cape Thompson Eskimos.		Aug. 24
				San Jose, Calif., defeats Kankeekee Ill. to win the Little League World Series final in Williamsport, Pa.	Aug. 25
			Vihjalmor Stefansson, 82, the last of the dog sled explorers of the Arctic, dies of a stroke in Hanover, New Hampshire. After his many expeditions, he was the formost authority on this area of the world.		Aug. 26
House joins the Senate in approving a Constitutional amendment to abolish the poll tax in federal elections. The measure still requires ratification by three-fourths of the states.	Sen. Homer Capehart (R, Ind.), speaking at a GOP rally, calls for a U.S. invasion of Cuba to prevent a possibly dangerous Soviet military buildup there.		U.S. launches a Mariner II spacecraft in its second effort to send a probe near Venus.		Aug. 27
Justice Dept. files suit in Jackson, Miss. charging that two sections of the Mississippi Constitution and six state laws are unconstitutionally designed to "perpetuate white political supremacy."	Atty. Gen. Robert Kennedy tells a group of federal employees that the U.S. must make significant progress to end racial discrimination if it is to maintain its moral leadership of the free world.			Antonio Maspes of Italy wins the speed title in the world professional bicycle championships in Milan, Italy.	Aug. 28

F	G	H	I	J
Includes elections, federal-state relations, civil rights and liberties, crime, the judiciary, education, health care, poverty, urban affairs and population.	*Includes formation and debate of U.S. foreign and defense policies, veterans' affairs and defense spending. (Relations with specific foreign countries are usually found under the region concerned.)*	*Includes business, labor, agriculture, taxation, transportation, consumer affairs, monetary and fiscal policy, natural resources, and pollution.*	*Includes worldwide scientific, medical and technological developments, natural phenomena, U.S. weather, natural disasters, and accidents.*	*Includes the arts, religion, scholarship, communications media, sports, entertainment, fashions, fads and social life.*

	World Affairs	Europe	Africa & the Middle East	The Americas	Asia & the Pacific
Aug. 29	Pres. Kennedy tells reporters that he supports the Soviet proposals for an end to nuclear testing by Jan. 1, but adds that the U.S. is unwilling to accept another unpoliced test moratorium.		Jordan and Saudi Arabia jointly announce a plan to merge their armed forces and to coordinate their national economic policies. . . . Congolese Foreign Min. Justine Bomboko publicly confirms that his government is aiding the Angolan rebels in their fight against Portugal.	Pres. Kennedy, at a Washington news conference, expresses his opposition to recent congressional calls for a U.S. invasion of Cuba.	Communist China closes its border with Hong Kong following recent terrorist attacks on Chinese customs officials and border guards.
Aug. 30			Algerian Political Bureau asks pro-Ben Bella military leaders to send troops to Algiers to put down dissident army units currently in control of the city. . . . The U.S. announces that a grant of $25 million worth of surplus food has been sent to Algeria to alleviate severe shortages caused by post-war economic disorganization.		
Aug. 31		Viggo Kampmann resigns as Danish premier after suffering his second heart attack in the past four months.		Trinidad and Tobago become an independent nation within the British Commonwealth. Eric Williams is sworn in as the nation's first prime minister. . . . The U.S. protests an alleged Cuban gunboat attack on an unarmed U.S. Navy plane flying on a training mission over international waters near Cuba.	
Sept. 1	The U.N.'s 1961 *Demographic Yearbook* reports that world population totaled more than three billion in mid-1961 and was increasing at an annual rate of 1.8%.		Serious fighting breaks out between rival factions in the Algerian armed forces.		
Sept. 2				The USSR makes public in Moscow an agreement for increased Soviet military aid to Cuba.	
Sept. 3		Foreign Min. Jens Otto Krag, a Social Democrat, is named Danish premier, succeeding Viggo Kampmann. . . . French Interior Ministry announces the outlawing of the underground rightist National Resistance Council headed by ex-Premier Georges Bidault.	Katanga Pres. Tshombe expresses enthusiasm for Secy. Gen. U Thant's Aug. 20 plan to settle the Congo problem.	Bolivia suspends relations with the OAS as a result of the organization's failure to fully support Bolivia in its dispute with Chile over the waters of the Lauca River.	The Indian Parliament approves legislation creating Nagaland as India's 16th state. Naga nationalists denounce the action.
Sept. 4	The USSR charges that a U.S. U-2 reconnaissance plane violated Soviet airspace in a flight over the Soviet island of Sakhalin in the north Pacific. The U.S. immediately acknowledges that an unintentional violation may have occurred "due solely to a navigation error."			Pres. Kennedy announces that the U.S. has confirmed that the USSR is providing Cuba with defensive missiles and related military equipment. Kennedy, however, says there is no evidence that Cuba has received weapons of "significant offensive capability."	
Sept. 5	Thirty-one nations pledge a total of $86 million to the U.N.'s new World Food Program.			U.S. State Secy. Rusk meets with 19 Latin American ambassadors in Washington to reaffirm the U.S.'s determination to prevent the export of communism from Cuba.	Four North Korean soldiers are killed in a brief gun battle with South Korean troops in the demilitarized zone.
	A	**B**	**C**	**D**	**E**
	Includes developments that affect more than one world region, international organizations and important meetings of major world leaders.	*Includes all domestic and regional developments in Europe, including the Soviet Union, Turkey, Cyprus and Malta.*	*Includes all domestic and regional developments in Africa and the Middle East, including Iraq and Iran and excluding Cyprus, Turkey and Afghanistan.*	*Includes all domestic and regional developments in Latin America, the Caribbean and Canada.*	*Includes all domestic and regional developments in Asia and Pacific nations, extending from Afghanistan through all the Pacific Islands, except Hawaii.*

U.S. Politics & Social Issues	U.S. Foreign Policy & Defense	U.S. Economy & Environment	Science, Technology & Nature	Culture, Leisure & Life Style	
Pres. Kennedy names Labor Secy. Arthur Goldberg to succeed retiring Supreme Court Justice Felix Frankfurter. Frankfurter, 79, suffered a mild stroke April 5. . . . An editorial prepared for the Sept. 1 issue of the Jesuit weekly journal *America*, warning U.S. Jews that their support for a constitutional ban of public school prayer may lead to anti-Semitism, draws sharp criticism from Jewish, Protestant and lay Catholic leaders.	Sen. Alexander Wiley (R, Wis.) proposes that Cuba be blockaded by an inter-American "peace fleet" to prevent it from receiving communist military supplies.				Aug. 29
Alabama Supreme Court upholds a $500,000 libel judgment awarded Montgomery Police Commissioner L. B. Sullivan against *The New York Times* for a pro-civil rights ad that appeared in 1960.		Pres. Kennedy names William Willard Wirtz to succeed Supreme Court nominee Arthur Goldberg as Secretary of Labor.			Aug. 30
A disappointingly small crowd of 830 persons attend a five-day anti-communism school held in New York by the Christian Anti-Communism Crusade.		National Farmers Organization members in 16 Midwestern states begin a "holding action" to keep livestock and soybeans off the market in an attempt to force higher prices. . . . A controversial administration-backed bill (HR 11040) authorizing creation of a private corporation to own and operate an international satellite communications network is signed into law by Pres. Kennedy.			Aug. 31
Ku Klux Klan stages cross-burning demonstrations in 15 Louisiana towns to protest racial integration efforts.	Pres. Kennedy sends GOP congressional leaders a letter denying their charges that the U.S. has done little to inform the world about the communist-built "wall of shame" in Berlin.		An earthquake—the worst in Iran's history—devastates a 23,000-square-mile region of northwest Iran, killing an estimated 10,000 people and injuring at least 10,000 others. . . . U.S. AEC announces that the July 9 high-altitude nuclear test has produced stronger radiation than anticipated and has either enlarged the natural Van Allen radiation belt or created a new artificial radiation envelope. . . . A typhoon from the South China Sea strikes Hong Kong, killing 128 people and leaving more than 27,000 homeless.		Sept. 1
	About 1,000 B-52 and B-47 bombers of the Strategic Air Command participate in a six-hour test of the U.S.'s continental air defense system.			Chicago Cubs second baseman Kenny Hubbs sets a new major league record by completing his 74th straight game without an error.	Sept. 2
		Census Bureau reports U.S. gold exports totaled $171 million in 1962's first half, down from $532.8 million from the same period a year ago.		American poet and painter (Edward Estlin) e.e. cummings dies in North Conway, N.H. at age 67.	Sept. 3
Token desegregation of scores of public and parochial schools in New Orleans, Atlanta, Dallas and elsewhere in the South is achieved without major incident as the new school year begins.		National Safety Council reports that Labor Day weekend auto accidents took the lives of a record 501 persons.	NASA scientists successfully complete a course correction in the flight path of the Venus-bound Mariner II satellite, raising hopes that the craft will pass within 9,000 miles of Venus.	Japan wins the fourth annual Asian Games in Jakarta, Indonesia.	Sept. 4
About 350 Negro pupils stay away from Lincoln School in Englewood, N.J. to protest alleged de facto segregation.		Labor Dept. reports that the seasonally adjusted unemployment rate rose in August to 5.8%, up slightly from the 20-month low of 5.3% recorded in July.	NASA officials announce they have learned that the USSR has failed in five of six attempts to send planetary probes toward Mars and Venus over the last two years.		Sept. 5
F	G	H	I	J	
Includes elections, federal-state relations, civil rights and liberties, crime, the judiciary, education, health care, poverty, urban affairs and population.	*Includes formation and debate of U.S. foreign and defense policies, veterans' affairs and defense spending. (Relations with specific foreign countries are usually found under the region concerned.)*	*Includes business, labor, agriculture, taxation, transportation, consumer affairs, monetary and fiscal policy, natural resources, and pollution.*	*Includes worldwide scientific, medical and technological developments, natural phenomena, U.S. weather, natural disasters, and accidents.*	*Includes the arts, religion, scholarship, communications media, sports, entertainment, fashions, fads and social life.*	

	World Affairs	Europe	Africa & the Middle East	The Americas	Asia & the Pacific
Sept. 6		USSR again rejects Western appeals for four-power talks on curbing violence along the Berlin border.		Argentine Pres. Guido, responding to military demands, issues decrees formally dissolving Congress and postponing presidential and Congressional elections until late October 1963.	
Sept. 7			Ghana's national Legislature adopts a motion extending Pres. Nkrumah's term of office for the remainder of his life.	The New York Times estimates that there are currently 4,000 Soviet-bloc troops serving in Cuba. . . . Pres. Kennedy, in an apparent effort to demonstrate American concern over Soviet buildup in Cuba, asks Congress to extend for one year his standby authority to call up to 150,000 reservists.	
Sept. 8			Albert Kalonji, self-proclaimed king of the Congo's South Kasai Province, is released from a Leopoldville prison after apparently pledging to support a unified Congo.	UPI reports that the U.S. has appealed to its NATO allies for cooperation in an economic boycott of Cuba.	
Sept. 9	U.S. Interior Secy. Stewart Udall concludes a 10-day tour of the Soviet hydroelectric facilities under the U.S.-Soviet exchange program.	French Pres. de Gaulle completes a historic and warmly received six-day state visit to West Germany. Observers view the trip as an impressive demonstration of the two nations' deepening commitment to an economic and political alliance of continental European states under Franco - German leadership.	Syria and Jordan restore diplomatic relations with France for the first time since the British-French invasion of the Suez Canal Zone in 1956. . . . A new threat of large-scale warfare between factions of the Algerian nationalist leadership is averted with the entry into Algiers of 4,000 troops supporting Vice Premier Ahmed (formerly Mohammed) Ben Bella and his ruling Political Bureau. . . . Three children are killed by a bomb explosion outside the palace of Ghana Pres. Kwame Nkrumah. Nkrumah escaped unhurt.		Communist China announces that it has shot down a U.S.-made nationalist Chinese U-2 reconnaissance jet on an alleged spy mission over the mainland.
Sept. 10	U.S. Defense Dept. announces plans to resume its temporarily suspended series of high-altitude nuclear tests in the vicinity of Johnston Island.		Ghanian Times newspaper accuses Britain, the U.S. and other Western states of complicity in recent assassination attempts on the life of Pres. Nkrumah.		Nationalist China acknowledges that one of its U-2's has failed to return from a "routine" reconnaissance flight over mainland China. . . . Cambodian officials charge that South Vietnamese troops yesterday sailed up the Mekong River and attacked Cambodian border villages. The incident comes amidst an intensification of Cambodia's long-standing border dispute with South Vietnam.
Sept. 11	USSR warns that a U.S. invasion of Cuba or interference with Soviet supply ships will result in nuclear war.	The USSR issues a statement saying that it will seek a resumption of Soviet-U.S. negotiations on Berlin and Germany following completion of U.S. congressional elections in November. . . . Striking Spanish coal miners return to work after mine owners agreed to negotiate on the workers' demands.	Pres. Leon Mba of Gabon is elected president of the 12-nation African-Malagasy Union.		
Sept. 12					

A	B	C	D	E
Includes developments that affect more than one world region, international organizations and important meetings of major world leaders.	Includes all domestic and regional developments in Europe, including the Soviet Union, Turkey, Cyprus and Malta.	Includes all domestic and regional developments in Africa and the Middle East, including Iraq and Iran and excluding Cyprus, Turkey and Afghanistan.	Includes all domestic and regional developments in Latin America, the Caribbean and Canada.	Includes all domestic and regional developments in Asia and Pacific nations, extending from Afghanistan through all the Pacific Islands, except Hawaii.

U.S. Politics & Social Issues	U.S. Foreign Policy & Defense	U.S. Economy & Environment	Science, Technology & Nature	Culture, Leisure & Life Style	
		A weakened version of the administration's tax reform bill (HR 10650) is passed by the Senate and sent to joint conference. The Senate version does not include administration-requested provisions to withhold the taxes on interest and dividends. . . . Pres. Kennedy signs a bill (S 476) establishing the Point Reyes National Seashore on the northern coast of Calif.		The Bolshoi Ballet opens in New York under the auspices of the recently expanded U.S.-Soviet cultural exchange program.	Sept. 6
HEW Secy. Anthony Celebrezze announces that a recently completed Public Health Service report on human birth control and reproduction will be made public by the end of the year. The announcement follows reports that the study might be suppressed to avoid public controversy and misunderstanding.	V.P. Lyndon Johnson completes a two-week tour of six Mediterranean and Middle Eastern countries during which he discussed the major goals of America's foreign aid program.				Sept. 7
Public schools in Prince Edward County (Va.) remain closed for the fourth consecutive school year despite a court order to reopen.				Jacquelyn Mayer of Sandusky, Ohio is named Miss America of 1963. . . . Andrey Tarkowski's *Childhood of Ivan* (USSR) and Valerio Zurlini's *Cronaca Familiare* (Italy) share top honors at the Venice Film Festival.	Sept. 8
Two Negro churches near Sasser, Ga., which had been used as the site of voter registration rallies, are burnt to the ground by arsonists.			U.N. Scientific Committee on the Effects of Atomic Radiation issues a report warning that test-caused fallout may eventually damage man's genetic heritage.	Jack Nicklaus defeats Arnold Palmer and Gary Player to win the first World Series of Golf in Akron, Ohio.	Sept. 9
Supreme Court Justice Hugo Black, upholding rulings by the Fifth Circuit Court, orders the University of Mississippi to admit Negro applicant James Meredith.				Rod Laver wins the men's national championship in Forest Hills (N.Y.) thus achieving the first "grand slam" in amateur tennis since Don Budge in 1938. . . . Auto-racer Glenn Leasher is killed in a crash of his jet-powered car during a test run at Bonneville Salt Flats, Utah.	Sept. 10
Senate confirms the nomination of Thurgood Marshall, a Negro, as a judge on the U.S. Second Circuit Court of Appeals. . . . Lunch counters in 15 New Orleans stores are integrated without serious incident.	Dr. Robert Soblen dies in London five days after taking an overdose of barbiturates to escape deportation to the U.S., where he was to face a life sentence for espionage.				Sept. 11
			Pres. Kennedy speaking in Houston, Tex., defends his administration's increased expenditures on space exploration saying that the U.S. must assure that a "banner of freedom and peace" rather than a "hostile flag of conquest" will govern space.		Sept. 12

F	G	H	I	J
Includes elections, federal-state relations, civil rights and liberties, crime, the judiciary, education, health care, poverty, urban affairs and population.	Includes formation and debate of U.S. foreign and defense policies, veterans' affairs and defense spending. (Relations with specific foreign countries are usually found under the region concerned.)	Includes business, labor, agriculture, taxation, transportation, consumer affairs, monetary and fiscal policy, natural resources, and pollution.	Includes worldwide scientific, medical and technological developments, natural phenomena, U.S. weather, natural disasters, and accidents.	Includes the arts, religion, scholarship, communications media, sports, entertainment, fashions, fads and social life.

	World Affairs	Europe	Africa & the Middle East	The Americas	Asia & the Pacific
Sept. 13	Pres. Kennedy discloses to reporters that the U.S. has modified plans for its remaining high-altitude nuclear tests in order to prevent a repetition of the unexpectedly high radiation produced by the July 9 test.		Congo sources report new outbreaks of fighting between Katangan units and U.N. forces. Each side blames the other for provoking the renewed violence.	In a prepared statement to reporters Pres. Kennedy warns that the presence of communist-supplied weapons in Cuba will not deter the U.S. from taking military action against Cuba should it prove necessary for U.S. security.	
Sept. 14					
Sept. 15			Izvestia reports that Iran has promised the USSR not to permit the establishment of foreign rocket bases on Iranian territory. . . . Abdel Khalek Hassouna of the UAR is unanimously reelected to a third term as secretary general of the Arab League.	Haitian assembly grants Pres. Francois Duvalier virtually unlimited power to cope with the nation's economic problems. . . . British Transport Ministry is reported to have advised the nation's merchant fleet not to carry strategic materials to Cuba.	
Sept. 16		National Association of British Manufacturers calls for a postponement of any final decision on whether to join the EEC.			
Sept. 17			Katanga Pres. Tshombe informs U.N. authorities that he remains willing to open talks on the U.N.'s Congo reunification plan despite the recurrence of U.N.-Katanga fighting.	Brazilian Pres. João Goulart names Hermes Lima as premier, succeeding Francisco Broachado da Rocha. Broachado resigned Sept. 14 in a dispute over a planned nationwide plebiscite on whether to restore strong executive powers to the Brazilian president.	
Sept. 18	U.N. General Assembly begins its 17th regular session. After electing Muhammad Zafrulla Khan of Pakistan to preside over the new session, the Assembly votes to accept four new members: Rwanda, Burundi, Jamaica and Trinidad-Tobago. . . . U.S. AEC reports monitoring the USSR's 18th nuclear detonation since it resumed atmospheric testing in August.	An official Soviet declaration, issued through Tass, accuses France and West Germany of conspiring to delay a German peace settlement.	Imam Ahmed, absolute monarch of Yemen dies and is immediately succeeded by his son, Crown Prince Saif-al-Islam Mohammed al Badr. . . . A Lebanese court in Beirut sentences 51 persons to death for their role in the unsuccessful Dec. 31, 1961 uprising.	Dissident Argentine army units, demanding quick elections and a return to constitutional rule, launch a rebellion against the government of Pres. José Guido.	
Sept. 19		The Soviet Central Council of Trade Unions urges an all-out campaign to promote atheism and eliminate the persisting popular "prejudice" in favor of religion.			U.S. Joint Chiefs Chmn. Gen. Maxwell Taylor, returning from a trip to South Vietnam, tells reporters in Manila that "the Vietnamese are on the road to victory."
Sept. 20	U.S. Amb.-to-U.N. Adlai Stevenson, addressing the General Assembly, stresses the urgent need for an arms agreement based on some form of "practical verification."	French Pres. de Gaulle announces plans to hold a national referendum on a proposal for amending the French Constitution to permit popular election of his successors. The proposal, apparently aimed at assuring a strong French executive after de Gaulle's death, is reportedly being submitted to the people in order to avoid a legal requirement that constitutional amendments be approved by the National Assembly.	Algerians, participating in their first national elections, choose members for a 196-seat National Assembly. The elections were limited to a ratification of a single list of candidates prepared by Ahmed Ben Bella's Political Bureau.	Formation of a Cuban revolutionary junta to overthrow Castro is announced in New York.	

A	B	C	D	E
Includes developments that affect more than one world region, international organizations and important meetings of major world leaders.	Includes all domestic and regional developments in Europe, including the Soviet Union, Turkey, Cyprus and Malta.	Includes all domestic and regional developments in Africa and the Middle East, including Iraq and Iran and excluding Cyprus, Turkey and Afghanistan.	Includes all domestic and regional developments in Latin America, the Caribbean and Canada.	Includes all domestic and regional developments in Asia and Pacific nations, extending from Afghanistan through all the Pacific Islands, except Hawaii.

U.S. Politics & Social Issues	U.S. Foreign Policy & Defense	U.S. Economy & Environment	Science, Technology & Nature	Culture, Leisure & Life Style	
Mississippi Gov. Ross Barnett, in a move to prevent the court-ordered integration of the University of Mississippi, proclaims that all institutions of higher learning will henceforth be operated under the exclusive supervision of state officials and state laws. . . . Pres. Kennedy, denouncing the recent burnings of Negro churches in Georgia, pledges to provide federal protection for voter registration workers.	Pres. Kennedy's request for standby authority to mobilize reservists receives unanimous approval of the Senate.		U.S. FDA reports that at least 10 deformed babies have been born in the U.S. to women who took Thalidomide. In Europe the number of Thalidomide-related birth defects is estimated to be well over 10,000.	Thirteen delegates from the U.S. National Council of Churches complete a three-week tour of the USSR as guests of the Russian Orthodox Church.	Sept. 13
	Sen. Barry Goldwater (R, Ariz.) says the American people are not satisfied with the administration's "do nothing" policy towards the Soviet build-up in Cuba.	A bill (HR 10113) authorizing $900 million for public works projects in heavy unemployment areas is signed by Pres. Kennedy.	Dr. E. G. Bowen, head of the Commonwealth Scientific and Research Organization, announces in Sydney, Australia the discovery of magnetic fields in intergalactic space.		Sept. 14
	U.S. Justice Dept. accuses two Russians formerly employed by the U.N. Secretariat of having engaged in "illegitimate intelligence activities" while at U.N. headquarters in New York.		U.S. Surgeon General's Office warns adults against further use of the Type III Sabin live-virus oral polio vaccine. Thirteen cases of polio have been reported among adults who took the Type III vaccine. . . . Harvard Medical School researchers report the development of new urine test for early detection of kidney and bladder cancers in Sept. 15 issue of the Journal of the American Medical Association.		Sept. 15
			World Health Organization reports that worldwide deaths from smallpox dropped from 358,456 in 1950 to 59,950 in 1960.	Graham Hill, driving a BRM, wins the Italian Grand Prix auto race.	Sept. 16
Justice Dept. files suit in Richmond, Va. to bar segregation in Prince Georges County public schools receiving federal aid under the "impacted areas" program.		HEW Secy. Anthony Celebrezze releases a Federal Radiation Council report asserting that test-caused fallout has not reached dangerous levels in the U.S. The report criticizes anti-radiation programs adopted in Utah and Minnesota as unnecessary and alarmist.	NASA announces the names of nine new astronauts: Neil Armstrong, Frank Borman, Charles Conrad, James Lovell, James McDivitt, Elliott See, Thomas Stafford, Edward White, and John Young.	Czechoslovakian news sources report the discovery of more than 50 "old masters" paintings in a 17th century Prague castle.	Sept. 17
Edward M. (Ted) Kennedy, 30, wins the Massachusetts Democratic nomination for Senator by an unexpectedly large margin. . . . Gallup Poll shows that 52% of Americans interviewed believed it "right" for a woman who had taken the drug Thalidomide to seek a legal abortion rather than risk the birth of a deformed baby; 32% thought it wrong.			A meteorological satellite, Tiros 6, is placed into orbit by means of a three-stage Delta rocket launched from Cape Canaveral. It is the 11th straight successful satellite launching by means of a Delta assembly, a new reliability record for U.S. launchings. . . . Corning Glass Works announces in New York the development of a new chemical process capable of producing glass five times stronger than existing types.		Sept. 18
	An administration-backed bill (S 2768) authorizing the U.S. to lend the U.N. up to $100 million is passed by the Senate and sent to the President.	The administration's Trade Expansion Act (HR11970) is passed by the Senate, 78-8, and sent to joint conference.			Sept. 19
Mississippi Gov. Ross Barnett, acting as a special university registrar, flies to the Mississippi campus at Oxford to personally reject James Meredith's application for admission. . . . House, by a 186-214 vote, rejects the administration's aid-to-colleges bill (HR 8900).	House passes a foreign aid authorization bill (HR13175), after cutting administration requests by over $1.1 billion. Administration officials hope for a restoration of at least some of the cuts when the bill reaches the Senate. . . . Pres. Kennedy tells a meeting of world finance officials in Washington that the U.S. has carried a disproportionate share of the free world's economic burden.				Sept. 20

F	G	H	I	J
Includes elections, federal-state relations, civil rights and liberties, crime, the judiciary, education, health care, poverty, urban affairs and population.	*Includes formation and debate of U.S. foreign and defense policies, veterans' affairs and defense spending. (Relations with specific foreign countries are usually found under the region concerned.)*	*Includes business, labor, agriculture, taxation, transportation, consumer affairs, monetary and fiscal policy, natural resources, and pollution.*	*Includes worldwide scientific, medical and technological developments, natural phenomena, U.S. weather, natural disasters, and accidents.*	*Includes the arts, religion, scholarship, communications media, sports, entertainment, fashions, fads and social life.*

	World Affairs	Europe	Africa & the Middle East	The Americas	Asia & the Pacific
Sept. 21		Soviet Pres. Leonid Brezhnev arrives in Yugoslavia for a 10-day visit reportedly aimed at winning Tito's acquiescence to a more disciplined Yugoslav Soviet bloc relationship. . . . French Defense Ministry discloses plans to radically transform France's armed forces into three nuclear armed commands by 1970.		Soviet Foreign Min. Gromyko, in an opening address to the U.N. General Assembly, denounces the U.S. for its allegedly threatening and bellicose attitude toward Cuba.	India announces tentative acceptance of a Sept. 13 China proposal to begin border negotiations in mid-October.
Sept. 22			Ghana Pres. Nkrumah declares a state of emergency in Accra following a recent wave of terrorist bombings.		
Sept. 23				Rebellious Argentine army units, described as constitutionalists, succeed in forcing Pres. José Maria Guido to appoint their own leaders to the nation's top military posts. Guido also agrees to rebel demands for national elections "within the briefest possible period."	
Sept. 24					
Sept. 25		The three Western allies deliver parallel notes denouncing as "unreasonable" the USSR's continued refusal to negotiate a lessening of tensions, in Berlin.		Castro announces that the USSR has agreed to build a port in Havana Bay as headquarters for a Cuban-Soviet fishing fleet.	
Sept. 26	The International Atomic Energy Agency concludes its sixth general conference in Vienna after adopting plans to advance the use of atomic power in areas of depleted conventional power sources.		A Yemeni military faction overthrows the week-old government of the new imam of Yemen, Saif-al-Islam Mohammed Bin Ahmed al-Badr. Rebel sources report that the imam was killed during the coup. . . . The newly installed Algerian Assembly elects Ahmed Ben Bella as premier. . . . U.S. announces that it has agreed to sell defensive missiles to Israel. The decision marks a reversal of earlier U.S. policy not to become a major supplier of weapons to the Middle East.	Congress adopts a joint resolution reaffirming U.S.'s determination to use "whatever means may be necessary, including the use of arms," to prevent Cuba from extending its "subversive activities to any part of this hemisphere.". . . Recently resigned Brazilian Premier Francisco Brochado da Rocha, 52, dies of a cerebral hemorrhage in Porto Alegre.	
Sept. 27	Swedish scientists report monitoring a Soviet atmospheric nuclear test with an estimated force of 32 megatons. It is the 17th reported test in the USSR's most recent series.			Turkey, responding to U.S. appeals, announces that it has asked its merchant fleet not to carry Soviet goods to Cuba. It is the first NATO nation to publicly honor the U.S. request.	Ex-South Korean Premier John Chang is sentenced to 10 years in prison for having allegedly conspired to overthrow the military junta of Gen. Chung Hee Park.

A	B	C	D	E
Includes developments that affect more than one world region, international organizations and important meetings of major world leaders.	*Includes all domestic and regional developments in Europe, including the Soviet Union, Turkey, Cyprus and Malta.*	*Includes all domestic and regional developments in Africa and the Middle East, including Iraq and Iran and excluding Cyprus, Turkey and Afghanistan.*	*Includes all domestic and regional developments in Latin America, the Caribbean and Canada.*	*Includes all domestic and regional developments in Asia and Pacific nations, extending from Afghanistan through all the Pacific Islands, except Hawaii.*

U.S. Politics & Social Issues	U.S. Foreign Policy & Defense	U.S. Economy & Environment	Science, Technology & Nature	Culture, Leisure & Life Style	
National Education Association reports that 12% of U.S. public elementary schools have adopted a "gradeless" system for early school years to encourage pupil progress based on individual ability.					Sept. 21
				USSR wins the team title at the world weight-lifting championships in Hungary.	Sept. 22
			New York Medical College announces plans to build the first U.S. center devoted entirely to research and treatment of heart disease.	Mrs. John F. Kennedy and other dignitaries attend a dedicatory concert formally opening Philharmonic Hall, the first unit of the Lincoln Center for the Performing Arts (N.Y.).	Sept. 23
Gov. Ross Barnett orders the summary imprisonment of any federal official seeking to arrest any Mississippi offical for defying court desegregation orders.	House passes and thus completes congressional action on the President's request for special power to call up 150,000 ready military reservists.				Sept. 24
Dr. Martin Luther King, addressing the annual convention of the Southern Christian Leadership Conference in Birmingham, Ala., pledges a vigorous campaign to enroll Negro students at the Universities of Alabama and Auburn. . . . Gov. Ross Barnett personally blocks the doorway to a university registrar's office in Jackson, Miss. to prevent James Meredith from registering for classes.				Charles (Sonny) Liston wins the world heavyweight championship by knocking out titleholder Floyd Patterson in the first round of their title bout in Chicago. . . . N.Y. Yankees beat the Washington Senators to clinch their third consecutive American League pennant. . . . The U.S. yacht *Weatherly* defeats Australia's *Grettel*, four races to one, to win the America's Cup.	Sept. 25
	Pres. Kennedy signs a bill (HR 12870) appropriating $1.3 billion in fiscal 1963 for military construction.	Pres. Kennedy says that strengthening the free market system and maintaining close relationships with business are the major objectives of his administration. . . . Kennedy signs a bill (HR 11974) appropriating $250 million to the AEC for fiscal 1963. The bill also authorizes the controversial sale of steam from the AEC's new Hanford (Wash.) atomic reactor to private power companies. . . . Joint Congressional Committee on Atomic Energy charges the executive branch with failing to develop adequate protective standards on fall-out problems.	Flash-flooding northwest of Barcelona, Spain takes the lives of 445 persons in what is described as the worst natural disaster in modern Spanish history.		Sept. 26
Civil Rights Commission urges issuance of an executive order barring racial discrimination in housing in Washington, D.C. and in federally assisted projects. . . . Justice Dept. postpones a planned attempt to register James Meredith at the Univ. of Mississippi after learning that a hostile crowd of 2,500 had gathered on the campus. . . . Ex-Pres. Eisenhower calls Mississippi's refusal to admit Meredith "absolutely unconscionable."		A conference committee-drafted omnibus farm bill (HR 12391), which narrowly passed in the House and the Senate over stiff GOP opposition, is signed by Pres. Kennedy.		International Olympic Committee bans government-subsidized "state amateurs" from competing in future Olympic Games.	Sept. 27

F	G	H	I	J
Includes elections, federal-state relations, civil rights and liberties, crime, the judiciary, education, health care, poverty, urban affairs and population.	*Includes formation and debate of U.S. foreign and defense policies, veterans' affairs and defense spending. (Relations with specific foreign countries are usually found under the region concerned.)*	*Includes business, labor, agriculture, taxation, transportation, consumer affairs, monetary and fiscal policy, natural resources, and pollution.*	*Includes worldwide scientific, medical and technological developments, natural phenomena, U.S. weather, natural disasters, and accidents.*	*Includes the arts, religion, scholarship, communications media, sports, entertainment, fashions, fads and social life.*

	World Affairs	Europe	Africa & the Middle East	The Americas	Asia & the Pacific
Sept. 28		U.S. Defense Secy. McNamara, just returned from an inspection tour of West Germany, tells reporters that the U.S. remains ready to use all means necessary including nuclear weapons to defend its postion in Berlin.	Algerian Premier Ben Bella pledges in an inagural address to the National Assembly to build a "Socialist Algeria" and to pursue a neutralist course in foreign policy. . . . Former Lumumba supporters and other leftist leaders in the Congo announce the formation of a unified National Movement of Resistance aimed at the ouster of the pro-Western Adoula regime.		
Sept. 29			The new Algerian government is formally recognized by the U.S.	U.S. Maritime Administration reports that merchant ships of at least 20 Western nations have carried supplies to Cuba during the past four months.	India and Communist China report minor casualties in recent skirmishes along the Tibet-Bhutan border.
Sept. 30			An Israeli border policeman is shot to death during a two-hour clash with Jordanian forces at Baka el Gharbia.	The first annual conference of the Alliance for Progress, sponsored by the OAS, begins in Mexico City.	Communist China's support for national liberation revolutions is reiterated by Premier Chou En-lai in ceremonies marking the 13th anniversary of the Communist regime.
Oct. 1	U.S. State Dept. discloses that Soviet Premier Khrushchev raised the possibility of a Moscow "summit" meeting with Interior Secy. Stewart Udall during the latter's recent visit to the USSR.				Dutch rule over Netherlands New Guinea is officially ended at ceremonies held in Hollandia.
Oct. 2	U.S. resumes its high altitude nuclear tests in the Pacific with the detonation of an airplane-dropped intermediate yield nuclear device above Johnston Island. . . . Official sources in Washington announce that the USSR has decided not to participate in the 1964-1965 New York World's Fair.		The U.N. Palestine Conciliation Commission presents Israel and the Arab states with a draft plan for the voluntary resettlement of Palestinian Arab refugees.		
Oct. 3		Sources in Yugoslavia report that Pres. Tito has refused to assure visiting Soviet Pres. Brezhnev of public Yugoslav support of Soviet threats to sign a separate East German peace treaty. . . . Soviet embassy officials in Washington, in a letter to the Jewish Nazi Victims Organization, flatly deny charges of anti-Semitism in the USSR. The letter asserts that Jews play a prominent role in all important areas of Soviet life.		A two-day meeting between Latin American foreign ministers and U.S. State Secy. Rusk results in a joint call for hemispheric measures to resist Soviet efforts to convert Cuba into a base "for communist penetration of the Americas."	Malayan Internal Security Min. Ismail bin Abdul Rahman, in an address to the General Assembly, warns that the Tibetan people's "identity as a distinctive Buddhist race is in danger of extinction" in wake of Communist China's "policy of genocide."
Oct. 4		French Pres. de Gaulle, in a nationwide TV address reaffirms his plans to hold a national referendum on the popular election of the president despite the National Assembly's opposition to the proposal.		Pres. Kennedy orders implementation of a four-point quasi-embargo program to halt the use of American or foreign ships in Cuban-Soviet bloc trade.	
Oct. 5		French National Assembly votes to censure the government of Premier Georges Pompidou for supporting Pres. de Gaulle's plan for holding a national referendum on direct election of the next French president.			The last of almost 1,000 U.S. military advisers are withdrawn from Laos 24 hours before the Oct. 6 deadline set by the 14-nation Geneva agreement.

A	B	C	D	E
Includes developments that affect more than one world region, international organizations and important meetings of major world leaders.	Includes all domestic and regional developments in Europe, including the Soviet Union, Turkey, Cyprus and Malta.	Includes all domestic and regional developments in Africa and the Middle East, including Iraq and Iran and excluding Cyprus, Turkey and Afghanistan.	Includes all domestic and regional developments in Latin America, the Caribbean and Canada.	Includes all domestic and regional developments in Asia and Pacific nations, extending from Afghanistan through all the Pacific Islands, except Hawaii.

U.S. Politics & Social Issues	U.S. Foreign Policy & Defense	U.S. Economy & Environment	Science, Technology & Nature	Culture, Leisure & Life Style	
The Fifth Circuit Court in New Orleans finds Mississippi Gov. Ross Barnett guilty of civil contempt for his resistance to court orders in the Meredith case.		A month-long strike against the Chicago & North Western Railway, the nation's third largest railroad, ends after both sides agree to Pres. Kennedy's request to submit the central issue of job security to binding arbitration. . . . A bill (S4) creating an 80-mile national park on Padre Island on the coast of Texas is signed by Pres. Kennedy. . . . Rep. Kathryn Granahan (D,Pa.) is named Treasurer of the U.S.	A Canadian satellite dubbed the Alouette, the first satellite completely designed and built by a nation other than the U.S. or USSR, is launched into orbit from Point Arguello, Calif. by means of a U.S. two-stage Thor-Agena rocket. . . . The launch of a scheduled six-orbit Project Mercury mission is cancelled after the discovery of a malfunction in the capsule's automatic control system.		Sept. 28
	U.S. demands the expulsion of two members of the Soviet U.N. mission for allegedly buying classified documents from an American sailor.			Soviet high jumper Valeri Brumel sets a new world record of 7 ft. 5 1/4 in. in Moscow. . . . Milwaukee Braves pitcher Warren Spahn, 41, wins his 327th game, setting a new major league record for left-handed pitchers.	Sept. 29
Thousands of rioting segregationists clash with federal law officers in Oxford, Miss., in a fierce protest against James Meredith's impending registration at the university. The violence occurs despite a nationally televised plea by Pres. Kennedy for peaceful compliance with federal law.					Sept. 30
James Meredith enrolls at the University of Mississippi and attends two classes under heavy federal protection. Meredith's registration followed a night and morning of violent segregationist demonstrations in which two persons were killed and 150 arrested. Among those charged is ex-Major Gen. Edwin Walker.					Oct. 1
House passes and sends to the President a bill (HR 8556) repealing the noncommunist affidavit requirements of the National Defense Education Act of 1958.	Dr. Edward Teller, U.S. atomic weapons scientist, claims that the USSR is currently ahead in the nuclear race.		U.S. scientists successfully orbit a satellite, Explorer 14, to collect data on how radiation, magnetic fields and solar particles affect man's daily life on earth.		Oct. 2
A nationwide Gallup Poll shows 72% of Americans favor making birth control information available to anyone who desires it. . . . About 50 students demonstrate near Meredith's Oxford campus residence and burn him in effigy.		Agriculture Dept. reports that its farm surplus investment dropped from $7.038 billion in fiscal 1961 to $6.657 billion in fiscal 1962.	U.S. Navy Cmndr. Walter Schirra Jr. completes a near perfect six-orbit flight in a Project Mercury capsule and safely returns to earth.	A Professional Golf Association poll names Arnold Palmer golfer of the year. Palmer also won the honor in 1960. . . . San Francisco Giants win the National League pennant by defeating the Los Angeles Dodgers, two games to one, in a post-season playoff.	Oct. 3
		The Trade Expansion Act of 1962 (HR 11970) - passes both houses of Congress and is sent to the President.	Pres. Kennedy signs a fiscal 1963 appropriation bill (HR 12711) authorizing $3.67 billion for NASA, more than twice the amount appropriated in fiscal 1962.	Ermer Robinson, an ex-Harlem Globetrotters star, is named coach of the American Basketball League's Oakland team, becoming one of the first Negroes to coach a major American pro club.	Oct. 4
					Oct. 5

F	G	H	I	J
Includes elections, federal-state relations, civil rights and liberties, crime, the judiciary, education, health care, poverty, urban affairs and population.	Includes formation and debate of U.S. foreign and defense policies, veterans' affairs and defense spending. (Relations with specific foreign countries are usually found under the region concerned.)	Includes business, labor, agriculture, taxation, transportation, consumer affairs, monetary and fiscal policy, natural resources, and pollution.	Includes worldwide scientific, medical and technological developments, natural phenomena, U.S. weather, natural disasters, and accidents.	Includes the arts, religion, scholarship, communications media, sports, entertainment, fashions, fads and social life.

	World Affairs	Europe	Africa & the Middle East	The Americas	Asia & the Pacific
Oct. 6		Premier Georges Pompidou's cabinet resigns following yesterday's National Assembly censure vote. It is the first time since the founding of the fifth Republic in 1958 that the French Parliament succeeded in reversing a government. . . . East German borderguards prevent a British military ambulance from entering East Berlin to aid a wounded refugee.			
Oct. 7			Yemeni sources report that fighting has erupted between forces of the ruling military junta and royalists loyal to the overthrown imam. Royalist leaders deny earlier reports that the imam had been killed during the Sept. 26 coup.		
Oct. 8	U.N. General Assembly votes by acclamation to admit Algeria as the 109th U.N. member.	*The New York Times* reports that serious rioting erupted in several southern Soviet cities during June as a protest against food shortages, price increases, and work speed-ups. As many as 500 persons are reported to have been killed in the disturbances. . . . The three Western allies formally protest East Germany's Oct. 6 refusal to admit a British ambulance into East Berlin.	Uganda becomes an independent nation within the British Commonwealth.	Cuban Pres. Osvaldo Dorticos Torrado, addressing the U.N. General Assembly, assails the U.S.'s Oct. 4 embargo plan as a virtual "naval blockade" deserving U.N. condemnation. . . . Venezuelan Pres. Romulo Betancourt suspends constitutional liberties following a week of leftist terrorist activities in Caracas.	Laotian National Assembly votes to grant Souvanna Phouma special decree powers to carry out the coalition government's program for integrating the three factions' military and administrative organizations. . . . U.S. Defense Dept. discloses that 46 American soldiers have been killed in South Vietnam since U.S.'s large scale intervention began in late 1961.
Oct. 9					Pres. Ngo Dinh Diem, addressing the South Vietnamese National Assembly, asserts that there has been an "incontestable turn" for the better in his government's war against the Viet Cong. . . . The U.S. announces that most of the troops sent to Thailand during the height of the Laotian crisis in May will be returned in the near future.
Oct. 10	Delegates from 43 nations gather in San Juan, Puerto Rico to attend a U.S. Peace Corps-sponsored conference on the problem of developing skilled manpower in developing countries.	French Pres. de Gaulle dissolves the National Assembly and orders new elections beginning Nov. 18.		Sen. Kenneth Keating (R, N.Y.) asserts in a Senate speech that Soviet technicians are beginning construction on "at least a half-dozen" tactical missile sites in Cuba. U.S. administration spokesmen deny the claim. . . . Alpha 66, an anti-Castro Cuban exile group, announces that a small group of its commandos attacked a military camp at the Cuban port of Isabella de Sagua, killing about 20 persons including some Soviet technicians.	
Oct. 11					*The New York Times* reports that as many as 4,000 North Vietnamese troops remain in Laos despite the Oct. 6 deadline for foreign troop withdrawals.
Oct. 12			U.N. General Assembly calls on Britain to seek the release of jailed opposition leaders in Southern Rhodesia.		
Oct. 13		France imposes a partial customs check on the border with its protectorate of Monaco. The move stems from Monaco's continuing rejection of French demands that it lift the tax-free privileges of its French and foreign residents.			
	A	**B**	**C**	**D**	**E**
	Includes developments that affect more than one world region, international organizations and important meetings of major world leaders.	*Includes all domestic and regional developments in Europe, including the Soviet Union, Turkey, Cyprus and Malta.*	*Includes all domestic and regional developments in Africa and the Middle East, including Iraq and Iran and excluding Cyprus, Turkey and Afghanistan.*	*Includes all domestic and regional developments in Latin America, the Caribbean and Canada.*	*Includes all domestic and regional developments in Asia and Pacific nations, extending from Afghanistan through all the Pacific Islands, except Hawaii.*

U.S. Politics & Social Issues	U.S. Foreign Policy & Defense	U.S. Economy & Environment	Science, Technology & Nature	Culture, Leisure & Life Style	
			U.S. Air Force bans cigarette gifts to patients in AF hospitals and clinics.		Oct. 6
Pres. Kennedy attacks what he calls Republican negativism during a three-day campaign swing through the Midwest.					Oct. 7
U.S. Supreme Court upholds an Oregon Supreme Court decision barring state grants of textbooks to parochial schools.	Senate passes the foreign aid appropriation bill (HR 3175), after restoring almost $300 million of the $1.1 billion which the House had cut from the President's original request. The bill bans aid to any country whose ships carry strategic materials to Cuba.	An eight-and-a-half year UAW strike against the Kohler Co. officially ends as company officials and the union sign a one-year contract. . . . An interstate compact to develop the Columbia River is signed in Portland, Ore. by representatives of seven Pacific Northwest and Rocky Mountain states.			Oct. 8
Southern School News reports that 234 of the 285 tax-supported colleges in the South have predominantly white or all-white enrollment, but that 146 of the predominantly white institutions have at least taken some steps toward desegregation.		Commerce Dept. reports that foreign investment in the U.S. totaled $7.5 billion at the end of 1961, while U.S. investment abroad totaled $35 billion. . . . Justice Dept. files an antitrust suit against Sinclair Oil, Cities Service and Richfield Oil, charging them with agreeing not to compete.			Oct. 9
Pres. Kennedy, speaking at a Democratic rally in Baltimore, praises the record of the 87th Congress as one of "positive and progressive accomplishment."	U.S. Senate joins the House in passing a resolution reaffirming U.S. readiness to defend allied rights in Berlin "by whatever means may be necessary."				Oct. 10
		Pres. Kennedy signs a postal rate increase bill (HR 7927) which will raise the per ounce rate for regular letters to 5¢.		Roman Catholic Church's 21st Ecumenical Council opens in St. Peter's Basilica in Rome. . . . Jewish Publication Society of America announces publication of a new and more accurate English translation of the *Torah*.	Oct. 11
Senate GOP leader Everett Dirksen, referring to the 87th Congress, says that never before has Congress "spent so much time accomplishing so little.". . . Pres. Kennedy signs a bill (S3361) permitting 23,000 aliens from countries with over-subscribed quotas to enter the U.S.				Pope John XXIII gives an unprecedented audience in the Vatican's Sistine Chapel to envoys of 80 governments and six international organizations. The Pope appeals for an end to "strife between men of different races."	Oct. 12
87th Congress formally adjourns after completing one of the longest second sessions since W.W. II.					Oct. 13

F	G	H	I	J
Includes elections, federal-state relations, civil rights and liberties, crime, the judiciary, education, health care, poverty, urban affairs and population.	Includes formation and debate of U.S. foreign and defense policies, veterans' affairs and defense spending. (Relations with specific foreign countries are usually found under the region concerned.)	Includes business, labor, agriculture, taxation, transportation, consumer affairs, monetary and fiscal policy, natural resources, and pollution.	Includes worldwide scientific, medical and technological developments, natural phenomena, U.S. weather, natural disasters, and accidents.	Includes the arts, religion, scholarship, communications media, sports, entertainment, fashions, fads and social life.

	World Affairs	Europe	Africa & the Middle East	The Americas	Asia & the Pacific
Oct. 14		West German Foreign Min. Gerhard Schroeder meets in Washington with State Secy. Rusk to discuss appropriate responses in the event of a new Soviet confrontation over Berlin. . . . Thousands of Dutch-speaking Flemings from northern Belgium march into Brussels and clash with French-speaking Walloons in a renewal of a long-standing dispute over language rights and political representation.			
Oct. 15					Sources in South Vietnam report that U.S. helicopter crewmen have begun to fire on any Viet Cong formations encountered during their missions. The U.S. Defense Dept. denies there has been any change in the orders governing the combat conduct of U.S. advisers.
Oct. 16		Soviet readiness to resume East-West negotiations on Berlin and Germany is reportedly stressed by Premier Khrushchev during a three-hour meeting with Foy Kohler, the new U.S. ambassador in Moscow. . . . The New York Times reports that the administration is planning to sell France a nuclear-powered submarine, an action promised by the Eisenhower administration in 1958 but dropped because of congressional opposition.	Ghana announces a relaxation of the national state of emergency imposed Sept. 22 to cope with an outbreak of anti-government terrorism. . . . Following a Washington meeting with Pres. Kennedy, Algerian Premier Ben Bella flies to Cuba where he praises the Castro revolution.		
Oct. 17	U.N. General Assembly elects Morocco, Brazil, Norway, and the Philippines to non-permanent seats on the 11-member Security Council.				
Oct. 18					
Oct. 19	Pres. Kennedy proposes a 1963 world conference on the reduction of international trade barriers.				
Oct. 20		Ukranian Supreme Court sentences six persons to death and nine to prison on charges of illegal currency speculation. All 15 defendants have identifiably Jewish names.			Full-scale fighting erupts between Indian and Communist Chinese troops at two points on the disputed India-Tibet border. Each side accuses the other of aggression.
Oct. 21					Indian forces are reportedly withdrawing from their forward posts on the Tibet border in the face of advancing Chinese troops. Casualties on both sides are described as heavy.

A	B	C	D	E
Includes developments that affect more than one world region, international organizations and important meetings of major world leaders.	Includes all domestic and regional developments in Europe, including the Soviet Union, Turkey, Cyprus and Malta.	Includes all domestic and regional developments in Africa and the Middle East, including Iraq and Iran and excluding Cyprus, Turkey and Afghanistan.	Includes all domestic and regional developments in Latin America, the Caribbean and Canada.	Includes all domestic and regional developments in Asia and Pacific nations, extending from Afghanistan through all the Pacific Islands, except Hawaii.

U.S. Politics & Social Issues	U.S. Foreign Policy & Defense	U.S. Economy & Environment	Science, Technology & Nature	Culture, Leisure & Life Style	
			Gale-force winds and torrential rains batter America's Pacific Northwest coast for the third straight day. At least 46 persons are known dead.		Oct. 14
A special Presidential panel releases a report urging creation of a domestic peace corps to help communities combat mental retardation and other social problems.		Agriculture Secy. Orville Freeman announces a cut in 1963 cotton-growing allotments to the legal minimum of 16 million acres. It is the smallest allotment since 1938.		The *Brooklyn Eagle*, a N.Y.C. newspaper founded in 1841, resumes publication after a seven-year suspension in operations.	Oct. 15
GOP National Chmn. William Miller asserts that Cuba is the "dominant issue of the 1962 campaign.". . . NAACP announces a legal assault upon barriers to Negro employment and job promotion. . . . Reps. Thomas Johnson (D, Md.) and Frank Boykin (D, Ala.) are indicted by a federal grand jury on charges of accepting money to interfere with a Justice Dept. prosecution.	A Thor IRBM carrying a nuclear device for a planned detonation 30 miles above the U.S.'s Pacific testing area veers off course and is destroyed on ground signal. It is the fourth time in five attempts that U.S. scientists have failed to carry out a high-altitude test over Johnston Island.	A compromise version (HR 10650) of the administration's tax-revision bill, including a 7% tax credit for businesses, is signed by Pres. Kennedy.		New York Yankees defeat the San Francisco Giants, 1-0, to win the seventh and deciding game of the World Series.	Oct. 16
James Meredith completes his second week of classes at the University of Mississippi without major incident. Most of the National Guardsmen and U.S. marshals sent to protect Meredith have been withdrawn.		An Agriculture Dept. study indicates that U.S. farmers receive less than $1 on every $5 worth of farm products sold.			Oct. 17
		Commerce Dept. reports that the U.S. GNP rose from an annual rate of $552 billion in the second quarter to a record $555 billion rate in the third quarter.	James Watson (Harvard), Maurice Wilkins (Kings College, London) and Francis Crick (Cambridge, England) are named winners of the 1962 Nobel Prize for medicine and physiology for their research into the structure of DNA.		Oct. 18
	A missile-borne, 20 kiloton nuclear device is detonated in the upper atmosphere over the U.S.'s central Pacific test site near Johnston Island. It is only the second successful high-altitude test in the last six U.S. attempts.				Oct. 19
Pres. Kennedy cuts short a two-week political campaign swing reportedly because he is suffering from a slight cold. Many observers attribute the cancellation to a deepening crisis in Cuba.	*Kill and Overkill: The Strategy of Annihilation* by Ralph Lapp is published in New York. The book claims that the U.S. currently has an atomic arsenal capable of "overkilling the Soviet Union at least 25 times."		An unmanned earth satellite of undisclosed mission is placed into orbit by Soviet scientists. It is the fourth successful Soviet satellite launch in the last 60 days.	The Roman Catholic ecumenical council, Vatican II, issues its first major pronouncement--a "message to humanity" proclaiming that "all men are brothers" irrespective of race or nationality. . . . USSR wins the world shooting championships in Cairo. The U.S. places second.	Oct. 20
			The Ranger Five lunar probe, launched from Cape Canaveral October 18, misses the moon by 450 miles and heads out into solar orbit.		Oct. 21
F	**G**	**H**	**I**	**J**	
Includes elections, federal-state relations, civil rights and liberties, crime, the judiciary, education, health care, poverty, urban affairs and population.	*Includes formation and debate of U.S. foreign and defense policies, veterans' affairs and defense spending. (Relations with specific foreign countries are usually found under the region concerned.)*	*Includes business, labor, agriculture, taxation, transportation, consumer affairs, monetary and fiscal policy, natural resources, and pollution.*	*Includes worldwide scientific, medical and technological developments, natural phenomena, U.S. weather, natural disasters, and accidents.*	*Includes the arts, religion, scholarship, communications media, sports, entertainment, fashions, fads and social life.*	

	World Affairs	Europe	Africa & the Middle East	The Americas	Asia & the Pacific
Oct. 22	Pres. Kennedy goes on nationwide TV to announce the imposition of a naval blockade against Cuba to turn back any vessels carrying offensive military weapons to the island. Kennedy says the action is based on the receipt of firm evidence that the USSR has begun constructing offensive ballistic missile installations in Cuba.	William Vassall, a British Admiralty clerk, is sentenced to 18 years in prison after pleading guilty to spying for the USSR. Vassall testified that he had been blackmailed into spying by agents who threatened to disclose evidence of homosexual activity.			
Oct. 23	U.N. Security Council convenes in emergency session to hear conflicting charges of aggression from the U.S., Cuba and the USSR. . . . USSR issues a statement warning that any U.S. aggressive actions toward Cuba may result in thermonuclear war. . . . According to U.S. Defense Secy. McNamara, at least 25 Russian and Soviet-bloc ships are currently enroute to Cuba.	Most NATO nations issue statements supporting the U.S. position in the Cuban crisis. France, however, remains noncommital and British Labor Party leaders publicly question the validity of U.S. evidence concerning a Soviet build-up in Cuba.		OAS Council unanimously approves a four-point U.S. resolution authorizing the "use of force" to carry out the U.S. arms quarantine against Cuba. . . . Castro denounces the U.S. blockade as a criminal violation of "the sovereign rights" of Cuba.	Indian military sources report that at least a dozen border outposts have fallen to the Chinese since fighting began Oct. 20.
Oct. 24	The U.S. quarantine on arms to Cuba officially begins at 10 a.m. Cuban time. . . . Actg. U.N. Secy Gen. U Thant calls for a temporary suspension of Soviet arms shipments to Cuba and of the U.S. naval counter-measures in order to permit time for a peaceful resolution of the crisis.			Six Latin American nations, including Brazil and Argentina, offer military aid to help the U.S. enforce its blockade of Cuba.	Communist China proposes direct talks between Premier Chou En-lai and Indian P.M. Nehru in an effort to resolve the border disputes that led to the current fighting.
Oct. 25	U.S. Amb.-to-U.N. Stevenson presents the Security Council with aerial photographs purporting to show offensive missile bases in Cuba. The introduction of the photo evidence followed a dramatic exchange in which Stevenson failed to get Soviet Amb. Valerian Zorin to confirm or deny the presence of Soviet missiles in Cuba. . . . Khrushchev informs U Thant that the USSR is willing to suspend arms shipments to Cuba in accord with Thant's Oct. 24 peace proposal. Pres. Kennedy also conveys his interest in the plan but makes no offer to lift the U.S. blockade.		By a General Assembly vote, Uganda is admitted as the U.N.'s 110th member.		Gen. Phoumi Nosavan, rightwing leader in the Laotian coalition government, claims that North Vietnam is increasing its forces in northwestern Laos. North Vietnamese officials insist they have no troops in Laos.
Oct. 26	Secy. Gen. U Thant receives assurances from Premier Khrushchev and Pres. Kennedy that both sides will try to avoid a direct naval confrontation. As yet there have been no reports of hostile contact between U.S. and Soviet vessels. . . . U.S. State Dept. officials indicate to newsmen that the U.S. may be forced to consider "further action" against Cuba if construction on the missile launch sites is not halted immediately.	For the second time in a week French Pres. de Gaulle threatens to resign if he is not given overwhelming support in the Oct. 28 referendum on his proposal for the popular election of future French presidents.	*The New York Times* reports that the U.S. has suspended aid negotiations with Algeria because of Pres. Kennedy's displeasure with anti-American speeches made by Premier Ben Bella during his recent visit to Cuba. State Dept. spokesmen deny the report.		Indian Pres. Sarvepalli Radhakrishnan declares a nationwide state of emergency to make gains on the northeastern and Ladakh fronts. . . . South Vietnamese National Assembly extends Pres. Diem's power to rule by decree for one year.
Oct. 27	A Khrushchev offer to withdraw Soviet missiles from Cuba if Pres. Kennedy promises to remove similar weapons from Turkey is rejected by the U.S. Later in the day, however, Kennedy discloses that the U.S. would accept a prior Soviet proposal to withdraw its missiles in exchange for an American pledge not to invade Cuba.	The publisher and five staff members of the West German news magazine *Der Spiegel* are arrested on charges of bribery and treason. The charges stem from the alleged disclosure of classified information in an October 10 *Der Spiegel* article on West Germany's current military preparedness. . . . A new round of negotiations on Britain's application to the EEC ends in Brussels without significant progress being reported.		U.S. Defense Dept. discloses that a U-2 reconnaissance plane, piloted by Maj. Rudolf Anderson, has failed to return from a mission over Cuba and is presumed lost.	Indian P.M. Nehru rejects an Oct. 24 Chinese proposal that both sides withdraw their forces 12 miles from the "line of actual control" as a first step toward cease-fire talks.

A	B	C	D	E
Includes developments that affect more than one world region, international organizations and important meetings of major world leaders.	Includes all domestic and regional developments in Europe, including the Soviet Union, Turkey, Cyprus and Malta.	Includes all domestic and regional developments in Africa and the Middle East, including Iraq and Iran and excluding Cyprus, Turkey and Afghanistan.	Includes all domestic and regional developments in Latin America, the Caribbean and Canada.	Includes all domestic and regional developments in Asia and Pacific nations, extending from Afghanistan through all the Pacific Islands, except Hawaii.

U.S. Politics & Social Issues	U.S. Foreign Policy & Defense	U.S. Economy & Environment	Science, Technology & Nature	Culture, Leisure & Life Style	
	Kennedy briefs congressional leaders on the crisis in Cuba. Several Senate leaders, including Richard Russell (D, Ga.), are reportedly urging an immediate U.S. invasion of Cuba.	A N.Y.C. minimum wage law providing for a $1.50 minimum by the end of 1963 is signed by Mayor Robert Wagner. The ordinance establishes a higher minimum than any current federal or state statute. . . . The Seattle World's Fair officially closes.			Oct. 22
Pres. Kennedy signs a bill (HR 8140) strengthening conflict-of-interest laws governing federal employees.	Defense Secy. McNamara discloses that U.S. military forces have been placed on worldwide alert and that the mobilization of a large naval-air task force to patrol Cuba's shipping lanes is nearly completed.			Dick Tiger of Nigeria captures the world middleweight championship by scoring a 15-round decision over title-holder Gene Fullmer in San Francisco.	Oct. 23
					Oct. 24
	Senate Preparedness Investigating Subcommittee issues a final report upholding the Defense Dept.'s right to require military officers to submit their speeches for policy review prior to delivery.	A special citizens advisory committee, reporting to HEW Secy. Anthony Celebrezze, calls for a reorientation of the U.S. FDA to emphasize constructive preventive measures instead of "after-the-fact enforcement.". . . Pres. Kennedy signs a bill (HR11586) providing for a two-year extension of federal cost-differential subsidies for domestic ship construction.	Tropical storm "Harriet" strikes southern Thailand leaving at least 769 persons dead and thousands homeless. . . . U.S. sources report that a Soviet nuclear device detonated over central Asia Oct. 22 had created a new artificial radiation belt around the earth.	The Nobel Prize in literature is awarded to American author John Steinbeck, 60, principally for his 1961 novel *The Winter of Our Discontent* . . . . USSR wins its fifth straight world pentathlon team championship in Mexico City. . . . The Nobel Foundation is named recipient of the Eugenio Balzan International Foundation's first annual peace prize.	Oct. 25
	Defense Secy. McNamara tells reporters that Pres. Kennedy had no firm evidence of Soviet missiles in Cuba until Oct. 16 when he received aerial reconnaissance photos showing the crated weapons near launch sites. The statement comes in apparent response to recent Republican charges that the administration dragged its feet in responding to Soviet activity in Cuba. . . . For the second time within a week the U.S. successfully tests a missile-borne nuclear device above its Johnston Island test site in the Pacific.	Bureau of Labor Statistics reports that the U.S. consumer price index jumped .6% in September, the highest monthly increase since February-March 1958.	Conflicting papers on the relationships between diet, blood cholesterol and heart disease highlight the annual meeting of the American Heart Association in Cleveland.	The Television Bureau of Advertising estimates that the number of U.S. homes with at least one TV set has increased from less than one million in 1949 to over 50 million in 1962.	Oct. 26
	Defense Dept. announces the immediate recall to active duty of over 14,000 Air Force Reservists. . . . About 1,000 Student Peace Union followers demonstrate in front of the White House to protest the U.S. blockade of Cuba.		U.S. Surgeon Gen. Luther Terry announces appointment of a 10-member committee to study and make recommendations on the possible health hazards of cigarette smoking.		Oct. 27

F	G	H	I	J
Includes elections, federal-state relations, civil rights and liberties, crime, the judiciary, education, health care, poverty, urban affairs and population.	Includes formation and debate of U.S. foreign and defense policies, veterans' affairs and defense spending. (Relations with specific foreign countries are usually found under the region concerned.)	Includes business, labor, agriculture, taxation, transportation, consumer affairs, monetary and fiscal policy, natural resources, and pollution.	Includes worldwide scientific, medical and technological developments, natural phenomena, U.S. weather, natural disasters, and accidents.	Includes the arts, religion, scholarship, communications media, sports, entertainment, fashions, fads and social life.

	World Affairs	Europe	Africa & the Middle East	The Americas	Asia & the Pacific
Oct. 28	Premier Khrushchev informs the U.S. that he has ordered the withdrawal of all Soviet missiles from Cuba and the dismantling of launch bases, under U.N. supervision. Khrushchev describes the action as a response to Pres. Kennedy's Oct. 27 assurance that the U.S. will not invade the island. Kennedy hails Khrushchev's decision as an "important and constructive contribution to peace."	De Gaulle's plan for direct election of future French presidents is supported by more than 62% of the voters in a nationwide referendum.		Cuban Premier Castro charges that the U.S. pledge not to invade Cuba will be meaningless unless the U.S. withdraws from its naval base at Guantanamo and lifts its "aggressive" trade embargo.	
Oct. 29		NATO's Permanent Council announces that Gen. Lauris Norstad will postpone his retirement as NATO commander until at least Jan. 1, 1963 because of the Cuban crisis. . . . The EEC Commission announces plans to complete the six-nation customs union by Jan. 1, 1967, three years ahead of the original timetable.		U.S. announces that its naval "quarantine" of Cuba will be lifted Oct. 30.	U.S. Amb.-to-India John Kenneth Galbraith announces that the U.S. will honor India's request for emergency American military aid in its border struggle with Communist China.
Oct. 30	By a 56-42 vote the U.N. General Assembly rejects a Soviet resolution calling for the admission of Communist China in place of Nationalist China.	USSR detonates an intermediate yield nuclear device in the atmosphere above its Novaya Zemlya test area in the Arctic. It is the 26th reported test since the Soviets resumed testing Aug. 5 and the seventh test in the last eight days.			British Commonwealth Office discloses that P.M. Macmillan has sent Pakistani Pres. Ayub Khan a message urging that Pakistan and India reconcile their differences in view of the "common danger."
Oct. 31	Actg. Secy. Gen. Thant ends two days of talks in Havana after failing to win Premier Castro's permission for U.N. observers to verify the removal of Soviet weapons from Cuba. . . . U.S. announces it will resume the naval blockade and aerial reconnaissance of Cuba in view of the refusal to permit verification.	West German Justice Min. Wolfgang Stammberger, a Free Democratic member of Adenauer's coalition cabinet, resigns in protest over not having been informed of the government's action against *Der Spiegel* magazine.			P.M. Nehru removes V.K. Krishna Menon as defense minister and assumes the post himself. The action comes amidst intense political criticism of the Indian military's apparent failure to anticipate the Chinese border assault that began Oct. 20.
Nov. 1					India's CP publicly urges all Indians to "unite in defense of the motherland against Chinese aggression."
Nov. 2	Pres. Kennedy reports in a TV address to the American people that the USSR has begun to dismantle its Cuban missile bases as promised. . . . U.S. and Soviet negotiators at the U.N. are reported to have reached agreement on a plan for Red Cross inspection of Soviet vessels enroute to Cuba.			Soviet Deputy Premier Anastas Mikoyan arrives in Havana for talks reportedly aimed at pressuring Castro to comply with the international inspection provisions of Khrushchev's Oct. 28 missile removal pledge.	UAR sources disclose that Communist China has rejected a UAR plan for settling the India-China border war. The proposal, which called for a withdrawal to pre-war positions, had been accpted by Indian P.M. Nehru.
Nov. 3		Barbara Salt is appointed British ambassador to Israel, becoming the first British woman to hold an ambassadorial post.		White House officials inform newsmen that Pres. Kennedy has decided to make on-site verification of Soviet missile base dismantling a precondition for a formal American pledge not to invade Cuba.	Indian military sources estimate that between 2,000 and 2,500 troops have been killed or reported missing since the intense border fighting with China began Oct. 20.

A	B	C	D	E
Includes developments that affect more than one world region, international organizations and important meetings of major world leaders.	*Includes all domestic and regional developments in Europe, including the Soviet Union, Turkey, Cyprus and Malta.*	*Includes all domestic and regional developments in Africa and the Middle East, including Iraq and Iran and excluding Cyprus, Turkey and Afghanistan.*	*Includes all domestic and regional developments in Latin America, the Caribbean and Canada.*	*Includes all domestic and regional developments in Asia and Pacific nations, extending from Afghanistan through all the Pacific Islands, except Hawaii.*

U.S. Politics & Social Issues	U.S. Foreign Policy & Defense	U.S. Economy & Environment	Science, Technology & Nature	Culture, Leisure & Life Style	
					Oct. 28
Ex-Narcotics Commissioner Harry Anslinger says that the number of U.S. narcotics addicts has fallen from one in 400 in 1909 to one in 4,000 currently. He also reports that the 1909 ratio of five female addicts to one male has now been reversed.	Ex-Pres. Eisenhower asserts that eight years of Republican leadership provided the "military readiness" and political backing which made Pres. Kennedy's successful Cuban policy possible.	Federal Reserve Board reports that the U.S. balance of payments deficit rose sharply from a seasonally-adjusted annual rate of $872 million in April-June to an estimated $2.6 billion in July-September.			Oct. 29
	Asst. Defense Secy. Arthur Sylvester, defending the administration from charges of withholding news during the Cuban crisis, asserts that news management is "part of the arsenal of weapons" available to an administration in dealing with crises.			Persons connected with the production of the film *Cleopatra* say the picture has already cost $35 million, easily the most expensive movie ever made.	Oct. 30
		The National Foreign Trade Convention, meeting in New York, adopts a resolution criticizing the 1962 federal tax revision law for requiring taxation of U.S. corporations' foreign income before profits are returned to the U.S.	U.S. civilian and military scientists successfully launch a 355-pound geodetic satellite designed to provide exact measurements of the earth's size and shape. The launch had been delayed for three days during the Cuban crisis for fear the USSR might mistake it for a ballistic missile.		Oct. 31
University of Mississippi Chancellor J. D. Williams warns that students participating in campus disorders will face "drastic disciplinary action, including expulsion." The warning comes after a week of sporadic demonstrations and acts of hooliganism directed against James Meredith, the school's lone Negro student. . . . New Jersey officials charge 60 companies and two hospitals with placing discriminatory job orders with private employment agencies in violation of the state's equal employment opportunity law.	AEC announces the successful detonation of a missile-borne "submegaton" nuclear device over the U.S.'s test area in the central Pacific. It was the 35th in the current series of U.S. atmospheric tests in the Pacific.		English chemists Drs. Max Perutz and John Kendrew share the Nobel Prize in chemistry for their development of an X-ray technique to map protein molecules. . . . Soviet scientist Lev Landau wins the Nobel Prize in physics for his theoretical work on condensed matter, especially liquid hydrogen. . . . Construction begins on a year-round U.S. scientific station at Ellsworth Land, Antarctica, about 850 miles from the South Pole. . . . Soviet scientists successfully launch a camera-equipped planetary probe designed to pass by Mars in June 1963.		Nov. 1
					Nov. 2
	The U.S. Agency for International Development announces that "needs, capabilities and commitment to development" will henceforth be used as the central criteria for processing foreign aid requests.	*Congressional Quarterly* reports that a peacetime record $92,266,154,659 was appropriated by the second session of the 87th Congress.			Nov. 3

F	G	H	I	J
Includes elections, federal-state relations, civil rights and liberties, crime, the judiciary, education, health care, poverty, urban affairs and population.	*Includes formation and debate of U.S. foreign and defense policies, veterans' affairs and defense spending. (Relations with specific foreign countries are usually found under the region concerned.)*	*Includes business, labor, agriculture, taxation, transportation, consumer affairs, monetary and fiscal policy, natural resources, and pollution.*	*Includes worldwide scientific, medical and technological developments, natural phenomena, U.S. weather, natural disasters, and accidents.*	*Includes the arts, religion, scholarship, communications media, sports, entertainment, fashions, fads and social life.*

	World Affairs	Europe	Africa & the Middle East	The Americas	Asia & the Pacific
Nov. 4	Pres. Kennedy announces that the U.S. has completed its current series of atmospheric tests in the Pacific and reaffirms American readiness to sign a treaty banning further tests. . . . USSR is reportedly continuing almost daily atmospheric nuclear tests.		King Hussein issues a decree approving an agreement to merge the military forces of Jordan and Saudi Arabia and to coordinate the two nations' economic policies.		
Nov. 5	A front page editorial in the *Peking People's Daily* condemns any "appeasement" of the U.S. in the Cuban situation. The article is the most direct expression to date of Chinese displeasure with Khrushchev's action in the missile crisis. . . . U.S. is reported to have protested the USSR's alleged failure to begin removing its 11-28 jet bombers from Cuban bases. . . . The Nobel Committee of the Norwegian Parliament announces its decision not to award a Peace Prize for 1962.	West German Chancellor Adenauer dismisses Dr. Walter Strauss as state secretary in the Justice Ministry. The firing follows a Free Democratic Party threat to withdraw from Adenauer's coalition cabinet unless action is taken against those responsible for the handling of the controversial crack down on *Der Spiegel* . . . . Bulgarian Premier Anton Yugov and seven other high-ranking government officials are expelled from the CP's Central Committee on charges of undermining party unity. The purge is viewed as a victory for Bulgarian supporters of Khrushchev's de-Stalinization programs.			Indian Defense Ministry reports the loss of the Ladakh post of Daulet Beg Oldi, a key position at the southern end of Karakorum Pass leading from China's Singkiang Province to Indian-controlled Kashmir. The statement estimates that Chinese troops have occupied 3,000 square miles of Indian-claimed territory since October 20. . . . Pakistani Pres. Ayub Khan criticizes U.S. and British military aid to India, claiming that it may have the effect of prolonging the India-China fighting.
Nov. 6	The U.N. General Assembly adopts two resolutions calling for immediate great power action to halt all nuclear tests by Jan. 1, 1963.	Soviet First Deputy Premier Aleksei Kosygin, delivering the traditional Kremlin address on the eve of the anniversary of the Bolshevik revolution, firmly defends Khrushchev's Cuban missile decision as the only sane course in the face of possible nuclear war.	U.N. General Assembly by 67-16 vote (23 abstentions) adopts a resolution calling for economic sanctions against South Africa in protest of its apartheid racial policies. . . . Saudi Arabia severs diplomatic relations with the UAR because of alleged attacks on Saudi territory by UAR naval units fighting with republican forces in Yemen.	A two-week London conference aimed at drafting a constitution for an independent British Guiana ends in deadlock after rival Guianian political groups failed to agree on critical election provisions.	Shipments of U.S. arms to aid India in its border fight with Communist China are reportedly arriving in Calcutta at the rate of a plane-load every three hours. . . . Prince Norodom Sihanouk publicly warns the U.S. that Cambodia will break diplomatic relations with South Vietnam if alleged border provocations are not halted immediately.
Nov. 7	Khrushchev tells a Kremlin reception that all the Soviet missiles sent to Cuba are now dismantled and on their way home. . . . A U.S.-Soviet agreement for U.S. observation at sea of Soviet missiles being removed from Cuba is reached in negotiations at the U.N. . . . Khrushchev tells Western newsmen that the USSR will end its current series of nuclear tests on Nov. 20.	West German Chancellor Adenauer, speaking in the Bundestag, vigorously defends the government's action against *Der Spiegel*, adding that the magazine "systematically commits treason to make money.". . . French Pres. de Gaulle appears on national television to ask support for Gaullist candidates in the forthcoming National Assembly elections scheduled to begin Nov. 18.			Neutralist Laotian Premier Souvanna Phouma says he may be forced to resign if right and left factions of the coalition continue to refuse to cooperate. Sporadic fighting between the factional forces has been reported over the last three months.
Nov. 8		The Conservative majority in the British Parliament turns back a Laborite motion demanding a stronger defense of British and Commonwealth interests in the ongoing EEC negotiations. . . . Thomas Galbraith, ex-civil lord of the Admiralty and currently joint undersecretary for Scotland, resigns from the British cabinet following public disclosure of controversial letters he had written to recently convicted spy William Vassall.	Ex-P.M. Julius Nyerere of the African National Union is elected president of Tanganyika following week-long nationwide balloting.	U.S. Defense Dept. announces that aerial surveillance of Cuba has shown that "all known. . .missile bases in Cuba have been dismantled."	
Nov. 9				Defense Dept. spokesmen tell reporters that a U.S. naval shipboard count of the Soviet missiles leaving Cuba has begun.	South Vietnam breaks relations with Laos after the Laotian neutralist government accepts credentials of an ambassador from North Vietnam.

A	B	C	D	E
Includes developments that affect more than one world region, international organizations and important meetings of major world leaders.	Includes all domestic and regional developments in Europe, including the Soviet Union, Turkey, Cyprus and Malta.	Includes all domestic and regional developments in Africa and the Middle East, including Iraq and Iran and excluding Cyprus, Turkey and Afghanistan.	Includes all domestic and regional developments in Latin America, the Caribbean and Canada.	Includes all domestic and regional developments in Asia and Pacific nations, extending from Afghanistan through all the Pacific Islands, except Hawaii.

U.S. Politics & Social Issues	U.S. Foreign Policy & Defense	U.S. Economy & Environment	Science, Technology & Nature	Culture, Leisure & Life Style	
			Tass reports the reception of natural radio signals from Venus by astronomers at the Pulkovo Observatory near Leningrad.		Nov. 4
Supreme Court denies a hearing to seven Black Muslim members appealing battery convictions in connection with disturbances during a church meeting in Monroe, La. The seven claimed they acted to prevent police deprivation of their right to freedom of worship.					Nov. 5
Democrats show impressive strength in mid-term elections. They gain four seats in the Senate, maintain their control of 34 gubernatorial posts and sustain only a minimal loss of six seats from their heavy majority in the House. . . . Ex-V.P. Nixon loses to incumbent Calif. Gov. Edmund Brown. Edward Kennedy easily defeats George Lodge (R) in the Mass. senatorial race. GOP presidential possibles George Romney (Mich.) and William Scranton (Pa.) win their respective gubernatorial contests.			British Navy reports that a record oceanic depth of 37,782 ft. was recorded by the survey ship Cook in the Mindanao trench, east of the Philippines.		Nov. 6
Nixon, conceding his Calif. defeat in what he termed his "last press conference," concludes with a bitter denunciation of the press, saying "You won't have Nixon to kick around any more.". . . A Texas state jury sentences agricultural financier Billie Sol Estes to eight years in prison on charges of arranging fraudulent mortgages. . . . Eleanor Roosevelt, widow of Pres. Franklin Roosevelt and world renowned humanitarian, dies of tuberculosis in New York at age 78.			NASA announces that Grumman Aircraft has been awarded a $350 million contract to build a lunar module designed to carry two astronauts from an orbiting Apollo spacecraft to the lunar surface and back.	U.N. General Assembly approves an international convention barring compulsory marriages and other abuses of women's rights in marital matters.	Nov. 7
Over 140 law school deans and college professors submit a statement to the Senate Judiciary Committee endorsing the Supreme Court's June 25 decision banning prayer in the N.Y. public schools.	The London-based Institute of Strategic Studies estimates that the U.S. has a vast superiority over the USSR in longrange missile strength, but not in numbers of medium and intermediate range missiles. . . . Roger Hillsman, chief of State Dept. intelligence, tells the Dallas World Affairs Council that the Sino-Soviet dispute is likely to persist for a long time and the U.S. world policy should be re-examined in view of this probability.			Catharina Lodders of the Netherlands wins the 1962 Miss World beauty contest in London.	Nov. 8
AFL-CIO Pres. George Meany charges Herbert Hill, labor secretary of the NAACP, of untruths and smears in accusing labor unions of racial bias. Hill's controversial anti-labor bias campaign has recently drawn criticism from Negro as well as labor leaders.				A. M. Sonnabend, head of the American Jewish Committee, tells the organization's national executive board that the Vatican II ecumenical council has opened a "new era of friendship" in Roman Catholic-Jewish relations. Sonnabend also lauds the Pope's removal from liturgy of offensive references to Jews.	Nov. 9

F	G	H	I	J
Includes elections, federal-state relations, civil rights and liberties, crime, the judiciary, education, health care, poverty, urban affairs and population.	Includes formation and debate of U.S. foreign and defense policies, veterans' affairs and defense spending. (Relations with specific foreign countries are usually found under the region concerned.)	Includes business, labor, agriculture, taxation, transportation, consumer affairs, monetary and fiscal policy, natural resources, and pollution.	Includes worldwide scientific, medical and technological developments, natural phenomena, U.S. weather, natural disasters, and accidents.	Includes the arts, religion, scholarship, communications media, sports, entertainment, fashions, fads and social life.

	World Affairs	Europe	Africa & the Middle East	The Americas	Asia & the Pacific
Nov. 10	Soviet CP newspaper *Izvestia* suggests that the East-West impasse over inspection of a nuclear test-ban might be solved by an agreement to use unmanned seismic devices that could be installed on the territories of the nuclear powers to record clandestine underground tests.		Mohammed al-Badr, deposed imam of Yemen, appears before newsmen at an undisclosed site in northeastern Yemen to extinguish rumors that he had been killed. . . . The UAR and the new republican regime in Yemen sign a five-year mutual defense pact in Sana.		U.S. State Dept. announces that its emergency airlift of some $5 million worth of military equipment to India has been completed.
Nov. 11			U.N. officials in the Congo report that U.N. troops are still being sporadically attacked by Katangan forces in violation of the existing truce agreement.	Deputy U.S. Defense Secy. Roswell Gilpatric discloses that naval units have counted 42 missiles on the decks of Soviet ships leaving Cuba. He says that while these include all the missiles believed to have been sent to Cuba, on-site inspection is still needed for final confirmation.	Indian P.M. Nehru tells a mass rally in New Delhi that the war with China may last for years.
Nov. 12					
Nov. 13	Proposals for Red Cross inspection of Soviet ships bound for Cuba are dropped after U.S., Soviet and Cuban negotiators repeatedly fail to agree on terms for implementing the plan. Talks on alternative inspection programs are expected to continue.	P.M. Macmillan names a high-level "tribunal of inquiry" to make a full investigation into the controversial case of William Vassall, a former Admiralty clerk convicted in October of spying for the Soviets. . . . West German Chancellor Adenauer flies to Washington to confer with Pres. Kennedy on Western policy toward Berlin in view of the Cuban crisis.	Israeli Knesset overwhelmingly approves a resolution reaffirming opposition to the return of Palestinian Arab refugees to Israel.		
Nov. 14			The Eritrean Assembly votes to end Eritrea's federated status and unite with Ethiopia.	*The New York Times* reports that the U.S. naval blockade of Cuba is continuing in effect, but that no action is being taken against Soviet vessels "carrying what are believed to be peaceful cargoes."	
Nov. 15		Following two days of Washington talks with Pres. Kennedy, West German Chancellor Adenauer tells U.S. newsmen that the Cuban crisis proved that USSR will negotiate only when forced.		Premier Castro informs Acting U.N. Secy. Gen. U Thant that Cuba intends to shoot down any U.S. military plane entering its airspace on a reconnaissance mission.	

A	B	C	D	E
Includes developments that affect more than one world region, international organizations and important meetings of major world leaders.	*Includes all domestic and regional developments in Europe, including the Soviet Union, Turkey, Cyprus and Malta.*	*Includes all domestic and regional developments in Africa and the Middle East, including Iraq and Iran and excluding Cyprus, Turkey and Afghanistan.*	*Includes all domestic and regional developments in Latin America, the Caribbean and Canada.*	*Includes all domestic and regional developments in Asia and Pacific nations, extending from Afghanistan through all the Pacific Islands, except Hawaii.*

U.S. Politics & Social Issues	U.S. Foreign Policy & Defense	U.S. Economy & Environment	Science, Technology & Nature	Culture, Leisure & Life Style	
U.S. Post Office Dept. announces that it has suspended the promotional authority of the Atlanta postmaster because of "clear evidence" of non-compliance with Pres. Kennedy's nondiscrimination policies.				A jury in Liege, Belgium acquits Suzanne Van De Put Coipel, mother of a Thalidomide-deformed child, on charges of murder in the mercy-killing of the infant.	Nov. 10
An interview with Alger Hiss on Howard K. Smith's ABC-TV documentary, *The Political Obituary of Richard M. Nixon*, gives rise to an intense national controversy. ABC V.P. James Hagerty, defending the program, says that Hiss' appearance was more than balanced by the pro-Nixon views expressed by Rep. Gerald R. Ford (R, Mich.) and other program participants. . . . Gallup Poll issues a report indicating that Democrats received 55.3% of the major party vote in the Nov. 6 Congressional elections. Nearly three out of four Negroes voted Democratic.				Golfers Arnold Palmer and Sam Snead retain the Canada Cup for the U.S. by defeating two-man teams from 33 countries.	Nov. 11
	Sen. Barry Goldwater (R, Ariz.), speaking in New York, calls for the firing of U.N. Amb. Stevenson and Presidential aides Chester Bowles and Arthur Schlesinger, alleging that the three have consistently urged "a soft policy toward communism."	AFL-CIO Pres. George Meany's opposition to a CIO union-backed candidate for a vacant seat on the Executive Council is prevented from becoming a potentially divisive issue by a council vote to refer the matter to private negotiation between Meany and AFL-CIO V.P. Walter Reuther.	Typhoon Karen strikes Guam leaving one dead and 45,000 homeless. It is the worst storm in Guam's history.		Nov. 12
		Budget Bureau estimates that the federal government will end fiscal 1963 with a $7.8 billion deficit instead of the $500 million surplus forecast in January. The Bureau attributes the deficit to the nation's "slower than assumed" economic recovery. . . . Post Office announces it will mass-produce misprinted 4¢ stamps commemorating the late Dag Hammarskjold. The decision is expected to reduce the collector value of the 400 originally misprinted stamps--estimated at from $1,000 to $10,000--back to 4¢.	NASA announces that Leroy Gordon Cooper has been chosen to pilot the next Mercury mission-- an 18-orbit full-day flight scheduled for April 1963.	A papal decree inserting the name of St. Joseph in the canon of the Roman Catholic mass is formally announced at the Vatican II ecumenical council. It is the first change in the canon since the seventh century.	Nov. 13
Southern Regional Council publicly criticizes the Kennedy administration for its alleged inactivity in the unsuccessful civil rights campaign against official segregation in Albany, Ga. . . . White House sources confirm reports that Pres. Kennedy has donated to charity his federal salaries received as a Congress member and as President.		Northern N. J. Teamsters local president Anthony (Tony Pro) Provenzano is indicted by a federal grand jury on charges of accepting gifts in violation of the Taft-Hartley law.	Canada lifts a two-month ban on the use of Sabin live-virus polio vaccine after an investigation of 31 recently reported polio cases revealed no significant link to the vaccine.		Nov. 14
Patrick Frawley Jr., chairman of Eversharp, Inc., and James Kemper, president of the Kemper Insurance Co., announce that their firms intend to withhold advertising from ABC-TV in protest against Alger Hiss's appearance on ABC's Nov. 11 documentary *The Political Obituary of Richard Nixon* . . . . Anti-discrimination pledges drafted by the President's Committee on Equal Employment Opportunity are formally signed by 119 of the AFL-CIO's 131 affiliated national unions.		Ex-State Secy. Christian Herter is named by Pres. Kennedy to the new post of Special Representative for Trade Negotiations. . . . Agriculture Secy. Orville Freeman announces a major reorganization of the Agriculture Stabilization and Conservation Service. . . . Justice Dept. announces that it has filed 72 antitrust suits in 1962. A total of 60 were filed in 1961.		Don Drysdale of the Los Angeles Dodgers wins the Cy Young Award as the best major league pitcher of 1962.	Nov. 15

F	G	H	I	J
Includes elections, federal-state relations, civil rights and liberties, crime, the judiciary, education, health care, poverty, urban affairs and population.	Includes formation and debate of U.S. foreign and defense policies, veterans' affairs and defense spending. (Relations with specific foreign countries are usually found under the region concerned.)	Includes business, labor, agriculture, taxation, transportation, consumer affairs, monetary and fiscal policy, natural resources, and pollution.	Includes worldwide scientific, medical and technological developments, natural phenomena, U.S. weather, natural disasters, and accidents.	Includes the arts, religion, scholarship, communications media, sports, entertainment, fashions, fads and social life.

	World Affairs	Europe	Africa & the Middle East	The Americas	Asia & the Pacific
Nov. 16					Indian Defense Ministry reports a renewed Chinese offensive in the eastern sector of the North East Frontier Agency. The advance ends a brief lull in the border fighting. . . . Thai government announces that all U.S. ground combat troops will be out of the country by Nov. 30.
Nov. 17		The latest round of talks in Brussels on conditions for British membership in the EEC ends in deadlock. The negotiations reportedly snagged on the question of EEC tariff rates to be applied to African members of the British Commonwealth.	French Defense Ministry reports that tens of thousands of Moslem Algerians who served with the French Army are fleeing Algeria to escape persecution by fellow countrymen.	Haitian government deports four French-born Roman Catholic priests accused of disrespect of the government and violations of local customs.	
Nov. 18	Soviet CP charges Chinese and Albanian critics of Khrushchev's Cuban missile policy with trying to push mankind "toward thermonuclear war."	Austria's ruling Conservative People's Party increases its Parliamentary plurality in nationwide elections.			
Nov. 19		West Germany's Free Democratic Party withdraws its five members from Chancellor Adenauer's coalition cabinet in protest against Defense Min. Franz Josef Strauss' recently acknowledged role in the raid on *Der Spiegel*. The action comes after Adenauer rejected FDP demands for Strauss' dismissal. . . . Bulgarian National Assembly names CP First Secy. Todor Zhivkov as new premier succeeding the recently purged Anton Yugov.		Chilean troops open fire on a crowd of 5,000 demonstrators gathered outside of Santiago to show support for a communist-sponsored general strike. Five persons are killed. . . . An Argentine electoral reform decree permitting limited participation by Peronist parties is announced by Interior Min. Rodolfo Martinez.	
Nov. 20	U.S. ends its naval quarantine of Cuba following the announcement by Pres. Kennedy that the USSR had agreed to withdraw all Soviet IL-28 jet bombers from the island. Cuban Premier Castro had earlier informed U.N. officials that he would no longer oppose the removal of the bombers.				Pres. Kennedy announces the dispatch of a special U.S. mission to New Delhi to determine what additional arms aid India needs to repel Chinese border advances. The announcement follows disclosure of a Nov. 19 request from Nehru for more military aid.
Nov. 21	*The New York Times* reports that Soviet Premier Khrushchev has recently informed the British government of his readiness to re-examine serious proposals for a nuclear test-ban.	USSR announces cancellation of the special military alert ordered for all Soviet and Warsaw Pact forces at the height of the Cuban missile crisis.		A federal grand jury in New York indicts three pro-Castro Cubans on charges of conspiring to commit sabotage in the U.S. Cuban officials dismiss the arrests as an attempt to offset the exposure of CIA activities in Cuba.	Communist China announces that it is ordering an immediate cease-fire along the India-China border and will withdraw all forces 20 miles from their current position. The order amounts to a unilateral imposition of Peking's Oct. 24 border proposals, previously rejected by India.
Nov. 22		EEC leaders meeting in Paris reject U.S. protests against what it considered unreasonable rate discrimination against American farm products. . . . René Jules Gustave Coty, 80, last president of the Fourth French Republic (1954-59), dies in Paris of heart complications.			Fighting along the India-China border is reportedly at a halt following imposition of China's unilateral cease-fire. Indian troops are apparently honoring the truce despite official Indian rejection of the terms contained in the Chinese cease-fire declaration. . . . U.N. command officials in Korea report North Korean troops Nov. 20 attacked a U.N. outpost killing one American soldier.
Nov. 23			A British-Nyasaland agreement providing for Nyasaland home rule as a preliminary step to full independence is announced in London.		Twelve American-manned U.S. transport planes arrive in New Delhi to help ferry Indian troops to forward fighting positions near the China border.

A	B	C	D	E
Includes developments that affect more than one world region, international organizations and important meetings of major world leaders.	Includes all domestic and regional developments in Europe, including the Soviet Union, Turkey, Cyprus and Malta.	Includes all domestic and regional developments in Africa and the Middle East, including Iraq and Iran and excluding Cyprus, Turkey and Afghanistan.	Includes all domestic and regional developments in Latin America, the Caribbean and Canada.	Includes all domestic and regional developments in Asia and Pacific nations, extending from Afghanistan through all the Pacific Islands, except Hawaii.

U.S. Politics & Social Issues	U.S. Foreign Policy & Defense	U.S. Economy & Environment	Science, Technology & Nature	Culture, Leisure & Life Style	
A LaFayette County (Miss.) grand jury blames federal officials for the University of Mississippi rioting during the registration of James Meredith. Atty. Gen. Kennedy rejects the finding, saying the jury "did not consider all the evidence about the riot."				Fifty-six modern French paintings--stolen from a Saint-Tropez museum on July 16, 1961--are discovered in a barn 50 miles west of Paris.	Nov. 16
Pres. Kennedy appoints a cabinet-level committee, headed by Atty. Gen. Robert Kennedy, to report on the feasibility of establishing a domestic peace corps.		Bureau of Labor Statistics reports that the purchasing power of the average U.S. consumer has increased 20-40% since 1947-1950. . . . Dulles International Airport, built to serve Washington D.C., is formally dedicated at ceremonies attended by Pres. Kennedy and ex-Pres. Eisenhower.			Nov. 17
		Four Teamsters locals in Pennsylvania and New Jersey retain their bargaining rights as representatives of 8,200 truck drivers and dock workers by narrowly defeating a rebel Teamsters reform group in a violence-marred NLRB election.	Dr. Neils Henrik David Bohr, Danish nuclear physicist, Nobel Prize winner (1922), and co-drafter of the theory of atomic fission, dies in Copenhagen at age 77.	Bruce McLaren of New Zealand, driving a Cooper Climax, wins the Australian Grand Prix.	Nov. 18
In a personal comment on the ABC-Hiss interveiw controversy, FCC Chmn. Newton Minow says that broadcasting must be free from censorship by "those few, fearful advertisers who seek to influence the professional judgment of broadcast newsmen."	Serious concern over an alleged overdependence upon computers and electronic equipment in military decision-making is voiced by government and industry experts attending an Air Force-sponsored conference in Hot Springs, Va.	Pres. Kennedy's Advisory Committee on Labor-Management Policy releases a report urging "prompt and significant" reductions be enacted in 1963 in personal and corporate income tax rates. . . . Commerce Dept. reports that U.S. personal income rose from a record rate of $443.5 billion in September to $445.6 billion in October, the largest monthly jump since April.		Prelates attending the Vatican II ecumenical council conclude a month-long study of proposals for reforming liturgical practices. Use of the vernacular instead of Latin in the recitation of the mass was among the possible changes discussed. . . . The Goncourt Prize is awarded in Paris to Anna Langfus for her novel Les Bagages de Sable.	Nov. 19
Pres. Kennedy issues a long-awaited executive order barring racial and religious discrimination in federal and federally aided housing. The action is hailed by civil rights leaders and denounced by Southern conservatives.	At a Washington news conference Pres. Kennedy defends administration handling of news during the Cuban crisis, but says steps will be taken to avoid unnecessary or inappropriate news restrictions in the future.	Commerce Dept. reports that U.S. GNP climbed from an annual rate of $552 billion in the second quarter to a $555.3 billion rate in the third quarter. The increase falls about $200 million short of the department's October prediction.			Nov. 20
					Nov. 21
For the fourth time in the past five years serious racial rioting mars the play-off game for the city high school football championship of Washington, D.C. At least 40 persons are injured and 15 arrested in the post-game fighting.		In a report to Pres. Kennedy, the AEC predicts that by 1970 nuclear power will be competitive with conventional fuels in most of the U.S.			Nov. 22
	Defense Dept. officially cancels its Cuban crisis order restricting information provided to reporters.			Los Angeles Dodger infielder Maury Wills is named the National League's most valuable player of 1962. Yankee outfielder Mickey Mantle was earlier selected as the American League's most valuable player.	Nov. 23
F	G	H	I	J	
Includes elections, federal-state relations, civil rights and liberties, crime, the judiciary, education, health care, poverty, urban affairs and population.	Includes formation and debate of U.S. foreign and defense policies, veterans' affairs and defense spending. (Relations with specific foreign countries are usually found under the region concerned.)	Includes business, labor, agriculture, taxation, transportation, consumer affairs, monetary and fiscal policy, natural resources, and pollution.	Includes worldwide scientific, medical and technological developments, natural phenomena, U.S. weather, natural disasters, and accidents.	Includes the arts, religion, scholarship, communications media, sports, entertainment, fashions, fads and social life.	

	World Affairs	Europe	Africa & the Middle East	The Americas	Asia & the Pacific
Nov. 24	U.S. delegate Arthur Dean, arriving in Geneva for the soon-to-be-reconvened disarmament talks, informally rejects Soviet press proposals for the use of automatic seismic devices as a substitute for on-site inspection of a nuclear test-ban treaty.			Havana sources report that Cuban militia units, mustered on special alert during the missile crisis, are being demobilized.	
Nov. 25	Correspondents at the Geneva disarmament talks report that Western officials believe the USSR is continuing nuclear tests despite Khrushchev's apparent pledge to suspend all tests by Nov. 20.	Final results from France's two-stage National Assembly elections reveal an overwhelming victory for candidates pledged to support Pres. de Gaulle. The Gaullist triumph marks the first time in modern French history that a single unified party has won full control of Parliament.	U.S. Pres. Kennedy is reported to have offered a plan for the settlement of the conflict in Yemen. The proposal reportedly calls for the withdrawal of UAR troops now serving with Yemen's republican regime and the suspension of Jordanian and Saudi Arabian aid to royalist forces.	Pro-government Guatemalan troops, led personally by Pres. Miguel Ydigoras Fuentes, crush a brief air force uprising outside of Guatemala City. Ydigoras blames pro-Castro leftists for inspiring the revolt. . . . Soviet First Deputy Premier Anastas Mikoyan concludes a three-and-a-half week visit to Cuba with a televised farewell address in which he pledged continued Soviet support and protection.	
Nov. 26	Soviet First Deputy Premier Mikoyan, in N.Y.C. for talks with U Thant, tells reporters that the flexibility shown by the USSR and U.S. in the Cuban crisis raises the possibility of a general improvement in Soviet-American relations. . . . The 17-nation Geneva disarmament talks resume after a two-and-a-half month recess. Despite recent optimism, opening statements indicate little likelihood for a quick end to the deadlock over major issues.				India announces that it is sending special delegations to nonaligned nation to explain its opposition to Communist China's border settlement proposals.
Nov. 27		Georges Pompidou is reappointed French premier by de Gaulle.	Rebel Yemeni royalists ask for a U.N. investigation into charges of UAR aggression in Yemen.	Cuba informs U.N. officials it will permit international inspection of the dismantling of Soviet missile bases only if similar inspection is made of bases in the U.S. where anti-Castro forces may be training for an invasion of Cuba.	India is reported to have shifted four of its eight divisions on the borders of East and West Pakistan to the northern border regions facing China. The move is believed to reflect a tacit understanding between Pakistan and India to cool the Kashmir dispute pending settlement of the China-India border crisis. . . . An agreement by the three Laotian factions to form a unified national army of 30,000 men is announced in Vientiane.
Nov. 28		West German Chancellor Adenauer, yielding to Free Democratic Party demands, announces his decision to form a new government without the controversial Franz-Josef Strauss as Defense Minister. . . . Princess Wilhelmina Helena Pauline Maria, Queen of the Netherlands from 1898 until her abdication in 1948, dies in Het Loo at age 82.	Saudi Arabian Premier Crown Prince Faisal rejects the U.S.'s recent Yemen peace proposal and asserts that the deposed imam is about to recover his role as the legitimate ruler of Yemen.		
Nov. 29		In notes to the Western allies, the USSR repeats demands for quick action to settle the Berlin problem, but significantly makes no reference to previous demands that such a settlement end allied occupation rights in the city.	Algerian government officially bans the Communist Party. The action follows an assertion by Premier Ben Bella that Algeria has room for only one party--his National Liberation Front.		India and Pakistan announce agreement to begin direct talks on disputed Kashmir. The action--a reversal of previous Indian policy--is believed to reflect a general easing of India-Pakistan tensions caused by a mutual apprehension over China's recent border offensive.
Nov. 30	U Thant is elected to a full four-year term as U.N. secretary general by unanimous vote of the Security Council and General Assembly. The USSR's support for Thant is viewed as a confirmation that Soviet leaders have abandoned (at least temporarily) their demand for a tripartite reorganization of the U.N. Secretariat.				

A	B	C	D	E
Includes developments that affect more than one world region, international organizations and important meetings of major world leaders.	Includes all domestic and regional developments in Europe, including the Soviet Union, Turkey, Cyprus and Malta.	Includes all domestic and regional developments in Africa and the Middle East, including Iraq and Iran and excluding Cyprus, Turkey and Afghanistan.	Includes all domestic and regional developments in Latin America, the Caribbean and Canada.	Includes all domestic and regional developments in Asia and Pacific nations, extending from Afghanistan through all the Pacific Islands, except Hawaii.

U.S. Politics & Social Issues	U.S. Foreign Policy & Defense	U.S. Economy & Environment	Science, Technology & Nature	Culture, Leisure & Life Style	
	Defense Dept. begins awarding contracts for the F-111, described as the biggest fighter plane program since W.W. II.			St. Louis University defeats the University of Maryland to win its third National Collegiate soccer championship in the last four years.	Nov. 24
	Defense Secy. McNamara announces that as a result of a restudy of the controversial RS-70 manned bomber he has decided to add $50 million to its development program.				Nov. 25
	Budget Dir. David Bell is named by Pres. Kennedy to succeed Hamilton Fowler as chief of the Agency for International Development.		Floods devastate towns and oases on the outskirts of the Tunisian Sahara leaving at least 50 dead.		Nov. 26
Calif. has surpassed N.Y. as the most populous state in the U.S. according to Calif. Gov. Edmund Brown.	A report by a special House Foreign Affairs subcommittee charges that the State Dept. and the Voice of America have not done enough to "sustain the spirit of resistance" in the communist nations of Eastern Europe.	Lloyd's Register of Shipping reports that the U.S. merchant ship fleet declined by nearly one million tons during fiscal 1962.	NASA discloses that budgetary and technical problems have forced postponement of the first two-man Gemini space flight from late 1963 to sometime in early 1964.	Terry Wayne Baker, Oregon State quarterback, wins the Heismann Memorial Trophy as the outstanding college football player of 1962.	Nov. 27
	Defense Dept. is reportedly tightening its "human reliability" regulations with regard to persons having access to atomic weapons. . . . For the fifth time an Air Force Skybolt air-to-ground missile fails to perform in a test firing near Cape Canaveral.	U.S. Seventh Circuit Court in Chicago upholds the right of U.S. railroads to make work-rule changes to eliminate "featherbedding" (unneeded jobs). . . . Bureau of Labor Statistics reports that the U.S. cost of living index declined slightly in October for the first time since December 1961.			Nov. 28
Virginia's 1962 state legislative reapportionment is ruled unconstitutional by a three-judge federal court in Alexandria. . . . Three Navajo Indians are convicted in San Bernardino, Calif. on narcotics charges for using peyote in a religious ceremony.					Nov. 29
Illinois Supreme Court upholds the right of the all-white suburb of Deerfield, Ill. to condemn the scheduled site of an interracial housing project for use as a park.	The U.S.'s 15th Polaris-firing submarine, U.S.S. Henry Clay, is launched at Newport News, Va.	Pres. Kennedy increases restrictions on oil imports in a move designed to allow domestic producers to share with foreign producers any increased U.S. market demand.			Nov. 30

F	G	H	I	J
Includes elections, federal-state relations, civil rights and liberties, crime, the judiciary, education, health care, poverty, urban affairs and population.	Includes formation and debate of U.S. foreign and defense policies, veterans' affairs and defense spending. (Relations with specific foreign countries are usually found under the region concerned.)	Includes business, labor, agriculture, taxation, transportation, consumer affairs, monetary and fiscal policy, natural resources, and pollution.	Includes worldwide scientific, medical and technological developments, natural phenomena, U.S. weather, natural disasters, and accidents.	Includes the arts, religion, scholarship, communications media, sports, entertainment, fashions, fads and social life.

	World Affairs	Europe	Africa & the Middle East	The Americas	Asia & the Pacific
Dec. 1					Communist Chinese troops begin withdrawing from some of their forward positions on the Indian border in apparent fulfillment of China's unilaterally declared cease-fire plan. Despite the pullback, India formally reiterates its rejection of China's proposed settlement.
Dec. 2	Newly elected U.N. Secy. Gen. U Thant, in a major policy address at Johns Hopkins University, chides Western leaders for not sufficiently responding to the "obvious change of political climate in the Soviet Union" brought about by Khrushchev.				India's Communist Party expresses full support for P.M. Nehru's rejection of China's border settlement proposals.
Dec. 3	The Soviet delegation at Geneva rejects various neutralist proposals for a new temporary moratorium on underground nuclear tests, saying they will endorse nothing short of a permanent ban on all tests. . . . Soviet representatives to the Italian CP congress openly criticize China's border conflict with India as an "adventurist position which has to do with Marxism." The denunciation comes in the wake of increasingly harsh Chinese attacks on Khrushchev's alleged "retreat" in the Cuban missile crisis.		Algerian troops take up positions in downtown Algiers and arrest an undisclosed number of Moslem and European opponents of the Ben Bella government.	U.S. Defense Dept. announces that the USSR has begun removing its IL-28 jet bombers from Cuba.	
Dec. 4		Yugoslav Pres. Tito arrives in Moscow to begin a two-week visit to the USSR.	France is reported to have agreed to provide Algeria with $50 million in emergency loans before the end of the year.	Argentine Economy Min. Alvaro Carlos Alsogaray resigns in the face of pressure from high-ranking military officers dissatisfied with his alleged failure to control Argentina's runaway inflation.	
Dec. 5		West European news sources report signs of a possible relaxation in international tensions over Berlin despite continuation of frequent incidents along the Berlin Wall.		Cuba nationalizes privately owned retail and wholesale stores dealing in clothing, shoes and hardware.	South Korea's state of martial law, in effect since the May 6, 1961 military coup, is formally terminated by order of junta chairman Gen. Chung Hee Park.

A	B	C	D	E
Includes developments that affect more than one world region, international organizations and important meetings of major world leaders.	Includes all domestic and regional developments in Europe, including the Soviet Union, Turkey, Cyprus and Malta.	Includes all domestic and regional developments in Africa and the Middle East, including Iraq and Iran and excluding Cyprus, Turkey and Afghanistan.	Includes all domestic and regional developments in Latin America, the Caribbean and Canada.	Includes all domestic and regional developments in Asia and Pacific nations, extending from Afghanistan through all the Pacific Islands, except Hawaii.

U.S. Politics & Social Issues	U.S. Foreign Policy & Defense	U.S. Economy & Environment	Science, Technology & Nature	Culture, Leisure & Life Style	
House Un-American Activities Committee begins hearings into possible communist infiltration of the Women-Strike-for-Peace organization. . . . The Southern Regional Council reports that over 27,000 Negroes were registered to vote during an April-June registration drive in key Southern areas.				Soviet high jumper Valeri Brumel is named international sportsman of the year for the 2nd straight year in a poll of sportswriters from 26 countries. . . . Australia wins the team title in the 35-nation Empire & Commonwealth Games held in Perth, Australia.	**Dec. 1**
	An article by Stewart Alsop written for the Dec. 8 issue of the *Saturday Evening Post* alleges that U.S. Amb.-to-U.N. Adlai Stevenson opposed the Cuban blockade decision and instead urged major concessions to the Soviets during administration deliberations at the height of the missile crisis. . . . Sen. Mike Mansfield, touring Southeast Asia, becomes the first major U.S. official to refuse to make an optimistic public comment on the military situation in South Vietnam.				**Dec. 2**
University of Alabama ends the processing of applicants for the 1963 spring semester without taking action on pending applications from three Negroes. . . . New Jersey and Illinois become the first two states to ratify the proposed 24th Constitutional amendment to bar the payment of poll taxes in federal elections. . . . HEW releases a study predicting that U.S. school enrollment will increase by one to one-and-a-half million students annually through 1980.	U.N. Amb. Stevenson meets with reporters to deny that he advocated compromise and appeasement during the Cuban missile crisis.			Carlos Ortiz of New York retains the world lightweight championship by knocking out Teruo Kosaka in a Tokyo title bout.	**Dec. 3**
Federal housing agencies make public new regulations designed to implement Pres. Kennedy's anti-bias housing order. The rules emphasize persuasion and negotiation, rather than sanctions, as the central means for gaining compliance with the order. . . . Union City, N.J. is the U.S.'s most densely populated city with 40,138 persons per square mile, according to figures published in the Census Bureau's *City and County Data Book*.	A controversial realignment and reorganization of the Army National Guard and Reserve forces is put into effect by Defense Secy. McNamara.	Internal Revenue Service announces a liberalization in proposed rules to curb abuses in business expense account tax deductions. The rules as originally proposed had been widely criticized as unreasonably stringent.			**Dec. 4**
U.S. District Judge Frank Ellis (New Orleans), reversing an earlier decision, rules that Tulane University cannot be forced by the court to accept Negro students.	Pres. Kennedy makes public a letter to U.N. Amb. Stevenson thanking him for his advice during the Cuban missile crisis and praising his performance at the U.N. Despite the apparent vote of confidence, some Washington observers believe Stevenson is about to be eased out of the administration. Pres. Walter Hallstein of the EEC Commission tells U.S. business leaders in New York that the European customs union will offer them greater trading opportunities but only at the price of reciprocal access to the U.S. market. . . . N.Y. Gov. Nelson Rockefeller (R), speaking to the annual meeting of the National Association of Manufacturers, criticizes the Kennedy administration for an alleged overreliance on deficit spending to stimulate the economy. U.S. and USSR announce agreement at the UN to cooperate in three peaceful areas of space—meteorology, a world geomagnetic survey and communications satellites. . . . Swedish scientists, visiting the USSR, report learning of a Soviet plan to send a manned spacecraft around the moon and back in late 1963.				**Dec. 5**

F	G	H	I	J
Includes elections, federal-state relations, civil rights and liberties, crime, the judiciary, education, health care, poverty, urban affairs and population.	Includes formation and debate of U.S. foreign and defense policies, veterans' affairs and defense spending. (Relations with specific foreign countries are usually found under the region concerned.)	Includes business, labor, agriculture, taxation, transportation, consumer affairs, monetary and fiscal policy, natural resources, and pollution.	Includes worldwide scientific, medical and technological developments, natural phenomena, U.S. weather, natural disasters, and accidents.	Includes the arts, religion, scholarship, communications media, sports, entertainment, fashions, fads and social life.

	World Affairs	Europe	Africa & the Middle East	The Americas	Asia & the Pacific
Dec. 6		The International Commission of Jurists releases a study in Geneva charging the Spanish government with pursuing political policies characteristic of a "totalitarian regime."		U.S. announces that 42 Soviet IL-28 jets, believed to be the entire bomber fleet sent to Cuba, have been observed on the decks of homeward-bound Russian ships.	India orders the closing of its consular offices in Shanghai and Lhasa, Tibet. A complete break in diplomatic relations with China, however, is not expected.
Dec. 7		Barbara Hunter Fell, an officer in the British Central Information Office, is sentenced to two years in prison for lending classified Foreign Office documents to a member of the Yugoslav embassy.	The Congo becomes the fourth African state to bar a visit by U.S. Sen. Allen Ellender (D,La.), currently on an African tour. The action follows publication of a Dec. 1 speech in which Ellender disparaged the leadership capability of the "average African."	Anti-Castro sources report that despite the removal of Soviet missiles a large number of Russian technicians are remaining in Cuba to help upgrade the island's conventional defense systems.	
Dec. 8					A widespread rebellion erupts in the British-protected territories of Brunei, Sarawak, and North Borneo. The insurgents, reputed in British circles to have Indonesian support, oppose British plans to merge the three territories with Malaya and Singapore to form the federation of Malaysia.
Dec. 9	U.S. State Dept. sources estimate that Soviet-Chinese trade declined in 1961 by as much as 45% over 1960. The figures are viewed as further evidence of the deterioration in Sino-Soviet relations.		Ceremonies are held in Dar-es-Salaam to mark Tanganyika's transformation into an independent republic within the British Commonwealth.		
Dec. 10	USSR informs the Geneva convention that it is prepared to accept an inspected test-ban policed by a small number of automatic seismic detection devices operated under international supervision.				
Dec. 11	Soviet delegation to the Geneva disarmament talks warns that unless Western powers cease nuclear testing by Jan. 1, 1963, the USSR will be forced to take "corresponding action."	West German Chancellor Adenauer and leaders of the Free Democratic Party (FDP) reach final agreement on the formation of a new coalition government. The accord ends a government crisis that began Nov. 19 when five FDP ministers resigned from the cabinet in protest against then Defense Min. Franz Josef Strauss's role in the arrest of *Der Spiegel* editors.	U.N. representatives in the Congo inform Pres. Tshombe that Secy. Gen. U Thant will ask for economic sanctions against Katanga unless immediate steps are taken to end its secession.		
Dec. 12	U.S. representatives at the Geneva talks propose installation of a direct "hot line" communication link between the White House and the Kremlin. USSR has previously advanced similar proposals. . . . In a televised address in defense of his Cuban missile decision, Soviet Premier Khrushchev explicitly rebuts the Chinese accusation of appeasement. The speech is believed to be the first public acknowledgement in the USSR of the deepened rift in Sino-Soviet relations caused by the Cuban crisis.	Supreme Soviet approves a fiscal 1963 defense budget of $15.3 billion, up $.6 billion over 1962.			In a Kremlin speech Soviet Premier Khrushchev warns against continued Western aid to India in its border conflict with China.

A	B	C	D	E
Includes developments that affect more than one world region, international organizations and important meetings of major world leaders.	*Includes all domestic and regional developments in Europe, including the Soviet Union, Turkey, Cyprus and Malta.*	*Includes all domestic and regional developments in Africa and the Middle East, including Iraq and Iran and excluding Cyprus, Turkey and Afghanistan.*	*Includes all domestic and regional developments in Latin America, the Caribbean and Canada.*	*Includes all domestic and regional developments in Asia and Pacific nations, extending from Afghanistan through all the Pacific Islands, except Hawaii.*

U.S. Politics & Social Issues	U.S. Foreign Policy & Defense	U.S. Economy & Environment	Science, Technology & Nature	Culture, Leisure & Life Style	
		Commerce Dept. reports that as of June 30 the bonded debt of local and state governments totaled $77.4 billion. . . . The Health Insurance Institute (U.S.) reports that per-capita health expenditures in the U.S. rose from $87 in 1956 to $116 in 1961. . . . An explosion at a U.S. Steel Corp. coal mine in Carmichaels, Pa. kills 37 miners.		A special report by FCC investigators calls for expanded federal supervision of U.S. TV network programming.	Dec. 6
Joseph McD. Mitchell, city manager of Newburgh, N.Y. who attracted national attention in 1961 for instituting strict welfare rules, is arrested on bribery charges.	Defense Dept. discloses that the Kennedy administration budget for fiscal 1964 will not include funds for continued development of the Skybolt air-to-ground missile.		Four days of heavy, smoke-laden fog is blamed for the deaths of 106 persons in London, England.	The first chapter of a draft constitution on sacred liturgy—granting bishops more power to authorize the use of modern languages in worship—is approved by delegates at the Vatican II ecumenical council. . . . Tom Tresh of the N.Y. Yankees and Ken Hubbs of the Chicago Cubs are named the American and National Leagues' rookies of the year.	Dec. 7
	A special advisory committee to the State Dept., headed by ex-State Secy. Christian Herter, calls for the establishment of a graduate Foreign Affairs College to train U.S. diplomats in cold war diplomacy.	A printers' strike results in the shut-down of New York City's nine daily newspapers.	NASA reports that data from free-world tracking stations indicates that at least seven Soviet cosmonauts have been killed in space. Rumors of fatalities have been repeatedly denied by Soviet space officials.	Pope John XXIII formally closes the first phase of the Vatican II ecumenical council with an expression of hope for more rapid progress on substantive issues during later sessions. . . . A football writers poll names John McKay of the University of Southern California as college coach of the year. . . . Emile Griffith retains the world welterweight championship by scoring a ninth round TKO over Argentine Jorge Fernandez in Las Vegas.	Dec. 8
	A Life magazine story asserts that the White House made available the information upon which the Saturday Evening Post based its controversial account of Adlai Stevenson's allegedly "soft" policy position during the Cuban crisis.				Dec. 9
The private Cosmos Club of Washington, D.C. accepts its first Negro member--Prof. John Hope Franklin of Brooklyn College. The club stirred controversy earlier in the year when it rejected the application of Asst. State Secy. Carl Rowan.	Pres. Kennedy appoints a special task force to review the political and economic effectiveness of existing U.S. foreign aid programs.		Pres. Kennedy's Science Advisory Committee calls for an expanded federal program to meet a projected national shortage of qualified scientists and engineers.		Dec. 10
		Labor Dept. reports that the U.S. unemployment rate averaged about 5.7% from September through November.			Dec. 11
Recently resigned Gary, Ind. Mayor George Chacharis pleads guilty to evading federal income tax on over $200,000 of alleged kickbacks from city contracts.	Pres. Kennedy at his Washington news conference once again lauds U.N. Amb. Stevenson's "distinguished service," but refuses to comment specifically on the truth of the Saturday Evening Post's characterization of Stevenson's position during the missile crisis. . . . Pres. Kennedy confirms press reports that the U.S. plans to curtail development of the Skybolt air-to-ground missile.			Dick Tiger of Nigeria is named fighter of the year in a New York Boxing Writers Association poll.	Dec. 12

F	G	H	I	J
Includes elections, federal-state relations, civil rights and liberties, crime, the judiciary, education, health care, poverty, urban affairs and population.	Includes formation and debate of U.S. foreign and defense policies, veterans' affairs and defense spending. (Relations with specific foreign countries are usually found under the region concerned.)	Includes business, labor, agriculture, taxation, transportation, consumer affairs, monetary and fiscal policy, natural resources, and pollution.	Includes worldwide scientific, medical and technological developments, natural phenomena, U.S. weather, natural disasters, and accidents.	Includes the arts, religion, scholarship, communications media, sports, entertainment, fashions, fads and social life.

	World Affairs	Europe	Africa & the Middle East	The Americas	Asia & the Pacific
Dec. 13		Visiting Yugoslav Pres. Tito, in a speech to the Supreme Soviet, praises Khrushchev's leadership in the Cuban crisis.			British military sources in Brunei say that considerable progress has been made in suppressing the recent uprising.
Dec. 14	Peking radio reports that Communist China has proposed a meeting of the world's Communist parties to resolve outstanding ideological disputes.		Northern Rhodesia receives its first African-dominated government as a result of legislative elections held under the territory's recently revised constitution. Leaders of the new government say they will seek a break-up of the Rhodesia-Nyasaland Federation.	Costa Rica, Nicaragua, Honduras, El Salvador and Guatemala sign a charter establishing an Organization of Central American States patterned after the OAS.	Indonesian government issues a statement disclaiming any role in the Brunei revolt, but praising the insurgents' struggle "against colonialism."
Dec. 15		NATO Ministerial Council ends three days of debate on the mounting controversy over proposals for reshaping the West's U.S.-controlled nuclear deterrent forces. Major issues of the discussions were France's determination to build an independent nuclear deterrent, and the U.S. decision to drop development of the Skybolt missile, a key weapon in Britain's planned nuclear arsenal.	U.N. General Assembly passes a U.S.-opposed resolution condemning Portugal for maladministration of Angola, Mozambique, and Portuguese Guinea. . . . The rightwing, pro-apartheid Rhodesian Front Party captures control of the Southern Rhodesian government by defeating the long-ruling United Federal Party in legislative elections. Most Africans boycotted the voting.		
Dec. 16		British P.M. Macmillan and French Pres. de Gaulle conclude two days of talks on Britain's negotiations to enter the EEC. No breakthroughs are reported in France's opposition to Britain's entry conditions.			Indian civilian officials begin reoccupying key border positions in the North East Frontier Agency following the withdrawal of Chinese forces.
Dec. 17	In a nationally televised interview, Pres. Kennedy cites the Communist-bloc's alleged desire to upset the existing balance of power as the chief obstacle to world stability.	France and West Germany announce reaching agreement on establishing "systemized" cooperation between the two governments in politics, culture and defense. . . . Pres. Kennedy reiterates U.S. opposition to the development of independent nuclear deterrents by America's Western European allies. . . . Monaco adopts a new constitution providing for female suffrage, continuation of the hereditary monarchy and abolition of capital punishment.	Algerian Premier Ben Bella publicly thanks the U.S. for its food relief program, which has helped feed an estimated four million Algerians. It is the first formal acknowledgement of the aid.	Pres. Kennedy says that Cuba's probable refusal to permit on-site inspection of its bases will require continued U.S. reliance on aerial reconnaissance. . . . U.S. Atty. Gen. Robert Kennedy meets with Brazilian Pres. João Goulart in Brasilia to discuss U.S. concern over the international consequences of Brazil's 50% annual inflation rate.	South Korean voters approve a new junta-drafted constitution providing for a strong presidential form of government.
Dec. 18	U.S. AEC confirms that the USSR is continuing atmospheric nuclear tests despite previously announced plans to suspend testing Nov. 20.	Pres. Kennedy and P.M. Macmillan arrive in Nassau for discussion of proposals on Europe's nuclear defense in the wake of the U.S. decision to drop the Skybolt missile program.	Senegalese Premier Mamadou Dia is arrested after an unsuccessful attempt to forcibly dissolve the National Assembly and seize power.		
Dec. 19	Chinese CP Central Committee member Liao Cheng-chin, in a Peking speech, accuses Soviet leaders of having "completely lost confidence in the revolutionary struggles of the peoples of the world."		The new republican government of Yemen is formally recognized by the U.S. after pledging to honor the previous Yemeni regime's international obligations. . . . Britain announces that it has accepted in principle Nyasaland's right to secede from the Rhodesia-Nyasaland Federation. The decision is denounced by Federation Premier Roy Welensky.		Pres. Kennedy is reported to have assured P.M. Nehru that the U.S. will seriously consider any Indian request for long-term U.S. military aid in its border conflict with China.
Dec. 20		The year's last scheduled round of talks on British membership in the EEC end without producing substantive settlement of any of the disputes blocking an agreement.	U.N. General Assembly unanimously passes a U.S.-sponsored resolution for a two-year extension of U.N. relief programs to Palestinian Arab refugees. . . . A preliminary agreement for the association of 18 African states with the EEC is signed in Paris.	Juan Bosch, candidate of the left-leaning Dominican Revolutionary Party, is elected president of the Dominican Republic in the nation's first free elections in 38 years.	
	A	**B**	**C**	**D**	**E**
	Includes developments that affect more than one world region, international organizations and important meetings of major world leaders.	*Includes all domestic and regional developments in Europe, including the Soviet Union, Turkey, Cyprus and Malta.*	*Includes all domestic and regional developments in Africa and the Middle East, including Iraq and Iran and excluding Cyprus, Turkey and Afghanistan.*	*Includes all domestic and regional developments in Latin America, the Caribbean and Canada.*	*Includes all domestic and regional developments in Asia and Pacific nations, extending from Afghanistan through all the Pacific Islands, except Hawaii.*

U.S. Politics & Social Issues	U.S. Foreign Policy & Defense	U.S. Economy & Environment	Science, Technology & Nature	Culture, Leisure & Life Style	
Defense Dept. reports that it has spent nearly $4 million in enforcing the court-ordered enrollment of James Meredith at the University of Mississippi.		The annual convention of the American Farm Bureau Federation backs a series of resolutions opposing Kennedy administration farm and fiscal policies.	The first experimental Project Relay communications satellite is launched successfully from Cape Canaveral, but lacks sufficient power to relay TV or telephone signals.		Dec. 13
	A satellite of undisclosed mission is launched into polar orbit from Vandenberg Air Base in California. It is the sixth "secret" satellite launched by the U.S. since Oct. 9.	Speaking before the Economic Club in New York, Pres. Kennedy reiterates his intention to seek an across-the-board tax cut in 1963. Kennedy adds that the "temporary" budget deficit entailed by the cut would be more than offset by the resulting boost in economic activity.	The U.S. Mariner 2 space probe passes within 22,000 miles of Venus and heads into solar orbit. The pass, closest ever by a manmade object, affords the transmission of valuable data on the planet's cloud cover and surface temperature.		Dec. 14
				Boston Celtic guard Bob Cousy sets a National Basketball Association career record of 5,926 field goals in a game against the Cincinnati Royals. . . . British-born character actor Charles Laughton, 63, dies of cancer in Hollywood, California. Laughton won an Academy Award in 1933 for his role in *The Private Life of Henry VIII*.	Dec. 15
	Several prominent Democratic Senators publicly criticize the administration's plans to cancel development of the Skybolt air-to-ground missile.		Explorer 16, a 222-pound satellite designed to report on micro-meteorites for the guidance of U.S. space vehicle designers, is successfully launched from Wallops Island, Va.		Dec. 16
Pres. Kennedy gives a personal report on his first two years in office in an unrehearsed, taped TV interview with leading network newsmen. . . . U.S. CP is fined $120,000 after being convicted of failing to register with the government as an agent of the USSR.	During his televised interview with network newsmen Pres. Kennedy accepts personal responsibility, for the ill-fated decision to back the Bay of Pigs invasion.				Dec. 17
					Dec. 18
	Air Force declares as operational the last of a planned 126 nuclear-armed Atlas missiles. The U.S.'s officially-reported nuclear ICBM strength now stands at 200 operational missiles.	Census Bureau reports that the number of U.S. manufacturing workers rose in the 1950s by 21% while the number of agricultural workers dropped 37%.	U.S. Public Health Service lifts its three month ban on Type III Sabin oral live-virus polio vaccine after an investigation established the drug's relative safety.		Dec. 19
Southern Education Reporting Service says that South Carolina and Alabama are the only states still with completely segregated schools. . . . Atty. Gen. Kennedy urges the Fourth Circuit Court of Appeals to order the reopening of the Prince Edward County, Va. public schools on a non-segregated basis.			National Science Foundation reports that U.S. federal spending for research and development in fiscal 1963 will total $14.7 billion, 31% more than in 1962.	Don Meyers, 22, sets a world indoor pole vault record of 16 ft. 1 1/4 in. at the University of Chicago's annual holiday track meet.	Dec. 20

F	G	H	I	J
Includes elections, federal-state relations, civil rights and liberties, crime, the judiciary, education, health care, poverty, urban affairs and population.	*Includes formation and debate of U.S. foreign and defense policies, veterans' affairs and defense spending. (Relations with specific foreign countries are usually found under the region concerned.)*	*Includes business, labor, agriculture, taxation, transportation, consumer affairs, monetary and fiscal policy, natural resources, and pollution.*	*Includes worldwide scientific, medical and technological developments, natural phenomena, U.S. weather, natural disasters, and accidents.*	*Includes the arts, religion, scholarship, communications media, sports, entertainment, fashions, fads and social life.*

	World Affairs	Europe	Africa & the Middle East	The Americas	Asia & the Pacific
Dec. 21	The 17th regular session of the U.N. General Assembly adjourns on schedule in New York.	Pres. Kennedy and P.M. Macmillan announce agreement on steps toward creating an integrated Western nuclear force. The envisioned force will be built around U.S.-made Polaris missiles rather than the recently abandoned Skybolt weapons.			The sultan of Brunei, Sir Omar Ali Saifuddin, suspends Brunei's constitution in the wake of the unsuccessful revolt against his British-protected regime. . . . Communist China's alleged claims to extensive territory in India, USSR and other countries is outlined in *India News*, a weekly publication of the Indian embassy in Washington.
Dec. 22					
Dec. 23		Nikolai Fedorenko replaces Valerian Zorin as Soviet amb.-to-the U.N. . . . P.M. Macmillan tells reporters in London that Pres. Kennedy's Dec. 21 pledge to provide Britain with Polaris missiles will assure British nuclear independence "for a generation."			An unidentified U.S. helicopter pilot is killed flying an airlift mission in South Vietnam. He is the fifth reported U.S. fatality since Nov. 3.
Dec. 24				The 1,113 prisoners captured in the 1961 invasion of Cuba are released in exchange for $53 million worth of medicine and baby food under an agreement reached Dec. 21 in Havana between Premier Castro and the U.S.-based Cuban Families Committee.	
Dec. 25					
Dec. 26		USSR accuses "several" unnamed members of the U.S. embassy of espionage and demands a halt to the activities.			Pakistan and Communist China announce an agreement on the demarcation of the border between China's Sinkiang Province and the Pakistan-controlled section of Kashmir.
Dec. 27		Official French sources report that Pres. de Gaulle has decided to reject Pres. Kennedy's offer to supply France and other allies with Polaris missiles for use in a unified nuclear force within NATO. De Gaulle reportedly opposes the decision as an obstacle to his plans for an independent French atomic force. . . . Soviet Premier Khrushchev is reported to have again asked West German Chancellor Adenauer to consider a Berlin settlement based on the creation of a U.N. presence in the city.			Preliminary Indian-Pakistani talks on disputed Kashmir begin on schedule in Rawalpindi despite Indian anger over yesterday's announcement of a Chinese-Pakistani border agreement.
Dec. 28					Indian sources report a massive build-up of Communist Chinese forces in Tibet.

A	B	C	D	E
Includes developments that affect more than one world region, international organizations and important meetings of major world leaders.	*Includes all domestic and regional developments in Europe, including the Soviet Union, Turkey, Cyprus and Malta.*	*Includes all domestic and regional developments in Africa and the Middle East, including Iraq and Iran and excluding Cyprus, Turkey and Afghanistan.*	*Includes all domestic and regional developments in Latin America, the Caribbean and Canada.*	*Includes all domestic and regional developments in Asia and Pacific nations, extending from Afghanistan through all the Pacific Islands, except Hawaii.*

U.S. Politics & Social Issues	U.S. Foreign Policy & Defense	U.S. Economy & Environment	Science, Technology & Nature	Culture, Leisure & Life Style	
		Atlantic and Gulf coast dock workers strike, closing down 54 major U.S. ports.		The National Board of Review selects *The Longest Day* as the best film of 1962.	Dec. 21
Atty. Gen. Kennedy names private attorney Leon Jaworski to prosecute contempt of court charges filed by the Justice Dept. against Miss. Gov. Ross Barnett for allegedly obstructing the court-ordered enrollment of James Meredith at the Univ. of Mississippi.	Air Force successfully tests a Skybolt missile in what is viewed as a last-minute attempt to demonstrate the controversial weapon's potential value.				Dec. 22
		District Judge William Miller in Nashville, Tenn. orders an investigation into possible jury tampering in the month-long trial of Teamsters Pres. James Hoffa on charges of violating the Taft-Hartley Act. Miller declared a mistrial prior to ordering the investigation.		Dallas Texans score a sudden death victory over the Houston Oilers to win the American Football League championship.	Dec. 23
				White House announces that Gen. of the Army Douglas MacArthur has agreed to arbitrate the continuing jurisdictional dispute between the Amateur Athletic Union and the National Collegiate Athletic Association.	Dec. 24
	It is learned today that a group including Attorney General Robert F. Kennedy raised a ransom of $2 million for the release of prisoners held by Cubans since the Bay of Pigs. This cash payment was in addition to a pledge of $53 million worth of food and drugs.				Dec. 25
		National Safety Council reports 632 U.S. traffic deaths during the Christmas weekend.			Dec. 26
		A final version of the newly tightened regulations governing tax-deductible business expense costs is released by the IRS. . . . American Telephone & Telegraph Co. reports that the number of telephones in the world total over 150 million. More than 50% are in the U.S.			Dec. 27
National Institute of Health reports that at least $6 million has been spent throughout the world for birth and population control studies. About 60% of the total was spent by the U.S. government.		Dr. Frances O. Kelsey, who played a key role in keeping Thalidomide off the U.S. market, is named director of a new investigational branch of the FDA.		Australia defeats Mexico to win its third straight Davis Cup tennis championship.	Dec. 28

F	G	H	I	J
Includes elections, federal-state relations, civil rights and liberties, crime, the judiciary, education, health care, poverty, urban affairs and population.	*Includes formation and debate of U.S. foreign and defense policies, veterans' affairs and defense spending. (Relations with specific foreign countries are usually found under the region concerned.)*	*Includes business, labor, agriculture, taxation, transportation, consumer affairs, monetary and fiscal policy, natural resources, and pollution.*	*Includes worldwide scientific, medical and technological developments, natural phenomena, U.S. weather, natural disasters, and accidents.*	*Includes the arts, religion, scholarship, communications media, sports, entertainment, fashions, fads and social life.*

	World Affairs	Europe	Africa & the Middle East	The Americas	Asia & the Pacific
Dec. 29			Troops of the U.N. Force in the Congo attack objectives in Elizabethville and other parts of Katanga in what appears to be a major attempt to end the Tshombe regime's secession from the central government. U.N. officials cite alleged recent truce violations by Katangan forces as the cause of the renewed fighting.	Pres. Kennedy reviews the 1,113 recently released members of the 1961 Cuban invasion Brigade 2506 during an emotional rally of 40,000 Cuban exiles in Miami.	
Dec. 30		Generalissimo Franco announces an increase in the daily minimum wage of Spain's unskilled workers from 60¢ to $1.	Katanga Pres. Tshombe flees to Southern Rhodesia to avoid capture by advancing U.N. troops.	The Dominican government reports that it has crushed an uprising of religious cultists in the town of Palma Sol near the Haitian border. . . . Cuban Premier Castro announces that remaining relatives of the recently-freed Bay of Pigs invaders will not be released unless the U.S. permits resumption of commercial air flights to Cuba, suspended since the missile crisis.	A Communist Chinese memo accuses India of stepping up preparations for a border offensive.
Dec. 31	In a New Year's Eve release by *Tass*, Premier Khrushchev is reported to have renewed his offer of an unpoliced nuclear test moratorium beginning Jan. 1, 1963.		U.N. Secy. Gen. U Thant releases an ultimatum demanding that Pres. Tshombe negotiate with the central government on Katanga's re-entry into the Congo within two weeks or else face "other measures" from the U.N. Force.		The first year of large-scale U.S. aid to South Vietnam ends without decisive gains for either the government or the Viet Cong. North Vietnamese leader Ho Chi Minh has reportedly vowed to outlast American aid and keep up guerrilla war for 10 years if necessary.

A	B	C	D	E
Includes developments that affect more than one world region, international organizations and important meetings of major world leaders.	*Includes all domestic and regional developments in Europe, including the Soviet Union, Turkey, Cyprus and Malta.*	*Includes all domestic and regional developments in Africa and the Middle East, including Iraq and Iran and excluding Cyprus, Turkey and Afghanistan.*	*Includes all domestic and regional developments in Latin America, the Caribbean and Canada.*	*Includes all domestic and regional developments in Asia and Pacific nations, extending from Afghanistan through all the Pacific Islands, except Hawaii.*

U.S. Politics & Social Issues	U.S. Foreign Policy & Defense	U.S. Economy & Environment	Science, Technology & Nature	Culture, Leisure & Life Style	
	Pres. Kennedy names ex-Texas reporter Bill Moyers to be deputy director of the Peace Corps.				Dec. 29
Housing and Home Finance Agency reports that despite an increase in Negroes' incomes over the past decade, Negroes still generally live in poorer quality housing than whites of comparable income.		U.S. Travel Service Director Voit Gilmore says that 559,000 persons have visited the U.S. from abroad since his office opened 11 months ago. The number represents a 19.4% increase over 1961.		Green Bay Packers defeat the New York Giants 16-7 to win their second straight National Football League championship.	Dec. 30
Census Bureau estimates U.S. population at 188,045,000, up 2,755,000 over Jan. 1, 1962.	Sens. Thomas Dodd (D, Conn.), Barry Goldwater (R, Ariz.) and other political conservatives denounce U.S. support for the U.N.'s current offensive against the Katanga regime. . . . *Newsweek* magazine reports that the U.S. has launched at least 35 reconnaissance satellites during the past year, including a recently developed model capable of "tapping Soviet microwave telephone links."	Negotiations in the 10-day old East coast dock strike are recessed until after the New Year by Labor Secy Willard Wirtz. Wirtz entered the talks Dec. 28.	Sir Charles Galton Darwin, 75, British theoretical physicist and grandson of the evolutionist Charles R. Darwin, dies near Cambridge, England.	Abe Saperstein, commissioner of the six-team American Basketball League, announces that the financially troubled ABL will suspend operations immediately.	Dec. 31

F	G	H	I	J
Includes elections, federal-state relations, civil rights and liberties, crime, the judiciary, education, health care, poverty, urban affairs and population.	*Includes formation and debate of U.S. foreign and defense policies, veterans' affairs and defense spending. (Relations with specific foreign countries are usually found under the region concerned.)*	*Includes business, labor, agriculture, taxation, transportation, consumer affairs, monetary and fiscal policy, natural resources, and pollution.*	*Includes worldwide scientific, medical and technological developments, natural phenomena, U.S. weather, natural disasters, and accidents.*	*Includes the arts, religion, scholarship, communications media, sports, entertainment, fashions, fads and social life.*

1963

Dr. Martin Luther King addresses thousands of civil rights demonstrators Aug. 28 from the steps of the Lincoln Memorial in Washington. In his address he announces, "I have a dream."

Valentina Tereshkova, the Soviet Union's first female cosmonaut, landed safely June 19, after orbiting the earth 48 times.

Night club owner Jack Ruby levels a pistol at Lee Harvey Oswald, the accused assassin of President Kennedy, on Nov. 23. Moments later Ruby shoots Oswald, who dies several hours later.

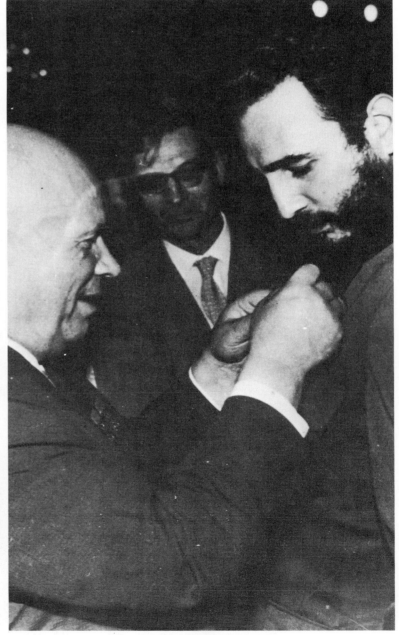

Soviet Premier Nikita Khrushchev examines a medal presented to Fidel Castro during the Cuban leader's visit to the USSR.

Mrs. John F. Kennedy with her children, Caroline and John, Jr., walk behind the casket of the slain president as it is carried up the steps of the Capitol to lie in state. Attorney General Robert Kennedy follows.

The day after his election, new West German Chancellor Ludwig Erhard (left) shakes hands with retiring Chancellor Konrad Adenauer, in the Palais Schaumburg in Bonn.

On June 5 John Profumo is forced to resign as Minister of War in the British Cabinet because of his affair with model Christine Keeler.

Devastation on a street in Skopje, Yugoslavia after a violent earthquake struck the city on July 26. Eighty percent of the city's structures were destroyed.

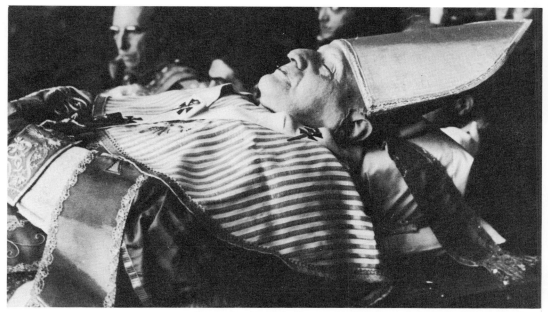

The body of the late Pope John XXIII is carried into St. Peter's Basilica on June 6.

Sir Winston Churchill doffs his hat before going for a ride in Monte Carlo. Churchill announced his retirement from public life on May 1.

	World Affairs	Europe	Africa & the Middle East	The Americas	Asia & the Pacific
Jan.	U.N. receives a Soviet-U.S. note saying that the two countries consider the Cuban missile crisis closed.	France and Germany sign a major treaty calling for close cooperation. . .France vetos Britain's entry into the Common Market.	U.N. troops occupy Kolwezi, the last major secessionist stronghold in Katanga.	More than 1,000 refugees leave Cuba for the U.S.	India says that Communist Chinese troops have withdrawn from most of the disputed territory captured during the 1962 border conflict.
Feb.	U.N. Undersecy. Ralph Bunche goes to Yemen as a mediator.	Seven NATO countries express support for a plan to establish a unified Western nuclear strike force.	Iraqi officers take power and execute P.M. Abdul Karim Kassem.	Canada accepts U.S. nuclear missiles on its territory.	Indonesia declares its opposition to the proposed federation of Malaysia.
March	U.N. African delegates criticize South Africa's aparteid policy.	Hungarian Premier Janos Kadar announces an amnesty for most political prisoners effective April 4.	France conducts an underground nuclear test in the Sahara despite Algeria's protests.	Peruvian Gen. Nicolas Lindley Lopez becomes the head of the ruling junta.	South Korea reimposes a ban on political activity.
April	U.N. Secy. Gen. U Thant says that Egypt and Saudi Arabia have approved a U.N. mediation plan.	Soviet Premier Nikita Khrushchev hints that he may retire because of old age.	Senegal accuses a Portuguese plane of strafing a Senegalese village.	Lester Pearson becomes premier of Canada.	80th U.S. soldier dies in Vietnam.
May	OAS calls for a peaceful solution of the dispute between the Dominican Republic and Haiti.	Sir Winston Churchill announces that he will retire from political life.	Baath Socialist party becomes dominant in Syria.	Dominican Republic withdraws its troops from the Haitian border.	Buddhists protest against the South Vietnamese government in Hue.
June	U.S. and the Soviet Union establish an emergency communications link between Moscow and Washington.	France withdraws its naval forces from the NATO fleet in the North Atlantic.	Levi Eshkol becomes Israeli premier.	Peruvian voters elect Fernando Belaunde Terry as president.	Laotian Communists make major advances in the Plain of Jarres.
July	U.S. Britain and the Soviet Union sign a treaty prohibiting nuclear tests in the atmosphere.	France refuses to sign the treat prohibiting nuclear tests in the atmosphere.	Observers report that African guerrilla activity is growing in the Portugese colonies.	OAS recommends new steps against Communist subversion emanating from Cuba.	Four British protectorates agree to form the Federation of Malaysia.
Aug.	U.N. Security Council votes for an arms embargo on South Africa.	Britain announces that Malta will become independent by May, 1964.	Israeli and Jordanian forces exchange gunfire in Jerusalem.	Canada makes a major wheat sale to Communist China.	South Vietnamese police raid Buddhist pagodas and arrest more than 100 Buddhist monks.
Sept.	At the U.N. Pres. Kennedy calls for a joint U.S.-Soviet moon program.	Turkey becomes an associate member of the Common Market.	Ben Bella becomes the first president of Algeria.	Dominican military overthrows Pres. Juan Bosch.	Indonesia declares its hostility to the newly independent Federation of Malaysia.
Oct.	U.N. calls on Britain not to transfer power to the white minority in Rhodesia.	Ludwig Erhard succeeds Konrad Adenauer as West German Chancellor.	Morocco and Algeria agree to a cease-fire after border clashes.	Honduran armed forces overthrow Pres. Ramon Villeda Morales.	South Korean voters elect Pres. Park Chung Hee to a four-year term.
Nov.	At the U.N. the Soviet Union criticizes the U.N.'s role in the Congo.	Former premier George Papandreou defeats Greek premier Constantine Caramanlis in national elections.	Somalia rejects a Western military aid proposal in favor of a larger Soviet proposal.	Argentina nationalizes its petroleum industry.	South Vietnamese military leaders overthrow Pres. Ngo Dinh Diem.
Dec.	At the U.N. Pres. Johnson calls for an end to the Cold War.	Hundreds of thousands of West Berliners cross the Wall to East Berlin for Christmas visits.	Zanzibar and Kenya become independent countries.	Venezuelan voters elect Raul Leoni as president despite a wave of leftist terrorism.	Cambodia recalls its ambassador to the U.S.

A	B	C	D	E
Includes developments that affect more than one world region, international organizations and important meetings of major world leaders.	*Includes all domestic and regional developments in Europe, including the Soviet Union, Turkey, Cyprus and Malta.*	*Includes all domestic and regional developments in Africa and the Middle East, including Iraq and Iran and excluding Cyprus, Turkey and Afghanistan.*	*Includes all domestic and regional developments in Latin America, the Caribbean and Canada.*	*Includes all domestic and regional developments in Asia and Pacific nations, extending from Afghanistan through all the Pacific Islands, except Hawaii.*

U.S. Politics & Social Issues	U.S. Foreign Policy & Defense	U.S. Economy & Environment	Science, Technology & Nature	Culture, Leisure & Life Style
Last state to maintain total university segregation, South Carolina, agrees to integrate Clemson college.	U.S. orders nuclear missiles to be withdrawn from Turkey and Italy.	Pres. Kennedy submits a federal budget with the largest deficit in history, $10 billion.	U.S. says it will concentrate on exploring Mars rather than Venus.	U.S. embassy in Moscow refuses entry to Siberian Evangelical Christians seeking refuge.
Supreme Court reverses conviction of 107 Negroes arrested in a 1961 Columbia, S.C. integration demonstration.	U.S. confirms reports that four U.S. civilians were killed in the 1961 Cuban invasion.	Pres. Kennedy intervenes in the 75-day-old New York City newspaper strike.	U.S. spacecraft indicates that the surface of Venus is of the order of 800 degrees fahrenheit.	Pope John says that the Vatican must adapt to changing times.
Civil rights demonstrations promoting voting rights take place in Greenwood, Miss.	U.S. warns Egypt not to attack Saudi Arabia.	Supreme Court rules that railroad companies can eliminate thousands of jobs.	U.S. space studies confirm the presence of water vapour in the Martian atmosphere.	Pope John beautifies Mother Elizabeth Ann Bayley Seton.
Alabama officials arrest civil rights leader Martin Luther King, Jr. after civil rights marches in Birmingham.	U.S. nuclear-powered submarine *Thresher* disappears in the Atlantic.	Pres. Kennedy praises the steel industry for price restraint.	U.S. doctors perform successful human nerve transplants in New York City.	Sir Winston Churchill becomes an honorary U.S. citizen.
Birmingham Ala. blacks riot after bombings in black neighborhoods.	U.S. says it will support India if it is attached by Communist China.	U.S. warns that certain pesticides may be dangerous.	U.S. astronaut Gordon Cooper orbits the earth several times.	William Carlos Williams wins the Pulitzer Prize in poetry.
Pres. Kennedy calls for racial integration in a nation-wide television address.	U.S. renews normal diplomatic relations with Haiti.	Pres. Kennedy intervenes directly in railroad workers' negotiations.	Soviet Union launches the first woman into orbit.	Pope Paul succeeds Pope John after he dies in Rome.
Blacks demonstrate for jobs at N.Y.C. construction sites.	U.S. agree to revise the Panama Canal Treaty.	Federal Reserve Board raises its basic lending rate from 3% to 3.5%.	Edwin McMillan wins the 1963 Atoms for Peace prize.	Sonny Liston knocks out Floyd Patterson to retain the heavyweight boxing title.
A massive civil rights march takes place in Washington D.C.	Pres. Kennedy submits the nuclear test-ban treaty to the Senate.	U.S. increases tariffs on Common Market goods in retaliation for tariffs on U.S. goods.	U.S. launches an advanced communications satellite.	New-born son of Pres. and Mrs. John Kennedy dies.
Pres. Kennedy orders the Alabama National Guard to enforce the integration of the University of Alabama.	U.S. Senate ratifies the nuclear test ban treaty by 80-19.	House of Representatives votes for a federal income tax reduction.	National Science Foundation announces a joint U.S.-Soviet project to measure cosmic rays.	Pope Paul opens the second session of the ecumenical council in Rome.
U.S. Labor Dept. orders an end to all discrimination in apprenticeship programs.	U.S. ends aid to the Dominican Republic and Honduras.	U.S. Steel Corporation announces major price increases.	Alan Hodgkins wins the 1963 Nobel Prize in physiology.	Giorgos Seferiades wins the 1963 Nobel Prize in literature.
Lee Harvey Oswald assassinates Pres. John Kennedy in Dallas, Tex.	V.P. Lyndon Johnson becomes President and promises to continue Pres. Kennedy's foreign policy.	U.S. steel unions agree to promote more jobs for blacks.	U.S. launches an advanced weather satellite.	Archeologists discover remains of a Viking settlement in Newfoundland dating back to circa 1,000 A.D.
Supreme Court rules that right-to-work laws are legal.	U.S. approves credits for wheat sales to communist countries.	Defense Secy. Robert McNamara orders the reduction of the number of domestic military bases.	Eighty-two passengers die in a plane crash near Elkton, Md.	Composer Paul Hindemith dies at 68 in Frankfurt, Germany.

F	G	H	I	J
Includes elections, federal-state relations, civil rights and liberties, crime, the judiciary, education, health care, poverty, urban affairs and population.	*Includes formation and debate of U.S. foreign and defense policies, veterans' affairs and defense spending. (Relations with specific foreign countries are usually found under the region concerned.)*	*Includes business, labor, agriculture, taxation, transportation, consumer affairs, monetary and fiscal policy, natural resources, and pollution.*	*Includes worldwide scientific, medical and technological developments, natural phenomena, U.S. weather, natural disasters, and accidents.*	*Includes the arts, religion, scholarship, communications media, sports, entertainment, fashions, fads and social life.*

	World Affairs	Europe	Africa & the Middle East	The Americas	Asia & the Pacific
Jan. 1	In an exchange of New Year's messages, Soviet Premier Nikita Khrushchev and U.S. Pres. John Kennedy pledge to redouble their efforts to preserve world peace in the coming year. Khrushchev's note also carried the signature of Soviet Pres. Leonid Brezhnev. . . . Leaders of the Chinese CP attack Khrushchev's doctrine of peaceful co-existence in a year-end statement published in the *Peking People's Daily* .	The municipal councils, governing local areas in Cyprus, are officially abolished by order of Cypriote Pres. Makarios. Turkish community leaders announce they will defy the decree.	Katanga Pres. Moise Tshombe calls for a cease-fire between Katanganese and U.N. forces.	Cuban Pres. Osvaldo Dorticos Torrado reports in the Jan. 1 issue of *Cuba Socialista* that the island's economy has grown by more than 80% since 1958.	An editorial in the *Peking People's Daily* reports that China's food shortage problems remain serious despite an improvement in the 1962 harvest. . . . Official Nationalist Chinese news sources confirm recent Peking reports that 172 Nationalist agents have been killed in landings on the Chinese coast during the past three months. The agents were reportedly sent to the mainland to train anti-Communist elements in guerilla warfare.
Jan. 2			U.N. Secy Gen. U Thant rejects Tshombe's appeal for a cease-fire and indicates that U.N. military action will continue until Katanga unequivocally abandons its secession.	Cuban Premier Fidel Castro hails the recent Cuban prisoner-food exchange with the U.S. as "the first time in history (that) imperialism has paid war indemnification."	Five U.S. helicopters are downed by Viet Cong gunfire while ferrying South Vietnamese troops to the village of Ap Bac 40 miles southeast of Saigon. Three U.S. advisers are killed, bringing to 26 the number of Americans known killed by Communist forces since large-scale U.S. aid began in late 1961.
Jan. 3		A group of 32 Siberian Evangelical Christians force their way into the U.S. embassy in Moscow and ask asylum from alleged Soviet religious persecution. U.S. officials, contending they have no jurisdiction in the matter, turn the group over to the Soviet Foreign Ministry.	Jadotville, one of the last strongholds of the Katanga secessionists, falls to U.N. forces without significant resistance.	Retiring NATO Commander Lauris Norstad, in a farewell call in Ottawa, says that Canada has failed its obligations to NATO by leaving its forces without U.S.-offered nuclear arms.	
Jan. 4		West Germany discloses that it offered East Germany $100 million in credits if it would agree to grant West Berliners visitation rights in East Berlin.	Cairo sources report that the UAR has reversed its decision to withdraw its troops from Yemen in view of alleged preparations by Saudi Arabia to increase aid to royalist forces. . . . Jordan's King Hussein joins with Saudi Arabian leaders in criticizing U.S. recognition of the republican regime in Yemen.		South Vietnam reports 65 troops killed and over 100 wounded in two days of fighting with the Viet Cong near the Mekong River village of Ap Bac. It is the second highest South Vietnamese casualty rate of the four-year guerrilla war.
Jan. 5				The ruling Peruvian military junta suspends constitutional guarantees after announcing that it had uncovered a leftist plot to overthrow the government. An estimated 800 persons have been arrested throughout Peru.	A U.S. civilian cargo plane is shot down--presumably by Pathet Lao forces--while dropping food supplies to anti-leftist Meo tribesmen in northwestern Laos. . . . A Communist Chinese-Pakistani trade agreement is signed in Karachi.
Jan. 6	Communist Chinese newspapers again carry editorials attacking the ideological foundations of recent Soviet foreign policy.			Voters in a Brazilian national plebiscite overwhelmingly approve the establishment of a presidential form of government to replace the current parliamentary system.	
Jan. 7	The Soviet CP, in a statement published in *Pravada*, denounces the major theses of recent Communist Chinese ideological criticism as expressions of "leftwing opportunism." The article warns that a continuation of Chinese attacks on Soviet policy may cause a major rift in world communism. . . . U.S. and USSR officially announce that they regard the Cuban missile crisis as closed and that they have ended their U.N. negotiations on it.	Six persons, apparently all Jews, are sentenced to death by a Ukrainian court for having engaged in illegal currency transactions.	Saudi Arabia calls for the immediate withdrawal of all foreign troops and military aid from Yemen as a first step toward the holding of an internationally supervised plebiscite to resolve Yemen's civil war.	U.S. State Dept. announces an emergency $30 billion loan to Brazil. . . . A new leftist Mexican peasant party, dedicated to the redistribution of foreign-owned land, is formed in Mexico City.	

A	B	C	D	E
Includes developments that affect more than one world region, international organizations and important meetings of major world leaders.	*Includes all domestic and regional developments in Europe, including the Soviet Union, Turkey, Cyprus and Malta.*	*Includes all domestic and regional developments in Africa and the Middle East, including Iraq and Iran and excluding Cyprus, Turkey and Afghanistan.*	*Includes all domestic and regional developments in Latin America, the Caribbean and Canada.*	*Includes all domestic and regional developments in Asia and Pacific nations, extending from Afghanistan through all the Pacific Islands, except Hawaii.*

U.S. Politics & Social Issues	U.S. Foreign Policy & Defense	U.S. Economy & Environment	Science, Technology & Nature	Culture, Leisure & Life Style	
Robert S. Kerr, 66, U.S. Senator (D, Okla.) since 1949 and powerful spokesman for conservative Democrats, dies in Washington of a coronary occlusion.		Dow Jones industrial average closes 1962 at 652.10. This compares to a record high of 734.91 in December 1961 and a low of 535.76 on June 26, 1962.		Southern California outlasts Wisconsin to win the Rose Bowl, 42-37. . . . Rod Laver, 24, of Australia signs a $110,000 contract with the new International Professional Tennis Players Association.	Jan. 1
Twenty-eight Methodist ministers in Mississippi issue a statement asserting that their church doctrine disapproves of all forms of racial discrimination.	Gen. Lyman Lemnitzer assumes command of NATO forces in Europe replacing retiring Gen. Lauris Norstad.	Census Bureau estimates that construction spending in the U.S. totalled a record $61.1 billion in 1962, up 7% from 1961. . . . National Fire Protection Association reports that U.S. fires took over 11,800 lives in 1962, 100 more than in 1961.	A new comet, known as Ikeya, is discovered by an amateur Japanese astronomer using a handmade eight-inch telescope.	The National Council of Churches reports that U.S. church membership increased by 1.4% in 1961.	Jan. 2
		Agriculture Secy. Orville Freeman reports to Pres. Kennedy that net U.S. farm income in 1961 and 1962 was $1.1 billion higher than in 1960. Income per farm reportedly climbed from $2,961 in 1960 to $3,470 in 1962.	U.S. scientists develop remedies for defects in the malfunctioning communications satellites, Telstar I and Relay I, and both begin successfully transmitting trans-Atlantic TV signals. . . . A research unit of the British Medical Research Council publishes evidence showing that the injection of a cold-causing virus stimulates the production of antibodies against the virus.	Bobby Fischer of New York defeats Arthur Bisguier to win the U.S. chess championship for the fifth time.	Jan. 3
Senate GOP leader Everett Dirksen (R, Ill.) predicts that the administration will have difficulty winning congressional approval of its foreign aid, tax-cut, aid-to-education and medical-care bills. . . . Congressional Quarterly study describes the "typical" member of the 88th Congress as a white male, 52.7-years-old, probably a lawyer and Methodist, with a record of military service.	Amb. Arthur Dean resigns as chief U.S. disarmament negotiator.	Food and Drug Administration issues newly tightened drug-testing regulations.		Pope John XXIII is named "man of the year" by Time magazine. . . . Doris Day is named the top audience-attracting film star of 1962 in a Motion Picture Herald poll of exhibitors.	Jan. 4
	Gen. Lucius Clay discloses in New York that he, Robert Kennedy and other U.S. officials personally helped raise funds to pay for the release of the captured Cuban Bay of Pigs invaders.		A fragment of the USSR's Sputnik 4, which fell in Wisconsin in 1962, is returned to a member of the Soviet embassy by the U.S. State Dept.	Rogers Hornsby, holder of National League batting record of .424 (1924) and member of the Hall of Fame, dies in Chicago at 66.	Jan. 5
	Ex-Rep. and John Birch Society member John Rousselot tells a crowd of 1,000 persons attending a conservative rally in Boston that the government is "selling us out" to the communists in the current disarmament negotiations.				Jan. 6
James Meredith, University of Mississippi's first Negro student, tells reporters that he will not return to the university next semester "unless. . .positive changes are made to make my situation more conducive to learning."	Air Force launches a "secret" satellite from Vandenberg Air Base in California.	Ward's Reports estimates that more than seven million cars were sold in the U.S. during 1962, including more than 300,000 imports. . . . The new 5¢-per-ounce postage rate goes into effect.			Jan. 7

F	G	H	I	J
Includes elections, federal-state relations, civil rights and liberties, crime, the judiciary, education, health care, poverty, urban affairs and population.	Includes formation and debate of U.S. foreign and defense policies, veterans' affairs and defense spending. (Relations with specific foreign countries are usually found under the region concerned.)	Includes business, labor, agriculture, taxation, transportation, consumer affairs, monetary and fiscal policy, natural resources, and pollution.	Includes worldwide scientific, medical and technological developments, natural phenomena, U.S. weather, natural disasters, and accidents.	Includes the arts, religion, scholarship, communications media, sports, entertainment, fashions, fads and social life.

	World Affairs	Europe	Africa & the Middle East	The Americas	Asia & the Pacific
Jan. 8	Premier Yumzhagin Tsedenbal of Outer Mongolia expresses his government's support for the USSR in its ideological dispute with Communist China.	A cabinet crisis, which threatened to bring down Italian Premier Amintore Fanfani's center-left government, ends after centrist factions agreed to compromise on leftist demands for the creation of local-autonomy governments in Italy's 15 remaining federally controlled regions.			
Jan. 9	U.S. and USSR jointly request that the meetings of the 17-nation Disarmament Committee, scheduled to resume Jan. 15, be postponed until at least Feb. 12. Observers regard the action as a sign that private Soviet-American disarmament talks may be underway.	Anti-government troops in Portugal announce agreement to form a unified exile committee to coordinate opposition policies.	Katanga Pres. Tshombe, who returned to Elizabethville yesterday, is placed under U.N. house arrest.		
Jan. 10		The Soviet newspaper *Izvestia*, in a front-page editorial, declares that East and West are closer to a settlement on Germany than on any other problem.		Pres.-elect Juan Bosch of the Dominican Republic meets in Washington with Pres. Kennedy following a two-week goodwill tour of the U.S.	Gen. Paul Harkins, commander of the U.S. Military & Advisory Group in South Vietnam, denounces recent press criticism of the fighting abilities of the South Vietnamese army.
Jan. 11			U.N. delegations of 31 African nations give Secy. Gen. U Thant assurances of their governments' support for his policies in the Congo.		
Jan. 12					
Jan. 13	The East German CP newspaper *Neues Deutschland* sharply denounces China for supporting Albania in views that are "a danger to the world communist movement."		Togo Pres. Sylvanus Olympio is assassinated in a military coup carried out by ex-soldiers opposed to his allegedly isolationist foreign policy.		Peking newspapers report that China has protested alleged Indian violations of Chinese territory near the China-Sinkiang boundary.
Jan. 14		French Pres. Charles de Gaulle, speaking at a Paris news conference, declares his firm opposition to both the U.S.'s proposal for a NATO nuclear force and to Britain's efforts to join the European Economic Community. . . . In his State of the Union address, Pres. Kennedy reaffirms U.S. determination to work for the creation of a multilateral nuclear force "within an increasingly intimate NATO alliance."		West Germany breaks diplomatic relations with Cuba following its Jan. 12 recognition of East Germany.	Pres. Kennedy, reporting to Congress on the state of the union, asserts that "the spearpoint of aggression has been blunted in Vietnam."
Jan. 15	Soviet Premier Khrushchev and delegates of 70 national Communist parties gather in East Berlin for the Sixth Congress of the East German CP. The meeting is expected to demonstrate worldwide Communist support for the USSR in its ideological disputes with China.	Representatives of all EEC members, except France, publicly disavow Pres. de Gaulle's Jan. 14 attack on the current negotiations for British membership in the Common Market. . . . U.S. State Undersecy. George Ball leaves Bonn to return to Washington after winning West German approval of Anglo-U.S. proposals for the creation of an integrated NATO nuclear force.	Katanga Pres. Moise Tshombe announces his formal surrender to U.N. demands that his government end its 30-month secession from the Congo Republic.		

A	B	C	D	E
Includes developments that affect more than one world region, international organizations and important meetings of major world leaders.	Includes all domestic and regional developments in Europe, including the Soviet Union, Turkey, Cyprus and Malta.	Includes all domestic and regional developments in Africa and the Middle East, including Iraq and Iran and excluding Cyprus, Turkey and Afghanistan.	Includes all domestic and regional developments in Latin America, the Caribbean and Canada.	Includes all domestic and regional developments in Asia and Pacific nations, extending from Afghanistan through all the Pacific Islands, except Hawaii.

U.S. Politics & Social Issues	U.S. Foreign Policy & Defense	U.S. Economy & Environment	Science, Technology & Nature	Culture, Leisure & Life Style	
In the House GOP party caucus, Rep. Charles Hoeven (Ia.) is ousted as House Republican conference chairman by Rep. Gerald Ford (Mich.). Ford's victory is viewed as a demonstration of power by the younger, less conservative element in GOP ranks.	Agriculture Secy. Orville Freeman warns that U.S. defense and aid commitments may be curtailed if the EEC imposes high trade barriers against U.S. farm exports.	Agriculture Dept. reports that U.S. farmers have agreed to cut winter wheat plantings by 5,200,000 acres from 1961 base levels.		Leonardo da Vinci's *Mona Lisa* —on loan to the U.S. from France—begins a three-week public display at Washington's National Gallery of Art. . . . National Collegiate Athletic Association reports that over 21 million people attended U.S. college football games in 1962 and that an average of 26 million watched Saturday games on TV. . . . Don Shula, 33, is signed as head coach of the NFL Baltimore Colts, replacing the fired Weeb Ewbank.	Jan. 8
88th Congress convenes with Democrats outnumbering Republicans by 67-33 in the Senate and 258-176 in the House. . . . A federal jury acquits J. Truman Bidwell, ex-chairman of the N.Y. Stock Exchange, of income tax evasion charges.		In a report to Pres. Kennedy, a National Academy of Sciences committee urges that overall U.S. natural resources policy be shifted from a concern over shortages to one of efficient management of a plenteous supply.		The American Football Coaches Association names John McKay of Southern California and Bill Edwards of Wittenberg as 1962's coaches of the year.	Jan. 9
Over 300 students, screaming "Go home, you nigger!", surround James Meredith at University of Mississippi's student cafeteria. Meredith said Jan. 7 that he would quit the university if harassment continued. . . . U.S. CP proclaims its support for Khrushchev in the current Sino-Soviet ideological dispute.					Jan. 10
	State Secy. Dean Rusk answers questions on U.S. policy toward Cuba during a lengthy appearance before the Senate Foreign Relations Committee. Rusk reportedly told the committee that Pres. Kennedy's missile crisis pledge not to invade Cuba was no longer in force because of Khrushchev's failure to fulfill his promise of on-site inspection.	Commerce Dept. reports that the value of U.S. exports rose from a record $19.9 billion total in 1961 to $20.8 billion in 1962. During the same period imports rose from $14.5 billion to a record $16.4 billion. . . . Commerce Dept. estimates that automatic vending machines dispense about $3 billion worth of goods in the U.S. annually.	Sixteen consecutive days of rain cause Morocco's worst floods in 50 years. At least 100 persons are believed dead and an estimated 100,000 homeless.	Australian swimmer Dawn Fraser is named 1962's "female athlete of the year" in an AP poll of sportswriters.	Jan. 11
	The U.S.'s 17th nuclear-powered Polaris missile submarine, the *John Adams*, is launched at the Portsmouth (N.H.) Naval Shipyard.			Pone Kingpetch of Thailand regains the world flyweight championship by winning a 15-round decision over title-holder Masahiko Harada of Japan.	Jan. 12
			The discovery of the new physical law by Soviet scientist Yevgeny Alexandrov (which reportedly modifies Newtonian physics) is announced in Moscow.	Gary Player wins the San Diego Open golf tournament.	Jan. 13
A pledge to fight for "segregation now, and. . .forever" is made by George C. Wallace as he is sworn in as governor of Alabama. . . . A 1956 Virginia law barring solicitation of legal business and aimed principally at the NAACP is nullified by the U.S. Supreme Court.	In his State of the Union Message Pres. Kennedy warns Americans not to take too much comfort in the current Sino-Soviet rift, explaining that the dispute is not over whether to oppose the free world, but how.	Pres. Kennedy highlights his State of the Union message with a call for a permanent reduction in federal income tax rates that would cut such levies $13.5 billion annually by 1965. Kennedy adds that the plan, the largest U.S. tax-cut in history, will require a reduction in all areas of federal spending except defense and space. . . . Commerce Secy. Luther Hodges estimates that U.S. GNP jumped from $518.7 billion in 1961 to almost $554 billion in 1962.			Jan. 14
Conservative Republican Sen. Barry Goldwater (R, Ariz.) introduces in the Senate an aid-to-education bill providing federal tax reductions to homeowners paying local school costs.			Major medical and dental health organizations endorse a statement urging controlled fluoridation of N.Y.C.'s water supply.	A poll of UPI sportswriters picks the NFL champion Green Bay Packers as the outstanding professional team of 1962. . . . The Film Critics Guild (London) chooses *Lawrence of Arabia* as the best British film of 1962.	Jan. 15

F	G	H	I	J
Includes elections, federal-state relations, civil rights and liberties, crime, the judiciary, education, health care, poverty, urban affairs and population.	Includes formation and debate of U.S. foreign and defense policies, veterans' affairs and defense spending. (Relations with specific foreign countries are usually found under the region concerned.)	Includes business, labor, agriculture, taxation, transportation, consumer affairs, monetary and fiscal policy, natural resources, and pollution.	Includes worldwide scientific, medical and technological developments, natural phenomena, U.S. weather, natural disasters, and accidents.	Includes the arts, religion, scholarship, communications media, sports, entertainment, fashions, fads and social life.

	World Affairs	Europe	Africa & the Middle East	The Americas	Asia & the Pacific
Jan. 16	Khrushchev, addressing delegates to the East German CP convention, attacks Communist Chinese leaders for irresponsibly underestimating the hazards and horror of nuclear war. Khrushchev concludes with a call for an immediate suspension in "polemics between Communist parties."	Soviet Premier Khrushchev, addressing the East German Congress, defends the building of the Berlin Wall as a step "toward the strengthening of the sovereignty of the German Democratic Republic." Khrushchev also reiterates his proposal for a U.N.-supervised free city in West Berlin.	The central Congolese government of Premier Cyrille Adoula begins taking over administrative functions from the disbanding Katanga regime. . . . Britain and Saudi Arabia announce agreement to resume diplomatic relations, severed since Britain's Suez invasion in 1956. . . . An agreement merging the British colony of Aden with the adjoining British-protected 11-state federation of South Arabia is signed in Al Ittihad.	Cuban Premier Castro, addressing a Havana rally, calls for a hemispheric-wide revolution against imperialism.	
Jan. 17		France formally asks for an immediate halt to the Brussels negotiations on British membership in the EEC.			In a note to Britain, Communist China lays claim to Kowloon City, a mainland enclave of Hong Kong.
Jan. 18	Delegates to the East German CP convention jeer and revile Chinese CP Central Committee member Wu Hsiu-chan as he attempts to reply to earlier speeches by Khrushchev and other European communist spokesmen. Wu repeats China's demand for a new world communist meeting to resolve outstanding doctrinal disputes.	France's demand for an end to British-EEC talk is strongly opposed by the other five Common Market nations. The French delegation reluctantly agrees to a 10-day postponement of any final decision on the fate of the Brussels negotiations. . . . Hugh Gaitskell, 56, British Labor Party leader since 1955, dies of kidney failure in a London hospital while being treated for pericarditis.	Tunisia recalls its ambassador from Algeria because of the Ben Bella government's alleged role in a December 1962 plot to assassinate Tunisian Pres. Habib Bourguiba.		
Jan. 19			A French agreement to provide Algeria extensive economic aid in 1963 is announced in Paris. . . . British Central African Affairs Min. Richard Butler arrives in the Rhodesia-Nyasaland Federation for talks with white and black leaders on the federation's future in view of African plans for secession.		
Jan. 20	U.S. makes public a letter from Soviet Premier Khrushchev in which he offers to allow two or three yearly inspections by international personnel of Soviet territory to enforce a nuclear test-ban treaty. The letter, considered a potential breakthrough in the test-ban deadlock, also confirms that the U.S. and USSR have undertaken private disarmament talks.	West German Chancellor Konrad Adenauer flies to Paris where he is scheduled to sign an historic French-West German treaty of reconciliation. He is also expected to seek a moderation of French Pres. de Gaulle's apparent determination to block British entry into the EEC.			
Jan. 21	Soviet Foreign Min. Andrei Gromyko tells reporters in Washington that the USSR will insist on French participation in any final nuclear disarmament pact.	In a speech to a Conservative Party meeting in Liverpool, P.M. Harold Macmillan accuses France of negotiating in bad faith, claiming that de Gaulle's opposition to British membership in the EEC should have been expressed one-and-a-half years ago when the Brussels talks began.	Troops of the U.N. Congo Force, acting with the cooperation of Pres. Tshombe, peacefully occupy Kolwezi, last major center of the secessionist Katanga government.		
Jan. 22	U.S. State Dept. spokesman Lincoln White says that the U.S. and Great Britain will make every effort to bring France into any disarmament agreement signed by the other nuclear powers.	Chancellor Adenauer and Pres. de Gaulle sign a treaty in Paris pledging cooperation and consultation between West Germany and France in foreign policy, defense, and cultural affairs. . . . Controversial former-West German Defense Min. Franz Joseph Strauss is elected Bundestag chairman of the Christian Social Union, Bavarian section of the ruling Christian Democratic Union.			

A	B	C	D	E
Includes developments that affect more than one world region, international organizations and important meetings of major world leaders.	Includes all domestic and regional developments in Europe, including the Soviet Union, Turkey, Cyprus and Malta.	Includes all domestic and regional developments in Africa and the Middle East, including Iraq and Iran and excluding Cyprus, Turkey and Afghanistan.	Includes all domestic and regional developments in Latin America, the Caribbean and Canada.	Includes all domestic and regional developments in Asia and Pacific nations, extending from Afghanistan through all the Pacific Islands, except Hawaii.

U.S. Politics & Social Issues	U.S. Foreign Policy & Defense	U.S. Economy & Environment	Science, Technology & Nature	Culture, Leisure & Life Style	
		Pres. Kennedy appoints a federal mediation board to seek settlement of the month-long East Coast dock strike, adding that the shutdown had passed the "point of public toleration."	The development of a new drug effective in treating cancer of the male reproductive system is announced by Dr. Joseph Burkhalter of the University of Michigan.	The Eastern Division defeats the West in the National Basketball Association's 13th all-star game. Celtic center Bill Russell is named the game's mvp. . . . *Wall Street Journal* reports that independent film production companies produced about 8% of all motion pictures made in the U.S. in 1962. The figures indicate a continuation of a steady decline in output by major Hollywood film companies.	Jan. 16
Pres. Kennedy's fiscal 1964 budget calls for holding social service expenditures at about the same level as 1963, although moderate increases are requested for health, education and job retraining programs. . . . *Congressional Quarterly* reports that the Democratic Party spent $3.17 million and the GOP $3.62 million in the congressional campaigns of 1962. The figures represent new records for both parties.	Pres. Kennedy's fiscal 1964 budget calls for defense expenditures of $55.4 billion, up $2.4 billion from 1963. Defense, foreign aid, and space spending together account for 51% of the total budget.	Pres. Kennedy sends Congress a fiscal 1964 budget calling for record expenditures of $98.8 billion, up $4.5 billion over 1963. The budget report, which assumes enactment of the administration's tax cut, forecasts a deficit of $11.9 billion. . . . Federal Reserve Bank of N.Y. reports that total U.S. Treasury gold stocks have dropped to $15.928 billion, the lowest level since May 24, 1939.	Pres. Kennedy's fiscal 1964 budget provides for space-related expenditures of $4.2 billion, up about 75% above the current year's spending. The increase is aimed principally at accelerating the U.S.'s manned lunar landing program.		Jan. 17
North Carolina Gov. Terry Sanford announces a statewide campaign to fight "unfair" job discrimination against Negroes. Justice Dept. files four suites in Alabama, Mississippi, and Louisiana in an effort to desegregate public schools in "impacted areas"-districts in which a large number of the students are dependents of federal employees.		Speaking at an annual *Printing Week* banquet in Philadelphia, White House Press Secy. Pierre Salinger describes the New York and Cleveland newspaper strikes as "intolerable" and urges renewed labor and management efforts to reach a responsible settlement. . . . Pres. Kennedy names Daniel Patrick Moynihan, 35, as Assistant Labor Secretary to succeed Jerry Holleman.	The U.N.'s World Health Organization proposes steps to speed the international dissemination of information regarding unsafe drugs.		Jan. 18
Gallup Poll reports that 76% of Americans interviewed approve Kennedy's performance as President.				Gen. Douglas MacArthur announces that the rival Amateur Athletic Union and the National Collegiate Athletic Association have agreed to a tentative settlement of their two-and-a-half year dispute over control of U.S. amateur sports.	Jan. 19
				Pope John XXIII proclaims as a saint Vincent Pallotti, an Italian priest who founded (in 1835) the Pallottine Fathers, a society credited with aiding Jews during World War II. . . . Billy Casper wins the $50,000 Bing Crosby golf tournament at Pebble Beach, Calif. U.S. Professional Golfers Association reports that Arnold Palmer won a record $81,448 in PGA-sponsored events in 1962.	Jan. 20
U.S. District Judge Claude Clayton dismisses all federal charges filed against ex-Maj. Gen. Edwin Walker in connection with the desegregation riots at the University of Mississippi in 1962.	Atty. Gen. Robert Kennedy, in a Knight Newspaper interview, denies that the U.S. had ever promised to provide air cover for the 1961 Cuban invasion. . . . Pres. Kennedy issues a special statement reaffirming U.S. support for recent U.N. actions against the Katanga regime in the Congo.	The 68-year-old Chicago, North Shore & Milwaukee Railway suspends operations after gaining approval from the ICC. . . . In his annual Economic Report to Congress, Pres. Kennedy stresses the "urgent" need for tax reduction and reform to stimulate economic growth. Kennedy also calls for greater export efforts to reduce the estimated $2 billion balance of payments deficit incurred in 1962.		Los Angeles Dodger shortstop Maury Wills is named winner of the $10,000 Hickok Award as "professional athlete of the year" (1962).	Jan. 21
Justice Dept. files a voter discrimination suit in Sunflower County, Miss., home of Senate Judiciary Committee Chmn. James Eastland.	A spokesman for the Miami-based anti-Castro Revolutionary Council tells reporters that U.S. military officers had assured the Bay of Pigs invaders they would have had U.S. "air support" in their attack.			*One Day in the Life of Ivan Denisovich*, by Russian novelist Alexander Solzhenitsyn, is published in the West.	Jan. 22

F	G	H	I	J
Includes elections, federal-state relations, civil rights and liberties, crime, the judiciary, education, health care, poverty, urban affairs and population.	Includes formation and debate of U.S. foreign and defense policies, veterans' affairs and defense spending. (Relations with specific foreign countries are usually found under the region concerned.)	Includes business, labor, agriculture, taxation, transportation, consumer affairs, monetary and fiscal policy, natural resources, and pollution.	Includes worldwide scientific, medical and technological developments, natural phenomena, U.S. weather, natural disasters, and accidents.	Includes the arts, religion, scholarship, communications media, sports, entertainment, fashions, fads and social life.

	World Affairs	Europe	Africa & the Middle East	The Americas	Asia & the Pacific
Jan. 23	Yugoslav Pres. Tito, in a Belgrade speech, accuses the Communist Chinese of following a "Genghis Khan policy" which threatens world peace. . . . Britain announces recognition of Outer Mongolia, thus becoming the first Western nation to establish diplomatic relations with that communist nation.	Adenauer returns to Bonn from Paris amidst criticism that he made only a token effort to dissuade de Gaulle from blocking further British-EEC talks.		*The New York Times* carries a report detailing what it describes as a considerable and continuing Soviet military presence in Cuba.	India and China announce tentative acceptance of the six-nation Colombo plan for ending the Indian-Chinese border dispute. The plan, first proposed in mid-December 1962, calls for a partial restoration of the status quo as of Sept. 8, 1962.
Jan. 24		Addressing the National Assembly, French Foreign Min. Maurice Couve de Murville reaffirms the official French view that Britain is not prepared to accept the discipline and conditions of membership in the EEC. . . . At his Washington news conference, Pres. Kennedy rejects French allegations that U.S. support for British membership in the EEC is based on a desire to perpetuate an American-dominated Atlantic power bloc.	Ten Tunisians are executed by firing squad for their role in a Dec. 22, 1962 plot to assassinate Pres. Habib Bourguiba.		Pakistani Industries Min. Zulfikar Bhutto is chosen foreign minister to replace the late Mohammed Ali.
Jan. 25		West Germany announces that it will present the EEC Commission with a compromise proposal aimed at ensuring continuation of the Brussels talks on possible British membership in the Common Market. . . . French Pres. de Gaulle reportedly tells a group of National Assembly deputies that Macmillan's signing of the Nassau accord on nuclear arms proved that Britain's primary allegiance is to the U.S. and not to Europe.		Canadian Liberal Party leader Lester Pearson charges that the Diefenbaker government is weakening Western defenses by delaying acceptance of U.S.-offered nuclear arms for Canada's NATO and North American armed forces.	India's lower House of Parliament gives final approval to P.M. Nehru's decision to accept the six-nation Colombo plan for ending the Indian-Chinese border conflict.
Jan. 26	Pres. Kennedy orders a temporary suspension of underground nuclear tests in an apparent gesture of good faith toward the current private Soviet-American test-ban talks in New York. . . . North Vietnamese Pres. Ho Chi Minh and visiting Pres. Antonin Novotny issue a joint communique in Hanoi supporting Khrushchev's doctrine of peaceful co-existence.		Iranian voters in a nationwide referendum overwhelmingly approve Shah Mohammad Riza Pahlevi's proposals for extensive economic, social and political reforms.		The U.S. embassy in Vientiane charges that the Communist Pathet Lao is threatening Laos's coalition government through its violent interference with the U.S.'s legitimate airlift aid programs.
Jan. 27	An editorial in the *Peking People's Daily* attributes the current Sino-Soviet dispute to Khrushchev's recent compromises with the "revisionism" of Yugoslav Pres. Tito. . . . U.N. sources report that France has refused to purchase its allotted share of the special 1961 U.N. bond issue designed to cover the costs of U.N. military operations in the Congo and Middle East.			Cuba announces that it has broken up two U.S. "spy networks" in Oriente Province.	
Jan. 28		French delegation at the resumed Brussels EEC talks rejects a West German proposal for a special EEC Executive Commission study of the major problems blocking British entry into the Common Market. . . . Preliminary talks on the U.S. proposal for forming a unified Western nuclear striking force begin at NATO Council headquarters in Paris.			Britain transfers 2,000 troops to the Far East in anticipation of a possible resumption of disorders in the British protectorate of Brunei.

A	B	C	D	E
Includes developments that affect more than one world region, international organizations and important meetings of major world leaders.	Includes all domestic and regional developments in Europe, including the Soviet Union, Turkey, Cyprus and Malta.	Includes all domestic and regional developments in Africa and the Middle East, including Iraq and Iran and excluding Cyprus, Turkey and Afghanistan.	Includes all domestic and regional developments in Latin America, the Caribbean and Canada.	Includes all domestic and regional developments in Asia and Pacific nations, extending from Afghanistan through all the Pacific Islands, except Hawaii.

U.S. Politics & Social Issues	U.S. Foreign Policy & Defense	U.S. Economy & Environment	Science, Technology & Nature	Culture, Leisure & Life Style	
	The New York Times reports that Pres. Kennedy met yesterday with leading administration officials and the National Security Council to request a detailed reassessment of the U.S. position in each foreign policy problem area. . . . Sen. Barry Goldwater (R, Ariz.) introduces a resolution calling for a Armed Services Committee investigation into the U.S. role in the Bay of Pigs invasion.		Dr. Daniel Baker Jr. of Columbia University reports on a new surgical treatment for larynx cancer which does not involve permanent damage to the victim's vocal chords.		Jan. 23
South Carolina Gov. Donald Russell announces that a court order to desegregate Clemson College will be met "peaceably, without violence, without disorder. . ."	Pres. Kennedy, speaking at a Washington news conference, again accepts responsibility for the failure of the 1961 Bay of Pigs invasion, but denies that the U.S. had ever planned to provide air support for the landing. . . . Senate Foreign Relations Committee Chmn. J. William Fulbright (D, Ark.) follows other congressional leaders in sharply criticizing French Pres. de Gaulle's opposition to British membership in the EEC.	Kennedy sends Congress a special tax message outlining his proposed three-year program for permanent reductions and reforms in personal and corporate income tax rates. Kennedy asks that the rate cuts and reform provisions be linked together in a single tax bill.	A theory asserting that all matter is composed not of 30 or more elementary particles but only two—the negatively charged electron and the positively charged positron—is advanced at the American Physical Society meeting in New York by Westinghouse researcher Ernest Sternglass.	Celebrations begin to mark the Chinese New Year 4661 (Year of the Rabbit).	Jan. 24
Five Negroes register without incident at the previously all-white Tulane University in New Orleans.		Bureau of Labor Statistics reports that the U.S. cost of living index in 1962 averaged 1.2% above the 1961 average.	Sir Isaac Shoenberg, Russian-born British scientist who pioneered the development of television, dies in London at age 82.	North and South Korea announce agreement to form a joint team for the 1964 Olympic Games in Tokyo.	Jan. 25
	Stewart Alsop, writing in the Jan. 26 issue of the Saturday Evening Post, attempts to clarify his controversial Dec. 8 Post story on Amb.-to-U.N. Adlai Stevenson's role in the Cuban missile crisis.	A 34-day strike of East and Gulf Coast longshoremen ends under terms recommended by a presidentially-appointed mediation board.		Dick Weber wins the $100,000 All-Star Bowling tournament in Kansas City.	Jan. 26
				The Italian team of Eugene Monti and Sergio Siopraes win the world two-men bobsled championship in Igls, Austria. . . . Former Washington Senator outfielder Sam Rice (1916-1933) heads a list of new inductees into the Baseball Hall of Fame.	Jan. 27
Harvey B. Gantt becomes the first Negro to attend school with whites in South Carolina as he enrolls without incident at Clemson College.		The Joint Economic Committee begins hearings on Pres. Kennedy's 1963 Economic Report. Presidential adviser Walter Heller testifies that Americans must overcome their "puritanical" aversion to deficit government spending. . . . General Motors Corp. announces that its net income rose from $893 million in 1961 to a record $1.459 billion in 1962, the highest profit ever recorded by a private company.	In a report to Congress, Pres. Kennedy asserts that the U.S. achieved a "greater rate of space progress" in 1962 than did the USSR. The report notes that the U.S. put 54 satellites into orbit in 1962, compared with 15 orbited by the Soviets.		Jan. 28

F	G	H	I	J
Includes elections, federal-state relations, civil rights and liberties, crime, the judiciary, education, health care, poverty, urban affairs and population.	Includes formation and debate of U.S. foreign and defense policies, veterans' affairs and defense spending. (Relations with specific foreign countries are usually found under the region concerned.)	Includes business, labor, agriculture, taxation, transportation, consumer affairs, monetary and fiscal policy, natural resources, and pollution.	Includes worldwide scientific, medical and technological developments, natural phenomena, U.S. weather, natural disasters, and accidents.	Includes the arts, religion, scholarship, communications media, sports, entertainment, fashions, fads and social life.

	World Affairs	Europe	Africa & the Middle East	The Americas	Asia & the Pacific
Jan. 29		France in effect vetoes Britain's application for EEC membership by refusing to withdraw its demand for a suspension in the Brussels negotiations. Representatives of the other five EEC nations express their extreme regret over the French action. Chief British negotiator Edward Heath attributes the collapse of the talks to French political aspirations unrelated to the unresolved economic issues.	U.N. Secy. Gen. Thant announces that the U.N.'s active military involvement in the Congo "is about over.". . . Joseph Ileo, the central Congolese government's new resident minister in Elizabethville, meets with Tshombe to discuss details of Katanga's reunification into the Congo.		
Jan. 30		British P.M. Macmillan, speaking on European TV, attributes France's veto of British membership in the EEC to Pres. de Gaulle's apparent desire for French domination of Western Europe. . . . Britain's negotiations to enter the European Atomic Energy Community (Euratom) are suspended following yesterday's rejection of Britain's application to the EEC.		U.S. State Dept. issues a statement asserting that the failure to deliver promised nuclear arms to Canada's NATO forces was due to the Canadian government's unwillingness to make practical arrangements for accepting such weapons.	
Jan. 31	Informal East-West negotiations on a nuclear test-ban are broken off at U.N. headquarters in New York. The talks are reportedly deadlocked over the West's refusal to accept Soviet proposals for an annual maximum of three on-site inspections.			Canadian P.M. John Diefenbaker denounces the Jan. 30 U.S. State Dept. statement on Canadian-American nuclear arms negotiations as unwarranted interference in Canadian affairs. . . . Sen. Kenneth Keating (R,N.Y.) asserts in a Senate speech that there is evidence of a continuing and dangerous Soviet military buildup in Cuba.	
Feb. 1	Pres. Kennedy orders preparations for a resumption of U.S. nuclear tests in the wake of the failure of the private Soviet-American test-ban talks.	The announcement of a new French-Soviet trade agreement rekindles recent press speculation that de Gaulle's foreign policy is aimed ultimately at a European rapprochement with the USSR. On Jan. 30 the French Foreign Ministry issued a statement saying that such reports were completely without foundation. . . . France and Monaco sign a compromise agreement on their long-standing dispute over the tax-free status afforded foreigners resident in Monaco.	Nyasaland's first African-dominated government, headed by P.M. Hastings Banda, is sworn-in in Zomba. In his inaugural address, Banda reaffirms Nyasaland's intention to secede from the Rhodesia-Nyasaland Federation.		Philippine claims to North Borneo are officially rejected by Britain following a week of talks in London.
Feb. 2					
Feb. 3		British P.M. Macmillan concludes two days of talks with Italian Premier Amintore Fanfani on possible alternative proposals for eventual British membership in the Common Market.	Yemeni Pres. Abdullah al Salal reports that 50 Saudi Arabians and Jordanians were killed in a battle with Yemeni republican forces Feb. 2 near the Saudi-Yemeni border.	Dr. Rene Schick Gutierrez, candidate of the governing Liberal Party, is overwhelmingly elected president of Nicaragua in nationwide elections.	
Feb. 4	A third conference of the Afro-Asian People's Solidarity Organization, attended by generally left-leaning delegates from 60 African and Asian countries, opens in Moshi, Tanganyika.	In an introduction to his government's annual report, Chancellor Adenauer reaffirms West Germany's support for NATO and U.S. leadership of the alliance. Adenauer also tells a Western newsman that French Pres. de Gaulle's opposition to U.S. leadership has been exaggerated. . . . A West German government report on the *Der Spiegel* affair indicates that ex-Defense Min. Franz Joseph Strauss had been more active in the controversial arrest of the magazine's editors than he had publicly acknowledged.		Canadian Defense Min. Douglas Harkness resigns in protest against P.M. John Diefenbaker's alleged failure to act promptly on the U.S. offer of nuclear arms for Canada's NATO forces. The resignation comes amidst mounting political controversy over Canada's defense policies.	

A	B	C	D	E
Includes developments that affect more than one world region, international organizations and important meetings of major world leaders.	*Includes all domestic and regional developments in Europe, including the Soviet Union, Turkey, Cyprus and Malta.*	*Includes all domestic and regional developments in Africa and the Middle East, including Iraq and Iran and excluding Cyprus, Turkey and Afghanistan.*	*Includes all domestic and regional developments in Latin America, the Caribbean and Canada.*	*Includes all domestic and regional developments in Asia and Pacific nations, extending from Afghanistan through all the Pacific Islands, except Hawaii.*

U.S. Politics & Social Issues	U.S. Foreign Policy & Defense	U.S. Economy & Environment	Science, Technology & Nature	Culture, Leisure & Life Style	
Pres. Kennedy sends Congress a $1.2 billion omnibus education bill calling for federal grants to states for public elementary and secondary schools.				Robert Frost, America's most popular 20th century poet and winner of four Pulitzer Prizes, dies in Boston at age 88. . . . Seventeen men are named charter members of the National Professional Football Hall of Fame, now under construction in Canton, Ohio.	Jan. 29
James Meredith announces that despite continuing harassment he will register for the second semester at the University of Mississippi.	Senate Armed Services Committee concludes its investigation into federal stockpiling of strategic materials. Chmn. Stuart Symington (D,Mo.) says the hearings revealed an urgent need for legislation against excessive profit-taking and favoritism.	The National Education Association reports that on the average U.S. school teachers now earn $5,735 per year. . . . National Safety Council reports that a record 41,000 persons died in U.S. traffic accidents in 1962.			Jan. 30
House Republicans introduce an omnibus civil rights bill to strengthen federal enforcement powers in voting rights and school desegregation cases. . . . U.S. House adopts resolutions to restrict federally financed junketing by Congress members.	In two days of testimony before the House Armed Services Committee, Defense Secy. Robert McNamara outlines the U.S.'s current "military posture" and defends his policy for primary reliance on missiles rather than manned bombers.	In a special farm message, Pres. Kennedy asks Congress for new feed-grains and milk production control programs based on voluntary participation by farmers. The message also urges expansion of the "eminently successful" food stamp program.	Explorer I, the U.S.'s first earth satellite, completes its fifth year in space.	The Fire Next Time, two essays on the U.S. race problem by Negro novelist James Baldwin, is published in New York.	Jan. 31
Florida Legislature approves an increase in its membership to comply with a court-ordered reapportionment.	Sen. Strom Thurmond (D, S.C.) declares in a Senate speech that Cuba has become a "formidable Soviet strategic military base," manned by as many as 40,000 Russian troops.	Federal Reserve Board Chmn. William McChesney Martin, appearing before the Joint Economic Committee, acknowledges that he is not "enthusiastic for deficit financing."			Feb. 1
				Pentti Nikula of Finland sets a world pole vault record of 16 ft. 8 3/4 in. in an indoor meet at Pajulahti, Finland.	Feb. 2
					Feb. 3
Mississippi Gov. Ross Barnett calls for a "compact" of states to create a common front against federal "usurpation.". . . Calif. Gov. Edmund Brown proposes a $3.25 billion budget, the largest state budget in U.S. history.	Rep. Donald Bruce (R, Ind.) tells the House that there are 40-50 offensive missiles in Cuba, "and the highest officials of the U.S. government know it.". . . Rep. William Cramer (R, Fla.) introduces in the House a resolution urging the U.S. "to take whatever steps are necessary to rid the hemisphere of the Castro-Communist threat."		About 2,000 persons from 80 countries attend a U.N. conference in Geneva on the application of science and technology to the problems of underdeveloped nations.	Jack Nicklaus defeats Gary Player in a playoff to win the Palm Springs golf classic.	Feb. 4

F	G	H	I	J
Includes elections, federal-state relations, civil rights and liberties, crime, the judiciary, education, health care, poverty, urban affairs and population.	Includes formation and debate of U.S. foreign and defense policies, veterans' affairs and defense spending. (Relations with specific foreign countries are usually found under the region concerned.)	Includes business, labor, agriculture, taxation, transportation, consumer affairs, monetary and fiscal policy, natural resources, and pollution.	Includes worldwide scientific, medical and technological developments, natural phenomena, U.S. weather, natural disasters, and accidents.	Includes the arts, religion, scholarship, communications media, sports, entertainment, fashions, fads and social life.

	World Affairs	Europe	Africa & the Middle East	The Americas	Asia & the Pacific
Feb. 5		Premier Georges Pompidou, speaking with Paris newsmen, acknowledges that France's veto of British admission to the EEC had been a reaction to Macmillan's negotiation of the Nassau accord with the U.S. . . . EEC Executive Commission Pres. Walter Hallstein, addressing the European Parliament in Strasbourg, declares that despite the French veto in the Brussels talks "Europe will never turn her back on England."		P.M. John Diefenbaker's Conservative Canadian government is overthrown in a no-confidence vote on a motion charging that the cabinet has failed "to give a clear statement of policy respecting Canada's national defense."	
Feb. 6		Spanish sources report that an agreement for close military cooperation between France and Spain has been reached in Madrid.		Canadian P.M. Diefenbaker dissolves Parliament and sets April 8 as the date for new elections. Diefenbaker will continue to govern on a caretaker basis. . . . Pres. Kennedy issues an order barring U.S. government-financed cargoes to foreign merchant ships engaged in trade with Cuba.	Laotian King Savang Vathana embarks on a three-month goodwill tour that will take him to the USSR, U.S. and Communist China.
Feb. 7	Sources at the Afro-Asian People's conference in Tanganyika report that Communist China has urged the expulsion of the Soviet delegation on the grounds that it is "neither African nor Asian."	Pres. Kennedy, at his first news conference since the collapse of the British-EEC talks, reaffirms strong U.S. support for eventual British membership in the Common Market. . . . Kennedy adds that those who object to the Nassau accord "really object to NATO.". . . Princess Margaret cancels a planned Paris goodwill visit scheduled for March on the advice of the Macmillan government.			Formal agreement by the British-protected government of Brunei to enter the Malaysian Federation is announced in Kuala Lumpur.
Feb. 8	Soviet Premier Khrushchev dismisses as impossible recent Western press predictions that the USSR and U.S. may someday unite in common opposition to the Chinese Communists.	Sources in London and other European capitals report that proposals are being studied for possible "associate" British membership in the EEC.	A coup led by anti-communist Iraqi air force officers overthrows the government of Premier Abdul Karim Kassim. Col. Abdel-Salam Mohammed Arif, an admirer of Nasser, is named provisional president of the revolutionary regime. . . . Ex-Katanga Pres. Tshombe leaves the Congo apparently to begin a life of exile in Europe.		South Vietnamese forces, supported by U.S.-piloted planes, launch a new offensive against Vietcong-held areas 130 miles southwest of Saigon. The drive is accompanied by the heaviest air strikes ever employed against the guerrillas. . . . U.S. Agency for International Development (AID) suspends aid to Ceylon because of its failure to compensate adequately for the 1962 seizure of two U.S. oil firms.
Feb. 9		U.S. State Dept. announces that U.S.-Spanish talks on renegotiating leases for U.S. military bases in Spain have been indefinitely postponed.	Deposed Iraqi Premier Abdul Karim Kassim is executed by rebels. As many as 1,000 persons are believed dead in the fighting that attended the military takeover.	Two more ministers resign from Canadian P.M. Diefenbaker's caretaker cabinet in protest against his policy of refusing U.S. nuclear arms.	
Feb. 10	The Soviet newspaper *Pravda*, in apparent reply to Chinese Communist criticism, defends Moscow's policy on Yugoslavia saying that despite "differences on some ideological questions" Yugoslavia rightfully belongs to the international communist movement. . . . The third Afro-Asian People's Solidarity conference concludes in Tanganyika after adopting resolutions denouncing U.S. "imperialism" in Cuba, Okinawa and South Vietnam.		Yemen demands the closing of the British legation in Taiz in apparent retaliation for Britain's refusal to recognize the new republican regime.	Gen. Alfredo Stroessner is overwhelmingly reelected to his third term as president of Paraguay.	The third round of the current Indian-Pakistani talks on disputed Kashmir end in Karachi with no progress being reported. . . . Laotian Premier Souvanna Phouma discloses that the government's neutralist, pro-communist and rightwing factions have agreed to speed talks on unification of their three armies.
Feb. 11	USSR issues a statement charging that the U.S. resumption of underground nuclear tests has given "impetus to a new nuclear arms race."	British P.M. Macmillan opens a House of Commons debate on the EEC crisis with a renewed denunciation of French Pres. de Gaulle's veto of Britain's membership. . . . French rightists, on trial for allegedly plotting to assassinate de Gaulle in 1962, testify that Finance Min. Valery Giscard d'Estaing had secretly agreed in 1961 to support a plan for the overthrow of the French government. D'Estaing denies the allegation.			U.S. Amb.-to-South Vietnam Frederick Nolting Jr. asks South Vietnamese officials to be less sensitive to constructive criticism from their U.S. allies.
	A	**B**	**C**	**D**	**E**
	Includes developments that affect more than one world region, international organizations and important meetings of major world leaders.	*Includes all domestic and regional developments in Europe, including the Soviet Union, Turkey, Cyprus and Malta.*	*Includes all domestic and regional developments in Africa and the Middle East, including Iraq and Iran and excluding Cyprus, Turkey and Afghanistan.*	*Includes all domestic and regional developments in Latin America, the Caribbean and Canada.*	*Includes all domestic and regional developments in Asia and Pacific nations, extending from Afghanistan through all the Pacific Islands, except Hawaii.*

U.S. Politics & Social Issues	U.S. Foreign Policy & Defense	U.S. Economy & Environment	Science, Technology & Nature	Culture, Leisure & Life Style	
Mississippi voters approve a new legislative reapportionment plan to give greater representation to urban areas. . . . A comprehensive program to combat mental illness and mental retardation is proposed to Congress by Pres. Kennedy in the first special presidential message on mental health. . . . Sen. John Williams (R, Del.) in a Senate speech attacks Rep. Adam Clayton Powell (D, N.Y.) for grossly misusing tax-payers' funds for personal recreation and private gain.					Feb. 5
New Orleans District Attorney Jim Garrison is convicted of defaming eight New Orleans Criminal Court Judges in connection with his accusations that they obstructed his anti-vice investigations.	CIA Dir. John McCone appears before Armed Services Subcommittee hearings on Cuba to deny recent congressional charges of a dangerous Soviet military buildup on the island.	National Safety Council estimates that 13,700 American workers lost their lives in on-the-job accidents.		Boy Scouts of America report that a record 5,322,067 persons participated in BSA activities in 1962.	Feb. 6
An attempt to reduce the number of votes required to apply cloture against a filibuster (from a two-thirds majority to a three-fifths) is defeated by a Southern filibuster.	Pres. Kennedy, responding to mounting congressional criticism, tells reporters that Soviet military personnel and equipment currently known to be in Cuba do not constitute a significant threat to U.S. security. Kennedy's statement was preceded by detailed presentations of the known facts concerning Soviet military involvement in Cuba.	Pres. Kennedy announces he will reappoint William McChesney Martin as Federal Reserve Board chairman.		The executive board of the International Olympic Games votes to bar Indonesia from Olympic competition, presumably because of Indonesia's refusal to allow Israel and Nationalist China to participate in the 1962 Asian games in Jakarta.	Feb. 7
	The U.S. AEC announces that an unspecified number of intermediate-yield nuclear detonations were set off earlier in the day at the Nevada proving grounds. The underground tests were the first by the U.S. since Dec. 1962.	FTC repots that the number of U.S. business mergers rose from 1,234 in 1961 to a record 1,260 in 1962.			Feb. 8
	N.Y. Gov. Nelson Rockefeller tells a GOP dinner in Chicago that the Kennedy administration has failed to maintain the unity and strength of the Western alliance.				Feb. 9
	State Undersecy. George Ball rebukes congressional critics of the administration for their refusal to accept Pres. Kennedy's word about Soviet military presence in Cuba.		Indian officials report that a smallpox epidemic in the state of Uttar Pradesh claimed over 600 victims in January.	Jack Brabham of Australia wins the 100-mile Australian Grand Prix auto race in Sidney.	Feb. 10
WOOK-TV, the first all-Negro operated TV station in the U.S., goes on the air in Washington D.C.	GOP congressional leaders issue a formal statement charging that anti-American sentiment has recently swept Britain, France and Canada because of the Kennedy administration's "inept conduct of our foreign policy affairs.". . . Pres. Kennedy asks Congress to establish a National Academy of Foreign Affairs to provide supplemental and graduate training for government personnel dealing with foreign policy.	A two-week series of City Hall bargaining sessions aimed at settling N.Y.C.'s newspaper strike ends without success.			Feb. 11
F	G	H	I	J	
Includes elections, federal-state relations, civil rights and liberties, crime, the judiciary, education, health care, poverty, urban affairs and population.	Includes formation and debate of U.S. foreign and defense policies, veterans' affairs and defense spending. (Relations with specific foreign countries are usually found under the region concerned.)	Includes business, labor, agriculture, taxation, transportation, consumer affairs, monetary and fiscal policy, natural resources, and pollution.	Includes worldwide scientific, medical and technological developments, natural phenomena, U.S. weather, natural disasters, and accidents.	Includes the arts, religion, scholarship, communications media, sports, entertainment, fashions, fads and social life.	

	World Affairs	Europe	Africa & the Middle East	The Americas	Asia & the Pacific
Feb. 12	The 17-nation U.N. Disarmament Committee, reconvening in Geneva, hears an opening Soviet plea for the barring of all foreign missile and nuclear submarine bases. The proposal, aimed in part at the recent Anglo-U.S. Nassau agreement, is immediately rejected by the West.	George Brown, Deputy Labor Party leader in Parliament, attacks the Macmillan government for allowing Britain to be "humiliated time after time" during the Brussels negotiations. . . . USSR orders the closing of NBC's Moscow news bureau in retaliation for what it calls "grossly distorted" broadcasts on Soviet politics. U.S. State Dept. protests the action.		A small group of pro-Castro Venezuelan rebels seize control of the Venezuelan freighter *Anzoategui* while en route to Houston, Tex. The action is reportedly aimed at forcing Pres. Romulo Betancourt to cancel his forthcoming visit to the U.S.	
Feb. 13					Indonesian Pres. Sukarno publicly declares his government's opposition to the formation of the proposed five-state Malaysian Federation. Pres. Sukarno says Indonesia will support rebel forces in Britain's Borneo territories opposed to the proposed union.
Feb. 14		French official sources inform Paris newsmen that France is willing to discuss proposals for some form of associate British membership in the EEC. . . . Foreign policy spokesman Harold Wilson defeats George Brown to become leader of the British Labor Party. . . . In a press conference statement reaffirming U.S. proposals for a multilateral NATO nuclear force, Pres. Kennedy makes clear that the U.S. intends no economic or political reprisals against France because of de Gaulle's opposition to the proposals.	Tunisia and Algeria agree to "normalize" their diplomatic relations which were disrupted Jan. 18 following Tunisian charges of Algerian participation in a plot to assassinate Tunisian Pres. Habib Bourguiba. . . . Many of the 300 African students attending schools in Bulgaria begin to leave the country in protest against alleged racial discrimination. Students charged that the government used extreme force to prevent the organization of an all-African Students' Union.	The formation of a Paris-based committee to promote the independence of Quebec from Canada and the eventual establishment of a French Republic of America is announced in Montreal.	
Feb. 15	USSR announces at the Geneva disarmament conference that it will not participate in three-nation subcommittee talks on nuclear weapons ban until the West accepts the latest Soviet proposal for no more than three on-site inspections per year.	Paris police arrest five persons for allegedly plotting to assassinate Pres. de Gaulle.			
Feb. 16			*The New York Times* publishes a detailed account of the Feb. 8 coup in Iraq.		
Feb. 17		West Berlin Mayor Willy Brandt's Social Democratic Party (SDP) increases its control of the city government in local elections.	Sources in Katanga report that recalcitrant Katanganese gendarmes are continuing to launch sporadic assaults on U.N. and central Congolese government forces. There are also reports of heavy fighting on the part of terrorist Baluba tribesmen in South Kasai Province.		
Feb. 18		British-U.S. negotiations on specific provisions of the Nassau accord begin in Washington. . . . The Italian Parliament is dissolved in preparation for new national elections scheduled for April 28.		USSR informs Pres. Kennedy that "several thousand" of its estimated 17,000 troops in Cuba will be withdrawn by March 15. . . . The leftist rebels who Feb 12 captured control of a Venezuelan freighter surrender the ship to Brazilian authorities after requesting political asylum in Brazil.	

A	B	C	D	E
Includes developments that affect more than one world region, international organizations and important meetings of major world leaders.	Includes all domestic and regional developments in Europe, including the Soviet Union, Turkey, Cyprus and Malta.	Includes all domestic and regional developments in Africa and the Middle East, including Iraq and Iran and excluding Cyprus, Turkey and Afghanistan.	Includes all domestic and regional developments in Latin America, the Caribbean and Canada.	Includes all domestic and regional developments in Asia and Pacific nations, extending from Afghanistan through all the Pacific Islands, except Hawaii.

U.S. Politics & Social Issues	U.S. Foreign Policy & Defense	U.S. Economy & Environment	Science, Technology & Nature	Culture, Leisure & Life Style	
In a Lincoln Day speech in N.Y.C. Gov. Nelson Rockefeller assails the Kennedy administration for failing to support concrete legislation to advance civil rights. . . . In a report to the President, the Civil Rights Commission suggests that the South's overt racial discrimination may be more quickly overcome than the "subtler forms of denial" that exist in the North.		International Air Transport Association reports that the number of passengers carried on scheduled flights over the north Atlantic rose from 1,919,434 in 1961 to 2,272,163 in 1962.	Soviet nuclear scientist Anapoly Alexandrov is awarded the Order of Lenin for his contribution to the peaceful uses of atomic energy. . . . U.S. Chief Justice Earl Warren says in Atlanta, Ga. that a "world order under law" must be established to prevent the destructive use of new scientific discoveries.		Feb. 12
Joe Tribble, running as a "Goldwater Republican," defeats three Democrats to win a Georgia Senate seat.	The Committee on the Foreign Student in American Colleges reports that foreign students in the U.S. currently number 60,000, about 75% more than in 1950.	Interior Dept. estimates the value of the 1962 U.S. commercial fish catch at a record $385 million.			Feb. 13
U.S. District Judge J. Robert Elliott in Columbus, Ga. rejects a suit brought by four Negroes seeking desegregation of public facilities in Albany. . . . Pres. Kennedy urges creation of a Youth Conservation Corps and a voluntary domestic peace corps in his first special message to Congress on the problems of U.S. youth.	Sen. Wayne Morse (D, Ore.) says in a Senate speech that he is against "trying to out-bid France for the leadership of Europe" and opposed to keeping American forces in Europe "if they are not wanted."	The Federal Deposit Insurance Corp. reports that no insured banks failed during 1962. This was the first fail-free year since the FDIC started operations in 1934. . . . A Presidential Committee on Federal Credit Programs recommends that federally financed loan programs should be used as a supplement rather than a substitute for private lending.	The U.S.'s first attempt to put a communications satellite (Syncom I) into an almost synchronous orbit (i.e., matching the earth's rotational speed) proves unsuccessful. NASA has announced that it is suspending development of the random-orbit communications satellites in favor of the potentially more efficient synchronous ones. . . . A team of English surgeons report that a successful transplant of a dead man's kidney into a living patient was performed in December 1962 at the Leeds General Infirmary. Spokesman for the Harvard Medical School of Boston reports that a similar operation was performed in 1961.		Feb. 14
Presidential adviser Chester Bowles, speaking at Lincoln University in Oxford, Pa., calls for a "policy of continued legal action backed by a persuasive militancy" to help end racial bias in the U.S.		In a report to the Joint Economic Committee, Walter Reuther, chairman of the AFL-CIO's economic policy committee, criticizes the administration's tax-cut plan as "too small and too late.". . . U.S. Chamber of Commerce, in a statement to the House Ways and Means Committee, says that the President's proposed 5% corporation tax cut is far too small. . . . Studebaker Corp. announces that it will begin March 1 installing seat belts in all its cars.	Delegates from 60 nations conclude a month-long U.N. conference in Geneva devoted to discussion of rules for the use of radio frequencies in satellite communications systems.	Jim Beatty sets a new world indoor mile record of three minutes 58.6 seconds at a N.Y. Athletic Club meet in Madison Square Garden. In the same competition Soviet highjumper Valeri Brumel breaks his own indoor record with a leap of 7 ft. 4 in.	Feb. 15
	Senate Foreign Relations Committee Chmn. J. W. Fulbright (D,Ark.) says that Republican critics of the administration's Cuban policy are guilty of "irresponsible" partisanship.			Bob Hayes of Florida A. & M. sets a new U.S. 70-yd. dash record of 6.9 seconds at the Mason-Dixon Games in Louisville, Ky.	Feb. 16
Over 400 integrationists demonstrate against the segregation policies of a Baltimore, Md. movie theater.	V.P. Lyndon Johnson tells an Atlantic City, N.J. audience that the U.S.'s "staying power is the key to our ultimate success" over the forces of international communism.		A Scientists' Institute for Public Information is founded in New York to provide the public with scientific information on environmental problems.	Dennis Ralston wins the men's U.S. indoor singles tennis championship in New York.	Feb. 17
By a 5-4 vote the Supreme Court invalidates two federal statutes providing for the revocation of citizenship of Americans who leave the country to avoid military service. . . . Supreme Court rules 8-1 that the Rhode Island Commission to Encourage Morality had gone "far beyond" its constitutional rights in its drive against obscene literature.	Barry Goldwater (R, Ariz.), in a Senate speech, calls for a total blockade of all goods shipped to Castro's Cuba. . . . House Inter-American Affairs Subcommittee opens hearing into communist subversion in Latin America.	Supreme Court upholds a section of the Robinson-Patman Act barring businesses from selling at "unreasonably" low prices for the purpose of destroying competition. . . . Pres. Kennedy sends Congress a bill authorizing a $500 million, three-year program of federal aid to urban transit systems. . . . *Editor & Publisher* reports that U.S. newspaper circulation totaled 59,848,688 in September 1962, up almost 600,000 from the year before.	The U.S.'s first National Medal of Science is presented by Pres. Kennedy to Theodore von Karman for his contributions to "applied mechanics, aerodynamics and astronautics."		Feb. 18
F	G	H	I	J	
Includes elections, federal-state relations, civil rights and liberties, crime, the judiciary, education, health care, poverty, urban affairs and population.	*Includes formation and debate of U.S. foreign and defense policies, veterans' affairs and defense spending. (Relations with specific foreign countries are usually found under the region concerned.)*	*Includes business, labor, agriculture, taxation, transportation, consumer affairs, monetary and fiscal policy, natural resources, and pollution.*	*Includes worldwide scientific, medical and technological developments, natural phenomena, U.S. weather, natural disasters, and accidents.*	*Includes the arts, religion, scholarship, communications media, sports, entertainment, fashions, fads and social life.*	

	World Affairs	Europe	Africa & the Middle East	The Americas	Asia & the Pacific
Feb. 19		The Ministerial Council of the British-led European Free Trade Association announces that the seven-member states have agreed to eliminate industrial tariffs by 1966, one year before the EEC's scheduled attainment of the same goal.		Pres. Kennedy warmly praises Venezuelan Pres. Romulo Betancourt for his "democratic leadership" upon the latter's arrival in the U.S. for a four-day state visit. . . . CIA Director John McCone tells the House Inter-American Affairs Subcommittee that Cuban premier Castro is actively supporting the revolutionary overthrow of Latin American governments. McCone estimates that at least 1,500 Latin Americans received geurrila warfare training in Cuba during 1962.	
Feb. 20		The State Dept. discloses that the U.S. has suggested substantial revisions in the original Nassau pact—among them the substitution of missile-armed surface vessels for submarines. The change reportedly reflects mounting Pentagon and congressional opposition to terms of the Nassau accord.	The Israeli Parliament defeats by narrow margins four opposition party motions to abolish military rule for 200,000 Israeli Arabs. P.M. David Ben-Gurion had threatened to resign if any of the four motions carried.	Visiting Venezuelan Pres. Romulo Betancourt, addressing the National Press Club, calls for a policy of increased "economic isolation" combined with assistance to "democratic resistance" elements as the best way to combat Cuba's Castro regime.	
Feb. 21		British Labor Party leader Harold Wilson announces formation of a "shadow cabinet" to formulate opposition strategy in Parliament.		U.S. Defense Dept. alleges that two Cuban-based MiG's yesterday attacked a U.S. shrimp boat in international waters north of Cuba. Kennedy orders the military to take "all necessary action" to prevent a recurrence of such attacks.	
Feb. 22				A special seven-nation committee of the OAS recommends the economic, political and cultural isolation of Cuba as part of a hemispheric effort to combat subversion in Latin America. . . . Soviet Defense Min. Rodion Malinovsky warns that an American attack on Cuba would result in a third world war.	In a note to Britain, Indonesia denounces the proposed Malaysian Federation as a threat to Indonesian security.
Feb. 23	U.S. and British delegations to the Geneva Disarmament Conference announce their willingness to reduce their proposed on-site inspection quota requirement from eight to seven inspections yearly. The USSR reaffirms its insistence on a maximum of three inspections annually.				
Feb. 24		Premier Khrushchev issues a statement dismissing Western charges of official Soviet anti-Semitism as "a crude falsehood."	Iraq's new revolutionary regime is reportedly engaged in a major crackdown against the nation's communists. An estimated 15,000 CP members have already been arrested.		
Feb. 25			Congo Premier Cyrille Adoula arrives in Brussels to discuss Belgian aid to the Congo. Adoula, the first Congolese head of government to visit Belgium since independence, is warmly received by Belgian officials.		Pres. Kennedy in Washington greets visiting Laotian King Savang Vathana with a promise of U.S. help to maintain Laos's independence and neutrality.

A	B	C	D	E
Includes developments that affect more than one world region, international organizations and important meetings of major world leaders.	Includes all domestic and regional developments in Europe, including the Soviet Union, Turkey, Cyprus and Malta.	Includes all domestic and regional developments in Africa and the Middle East, including Iraq and Iran and excluding Cyprus, Turkey and Afghanistan.	Includes all domestic and regional developments in Latin America, the Caribbean and Canada.	Includes all domestic and regional developments in Asia and Pacific nations, extending from Afghanistan through all the Pacific Islands, except Hawaii.

U.S. Politics & Social Issues	U.S. Foreign Policy & Defense	U.S. Economy & Environment	Science, Technology & Nature	Culture, Leisure & Life Style	
Sen. Joseph Clark (D, Pa.) criticizes the Democratic, Steering Committee for allegedly favoring anti-administration Southern Democrats in committee assignments.	Washington sources report that the Kennedy administration has conducted a series of high-level meetings to reconsider provisions in the Nassau accord and to review general policy toward the rift in the Western alliance caused by France. . . . Amb.-to-U.N. Stevenson, addressing the Chicago Council on Foreign Relations, says he is "far more concerned" about the training of Latin American revolutionaries in Cuba than he is about the presence of Russian troops there.	Labor Secy. W. Willard Wirtz proposes that the N.Y.C. and Cleveland newspaper strikes be submitted to some form of third-party arbitration.			Feb. 19
Rep. Adam Clayton Powell (D, N.Y.) tells reporters that recent charges against him are racially motivated and based on deliberate inaccuracies.				San Francisco Giants outfielder Willie Mays signs a 1963 contract for an estimated $100,000, thus becoming baseball's highest-salaried player.	Feb. 20
The first Presidential message on ageing is sent to Congress by Pres. Kennedy. In it Kennedy renews his request for enactment of an aged health care plan financed through Social Security. . . . HEW announces that it will build and operate integrated public elementary schools at six military bases in three Southern states by Sept. 1.		In an opening statement at his news conference, Pres. Kennedy criticizes leaders of N.Y.C.'s striking typographical union for seeking to impose a settlement which could shut down several newspapers.			Feb. 21
Walt Disney is named winner of the George Washington Award by the Freedoms Foundation in Valley Forge, Pa.			Over 300 persons are reported dead in the wake of a series of three earthquakes which shook northeastern Libya. About 15,000 survivors are homeless.	Norwegian explorer Helge Ingstad reports the discovery in Lance Aux Meadows, Newfoundland of numerous Nordic artifacts, all dating about A.D. 1,000. Ingstad says the discovery is positive proof of a Viking settlement in America 500 years before Columbus. . . . Pro golfer Lee Elders wins the men's title in the north-south Negro tournament in Miami. Tennis star Althea Gibson wins the women's title.	Feb. 22
		Ford Foundation announces a $4 million program to improve college teacher preparation.		Dick Tiger retains the world middleweight championship by fighting a 15-round draw with Gene Fullmer in Las Vegas.	Feb. 23
	A special Senate panel headed by majority leader Mike Mansfield (D, Mont.) issues a report openly questioning the current high level of U.S. aid to the South Vietnamese government. The report concludes "there is no interest of the U.S. in Vietnam which would justify. . . conversion of the war into an American war."				Feb. 24
Supreme Court, citing First Amendment rights of assembly and speech, overturns breach-of-peace convictions against 187 Negroes arrested in March 1961 for demonstrating on State Capitol grounds in Columbia, S.C.		Pres. Kennedy tells an American Bankers Association Symposium that if it is necessary to choose between the reform and reduction components of his tax package, he will give priority to a tax cut.			Feb. 25

F	G	H	I	J
Includes elections, federal-state relations, civil rights and liberties, crime, the judiciary, education, health care, poverty, urban affairs and population.	Includes formation and debate of U.S. foreign and defense policies, veterans' affairs and defense spending. (Relations with specific foreign countries are usually found under the region concerned.)	Includes business, labor, agriculture, taxation, transportation, consumer affairs, monetary and fiscal policy, natural resources, and pollution.	Includes worldwide scientific, medical and technological developments, natural phenomena, U.S. weather, natural disasters, and accidents.	Includes the arts, religion, scholarship, communications media, sports, entertainment, fashions, fads and social life.

	World Affairs	Europe	Africa & the Middle East	The Americas	Asia & the Pacific
Feb. 26		Icelandic officials order the recall of two Soviet embassy officials for allegedly organizing espionage activities against the U.S. military base at Keflavik.	U.N. officials announce that U.N. Undersecy. Ralph Bunche has been sent to Yemen in an effort to resolve the continuing civil strife between Yemeni republican troops and loyalist rebels.	The signing of a 1963-1964 Cuban-Chinese Communist trade and credit agreement is announced in Havana.	U.S. helicopter crews assisting South Vietnamese troops are authorized to shoot immediately upon sighting enemy soldiers. Heretofore, the crews had been required to refrain from shooting until fired upon.
Feb. 27				Soviet Premier Khrushchev warns that a U.S. invasion of Cuba would provoke a full-scale counteraction by the USSR. . . . Juan Bosch is sworn-in as the Dominican Republic's first constitutionally-elected president in 39 years. U.S. V.P. Lyndon Johnson is among the foreign dignitaries attending inaugural ceremonies.	
Feb. 28		Representatives of Italy, West Germany, Greece, Belgium, the Netherlands and Turkey, attending NATO meetings in Paris, express support for the Anglo-U.S. plan to establish a unified Western nuclear striking force. . . . Paris police arrest nine right-wing terrorists for allegedly planning to assassinate Premier Georges Pompidou.	Yemeni Republic Pres. Abdullah al-Salal asks the U.N. Security Council to halt alleged British "aggression" on behalf of royalists in Yemen's civil war.	Defense Secy. Robert McNamara declares at a Washington news conference that the U.S. would "not accept" the use of Soviet troops to put down an anti-Castro revolt in Cuba.	
March 1	The Communist Chinese news service Hsinhua accuses the USSR of jamming international Chinese broadcasts to "prevent people from listening" to Peking's viewpoint on ideological disputes. Soviet officials deny the charge. . . . The Balzan Foundation of Zurich, Switzerland awards its 1963 world peace prize to Pope John XXIII.	French coal miners begin a nationwide strike for higher wages.	Congolese government officials report the successful repression of the two-month terrorist uprising by Baluba tribesmen in South Kasai. Military spokesmen report that as many as 3,000 Balubas were killed in the fighting.	Daniel Fernandez Crespo, head of the nine-man ruling Executive Council, is inaugurated as president of Uruguay.	Communist China's Defense Ministry announces that its frontier guards have "completed their plan of withdrawal along the entire Sino-Indian border."
March 2			USSR asks Secy. Gen. U Thant to withdraw U.N. troops from the Congo and let the Congolese army police the country.	Reuters news agency reports that a Soviet liner has left Cuba with what are believed to be several hundred Russian troops aboard.	Pakistani Foreign Min. Zulfikar Bhutto signs a provisional agreement in Peking demarcating the frontier between China's Sinkiang province and the Pakistani-controlled section of disputed Kashmir. . . . Singapore police arrest over 100 left-wing leaders for allegedly conspiring to block Singapore's merger with the proposed Malaysian Federation.
March 3		French Pres. de Gaulle signs a special order requiring striking miners to return to work or face dismissal and imprisonment. Miners pledge to defy the decree.		In an election speech in Prince Albert, Canadian P.M. Diefenbaker declares that he will not allow Canada to be used as a "storage dump" for U.S. nuclear weapons. Diefenbaker has repeatedly accused the Liberals of a slavish submission to U.S. interests and policy. . . . Gen. Ricardo Perez Godoy is ousted as Peruvian chief of state in a dispute with other members of the ruling military junta.	
March 4	An article carried by the Communist Chinese news service Hsinhua asserts that the USSR's rejection of China's "paper tiger" thesis on imperialists amounts to a startling departure from obvious Marxist-Leninist doctrine.	Three members of the right-wing terrorist Secret Army Organization are sentenced to death in Vincennes for the Aug. 22, 1962 attempt to assassinate French Pres. Charles de Gaulle. Three others are condemned in absentia.	For the second straight day UAR warships are reported to have shelled the Saudi Arabian port of Jizan.		

A	B	C	D	E
Includes developments that affect more than one world region, international organizations and important meetings of major world leaders.	Includes all domestic and regional developments in Europe, including the Soviet Union, Turkey, Cyprus and Malta.	Includes all domestic and regional developments in Africa and the Middle East, including Iraq and Iran and excluding Cyprus, Turkey and Afghanistan.	Includes all domestic and regional developments in Latin America, the Caribbean and Canada.	Includes all domestic and regional developments in Asia and Pacific nations, extending from Afghanistan through all the Pacific Islands, except Hawaii.

U.S. Politics & Social Issues	U.S. Foreign Policy & Defense	U.S. Economy & Environment	Science, Technology & Nature	Culture, Leisure & Life Style	
In an address to the Black Muslims convention in Chicago, New York leader Malcolm X departs from his generally separatist theme to appeal for cooperation with Negro integrationists in the fight for civil rights. . . . The House Rules Committee votes 12-1 to table a proposal to transfer functions of the House Un-American Activities Committee to the Judiciary Committee.	Sen. Mike Mansfield (D,Mont.) confirms that four U.S. civilian airmen were killed while flying air support missions in the 1961 Bay of Pigs invasion.	Commerce Dept. reports that the value of U.S. goods exported to the USSR and European communist countries dropped over 12% in 1962. . . . The AFL-CIO Executive Council, meeting in Bal Harbour, Fla., reiterates its support for a 35-hour workweek.	Scientists at a NASA press conference report on data concerning Venus made available by the Mariner II interplanetary probe which passed the planet Dec. 14, 1962.		Feb. 26
The House passes an anti-junketing rule limiting spending by Congress members traveling abroad to the per diem amount allowed other federal employees.	The U.S. Information Agency releases 34 previously secret overseas public opinion polls under a new public disclosure policy.	Treasury Secy. Douglas Dillon reassures the House Ways & Means Committee that Pres. Kennedy has not "lost interest in" tax reform despite his recent statement that "nothing should stand" in the way of a tax cut.	White House confirms that Leo Welch has been chosen as chairman of the new, privately-owned Communications Satellite Corp.		Feb. 27
In his first special messages on civil rights, Pres. Kennedy asks Congress to enact measures to strengthen enforcement of the voting rights provisions of the 1957 and 1960 Civil Rights Acts.			Soviet mathematician Andrei Nikolaye-vich Kolomogrov is among the winners of the Balzan Foundation prizes for scientific achievement.		Feb. 28
Roman Catholic Archbishop Lawrence Shehan bans racial discrimination from Catholic schools, churches, social organizations and charities in his Maryland archdiocese. . . . A massive Negro voter registration drive begins in Greenwood, Miss.			U.S. scientists send up a telescope-bearing balloon to an altitude of 77,000 feet in an effort to gather data on possible life-support conditions on the planet Mars.		March 1
				Frithiof Prydz of Norway wins the North American ski jumping championship at Iron Mountain, Mich.	March 2
The Ford Foundation announces three grants, amounting to $2.6 million, to improve legal services to the indigent.			Dr. Stuart Finch of Yale University reports on a study of pregnancies in Hiroshima and Nagasaki which indicates that parental exposure to radiation may affect determination of sex in their offspring.	Sjoukje Dijkstra of the Netherlands wins her second straight women's world figure skating championship in Cortina, Italy. . . . Charles Sifford, a Los Angeles Negro pro, wins the Puerto Rico open golf tournament in San Juan.	March 3
In separate statements Gov. George Romney (Mich.) and Gov. William Scranton (Pa.) both disclaim any intention to seek the GOP presidential nomination in 1964. . . . Gov. Nelson Rockefeller, addressing an NAACP rally in Albany, N.Y., criticizes Pres. Kennedy for appointing four allegedly "segregationist" judges to federal posts in the South. . . . NAACP files suit in federal court to desegregate public schools in Jackson, Miss.	The New York Times reports that the widows of four U.S. civilian fliers killed in the Bay of Pigs invasion have been receiving regular support checks from an anonymous source. . . . Asst. State Secy. W. Averell Harriman is designated by Pres. Kennedy to be State Undersecretary for Political Affairs.	Twenty GOP Congress members hold a televised news conference to announce their intent to cut $10-$15 billion from Pres. Kennedy's proposed fiscal 1964 budget. . . . Supreme Court upholds a lower court decision supporting the right of U.S. railroads to institute job-reducing work rules. . . . The New York Post resumes publication, marking the first break in the 97-day old N.Y.C. newspaper strike. The Post is being produced under terms of the old contract.		Dr. William Carlos Williams, 79, American poet, novelist and physician dies in Rutherford, N.J.	March 4
F	G	H	I	J	
Includes elections, federal-state relations, civil rights and liberties, crime, the judiciary, education, health care, poverty, urban affairs and population.	Includes formation and debate of U.S. foreign and defense policies, veterans' affairs and defense spending. (Relations with specific foreign countries are usually found under the region concerned.)	Includes business, labor, agriculture, taxation, transportation, consumer affairs, monetary and fiscal policy, natural resources, and pollution.	Includes worldwide scientific, medical and technological developments, natural phenomena, U.S. weather, natural disasters, and accidents.	Includes the arts, religion, scholarship, communications media, sports, entertainment, fashions, fads and social life.	

	World Affairs	Europe	Africa & the Middle East	The Americas	Asia & the Pacific
March 5		Thousands of workers throughout France stage brief work stoppages to demonstrate sympathy for coal miners striking in defiance of a presidential return-to-work order.		Cuban Foreign Min. Raul Roa, in a letter to U.N. Secy. Gen. U Thant, accuses the U.S. of making preparations for renewed aggression against Cuba.	
March 6	The U.S. announces that it will discontinue making special voluntary contributions above its regular assessments for the U.N.'s Middle East and Congo operations if other U.N. nations do not pay their share.	At his Washington news conference Pres. Kennedy confirms that the U.S. now favors creation of a multilateral NATO nuclear force based on Polaris-armed surface ships rather than the nuclear submarines envisaged in the original Nassau pact.		At his press conference Pres. Kennedy refuses to confirm or deny whether four American airmen who died during the 1961 Cuban invasion were in the employ of the U.S. government. . . . Pres. Kennedy calls on Latin American countries to prevent their citizens from traveling to Cuba for training in guerrilla warfare. Kennedy also says that the U.S. is satisfied with the rate of Soviet troop withdrawals from Cuba.	The South Vietnamese navy, consisting of 30 destroyer-type patrol boats, is reported to have taken over routine coastal patrol duties from the U.S. Seventh Fleet. The Seventh Fleet will remain in the area.
March 7		Pope John XXIII grants a private audience to Alexei Adzhubei, editor of *Izvestia* and son-in-law of Soviet Premier Khrushchev. The meeting prompts speculation about possible establishment of diplomatic relations between the Vatican and the USSR. . . . Poland and West Germany sign a three-year trade agreement in Warsaw.	The U.S. formally warns the UAR that Egyptian attacks on Saudi Arabian territory threaten U.S.-UAR relations. Mohammad Habib, UAR press attaché in Washington, says the attacks are legitimately aimed at destroying Yemeni royalist supply lines in Saudi territory.		
March 8	The Chinese Communist Party newspaper, the *Peking People's Daily*, assails the U.S. CP for supporting Khrushchev's policies in Cuba.	Soviet Premier Khrushchev warns CP cultural leaders that his de-Stalinization policies should not be viewed as an excuse for ideological irresponsibility in the arts. Khrushchev singles out Ilya Ehrenburg and poet Yevgeny Yevtushenko in charging that Soviet writers have focused too much on the negative aspects of the Stalin era. . . . Striking French miners ignore a televised back-to-work appeal by Premier Georges Pompidou.	An army coup led by pro-Nasser Syrian military elements overthrows the government of Premier Khaled el-Azem. Salah ed-Din Bitar is named prime minister of the new regime, which is immediately recognized by the UAR and Iraq. . . . British Colonial Secy. Duncan Sandys announces that Kenya will be granted internal self-government following parliamentary elections in mid-May.		
March 9	Communist China formally invites Soviet Premier Khrushchev to Peking for bilateral talks to settle the Sino-Soviet ideological dispute.		The UAR and the new Syrian government exchange messages stressing the restoration of friendly relations between the two nations.	Premier Khrushchev, in a Canadian newspaper interview, denies that the USSR is building up an offensive military capability in Cuba.	Communist China accuses the U.S. forces in South Vietnam of using poison chemicals to kill civilians and devastate crops. U.S. officials describe the chemical as a defoliant, harmless to human and animal life.
March 10		Georges Bidault, fugitive leader of the anti-Gaullist French National Council of Resistance is arrested by West German police in Bavaria.	The ruling Iraqi Revolutionary Council proposes the establishment of a joint military command consisting of Iraq, Syria, the UAR, Algeria and Yemen.		
March 11		The West Berlin Parliament approves Mayor Willy Brandt's coalition government of nine Social Democrats and three Free Democrats. It is the first West Berlin government in 15 years not to include a Christian Democrat. . . . Lt. Col. Jean Marie Bastien-Thiry is executed in Paris for his part in the Aug. 22, 1962 attempt to assassinate French Pres. de Gaulle. De Gaulle commutes to life imprisonment the sentences of two other defendants.			

A	B	C	D	E
Includes developments that affect more than one world region, international organizations and important meetings of major world leaders.	*Includes all domestic and regional developments in Europe, including the Soviet Union, Turkey, Cyprus and Malta.*	*Includes all domestic and regional developments in Africa and the Middle East, including Iraq and Iran and excluding Cyprus, Turkey and Afghanistan.*	*Includes all domestic and regional developments in Latin America, the Caribbean and Canada.*	*Includes all domestic and regional developments in Asia and Pacific nations, extending from Afghanistan through all the Pacific Islands, except Hawaii.*

U.S. Politics & Social Issues	U.S. Foreign Policy & Defense	U.S. Economy & Environment	Science, Technology & Nature	Culture, Leisure & Life Style	
	The Joint Congressional Committee on Atomic Energy opens hearings on the scientific reliability of U.S.-proposed policing systems for a nuclear test-ban agreement.	Pres. Kennedy resubmits to Congress his 1962 transportation proposals aimed at creating a modern national transportation system.			March 5
The city commission of Albany, Ga. officially rescinds its local racial segregation ordinances. The action follows a two-year Negro-led civil rights campaign in the community. . . . Four Negro voter registration workers are shot and wounded by a group of unidentified whites in Greenwood, Miss. . . . Pres. Kennedy, responding to reporters' questions, acknowledges that his administration has recently experienced some disappointments in both domestic and foreign affairs.	A House Armed Services Committee report on the administration's requested defense budget criticizes the Defense Dept. for over-emphasizing missiles at the expense of manned strategic systems, such as the RS-70 bomber. . . . The Senate Permanent Investigations Subcommittee completes 10 days of hearings into charges that the Defense Dept. revealed undue favoritism in the November 1962 award of the contract for the TFX fighter planes to the General Dynamics Corp. instead of the Boeing Co.	Pres. Kennedy at his news conference challenges Republican budget critics to specify where drastic budget cuts can be made without endangering U.S. security or space efforts.			March 6
A Civil Rights Commission study charges that discrimination in Rapid City, S.D. has caused serious "hardship" to Negro servicemen stationed at nearby Ellsworth Air Force Base.		Labor Dept. reports that unemployment in February climbed to 6.1%, the highest point since November 1961. . . . Treasury Secy. Douglas Dillon tells an American Bankers Association conference that the administration was disappointed by the $2.2 billion deficit in the U.S.'s 1962 balance of payments, even though it was the smallest deficit in five years. . . . The $100 million Pan Am Building, the world's largest commercial office building, is dedicated in New York.			March 7
Kennedy sends Congress a draft bill to establish a public defender system for needy defendants in federal criminal cases.				Jim Beatty sets a world indoor two-mile record of eight minutes 30.7 seconds in Chicago.	March 8
Mississippi State Univ. Board votes to allow the school's basketball team to participate in the NCAA tournament, thus departing from its policy of not playing against schools with Negro players. Gov. Ross Barnett opposes the decision.	Pres. Kennedy names ex-Sen. William Benton as chief U.S. representative to UNESCO.			*Sporting News* names Bill Russell of the Boston Celtics as NBA player of the year for the third straight year.	March 9
Population Reference Bureau, Inc. reports that rural population in the U.S. declined 425,000 during the 1950s.					March 10
	The House passes and sends to the Senate a bill (HR2438) to extend the military draft for four years.	Pres. Kennedy submits to Congress a manpower report in which he calls unemployment "our number one economic problem." He warns that unemployment may rise to 7% by 1967 if Congress does not act on his tax and economic proposals. . . . Agriculture Dept. reports that the number of farms in the U.S. dropped 3% in 1962 to a total of 3,688,000, almost two million fewer than in 1950.	NASA and the French National Center for Space Studies announce plans for a cooperative program to investigate the propagation of very low frequency (VLF) electromagnetic waves in space. . . . Tornados touch down in Mississippi, Alabama and Tennessee, leaving at least five persons dead.		March 11

F	G	H	I	J
Includes elections, federal-state relations, civil rights and liberties, crime, the judiciary, education, health care, poverty, urban affairs and population.	*Includes formation and debate of U.S. foreign and defense policies, veterans' affairs and defense spending. (Relations with specific foreign countries are usually found under the region concerned.)*	*Includes business, labor, agriculture, taxation, transportation, consumer affairs, monetary and fiscal policy, natural resources, and pollution.*	*Includes worldwide scientific, medical and technological developments, natural phenomena, U.S. weather, natural disasters, and accidents.*	*Includes the arts, religion, scholarship, communications media, sports, entertainment, fashions, fads and social life.*

	World Affairs	Europe	Africa & the Middle East	The Americas	Asia & the Pacific
March 12			Ex-Katanga Pres. Moise Tshombe returns to Elizabethville after undergoing six weeks of medical treatment and rest in France.		
March 13	USSR charges that U.S. warships fired March 8 on a Russian trawler 70 miles east of Norfolk, Va. The U.S. denies any such incident.	The discontinuation of the USSR's current seven-year economic plan and the establishment of a new Supreme Council of National Economy to draft a new five-year plan are announced in Moscow. The new plan reportedly will be aimed at achieving a "substantial" increase in Soviet living standards.		Cuban Premier Castro asserts that his government has received sufficient military armaments to repel any U.S. invasion against the island.	
March 14		In a statement to the press, Premier Khrushchev declares that despite recent farm reforms, greater administrative and organizational efficiency is still needed to raise Soviet agricultural production.	Over 1,500 persons demonstrate in front of the Iraqi embassy in Moscow to protest the new Iraqi government's current anti-communist campaign. . . . U.N. sources report that Congo Premier Cyrille Adoula has asked Secy. Gen. U Thant to coordinate an international program to reorganize and train the Congolese army.		
March 15	The 17-nation U.N. Disarmament Committee begins its second year in Geneva with no immediate prospect of an agreement.			Caribbean sources report that an estimated 3,800 Soviet troops have departed Cuba since Feb. 5. According to the Soviet newspaper *Pravda*, the troops are leaving because they have finished their mission of technical aid to Cuban armed forces.	Allegations that Nationalist Chinese and Communist North Vietnamese troops are remaining in Laos in violation of international accords are officially dismissed as untrue by the International Control Commission.
March 16	In a formal protest note the U.S. State Dept. charges that two Soviet aircraft yesterday violated U.S. airspace over Alaska. The protest marks the first official report of a Soviet overflight of American territory.		Representatives of Syria, Iraq and the UAR conclude two days of meetings in Cairo on a proposed military, political and economic merger of the three nations. . . . Algeria formally protests reported French plans to test another nuclear device in the Sahara.		South Korean junta chairman Gen. Chung Hee Park reimposes a ban on all civilian political activity. Park also discloses plans for a national referendum on extension of the junta's rule for another four years. . . . In a note to the U.N. Security Council India protests Pakistan's provisional March 2 border agreement with Communist China, claiming that the pact "unlawfully apportioned" part of Indian Kashmir.
March 17				Pres. João Goulart and other top Brazilian leaders are reportedly indignant over the release of a U.S. State Dept. statement asserting that Communists exercise "substantial influence" in Brazil's government.	

A	B	C	D	E
Includes developments that affect more than one world region, international organizations and important meetings of major world leaders.	Includes all domestic and regional developments in Europe, including the Soviet Union, Turkey, Cyprus and Malta.	Includes all domestic and regional developments in Africa and the Middle East, including Iraq and Iran and excluding Cyprus, Turkey and Afghanistan.	Includes all domestic and regional developments in Latin America, the Caribbean and Canada.	Includes all domestic and regional developments in Asia and Pacific nations, extending from Afghanistan through all the Pacific Islands, except Hawaii.

U.S. Politics & Social Issues	U.S. Foreign Policy & Defense	U.S. Economy & Environment	Science, Technology & Nature	Culture, Leisure & Life Style	
	In a published letter to the Senate Investigations Subcommittee, Defense Secy. Robert McNamara charges that the committee's recent hearings into the TFX contract had "needlessly undermined public confidence in top Defense officials."	Democrats and Republicans on the Joint Economic Committee join in advocating a larger tax cut for 1963 than that proposed by Pres. Kennedy. The Democratic majority also criticizes the administration's failure to increase spending on education, health and other domestic priority areas. . . . For the second time in 11 years, Seattle voters reject a proposal to fluoridate the city's water supply.	Floods ravage parts of West Virginia, Tennessee, Virginia, Kentucky and Alabama. At least 13 persons are known dead.	Poet William Stafford is presented a National Book Award for his 1962 book, *Traveling through the Dark*.	March 12
	House passes and sends to the Senate a bill (HR2440) authorizing a record $15.85 billion program of military procurement in fiscal 1964. The measure includes $363 million (not requested by the administration) to build two RS-70 bombers. . . . The U.S. Information Agency releases a number of opinion polls indicating an increase in U.S. prestige in Britain, West Germany and France. . . . Amb.-to-U.N. Adlai Stevenson tells a Senate subcommittee that the U.N. has served U.S. interests well in the Cuban, Congo, and other world crises.	House Anti-trust Subcommittee opens hearings on the increasing concentration of ownership in the U.S. press and other news media.			March 13
					March 14
			Dr. James Van Allen concedes that the U.S.'s July 9, 1962 high-altitude nuclear test might have created a fairly durable artifical radiation belt around the earth.		March 15
		U.S. Chamber of Commerce urges a $9.1 billion cut in the administration's proposed fiscal 1964 budget.			March 16
				Mother Elizabeth Ann Bayley Seton (1774-1821), founder of the 11,000-member Sisters of Charity of St. Joseph (Maryland) is beatified by Pope John XXIII. If canonized, she would become the first American-born saint. . . . USSR wins the world amateur ice hockey championship in Stockholm, Sweden.	March 17

F	G	H	I	J
Includes elections, federal-state relations, civil rights and liberties, crime, the judiciary, education, health care, poverty, urban affairs and population.	Includes formation and debate of U.S. foreign and defense policies, veterans' affairs and defense spending. (Relations with specific foreign countries are usually found under the region concerned.)	Includes business, labor, agriculture, taxation, transportation, consumer affairs, monetary and fiscal policy, natural resources, and pollution.	Includes worldwide scientific, medical and technological developments, natural phenomena, U.S. weather, natural disasters, and accidents.	Includes the arts, religion, scholarship, communications media, sports, entertainment, fashions, fads and social life.

	World Affairs	Europe	Africa & the Middle East	The Americas	Asia & the Pacific
March 18		France detonates an underground nuclear device at its testing site in the Sahara. The test marks France's eighth nuclear detonation. . . . West Berlin Mayor Willy Brandt, in a statement to the new city Parliament, calls Soviet proposals for a U.N. take-over of Berlin unrealistic and dangerous.		"Commando Units" of two anti-Castro organizations attack a Soviet army installation and ship at the port of Isabela de Sague, about 130 miles east of Havana, reportedly leaving 12 Russians wounded. . . . Pres. Kennedy and six Central American presidents meet in San Jose, Costa Rica to discuss the U.S.'s Alliance for Progress and the economic integration of Central America. Kennedy pledges increased U.S. aid for the region's economic development programs.	
March 19			Tunisia, Syria, Ghana and several other African governments join Algeria in protesting yesterday's test of a French nuclear device in the Sahara Desert.	U.S. State Dept. sharply criticizes yesterday's anti-Castro raid on Soviet personnel in Cuba, claiming that such hit-and-run attacks may strengthen rather than weaken the Castro regime. . . . The Central American presidents' conference in Costa Rica ends with the issuance of a Declaration of San Jose. The communique outlines U.S. aid commitments and pledges joint efforts to halt Soviet aggression and communist subversion in the Western Hemisphere.	Civilian politicians in South Korea openly defy the government's ban on political activity and vow to oppose the junta's apparent intention to extend military rule. . . . Mohammed Yousuf is sworn-in as premier of Afghanistan, replacing Sardar Mohammed Daud Khan who resigned March 3. Yousuf announces formation of new cabinet which excludes members of the royal family.
March 20			Israeli Foreign Min. Golda Meir formally calls upon West Germany to bar its scientists from helping the UAR develop rockets which allegedly threaten Israeli security. . . . The Southern Rhodesian Parliament adopts an anti-subversion bill mandating the death penalty for anyone convicted of arson or sabotage.	Cuba claims that the March 17 exile raid on Isabela de Sagua was launched from U.S. territory. . . . Brazilian Pres. João Goulart is reported to have accepted "with satisfaction" a U.S. State Dept. letter retracting recent U.S. claims of excessive Communist influence in the Brazilian government.	
March 21		Hungarian Premier Janos Kadar announces an amnesty for political prisoners, including many of those who participated in the 1956 revolt. Kadar also promises a normalization of relations with the Roman Catholic Church.		Pres. Kennedy tells reporters at a news conference that the U.S. opposes hit-and-run attacks upon Cuba and had no part whatever in the March 18 raid. . . . Kennedy also praises the recent San Jose conference for its resolve to resist Cuban-sponsored subversion in Central America.	
March 22			The West German Justice Ministry, responding to recent Israeli demands, says that it has no power to bar law-abiding German nationals from working for the UAR.	The Paris newspaper Le Monde publishes a two-part interview in which Cuban Premier Fidel Castro criticizes Soviet Premier Khrushchev's treatment of Cuba during the October 1962 missile crisis. Castro denies the specific statements attributed to him in the interview.	
March 23					
March 24		Negotiations in the nationwide strike of 170,000 French coal miners collapse in Paris as union officials reject a new wage offer by the government's coal board.			South Vietnamese Pres. Ngo Dinh Diem attacks a Feb. 24 U.S. Senate report criticizing his government for failing to achieve political democracy.

	A	B	C	D	E
	Includes developments that affect more than one world region, international organizations and important meetings of major world leaders.	*Includes all domestic and regional developments in Europe, including the Soviet Union, Turkey, Cyprus and Malta.*	*Includes all domestic and regional developments in Africa and the Middle East, including Iraq and Iran and excluding Cyprus, Turkey and Afghanistan.*	*Includes all domestic and regional developments in Latin America, the Caribbean and Canada.*	*Includes all domestic and regional developments in Asia and Pacific nations, extending from Afghanistan through all the Pacific Islands, except Hawaii.*

U.S. Politics & Social Issues	U.S. Foreign Policy & Defense	U.S. Economy & Environment	Science, Technology & Nature	Culture, Leisure & Life Style	
The Supreme Court, responding to a hand-written petition from Florida convict Clarence Gideon, unanimously rules that states must supply free counsel to indigent defendants facing serious criminal charges. The decision overturns a 1942 Supreme Court ruling (Betts v. Brady). . . . The Supreme Court upholds a lower court decision invalidating Ga.'s county unit vote system as a violation of the one-man, one-vote principle.		Pres. Kennedy asks Congress to cut some $125 million from his fiscal 1963 and 1964 budgets. Specific reductions were asked in VA benefit funds, elderly housing programs and public assistance grants.			March 18
	The House Government Information Subcommittee hears testimony from seven leading newsmen on the administration's handling of information during the 1962 Cuban missile crisis.	The 63rd annual convention of the National Farmers Union, meeting in New York, expresses overall approval of the Kennedy administration's farm program. . . . Commerce Dept. reports that the U.S. continued to lead the world in steel production during 1962 with a total of more than 98 million tons (25.7% of total world output). The USSR ranked second with 84.1 million tons.		For the fourth straight year NBA statistics show San Francisco Warrior center Wilt Chamberlain as the league's scoring champion with an average of 44.8 points per game. Chamberlain's field goal percentage of .528 also marks a new NBA record.	March 19
	A special foreign aid study group headed by Gen. Lucius Clay reports to Pres. Kennedy that the application of more realistic guidelines could increase the effectiveness of U.S. aid programs while substantially lowering the cost. The report specifically advised against aid programs which enable recipient nations to postpone needed fiscal, economic and political reforms.		An agreement on details for joint U.S.-Soviet weather and communications satellite projects is announced by negotiators in Rome. The plan calls for coordinated satellite monitoring and the sharing of meteorological data. . . . Dr. C. H. Li of the University of California reports on the successful artificial synthesis of a hormone resembling natural ACTH.		March 20
The 54-year old federal prison on Alcatraz Island in San Francisco Bay is officially closed after prison authorities determined that needed renovations would be too expensive.	Pres. Kennedy tells newsmen that he expects the Senate Permanent Investigations Subcommittee to fully exonerate the Defense Dept. in its current inquiry into the controversial decision toward the TFX fighter plane contract to General Dynamics Corp. despite military recommendations favoring a Boeing Co. design.	Pres. Kennedy tells reporters that February economic indicators support his belief that there will be no recession in 1963.	U.S. Public Health Service announces the licensing of two measles vaccines—a killed-virus type and a live-virus type. . . . Eruptions of lava from the Agung volcano on the Indonesian island of Bali kill an estimated 1,500 persons.	Louis Rodriguez of Cuba wins the world welterweight championship by a 15-round decision over Emile Griffith of New York. . . . Ex-world featherweight champion Davey Moore collapses into a coma in his dressing room after losing his title by TKO to Ultiminio Ramos of Cuba in Los Angeles.	March 21
In a letter to 23 state governors Pres. Kennedy appeals for quick ratification of the anti-poll tax amendment. Twenty-four states have already ratified the measure. . . . Doris Stevens, long-time campaigner for equal rights for women, dies in New York.		Speaking in New York, Sen. Barry Goldwater denounces Pres. Kennedy's spending and tax reduction proposals as "another gimmick."	Meteorological experts report that the 1962-1963 winter was the "most severe" of the past 100 years in Europe, Japan and parts of the U.S.	Members of six major U.S. Protestant denominations (Presbyterian, Methodist, Episcopal, United Church of Christ, Disciples of Christ, and Evangelical United Brethren) conclude three days of preliminary talks in Oberlin, Ohio on their possible merger in to a 22-million member church. . . . Gov. Edmund Brown calls for the abolition of boxing in California following last night's serious injury to featherweight champion Davey Moore.	March 22
Rep. Adam Clayton Powell (D, N.Y.), attending a New York rally with Malcolm X of the Black Muslims, urges Negroes to boycott civil rights organizations led in part by whites. The statement draws criticism from the NAACP.				Loyola Univ. wins the NCAA basketball championship in Louisville, Ky. with an overtime victory over defending champion Cincinnati. . . . Providence (R.I.) College wins the National Invitational Basketball Tournament in New York. . . . Mrs. Richard duPont's Kelso wins the $100,000 Campbell Handicap in Bowey, Md. to become the third greatest money winning horse in racing history. . . . Oxford defeats Cambridge in the Thames rowing races in London.	March 23
				Pope John XXIII issues a statement describing professional boxing as "barbarous" and "contrary to natural principles."	March 24

F	G	H	I	J
Includes elections, federal-state relations, civil rights and liberties, crime, the judiciary, education, health care, poverty, urban affairs and population.	Includes formation and debate of U.S. foreign and defense policies, veterans' affairs and defense spending. (Relations with specific foreign countries are usually found under the region concerned.)	Includes business, labor, agriculture, taxation, transportation, consumer affairs, monetary and fiscal policy, natural resources, and pollution.	Includes worldwide scientific, medical and technological developments, natural phenomena, U.S. weather, natural disasters, and accidents.	Includes the arts, religion, scholarship, communications media, sports, entertainment, fashions, fads and social life.

	World Affairs	Europe	Africa & the Middle East	The Americas	Asia & the Pacific
March 25				Dr. Manuel Urrutia Lleo, Cuba's first president after the Castro revolution, is allowed to leave the Mexican embassy where he had lived as an anti-communist political refugee since November 1961. . . . Guatemalan Pres. Miguel Ydigoras temporarily suspends constitutional rights in response to an alleged increase in pro-communist agitation and subversion.	U.S. State Dept. issues a statement criticizing the continuation of military rule in South Korea.
March 26		London police clash with an estimated 7,000 unemployed workers from Scotland and Northern Ireland during a demonstration before the House of Parliament. . . . U.S. State Secy. Dean Rusk meets with Soviet Amb.-to-U.S. Anatoly Dobrynin in Washington to resume bilateral talks on Berlin for the first time since the Cuban missile crisis.			South Korea's ruling junta offers a compromise political settlement which would allow civilians a limited role in governing the country over the next two years. Under the plan Gen. Chung Hee Park would remain head of state.
March 27	The Soviet delegation at the Geneva disarmament talks proposes a land and submarine missile disarmament pact based on international inspection of missile stockpiles at launching sites.	Delegates to the Union of Writers conference in Moscow denounce poet Yevgeny Yevtushenko for allowing the publication in the West of uncleared selections from his book *Precocious Autobiography* . The attacks appear to be part of a growing campaign against "liberalism" among Soviet intellectuals.		The USSR formally protests alleged U.S. complicity in the March 17 Cuban exile raid on Soviet personnel at Isabela de Sagua. . . . A Cuban exile splinter group, known as Commando L, announces in Miami that its members yesterday attacked and damaged a Soviet vessel at the port of Caibarien.	
March 28		Marshal Sergei Semenovitch Biryuzov is reported to have replaced Marshal Matvei Zakharov as chief of staff of the Soviet armed forces.	The British cabinet officially endorses the principle that any member of the Rhodesia-Nyasaland Federation has the right to secede. The decision is expected to ensure the eventual dissolution of the federation.	The U.S. State Dept. reports that two Cuban-piloted MiG jets fired on but missed the U.S. motor ship *Floridian* in international waters off Key West.	
March 29	Britain's Geneva delegation announces the West's rejection of a March 27 Soviet missile disarmament proposal.	U.S. Dept. of Agriculture reports that western Europe's wheat crop rose from 37.5 million short tons in 1961 to a record 48 million tons in 1962.	Southern Rhodesian P.M. Sir Winston Field says that his country will seek independence from Britain in view of the probable collapse of the Rhodesia-Nyasaland Federation. . . . Pres. Kennedy publicly confirms that the U.S. will fulfill a 1959 agreement to evacuate four U.S. military bases in Morocco by the end of 1963. The statement comes at the conclusion of three days of Washington talks with visiting Moroccan King Hassan II.	The Cuban government admits and apologizes for the March 28 attack on the U.S. ship *Floridian* .	Communist China releases a protest note to India charging that country with interfering in China's internal affairs by aiding Tibetan rebels.
March 30			Algerian P.M. Mohammed Ben Bella announces the nationalization of all agricultural and industrial property owned by Frenchmen who fled Algeria after its independence.	The U.S. announces that it will take "every step necessary" to make sure that Cuban exile attacks against "targets in Cuba" are not launched, manned-equipped on U.S. territory. . . . An army coup led by Col. Enrique Peralta Azurdia, overthrows the Guatemalan regime of Pres. Miguel Ydigoras Fuentes and forms a military government. Coup leaders say the action was necessary to ensure a more effective campaign against communist subversion.	Laotian sources report an eruption of serious fighting in the Plaine des Jarres between Pathet Lao forces and troops led by neutralist Gen. Kong Le.

A	B	C	D	E
Includes developments that affect more than one world region, international organizations and important meetings of major world leaders.	Includes all domestic and regional developments in Europe, including the Soviet Union, Turkey, Cyprus and Malta.	Includes all domestic and regional developments in Africa and the Middle East, including Iraq and Iran and excluding Cyprus, Turkey and Afghanistan.	Includes all domestic and regional developments in Latin America, the Caribbean and Canada.	Includes all domestic and regional developments in Asia and Pacific nations, extending from Afghanistan through all the Pacific Islands, except Hawaii.

U.S. Politics & Social Issues	U.S. Foreign Policy & Defense	U.S. Economy & Environment	Science, Technology & Nature	Culture, Leisure & Life Style	
By a 5-4 vote, the Supreme Court holds that legislative investigators must first prove that an organization is involved in subversive activities before being allowed access to its membership lists. . . . A voter registration headquarters in Greenwood, Miss. is damaged by arson.				Ex-featherweight champion Davey Moore dies in Los Angeles of injuries suffered in his March 21 title bout with Ultiminio Ramos. Moore's ring injury had already spurred renewed demands for the abolition of boxing. . . . Univ. of Oklahoma wins its sixth NCAA wrestling championship in Kent, Ohio. . . . The Univ. of Denver wins its third straight NCAA ski championship.	March 25
				Henry Cooper retains the British heavyweight championship by knocking out Dick Richardson of Wales in the fifth round of their title bout in London. . . . Glenn Hall of the Chicago Blackhawks wins the Vezina Trophy as the NHL's outstanding goalie of the year.	March 26
Police disperse groups of Negroes as they march on the Greenwood, Miss. courthouse in an attempt to register to vote.					March 27
Republican liberals introduce in the Senate a package of proposed civil rights bills. In addition to strengthening enforcement of voting rights, the measures would bar bias in interstate public accommodations and would provide curbs against police brutality. . . . An article by Jack Anderson in the March 24 edition of *Parade* magazine, alleging widespread misuse of government funds by Congress members, evokes angry criticism from Capitol Hill.			The California Medical Association becomes the first U.S. state medical society to publicly declare that cigarette smoking is a health hazard. . . . The U.S.'s Saturn I super rocket booster is test flown successfully for the fourth consecutive time.		March 28
A Rockefeller-for-President headquarters, opened in Los Angeles, is closed at Gov. Rockefeller's request.	Pres. Kennedy signs a bill (HR2438) providing for a four-year extension of the draft law. The Army, the only service currently using the draft, is expected to call 90,000 men in the coming year. . . . A House Appropriations subcommittee releases the Feb. 7 testimony of Defense Secy. McNamara, in which he attempted to explain why it took so long for U.S. intelligence to confirm the building of Soviet missile sites in Cuba.	In a published letter, ex-Pres. Eisenhower says that $10-12 billion must be cut from the fiscal 1964 Kennedy budget if the U.S. is to avoid "a vast wasteland of debt and financial chaos."	In a letter attacking the 1964 Kennedy budget, ex-Pres. Eisenhower criticizes the U.S. moon program as "not worth the added tax burden.". . . The British Aviation Ministry announces that it intends to pursue its own national space program and is considering starting a British satellite communications system. . . . The U.S. FDA bans the use of menadione—vitamin K3—in foods and food supplements. Menadione is suspected as a possible cause of mental defects in infants.		March 29
The Justice Dept. files suit in federal court to bar interference with Negro voter registrations in Greenwood, Miss. . . . Pres. Kennedy establishes a special commission to study why so many Americans fail to vote.			Fifteen more pilots, including the program's first Negro, Edward J. Dwight Jr., are chosen by NASA for astronaut training.	Univ. of Michigan wins the NCAA gymnastics championship in Pittsburgh, Pa.	March 30

F	G	H	I	J
Includes elections, federal-state relations, civil rights and liberties, crime, the judiciary, education, health care, poverty, urban affairs and population.	Includes formation and debate of U.S. foreign and defense policies, veterans' affairs and defense spending. (Relations with specific foreign countries are usually found under the region concerned.)	Includes business, labor, agriculture, taxation, transportation, consumer affairs, monetary and fiscal policy, natural resources, and pollution.	Includes worldwide scientific, medical and technological developments, natural phenomena, U.S. weather, natural disasters, and accidents.	Includes the arts, religion, scholarship, communications media, sports, entertainment, fashions, fads and social life.

	World Affairs	Europe	Africa & the Middle East	The Americas	Asia & the Pacific
March 31				Ex-Guatemalan Pres. Miguel Ydigoras Fuentes tells reporters in Managua, Nicaragua that the coup which overthrew him yesterday was probably good for Guatemala. . . . The U.S. Justice Dept. places travel restrictions on 18 Cuban exile leaders in the Miami area.	
April 1			Syria's ruling Revolutionary Council decrees a state of emergency to curb extreme pro-Nasser demonstrators demanding an immediate Syrian-UAR union.		Laotian Foreign Min. Quinim Pholsena is assassinated by a neutralist soldier guarding his home in Vientiane. Although officially a neutralist, Quinim Pholsena was believed to be sympathetic to the Communist Pathet Lao.
April 2	In a letter to Chinese Premier Chou En-lai, Soviet Premier Khrushchev declines a March 9 Chinese invitation to participate in bilateral ideological talks in Peking. Khrushchev instead invites Mao Tse-tung to visit Moscow for discussions in spring or summer.	A Soviet fighter plane fires at a private twin-engine plane flying in the southernmost air corridor to West Berlin. It is the first Soviet attack on a Western plane in the corridors since 1953. . . . Editorials carried in the Soviet press urge a ban on foreign travel by writers who have not yet demonstrated their political "maturity."			In a letter to South Korean Gen. Chung Hee Park, Pres. Kennedy reiterates U.S. opposition to indefinite continuation of military rule in South Korea.
April 3		French coal miners end their nationwide walkout after accepting a government offer for a 12.5% wage increase over the next year. . . . British Chancellor of the Exchequer Reginald Maudling presents Parliament with a fiscal 1964 budget calling for a $753 million tax cut.		In a statement to his Washington news conference, Pres. Kennedy reiterates firm U.S. opposition to Cuban exile raids. He also reports that an estimated 4,000 Soviet troops left Cuba in March. . . . Argentinian government troops report that they have virtually suppressed a two-day rebellion by anti-Peronist naval units aimed at overthrowing the government of Pres. José Maria Guido.	
April 4		Responding to Western protests over the April 2 attack on a private plane, the USSR declares that it will "not guarantee the safety of such flights to and from West Berlin in the future."	France announces a resumption of diplomatic relations with the UAR. French-UAR relations have been broken since the 1956 Suez crisis.		
April 5	The USSR announces acceptance of U.S. proposals for a direct communications link between Washington and Moscow.		France protests the disregard for French interests in Algeria's March 30th decision to nationalize all absentee French-owned property.	U.S. military authorities announce the reinforcing of sea and air surveillance against potential Cuban exile raiders in the Florida straits.	
April 6					U.S. State Dept. angrily protests recent Pathet Lao accusations that it had a role in the April 1 assassination of Foreign Min. Quinim Pholsena. . . . South Korean junta chairman Gen. Chung Hee Park, under pressure from domestic political leaders and the U.S. agrees to lift his ban on civilian political activity and to permit elections in the fall.

A	B	C	D	E
Includes developments that affect more than one world region, international organizations and important meetings of major world leaders.	*Includes all domestic and regional developments in Europe, including the Soviet Union, Turkey, Cyprus and Malta.*	*Includes all domestic and regional developments in Africa and the Middle East, including Iraq and Iran and excluding Cyprus, Turkey and Afghanistan.*	*Includes all domestic and regional developments in Latin America, the Caribbean and Canada.*	*Includes all domestic and regional developments in Asia and Pacific nations, extending from Afghanistan through all the Pacific Islands, except Hawaii.*

U.S. Politics & Social Issues	U.S. Foreign Policy & Defense	U.S. Economy & Environment	Science, Technology & Nature	Culture, Leisure & Life Style	
		N.Y.C.'s longest newspaper strike ends in its 114th day. Settlement comes on the basis of proposals introduced into negotiations March 8 by N.Y.C. Mayor Robert F. Wagner. . . . The non-profit Resources for the Future organization predicts that the U.S. will have sufficient natural resources for the rest of the century and "for a long time thereafter."			March 31
Nationally known comedian Dick Gregory arrives in Greenwood, Miss. to add his support to the current voter registration drive.		A federal grand jury in New York returns two indictments charging seven major U.S. steel companies with conspiring to fix prices on specialized steel products between 1948-1961.	Nobel Prize-winner Peter Debye of Cornell Univ. is awarded the Priestly Medal, the highest U.S. honor in chemistry.		April 1
Richard Daley outpolls Republican challenger Ben Adamowski to win a third term as mayor of Chicago. . . . Albert Boutwell is elected mayor of Birmingham, Ala., defeating Police Commissioner Eugene (Bull) Connors. . . . A major Negro campaign against segregation is launched in Birmingham, Ala.	Pres. Kennedy asks Congress for a fiscal 1964 foreign aid appropriation of $4.525 billion, $600 million more than Congress appropriated in fiscal 1963. Kennedy also proposes enactment of tax incentives to encourage private investment in underdeveloped nations.	Speaking to the convention of the National Association of Broadcasters, FCC Chmn. Newton Minow urges federal legislation to curb excessive advertising on radio and TV.	A space probe, designated Lunik 4, is launched toward the moon by Soviet scientists. It is the first Soviet moon probe since three USSR launchings in 1959.	Georgia Atty. Gen. Eugene Cook releases evidence tending to confirm a March 23 *Saturday Evening Post* claim that the University of Alabama's September 22, 1962 football win over Georgia had been "rigged." The *Post* story claimed that Georgia coach Wally Butts had given his team's plays and strategy to Alabama coach Paul Bryant before the game. Both men deny any wrongdoing.	April 2
	Pres. Kennedy tells reporters that ex-Pres. Eisenhower's recent call for a $10 billion budget cut would "cut the heart out" of military spending.	Pres. Kennedy appoints an emergency board to investigate the work-rules dispute between the nation's railroads and five unions representing about 200,000 on-train employees. On March 4, the Supreme Court upheld the railroads' right to make work-rule changes. . . . U.S. Securities & Exchange Commission proposes new laws and sterner self-regulation by the securities industry to correct "grave abuses" uncovered in the SEC's 15-month investigation of the stock market.			April 3
In a report to the President, the Advisory Commission on Narcotic and Drug Abuse urges a "massive attack" against importers and distributors of hard narcotics.		The 127-day old strike against Cleveland newspapers, the longest in U.S. history, ends as typographical workers agree to a new 26-month contract. . . . A bill (S6) to create a $750 million aid program for mass transit is passed by the Senate and sent to the House. It is the first major administration bill to clear either house so far in 1963.			April 4
	Julius Robert Oppenheimer, atomic scientist who was declared an AEC security risk in 1954, is awarded the Enrico Fermi Award, the AEC's top honor, for his contributions to nuclear energy. The announcement is viewed as part of a Kennedy administration move to clear Oppenheimer's name.				April 5
	Chester Bowles, Pres. Kennedy's special adviser on third world affairs, is named ambassador to India, succeeding J. Kenneth Galbraith.	Speaking in Omaha, Neb. Gov. Rockefeller (N.Y.) attacks the Kennedy administration for failing to increase the nation's rate of economic growth, adding that if present policies continue, unemployment may climb to 8.4% by 1967.	The Soviet lunar probe Lunik 4 passes the moon at a distance of about 5,270 miles and then swings back into orbit around the earth. Although Russian sources describe the mission as a success, Western observers speculate that the probe was intended for a soft landing or a least a much closer lunar pass.	Australian boxer Norman Smith dies following a fight in Gympio, Australia. *Ring Magazine* estimates there have been 14 ring deaths in 1962 and 217 since 1946. . . . Scotland defeats England to win the British soccer championship in London.	April 6

F	G	H	I	J
Includes elections, federal-state relations, civil rights and liberties, crime, the judiciary, education, health care, poverty, urban affairs and population.	*Includes formation and debate of U.S. foreign and defense policies, veterans' affairs and defense spending. (Relations with specific foreign countries are usually found under the region concerned.)*	*Includes business, labor, agriculture, taxation, transportation, consumer affairs, monetary and fiscal policy, natural resources, and pollution.*	*Includes worldwide scientific, medical and technological developments, natural phenomena, U.S. weather, natural disasters, and accidents.*	*Includes the arts, religion, scholarship, communications media, sports, entertainment, fashions, fads and social life.*

	World Affairs	Europe	Africa & the Middle East	The Americas	Asia & the Pacific
April 7		The Yugoslav Parliament approves a new constitution making Marshal Tito president for life.	The Israeli Parliament defeats an opposition motion calling for a full debate on the presence of West German scientists in the UAR. The motion comes amidst accusations that the Ben-Gurion government has been weak in pressing Israel's protests to the Bonn government.		
April 8				Parliamentary elections in Canada give Lester Pearson's Liberal Party a 128-96 plurality over P.M. John Diefenbaker's Conservative Party. Liberals, however, remain five seats short of a working majority.	In a message to neutralist Premier Souvanna Phouma, Britain and the USSR, co-chairmen of the Geneva conference, appeal for an immediate restoration of a cease-fire between neutralist and Pathet Lao factions in Laos.
April 9		Pres. Kennedy proclaims Sir Winston Churchill, 88, an honorary citizen of the U.S. Authorization for the unprecedented honor passed Congress on April 2. . . . Exiled ex-French Premier Georges Bidault, head of the outlawed National Council of Resistance, arrives in Rio de Janeiro, Brazil where he has been granted a temporary visa.		José Miro Cardona resigns as head of the anti-Castro Cuban Revolutionary Movement in Miami after reportedly failing to win a U.S. government promise of support for a future Cuban invasion.	
April 10				Guatemala's new ruling junta promulgates an interim national constitution providing for heavy penalties against pro-communist political activities.	
April 11			The heads of the UAR, Syrian and Iraqi governments announce agreement on the merger of their three nations into a federal United Arab Republic. The announcement follows four days of constitutional talks in Cairo. . . . Britain discloses that it has denied a formal Southern Rhodesian request for independence (submitted April 1).		U.N. Secy. Gen. U Thant suggests that the Geneva conference on Laos reconvene to discuss the renewed Laotian fighting. . . . Saigon sources report that an additional 100 troops from the U.S. 25th Infantry Division have been sent to Vietnam. The reinforcements bring the number of U.S. personnel in South Vietnam to almost 12,000.
April 12		The Soviet press carries letters demanding that poet Yevgeny Yevtushenko be expelled from the National Union of Writers. . . . British police seize copies of a pamphlet purporting to reveal the government's nuclear war emergency plans as they were being distributed to demonstrators preparing for a 50-mile peace march from Aldermaston to London. . . . U.S. Secy. of State Rusk and Soviet Amb.-to-U.S. Dobrynin meet in Washington for their 25th informal conference on Berlin problems.			The U.S. State Dept. publicly expresses its opposition to a reconvening of the Geneva conference on Laos, suggesting instead that the International Control Commission be strengthened to enforce existing accords.
April 13			Gen. Joseph Mobutu says the Congo will go ahead with a plan to have European advisers help in the retraining of its army despite criticism from African and Asian nations.		Nepal King Mahendra Bir Bikra Shah Diva relaxes the state of emergency in effect since he took personal control of the government in December 1960.
April 14					Premier Souvanna Phouma announces achievement of an interim cease-fire between contending neutralist troops and Pathet Lao forces in northeast Laos.

A	B	C	D	E
Includes developments that affect more than one world region, international organizations and important meetings of major world leaders.	Includes all domestic and regional developments in Europe, including the Soviet Union, Turkey, Cyprus and Malta.	Includes all domestic and regional developments in Africa and the Middle East, including Iraq and Iran and excluding Cyprus, Turkey and Afghanistan.	Includes all domestic and regional developments in Latin America, the Caribbean and Canada.	Includes all domestic and regional developments in Asia and Pacific nations, extending from Afghanistan through all the Pacific Islands, except Hawaii.

U.S. Politics & Social Issues	U.S. Foreign Policy & Defense	U.S. Economy & Environment	Science, Technology & Nature	Culture, Leisure & Life Style	
				Jack Nicklaus, 23, wins the Masters golf championship at Augusta, Ga. He is the youngest ever to win the tourney.	April 7
A National Draft Goldwater for President Committee is organized in Texas.			A program of coordinated Western European space exploration is proposed in Paris by the 125 companies and scientific organizations forming the nine-nation Eurospace group.	Motion Picture Academy Award winners for achievements in 1962 include: best film, *Lawrence of Arabia* ; best actress, Anne Bancroft (*The Miracle Worker*); best actor, Gregory Peck (*To Kill a Mockingbird*); best supporting actress, Patty Duke (*The Miracle Worker*).	April 8
		The Wheeling Steel Corp., the 11th largest U.S. producer, announces a $5- to $10-a-ton price increase. . . . An administration bill to establish a National Wilderness Preservation System passes the Senate and is sent to the House. A similar bill died in the House in 1961.			April 9
		The House passes a $1.44 billion supplemental appropriations bill for fiscal 1963 after overcoming Republican attemtps to cut $450 million designated for public works projects.		A plea for world peace, political unity and disarmament is issued by Pope John XXIII in his eighth encyclical letter, *Pacem in Terris* . The encyclical is the first to be addressed not only to Roman Catholics but to "all men of good will."	April 10
	The Navy announces that the 129-man, atomic-powered *U.S.S. Thresher*, the U.S.'s deepest-diving submarine, has been lost after making a deep dive in the North Atlantic on April 10. It is the worst submarine disaster in U.S. history. . . . Kennedy administration spokesmen, responding to recent congressional criticism, warn that efforts to curb Western technical assistance to Arab nations might only encourage an increased Soviet presence in the Middle East.	Pres. Kennedy, commenting on an expected round of steel price increases, says the administration strongly opposes an across-the-board rise, but appreciates the possible need for price adjustments on selected steel products.		Pope John XXIII's peace encyclical draws praise from religious and political leaders throughout the world.	April 11
Martin Luther King is among more than 60 persons arrested during an anti-segregation march in Birmingham, Ala.	Navy Secy. Fred Korth announces that construction of 22 *Thresher* -type nuclear submarines will continue, although the Navy intends a new study of the vessel's structural design, in view of the recent disaster.		Explorer XVII, a scientific satellite equipped to study the earth's rarified atmosphere at satellite altitudes, is successfully launched from Cape Canaveral.		April 12
	In a Washington TV interview, State Secy. Dean Rusk asserts that "an important corner has been turned" in the South Vietnamese war. Rusk adds, however, that the U.S. will face some very "harsh decisions" should the Viet Cong step up their guerrilla campaign.				April 13
		The SEC estimates that the net working capital of U.S. corporations rose by $7.1 billion in 1962 to a record $144.5 billion.		Chuang Tse-tung of Communist China wins his second straight world table tennis championship in Prague, Czechoslovakia.	April 14
F	**G**	**H**	**I**	**J**	
Includes elections, federal-state relations, civil rights and liberties, crime, the judiciary, education, health care, poverty, urban affairs and population.	*Includes formation and debate of U.S. foreign and defense policies, veterans' affairs and defense spending. (Relations with specific foreign countries are usually found under the region concerned.)*	*Includes business, labor, agriculture, taxation, transportation, consumer affairs, monetary and fiscal policy, natural resources, and pollution.*	*Includes worldwide scientific, medical and technological developments, natural phenomena, U.S. weather, natural disasters, and accidents.*	*Includes the arts, religion, scholarship, communications media, sports, entertainment, fashions, fads and social life.*	

	World Affairs	Europe	Africa & the Middle East	The Americas	Asia & the Pacific
April 15		Over 14,000 anti-nuclear weapons marchers arrive in London where they are joined by 56,000 other protesters for a mass peace rally in Hyde Park.	The Soviet C.P. in a *Pravda* editorial urges African nations to oppose further French nuclear tests in the Sahara and to turn Africa into an "atom-free zone."		Laotian sources report that despite yesterday's cease-fire announcement sporadic fighting continues between neutralists and Pathet Lao troops.
April 16				The Haitian government announces a crackdown against an alleged plot to overthrow the regime of Pres. Francois Duvalier. Officials imply that certain Dominican Republican citizens are connected with the conspiracy.	Indian P.M. Nehru rejects an unofficial U.S.-sponsored proposal to partition the Vale of Kashmir as a first step toward resolving the India-Pakistan dispute over Kashmir.
April 17	The 17-nation disarmament committee resumes meetings in Geneva after a week-long Easter recess.		Congolese P.M. Cyrille Adoula announces formation of a new "National Reconciliation" cabinet. The new cabinet includes a wide spectrum of political groups, ranging from former Lumumba supporters to former Katanganese secessionists. . . . Algerian Premier Ahmed Ben Bella assumes exclusive leadership of the ruling National Front after forcing Mohammed Khider to resign as leader of the Front's Political Bureau. According to observers, Khider favored a more doctrinaire approach to "Algerian Socialism" than did Ben Bella.	U.S. recognizes the Guatemalan military regime of Enrique Peralta Azurdia, which seized power March 30. . . . Canadian P.M. John Diefenbaker resigns after final election returns gave the Liberals a virtual working majority.	South Vietnamese Pres. Diem promises Vietcong guerrillas clemency and material benefits if they abandon their war against his regime. Over 2,700 persons reportedly defected from Communist ranks as a result of a similar clemency offer in February.
April 18				Cuban exile leader José Miro Cardona releases a detailed statement accusing Pres. Kennedy of breaking repeated promises to help organize and launch a second military invasion of Cuba.	Pathet Lao troops capture the neutralist stronghold of Phongsavan in their continuing advance against neutralist forces in the Plaine des Jarres.
April 19				Pres. Kennedy flatly denies that he or anyone in his administration ever promised another invasion of Cuba.	
April 20		Julian Garcia Grimau, leader of the Spanish Communist underground, is executed by firing squad in Madrid for his alleged "crimes against humanity" during the Spanish Civil War (1936-1939).	Samir el-Rifai resigns as prime minister of Jordan after a majority in the House of Deputies expressed opposition to his policies on Arab unity.	Fidel Castro claims that the U.S. has given up its plans for a second invasion of Cuba and is instead concentrating on a plot to assassinate Cuba's leaders. . . . British Guiana's powerful Trade Union Council launches a nationwide general strike to protest the labor policies of Prime Minister Cheddi Jagan's ruling People's Progressive Party. . . . A night watchman at a Montreal armory is killed in a terrorist bomb explosion attributed to members of the separatist Quebec Liberation Front.	
	A	**B**	**C**	**D**	**E**
	Includes developments that affect more than one world region, international organizations and important meetings of major world leaders.	Includes all domestic and regional developments in Europe, including the Soviet Union, Turkey, Cyprus and Malta.	Includes all domestic and regional developments in Africa and the Middle East, including Iraq and Iran and excluding Cyprus, Turkey and Afghanistan.	Includes all domestic and regional developments in Latin America, the Caribbean and Canada.	Includes all domestic and regional developments in Asia and Pacific nations, extending from Afghanistan through all the Pacific Islands, except Hawaii.

U.S. Politics & Social Issues	U.S. Foreign Policy & Defense	U.S. Economy & Environment	Science, Technology & Nature	Culture, Leisure & Life Style	
The Urban League of Greater New York charges that there has been almost no progress in its four-year campaign to gain greater Negro job representation in the city's advertising agencies. . . . Texas financier Billie Sol Estes is sentenced to 15 years in prison following his March 28 mail fraud conviction by a federal jury in El Paso, Tex. . . . White House announces that Mrs. John Kennedy is expecting her third child in August.			Researchers at UCLA and Syracuse University publish in *Physical Review Letters* the results of experiments which confirm the existence of the short-lived Phi-meson atomic particle. Theoretical predictions of the particle's existence had been advanced in 1962 by Jun John Sakurai of the Univ. of Chicago. . . . Spokesmen for the kidney research center of Swedish Hospital in Seattle report that artificial kidney machines have been used with great success in the treatment of critical kidney disorders.		April 15
The Civil Rights Commission urges Pres. Kennedy to explore the possibility of cutting off federal funds to Mississippi until the state demonstrates compliance with the federal Constitution and laws. . . . Sen. Clifford Case (R, N.J.) says he will support Gov. Nelson Rockefeller for the GOP presidential nomination.		U.S. Steel Corp. joins seven other major U.S. producers in announcing price increases on selected steel products.	Private U.S.-Soviet talks on a proposed U.N. declaration governing space exploration are broken-off in New York. The negotiations are reportedly deadlocked over U.S. opposition to Soviet proposals for a ban against military reconnaissance. . . . Researchers at the American Home Products' Wyeth Laboratories report the discovery of a new, highly effective pain-killing drug, known as WY-535. The drug is reportedly related to Demerol, but without its addictive characteristics.	An Alabama legislative committee reports that it has found no evidence to support a *Saturday Evening Post* charge that the September 22, 1962 Alabama-Georgia football game had been rigged.	April 16
Southern Congressmen denounce yesterday's Civil Rights Commission proposal for a federal fund cut-off to Mississippi. . . . The renting of an apartment to a Negro family in an all-white section of Chicago's South Side provokes an angry demonstration by over 1,000 whites.	The National Academy of Sciences publishes a report urging U.S. support for international birth control studies. The report cites population growth as a major problem in the search for world peace.			NFL Commissioner Pete Rozelle indefinitely suspends Green Bay Packer halfback Paul Hornung and Detroit Lion tackle Alex Karras for allegedly betting on NFL games.	April 17
	Secy. of State Dean Rusk defends the administration's Cuban policy in a speech to the American Society of Newspaper Editors. Rusk says the U.S. will press for further Soviet troop withdrawals and will continue its effort to isolate Cuba economically and politically from the rest of the Western Hemisphere.			The Toronto Maple Leafs defeat the Detroit Red Wings, four games to one, to win their second straight National Hockey League Stanley Cup championship. . . . The Women's National Press Club announces the establishment of an annual Eleanor Roosevelt Memorial Award to honor humanitarian contributions by American women.	April 18
Pres. Kennedy says he is opposed to a general fund cut-off "as a disciplinary measure" against states resisting enforcement of civil rights.		Pres. Kennedy defends his administration's deficit budget in a speech to the American Society of Newspaper Editors in Washington. . . . The ICC reports that net income of U.S. railroads rose from $538 million in 1961 to $726 million in 1962. . . . Pres. Kennedy praises U.S. steel companies for showing "some restraint" in the recent round of selective price increases.	At least 110 persons are reported killed in the wake of 2 cyclones which struck eastern India.		April 19
	Richard Nixon, speaking to the American Society of Newspaper Editors, criticizes the Kennedy administration for failing to give open support to all opponents of communist regimes, including Cuban exiles.				April 20

F	G	H	I	J
Includes elections, federal-state relations, civil rights and liberties, crime, the judiciary, education, health care, poverty, urban affairs and population.	*Includes formation and debate of U.S. foreign and defense policies, veterans' affairs and defense spending. (Relations with specific foreign countries are usually found under the region concerned.)*	*Includes business, labor, agriculture, taxation, transportation, consumer affairs, monetary and fiscal policy, natural resources, and pollution.*	*Includes worldwide scientific, medical and technological developments, natural phenomena, U.S. weather, natural disasters, and accidents.*	*Includes the arts, religion, scholarship, communications media, sports, entertainment, fashions, fads and social life.*

	World Affairs	Europe	Africa & the Middle East	The Americas	Asia & the Pacific
April 21					Premier Souvanna Phouma announces that he has arranged the second cease-fire in eight days between neutralist and Pathet Lao forces in northeast Laos. Pathet Lao troops reportedly gained almost complete control of Plaine des Jarres in recent fighting.
April 22				Liberal Party leader Lester Pearson is sworn-in as prime minister of Canada. . . . Twenty-seven Americans imprisoned in Cuba for the past two-to-three-a-half years are released following negotiations in Havana between N.Y. attorney James Donovan and Premier Castro.	The U.S. Seventh fleet is reported to have begun maneuvers in the Gulf of Siam to emphasize American concern over recent Laotian fighting.
April 23		West German Economy Min. Ludwig Erhard is nominated by the ruling Christian Democratic Union-Christian Social Union to succeed Konrad Adenauer as chancellor when he retires in the fall.	Itzhak Ben-Zvi, 78, president of Israel since 1952, dies of stomach cancer in Jerusalem. . . . Jordanian police clash with pro-Nasser, anti-monarchist demonstrators demanding Jordan's entry into the proposed United Arab Republic.	By a vote of 13 to 1 (six abstentions), the OAS approves a U.S. proposal empowering the OAS Council to investigate possible Cuban subversion in the Western Hemisphere, with or without permission of the member governments.	USSR refuses to sign a British-proposed joint appeal for observance of the 1962 Geneva accords on Laos because of Britain's refusal to include a condemnation of alleged U.S. interference.
April 24	Soviet Premier Khrushchev rejects Western proposals to consider nuclear test-ban issues other than the number-of-inspections question which has stalled disarmament discussions. Pres. Kennedy says the Soviet position dims hopes for an agreement.	In a Moscow speech to Communist Party members, Premier Khrushchev hints that his age (69) may soon oblige him to relinquish some of his duties as Soviet premier and CP first secretary.	Senegalese allegations of Portuguese air raids on its territory from neighboring Portuguese Guinea are supported in a unanimous U.N. Security Council resolution deploring the attacks. Portugal has denied the charges.		Pres. Kennedy announces that he is sending State Undersecy. W. Averell Harriman to Moscow for talks with Soviet leaders on the Laos situation.
April 25		A special British tribunal investigating military security issues arising from the 1962 espionage conviction of Admiralty clerk William Vassal issues its final report. The report generally exonerates the security policies of the Conservative government, but urges greater caution in the hiring of sensitive personnel.			
April 26		In a speech published in the Soviet press, Premier Khrushchev says that "healthy criticism" will help hitherto non-conforming Russian writers to reaffirm true communist goals. . . . Dr. Giuseppe Martelli, an Italian nuclear physicist working in England, is arrested at London airport on charges of spying for the USSR.		Haitian police break into the Dominican Republic embassy in Port-au-Prince and seize 22 Haitian political refugees who had been granted asylum there. . . . A Miami-based Cuban exile group announces that it yesterday carried out an air attack on an oil refinery near Havana. Cuban officials confirm the attack and blame the U.S. for permitting it.	The USSR joins the U.S. in a public reaffirmation of support for the 1962 Geneva agreements for a neutral and independent Laos. The statement follows Moscow talks between U.S. State Undersecy. W. Averell Harriman and Soviet Premier Khrushchev. . . . Saigon sources report a growing controversy between U.S. and South Vietnamese officials arising from Pres. Diem's opposition to a U.S. plan to increase the number of military advisers in Vietnam.
April 27			Anti-Hussein Jordanian students, proclaiming a commitment to Arab unity, briefly occupy the Jordan embassy in Baghdad, Iraq.	Premier Castro leaves Havana for a month-long state visit to the USSR.	Forty-one South Vietnamese soldiers and a U.S. Army sergeant are killed in a Vietcong attack northeast of Kontun, bringing to 80 the number of Americans killed in South Vietnam. . . . Laotian Deputy Premier Souphanouvong, leader of the Pathet Lao, accuses the U.S. of having directly aided neutralist forces during recent clashes with the Pathet Lao.
	A	B	C	D	E
	Includes developments that affect more than one world region, international organizations and important meetings of major world leaders.	Includes all domestic and regional developments in Europe, including the Soviet Union, Turkey, Cyprus and Malta.	Includes all domestic and regional developments in Africa and the Middle East, including Iraq and Iran and excluding Cyprus, Turkey and Afghanistan.	Includes all domestic and regional developments in Latin America, the Caribbean and Canada.	Includes all domestic and regional developments in Asia and Pacific nations, extending from Afghanistan through all the Pacific Islands, except Hawaii.

U.S. Politics & Social Issues	U.S. Foreign Policy & Defense	U.S. Economy & Environment	Science, Technology & Nature	Culture, Leisure & Life Style	
			Nuclear scientist Bruno Pontecorvo, a Britisher who defected to the USSR in 1950, is named winner of a 1963 Lenin Prize for his contributions to atomic research.		April 21
Supreme Court upholds the constitutionality of a Colorado law prohibiting racial discrimination in hiring by interstate carriers. The case involves Continental Air Lines' alleged refusal to hire a qualified Negro pilot.	Pres. Kennedy meets with the National Security Council to discuss the current military situation in Laos.	A special U.S. government committee headed by Walter Heller recommends to Pres. Kennedy that all U.S. commercial banks be required to have reserve funds on deposit with the Federal Reserve System.	Donald Clayton of California Institute of Technology reports to the American Physical Society in Washington on a new method of radioactive dating to determine a chemical element's age. According to the method, the earth's gold and other heavy elements were formed 10-15 billion years ago, six-10 billion years before the evolution of the solar system.		April 22
William Moore, a white who embarked April 22 on a personal anti-segregation protest march across the South, is found shot to death on a road near Attalla, Ala. . . . Joseph Mitchell, controversial city manager of Newburgh, N.Y., is acquitted of bribery charges by a State Supreme Court jury in N.Y.C.	Clark Clifford is named chairman of Pres. Kennedy's Foreign Intelligence Advisory Board, succeeding James Killian Jr.	Delegates to the annual convention of the American Newspaper Publishers Association agree to meet with Labor Secy. Willard Wirtz to explore "new approaches" to the industry's recent labor problems.	The National Academy of Sciences formally proposes the creation of a coequal U.S. National Academy of Engineering.		April 23
Alabama Gov. George Wallace offers a $1,000 reward for the conviction of the killer of white integrationist William Moore. . . . An investigating committee of the Mississippi legislature charges that federal marshals were guilty of brutality during the University of Mississippi segregation crisis in 1962. The Justice Dept. denounces the accusation.	Pres. Kennedy tells reporters that Republican critics of his Cuban policy consistently avoid the key question of whether the U.S. "should go to war. . . to remove Castro.". . . Pres. Kennedy tells reporters that he is not opposed to U.S. government support for birth control research programs, saying that they may help the world make an informed judgement on the problem.	The President's Committee on Youth Employment submits a four-point program to combat joblessness among persons aged 16-21. . . . The House passes and sends to the Senate a key administration bill (HR12) to authorize a three-year, $206 million program of aid to medical schools. . . . A U.S. Public Health Service study indicates that about 43 billion Americans use municipally-fluoridated water.	Pravda reports that Soviet scientists have produced a stable plasma at a temperature of 40 million degrees C. Commentators describe the achievement as a major step toward harnessing the hydrogen bomb for industrial uses.	The Boston Celtics win their fifth straight National Basketball Association championship by defeating the Los Angeles Lakers, four games to two.	April 24
The President's Committee on Equal Opportunity in Housing recommends that government facilities not be built in communities practicing housing discrimination.	Rep. Bob Wilson (R, Calif.) attacks the administration's Cuban policy and calls for U.S. recognition of a Cuban exile government. . . . Gov. Nelson Rockefeller, speaking to the American Newspaper Publishers convention in New York, says he favors formation of a "combined European nuclear force related to the American nuclear force on a basis of genuine partnership."	A group of business leaders meets with Pres. Kennedy to express their support for a rapid $10 billion tax cut.	Floods kill 107 persons in the western Afghanistan city of Herat.	Edward Albee's Who's Afraid of Virginia Woolf is honored as the best play of the 1962-1963 New York theater season at the 17th annual Antoinette Perry (Tony) Awards.	April 25
Martin Luther King is among 11 Negro leaders convicted in Birmingham, Ala. for violating a state injunction barring demonstrations. . . . Civil rights leaders attending a Washington conference on housing criticize Pres. Kennedy for not implementing his anti-housing bias edict. . . . Atty. Gen. Robert Kennedy completes a three-day "courtesy" tour through the South. The trip, which included a meeting April 25 with Alabama Gov. George Wallace, was marked by several pro-segregationist demonstrations.		The Senate Antitrust and Monopoly Subcommittee concludes six weeks of hearings on a bill to strengthen curbs on the deceptive labeling and packaging of consumer items.		Delegates to the U.S. Conference of the World Council of Churches emphasize interfaith unity during a three-day meeting in Buck Hill Falls, Pa. Roman Catholic priests attend the conference for the first time.	April 26
Rep. Adam Clayton Powell (D,N.Y.) tells reporters that he will resume his practice of introducing anti-discrimination amendments to administration legislation. In 1961 Powell had promised to dispense with the amendments as long as the administration pursued a vigorous civil rights policy.				Bob Hayes of Florida A&M, competing in a Walnut, Calif. meet, runs the 100-meters in 9.9 seconds, fastest time ever recorded. The time, however, will not be recognized as a world record because of an 11-mph trailing wind. . . . Al Oerter's discus throw of 205 ft. 5 1/2 in. and Arizona State University's one-mile relay time of 3 minutes 4.5 seconds established new world records at the same meet.	April 27
F	G	H	I	J	
Includes elections, federal-state relations, civil rights and liberties, crime, the judiciary, education, health care, poverty, urban affairs and population.	Includes formation and debate of U.S. foreign and defense policies, veterans' affairs and defense spending. (Relations with specific foreign countries are usually found under the region concerned.)	Includes business, labor, agriculture, taxation, transportation, consumer affairs, monetary and fiscal policy, natural resources, and pollution.	Includes worldwide scientific, medical and technological developments, natural phenomena, U.S. weather, natural disasters, and accidents.	Includes the arts, religion, scholarship, communications media, sports, entertainment, fashions, fads and social life.	

	World Affairs	Europe	Africa & the Middle East	The Americas	Asia & the Pacific
April 28			Israeli Prime Minister David Ben-Gurion charges that the new federation of Egypt, Syria, and Iraq has the destruction of Israel as one of its principal aims.	Cuban Premier Castro, arriving in the USSR for a month-long state tour, tells a welcoming crowd in Moscow that "Soviet arms and economic aid had prevented the destruction of the Socialist revolution in Cuba."	
April 29	Semyon Tsarapkin, chief Soviet delegate to the Geneva disarmament talks, says that efforts to reach a test-ban agreement have become "a waste of time."	Italy's ruling Christian Democratic Party loses 13 seats in parliamentary elections, but retains its position as the single largest party. Communists, Liberals, and Leftwing Socialists make moderate gains at the expense of conservative parties.	Jordan declares a state of emergency along its borders in an apparent move to prevent anti-Hussein infiltrators from entering the country.	Haitian police surrender control of the Dominican embassy and promise to release 22 political refugees seized there on April 26. The action follows a Dominican threat of military action to force Haitian observance of its diplomatic rights and sovereignty.	U.S. Secy. of State Dean Rusk arrives in Karachi, Pakistan for discussions with foreign ministers attending the annual conference of the Central Treaty Organization (CENTO).
April 30			U.N. Secy. Gen. U Thant announces that the UAR and Saudi Arabia have tentatively accepted a U.N. plan for the withdrawal of their forces from Yemen. Yemen has also endorsed the proposal.	The ending of U.S. government financial aid to the Miami-based anti-Castro Cuban Revolutionary Council is disclosed in Miami. The council had reportedly received more than $100,000 a month in U.S. aid.	Neutralist and Pathet Lao representatives at cease-fire talks agree to the formation of a new civil committee to work out a permanent Laotian truce. . . . Pakistani Foreign Min. Zulfikar Ali Bhutto, addressing the CENTO conference, voices his government's concern over the U.S.'s apparent indifference to the needs of Pakistan when measured against the extent of American aid to India.
May 1	French news sources report that the government is planning to build a nuclear test center in the Tahitian islands.	Sir Winston Churchill, 88, announces that due to his health he will not seek re-election to his Commons seat at the next general election--to be held before October 1964. Churchill has sat in the House for all but three of the last 63 years.	Mali Pres. Modibo Keita is among the recipients of the USSR's 1963 Lenin Peace Prize.		Laotian sources report that the Polish member of the International Control Commission has refused to accompany his Canadian and Indian counterparts on an inspection of positions in the Plaine des Jarres where neutralists have claimed unprovoked Pathet Lao attacks. . . . U.N. officials formally transfer to Indonesia the administration of the former Netherlands New Guinea, now called West Irian.
May 2			France and Algeria agree on a revision of the 1962 Evian peace accords stipulating the date of final French troop withdrawals and laying ground rules for the protection of French property interests in Algeria. . . . A South African anti-sabotage bill, aimed at greatly increasing the government's power to suppress African nationalist groups, becomes law with the signature of Pres. Charles Swart.	A special OAS fact-finding commission departs Port-au-Prince after failing to secure the promised release of 22 Haitian refugees whose April 26 seizure in the Dominican embassy precipitated the current Haitian-Dominican crisis.	
May 3			Pro-Nasserite ministers resign from Syria's Baathist Party-dominated government amidst a growing dispute over which faction will represent Syria in the proposed federation with Iraq and Egypt. A similar crisis between Nasserite and Baathist factions is reported in Iraq. . . . Congo sources report that special troops under the command of Gen. Joseph Mobutu have put down a mutiny by 3,000 Leopoldville policemen.	Dominican Republic Pres. Juan Bosch reiterates a threat to take military action against Haiti unless the Duvalier regime grants safe conduct to 22 refugees arrested in the Dominican embassy.	Two International Control Commission helicopters are hit by machine gun fire near Phongsavan in the Plaine des Jarres. Four persons are injured.
May 4		Dean Rusk, the first U.S. Secy. of State to visit Yugoslavia since 1955, arrives in Belgrade. Rusk reportedly will try to reassure Pres. Tito of the Kennedy administration's opposition to congressional efforts to end Yugoslavia's most-favored-nation trade status.	Cairo reports an indefinite postponement of military unity talks among the UAR, Syria and Iraq. The talks were to have begun May 12.		Laotian Premier Souvanna Phouma blames Pathet Lao troops for yesterday's attack on two International Control Commission helicopters in the Plaine des Jarres. . . . Thai provincial officials charge that pro-communists have increased their infiltration of Thailand from a new Pathet Lao base in Laos.
May 5			Nicholas Grunitzky, running unopposed, is reconfirmed as president of Togo in nationwide balloting.		
	A	**B**	**C**	**D**	**E**
	Includes developments that affect more than one world region, international organizations and important meetings of major world leaders.	*Includes all domestic and regional developments in Europe, including the Soviet Union, Turkey, Cyprus and Malta.*	*Includes all domestic and regional developments in Africa and the Middle East, including Iraq and Iran and excluding Cyprus, Turkey and Afghanistan.*	*Includes all domestic and regional developments in Latin America, the Caribbean and Canada.*	*Includes all domestic and regional developments in Asia and Pacific nations, extending from Afghanistan through all the Pacific Islands, except Hawaii.*

U.S. Politics & Social Issues	U.S. Foreign Policy & Defense	U.S. Economy & Environment	Science, Technology & Nature	Culture, Leisure & Life Style	
					April 28
Supreme Court unanimously rules that racial segregation in a courtroom is unconstitutional. . . . Floyd Simpson, a white grocery store operator in Collbran, Ala., is formally charged with the April 24 murder of integrationist marcher William Moore.	Adm. Robert Dennison is awarded a Distinguished Service Medal by Pres. Kennedy for his command of the mobilization of U.S. naval forces during the 1962 Cuban crisis.	SEC Chmn. William Cary asks for congressional legislation to increase the SEC's regulatory power over independent securities dealers.			April 29
Birmingham, Ala. officials turn down requests from Negro leaders for permits to stage peaceful protests against segregation. Negro spokesmen say they will defy the ban. . . . Pres. Kennedy sends Congress draft bills to require full disclosure of political campaign financing and to encourage political contributions by giving tax benefits to contributors.	In-a Senate floor attack on the Kennedy administration's Middle East policy, Sen. Jacob Javits (R,N.Y.) calls for a cut-back in U.S. aid to Egypt and a general realignment of American policy to assure Israel's security.	New Hampshire Gov. John King signs a bill legalizing a state sweepstakes lottery, the proceeds of which are to go to a state education fund. It is the first legal state lottery in the U.S. since 1894.		John Pennel sets a world pole vault record of 16 ft 6 3/4 in. at an outdoor meet in Monroe, La.	April 30
		A $1.49 billion supplemental appropriation bill (HR5517) is passed by the Senate and sent to joint conference. The measure includes $459 billion requested by Pres. Kennedy for accelerated public works.	Indian officials report that a cholera epidemic has killed more than 700 people in Calcutta since January 1.	A U.S. climbing expedition, headed by Norman Dyhrenfurth of Santa Monica, Calif., completes the first successful American-directed ascent of Mt. Everest. . . . Former Stamford, Conn. Mayor J. Walter Kennedy is elected president of the National Basketball Association.	May 1
Richard Nixon discloses that he is moving from California to N.Y.C. to join a private law firm. . . . In a Senate speech GOP whip Thomas Kuchel (Calif.) angrily assails the John Birch Society and other right-wing groups, charging that they "defile the honorable philosophy of conservatism."				Van Wyck Brooks, 77, American historian, biographer and literary critic, dies in Bridgeport, Conn.	May 2
Birmingham, Ala. police use fire hoses and police dogs to disperse groups of Negro youths participating in a growing campaign against racial discrimination in that city. More than 250 arrests are reported. . . . Alabama police arrest on breach-of-peace charges a group of integrationists as they attempt to complete the slain William Moore's "Freedom Walk" to Jackson, Miss.					May 3
N.Y. Gov. Nelson Rockefeller marries Mrs. Margaretta (Happy) Murphy, a recent divorcee.				John W. Galbreath's Chateaugay, Braulio Baeza up, wins the 89th running of the Kentucky Derby. Chateaugay was a 15-to-1 shot.	May 4
				Jack Nicklaus wins the $60,000 Tournament of Champions in Las Vegas.	May 5

F	G	H	I	J
Includes elections, federal-state relations, civil rights and liberties, crime, the judiciary, education, health care, poverty, urban affairs and population.	Includes formation and debate of U.S. foreign and defense policies, veterans' affairs and defense spending. (Relations with specific foreign countries are usually found under the region concerned.)	Includes business, labor, agriculture, taxation, transportation, consumer affairs, monetary and fiscal policy, natural resources, and pollution.	Includes worldwide scientific, medical and technological developments, natural phenomena, U.S. weather, natural disasters, and accidents.	Includes the arts, religion, scholarship, communications media, sports, entertainment, fashions, fads and social life.

	World Affairs	Europe	Africa & the Middle East	The Americas	Asia & the Pacific
May 6			The Soviet CP in a *Pravda* editorial expresses support for the efforts of Kurdish tribesmen to establish an autonomous state in Iraq. Observers say the policy reflects the USSR's displeasure over the anti-Soviet actions of the new Iraqi regime.	Dominican Pres. Juan Bosch informs the OAS that his government will defer any military action at least until the OAS completes its investigation of the Haitian-Dominican dispute.	
May 7	An agreement providing for the continuation of Soviet-Chinese cultural exchange programs is signed in Peking.				
May 8			At least 50 persons are killed in Aleppo as Syrian police attempt to disperse pro-Nasserite mobs demanding the ouster of the ruling Baathist Party. . . . Pres. Kennedy tells a Washington news conference that the U.S. remains firmly opposed to the use of force in the Middle East and will continue its policy of limiting arms shipments to that region.	U.N. Security Council convenes in emergency session to hear Haitian charges of Dominican interference in its internal affairs. The Dominican delegation asks that investigations into the dispute be left to the OAS. . . . The OAS Council votes to instruct its special investigating commission to return to Haiti and the Dominican Republic to perform "whatever service is necessary" to settle the dispute.	Pres. Kennedy tells his Washington news conference that he hopes Soviet Premier Khrushchev will use his utmost influence to restore peace in Laos.
May 9	U.S. and Soviet telecommunications experts hold their second meeting in Geneva to work out technical arrangements for the proposed "hot-line" link between Washington and Moscow. . . . Premier Chou En-lai discloses China's acceptance of a March 30 Soviet invitation to send a delegation to Moscow in midsummer to discuss the Sino-Soviet ideological dispute.	Laborites completely overwhelm Conservative candidates in local elections for Borough Council seats held throughout England and Wales.		The U.N. Security Council suspends hearings on the Haitian-Dominican dispute after agreeing to let the OAS continue to handle the matter.	South Vietnamese Pres. Diem discloses that after negotiations with the U.S. his government has agreed to drop demands for a reduction in the number and influence of U.S. military advisers serving on local and provincial levels.
May 10		British Labor Party leader Harold Wilson calls for the resignation of P.M. Macmillan's Conservative government in view of the results of yesterday's borough council elections.		ABC-TV broadcasts an April 24 interview with Cuban Premier Castro in which he praises the U.S. government for trying to curb anti-Castro exile raids.	Britain refuses to endorse a Soviet-drafted statement protesting the presence of Indian and Canadian members of the International Control Commission in the Plaine des Jarres.
May 11		Oleg Penkovsky, an ex-Soviet government official, and Greville Wynne, a British businessman, are convicted in Moscow on charges of spying for the West. Penkovsky is sentenced to death and Wynne is given an eight-year prison term.		Canada's intention to accept U.S. nuclear warheads for use by its forces serving with NATO and in NORAD is confirmed by P.M. Lester Pearson following a two-day meeting with Pres. Kennedy in Hyannisport, Mass. Acceptance of the weapons had been a major issue in Pearson's election victory over Conservative P.M. Diefenbaker.	
May 12				Argentine Pres. José Maria Guido's entire cabinet resigns in an intra-government dispute over to what extent Peronists ought to be allowed to participate in upcoming national elections. . . . Haitian exiles in San Juan, P.R. announce the formation of a Haitian government-in-exile.	

A	B	C	D	E
Includes developments that affect more than one world region, international organizations and important meetings of major world leaders.	Includes all domestic and regional developments in Europe, including the Soviet Union, Turkey, Cyprus and Malta.	Includes all domestic and regional developments in Africa and the Middle East, including Iraq and Iran and excluding Cyprus, Turkey and Afghanistan.	Includes all domestic and regional developments in Latin America, the Caribbean and Canada.	Includes all domestic and regional developments in Asia and Pacific nations, extending from Afghanistan through all the Pacific Islands, except Hawaii.

U.S. Politics & Social Issues	U.S. Foreign Policy & Defense	U.S. Economy & Environment	Science, Technology & Nature	Culture, Leisure & Life Style	
Increasing national attention is focused on Birmingham, Ala. where thousands of Negroes and white integrationists are continuing massive protests against segregation. Sens. John Sherman Cooper (R, Ky.) and Wayne Morse (D, Ore.) are among a growing number of prominent figures who have publicly denounced the conduct of Birmingham police during the demonstrations.	Pres. Kennedy names Adm. David McDonald to succeed Adm. George Anderson as chief of naval operations and extends Gen. Curtis LeMay's term as Air Force chief of staff.			Pulitzer Prizes for letters are awarded posthumously to William Faulkner for *The Reivers* and to late poet William Carlos Williams for *Pictures from Breughel* . . . . Pittsburgh Steeler quarterback Bobby Layne, 35, holder of several NFL passing records, announces his retirement from pro football.	May 6
Another day of civil rights demonstrations in Birmingham ends with a rock-throwing disturbance by about 3,000 Negroes in the downtown business district. Arrests in connection with the demonstrations that began May 2 now number 2,453.	Gen. William Draper Jr., former adviser to ex-Pres. Eisenhower, tells the Planned Parenthood Federation that the U.S. should support world efforts to control population, adding that underdeveloped nations will not be "off our backs" until the population problem is solved.		Telstar 2, an experimental communications satellite built and owned by American Telephone & Telegraph Co., successfully relays a trans-Atlantic TV signal after being launched earlier in the day by NASA.		May 7
Rev. Martin Luther King is released on bond from a Birmingham jail after being arrested earlier in the day for organizing a parade without a permit. King's arrest had threatened to upset a temporary truce agreement worked out in the morning between Negro and white leaders of the racially tense city. . . . The final report of a special Mississippi legislative committee charges the federal government with full responsibility for the 1962 desegregation rioting at the University of Mississippi.	A bill (HR5555) providing for military pay increases of 12-14% and authorizing combat pay to U.S. personnel in South Vietnam passes the House and is sent to the Senate.				May 8
	A U.S.-Australian agreement for the establishment of a U.S. Navy communications base in Western Australia is signed in Canberra.	A federal grand jury in Nashville, Tenn. indicts Teamsters Pres. James Hoffa on charges of conspiring to influence the jury during his 1962 trial on Taft-Hartley law violations. . . . In an appearance before the Committee for Economic Development, Pres. Kennedy cites irreducible expenditures for defense and space as the basic reason for the current high level of federal spending.			May 9
Birmingham, Ala. business and Negro leaders announce tentative agreement on a plan to gradually eliminate racial discrimination in the operation of the city's retail stores and restaurants. Martin Luther King calls the agreement the "most significant victory for justice . . . in the Deep South."			In a paper to the American Psychiatric Association meeting in St. Louis, Dr. Peter Lindstrom reports significant successes in treating severely disturbed mental patients by means of ultrasound applications to the brain.	Gene (Big Daddy) Lipscomb, 31, star defensive tackle for the Pittsburgh Steelers, is found dead in Baltimore of an apparent drug overdose. . . . For the sixth time in his career Gordie Howe of the Detroit Red Wings wins the Hart Trophy as the NHL's most valuable player.	May 10
A bomb rips through the Birmingham home of Rev. A.D. King, younger brother of Martin Luther King and himself a prominent leader in the current Birmingham anti-segregation drive. No one is injured. . . . The formation of a biracial committee to consider Negro grievances marks the climax of a three-day anti-segregation campaign in Nashville, Tenn.				Los Angeles Dodgers' Sandy Koufax pitches an 8-0 no-hit victory over the San Francisco Giants, the second no-hitter of his career. . . . Everton defeats Fulham to win the English Football League championship in London.	May 11
A three-day-old truce in racially troubled Birmingham, Ala. collapses as about 2,500 Negroes stage a violent and disorderly protest against last night's bombing of the Rev. A. D. King's home. Fifty persons are reported injured. . . . Pres. Kennedy, in a televised statement, announces the dispatching of federal troops to bases near Birmingham, Ala. for possible use in the event of renewed racial violence. Alabama Gov. Wallace deplores the action.			MIT's Lincoln Laboratory discloses that 400 million copper dipoles (needles) have been successfully released in space by a U.S. Air Force satellite launched May 9. The experiment, aimed at creating a wide orbital belt for the relay of radio signals, raised controversy when first proposed in 1961 because of fears that it would "pollute space and interfere with other space projects." . . . Betty Miller of Santa Monica, Calif. becomes the first woman to fly solo across the Pacific from east to west.		May 12

F	G	H	I	J
Includes elections, federal-state relations, civil rights and liberties, crime, the judiciary, education, health care, poverty, urban affairs and population.	Includes formation and debate of U.S. foreign and defense policies, veterans' affairs and defense spending. (Relations with specific foreign countries are usually found under the region concerned.)	Includes business, labor, agriculture, taxation, transportation, consumer affairs, monetary and fiscal policy, natural resources, and pollution.	Includes worldwide scientific, medical and technological developments, natural phenomena, U.S. weather, natural disasters, and accidents.	Includes the arts, religion, scholarship, communications media, sports, entertainment, fashions, fads and social life.

	World Affairs	Europe	Africa & the Middle East	The Americas	Asia & the Pacific
May 13	U.S. cancels three low-power nuclear tests scheduled for the Nevada test site later in May. The announcement follows reports that Pres. Kennedy has received a letter regarding the current test-ban talks from Soviet Premier Khrushchev.		Syrian Premier Salah el-Bitar undertakes a complete reorganization of his cabinet in an attempt to cope with the growing struggle between Baathists and Nasserites for government control. Iraqi Premier Ahmad Hassan al-Bakr likewise reorganizes his government in a move prompted by the resignation May 11 of five pro-Nasserite ministers. . . . Israeli Premier David Ben-Gurion criticizes the U.S. policy of limiting the Middle East arms race, saying that it does not take into account Soviet-bloc aid to Arab states.	An OAS fact-finding commission, returning to the Dominican Republic in a renewed effort to resolve the Haitian-Dominican crisis, reports a general easing of tensions following the withdrawal of Dominican forces from positions along the Haitian border.	
May 14				Haiti Pres. Francois Duvalier informs the OAS Council that he will permit the safe departure of some 40 political opponents who had been granted asylum in Port-au-Prince; Duvalier, however, says he will deny the passage of persons who conspired to assassinate him.	A fresh outbreak of fighting in Laos's Plaine des Jarres is reported by Pathet Lao spokesmen who charge that rightist and neutralist troops yesterday attacked a group of pro-Pathet Lao neutralist dissidents near Xiengkhouang.
May 15		Prague sources report that two prominent Stalinists have been ousted from the Czech CP. . . . The Roman Catholic People's Party remains the strongest party in the Netherlands' lower house of Parliament following general elections.		Duvalier tells newsmen in Port-au-Prince that he plans on May 22 to begin his second term as Haiti's president. The statement is intended to quash persistent rumors that Duvalier is preparing to step down and flee the country.	
May 16		Amintore Fanfani, leader of the Christian Democratic party, resigns as Premier of Italy. Fanfani has been blamed for his party's heavy losses in the April 28-29 general elections.			India and Pakistan break off their fifth and apparently final round of ministerial talks on disputed Kashmir. Both sides express a willingness to consider outside mediation should negotiations be resumed. . . . At least eight persons are reported dead following a week of rioting against Chinese residents of Indonesia.
May 17	In a Hanoi communique North Vietnamese Pres. Ho Chi Minh indicates his support for Communist China in its doctrinal dispute with the USSR.		Supporters of King Hassan II emerge triumphant in the wake of Morocco's first parliamentary elections since gaining independence in 1956.	Six bombs, believed to have been placed by the Quebec Liberation Front, explode in mailboxes in an English-speaking suburb of Montreal. . . . Argentine Pres. José Maria Guido signs a decree barring Peronist candidates from running for any national, state or local executive positions. Peronists will still be permitted to enter for legislative offices.	Indonesian Pres. Sukarno imposes restrictions on political meetings in a move reportedly aimed at preventing opposition groups from capitalizing on the recent outbreak of anti-Chinese riots. . . . Two U.S. Army captains are reported captured after their helicopter was downed by North Korean groundfire.
May 18					Malayan radio reports that British security forces killed two rebels in the most recent of a continuing series of skirmishes with dissidents in Britain's Borneo territories of Brunei, North Borneo and Sarawak. . . . Indonesia's appointed Provisional People's Congress elects Sukarno president for life.
May 19		French Pres. de Gaulle concludes a three-day state tour of Greece.			Nationalist China calls upon Indonesian Pres. Sukarno to halt anti-Chinese violence and to compensate the victims of recent attacks. Communist China earlier issued a statement blaming the riots on "U.S. imperialism."

A	B	C	D	E
Includes developments that affect more than one world region, international organizations and important meetings of major world leaders.	Includes all domestic and regional developments in Europe, including the Soviet Union, Turkey, Cyprus and Malta.	Includes all domestic and regional developments in Africa and the Middle East, including Iraq and Iran and excluding Cyprus, Turkey and Afghanistan.	Includes all domestic and regional developments in Latin America, the Caribbean and Canada.	Includes all domestic and regional developments in Asia and Pacific nations, extending from Afghanistan through all the Pacific Islands, except Hawaii.

U.S. Politics & Social Issues	U.S. Foreign Policy & Defense	U.S. Economy & Environment	Science, Technology & Nature	Culture, Leisure & Life Style	
		Supreme Court reverses an appeals court decision and rules that companies cannot grant extra seniority to employees who refuse to participate in a strike.			May 13
		White House announces the resignation of Newton Minow as FCC chairman. Minow will be succeeded by FCC member E. William Henry. . . . A report of the Presidential emergency board investigating the railroad work-rules dispute recommends the elimination of locomotive firemen's jobs except where safety considerations warrant their retention.	A radar failure forces a last-minute postponement of the U.S.'s seventh Project Mercury space flight.		May 14
		Pres. Kennedy releases a report of his Science Advisory Committee recommending "more judicious use of pesticides." The report stresses the need for research into possible health and environmental hazards of DDT and related pest control chemicals. . . . The House, over unified GOP opposition, passes a bill (HR6009) to increase the temporary national debt ceiling by $4 billion to a record $309 billion.	Air Force Maj. Leroy Gordon Cooper, riding in a Project Mercury capsule dubbed Faith 7, is launched into earth orbit to begin a projected 22-orbit mission.	Jacques Anquetil of France wins the 15-day Tour de Spain bicycle race.	May 15
New Jersey Commissioner of Education Frederick Raubinger orders the Orange, N.J. school board to submit a plan to end de facto segregation in its public schools.			Project Mercury astronaut Leroy Gordon Cooper is picked up in the Pacific recovery area after successfully completing 22 orbits of the earth. Cooper was forced to control manually the capsule's re-entry flight because of a malfunction in the automatic guidance system. NASA spokesmen say the mission proved the Mercury-type capsule's suitability for even longer missions.		May 16
Senate passes and sends to the House an administration bill requiring equal pay for equal work regardless of sex. . . . The President's Council on Aging reports that the situation of many elderly Americans is approaching that of "second-class citizens." The council cites "a basic plan of hospital insurance" as the primary need of older Americans.	U.S. embassy in Port-au-Prince announces the temporary suspension of U.S. Diplomatic relations with Haiti. The move reflects U.S. opposition to Duvalier's announced intention to remain in office beyond the expiration of his constitutional term.	Commerce Dept. reports that private housing starts rose to a record annual rate of 1,627,000 in April, easily topping the previous high set in November 1962.	Tass reports that Soviet scientists lost radio contact with the USSR's Mars I interplanetary probe on March 21 after it had traveled some 66 million miles from the time of its launch Nov. 1, 1962. According to Tass the distance set a new record for two-way radio communication.		May 17
Alabama Gov. George Wallace asks the U.S. Supreme Court to declare unconstitutional Pres. Kennedy's recent order dispatching federal troops to Alabama because of the Birmingham racial strife. . . . A three-judge U.S. court in New Orleans rules that a Louisiana law sanctioning segregated hotels is unconstitutional. . . . NAACP general counsel Robert Carter announces a major drive against De Facto school segregation throughout the North.				Rex Ellsworth's Candy Spots, with Willie Shoemaker up, edges out Derby-winner Chateaugay to win the 87th Preakness Stakes in Baltimore.	May 18
A third attempt by integrationists to complete the Freedom Walk to Mississippi begun by the slain William Moore ends with arrest of the 11 participants.	GOP National Committee Chmn. Rep. William Miller (R,N.Y.) challenges Pres. Kennedy to respond to "reports" that the USSR is building a large naval base in Cuba.				May 19
F	G	H	I	J	
Includes elections, federal-state relations, civil rights and liberties, crime, the judiciary, education, health care, poverty, urban affairs and population.	Includes formation and debate of U.S. foreign and defense policies, veterans' affairs and defense spending. (Relations with specific foreign countries are usually found under the region concerned.)	Includes business, labor, agriculture, taxation, transportation, consumer affairs, monetary and fiscal policy, natural resources, and pollution.	Includes worldwide scientific, medical and technological developments, natural phenomena, U.S. weather, natural disasters, and accidents.	Includes the arts, religion, scholarship, communications media, sports, entertainment, fashions, fads and social life.	

	World Affairs	Europe	Africa & the Middle East	The Americas	Asia & the Pacific
May 20			Loyal Turkish troops crush an attempt by a group of former officers at the War College in Ankara to overthrow the government of Premier Ismet Inonu. At least 10 persons are reported killed.	An agreement to provide the British colony of the Bahama Islands with internal self-rule by 1964 is signed in London.	
May 21			Schneor Zalman Shazar, 73, of the Mapai party is elected president of Israel, succeeding the late Itzhak Ben-Zvi.	Canada's Parliament upholds P.M. Pearson's decision to accept U.S. nuclear weapons by defeating a Conservative-sponsored no-confidence motion, 124-113.	The Laotian government reports an ongoing battle between neutralist and Pathet Lao troops just north of the Plaine des Jarres. . . . A published Indian note to Communist China charges that Chinese forces crossed into Indian territory April 27, May 4, and May 5.
May 22		Dissident Greek Parliament member Gregory Lambrakis is struck and killed by a motorcycle in Athens in an apparently deliberate attack. Leftist political leaders accuse the government of moral responsibility for the incident.	Syrian government reports thwarting an attempted coup by a group of pro-Nasser military officers.	Over 50,000 persons attend the inauguration of Francois Duvalier for a second term as president of Haiti.	
May 23					The International Control Commission for Laos urges Britain and the USSR to make a joint appeal for a halt in the renewed Plaine des Jarres fighting between neutralist and Pathet Lao forces.
May 24		NATO foreign ministers announce their approval of measures intended to lead to the creation of an inter-allied nuclear striking force. The announcement, which in effect endorsed the Anglo-American Nassau agreement, was drafted in vague language, reportedly at France's request.	About 400 U.N. troops disarm the personal guard of Katanga Pres. Tshombe in a pre-dawn raid at the presidential palace in Elizabethville.	Soviet Premier Khrushchev and visiting Cuban Premier Castro issue a joint communique in Moscow reaffirming the USSR's promise to defend Cuba's independence "with all the means at its disposal."	An Indian delegation, in Washington for consultations with Pres. Kennedy, discloses that the U.S. has promised to provide India long-term military aid to cope with any renewed military attack by Communist China.
May 25		Italian Pres. Antonio Segni appoints Christian Democrat Aldo Moro to form a new government.	A pro-Nasser plot aimed at overthrowing the Iraqi government is crushed, according to a Baghdad radio report.	The Ecuadoran Navy detains two U.S. tuna boats for allegedly fishing in Ecuadoran waters without a license.	USSR asks for a resumption of British-Soviet talks on drafting a joint Laotian peace appeal.
May 26		Swiss voters in a national referendum reject a proposal to require electorate ratification of any government decision to equip the Swiss army with nuclear weapons.	The Kenya African National Union, headed by Jomo Kenyatta, captures a majority of seats in Kenya's first parliamentary elections. The new parliament will be responsible for the colony's internal affairs under a recent agreement with Britain. . . . The Iraqi government announces that 11 of 26 persons arrested in yesterday's alleged coup attempt have been executed.		

A	B	C	D	E
Includes developments that affect more than one world region, international organizations and important meetings of major world leaders.	Includes all domestic and regional developments in Europe, including the Soviet Union, Turkey, Cyprus and Malta.	Includes all domestic and regional developments in Africa and the Middle East, including Iraq and Iran and excluding Cyprus, Turkey and Afghanistan.	Includes all domestic and regional developments in Latin America, the Caribbean and Canada.	Includes all domestic and regional developments in Asia and Pacific nations, extending from Afghanistan through all the Pacific Islands, except Hawaii.

U.S. Politics & Social Issues	U.S. Foreign Policy & Defense	U.S. Economy & Environment	Science, Technology & Nature	Culture, Leisure & Life Style	
In six separate cases, the Supreme Court rules that a city cannot prosecute Negroes for seeking service in stores governed by unconstitutional municipal segregation ordinances. . . . At least 1,400 Negroes in Durham, N.C. are reported to have been arrested during three days of demonstrations against segregated public facilities.	State Dept. says it has "absolutely no evidence" on an alleged Soviet-built naval base in Cuba.			The USSR's Tigran Petrosian, 33, an Armenian, wins the world chess championship from defending title-holder Mikhail Botvinnik, 52, of Leningrad, in Moscow.	May 20
The June 10 admission of two Negro students to the all-white University of Alabama is ordered by U.S. District Judge Hobart Grooms in Birmingham. Gov. Wallace tells newsmen in Montgomery that he "will be present to bar the entrance of any Negro."		The administration's new wheat control program is defeated by a record number of farmers voting in the wheat referendum. It is the first defeat for controls in 13 wheat referendums.	A three-year U.S.-Soviet agreement for a cooperative program of nuclear research is signed in Moscow.		May 21
Pres. Kennedy, referring to growing tensions over civil rights, tells reporters that his administration is seeking ways to "provide a legal outlet" for "those who feel themselves . . . denied equal rights.". . . Pres. Kennedy tells a Washington news conference that he hopes it will not be necessary to send federal troops to enforce the court-ordered desegregation of the University of Alabama.	Pres. Kennedy tells his news conference that there is no truth to recent Republican charges that the administration is planning to abandon the U.S. naval base at Guantanamo.		The seven Project Mercury astronauts are reported to have urged the scheduling of at least one more Mercury space flight during a White House dinner with Pres. Kennedy. At present, no further Mercury flights are planned.	The 175th General Assembly of the United Presbyterian Church (U.S.A.) concludes its week-long session in Des Moines, Ia. after resolving the following: to increase racial integration efforts, to oppose prayer reading in public schools, and to open areas of cooperation with Roman Catholics.	May 22
The President's Committee on Juvenile Delinquency announces plans for a trial program to send former Peace Corps volunteers to work with high school youths in the Washington, D.C. area. . . . A bipartisan group of 20 Senators join in introducing two bills to eliminate segregation in public businesses and to accelerate school integration.	Pres. Kennedy signs a bill (HR2440) authorizing $15,314,291,000 in fiscal 1964 for missiles, aircraft, ships, and military research.				May 23
Novelist James Baldwin and several other prominent Negro artists and entertainers hold a lengthy private conference in New York with Atty. Gen. Robert Kennedy. Baldwin afterwards tells reporters that Kennedy does not appreciate "the extremity of the racial situation" in the North. . . . Justice Dept. files suit in Birmingham, Ala. to prevent Gov. George Wallace from interfering in the court-ordered desegregation of the University of Alabama.			*Tass* reports the successful launch of Cosmos 18, the third unmanned Soviet satellite placed in orbit in the last month.		May 24
		An advisory labor-management panel, authorized by the 1947 Taft-Hartley Act, but long unused, is reactivated by Pres. Kennedy to assist existing federal mediation services.		Brian Sternberg of the University of Washington sets a world outdoor pole vault record of 16 ft. 7 in. at the California Relays in Modesto. Peter Snell of New Zealand, competing in the same meet, ran the mile in three minutes 54.9 seconds, fastest time ever recorded in the U.S. . . . A U.S. golf team defeats Britain in Turnberry, Scotland to win the Walker Cup for the 18th time in 19 tries.	May 25
Martin Luther King addresses a Los Angeles "Freedom Rally for Birmingham," attended by over 30,000 people. A similar rally in San Francisco drew about 20,000.				Television programs cited for outstanding achievement during the 1962-1963 season at the annual Emmy Awards include: for news, *The Huntley-Brinkley Report*; for comedy, *The Dick Van Dyke Show*; for drama, *The Defenders*; and for variety, *The Andy Williams Show* . . . . John Kelley wins the AAU marathon in Yonkers, N.Y. for the eighth straight year.	May 26

F	G	H	I	J
Includes elections, federal-state relations, civil rights and liberties, crime, the judiciary, education, health care, poverty, urban affairs and population.	*Includes formation and debate of U.S. foreign and defense policies, veterans' affairs and defense spending. (Relations with specific foreign countries are usually found under the region concerned.)*	*Includes business, labor, agriculture, taxation, transportation, consumer affairs, monetary and fiscal policy, natural resources, and pollution.*	*Includes worldwide scientific, medical and technological developments, natural phenomena, U.S. weather, natural disasters, and accidents.*	*Includes the arts, religion, scholarship, communications media, sports, entertainment, fashions, fads and social life.*

	World Affairs	Europe	Africa & the Middle East	The Americas	Asia & the Pacific
May 27			Ex-West German Defense Min. Franz-Josef Strauss arrives in Israel for a 10-day visit despite widespread demonstrations protesting the trip.		In a note to India, Communist China protests alleged border provocations by Indian troops and warns that a continuation of such incidents may rekindle fighting.
May 28		French information Min. Alain Peyrefitte declares in Paris that France's nuclear policies are directed toward creating a European nuclear force independent of the U.S. . . . The European Investment Bank reports that the GNP of the six-nation European Economic Community increased 4.9% in 1962. This compares with a growth rate of 5.2% in 1961 and 7.1% in 1960.	Yemeni royalist forces launch an offensive against Yemeni republican troops, thus breaking a tacit cease-fire in effect since an April 30 U.N. agreement providing for the withdrawal of Saudi Arabia and the UAR from the civil conflict. . . . U.S. officials urge Secy. Gen. U Thant to renew U.N. peace efforts in Yemen.		
May 29		*Izvestia* reports that Chief Marshall of Artillery Sergei Varentsov has been stripped of his position for having helped executed spy Oleg Penkovsky get his sensitive post with the State Committee for the Coordination of Scientific Research.		Cuba charges that a U.S. Navy plane fired on a Cuban-Soviet crew digging for oil on the islet of Cayo Frances, 200 miles east of Havana. U.S. denies the charge.	Pakistan and Afghanistan resume diplomatic relations broken since September 1961 in a dispute over contested Pushtoonistan.
May 30					
May 31		The French delegation to the EEC council vetoes a formal proposal sponsored by the other four EEC members for a renewal of contacts between Britain and the Common Market states.			
June 1			Jomo Kenyatta is sworn-in as Kenya's first home rule prime minister.		Indonesian Pres. Sukarno and Malayan P.M. Abdul Rahman conclude two days of talks in Tokyo on Indonesia's opposition to the proposed Malaysian Federation of Malaya, Singapore and Britain's three Borneo territories. . . . An Indonesian threat to impose confiscatory restrictions on American and British oil companies is averted as the companies agree to accept a new government contract on the continuation of their concession. . . . The Japanese government estimates the population of Tokyo, the world's largest city, at 10,393,666.
June 2			African nationalist parties in Swaziland denounce a new British-drafted constitution which would ensure a permanent position in the legislature for Swaziland's white minority.		

A	B	C	D	E
Includes developments that affect more than one world region, international organizations and important meetings of major world leaders.	*Includes all domestic and regional developments in Europe, including the Soviet Union, Turkey, Cyprus and Malta.*	*Includes all domestic and regional developments in Africa and the Middle East, including Iraq and Iran and excluding Cyprus, Turkey and Afghanistan.*	*Includes all domestic and regional developments in Latin America, the Caribbean and Canada.*	*Includes all domestic and regional developments in Asia and Pacific nations, extending from Afghanistan through all the Pacific Islands, except Hawaii.*

U.S. Politics & Social Issues	U.S. Foreign Policy & Defense	U.S. Economy & Environment	Science, Technology & Nature	Culture, Leisure & Life Style	
The Supreme Court unanimously rules that the "all deliberate speed" clause in its 1954 and 1955 school desegregation decisions cannot be interpreted to countenance indefinite delay in the integration of schools or other public facilities. . . . Supreme Court rejects Alabama Gov. George Wallace's suit challenging Pres. Kennedy's sending of federal troops to Alabama during the Birmingham racial crisis.	State Secy. Dean Rusk, commenting on the growing civil rights controversy, says that discrimination in the U.S. "deeply affects the conduct of our foreign relations."		*The New York Times* reports that some U.S. scientists believe that the basic purpose of the USSR's recent series of unmanned satellite missions is "paramilitary."		May 27
NAACP Legal Defense Fund files suit in Washington, D.C. asking for a reduction in House representation of those states denying Negroes the right to vote. The suit is based on provisions of the 14th Amendment.		The Senate passes and sends to the President a bill to increase the temporary national debt limit to $309 billion. . . . Pres. Kennedy signs a bill (S20) authorizing creation of a permanent Outdoor Recreation Bureau within the Interior Dept.		Rumors, dating from late 1962, that Pope John XXIII is suffering from stomach cancer are confirmed in a brief Vatican announcement.	May 28
Pres. Kennedy asks nine northern and border state governors attending a Presidential luncheon to lead drives in their states to assure equal opportunities regardless of race.		Gary, Ind. public school teachers end a one-day strike after the city's school board agreed to recognize their union.	A cyclone batters a 178-mile strip of the East Pakistan coast, leaving thousands dead.		May 29
V.P. Lyndon Johnson tells a Memorial Day audience in Gettysburg, Pa. that Negroes should no longer be asked "to be patient" in their quest for equal rights. . . . Police using tear gas disperse a CORE-sponsored anti-segregation demonstration in Tallahassee, Fla. Thirty-seven persons are arrested.					May 30
		The Dow Jones industrial average climbs 6.43 points to close the day at a 1963 record 726.96. . . . AP reports that traffic accidents over the one-day Memorial Day holiday took a record 159 lives.			May 31
					June 1
		Official sources list the death toll from the May 29 East Pakistan cyclone at about 22,000.		USSR wins the 15th world free-style wrestling championship in Sofia, Bulgaria.	June 2

F	G	H	I	J
Includes elections, federal-state relations, civil rights and liberties, crime, the judiciary, education, health care, poverty, urban affairs and population.	*Includes formation and debate of U.S. foreign and defense policies, veterans' affairs and defense spending. (Relations with specific foreign countries are usually found under the region concerned.)*	*Includes business, labor, agriculture, taxation, transportation, consumer affairs, monetary and fiscal policy, natural resources, and pollution.*	*Includes worldwide scientific, medical and technological developments, natural phenomena, U.S. weather, natural disasters, and accidents.*	*Includes the arts, religion, scholarship, communications media, sports, entertainment, fashions, fads and social life.*

	World Affairs	Europe	Africa & the Middle East	The Americas	Asia & the Pacific
June 3				Cuban Premier Castro returns to Havana after a month-long visit to the USSR, during which he was honored as a Hero of the Soviet Union. . . . U.S. resumes "normal diplomatic business" with Haiti and simultaneously withdraws an American naval task force which had been sent into Haitian waters at the outset of the Haitian-Dominican crisis.	
June 4		U.S. Adm. Claude Ricketts meets with British officials in London to present the Kennedy administration's case for a multilateral nuclear force fleet of service vessels manned by crews of mixed nationality.		*The New York Times* reports that the U.S. had planned a possible Marine landing in Haiti to demonstrate American support of a new regime in anticipation of the then expected departure from Haiti of Pres. Francois Duvalier. . . . Santo Domingo sources report that Haitian troops have secured the 129-mile Dominican border area to prevent Haitians from fleeing to the Dominican Republic.	
June 5		Soviet-bloc sources report growing opposition by Rumania to Soviet proposals for more central economic planning and industrial specialization among the Communist nations of East Europe.		An OAS investigating committee charges that Cuba is serving as a base for increased communist subversion in Latin America. The committee report identifies Venezuela as the "primary objective" of the Castro regime's subversive efforts. . . . The U.S. State Dept. discloses that the U.S. and Ecuador have agreed to open negotiations on a dispute over fishing rights off Ecuador's coast.	
June 6					Saigon sources report that B-57 bombers, flown by U.S. Air Force pilots, have gone into action for the first time against Viet Cong troops.
June 7					
June 8					
June 9			Saudi Arabian officials charge that UAR planes from Yemen yesterday bombed the Saudi Red Sea port of Quizan, killing 30 persons. . . . U.S. Defense Dept. reports that the Saudi government has lifted its ban against Jewish U.S. servicemen being stationed in Saudi Arabia. . . . Mali announces that it has signed a five-year agreement with Senegal to end the rift that has existed since the 1960 break-up of the Mali-Senegal Federation.	Fernando Belaunde Terry, candidate of the coalition Popular Action-Christian Democratic Party, is elected to a six-year term as president of Peru.	

A	B	C	D	E
Includes developments that affect more than one world region, international organizations and important meetings of major world leaders.	*Includes all domestic and regional developments in Europe, including the Soviet Union, Turkey, Cyprus and Malta.*	*Includes all domestic and regional developments in Africa and the Middle East, including Iraq and Iran and excluding Cyprus, Turkey and Afghanistan.*	*Includes all domestic and regional developments in Latin America, the Caribbean and Canada.*	*Includes all domestic and regional developments in Asia and Pacific nations, extending from Afghanistan through all the Pacific Islands, except Hawaii.*

U.S. Politics & Social Issues	U.S. Foreign Policy & Defense	U.S. Economy & Environment	Science, Technology & Nature	Culture, Leisure & Life Style	
Supreme Court rules unconstitutional a school desegregation plan permitting pupils to transfer if their race is in the minority in their school or grade. . . . Supreme Court rules that the city-wide TV broadcast of an alleged murderer's confession to police entitles the defendant to a change of venue.		Supreme Court issues its decision in the 40-year-old controversy over apportioning water from the Colorado River's lower basin.		Pope John XXIII (Angelo Giuseppe Roncalli), 81, 261st Pope of the Roman Catholic Church, dies in the Vatican Palace of peritonitis brought on by a malignant stomach tumor. Pope John XXIII earned worldwide attention for his unprecedented efforts to increase the church's communication with non-Roman Catholic Christians.	June 3
Pres. Kennedy announces that he will soon issue an executive order barring job bias in all federal construction programs. Kennedy also met with about 100 hotel, theater and chain store owners, who reportedly assured him of their cooperation in efforts to end discrimination. . . . A biracial committee in Gainesville, Fla. meets to negotiate Negro demands for an end to segregation in local public buildings and businesses.		A bill (HR5389) changing the backing of $1 and $2 bills from silver to gold is signed by Pres. Kennedy. . . . Teamsters Pres. James Hoffa and seven others are indicted in Chicago on charges of fraudulently obtaining $20 million in loans from the Central States Teamster Pension Fund.			June 4
Rep. Edwin Willis (D, La.) is elected chairman of the House Committee on Un-American Activities to succeed the late Rep. Francis Walter (D, Pa.). . . . Fred Link, a white, is killed by gun shots as a group of 500 whites clash with Negroes in the black section of Lexington, N.C. The incident follows a day of Negro demonstrations against segregation.		The Florida Supreme Court rules that a cigarette manufacturer can be held liable if a person's death is caused by the company's product.			June 5
Mass Negro demonstrations resume in Greensboro, N.C. following the arrest of North Carolina A&T student leader Jesse Jackson during a peaceful demonstration the night before. . . . A coalition of Negro and white organizations meet with Los Angeles officials to demand a quick elimination of racial discrimination in the city.		Labor Dept. reports that the unemployment rate climbed to 5.9% in May after falling to a low point of 5.6% in March. The jobless rate for teenagers is estimated at 15%.		Michel Jazy of France sets a world record of 8 minutes 29.6 seconds for the two-mile run in a Paris meet.	June 6
				Brian Sternberg of the University of Washington sets a world pole vault record of 16 ft. 8 in. in a Compton (Calif.) Invitational Meet.	June 7
			The American Heart Association adopts a resolution urging "joint educational efforts with other voluntary and official health groups" to discourage smoking. The AHA is the first voluntary public agency to open a major drive against cigarette smoking.	John Galbreath's Chateaugay wins the 95th Belmont Stakes at Aqueduct (N.Y.). . . . Emile Griffith regains the world welterweight boxing championship by winning a 15-round split decision in New York over Luis Rodriguez.	June 8
National Urban League director Whitney Young warns that the racial incidents in the South may appear "mild in comparison" with the unrest that could soon erupt in Northern cities.					June 9

F	G	H	I	J
Includes elections, federal-state relations, civil rights and liberties, crime, the judiciary, education, health care, poverty, urban affairs and population.	Includes formation and debate of U.S. foreign and defense policies, veterans' affairs and defense spending. (Relations with specific foreign countries are usually found under the region concerned.)	Includes business, labor, agriculture, taxation, transportation, consumer affairs, monetary and fiscal policy, natural resources, and pollution.	Includes worldwide scientific, medical and technological developments, natural phenomena, U.S. weather, natural disasters, and accidents.	Includes the arts, religion, scholarship, communications media, sports, entertainment, fashions, fads and social life.

	World Affairs	Europe	Africa & the Middle East	The Americas	Asia & the Pacific
June 10			The Iraqi government announces that it has launched a major offensive against Kurdish tribesmen in Iraq's northern provinces.		Gen. Paul Harkins, head of the U.S. military mission in Vietnam is reported to have warned U.S. military personnel to shun duty with Vietnamese military units involved in the suppression of Buddhist demonstrations.
June 11			The U.N. Security Council approves Secy. Gen. U Thant's plan to send a 200-man U.N. observation team to Yemen to supervise the withdrawal of UAR troops and Saudi Arabia aid.		A Buddhist priest, Quang Duc, 73, commits suicide by burning himself in a Saigon street in protest against the South Vietnamese government's Buddhist policies. . . . Indonesian and Philippine opposition to the proposed Malaysian Federation is reportedly lessened as a result of a three-day meeting in Manila between Malayan, Indonesian and Philippine officials.
June 12			Two alleged Israeli agents are convicted in Switzerland on charges of coercion in trying to stop West German rocket expert Paul Gorcke from working for the UAR.	An OAS fact-finding committee asserts that Haitian compliance with OAS principles on human rights would contribute greatly to the relaxation of tensions between Haiti and the Dominican Republic.	
June 13					American diplomatic officials in Saigon inform South Vietnamese Pres. Diem of U.S. opposition to his treatment of Buddhist dissidents. . . . Laotian sources report that hostilities are spreading from the Plaine des Jarres in northern Laos to southern and central regions and that rightist forces are becoming increasingly involved in the clashes.
June 14	Pres. Kennedy's recent appeal for a fresh start in negotiations on the nuclear test-ban and other East-West Cold War questions is rebuffed by Premier Khrushchev in a statement to Soviet newsmen.	British lawyers for Christine Keeler issue a statement denying that she had ever been asked to get military information from ex-War Secy. John Profumo.			
June 15		Hans Merten, a Social Democratic member of the West German Bundestag, claims that soldiers from Israel and other non-European countries are being trained in West Germany.	Baghdad radio announces that the Iraqi army has captured 14 Kurdish villages.		A five-point compromise agreement aimed at ending the dispute between the South Vietnamese government and the country's Buddhists is reached in Saigon.
June 16	In a published letter, the Chinese CP Central Committee criticizes Soviet Premier Khrushchev for pursuing a peaceful co-existence policy at the expense of the revolutionary aims of world communism. Observers say the letter lessens chances of a Sino-Soviet reconciliation at the forthcoming ideological discussions in Moscow.		David Ben-Gurion, 76, citing personal reasons, unexpectedly resigns as prime minister of Israel. . . . The New York Times quotes diplomatic sources as estimating that the number of Soviet military technicians in Yemen now exceeds 1,000. . . . Two Kurdish members of the Iraqi cabinet resign in protest against the government's resumption of hostility against the Kurds.		Thousands of Buddhists riot in Saigon as they attempt to break through police lines to attend funeral services for the martyred priest, Quang Duc.

A	B	C	D	E
Includes developments that affect more than one world region, international organizations and important meetings of major world leaders.	Includes all domestic and regional developments in Europe, including the Soviet Union, Turkey, Cyprus and Malta.	Includes all domestic and regional developments in Africa and the Middle East, including Iraq and Iran and excluding Cyprus, Turkey and Afghanistan.	Includes all domestic and regional developments in Latin America, the Caribbean and Canada.	Includes all domestic and regional developments in Asia and Pacific nations, extending from Afghanistan through all the Pacific Islands, except Hawaii.

U.S. Politics & Social Issues	U.S. Foreign Policy & Defense	U.S. Economy & Environment	Science, Technology & Nature	Culture, Leisure & Life Style	
Pres. Kennedy signs an administration bill (S1409) requiring equal pay for equal work regardless of sex. . . . A biracial committee in Nashville, Tenn. announces that the city's leading hotels and restaurants have agreed to desegregate. . . . Danville, Va. police use fire hoses to break up a desegregation demonstration by about 150 Negroes. Massive civil rights protests began in Danville June 1.	Richard Phillips replaces Lincoln White as official spokesman for the U.S. State Dept.				June 10
Pres. Kennedy begins holding a series of meetings with political leaders in an attempt to gain a bipartisan support for his civil rights proposals. . . . About 3,000 Negroes march into downtown Savannah, Ga. in an anti-segregation demonstration that ends in the arrest of over 50 Negroes.				A collection of French impressionist paintings is auctioned in London for $2,922,852, a record sum for a modern art sale. . . . The opening of an experimental Quaker-sponsored World College, staffed by an international faculty, is announced in New York.	June 11
The Defense Dept. announces a program to end discrimination in its hiring of civilian personnel.		Southern Democrats, reportedly unhappy with the administration's civil rights activity, join Republicans to defeat an administration measure to strengthen the redevelopment program for economically distressed areas.	Moscow sources report that a woman has been selected for a Soviet space flight to take place in the very near future. . . . NASA officially announces the end of the Project Mercury manned space flight program.	The extremely costly motion picture epic, Cleopatra, is released in New York.	June 12
Ex-Reps. Thomas Johnson (D,Md.) and Frank Boykin (D,Ala.) are convicted by a federal grand jury of conspiracy and conflict of interest charges. . . . Dave McGalthery becomes the third Negro to enroll and attend classes at the University of Alabama.					June 13
National Guard troops are ordered into Cambridge, Md., where anti-segregation demonstrations have led to violence between Negroes and whites. . . . Several thousand Negroes and whites participate in a Washington D.C. "freedom march" against racial discrimination.	A Gallup Poll shows that 65% of Americans favor having the U.N. provide birth control information to nations desiring it.	The Federal Reserve Board reports that U.S. industrial production climbed in May for the fifth consecutive month.			June 14
Nearly 3,000 people attend Jackson, Miss. funeral services for slain civil rights leader Medgar Evers. In a eulogy NAACP Executive Secy. Roy Wilkins says that ultimate responsibility for Evers' death lies with the "Southern political system.". . . The Justice Dept. reports that in the last three weeks 143 Southern cities have taken some form of action toward the voluntary removal of racial barriers.		Pres. Kennedy issues a statement criticizing railroad and union negotiators for not heeding presidential board recommendations concerning their still unresolved dispute over work-rules.	Lt. Col. Valery Fyodorovich Bykovski is successfully launched into orbit from the USSR's Vaikonour Cosmodrome in Kazakhstan.		June 15
				Special presidential consultant on the arts August Heckscher resigns after submitting a report criticizing the government for inadequate efforts to stimulate artistic achievement in the U.S. . . . Lorenzo Bandini and Ludovico Scarfiotti of Italy, driving a Ferrari, win the 24-hour Le Mans endurance race.	June 16

F	G	H	I	J
Includes elections, federal-state relations, civil rights and liberties, crime, the judiciary, education, health care, poverty, urban affairs and population.	Includes formation and debate of U.S. foreign and defense policies, veterans' affairs and defense spending. (Relations with specific foreign countries are usually found under the region concerned.)	Includes business, labor, agriculture, taxation, transportation, consumer affairs, monetary and fiscal policy, natural resources, and pollution.	Includes worldwide scientific, medical and technological developments, natural phenomena, U.S. weather, natural disasters, and accidents.	Includes the arts, religion, scholarship, communications media, sports, entertainment, fashions, fads and social life.

	World Affairs	Europe	Africa & the Middle East	The Americas	Asia & the Pacific
June 17		The British House of Commons by a 321-252 vote defeats a no-confidence motion over P.M. Macmillan's handling of the security aspects involving Ex-War Secy. John Profumo and Christine Keeler. Twenty-seven Conservative Party members abstain from voting. . . . King Paul designates ex-Trade Min. Panayotis Pipinelis as prime minister of Greece. He replaces Constantine Caramanlis who resigned June 11.		Bolivia withdraws from participation on the Council of the OAS in protest against the OAS's handling of a river dispute between Chile and Bolivia.	
June 18		Italian Premier-designate Aldo Moro abandons his efforts to form a new cabinet after failing to win left-wing Socialist support for a proposed center-left coalition government.		Premier Castro warns Britain and France not to permit their Caribbean islands to be used by Cuban exiles for raids on Cuba.	
June 19		Italian Chamber of Deputies Speaker Giovanni Leone, a Christian Democrat, accepts Pres. Antonio Segni's invitation to attempt to form a new cabinet.	Israeli Pres. Zalman Shazar designates Finance Min. Levi Eshkol as prime minister to replace David Ben-Gurion who resigned June 16.		
June 20	A "Memorandum of Understanding" on the creation of a Washington-Moscow teletype system is signed in Geneva by the chief U.S. and Soviet delegates to the Geneva arms conference.	Italian P.M.-designate Giovanni Leone announces formation of a cabinet composed entirely of Christian Democrats. . . . France announces that it will shortly withdraw to national control the French naval units presently assigned for wartime NATO service in the English Channel. The action is viewed as a sign of continuing French hesitation to participate in a U.S.-dominated NATO alliance.	The U.N. names Ralph Bunche of the U.S. to head its civilian operations in the Congo.	The Miami-based Cuban Revolutionary Council announces that an unspecified number of exile commandos have landed in Cuba to begin a "war of liberation" against the Castro regime.	
June 21	The 17-nation Geneva disarmament conference begins a tentative month-long recess.	British P.M. Macmillan announces in the House of Commons that a high-level judicial inquiry will be held on the security aspects of the Profumo affair. Labor Party leader Harold Wilson assails the proposed inquiry as a potential "cover-up." . . . The West German Parliament approves a record $13.2 billion federal budget for 1963.		U.S. State Dept. denounces as "inaccurate" yesterday's announcement of a Cuban exile invasion and accuses Cuban Revolutionary Council leaders of deceiving "the hopes of the anti-Castro elements within Cuba."	The British Foreign Office reports that Britain has been unable to reach an agreement with the USSR on framing a new appeal to end fighting in northern Laos.
June 22		British P.M. Macmillan tells a Conservative Party rally that he will not let the Profumo scandal force his early resignation. . . . Pres. Kennedy leaves Washington for West Germany to begin a 10-day European trip. The trip is reportedly aimed at easing dissention within the NATO alliance and at reaffirming the U.S. commitment to European freedom.	A British Army group from Aden is attacked by Yemeni tribesmen after the Britons accidently crossed into the Yemen territory. Four British soldiers are reported killed.		The Laotian National Assembly adopts a resolution asking the signatory nations of the 1962 Geneva Conference on Laos to halt North Vietnam's "direct military intervention" in Laos.
June 23		West German Chancellor Konrad Adenauer welcomes Pres. Kennedy upon his arrival in Bonn. Adenauer calls Kennedy's visit proof that the U.S. will "make no deal with the Soviet Union at the expense of others."	Twenty-eight Communists are executed by the Iraqi government for their alleged role in atrocities during the abortive 1959 coup in Mosul.		

	A	B	C	D	E
	Includes developments that affect more than one world region, international organizations and important meetings of major world leaders.	*Includes all domestic and regional developments in Europe, including the Soviet Union, Turkey, Cyprus and Malta.*	*Includes all domestic and regional developments in Africa and the Middle East, including Iraq and Iran and excluding Cyprus, Turkey and Afghanistan.*	*Includes all domestic and regional developments in Latin America, the Caribbean and Canada.*	*Includes all domestic and regional developments in Asia and Pacific nations, extending from Afghanistan through all the Pacific Islands, except Hawaii.*

U.S. Politics & Social Issues	U.S. Foreign Policy & Defense	U.S. Economy & Environment	Science, Technology & Nature	Culture, Leisure & Life Style	
The Supreme Court reaffirms its decision that state and local rules requiring recitation of the Lord's Prayer or of Bible verses in U.S. public schools violate the First Amendment. The decision involves a suit brought against the Baltimore, Md. school board by two atheists, Mrs. Madalyn Murray and her son, William Murray.		The Supreme Court rules that the Singer Manufacturing Co. violated the Sherman Antitrust Act by conspiring with European manufacturers to "suppress imports of Japanese sewing machines."	Valentina Vladimirovna Tereshkova, a former textile mill worker, becomes the first woman in space as she is successfully launched into an orbit similar to that of her fellow cosmonaut, Valery Bykovski. According to a statement accompanying the launch announcement, the purpose of the twin-orbit mission is to provide a comparative analysis of the impact of space flight factors on a man and a woman.		June 17
About 3,000 Negro students participate in a Boston public school boycott to protest de facto segregation. . . . NAACP leaders warn N.Y.C. officials that mass demonstrations will be held if Negroes are not given enough opportunity to air their grievances about discrimination in housing, jobs and political representation.					June 18
Pres. Kennedy sends Congress a draft Civil Rights Act of 1963 providing for the desegregation of public facilities, the banning of bias in federally aided construction projects, and authorizing federal officials to initiate public school desegregation suits. . . . Federal Bureau of Prisons reports that 47 persons were executed by civil authorities in 18 states in 1962. Forty-two persons were executed in 1961.		Major U.S. cigarette manufacturers announce that they have voluntarily decided to discontinue advertising and promotional activities in college publications. . . . A proposed merger of the domestic routes of American Airlines Inc. and Eastern Air Lines Inc. is barred by the CAB.	The USSR's twin-orbiting male and female cosmonauts return to earth after setting new records in every space endurance category. Both are reported in good condition. . . . A Tiros weather satellite is successfully launched from Cape Canaveral by means of a Thor-Delta rocket. It is the Thor-Delta system's 18th successful satellite launching.		June 19
Delegates to the annual CORE convention elect Floyd McKissick as national chairman. He is the first Negro to hold that post. . . . Jackson, Miss. hires its first Negro policeman.		United Steelworkers of America and 11 steel companies agree on a new two-year labor contract which provides for job security measures in lieu of wage increases. It is the first time that a steel industry contract has been settled without a major strike threat.		A Los Angeles Superior Court judge declares nightclub comedian Lenny Bruce, 37, a narcotics addict and orders him confined to a California rehabilitation center. Bruce was earlier convicted of possession of heroin.	June 20
A municipal court grand jury in Danville, Va. indicts 10 civil rights leaders on charges of "inciting the colored population to acts of violence." The defendants will be represented by William Kunstler, a lawyer for the Ghandi Society of New York.				Cardinal Giovanni Batista Montini, 65, archbishop of Milan, is elected 263d pope of the Roman Catholic Church to succeed the late John XXIII. The new pope will assume the name Paul VI. . . . Bob Hayes, 20, sets a new world 100-yard dash record of 9.1 seconds at the AAU national track championships in St. Louis.	June 21
Pres. Kennedy meets with Martin Luther King and other prominent Negro leaders to discuss his civil rights program and proposals. Following the meeting, Dr. King tells reporters he will lead a non-violent peaceful demonstration in Washington if there is a Senate filibuster on rights legislation. . . . Pres. Kennedy issues an executive order authorizing withdrawal of federal funds from construction projects where racial discrimination is practiced.	The U.S. Navy launches four nuclear powered submarines—three of them designed for carrying Polaris missiles.		The USSR's two newest cosmonauts, Valentina Tereshkova and Valery Bykovski are flown to Moscow for a hero's welcome after their record-breaking flights in twin orbits.	In his first public address, Pope Paul announces his intention to continue Vatican II, the recessed ecumenical council opened in October 1962 by John XXIII. . . . Dennis Ralston of Southern California defeats Martin Riessen of Northwestern to win the NCAA singles tennis championship in Princetown, N.J.	June 22
Byron de la Beckwith, 42, of Greenwood, Miss. is charged in Jackson with murder in the ambush slaying of Negro leader Medgar Evers. . . . An estimated 125,000 Negroes and whites participate in a massive pro-civil rights freedom parade in Detroit, Mich. Mayor Jerome Cavanaugh had endorsed the parade.			*Pravda* quotes high-level Soviet space officials as saying that rendezvous and docking will be major goals in forthcoming Soviet flights.	Julius Boros defeats Jacky Cupit and Arnold Palmer in an 18-hole play-off to win the 63d U.S. Open golf championship in Brookline, Mass.	June 23
F	G	H	I	J	
Includes elections, federal-state relations, civil rights and liberties, crime, the judiciary, education, health care, poverty, urban affairs and population.	*Includes formation and debate of U.S. foreign and defense policies, veterans' affairs and defense spending. (Relations with specific foreign countries are usually found under the region concerned.)*	*Includes business, labor, agriculture, taxation, transportation, consumer affairs, monetary and fiscal policy, natural resources, and pollution.*	*Includes worldwide scientific, medical and technological developments, natural phenomena, U.S. weather, natural disasters, and accidents.*	*Includes the arts, religion, scholarship, communications media, sports, entertainment, fashions, fads and social life.*	

	World Affairs	Europe	Africa & the Middle East	The Americas	Asia & the Pacific
June 24	A Communist-sponsored World Women's Congress opens in Moscow.	In a Bonn press conference, visiting U.S. Pres. Kennedy reiterates his plea for NATO unity and for East-West action to prevent a further spread of nuclear weapons.	The British protectorate of Zanzibar receives internal self-rule as P.M. Mohammed Shamte is sworn-in to head an eight-man coalition government. Members of the new government say they will seek the closing of a small U.S. military base in Zanzibar. . . . Israeli P.M.-designate Levi Eshkol announces formation of a three-party coalition cabinet, similar to Ben-Gurion's.	The Canadian Parliament defeats a Conservative Party motion of no-confidence in P.M. Pearson's Liberal government. The motion was prompted by a dispute over alleged anti-foreigner tax provisions in the Liberal government's proposed 1963-1964 budget.	
June 25		In a speech to cheering crowds in the Frankfurt City Hall Square, Pres. Kennedy says that "those who would separate Europe from America or split one ally from another. . .only give aid and comfort to. . .our adversaries." Observers view the remark as a reference to French Pres. de Gaulle's opposition to a tightening of the Atlantic alliance. . . . Czechoslovakian CP leader Alexander Dubcek announces the posthumous rehabilitation of executed ex-Czech Foreign Min. Vladimir Clementis who was condemned in 1952 on charges of economic sabotage and Titoism.	Algerian Premier Ahmed Ben Bella announces the arrest of four prominent political figures accused of plotting against his regime. . . . The U.S. signs an agreement to provide Algeria with an estimated $1 million in food and technical assistance.		
June 26		Pres. Kennedy's arrival in West Berlin is marked by an enthusiastic welcome by nearly all of the city's two-and-a-half million residents. Later in the day he addresses a cheering crowd of 150,000 West Berliners, concluding with the statement: "As a free man, I take pride in the words 'Ich bin ein Berliner.'". . . Thousands of Dubliners turn out to welcome Pres. Kennedy on his arrival for a four-day visit to Ireland.	Kurdish sources charge in Beirut that Syrian MiG's are assisting the Iraqi air force in its renewed campaign to suppress Kurdish rebels. . . . An agreement to provide $200 million in French financial aid for Algeria's development is signed in Paris.		
June 27	The USSR ousts three Chinese embassy officials for distributing an allegedly anti-Soviet letter outlining China's proposed agenda for the upcoming ideological talks in Moscow.	French Information Min. Alain Peyrefitte expresses doubt over the value of U.S. pledges to come to the defense of Europe despite Pres. Kennedy's Frankfurt speech reiterating these assurances. . . . Pres. Kennedy confers with Irish P.M. Sean Lemass before leaving Dublin to visit County Wesford, ancestral home of the Kennedy family.			
June 28		In an address to the Irish Parliament, Pres. Kennedy stresses the major role played in U.S. history by citizens of Irish descent.	U.S. Defense Dept. discloses an agreement permitting Israel to buy about $25 million worth of U.S.-manufactured Hawk anti-aircraft missiles.		
June 29	Soviet CP officials make public a June 21 Khrushchev speech in which he attacked Chinese leaders for "extremely aggravating their differences" with the USSR.		The Congo government recognizes the National Front for the Liberation of Angola (NFL) as Angola's only legitimate government. The action draws protest from Portugal and from the Popular Movement for the Liberation of Angola (PML), a rival rebel organization. . . . The UAR breaks off diplomatic relations with Portugal to protest the latter's continuing colonial presence in Africa.		
June 30		Following two days of talks, British P.M. Macmillan and visiting Pres. Kennedy announce full agreement on the position to be taken by their delegates to the U.S.-British-Soviet talks on a nuclear test-ban, to open in Moscow in mid-July.		About 60 U.S. students, defying a U.S. travel ban, arrive in Havana to begin a two-month Castro-sponsored tour of Cuba.	

A	B	C	D	E
Includes developments that affect more than one world region, international organizations and important meetings of major world leaders.	*Includes all domestic and regional developments in Europe, including the Soviet Union, Turkey, Cyprus and Malta.*	*Includes all domestic and regional developments in Africa and the Middle East, including Iraq and Iran and excluding Cyprus, Turkey and Afghanistan.*	*Includes all domestic and regional developments in Latin America, the Caribbean and Canada.*	*Includes all domestic and regional developments in Asia and Pacific nations, extending from Afghanistan through all the Pacific Islands, except Hawaii.*

U.S. Politics & Social Issues	U.S. Foreign Policy & Defense	U.S. Economy & Environment	Science, Technology & Nature	Culture, Leisure & Life Style	
Sen. Richard Russell (Ga.), leader of the Southern Democratic bloc, denounces Pres. Kennedy's recent civil rights proposals, claiming they in effect encourage civil rights demonstrations and disorder.		Pres. Kennedy asks Congress for $60 million to finance a design competition for the development of a commercial supersonic airliner. Kennedy has estimated that the total federal share of the plane's long-run development cost can be held to less than $750 million.			June 24
The Democratic Party selects Atlantic City, N.J. as the site for its 1964 nominating convention.	Twenty-seven African ambassadors send a joint letter to Pres. Kennedy protesting Sen. Allen Ellender's (D,La.) June 16 statement suggesting that U.S. and African Negroes have shown an inability to govern their own affairs. Ellender's remarks, made in an ABC-TV interview, were previously disowned by the U.S. State Dept.		The U.S. Surgeon General's Office announces the licensing of a three-in-one oral polio vaccine to provide simultaneous immunity against the three types of polio. . . . Landslides, caused by a week of torrential rainfall, are responsible for the death of at least 116 persons in South Korea.		June 25
The House Judiciary Subcommittee begins hearings on the administration's draft civil rights bill (HR7152). Atty. Gen. Robert Kennedy tells the subcommittee that the administration favors exempting small stores and rooming houses from the public accommodations section of the proposed bill. . . . Kentucky Gov. Bert Combs signs an executive order barring racial bias in state-licensed businesses.	The Air Force launches a "secret" satellite from its Vandenberg Base, Calif. missile center.				June 26
The Defense Dept. announces a major effort to integrate the armed forces reserves. The statement says that 10 southern states do not yet have Negroes in their National Guard units.	Pres. Kennedy announces the appointment of Henry Cabot Lodge Jr. as ambassador to South Vietnam, succeeding Frederic Nolting Jr.				June 27
	Navy Secy. Fred Korth is among the most recent witnesses in the continuing Senate Permanent Investigations Subcommittee inquiry into the award of the TFX fighter plane contract to the General Dynamics Corp.				June 28
The Senate Commerce Committee opens hearings on the administration's bill (S1732) to bar racial discrimination in public accommodations.		A bill (HR6755) extending until June 30, 1964 temporary excise and corporation income taxes at current rates is signed by Pres. Kennedy.		Yuri Vlasov of the USSR is reported to have set a world weight-lifting record by pressing 418.5 pounds in a Vienna competition.	June 29
CORE adopts a resolution accusing the Kennedy administration of failing to appreciate the frustration and potential for violence within the Negro community resulting from un-met demands for equality. . . . Eggs are thrown at Martin Luther King's car as he is driven through N.Y. City's Harlem area enroute to a speaking engagement. Police attribute the incident to Black Muslim sympathizers.				Pope Paul VI is crowned in an outdoor ceremony in St. Peter's Square in Rome. . . . Scottish race driver Jim Clark, driving a Lotus, wins the French Grand Prix at Rheims.	June 30

F	G	H	I	J
Includes elections, federal-state relations, civil rights and liberties, crime, the judiciary, education, health care, poverty, urban affairs and population.	Includes formation and debate of U.S. foreign and defense policies, veterans' affairs and defense spending. (Relations with specific foreign countries are usually found under the region concerned.)	Includes business, labor, agriculture, taxation, transportation, consumer affairs, monetary and fiscal policy, natural resources, and pollution.	Includes worldwide scientific, medical and technological developments, natural phenomena, U.S. weather, natural disasters, and accidents.	Includes the arts, religion, scholarship, communications media, sports, entertainment, fashions, fads and social life.

		World Affairs	Europe	Africa & the Middle East	The Americas	Asia & the Pacific

July 1

World Affairs: The Chinese CP Central Committee announces that it will go through with the planned Moscow ideological talks despite the USSR's recent expulsion of three Chinese embassy officials. The statement denounces the Soviet action as a "serious step in further worsening Sino-Soviet relations."

Europe: Pres. Kennedy arrives in Rome for talks with Italian leaders on issues related to the overall unity of the NATO alliance.

July 2

World Affairs: Soviet Premier Khrushchev calls for the simultaneous signing of an East-West non-aggression pact and an agreement banning all nuclear weapons tests except those conducted underground. It is the first time that Khrushchev has linked the nuclear-test question to repeated Soviet proposals for a non-aggression treaty between NATO and the Warsaw Pact. . . . FBI agents arrest four Soviet citizens in New York and Washington on charges of conspiring to spy for the USSR.

Europe: Violent farmer demonstrations erupt in southern France in protest against falling prices and foreign competition.

Africa & the Middle East: British Colonial Secy. Duncan Sandys announces that Britain will grant Kenya its full independence on December 12. . . . Seyyid Iamshid bin Abdullah succeeds his late father as sultan of the British protectorate of Zanzibar.

The Americas: British troops are called upon to quell racial clashes between Negroes and East Indians which have erupted amidst British Guiana's 10-week-old general strike.

July 3

World Affairs: Kennedy administration officials tell newsmen that the U.S. remains ready to sign a limited nuclear-test ban treaty, but not one linked to a general non-aggression pact.

Africa & the Middle East: The Iraqi government announces that it has crushed an armed attempt by a group of Kurdish tribesmen and "Moscow agents" to take over military installations near Baghdad.

The Americas: The U.S.-Cuban arrangement to exchange Cuban refugees for $53 million worth of U.S. food and drugs comes to an end with the arrival of the last 1,204 Cuban refugees in Miami. A total of 9,703 persons have been brought out of Cuba under terms of the exchange. . . . The Council of the OAS approves a series of measures aimed at combating Cuban-sponsored communist subversion.

July 4

World Affairs: Pres. Kennedy and Premier Khrushchev use their traditional exchange of July 4th messages to stress hopes for continued world peace.

Europe: The French government announces an expansion of its wheat price-support program in an effort to quell mounting farmer unrest.

Africa & the Middle East: The New York Times confirms reports that the USSR suspended aid to Iraq following the February 8th coup by Baathist partisans.

July 5

World Affairs: Delegations from the Central Committees of the Soviet and Chinese Communist parties open ideological reconciliation talks in Moscow despite an intensifying exchange of propaganda charges between Soviet and Chinese leaders.

Europe: Pres. Kennedy tells the American people that his recent Western European tour has further strengthened ties between the Old World and New.

Africa & the Middle East: Iraqi soldiers report that they have driven dissident Kurdish tribesmen to within 20 miles of the Iranian border.

July 6

World Affairs: A Peking radio broadcast charges that the preaching of "peaceful co-existence between the oppressors and the oppressed" has become the chief ideological preoccupation of Soviet Premier Khrushchev.

The Americas: British Guiana's 11-week-old crippling general strike ends after the striking Trade Unions Council agrees to a compromise formula to settle its dispute with P.M. Cheddi Jagan's labor policies.

July 7

World Affairs: Chinese Foreign Min. Chen Yi tells a Peking rally honoring the three Chinese ousted by the USSR that Soviet leaders are entirely responsible for the current Sino-Soviet rift.

A	B	C	D	E
Includes developments that affect more than one world region, international organizations and important meetings of major world leaders.	Includes all domestic and regional developments in Europe, including the Soviet Union, Turkey, Cyprus and Malta.	Includes all domestic and regional developments in Africa and the Middle East, including Iraq and Iran and excluding Cyprus, Turkey and Afghanistan.	Includes all domestic and regional developments in Latin America, the Caribbean and Canada.	Includes all domestic and regional developments in Asia and Pacific nations, extending from Afghanistan through all the Pacific Islands, except Hawaii.

U.S. Politics & Social Issues	U.S. Foreign Policy & Defense	U.S. Economy & Environment	Science, Technology & Nature	Culture, Leisure & Life Style	
The 54th annual convention of the NAACP begins in Chicago.				Golfer Arnold Palmer wins the Cleveland Open to raise his 1963 tournament earnings to a single-year record of $85,545.	July 1
Martin Luther King, Roy Wilkins, James Farmer, Whitney Young and other prominent Negro leaders confer in New York on plans to stage a mass civil rights march on Washington, Aug. 28.	AEC Chmn. Glenn Seaborg confirms in a Voice of America interview that the U.S. is considering curtailing its nuclear weapons production. The remark follows reports of congressional and administration concern over the growth in the U.S.'s already large stockpile of nuclear weapons.	A federal grand jury in New York indicts eight steel companies on charges of conspiring to fix prices on heavy steel castings between 1956 and 1961.		U.S. Pres. Kennedy is received by Pope Paul VI in private audience in the Vatican. . . . World pole-vault record holder Brian Sternberg is seriously injured and possibly paralyzed in an accident while practicing in Seattle.	July 2
Sen. Philip Hart (D, Mich.) tells fellow members of the Senate Commerce Committee that he opposes any exemptions from the administration's proposed ban on discrimination in public accommodations. Hart adds that the commerce clause provides adequate constitutional authority for such a measure.		Negotiators for major U.S. railroads announce that their companies will put disputed new work-rules into effect July 11. Union leaders say that institution of the rules will result in an immediate strike.		The National League beats the American League 5-3 in baseball's 1963 All-Star game. . . . The USSR wins the team championship in the world Greco-Roman wrestling championships in Helsingborg, Sweden.	July 3
Hecklers prevent Mayor Richard Daley from delivering an address to an NAACP outdoor rally in Chicago's Grant Park.				Contralto Marian Anderson, cellist Pablo Casals, architect Ludwig Mies van der Rohe, pianist Rudolf Serkin, photographer Edward Steichen, playwright Thornton Wilder, literary critic Edmund Wilson and artist Andrew Wyeth are among 31 persons named by Pres. Kennedy as winners of the new Presidential Medal of Freedom. . . . Bohemia Stable's Kelso wins the suburban handicap at Aqueduct (N.Y.) to boost his all-time earnings to $1,307,037, second only to Travis Kerr's Round Table.	July 4
The NAACP convention, meeting in Chicago, votes to extend its "direct action policy" by urging all NAACP local units to implement anti-discrimination programs including "picketing, sit-ins, mass action protests and selective buying campaigns."	The U.S. Coast Guard announces organization of a special Coastal Force to "prevent clandestine entry of saboteurs and espionage agents" into the U.S. from the sea.		The Ford Foundation announces grants totalling $7.5 million for birth control research programs in the U.S., Britain, India and Tunisia.		July 5
Over 100 deans and professors at 22 law schools in 11 Southern states sign a statement supporting the Supreme Court's civil rights decisions.	Pres. Kennedy is reported to have rejected a British Guiana request for American economic aid. The decision is said to be based on U.S. displeasure with P.M. Jagan's apparent pro-communist sympathies and on the belief that aid will be useless during British Guiana's current racial and political strife.		The world's 16 major whaling nations agree in London to restrict their annual catches of blue whales to 10,000 units per country (15,000 previously allowed).	Chuck McKinley of Texas defeats Fred Stolle of Australia to win the men's singles finals of the All-England tennis tourney in Wimbledon.	July 6
Integrationists conduct their second major demonstration within the week to protest segregation at the Gwynn Oak Amusement Park near Baltimore. Over 380 persons have been arrested, including some of the nation's most prominent clergymen.		The AP reports that 510 persons died in traffic accidents during the July 4th holiday—a new record for a four-day July 4 weekend.		The two million-member United Church of Christ, meeting in Denver, approves further study of a plan to merge six major U.S. Protestant denominations into a single church.	July 7
F	G	H	I	J	
Includes elections, federal-state relations, civil rights and liberties, crime, the judiciary, education, health care, poverty, urban affairs and population.	*Includes formation and debate of U.S. foreign and defense policies, veterans' affairs and defense spending. (Relations with specific foreign countries are usually found under the region concerned.)*	*Includes business, labor, agriculture, taxation, transportation, consumer affairs, monetary and fiscal policy, natural resources, and pollution.*	*Includes worldwide scientific, medical and technological developments, natural phenomena, U.S. weather, natural disasters, and accidents.*	*Includes the arts, religion, scholarship, communications media, sports, entertainment, fashions, fads and social life.*	

	World Affairs	Europe	Africa & the Middle East	The Americas	Asia & the Pacific
July 8	The Soviet CP issues a statement accusing Chinese leaders of deliberately kindling popular hostility against the USSR.			The U.S. bans virtually all financial dealings with Cuba in a move to further isolate the Castro government. The U.S. State Dept. describes the action as a fulfillment of the counter-subversion recommendation adopted by the OAS on July 3.	
July 9			The USSR formally protests what it calls Iraq's "genocidal" campaign against Kurdish tribesmen.		An agreement formally establishing the Federation of Malaysia is signed in London by officials of the four member-nations: Malaya, Singapore, Sarawak and North Borneo. The fifth proposed member, Brunei, withdrew from federation talks July 8 after the sultan of Brunei protested that the precedence of his title had not been fully recognized.
July 10	*Tass* reports that the emergency communications teletype system linking the White House and the Kremlin will be in operation by Sept. 1.				
July 11		The Italian Chamber of Deputies narrowly approves the cabinet of P.M. Giovanni Leone. . . . King Paul and Queen Frederika of Greece conclude a three-day British visit marked by frequent leftist demonstrations against alleged political repression in Greece.		The Ecuadoran Army ousts Carlos Arosemena Monroy as president and establishes a four-man ruling military junta. Army communiques cite Arosemena's alleged heavy drinking and sympathy for communism as the reason for his overthrow.	
July 12		Anti-government demonstrations and disorders by farmers are reportedly continuing throughout southern France.			
July 13	An editorial in the Z2 Peking People's Daily asserts that the current Moscow ideological talks have "gone contrary to our hopes," adding that there is reason to believe that "the Soviet Central Committee wants to push Sino-Soviet relations to the point of rupture."				
July 14	The Soviet CP publishes a long open letter criticizing China's leaders for their reckless disregard of the horrible cost of a nuclear war.				

A	B	C	D	E
Includes developments that affect more than one world region, international organizations and important meetings of major world leaders.	Includes all domestic and regional developments in Europe, including the Soviet Union, Turkey, Cyprus and Malta.	Includes all domestic and regional developments in Africa and the Middle East, including Iraq and Iran and excluding Cyprus, Turkey and Afghanistan.	Includes all domestic and regional developments in Latin America, the Caribbean and Canada.	Includes all domestic and regional developments in Asia and Pacific nations, extending from Afghanistan through all the Pacific Islands, except Hawaii.

U.S. Politics & Social Issues	U.S. Foreign Policy & Defense	U.S. Economy & Environment	Science, Technology & Nature	Culture, Leisure & Life Style	
Byron de la Beckwith pleads not guilty in Jackson, Miss. to charges that he murdered Negro integration leader Medgar Evers.				Margaret Smith of Australia defeats Billy Jean Moffitt of California to win the women's singles tennis championship at Wimbledon.	**July 8**
Connecticut Gov. John Dempsey signs a bill prohibiting discrimination in the sale or renting of most housing units. . . . Biracial negotiators in Chattanooga, Tenn. announce that most of the city's leading restaurants have agreed to desegregate. . . . Labor leaders in Trenton, N.J. sign an agreement to accept qualified journeymen and apprentices regardless of race on state construction projects.		Commerce Secy. Luther Hodges reports that corporate income taxes were reduced by about $2.3 billion in 1962 as a result of new rules on depreciation and tax credits for new investment in equipment.			**July 9**
U.S. District Judge J. Robert Martin, in two separate decisions, orders the University of South Carolina to enroll a Negro applicant and directs state officials to integrate South Carolina's state parks. . . . State Secy. Rusk tells the Senate Commerce Committee that failure to enact the civil rights bill will evoke worldwide questioning of the "real convictions of the American people."		A threatened nationwide rail strike over the continuing work-rules dispute is postponed until at least July 29 at the request of Pres. Kennedy. Kennedy says he will use the time to send Congress legislative proposals aimed at settling the controversy.	After two weeks of debate, the House Science & Astronautics Committee votes to cut 8% from the $5.7 billion requested by the administration for civilian space projects in fiscal 1964.	The N.Y. Court of Appeals rules 4-3 that Henry Miller's novel, *Tropic of Cancer*, is "flagrantly obscene."	**July 10**
Civil rights demonstrations are launched at various construction sites in N.Y.C. in an effort to force hiring of more Negroes and Puerto Ricans. . . . AFL-CIO Brotherhood of Locomotive Firemen and Enginemen's convention votes to remove their constitutional ban on Negro membership. . . . Pres. Kennedy meets with U.S. Business Council in the sixth of a series of meetings aimed at consolidating support for his civil rights proposals.					**July 11**
Mississippi Gov. Ross Barnett, testifying against the administration's proposed civil rights bill before the Senate Commerce Committee, accuses Pres. Kennedy of aiding a "world communist conspiracy to divide and conquer" the U.S. by fomenting racial strife. . . . The U.S. Fifth Circuit Court of Appeals in New Orleans orders the Birmingham, Ala. school board to submit a desegregation plan by this fall.					**July 12**
The Southern Regional Council denounces "token" school integration as an example of "bad faith" in race relations. A council report says that 92 out of every 100 Negroes in 17 southern states still attend segregated schools.	Washington sources report that the Joint Chiefs of Staff have informed the Senate Preparedness Subcommittee that they oppose the partial test-ban agreement said to be receiving serious consideration by the Kennedy administration.			John Pennel of Miami, Fla. sets a world pole-vault record of 16 ft. 8 2/3 in. at the British track and field championships in London. . . . Bob Charles of New Zealand wins the British Open golf tournament at Lytham-Saint Ann's England. . . . Right-handed pitcher Early Wynn, 43, of the Cleveland Indians becomes the 14th major league pitcher to win 300 games.	**July 13**
N.Y. Gov. Rockefeller (R) issues a statement condemning "the radical right" of the Republican Party. The statement is viewed as an indirect attack upon ultraconservative supporters of Sen. Barry Goldwater.				Jacques Anquetil wins the 2,570-mile Tours de France bicycle race for the fourth time.	**July 14**

F	G	H	I	J
Includes elections, federal-state relations, civil rights and liberties, crime, the judiciary, education, health care, poverty, urban affairs and population.	Includes formation and debate of U.S. foreign and defense policies, veterans' affairs and defense spending. (Relations with specific foreign countries are usually found under the region concerned.)	Includes business, labor, agriculture, taxation, transportation, consumer affairs, monetary and fiscal policy, natural resources, and pollution.	Includes worldwide scientific, medical and technological developments, natural phenomena, U.S. weather, natural disasters, and accidents.	Includes the arts, religion, scholarship, communications media, sports, entertainment, fashions, fads and social life.

	World Affairs	Europe	Africa & the Middle East	The Americas	Asia & the Pacific
July 15	The U.S., Britain and the USSR reconvene private three-power talks in Moscow in a major new effort to end the five-year-old deadlock over a nuclear test-ban treaty. Premier Khrushchev personally heads the Soviet delegation at the opening session. . . . A federal grand jury in N.Y.C. indicts two Soviet couples on conspiring to transmit U.S. nuclear and rocket secrets to the USSR.	A London jury acquits Italian physicist Giuseppe Martelli of charges that he had spied in Britain for the USSR.			South Vietnamese Buddhist leaders announce a renewal of their campaign to protest the Diem government's alleged discrimination against their religion.
July 16	Moscow sources report that the Soviet, British and American test-ban conferees are focusing attention on a limited agreement excluding underground tests. Such a limited pact had been proposed by Khrushchev in a July 2 East Berlin speech.			Manuel Artime of the anti-Castro Revolutionary Recovery Movement says that his group will leave Miami to re-establish headquarters "somewhere" in Central America. Artime cites U.S. government opposition to Cuban exile activities as the reason for the move.	
July 17	The three delegations at the Moscow test-ban talks report making progress "in drafting some provisions of a test-ban treaty covering. . .the atmosphere, outerspace and under water." Pres. Kennedy expresses satisfaction over the Moscow negotiations in a statement to Washington newsmen.		Portugal claims that armed rebels, using neighboring Senegal and Guinea bases, have gained control of about 15% of Portuguese Guinea.	Pres. Kennedy tells a Washington news conference that peaceful relations between U.S. and Cuba are impossible as long as Cuba remains a "Soviet satellite in the Caribbean."	South Vietnamese riot police, wielding clubs, forcibly disperse a Saigon sit-down demonstration by about 1,000 Buddhists.
July 18			The Syrian army crushes an attempt by pro-Nasser elements to overthrow the ruling Baathist government. As many as 70 persons are reported killed and several hundred others arrested. . . . A special commission of the recently formed Organization of African Unity recommends that all Angolan nationalist groups join together under the leadership of the National Front for the Liberation of Angola, headed by Holden Roberto.	The U.S. and Mexico agree on a settlement on the long-disputed El Chamizal border area between El Paso, Tex. and Ciudad Juarez, Chihuahua.	
July 19	Soviet Premier Khrushchev says that progress in the nuclear test-ban talks opens the way for further negotiations on a broad range of cold war issues. . . . In a Kremlin address Premier Khrushchev denounces China's attack on his leadership and policies. He accuses China of attempting to return the world communist movement to the period of Stalinist rule-by-terror.	Another major coal strike, the third in the last 15 months, breaks out in Spain's northwest province of Asturias.			
July 20	The Soviet-Chinese ideological talks underway in Moscow since July 5 are ended after apparently failing to reconcile any of the outstanding differences. . . . The *Peking People's Daily* denounces the current Moscow test-ban treaty talks claiming that any prospective accord will amount to "capitulation in the face of imperialist nuclear blackmail."				

A	B	C	D	E
Includes developments that affect more than one world region, international organizations and important meetings of major world leaders.	Includes all domestic and regional developments in Europe, including the Soviet Union, Turkey, Cyprus and Malta.	Includes all domestic and regional developments in Africa and the Middle East, including Iraq and Iran and excluding Cyprus, Turkey and Afghanistan.	Includes all domestic and regional developments in Latin America, the Caribbean and Canada.	Includes all domestic and regional developments in Asia and Pacific nations, extending from Afghanistan through all the Pacific Islands, except Hawaii.

U.S. Politics & Social Issues	U.S. Foreign Policy & Defense	U.S. Economy & Environment	Science, Technology & Nature	Culture, Leisure & Life Style	
					July 15
The Senate Judiciary Committee begins hearings on the administration's omnibus civil rights measures as incorporated in Senate bill 1731. Sen. Sam Ervin Jr. says the proposals are unconstitutional whether based on the commerce clause or the 14th Amendment. . . . A U.S. Civil Service Commission spokesman confirms that 12 Black Muslims have been fired from federal jobs for admitting that their first allegiance was not to the U.S., but to the projected State of Islam.		The Federal Reserve System announces an increase in the discount rate charged FRB member banks from 3% to 3 1/2%. The move is aimed at "minimizing short-term capital outflows prompted by higher interest rates in other countries."		*Blitzen*, a 56-foot sloop owned by Bill and Tom Schoendor of Milwaukee, Wis. wins the 333-mile Chicago to Mackinac Island yacht race.	July 16
Pres. Kennedy tells a Washington news conference that the planned Negro March on Washington is in "the great tradition of peaceable assembly.". . . A plan endorsed by Mayor Robert Wagner to increase the number of Negroes in the N.Y.C. construction trades is rejected by the AFL-CIO Building & Construction Trades Council. Council Pres. Peter Brennan says the unions will not accept "dictation by any outside group."	Pres. Kennedy says that the U.S., despite its concern over the handling of Buddhist disorders, will not withdraw its military support from South Vietnam, explaining that withdrawal "would mean a collapse not only of South Vietnam but Southeast Asia."	The SEC sends Congress a report recommending reforms for various alleged abuses in the operations of the nation's securities markets.	The U.S. FDA bans further interstate distribution of the controversial anti-cancer drug Krebiozen. The FDA had earlier refused to approve the drug for commercial sale on the grounds that it was ineffective. The FDA's decision has been supported by the National Cancer Institute and the American Medical Association.		July 17
A Gallup Poll indicates that three out of four Southern Negro and white voters believe that widespread integration will come to the South within 10 years.	In a Miami Beach speech to the Inter-American Press Association, Pres. Kennedy reaffirms his support for continuation of Alliance for Progress aid to Latin America.	Labor Dept. statistics indicate that the average wages of U.S. factory workers have exceeded $100 a week for the first time. . . . In a special message to Congress on the U.S.'s payments position, Pres. Kennedy proposes a tax on foreign investments as a means of decreasing the U.S. deficit.			July 18
White House discloses that Pres. Kennedy mailed letters to the presidents of thousands of school boards asking their help "in solving the grave civil rights problems faced by this nation.". . . The Justice Dept. files suits charging discrimination against Negro voters in two Alabama counties.	Defense Secy. McNamara, commenting on the arrest of Soviet agents in the U.S. and other Western countries, says he knows of no recent case in which a foreign spy obtained any critical military or policy secrets. . . . U.S. Navy Yeoman Nelson Drummond is convicted by a federal jury in New York of conspiracy to spy for the USSR.		NASA research pilot Joseph Walker flies the experimental X-15 rocket plane to a record altitude of 66.3 miles.		July 19
		Budget Bureau preliminary report estimates that government spending in fiscal 1963 exceeded revenues by $6.2 billion, $2.6 billion less than the deficit estimated by the administration in January.	The world's largest known rocket engine, a prototype for the Air Force's Titan 3C space vehicle, is fired successfully in a static test in Coyote, Calif. The motor reportedly developed more than 1,000,000 pounds of thrust during the test.		July 20

F	G	H	I	J
Includes elections, federal-state relations, civil rights and liberties, crime, the judiciary, education, health care, poverty, urban affairs and population.	*Includes formation and debate of U.S. foreign and defense policies, veterans' affairs and defense spending. (Relations with specific foreign countries are usually found under the region concerned.)*	*Includes business, labor, agriculture, taxation, transportation, consumer affairs, monetary and fiscal policy, natural resources, and pollution.*	*Includes worldwide scientific, medical and technological developments, natural phenomena, U.S. weather, natural disasters, and accidents.*	*Includes the arts, religion, scholarship, communications media, sports, entertainment, fashions, fads and social life.*

	World Affairs	Europe	Africa & the Middle East	The Americas	Asia & the Pacific
July 21					
July 22			UAR Pres. Gamal Abdel Nasser renounces the April 17 agreement to merge Egypt, Syria and Iraq into a new United Arab Republic. Nasser cites continued rule in Syria by what he calls the "fascist" Baath party as the reason for his action.	British Colonial Office announces that British Honduras will be granted internal self-rule Jan. 1, 1964. . . . Guatemala breaks diplomatic relations with Britain because of Britain's decision to grant home-rule to British Honduras. The action is intended as a reaffirmation of Guatemala's claim to British Honduras.	India announces acceptance of a plan for the temporary stationing in India of American and British aircraft to guard against a possible "large scale air attack by Communist China."
July 23					
July 24	Moscow sources report considerable progress in the U.S.-British-Soviet negotiations on a nuclear test-ban treaty. Observers say that the growing concern of both sides over the spread of nuclear armaments is the principle factor underlying the recent breakthrough in the long-deadlocked talks.	Victor Marijnen is sworn-in as the new prime minister of the Netherlands, replacing retiring P.M. Jan Eduard de Quay.		The Cuban government issues a decree expropriating the U.S. embassy building in Havana. Swiss diplomatic officials, who currently occupy the building, say they will defy a Cuban evacuation order.	
July 25	The USSR, Britain and the U.S. initial, in Moscow, a treaty prohibiting nuclear weapons tests in the atmosphere, outer-space and under water. The agreement also expresses hopes for a future accord on underground tests. The participating nations further pledge to pursue negotiations toward a non-aggression treaty between NATO and Warsaw Pact powers.	The French National Assembly approves a government bill limiting the strike rights of transport and public utility workers. Over 10,000 Parisians participate in a mass protest against the measure.			
July 26	In a nationally televised address, Pres. Kennedy hails yesterday's nuclear test-ban agreement as "a step away from war" and "a victory for mankind." A similar expression of approval by Premier Khrushchev is carried in the Soviet press.				The Indian Foreign Ministry reports a build-up of Chinese Communist military forces along the India-China border.
July 27	State Undersecy. W. Averell Harriman, recently returned U.S. negotiator of the Moscow test-ban treaty, tells reporters in Hyannisport, Mass. that Khrushchev had agreed to the treaty because he "wanted to show the Chinese that his policy of co-existence could produce some results."				

A	B	C	D	E
Includes developments that affect more than one world region, international organizations and important meetings of major world leaders.	Includes all domestic and regional developments in Europe, including the Soviet Union, Turkey, Cyprus and Malta.	Includes all domestic and regional developments in Africa and the Middle East, including Iraq and Iran and excluding Cyprus, Turkey and Afghanistan.	Includes all domestic and regional developments in Latin America, the Caribbean and Canada.	Includes all domestic and regional developments in Asia and Pacific nations, extending from Afghanistan through all the Pacific Islands, except Hawaii.

U.S. Politics & Social Issues	U.S. Foreign Policy & Defense	U.S. Economy & Environment	Science, Technology & Nature	Culture, Leisure & Life Style	
		The Commerce Dept. reports that total U.S. personal incomes rose to a record annual rate of $462.1 billion in June.	Dr. George Mueller is named by NASA to head the U.S. lunar landing program.	Valery Brumel of the USSR sets a new world high-jump record of 7 ft. 5 3/4 in. in Moscow during a two-day dual U.S.-Soviet track meet, won by the U.S. 119 to 114. . . . Richard Petty wins the 100-mile Grand National Stock Car race at Bridgehampton, N.Y. . . . Jack Nicklaus wins the 45th PGA golf championship in Dallas.	**July 21**
	The Navy discloses that it has orbited a boom-type satellite designed to keep one face always directed at the earth. Date of launch and purpose of satellite are not revealed. . . . *Izvestia* reports that Victor Norris Hamilton, a former U.S. National Security Agency employee, has requested political asylum in the USSR.	Pres. Kennedy asks Congress to empower the ICC to settle the nation's railroad work-rules dispute. The President's proposed legislation would bar strikes and lockouts during implementation of ICC recommendations. . . . The U.S. Geological Survey reports that tritium-a radioactive substance-has been found in record quantities in U.S. rainwater during the past year as a result of nuclear testing.		Charles (Sonny) Liston, 30, retains his world heavyweight boxing championship by knocking out ex-champ Floyd Patterson in the first minutes of a scheduled 15-round bout in Las Vegas.	**July 22**
Civil rights dominate the 55th National Governors' Conference, being held in Miami Beach, Fla. Democrats turn back Republican efforts to get the conference to consider a strong civil rights resolution. . . . AFL-CIO Building & Construction Trades Council Pres. Peter Brennan announces the establishment of a biracial committee, with some outside members, to pass on the qualifications of Negroes applying to be apprentices or journeymen. . . . The recently-elected Birmingham, Ala. city council repeals all six of its existing racial segregation ordinances.	Navy Secy. Fred Korth appears before the Senate Permanent Investigations Subcommittee to deny that he showed any favoritism in the awarding of the TFX fighter plane contract to General Dynamics Corp. Korth is a former resident of Fort Worth Texas, site of the General Dynamics TFX project. . . . State Secy. Rusk gives a closed-door briefing to the Senate Foreign Relations Committee on the progress being made at the Moscow test-ban talks.	The American Association of Railroads announces its support of the President's proposed legislation for settling the railroad work-rules controversy. . . .			**July 23**
Harvard Law School Dean Erwin Griswold tells the Senate Commerce Committee that the Constitution's commerce clause and the 14 Amendment both support Congress's right to ban bias in public accommodations.	The Air Force discloses that two secret satellites were sent into polar orbit by means of a single Thor-Agena rocket fired from Vandenberg Air Force Base June 27.	The Commerce Clearing House reports that state tax collections totalled $20.6 billion in 1962, up 7.9% from 1961.			**July 24**
		The nation's railroads announce that they will postpone until August 29 work-rules changes that they had scheduled to put into effect July 30. The delay is designed to give Congress more time to consider Pres. Kennedy's proposals for resolving the work-rules dispute.	Dr. Ugo Cerletti, 85, Italian neuro-psychiatrist and developer of electroshock therapy for mental ailments, dies in Rome.		**July 25**
The Labor Dept.'s Bureau of Apprenticeship issues new rules barring racial discrimination in federally sponsored apprenticeship programs. . . . Defense Secy. Robert McNamara authorizes military commanders to designate as "off limits" areas near bases where "relentless discrimination" is practiced against Negroes.		The Bureau of Labor Statistics reports that the average weekly take-home pay of a factory worker with three dependants rose in June to a record $88.37. . . . Pres. Kennedy signs a fiscal 1964 Interior Dept. appropriation bill totalling $958,456,500, about $70 million less than he initially requested.	The Yugoslav city of Skoplje is devastated by a series of severe earthquakes. First reports indicate that as many as 2,000 of the city's 170,000 inhabitants may have been killed. . . . An experimental Syncom II communications satellite, designed to achieve a "synchronous" orbit matching the speed of the earth's rotation, is successfully launched from Cape Canaveral.	A two-week World Council of Churches conference concludes in Montreal after devoting most of its time to an examination of the historical and doctrinal issues which separate Christian churches.	**July 26**
National Urban League director Whitney Young tells the group's annual convention in Los Angeles that past racial discrimination entitles Negroes to "indemnification" in the form of needed social services and economic preferment.		For the fourth day, railroad union leaders appear before the Senate Commerce Committee to express their opposition to Pres. Kennedy's proposed legislation to settle the work-rules dispute.			**July 27**

F	G	H	I	J
Includes elections, federal-state relations, civil rights and liberties, crime, the judiciary, education, health care, poverty, urban affairs and population.	*Includes formation and debate of U.S. foreign and defense policies, veterans' affairs and defense spending. (Relations with specific foreign countries are usually found under the region concerned.)*	*Includes business, labor, agriculture, taxation, transportation, consumer affairs, monetary and fiscal policy, natural resources, and pollution.*	*Includes worldwide scientific, medical and technological developments, natural phenomena, U.S. weather, natural disasters, and accidents.*	*Includes the arts, religion, scholarship, communications media, sports, entertainment, fashions, fads and social life.*

	World Affairs	Europe	Africa & the Middle East	The Americas	Asia & the Pacific
July 28	Japan joins Australia, India, Iran, the UAR, Finland and Denmark in announcing its readiness to accept the Moscow nuclear test-ban treaty.			Fernando Belaunde Terry is inaugurated as Peru's 34th constitutional president. Belaunde, described as a political moderate, takes over from a Peruvian military junta which has ruled since July 1962.	Peking radio denies recent Indian claims of a Chinese troop build-up on the Sino-Indian border.
July 29	French Pres. de Gaulle confirms that France will not sign the limited test-ban agreement reached by the U.S., Britain and the USSR July 25. He also denounces the Anglo-U.S. agreement to discuss with the USSR an East-West non-aggression pact and other issues concerning Europe.			Peru and Venezuela resume diplomatic relations. Venezuela severed diplomatic relations July 17, 1962 after the military junta seized control in Peru.	Two U.S. soldiers are killed by a small group of North Koreans allegedly operating in the South Korean section of the demilitarized zone.
July 30					Over 60,000 South Vietnamese Buddhists participate in countrywide demonstrations in memory of Quang Duc, a Buddhist priest who burned himself in protest against government policies. . . . A serious clash between U.S. and North Korean troops is reported along the Korean demilitarized zone. Eight soldiers on both sides are reported killed.
July 31	Communist China issues a statement denouncing the Moscow test-ban treaty as "dirty fraud" perpetrated by the U.S., Britain and the USSR to "consolidate their nuclear monopoly."	Dr. Stephen Ward, a central figure in the so-called "call girl" scandal exposed by the Profumo investigations, is convicted in London of having lived off the earnings of prostitution.	The U.N. Security Council votes 8-0 (U.S., Britain and France abstaining) to impose a partial ban on arms sales to Portugal. The action follows a lengthy debate on alleged Portuguese repression in its African colonies.		The Argentine Electoral College elects Arturo Illia of the moderate Popular Radical Party to succeed José Maria Guido as Argentina's president on expiration of the latter's term in October.
Aug. 1		A young East German couple is shot down by Communist border guards in full view of hundreds of vacationers and foreign tourists near the West German resort of Hohegeiss. . . . British Colonial Secy. Duncan Sandys says that Malta would be granted its independence by May 31, 1964 even if Maltese leaders have not agreed on a constitution by that date.			
Aug. 2	The Canadian Trade Ministry announces that Communist China has agreed to buy three to five million long tons of wheat over the next three years.			The U.S. announces the end of all American assistance to the Duvalier regime in Haiti.	
Aug. 3	The USSR issues a statement denouncing Communist China's criticism of the Moscow test-ban treaty as tantamount to "actual connivance with those who advocate world thermonuclear war."	Dr. Stephen Ward, a central figure in the Profumo-Keeler vice scandal, dies of a drug overdose taken after his July 31 conviction on morals charges.			The U.N. Korean Command warns of sharp reprisals if North Korea continues its recent attacks on U.S. forces in the demilitarized zone.
Aug. 4			Government communiques issued in Baghdad claim that Iraqi troops have driven Kurdish guerrillas from large sections of northwest Iraq.		

A	B	C	D	E
Includes developments that affect more than one world region, international organizations and important meetings of major world leaders.	*Includes all domestic and regional developments in Europe, including the Soviet Union, Turkey, Cyprus and Malta.*	*Includes all domestic and regional developments in Africa and the Middle East, including Iraq and Iran and excluding Cyprus, Turkey and Afghanistan.*	*Includes all domestic and regional developments in Latin America, the Caribbean and Canada.*	*Includes all domestic and regional developments in Asia and Pacific nations, extending from Afghanistan through all the Pacific Islands, except Hawaii.*

U.S. Politics & Social Issues	U.S. Foreign Policy & Defense	U.S. Economy & Environment	Science, Technology & Nature	Culture, Leisure & Life Style	
	George F. Kennan, 59, retires as U.S. ambassador to Yugoslavia.				July 28
	Sen. Barry Goldwater (R, Ariz.) tells reporters in New York that he has serious "reservations" about the nuclear test-ban pact.		The White House Office of Science & Technology proposes a $2.3 billion program of oceanographic research. . . . NASA officials report that Syncom II communications satellite launched July 27 is performing "extremely well" although it has not precisely achieved the planned synchronous orbit.	Arnold Palmer defeats Jack Nicklaus in an 18-hole playoff to win the Western Open in Chicago.	July 29
Demonstrators protesting alleged job discrimination in N.Y.C.'s building trades lie down in front of heavy equipment to disrupt construction at a hospital site. The action is viewed as a potentially significant turning point in the tactics of the non-violent civil rights movement.			Edwin McMillan of the University of California's Lawrence Radiation Laboratory and Vladimir Veksler of the Moscow Joint Institute for Nuclear Research are named co-winners of the sixth annual Atoms for Peace Award.	The N.Y. Mets end a 22-game losing streak with a five-run win over the Los Angeles Dodgers.	July 30
The Census Bureau reports that in 1962 the average Negro male worker earned about 51% of the amount earned by the average white worker. In 1951 Negroes averaged about 62% of the income received by their white counterparts.	The Federation of American Scientists, formed after World War II by scientists who had worked on the first A-bomb project, announce their support for ratification of the Moscow treaty. . . . The White House says that Pres. Kennedy's mail is running 12-1 in favor of the nuclear test-ban treaty.				July 31
A three-judge federal court in New Orleans orders the desegregation of the city's public parks, playgrounds and cultural facilities. . . . Pres. Kennedy tells his Washington news conference that a subsiding of civil rights demonstrations, "particularly in that extreme form," would be "a good thing.". . . Henry Steeger, white publisher of *Argosy* magazine, is elected to a fourth term as president of the National Urban League.		Pres. Kennedy, speaking at a Washington news conference, appeals for a greater public effort to reduce the high school student drop-out rate.			Aug. 1
	Democratic Sen. J. William Fulbright launches a Senate floor attack on the foreign policy views of Republican Sen. Barry Goldwater, claiming that Goldwater favors a "bold policy of co-annihilation."			The College All-Stars defeat NFL-champion Green Bay Packers, 20-17, in Chicago.	Aug. 2
	Pres. Kennedy accepts the resignation of U.S. Amb.-to-Panama Joseph Farland. Farland reportedly disagreed with U.S. foreign aid policies.		The U.S. FDA announces that Enovid, a progesterone hormone birth control pill, has been proven safe enough to remain on the market. The FDA estimates that more than two million American women are currently using some type of birth control pill.		Aug. 3
A job agreement opening Cleveland construction unions to Negro journeymen and trainees is signed by labor, Negro and construction industry representatives. . . . The Republican Citizens Committee announces creation of a Critical Issues Council to develop position papers on major national issues. The council is to be headed by Milton S. Eisenhower.		Chemical workers end a year-long strike against the Shell Oil Co.'s Houston facility. The dispute involved company plans to institute work-rule changes at the newly automated plant.		New York Mets pitcher Roger Craig absorbs his 18th straight loss, to tie a modern National League record. . . . West Ham United of London defeats Gornik of Poland to win the International Soccer League Championship in New York.	Aug. 4

F	G	H	I	J
Includes elections, federal-state relations, civil rights and liberties, crime, the judiciary, education, health care, poverty, urban affairs and population.	*Includes formation and debate of U.S. foreign and defense policies, veterans' affairs and defense spending. (Relations with specific foreign countries are usually found under the region concerned.)*	*Includes business, labor, agriculture, taxation, transportation, consumer affairs, monetary and fiscal policy, natural resources, and pollution.*	*Includes worldwide scientific, medical and technological developments, natural phenomena, U.S. weather, natural disasters, and accidents.*	*Includes the arts, religion, scholarship, communications media, sports, entertainment, fashions, fads and social life.*

	World Affairs	Europe	Africa & the Middle East	The Americas	Asia & the Pacific
Aug. 5	The three-power nuclear test-ban treaty is formally signed in Moscow by U.S. State Secy. Dean Rusk, Soviet Foreign Min. Andrei Gromyko and British Foreign Secy. Lord Home. At least 33 other nations have publicly announced their support for the treaty.	Six bombs explode in Italy's South Tyrol area. The bombings are attributed to terrorists seeking self-rule for the region.		Haitian exiles announce the landing of an anti-Duvalier invasion force somewhere in northern Haiti. Details of the mission are not disclosed.	
Aug. 6	Moscow sources report that State Secy. Rusk has informed Foreign Min. Gromyko that the U.S. is ready to begin talks on Soviet proposals to prevent surprise attack, but that negotiations on NATO-Warsaw Pact non-aggression treaty must be postponed until all NATO members have been fully consulted.	Kennedy administration sources report that Pres. de Gaulle has rejected a U.S. offer to help in the development of a French nuclear striking force if France will agree to sign the test-ban treaty.		An emergency session of the OAS Council is called in Washington to hear Haitian charges that yesterday's reported rebel invasion had been staged with the Dominican Republic's "complicity." Dominican officials deny the charge.	Pakistan and India agree on the demarcation line of Berubari, a small Indian enclave which jutts into East Pakistan.
Aug. 7		West Germany reports that 16,456 East Germans have escaped to the West since construction of the Berlin Wall in August 1961. The report says that 65 persons are known to have been killed in escape attempts. . . . Yevgeny Yevtushenko's *A Precocious Autobiography* is published in the West without Soviet government authorization.	The U.N. Security Council votes 9-0 (Britain and France abstaining) to recommend a complete embargo on arms shipments to South Africa. A second resolution urging a trade boycott of South Africa failed to receive the necessary seven votes for passage.	The Haitian embassy in Washington reports that the Aug. 5 anti-government invaders have been completely routed from their positions in northeast Haiti.	Madame Ngo Dinh Nhu, wife of the South Vietnamese secret police chief and sister-in-law of President Diem, says that the Saigon government should ignore Communist-sponsored Buddhist troublemakers.
Aug. 8	East Germany signs the Soviet copy of the limited test-ban treaty. The U.S. and Britain say the signing does not imply any Western recognition of the East German regime.	The West German Interior Ministry acknowledges that its security division employs "about 16 former Nazis who cannot be dismissed because of the security risk."			
Aug. 9			A joint Syrian-Iraqi communique calls on UAR Pres. Nasser to cooperate in stopping a deterioration of relations among Arab states.		Burma's ruling Revolutionary Council, headed by Gen. Ne Win, announces that 11 prominent political leaders have been arrested in the interest of "preserving internal order". The 11 are believed to have been the last major active opponents of the Ne Win regime.
Aug. 10			Spain announces that its African territories, known collectively as Spanish Guinea, will receive partial autonomy in the near future.		
Aug. 11	Washington sources report that the U.S-Soviet contacts which led to the test-ban treaty are continuing on an intermittent basis.		A gradualist approach to African unity is reported to have prevailed in the first foreign ministers' conference on the new 32-nation Organization of African Unity. The meeting, held in Dakar, Senegal, began Aug. 2.		
Aug. 12			Portuguese Premier Antonio de Oliveira Salazar declares that Portugal is prepared to fight "to the limit" to defend its African territories of Angola, Mozambique and Portuguese Guinea. . . . The industry ministry of the UAR announces the nationalization of 240 industries—embracing domestic and foreign firms.	The U.S. State Dept. approves the extradition to Venezuela of ex-Venezuelan Pres. Marcos Perez Jimenez. Perez Jimenez, who has been in the U.S. since his overthrow in 1958, faces charges of embezzling more than $13 million.	
	A	**B**	**C**	**D**	**E**
	Includes developments that affect more than one world region, international organizations and important meetings of major world leaders.	*Includes all domestic and regional developments in Europe, including the Soviet Union, Turkey, Cyprus and Malta.*	*Includes all domestic and regional developments in Africa and the Middle East, including Iraq and Iran and excluding Cyprus, Turkey and Afghanistan.*	*Includes all domestic and regional developments in Latin America, the Caribbean and Canada.*	*Includes all domestic and regional developments in Asia and Pacific nations, extending from Afghanistan through all the Pacific Islands, except Hawaii.*

U.S. Politics & Social Issues	U.S. Foreign Policy & Defense	U.S. Economy & Environment	Science, Technology & Nature	Culture, Leisure & Life Style	
The Alabama State Board of Education orders Bible reading as part of the regular course of study in the public schools.			Yugoslav officials report that the final death toll from the July 26 earthquake in Skoplje numbers 1,011.	Craig Breedlove, driving a jet-car named Spirit of America, sets a world land-speed record of 407.45 mph. at Bonneville Salt Flats, Utah. . . . John Pennel of Miami, Fla. sets a new world pole-vault record of 16 ft. 10 1/4 in. at a U.S.-British track meet in London.	Aug. 5
Sen. Barry Goldwater (R, Ariz.) says that Gov. Nelson Rockefeller's recent attacks on allegedly pro-Goldwater right-wing extremists is an example of "the old Democratic technique of guilt by association." Goldwater adds that while he disagrees with some objectives of the John Birch Society he will not "disavow their support on that account."	Pres. Kennedy appoints William Rogers, 36, as deputy U.S. coordinator of the Alliance for Progress.	The House passes a bill (HR4955) intended to more than triple federal aid to vocational education. Republicans fail in an effort to add an anti-race bias amendment to the measure.			Aug. 6
Mrs. John F. Kennedy gives birth to a 4 pound 10 1/2 ounce boy—Patrick Bouvier Kennedy—by Caesarean section at Otis Air Force Base Hospital on Cape Cod. The baby, five and-a-half weeks premature, is rushed to Boston Children's Hospital for treatment of prematurity and hyaline membrane disease.				Dukla of Czechoslovakia defeats West Ham United of London to win the American Challenge Soccer Cup for the third straight year.	Aug. 7
The NAACP describes the Aug. 5 Cleveland agreement on increasing minorities in construction trades as the "most significant breakthrough" since Negro job-picketing began.	Pres. Kennedy submits the Moscow test-ban treaty to the Senate for ratification. In an accompanying message Kennedy asserts that acceptance of the treaty will in no way endanger U.S. national security or affect the West's superiority in the balance of atomic strength. . . . The House Foreign Affairs Committee releases a report on the efficacy of U.S. aid programs. The report recommends cuts in U.S. aid to the Middle East, India and Pakistan, and Indonesia.	The special investigating commission of the SEC recommends that contractual mutual fund purchase plans be outlawed on the grounds that they are unfair to small investors.		A gang of 20-30 masked robbers steal more than $7 million from a Glasgow-to-London mail train in what is described as the largest theft in history.	Aug. 8
The two-day-old son of Pres. and Mrs. Kennedy dies in Boston of hyaline membrane disease. It is the third such loss for Mrs. Kennedy who had suffered a miscarriage in 1955 and had been delivered of a stillborn child in 1956.	Sen. Henry M. Jackson (D, Wash.) says that he has serious concerns about the effect of the Moscow test-ban treaty on U.S. military security.				Aug. 9
Estes Kefauver, 60, U.S. Senator (D, Tenn.) since 1949 and Democratic vice presidential candidate in 1956, dies in Bethesda, Md. following a heart attack.			A landslide destroys four Nepalese villages, killing at least 150 persons.	Dick Tiger of Nigeria retains the world middleweight championship by scoring a seventh-round TKO over ex-titleholder Gene Fullmer in Nigeria. . . . Don Schollander, 17, of Santa Clara Calif. sets a world 200-meter freestyle record of one minute 59 seconds at the AAU outdoor swimming championships in Chicago.	Aug. 10
James Hood, one of the first two Negroes admitted to the University of Alabama, withdraws from the school "to avoid a complete mental and physical breakdown."			U.S. Agricultural Secy. Orville Freeman, meeting with Yugoslav Pres. Tito, discloses that the U.S. will furnish $50 million to help rebuild the earthquake-devastated city of Skoplje.	Tom Weiskopf, 20, wins the 61st Western Amateur golf championship in Benton Harbor, Mich.	Aug. 11
U.S. District Judge H. Hobart Grooms orders the Huntsville, Ala. school board to accept four Negro children into its all-white public schools.	The Senate Foreign Relations Committee opens hearings on ratification of the U.S.-British-Soviet nuclear test-ban treaty.	Treasury Secy. Douglas Dillon presents the House Ways and Means Committee with a revised version of the administration's tax-cut program. The proposed revisions would lessen tax-cuts for lower income persons and would slightly increase the reductions for upper income brackets.		Long-time St. Louis Cardinal star Stan Musial, 42, announces that he will retire from baseball at the end of this season.	Aug. 12

F	G	H	I	J
Includes elections, federal-state relations, civil rights and liberties, crime, the judiciary, education, health care, poverty, urban affairs and population.	Includes formation and debate of U.S. foreign and defense policies, veterans' affairs and defense spending. (Relations with specific foreign countries are usually found under the region concerned.)	Includes business, labor, agriculture, taxation, transportation, consumer affairs, monetary and fiscal policy, natural resources, and pollution.	Includes worldwide scientific, medical and technological developments, natural phenomena, U.S. weather, natural disasters, and accidents.	Includes the arts, religion, scholarship, communications media, sports, entertainment, fashions, fads and social life.

	World Affairs	Europe	Africa & the Middle East	The Americas	Asia & the Pacific
Aug. 13		A brief riot by a group of West Berlin youths marks an otherwise "quiet" observance of the second anniversary of the Berlin Wall.	Ferhat Abbas resigns as president of the Algerian National Assembly to protest what he calls Premier Ahmed Ben Bella's constitutional proposal for "one-man rule."		Indian P.M. Nehru announces that the "generous concessions" that India had offered Pakistan in the March-May talks on Kashmir have been officially withdrawn. India had reportedly proposed a division of Kashmir along the U.N. cease-fire line of 1948.
Aug. 14	Charles Stelle, chief U.S. delegate to the Geneva disarmament talks, discloses that the USSR has rejected an American proposal for an immediate joint-halt in the production of missile materials for weapons purposes.				
Aug. 15		English police arrest five persons in connection with the Aug. 8 Glasgow-to-London mail train robbery. About $800,000 of the more than $7 million taken in the robbery has been recovered. . . . Stefan Cardinal Wyszynski, Roman Catholic primate of Poland, renews his denunciation of government efforts to curtail church activities.	Fulbert Youlou resigns as president of the Congo Republic (Brazzaville) in the face of violent worker opposition to his economic and political policies. Ex-Planning Min. Alphonse Massamba-Debat succeeds as premier.	Gen. Alfredo Stroessner is sworn-in for his third term as president of Paraguay.	
Aug. 16	U.S. State Secy. Rusk says that American and Soviet negotiators will soon begin discussions of proposals for an agreement to prevent surprise attacks.			Three anti-Castro Cubans are executed by firing squad on charges of attempting to carry out CIA-planned sabotage.	U.S. State Secy. Rusk tells Washington newsmen that the U.S. is concerned that the South Vietnamese Buddhist crisis is undermining the government's war against Viet Cong guerrillas. . . . A 71-year-old Buddhist monk burns himself to death in protest against the religious policies of South Vietnam's Diem regime. It is the fifth self-immolation protest in the last six days.
Aug. 17					
Aug. 18				Haitian Foreign Min. Rene Chalmers says in Washington that government troops Aug. 15 repulsed a new exile invasion of Haiti.	
Aug. 19	West Germany signs the Moscow test-ban treaty after being given repeated U.S. assurances that East Germany would gain no recognition by its participation in the accord.			Haiti asks the OAS to appoint a military committee to supervise the Dominican Republic-Haiti border to prevent infiltration by anti-Duvalier subversives.	
Aug. 20		Soviet Premier Khrushchev arrives in Yugoslavia for a two-week working vacation that is expected to include extensive political consultations with Pres. Tito. . . . British Laborite Anthony Wedgewood Benn wins a Commons seat in a Bristol by-election. Benn, who succeeded his father as Viscount Stansgate, is the first person to seek a Commons seat under a new law (passed July 31) permitting peers to relinquish their titles for life.	The Israeli government blames Syrian agents for the ambush slaying of two Israeli farmers near the northern tip of the Sea of Galilee. It is the latest in a recent series of Syrian-Israeli border incidents.	Pres. Kennedy tells reporters that the number of Soviet troops in Cuba has declined since June.	

A	B	C	D	E
Includes developments that affect more than one world region, international organizations and important meetings of major world leaders.	Includes all domestic and regional developments in Europe, including the Soviet Union, Turkey, Cyprus and Malta.	Includes all domestic and regional developments in Africa and the Middle East, including Iraq and Iran and excluding Cyprus, Turkey and Afghanistan.	Includes all domestic and regional developments in Latin America, the Caribbean and Canada.	Includes all domestic and regional developments in Asia and Pacific nations, extending from Afghanistan through all the Pacific Islands, except Hawaii.

U.S. Politics & Social Issues	U.S. Foreign Policy & Defense	U.S. Economy & Environment	Science, Technology & Nature	Culture, Leisure & Life Style	
The AFL-CIO Executive Council, meeting in Unity House, Pa. backs a generally worded civil rights resolution, but stops short of endorsing the Aug. 28 march on Washington. The failure to take a stronger stand draws protest from UAW Pres. Walter Reuther and from A. Philip Randolph.	Defense Secy. McNamara assures the Senate Foreign Relations Committee that the Moscow nuclear test-ban treaty has the full approval of the Joint Chiefs of Staff. McNamara stresses that the accord will not reduce the U.S.'s nuclear superiority.			The Wisconsin Evangelical Lutheran Synod, with 250,000 members in 17 states, votes to withdraw from the Lutheran Synodical Conference in protest against alleged doctrinal liberalism in the Lutheran Church-Missouri Synod.	Aug. 13
The Senate, by a 37-44 vote, passes and sends to the House an administration-backed bill (S1321) to establish a domestic peace corps called the National Service Corps. . . . Virginia Gov. Albertis Harrison announces the formation of a privately financed organization to provide schooling for Negro children in Prince Edward County, where public schools have been closed since 1959 to avoid court-ordered desegregation.			A discovery of the 34th and last elementary particle in the atom's nucleus, the anti-XI-O, is announced in *Physical Review Letters*.		Aug. 14
		The AFL-CIO Executive Council urges increased federal expenditures for public works and lower interest rates in order to prevent another economic recession in 1964.		Playwright and movie writer Clifford Odets, 57, dies of cancer in Los Angeles.	Aug. 15
The American Bar Association, meeting in annual convention in Chicago, declares opposition to three "states' rights" amendments to the U.S. Constitution currently being circulated among the states. One of the proposed amendments would create a special court made up of state chief justices with power to review and reverse Supreme Court decisions.	CIA Director John McCone testifies before the Senate Foreign Relations Committee that the test-ban pact presents no threat to continued U.S. superiority over the USSR.	A six-year contract containing a no-strike pledge is signed in New York by the AFL-CIO National Maritime Union and representatives of 34 shipping lines.	The U.S. and the USSR announce final approval of an agreement to cooperate in weather, communications and magnetic satellite programs.		Aug. 16
			Fifty-five people are lost when the ferry boat Midori Maru sinks in the China Sea off Naha, Okinawa. Local fisherman and military aircraft pick up 185 survivors.		Aug. 17
James Meredith becomes the first Negro to graduate from the University of Mississippi in its 115-year history.					Aug. 18
N.Y.C. Mayor Robert Wagner issues an order granting a one-day paid vacation to city employees wishing to participate in the Aug. 28 march on Washington.		The Commerce Dept. reports that the deficit in the U.S. balance of payments rose to a record annual rate of $5.2 billion in the second quarter of 1963.			Aug. 19
In answer to a press question, Pres. Kennedy says that he is opposed to establishment of racial quotas to ensure minorities a fair proportion of jobs in specific industries. . . . Pres. Kennedy confirms at his news conference that he has agreed to meet with leaders of the civil rights march on Washington scheduled to take place Aug. 28.	Nuclear scientist Edward Teller voices his opposition to the test-ban treaty in an appearance before the Senate Foreign Relations Committee. Teller says the U.S. needs to continue atmospheric testing to complete development of an anti-missile, an area in which he claims the USSR has a substantial lead. . . . Pres. Kennedy tells reporters that the cut in foreign aid voted recently by the House "involves the security" of the U.S. and "the balance of power all over the world."	Pres. Kennedy tells his news conference that the increasing health of the economy depends on prompt congressional approval of his tax-cut proposals. . . . The Licensed Beverages Industries, Inc. report that per capita consumption of liquor in the U.S. averaged 1.37 gallons in 1962, about 30% less than the average established for the years 1920-1933.		A federal grand jury in Atlanta awards ex-University of Georgia athletic director Wally Butts a $3 million libel award arising from a March 23 *Saturday Evening Post* article accusing him of "rigging" the Georgia-Alabama football game of Sept. 22, 1962.	Aug. 20
F	**G**	**H**	**I**	**J**	
Includes elections, federal-state relations, civil rights and liberties, crime, the judiciary, education, health care, poverty, urban affairs and population.	*Includes formation and debate of U.S. foreign and defense policies, veterans' affairs and defense spending. (Relations with specific foreign countries are usually found under the region concerned.)*	*Includes business, labor, agriculture, taxation, transportation, consumer affairs, monetary and fiscal policy, natural resources, and pollution.*	*Includes worldwide scientific, medical and technological developments, natural phenomena, U.S. weather, natural disasters, and accidents.*	*Includes the arts, religion, scholarship, communications media, sports, entertainment, fashions, fads and social life.*	

	World Affairs	Europe	Africa & the Middle East	The Americas	Asia & the Pacific
Aug. 21		The NATO Permanent Council begins consideration of proposals for formal negotiations on an East-West non-aggression pact and for an agreement to reduce the danger of surprise attack.	The UAR, Iraq, Saudia Arabia and Jordan pledge full support to Syria in the wake of heightened Israeli-Syrian border tensions.		South Vietnamese troops, acting under a martial law order, attack and occupy Buddhist pagodas throughout the country. Hundreds of Buddhist priests are said to have been beaten and arrested. The U.S. denounces the action as a violation of the Diem government's pledge to seek a reconciliation with dissident Buddhists.
Aug. 22		The Association for Christian-Jewish Cooperation in Germany criticizes West German courts for allegedly giving lenient sentences to convicted Nazi war criminals. . . . The official Czech news agency reports that Rudolf Slansky, ex-Czech CP leader hanged for treason in 1952, has been officially absolved of any treasonable offense.		The Haitian Legislature authorizes Pres. Francois Duvalier to rule by decree for six months.	
Aug. 23			Secy. Gen. U Thant informs an emergency session of the U.N. Security Council that Israel and Syria have accepted a cease-fire agreement worked out by the U.N. Truce Supervision Organization in Palestine.		
Aug. 24					
Aug. 25			An Israeli soldier is killed in an exchange of gunfire with Jordanian troops along the wall of Jerusalem's Jordanian-held Old City.		South Vietnamese sources report that the focus of anti-government unrest is shifting from Buddhists to university students in Saigon and elsewhere. Student-sponsored demonstrations began Aug. 22 and have increased daily. Arrests are said to number in the thousands.
Aug. 26					A U.N. observation team begins a survey in Sarawak and North Borneo to determine whether recent elections in the two British colonies represent a genuine majority support for their membership in the proposed Malaysian Federation. The survey had been requested July 31 by leaders of Indonesia and Malaya.
Aug. 27	Officials report that Yugoslav Pres. Tito and visiting Soviet Premier Khrushchev have completed three days of talks on the Sino-Soviet dispute and on terms for closer Yugoslav relations with the Soviet bloc.				Cambodia severs diplomatic relations with South Vietnam in protest against alleged border violations and the Diem regime's persecution of Buddhists.

A	B	C	D	E
Includes developments that affect more than one world region, international organizations and important meetings of major world leaders.	Includes all domestic and regional developments in Europe, including the Soviet Union, Turkey, Cyprus and Malta.	Includes all domestic and regional developments in Africa and the Middle East, including Iraq and Iran and excluding Cyprus, Turkey and Afghanistan.	Includes all domestic and regional developments in Latin America, the Caribbean and Canada.	Includes all domestic and regional developments in Asia and Pacific nations, extending from Afghanistan through all the Pacific Islands, except Hawaii.

U.S. Politics & Social Issues	U.S. Foreign Policy & Defense	U.S. Economy & Environment	Science, Technology & Nature	Culture, Leisure & Life Style	
	Pres. Kennedy meets with top administration officials to review the South Vietnamese situation in light of the Diem government's attack on Buddhists. . . . Two leading nuclear weapons experts appear before the Senate Foreign Relations Committee to rebut the anti-test-ban treaty testimony given yesterday by Edward Teller.		The *Federal Register* reports that the FDA has tentatively approved the use of radiation to kill insects in wheat and wheat products.		Aug. 21
	Pres. Kennedy attends unveiling ceremonies in Marietta, Ga. to dedicate the new Lockheed C-141 Starlifter, considered the ultimate in military air transportation.		NASA test pilot Joseph Walker pilots the X-15 rocket plane to a record altitude of 67 miles.		Aug. 22
	The Kennedy administration suffers a major setback as the House approves a foreign aid authorization bill (HR7885) after cutting over $1 billion of the $4.5 billion originally requested by the President. . . . In a Senate speech Sen. Goldwater denies administration claims that the limited test-ban treaty will increase U.S. atomic superiority.				Aug. 23
				Don Schollander sets a 200-meter freestyle world record of one minute 58.4 seconds at a U.S.-Japanese swimming meet in Osaka, Japan. . . . William Lombardy, 25, of New York wins the U.S. Open chess championship in Chicago. . . . John Pennel sets a world pole-vault record of 17 ft. 3/4 in. in Miami. He is the first man to clear 17 ft.	Aug. 24
				Arnold Palmer, following a second-place finish at the American Golf Classic in Akron, O., becomes the first pro golfer to win more than $100,000 in a single year.	Aug. 25
	Sen. William Fulbright announces that ex-Presidents Eisenhower and Truman have informed the Foreign Relations Committee of their personal support for the ratification of the test-ban treaty. . . . The U.S. State Dept. releases a statement blaming South Vietnamese Secret Police chief Ngo Dinh Nhu, Pres. Diem's brother, for having engineered the "brutal" crackdown on Buddhist dissidents.	Interior Secy. Stewart Udall proposes a 30-year, $4 billion plan for developing the water resources of the five-state lower Colorado River basin.			Aug. 26
William E. B. DuBois, 95, one of the major U.S. Negro leaders of the 20th century, author, sociologist and co-founder of the NAACP (1909), dies in Accra, Ghana. DuBois moved to Ghana in 1961 and became a naturalized Ghanaian citizen shortly before his death.		The Bureau of Labor Statistics reports that the U.S. cost of living rose in July to a record 107.1% of the 1957-1959 average.			Aug. 27

F	G	H	I	J
Includes elections, federal-state relations, civil rights and liberties, crime, the judiciary, education, health care, poverty, urban affairs and population.	Includes formation and debate of U.S. foreign and defense policies, veterans' affairs and defense spending. (Relations with specific foreign countries are usually found under the region concerned.)	Includes business, labor, agriculture, taxation, transportation, consumer affairs, monetary and fiscal policy, natural resources, and pollution.	Includes worldwide scientific, medical and technological developments, natural phenomena, U.S. weather, natural disasters, and accidents.	Includes the arts, religion, scholarship, communications media, sports, entertainment, fashions, fads and social life.

	World Affairs	Europe	Africa & the Middle East	The Americas	Asia & the Pacific
Aug. 28			The Algerian Assembly approves a Ben Bella-backed constitution providing for a strong presidential form of government within a single-party political system.	Bolivian miners end a two-week general strike against the nation's tin mining facilities.	A South Vietnamese government communique denounces the Aug. 26 U.S. State Dept. statement on the current Buddhist crisis. The communique says that responsibility for the Aug. 21 attack on Buddhist pagodas lies entirely with military commanders and not Saigon political officials.
Aug. 29	The 17-nation U.N. Committee on Disarmament recesses its Geneva talks for two months to permit the General Assembly to take up the disarmament question.	*The New York Times* reports that East Germany has mined nearly one-half of its 860 mile border with West Germany.		The U.S. Federal Maritime Administration reports that 164 ships from 13 nations have disregarded the U.S.'s informal embargo on trade with Cuba since Jan. 1. Forty-nine of the vessels were British.	Pres. Charles de Gaulle declares that France is prepared to help form a unified, neutral Vietnam, free of interference from the U.S. and communist nations. . . . An airline agreement is signed between Pakistan and Communist China.
Aug. 30	The direct communication teletype link or "hot line" between Washington and Moscow is declared operational.	The *New York Herald Tribune* reports that France, Greece, Turkey and West Germany voiced opposition to proposals for an East-West non-aggression pact during the recent NATO debate on the question.			
Aug. 31			Belgium formally agrees to provide the Congo with more than $1 billion in investment aid and technical assistance.		Britain grants internal self-rule to Sarawak and North Borneo as a prelude to their joining the Malaysian Federation.
Sept. 1					Three Buddhist monks request and are granted asylum in the U.S. embassy in Saigon.
Sept. 2					Indian Defense Min. Y.B. Chavan tells Parliament that Indian reverses in the 1962 Chinese border war resulted from poor military leadership and high level interference in tactical decisions. . . . Pres. Kennedy, in a TV interview, describes South Vietnam's repression of Buddhists as "very unwise." Kennedy adds that "changes in . . . personnel" may be necessary to restore public confidence in the South Vietnamese government. . . . Saigon's pro-government English newspaper, the *Times of Vietnam*, charges that CIA agents are planning a coup against Pres. Diem's government. . . . U.S. Pres. Kennedy dismisses as irrelevant an Aug. 29 proposal by French Pres. de Gaulle to help create a unified, neutral Vietnam.
Sept. 3		U.S. V.P. Lyndon Johnson arrives in Sweden to begin a two-week goodwill tour of five Scandinavian countries. . . . France and Monaco formally resume relations following settlement of a long disagreement over taxes and customs.	The USSR vetoes a U.N. Security Council Resolution condemning Syria for the Aug. 20 slaying of two Israeli farmers near the Sea of Galilee. The U.S.-British-sponsored resolution had passed the Council by vote of 8-2.		U.S. State Undersecy. George Ball meets with Pakistani Pres. Ayub Khan in Rawalpindi to express American conern over Pakistan's recent moves toward a closer relationship with Communist China.

A	B	C	D	E
Includes developments that affect more than one world region, international organizations and important meetings of major world leaders.	*Includes all domestic and regional developments in Europe, including the Soviet Union, Turkey, Cyprus and Malta.*	*Includes all domestic and regional developments in Africa and the Middle East, including Iraq and Iran and excluding Cyprus, Turkey and Afghanistan.*	*Includes all domestic and regional developments in Latin America, the Caribbean and Canada.*	*Includes all domestic and regional developments in Asia and Pacific nations, extending from Afghanistan through all the Pacific Islands, except Hawaii.*

U.S. Politics & Social Issues	U.S. Foreign Policy & Defense	U.S. Economy & Environment	Science, Technology & Nature	Culture, Leisure & Life Style	
About 200,000 Negroes and thousands of whites participate in a massive non-violent civil rights march in Washington. Organizers of the march, including Martin Luther King, meet with congressional leaders and later with Pres. Kennedy. . . . King, speaking from the steps of the Lincoln Memorial, tells the marchers "we will not be satisfied until justice rolls down like water and righteousness like a mighty stream." Pres. Kennedy praises the "orderly" and dignified conduct of the demonstrators.		The House adopts a joint resolution barring a railroad strike for 180 days and providing for government arbitration of the key work-rules issues. The action comes only hours before a nationwide rail strike was to begin. . . . Pres. Kennedy signs a bill (HR7824) extending the temporary $309 billion national debt limit till Nov. 30.			Aug. 28
	The Senate Foreign Relations Committee votes 16-1 (Democrat Russell Long of Louisiana opposing) to recommend ratification of the limited nuclear test-ban treaty.				Aug. 29
A Negro couple moves into the white Philadelphia suburb of Folcroft despite violent demonstrations by white mobs.					Aug. 30
		ALF-CIO Pres. George Meany issues a Labor Day message urging stronger administration action to reduce unemployment. Meany reiterates his proposals for a 35-hour work week.		French painter Georges Braque, 81, a pioneer of the "cubist" style, dies in Paris. . . . Michelle Metrinko, 18, is crowned Miss U.S.A. of 1963 in Hutington, W. Va.	Aug. 31
					Sept. 1
Alabama Gov. Wallace issues an order delaying the opening of public schools in Tuskegee and Huntsville. The two cities have been ordered to begin desegregation of their schools.		The American Association of Fund-Raising Council estimates that Americans contributed a record $9.3 billion to philanthropic causes in 1962.	An earthquake rocks the Kashmir Valley leaving an estimated 100 persons dead.	Donna Mims, driving an Austin Healey, becomes the Sports Car Club of America's first woman class champion by winning the class H Production Race at Thompson, Conn.	Sept. 2
Eleven Negroes attend previously all-white public schools in Charleston, S.C., marking the state's first school desegregation. The desegregation is also effected quietly in many other southern cities.		The AP reports that a record 556 persons died in U.S. traffic accidents during the Labor Day weekend. . . . The 1961 Wage-Hour Law enters its second phase. The measure raises the minimum wage from $1.15 to $1.25 an hour and provides for a 40-hour work week with time-and-a-half for overtime.	The National Science Foundation announces a joint U.S.-USSR research project to make indirect measurements of solar cosmic rays by studying changes in radio reception. . . . NASA announces that a photo taken during the July 20 solar eclipse disclosed the existence of a faint comet near the sun. The announcement attributes the discovery to Belgian astrophysicist Francois Dossin.		Sept. 3
F	**G**	**H**	**I**	**J**	
Includes elections, federal-state relations, civil rights and liberties, crime, the judiciary, education, health care, poverty, urban affairs and population.	*Includes formation and debate of U.S. foreign and defense policies, veterans' affairs and defense spending. (Relations with specific foreign countries are usually found under the region concerned.)*	*Includes business, labor, agriculture, taxation, transportation, consumer affairs, monetary and fiscal policy, natural resources, and pollution.*	*Includes worldwide scientific, medical and technological developments, natural phenomena, U.S. weather, natural disasters, and accidents.*	*Includes the arts, religion, scholarship, communications media, sports, entertainment, fashions, fads and social life.*	

	World Affairs	Europe	Africa & the Middle East	The Americas	Asia & the Pacific
Sept. 4			Secy. Gen. U Thant reports that the U.N. Yemen observation mission has thus far failed in its efforts to end fighting between Yemeni republican troops and royalist rebel forces.	U.N. officials report that Haiti has withdrawn an Aug. 30 request for a Security Council meeting on alleged "aggression" by the Dominican Republic.	Ex-South Korean Premier Song Yo Chan is arrested in Seoul on charges of slandering Gen. Chung Hee Park's military government.
Sept. 5	France confirms that it is planning hydrogen bomb tests in the Pacific Ocean within the next few years. The French Foreign Ministry announces that it will disregard protests against the tests from New Zealand, Australia, Chile and other Pacific nations.	A Turkish military court sentences six ex-army officers to death for their role in the unsuccessful May 21 attempt to overthrow the government of Pres. Ismet Inonu.			South Vietnamese Pres. Diem denies allegations that his brother, Ngo Dinh Nhu, has assumed actual control of the government.
Sept. 6	Communist China issues an official statement accusing Soviet leaders of having "pushed Sino-Soviet relations to the brink of a split." The statement gives China's version of the development of ideological differences which it traces directly to Soviet Premier Khrushchev's denunciation of Stalin before the Soviet CP's Congress in 1956.			Havana radio reports that Cuban anti-aircraft fire yesterday drove off two bombers attempting to attack an air force base at Santa Clara.	The U.S. State Dept. says that the arrest of former Premier Song Yo Chan raises "serious doubts" about the South Korean junta's intention to hold free presidential elections. . . . The USSR discloses that it has asked the International Control Commission for Laos to investigate charges that the U.S. is providing training planes and ammunition to the pro-Western rightist forces of Laotian Gen. Phoumi Nosavan.
Sept. 7					At least 800 persons are arrested in Saigon during student-sponsored anti-government demonstrations. The protesters criticized U.S. support of the Diem government and praised the Vietnamese regular army for its refusal to suppress government critics.
Sept. 8			Algerian voters in a nation-wide referendum overwhelmingly approve Premier Ben Bella's proposed one-party constitution.		
Sept. 9			Jewish religious zealots raid Christian missions in three Israeli cities in protest against the missions' efforts to convert Jews to Christianity.		Pres. Kennedy, in a TV interview, says the U.S. does not intend to reduce aid to South Vietnam despite its displeasure over policies of the Diem government. Kennedy denies reports that the CIA has plans to intervene in Vietnamese politics.
Sept. 10		U.S. V.P. Johnson completes a five-day visit to Finland marked by unexpectedly large and warm pro-American demonstrations.	Israeli Premier Levi Eshkol expresses anger and regret over yesterday's attacks on Christian missions in Israel.	Havana radio claims that the USSR has warned the U.S. that it will not tolerate further raids on Cuba by American-supplied anti-Castro exiles. The U.S. State Dept. says it has received no such communication.	The AP reports that South Vietnamese government censors have begun deleting all unfavorable references to the war and to government casualties from dispatches filed by foreign newsmen. . . . Pope Paul VI cancels a scheduled audience with Vietnamese Roman Catholic archbishop Ngo Dinh Thuc, brother of Pres. Diem.

A	B	C	D	E
Includes developments that affect more than one world region, international organizations and important meetings of major world leaders.	*Includes all domestic and regional developments in Europe, including the Soviet Union, Turkey, Cyprus and Malta.*	*Includes all domestic and regional developments in Africa and the Middle East, including Iraq and Iran and excluding Cyprus, Turkey and Afghanistan.*	*Includes all domestic and regional developments in Latin America, the Caribbean and Canada.*	*Includes all domestic and regional developments in Asia and Pacific nations, extending from Afghanistan through all the Pacific Islands, except Hawaii.*

U.S. Politics & Social Issues	U.S. Foreign Policy & Defense	U.S. Economy & Environment	Science, Technology & Nature	Culture, Leisure & Life Style	
The *Wall Street Journal* reports that Bible reading or prayer recitations continue in the public schools of nine states despite the June 17 Supreme Court ruling barring such practices. . . . Negroes demonstrate at six Chicago schools to protest alleged de facto segregation. . . . Two Negro students register in a Birmingham, Ala. school without incident.		The Senate passes and sends to the House a bill to continue complete federal financing of the Manpower Development and Training Program.		Ezra Pound, 77, is chosen by the Academy of American Poets as the winner of its $5,000 fellowship for "distinguished poetic achievement."	**Sept. 4**
A threatened Negro boycott of N.Y.C. schools is cancelled after the Board of Education agrees to submit a specific timetable for reducing de facto segregation.		Thirty-seven U.S. drug companies file suit to challenge a June 20 FDA regulation requiring use of the generic name in the labeling and advertising of prescription drugs.			**Sept. 5**
Gov. Wallace uses state troopers to block the already delayed opening of four white Huntsville, Ala. schools under orders to accept one Negro student each.		The Labor Dept. reports that unemployment in the U.S. fell 5.5% in August.	The U.S. FDA announces that the controversial "anti-cancer" drug Krebiozen has been identified as creatine, a common and easily synthesized amino acid produced by the human body.		**Sept. 6**
Integrationists in Boston conclude a 36-hour sit-in demonstration against de facto school segregation.			Dr Andrew Ivy of the University of Illinois, chief scientific backer of Krebiozen, denies that Krebiozen is simply creatine. . . . Raging forest fires in Brazil's coffee-rich state, Parana, are reported to have caused 250 deaths and left 300,000 people homeless.	Donna Axum of El Dorado, Ark. is named Miss America of 1964 in Atlantic City, N.J. . . . The National Professional Football Hall of Fame is officially dedicated in Canton, Ohio. . . . Ines Cuervo de Prieto, 34, gives birth to quintuplets—all boys—in Maracaibo, Venezuela.	**Sept. 7**
		A threatened strike by N.Y.C. public school teachers is averted by a last-minute agreement on outstanding wage and class-size disputes.		Jack Nicklaus wins the second World Series of Golf tournament at Akron, Ohio.	**Sept. 8**
	GOP presidential contender Barry Goldwater says that foreign policy and especially "the stupidity of Cuba" will be major issues in the 1964 presidential campaign.	Pres. Kennedy designates Wisconsin Tax Commissioner John Gronouski to be Postmaster General.			**Sept. 9**
Negro students, beginning Sept. 9, attend nine previously all-white public schools in Birmingham and three other Alabama cities. The desegregation was attended by presidential order prohibiting Gov. Wallace from further interference with federal court orders.	Secy. of State Rusk, addressing the American Legion convention in Miami, says that Cuba remains a "major obstacle to the improvement of U.S.-Soviet relations.". . . Pres. Kennedy signs an executive order halting the drafting of married men into the armed forces.	A Senate-passed bill to authorize an $850 million program to combat mental retardation is slashed by 75% and then passed by the House. The amended bill is sent back to the Senate.	Significant discoveries in the mechanism of inheritance highlight the 11th International Congress of Genetics which began in The Hague Sept. 2.		**Sept. 10**

F	G	H	I	J
Includes elections, federal-state relations, civil rights and liberties, crime, the judiciary, education, health care, poverty, urban affairs and population.	*Includes formation and debate of U.S. foreign and defense policies, veterans' affairs and defense spending. (Relations with specific foreign countries are usually found under the region concerned.)*	*Includes business, labor, agriculture, taxation, transportation, consumer affairs, monetary and fiscal policy, natural resources, and pollution.*	*Includes worldwide scientific, medical and technological developments, natural phenomena, U.S. weather, natural disasters, and accidents.*	*Includes the arts, religion, scholarship, communications media, sports, entertainment, fashions, fads and social life.*

	World Affairs	Europe	Africa & the Middle East	The Americas	Asia & the Pacific
Sept. 11			*The New York Times* reports that South Africa's intensified immigration efforts have resulted in a net gain of 11,972 white settlers during the first six months of 1963.		Mrs. Ngo Dinh Nhu, wife of Pres. Diem's chief adviser, assails U.S. Pres. Kennedy as an "appeaser."
Sept. 12		The World Jewish Congress charges Soviet authorities with applying "exceptional ferocity" against Jews convicted of minor economic crimes.		The Brazilian War Ministry announces that government troops had earlier in the day crushed a revolt of navy and air force non-commissioned officers in Brasilia. The uprising reportedly related to a contested local election. . . . Pres. Kennedy, responding to conservative demands for a tougher policy, says it is not "in the interest" of the U.S. to launch a military invasion of Cuba.	U.N. Secy. Gen. U Thant denounces South Vietnam's Diem government at a news conference in New York. . . . *The New York Times reports that U.S. Amb. Henry Cabot Lodge has informed South Vietnamese Pres. Diem that the U.S. believes it vital that he remove his brother, Ngo Dinh Nhu, from politics.*
Sept. 13		The West German Justice Ministry discloses that 10,551 Nazi war criminals have been convicted and sentenced since the end of World War II. Of these 489 were executed for their crimes.	Britain vetoes a Security Council resolution calling on Britain to refrain from transferring governmental powers to Southern Rhodesia's white-dominated regime. It is only the third time Britain has exercised its veto.		
Sept. 14					U Thant reports that a U.N. survey in Sarawak and North Borneo confirmed that "a sizeable majority" of persons in the two territories approve the proposed Malaysian Federation.
Sept. 15			Premier Ahmed Ben Bella, running unopposed, is elected Algeria's first constitutional president in nation-wide balloting.		Indonesia and the Philippines announce their refusal to recognize the new Malaysian Federation.
Sept. 16				Canada agrees to sell the USSR $500 million worth of wheat and flour by July 1964. It is the largest one-year grain sale ever contracted.	The Federation of Malaysia is formally proclaimed in ceremonies at Kuala Lumpur. Malayan Premier Abdul Rahman is inaugurated as premier of the new federation.
Sept. 17	The 18th regular session of the U.N. General Assembly opens at U.N. headquarters in New York. Carlos Sosa Rodriguez of Venezuela is elected president of the new session.		Iranian supporters of the reform policies of Shah Mohammed Riza Pahlevi win an overwhelming majority in nationwide parliamentary elections.		

A	B	C	D	E
Includes developments that affect more than one world region, international organizations and important meetings of major world leaders.	*Includes all domestic and regional developments in Europe, including the Soviet Union, Turkey, Cyprus and Malta.*	*Includes all domestic and regional developments in Africa and the Middle East, including Iraq and Iran and excluding Cyprus, Turkey and Afghanistan.*	*Includes all domestic and regional developments in Latin America, the Caribbean and Canada.*	*Includes all domestic and regional developments in Asia and Pacific nations, extending from Afghanistan through all the Pacific Islands, except Hawaii.*

U.S. Politics & Social Issues	U.S. Foreign Policy & Defense	U.S. Economy & Environment	Science, Technology & Nature	Culture, Leisure & Life Style	
Southern School News reports that 150 additional Southern school districts were desegregated at the begining of the current school term. Over 1,100 of the 3,053 Southern districts have now begun some measure of desegregation. . . . The Chicago City Council passes an ordinance barring racial discrimination in the sale or rental of real estate, despite a march on city hall by more than 4,000 whites opposing the measure. . . . The non-profit National Association for the Prevention of Addiction to Narcotics announces in New York that it is sponsoring two pilot projects for out-patient treatment of addicts. The American Medical Association and the Federal Narcotics Bureau have opposed such out-patient programs in the past. . . . The Virginia Supreme Court rules that a state law requiring segregated seating is unconstitutional under the 14th Amendment.	In a letter to congressional leaders, Pres. Kennedy promises that his administration will take every step to safeguard U.S. security under the provisions of the nuclear test-ban treaty signed in Moscow Aug. 5.	In a speech to a Republican women's group in Chicago, Sen. Barry Goldwater accuses the Kennedy administration of leading the U.S. toward "a socialized welfare state."	The U.S. House approves the establishment of a panel to investigate the government's scientific research programs.	Santos of Brazil defeats Boca Juniors of Argentina to win the South American soccer championship for the second straight year in Buenos Aires.	Sept. 11
Pres. Kennedy, responding to a reporter's question, says he would not approve a program to transport children away from their neighborhood to far-away schools to achieve racial balance.	Sen. Frank Church (D, Ida.) urges an end to U.S. aid to South Vietnam if the government's repressive policies are continued. . . . The American Legion concludes its 45th national convention in Miami after adopting a resolution favoring ratification of the nuclear test-ban treaty. In another resolution the Legion urges the administration to consider use of armed force "to free Cuba."	The Senate passes and sends to the President an administration bill authorizing a three-year $263 million program to provide medical facilities and loans to medical students.			Sept. 12
Pres. Kennedy, in a memo to federal agencies, urges "full consideration" to the hiring of mentally retarded persons wherever possible. . . . A grand jury in Gadsden, Ala. refuses to indict Floyd Simpson who had been arrested for the murder of integrationist William Moore.	Sen. Henry Jackson (D, Wash.), heretofore considered a opponent of the nuclear test-ban treaty, announces his support for the pact despite what he calls "serious disadvantages.". . . A House Un-American Activities Committee hearing into unauthorized U.S. student visits to Cuba is recessed in disorder after students heckle Southern committee members as "racists."			The Greek Orthodox Church's decision not to send observers to the forthcoming resumption of the Vatican II meetings is explained by Archbishop Chrysostomos, primate of Greece. Chrysostomos says that Orthodoxy "will never be disposed to accept the infallibility of the pope.". . . The N.Y. Yankees defeat the Minnesota Twins to clinch their 28th American League pennant.	Sept. 13
		A newly established Republican Governors' Association issues a statement asserting that full employment is the single most important domestic issue facing the nation.		Mrs. Andrew Fischer, 30, of Aberdeen, S.D. gives birth to quintuplets—four girls and a boy. . . . Deane Beman, 25, wins the U.S. amateur golf championship in Des Moines for a second time.	Sept. 14
A bomb explodes during Sunday school classes at a Negro church in Birmingham, Ala. Four Negro girls are killed and 14 others are injured. Martin Luther King cables Pres. Kennedy urging federal action to prevent "a racial holocaust." King also cables Gov. Wallace accusing him of indirect responsibility for the violence.			MIT scientists report that Project West Ford has proved that bands of orbiting copper "needles" can provide a "jam-proof" global communications system.		Sept. 15
	Pres. Kennedy sends Congress a detailed report on the distribution of the $4.5 billion appropriated for foreign aid in fiscal 1962.				Sept. 16
The first issue of *Realm*, a monthly magazine for American professional and business women with incomes of more than $10,000 appears on newsstands in Chicago and New York.	The House passes and sends to the Senate an administration-backed bill (HR8200) to authorize in fiscal 1964 $175 million for construction of fall-out shelters.				Sept. 17

F	G	H	I	J
Includes elections, federal-state relations, civil rights and liberties, crime, the judiciary, education, health care, poverty, urban affairs and population.	*Includes formation and debate of U.S. foreign and defense policies, veterans' affairs and defense spending. (Relations with specific foreign countries are usually found under the region concerned.)*	*Includes business, labor, agriculture, taxation, transportation, consumer affairs, monetary and fiscal policy, natural resources, and pollution.*	*Includes worldwide scientific, medical and technological developments, natural phenomena, U.S. weather, natural disasters, and accidents.*	*Includes the arts, religion, scholarship, communications media, sports, entertainment, fashions, fads and social life.*

	World Affairs	Europe	Africa & the Middle East	The Americas	Asia & the Pacific
Sept. 18					Indonesia announces a protective seizure of the British embassy in Jakarta after more than 10,000 demonstrators had sacked and burned the building to protest the formation of the British-sponsored Malaysian Federation. Pres. Sukarno declares martial law in an attempt to curb attacks on British property and citizens throughout Indonesia.
Sept. 19	In an address to the U.N. General Assembly, Soviet Foreign Min. Andrei Gromyko calls for a new summit meeting to negotiate a treaty on general and complete disarmament.	The French government submits a record 1964 $18.5 billion budget. Military expenditures are set at about $4 billion, 7.1% over 1963.			Indonesia, responding to British protests, apologizes for yesterday's attack on the British embassy and other British properties.
Sept. 20	Pres. Kennedy, addressing the U.N. General Assembly, says that the hope for relaxed world tensions raised by the test-ban treaty should be directed toward the solution of other outstanding East-West differences.				In a speech to the U.N. Gen. Assembly, Laotian Premier Souvanna Phouma appeals to the great powers to reaffirm the Geneva accords for a neutral and independent Laos.
Sept. 21	The Tass news agency releases a two-part government statement reiterating the USSR's total rejection of the central doctrines underlying Communist China's foreign policy.	Czech Pres. Antonin Novotny dismisses Viliam Siroky as premier and ousts six other prominent government officials. The ousted leaders were generally regarded as "Stalinist.". . . Norwegian P.M. John Lyng's Conservative coalition government resigns in the wake of a parliamentary no-confidence vote yesterday.			Indonesian Pres. Sukarno decrees an embargo of all trade with Malaysia, a normally important outlet of Indonesian exports.
Sept. 22					
Sept. 23		The French government announces that Georges Paques, a NATO headquarters press officer in Paris, has been arrested on charges of spying for "an Eastern European power.". . . A French offer to place its nuclear force at the disposal of an eventually united and independent Europe is submitted to the European Assembly in Strasbourg. The action reportedly fails to win the support of any other European nation.			
Sept. 24				Peruvian Foreign Min. Fernando Lopez Aldana asserts in an address to the U.N. General Assembly that "excessive red tape" has prevented the U.S.'s Alliance for Progress from achieving significant results in Latin America.	The U.S. announces a temporary suspension of economic aid to Indonesia in view of Jakarta's anti-British riots and the government's severance of diplomatic relations with Malaysia.

A	B	C	D	E
Includes developments that affect more than one world region, international organizations and important meetings of major world leaders.	Includes all domestic and regional developments in Europe, including the Soviet Union, Turkey, Cyprus and Malta.	Includes all domestic and regional developments in Africa and the Middle East, including Iraq and Iran and excluding Cyprus, Turkey and Afghanistan.	Includes all domestic and regional developments in Latin America, the Caribbean and Canada.	Includes all domestic and regional developments in Asia and Pacific nations, extending from Afghanistan through all the Pacific Islands, except Hawaii.

U.S. Politics & Social Issues	U.S. Foreign Policy & Defense	U.S. Economy & Environment	Science, Technology & Nature	Culture, Leisure & Life Style	
		Pres. Kennedy appears on national television to urge the public to support congressional approval of his tax-cut proposal.		Hiroyuki Ebihara of Japan wins the world flyweight championship by knocking out titleholder Pone Kingpetch of Thailand in the first round of their Tokyo title fight.	Sept. 18
Sen. Barry Goldwater says in a *Congressional Quarterly* interview that he favors using federal troops under certain conditions to enforce court-ordered school desegregation. Goldwater reiterates his opposition to the administration's proposed ban on discrimination in public accommodations. . . . Pres. Kennedy meets with Martin Luther King and six other Negro leaders to discuss the racial crisis in Birmingham. CORE national director James Farmer is jailed in Plaquemine, La. for leading anti-segregation marches in the city.	Sen. Barry Goldwater explains on the Senate floor that he will vote against the nuclear test-ban treaty because "I feel it is detrimental to the strength of my country."			British political cartoonist Sir David Low, 72, creator of the pompous "Colonel Blimp" as a symbol of unyielding English conservatism, dies in London.	Sept. 19
		Rep. John Byrnes (R, Wis.) appears on national television (under equal time provisions) to express the GOP response to Pres. Kennedy's Sept. 18 appeal for public support for his tax-cut. Byrnes contends that cuts should be linked to limits on federal spending.	In a speech to the U.N. General Assembly, U.S. Pres. Kennedy unexpectedly outlines a proposal for a joint U.S.-Soviet manned expedition to the moon.		Sept. 20
	Pres. Kennedy orders Defense Secy. McNamara and Joint Chiefs of Staff member Maxwell Taylor to leave for South Vietnam Sept. 24 for a detailed review of the military and political situation there.				Sept. 21
Massive demonstrations are staged throughout the U.S. to express grief over the Sept. 15 Birmingham church bombing which took the lives of four Negro children.					Sept. 22
					Sept. 23
Cleve McDowell, the only Negro currently enrolled at the University of Mississippi, is suspended after being arrested for carrying a concealed weapon.	The Senate ratifies the U.S.-British-Soviet nuclear test-ban treaty by a vote of 80 to 19. Attempts by conservative members to attach reservations to the treaty were defeated by overwhelming majorities. . . . Kennedy designates Lt. Gen. Wallace Greene to succeed retiring Gen. David Shoup as Marine Corps Commandant. . . . The Senate unanimously passes a bill (HR7179) to appropriate $47.3 billion in fiscal 1964 for defense.				Sept. 24

F	G	H	I	J
Includes elections, federal-state relations, civil rights and liberties, crime, the judiciary, education, health care, poverty, urban affairs and population.	*Includes formation and debate of U.S. foreign and defense policies, veterans' affairs and defense spending. (Relations with specific foreign countries are usually found under the region concerned.)*	*Includes business, labor, agriculture, taxation, transportation, consumer affairs, monetary and fiscal policy, natural resources, and pollution.*	*Includes worldwide scientific, medical and technological developments, natural phenomena, U.S. weather, natural disasters, and accidents.*	*Includes the arts, religion, scholarship, communications media, sports, entertainment, fashions, fads and social life.*

	World Affairs	Europe	Africa & the Middle East	The Americas	Asia & the Pacific
Sept. 25	The Presidium of the Supreme Soviet unanimously approves ratification of the limited nuclear test-ban treaty.			The Dominican Republic's armed forces oust Pres. Juan Bosch in a right-wing bloodless coup. A military broadcast announcing the take-over condemns the former Bosch government as "corrupt and pro-communist.". . . The U.S. suspends diplomatic relations with the Dominican Republic following news of the military coup.	Indonesian Pres. Sukarno charges that his country is threatened by "Malaysian neo-colonialism," adding that Indonesia is prepared "to fight and destroy" the new four-nation federation.
Sept. 26		A British high court inquiry into the Profumo affair concludes that there is no evidence of any security "leakage" in the Profumo-Keeler relationship. The report, however, criticizes the Macmillan government's handling of the scandal. . . . Spain and the U.S. agree on a five-year extension of the 1953 pact granting the U.S. air and naval bases on Spanish territory.	Britain announces that it will grant independence to Nyasaland on July 6, 1964.	A three-man rightist civil junta, headed by Emilio da Los Santos, is sworn-in as the Dominican Republic's ruling government.	
Sept. 27	Unofficial sources in Ottawa, Canada report that informal discussions between U.S. grain producers and Soviet officials on a possible American wheat sale to Russia have been suspended in view of the Kennedy administration's disinclination to lift U.S. prohibitions on such grain sales.	In a speech to Ukrainian farm officials, Premier Khrushchev acknowledges that the USSR had a very poor grain harvest this year.			
Sept. 28	U.S. State Secy. Rusk and Soviet Foreign Min. Gromyko meet in New York in the first of a planned series of informal discussions on disarmament and other East-West issues. . . . *Izvestia* charges that Soviet officials and their families have been victims of harassment in the Chinese port city of Dairen.				The U.S. signs an agreement in Karachi to give Pakistan a $70.5 million 30-year interest-free loan for industrial development.
Sept. 29		A heavy emphasis on France's independence in world affairs marks a four-day political tour of the provinces by Pres. de Gaulle.	Outlawed Algerian Front of Socialist Forces, headquartered in the Kabylia Mountain region east of Algiers, publicly proclaims opposition to continued rule by Pres. Ben Bella.		
Sept. 30			Algerian Pres. Ben Bella charges that Moroccan troops are massing on the Algerian border to support Kabyle Berbers' opposition to his government.		

A	B	C	D	E
Includes developments that affect more than one world region, international organizations and important meetings of major world leaders.	*Includes all domestic and regional developments in Europe, including the Soviet Union, Turkey, Cyprus and Malta.*	*Includes all domestic and regional developments in Africa and the Middle East, including Iraq and Iran and excluding Cyprus, Turkey and Afghanistan.*	*Includes all domestic and regional developments in Latin America, the Caribbean and Canada.*	*Includes all domestic and regional developments in Asia and Pacific nations, extending from Afghanistan through all the Pacific Islands, except Hawaii.*

U.S. Politics & Social Issues	U.S. Foreign Policy & Defense	U.S. Economy & Environment	Science, Technology & Nature	Culture, Leisure & Life Style	
	Sen. Stuart Symington (D, Mo.) releases a final report on the 1962 Senate hearings on federal stockpiling programs. The report criticizes ex-Treasury Secy. George Humphrey and former H.E.W. Secy. Arthur Flemming for maladministration of stockpiling during the Eisenhower years.	The House, by a 271-155 vote, passes a modified version of Pres. Kennedy's tax-cut program. The bill provides for an overall $11.1 billion reduction in individual and corporate taxes, but excludes most of the reform proposals designed by the administration to raise $3.3 billion in additional annual revenue.			Sept. 25
	Pres. Kennedy, speaking in Salt Lake City, defends the administration's foreign policy record in what many observers view as a response to the foreign policy positions associated with Sen. Barry Goldwater. Kennedy says that foreign policy in the modern world "does not lend itself to simple black and white choices of good or evil.". . . International Longshoremen's Association Pres. Thomas Gleason says that his union's membership opposes reported proposals that the U.S. sell wheat to the USSR. . . . The House Foreign Operations Subcommittee criticizes the U.S. State Dept. for allegedly under-informing and sometimes mis-informing the American public on the situation in Vietnam.				Sept. 26
Joseph Michael Valachi, confessed member of what he calls the nationwide Cosa Nostra crime syndicate, describes the Mafia-related organization's structure and operations in public hearings before the Senate Permanent Investigations Subcommittee. . . . The Southern Christian Leadership Conference concludes its seventh annual convention in Richmond, Va. after endorsing plans for a drive to secure civil rights in Danville, Va. and for a possible renewal of demonstrations in Birmingham, Ala.		The Census Bureau estimates that the U.S. population today reached the 190 million mark.			Sept. 27
		Pres. Kennedy completes a five-day tour of 11 states during which he discussed various aspects of the administration's conservation policies.			Sept. 28
Ex-Pres. Dwight Eisenhower in a *New York Herald Tribune* article, denies as untrue reports that he is "anti-Goldwater." He explains that he is withholding judgment until he fully understands Goldwater's views.	Defense Secy. McNamara and Gen. Maxwell Taylor, in South Vietnam for a week-long review of the war against the Viet Cong, confer in Saigon with Pres. Diem.			The second session of the Roman Catholic Church's 21st Ecumenical Council, Vatican II, is convened in Rome. Pope Paul VI declares that Christian unity will remain as the council's chief objective.	Sept. 29
The Civil Rights Commission, in its third biennial report, recommends a broad range of measures to eliminate discrimination in voting, education, employment, the administration of justice, health care and the armed forces.			The U.S. AEC discloses that a nuclear-powered electrical generator has been successfully used in an orbiting U.S. satellite. The statement does not identify the satellite or the date of its launch.		Sept. 30

F	G	H	I	J
Includes elections, federal-state relations, civil rights and liberties, crime, the judiciary, education, health care, poverty, urban affairs and population.	Includes formation and debate of U.S. foreign and defense policies, veterans' affairs and defense spending. (Relations with specific foreign countries are usually found under the region concerned.)	Includes business, labor, agriculture, taxation, transportation, consumer affairs, monetary and fiscal policy, natural resources, and pollution.	Includes worldwide scientific, medical and technological developments, natural phenomena, U.S. weather, natural disasters, and accidents.	Includes the arts, religion, scholarship, communications media, sports, entertainment, fashions, fads and social life.

	World Affairs	Europe	Africa & the Middle East	The Americas	Asia & the Pacific
Oct. 1	Soviet news dispatches arriving in Moscow claim that Chinese troops machine-gunned a crowd of about 300 non-Chinese in May 1962 as they sought permission to emigrate to the USSR.	British Labor leader Harold Wilson tells the party's annual conference that Britain must take steps to keep its scientists and technicians from leaving the country.	Nigeria becomes an independent republic within the British Commonwealth. Nnamdi Azikiwe is sworn-in as the country's first president.		
Oct. 2					
Oct. 3	U.S. Secy. of State Rusk and Soviet Foreign Min. Gromyko, meeting in New York, disclose a tentative agreement on the banning of nuclear weapons from earth satellites.	Vatican sources report that the Czech government has released the Most Rev. Josef Beran, Roman Catholic primate of Czechoslovakia. Beran has been under detention since 1954.	Britain grants Gambia full internal self-government.	The Honduran armed forces, led by Col. Osvaldo Lopez Arellano, oust Ramon Villeda Morales as president in a violent right-wing coup. Over 100 persons are reported killed in fighting throughout the country.	
Oct. 4			Iraq signs an agreement formally recognizing Kuwait's right to "full sovereignty" over its current territory. . . . The Uganda Legislature elects Uganda King Mutesa II to a five-year term as Uganda's first president.	The U.S. suspends diplomatic relations with Honduras to protest yesterday's military coup. Pres. Kennedy also orders the withdrawal of all U.S. aid and military personnel from Honduras and the Dominican Republic. . . . Caracas sources report a major government crackdown on Communists and leftists throughout Venezuela.	
Oct. 5		Appearing at a Munich rally in his honor, soon-to-retire West German Chancellor Adenauer speaks scornfully of "all this talk about relaxing tension between East and West."			*The New York Times* writer David Halberstam and two NBC correspondents are severely beaten by South Vietnamese police after they witness a protest self-immolation by a Buddhist monk in Saigon. The U.S. embassy vigorously protests the attack.
Oct. 6	The Population Reference Bureau estimates world population in mid-1963 at 3.18 billion. Communist China is listed as the most populous nation with an estimated 731 million.			Exiled Dominican Pres. Juan Bosch, interviewed in Puerto Rico, appeals to his compatriots to fight for the "restoration of freedom and legality in our country."	
Oct. 7				The Dominican Republican junta declares a state of siege following clashes between police and thousands of pro-Bosch university students.	Saigon sources report that the U.S. has suspended commercial export assistance to South Vietnam to protest the government's anti-Buddhist actions.

A	B	C	D	E
Includes developments that affect more than one world region, international organizations and important meetings of major world leaders.	*Includes all domestic and regional developments in Europe, including the Soviet Union, Turkey, Cyprus and Malta.*	*Includes all domestic and regional developments in Africa and the Middle East, including Iraq and Iran and excluding Cyprus, Turkey and Afghanistan.*	*Includes all domestic and regional developments in Latin America, the Caribbean and Canada.*	*Includes all domestic and regional developments in Asia and Pacific nations, extending from Afghanistan through all the Pacific Islands, except Hawaii.*

U.S. Politics & Social Issues	U.S. Foreign Policy & Defense	U.S. Economy & Environment	Science, Technology & Nature	Culture, Leisure & Life Style	
The Senate passes and sends to the House a bill providing for a one-year extension of the Civil Rights Commission. Most Southern senators oppose the extension.	*The New York Times* reports that the administration is considering a 40,000-man reduction in the U.S.'s 230,000-man military force currently stationed in Germany.	The Justice Dept. discloses its opposition to a proposed merger of the N.Y. Central and the Pennsylvania Railroads. . . . The Senate passes and sends to the House a bill (S1988) to prohibit foreign ships from fishing within U.S. territorial waters or from taking "fishery resources" from the Continental Shelf extending out from the U.S.			Oct. 1
The House Judiciary Subcommittee No. 5 approves a tough civil rights bill including public accommodations and police brutality provisions which go far beyond the administration's original proposals. Administration officials are expected to oppose full committee approval of the bill in its present form.	Defense Secy. McNamara and Gen. Maxwell Taylor report to Pres. Kennedy on their just completed trip to South Vietnam. A White House statement issued after the meeting indicates that the U.S. will continue its military support of South Vietnam. The statement adds that McNamara and Gen. Taylor believe that the major part of the U.S. military task in South Vietnam can be completed by the end of 1965. . . . Pres. Kennedy signs a bill authorizing an approximate 17% increase in military pay.	The President's Council of Economic Advisers reports that U.S. GNP rose to a record annual rate of $588.5 in 1963's third quarter.			Oct. 2
	In a political appearance in Coronado, Calif., Sen. Barry Goldwater implies that the Kennedy administration is soft toward Soviets and tough toward "our tried and proven allies."		The U.S. G.A.O. releases a report charging that mismanagement by NASA and private contractors has delayed the lunar landing program by two years and has cost $100 million in federal money.		Oct. 3
			Hurricane Flora batters Haiti, causing more than 5,000 deaths. . . . Soviet cosmonaut Valentina Tereshkova asserts in a Havana, Cuba interview that the USSR has already selected a crew for its first expedition to the moon.		Oct. 4
	John Richardson, CIA chief in South Vietnam, is recalled to Washington amid reports of a policy dispute over the military and political situation in Vietnam between himself and U.S. Amb. Henry Cabot Lodge.				Oct. 5
		The *Mexico City Excelsior* reports that the U.S. has overtaken Mexico as the world's largest silver producer. 1962 U.S. output is estimated at over 54 million ounces.		The Los Angeles Dodgers defeat the N.Y. Yankees in four straight games to win the 1963 World Series. . . . Arnold Palmer wins $26,000 first prize at the Whitemarsh (Pa.) open golf tournament. It is the largest prize ever offered in a PGA-sponsored event.	Oct. 6
Police in Plaquemine, La. use tear gas and cattle prods to break up a demonstration by Negro high school students protesting segregation in local schools. . . . Robert G. (Bobby) Baker resigns as Senate majority secretary in the face of charges of "influence peddling" and conflicts of interest arising from his outside business activities.		Pres. Kennedy signs a bill (HR8100) designed to improve the financial condition of the railroad retirement and railroad unemployment insurance systems.		The British-produced motion picture *Tom Jones* is released in New York.	Oct. 7

F	G	H	I	J
Includes elections, federal-state relations, civil rights and liberties, crime, the judiciary, education, health care, poverty, urban affairs and population.	Includes formation and debate of U.S. foreign and defense policies, veterans' affairs and defense spending. (Relations with specific foreign countries are usually found under the region concerned.)	Includes business, labor, agriculture, taxation, transportation, consumer affairs, monetary and fiscal policy, natural resources, and pollution.	Includes worldwide scientific, medical and technological developments, natural phenomena, U.S. weather, natural disasters, and accidents.	Includes the arts, religion, scholarship, communications media, sports, entertainment, fashions, fads and social life.

	World Affairs	Europe	Africa & the Middle East	The Americas	Asia & the Pacific
Oct. 8	In an address to the General Assembly, Belgian Foreign Min. Paul-Henri Spaak urges Western leaders to appreciate and support Soviet Premier Khrushchev in his role as the Soviet-bloc's "apostle of peaceful co-existence."		Syria and Iraq formally proclaim the merger of their armed forces. . . . Congolese Premier Cyrille Adoula asks the U.N. General Assembly to keep the U.N. force in the Congo until the Congolese army is capable of ensuring internal peace.		The U.N. General Assembly votes to send a fact-finding commission to South Vietnam to investigate charges of anti-Buddhist repression.
Oct. 9	Pres. Kennedy announces that he has authorized the private sale to Russia of more than $250 million worth of U.S. wheat. If carried out, it will be the largest commercial transaction ever made between the U.S. and USSR. . . . Pres. Kennedy denies at his news conference that there has been any formal accord on the banning of nuclear weapons from space. Kennedy characterizes the Oct. 3 announcement of such an agreement as merely a joint declaration of existing policy.	Harold Macmillan, 69, announces that he will retire as British prime minister for health reasons in a letter to the Conservative Party's annual conference in Blackpool. . . . The French cabinet indirectly confirms that the first elements of France's planned nuclear striking force are now operational.		An American Red Cross offer of aid to hurricane victims in Cuba is rejected as "hypocritical" by Premier Castro.	U.S. officials in Saigon report that 60 Americans have been killed in Vietnamese combat since Jan. 1, 1961.
Oct. 10	U.S.-British-Soviet treaty banning all nuclear tests except those conducted underground enters into force with the exchange of ratification instruments in Washington, London and Moscow. . . . The Nobel Peace Prize Committee announces that its previously withheld 1962 Peace Prize will be awarded to American nuclear-test opponent Linus Pauling. The committee simultaneously announces that the 1963 Nobel Peace Prize will be shared by two Geneva-based Red Cross agencies.	Soviet troops detain a U.S. Army convoy on the autobahn linking West Berlin with West Germany after U.S. officers refused Russian demands that the convoy's passengers dismount and be counted by checkpoint personnel. . . . The New York Times reports that France is believed to have armed six Mirage-type jet bombers with 30 kiloton plutonium bombs as a first phase of its proposed nuclear strike force.			
Oct. 11	The U.S. State Dept. discloses that two accused Soviet agents held by the U.S. have been exchanged for two Americans convicted in the USSR on espionage charges.	Representatives of the U.S., West Germany, Italy, Greece, Turkey, Britain and Belgium open talks in Paris on the military and technical problems posed by the creation of a multi-lateral nuclear fleet made up of internationally-manned missile vessels.	The U.N. General Assembly votes 106-1 to ask South Africa to cancel its planned prosecution of 11 African nationalists accused of conspiring violence against the government of P.M. Hendrik Verwoerd.		Chief Indian U.N. delegate Vijaya Lakshmi Pandit, in a speech to the General Assembly, condemns Communist China for its "wanton aggression" against India and denounces Pakistan for "opportunistic" collusion with China.
Oct. 12		Soviet officers, apparently responding to U.S. protests, withdraw their demands for a troop count and permit a detained U.S. convoy to proceed to West Berlin.	Algerian Pres. Ben Bella proclaims victory over the rebel Kabyle Berbers after learning that government troops had successfully occupied Socialist Forces Front headquarters at Michelet.	Arturo Illia is sworn-in as president of Argentina. In his inaugural address Illia declares his intention to cancel foreign oil company concessions.	
Oct. 13					
Oct. 14			Official Algerian sources report that serious fighting has erupted between Moroccan and Algerian forces in the disputed Sahara border region. . . . The U.N. General Assembly calls upon Britain not to carry out its intended transfer of political sovereignty to Southern Rhodesia's white-dominated government. Britain vetoed a similar resolution passed in the Security Council.		

A	B	C	D	E
Includes developments that affect more than one world region, international organizations and important meetings of major world leaders.	Includes all domestic and regional developments in Europe, including the Soviet Union, Turkey, Cyprus and Malta.	Includes all domestic and regional developments in Africa and the Middle East, including Iraq and Iran and excluding Cyprus, Turkey and Afghanistan.	Includes all domestic and regional developments in Latin America, the Caribbean and Canada.	Includes all domestic and regional developments in Asia and Pacific nations, extending from Afghanistan through all the Pacific Islands, except Hawaii.

U.S. Politics & Social Issues	U.S. Foreign Policy & Defense	U.S. Economy & Environment	Science, Technology & Nature	Culture, Leisure & Life Style	
		The President's Consumer Advisory Council urges Congress to act on pending legislation requiring a clear statement of interest on consumer loans.	As many as 1,000 Cubans are believed killed in the wake of devastation caused by hurricane Flora, which hit the island Oct. 5. . . . The International Telephone & Telegraph Corp. discloses that a new infrared telescope at the Air Force's Cambridge, Mass. laboratories has uncovered several invisible stars. The telescope was originally designed to trace non-broadcasting satellites.		Oct. 8
	Ex-V.P. Richard Nixon describes Pres. Kennedy's authorization of wheat sales to Russia as "the major foreign policy mistake of this administration."		A huge wall of water, caused by a rockslide, pours over the top of northern Italy's 873-foot-high Vaiont Dam, inundating 11 Alpine villages. Death estimates run as high as 2,000. . . . NASA Administrator James Webb announces that the space agency will undergo a major reorganization in an effort to improve central control and coordination of all NASA research and development programs.		Oct. 9
The Senate adopts a resolution calling for an investigation into the financial or business interests of Senate employees or former employees to reveal any "impropriety.". . . Joseph Valachi, former member of the Cosa Nostra crime syndicate, completes 10 days of public testimony before the Senate Permanent Investigations Subcommittee.	In a letter to Congress, Pres. Kennedy defends the proposed Soviet wheat sale as the best way to advertise "the success of free agriculture.". . . Ten Republican members of the House Agriculture Committee say they will oppose the proposed wheat sale to Russia on the grounds that "trading with the enemy is morally wrong."	The Senate passes and sends to the House a bill aimed at raising dairy incomes by linking increased price supports with incentives for reduced production.	The House passes a 1964 NASA appropriation bill totaling $5.1 billion, over $600 million less than Pres. Kennedy had budgeted. The House measure also bars use of any funds for a joint manned U.S.-Soviet flight to the moon. . . . Pres. Kennedy presents the Robert Collier Trophy (for outstanding contributions to aviation) to the seven original Project Mercury astronauts.		Oct. 10
In a report to Pres. Kennedy, the Commission on the Status of Women identifies jury status and personal property rights as the two major areas of injustice to women under present law.		Pres. Kennedy signs a bill (HR5888) appropriating $5.47 billion in fiscal 1964 for the Labor and HEW Depts. The total is $288 million less than Pres. Kennedy requested and $100 million less than appropriated in fiscal 1963.		Jean Cocteau, French poet, playwright, novelist and motion picture director, dies in France at age 74. . . . French singer Edith Piaf, 47, dies in Paris. . . . Kingman Brewster Jr. is unanimously elected to be Yale University's 17th president.	Oct. 11
Gov. Nelson Rockefeller challenges Sen. Barry Goldwater to a series of debates on issues facing the Republican Party and the nation. Goldwater rejects the invitation, saying it would have a divisive effect on the party.					Oct. 12
	Agriculture Secy. Orville Freeman says in an ABC-TV interview that he has found that 99% of American farmers in the wheat belt states favor the sale of U.S. grain to the USSR.			Mrs. John F. Kennedy concludes a two-week vacation during which she toured the Aegean Sea aboard a yacht owned by Greek shipping magnate Aristotle Onassis. . . . Mickey Wright wins the Ladies' PGA golf championship in Las Vegas.	Oct. 13
The Supreme Court directs the Florida Supreme Court to review the convictions of 10 unrepresented defendants in light of the U.S. Supreme Court's March decision requiring states to provide lawyers for accused persons who cannot afford counsel.	The White House announces the resignation of Navy Secy. Fred Korth and the appointment of Paul Nitze to succeed him. Korth reportedly resigned to protest Defense Secy. McNamara's decision against atomic propulsion for a new aircraft carrier.				Oct. 14

F	G	H	I	J
Includes elections, federal-state relations, civil rights and liberties, crime, the judiciary, education, health care, poverty, urban affairs and population.	Includes formation and debate of U.S. foreign and defense policies, veterans' affairs and defense spending. (Relations with specific foreign countries are usually found under the region concerned.)	Includes business, labor, agriculture, taxation, transportation, consumer affairs, monetary and fiscal policy, natural resources, and pollution.	Includes worldwide scientific, medical and technological developments, natural phenomena, U.S. weather, natural disasters, and accidents.	Includes the arts, religion, scholarship, communications media, sports, entertainment, fashions, fads and social life.

	World Affairs	Europe	Africa & the Middle East	The Americas	Asia & the Pacific
Oct. 15		Konrad Adenauer, 87, formally resigns as West German chancellor. In his fare-well Bundestag speech, Adenauer cites German reunification as the outstanding unachieved goal of the post-war period.	Algerian Pres. Ben Bella orders a gener-al military mobilization in response to what he calls "collusion" between Mor-occan aggressors and Algerian dissi-dents. . . . Tunisian Pres. Habib Bour-guiba announces that France has com-pleted evacuation of its big naval base at Bizerte.		South Korean junta chmn. Chung Hee Park narrowly outpolls ex-Pres. Posun Yun of the Civil Rule Party to win a four-year term as president.
Oct. 16		Ludwig Erhard, 66, is elected by a 279-180 Bundestag vote to succeed Ade-nauer as chancellor of West Germany. . . . Visiting Irish P.M. Sean Lemass tells the National Press Club in Washington that Britain will soon permit reunification of Ireland with the six Brit-ish-ruled northern Ireland counties.			
Oct. 17	The U.N. General Assembly adopts by acclamation a resolution calling on all states to refrain from placing nuclear arms in space. The resolution is viewed as a formal confirmation of the tentative U.S.-Soviet agreement announced Oct. 3.	Visiting Yugoslav Pres. Tito confers in Washington with Pres. Kennedy. A sub-sequent joint communique expresses hopes for expanded trade and cultural contacts between the two countries.	Algerian and Moroccan officials con-clude two days of talks in Marrakesh in an apparently unsuccessful effort to end their border fighting.		
Oct. 18	In remarks to British newsmen, Soviet Foreign Min. Gromyko says little prog-ress has been made in recent U.S.-British-Soviet talks on lessening East-West tensions.	Newly elected West German Chancellor Ludwig Erhard tells Parliament that he intends to continue Adenauer's policy of close relations with France.	Moroccan sources assert that Algerian troops have greatly expanded the cur-rent border fighting by launching air attacks on Moroccan positions 230 miles north of the original battle zone. . . . The General Assembly ap-proves an $18 million appropriation to pay the cost of keeping the U.N. Force in the Congo through the first half of 1964.		
Oct. 19		Foreign Secy. Lord Home (Alexander Douglas-Home) is named British prime minister on the recommendation of out-going P.M. Macmillan. Home's selection drew considerable criticism within the Conservative Party.	Three Lebanese soldiers are killed in a clash with Syrian border patrols in the worst of 17 such incidents which have been reported in the last two months.		South Vietnamese officials announce that the government has smashed a student rebellion aimed at overthrowing the Diem government.
Oct. 20		The Spanish government launches a four-year, $5.5 billion economic develop-ment plan aimed at increased produc-tion and full employment by 1967.	The Arab League appeals to Morocco and Algeria for a cease-fire based on a mutual withdrawal of their troops to pre-war positions. . . . The Iraq government confirms that 5,000 Syrian troops are aiding the Iraqi army in its fight against rebellious Kurdish guerrillas in northern Iraq.	Dominican police disperse a massive anti-government demonstration in Santo Domingo.	
Oct. 21	The U.N. General Assembly votes 57-41 to defeat an Albanian proposal to admit Communist China in the place of the Nationalist Chinese delegation. It is the first time that the perennial motion was not introduced by the USSR.			Cuban Premier Castro, referring to re-cent hurricane-caused devastation, urges an "end to the (U.S.) economic blockade of our country, especially at this moment."	The U.S. is reported to have withdrawn financial aid to certain South Vietnam-ese military units in a further effort to force Pres. Diem to make political re-forms.

A	B	C	D	E
Includes developments that affect more than one world region, international or-ganizations and important meetings of major world leaders.	*Includes all domestic and regional de-velopments in Europe, including the Soviet Union, Turkey, Cyprus and Malta.*	*Includes all domestic and regional de-velopments in Africa and the Middle East, including Iraq and Iran and exclud-ing Cyprus, Turkey and Afghanistan.*	*Includes all domestic and regional de-velopments in Latin America, the Carib-bean and Canada.*	*Includes all domestic and regional developments in Asia and Pacific nations, extending from Afghanistan through all the Pacific Islands, except Hawaii.*

U.S. Politics & Social Issues	U.S. Foreign Policy & Defense	U.S. Economy & Environment	Science, Technology & Nature	Culture, Leisure & Life Style	
Atty Gen. Robert Kennedy appears before the House Judiciary Committee to urge a less comprehensive ban on discrimination in public accommodations than has been approved by Subcommittee No. 5. Kennedy claims that the bill in its present form will be defeated by Congress. . . . Martin Luther King addresses a voter registration rally in Selma, Ala. More than 300 Negroes have been arrested since the Selma voter drive began Sept. 16.		An administration-backed bill authorizing an additional $50 billion for federal aid to housing for low-income elderly is passed by the Senate and sent to the President.	The National Cancer Institute reports in Washington that a panel of 23 cancer experts have unanimously found that the drug Krebiozen is wholly ineffective against cancer in man. . . . At a New York press conference for visiting Soviet cosmonauts Yuri Gagarin and Valentina Tereshkova, Soviet Amb.-to-U.S. Dobrynin confirms that the USSR plans to land a man on the moon before 1970.		Oct. 15
	Unofficial sources report the successful launching from Cape Canaveral of two experimental Project Vela Hotel satellites equipped to detect man-made nuclear explosions in space.	The *New York Daily Mirror*, the second highest daily circulation paper in the U.S., ends publication. The Hearst Corp., publisher of the *Mirror*, blames rising costs and the recent newspaper strike for the paper's demise.		Boxer Ernie Knox, 26, dies of brain injuries suffered in a Oct. 14 heavyweight fight in Baltimore, Md.	Oct. 16
Pres. Kennedy signs a compromise measure to extend the life of the Civil Rights Commission for one year.	Pres. Kennedy signs a 1964 Defense Dept. appropriation bill (HR7179) for $47.2 billion. The final total was $1.8 billion less than the administration had requested, marking the largest such congressional cut since 1957. . . . Sen. Barry Goldwater denounces the U.N. resolution barring nuclear weapons from space as a "flagrant assault" on American defenses which seriously "weakens the last great bulwark against communist domination of the world."		The U.S. Defense Dept. and NASA announce they have agreed to consolidate their research programs aimed at the development of a manned orbital space station.		Oct. 17
	Ex-Pres. Eisenhower, in a *Saturday Evening Post* article, asserts that the time has come for a reduction of U.S. troop strength in Europe and for a greater European role in its own defense.	The Commerce Dept. reports that U.S. personal incomes rose to a new record annual rate of $466.4 billion in September.	The French Armed Forces Ministry announces that a cat was launched into space and brought safely back to earth as part of a French program of space biology research. . . . NASA officials appear before a Senate Appropriation subcommittee to urge Senate restoration of House-voted cuts in NASA funding. . . . Air Force Maj. Edwin Aldrin and Navy Lts. Alan Bean, Eugene Cernan, and Roger Chaffee are among 14 more jet pilots designated by NASA for astronaut training.	The International Olympic Committee votes to hold the 1968 summer Olympic Games in Mexico City, the first Latin American city to host the games.	Oct. 18
The Labor Dept. issues revised standards aimed at eliminating racial discrimination in federally aided apprenticeship programs.	Kennedy, speaking at Orono, Maine, defends recent administration moves toward easing Cold War tensions, particularly the atmospheric nuclear test-ban and the decision to authorize the private sale of U.S. wheat to the USSR.	Treasury Secy. Douglas Dillon tells a U.S. Business Council meeting in Hot Springs, Va. that a recession in 1964 is probable unless action is taken on the administration's tax-cut proposals.			Oct. 19
Sen. Barry Goldwater, answering an AP written questionnaire, says he is "completely opposed" to legislation barring bias in public accommodations. N.Y. Gov. Rockefeller voices strong support for a public accommodations measure in answer to the same question. . . . Gov. William Scranton (Pa.) says that he will not seek the 1964 GOP presidential nomination but would accept an "honest and sincere" draft.				Cleveland Browns fullback Jimmy Brown sets a NFL career rushing mark of 8,390 yards in a game against the Philadelphia Eagles.	Oct. 20
The Senate passes and sends to joint conference an amended House bill (HR6143) to authorize a $1.9 billion program of construction grants and loans to colleges and universities.				Ralph Houk, manager of the N.Y. Yankees, is named American League manager of the year in AP and UPI writers' polls.	Oct. 21

F	G	H	I	J
Includes elections, federal-state relations, civil rights and liberties, crime, the judiciary, education, health care, poverty, urban affairs and population.	Includes formation and debate of U.S. foreign and defense policies, veterans' affairs and defense spending. (Relations with specific foreign countries are usually found under the region concerned.)	Includes business, labor, agriculture, taxation, transportation, consumer affairs, monetary and fiscal policy, natural resources, and pollution.	Includes worldwide scientific, medical and technological developments, natural phenomena, U.S. weather, natural disasters, and accidents.	Includes the arts, religion, scholarship, communications media, sports, entertainment, fashions, fads and social life.

	World Affairs	Europe	Africa & the Middle East	The Americas	Asia & the Pacific
Oct. 22		British P.M. Home announces that he has postponed the reopening of parliament from Oct. 29 to Nov. 12 to permit him to run in a by-election for a Commons seat. Tradition requires a prime minister to be a Commons member. . . . Member nations of the Soviet bloc Council of Economic Mutual Assistance (Comecon) agree in Moscow on the creation of an international bank to provide increased trade among member states.			
Oct. 23	A Soviet trade delegation begins talks in Washington with U.S. officials on conditions for the planned sale of $250 million worth of U.S. wheat to Russia. . . . An article in the Soviet theoretical journal *Kommunist* appeals to Communist parties throughout the world to oppose Chinese efforts to replace "Leninism with Maoism."	British P.M. Lord Home adopts the new name, Alec Douglas-Home, after formally renouncing his peerage in preparation to run for a Commons seat.		The U.S. State Dept. declares that the U.S. will "maintain the present economic" isolation of Cuba as long as the Castro government continues its "aggressive" course.	Japanese Premier Hayato Ikeda dissolves Parliament and calls for national elections to test public support of his economic programs and pro-Western foreign policies.
Oct. 24		An entire U.S. army division is airlifted from Ft. Hood, Tex. to Frankfurt, West Germany in a widely-publicized demonstration of the U.S.'s ability to carry combat-ready troops to Europe within a few days. Some observers view the maneuver as an effort to reduce opposition to a possible future reduction in U.S. troop levels in Europe.			
Oct. 25		U.S. State Secy. Rusk confers in Bonn with Chancellor Ludwig Erhard to convey assurances that U.S. intends no troop reductions in Europe within the foreseeable future.			
Oct. 26	Soviet Premier Khrushchev warns in an *Izvestia* interview that the USSR may cancel its planned purchase of American wheat unless the U.S. drops its requirement that the grain be transported in available U.S. ships.				
Oct. 27			*The London Times* reports that Soviet weapons and Egyptian troops have been offered to Algeria in its border war with Morocco.		
Oct. 28	Talks between Soviet officials and representatives of private U.S. grain firms end without agreement. The negotiations are reportedly deadlocked over Russian opposition to U.S. demands that the wheat be shipped in American vessels.				Communist Chinese Foreign Min. Chen Yi tells visiting Japanese newsmen in Peking that China will not be prepared to test its first nuclear bomb for several years. Many Western experts had predicted that China would test its first nuclear device next year.

A	B	C	D	E
Includes developments that affect more than one world region, international organizations and important meetings of major world leaders.	Includes all domestic and regional developments in Europe, including the Soviet Union, Turkey, Cyprus and Malta.	Includes all domestic and regional developments in Africa and the Middle East, including Iraq and Iran and excluding Cyprus, Turkey and Afghanistan.	Includes all domestic and regional developments in Latin America, the Caribbean and Canada.	Includes all domestic and regional developments in Asia and Pacific nations, extending from Afghanistan through all the Pacific Islands, except Hawaii.

U.S. Politics & Social Issues	U.S. Foreign Policy & Defense	U.S. Economy & Environment	Science, Technology & Nature	Culture, Leisure & Life Style	
N.Y. Gov. Rockefeller tells a Salt Lake City audience that U.S. voters deserve a better choice than the two "extremes" that would confront them in a Gold-water-Kennedy presidential race. . . . About 225,000 students participate in a one-day boycott of Chicago public schools to protest de facto segregation.			Nobel Peace Prize winner Linus Pauling attacks the U.S. lunar landing program as a waste of "billions of dollars" which could be used for more beneficial scientific projects.		Oct. 22
			NASA announces that the launching of the Ranger 6 lunar probe has been postponed from late 1963 to early 1964 because of the discovery of possible technical defects.		Oct. 23
Pres. Kennedy signs a $329 million bill (S1576) embodying part of his proposed program to combat mental retardation. Kennedy had asked for an $800 million program.	About 100 anti-U.N. demonstrators in Dallas, Tex. jeer and spit upon U.S. Amb.-to-U.N. Adlai Stevenson following a speech to a U.N. Day celebration.	Pres. Kennedy signs a bill (HR7195) extending for two years the program of federal incentives for state billboard control.	Dr. Fred Whipple of Harvard's Smithsonian Astrophysical Observatory reports that most meteoroids appear to be flakes of powder from decaying meteors rather than the solid rocks which scientists feared would endanger future space travelers. The findings are based on data from the U.S. satellite Explorer 16.	The Royal Swedish Academy awards the 1963 Nobel Prize in literature to Greek poet Stylianou Seferiades. . . . Los Angeles Dodger Sandy Koufax is named Cy Young Award winner as the best major league pitcher of 1963.	Oct. 24
Dallas Mayor Earle Cabell and civic leaders telegram an apology to Adlai Stevenson for the insults he suffered during his appearance in the city yesterday.					Oct. 25
The Civil Rights Commission calls on the Defense Dept. to take stronger action to eliminate racial discrimination in the off-base housing available to servicemen stationed in the South.	The AEC discloses that the U.S. has conducted 14 underground nuclear tests in Nevada since May 23. Most of the tests are described as low yield.		Soviet Premier Khrushchev, in an *Izvestia* interview, says the USSR will not compete with the U.S. in a race to the moon. He explains that such competition encourages inadequate preparation which may risk scientific benefits as well as the safety of astronauts.		Oct. 26
The N.Y. City Commission on Human Rights issues a policy statement calling for "preferential" hiring of qualified Negroes as an appropriate solution to the "historic and existing exclusion pattern of our society.". . . About 10,000 persons participate in a massive civil rights rally in Cincinnati, Ohio. The day had been proclaimed "Jobs and Freedom Day" by Mayor Walton Bachrach.	Sen. Hubert Humphrey (D, Minn.), in a Washington speech, calls for a total reshaping of U.S. policy on trade with the USSR and its Eastern European allies.		The first successful attempt to supplement the pumping action of the human heart with an artificial device implanted in the body is reported by Dr. Michael DeBakey of Baylor University Medical School. DeBakey says the device kept a severely heart-damaged patient alive for four days.		Oct. 27
Thomas Connally, powerful Democratic Senator from Texas, 1929-1953 and leading figure in the formation of the United Nations, dies in Washington at age 86.				A U.S. team of Jack Nicklaus and Arnold Palmer defeats golf teams from 32 other countries to retain the Canada Cup for the U.S.	Oct. 28

F	G	H	I	J
Includes elections, federal-state relations, civil rights and liberties, crime, the judiciary, education, health care, poverty, urban affairs and population.	Includes formation and debate of U.S. foreign and defense policies, veterans' affairs and defense spending. (Relations with specific foreign countries are usually found under the region concerned.)	Includes business, labor, agriculture, taxation, transportation, consumer affairs, monetary and fiscal policy, natural resources, and pollution.	Includes worldwide scientific, medical and technological developments, natural phenomena, U.S. weather, natural disasters, and accidents.	Includes the arts, religion, scholarship, communications media, sports, entertainment, fashions, fads and social life.

	World Affairs	Europe	Africa & the Middle East	The Americas	Asia & the Pacific
Oct. 29	U.S. Senate Foreign Relations Committee chmn. J.W. Fulbright warns that France's persisting criticism of the Atlantic alliance may someday lead to an American withdrawal from Europe.		Moroccan King Hassan II and Algerian Pres. Ahmed Ben Bella arrive in Bamako, Mali to open talks aimed at ending the Algerian-Moroccan border conflict. Mali Pres. Modibo Keita and Ethiopian Emperor Selassie are acting as mediators.	Canadian P.M. Lester Pearson easily survives two parliamentary no-confidence votes over his policy of close defense cooperation with the U.S.	The U.S. accuses North Vietnam of having renewed massive military aid to pro-Communist forces in northern Laos.
Oct. 30			A cease-fire agreement to halt the Algerian-Moroccan border fighting is signed in Bamako, Mali. The accord provides for the creation of a special committee of the Organization of African Unity to seek a solution of the disputed border claims.	Cuban Premier Castro claims the capture of several U.S. CIA agents engaged in a raid on Cuba.	
Oct. 31		Persistent reports of an impending U.S. troop reduction in Europe are firmly denied by Pres. Kennedy at a Washington news conference.		Pres. Kennedy discloses that the U.S. is seeking assurances of a restoration of constitutional government in the Dominican Republic as a pre-condition to resuming normal diplomatic relations. . . . British Colonial Secy. Duncan Sandys announces that Britain will not grant independence to British Guiana until general elections are held under a proportional representation system.	Britain suspends aid to Indonesia under the Columbo Plan in protest against Indonesia's opposition to the Malaysian Federation.
Nov. 1					South Vietnamese army units overthrow the Diem government in a violent coup d'etat. The coup leaders are identified as Maj. Gen. Duoung Van Minh, Maj. Gen. Tran Van Don, and Maj. Gen. Ton Taht Dinh.
Nov. 2		Roman Catholic Church sources report that the Polish government has ordered seminary students hitherto exempt from military service to report for army duty.			Deposed South Vietnamese Pres. Ngo Dinh Diem and secret police chief Ngo Dinh Nhu are found dead. Rebel leaders say both committed suicide; other reports indicate they were executed. . . . South Vietnamese Buddhist leaders imprisoned under the Diem regime are released by leaders of yesterday's revolt.
Nov. 3		The New York Herald Tribune reports that France secretly conducted a new series of underground nuclear tests in the Sahara during October.			
Nov. 4		For the second time in a month, Soviet troops detain a U.S. Army convoy enroute to West Berlin after the Americans refused to submit to a Soviet personnel count. . . . The Greek Center Union Party, led by ex-Premier George Papandreou, defeats the National Radical Union, headed by Constantine Caramanlis, in nationwide elections.			South Vietnam's new provisional government promises a return to "democracy and liberty" and renewed efforts "to fight communism." . . . The Communist Chinese Security Ministry claims that 461 Nationalist Chinese guerrillas have been killed or captured in coastal raids over the past five months.
Nov. 5		Giovanni Leone resigns as Italian prime minister after his four-month Christian Democratic government proved incapable of maintaining a working parliamentary majority.		Britain is reported to have postponed the sale of 12 jet fighters to the Dominican Republic in view of that country's political situation.	

A	B	C	D	E
Includes developments that affect more than one world region, international organizations and important meetings of major world leaders.	Includes all domestic and regional developments in Europe, including the Soviet Union, Turkey, Cyprus and Malta.	Includes all domestic and regional developments in Africa and the Middle East, including Iraq and Iran and excluding Cyprus, Turkey and Afghanistan.	Includes all domestic and regional developments in Latin America, the Caribbean and Canada.	Includes all domestic and regional developments in Asia and Pacific nations, extending from Afghanistan through all the Pacific Islands, except Hawaii.

U.S. Politics & Social Issues	U.S. Foreign Policy & Defense	U.S. Economy & Environment	Science, Technology & Nature	Culture, Leisure & Life Style	
A compromise civil rights bill with bipartisan backing is approved by the House Judiciary Committee. The bill is a compromise between the administration's original measure and stronger legislation backed by the committee's Subcommittee No. 5. Negro leaders criticize abandonment of the tougher measure. . . . In a Washington speech Sen. Barry Goldwater says he favors putting the TVA under private ownership.	An American engineer and a Soviet trade mission employee are arrested in Englewood, N.J. on charges of conspiring to spy for the USSR.				Oct. 29
	The U.S. orders the expulsion of three members of the Soviet mission to the U.N. for alleged espionage.	The U.S. Internal Revenue Service reports that a record $105.9 billion in federal taxes was collected in fiscal 1963.			Oct. 30
Pres. Kennedy, responding to a news conference question, says he wants and expects V.P. Johnson to be his running mate in 1964.			Pres. Kennedy tells a Washington news conference that the U.S. should not be deterred from its announced space goals by Soviet Premier Khrushchev's apparent renunciation of participation in the moon race.		Oct. 31
The U.S. fourth Circuit Court of Appeals rules in Richmond, Va. that federal aid to segregated hospitals violates the Fifth and 14th Amendments.	Madame Ngo Dinh Nhu, touring in the U.S., accuses the U.S. government of responsibility for the coup in Vietnam.		Soviet scientists launch an unmanned space vehicle into orbit and then, by ground radio signal, guide it through a series of orbit-changing maneuvers. The experiment is viewed as a key step toward the achievement of docking and rendezvous capabilities.		Nov. 1
	The New York Times reports that administration officials welcome South Vietnamese Pres. Diem's overthrow, but have denied any direct role in the coup. . . . The Navy's 51st operational nuclear submarine (and its 25th Polaris submarine) the Ulysses S. Grant, is launched in Groton, Conn.				Nov. 2
The AP releases a poll of Republican state and county leaders showing that Barry Goldwater is considered the GOP's "strongest candidate" against President Kennedy in 1964.			Valentina Tereshkova, first woman in space, marries fellow Soviet cosmonaut Andrian Nikolayev in Moscow.		Nov. 3
				The U.S. defeats India in the interzone Davis Cup tennis finals in Bombay.	Nov. 4
Louise Day Hicks, who has become prominent for her denial of charges of de facto school segregation in Boston, leads the entire city ticket in winning an easy re-election to the Boston School Committee.		The Federal Reserve Board raises the margin requirement for stock purchases from 50% to 70%. It is the first increase requirement since October 1958. . . . Rep. Melvin Price (D, Ill.) chairman of the Joint Congressional Research Subcommittee, criticizes the "ill-defined objectives" and "gross overruns" which he says characterize many government research programs.	Professor Eugene Wigner of Princeton University, Prof. Maria Mayer of the University of California and Dr. J. Hans Jenson of the University of Heidelberg are named co-winners of the Nobel Prize in physics.		Nov. 5

F	G	H	I	J
Includes elections, federal-state relations, civil rights and liberties, crime, the judiciary, education, health care, poverty, urban affairs and population.	Includes formation and debate of U.S. foreign and defense policies, veterans' affairs and defense spending. (Relations with specific foreign countries are usually found under the region concerned.)	Includes business, labor, agriculture, taxation, transportation, consumer affairs, monetary and fiscal policy, natural resources, and pollution.	Includes worldwide scientific, medical and technological developments, natural phenomena, U.S. weather, natural disasters, and accidents.	Includes the arts, religion, scholarship, communications media, sports, entertainment, fashions, fads and social life.

	World Affairs	Europe	Africa & the Middle East	The Americas	Asia & the Pacific
Nov. 6	The Institute of Strategic Studies reports that NATO nations outpace the Soviet bloc five to one in numbers of intercontinental ballistic missiles.	A Berlin-bound U.S. Army convoy, detained by Soviet troops for 41 hours, is released without explanation. The U.S. had vigorously protested the action. . . . Soviet Premier Khrushchev tells a group of visiting U.S. businessmen that only Soviet restraint prevented the most recent U.S.-Soviet convoy incident on the autobahn to West Berlin from becoming a violent confrontation.	The General Assembly calls on Britain to refuse independence to Southern Rhodesia until that country institutes majority rule. Britain vetoed a similar resolution passed by the Security Council.		
Nov. 7	Western newsmen attending a Kremlin reception report an unusually sharp and aggressive tone to Premier Khrushchev's remarks about Cuba, co-existence and the general state of East-West relations.	Four rockets, unofficially described as anti-missile missiles, are displayed for the first time in the USSR's traditional Nov. 7 military parade through Red Square. . . . British P.M. Alec Douglas-Home wins a House of Commons seat in a by-election in Kinross, Scotland.			The U.S. formally recognizes the new provisional government of South Vietnam. . . . The South Vietnamese ruling council removes the nationwide curfew it had imposed following the Nov. 1 coup. It also orders an end to news censorship.
Nov. 8		The annual conference of NATO parliamentarians, meeting in Paris, urges the establishment of a system of joint control over the U.S. nuclear forces currently at the service of the Atlantic alliance. The action is viewed as support for the multilateral nuclear force concept of a single integrated atomic unit, which has evolved out of the original Anglo-American proposal for NATO coordination of separate national units. . . . George Papandreou is sworn-in as Greek prime minister.			
Nov. 9					Over 450 miners are killed in an explosion in a coal mine on Japan's southernmost island of Kyushu. A train accident near Yokohama later in the day claims 162 lives.
Nov. 10			Somalia is reported to have accepted a Soviet offer to provide military equipment for a greatly expanded 20,000-man army after previously rejecting U.S. and West German offers of limited military assistance.	The New York Times reports that U.S. government officials believe that there are now only about 5,000 Soviet troops remaining in Cuba.	
Nov. 11		Italian Pres. Antonio Segni designates Christian Democrat Aldo Moro to form a new government.	The Kabyle Berber revolt against the Algerian government is formally ended by an agreement between Pres. Ahmed Ben Bella and Col. Mohand Ou el Hadj, military leader of the rebellious Socialist Forces Front.	The second annual review meeting of the Alliance for Progress opens in Sao Paulo, Brazil. In an opening address Brazilian Pres. João Goulart warns that U.S. aid alone cannot solve Latin America's economic and social problems.	
Nov. 12	Tass reports that the USSR has arrested Prof. Frederick Barghoorn, chairman of Yale University's Soviet Studies Department, on charges of espionage.	P.M. Alec Douglas-Home challenges the opposition Labor Party to debate Britain's new nuclear defense policies in next year's general election.			Cambodian Prince Norodom Sihanouk declares that his country will refuse further U.S. economic and military aid to protest alleged U.S. financing of South Vietnamese and Thai subversion of his government.
Nov. 13				U.S. State Undersecy. Averell Harriman, addressing the Alliance for Progress meeting in Sao Paulo, asserts that the failure of the Alliance program to achieve hoped-for changes is largely the fault of recipient nations.	

A	B	C	D	E
Includes developments that affect more than one world region, international organizations and important meetings of major world leaders.	Includes all domestic and regional developments in Europe, including the Soviet Union, Turkey, Cyprus and Malta.	Includes all domestic and regional developments in Africa and the Middle East, including Iraq and Iran and excluding Cyprus, Turkey and Afghanistan.	Includes all domestic and regional developments in Latin America, the Caribbean and Canada.	Includes all domestic and regional developments in Asia and Pacific nations, extending from Afghanistan through all the Pacific Islands, except Hawaii.

U.S. Politics & Social Issues	U.S. Foreign Policy & Defense	U.S. Economy & Environment	Science, Technology & Nature	Culture, Leisure & Life Style	
A U.S. Court of Appeals in Chicago rules that the Black Muslim movement in the U.S. is not a religion and hence not covered by the constitutional guarantee of religious freedom.		Teamsters Pres. James Hoffa announces that the union will seek a 30¢-an-hour wage increase in the forthcoming contract negotiations. The demand is well above the 3% levels recommended as a non-inflationary guideline by the administration. . . . The U.S. Public Health Service says that, barring the resumption of atmospheric nuclear testing, the level of radioactive substances in U.S. milk supplies should never again exceed the levels recorded in June 1963.	Soviet Premier Khrushchev indicates that the USSR has not abandoned its lunar landing program, despite the impression created by his Oct. 26 denunciation of a "moon race" with the U.S.		Nov. 6
Gov. Nelson Rockefeller (N.Y.) formally announces in Albany, N.Y. his candidacy for the Republican nomination for President. In his announcement Rockefeller indicts the Kennedy administration for failing to "understand and meet the menace of international communism."		The report of the Senate Internal Security Subcommittee charges that the administration has ignored the "serious deterioration" of the U.S. merchant fleet. The report says that over the past year the number of U.S. merchant ships fell almost 5%, while the Soviet fleet increased nearly 20%.	The U.S. Apollo capsule, the craft designed to take three astronauts to the moon, is launched to an altitude of one mile above the White Sands Missile Range in New Mexico in a successful test of its escape system.	N.Y. Yankee catcher Elston Howard becomes the first Negro to win the American League's Most Valuable Player honors.	Nov. 7
		The Justice Dept. files suit against the Hanna Mining Co. and the Hanna Nickel Smelting Co. to recover nearly $2 million in overcharges for nickel sold to the federal government.	Delegates from the U.S., USSR and other nations, attending an International Telecommunications Union conference in Geneva, announce agreement on the allocation of radio bands for use by communications satellites.		Nov. 8
Repeal of a 61-year-old Texas poll tax is rejected by voters in a statewide referendum.	V.P. Lyndon Johnson completes a five-day goodwill tour to the Benelux countries. Johnson has now visited 34 countries since becoming vice president.				Nov. 9
			The U.S. Air Force announces the successful testing of a satellite propulsion engine in which sunlight generates thrust by expanding hydrogen gas and forcing it through a nozzle.		Nov. 10
Former V.P. Richard Nixon reiterates that he is not a candidate for the GOP 1964 presidential nomination.			Soviet scientists announce the launch of an unmanned satellite, Cosmos 21. No details are given.	Gordie Howe of the Detroit Red Wings sets a National Hockey League career record by scoring his 545th goal in a game against the Montreal Canadiens.	Nov. 11
		The Commerce Clearing House reports that a record $105.9 billion in taxes were collected by the federal government in fiscal 1963. . . . The Supreme Court rejects a request by Teamsters Pres. James Hoffa for dismissal of his Nashville jury-tampering indictment.			Nov. 12
		Pres. Kennedy announces plans to extend emergency aid to the poverty-stricken people in eastern Kentucky's Appalachia region.			Nov. 13

F	G	H	I	J
Includes elections, federal-state relations, civil rights and liberties, crime, the judiciary, education, health care, poverty, urban affairs and population.	*Includes formation and debate of U.S. foreign and defense policies, veterans' affairs and defense spending. (Relations with specific foreign countries are usually found under the region concerned.)*	*Includes business, labor, agriculture, taxation, transportation, consumer affairs, monetary and fiscal policy, natural resources, and pollution.*	*Includes worldwide scientific, medical and technological developments, natural phenomena, U.S. weather, natural disasters, and accidents.*	*Includes the arts, religion, scholarship, communications media, sports, entertainment, fashions, fads and social life.*

	World Affairs	Europe	Africa & the Middle East	The Americas	Asia & the Pacific
Nov. 14	In a press conference statement, Pres. Kennedy strongly denounces the USSR's arrest of Prof. Frederick Barghoorn. Kennedy asserts that Barghoorn was not "on an intelligence mission of any kind."	Bjarni Benediktsson is named prime minister of Iceland to succeed the ailing Olafur Thors.			The U.N. South Korea command charges that North Korean soldiers yesterday attacked an unarmed eight-man group of U.S. and South Korean soldiers in the demilitarized zone.
Nov. 15	Sources close to the U.S.-Soviet negotiations on the proposed wheat sale say that differences over shipping costs and financing remain major obstacles to an agreement.			Argentine Pres. Arturo Illia signs decrees cancelling unexpired oil contracts with eight U.S. and two European firms. The action is viewed as a first step toward complete nationalization of the petroleum industry.	
Nov. 16	The USSR releases and deports Yale University Prof. Frederick Barghoorn, who had been arrested in Moscow on espionage charges. The Soviet action follows an unusual personal protest by Pres. Kennedy.			Several U.S. Senators express anger over Argentina's Nov. 15 decision to cancel the unexpired oil concessions of U.S. firms. Democratic Majority Leader Mike Mansfield (Mont.) calls for a suspension of U.S. aid to Argentina "pending a just settlement."	Loatian neutralist and Pathet Lao representatives announce the signing of an informal cease-fire agreement to halt the fighting in the Plaine de Jarres.
Nov. 17					
Nov. 18		The U.S. asks fellow NATO countries to coordinate their policies on trade with the USSR and its allies.	A military coup led by pro-Nasser Pres. Abdel Salam Arif ousts Iraq's Baathist government. Arif, viewed as a figurehead under the previous government, seized control by capitalizing on a violent split between moderate and extremist factions of the Baathist party. . . . The Organization of African States meeting in Addis Ababa, appoints a seven-nation commission to recommend proposals for settling the Morocco-Algeria border dispute.		
Nov. 19	*The New York Times* reports that Russian and Chinese representatives have begun consultations in Moscow on a reconvening of the two countries' unsuccessful July conference on their ideological differences.				Cambodia severs all economic and military relations with the U.S. to protest alleged American complicity in attacks on the Sihanouk regime.
Nov. 20	A U.N. declaration calling for the abolition of all forms of racial discrimination is adopted by the General Assembly with the unanimous vote of all member states except South Africa.				Communist Chinese Foreign Min. Chen Yi publicly pledges to provide Cambodia with support in its "just and patriotic struggle" against U.S.-sponsored "subversive activities."
Nov. 21	The U.N. General Assembly approves a resolution designating 1965 as International Cooperation Year.	The USSR rejects a U.S. diplomatic protest against the Nov. 4 delay of a Berlin-bound U.S. convoy.	The Congolese government expels the entire Soviet embassy staff following the arrest of two embassy members on charges of attempting to undermine the Adoula government. . . . Baathist-ruled Syria publicly denounces the Nov. 18 anti-Baathist coup in Iraq. . . . New Iraqi Premier Taher Yahya says that his government will seek to fulfill the pact providing for the merger of Iraq, Syria and the UAR into one nation.		Cambodian Prince Sihanouk is reported to have asked France to provide funds and assistance to replace the just-canceled U.S. assistance program.

A	B	C	D	E
Includes developments that affect more than one world region, international organizations and important meetings of major world leaders.	*Includes all domestic and regional developments in Europe, including the Soviet Union, Turkey, Cyprus and Malta.*	*Includes all domestic and regional developments in Africa and the Middle East, including Iraq and Iran and excluding Cyprus, Turkey and Afghanistan.*	*Includes all domestic and regional developments in Latin America, the Caribbean and Canada.*	*Includes all domestic and regional developments in Asia and Pacific nations, extending from Afghanistan through all the Pacific Islands, except Hawaii.*

U.S. Politics & Social Issues	U.S. Foreign Policy & Defense	U.S. Economy & Environment	Science, Technology & Nature	Culture, Leisure & Life Style	
Pres. Kennedy concedes in his press conference that he does not really expect Congress to pass his tax-cut or civil rights bills before the end of 1963. . . . Sen. Barry Goldwater says that his proposal to reorganize the TVA has been subjected to partisan distortion and misrepresentation.		AFL-CIO Pres. George Meany opens the federation's fifth biennial convention in New York with a speech denouncing automation as "a curse to society."			Nov. 14
	The Senate passes and sends to joint conference a drastically amended bill (HR7885) authorizing a $3.7 billion foreign aid program for fiscal 1964. Although higher than the House-passed bill, the Senate version is still $800 million less than Pres. Kennedy requested and includes several restrictive amendments opposed by the administration.	Pres. Kennedy tells the AFL-CIO convention in New York that economic security and jobs remain the top domestic issues of 1963, eclipsing civil rights and education.			Nov. 15
	GOP presidential hopeful Nelson Rockefeller charges the Kennedy administration with failing to understand the nature "of the communist challenge."				Nov. 16
			The USSR orbits its 22d unmanned satellite in the Cosmos series.		Nov. 17
	Defense Secy. McNamara asserts, in a New York speech, that the U.S. strategic nuclear forces remain far superior to USSR. . . . The Senate Permanent Investigation Subcommittee resumes hearings into the controversial award of the TFX fighter plane contract to the General Dynamics Corp.	The AFL-CIO convention in New York elects George Meany to a fifth term as president and approves a resolution urging an increase in the minimum wage from $1.25 an hour to $2.00. The convention also urges passage of the administration's civil rights bill. . . . Pres. Kennedy, speaking to the Florida Chamber of Commerce at Tampa, denies that his administration has been "anti-business."		A long-awaited document absolving Jews of guilt for Christ's death is formally introduced at the second session of the Roman Catholic Church's Vatican II Ecumenical Council. The document draws wide praise from Jewish and interfaith groups, but is criticized by Catholic patriarchs representing churches in Arab nations.	Nov. 18
				The Goncourt Prize is awarded in Paris to Armand Lanoux for his novel *Quand La Mer se Retire* .	Nov. 19
	State Secy. Rusk, Defense Secy. McNamara and U.S. Amb. to South Vietnam Henry Cabot Lodge confer in Honolulu on general questions of U.S. policy in Vietnam. . . . Treasury Secy. Douglas Dillon tells the Senate Banking & Currency Committee that Export-Import Bank credit guarantees will be necessary to complete the Soviet wheat sale. Senate critics of the proposed sale are expected to oppose the extension of guarantees.		Pres. Kennedy issues a statement inviting other countries to participate in establishing a global communication satellite system.		Nov. 20
Pres. Kennedy, accompanied by his wife, flies to San Antonio to begin a two-day Texas tour reportedly aimed at healing the rift between the state's liberal and conservative Democrats.	A House Republican task force on aeronautics warns that a "military space gap" may be developing between the U.S. and the USSR because of administration neglect of the military aspects of space.	The Commerce Dept. reports that U.S. steel production in the first nine months of 1963 rose to 83.5 million tons, about 28% of the world total.			Nov. 21

F	G	H	I	J
Includes elections, federal-state relations, civil rights and liberties, crime, the judiciary, education, health care, poverty, urban affairs and population.	Includes formation and debate of U.S. foreign and defense policies, veterans' affairs and defense spending. (Relations with specific foreign countries are usually found under the region concerned.)	Includes business, labor, agriculture, taxation, transportation, consumer affairs, monetary and fiscal policy, natural resources, and pollution.	Includes worldwide scientific, medical and technological developments, natural phenomena, U.S. weather, natural disasters, and accidents.	Includes the arts, religion, scholarship, communications media, sports, entertainment, fashions, fads and social life.

	World Affairs	Europe	Africa & the Middle East	The Americas	Asia & the Pacific
Nov. 22	U.S. Pres. John Fitzgerald Kennedy is assassinated in Dallas, Tex. V.P. Lyndon Baines Johnson is sworn-in as President later in the day.	West German Chancellor Erhard meets in Paris with French Pres. de Gaulle in his first regular consultation under the terms of the 1962 French-German cooperation treaty. Erhard is said to have stressed West Germany's fundamental reliance on the U.S. involvement in Europe's defense despite continued French efforts to use the French-West German treaty as a basis for an independent Europe under Franco-German leadership.			South Vietnam's ruling revolutionary council, dismisses 31 high-ranking military officers accused of supporting the late Pres. Diem's government.
Nov. 23	Soviet Premier Khrushchev joins leaders from throughout the world in expressing grief and sorrow over the assassination of U.S. Pres. John F. Kennedy.			Cuban Premier Fidel Castro declares in a TV address that the death of Pres. Kennedy, although an enemy, cannot "cause us joy."	
Nov. 24					A U.S. official in South Vietnam reports that 78 Americans have been killed in combat action and 63 others in non-combat accidents.
Nov. 25					Cambodia appeals to Britain and the USSR to convene a nine-nation meeting to guarantee Cambodia's independence and neutrality. . . . The U.S. suspends arms shipments to Indonesia in view of its hostility toward the Malaysian Federation.
Nov. 26	U.S. Pres. Johnson meets with a number of world leaders who came to Washington to attend the funeral of John Kennedy. Pledges of continuity in U.S. policy are said to be the main theme of the discussions. . . . The U.N. General Assembly holds a memorial meeting for the late Pres. John Kennedy.				South Korean Pres. Chung Hee Park's ruling Democratic Republican Party wins a majority of seats in the national assembly in nationwide elections.
Nov. 27	The U.N. General Assembly votes resolutions calling for the suspension of underground nuclear tests, the reconvening of the 18-nation U.N. Disarmament Committee and the creation of a "nuclear-free zone" in Latin America.				

A	B	C	D	E
Includes developments that affect more than one world region, international organizations and important meetings of major world leaders.	Includes all domestic and regional developments in Europe, including the Soviet Union, Turkey, Cyprus and Malta.	Includes all domestic and regional developments in Africa and the Middle East, including Iraq and Iran and excluding Cyprus, Turkey and Afghanistan.	Includes all domestic and regional developments in Latin America, the Caribbean and Canada.	Includes all domestic and regional developments in Asia and Pacific nations, extending from Afghanistan through all the Pacific Islands, except Hawaii.

U.S. Politics & Social Issues	U.S. Foreign Policy & Defense	U.S. Economy & Environment	Science, Technology & Nature	Culture, Leisure & Life Style	
Pres. John Kennedy is killed by an assassin's bullets riding in a mid-day motorcade through Dallas, Texas. V.P. Lyndon Johnson, 55, who was riding two cars behind Kennedy, is sworn-in as President at 2:39 P.M. aboard the presidential jet at Love Field in Dallas. . . . Lee Harvey Oswald, 24, an ex-Marine who lived briefly in the USSR, is arrested in Dallas and charged with the President's murder.	An anti-communist organization in Miami announces that 22 U.S. cities and towns (mainly in the South and Southwest) have enacted ordinances prohibiting the local sale of goods made in the USSR and its satellites.	The Dow Jones Industrial average drops 21.16 points upon receiving news of Pres. Kennedy's assassination. . . . The U.S. Bureau of Mines reports that crude petroleum production in the U.S. totaled a record 7,332,000 barrels a day in 1962, up 149,000 barrels from the 1961 daily output.		British novelist, philosopher and historian Aldous Huxley dies of cancer in Los Angeles at the age of 69.	Nov. 22
Pres. Johnson confers with ex-Presidents Eisenhower and Truman, members of the cabinet and other high administration officials. Cabinet members pledge to serve the new President as long as they are needed. . . . Pres. Johnson proclaims Nov. 25 as a national day of mourning. . . . Observers say the extent of U.S. public shock and grief exceeds that of any tragedy in this century, including the death of Franklin Roosevelt.					Nov. 23
Lee Harvey Oswald, accused assassin of Pres. Kennedy, is shot and killed in Dallas's municipal building as police transfer him to the county jail. Oswald's assailant, arrested immediately, is Jack Rubenstein (known as Jack Ruby), a Dallas night-club operator said to have been an admirer of Pres. Kennedy. . . . Millions of Americans witness the shooting of Oswald via a live TV broadcast.	Pres. Johnson pledges that his administration will continue the U.S. policies on South Vietnam that have been established by the late Pres. Kennedy. The statement follows a White House meeting with high administration officials.				Nov. 24
Hundreds of thousands of Americans file past the closed coffin of John Kennedy, lying in state in the Capitol. The remains of the late President are later interred at Arlington National Cemetary in the presence of leaders from nearly 100 countries. . . . Pres. Johnson orders the Justice Dept. and FBI to conduct a prompt investigation of circumstances surrounding the assassination of Pres. Kennedy and Oswald's subsequent murder.					Nov. 25
The Republican and Democratic National Committees declare a moritorium on partisan politics during the 30-day official mourning period for the late Pres. Kennedy.	The Senate defeats a bill which would have prevented the Export-Import Bank from guaranteeing credit for the USSR's proposed purchase of U.S. wheat. The vote followed the reading of a letter from late Pres. Kennedy requesting that the Senate reject the measure.	The congressionally created arbitration board in the railroad dispute rules that 90% of diesel locomotive firemen's jobs are unnecessary and could be eliminated as current job holders quit, die or retire. . . . The Dow Jones industrial average climbs a record 32.03 points to close the day at 743.52.	The satellite Explorer 18 or IMP, (Interplanetary Monitoring Platform), is successfully launched from Cape Canaveral. The Explorer 18 is designed to assess radiation hazards from solar flares that astronauts would face in travels between the earth and moon.		Nov. 26
Pres. Lyndon Johnson appears before a joint session of Congress to urge the "earliest possible passage" of the civil rights bill and "early passage" of a tax bill. Johnson calls quick action on the civil rights measure the most appropriate memorial to the late John Kennedy.	In an address to a joint session of Congress, Pres. Johnson pledges uninterrupted continuation of the Kennedy administration foreign policies and programs.		The U.S. conducts its first successful test flight of the two-stage Atlas-Centaur launching vehicle. The launching marks the first known flight of a rocket using liquid hydrogen as fuel. . . . Astronomers at the Lowell Observatory report observing a dull red flash on the lunar surface. The observation tends to strengthen previously discounted reports of eruptive activity on the moon.		Nov. 27

F	G	H	I	J
Includes elections, federal-state relations, civil rights and liberties, crime, the judiciary, education, health care, poverty, urban affairs and population.	Includes formation and debate of U.S. foreign and defense policies, veterans' affairs and defense spending. (Relations with specific foreign countries are usually found under the region concerned.)	Includes business, labor, agriculture, taxation, transportation, consumer affairs, monetary and fiscal policy, natural resources, and pollution.	Includes worldwide scientific, medical and technological developments, natural phenomena, U.S. weather, natural disasters, and accidents.	Includes the arts, religion, scholarship, communications media, sports, entertainment, fashions, fads and social life.

	World Affairs	Europe	Africa & the Middle East	The Americas	Asia & the Pacific
Nov. 28		West Berlin Mayor Willy Brandt, just returned from the U.S., says that he received assurances from Pres. Johnson that the late Pres. Kennedy's pledges on Berlin would be honored by the new administration. . . . The seven-nation NATO meetings on the formation of a multi-lateral force of missile-armed service vessels is reported to have received assurances that the new Johnson administration will stand by the MLF proposals previously advanced by the Kennedy administration.	An Algerian-Tunisian agreement for joint exploitation of Saharan gas and petroleum resources is signed in Algiers.	Venezuelan spokesmen publicly charge that Cuba is supplying weapons to pro-communist Venezuelan terrorists.	
Nov. 29		P.M. Douglas-Home, speaking at a news conference, rejects suggestions that Britain take advantage of the change in American leadership to assume a more dominant role in international affairs. Home asserts that Britain's influence depends upon its loyalty as an ally.			
Nov. 30	In an unprecedented action the USSR provides the U.S. with its Soviet consular files on Lee Harvey Oswald. The papers reportedly deal with Oswald's stay in the USSR and his attempts to gain visas to return there.	The square before West Berlin's City Hall, where Pres. Kennedy made his famous "Ich bin ein Berliner" declaration, is renamed the John F. Kennedy Plaza at a ceremony attended by more than 200,000 West Berliners.			
Dec. 1				Raul Leoni, candidate of outgoing Pres. Romulo Betancourt's Democratic Action party, is elected president of Venezuela in nationwide balloting. The presidential campaign was marked by extensive violence attributed to leftist terrorists.	U.S. sources in Vietnam report that government casualties in November were the highest of any month in 1963. An estimated 1,400 U.S.-made weapons are reported to have fallen into Viet Cong hands. . . . New Zealand P.M. Keith Holyoake's National Party government is elected to another three-year term.
Dec. 2		British businessman Lord Mancroft, a Jew, resigns from the Advisory Board of the Norwich Union Insurance Societies in the face of boycott threats against the company by the Arab League Office in London.			South Vietnam's ruling Revolutionary Council, headed by Maj. Gen. Duong Van Minh, announces temporary suspension of the U.S.-originated strategic hamlets program aimed at providing rural villagers with defense against the Vietcong. The statement asserts that the program tended to alienate uprooted peasants.
Dec. 3	Soviet Premier Khrushchev, speaking in Moscow, says that the USSR will cooperate with the new U.S. President in a continued search for a reduction in East-West tensions. . . . Delegates to the 80-nation pro-communist World People's Council in Warsaw overwhelmingly reject a Chinese resolution calling for world communist support of Peking's anti-Western policies. Only Albania, North Korea, North Vietnam and Indonesia side with the Chinese.	West German Chancellor Erhard declares at a Bonn news conference that "West Germany can rely unconditionally on the United States" to carry out its pledges for the defense of Germany and Western Europe. Erhard says he conveyed this confidence in his recent consultation meeting with French Pres. de Gaulle.		The OAS votes to investigate Venezuelan charges that Cuba has smuggled arms into Venezuela for use by the outlawed pro-communist Armed Forces of National Liberation (FALN).	
Dec. 4		Italian P.M. designate Aldo Moro announces formation of a center-left coalition government made up of Christian Democrats and Socialists. Socialist leader Pietro Nenni is named vice prime minister. . . . The Assembly of the Western European Union, meeting in Paris, rejects a resolution supporting creation of a multilateral nuclear force as proposed by the U.S.	The U.N. Security Council votes unanimously to repeat its previous condemnations of South Africa's apartheid policy and to recommend stricter military embargo measures against the country's nationalist government.		

A	B	C	D	E
Includes developments that affect more than one world region, international organizations and important meetings of major world leaders.	Includes all domestic and regional developments in Europe, including the Soviet Union, Turkey, Cyprus and Malta.	Includes all domestic and regional developments in Africa and the Middle East, including Iraq and Iran and excluding Cyprus, Turkey and Afghanistan.	Includes all domestic and regional developments in Latin America, the Caribbean and Canada.	Includes all domestic and regional developments in Asia and Pacific nations, extending from Afghanistan through all the Pacific Islands, except Hawaii.

U.S. Politics & Social Issues	U.S. Foreign Policy & Defense	U.S. Economy & Environment	Science, Technology & Nature	Culture, Leisure & Life Style	
In a nationally televised Thanksgiving address, Pres. Johnson calls for an end to "injustice or intolerance or oppression to any of our fellow Americans whatever their opinion, whatever the color of their skins."			Pres. Johnson announces that Cape Canaveral, Fla. will be renamed Cape Kennedy and its space installations will be called the John F. Kennedy Space Center.		Nov. 28
Pres. Johnson appoints a special commission headed by Chief Justice Earl Warren to investigate Pres. Kennedy's assassination and the murder of his alleged assassin, Lee Harvey Oswald.			The USSR announces that it is reserving two mid-Pacific impact areas for the December testing of "new improved versions of booster rockets for space vehicles."	Pope Paul VI announces that a third session of the Ecumenical Council Vatican II, will begin Sept. 14, 1964.	Nov. 29
Pres. Johnson announces his support for home-rule in the District of Columbia.				The Hamilton Tiger Cats defeat the British Columbia Lions to win Canada's professional football championship.	Nov. 30
Bayard Rustin, principal organizer of the August civil rights march on Washington, calls for a broadened social reform movement to embrace not only Negroes but all economically disadvantaged Americans.					Dec. 1
The Virginia Supreme Court upholds the right of Prince Edward County not to operate a public school system. Prince Edward Schools have been closed since the issuing in 1959 of a court desegregation order.			Adlai Stevenson announces at the U.N. that Pres. Johnson has instructed him to reaffirm the late Pres. Kennedy's proposal for a joint U.S.-Soviet expedition to the moon.		Dec. 2
Pres. Johnson meets with Martin Luther King in one of a number of White House conferences with Negro leaders. King later tells reporters that Johnson promised to press for congressional civil rights action before Christmas.	About 220 U.S. troops leave South Vietnam for the U.S. They are part of a 1,000-man force that is to be withdrawn by Dec. 25.			Pope Paul VI issues an apostolic letter, *The Pastoral Office*, increasing the authority of Roman Catholic bishops. . . . Sen. J. W. Fulbright (D, Ark.) introduces in the Senate a bill to name the proposed U.S. national cultural center the John Fitzgerald Kennedy Memorial Center.	Dec. 3
Black Muslim leader Elijah Muhammad announces that he has officially silenced Malcolm X's public statements expressing satisfaction at Pres. Kennedy's assassination.		Pres. Johnson meets separately with leaders of the AFL-CIO and representatives of the National Association of Manufacturers in an effort to rally support for the administration's tax-cut and other pending economic proposals. Both groups reportedly pledged to cooperate with the new President.	The American Cancer Society releases a statistical study clearly establishing a link between cigarette smoking and early death.	The second session of the Roman Catholic Church's Ecumenical Council concludes in Rome with Pope Paul's promulgation of a reform of the sacred liturgy permitting the use of the vernacular in parts of the mass and in the sacraments.	Dec. 4

F	G	H	I	J
Includes elections, federal-state relations, civil rights and liberties, crime, the judiciary, education, health care, poverty, urban affairs and population.	Includes formation and debate of U.S. foreign and defense policies, veterans' affairs and defense spending. (Relations with specific foreign countries are usually found under the region concerned.)	Includes business, labor, agriculture, taxation, transportation, consumer affairs, monetary and fiscal policy, natural resources, and pollution.	Includes worldwide scientific, medical and technological developments, natural phenomena, U.S. weather, natural disasters, and accidents.	Includes the arts, religion, scholarship, communications media, sports, entertainment, fashions, fads and social life.

	World Affairs	Europe	Africa & the Middle East	The Americas	Asia & the Pacific
Dec. 5		East Germany offers to negotiate arrangements for holiday visits to East Berlin by West Berlin residents in a letter to West Berlin Mayor Willy Brandt.	A private West German firm conducts demonstration test-firings of four military rockets. Jordanian and Saudi Arabian military attachés observe the tests. A Bonn government spokesman says there are no plans to issue export licenses for the sale of military rockets abroad.		
Dec. 6				Three U.S. officials and a Peace Corps volunteer are seized by insurgent Bolivian tin miners at a mine center about 150 miles south of La Paz.	
Dec. 7					The U.S. signs an agreement in New Delhi to provide India with a $80 million loan to help build an atomic reactor plant.
Dec. 8			Arab League representatives begin a three-day conference in Cairo devoted to discussing means of blocking an Israeli project to divert Jordan River waters for irrigating the Negev desert.		P.M. Sarit Thanarat of Thailand dies in Bangkok.
Dec. 9		The British Foreign Office issues a statement criticizing Arab pressures to force British firms to discriminate against Jewish members.			Hayato Ikeda, is re-elected as Japanese prime minister by the Diet. Ikeda's Liberal-Democratic Party retained its parliamentary majority in elections held Nov. 21. . . . South Vietnam's ruling Revolutionary Council announces that pro-Communists exiled during the Diem regime will not be permitted to return to South Vietnam.
Dec. 10	Communist Chinese leaders reject an Oct. 26 appeal by Soviet Premier Khrushchev for an end to ideological polemics.		The British protectorate of Zanzibar becomes an independent country within the British Commonwealth. . . . A state of emergency is declared in the British-sponsored federation of South Arabia following an attack on British officials at Aden airport. Federation officials blame the assault on Yemeni terrorists.	Bolivia asks the U.S. for arms and planes for possible use against defiant tin miners holding four U.S. hostages.	Cambodia announces that most Western newsmen will be barred from the country because of recent, allegedly anti-Cambodian articles.
Dec. 11	American chemist Dr. Linus Carl Pauling, in a speech accepting the 1962 Nobel Peace Prize in Oslo, calls for an end to research, development and use of all biological and chemical weapons.		The U.N. Security Council votes 10-0 to call on Portugal to apply U.N. self-determination criteria to all its colonies and territories. . . . The General Assembly votes to create a special U.N. committee to investigate conditions in Oman, a British-protected sultanate on the Arabian Sea.		The South Vietnamese government indefinitely suspends three Vietnamese-language newspapers in Saigon for allegedly "slandering the army.". . . Gen. Thanom Kittikachorn is sworn-in as the new prime minister of Thailand. Kittikachorn succeeds P.M. Sarit Thanarat, who died Dec. 8.
Dec. 12		The Swiss Parliament elects Ludwig von Moos, a Conservative, as president of Switzerland for 1964. . . . British P.M. Alec Douglas-Home says in Commons that his government will help any British company facing difficulties because of Arab League boycotts.			

A	B	C	D	E
Includes developments that affect more than one world region, international organizations and important meetings of major world leaders.	*Includes all domestic and regional developments in Europe, including the Soviet Union, Turkey, Cyprus and Malta.*	*Includes all domestic and regional developments in Africa and the Middle East, including Iraq and Iran and excluding Cyprus, Turkey and Afghanistan.*	*Includes all domestic and regional developments in Latin America, the Caribbean and Canada.*	*Includes all domestic and regional developments in Asia and Pacific nations, extending from Afghanistan through all the Pacific Islands, except Hawaii.*

U.S. Politics & Social Issues	U.S. Foreign Policy & Defense	U.S. Economy & Environment	Science, Technology & Nature	Culture, Leisure & Life Style	
Following a meeting with Pres. Johnson, House GOP leader Charles Halleck announces support for the civil rights bill and says that Republicans will work for quick floor action on the measure. House Rules Committee Chmn. Howard Smith (D, Va.) indicates that he has abandoned a previously declared effort to trap the bill in committee.		Senate GOP leader Everett Dirksen (Ill.) pledges Republican efforts for early congressional action on the tax-cut bill following a White House meeting with Pres. Johnson.			Dec. 5
Pres. Johnson announces that he and House Speaker John McCormack (D, Mass.) have made an informal agreement on temporary succession to the presidency should Johnson become disabled.		The Labor Dept. reports that the seasonally-adjusted unemployment rate rose to a six-month high of 5.9% in November.			Dec. 6
Pres. Johnson tells his first presidential news conference that his primary task is "to establish a continuity in government," adding that good progress has been made so far.	Pres. Johnson, following a meeting with Defense Secy. McNamara, announces that the Defense Dept.'s civilian employment will be reduced by 25,000 by mid-1965.				Dec. 7
		Four unions representing locomotive firemen, trainmen and engineers file suit in federal court to challenge the federal arbitration ruling in the railroads' work-rules dispute.			Dec. 8
The FBI's report on its investigation of Pres. Kennedy's assassination is turned over to the special investigation commission headed by Chief Justice Earl Warren. The report, disclosed in part, names Lee Harvey Oswald as Pres. Kennedy's lone assassin.		The Studebaker Corp. announces the closing of its South Bend, Ind. plant because of financial losses. Studebaker's remaining auto production will be limited to a Canadian plant in Hamilton, Ont. . . . The *Wall Street Journal* reports that several Teamsters union leaders have resigned in protest against Teamsters Pres. Hoffa's alleged opposition to any official union expressions of mourning over the assassination of Pres. Kennedy.	Three NASA scientific advisers report that U.S. scientists may not be able to develop the technology to provide adequate radiation shielding for the project Apollo crew in time for their first scheduled flight to the moon in 1970.		Dec. 9
The Warren Commission investigating Pres. Kennedy's assassination announces the appointment of James Lee Rankin as its general counsel. . . . Pres. Johnson asks Congress to approve the minting of 50¢ coins bearing the portrait of the late Pres. Kennedy.		The N.Y.C. Council renames Idlewild Airport the John F. Kennedy International Airport.	U.S. Defense Secy. Robert McNamara discloses that he has ordered the Air Force to begin development of a manned orbiting space station to be ready for launch by early 1968. He simultaneously announces the cancellation of further development of the Dyna-Soar space glider.	British police report that 21 persons have now been arrested in connection with the Aug. 8, $7 million British train robbery. Almost $1 million of the stolen money has been recovered.	Dec. 10
		Pres. Johnson issues a statement directing federal agency heads to hold civilian employment below 1964 and 1963 budget levels. Johnson stresses the special need to cut costs in the Defense Dept.		Frank Sinatra Jr., 19, son of actor-singer Frank Sinatra, is released unharmed by kidnappers after his father reportedly payed a $240,000 ransom. The young Sinatra had been held for three days.	Dec. 11
Speaking to a meeting sponsored by the President's Committee on Equal Employment Opportunity, Pres. Johnson hails statistics showing an increase of Negro employment in management, sales, and technical jobs.	Defense Secy. McNamara discloses plans to close or curtail operations at 26 military posts in 14 states.	The American Farm Bureau Federation concludes its annual convention in Chicago after adopting resolutions opposing compensatory payments for agriculture and other policies "restricting production."			Dec. 12

F	G	H	I	J
Includes elections, federal-state relations, civil rights and liberties, crime, the judiciary, education, health care, poverty, urban affairs and population.	Includes formation and debate of U.S. foreign and defense policies, veterans' affairs and defense spending. (Relations with specific foreign countries are usually found under the region concerned.)	Includes business, labor, agriculture, taxation, transportation, consumer affairs, monetary and fiscal policy, natural resources, and pollution.	Includes worldwide scientific, medical and technological developments, natural phenomena, U.S. weather, natural disasters, and accidents.	Includes the arts, religion, scholarship, communications media, sports, entertainment, fashions, fads and social life.

	World Affairs	Europe	Africa & the Middle East	The Americas	Asia & the Pacific
Dec. 13		The West German Defense Ministry discloses that the U.S. and West Germany have reached agreement on manning a missile-firing destroyer with a mixed crew to test the controversial U.S. plan for NATO formation of a multi-lateral nuclear vessel force.			Communist Chinese Premier Chou En-lai leaves Peking to begin a two-month tour of African nations. . . . U.S. and Cambodia suspend diplomatic ties following a further deterioration in relations caused by a Cambodian government broadcast which allegedly implied satisfaction at Pres. Kennedy's assassination. Cambodia denies the allegation.
Dec. 14	In a speech carried in *Izvestia*, Premier Khrushchev announces a 5% reduction in the USSR's 1964 military budget. Khrushchev challenges Western nations to match Soviet arms cuts.			The U.S. recognizes the new military governments in the Dominican Republic and Honduras.	
Dec. 15		French Pres. de Gaulle pardons about 100 former members of the right-wing Secret Army Organization who had been jailed on subversion and terrorism charges.			
Dec. 16	The U.N.'s membership increases from 111 to 113 with the admission of Zanzibar and Kenya, former British colonial possessions in East Africa.	The regular meeting of NATO foreign ministers opens in Paris with the reading of a letter from Pres. Johnson reaffirming the U.S.'s commitment to the defense of Western Europe.	The last U.S. military base in Morocco is officially turned over to the Moroccan government.	Rebellious Bolivian tin miners, surrounded by government troops, release four U.S. officials held as hostages since Dec. 6. . . . The U.S. State Dept. issues tightened regulations barring Western ships trading with Cuba from carrying U.S. government-financed cargoes.	
Dec. 17	U.S. Pres. Lyndon Johnson, addressing the concluding meeting of the 18th regular session of the General Assembly, calls for U.N. leadership in a world wide peaceful revolution to wipe out poverty, hunger and disease. . . . *The New York Times* reports that Western leaders have been favorably impressed with USSR's Dec. 14 announcement of military expenditure cuts, despite some skepticism over the reliability of Soviet budget figures.	A special holiday pass agreement is signed by West Berlin and East German officials. It is the first bilateral agreement concluded between West Berlin and the East German government. . . . Defense Secy. McNamara warns NATO foreign ministers meeting in Paris that the U.S. expects its European allies to fulfill their obligations to raise the conventional force levels available to NATO.		The U.S. Senate ratifies the El Chamizal Treaty settling the boundary dispute between the U.S. and Mexico.	South Korea's third republic is formally established with the opening of the newly elected National Assembly and the inauguration of Pres. Chung Hee Park. . . . An effort to open negotiations on the deteriorating relations between the U.S. and Cambodia collapses in the face of a Cambodian demand for a prior U.S. apology. . . . The USSR informs Britain that it will support Cambodia's call for an international conference on Cambodian neutrality.
Dec. 18	Adlai Stevenson tells a U.N. news conference that the U.S. will press for suspension of the USSR's General Assembly voting rights in 1964 when its arrears will exceed twice its regular U.N. assessment—the point at which the U.N. Charter provides for forfeiture of a debtor nation's voting rights.	About 500 African students clash with Moscow police in a mass demonstration protesting alleged racial discrimination against African students in the USSR.			
Dec. 19	*The New York Times* reports that the USSR currently owes more than $50 million in unpaid assessments for U.N. operations in the Congo and the Middle East.	U.S. Secy. of State Rusk completes nine days of meetings with Western European leaders in a reported effort to gain broad support for new negotiations with the USSR on disarmament and other East-West problems. . . . The Supreme Soviet approves a $100.4 billion fiscal 1964-1965 state budget. The budget includes greatly increased expenditures for agricultural research and fertilizer production designed to boost the USSR's lagging farm economy.			U.S. Defense Secy. McNamara arrives in Saigon to make a personal assessment of the new South Vietnam government's military efforts against the Viet Cong.

A	B	C	D	E
Includes developments that affect more than one world region, international organizations and important meetings of major world leaders.	*Includes all domestic and regional developments in Europe, including the Soviet Union, Turkey, Cyprus and Malta.*	*Includes all domestic and regional developments in Africa and the Middle East, including Iraq and Iran and excluding Cyprus, Turkey and Afghanistan.*	*Includes all domestic and regional developments in Latin America, the Caribbean and Canada.*	*Includes all domestic and regional developments in Asia and Pacific nations, extending from Afghanistan through all the Pacific Islands, except Hawaii.*

U.S. Politics & Social Issues	U.S. Foreign Policy & Defense	U.S. Economy & Environment	Science, Technology & Nature	Culture, Leisure & Life Style	
	A bill (HR9009) authorizing $102 million for the Peace Corps in 1964 is signed by Pres. Johnson. The total represents a $38 million increase over the fiscal 1963 authorization. . . . Asst. State Secy. Roger Hilsman says that the U.S. favors keeping "the door open" to negotiations with Communist China in the event the Peking government ever abandons its public hostility toward the U.S.	The National Policy Committee on Pockets of Poverty, meeting in Washington, estimates that at least 46 million Americans live at "minimum adequacy" levels or below. . . . Pres. Johnson signs an administration-backed bill (HR134) establishing federal safety standards for automobile seat belts.	Congress passes and sends to the President a bill (HR8747) appropriating $5.1 billion for NASA in fiscal 1964. Although over $600 million less than the administration requested, it is $1.4 billion more than the fiscal 1963 NASA appropriation. . . . The U.N. General Assembly approves a resolution outlining legal principles to assure the peaceful exploration of space.		**Dec. 13**
A Gallup Poll of presidential nominees preferred by Republicans shows 29% favoring Richard Nixon, 27% for Goldwater, 16% for Lodge and 13% for Rockefeller.				The FBI announces the arrest of three men for the Dec. 8 kidnapping of Frank Sinatra Jr.	**Dec. 14**
About 2,500 Negroes, including Martin Luther King, participate in a civil rights march and demonstration in Atlanta, Ga.			U.S. scientists begin a three-day symposium in Dallas, Tex devoted to discussions of the Hoyle-Fowler theory that recently discovered celestial objects known as "radio stars" were created by a process of "gravitational collapse."		**Dec. 15**
	Pres. Johnson signs a compromise bill (HR7885) authorizing $3.6 billion for foreign aid programs in fiscal 1964. At about the same time, the House approves a bill to appropriate $800 million less than the sum authorized.	Pres. Johnson signs a compromise bill (HR6143) authorizing a $1.195 billion five-year program of federal grants and loans for college and university construction. Johnson calls it the most significant education bill "in the history of the republic."		A 13-man U.S. parachute team sets a world free-fall record of nearly eight miles near El Centro, Calif. . . . Welsh-born movie star Richard Burton is divorced by Sybil Burton. Burton has been involved in a widely publicized romance with actress Elizabeth Taylor.	**Dec. 16**
A special Senate investigating committee opens the public phase of its hearings into the outside business activities of dismissed Senate Democratic Party secretary Robert Baker.	Pres. Johnson sends a letter to Senate leaders urging restoration of House-passed cuts in the 1964 foreign aid appropriation bill. Johnson warns that the reductions risk "our security and future well-being."	Pres. Johnson signs into law a Clean Air Act (HR6518) authorizing a $95 million four-year program to prevent air pollution.		Northwestern University football coach Ara Parseghian is signed to a four-year contract as head coach at Notre Dame.	**Dec. 17**
The *Washington Post* carries an article summarizing the findings of an autopsy performed on Pres. Kennedy. According to the article, investigations showed that all three shots fired at the car (two of which mortally wounded the president) "had trajectories that would line them up with the sixth floor window of the Texas School Book Depository building, where the assassin has been traced.". . . Pres. Johnson tells an informal news conference that "poverty legislation for the lowest income groups" will be given high priority in the future legislative plans of his administration.		Pres. Johnson signs an administration-backed bill (HR4955) expanding vocational education programs.		The National Collegiate Athletic Association reports that a record 22,237,094 persons attended college football games in 1963.	**Dec. 18**
			Pres. Johnson criticizes Congress's action to ban use of appropriate space funds for a joint manned lunar landing with the USSR.		**Dec. 19**

F	G	H	I	J
Includes elections, federal-state relations, civil rights and liberties, crime, the judiciary, education, health care, poverty, urban affairs and population.	*Includes formation and debate of U.S. foreign and defense policies, veterans' affairs and defense spending. (Relations with specific foreign countries are usually found under the region concerned.)*	*Includes business, labor, agriculture, taxation, transportation, consumer affairs, monetary and fiscal policy, natural resources, and pollution.*	*Includes worldwide scientific, medical and technological developments, natural phenomena, U.S. weather, natural disasters, and accidents.*	*Includes the arts, religion, scholarship, communications media, sports, entertainment, fashions, fads and social life.*

	World Affairs	Europe	Africa & the Middle East	The Americas	Asia & the Pacific
Dec. 20			The British colony of Kenya becomes an independent country within the British Commonwealth at Nairobi ceremonies presided over by Prince Philip and Kenya Premier Jomo Kenyatta.		In remarks to Cairo newsmen, touring Chinese Premier Chou En-lai describes the assassination of Pres. Kennedy as a "despicable, shameful act.". . . The Asian Population Conference, meeting in New Delhi, adopts a resolution calling on Asian nations to take immediate steps to reduce population growth.
Dec. 21		Violent communal clashes erupt between Greek and Turkish Cypriotes on the island of Cyprus. The fighting reportedly stems from Turkish opposition to constitutional proposals by Cypriote Pres. Archbishop Makarios which would eliminate the Turkish minority's legislative veto rights.			Defense Secy. McNamara, just returned from Vietnam, reports to Pres. Johnson on recent military success scored by Viet Cong guerrillas. Following the meeting, the administration confirms that it has abandoned its previously announced goal of withdrawing most U.S. military personnel from South Vietnam by the end of 1965. . . . UAR Pres. Nasser issues a statement pledging support for China's claims to Formosa.
Dec. 22			The U.N. confirms that Ghana Pres. Nkrumah has asked that U.N. troops in the Congo be replaced by an all-African force. . . . Baghdad radio reports the withdrawal of a 5,000-man Syrian brigade that had been sent to northern Iraq to help fight Kurdish rebels.		
Dec. 23		At least 16 persons are reported to have been killed in the continuing fighting between the Greek and Turkish Cypriotes. . . . The six EEC nations conclude a two-week meeting in Brussels after agreeing on the creation of a Europe-wide market in basic foodstuffs and on a unified policy in the forthcoming world tariff reduction talks.			
Dec. 24		Britain, Greece, and Turkey, as guarantors of Cyprus's independence, issue a joint appeal for an immediate cease-fire between Greek and Turkish Cypriotes. . . . George Papandreou resigns as Prime Minister of Greece after his coalition government narrowly survived a parliamentary no-confidence vote earlier in the day.	Ghana Pres. Kwame Nkrumah declares "null and void" the Dec. 9 acquittals of three defendants charged with conspiracy against his regime.		
Dec. 25	New Delhi sources report that Communist China has reinforced its Sinkiang Province border opposite the USSR Republic Kazakhstan, scene of recent frontier tensions.	An estimated 500,000 West Berliners are visiting relatives in East Berlin under a special agreement granting them temporary passes during the Christmas-New Year holiday. It marks the first time since Aug. 13, 1961 that residents of West Berlin have been permitted to enter the Communist sector of the city.			South Vietnamese government forces reject a Viet Cong unilateral 24-hour Christmas cease-fire and continue operations.
Dec. 26	The U.S. Commerce Dept. announces approval of two licenses for the export of 500,000 tons of wheat to the USSR. The announcement is the first indication that suspended Soviet-U.S. wheat negotiations have been resumed.				New Delhi sources report that talks are underway in Peking between Chinese and French representatives seeking an accord on increased trade between the two countries.

A	B	C	D	E
Includes developments that affect more than one world region, international organizations and important meetings of major world leaders.	*Includes all domestic and regional developments in Europe, including the Soviet Union, Turkey, Cyprus and Malta.*	*Includes all domestic and regional developments in Africa and the Middle East, including Iraq and Iran and excluding Cyprus, Turkey and Afghanistan.*	*Includes all domestic and regional developments in Latin America, the Caribbean and Canada.*	*Includes all domestic and regional developments in Asia and Pacific nations, extending from Afghanistan through all the Pacific Islands, except Hawaii.*

U.S. Politics & Social Issues	U.S. Foreign Policy & Defense	U.S. Economy & Environment	Science, Technology & Nature	Culture, Leisure & Life Style	
Proposals for the abolition of literacy tests and poll taxes and for an 18-year-old voting age are among 19 recommendations included in a report of the President's Commission on Registration and Voting Participation.		A federal grand jury in Washington indicts the William S. Merrill Co. on charges of filing false information about the harmful effects of anti-cholesterol drug MER-29 (triparanol).			Dec. 20
	Defense Secy. McNamara, just returned from Vietnam, reports to Pres. Johnson on a recent military success scored by Viet Cong guerrillas. Following the meeting, the administration confirms that it has abandoned its previously announced goal of withdrawing most U.S. military personnel from South Vietnam by the end of 1965. . . . Pres. Johnson signs a bill (HR9139) appropriating nearly $1.6 billion for fiscal 1964 construction at military bases in the U.S. and abroad.		A Tiros 8 weather satellite is successfully orbited from Cape Kennedy. The satellite is equipped with experimental camera equipment designed to transmit instant weather pictures to inexpensive ground stations that could be set up anywhere in its path.		Dec. 21
Pres. Johnson attends a candlelight service at the Lincoln Memorial to mark the end of the 30-day official mourning period for the late Pres. Kennedy.			The U.S. Communications Satellite Corp. announces that it hopes to begin trans-Atlantic service in 1965, about a year earlier than previously planned.	Paul Robeson, Negro basso and actor, arrives in New York, ending a five-year self-exile from the U.S.	Dec. 22
	Pres. Johnson signs a bill (HR7044) to make Corregidor Island in Manila Bay a World War II memorial.				Dec. 23
					Dec. 24
					Dec. 25
		The National Safety Council reports that traffic accidents during the 30-hour Christmas holiday caused 226 U.S. deaths.		Gallup Poll finds Pres. Johnson as the living man "most admired" by Americans in 1963.	Dec. 26

F	G	H	I	J
Includes elections, federal-state relations, civil rights and liberties, crime, the judiciary, education, health care, poverty, urban affairs and population.	Includes formation and debate of U.S. foreign and defense policies, veterans' affairs and defense spending. (Relations with specific foreign countries are usually found under the region concerned.)	Includes business, labor, agriculture, taxation, transportation, consumer affairs, monetary and fiscal policy, natural resources, and pollution.	Includes worldwide scientific, medical and technological developments, natural phenomena, U.S. weather, natural disasters, and accidents.	Includes the arts, religion, scholarship, communications media, sports, entertainment, fashions, fads and social life.

	World Affairs	Europe	Africa & the Middle East	The Americas	Asia & the Pacific
Dec. 27		The U.N. Security Council meets in emergency session to hear Cypriote charges that Turkey is preparing to forcibly intervene in Cyprus's internal affairs. . . . West German Chancellor Ludwig Erhard meets with Pres. Johnson at the latter's LBJ ranch in Texas. Erhard is reported to have assured Pres. Johnson that Bonn will support American efforts to seek new negotiations with the USSR on easing East-West tensions.			Philippine Foreign Secy. Salvador Lopez announces that the U.S. and Cambodia have accepted a Philippine offer to mediate their current dispute. . . . Soviet Premier Khrushchev, speaking at a Kremlin reception, predicts that the U.S. will someday be ousted from South Vietnam.
Dec. 28					
Dec. 29			A Soviet agreement to provide additional economic assistance to Algeria is disclosed in Moscow by *Tass*.		
Dec. 30	In a traditional year-end interview Soviet Premier Khrushchev calls for intensified Soviet-U.S. efforts to make 1964 "a year of decisive change for the better in the entire international situation.". . . Premier Chou En-lai, in a French TV interview taped in Rabat, Morocco, proposes a "normalization" of relations between Communist China and France.				
Dec. 31		British Commonwealth Secy. Duncan Sandys announces in Nicosia that Greek and Turkish Cypriotes have agreed to a number of cease-fire proposals, including the creation of a British-patrolled demilitarized zone in Nicosia and an exchange of prisoners taken in recent fighting. . . . The Bulgarian Supreme Court sentences to death a former member of the Bulgarian U.N. mission, Ivan Khristov Georgiev, on charges of having spied for the U.S.			

A	B	C	D	E
Includes developments that affect more than one world region, international organizations and important meetings of major world leaders.	Includes all domestic and regional developments in Europe, including the Soviet Union, Turkey, Cyprus and Malta.	Includes all domestic and regional developments in Africa and the Middle East, including Iraq and Iran and excluding Cyprus, Turkey and Afghanistan.	Includes all domestic and regional developments in Latin America, the Caribbean and Canada.	Includes all domestic and regional developments in Asia and Pacific nations, extending from Afghanistan through all the Pacific Islands, except Hawaii.

U.S. Politics & Social Issues	U.S. Foreign Policy & Defense	U.S. Economy & Environment	Science, Technology & Nature	Culture, Leisure & Life Style	
Pres. Johnson, spending a working vacation at the LBJ ranch near Austin, Tex., holds an outdoor barbecue for 200 reporters and photographers.	The New York-based Fair Play for Cuba Committee announces that it is disbanding in the wake of unfavorable publicity arising from Lee Harvey Oswald's brief association with the group. . . . Newly appointed Asst. State Secy. Thomas Mann is named by Pres. Johnson as the coordinator of all Alliance for Progress programs.				Dec. 27
				A U.S. tennis team of Chuck McKinley and Dennis Ralston defeats an Australian team of Roy Emerson, Neale Fraser and John Newcombe to win the Davis Cup in Adelaide, Australia.	Dec. 28
	A *New York Times* article estimates that U.S. military authorities launched 46 "secret" satellites during 1963.		The USSR's Institute of Radio Engineering reports that Soviet scientists have successfully bounced a radio signal off the planet Jupiter.	The Chicago Bears defeat the New York Giants to win the 1963 National Football League championship in Chicago.	Dec. 29
Congress adjourns after its longest peacetime session in history.	Congress passes a greatly reduced $3 billion foreign aid appropriation bill for fiscal 1964. The bill includes a much-debated provision to allow the President to approve credit for sales of wheat and other products to communist nations.	Pres. Johnson signs a bill (HR6754) appropriating $6.2 billion for the Agriculture Dept. in fiscal 1964. The total is $144 million less than requested by the administration. . . . The U.S. Agriculture Dept. reports that the farm parity ratio dropped from 79 in 1962 to 78 in 1963, the lowest level since 1939.		The N.Y. Film Critics pick the British film *Tom Jones* as the best motion picutre of 1963. . . . Bobby Fischer, 20, wins the U.S. chess championship for the sixth time.	Dec. 30
The District of Columbia approves a broad anti-discrimination housing measure.		The Dow Jones average of industrial stock prices closed the year 762.95, up 110.85 from Dec. 31, 1962.			Dec. 31

F	G	H	I	J
Includes elections, federal-state relations, civil rights and liberties, crime, the judiciary, education, health care, poverty, urban affairs and population.	*Includes formation and debate of U.S. foreign and defense policies, veterans' affairs and defense spending. (Relations with specific foreign countries are usually found under the region concerned.)*	*Includes business, labor, agriculture, taxation, transportation, consumer affairs, monetary and fiscal policy, natural resources, and pollution.*	*Includes worldwide scientific, medical and technological developments, natural phenomena, U.S. weather, natural disasters, and accidents.*	*Includes the arts, religion, scholarship, communications media, sports, entertainment, fashions, fads and social life.*

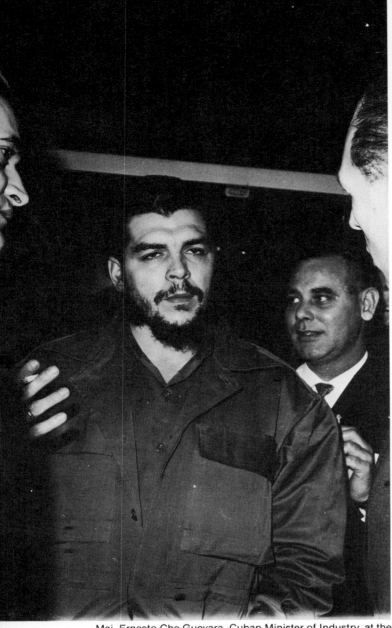

Maj. Ernesto Che Guevara, Cuban Minister of Industry, at the
United Nations Dec. 10.

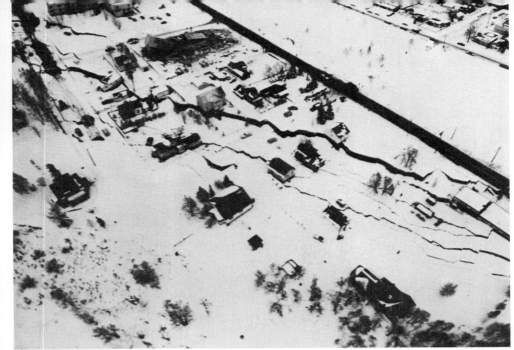

Aerial scene showing damage in Anchorage, Alaska. The area was
devastated by a powerful earthquake on March 27.

Cassius Clay connects with a left to Sonny Liston's right eye in the third
round of their championship fight in Miami Beach, Florida on Feb. 26.
Clay won on a technical knockout in the seventh round.

The Unisphere, symbol of the New York World's Fair.

Delegates demonstrate for President Johnson after he receives
the presidential nomination at the Democratic National Convention.

Members of the Warren Commission examine the scene of President
Kennedy's assassination in Dallas. They are (left to right) Rep. Hale
Boggs, Secret Service Agent John Joe Howlett, Sen. Richard Russell
and Sen. John Sherman Cooper.

King Constantine of Greece takes the oath as new Monarch of the Hellenes following the death of his father, King Paul. At the King's left is Prime Minister George Papandreou.

James R. Hoffa leaves the U.S. District Court in Chicago after he and six co-defendents were convicted on fraud charges.

A Greek Orthodox priest examines the remains of his church at Pahyamos, Cyprus, after it was bombed by the Turkish Air Force during the Greek-Cypriot war.

Southern Rhodesia's newly appointed prime minister, Ian Smith, addresses local cattlemen in Gwanda.

	World Affairs	Europe	Africa & the Middle East	The Americas	Asia & the Pacific
Jan.	Seventeen-nation disarmament conference reconvenes in Geneva.	Soviet fighters shoot down an unarmed U.S. jet training plane over East Germany.	Kenneth Kuanda becomes the first prime minister of Zambia after winning parliamentary elections.	Anti-U.S. riots leave 20 Panamanians and four U.S. soldiers dead in the Canal Zone.	Major Gen. Nguyen Khanh overthrows the ruling South Vietnamese military junta.
Feb.	U.N. calls on Ethiopia and Somalia to end their border hostilities.	Greece says it opposes an independent Cyprus.	Libya says it will not renew the leases of the U.S. and British military bases on its territory.	OAS charges that Cuba smuggled arms into Venezuela during the 1963 presidential elections.	Malaysia asks Britain to defend it against any attack from Indonesia.
March	U.N. votes to send an international peace force to Cyprus.	Soviet planes shoot down a U.S. jet reconnaissance plane over East Germany.	Royal Saudi family indicates that it will replace King Saud with Prince Faisal.	Raul Leoni succeeds Romulo Betancourt as president of Venezuela thereby becoming the nation's first popularly elected president to succeed a popularly elected president who had fulfilled his term.	Cambodian officials arrive in Communist China for arms purchases talks.
April	Cuba withdraws from the International Monetary Fund.	Cyprus unilaterally ends its treaty of association with Greece and Turkey.	Ian Smith becomes Prime Minister of Southern Rhodesia.	Brazilian Army overthrows Pres. Joào Goulart and names Gen. Humberto Castelo Branco as president.	Right-wing military junta overthrows the coalition government of Laos.
May	Kennedy round of trade negotiations begins in Geneva.	Britain flies in troops to Aden after violent unrest by Arab nationalists breaks out.	Iraq says it plans to join Egypt's United Arab Republic.	Canada makes a major wheat sale to Communist China.	Indian P.M. Jawaharlal Nehru dies.
June	U.N. ends its four-year military operation in the Congo.	Turkey draws back from invading Cyprus.	Rebel forces capture Albertville, the capital of the Congo's North Katanga Province.	Brazil suspends the political rights of former Pres. Juscelino Kubitschek.	South Korea declares martial law in the Seoul area in the wake of rioting.
July	OAS votes for economic sanctions against Cuba.	Britain agrees to grant Gambia its independence in 1965.	Malawi becomes an independent country.	Haiti accuses the Dominican Republic of supporting an armed invasion of its territory.	Viet Cong inflict a major defeat on South Vietnamese forces during a two-day battle.
Aug.	U.N. calls for an end to minor clashes between Turkey and Cyprus.	Cyprus agrees to lift a blockade imposed on Turkish Cypriots.	Rebel forces capture Stanleyville, the Congo's third largest city.	Bolivia breaks diplomatic relations with Cuba.	U.S. planes bomb North Vietnam after North Vietnamese patrol boats attack U.S. destroyers in international waters.
Sept.	U.N. votes to keep its forces in Cyprus for another three months.	Italian CP publishes a wide-ranging critique of the Soviet Union.	Saudi Arabia and Egypt agree to try to reach a settlement of their dispute in Yemen.	Eduardo Frei wins the Chilean presidential election.	Indonesia parachutes small groups of guerrillas into Malaysia.
Oct.	Second conference of unaligned nations opens in Cairo.	Soviet CP forces Premier Nikita Khrushchev to retire and replaces him with Aleksei Kosygin and Leonid Brezhnev.	Zambia becomes an independent country.	Marco Aurelio Robles becomes president of Panama.	Communist China conducts its first nuclear test.
Nov.	Kennedy-round tariff negotiations for reduced tariffs reconvene in Geneva.	West Germany calls for increased efforts for European unity.	Saudi ruling family dethrowns King Saud and replaces him with Prince Faisal.	Bolivian military overthrows Victor Pres. Paz Estenssoro and replaces him with Gen. Rene Bavientos Ortuno.	South Vietnam imposes martial low on Saigon following anti-government rioting.
Dec.	U.N. extends its Cypriote peace-keeping mission for another three months.	Belgian notifies the U.N. that its military intervention in the Congo has ended.	Egypt says that it is aiding Congolese rebels.	Brazil sends former Argentine dictator Juan Peron back to Spain after he lands in Brazil enroute to Argentina.	South Vietnamese leaders arrest scores of civilian political leaders.

A	B	C	D	E
Includes developments that affect more than one world region, international organizations and important meetings of major world leaders.	Includes all domestic and regional developments in Europe, including the Soviet Union, Turkey, Cyprus and Malta.	Includes all domestic and regional developments in Africa and the Middle East, including Iraq and Iran and excluding Cyprus, Turkey and Afghanistan.	Includes all domestic and regional developments in Latin America, the Caribbean and Canada.	Includes all domestic and regional developments in Asia and Pacific nations, extending from Afghanistan through all the Pacific Islands, except Hawaii.

U.S. Politics & Social Issues	U.S. Foreign Policy & Defense	U.S. Economy & Environment	Science, Technology & Nature	Culture, Leisure & Life Style
Pres. Johnson calls for wide-ranging programs to end discrimination in his State of the Union Message.	U.S. makes its first wheat sale to the Soviet Union.	Teamsters Union agrees to a nationwide trucking contract.	U.S. FTC proposes stringent curbs on cigarette advertising.	Pope Paul and Athenagoras I, ecumenical patriarch of Constantinople, meet on the Mount of Olives in Jerusalem.
Supreme Court rules that congressional districts within each state must be substantially equal in population.	Pres. Johnson says that the U.S. has a plane capable of flying more than 2,000 m.p.h.	U.S. Treasury Dept. announces the first U.S. drawing from the International Monetary Fund.	British scientists detect an omega-minus sub-atomic particle.	Cassius Clay wins the heavyweight boxing championship from Sonny Liston.
Two-day race riots take place in Jacksonville, Fla.	Defense Secy. Robert McNamara announces large aid increases to South Vietnam.	Pres. Johnson calls for the creation of a national commission on automation and technological change.	Pres. Johnson declares Alaska a disaster area after an earthquake rocks the Anchorage area.	Pope Paul calls for a dialogue between Roman Catholic and Protestants.
Supreme Court refuses to consider a union challenge to an arbitration award allowing the elimination of thousands of railroad jobs.	U.S. resumes diplomatic relations with Panama.	U.S. indicts eight steel companies for price-fixing.	U.S. launches Gemini spacecraft into orbit.	Britain celebrates the 400th anniversary of the birth of William Shakespeare.
Supreme Court orders Prince Edward County, Va. to reopen its public schools which were closed in 1959 to avoid desegregation.	Defence Secy. Robert McNamara arrives in Saigon on his fifth fact-finding mission.	AFL-CIO states its opposition to the Johnson administration's wage and price guidelines policy.	World's first nuclear-powered lighthouse begins operation in Chesapeake Bay.	Pulitzer Prizes fail to include a selection in the arts for the first time since 1917.
U.S. Senate inokes cloture and then passes a major civil rights bill.	Pres. Johnson warns Turkey not to invade Cyprus.	U.S. steel companies agree to promote racial equality in the steel industry.	U.S. and the Soviet Union agree to exchange meteorological information.	Pope Paul says the Church is making a major study of its position on birth control.
Republican party nominates Senator Barry Goldwater (R. Ariz.) as its presidential nominee.	U.S. warns North Vietnam to stop its infiltration of South Vietnam.	NLRB votes that racial discrimination by a union constitutes an unfair labor practice.	U.S. spacecraft Ranger 7 transmits 4,000 photos of the moon back to the earth.	Pope Paul says that reconciliation with other Christian churches is imperative.
Pres. Johnson chooses Sen. Hubert Humphrey as his vice-presidential candidate.	Congress gives its near unanimous approval for the U.S. bombing of North Vietnam.	Senate passes a bill providing additional safeguards for stock investors.	U.S. launches the meteorological satellite Nimbus.	Pope Paul states his readiness to mediate any international disputes.
F.B.I. reports that it has found no systematic organization behind the 1964 summer racial riots in nine northern cities.	U.S. agrees to send India free wheat in the wake of a food crisis.	UAW begins a strike against General Motors.	U.S. postpones a projected two-man Gemini spaceflight until 1965.	Hungary agrees to allow the Vatican to appoint Hungarian bishops.
F.B.I. arrests four Philadelphia, Miss. officials on charges of depriving blacks of their civil rights.	Pres. Johnson confers with Philippine Pres. Diosdado Macapagal about Vietnam.	UAW votes to end their strike against General Motors.	Three Soviet cosmonauts make the world's first multiseat spacecraft orbit.	Jean Paul Sartre wins the 1964 Nobel Prize in Literature.
Pres. Johnson wins 44 states in a decisive victory over Republican candidate Barry Goldwater.	U.S. planes parachute Belgian paratroopers over Stanleyville, the Congo.	U.S. closes 95 domestic military cases in an economy move.	U.S. launches Mariner 4 to take close-up television pictures of Mars.	Vatican Council denies any special Jewish guilt in the crucifixion of Jesus.
F.B.I. arrests 21 white men in Miss. in connection with the murder of three civil rights workers in June.	Pres. Johnson presents the first Medal of Honor for heroism in South Vietnam.	U.S. Secy. of Commerce Luther Hodges resigns.	Soviet Union launches an advanced communications satellite.	One million people warmly welcome Pope Paul in Bombay, India.

F	G	H	I	J
Includes elections, federal-state relations, civil rights and liberties, crime, the judiciary, education, health care, poverty, urban affairs and population.	Includes formation and debate of U.S. foreign and defense policies, veterans' affairs and defense spending. (Relations with specific foreign countries are usually found under the region concerned.)	Includes business, labor, agriculture, taxation, transportation, consumer affairs, monetary and fiscal policy, natural resources, and pollution.	Includes worldwide scientific, medical and technological developments, natural phenomena, U.S. weather, natural disasters, and accidents.	Includes the arts, religion, scholarship, communications media, sports, entertainment, fashions, fads and social life.

	World Affairs	Europe	Africa & the Middle East	The Americas	Asia & the Pacific
Jan. 1	U.S. Pres. Lyndon Johnson, in a New Year's message to the USSR, says that 1964 should be a year of concrete action toward the goal of relaxed East-West tensions. . . . A New Year's editorial in the *Peking People's Daily* declares that China will continue to "resolutely oppose the policy of war and aggression of imperialism headed by the United States."	Archbishop Makarios, President of Cyprus and leader of the Greek Cypriotes, announces that he will seek abrigation of existing treaties which permit Turkey, Greece and Britain to station troops in Cyprus to guarantee its independence.		Cuban Premier Fidel Castro in an ABC-TV interview expresses hope for improvement in U.S.-Cuban relations. Castro asserts that Pres. John Kennedy indicated before his death a willingness to normalize relations with Cuba.	U.S. Pres. Lyndon Johnson, in a message to South Vietnamese junta chairman Gen. Duong Van Minh, promises continued U.S. aid in the fight against Viet cong guerrillas. . . . The *Peking People's Daily*, the official Communist Party newspaper, reports that increased agricultural production will be China's primary economic goal in 1964.
Jan. 2	Soviet Premier Khrushchev, in a message to world leaders, proposes a worldwide treaty denouncing war as a means of settling territorial disputes. Khrushchev also urges the withdrawal of U.S. troops from Germany, Korea and Vietnam as a first step toward reunification of those countries.	Greek and Turkish Cypriote leaders agree to a British proposal for an international conference in London on resolving the communal disputes that have led to bloody clashes between ethnic groups on Cyprus.	Ghana Pres. Kwame Nkrumah escapes unhurt after being shot at by a lone assassin outside his presidential palace. It is the fifth attempt on Nkrumah's life since 1956.	U.S. Secy. of State Dean Rusk, commenting on a Jan. 1 interview with Fidel Castro, denies that Pres. Kennedy had ever expected an early improvement in U.S.-Cuban relations.	
Jan. 3	The U.S. State Dept. says it will give careful study to Soviet Premier Khrushchev's Jan. 2 proposal on renouncing war, but indicates disappointment at the allegedly propagandistic purposes and tone of his message. . . . U.S. and Soviet officials jointly announce completion of the first of a series of Soviet purchases of U.S. wheat expected eventually to total more than four million metric tons, worth about $250 million.	West German sources report that the U.S., Britain and France have agreed to allow West Berlin Mayor Willy Brandt to pursue contacts with East German authorities on extending the current holiday pass agreement due to expire at midnight Jan. 5. Such contacts have been officially opposed by West German political leaders. . . . Cyprus V.P. Fazil Kutchuk, leader of the Turkish Cypriotes, declares that partition is the only way to guarantee the minority rights of Turkish Cypriotes.	Holden Roberto, leader of a major Angolan rebel group, says that his organization has decided to accept offers of aid from Communist China "and other communist nations."		
Jan. 4					U.S. military spokesmen in South Vietnam report an increase over the past six months in Communist arms shipments to the Viet Cong. Most of the increased arms are said to be entering South Vietnam through Cambodia.
Jan. 5			Ghana Pres. Nkrumah issues a declaration calling for the expulsion of "capitalists" and "reactionaries" from the country's civil service, judiciary and army.		
Jan. 6		Communist border guards close the Berlin Wall following the expiration of a Christmas pass agreement under which 1.25 million West Berliners had entered the city's Communist sector for one day visits with relatives. . . . The government of Cyprus announces its approval of the stationing of a U.N. observer in Cyprus to supervise the cease-fire that had been negotiated Dec. 24, 1963 to end Greek-Turkish Cypriote clashes.			Maj. Gen. Duong Van Minh, chairman of South Vietnam's ruling military junta, signs a series of decrees formalizing the junta's military and political control of the nation.

A	B	C	D	E
Includes developments that affect more than one world region, international organizations and important meetings of major world leaders.	*Includes all domestic and regional developments in Europe, including the Soviet Union, Turkey, Cyprus and Malta.*	*Includes all domestic and regional developments in Africa and the Middle East, including Iraq and Iran and excluding Cyprus, Turkey and Afghanistan.*	*Includes all domestic and regional developments in Latin America, the Caribbean and Canada.*	*Includes all domestic and regional developments in Asia and Pacific nations, extending from Afghanistan through all the Pacific Islands, except Hawaii.*

U.S. Politics & Social Issues	U.S. Foreign Policy & Defense	U.S. Economy & Environment	Science, Technology & Nature	Culture, Leisure & Life Style	
The Census Bureau estimates that U.S. population grew 2,633,000 during 1963 to a current total of 190,695,000.	Pres. Lyndon Johnson promises continued aid to South Vietnam in a message to junta chairman Gen. Duong Van Minh. Johnson asserts that recent proposals for the neutralization of South Vietnam "would be another name for Communist takeover."			The University of Illinois defeats the University of Washington, 17-7, in the Rose Bowl football classic.	**Jan. 1**
In an article in the *Journal of the National Education Association*, Pres. Lyndon Johnson calls for a national education program "of massive proportions that will help master the problems of our age."	Pres. Johnson designates ex-Amb.-to-India Ellsworth Bunker as ambassador to the OAS.	Final legislative figures show that the first session of the 88th Congress approved a total of $102,576,952,132 in appropriations during 1963. The administration had requested a total of $109,094,256,136. . . . The Labor Dept. reports that 3,400 strikes involving just over 1 million workers began in 1963. . . . The Russell Sage Foundation reports that the assets of U.S. philanthropic foundations total $14.5 billion, a $3 billion increase over 1960.			**Jan. 2**
Sen. Barry Goldwater formally announces his candidacy for the Republican presidential nomination. Goldwater says he is running to give the American people "a clear choice" between a party emphasizing "individual liberty" and one emphasizing "the extension of government power."		The Justice Dept. reports that the number of racketeering indictments brought in 1963 numbered 262, almost six times as many as 1961.	Astronomers at the University of Arizona's Stewart Observatory report in *Science* magazine that bright clouds seen in the U.S. southwest long after sunset are probably produced by rockets launched from the Pacific Missile Range.		**Jan. 3**
Auburn (Ala.) University enrolls its first Negro student without serious incident.	Pres. Lyndon Johnson orders a voluntary program for rehabilitating persons rejected by the draft for physical or mental reasons. Johnson estimates that one-third of all youths becoming 18 would be found unqualified for induction into the armed forces.			John Pennel, the first man to pole-vault over 17 feet, is named winner of AAU's Sullivan Memorial Trophy as the outstanding athlete of 1963. . . . An AP poll of sports writers names Mary (Mickey) Wright as 1963's woman athlete of the year.	**Jan. 4**
	In an NBC-TV interview, GOP presidential hopeful Barry Goldwater says that Soviet Premier Khrushchev should be induced to permit self-determination in Eastern Europe and calls for a naval blockade of Cuba to compel withdrawal of remaining Soviet troops.	The American Tobacco Co. introduces a new brand of cigarettes, called Carltons, which prominently states the tar and nicotine contents on every package.		The San Diego Chargers defeat the Boston Patriots, 51-10, to win the American Football League championship.	**Jan. 5**
Dallas District Atty. Henry Wade reports that an inquiry has disclosed "no evidence whatever" of alleged collusion between Jack Ruby and Dallas police officers in Ruby's slaying of accused assassin Lee Harvey Oswald. . . . Mrs. Anna Campbell Kelton Wiley, women's rights campaigner and pioneer in the area of consumer protection, dies in Washington at age 86.		The Consolidated Edison Co. announces that it has abandoned plans for a nuclear power plant on Long Island (N.Y.) in the face of strong public opposition to the site. . . . The Supreme Court reverses a Tennessee court injunction against picketing of a construction site by non-employees.		Pope Paul VI concludes a three-day historic visit to the holy lands of Jordan and Israel. The trip marked the first papal excursion outside of Italy since 1809 and the first air flight ever made by a Roman Catholic pope.	**Jan. 6**

F	G	H	I	J
Includes elections, federal-state relations, civil rights and liberties, crime, the judiciary, education, health care, poverty, urban affairs and population.	Includes formation and debate of U.S. foreign and defense policies, veterans' affairs and defense spending. (Relations with specific foreign countries are usually found under the region concerned.)	Includes business, labor, agriculture, taxation, transportation, consumer affairs, monetary and fiscal policy, natural resources, and pollution.	Includes worldwide scientific, medical and technological developments, natural phenomena, U.S. weather, natural disasters, and accidents.	Includes the arts, religion, scholarship, communications media, sports, entertainment, fashions, fads and social life.

	World Affairs	Europe	Africa & the Middle East	The Americas	Asia & the Pacific
Jan. 7	Talks open in Moscow on the fourth two-year renewal of the U.S.-Soviet cultural exchange program.		U.N. Secy. Gen. U Thant, speaking at Columbia Univ., singles out the Middle East as one of the world's major trouble spots of 1964. Thant calls for continued U.N. efforts to control tensions growing out of the Yemeni civil war and the continued Arab-Israeli hostility.	British officials announce the sale of 450 English buses to the Cuban government. The transaction is criticized by the U.S. State Dept. . . . Britain grants the Bahamas internal self-government. Sir Roland Symonette is inaugurated as the Bahamas' first prime minister.	Indian P.M. Jawaharal Nehru, 74, is reported to have fallen seriously ill on the eve of the Congress Party's annual convention. Official sources describe Nehru's condition as extreme fatigue and high blood pressure, but others report he has suffered a mild stroke. . . . British forces in Malaysia report sporadic clashes with armed Indonesian infiltrators in the federation states of Sarawak and Sabah.
Jan. 8	The U.S. representatives to the Soviet-U.S. cultural exchange talks in Moscow propose a freer and expanded program of cultural contacts between the American and Soviet peoples.				
Jan. 9	Communist Chinese Premier Chou En-lai concludes a nine-day state visit to Albania, marked by extensive talks with Communist Party chief Enver Hoxha.	West German Chancellor Ludwig Erhard proposes that EEC leaders meet to discuss the group's internal divisions over the admission of Britain and over the future political organization of Western Europe. . . . CIA analysts assert at a Washington press conference that the USSR's economic growth has slowed down from a post-war annual average of 6%-10% to less than 2.5% a year during 1962 and 1963.		A dispute over flag-flying, a focal point of mounting U.S.-Panamanian tensions over the 60-year-old Canal Zone treaty erupts into widespread violence. At least 20 persons, including four U.S. soldiers, are killed and more than 300 wounded in clashes between Panamanian mobs and American troops within the Canal Zone. . . . Panama severs diplomatic relations with the U.S. in protest against alleged brutality of U.S. troops against Panamanian demonstrators.	Viet cong guerrillas overrun two strategic hamlets in South Vietnam's Pleiku Province, 250 miles north of Saigon. It is one of several recent victories scored by the pro-Communist forces.
Jan. 10	Two more U.S. grain trading firms are granted Commerce Dept. licenses for the export of wheat to the USSR. . . . U.S. Secy. of State Rusk proposes a thorough reform of the U.N. General Assembly's growing role in world peace-keeping efforts.	Officials in West Berlin and East Germany resume talks on proposals for re-opening East Berlin to visits by West Berliners.		The U.S. and Panama agree to use the good offices of the OAS in an effort to settle their current Canal dispute. . . . Panamanian Pres. Roberto Chiari declares that "a complete revision" of the treaty governing U.S. operation of the Panama Canal will be a pre-condition to resuming relations with Washington.	
Jan. 11				The U.N. Security Council, following an emergency session, urges the U.S. and Panama to halt the bloodshed in the Canal Zone. . . . U.S. and Panamanian officials begin meeting with the OAS Inter-American Peace Committee in Panama City.	
Jan. 12			The predominantly Arab government of Zanzibar under P.M. Sheik Mohammed Shamte Hamadi is overthrown by an armed revolt led by a coalition of African (Negro) nationalist groups.		
Jan. 13			U.N. Secy. Gen. U Thant appoints an expert committee to try to devise a peaceful resolution of South Africa's racial strife.	U.S. State Secy. Rusk charges in an ABC-TV interview that Castro agents played a direct role in instigating the recent Panama Canal Zone rioting. . . . Cuban Premier Castro arrives in Moscow for discussions of Soviet-Cuban relations.	

A	B	C	D	E
Includes developments that affect more than one world region, international organizations and important meetings of major world leaders.	Includes all domestic and regional developments in Europe, including the Soviet Union, Turkey, Cyprus and Malta.	Includes all domestic and regional developments in Africa and the Middle East, including Iraq and Iran and excluding Cyprus, Turkey and Afghanistan.	Includes all domestic and regional developments in Latin America, the Caribbean and Canada.	Includes all domestic and regional developments in Asia and Pacific nations, extending from Afghanistan through all the Pacific Islands, except Hawaii.

U.S. Politics & Social Issues	U.S. Foreign Policy & Defense	U.S. Economy & Environment	Science, Technology & Nature	Culture, Leisure & Life Style	
The second session of the 88th Congress convenes with Democrats outnumbering Republicans 67-33 in the Senate and 255-177 in the House. . . . Gov. George Romney (R, Mich.) tells a National Press Club luncheon that he is not an active candidate for the GOP presidential nomination but would accept a draft. . . . Howard H. Baker, 61, U.S. Representative (Tenn.) since 1950 and a powerful GOP congressional leader, dies in Knoxville of a heart attack.	Pres. Johnson signs a severely reduced fiscal 1964 foreign aid appropriations bill (HR9499) totaling $3 billion ($2 billion for economic aid, $1 billion for military assistance).			Johnny Kerr of the Philadelphia 76ers sets an NBA record of 711 consecutive games.	Jan. 7
Pres. Lyndon Johnson appears before a joint session of Congress to deliver his first State of the Union Message. Johnson, emphasizing domestic issues, calls for a general "war on poverty" and reiterates earlier demands for quick congressional action on pending civil rights and tax-cut measures. . . . Sen. Barry Goldwater accuses Pres. Johnson of having "out-Roosevelted Roosevelt" in his State of the Union speech.	In his State of the Union Message, Pres. Johnson pledges to maintain and use U.S. strength in a continuing effort to achieve world peace.	In his first State of the Union Message, Pres. Johnson says he will submit to Congress a "frugality" budget calling for expenditures of $97.9 billion.	Pres. Johnson, in his State of the Union Message pledges policies to assure U.S. "pre-eminence in the peaceful exploration of outer space, focusing on an expedition to the moon in this decade.". . . Researchers at the University of Maryland announce that the Food and Drug Administration has approved Indoklon (hexafluorodiethyl ether), an inhalant drug that may replace electric shock therapy in treating acute depression.		Jan. 8
The Senate Rules Committee resumes closed hearings on the business activities of Robert Baker, ex-secretary to Senate Democrats.	Sen. Barry Goldwater, campaigning in the New Hampshire GOP presidential primary, charges that U.S. ICBM missiles are "not dependable" and says the Defense Dept. should "tell the American people" about it. . . . Deputy Defense Secy. Roswell Gilpatric announces his resignation, effective Jan. 20. Pres. Johnson designates Army Secy. Cyrus Vance to succeed Gilpatric and Army Undersecy. Stephen Ailes to replace Vance.	The Commerce Clearing House reports that total annual state tax collections exceeded $22 billion for the first time in 1963.			Jan. 9
Gov. Nelson Rockefeller (R, N.Y.) asserts that Pres. Johnson in his State of the Union Message "held out to the people a package of promises that simply will not be delivered at the quoted price."					Jan. 10
Chief counsel J. Lee Rankin announces that the Warren Commission inquiry into the assassination of Pres. John Kennedy will focus on three main areas: Lee Harvey Oswald, Jack Ruby, and the security measures taken to protect the President. . . . Atlanta Mayor Ivan Allen announces that 14 major Atlanta hotels and motels have agreed to accept reservations regardless of race.			U.S. Surgeon Gen. Luther Terry releases a federal report entitled *Smoking and Health* that describes cigarettes as a definite "health hazard" far outweighing "all other factors" as a cause of lung disease. The report estimates that 70 billion Americans smoked cigarettes during 1963.	Peggy Fleming, 15, of Pasadena, Calif. wins the women's senior title in the U.S. figure skating championships in Cleveland. . . . Charles (Bud) Wilkinson, 47, resigns as head football coach at the University of Oklahoma after 17 years. Wilkinson is said to be considering running for the U.S. Senate.	Jan. 11
					Jan. 12
Pres. Johnson meets with congressional leaders to urge the removal of discriminatory provisions from U.S. immigration laws. . . . The Supreme Court invalidates a Louisiana law requiring that the race of a political candidate be printed on the ballot.		The Supreme Court rules it an unfair labor practice for an employer to grant unilateral benefits to employees shortly before a union representation election.	The Federal Trade Commission announces plans to require that every cigarette pack contain a warning to the public on possible health hazards of smoking. The FTC also discloses plans to impose restrictions on cigarette advertising.		Jan. 13

F	G	H	I	J
Includes elections, federal-state relations, civil rights and liberties, crime, the judiciary, education, health care, poverty, urban affairs and population.	Includes formation and debate of U.S. foreign and defense policies, veterans' affairs and defense spending. (Relations with specific foreign countries are usually found under the region concerned.)	Includes business, labor, agriculture, taxation, transportation, consumer affairs, monetary and fiscal policy, natural resources, and pollution.	Includes worldwide scientific, medical and technological developments, natural phenomena, U.S. weather, natural disasters, and accidents.	Includes the arts, religion, scholarship, communications media, sports, entertainment, fashions, fads and social life.

	World Affairs	Europe	Africa & the Middle East	The Americas	Asia & the Pacific
Jan. 14				Western newsmen in Moscow report that the Soviet press has treated recent U.S.-Panamanian clashes with an unexpected caution that contrasts sharply with the violent denunciations appearing in the Communist Chinese press.	A U.S. agreement to provide South Vietnam with additional economic assistance is signed in Saigon.
Jan. 15		Visiting Italian Pres. Antonio Segni addresses a joint session of the U.S. Congress to reaffirm Italy's commitment to a Europe linked with the U.S. in an "indissoluble" Atlantic partnership.	The leaders of the 13 member Arab League, meeting in Cairo, announce an agreement on the establishment of a unified military command for possible future use in a war against Israel.	The OAS Inter-American Peace Committee announces that the U.S. and Panama have agreed to restore diplomatic relations and to renegotiate differences over the Canal Zone beginning 30 days after relations are resumed.	Indian sources report that as many as 163 persons have been killed in a week of violent clashes between Hindus and Moslems in and around Calcutta.
Jan. 16			Zanzibar Pres. Abeid Karume announces that his rebel government has severed diplomatic relations with the U.S. because of Washington's refusal to recognize it.		
Jan. 17			Arab League leaders conclude a five-day Cairo meeting after agreeing to end their political differences and halt propaganda campaigns heretofore directed against each other.	Panama breaks all remaining diplomatic ties with the U.S. following the collapse of OAS-sponsored talks on Panama's demand that the U.S. agree to renegotiate the Panama Canal Zone treaty. . . . Soviet Premier Khrushchev declares his support for the Panamanian people's struggle against the "United States imperialists."	
Jan. 18	Pres. Johnson informs Soviet Premier Khrushchev that the U.S. is willing to discuss recent Soviet proposals for a world treaty outlawing territorial aggression provided that the pact be extended to cover guerrilla warfare and other forms of forcible subversion.		Unofficial reports from Zanzibar indicate that as many as 3,000 persons have died in the clashes that attended and followed the Jan. 12 revolt.		
Jan. 19			A *New York Times* dispatch reports that the Zanzibar rebels who seized government control Jan. 12 had received training and support from Cuban and Communist Chinese agents.		
Jan. 20			Mutinous Tanganyikan soldiers, demanding higher pay and the ouster of white British officers, forcibly seize control of the capital city of Dar es Salaam.	The U.S. State Dept. announces the suspension of American economic assistance to Panama.	

A	B	C	D	E
Includes developments that affect more than one world region, international organizations and important meetings of major world leaders.	Includes all domestic and regional developments in Europe, including the Soviet Union, Turkey, Cyprus and Malta.	Includes all domestic and regional developments in Africa and the Middle East, including Iraq and Iran and excluding Cyprus, Turkey and Afghanistan.	Includes all domestic and regional developments in Latin America, the Caribbean and Canada.	Includes all domestic and regional developments in Asia and Pacific nations, extending from Afghanistan through all the Pacific Islands, except Hawaii.

U.S. Politics & Social Issues	U.S. Foreign Policy & Defense	U.S. Economy & Environment	Science, Technology & Nature	Culture, Leisure & Life Style	
Mrs. Marguerite Oswald, mother of accused assassin Lee Harvey Oswald, announces that she has retained ex-N.Y. Assemblyman Mark Lane as an unpaid attorney to prove Oswald's innocence before the Warren Commission.			NASA announces that the U.S. has agreed to provide rockets for the launching of four Canadian-built satellites in a joint program of ionospheric research.		Jan. 14
Theodore Sorensen, a key adviser to the late John Kennedy, resigns as special counsel to the President. Sorensen says he will write a book about his years with Pres. Kennedy. . . . GOP Presidential contender Barry Goldwater, speaking to the Economic Club of New York, suggests that many welfare recipients are getting more help than they need or deserve.				San Francisco Giants outfielder Willie Mays, 32, signs a 1964 contract for an estimated $105,000, making him baseball's highest-salaried player. . . . Jazz trombonist Jack Teagarden, one of the first white musicians to popularize Negro blues music, dies in New Orleans at age 58.	Jan. 15
		Negotiators for the International Brotherhood of Teamsters and four major U.S. trucking concerns reach agreement in Chicago on a nationwide three-year contract. The new pact provides for a 45¢ per hour increase in wages and benefits over the next three years.	Researchers at the Harvard School of Public Health report in *Science* that radioactive polonium, found in tobacco and other green plants, may be the cause of cigarette-related lung cancer.	The musical comedy *Hello Dolly!* opens in New York.	Jan. 16
Gov. Nelson Rockefeller, campaigning in New Hampshire, says that Barry Goldwater's recent criticism of welfare recipients reveals a "lack of understanding" of the basic causes of poverty. . . . Lt. Col. John Glenn, the first American to orbit the earth, announces that he will seek the Ohio Democratic nomination to the U.S. Senate.				Sjoukje Dijkstra, 22, of the Netherlands wins the European women's figure skating championship for the fifth straight year in Grenoble, France.	Jan. 17
Pres. Johnson calls Martin Luther King and other prominent Negro leaders to the White House to report on his continuing efforts to win House approval of the civil rights bill before the end of the month.		The Port of New York Authority announces plans to build in downtown Manhattan the world's tallest buildings--two 110-story, 1,350-foot towers to serve as the headquarters of the World Trade Center. . . . The Federal Trade Commission proposes rules that would require health hazard warnings on all cigarette packs and on cigarette advertisements.	An earthquake strikes southern Taiwan, killing about 400 persons.		Jan. 18
					Jan. 19
	The U.S. Second Circuit Court of Appeals in New York rules unconstitutional the provision of the Selective Service Act which requires a conscientious objector seeking deferment to prove his religious belief in a supreme being. The ruling reverses the conviction of Andrew Seeger, a self-described "religious agnostic" who refused induction into the army.	In his first annual economic report, Pres. Johnson predicts record-breaking economic growth if Congress enacts the administration's tax cut proposals. The report also stresses the need to combat the poverty afflicting one-fifth of "our fellow citizens."		*Publisher's Weekly* reports that Morris West's *The Shoes of the Fisherman* was the best-selling fiction book in the U.S. in 1963. Mary McCarthy's *The Group* is listed second. . . . Lefthanded pitcher Sandy Koufax, 28, of the Los Angeles Dodgers receives the Hickok Award as the "professional athlete of the year (1963)."	Jan. 20

F	G	H	I	J
Includes elections, federal-state relations, civil rights and liberties, crime, the judiciary, education, health care, poverty, urban affairs and population.	Includes formation and debate of U.S. foreign and defense policies, veterans' affairs and defense spending. (Relations with specific foreign countries are usually found under the region concerned.)	Includes business, labor, agriculture, taxation, transportation, consumer affairs, monetary and fiscal policy, natural resources, and pollution.	Includes worldwide scientific, medical and technological developments, natural phenomena, U.S. weather, natural disasters, and accidents.	Includes the arts, religion, scholarship, communications media, sports, entertainment, fashions, fads and social life.

	World Affairs	Europe	Africa & the Middle East	The Americas	Asia & the Pacific
Jan. 21	The U.S. delegation to the opening 1964 session of the Geneva disarmament conference proposes a general "freeze" on the production and the development of nuclear-armed strategic missiles and bombers. . . . Washington officials report that the U.S. has completed the first Western disarmament inspection of Soviet scientific posts in Antarctica under the terms of a 1959 treaty banning military activities on that continent.		Congolese Pres. Joseph Kasavubu declares a state of emergency in Kwilu Province where rebellious Bapende and Babunda tribesmen have seized control of one-half of the territory. Several European missionaries are reported to have fallen victim to the rebels.		Japanese P.M. Hayato Ikeda, in a speech to the Diet, calls for a "realistic" trade policy with Communist China, but reaffirms his government's opposition to diplomatic recognition of the Peking regime.
Jan. 22			Kenneth Kaunda is sworn in as the first home-rule prime minister of Northern Rhodesia, a British protectorate formerly part of the dissolved Federation of Rhodesia and Nyasaland.		
Jan. 23	Semyon Tsarapkin, chief Soviet delegate to the 17-nation disarmament conference, tells a Geneva news conference that U.S.-sponsored plans for a multilateral Western nuclear force will have to be dropped before there can be any agreement curbing the spread of atomic weapons. . . . Cuban Premier Castro, concluding a nine-day visit to the USSR, publicly proclaims his support for Moscow's position in its ideological dispute with China. Observers link the declaration with a recent Soviet offer to increase economic assistance to Cuba.				Pro-communist Pathet Lao forces, allegedly supported by North Vietnamese troops, launch a new military drive in central Laos. . . . Indonesian Pres. Sukarno, following talks with touring U.S. Atty. Gen. Robert Kennedy, announces a cease-fire halting Indonesian guerrilla activities in the Malaysian Federation states of Sarawak and Sabah. Kennedy had previously conferred with Malaysian and Philippine leaders and is personally credited with arranging the truce.
Jan. 24					
Jan. 25			About 5,000 British troops are mobilized to suppress three simultaneous army mutinies in the former British East African territories of Tanganyika, Kenya and Uganda. Leaders of the three nations had formally requested Britain's intervention.		
Jan. 26					Indian Prime Minister Jawaharlal Nehru makes his first public appearance since a paralytic stroke on January 7th affected his right side. He attends the two-hour Republic Day parade.
Jan. 27	France announces plans to establish diplomatic relations with Communist China, thus becoming the first major Western power to recognize the Peking government since 1950. The U.S. State Dept. calls the move "unfortunate," particularly in the light of alleged Red Chinese subversion in Southeast Asia. . . . The French decision to recognize Communist China is officially lauded in Soviet bloc nations and Pakistan, but draws sharp criticism from West German and Indian leaders.				U.S. Defense Secy. McNamara informs a House Armed Services subcommittee that Viet cong guerrillas have "made considerable progress" in their war against the South Vietnamese government since the November 1963 coup which overthrew the Diem government.

A	B	C	D	E
Includes developments that affect more than one world region, international organizations and important meetings of major world leaders.	*Includes all domestic and regional developments in Europe, including the Soviet Union, Turkey, Cyprus and Malta.*	*Includes all domestic and regional developments in Africa and the Middle East, including Iraq and Iran and excluding Cyprus, Turkey and Afghanistan.*	*Includes all domestic and regional developments in Latin America, the Caribbean and Canada.*	*Includes all domestic and regional developments in Asia and Pacific nations, extending from Afghanistan through all the Pacific Islands, except Hawaii.*

U.S. Politics & Social Issues	U.S. Foreign Policy & Defense	U.S. Economy & Environment	Science, Technology & Nature	Culture, Leisure & Life Style	
The Senate Rules Committee releases testimony from its closed hearings into the Bobby Baker case revealing that Baker once gave Pres. Johnson an expensive phonograph system as a gift.	Pres. Johnson's fiscal 1965 budget estimates defense expenditures at $51.2 billion, a $1.1 billion decrease from fiscal 1964. The figure includes $3.4 billion for foreign aid, $300 million less than 1964 and the lowest aid request since 1948. . . . Pres. Johnson appoints Carl T. Rowan as director of the U.S. Information Agency to replace the ailing Edward R. Murrow. Rowan will be the first Negro to serve on the National Security Council.	Pres. Johnson sends Congress a 1965 budget proposing $97.9 billion in expenditures and estimating receipts of $93 billion, leaving a deficit of $4.9 billion. The proposed expenditures, which are $500 million less than last year, request $51.2 billion for defense, about $1.1 billion below current defense spending levels. . . . Pres. Johnson's 1965 fiscal budget allocates nearly $1 billion for new or expanded anti-poverty programs.	An experimental Relay 2 communications satellite, an improved version of the still-transmitting Relay 1, is successfully orbited from Cape Kennedy.		Jan. 21
The FCC foreswears any right to use its licensing authority to censor sexually or politically "provocative" radio and TV programming which "may offend some listeners."			Dr. Richard Wilson, addressing the American Physical Society convention in New York, reports on research which indicates that the proton has no core or internal parts.		Jan. 22
The 24th Amendment to the Constitution, barring the use of a poll tax in federal elections, is formally ratified as South Dakota becomes the 38th state to approve the measure. . . . Pres. Johnson tells reporters that the phonograph he received from "the Baker family" was simply a gift and had no bearing whatever on his conduct as an elected official.		The Senate Finance Committee, by a 12-5 vote, approves the administration's tax cut bill (HR8363).		Pone Kingpetch of Thailand regains the world flyweight boxing championship by scoring a 15-round decision over titleholder Hiroyuki Ebihara in Bangkok.	Jan. 23
An order to end de facto segregation in Manhasset, N.Y. elementary schools is issued by U.S. District Judge Joseph Zavatt. . . . A three-judge federal court in New York upholds a provision of the 1950 Subversive Activities Control Act which allows the denial of a passport to any citizen refusing to sign a non-communist affidavit.					Jan. 24
Pres. Johnson declines comment at a news conference on Republican charges concerning his receipt of a gift from controversial ex-Democratic Senate secretary Robert Baker.		The AEC issues a report asserting that nuclear power plants "may be safely operated under all normal conditions."	A 135-foot spherical balloon dubbed Echo 2 is successfully launched into polar orbit from Vandenberg Air Force Base in California. The U.S. and USSR plan to transmit radio signals via the reflecting satellite in the first of a proposed series of cooperative space projects.		Jan. 25
					Jan. 26
Sen. Margaret Chase Smith (R, Me.) announces at a Women's National Press Club luncheon that she will enter the New Hampshire and Illinois presidential primaries.	Defense Secy. McNamara appears before the House Armed Services Committee to present his annual briefing on the U.S. defense posture. In his annual report to Congress on space activities, Pres. Johnson discloses that two experimental "early warning" (Midas) satellites, launched May 9 and July 12, 1963, had detected the launching of missiles from both the Pacific and Atlantic coasts. The satellites are part of a projected global missile alarm system.	Pres. Johnson sends Congress a special housing message proposing programs ranging from low-income public housing to massive urban renewal. . . . General Motors Corp. reports its 1963 net earnings at $1.592 billion, a new record for any single company.		U.S. pole vaulter Brian Sternberg is one of six athletes chosen by the Helms Athletic Foundation as the world's outstanding amateurs of 1963.	Jan. 27
F	G	H	I	J	
Includes elections, federal-state relations, civil rights and liberties, crime, the judiciary, education, health care, poverty, urban affairs and population.	Includes formation and debate of U.S. foreign and defense policies, veterans' affairs and defense spending. (Relations with specific foreign countries are usually found under the region concerned.)	Includes business, labor, agriculture, taxation, transportation, consumer affairs, monetary and fiscal policy, natural resources, and pollution.	Includes worldwide scientific, medical and technological developments, natural phenomena, U.S. weather, natural disasters, and accidents.	Includes the arts, religion, scholarship, communications media, sports, entertainment, fashions, fads and social life.	

	World Affairs	Europe	Africa & the Middle East	The Americas	Asia & the Pacific
Jan. 28	The USSR, in a memo to the Geneva disarmament conference, proposes the worldwide destruction of all bomber aircraft in advance of a general disarmament agreement. The U.S. has suggested the mutual destruction of obsolescent bombers.	A U.S. Air Force T-39 training plane is attacked and downed by Soviet fighters near Erfurt, East Germany after its pilot failed to respond to warnings that he was intruding into Communist air space. All 3 crewmen are believed dead.	Ghanaian voters overwhelmingly approve a referendum granting virtual dictatorial authority to Pres. Nkrumah.		
Jan. 29	The French government issues a statement disclaiming any intent to pursue a "two Chinas" policy. No direct action, however, has yet been taken to sever French-Nationalist Chinese relations.	The U.S. formally protests yesterday's Soviet attack on an American training plane as "a brutal act of violence against an unarmed aircraft that accidentally strayed over the demarcation line between West and East Germany." The USSR rejects the note.		Renewed OAS-sponsored talks between the U.S. and Panama end in deadlock after a week of discussions fail to resolve U.S. opposition to Panamanian demands for a formal renegotiation of the Panama Canal treaty.	
Jan. 30		Ewald Peters, personal security chief for West German Chancellor Erhard, commits suicide in a Bonn prison four days after being arrested on charges of participating in the mass murder of Soviet Jews as a member of the Nazi SS.			South Vietnam's ruling junta is overthrown in a bloodless military coup headed by Maj. Gen. Nguyen Khanh. Coup leaders claim that old junta members were conspiring with French agents in a plan for the neutralization of South Vietnam.
Jan. 31		Britain and the U.S. propose creation of 10,000-man NATO force to keep the peace between Turkish and Greek Cypriotes on Cyprus. Greece and Turkey indicate support, but Cypriote Pres. Makarios says he will oppose the plan.	The central Congolese government begins airlifting reinforcements to Kwilu Province to combat a growing tribal revolt. U.N. troops are being used to evacuate white missionaries, principal targets of the rebel attacks.	The OAS Council meets in emergency session in Washington to consider a Panamanian request that it fully investigate alleged U.S. aggression during the Jan. 9-10 Canal Zone riots.	French Pres. de Gaulle stresses at a Paris news conference his government's continuing interest in proposals for the "neutralization" of Southeast Asia. De Gaulle makes clear that the recognition of Communist China is linked to wider French hopes for a settlement of fighting in Vietnam, Laos and Cambodia. . . . Neutralist Laotian Premier Souvanna Phouma reveals that he has asked Britain and the USSR, as co-chairmen of the 1962 Geneva conference on Laos, to intervene to halt the renewed central Laos fighting.
Feb. 1	A U.S.-controlled radio station in West Berlin suspends long-range propaganda broadcasts to East Germany in apparent reciprocity for a 1963 Soviet decision to end the jamming of Voice of America broadcasts reaching Eastern Europe.				Pres. Johnson tells a Washington news conference that he regards French Pres. de Gaulle's recent proposals for neutralization of Southeast Asia as unrealistic, adding that the U.S. intends to pursue "diligently" its current policies in that part of the world.
Feb. 2		Cypriote Pres. Makarios says he will consider a proposed NATO peace-keeping force on Cyprus if Turkey, Britain and Greece agree to the cancellation of a 1960 treaty giving them the right to intervene in the island's affairs. Turkey is known to oppose any modification in the 1960 accord.		U.S. Coast Guard seizes four Cuban fishing boats after they allegedly refused to leave U.S. territorial waters.	
Feb. 3	The Chinese Communist Party publishes the seventh in its series of formal statements on the Sino-Soviet ideological dispute. Observers regard the statement's emphasis on Lenin's break with the Socialist Second International as a possible sign that Peking is considering an open rejection of Moscow's leadership.		Communist Chinese Premier Chou En-lai, on the final leg of his two-month African tour, tells reporters in Somalia that "revolutionary prospects are excellent throughout Africa."		Touring Chinese Premier Chou En-lai tells newsmen in Somalia that France will not be permitted to retain ties with Nationalist China after exchanging envoys with the Peking government.

A	B	C	D	E
Includes developments that affect more than one world region, international organizations and important meetings of major world leaders.	*Includes all domestic and regional developments in Europe, including the Soviet Union, Turkey, Cyprus and Malta.*	*Includes all domestic and regional developments in Africa and the Middle East, including Iraq and Iran and excluding Cyprus, Turkey and Afghanistan.*	*Includes all domestic and regional developments in Latin America, the Caribbean and Canada.*	*Includes all domestic and regional developments in Asia and Pacific nations, extending from Afghanistan through all the Pacific Islands, except Hawaii.*

U.S. Politics & Social Issues	U.S. Foreign Policy & Defense	U.S. Economy & Environment	Science, Technology & Nature	Culture, Leisure & Life Style	
Former key policy adviser to the late Pres. Kennedy, Arthur Schlesinger Jr., resigns as special assistant to the President.	GOP congressional leaders at a joint press conference criticize Pres. Johnson for compiling "a losing record" in the Cold War.			The International Olympic Committee names Grenoble, France to host the 1968 Winter Olympic Games.	Jan. 28
Mary Anderson, 91, first director of the U.S. Labor Dept's. Women's Bureau (1920-1944), dies in Washington.		The Bureau of Labor Statistics reports that the cost of living index rose 1.7% in 1963, the largest annual increase since 1958.	The first complete, fully-fueled Saturn rocket-booster is successfully launched from Cape Kennedy with the heaviest payload ever carried into orbit (20,000 pounds). The experimental Saturn is a forerunner of the booster rocket to be used in the U.S.'s Apollo lunar landing program.	Winter Olympic Games open in Innsbruck, Austria. . . . The film *Dr. Strangelove*, a satirical denunciation of the nuclear arms race, premiers in New York.	Jan. 29
		Pres. Johson sends Congress draft bills requiring double pay for overtime work in specified industries and extending minimum wage coverage to over 700,000 additional workers.	An 800-pound Ranger 6 lunar probe, designed to transmit close-up TV photos of the moon's surface before impact, is successfully launched from Cape Kennedy. . . . Two satellites, equipped to study the earth's radiation belts, are successfully put in orbit by a single Soviet booster rocket. It is the first multiple satellite launch reported by the USSR.		Jan. 30
Tuskegee (Ala.) High School, currently attended by only 12 Negro students, is ordered closed by Gov. George Wallace. Tuskegee's white pupils withdrew following the school's desegregation in September 1963.	Administration officials inform newsmen that the U.S. regards its recognition of the South Vietnamese government to be uninterrupted despite the Khanh coup.	Pres. Johnson sends Congress a special message recommending increased aid to improve farm incomes and an inquiry into the effects of supermarket chains on agricultural marketing.			Jan. 31
	At his Washington news conference, Pres. Johnson defends his administration's foreign policy record from recent charges of inconsistency and misdirection.	Auto industry sources report that 7,637,119 cars were manufactured in the U.S. in 1963, second only to the 1955 record of 7,941,372.		J. Robert Atkinson, blind founder of the Braille Institute of America (1919), dies in Los Angeles at age 76.	Feb. 1
			The U.S. Ranger 6 crashes on target in the moon's Sea of Tranquility, but fails to relay a single TV photo as planned. Although Ranger 6 is only the third man-made object known to have hit the moon, the TV failure prompts NASA scientists to label the mission unsuccessful.	Lidiya Skoblikova of the USSR captures her fourth gold medal in speed skating events at the Winter Olympics in Innsbruck and thus becomes the first person to win four gold medals in any single games competition, winter or summer.	Feb. 2
Negro and Puerto Rican students stage a one-day massive boycott of N.Y.C.'s public schools in protest against alleged *de facto* segregation. About 45% of the system's 1,037,757 students reportedly stayed home. . . . A three-judge federal court in Baltimore advises the State of Maryland that there is "no justification for the existing imbalance" of population in the state's congressional districts.			Dr. Joseph Melnick of Baylor University reports the discovery of large amounts of virus-like particles in the blood of about 80% of leukemic children studied.	Tom O'Hara, a Loyola University senior, sets a world indoor mile record of three minutes 56.6 seconds at the New York Athletic Club meet in Madison Square Garden. . . . American philosopher and social commentator Clarence Irving Lewis dies in Menlo Park, Calif.	Feb. 3

F	G	H	I	J
Includes elections, federal-state relations, civil rights and liberties, crime, the judiciary, education, health care, poverty, urban affairs and population.	*Includes formation and debate of U.S. foreign and defense policies, veterans' affairs and defense spending. (Relations with specific foreign countries are usually found under the region concerned.)*	*Includes business, labor, agriculture, taxation, transportation, consumer affairs, monetary and fiscal policy, natural resources, and pollution.*	*Includes worldwide scientific, medical and technological developments, natural phenomena, U.S. weather, natural disasters, and accidents.*	*Includes the arts, religion, scholarship, communications media, sports, entertainment, fashions, fads and social life.*

	World Affairs	Europe	Africa & the Middle East	The Americas	Asia & the Pacific
Feb. 4		A bomb blast rocks the U.S. embassy in Nicosia, Cyprus. The incident is linked to Greek Cypriote anger over U.S. support for a proposed NATO peace force on Cyprus. Preparations for the evacuation of U.S. dependents are reportedly underway.		The OAS Council approves a Panamanian request for a full-scale investigation into the Jan. 9-10 Canal Zone riot which has caused a still unresolved rift in U.S.-Panamanian relations.	
Feb. 5			U.S. Amb.-to-Ghana William Mahoney is recalled to Washington following two days of government-organized anti-American demonstrations in Accra. The disorders are said to be the result of official Ghanaian news releases linking the CIA and Peace Corps to assassination attempts against Pres. Nkrumah.		South Vietnamese sources report a continuing intensification of Vietcong military activity and an increase in terrorist assassinations.
Feb. 6	U.S. delegation at the Geneva disarmament talks calls for a joint Soviet-American pledge to refrain from providing nuclear weapons or relevant technological information to nations not now possessing an atomic capability.	Britain and the U.S. make public a revised Cyprus peace-force plan calling for U.N. consultations on the operations of the projected 10,000-man NATO truce army. The new plan is seen as a response to Cypriote Pres. Makarios' recent demands that any outside force sent to Cyprus be under direct U.N. command. Cypriote leaders indicate little interest in the compromise proposal.	Pres. Johnson discloses that U.S. and Israeli officials have begun discussions on joint research for using nuclear power to convert salt water into fresh water to solve Israeli irrigation problems. The announcement provokes sharp criticism in Arab states.	Cuba cuts the normal water supply to the U.S. naval base at Guantanamo in reprisal for the Feb. 2 seizure in U.S. territorial waters of four Cuban fishing boats and their crews. U.S. officials indicate that alternative water supplies will prevent the Cuban action from causing any hardship at the base.	Gen. Emilio Aguinaldo, leader of the Philippine's revolt against Spain and subsequently of an unsuccessful insurrection against the U.S., dies in Manila at age 94.
Feb. 7		Soviet Premier Khrushchev, in notes to Western leaders, warns that the USSR will not tolerate forcible NATO intervention in the affairs of "neutral" Cyprus.			U.S. State Secy. Rusk tells reporters in Washington that he has found no real substantive proposals for the neutralization of Southeast Asia in any of Pres. de Gaulle's recent statements on the matter.
Feb. 8		British P.M. Alec Douglas-Home denounces Soviet Premier Khrushchev's "unfounded" charges and threats regarding Western efforts to restore peace on Cyprus.	The Ethiopian government reports that 2,000 Somali troops yesterday invaded Ethiopian territory and that more than 100 were killed in the subsequent fighting. Other clashes along the two nations' disputed border have also been reported.		
Feb. 9		Princess Irene, second in line to the traditionally Protestant Dutch throne, renounces her royal claims following the disclosure of her engagement to Spanish Prince Carlos Hugo and her conversion to Roman Catholicism.			A bomb blast in a Saigon stadium kills two U.S. soldiers and injures 20 other Americans. It is the latest in a recent rash of terrorist attacks aimed directly at American personnel in South Vietnam. . . . Indonesian, Malaysian and Philippine foreign officers complete a fourth day of talks in Bangkok after tentatively agreeing to have Thailand supervise a Malaysian-Indonesian border cease-fire.
Feb. 10		Ex-British P.M. Harold Macmillan announces his retirement from active political life.	A cease-fire between Iraqi troops and rebel Kurdish tribesmen is announced by the leaders of both sides. Pledges to resume negotiations on final settlement are also exchanged.	U.S. Defense Dept. announces plans to build a $5 million permanent salt water conversion plant at the Guantanamo Naval Base in Cuba.	Nationalist China breaks diplomatic relations with France because of the latter's recognition of Communist China. The action comes only hours after the de Gaulle government indicated that it would no longer consider the Nationalist Chinese embassy in Paris as the diplomatic representative of China.

A	B	C	D	E
Includes developments that affect more than one world region, international organizations and important meetings of major world leaders.	*Includes all domestic and regional developments in Europe, including the Soviet Union, Turkey, Cyprus and Malta.*	*Includes all domestic and regional developments in Africa and the Middle East, including Iraq and Iran and excluding Cyprus, Turkey and Afghanistan.*	*Includes all domestic and regional developments in Latin America, the Caribbean and Canada.*	*Includes all domestic and regional developments in Asia and Pacific nations, extending from Afghanistan through all the Pacific Islands, except Hawaii.*

U.S. Politics & Social Issues	U.S. Foreign Policy & Defense	U.S. Economy & Environment	Science, Technology & Nature	Culture, Leisure & Life Style	
A Gallup Poll indicates that 63% of adult Americans drink alcoholic beverages, an increase of 8% over a similar poll taken in 1958.			NASA Administrator James Webb tells the House Science and Astronautics Committee that any major cuts in NASA's 1965 budget request will seriously jeopardize the U.S.'s chance of landing a man on the moon before 1970. . . . Navy scientists disclose that a satellite designed to monitor solar X-rays was launched from Vandenberg Air Force Base January 11. Data from the satellite is said to have confirmed that the sun is nearing the two-year period of minimum sunspot activity in its 11-year cycle.	Terry McDermott of Essexville, Mich. wins the 500-meter speed-skating event for the U.S.'s only gold medal of the Winter Olympic Games.	Feb. 4
All-white students at Notasulga (Ala.) High School withdraw after a federal court orders the school to admit six Negro transfer students from the recently closed Tuskegee High School.		Pres. Johnson sends Congress a consumer affairs message stressing the need for truth-in-packaging and truth-in-lending legislation.			Feb. 5
Marina Oswald, 22, widow of Lee Harvey Oswald, completes three days of questioning by the Warren Commission. Mrs. Oswald, whose testimony was not disclosed, had said in a Jan. 27 Dallas TV interview that "the facts tell me Lee shot Kennedy."			Britain and France announce an agreement to build a 32-mile railroad tunnel under the English Channel. Estimated cost: $400 million. . . . The American Medical Association announces acceptance of $10 million offered by six tobacco companies for research on the relationship between smoking and health.		Feb. 6
The trial of Byron de la Beckwith for the 1963 murder of civil rights leader Medgar Evers is declared a mistrial. The all-white Jackson, Miss. jury reported its inability to reach a verdict after repeatedly voting 7-5 for acquittal.	Pres. Johnson names C. McMurtrie Godley as ambassador to the Congo to succeed Edmund Gullion.	The Senate, by a 77-21 vote, passes the administration's $11.6 billion tax cut bill. The measure will go to joint conference for resolution of minor differences with the House-passed version.		According to a Gallup Poll, 48% of Americans attend church regularly, 27% occasionally, and 20% never attend. Only 6% of those interviewed say they never pray.	Feb. 7
More than 90 Negroes are arrested in connection with three anti-segregation marches in Chapel Hill, N.C. The arrests bring to 436 the total number arrested since the anti-segregation drive began Dec. 31, 1963.					Feb. 8
				The USSR, dominating speed skating and skiing, wins the unofficial team championship of the 1964 Winter Olympic Games at Innsbruck with a total of 25 medals. The U.S. finishes eighth with six medals.	Feb. 9
The administration's civil rights bill (HR 7152) is passed by the House on a vote of 290-130. The measure, which awaits Senate action, bars discrimination in public accommodations, strengthens guarantees of Negro voting rights and increases the federal government's authority to initiate school desegregation action. . . . A new appeal for passage of a Social Security-financed program of health care for the elderly is made by Pres. Johnson in a special health message to Congress.	The State Dept. announces that Yuri Nossenko, a senior officer of the Soviet secret police (KGB), has defected to the U.S.		The North American Defense Command reports that 60 U.S. and 17 Soviet payloads were sent into space during 1963.		Feb. 10
F	G	H	I	J	
Includes elections, federal-state relations, civil rights and liberties, crime, the judiciary, education, health care, poverty, urban affairs and population.	*Includes formation and debate of U.S. foreign and defense policies, veterans' affairs and defense spending. (Relations with specific foreign countries are usually found under the region concerned.)*	*Includes business, labor, agriculture, taxation, transportation, consumer affairs, monetary and fiscal policy, natural resources, and pollution.*	*Includes worldwide scientific, medical and technological developments, natural phenomena, U.S. weather, natural disasters, and accidents.*	*Includes the arts, religion, scholarship, communications media, sports, entertainment, fashions, fads and social life.*	

	World Affairs	Europe	Africa & the Middle East	The Americas	Asia & the Pacific
Feb. 11		The New York Times reports that West Germany's initial "dismay" at France's recognition of Communist China has given way to respect for the impact and independence of the move.			The political wing of the Viet Cong, the National Liberation Front, announces its willingness to consider French Pres. de Gaulle's proposals "for the realization of peace and neutrality in South Vietnam.". . . Cambodian Prince Sihanouk charges the U.S. with partial responsibility for a Feb. 6 South Vietnamese air attack on two Cambodian villages that left five persons dead. Sihanouk's charges are viewed as a threat to the recent progress made in Philippine-sponsored mediation talks aimed at normalizing U.S.-Cambodian relations.
Feb. 12		As many as 50 Cypriotes are reported to have been killed in recent clashes that have marred the tenuous truce between the island's Greek and Turkish communities.		U.S. Defense Dept. orders a gradual reduction in the number of civilians and dependents at the U.S. Guantanamo Naval Base.	
Feb. 13	William Foster, chief U.S. disarmament delegate at the Geneva talks, reiterates U.S. proposals for an immediate reduction in the production of missile materials for weapons purposes.	British P.M. Alec Douglas-Home concludes two days of talks in Washington with Pres. Johnson. The two leaders reportedly agreed to a policy of mutual support for each nation's position in Southeast Asia (specifically, Vietnam and Malaysia), but failed to resolve Anglo-U.S. differences over trade with Cuba. . . . East Germany proposes a temporary travel accord giving West Berliners special passes to visit East Berlin for 10 days at Easter. . . . Cypriote Pres. Makarios formally rejects Anglo-U.S. proposals for a U.N.-"linked" NATO peace-keeping force on Cyprus.	The Organization of African Unity at an emergency meeting in Dar es Salaam agrees to a Tanganyikan request to send three battalions of African soldiers to keep the peace while Tanganyika reorganizes its army. The African units will replace British troops who had been called in to quell an army mutiny.		Asians begin 10 days of celebrations to mark the Chinese New Year 4662 (Year of the Dragon).
Feb. 14	Premier Khrushchev declares that the Soviet CP has launched a major effort to restore "the monolithic unity of the world socialist system" on the basis of the ideological declaration adopted at the 1960 world communist congress in Moscow.	The West Berlin Senate and the West German government reject yesterday's special Easter pass offer from East Germany, contending that the wording of the proposed pact implies recognition of East German sovereignty.			The U.S. Military Assistance Command in Saigon reports that 12 Americans have been killed and 87 wounded in South Vietnamese fighting since Jan. 1, 1964. . . . Communist Chinese Premier Chou En-lai, just returned from a 50-day African tour, leaves Peking to begin a two-week swing through Southeast Asia.
Feb. 15		West German Chancellor Ludwig Erhard meets in Paris with French Pres. de Gaulle in one of the periodic consultative meetings required by the 1962 Franco-German treaty of cooperation. No statement is issued, but talks reportedly centered on French proposals for the neutralization of Southeast Asia.	Somalia and Ethiopia tentatively agree to a cease-fire in their recently renewed border fighting.	U.S. Secy. of State Rusk warns that foreign firms trading with Cuba may be risking a loss of U.S. sales because of possible "consumer reaction" against their activities.	
Feb. 16		Recently resigned Greek Premier George Papandreou's Center Union Party wins a comfortable working majority in nationwide parliamentary elections.		A special OAS commission assigned to investigate the Jan. 9-10 Panama Canal Zone riots reports finding little evidence to support U.S. claims of Castro-Communist influence in the disorders. The commission also concludes that while American soldiers used "disproportionate" force, Panama's charge of U.S. "aggression" was unwarranted.	

A	B	C	D	E
Includes developments that affect more than one world region, international organizations and important meetings of major world leaders.	Includes all domestic and regional developments in Europe, including the Soviet Union, Turkey, Cyprus and Malta.	Includes all domestic and regional developments in Africa and the Middle East, including Iraq and Iran and excluding Cyprus, Turkey and Afghanistan.	Includes all domestic and regional developments in Latin America, the Caribbean and Canada.	Includes all domestic and regional developments in Asia and Pacific nations, extending from Afghanistan through all the Pacific Islands, except Hawaii.

U.S. Politics & Social Issues	U.S. Foreign Policy & Defense	U.S. Economy & Environment	Science, Technology & Nature	Culture, Leisure & Life Style	
	Sen. Barry Goldwater, speaking in Portland, Ore., accuses the Johnson administration of pursuing an "appeasement policy" in its failure to respond directly to Cuba's cut-off of water to the U.S. naval base at Guantanamo. . . . Pres. Johnson, in remarks to a meeting of IRS employees, calls his GOP foreign policy critics "alarmists" who have an oversimplified view of world problems.			Ch. Courtenay Fleetfoot, a whippet owned by Pennyworth Kennels of Newington, N.H., is chosen best-in-show at the annual Westminster Kennel Club show in New York.	Feb. 11
Following three days of secret testimony before the Warren Commission, Marguerite Oswald, mother of the accused assassin of John Kennedy, tells reporters she still believes her son innocent, adding that she thinks Oswald was a CIA agent "set up to take the blame.". . . The Southern Regional Council reports that its 20-month voter registration drive, ending Dec. 31, 1963, resulted in the registration of 265,000 Negroes and 60,000 Mexican-Americans (in Texas).		The Commerce Dept. reports that the U.S. balance of payments deficit totaled $3.02 billion in 1963, down $350 million from 1962.			Feb. 12
CIA chief John McCone issues a statement asserting that Lee Harvey Oswald "was never directly or indirectly linked with the CIA."		The Treasury Dept. announces the U.S.'s first borrowing from the International Monetary Fund. The $125 million loan is described as a "technical" move to ease pressure on the U.S. gold reserves.		Pres. Johnson asks Congress to appropriate $15.5 million for the federal share of the John F. Kennedy Center for the Performing Arts, to be built in Washington.	Feb. 13
Texas District Judge Joseph Brown rules that Jack Ruby must go on trial in Dallas beginning Feb. 17 on charges of murdering Lee Harvey Oswald. Ruby's attorney Melvin Belli had requested a delay and a change of venue, claiming that his client could not get a fair trial in Dallas.					Feb. 14
				Chicago Cubs second baseman Ken Hubbs, 1962 National League Rookie of the Year, dies in a plane crash in Provo, Utah. . . . Carlos Ortiz of New York retains his world lightweight boxing championship by scoring a TKO over Gabriel Elorde in the 14th round of their Manila title bout.	Feb. 15
				Lidiya Skoblikova, 26, of the USSR wins the women's world speed skating championship in Kristinehamn, Sweden. . . . Some of the Roman Catholic liturgical reforms approved at the second session of the Vatican II Ecumenical Council officially go into effect.	Feb. 16

F	G	H	I	J
Includes elections, federal-state relations, civil rights and liberties, crime, the judiciary, education, health care, poverty, urban affairs and population.	Includes formation and debate of U.S. foreign and defense policies, veterans' affairs and defense spending. (Relations with specific foreign countries are usually found under the region concerned.)	Includes business, labor, agriculture, taxation, transportation, consumer affairs, monetary and fiscal policy, natural resources, and pollution.	Includes worldwide scientific, medical and technological developments, natural phenomena, U.S. weather, natural disasters, and accidents.	Includes the arts, religion, scholarship, communications media, sports, entertainment, fashions, fads and social life.

	World Affairs	Europe	Africa & the Middle East	The Americas	Asia & the Pacific
Feb. 17		British Commonwealth Secy. Duncan Sandys charges the Cypriote government with permitting the smuggling of arms into Cyprus for use by Greek Cypriote soldiers.	The French-backed Gabonese government of Pres. Leon Mba is overthrown in a bloodless military coup. The uprising is traced to Mba's January decision to dissolve Gabon's National Assembly on the ground that the government could not afford the cost of a legislature.		The U.N. Security Council concludes two weeks of debate on the India-Pakistan dispute over Kashmir without taking any substantive action.
Feb. 18	Chief Soviet disarmament negotiator Semyon Tsarapkin tells the Geneva conference that the U.S. plan for freezing strategic weapons at current levels is unacceptable to the USSR because it fails to remove the danger of nuclear war at an early stage of disarmament. He concludes by reiterating Soviet proposals for the immediate scrapping of all but a few strategic missiles.	The U.N Security Council opens debate on the Cyprus crisis. Britain and Cyprus had requested the meeting after they failed to agree on any previously outlined international peace force plans.		The U.S. State Dept. announces termination of its nominal military aid programs to Britain, France and Yugoslavia. The action was required under provisions of the 1963 Foreign Aid Act barring military assistance to nations permitting trade with Cuba.	
Feb. 19					
Feb. 20			Leon Mba is restored as president of Gabon by French forces who intervened Feb. 18 to suppress an army-led rebellion. . . . Algeria and Morocco announce an agreement ending their border dispute which had led to military clashes in Oct. 1963.	The U.S. State Dept. announces that it opposes consumer boycotts of the goods of nations trading with Cuba. The statement is apparently aimed at counteracting the adverse reaction of U.S. allies to State Secy. Rusk's Feb. 15 warning that foreign firms doing business with Cuba risked alienating U.S. customers. . . . Twenty-nine Cuban fishermen, seized Feb. 2 in U.S. territorial waters, are released after paying a Florida state fine for fishing without a license.	
Feb. 21	The U.S. ship *Exilona* arrives in Odessa with the first shipment of wheat to be delivered under the recently negotiated Soviet-American grain deal.				U.S. Pres. Johnson, speaking in Los Angeles, warns North Vietnam that continuation of its aid to the Viet Cong "is a deeply dangerous game." Observers view the speech as a signal that consideration is being given to extending South Vietnam's anti-guerrilla campaign into North Vietnam. . . . Serious fighting flares briefly between Pakistani and Indian forces along the Kashmir cease-fire line.
Feb. 22	The USSR and the U.S. sign a new two-year cultural exchange agreement providing for increased contacts in the fields of industry, agriculture, medicine and the performing arts.	The U.S. State Dept. is reportedly reconsidering a threatened military aid cut-off to Spain because of its continued trade with Cuba. Spanish officials have indicated they would regard the action as a violation of the treaties granting U.S. bases in Spain.	More than 20 persons are killed in Homs, Syria as police attempt to disperse pro-Nasser demonstrations marking the sixth anniversary of the defunct Egyptian-Syrian union.	Pres. Johnson concludes two days of discussions in California with Mexican Pres. Adolfo Lopez Mateos. A final communique stresses on-going efforts to expand U.S.-Mexican trade.	Malaysia charges that Indonesian guerrillas have violated the recently-concluded cease-fire in the Federation states of Sarawak and Sabah.
Feb. 23	A six-member Communist Chinese delegation arrives in Paris to establish formal diplomatic relations with the French government.		Libya announces that it will not renew or extend the leases of U.S. and British military bases on their expiration. The Libyan action had been publicly urged in recent speeches by UAR Pres. Nasser. . . . U.S. and Britain recognize the new revolutionary government of Zanzibar.		After conferring with Pakistani Pres. Ayub Khan, visiting Chinese Premier Chou En-lai announces that Peking has abandoned its traditional neutrality on the Kashmir question and will in the future support Pakistan's position in the dispute.
	A	**B**	**C**	**D**	**E**
	Includes developments that affect more than one world region, international organizations and important meetings of major world leaders.	*Includes all domestic and regional developments in Europe, including the Soviet Union, Turkey, Cyprus and Malta.*	*Includes all domestic and regional developments in Africa and the Middle East, including Iraq and Iran and excluding Cyprus, Turkey and Afghanistan.*	*Includes all domestic and regional developments in Latin America, the Caribbean and Canada.*	*Includes all domestic and regional developments in Asia and Pacific nations, extending from Afghanistan through all the Pacific Islands, except Hawaii.*

U.S. Politics & Social Issues	U.S. Foreign Policy & Defense	U.S. Economy & Environment	Science, Technology & Nature	Culture, Leisure & Life Style	
The Supreme Court rules 6-3 that congressional districts should be as equal in population as practicable so as to assure that "one man's vote is . . . worth as much as another's." The decision involves a case (Wesberry vs. Sanders) brought by two Atlanta residents who claimed that Georgia's congressional districting deprived them of the full benefit of their voting rights.	Members of the International Longshoremen's Association stop loading wheat for shipment to the USSR to protest the Johnson administration's alleged failure to enforce the condition that at least 50% of the wheat be carried in U.S. vessels.	The Dow Jones industrial stock price average briefly exceeds 800 for the first time and then dips to close the day at a record 796.19.	Southern Rhodesian archeologists report the discovery of the remains of a civilization (dating about 850 A.D.) near Ingombe Ilede in Northern Rhodesia.	Chicago White Sox shortstop Luke Appling (1930-1950) becomes the 101st member of baseball's Hall of Fame.	Feb. 17
	The House Armed Services Committee releases Jan. 27 testimony of Defense Secy. McNamara in which he asserts that the U.S. still hopes to withdraw most of its 15,000 troops from South Vietnam before the end of 1965. . . . The Defense Dept. discloses that the Air Force Jan. 11 successfully launched a new Army mapping satellite called Secor. The Secor is reportedly designed to precisely locate targets for ICBMs.				Feb. 18
Ex-Senate Democratic secretary Bobby Baker, invoking constitutional immunity against self-incrimination, refuses to answer any questions during an appearance before a closed session of the Senate Rules Committee.			The discovery by scientists at the Brookhaven National Laboratory (N.Y.) of a previously undetected, short-lived, subatomic particle, the omega-minus, is reported in the British journal *New Scientist*.	Luke Hart, 83, chief sponsor of the inclusion of the words "under God" in the U.S. Pledge of Allegiance, dies in New Haven, Conn.	Feb. 19
Several hundred Negroes and whites in Stamford, Conn. demonstrate before city hall to protest high rents and slum conditions.		The U.S. Court of Appeals in Washington upholds a federal arbitration board's ruling permitting U.S. railroads to gradually eliminate unnecessary jobs. . . . AFL-CIO Pres. George Meany tells the Executive Council's mid-winter meeting that forthcoming contract negotiations will not be "straight-jacketed" by the Johnson administration's wage guidelines.			Feb. 20
	A three-judge federal court in New Haven, Conn. upholds the constitutionality of the U.S. State Dept.'s ban on travel to Cuba.	National Safety Council estimates that 100,500 persons were killed and 10 million injured in U.S. accidents during 1963. Traffic accidents accounted for 43% of the deaths. . . . Labor Secy. Willard Wirtz appears before the AFL-CIO Executive Council meeting in Bal Harbour, Fla. to reiterate the administration's opposition to council proposals for a 35-hour work week.	A radio signal broadcast from England is bounced off the U.S. Echo 2 communications satellite and picked up by Soviet scientists at the Zimenki Observatory near Gorki. It marks the first joint U.S.-British-Soviet experiment in space. . . . NASA official George Mueller tells an engineers' meeting in Los Angeles that despite reports to the contrary there are no technological problems or radiation hazards that would prevent a manned lunar landing in the current decade.		Feb. 21
	Ex-V.P. Richard Nixon, speaking in Peoria, Ill., calls for congressional action to deny American markets to foreign firms who persist in trading with Cuba.	The AFL-CIO Executive Council adopts a resolution urging support for and expansion of Pres. Johnson's proposed "war on poverty" programs.	The American Heart Association reports that the death rate from cardiovascular diseases among American men aged 45-64 declined 6% during the 1950's.	Bob Hayes sets a world record of 5.9 seconds for the indoor 60-yard dash at the AAU national indoor championships in New York.	Feb. 22
	The New York Times reports that the Johnson administration is considering new steps to end the Viet Cong military successes in South Vietnam. An increased American military commitment to South Vietnam is reportedly among the options being reviewed.				Feb. 23

F	G	H	I	J
Includes elections, federal-state relations, civil rights and liberties, crime, the judiciary, education, health care, poverty, urban affairs and population.	*Includes formation and debate of U.S. foreign and defense policies, veterans' affairs and defense spending. (Relations with specific foreign countries are usually found under the region concerned.)*	*Includes business, labor, agriculture, taxation, transportation, consumer affairs, monetary and fiscal policy, natural resources, and pollution.*	*Includes worldwide scientific, medical and technological developments, natural phenomena, U.S. weather, natural disasters, and accidents.*	*Includes the arts, religion, scholarship, communications media, sports, entertainment, fashions, fads and social life.*

	World Affairs	Europe	Africa & the Middle East	The Americas	Asia & the Pacific
Feb. 24		*Izvestia* reports that Albanian authorities have seized the Soviet embassy in Tirana. The embassy buildings had been occupied only by caretakers since the suspension of Soviet-Albanian relations in 1961.		A special committee of the OAS makes public a report confirming Venezuelan charges that Cuba had smuggled arms to pro-communist Venezuelan guerrillas in November 1963.	
Feb. 25		U.N. Secy. Gen. U Thant informs the Security Council that an impasse has been reached in his efforts to establish a peace-keeping force on Cyprus. The deadlock reportedly involves Cypriote insistence on the abrogation of the 1960 treaty (giving Turkey intervention rights) as pre-condition to the creation of an international peace force.			Pathet Lao troops overrun strategic right-wing positions near the southeastern gateway to the Plaine des Jarres in north-central Laos. Right-wing spokesmen claim that six North Vietnamese battalions took part in the attack. . . . Visiting Communist Chinese Premier Chou En-lai tells a news conference in Dacca, East Pakistan that a relaxation in China-U.S. tensions can come only after the U.S. abandons its commitment to the Nationalist government on Taiwan and withdraws its troops from Vietnam.
Feb. 26					The Viet Cong's 514th Battalion kills 16 South Vietnamese soldiers while successfully breaking out of a government trap near Long Dinh, 40 miles southwest of Saigon. The action marks the first time that the Viet Cong have employed the classic infantry tactic of frontal assault.
Feb. 27		East German, West Berlin and West German negotiators announce they are temporarily abandoning efforts to reach an agreement on visits to East Berlin by residents of West Berlin.	The Sudanese government orders the deportation of 300 Roman Catholic and Protestant missionaries for allegedly supporting anti-government activity in the province of Bahr-el-Ghazal.		
Feb. 28		A report submitted to the U.N. Security Council estimates that more than 800 Turkish Cypriotes have been killed or wounded since the fighting began on Cyprus Dec. 21, 1963.		Paris sources report that British merchant ships made 132 trips to Cuba during 1963.	North Vietnamese Defense Min. Vo Nguyen Giap warns that his nation will respond appropriately if the Vietnamese fighting is extended to North Vietnamese territory.
Feb. 29	The Polish government calls for a treaty freezing the current levels of nuclear armaments on the territories of East and West Germany, Poland and Czechoslovakia.	Several thousand students stage anti-U.S. demonstrations in Greece to protest alleged U.S. bias in favor of the Turkish Cypriote minority on Cyprus.			
March 1			Foreign ministers of the 33-nation Organization of African Unity conclude a week-long conference in Lagos, Nigeria after voting to create a permanent commission to mediate border disputes among member states.		South Vietnamese Premier Nguyen Khanh accuses French agents of having plotted to assassinate him to impose "a neutralist settlement" in Vietnam.

A	B	C	D	E
Includes developments that affect more than one world region, international organizations and important meetings of major world leaders.	*Includes all domestic and regional developments in Europe, including the Soviet Union, Turkey, Cyprus and Malta.*	*Includes all domestic and regional developments in Africa and the Middle East, including Iraq and Iran and excluding Cyprus, Turkey and Afghanistan.*	*Includes all domestic and regional developments in Latin America, the Caribbean and Canada.*	*Includes all domestic and regional developments in Asia and Pacific nations, extending from Afghanistan through all the Pacific Islands, except Hawaii.*

U.S. Politics & Social Issues	U.S. Foreign Policy & Defense	U.S. Economy & Environment	Science, Technology & Nature	Culture, Leisure & Life Style	
	The State Dept. announces establishment of an inter-agency committee, headed by William Sullivan, to coordinate the U.S. Vietnam policy.			Henry Cooper, 29, wins the vacant European heavyweight boxing championship by scoring a 15-round decision over Brian London in Manchester, England.	Feb. 24
Bobby Baker, making his second appearance before the Senate Rules Committee—this time in public session—again invokes constitutional immunities in declining to answer the committee's questions.	Recent flexibility in U.S. policy toward communist countries is defended by Secy. of State Dean Rusk as the best way to promote greater internal independence and diversity within the communist bloc. . . . A nine-day boycott of the loading of Russian-bound wheat is ended by the International Longshoremen's Association after the Johnson administration assures the union that 50% of the wheat sent to the USSR under future contracts would be shipped in U.S. vessels.		NASA official Homer Newell Jr. asserts in a *Christian Science Monitor* interview that putting a man on the moon is not a "stunt" but a scientifically necessary and economically defensible step in the conquest of space.	Cassius Clay, 22, a 7-1 underdog, wins the world heavyweight boxing championship in Miami Beach by scoring a TKO over titleholder Charles (Sonny) Liston, who failed to come out for the seventh round due to a dislocated shoulder. The Miami Beach Boxing Association says it will withhold Liston's share of the purse pending confirmation of his injury. . . . Grace de Repentigny Metalious, 39, author of the controversial 1956 bestseller *Peyton Place*, dies in Boston of chronic liver disease.	Feb. 25
The Senate votes 54-37 to put the House-passed civil rights bill (HR 7152) directly on the floor calendar instead of referring it to the Judiciary Committee, headed by Sen. James Eastland (D, Miss.), a foe of rights legislation. . . . Police use dogs and fire hoses on an unruly anti-segregation demonstration in Princess Anne, Md. Sixty-two Negroes are reported injured, including 14 with dog bites.		The conference version of the administration's $11.5 billion tax cut bill is signed into law by Pres. Johnson. The bill, which Johnson describes as "the single most important step . . .to strengthen our economy since World War II," received final House approval yesterday and Senate passage earlier today.		*The Deputy,* a controversial play by Rolf Hochuth indhcting Pope Pius XII for his alleged failure to resist Nazi persecution of Jews, opens in New York.	Feb. 26
Pres. Johnson stresses the need for continued civil rights action in a speech to a Democratic fund-raising dinner in Miami Beach, Fla. Johnson asserts that "full participation in our society can no longer be reserved to men of one color."				The Appellate Division of the N.Y. Supreme Court, in a 3-2 decision, adjudges John Cleland's 1749 novel *Fanny Hill* "obscene" and enjoins G.P. Putnam's Sons from publishing it.	Feb. 27
	Sen. Barry Goldwater tells the National Press Club that French Pres. de Gaulle's decision to recognize Communist China was due in part to shortcomings in the administration's policies regarding NATO.	The U.S. FDA issues new guidelines governing the tests used to determine a drug's safety and effectiveness.			Feb. 28
Pres. Johnson tells reporters at a Washington news conference that he was "deeply impressed by the spirit of unity in this country" during his first 100 days as President.	Newspaper reports that the U.S. is considering an intensification of the Vietnam War are denied by Pres. Johnson at his regular news conference. . . . Pres. Johnson designates William Bundy to replace the resigning Roger Hilsman as Assistant State Secretary for Far Eastern Affairs. Like Hilsman in the past, Bundy is expected to play a key role in the formulation of U.S. Vietnam policies.	In a press conference statement disclosing the U.S.'s development of the A-11 high-speed military aircraft, Pres. Johnson notes that "the development of a supersonic commercial transport aircraft will be greatly assisted by the lessons learned from this A-11 program."		Dawn Fraser of Australia sets her 36th world record by swimming the 100-meter free-style in 58.9 seconds at the Australian national championships in Sydney.	Feb. 29
			Anthropological journals are reporting the discovery by Dr. Louis Leakey of the remains of tool-making creatures thought to have lived 1.75 million years ago. The bones were discovered in northern Tanganyika and are older than any previously found.		March 1

F	G	H	I	J
Includes elections, federal-state relations, civil rights and liberties, crime, the judiciary, education, health care, poverty, urban affairs and population.	Includes formation and debate of U.S. foreign and defense policies, veterans' affairs and defense spending. (Relations with specific foreign countries are usually found under the region concerned.)	Includes business, labor, agriculture, taxation, transportation, consumer affairs, monetary and fiscal policy, natural resources, and pollution.	Includes worldwide scientific, medical and technological developments, natural phenomena, U.S. weather, natural disasters, and accidents.	Includes the arts, religion, scholarship, communications media, sports, entertainment, fashions, fads and social life.

	World Affairs	Europe	Africa & the Middle East	The Americas	Asia & the Pacific
March 2					The French embassy in Saigon formally denies South Vietnamese Premier Khanh's allegation of a French plot to overthrow him.
March 3	The French delegate to the Geneva meeting of the World Health Organization votes for the seating of a Communist Chinese delegation in the place of the Nationalist Chinese representatives. The move is seen as an indication of future French support for Communist China's admission to the U.N. in the place of the Nationalists.		Gabonese demonstrators riot in Libreville in protest against the continued presence in Gabon of the French troops who recently intervened to restore the government of Pres. Leon Mba.		The UPI estimates that 190 Americans have been killed in South Vietnam, 110 in combat.
March 4	An editorial in the *Peking People's Daily* declares that the Viet Cong's recent successes in South Vietnam prove the correctness of China's call for direct revolutionary struggles against the imperialist "paper tiger" in Asia, Africa and Latin America.	The U.N. Security Council unanimously approves a resolution creating a U.N.-supervised, temporary, international peace-keeping force on Cyprus. The proposal is reportedly supported by all the principals in the dispute. . . . *The New York Times* quotes European diplomatic sources as saying that France is considering a new and significantly expanded economic accord with the USSR.			
March 5					U.S. Defense Secy. McNamara tells a Washington news conference that "North Vietnamese support of the Viet Cong" has increased over the last six months. . . . Malaysian, Indonesian and Philippine foreign ministers, holding their second conference on the Malaysian dispute, conclude three days of talks in Bangkok without reaching agreement on a permanent settlement of their differences.
March 6		King Paul of Greece, 62, dies in Athens of complications resulting from a Feb. 21 operation for a stomach ulcer. Crown Prince Constantine, 23, is proclaimed king.			
March 7		An unusually harsh denunciation of West Germany is the subject of an official Soviet statement released by *Tass* . The statement compares the policies of the current Bonn government to those of Hitler on the eve of W.W. II.	Algerian Premier Ahmed Ben Bella decrees a major reorganization of the army in a move apparently aimed at strengthening his personal control over the nation's military forces.		South Vietnamese Premier Nguyen Khanh announces a comprehensive program of military, political and economic reforms designed to solidify popular support for the government's war against the Viet Cong.
March 8			Zanzibar Pres. Abeid Amani Karume announces the government's nationalization of all commercial farms and plantations.		U.S. Defense Secy. McNamara arrives in Saigon on his fourth fact-finding mission to South Vietnam. McNamara promises a welcoming crowd that the U.S. will support the South Vietnamese government for "as long as it takes to defeat the Viet Cong."

A	B	C	D	E
Includes developments that affect more than one world region, international organizations and important meetings of major world leaders.	Includes all domestic and regional developments in Europe, including the Soviet Union, Turkey, Cyprus and Malta.	Includes all domestic and regional developments in Africa and the Middle East, including Iraq and Iran and excluding Cyprus, Turkey and Afghanistan.	Includes all domestic and regional developments in Latin America, the Caribbean and Canada.	Includes all domestic and regional developments in Asia and Pacific nations, extending from Afghanistan through all the Pacific Islands, except Hawaii.

U.S. Politics & Social Issues	U.S. Foreign Policy & Defense	U.S. Economy & Environment	Science, Technology & Nature	Culture, Leisure & Life Style	
The Supreme Court upholds a 1963 district court ruling that Texas congressional districts are unconstitutionally disparate in population and must be redrawn.		The White House releases a report on the U.S. program to develop a commercial supersonic airplane, scheduled to begin passenger service in 1970, comparable to the Anglo-French Concorde currently being developed. . . . Democratic members of the Joint Economic Committee describe the economic outlook for 1964 as "encouraging." The Republican minority, in a separate report, warns that the administration's "boom and bust" policy will hasten "the persistent, creeping inflation of recent years."			March 2
N.Y. Gov. Nelson Rockefeller signs two controversial law enforcement bills: a "stop-and-frisk" measure permitting temporary police detention of suspects and a "no-knock" bill permitting police in certain cases to use special search warrants to enter premises without giving advance notice to the occupants.	After testifying on the South Vietnamese situation before a closed hearing of the Senate Foreign Relations Committee, Secy. of State Dean Rusk tells waiting reporters, "It is a mean, frustrating and difficult struggle, but we think it can be won."			*Pravda* reports that the Soviet CP's Central Committee has established a nationwide program to discourage religion in Soviet life.	March 3
Pres. Johnson announces the appointment of 10 women to major government posts. The action is viewed as a partial fulfillment of his pledge to end "stag government" in Washington. . . . A federal court in Jackson, Miss. orders school boards in Biloxi and Jackson to submit school desegregation plans for the fall term. It is the first Mississippi integration order below the college level.		Teamsters Pres. James Hoffa is convicted by a federal grand jury in Chattanooga, Tenn. of tampering with the jury in his 1962 Nashville trial on charges of accepting illegal payments from an employer. Four other persons are also convicted on related charges. . . . Nearly half of Jersey City's 1,500 public school teachers stage a one-day strike to protest a $700,000 cut in the city's education budget.			March 4
Over 10,000 Kentuckyans participate in a peaceful march to the state Capitol to demonstrate support for passage of a state public accommodations law.			The National Institutes of Health reports the successful use of a drug in the phenothiazine family for the treatment of acute schizophrenia.	Elizabeth Taylor, 32, is divorced from singer Eddie Fisher amidst reports that she plans to marry British actor Richard Burton.	March 5
		The Senate passes and sends to joint conference an administration farm bill (HR 6196) establishing semi-voluntary programs to control wheat and cotton production.		Tom O'Hara sets a new world indoor mile record of three minutes, 54.6 seconds at the *Chicago Daily News* Relays.	March 6
Pres. Johnson signs a compromise bill (HR 4638) to provide for an orderly transfer of power from an incumbent President to a newly elected one.				The University of Denver wins its fourth straight NCAA skiing championship at Cannon Mt., N.H.	March 7
Suspended Black Muslim leader Malcolm X discloses plans to form an independent organization to promote the black nationalist movement among "America's 22 million non-Muslim Negroes."	The magazine *Aviation Week & Space Technology* reports that the high-altitude A-11 interceptor had flown long-range reconnaissance missions over Communist territory for at least two years before its existence was officially disclosed by Pres. Johnson Feb. 29.				March 8

F	G	H	I	J
Includes elections, federal-state relations, civil rights and liberties, crime, the judiciary, education, health care, poverty, urban affairs and population.	Includes formation and debate of U.S. foreign and defense policies, veterans' affairs and defense spending. (Relations with specific foreign countries are usually found under the region concerned.)	Includes business, labor, agriculture, taxation, transportation, consumer affairs, monetary and fiscal policy, natural resources, and pollution.	Includes worldwide scientific, medical and technological developments, natural phenomena, U.S. weather, natural disasters, and accidents.	Includes the arts, religion, scholarship, communications media, sports, entertainment, fashions, fads and social life.

	World Affairs	Europe	Africa & the Middle East	The Americas	Asia & the Pacific
March 9		At least 30 Cypriots are dead following three days of renewed clashes between Greek and Turkish Cypriotes near Paphos on the southeast coast of Cyprus.			Cambodian Prince Sihanouk charges that U.S. "hostility" has "torpedoed" his repeated proposals for an international conference to guarantee Cambodia's neutrality and territorial integrity.
March 10	Soviet air defenses shoot down an unarmed U.S. Air Force RB-66 jet reconnaissance plane over East Germany. The three crew members are reported to have parachuted to safety. It is the second time in six weeks that a U.S. plane has been downed by the Russians over East Germany.	Cyprus V.P. Fazil Kutchuk urges prompt U.N. intervention to save the Turkish Cypriotes "from complete annihilation.". . . Greek Cypriotes inform British authorities that they will no longer recognize the December 1963 truce line dividing the Greek and Turkish sectors of Nicosia. . . . British Queen Elizabeth II gives birth to her fourth child and third son.			
March 11	Rumanian C.P. leaders conclude eight days of talks with Communist Chinese officials in Peking in a reported effort to avert an open break between China and the USSR. No specifics are mentioned in the final communique. . . . A Soviet protest note charges that the downed U.S. RB-66 had been on a military reconnaissance mission over East Germany. The U.S. insists that the plane had inadvertently strayed across the East German border.			Raul Leoni of the Democratic Action Party is sworn in as president of Venezuela, succeeding Romulo Betancourt.	Anti-U.S. riots erupt in the Cambodian capital of Pnompenh. The disorders are linked to U.S. opposition to Prince Sihanouk's proposal for an international conference on Cambodian neutrality.
March 12				The U.S. and Panama reach tentative agreement on an OAS-sponsored formula for resolving their dispute over the Canal Zone treaty.	
March 13		Turkey warns Cyprus that it is prepared to exercise its intervention rights if Greek Cypriotes do not end alleged "aggression" against the island's Turkish minority.		Brazilian Pres. João Goulart signs two decrees expropriating several privately owned oil refineries and a number of "untilled" farms.	Cambodian Defense Min. Lon Nol arrives in Peking on what is reported to be an arms-buying mission. Communist Chinese sources quote Nol as having "condemned U.S. imperialism" in South Vietnam and Thailand.
March 14		The first contingent of the U.N.'s special peace-keeping force arrives in Cyprus. The dispatch of the troops prompts Turkey to withdraw its March 13 threat to intervene on behalf of the Turkish Cypriotes.			
March 15		West Berlin authorities report that 17 teenage students of East Berlin's Max Plank school escaped to the West by jumping into open westbound railroad cars from an East Berlin overpass.	French sources in Algiers report that France will end its nuclear testing program in the Algerian Sahara during 1964.	French Pres. de Gaulle leaves Paris to begin a 10-day Latin American tour that will include Mexico and French possessions in the Caribbean. The trip is described as the first in a series of moves to increase French economic and political involvement in the Western Hemisphere.	

A	B	C	D	E
Includes developments that affect more than one world region, international organizations and important meetings of major world leaders.	Includes all domestic and regional developments in Europe, including the Soviet Union, Turkey, Cyprus and Malta.	Includes all domestic and regional developments in Africa and the Middle East, including Iraq and Iran and excluding Cyprus, Turkey and Afghanistan.	Includes all domestic and regional developments in Latin America, the Caribbean and Canada.	Includes all domestic and regional developments in Asia and Pacific nations, extending from Afghanistan through all the Pacific Islands, except Hawaii.

U.S. Politics & Social Issues	U.S. Foreign Policy & Defense	U.S. Economy & Environment	Science, Technology & Nature	Culture, Leisure & Life Style	
The Supreme Court rules unanimously that the First Amendment "prohibits a public official from recovering damages for a defamatory falsehood relating to his official conduct" unless he can prove deliberate malice. The decision reverses a $500,000 Alabama libel judgment awarded to Montgomery city commissioner L.B. Sullivan against *The New York Times* for an ad that appeared in the March 29, 1960 edition.		Pres. Johnson sends Congress a special employment message stressing the need for strengthened educational and related programs to combat joblessness among youth.			March 9
Amb.-to-South Vietnam Henry Cabot Lodge, a non-campaigning write-in candidate, captures 35.4% of the vote to win the New Hampshire Republican presidential primary, outpolling declared candidates Sen. Barry Goldwater (23%) and Gov. Nelson Rockefeller (20%). . . . Seattle, Washington voters reject a municipal "open" housing ordinance by a more than 2-1 margin.	In a Senate floor speech, Sen. Ernest Gruening (D, Alaska) calls for the withdrawal of American forces from the "bloody and wanton stalemate" in Vietnam, adding that "the time has come to cease the useless and senseless losses of American lives in an area not essential to the security of the U.S." Gruening's appeal is backed by Sen. Wayne Morse (D, Ore.).			The National Book Award for U.S. fiction in 1963 is awarded to John Updike for his novel, *The Centaur*.	March 10
	Sen. Thomas Dodd, a supporter of the administration's Vietnam policies, dismisses recent criticism on the part of Sens. Morse and Gruening as "the faint-hearted chorus of those who always ask the price of victory."	Pres. Johnson signs a compromise bill (S 1153) extending until mid-1967 the $75 million annual authorization for federal aid to airports. . . . A federal grand jury in New York indicts Dr. Herman Taller, author of the 1961 best seller *Calories Don't Count*, on charges of fraudulently promoting ineffective weight-reducing pills.			March 11
Malcolm X tells newsmen that Negroes should use force to defend themselves "whenever and wherever" they are unjustly attacked. . . . Atty. Gen. Robert Kennedy issues a statement urging Wisconsin supporters to end efforts to draft him for the vice presidency. Kennedy received 25,000 write-in votes for vice president in the March 10 New Hampshire Democratic primary.		A U.S. district court in Chattanooga, Tenn. sentences Teamsters Pres. James Hoffa to eight years in prison for attempting to influence a federal jury. . . . An administration-backed bill (HR 8986) to authorize $545 million a year in federal pay raises, including a $10,000 annual raise for Congress members, is defeated by a House vote of 222-184. Southern Democrats joined Republicans in opposing the measure.			March 12
			Pres. Johnson makes an aerial inspection tour of the flood-devastated Ohio River valley. The floods are credited with causing 11 deaths in the seven-state affected area.		March 13
A Dallas, Tex. jury convicts Jack Ruby of the malicious murder of Lee Harvey Oswald and recommends a death sentence. . . . Republican presidential contender Barry Goldwater says that he has disagreed "completely, roundly and loudly for years" with John Birch Society founder Robert Welch. . . . Police in Yellow Springs, Ohio use fire hoses and tear gas to break up a crowd of college students demonstrating against a segregated barber shop. Over 100 persons are arrested.		U.S. Census Bureau reports that U.S. exports jumped sharply in February to a record $2.13 billion. The rise reflects the settlement of the East Coast dock strike in January.			March 14
Pres. Johnson cites the conquest of poverty and the enactment of the civil rights bill as his foremost domestic goals. . . . Johnson dismisses reports of a personal feud between himself and Atty. Gen. Robert Kennedy as mere "newspaper talk."	During a nationally televised interview, Pres. Johnson stresses the need for continuing U.S. support of South Vietnam, saying that "We must stay there and help them, and that is what we are going to do."			Elizabeth Taylor, 32, marries actor Richard Burton, 38, in Montreal (her fifth marriage, his second).	March 15

F	G	H	I	J
Includes elections, federal-state relations, civil rights and liberties, crime, the judiciary, education, health care, poverty, urban affairs and population.	*Includes formation and debate of U.S. foreign and defense policies, veterans' affairs and defense spending. (Relations with specific foreign countries are usually found under the region concerned.)*	*Includes business, labor, agriculture, taxation, transportation, consumer affairs, monetary and fiscal policy, natural resources, and pollution.*	*Includes worldwide scientific, medical and technological developments, natural phenomena, U.S. weather, natural disasters, and accidents.*	*Includes the arts, religion, scholarship, communications media, sports, entertainment, fashions, fads and social life.*

	World Affairs	Europe	Africa & the Middle East	The Americas	Asia & the Pacific
March 16		The Turkish congress approves Pres. Ismet Inonu's request for stand-by authorization to implement Turkey's right under the 1960 Cyprus treaty of guarantee to intervene if he considers it necessary.	Pres. Leon Mba of Gabon exonerates the U.S. of any role in the Feb. 17 uprising that temporarily deposed him. Rumors of American involvement have been circulated by French residents in Gabon.	Speaking at OAS headquarters in Washington, Pres. Johnson pledges continued U.S. support of the Alliance for Progress.	
March 17	U.S. delegation to the Geneva disarmament conference rejects the USSR's plan for an immediate scrapping of most strategic weapons. The U.S. says the proposal would radically alter the East-West power balance in favor of the Soviets.			The OAS reports that the March 12 U.S.-Panama agreement has collapsed in the face of differing interpretations of the accord. Panama views the pact as a pledge to "negotiate" a new canal treaty; the U.S. insists that it merely agreed to "discuss" all disputed issues.	The White House announces that the U.S. will provide increased military and economic aid to support South Vietnamese Premier Khanh's new plans for intensifying the government's war against the Viet Cong. The announcement comes only hours after Defense Secy. McNamara briefed Pres. Johnson and the National Security Council on his recent fact-finding trip to South Vietnam. . . . The U.N. Security Council resumes its debate on disputed Kashmir. Pakistan again charges that India is preparing "to annex" Kashmir even if it means "the wholesale imprisonment of an entire people."
March 18	U.S. protests the USSR's detention of three U.S. airmen who had parachuted from their RB-66 jet when it was shot down March 10 over East Germany. The note warns that delay in return of the crewmen may jeopardize current efforts to expand Soviet-American cooperation.		Congolese troops under the command of army chief Joseph Mobutu continue their offensive against rebel tribesmen in Kwilu Province.	Following three days of talks, French Pres. de Gaulle and Mexican Pres. Adolfo Lopez Mateos issue a joint communique urging increased economic contacts between Europe and Latin America.	
March 19	The American delegation to the Geneva disarmament conference announces that the U.S. is prepared to destroy 480 of its older B-47 jet bombers, if the USSR will destroy an equal number of its comparable TU-16 bombers. The Soviets denounce the proposal as an effort to pass off the retirement of obsolete aircraft as disarmament.	A 10-day lull in Cyprus's communal fighting ends as Greek Cypriotes, armed with mortars, attack Turkish Cypriotes in the northern coastal town of Ghaziveran. Three Turks are reported killed.	South Africa walks out of the World Health Organization after the body adopts a resolution banning membership to nations enforcing racial discrimination. It is the seventh international organization South Africa has left in recent years.		South Vietnamese troops, accompanied by U.S. personnel, attack the Cambodian border village of Chantrea, killing 17 residents. The incident comes on the eve of scheduled border dispute talks between Cambodia and South Vietnam.
March 20		Turkish Pres. Ismet Inonu warns that his government will have "no choice but to intervene" if heavy fighting is resumed on Cyprus.	An agreement providing for long-term Belgian aid to the Congo is announced in Leopoldville.	Addressing a rally in Guadaloupe, French Pres. de Gaulle says that France's new initiatives in Latin America are in no way intended to undermine the traditional hemispheric role played by the U.S.	
March 21	An injured member of the crew of a U.S. Air Force RB-66 reconnaissance plane shot down March 10 over East Germany is released to U.S. medical personnel in West Berlin by Soviet authorities. The plane's other two crew members are still being held.		Yemen signs a five-year friendship treaty with the USSR.	The U.S. refuses to return two Cuban defectors who yesterday hijacked a Cuban helicopter and flew it to Key West, Fla.	The U.S. and South Vietnam apologize to Cambodia for the March 19 attack on the border village of Chantrea. The incident is attributed to faulty map reading. Cambodian Prince Sihanouk dismisses the American apology as insufficient and reiterates his demand for U.S. backing of an international conference on Cambodian neutrality.
	A	B	C	D	E
	Includes developments that affect more than one world region, international organizations and important meetings of major world leaders.	Includes all domestic and regional developments in Europe, including the Soviet Union, Turkey, Cyprus and Malta.	Includes all domestic and regional developments in Africa and the Middle East, including Iraq and Iran and excluding Cyprus, Turkey and Afghanistan.	Includes all domestic and regional developments in Latin America, the Caribbean and Canada.	Includes all domestic and regional developments in Asia and Pacific nations, extending from Afghanistan through all the Pacific Islands, except Hawaii.

U.S. Politics & Social Issues	U.S. Foreign Policy & Defense	U.S. Economy & Environment	Science, Technology & Nature	Culture, Leisure & Life Style	
Negro and Puerto Rican students in N.Y.C. stage a second boycott against *de facto* school segregation. The action is said to have less support than the initial boycott Feb. 3.		Pres. Johnson sends Congress a special message outlining plans for a $962 million "war on poverty." The proposed programs, to be overseen by an Office of Economic Opportunity, include a Job Corps for unemployed youth and a Volunteers-for-America Corps to serve as a domestic peace corps.		National Football League commissioner Pete Rozelle reinstates Paul Horning of the Green Bay Packers and Alex Karras of the Detroit Lions following an 11-month suspension for betting on games.	March 16
	Defense Secy. McNamara and Gen. Maxwell Taylor brief Pres. Johnson and the National Security Council on their recent fact-finding mission to South Vietnam. McNamara is reported to have been impressed by South Vietnamese Premier Khanh's military and economic reform proposals. . . . Pres. Johnson signs a bill (S 2455) authorizing $115 million for the Peace Corps in fiscal 1965. The bill provides for a doubling of Peace Corps strength from 7,000 to 14,000 by the end of 1965.	The FCC grants the American Telephone & Telegraph Co. permission to lay the fourth trans-Atlantic cable (from New Jersey to France).			March 17
		The Labor Dept. reports that unemployment fell in February to 5.4%, a 15-month low.	The USSR announces the launch of an unmanned Cosmos 26 satellite. No details are given.		March 18
Pierre Salinger resigns as White House press secretary to campaign for the Democratic senatorial nomination in California. Pres. Johnson names George Reedy as Salinger's successor.	Pres. Johnson sends Congress a special message outlining a $3.4 billion foreign aid program for fiscal 1965. Johnson says the requested sum ($1.1 billion less than the final request of last year) is the minimum needed to serve U.S. interests and commitments abroad. . . . Secy. of State Dean Rusk, speaking in Salt Lake City, assails critics of the administration's Vietnam policy as "quitters" whose stand could encourage the enemy.		The first automobile tunnel through the Alps, the 3.4 mile-long Great St. Bernard Tunnel connecting St. Rhemy, Italy and Canton d'en Haute, Switzerland, is officially opened. The project cost $35 million, took five years to build and the lives of 17 workmen.		March 19
A book entitled *The Conservative Papers* is published in New York under the sponsorship of nine GOP congressmen, including Rep. Gerald Ford (Mich.) and Rep. Melvin Laird (Wis.). The essays, conceived as a reply to the 1962 *Liberal Papers*, include contributions from Chicago Prof. Milton Friedman and Harvard Prof. Henry Kissinger.	In a speech assailing the Johnson administration's disarmament policies, GOP presidential hopeful Barry Goldwater says he wants to protect American voters "against softheaded people who believe in co-existence with communism.". . . Pres. Johnson signs a compromise bill (HR 9637) authorizing $16,976,620,000 in fiscal 1965 for defense procurement and research. The total authorization is over $208 million less than the administration had requested and includes $47 million in unrequested funds for the development of a high-speed manned bomber to succeed the existing B-52.	UAW Pres. Walter Reuther tells delegates to the union's constitutional convention in Atlantic City that improved working conditions and early retirement will be top priorities in the forthcoming contract talks with the auto industry.		Irish playwright Brendan Francis Behan, 41, dies in Dublin of a combination of ailments aggravated by excessive drinking.	March 20
				UCLA defeats Duke University, 98-83, to win the National Collegiate Athletic Association basketball championship in Kansas City. . . . Bradley Univ. wins the National Invitational (basketball) Tournament in New York. . . . *Team Spirit*, Willie Robinson up, wins the 123rd Grand National Steeplechase in Aintree, England, becoming the first American-owned horse to win the event since 1938.	March 21

F	G	H	I	J
Includes elections, federal-state relations, civil rights and liberties, crime, the judiciary, education, health care, poverty, urban affairs and population.	Includes formation and debate of U.S. foreign and defense policies, veterans' affairs and defense spending. (Relations with specific foreign countries are usually found under the region concerned.)	Includes business, labor, agriculture, taxation, transportation, consumer affairs, monetary and fiscal policy, natural resources, and pollution.	Includes worldwide scientific, medical and technological developments, natural phenomena, U.S. weather, natural disasters, and accidents.	Includes the arts, religion, scholarship, communications media, sports, entertainment, fashions, fads and social life.

	World Affairs	Europe	Africa & the Middle East	The Americas	Asia & the Pacific
March 22					Cambodian Prince Sihanouk warns that if Britain and the U.S. persist in opposing an international conference on Cambodia, he will "go to Peking to discuss our problems with our good Chinese friends.". . . South Vietnam's 53-member ruling Revolutionary Council unanimously confirms Nguyen Khanh as national premier. Previous junta leader Maj. Gen. Duong Van Minh is retained as the council's supreme adviser.
March 23	Delegates from 116 nations gather in Geneva to convene a U.N. Conference on Trade and Development. The discussions are expected to focus on ways of expanding world trade so as to spur the economic development of "have-not" countries.				Indian sources report that 200 persons, mostly Moslems, have been killed in a week-long wave of violent Hindu attacks upon Moslems in eastern India.
March 24	French Finance Min. Valery Giscard d'Estaing presents the U.N. Conference on Trade with a French plan for a "massive" effort to end the division between rich and poor nations by reorganizing world markets to assure high and consistent prices for raw materials and farm products. . . . Vishnu Trivedi, Indian delegate to the Geneva disarmament conference, declares his country's support for Soviet proposals to destroy all but a limited number of strategic missiles in the first stage of disarmament.				New Delhi sources report that Indian troops yesterday killed 24 members of a Pakistani force after it had allegedly crossed the cease-fire line near Uri. . . . French Pres. de Gaulle offers to help Cambodia arrange international guarantees of its borders and neutrality. . . . U.S. Amb.-to-Japan Edwin Reischauer, 53, is reported in good condition after being stabbed outside the U.S. embassy in Tokyo by a mentally disturbed Japanese teenager.
March 25		Secy. Gen. U Thant designates former Finnish Premier Sakari Severi Tuomioja as U.N. mediator in Cyprus.			Cambodia demands that the U.S. pay reparations for its role in the killing of 17 Cambodians during a South Vietnamese raid on the village of Chantrea March 19.
March 26	The Soviet delegation to the Geneva disarmament talks rejects a March 24 British proposal for the establishment of military observation posts throughout Europe, Russia, Britain and the U.S. Chief delegate Semyon Tsarapkin calls it another Western attempt to create an espionage system before making any real commitment to disarmament.	Pres. Johnson restores most-favored-nation status to imports from Yugoslavia and Poland. Congress had deprived such treatment from the two Communist states in 1962 under the Trade Expansion Act. . . . A British court convicts 10 men of involvement in the $7 million 1963 mail train robbery.	A renewal of heavy fighting erupts between Ethiopian and Somali forces along their disputed border.		In a White House-drafted address to a Washington meeting of leading defense contractors, Defense Secy. McNamara reaffirms U.S. determination to increase military and economic aid to South Vietnam. McNamara identifies North Vietnam as the "prime aggressor" in South Vietnam and charges Communist China with encouraging its aggressive course.
March 27	The USSR returns the two remaining crewmen of an American RB-66 reconnaissance jet shot down over East Germany March 10. Return of the U.S. fliers had been the subject of several notes exchanged by the U.S. and USSR and of at least two private diplomatic meetings.			Brazilian Pres. João Goulart grants amnesty to about 1,000 left-wing sailors and marines who launched a protest mutiny March 25. The action is denounced by right-wing military leaders.	Soviet news agency Tass reports that Premier Khrushchev has assured Cambodian Prince Sihanouk of complete support should Sihanouk decide to bring the "brutal" attack on Chantrea to the attention of the U.N. Security Council.

A	B	C	D	E
Includes developments that affect more than one world region, international organizations and important meetings of major world leaders.	Includes all domestic and regional developments in Europe, including the Soviet Union, Turkey, Cyprus and Malta.	Includes all domestic and regional developments in Africa and the Middle East, including Iraq and Iran and excluding Cyprus, Turkey and Afghanistan.	Includes all domestic and regional developments in Latin America, the Caribbean and Canada.	Includes all domestic and regional developments in Asia and Pacific nations, extending from Afghanistan through all the Pacific Islands, except Hawaii.

U.S. Politics & Social Issues	U.S. Foreign Policy & Defense	U.S. Economy & Environment	Science, Technology & Nature	Culture, Leisure & Life Style	
			British astronomer Bernard Lovell asserts that Soviet space scientists are working intensively on a manned lunar mission.		March 22
The New York Times reports that the largest of the Ku Klux Klan groups, the United Klans of America, is planning to organize and build its own private communities in order to escape racial integration.	The Supreme Court rules 8-1 that U.S. courts cannot contest the legality of a foreign government's expropriation of property on its territory. The case involved Cuba's nationalization of a sugar company.	In an address to the United Auto Workers convention in Atlantic City, Pres. Johnson appeals for responsible wage negotiations on the part of American labor so as to avoid a new price-wage spiral. . . . The first new labor contract in the soft coal industry since 1958 is signed in Pittsburgh by the United Mine Workers and the Bituminous Coal Operators Association. The pact provides for a $2-a-day wage hike over the next year.		Hungarian-born character actor Peter Lorre dies of a stroke in Hollywood at age 59.	March 23
One person is dead and dozens injured following two days of racial rioting in Jacksonville, Fla.	Pres. Johnson, speaking of foreign policy to labor leaders in Washington, says that "in this nuclear world" responsible men "must follow the Prophet Isaiah and say 'Come now and let us reason together'."				March 24
The Senate Rules Committee votes to end its inquiry into the business affairs of ex-Senate Democratic secretary Bobby Baker, despite Republican charges that termination of the hearings amounts to a cover-up. . . . Pres. Johnson asks 150 Southern Baptist leaders attending a White House reception to support the administration's pending civil rights bill.	Sen. J. William Fulbright (D, Ark.), in a major Senate floor speech, calls for a fundamental reshaping of American foreign policy to meet the "new realities of our times." Fulbright specifically urges: 1) increasing trade with the USSR to promote the emerging East-West detente; 2) an end to the "monolithic" conception of the communist bloc; 3) de-sanctification of the U.S. attitude toward the Panama Canal treaty; 4) abandonment of the Cuban boycott and acceptance of the probable permanence of the Castro regime.		Drs. Pentti Eelis Eskola of Finland and Arthur Holmes of England share the 1964 Vetlesen Prize for earth science.		March 25
The Senate votes to take up debate on the House-passed civil rights bill (HR 7152). Martin Luther King warns that nationwide demonstrations will be launched if an expected Southern filibuster persists past May 1.	Sen. Fulbright's March 25 foreign policy speech prompts intense and varied reaction. Senate GOP leader Everett Dirksen attacks Fulbright's Cuban proposals as a "good" way "to enhance communism in the Western Hemisphere." Rep. Donald Fraser (D, Minn.) describes the speech as courageous. . . . In a White House-approved speech, Defense Secy. McNamara tells leading defense contractors that the U.S. "role in South Vietnam" includes proving "that the free world can cope with communist 'wars of liberation.'"	Census Bureau estimates that 18% of all U.S. families own some common stock.		The American Academy of Arts & Letters names John O'Hara as the winner of its "award of merit for the novel," a prize presented once every five years. . . . *Funny Girl*, a musical starring Barbra Streisand, opens in New York.	March 26
	Secy. of State Rusk says at a Washington news conference that Sen. Fulbright's March 25 speech should not be interpreted as an expression of Johnson administration policies.		An earthquake measuring 8.4 on the Richter scale devastates southern Alaska, causing 66 deaths. It is one of the most severe quakes ever recorded. . . . A British scientific satellite, Ariel 2, designed to gather data on galactic radio noise and ozone distribution in the upper atmosphere, is launched by NASA from Wallops Island, Va.	Oklahoma State wins its 24th NCAA wrestling championship.	March 27

F	G	H	I	J
Includes elections, federal-state relations, civil rights and liberties, crime, the judiciary, education, health care, poverty, urban affairs and population.	Includes formation and debate of U.S. foreign and defense policies, veterans' affairs and defense spending. (Relations with specific foreign countries are usually found under the region concerned.)	Includes business, labor, agriculture, taxation, transportation, consumer affairs, monetary and fiscal policy, natural resources, and pollution.	Includes worldwide scientific, medical and technological developments, natural phenomena, U.S. weather, natural disasters, and accidents.	Includes the arts, religion, scholarship, communications media, sports, entertainment, fashions, fads and social life.

	World Affairs	Europe	Africa & the Middle East	The Americas	Asia & the Pacific
March 28		Ex-French Premier Edgar Faure confers in Moscow with Soviet Premier Khrushchev amidst what some observers are describing as an intensified diplomatic search for possible new directions in Franco-Soviet relations.	British planes stationed in the South Arabian Federation launch an air raid on a military base near Harib, Yemen in reprisal for alleged Yemeni and Egyptian attacks on federation territory during past two weeks. . . . The Saudi Arabian royal family council votes to reduce King Saud to the status of a figure-head monarch. The move gives full control of the kingdom to Premier Crown Prince Faisal, King Saud's half-brother.		Burma's ruling military government bans all political parties except the government-sponsored Burma Socialist Program party.
March 29		An estimated 110,000 West Germans begin returning from two-day Easter weekend visits to friends and relatives in East Berlin. West Berlin residents were not among those permitted to enter the Communist sector due to the failure in February of special pass negotiations between East Germany and West Berlin.			U.S. Defense Secy. McNamara announces that the U.S. will provide South Vietnam with an additional $50 million (above the current yearly assistance of $500 million) to finance the expansion of its armed forces.
March 30			Ethiopia and Somali announce a truce in their recent border war.		
March 31	The Chinese CP issues a formal statement calling on communists everywhere to repudiate Khrushchev and Soviet leadership and to join China in a united struggle for world revolution.		British sources report that Soviet military advisers and Communist Chinese technicians have recently arrived in Zanzibar to assist the new government.	Brazilian army chiefs launch a nation-wide revolt reportedly aimed at deposing Pres. João Goulart for his allegedly pro-communist sympathies.	
April 1	Soviet Premier Khrushchev, visiting Hungary, publicly ridicules the ideological impracticality of the Chinese Communists, saying that they prefer "revolution to goulash."	Most of Belgium's 10,000 physicians go on strike to protest a 1963 national health insurance law.		Brazilian Pres. Goulart flees the capital city of Brasilia, but pledges to resist the spreading army revolt. . . . Haitian ruler Francois Duvalier officially decrees himself president for life.	
April 2		Joseph Klaus of the Conservative People's Party succeeds the resigning Alfons Gorbach as chancellor of Austria.		Dr. Paschoal Ranieri Mazzilli is sworn in as interim president of Brazil, succeeding the deposed João Goulart. The U.S. announces almost immediate recognition of the new government. . . . Marcos Rodriguez Alfonso, 26, a prominent member of the Cuban CP, is executed on charges of having conspired to thwart Fidel Castro's revolutionary movement in 1957. Rodriguez is the first known Communist sentenced to death under the Castro regime.	
April 3	The USSR publishes a report in which Soviet CP Secy. Mikhail A. Suslov, the party's leading ideologist, declares that China's betrayal of Marxist principles has made it an "enemy" of the Soviet camp.	Moscow sources confirm that ex-Premier Georgi Malenkov and ex-Foreign Min. Vyacheslav Molotov have been officially expelled from the Soviet CP for their role in the Stalinist purges of the 1930s.		The U.S. and Panama agree to resume diplomatic relations and to begin talks "on the prompt elimination of the causes of conflict between the two countries without limitations or preconditions of any kind." The agreement comes after several weeks of OAS-sponsored mediation in Washington.	More than 1,000 Moslems are reported to have been killed in religious violence in eastern India.
April 4		Pres. Makarios announces that Cyprus has terminated a 1960 treaty giving Turkey and Greece the right to station a limited number of troops on the island.		Venezuela is reported to have requested a special OAS meeting to consider adoption of mandatory sanctions against Cuba.	
	A	**B**	**C**	**D**	**E**
	Includes developments that affect more than one world region, international organizations and important meetings of major world leaders.	*Includes all domestic and regional developments in Europe, including the Soviet Union, Turkey, Cyprus and Malta.*	*Includes all domestic and regional developments in Africa and the Middle East, including Iraq and Iran and excluding Cyprus, Turkey and Afghanistan.*	*Includes all domestic and regional developments in Latin America, the Caribbean and Canada.*	*Includes all domestic and regional developments in Asia and Pacific nations, extending from Afghanistan through all the Pacific Islands, except Hawaii.*

U.S. Politics & Social Issues	U.S. Foreign Policy & Defense	U.S. Economy & Environment	Science, Technology & Nature	Culture, Leisure & Life Style	
Pres. Johnson appoints Mrs. Mary Bunting as the first woman member of the Atomic Energy Commission.	Pres. Johnson tells newsmen at his Texas ranch that the administration does not share the views on Cuba and Panama expressed by Sen. Fulbright in his March 25 foreign policy speech.			Cambridge defeats Oxford in their annual race on the Thames in London.	March 28
			Thomas Matthews and Maarten Schmidt, California astronomers, report that the recently identified "quasi-stellar radio source," 3C-147, is the most distant celestial object yet found.		March 29
The Supreme Court nullifies the contempt of court conviction of a Negro woman who refused to answer an Etowah County, Ala. court solicitor when he insisted on addressing her by her first name only. . . . Senate debate on the House-passed civil rights bill is opened by the bill's Senate floor manager Hubert Humphrey (D, Minn.).	Vice Adm. John Hoskins, World War II and Korean War naval commander, dies in Falls Church, Va.				March 30
Mrs. Malcolm Peabody, 72, mother of Mass. Gov. Endicott Peabody, is among 283 persons arrested and jailed in connection with anti-segregation demonstrations in St. Augustine, Fla.	GOP Presidential hopeful Barry Goldwater accuses Sen. J. William Fulbright of espousing the "reality of a Munich" in his recent recommendations for a more "realistic" American foreign policy.	U.S. economists report that federal tax collections rose during the first quarter of 1964 despite the tax cut which went into effect March 1.			March 31
		A White House task force reports that huge nuclear power plants probably can be built by 1975 to supply cheap electricity and simultaneously produce large amounts of fresh water from the oceans.	The New York Times reports that USSR has failed in its two most recent attempts to send interplanetary probes to Venus. The Times says the latest failures bring to "more than 15" the number of unsuccessful Soviet interplanetary probe missions.		April 1
	Sen. Thomas Dodd (D, Conn.) criticizes the administration's "passive acceptance of the Castro regime" and urges the provision of moral and material support for anti-Castro "freedom fighters."		An unmanned Soviet satellite is shot out into space from an orbiting launch platform. The purpose and destination of the probe, known as Zond I, are not disclosed.	Tamara Press of the USSR breaks the women's indoor shot-put record in a Leningrad meet with a toss of 56 ft. 1/2 in.	April 2
		Pres. Johnson informs Congress that U.S. farm exports totaled a record $5.6 billion in 1963.	The New York Times reports that U.S. scientists working on the Project Vela nuclear detection program have found methods of detecting underground atomic blasts with greater precision and at greater distances than heretofore acknowledged by the U.S. government.		April 3
	Pres. Johnson nominates Jack Vaughn, Latin American director of the Peace Corps, as the new U.S. ambassador to Panama.			Dallas Long breaks his own 1962 world shot-put record with a toss of 65 ft. 11 1/2 in. at the Pasadena, Calif. meet. . . . Northern Dancer, owned by E.P. Taylor of Toronto, wins the Florida Derby.	April 4

F	G	H	I	J
Includes elections, federal-state relations, civil rights and liberties, crime, the judiciary, education, health care, poverty, urban affairs and population.	Includes formation and debate of U.S. foreign and defense policies, veterans' affairs and defense spending. (Relations with specific foreign countries are usually found under the region concerned.)	Includes business, labor, agriculture, taxation, transportation, consumer affairs, monetary and fiscal policy, natural resources, and pollution.	Includes worldwide scientific, medical and technological developments, natural phenomena, U.S. weather, natural disasters, and accidents.	Includes the arts, religion, scholarship, communications media, sports, entertainment, fashions, fads and social life.

	World Affairs	Europe	Africa & the Middle East	The Americas	Asia & the Pacific
April 5		Turkey rejects Cyprus's unilateral nullification of a 1960 troop stationing accord, calling the action illegal.		Deposed Brazilian Pres. Goulart, speaking to newsmen in Montivideo, Uruguay, expresses "mystification" at his overthrow, adding "Everyone knows that I have never been a communist."	South Vietnam adopts a military conscription system in a move to compensate for a drop-off in the volunteer rate and an increase in desertions. . . . Premier Jigme Dorji of Bhutan is assassinated in Punchholing near the Indian frontier.
April 6	The New York Herald Tribune reports that Soviet intelligence agents have thwarted a recent Communist Chinese plot to assassinate Premier Khrushchev.				
April 7		The Greek-dominated Cypriote government warns that it is prepared to take direct action to remove Turkish troops from the island. The Turks were sent to Cyprus under terms of a 1960 accord no longer recognized by the Cypriote government. . . . Belgium's nationwide doctors' strike enters its seventh day. At least six deaths have so far been attributed to the absence of physicians.			Indian Home Min. Gulzarilal Nanda confers with Pakistani Home Min. Khan Habibullah Khan in New Delhi on measures to end the current wave of religious clashes between Hindus and Moslems in both countries.
April 8					Sheik Mohammed Abdullah, ex-prime minister of the Indian-held part of Kashmir and a proponent of self-determination, is released by India after spending 11 years in prison.
April 9	The U.S. delegation at the Geneva arms talks says it needs a much more detailed accounting of Soviet defense spending before it can seriously consider the USSR's proposals for matched reductions in the military budgets of all states. . . . In a farewell address marking the end of his Hungarian tour, Soviet Premier Khrushchev assails Chinese leaders for "slipping into the quagmire of Trotskyism and big-China chauvinism."	British P.M. Alec Douglas-Home announces the government's decision to hold general elections in October rather than June as previously expected. Labor Party leader Harold Wilson assails the announcement as a Conservative Party effort to avoid the voters.	The U.N. Security Council adopts a resolution deploring a March 28 British air raid on a Yemeni base, which reportedly resulted in the death of 25 persons.		
April 10				The Brazilian government launches a new crackdown on alleged leftists under terms of a newly decreed Institutional Act.	
April 11		Cypriote Pres. Makarios arrives in Athens for talks with Greek Premier George Papandreou.		The Brazilian Congress elects army chief Gen. Humberto de Alecar Castelo Branco to a full term as president of Brazil. Castelo succeeds deposed Pres. João Goulart and interim Pres. Paschoal Mazzilli.	

A	B	C	D	E
Includes developments that affect more than one world region, international organizations and important meetings of major world leaders.	Includes all domestic and regional developments in Europe, including the Soviet Union, Turkey, Cyprus and Malta.	Includes all domestic and regional developments in Africa and the Middle East, including Iraq and Iran and excluding Cyprus, Turkey and Afghanistan.	Includes all domestic and regional developments in Latin America, the Caribbean and Canada.	Includes all domestic and regional developments in Asia and Pacific nations, extending from Afghanistan through all the Pacific Islands, except Hawaii.

U.S. Politics & Social Issues	U.S. Foreign Policy & Defense	U.S. Economy & Environment	Science, Technology & Nature	Culture, Leisure & Life Style	
Sen. J. William Fulbright, speaking in Chapel Hill, N.C., calls for a reassessment of domestic and foreign policy priorities to determine whether excessive concern with Cold War issues has led to a neglect of social, economic and cultural problems at home.	Gen. of the Army Douglas MacArthur, 84, heroic leader of the Pacific campaign in W.W. II and controversial commander of U.N. forces in the Korean War, dies in Washington of acute kidney failure.				April 5
The Supreme Court rules 5-4 that the Constitution's jury trial requirement does not apply to criminal-contempt cases. The ruling involves Miss. Gov. Ross Barnett's request for a jury trial on federal contempt charges brought against him for his alleged obstruction of the court-ordered desegregation of the Univ. of Mississippi.	Leaders of 24 U.S. Jewish organizations hold a two-day emergency conference in Washington to voice their concern over alleged Soviet efforts "to crush the spirit of Soviet Jews and sever their ties to Judaism."	The Supreme Court rules that the proposed merger of the First National Bank and the Security Trust Co., both of Lexington, Ky., violates the Sherman Antitrust Act. The case marks the first application of the Sherman Act against banks.			April 6
Ala. Gov. George Wallace, campaigning on an anti-civil rights platform, captures a surprising 34% of the vote in Wisconsin's Democratic presidential primary. The remainder of the vote goes to Gov. John Reynolds, running as a favorite son pledged to Pres. Johnson. . . . Rev. Bruce Klunder, a white Presbyterian minister, is accidentally run over and killed by a bulldozer while participating in a civil rights sit-down demonstration at a Cleveland school construction site.	A Republican Citizens' Committee, headed by Milton Eisenhower, issues a Panama Canal position paper calling for the building of a new canal and revision of the existing treaty to last until the new facility is completed.	FCC Chmn. E. William Henry says that cable TV systems should be subject to the same federal controls as regular air transmitting systems.	A warning on the need for more research into possible cancer-causing effects of the new live-virus vaccines is issued by Robert Huebner at the American College of Physicians meeting in Atlantic City.		April 7
	In two posthumously published interviews, Gen. of the Army Douglas MacArthur is quoted as saying that "interference from Washington" thwarted his plans to win the Korean War. MacArthur asserts that the Truman administration vetoed both his proposal for atomic bombing of Communist Chinese air bases in Manchuria and his plan for entrapping Red forces by spreading a belt of radioactive cobalt between them and sources of supply. . . .		NASA scientists successfully launch and orbit an unmanned 7,000-pound Gemini capsule. It was the first full test of the Gemini, a two-man vehicle designed to succeed the Mercury capsules. . . . The Health Insurance Institute reports that the incidence in the U.S. of 10 major communicable diseases has declined markedly in the past decade and that three of the diseases—polio, diphtheria, and typhoid fever—appear to be vanishing.		April 8
Sen. Edward Kennedy (D, Mass.), in his first major Senate speech, calls for enactment of the civil rights bill as a memorial to the late Pres. Kennedy.	Ex-Pres. Truman and Eisenhower decline comment on Gen. MacArthur's posthumously published criticism of their Korean War policies.	Pres. Johnson's Appalachian Regional Commission issues a report recommending a five-year, $4.3 billion plan to rejuvenate the nine-state Appalachian area. . . . By a narrow 211-203 vote the House passes and sends to the President the Senate version of the administration's farm bill (HR 6196). In addition to establishing new wheat and cotton production programs, the bill expands and makes permanent the food stamp program.			April 9
			The British Medical Journal reports that an Italian researcher, Dr. Gavino Negroni, has isolated a specific virus in the bone marrow of 10 of 25 leukemia victims studied.	Willie Pastrano retains the world lightheavyweight boxing championship by scoring a sixth round TKO over Argentina's Gregorio Peralta in New Orleans.	April 10
Teamsters Pres. James Hoffa denounces as a "lie" rumors that he had threatened to kill Atty. Gen. Robert F. Kennedy.		A modified version of the administration's farm bill (HR 6196) is signed into law by Pres. Johnson.			April 11

F	G	H	I	J
Includes elections, federal-state relations, civil rights and liberties, crime, the judiciary, education, health care, poverty, urban affairs and population.	*Includes formation and debate of U.S. foreign and defense policies, veterans' affairs and defense spending. (Relations with specific foreign countries are usually found under the region concerned.)*	*Includes business, labor, agriculture, taxation, transportation, consumer affairs, monetary and fiscal policy, natural resources, and pollution.*	*Includes worldwide scientific, medical and technological developments, natural phenomena, U.S. weather, natural disasters, and accidents.*	*Includes the arts, religion, scholarship, communications media, sports, entertainment, fashions, fads and social life.*

	World Affairs	Europe	Africa & the Middle East	The Americas	Asia & the Pacific
April 12	In a TV address to the Russian people, Premier Khrushchev discloses that the USSR has asked other Communist states to join in a "resolute rebuff" to Communist China.	Turkish and Greek Cypriotes in the Kyrenia mountain area continue to exchange sporadic gunfire despite U.N. truce team efforts to halt the shooting. . . . The Belgian government drafts 6,000 physicians into the army in an effort to cope with the nationwide health care crisis resulting from the continuing doctors' strike.			
April 13	Mistaken reports of Khrushchev's death are broadcast throughout the world as a result of an erroneous dispatch transmitted by a West German news agency.	U.N. Secy. General Thant publicly instructs the U.N.'s Cyprus force to use the "minimum" force needed to protect themselves in the performance of their peace-keeping duties. The U.N. troops are expected to try to interpose themselves between rival forces whenever violence appears imminent.	Conservative ex-Treasury Min. Ian Smith is appointed prime minister of Southern Rhodesia after a rightwing faction of the all-white Rhodesian Front Party forces moderate P.M. Winston Field to resign.		In an address to the opening session of SEATO's annual meeting in Manila, French Foreign Min. Maurice Couve de Murville calls for a neutralist "political solution" in South Vietnam. He says that despite the praiseworthy help from the U.S. the Saigon government will never gain sufficient popular support to defeat the Viet Cong. . . . U.S. military sources in Saigon report that the U.S. casualty rate in Vietnam combat is up somewhat from the same period one year ago. Thirty-one Americans are listed as killed in action since Jan. 1.
April 14		British Chancellor of the Exchequer Reginald Maulding presents Parliament with a $20.8 billion budget for fiscal 1965, a 6.6% increase over last year's spending. The budget, which includes an 8.8% increase in defense expenditures, anticipates a deficit of $2.5 billion, the highest in British peacetime history.			
April 15	In remarks to a Polish delegation visiting the Kremlin, Soviet Premier Khrushchev ridicules China's industrial decentralization programs and its network of rural and urban communes.	Cypriote Pres. Makarios accuses Turkey of having "encouraged and directed" Turkish Cypriote "provocations" aimed at partition of the island. . . . Turkey asks the U.N. Security Council to investigate an alleged continuation of Greek Cypriote government attacks upon the island's Turkish minority.	Jordanian King Hussein, in the U.S. for talks with Pres. Johnson, asks American Jews to reappraise "their attitude toward this whole problem of Zionism." . . . Syrian sources report an uprising in central Syria against the socialist and land reform policies of the ruling Baathist regime.		A four-day engagement between South Vietnamese troops and a Viet Cong force (estimated at three battalions) ends with the arrival of U.S.-accompanied government reinforcements. The retiring Viet Cong force is described as the largest coordinated rebel unit yet encountered in the four years of civil war. . . . SEATO, meeting in Manila, adopts a resolution pledging its support for South Vietnam's war against the Viet Cong. France abstains.
April 16	The U.S. presents the Geneva disarmament conference with the details of Pres. Johnson's Jan. 21 proposal for a freeze of nuclear-armed missile and bomber forces.		Africans stage violent demonstrations in Southern Rhodesia in protest against the new all-white government's banishment of Joshua Nkomo and three other African nationalist leaders.	Pres. Johnson announces at a Washington news conference that the U.S. and Colombia have agreed to study the feasibility of a sea-level canal through Colombia.	
April 17		French Pres. de Gaulle is reported in good condition following surgery on a diseased prostate gland.		A Panamanian Foreign Ministry spokesman, commenting on Pres. Johnson's announcement of a Colombian canal study, says "We are bored with the U.S. threatening to take its canal somewhere else.". . . Venezuela breaks diplomatic relations with Brazil in line with its policy of not recognizing governments that overthrow elected governments.	U.S. Secy. of State Rusk arrives in South Vietnam for a four-day visit to demonstrate U.S. support for the Khanh government's war against the Viet Cong.
April 18		Belgian doctors end their 18-day-old strike after the government offered to negotiate their grievances against a new national health insurance program.			More than 250,000 persons turn out to greet the recently freed Sheik Abdullah of Kashmir upon his return to his native city of Srinigar.
	A	**B**	**C**	**D**	**E**
	Includes developments that affect more than one world region, international organizations and important meetings of major world leaders.	*Includes all domestic and regional developments in Europe, including the Soviet Union, Turkey, Cyprus and Malta.*	*Includes all domestic and regional developments in Africa and the Middle East, including Iraq and Iran and excluding Cyprus, Turkey and Afghanistan.*	*Includes all domestic and regional developments in Latin America, the Caribbean and Canada.*	*Includes all domestic and regional developments in Asia and Pacific nations, extending from Afghanistan through all the Pacific Islands, except Hawaii.*

U.S. Politics & Social Issues	U.S. Foreign Policy & Defense	U.S. Economy & Environment	Science, Technology & Nature	Culture, Leisure & Life Style	
				Arnold Palmer wins his fourth Masters golf championship at Augusta, Ga. . . . Olympic skier Wallace Werner of Steamboat Springs, Colo. is killed in an avalanche near St. Moritz, Switzerland.	April 12
	In a *Life* magazine article U.S. Amb.-to-South Vietnam Henry Cabot Lodge predicts that the Mekong Delta may be "totally cleared of Communist guerrilla forces by the end of 1965."			Sidney Poitier is named "best actor" for his role in *Lilies of the Field* at the 36th annual American Academy of Motion Picture Arts & Sciences awards. Oscar for the best film of 1963 goes to *Tom Jones*.	April 13
Sen. Barry Goldwater captures 64% of the vote to win the Illinois GOP presidential primary over Sen. Margaret Chase Smith, the only other candidate on the ballot. Ex-Bell & Howell executive Charles Percy wins the state's GOP gubernatorial nomination.		Five U.S. cigarette makers report that their earnings so far in 1964 have suffered far less than they expected as a result of the Public Health Service report on the hazardous health effects of smoking. . . . Rachel Louise Carson, American biologist and science writer whose 1962 book *Silent Spring* initiated a controversy over the uncontrolled use of pesticides, dies of cancer in Silver Spring, Md. at age 56.			April 14
		N.Y.C. Mayor Robert Wagner submits an "austerity budget" proposing record expenditures of $3.35 billion in fiscal 1975.			April 15
	Ex-V.P. Richard Nixon tells the N.Y. Chamber of Commerce that the U.S. should support extension of the Vietnam War to guerrilla sanctuaries in North Vietnam and Laos. Nixon has just returned from a 24-day Asian tour.	Pres. Johnson urges U.S. business to hold the line on prices in remarks at a Washington news conference.			April 16
A second mistrial is declared in Jackson, Miss. in the trial of Byron de la Beckwith for the 1963 murder of Negro leader Medgar Evers. As in the previous trial, the all-white jury found it impossible to agree on a verdict.		Commerce Dept. reports that the U.S. GNP climbed to a record annual rate of $608.5 billion during the first quarter of 1964.	The Alaska Civil Defense Office says the final death toll from the March 27 earthquake may reach 120.	Shea Stadium, new home of the New York Mets, opens in Flushing near the site of the World's Fair. . . . Mrs. Jerrie Mock of Columbus, O. completes the first world solo flight by a woman.	April 17
	Pres. Johnson orders a comprehensive review of the military draft system, including a study into the possibility of an all-volunteer army.				April 18
F	**G**	**H**	**I**	**J**	
Includes elections, federal-state relations, civil rights and liberties, crime, the judiciary, education, health care, poverty, urban affairs and population.	*Includes formation and debate of U.S. foreign and defense policies, veterans' affairs and defense spending. (Relations with specific foreign countries are usually found under the region concerned.)*	*Includes business, labor, agriculture, taxation, transportation, consumer affairs, monetary and fiscal policy, natural resources, and pollution.*	*Includes worldwide scientific, medical and technological developments, natural phenomena, U.S. weather, natural disasters, and accidents.*	*Includes the arts, religion, scholarship, communications media, sports, entertainment, fashions, fads and social life.*	

	World Affairs	Europe	Africa & the Middle East	The Americas	Asia & the Pacific
April 19			Maj. Gen. Amin el-Hafez, chairman of Syria's ruling Revolutionary Council, accuses the UAR of partial responsibility for recent anti-Baathist disorders in central Syria.	Cuban Premier Castro denounces the U.S.'s regular reconnaissance flights over Cuba as a violation of the island's sovereignty and warns that ground-to-air missiles may be employed to combat future flights.	The tripartite Laotian coalition government, headed by Prince Souvanna Phouma, is overthrown in a right-wing military coup directed by Brig. Gen. Kouprasith Abhay. The coup comes only hours after the complete collapse of the latest attempt to settle the outstanding differences between the three factions of the old coalition.
April 20	Soviet Premier Khrushchev and U.S. Pres. Johnson issue simultaneous statements pledging equal cutbacks in the production of fissionable material for nuclear weapons. The pledges are considered unilateral and are not subject to verification.			In a speech to an annual AP meeting in New York, Pres. Johnson pledges continuation of U.S. efforts "to isolate Cuba from the inter-American system."	In separate statements Britain, USSR, U.S. and Communist China all denounce yesterday's right-wing coup against Laos's coalition government.
April 21		Belgian Premier Theo Lefevre proposes in Parliament amendments to the national health insurance program, including increased fee schedules for the nation's recently striking doctors.		Argentine Pres. Arturo Illia sends Congress a bill to relax political restrictions placed on the Peronist and Communist parties.	U.S. Asst. State Secy. William Bundy flies to Vientiane in a reported effort to persuade right-wing coup leaders not to overthrow Laos's coalition government. . . . U.S. military sources in Saigon report that South Vietnamese government forces suffered their heaviest casualties of the war in the week April 12-18. Casualty estimates list 200 killed, 140 missing. Vietcong losses are put at 660 dead, 50 captured.
April 22	Exhibitors from 66 countries attend ceremonies marking the opening of the New York World's Fair. In his dedicatory address, Pres. Johnson stresses the Fair's theme of "Peace through Understanding."	Cypriote Pres. Makarios announces that amnesty will be granted to Turkish Cypriotes who join with Greek Cypriotes in a program of mutual disarmament under U.N. supervision. Turkish Cypriote leaders reject the bid as "propaganda."	Tanganyikan Pres. Julius Nyerere and Zanzibar Pres. Abeid Amani Karume sign an agreement merging their two nations into a single United Republic of Tanzania. Observers say the merger is motivated in part by a desire to check growing communist influence in the current Zanzibar government.	The agrarian Socialist government of Saskatchewan, in power for 20 years, is ousted by the Liberal Party in provincial elections.	
April 23		*Izvestia* publishes a lengthy memorandum from Premier Khrushchev demanding that Soviet agriculture adopt the efficient farm techniques commonly used in the West. . . . USSR and Britain sign an agreement to extend their current liberal trade accord for five years.	UAR Pres. Nasser, arriving in Yemen for a goodwill visit, pledges unceasing efforts "to expel Britain from all parts of the Arab world."	U.S. Defense Dept. warns that "swift countermeasures" will be taken if Cuba attempts to down American U-2 planes on reconnaissance missions over the island.	The rightist military committee that seized power in Laos April 19 fails to carry out its declared aim of ousting the Souvanna Phouma government. Instead they are reportedly asking Souvanna Phouma to remain as head of a new, more right-oriented coalition. . . . A Malaysian government white paper accuses Indonesian agents of plotting to assassinate leaders of the Malaysian Federation.
April 24	Cuba calls on the World Trade and Development Conference in Geneva to censure the use of economic sanctions as a violation of the U.N. Charter.				Laotian Premier Souvanna Phouma announces his acceptance of a rightist offer to remain as leader of a revised coalition government.
April 25					

A	B	C	D	E
Includes developments that affect more than one world region, international organizations and important meetings of major world leaders.	*Includes all domestic and regional developments in Europe, including the Soviet Union, Turkey, Cyprus and Malta.*	*Includes all domestic and regional developments in Africa and the Middle East, including Iraq and Iran and excluding Cyprus, Turkey and Afghanistan.*	*Includes all domestic and regional developments in Latin America, the Caribbean and Canada.*	*Includes all domestic and regional developments in Asia and Pacific nations, extending from Afghanistan through all the Pacific Islands, except Hawaii.*

U.S. Politics & Social Issues	U.S. Foreign Policy & Defense	U.S. Economy & Environment	Science, Technology & Nature	Culture, Leisure & Life Style	
			The National Academy of Sciences presents its Comstock Award (in electricity and radiation research) to Chien-shiung Wu of Columbia University for her experimental confirmation of the violation of the law of "parity conservation" in the nucleus. She is the first woman to receive the honor.		April 19
Over 85% of Cleveland's Negro public school pupils participate in a one-day protest boycott against alleged de facto segregation.					April 20
Sen. Herman Talmadge (D, Ga.) introduces an amendment to the civil rights bill to entitle criminal contempt defendants to jury trials. The amendment is regarded as part of a Southern effort to delay final action on the main bill. . . . Testimony by FBI Director J. Edgar Hoover that "communist influence does exist in the Negro movement" is released by a House Appropriations subcommittee. Hoover appeared before the subcommittee Jan. 29.	GOP congressional leaders Sen. Everett Dirksen and Rep. Charles Halleck, in a joint statement, accuse the Johnson administration of concealing the extent and character of the U.S.'s combat role in Vietnam.				April 21
Several hundred persons participate in civil rights demonstrations at the opening of New York World's Fair in an effort to focus attention on continuing discrimination against Negroes in N.Y.C. and the U.S. . . . The House Judiciary Committee opens hearings on some 150 proposed constitutional amendments to permit prayers in public schools.	The House unanimously passes and sends to the Senate a bill (HR 10939) appropriating nearly $46.8 billion for the Defense Dept. in fiscal 1965. The bill does not cover foreign aid, military construction or civil defense expenditures.	A "just and fair" settlement of the last remaining issues in the four-and-a-half-year-old railroad work-rules dispute is announced by Pres. Johnson in a nationally televised broadcast. Johnson is reported to have played a personal role in the final phases of the negotiations. . . . The New York World's Fair opens in Flushing Meadows, N.Y. The Fair, constructed at a cost of $500 million, is expected to run for two years.			April 22
Pres. Johnson criticizes yesterday's civil rights demonstrations at the New York World's Fair as "rudeness" which "served no good purpose."	Pres. Johnson criticizes Republican leaders for allegedly offering inconsistent and even contradictory recommendations regarding U.S. policy in Vietnam.			Houston Colts pitcher Ken Johnson throws a no-hitter against the Cincinnati Reds, but loses the game 1-0 on an unearned run in the ninth inning. It is the first nine-inning no-hit loss in major league history. . . . Blues for Mr. Charlie, a play by Negro author James Baldwin, opens in New York.	April 23
CORE National Director James Farmer predicts an increase in civil rights demonstrations throughout the nation, adding that the U.S. faces "a longer and hotter summer than this country has ever seen."	Defense Secy. McNamara indicates at a Pentagon press conference that the Johnson administration has dropped or at least amended its plans to withdraw most U.S. military personnel from South Vietnam by the end of 1965. . . . Defense Secy. McNamara announces cost-saving plans to reduce or discontinue activities at 63 military facilities in 29 states.				April 24
The General Assembly of the Southern Presbyterian Church adopts a resolution acknowledging the legitimacy of Negro protest demonstrations.	Pres. Johnson announces the appointment of Lt. Gen. William Westmoreland, 50, to replace retiring Gen. Paul Harkins as head of the U.S. Military Assistance Command in South Vietnam.		British physicist Keith Runcorn reports in London the discovery of a new method of measuring the rise and fall of mid-ocean tides by plotting variations in electrical impulses carried on trans-oceanic cables.	The Toronto Maple Leafs win their third consecutive Stanley Cup hockey championship by defeating the Detroit Red Wings, four games to three. . . . Al Oerter of New York sets a world discus record of 206 ft. 6 in. in Walnut, Calif.	April 25
F	G	H	I	J	
Includes elections, federal-state relations, civil rights and liberties, crime, the judiciary, education, health care, poverty, urban affairs and population.	Includes formation and debate of U.S. foreign and defense policies, veterans' affairs and defense spending. (Relations with specific foreign countries are usually found under the region concerned.)	Includes business, labor, agriculture, taxation, transportation, consumer affairs, monetary and fiscal policy, natural resources, and pollution.	Includes worldwide scientific, medical and technological developments, natural phenomena, U.S. weather, natural disasters, and accidents.	Includes the arts, religion, scholarship, communications media, sports, entertainment, fashions, fads and social life.	

	World Affairs	Europe	Africa & the Middle East	The Americas	Asia & the Pacific
April 26		A Turkish Cypriote mob attacks a group of U.N. peace team officials in Nicosia. Turkish Cypriote leaders have accused the U.N. force of deliberately failing to halt Greek Cypriote attacks on Turkish communities.			
April 27		The Greek government grants amnesty to 421 imprisoned communists convicted of sedition during the communists' struggle to seize power in the late 1940s.	Sierra Leone P.M. Sir Milton Augustus Strieby Margai dies in Freetown at age 68.	Bolivian V.P. Juan Lechin Oquendo publicly accuses the U.S. of giving money to the government of Pres. Victor Paz Estenssoro to subsidize pro-government propaganda and demonstrations.	Pathet Lao troops break the shaky Laotian truce by launching a major offensive against neutralist and right-wing positions in northern Laos. The renewed fighting is attributed in part to the confusion that has characterized the Laotian political situation since the April 19 right-wing coup.
April 28	Delegates to the Geneva disarmament conference begin a five-week recess to allow for consultations with their governments.	U.N. peace-keeping troops succeed in halting a four-day Greek Cypriote offensive against remaining Turkish Cypriote strongholds in the Kyrenia Mountains of northern Cyprus. The attacks were reportedly undertaken with the implicit approval of the Greek-dominated Cyprus government.			
April 29		U.N. Secy. Gen. U Thant asserts that a negotiated settlement between Greek and Turkish Cypriotes is urgently needed if Cyprus "is to avoid utter disaster." Thant rules out proposals for increased armed action by U.N. peace-keeping troops, saying it would contribute nothing to the long-range solution of the island's problems.			
April 30		West German Chancellor Ludwig Erhard pledges to continue prosecution of Nazi war criminals, saying there must always be "atonement for murder and atrocities."		Brazilian sources report continuation of the new government's anti-leftist purge. At least 150 allegedly pro-communist Brazilian politicians have been deprived of their political rights.	
May 1		An estimated 3,000 Czech college students demonstrate in Prague against alleged "political indoctrination" in the nation's universities.	Ghana Pres. Kwame Nkrumah decrees to himself authority to detain any person "acting in a manner prejudicial to Ghana's defense."	Soviet Premier Khrushchev, in a May Day speech, dismisses as "fabrications" recent American assertions that he had acknowledged the U.S.'s right to fly reconnaissance missions over Cuba during the 1962 missile crisis.	Indonesian Pres. Sukarno warns in a May Day speech that there are "21 million Indonesian volunteers" awaiting his order to crush the Malaysian Federation.
May 2				The Cuban Refugee Center in Miami reports that 171,606 Cuban refugees have registered in the U.S. since June 1961.	Laotian Premier Souvanna Phouma announces that the neutralist and rightist wings of the coalition government have formally merged under his leadership. . . . The Indonesian government marks "education day" by burning 500 European-language books which allegedly symbolize "cultural subversion through ideas. . .contrary to Indonesian ideas and theories.". . . The *U.S.N.S. Card*, a helicopter transport vessel, is sunk by an underwater bomb while docked in Saigon harbor. No injuries are reported.
May 3		Hundreds of Bulgarian Christians are reported to have clashed with Sofia police who tried to block them from attending church ceremonies in observance of Orthodox Easter.			A reported easing in Malaysian-Philippine tensions is confirmed by the announcement of resumed diplomatic relations. . . . Indonesian Pres. Sukarno publicly reiterates his scorn for American threats to suspend aid because of Indonesia's anti-Malaysian policies.
	A	B	C	D	E
	Includes developments that affect more than one world region, international organizations and important meetings of major world leaders.	*Includes all domestic and regional developments in Europe, including the Soviet Union, Turkey, Cyprus and Malta.*	*Includes all domestic and regional developments in Africa and the Middle East, including Iraq and Iran and excluding Cyprus, Turkey and Afghanistan.*	*Includes all domestic and regional developments in Latin America, the Caribbean and Canada.*	*Includes all domestic and regional developments in Asia and Pacific nations, extending from Afghanistan through all the Pacific Islands, except Hawaii.*

U.S. Politics & Social Issues	U.S. Foreign Policy & Defense	U.S. Economy & Environment	Science, Technology & Nature	Culture, Leisure & Life Style	
Rev. Thomas Toolen, archbishop of the Mobile-Birmingham archdiocese, orders the desegregation of all Roman Catholic schools in Ala.		General Electric Co. announces the payment of $26.5 million to 44 Eastern utilities in settlement of suits arising from GE's 1960 conviction for conspiracy to fix prices in the sale of electrical equipment.		The Boston Celtics defeat the San Francisco Warriors, four games to one, to win their sixth consecutive National Basketball Association championship.	April 26
		The Supreme Court upholds (by declining to review) the constitutionality of the compulsory arbitration law passed by Congress in 1963 in the railroad work-rules dispute.	Nine major U.S. cigarette makers adopt a voluntary ban on youth-oriented advertising.		April 27
Gov. William Scranton wins the Republican presidential preference primary in Pa. with a record 220,000 (58%) write-in votes. Goldwater finishes fourth with 8.5%. . . . Gov. Nelson Rockefeller, campaigning in Calif., says that Goldwater's "irresponsibility and extremism" will not appeal to American voters in November.		Pres. Johnson sends Congress a special message outlining a $228 million program for the economic revitalization of chronic poverty areas in Appalachia.		The New York Drama Critics Circle names *Hello Dolly!* as the best musical of the 1963-1964 theater season.	April 28
Spokesmen for the National Council of Churches testify before the House Judiciary Committee in support of the Supreme Court's ruling against prayer in public schools.			In a paper to the National Academy of Sciences, Dr. Edward Anders hypothesizes that more than half of all observed meteorites were produced by a single collision of two large asteroids about 400 million years ago.		April 29
	The Republican Citizens Committee issues a position paper on Cuba urging the formation of an anti-Castro government-in-exile with U.S. support.	The Bureau of Labor Statistics reports that the U.S. economy expanded in April, marking the 38th consecutive month of economic growth. The achievement breaks the old 37-month growth record set in 1945-1948.			April 30
	Over 1,000 American college students demonstrate in front of the Soviet U.N. mission in New York to protest reported anti-Semitism in the USSR.				May 1
Sen. Goldwater wins the GOP presidential preference primary in Texas. He was the only candidate to actively campaign in the state.				E.P. Taylor's Northern Dancer, Billy Hartack up, wins the 90th running of the Kentucky Derby. . . . A Communist Chinese team scales the previously unclimbed 26,291-foot Shisha Pangma peak in the Himalayas near the Tibet-Nepal border.	May 2
CORE announces plans for staging civil rights demonstrations at the Republican and Democratic national conventions later this summer.			Dr. Muriel Roger of the Rockefeller Institute reports that she has successfully transplanted individual genes to new host cells which subsequently displayed the specific hereditary trait governed by the transplanted gene. It is the first such transference of single hereditary traits.	Jack Nicklaus wins his second consecutive Tournament of Champions golf tournament in Las Vegas.	May 3

F	G	H	I	J
Includes elections, federal-state relations, civil rights and liberties, crime, the judiciary, education, health care, poverty, urban affairs and population.	Includes formation and debate of U.S. foreign and defense policies, veterans' affairs and defense spending. (Relations with specific foreign countries are usually found under the region concerned.)	Includes business, labor, agriculture, taxation, transportation, consumer affairs, monetary and fiscal policy, natural resources, and pollution.	Includes worldwide scientific, medical and technological developments, natural phenomena, U.S. weather, natural disasters, and accidents.	Includes the arts, religion, scholarship, communications media, sports, entertainment, fashions, fads and social life.

	World Affairs	Europe	Africa & the Middle East	The Americas	Asia & the Pacific
May 4		Soviet Premier Khrushchev charges that Cyprus's internal strife is the direct result of NATO intervention in the island's affairs. . . . Maltese voters narrowly approve a referendum on the government's plan for an independent Malta within the British Commonwealth.	The Israeli Knesset adopts a resolution urging the West German government to prohibit German scientists from working in the UAR.		Pathet Lao chief Prince Souphanouvong rejects an invitation to rejoin Premier Souvanna Phouma's reorganized coalition government. . . . The U.S. State Dept. announces an expansion of the U.S. military police force in Vietnam in an effort to curb increasing Viet Cong terrorist attacks on U.S. personnel.
May 5			Israel announces that it has already begun a limited diversion of Jordan River waters in a test of its controversial plan for the irrigation of the Negev Desert. The announcement prompts angry denunciations in the Arab press.		Saigon sources report a continuing sharp increase in South Vietnamese fighting.
May 6		The EEC signs an agreement with Israel cutting tariffs on Israeli goods by an average of 20%.	At a Moscow farewell dinner marking the end of his two-week Russian visit, Algerian Premier Ben Bella thanks the USSR for doing "more than anyone else" to help Algeria.		
May 7		British Labor Party candidates swamp Conservatives and Liberals in town council elections held throughout England and Wales.	British P.M. Alec Douglas-Home reiterates in a Commons speech Britain's determination to defend South Arabia and Aden from attacks by dissident tribesmen and Yemeni border forces.	Brazilian Pres. Castelo Branco suspends the political rights of 34 members of ousted Pres. Goulart's Brazilian Labor Party as part of continuing crackdown against alleged communist sympathizers.	
May 8		U.N. troops intervene to halt an outbreak of heavy fighting between Greek and Turkish Cypriotes near the village of Louroujina, southeast of Nicosia.		More than 800 persons are said to have been arrested following six days of demonstrations and strikes in the Dominican Republic.	
May 9			Enthusiastic Egyptian crowds greet Soviet Premier Khrushchev upon his arrival in Alexandria for a two-week visit to the UAR to mark completion of the first stage of Soviet-aided Aswan High Dam project.		South Korean Pres. Chung Hee Park announces a cabinet reorganization amidst anti-government student demonstrations protesting his government's efforts to restore diplomatic and trade relations with Japan.
May 10					
May 11			In an address to the UAR National Assembly, visiting Premier Khrushchev reaffirms total Soviet support for the Arab states in their dispute with Israel. . . . The U.N. Special Committee on Colonialism adopts a resolution asking Britain to halt its military activity in the Federation of South Arabia.		
May 12				Brazil's new anti-communist regime breaks diplomatic relations with Cuba. . . . Chile's 5000-member Nazi Party disbands under government order.	

A	B	C	D	E
Includes developments that affect more than one world region, international organizations and important meetings of major world leaders.	*Includes all domestic and regional developments in Europe, including the Soviet Union, Turkey, Cyprus and Malta.*	*Includes all domestic and regional developments in Africa and the Middle East, including Iraq and Iran and excluding Cyprus, Turkey and Afghanistan.*	*Includes all domestic and regional developments in Latin America, the Caribbean and Canada.*	*Includes all domestic and regional developments in Asia and Pacific nations, extending from Afghanistan through all the Pacific Islands, except Hawaii.*

U.S. Politics & Social Issues	U.S. Foreign Policy & Defense	U.S. Economy & Environment	Science, Technology & Nature	Culture, Leisure & Life Style	
The U.S. Supreme Court sustains a court of appeals decision upholding Gary, Indiana's neighborhood school policy despite its consequent *de facto* segregation.	Z2The New York Times journalist David Halberstam, 30, wins a Pulitzer Prize for his coverage of the Vietnam conflict.	Pres. Johnson, speaking to a White House meeting of labor leaders, predicts another tax cut in the next few years if economic conditions continue to improve.		The International Olympic Committee bars Indonesia from the 1964 Games because of its refusal to observe rules forbidding political and racial discrimination in sports. Israel has been repeatedly barred from competitions hosted in Indonesia.	May 4
Pres. Johnson appoints a 32-member women's advisory committee to the Federal Aviation Agency.		The Health Insurance Institute reports that health benefit payments increased from $7.1 billion in 1962 to $7.8 billion in 1963.			May 5
Pres. Johnson tells reporters he would consider calling an extra congressional session if Congress deliberately delays action on civil rights, anti-poverty, health care and other priority measures pending in the current session.					May 6
		U.S. railroads dismiss more than 3,000 locomotive firemen under new work rules authorized by a federal arbitration award. . . . The Dow Jones average of industrial stock prices climbs to a closing record of 830.17.		An official spokesman for Britain's Roman Catholic bishops issues a statement denouncing all contraceptive devices, including birth control pills. The statement comes in the midst of a national controversy over the Catholic Church's views on birth control.	May 7
Pres. Johnson addresses Ga. legislators at an integrated breakfast meeting in Atlanta.	The Methodist Church's general conference, meeting in Pittsburgh, urges a more open and flexible U.S. policy toward Communist China and Cuba.				May 8
Pres. Johnson stresses anti-poverty and civil rights goals in speeches given during his second visit to the New York World's Fair.				Ultiminio Ramos of Cuba retains his world flyweight championship in Accra, Ghana by scoring a disputed 15-round split decision over Ghanaian Floyd Robertson.	May 9
Bernice Pyke, fighter for women's suffrage and first women delegate to a national political convention (Democrat-1920), dies in Lakewood, O. at age 84.				U.S. shot-putter Dallas Long breaks his own five-week-old world record in Fresno, Calif. with a toss of 66 ft. 7 1/2 in.	May 10
Sen. Hubert Humphrey (D, Minn.) assails the Senate debate on the civil rights bill--now in its 52nd day. Humphrey directs his attack on Northern and Western backers of the bill, who he claims are permitting Southern obstruction by refusing to support cloture. . . . The Connecticut Supreme Court of Errors upholds the constitutionality of an 85-year-old state law prohibiting the distribution of information about and use of contraceptive devices.		The American Federation of Teachers defeats the National Education Association in an NLRB election for the right to represent Detroit's 9,600 public school teachers.		Margaret Smith of Australia wins her third consecutive international women's singles tennis championship in Rome.	May 11
New York State Education Commission releases a task force report recommending the limited busing of students to reduce racial imbalance in N.Y.C. public schools. Civil rights leaders hail the proposal. . . . In a Madison Square Garden speech, GOP presidential contender Goldwater assails the administration's civil rights proposals, saying "You can not pass a law that will make me like you or you like me."	Defense Secy. McNamara arrives in Saigon on his fifth fact-finding mission to South Vietnam.	Pres. Johnson outlines the commodity support, community development and consumer protection goals of his farm program at a meeting with members of the Newspaper Farm Editors Association. . . . Pres. Johnson signs a bill authorizing the Agriculture Dept. to prevent the sale of a pesticide until its safety has been established.			May 12

F	G	H	I	J
Includes elections, federal-state relations, civil rights and liberties, crime, the judiciary, education, health care, poverty, urban affairs and population.	Includes formation and debate of U.S. foreign and defense policies, veterans' affairs and defense spending. (Relations with specific foreign countries are usually found under the region concerned.)	Includes business, labor, agriculture, taxation, transportation, consumer affairs, monetary and fiscal policy, natural resources, and pollution.	Includes worldwide scientific, medical and technological developments, natural phenomena, U.S. weather, natural disasters, and accidents.	Includes the arts, religion, scholarship, communications media, sports, entertainment, fashions, fads and social life.

	World Affairs	Europe	Africa & the Middle East	The Americas	Asia & the Pacific
May 13				Panamanian election officials declare government candidate Marco Robles winner of the May 10 presidential election. Final returns show Robles with about 40% of the total vote in the four-man race.	In a statement summarizing his two-day fact-finding visit to Saigon, U.S. Defense Secy. McNamara predicts that despite "excellent progress" it "is going to be a long war."
May 14				U.S. Commerce Dept. tightens curbs on trade with Cuba by issuing an order requiring export licenses for the sale of food and medicine to Cuba.	After conferring with Pres. Johnson, Defense Secy. McNamara meets with newsmen to report on his South Vietnam fact-finding mission. He says the trip confirmed the necessity for a rapid and substantial increase in South Vietnamese forces as well as a possible need for "certain additional U.S. personnel" to expand "training."
May 15					
May 16		The U.N. Cyprus command is reported to have authorized its troops to shoot if necessary to protect Cypriote civilians.	In a speech at the UAR's Aswan High Dam, visiting Soviet Premier Khrushchev chides Arab leaders for overemphasizing "Arab unity and nationalism" instead of stressing their fraternal unity with socialist movements throughout the world.		
May 17			Premier Ben Bella announces that the USSR, Bulgaria and Czechoslovakia have agreed to give Algeria a total of $140 million in aid.		Laotian neutralist and rightist troops are reported in full retreat in the face of an intensified Pathet Lao offensive in the strategic Plaine des Jarres.
May 18		The Greek Cypriote-dominated government of Cyprus confirms that it has taken the first steps toward establishing a military draft and toward purchasing foreign arms. The actions are described as a precaution against "possible Turkish aggression."			Neutralist Laotian Premier Souvanna Phouma denounces his half-brother Prince Souphanouvong, Pathet Lao leader, for ordering the stepped-up offensive "with the help of the Viet Minh (North Vietnamese) Communists.". . . The U.N. Security Council concludes a second session devoted to the Kashmir dispute without achieving any significant reconciliation of Indian-Pakistani differences.
May 19			British Colonial Secy. Duncan Sandys announces that the British protectorate of Northern Rhodesia will become the independent nation of Zambia on Oct. 24.		The U.N. Security Council meets in special session to hear Cambodian charges of U.S.-South Vietnamese aggression.
May 20		A Finnish soldier on patrol northwest of Nicosia becomes the first U.N. force member to be killed in the performance of peace-keeping duties on Cyprus.		Cuban exile groups claim that prominent anti-Castro leader Manuel Ray has landed in Cuba with a small force to launch a guerrilla war against the Castro regime. . . . Pres. Johnson says the U.S. economic boycott of Cuba has been very successful despite non-compliance by several of America's European allies.	French Pres. de Gaulle proposes that the 14-nation Geneva conference on Laos reconvene to consider the latest political and military crisis in that country.

A	B	C	D	E
Includes developments that affect more than one world region, international organizations and important meetings of major world leaders.	Includes all domestic and regional developments in Europe, including the Soviet Union, Turkey, Cyprus and Malta.	Includes all domestic and regional developments in Africa and the Middle East, including Iraq and Iran and excluding Cyprus, Turkey and Afghanistan.	Includes all domestic and regional developments in Latin America, the Caribbean and Canada.	Includes all domestic and regional developments in Asia and Pacific nations, extending from Afghanistan through all the Pacific Islands, except Hawaii.

U.S. Politics & Social Issues	U.S. Foreign Policy & Defense	U.S. Economy & Environment	Science, Technology & Nature	Culture, Leisure & Life Style	
Sen. Barry Goldwater denounces the Republican Party's liberal wing as its "blight." . . . Rev. Carl McIntire of Collingwood, N.J. appears before the House Judiciary Committee to support constitutional proposals permitting prayer reading in public schools.	Air Force Secy. Eugene Zucert denies recent congressional charges that U.S. forces in Vietnam are forced to fly ill-equipped and defective T-28 training planes.				May 13
Republican Reps. David Martin (Neb.) and M.G. Snyder (Ky.) show newsmen photographs of rundown tenant houses on Alabama land owned by Mrs. Lyndon Johnson in an effort to dramatize the alleged political hypocrisy of Pres. Johnson's anti-poverty proposals.	Washington sources estimate current U.S. armed strength in Vietnam at about 15,500 uniformed personnel, down about 1,000 since late 1963. Further immediate reductions, however, are not expected in view of recent administration policy statements.			The French film, *The Umbrellas of Cherbourg*, wins the grand prize at the Cannes Film Festival.	May 14
Gov. Nelson Rockefeller captures 33% of the vote to score an upset victory in the Ore. GOP presidential primary over Henry Cabot Lodge (25%) and Barry Goldwater (20%).	Some congressional leaders, leaving a National Security Council briefing on Defense Secy. McNamara's recent South Vietnamese trip, describe McNamara's report as "very gloomy."				May 15
			Researchers at the California Institute of Technology disclose significant new data on the atmosphere of Jupiter.	Northern Dancer, ridden by Bill Hartack, wins the Preakness at Pimlico Race Course in Baltimore.	May 16
Residents of the largely Jewish Crown Heights section of Brooklyn announce the formation of a biracial citizens' radio-car patrol to cope with a recent wave of attacks and muggings. Most of the attacks have been attributed to Negro teenagers living in nearby Bedford-Stuyvesant.					May 17
The Supreme Court rules 6-3 that voluntary incriminating statements by an indicted criminal defendant, obtained by federal agents in the absence of counsel, are inadmissible as evidence because of the Sixth Amendment's guarantee of the right to counsel.	Pres. Johnson asks Congress to provide South Vietnam with an additional $125 million in U.S. economic and military aid to combat the Viet Cong. Over $500 million has already been appropriated for fiscal 1965.	More than 10,000 Utah teachers begin a second-day strike to press demands for more state aid to education.			May 18
Ala. Gov. George Wallace gets nearly 43% of the vote in losing Md.'s Democratic presidential primary to Sen. Daniel Brewster, a stand-in for Pres. Johnson.	A State Dept. spokesman discloses that at least 40 microphones have been found hidden in the walls of the U.S. embassy in Moscow.	The National Education Association urges its members not to accept jobs in Utah until the state increases its aid to education.	The Soviet and U.S. academies of science announce an agreement under which each country is allowed to send 55 scientists on inspection or research visits to the other country.		May 19
		The Critical Issues Council of the Republican Citizens Committee recommends intensified export efforts and a greater sharing of the West's foreign aid burden as urgently needed steps to reduce the U.S. balance of payments deficit.			May 20

F	G	H	I	J
Includes elections, federal-state relations, civil rights and liberties, crime, the judiciary, education, health care, poverty, urban affairs and population.	Includes formation and debate of U.S. foreign and defense policies, veterans' affairs and defense spending. (Relations with specific foreign countries are usually found under the region concerned.)	Includes business, labor, agriculture, taxation, transportation, consumer affairs, monetary and fiscal policy, natural resources, and pollution.	Includes worldwide scientific, medical and technological developments, natural phenomena, U.S. weather, natural disasters, and accidents.	Includes the arts, religion, scholarship, communications media, sports, entertainment, fashions, fads and social life.

	World Affairs	Europe	Africa & the Middle East	The Americas	Asia & the Pacific
May 21			A Communist Chinese agreement to give Kenya $3 million in aid and a $15 million interest-free loan is announced in Nairobi.		U.S. State Dept. discloses that U.S. planes are flying reconnaissance missions over Pathet Lao territory at the request of the Laotian government. . . . U.S. Amb. Adlai Stevenson explains American opposition to a reconvening of a Geneva conference on Indochina in a speech to the U.N. Security Council. Soviet Amb. Nikolai Fedorenko replies by denouncing the U.S. for "waging a very cruel and dirty war" against the Vietnamese people.
May 22				Cuban Vice Premier Raul Castro charges that U.S. CIA agents have infiltrated high provincial government posts. He warns of a thorough investigation.	In a Washington speech apparently aimed at North Vietnam, U.S. State Secy. Rusk says the Vietnamese War could be expanded "if the Communists persist in their course of aggression."
May 23					The USSR announces its support of French Pres. de Gaulle's recent call for a reconvening of the 14-nation Geneva Conference on Laos. . . . The South Vietnamese government closes three Saigon daily newspapers on charges of printing anti-government articles.
May 24			A Soviet agreement to lend the UAR $277 million is announced by Pres. Nasser at a farewell dinner marking the end of Soviet Premier Khrushchev's two-week visit to Egypt.		
May 25					
May 26		Swedish ex-Col. Stig Wennerstrom, an accused Soviet spy, admits in pre-trial testimony that he sold to the USSR secret information on the U.S. Strategic Air Command while serving as a Swedish military attaché in Washington.	UAR and Iraqi leaders announce the formation of a special council to explore means of unifying their two governments.	Racial and political clashes between British Guiana's East Indian and Negro populations are reportedly growing in violence and frequency despite increased intervention by British police.	Saigon sources report that South Vietnamese Premier Nguyen Khanh has informed U.S. officials that he would consider expansion of the war to North Vietnam only if the U.S. guarantees South Vietnam's protection through commitment of additional American combat troops. . . . Recently freed ex-Kashmiri P.M. Sheik Mohammed Abdullah completes a series of separate talks with Pakistani and Indian leaders in an apparently unsuccessful effort to find a basis for settling the Kashmir question.
May 27	World leaders, including Pakistani Pres. Ayub Khan and Communist Chinese Premier Chou En-lai, express condolences on the death of Indian P.M. Nehru. Many of the expressions laud Nehru's contribution to world peace as the architect of developing nations' nonalignment.		The U.N. Special Committee on Apartheid urges the Security Council to apply mandatory economic sanctions against South Africa until it abandons its policy of racial separation.	A controversial proposal to replace the Union Jack with a flag of purely Canadian design and to recognize *Oh, Canada* instead of *God Save the Queen* as the national anthem is submitted to Parliament by Liberal P.M. Lester Pearson. The changes, long sought by French-Canadians, are opposed by many English-speaking citizens, including Conservative leader John Diefenbaker.	Jawaharlal Nehru, prime minister of India and the nation's undisputed leader since the death of Gandhi in 1948, dies of a heart attack in New Delhi at age 74. . . . The U.S. State Dept. announces that the Laotian government will be given several U.S. T-28 training planes for use against the Pathet Lao.
	A	B	C	D	E
	Includes developments that affect more than one world region, international organizations and important meetings of major world leaders.	Includes all domestic and regional developments in Europe, including the Soviet Union, Turkey, Cyprus and Malta.	Includes all domestic and regional developments in Africa and the Middle East, including Iraq and Iran and excluding Cyprus, Turkey and Afghanistan.	Includes all domestic and regional developments in Latin America, the Caribbean and Canada.	Includes all domestic and regional developments in Asia and Pacific nations, extending from Afghanistan through all the Pacific Islands, except Hawaii.

U.S. Politics & Social Issues	U.S. Foreign Policy & Defense	U.S. Economy & Environment	Science, Technology & Nature	Culture, Leisure & Life Style	
		The White House releases revised budget estimates indicating a federal deficit in fiscal 1964 of $8.8 billion, $1.2 billion below the January estimate.		Rev. Edler Hawkins of New York is elected as the first Negro moderator of the 3.2 million-member United Presbyterian Church, U.S.A.	**May 21**
In a commencement address at the Univ. of Michigan, Pres. Johnson urges a massive national effort to build a "great society" marked by revitalized cities, expanded educational and economic opportunity, and a carefully protected natural environment.		Commerce Dept. estimates that U.S. corporate profits after taxes rose from an annual rate of $28.6 billion in the final quarter of 1963 to $31.1 billion in the first quarter of 1964.			**May 22**
	Pres. Johnson outlines his Eastern European policies in a speech dedicating the George C. Marshall Library at Virginia Military Institute in Lexington, Va. Johnson proposes an expansion of U.S. contacts to promote the increasing diversity and national independence among the communist states of Eastern Europe.				**May 23**
	Sen. Barry Goldwater, appearing on the ABC program *Issues and Answers*, proposes that "low-yield nuclear weapons" be used to defoliate South Vietnamese border jungles affording cover for Communist supply lines to the Viet Cong.	The Bureau of Labor Statistics reports that union membership increased from 16,303,000 (22% of the labor force) in 1961 to 16,586,000 (22.2%) in 1962. It is the first such proportional gain in union strength since 1956 when total membership stood at 17,900,000.		Over 300 people are killed and 500 injured in a riot at a disputed Peru-Argentina Olympic soccer elimination match in Lima's National Stadium. . . . The musical *Hello Dolly!* gains a near sweep of the annual Antoinette Perry (Tony) Awards for "distinguished achievement" in the New York theater.	**May 24**
Ex-Pres. Eisenhower says in a *New York Herald Tribune* article that he will remain neutral in the race for the GOP presidential nomination, but adds that he hopes the nominee will recognize that there is no room for "impulsiveness" in "today's nuclear-age diplomacy." The proviso is viewed as a mild rebuke to the Goldwater campaign. . . . The Supreme Court unanimously rules that the closing of Prince Edward County, Va. public schools to avoid desegregation is unconstitutional.				*The Making of the President, 1960* is named the outstanding TV program of 1963-1964 at the annual Emmy awards presented by the National Academy of Television Arts and Sciences. Dick Van Dyke and Mary Tyler Moore win acting honors for their co-starring roles on *The Dick Van Dyke Show*.	**May 25**
	U.N. Secy. Gen. U Thant, in an apparent reference to U.S. Sen. Barry Goldwater, tells reporters that anyone who favors use of atomic weapons in South Vietnam must be "out of his mind."				**May 26**
			The U.S. and the European Atomic Energy Community agree in Brussels to exchange information on the development of fast breeder reactors.	Internazionale of Milan defeats Real Madrid of Spain to win the European Soccer Cup in Vienna.	**May 27**

F	G	H	I	J
Includes elections, federal-state relations, civil rights and liberties, crime, the judiciary, education, health care, poverty, urban affairs and population.	Includes formation and debate of U.S. foreign and defense policies, veterans' affairs and defense spending. (Relations with specific foreign countries are usually found under the region concerned.)	Includes business, labor, agriculture, taxation, transportation, consumer affairs, monetary and fiscal policy, natural resources, and pollution.	Includes worldwide scientific, medical and technological developments, natural phenomena, U.S. weather, natural disasters, and accidents.	Includes the arts, religion, scholarship, communications media, sports, entertainment, fashions, fads and social life.

	World Affairs	Europe	Africa & the Middle East	The Americas	Asia & the Pacific
May 28			The central Congolese government mobilizes additional troops to cope with growing tribal and political rebellions which have spread to at least three provinces.		An estimated 1.5 million Indians attend final cremation rites in New Delhi for the late P.M. Nehru.
May 29	The U.N. Trade & Development Conference adopts a resolution urging industrial nations to earmark at least 1% of their national incomes for aid to lesser developed nations.		Delegates to a meeting of the Palestine National Congress in the Jordanian sector of Jerusalem announce the formation of a Palestine Liberation Organization, dedicated to the recovery of the Palestinian people's "usurped home."	Soviet Premier Khrushchev is reported to have urged the U.S. to substitute satellite observation in the place of its controversial aerial reconnaissance flights over Cuba.	The Pathet Lao announces that it has withdrawn recognition of Souvanna Phouma as the premier of a legitimate Laotian coalition government.
May 30		Pan American Airlines begins direct passenger service between New York and West Berlin.		Representatives of 55 Cuban exile groups meet in Miami to form a single anti-Castro Cuban Assembly.	
May 31			Congolese rebels are reported to have completely routed two central government army units near Lake Tanganyika.	Bolivian Pres. Victor Paz Estenssoro is elected to a third four-year term in an uncontested national election.	A Tokyo court announces the sentencing of eight right-wing extremists convicted of plotting a mass assassination of Japanese leaders.
June 1				Cuban exile leader, Manuel Ray, who was reported to have landed in Cuba with a guerrilla band May 20, is arrested by British authorities on a remote island in the Bahamas. Ray explains that he postponed his pledged May 20 Cuban landing because of the Castro government's nationwide alert against an invasion.	
June 2			Levi Eshkol, the first Israeli prime minister to make an official U.S. visit, confers in Washington with Pres. Johnson. A final communique reaffirms U.S. "support for the territorial integrity and political integrity of all countries in the Near East."		India's Congress Party elects Lal Bahadur Shastri to succeed Nehru as Indian prime minister. Shastri had served as an unofficial prime minister during Nehru's convalescence from a stroke in January. . . . Representatives of Britain, U.S., South Vietnam, Thailand, India and Canada meet in Vientiane, Laos to support the Laotian government's demand that the Pathet Lao agree to a cease-fire and a withdrawal from neutralist territory.
June 3		The government of Cyprus indicates that it intends to implement a recently passed military expansion program, despite a veto of the measure by Turkish Cypriote V.P. Fazil Kutchuk. The alleged circumvention of the Cypriote Constitution prompts renewed intervention threats from Turkey.			Martial law is declared in South Korea to cope with continuing student demonstrations against the government of Pres. Chung Hee Park.

A	B	C	D	E
Includes developments that affect more than one world region, international organizations and important meetings of major world leaders.	Includes all domestic and regional developments in Europe, including the Soviet Union, Turkey, Cyprus and Malta.	Includes all domestic and regional developments in Africa and the Middle East, including Iraq and Iran and excluding Cyprus, Turkey and Afghanistan.	Includes all domestic and regional developments in Latin America, the Caribbean and Canada.	Includes all domestic and regional developments in Asia and Pacific nations, extending from Afghanistan through all the Pacific Islands, except Hawaii.

U.S. Politics & Social Issues	U.S. Foreign Policy & Defense	U.S. Economy & Environment	Science, Technology & Nature	Culture, Leisure & Life Style	
N.Y.C. School Supt. Calvin Gross announces adoption of a modified State Education Commission plan for the busing of students to reduce racial imbalance in the city's schools. A white parents group is formed to oppose the involuntary transfer plan.		The Federal Reserve Board reports a sharp improvement in April in the U.S. balance of payments. . . . Michigan Gov. George Romney orders National Guard troops to Hillsdale, Mich. to cope with increasing violence in a three-month-old Electrical Workers strike against the Essex Wire Corp.	A 17,000-pound mock-up model of the U.S. Apollo lunar spacecraft is successfully orbited by means of a Saturn I a rocket launched from Cape Kennedy.		May 28
					May 29
Pres. Johnson, addressing graduates at the Univ. of Texas at Austin, says the achievement of a "broad national consensus" is one of the major tasks of his political leadership.			Dr. Leo Szilard, 66, Hungarian-born nuclear physicist who collaborated with Enrico Fermi in creating the first sustained nuclear chain reaction (1942), dies in La Jolla, Calif. of a heart attack.	Pope Paul VI, in an audience with members of the Italian Association of War Prisoners, defends the late Pope Pius XII against charges (made in Rolf Hochhuth's play *The Deputy*) that he failed to use his papal influence to stop Nazi persecution of Jews. . . . A.J. Foyt, 29, driving an Offenhauser, wins the Indianapolis 500 Memorial Day auto race, averaging a record speed of 147.3 mph. The event was marred by a seven-car crash on the second lap which took the lives of drivers Dave MacDonald and Eddie Sachs.	May 30
			The U.S.'s dummy Apollo moon craft successfully completes 50 earth orbits before burning on re-entry into the atmosphere.		May 31
The U.S. Supreme Court, citing its June 17, 1963 decision, bars Bible reading and prayers in Fla. public schools. The Fla. Supreme Court, on two recent occasions, has upheld the practice. . . . The Supreme Court votes 7-2 to invalidate as "too vague" two Washington State laws requiring sworn loyalty oaths from public employees and school teachers. . . . U.S. Public Health Service reports a decline in the American birth rate during the year ending March 31, 1963.	Top ranking administration and military leaders meet in Honolulu, Hawaii to map U.S. strategy in the face of the mounting crisis in Southeast Asia.				June 1
Sen. Barry Goldwater outpolls Nelson Rockefeller by less than 60,000 votes to win the pivotal Calif. GOP presidential primary. Goldwater now has 438 of the 655 delegate votes needed for the nomination.	Pres. Johnson, in a statement to newsmen, cites honor, containment, peace and freedom as the four major goals of U.S. involvement in South Vietnam.				June 2
	Pres. Johnson, addressing graduates of the U.S. Coast Guard Academy, asserts that the U.S. current military strength exceeds "the combined might of all the nations in the history of the world." The President also notes that America's special forces for combating subversion have been increased eight-fold since 1961.			Santa Claus, Scobie Breasley up, wins the Epsom Downs (England) Derby.	June 3

F	G	H	I	J
Includes elections, federal-state relations, civil rights and liberties, crime, the judiciary, education, health care, poverty, urban affairs and population.	Includes formation and debate of U.S. foreign and defense policies, veterans' affairs and defense spending. (Relations with specific foreign countries are usually found under the region concerned.)	Includes business, labor, agriculture, taxation, transportation, consumer affairs, monetary and fiscal policy, natural resources, and pollution.	Includes worldwide scientific, medical and technological developments, natural phenomena, U.S. weather, natural disasters, and accidents.	Includes the arts, religion, scholarship, communications media, sports, entertainment, fashions, fads and social life.

	World Affairs	Europe	Africa & the Middle East	The Americas	Asia & the Pacific
June 4		The U.S. strongly urges Turkey not to follow through on a reported Turkish plan to invade Cyprus June 6.			U.N. Security Council votes to send a three-man inspection team to investigate Cambodian charges of South Vietnamese border violations.
June 5		A Soviet Defense Ministry newspaper accuses six U.S. military attachés in the Moscow embassy of engaging in illegal espionage.			USSR announces its support of a May 28 Polish proposal for the convening of a six-nation preliminary conference on Laos that would include Britain, USSR, India, Canada, Poland and the leaders of the three Laotian factions.
June 6					Britain announces its tentative approval of a Polish plan for holding a six-nation conference on Laos.
June 7					The U.S. State Dept. discloses that two U.S.-piloted planes have been shot down in the last 48 hours while flying reconnaissance missions over Pathet Lao territory. . . . More than 35,000 South Vietnamese Roman Catholics demonstrate in Saigon against alleged government partiality toward Buddhists.
June 8			Zanzibar officials announce that Communist China has agreed to provide a $14 million interest-free loan for Zanzibar's economic development.		Australia announces a moderate increase in its military assistance to South Vietnam.
June 9	The 17-nation U.N. Disarmament Committee reconvenes in Geneva. The U.S., in an opening statement, urges agreement on proposals to halt production of fissile materials for weapons, to halt proliferation of atomic weapons, and to conduct a mutual destruction of reserve bombers. The Soviet delegation promises serious consideration of the proposals, but insists that the U.S. abandon plans for a NATO nuclear force as a precondition to a non-proliferation pact.		U.N. Security Council adopts a resolution calling on South Africa to cease its criminal prosecutions of apartheid foes.	The International Commission of Jurists rules in Geneva that U.S. troops who fired on Panama Canal rioters Jan. 9-10 may have used excessive force, but did not violate human rights.	Washington sources report that U.S. Navy planes earlier in the day bombed a Pathet Lao gun position in north-central Laos in retaliation for the recent downing of two U.S. planes.
June 10					Official French sources reveal that U.S. State Undersecy. George Ball conferred privately with Pres. de Gaulle June 5 in an apparently unsuccessful effort to resolve French-American differences over how best to stabilize the political and military situation in Southeast Asia.

A	B	C	D	E
Includes developments that affect more than one world region, international organizations and important meetings of major world leaders.	Includes all domestic and regional developments in Europe, including the Soviet Union, Turkey, Cyprus and Malta.	Includes all domestic and regional developments in Africa and the Middle East, including Iraq and Iran and excluding Cyprus, Turkey and Afghanistan.	Includes all domestic and regional developments in Latin America, the Caribbean and Canada.	Includes all domestic and regional developments in Asia and Pacific nations, extending from Afghanistan through all the Pacific Islands, except Hawaii.

U.S. Politics & Social Issues	U.S. Foreign Policy & Defense	U.S. Economy & Environment	Science, Technology & Nature	Culture, Leisure & Life Style	
	The Republican Citizens Committee releases a position paper urging a more politically selective and cost-effective foreign aid program.			Sandy Koufax of the Los Angeles Dodgers pitches his third major league no-hitter against the Philadelphia Phillies.	June 4
				Jim Ryun, 17, of Wichita, Kansas runs the mile in 3:59.0, becoming the first high school athlete to break the four-minute barrier.	June 5
In a speech to a New York meeting of the International Ladies Garment Workers Union, Pres. Johnson predicts that the U.S. will make greater gains "toward justice and social progress" in the next decade than ever before in the nation's history.		The International Union of Electrical Workers and the Essex Wire Corp. reach an agreement ending a violence-marred three-and-a-half-month strike.		Paul Mellon's Quadrangle, Manuel Ycaza up, wins the 96th running of the Belmont Stakes at Aqueduct (N.Y.).	June 6
In a CBS-TV interview, Gov. William Scranton stresses his availability for the GOP presidential nomination, but refuses to characterize his candidacy as a "Stop Goldwater" move. A much firmer anti-Goldwater statement is issued by Mich. Gov. George Romney who says the Ariz. Senator's nomination would "commence the suicidal destruction of the Republican Party."	In a commencement address at Pennsylvania Military College, Sen. Goldwater warns Americans against "being beguiled by the illusions of co-existence and peaceful accommodations."				June 7
An active role for the federal government in today's society is defended by Pres. Johnson in a commencement address at Swarthmore College, Pa. . . . Louisiana State Univ. admits its first Negro undergraduate. . . . *Why We Can't Wait*, Martin Luther King's autobiographical account of the U.S. civil rights movement, is published in New York.				Debbie Thompson, a 16-year-old Md. high school student, sets a women's world record of 10.2 seconds for the 100-yard dash in Baltimore.	June 8
	A federal jury in Kansas City, Mo. convicts George Gessner, a former nuclear weapons technician, of giving U.S. atomic secrets to the USSR in 1960-1961. The jury recommends a life sentence.				June 9
The Senate votes 71-29 to limit debate on the civil rights bill (HR 7152). It is the first time the Senate has successfully invoked cloture against a Southern filibuster of a civil rights measure. Minority leader Everett Dirksen (Ill.) is credited with marshalling the broad Republican support needed for the action. . . . GOP National Chmn. Rep. William Miller (N.Y.), dismissing liberal anti-Goldwater moves, says "the battle is over" and the party should "unite behind Goldwater."	The House, by a 230-175 vote, approves the administration's $3.5 billion foreign aid request for fiscal 1965. It is the first time in the foreign aid program's 17-year history that the House declined to make any cuts in the administration's authorization request.		U.S. Surgeon Gen. Luther Terry tells a New York conference on smoking that more research is now needed on "how cigarette smoking produces lung cancer, bronchitis and other diseases, not whether it produces them." Terry predicts it may take 10 years to change American smoking habits.		June 10

F	G	H	I	J
Includes elections, federal-state relations, civil rights and liberties, crime, the judiciary, education, health care, poverty, urban affairs and population.	*Includes formation and debate of U.S. foreign and defense policies, veterans' affairs and defense spending. (Relations with specific foreign countries are usually found under the region concerned.)*	*Includes business, labor, agriculture, taxation, transportation, consumer affairs, monetary and fiscal policy, natural resources, and pollution.*	*Includes worldwide scientific, medical and technological developments, natural phenomena, U.S. weather, natural disasters, and accidents.*	*Includes the arts, religion, scholarship, communications media, sports, entertainment, fashions, fads and social life.*

	World Affairs	Europe	Africa & the Middle East	The Americas	Asia & the Pacific
June 11		U.S. Undersecy. of State George Ball holds separate talks with Greek and Turkish leaders to convey the American view that the Cyprus dispute should not be permitted to lead to a direct Turkish-Greek confrontation.		Ten persons are killed and over 100 injured in a series of ammunition dump explosions outside Santo Domingo. The explosions are attributed to terrorist opponents of the Dominican Republic's ruling junta.	
June 12		USSR and East Germany sign a 20-year friendship treaty in Moscow. While the pact asserts the legal existence of the East German state, it also explicitly acknowledges the USSR's 1945 Potsdam commitments regarding the four-power occupation of Germany and Berlin. . . . West German Chancellor Erhard confers in Washington with U.S. Pres. Johnson. A joint communique reaffirms the West's determination to seek "the reunification of Germany through self-determination."	South Africa's Supreme Court sentences seven African and one white opponent of apartheid to life imprisonment on charges of conspiring to promote revolution. The action defies recent U.N. demands for a suspension of South Africa's prosecution of apartheid critics.		
June 13		Britain, France and the U.S. inform the USSR that they regard their occupation rights in Germany and Berlin as wholly unaffected by yesterday's Soviet-East German friendship treaty.		British Guiana Gov. Sir Richard Luyt assumes complete emergency powers to cope with the continuing racial violence between East Indians and Negroes. The British action is assailed by Premier Cheddi Jagan and other British Guianaian leaders.	
June 14					
June 15			The last remaining French troops leave Algeria.	The Brazilian government announces that it has completed its purge of pro-communist office-holders and politicians. Several hundred persons have been barred from political activity since the crackdown began following the April 1 overthrow of Pres. Goulart.	Laotian Premier Souvanna Phouma urges Pathet Lao chief Souphanouvong to meet with him in a neutral country to seek ways of preventing a further deterioration of Laos's political situation.
June 16	The 120-nation U.N. Conference on Trade and Development ends its three-month meeting in Geneva after agreeing on steps to establish a new world trade agency to stimulate the economic growth of lesser developed countries.	U.N. Secy. Gen. U Thant urges the Security Council to extend the life of the 6,400-man Cyprus peace-keeping force for another three months--to Sept. 27. . . . Soviet Premier Khrushchev arrives in Denmark to begin a two-and-a-half-week tour of Scandinavia.			
June 17			The U.S. State Dept. confirms reports that American civilian pilots have been hired by the central Congolese government to fly combat missions against rebel forces. The State Dept. says the practice will be discontinued.		

A	B	C	D	E
Includes developments that affect more than one world region, international organizations and important meetings of major world leaders.	Includes all domestic and regional developments in Europe, including the Soviet Union, Turkey, Cyprus and Malta.	Includes all domestic and regional developments in Africa and the Middle East, including Iraq and Iran and excluding Cyprus, Turkey and Afghanistan.	Includes all domestic and regional developments in Latin America, the Caribbean and Canada.	Includes all domestic and regional developments in Asia and Pacific nations, extending from Afghanistan through all the Pacific Islands, except Hawaii.

U.S. Politics & Social Issues	U.S. Foreign Policy & Defense	U.S. Economy & Environment	Science, Technology & Nature	Culture, Leisure & Life Style	
Martin Luther King and 17 other integrationists are arrested during a sit-in demonstration at a segregated restaurant in St. Augustine, Fla. St. Augustine has been the scene of an intensive two-week anti-segregation drive.		Labor Dept. reports that unemployment fell in May to 5.1%, the lowest since February 1960. . . . The Bureau of Labor Statistics reports that 941,000 U.S. workers were involved in labor strikes during 1963. This was the lowest total since 1942. Only seven 1963 strikes were classified as major. . . . The House passes and sends to the Senate a bill (HR 11049) authorizing pay increases for 1,700,000 federal employees. The measure provides for a $7,500 increase in the salary of members of Congress (to $30,000 annually).	Melting snow from the Continental Divide bursts reservoir dams, causing massive flash floods in northwestern Montana. At least 30 persons are believed dead.		June 11
Pa. Gov. William Scranton, addressing the Maryland State Republican Convention, formally announces his active candidacy for the GOP presidential nomination under a banner of "progressive Republicanism." Scranton asserts that the voice of "fear and of reaction" should not be allowed to speak for the Republican Party.					June 12
Newly announced GOP presidential contender William Scranton assails Goldwater's "shoot-from-the-hip" approach to foreign policy in a speech to the Conn. GOP convention.					June 13
Supporters of Amb. Henry Cabot Lodge announce they are shifting their support to Gov. William Scranton. Ex-Pres. Eisenhower and ex-V.P. Nixon each issued June 12 statements "welcoming" Scranton's candidacy, but neither offered an explicit endorsement.			Torrential rain and wind storms batter West Pakistan, killing more than 330 people.	Scottish auto racer Jim Clark, driving a Lotus, wins the Belgian Grand Prix.	June 14
The Supreme Court rules 6-3 that both houses of a state legislature must be apportioned according to population. All states currently have at least one house apportioned geographically. . . . N.Y. Gov. Nelson Rockefeller announces that he is withdrawing from the GOP presidential race to support Gov. William Scranton.					June 15
Masked white men beat three Negroes and burn a Negro church outside of Philadelphia, Miss.			Japan's worst earthquake since 1923 shakes the northern island of Honshu, killing at least 30 persons.		June 16
In a speech to the AFL-CIO Communications Workers convention in Cleveland, Pres. Johnson predicts "we are going to build a great society, where no man is the victim of fear or poverty or hatred."				World boxing authorities report that three fighters have died of ring injuries in the last two days.	June 17

F	G	H	I	J
Includes elections, federal-state relations, civil rights and liberties, crime, the judiciary, education, health care, poverty, urban affairs and population.	Includes formation and debate of U.S. foreign and defense policies, veterans' affairs and defense spending. (Relations with specific foreign countries are usually found under the region concerned.)	Includes business, labor, agriculture, taxation, transportation, consumer affairs, monetary and fiscal policy, natural resources, and pollution.	Includes worldwide scientific, medical and technological developments, natural phenomena, U.S. weather, natural disasters, and accidents.	Includes the arts, religion, scholarship, communications media, sports, entertainment, fashions, fads and social life.

	World Affairs	Europe	Africa & the Middle East	The Americas	Asia & the Pacific
June 18					Gen. Kong Le, neutralist force commander in Laos, displays Chinese-made weapons allegedly captured from the Pathet Lao to newsmen in Vientiane.
June 19		West German Chancellor Ludwig Erhard tells newsmen in Bonn that West Germany will support the U.S. in Southeast Asia just as it expects the U.S. to support West Germany in Europe.	Congolese rebels capture the North Katanga Province capital of Albertville, routing the city's 900-man government garrison.		
June 20	In a statement to an Asian Economic Seminar in North Korea, Communist China warns African and Asian nations that acceptance of Soviet aid will bring them under Moscow's exploitative domination.	The USSR protests the inauguration, May 30, of direct passenger service between New York and West Berlin, claiming that the flights are "unlawful" without the consent of East Germany. . . . U.N. Security Council unanimously approves a three-month extension of the U.N. peacekeeping force in Cyprus.			A one-day conciliation conference in Tokyo between Malaysian P.M. Abdul Rahman and Indonesian Pres. Sukarno ends in failure after the two leaders refuse to accept a Philippine proposal for the creation of an Afro-Asian commission to mediate their dispute.
June 21	The Soviet CP issues a statement challenging the sincerity of Communist Chinese pledges to support the unity of world communism in light of its "dirty anti-Soviet campaign."				
June 22					The U.S. State Dept. issues a formal statement strongly reaffirming U.S.'s unlimited determination "to resist aggression" in Southeast Asia. It is the latest in a recent series of American "commitment" announcements which are reportedly intended to dispel any Communist doubts about the U.S. position in the area and, thereby, to avert "another Korea.". . . Laotian Premier Souvanna Phouma defends U.S. reconnaissance flights, claiming they have proved North Vietnamese support of the Pathet Lao.
June 23				Cuban underground sources report that former world welterweight boxing champion Kid Gavilan has been imprisoned in Cuba for "anti-state" activity.	
June 24		Greek P.M. George Papandreou arrives in Washington for talks with Pres. Johnson. Johnson, who met June 22-23 with Turkish P.M. Ismet Inonu, is reportedly attempting to use his personal influence to avert a full-scale Turkey-Greece conflict over Cyprus.	Communist China declares its support for the continuing provincial rebellion against the central Congolese government.		Communist Chinese Foreign Min. Chen Yi denounces U.S. involvement in Vietnam and Laos and reiterates warnings that China will not tolerate continued American disregard for the Geneva agreements on Southeast Asia.

A	B	C	D	E
Includes developments that affect more than one world region, international organizations and important meetings of major world leaders.	Includes all domestic and regional developments in Europe, including the Soviet Union, Turkey, Cyprus and Malta.	Includes all domestic and regional developments in Africa and the Middle East, including Iraq and Iran and excluding Cyprus, Turkey and Afghanistan.	Includes all domestic and regional developments in Latin America, the Caribbean and Canada.	Includes all domestic and regional developments in Asia and Pacific nations, extending from Afghanistan through all the Pacific Islands, except Hawaii.

U.S. Politics & Social Issues	U.S. Foreign Policy & Defense	U.S. Economy & Environment	Science, Technology & Nature	Culture, Leisure & Life Style	
Sen. Barry Goldwater meets with newsmen to announce his decision to vote against the civil rights bill. Goldwater contends that effective enforcement of the bill's public accommodation provisions will require creation of "a police state."	May 4 testimony in which Asst. State Secy. William Bundy asserted that the U.S. would have no choice but to commit troops if the Pathet Lao gained a decided military advantage in Laos is released by the House Appropriations Committee.				June 18
The Senate, by a vote of 73-27, passes the administration's omnibus civil rights bill. The measure, which differs slightly from the House-passed bill, will be sent to joint conference for reconciliation. . . . Barry Goldwater votes against the bill. . . . Sen. Edward Kennedy (D, Mass.) suffers severe back injuries in the crash of a two-engine plane near West Springfield, Mass.		The SEC estimates that the net working capital of all U.S. corporations climbed to a record $154.7 billion by the end of 1964's first quarter.			June 19
				Ken Venturi wins the U.S. Open golf tournament in Washington, D.C.	June 20
				Jim Bunning of the Philadelphia Phillies pitches a perfect game against the New York Mets in New York. It is the first perfect game ever recorded in the National League. . . . Jean Guichet of France and Nino Vacarella of Italy, driving a Ferrari, win the 24-hour Le Mans (France) auto endurance race.	June 21
Three civil rights workers participating in a Mississippi summer voter registration project are reported missing near Philadelphia, Miss. The three men are identified as Michael Schwerner, Andrew Goodman (both white) and James Chaney, a Negro. Atty. Gen. Kennedy orders a full-scale FBI investigation. . . . The U.S. Supreme Court, in a 5-4 decision, rules as inadmissible confessions obtained from a suspect who has not been fully informed of his right to counsel or that his statements to police may be used against him. The decision comes in the Illinois murder case of Danny Escobedo.				In four separate cases the Supreme Court rules against local government censorship of allegedly obscene books and movies.	June 22
Henry Cabot Lodge resigns as ambassador to South Vietnam to actively support Gov. William Scranton's candidacy for the Republican presidential nomination.	Pres. Johnson appoints Gen. Maxwell Taylor to succeed Henry Cabot Lodge as U.S. ambassador to South Vietnam. In a statement accompanying the announcement, Johnson says the U.S. "seeks no wider war," but remains determined to help South Vietnam resist "aggression."			Pope Paul VI discloses that the Roman Catholic Church is currently engaged in "a wide and profound" study of the "grave" question of birth control.	June 23
The annual convention of the NAACP, meeting in Washington, urges Atty. Gen. Kennedy to increase federal protection of civil rights workers in the South.	Speaking with newsmen in Saigon, retiring U.S. Amb. Lodge says he cannot see how Vietnam "could possibly be" a presidential campaign issue. . . . Pres. Johnson names Gen. Harold Johnson to succeed Gen. Earle Wheeler as Army chief of staff. Wheeler has been nominated chairman of the Joint Chiefs of Staff, replacing Maxwell Taylor.	The Air Traffic Conference reports that U.S. airlines in 1963 achieved a new record safety mark of .23 fatalities per 100 million revenue passenger miles. . . . Federal Trade Commission Chmn. Paul Dixon, testifying before the House Interstate Commerce Committee, suggests that health warnings be required on all cigarette packs and advertisements by Jan. 1, 1975.	The American Medical Association's House of Delegates, meeting in San Francisco, adopts a resolution affirming evidence "that cigarette smoking is a serious health hazard."	Stuart Davis, 69, American abstract painter and recognized forerunner of pop art, dies of a heart attack in New York.	June 24

F	G	H	I	J
Includes elections, federal-state relations, civil rights and liberties, crime, the judiciary, education, health care, poverty, urban affairs and population.	Includes formation and debate of U.S. foreign and defense policies, veterans' affairs and defense spending. (Relations with specific foreign countries are usually found under the region concerned.)	Includes business, labor, agriculture, taxation, transportation, consumer affairs, monetary and fiscal policy, natural resources, and pollution.	Includes worldwide scientific, medical and technological developments, natural phenomena, U.S. weather, natural disasters, and accidents.	Includes the arts, religion, scholarship, communications media, sports, entertainment, fashions, fads and social life.

	World Affairs	Europe	Africa & the Middle East	The Americas	Asia & the Pacific
June 25	Soviet disarmament negotiator Valerian Zorin calls for positive and prompt action on the USSR's plan for joint military budget cuts.				
June 26		U.S., Britain and France jointly denounce the June 12 Soviet-East German friendship treaty as another attempt to keep Germany divided and to obstruct efforts for a peaceful settlement of European problems. . . . Italian Premier Aldo Moro and his center-left cabinet resign after oppositionists defeat a government aid-to-Catholic schools bill. . . . Over 300,000 West Berliners greet U.S. Atty. Gen. Robert Kennedy on his arrival in the city during a three-day goodwill trip to West Germany.			Cambodian Prince Norodom Sihanouk declares his support for France's policy aims in Southeast Asia following three days of Paris talks with French Pres. de Gaulle.
June 27		Visiting U.S. Atty. Gen. Robert Kennedy, speaking at the University of Heidelberg, asks West Germany to assist the U.S. in fulfilling its Berlin-like commitment to the government of South Vietnam.	Ex-Katanga Pres. Moise Tshombe, responding to an invitation from the central Congolese government, ends a year-long European exile and returns to Leopoldville. Tshombe is expected to participate in the formation of a new Congo government of national reconciliation.		
June 28		Greece and Bulgaria agree in Sofia on a formula for settlement of post-war differences between the two countries.			
June 29				Juana Castro Ruz, sister of Fidel Castro, announces on Mexico City television that she has defected from Cuba and has requested political asylum in Mexico. She accuses her brother of betraying the Cuban revolution to "Russian imperialism."	
June 30		U.S. Atty. Gen. Robert Kennedy concludes a three-day goodwill trip to Poland, highlighted by a controversial meeting with Stefan Cardinal Wyszynski, Roman Catholic primate of Poland and prominent critic of the government.	The U.N. officially ends its four-year military operation in the Congo with the departure of the last U.N. Force contingent from Leopoldville. . . . Congo Premier Cyrille Adoula resigns upon the expiration of his term. Pres. Kasavubu immediately reappoints Adoula to head a caretaker government pending formation of a new national reconciliation government.		
July 1		The West German Federal Assembly holds its quintennial meeting in West Berlin despite Russian protests. . . . The Belgian Parliament approves an amended national health insurance program, tailored to meet the objections of the nation's recently striking physicians.	Secy. Gen. U Thant reports that 126 U.N. troops were killed in connection with the U.N.'s four-year, $381 million peace-keeping mission in the Congo. . . . Algerian Premier Ben Bella confirms the existence of an anti-government uprising by army units in the Aures Mountain region and in the eastern Sahara.		

A	B	C	D	E
Includes developments that affect more than one world region, international organizations and important meetings of major world leaders.	Includes all domestic and regional developments in Europe, including the Soviet Union, Turkey, Cyprus and Malta.	Includes all domestic and regional developments in Africa and the Middle East, including Iraq and Iran and excluding Cyprus, Turkey and Afghanistan.	Includes all domestic and regional developments in Latin America, the Caribbean and Canada.	Includes all domestic and regional developments in Asia and Pacific nations, extending from Afghanistan through all the Pacific Islands, except Hawaii.

U.S. Politics & Social Issues	U.S. Foreign Policy & Defense	U.S. Economy & Environment	Science, Technology & Nature	Culture, Leisure & Life Style	
Pres. Johnson orders U.S. naval personnel to join in the search for three missing civil rights workers last seen near Philadelphia, Miss. . . . Over 30 Negroes are hospitalized in St. Augustine, Fla. after a mob of 800 whites attacked an integrationist parade as it approached the city square.	Pres. Johnson signs a bill (HR 10669) extending the Renegotiation Act of 1951 through June 30, 1966. The measure authorizes government recovery of excess profits on certain defense and space contracts.	The GOP Critical Issues Council releases a report urging a "new and constructive federal" energy policy aimed at reducing power costs. . . . Travelers Insurance Co. reports that a record 42,700 persons died in U.S. traffic accidents in 1963, a 5.5% increase over 1962.			June 25
GOP congressional leaders announce they will lead efforts to overturn or limit the recent Supreme Court decision barring geographic-based apportionment in state legislatures.				The International Olympic Committee votes to re-admit Indonesia to the 1964 Games if it pledges to end political discrimination in sports. The 12-nation Arab League had threatened to boycott the games if Indonesia were not reinstated.	June 26
NAACP's annual convention adjourns in Washington after delegates vote to denounce Sen. Barry Goldwater's opposition to the civil rights bill and to urge Republicans not to grant him the party's nomination.					June 27
	Speaking to a political rally in Minneapolis, Pres. Johnson declares that the U.S. wants peace, but it is "prepared to risk war to keep its freedom." Johnson links the strong declaration with a reaffirmation of the U.S. commitment to South Vietnam.	The Senate Government Reorganization Subcommittee opens hearings on the role of the pesticide Endrin in the massive killing of Mississippi River fish in 1963.			June 28
	Retiring U.S. Amb.-to-South Vietnam Henry Cabot Lodge gives Johnson administration officials and later the press a generally optimistic report on the U.S.-Vietnamese campaign against the Viet Cong. Lodge asserts that U.S. withdrawal from Southeast Asia is "utterly unthinkable."	A bill (HR 11375) raising the temporary national debt limit to $324 billion through June 30, 1965 is signed by Pres. Johnson. . . . Fortune magazine reports that combined sales of the 500 largest U.S. industrial corporations totaled a record $245 billion in 1963, up 7% from 1962. Profits increased 10.1% to a record $14.8 billion.			June 29
Florida Gov. Farris Bryant appoints a biracial committee to try "to restore communications" between whites and Negroes in racially torn St. Augustine.		Pres. Johnson signs a bill (HR 11376) providing for a one-year extension of existing excise taxes.	Typhoon Winnie strikes Manila and most of Luzon Island in the northern Philippines, killing 43 and leaving 370,000 persons homeless.		June 30
Influential Senate minority leader Everett Dirksen endorses Sen. Barry Goldwater for the GOP Presidential nomination.					July 1

F	G	H	I	J
Includes elections, federal-state relations, civil rights and liberties, crime, the judiciary, education, health care, poverty, urban affairs and population.	Includes formation and debate of U.S. foreign and defense policies, veterans' affairs and defense spending. (Relations with specific foreign countries are usually found under the region concerned.)	Includes business, labor, agriculture, taxation, transportation, consumer affairs, monetary and fiscal policy, natural resources, and pollution.	Includes worldwide scientific, medical and technological developments, natural phenomena, U.S. weather, natural disasters, and accidents.	Includes the arts, religion, scholarship, communications media, sports, entertainment, fashions, fads and social life.

	World Affairs	Europe	Africa & the Middle East	The Americas	Asia & the Pacific
July 2	Soviet Deputy Foreign Min. Valerian Zorin, in a speech to the Geneva arms conference, condemns NATO plans for a multi-lateral nuclear force as a major obstacle to disarmament, inspired by a desire to quench "the nuclear thirst of West German revenge seekers."	Cypriote V.P. Fazil Kutchuk accuses senior U.N. officials in Cyprus of bias against the Turkish Cypriote minority.			
July 3		Gen. George Grivas, an heroic leader of the Greek Cypriotes' resistance to British rule, declares in a Nicosia speech that *enosis* (union with Greece) is the only solution to the Cyprus crisis. *Enosis* is opposed by Cypriote Pres. Makarios, but has strong appeal in the Greek Cypriote community.	Secy. Gen. U Thant announces a two-month extension of the U.N. observation mission in Yemen, where civil strife between UAR-assisted republicans and Saudi-supported royalists continues.		
July 4		French Pres. de Gaulle concludes a two-day consultation conference in Bonn with West German Chancellor Ludwig Erhard. Unlike his predecessor, Konrad Adenauer, Erhard is reported to have shown little enthusiasm for de Gaulle's vision of a loosely confederated Europe under Franco-German leadership.	The British government pledges to grant independence to the Federation of South Arabia "not later than 1968."		The National Liberation Front, political arm of the Viet Cong, declares that the South Vietnamese fighting has entered a new phase and urges its supporters to press their recently gained military successes against the government.
July 5				Gustavo Diaz Ordaz, candidate of the ruling Institutional Revolutionary party, is overwhelmingly elected to a six-year term as President of Mexico. Diaz will replace Pres. Adolfo Lopez Mateos on the expiration of his term in December.	
July 6			The British protectorate of Nyasaland becomes the independent nation of Malawi.	Premier Castro suggests in a *New York Times* interview that Cuba might agree to end its direct support of Latin American revolutionary movements if the OAS agreed to drop its anti-Cuban policies.	Communist China declares its readiness to defend North Vietnam from a U.S.-South Vietnamese attack.
July 7	The USSR, reversing its traditional position, expresses support for the creation of a permanent U.N. military force to serve under Security Council orders in future peace keeping operations. The Soviet proposal would replace existing resolutions that give the General Assembly the authority to order U.N. military actions.			Cuban Premier Fidel Castro invites U.S. newsmen to cover July 26 celebrations marking the 11th anniversary of the Cuban revolution. The U.S. State Dept. says it will validate passports of newsmen sent to cover the event. . . . Prominent Argentine Peronist leaders call for a congressional investigation into alleged "anti-national attitudes" among the country's 450,000 Jews.	
July 8	Secy. Gen. U Thant welcomes the USSR's July 7 proposal as a breakthrough in the long deadlock over creation of a permanent U.N. peace keeping force. . . . A conference of the 18-nation British Commonwealth opens in London.	Rumania signs a new, liberalized trade and technical exchange agreement with Communist China. . . . The International Commission of Jurists in Geneva condemns the USSR for anti-Semitism.			U.N. Secy. Gen. U Thant calls for the reconvening of the 1954 Geneva Conference on Indochina to negotiate an end to the war in South Vietnam. . . . U.S. military sources in Saigon report that American combat casualties in Vietnam have now passed 1,000: 152 killed-in-action; 971 wounded-in-action; 17 missing.
July 9		West German Chancellor Erhard's opposition to French Pres. de Gaulle's plan for a confederal European organization is publicly attacked by ex-Chancellor Adenauer and other leaders of the so-called Gaullist faction of the Christian Democratic Party.	Moise Tshombe, recently returned former leader of Katanga Province, is named Prime Minister of the central Congolese government by Pres. Joseph Kasavubu. Tshombe is charged with forming a coalition government of national reconciliation to prepare for general elections within nine months.		

A	B	C	D	E
Includes developments that affect more than one world region, international organizations and important meetings of major world leaders.	Includes all domestic and regional developments in Europe, including the Soviet Union, Turkey, Cyprus and Malta.	Includes all domestic and regional developments in Africa and the Middle East, including Iraq and Iran and excluding Cyprus, Turkey and Afghanistan.	Includes all domestic and regional developments in Latin America, the Caribbean and Canada.	Includes all domestic and regional developments in Asia and Pacific nations, extending from Afghanistan through all the Pacific Islands, except Hawaii.

U.S. Politics & Social Issues	U.S. Foreign Policy & Defense	U.S. Economy & Environment	Science, Technology & Nature	Culture, Leisure & Life Style	
The Civil Rights Act of 1964 is signed into law by Pres. Johnson during nationally televised ceremonies. The House and Senate completed final action on the bill (HR 7152) earlier in the day. . . . Malcolm X, leader of a new Muslim splinter group, cables Martin Luther King, offering to send armed Negroes to protect civil rights demonstrators in violence-torn St. Augustine, Fla.		The NLRB rules that racial discrimination by a labor union is an unfair labor practice under the Taft-Hartley law.		Leading U.S. stock car driver, Glenn (Fireball) Roberts, 37, dies of injuries suffered May 24 in the world 600-mile stock car race in Charlotte, N.C.	July 2
Formerly segregated restaurants and hotels throughout the South accept their first Negro patrons in compliance with the newly passed Civil Rights Act. In Atlanta, Ga., however, restaurant owner Lester Maddox distributes ax handles to white customers and urges them to help drive off three Negroes seeking to enter his place.					July 3
					July 4
		U.S. auto makers report producing 4,431,856 passenger cars in the first half of 1964. The mark surpasses the old first-half record set in 1955.	The American Institute of Physicists warns that if current trends continue the U.S. will face an acute shortage of trained physicists by 1970.		July 5
Gov. William Scranton announces that his name will be placed in nomination at the Republican convention in San Francisco by Milton S. Eisenhower, brother of the ex-President.		AP reports that traffic deaths over the three-day July 4th weekend set a national record of 504.			July 6
The Georgia Court of Appeals rules that systematic exclusion of Negroes from juries violates the constitutional rights of defendants. . . . In an interview transcript released by his campaign headquarters, Barry Goldwater asserts that "no Republican" can beat Pres. Johnson without "the support of the South."	Maxwell Taylor arrives in Saigon to assume his new duties as Ambassador-to-South Vietnam.	Pres. Johnson signs a bill (S 2) authorizing federal grants for water resource research.		The National League outscores the American League, 7-4, to win baseball's 1964 All-Star Game.	July 7
The Senate Rules Committee issues a report on its investigations into the business dealings of Senate Democratic secretary Bobby Baker. The report says Baker was "guilty of many gross improprieties," but not in technical violation of conflict-of-interest statutes. The Republican minority on the committee issues a dissenting report accusing the majority of blocking a full inquiry into the Baker affair.					July 8
		Pres. Johnson asks Congress to authorize $29 million for the study of safer pest control methods and materials. . . . Pres. Johnson signs the Urban Mass Transportation Act of 1964, which authorizes $375 million to improve and expand municipal train and bus systems.		The League of New York Theaters issues a code of ethics to govern the financial operations of Broadway theatrical productions.	July 9

F	G	H	I	J
Includes elections, federal-state relations, civil rights and liberties, crime, the judiciary, education, health care, poverty, urban affairs and population.	Includes formation and debate of U.S. foreign and defense policies, veterans' affairs and defense spending. (Relations with specific foreign countries are usually found under the region concerned.)	Includes business, labor, agriculture, taxation, transportation, consumer affairs, monetary and fiscal policy, natural resources, and pollution.	Includes worldwide scientific, medical and technological developments, natural phenomena, U.S. weather, natural disasters, and accidents.	Includes the arts, religion, scholarship, communications media, sports, entertainment, fashions, fads and social life.

	World Affairs	Europe	Africa & the Middle East	The Americas	Asia & the Pacific
July 10	Soviet and American delegations to the Geneva disarmament talks report that a recent series of private discussions has failed to produce a compromise between their rival plans for missile and warhead reductions. The Geneva talks have been deadlocked over the issue since they resumed June 9.		The Congo's new cabinet, headed by Moise Tshombe, orders the releases of all political prisoners in an apparent move to appease left-wing critics of Tshombe's power.		Japanese Premier Hayato Ikeda is re-elected head of the ruling Liberal-Democratic Party, overcoming a leadership challenge by ex-State Min. Eisaku Sato.
July 11		A U.N. spokesman in Nicosia says that Greece has illegally landed 3,000 troops in Cyprus and that Turkey has sent at least 500. . . . Maurice Thorez, pro-Stalinist leader of the French CP since 1930, dies at age 64.			
July 12	U.N. sources report that the U.S. has privately voiced opposition to the exclusive Security Council control provisions of the USSR's recent proposal for a permanent U.N. peace force.				
July 13			UAR and Yemen sign a policy coordination agreement "as a step toward complete unity.". . . Algerian Premier Ben Bella reports progress in government efforts to suppress army rebels in the Aures Mountain region.		
July 14					U.S. sends 300 more special forces troops to Vietnam, bringing total American military manpower up to a reported 16,000.
July 15		Soviet Pres. Leonid Brezhnev relinquishes his post as Presidium chairman to concentrate on his duties as deputy chief of the Soviet CP. Deputy Premier Anastas Mikoyan is elected to succeed Brezhnev as President of the Presidium of the Supreme Soviet.	P.M. Alec Douglas-Home announces at the British Commonwealth conference in London that Britain has agreed to African demands that it use its influence to end all-white government in Southern Rhodesia. Douglas-Home also pledges not to grant independence to Southern Rhodesia until majority rule has been achieved. . . . Congo Pres. Moise Tshombe announces that he will boycott the forthcoming Cairo meeting of the Organization for African Unity.		Pakistan and Communist China are reported to have begun the physical demarcation of their mutual border in fulfillment of previously reached agreements.
July 16			Former Congolese leftist leader Antoine Gizenga is released from prison by Tshombe as part of a continuing program to achieve a political reconciliation of the Congo's opposing factions.		

A	B	C	D	E
Includes developments that affect more than one world region, international organizations and important meetings of major world leaders.	Includes all domestic and regional developments in Europe, including the Soviet Union, Turkey, Cyprus and Malta.	Includes all domestic and regional developments in Africa and the Middle East, including Iraq and Iran and excluding Cyprus, Turkey and Afghanistan.	Includes all domestic and regional developments in Latin America, the Caribbean and Canada.	Includes all domestic and regional developments in Asia and Pacific nations, extending from Afghanistan through all the Pacific Islands, except Hawaii.

U.S. Politics & Social Issues	U.S. Foreign Policy & Defense	U.S. Economy & Environment	Science, Technology & Nature	Culture, Leisure & Life Style	
FBI Director J. Edgar Hoover discloses that 140 federal agents have been assigned to Mississippi to protect civil rights workers. An increase in violence against Negroes has been reported in a number of Southern states.		Manuel Cohen is named chairman of the Securities and Exchange Commission, succeeding the resigned William Cary.		Tony Lema wins the British Open golf tournament in St. Andrews, Scotland.	July 10
Asst. Washington, D.C. School Superintendent Lemuel Penn, a Negro, is killed by gunshots from a passing car on a Ga. highway while driving home to Washington from two weeks army reserve training at Ft. Benning, Ga.			The USSR successfully orbits two unmanned earth satellites by means of a single booster rocket. The two satellites, dubbed Elektron 3 and Elektron 4, are designed to gather data on radiation and magnetic fields in the earth's upper atmosphere.		July 11
In an open letter Gov. William Scranton charges that "Goldwaterism has come to stand for nuclear irresponsibility." The letter prompts indignation among Goldwater backers. . . . Hotels, motels and restaurants in Jackson, Miss. are reported to have integrated peacefully in compliance with the public accommodations section of the 1964 Civil Rights Act.				Mickey Wright captures the $2,200 first prize in winning her fourth U.S. Women's Open golf tournament in San Diego.	July 12
The GOP National Convention opens in San Francisco. Gov. Mark Hatfield (Ore.) urges a repudiation of extremism and strong support for civil rights in his keynote address to the convention. . . . The mutilated corpses of two Negroes are discovered near Tallulah, La. Local civil rights leaders say that at least five other area Negroes have been murdered in the past six months.		A strike shuts down publication of Detroit's two daily papers: the *Detroit News* and the *Detroit Free Press*.	Pres. Johnson signs a compromise bill (HR 10456) authorizing $5.23 billion for NASA in fiscal 1965. The total is $76 million less than the administration had requested for space projects.		July 13
Pro-Goldwater forces reveal their overwhelming convention strength by easily defeating "liberal" Republican efforts to strengthen the party's civil rights plank and to add a provision repudiating extremism. The platform in its adopted form calls for: a strengthened world stand against communism; the lifting of limits on the U.S. Vietnam war effort; support for a prayer-in-schools amendment; and a $5 billion reduction in federal spending.		The Republican national platform, approved at the San Francisco convention, assails the Johnson administration for "fiscal irresponsibility" and for unwarranted federal intrusion in the free enterprise system.		Jacques Anquetil wins his fourth consecutive Tour de France bicycle race.	July 14
Sen. Barry Goldwater of Arizona is nominated as the Republican candidate for President on the first ballot at the GOP National Convention in San Francisco. Goldwater receives 883 delegate votes to 214 for his nearest rival, Gov. William Scranton. . . . Federal Judge Carl Weinman orders that Dr. Samuel Sheppard, convicted in 1954 of his wife's murder, be released from the Ohio State Penitentiary. Weinman rules that Sheppard's 1954 trial was "a mockery of justice."					July 15
In an acceptance speech marked by an absence of conciliation gestures toward the party's liberal wing, GOP presidential candidate Goldwater declares that "extremism in the pursuit of freedom is no vice" and "moderation in the pursuit of justice is no virtue.". . . Rep. William Miller, a conservative Roman Catholic from New York, is nominated as the Republican vice presidential candidate. Miller and Rep. Gerald Ford (Mich.) were reportedly Goldwater's first two choices for a running mate.	In his nomination acceptance speech, GOP candidate Goldwater assails the Johnson administration for being overly "eager to deal with communism."				July 16
F	G	H	I	J	
Includes elections, federal-state relations, civil rights and liberties, crime, the judiciary, education, health care, poverty, urban affairs and population.	*Includes formation and debate of U.S. foreign and defense policies, veterans' affairs and defense spending. (Relations with specific foreign countries are usually found under the region concerned.)*	*Includes business, labor, agriculture, taxation, transportation, consumer affairs, monetary and fiscal policy, natural resources, and pollution.*	*Includes worldwide scientific, medical and technological developments, natural phenomena, U.S. weather, natural disasters, and accidents.*	*Includes the arts, religion, scholarship, communications media, sports, entertainment, fashions, fads and social life.*	

	World Affairs	Europe	Africa & the Middle East	The Americas	Asia & the Pacific
July 17		Denmark and Sweden warn they will withdraw their contingents from the U.N. peace force on Cyprus if Greece and Turkey continue to ignore U.N. appeals to stop smuggling men and arms onto the island.			USSR reaffirms its pledge to provide Indonesia with material support in its campaign against Malaysia.
July 18			Portugal and South Africa are bitterly denounced by African leaders at the Organization of African Unity meeting in Cairo.		
July 19		The Cyprus government authorizes an economic blockade of selected Turkish Cypriote communities.	Ghana Pres. Nkrumah renews his call for a federal union of all African nations, describing it as the only reliable safeguard against re-colonization.		South Vietnamese Premier Nguyen Khanh, reportedly disregarding U.S. objections, publicly calls for a full-scale military attack on North Vietnam.
July 20			Pres. Julius Nyerere of Tanganyika and Zanzibar assails Ghana Pres. Nkrumah's appeal for an African federation, charging that Nkrumah preaches unity while practicing dissension.	Cuban Premier Castro compares U.S. Republican Party presidential candidate Barry Goldwater to Adolf Hitler.	
July 21		Resigned Italian Premier Aldo Moro succeeds in reorganizing a new center-left coalition government.	Representatives of the 34-nation Organization of African Unity conclude a four-day conference in Cairo after resolving to urge member states to sever trade relations with Portugal and South Africa in protest against their racial policies.	The newly-formed Inter-American Committee for the Alliance for Progress concludes a week-long meeting in Mexico City after agreeing to arrange financing for 35 selected hemispheric development projects.	South Vietnamese students damage the French embassy in Saigon to protest Pres. de Gaulle's proposals for the neutralization of Southeast Asia.
July 22		The Soviet government reports that industrial production in the USSR climbed 7.5% during the first half of 1964. It is the lowest reported first-half gain in 20 years.		U.S. Secy. of State Rusk urges an OAS foreign ministers meeting in Washington to demonstrate their united opposition to Cuba's "efforts to export revolution.". . . The Brazilian Congress approves a constitutional amendment extending Pres. Humberto de Castelo Branco's term for 18 months until March 1967.	South Vietnamese Air Commodore Nguyen Cao Ky tells Saigon newsmen that his forces are fully prepared to launch an attack on North Vietnamese territory.
July 23		Pres. de Gaulle tells a Paris press conference that France will not participate in any European political unification program which limits the sovereignty of member states.	More than 100 persons are killed by a series of explosions aboard a UAR freighter in the Algerian port of Bone.		U.S. Amb. Maxwell Taylor meets with South Vietnamese Premier Khanh to express U.S. displeasure over recent public threats by South Vietnamese leaders to extend the war to North Vietnam. . . . French Pres. de Gaulle proposes that France, USSR, U.S. and Communist China meet to work out an agreement guaranteeing the neutrality and independence of the Indochinese nations.
July 24					The International Control Commission for Laos warns that continuation of the current fighting could soon lead to a renewal of full-scale civil war. . . . In a statement to newsmen, Pres. Johnson rejects de Gaulle's proposal for a great power meeting on Indochina, saying that the U.S. does not "believe in conferences called to ratify terror."
	A	B	C	D	E
	Includes developments that affect more than one world region, international organizations and important meetings of major world leaders.	Includes all domestic and regional developments in Europe, including the Soviet Union, Turkey, Cyprus and Malta.	Includes all domestic and regional developments in Africa and the Middle East, including Iraq and Iran and excluding Cyprus, Turkey and Afghanistan.	Includes all domestic and regional developments in Latin America, the Caribbean and Canada.	Includes all domestic and regional developments in Asia and Pacific nations, extending from Afghanistan through all the Pacific Islands, except Hawaii.

U.S. Politics & Social Issues	U.S. Foreign Policy & Defense	U.S. Economy & Environment	Science, Technology & Nature	Culture, Leisure & Life Style	
Gov. Nelson Rockefeller issues a statement criticizing the references to extremism in Barry Goldwater's nomination acceptance speech. Ex-Pres. Eisenhower has reportedly asked for a clarification of the extremism passage as a condition of his active support for the Goldwater-Miller ticket. . . . Arizonian Dean Burch, a Goldwater campaign official, is elected to succeed William Miller as chairman of the Republican National Committee.			Three U.S. atomic-detection satellites are orbited from Cape Kennedy by means of a single Atlas-Agena rocket. The satellites are part of a system designed to detect nuclear blasts in space in violation of the 1963 test-ban treaty.	British racer Donald Campbell drives his jet car Bluebird to a new world auto speed record of 403.1 mph. on a salt flat track near Lake Eyre, Australia.	July 17
		Pres. Johnson reports that the fiscal 1964 federal budget deficit proved to be $3.6 billion less than originally estimated due to a $1 billion cut in expenditures and $2 billion increase in revenues.			July 18
			Over 100 persons are reported dead following a series of floods and landslides in central and western Japan.	Golfer Bobby Nichols wins the 1964 PGA championship in Columbus, O. . . . Dennis Ralston wins the U.S. clay courts tennis championship at River Forest, Ill.	July 19
FBI reports that serious crime increased in the U.S. by 10% in 1963. Reported crimes included 8,500 murders and 16,400 rapes.	A military pay raise bill (S 3001) passes the Senate and is sent to the House.				July 20
					July 21
At least 100 persons, including 35 policemen, are injured following four nights of rioting and looting in Negro sections of N.Y.C. The disorders are attributed to racial tensions, heightened by anger over the July 16 fatal shooting of a Negro teenager by an off-duty white policeman. Mayor Robert Wagner returns from a European vacation to appeal for calm. . . . A three-judge federal court in Atlanta, in the first judicial test of the 1964 Civil Rights Act, upholds the law's public accommodations section and orders the Pickrick Restaurant (owned by Lester Maddox) to admit Negroes.					July 22
Rioting continues in Brooklyn's predominantly-Negro Bedford-Stuyvesant section, despite efforts of Negro and white leaders. . . . The FBI arrests three whites in Greenwood, Miss. on charges of violating the 1964 Civil Rights Act by beating a Negro who attempted to desegregate a previously all-white movie theater. The action marks the first arrests under the new law.		The Senate passes the administration's anti-poverty bill (S 2642) by a 61-34 vote. The bill provides $947 million for 10 separate anti-poverty programs to be coordinated by an Office of Economic Opportunity.			July 23
	Pres. Johnson asserts at a Washington news conference that final responsibility on the use of nuclear weapons "must rest" with the President alone. The remark is in apparent response to Goldwater's recent statement that he would allow generals to decide how to win the Vietnamese War, including whether or not to use nuclear weapons.		Representatives of 18-nations agree at a Washington meeting on a formula for sharing the ownership and management of the U.S.-proposed international communications satellite system.		July 24
F	**G**	**H**	**I**	**J**	
Includes elections, federal-state relations, civil rights and liberties, crime, the judiciary, education, health care, poverty, urban affairs and population.	Includes formation and debate of U.S. foreign and defense policies, veterans' affairs and defense spending. (Relations with specific foreign countries are usually found under the region concerned.)	Includes business, labor, agriculture, taxation, transportation, consumer affairs, monetary and fiscal policy, natural resources, and pollution.	Includes worldwide scientific, medical and technological developments, natural phenomena, U.S. weather, natural disasters, and accidents.	Includes the arts, religion, scholarship, communications media, sports, entertainment, fashions, fads and social life.	

	World Affairs	Europe	Africa & the Middle East	The Americas	Asia & the Pacific
July 25					Saigon sources report that Premier Khanh has personally appealed to the leaders of 34 countries for material help in his country's fight against the Viet Cong.
July 26				OAS foreign ministers, meeting in Washington, vote to impose the following mandatory sanctions against Cuba: (a) suspension of all trade with Cuba except food and medicine; (b) suspension of all sea transportation to Cuba; and (c) termination of diplomatic and consular relations. Of the 20 OAS member states only Mexico, Chile, Bolivia and Uruguay oppose the action. . . . Cuban Premier Castro denounces the OAS as the "ministry of the Yankee colonies."	
July 27		Cypriote Pres. Makarios declares in Nicosia that he has lost hope for a negotiated solution to the Cyprus crisis and asks that the problem be placed before the forthcoming session of the U.N. General Assembly.		Premier Castro tells newsmen that Cuba is very interested in improving relations with the U.S., but not if it means sacrificing the goals of the revolution.	Saigon sources report that the U.S. has agreed to commit about 5,000 more men to its current 16,000-man military mission in South Vietnam. . . . The Indian government imposes strict rationing and anti-hoarding measures in an effort to cope with an increasingly critical grain shortage. briefing on the U.S. defense posture.
July 28	Sweden asks the Geneva disarmament conference to consider creating a permanent international peace keeping force.	The British House of Commons extends Winston Churchill, 89, a rare official motion of gratitude upon his retirement from Parliament.	Algerian Pres. Ben Bella charges "counter-revolutionary" groups with responsibility for the July 23 bombing of a UAR freighter which took the lives of nearly 100 people.	British Guianaian sugar workers are reported returning to their plantation jobs after ending a 171-day strike. Almost 200 people were killed in racial clashes related to the strike.	
July 29			Anti-government uprisings in the Congo are reportedly increasing in strength despite stepped-up government efforts to suppress them.		U.S. Military Assistance Command in Saigon estimates that Viet Cong currently have 28,000-34,000 regular troops and 60,000-80,000 part-time irregulars. The figures are considerably above previous estimates.
July 30					Anti-French South Vietnamese soldiers dismantle a French war memorial in Saigon. The French embassy issues an angry protest.
July 31					

A	B	C	D	E
Includes developments that affect more than one world region, international organizations and important meetings of major world leaders.	Includes all domestic and regional developments in Europe, including the Soviet Union, Turkey, Cyprus and Malta.	Includes all domestic and regional developments in Africa and the Middle East, including Iraq and Iran and excluding Cyprus, Turkey and Afghanistan.	Includes all domestic and regional developments in Latin America, the Caribbean and Canada.	Includes all domestic and regional developments in Asia and Pacific nations, extending from Afghanistan through all the Pacific Islands, except Hawaii.

U.S. Politics & Social Issues	U.S. Foreign Policy & Defense	U.S. Economy & Environment	Science, Technology & Nature	Culture, Leisure & Life Style	
The Civil Rights Commission releases a study in Washington charging that North Carolina made "little progress" toward school desegregation over the past year; 155 of the state's 173 school districts remain totally segregated.				Gedney Farm's Gun Bow wins the Brooklyn Handicap at Aqueduct.	July 25
One white man is dead and more than 350 persons injured after three nights of racial rioting in Rochester, N.Y. The violence is traced to Negro anger over alleged police brutality and white reaction to Black Muslim activities. N.Y. Gov. Rockefeller sends 1,000 National Guardsmen to restore order.		A federal jury in Chicago convicts Teamsters Pres. James Hoffa of fraud and conspiracy in connection with the misuse of union pension funds.		U.S. men defeat the Soviets in the annual U.S.-USSR track and field competition in Los Angeles. Soviets outscored the Americans to win the women's team championship.	July 26
					July 27
Marfin Luther King meets with N.Y.C. Mayor Robert Wagner to discuss ways of preventing further racial violence in the city.		Congress passes and sends to the President a bill (HR 10532) appropriating $5 billion for the U.S. Post Office in fiscal 1965.			July 28
Negro leaders Martin Luther King, Whitney Young, Roy Wilkins and A. Philip Randolph issue a statement calling for a suspension (until after the November elections) of mass civil rights demonstrations in favor of political activity and increased voter registration efforts. CORE Director James Farmer refuses to support the appeal.		Pres. Johnson approves a regional public power plan to connect the federal, private and municipal power systems of 11 Rocky Mountain and Pacific Northwest states.			July 29
Pres. Johnson announces that he has ruled out Atty. Gen. Robert Kennedy and other cabinet members as potential running mates in the forthcoming presidential campaign. Johnson, who says he has made no decision on a vice presidential candidate, is reportedly leaning toward Sen. Hubert Humphrey or Sen. Eugene McCarthy, both of Minnesota. . . . Sen. Clair Engle (D, Calif.) succumbs to a brain tumor at age 52. Engle appeared in the Senate for the last time June 26 to nod his affirmative vote on the civil rights bill.			Tass announces the launching of an unmanned Soviet scientific satellite, Cosmos 36.		July 30
The Pleasant Grove Missionary Baptist Church, outside of Jackson, Miss., is destroyed by fire. The suspected arson brings to at least 15 the number of Negro churches burned in Mississippi since June 15.			The U.S.'s Ranger 7, launched July 28 from Cape Kennedy, televises back to earth 4,316 close-up photos of the lunar surface before crashing on the moon near the Sea of Clouds. The mission, the first of 13 U.S. lunar shots to be described as completely successful, is said to have indicated that large portions of the moon's surface are suitable for manned landings.	American country music singer Jim Reeves, 39, dies in a plane crash south of Nashville, Tenn.	July 31

F	G	H	I	J
Includes elections, federal-state relations, civil rights and liberties, crime, the judiciary, education, health care, poverty, urban affairs and population.	Includes formation and debate of U.S. foreign and defense policies, veterans' affairs and defense spending. (Relations with specific foreign countries are usually found under the region concerned.)	Includes business, labor, agriculture, taxation, transportation, consumer affairs, monetary and fiscal policy, natural resources, and pollution.	Includes worldwide scientific, medical and technological developments, natural phenomena, U.S. weather, natural disasters, and accidents.	Includes the arts, religion, scholarship, communications media, sports, entertainment, fashions, fads and social life.

	World Affairs	Europe	Africa & the Middle East	The Americas	Asia & the Pacific
Aug. 1		Manlio Brosio of Italy replaces Dirk Stikker of the Netherlands as secretary general of NATO.	Congo Premier Tshombe displays propaganda literature to newsmen which allegedly proves that anti-government rebels are being supported by communists and by neighboring African states. . . . Nigerian sources report that as many as 1,000 persons have been killed in recent tribal and religious fighting in the northeastern part of the nation.		
Aug. 2					U.S. Defense Dept. reports that three North Vietnamese PT-boats earlier in the day attacked a U.S. destroyer in the Gulf of Tonkin 30 miles off the coast of North Vietnam. North Vietnam says the American ship, which suffered no serious damage, had violated its territorial waters.
Aug. 3				Mexico announces that it intends to maintain diplomatic relations with Cuba despite the OAS's July 26 call for a severing of all ties with the Castro government.	
Aug. 4					U.S. Defense Dept. reports that two U.S. destroyers, the *Maddox* and the *C. Turner Joy*, were attacked earlier in the day by North Vietnamese PT-boats while cruising in international waters in the Gulf of Tonkin. Neither destroyer was damaged. . . . Pres. Johnson announces on national television that he has ordered U.S. air raids on North Vietnamese naval installations in retaliation for the alleged PT-boat attacks.
Aug. 5			A rebel Congolese army, led by Nicholas Olenga, captures Stanleyville, the nation's third largest city. An undetermined number of Europeans are reportedly being held as hostages.		U.S. Navy planes conclude a five-hour air attack on North Vietnamese coastal bases and patrol boats in retaliation for an Aug. 4 PT-boat attack on two U.S. destroyers in the Gulf of Tonkin. North Vietnamese officials denounce the attack, claiming that the alleged Aug. 4 attacks never took place.
Aug. 6					Communist China declares that the blame for any future widening of the Indochina War rests entirely with the U.S. because of its "unprovoked" Aug. 4-5 air attack on North Vietnam.
Aug. 7		Turkish warplanes launch attacks on widespread targets in northwestern Cyprus in an effort to relieve Turkish Cypriote communities under heavy Greek Cypriote assault.			South Vietnamese Premier Khanh declares nationwide martial law to cope with what he describes as increasing pressures from Communist China and North Vietnam. . . . Referring to North Vietnam Soviet Premier Khrushchev warns that the USSR will "stand up for...other socialist countries if the imperialists impose war on them."

A	B	C	D	E
Includes developments that affect more than one world region, international organizations and important meetings of major world leaders.	*Includes all domestic and regional developments in Europe, including the Soviet Union, Turkey, Cyprus and Malta.*	*Includes all domestic and regional developments in Africa and the Middle East, including Iraq and Iran and excluding Cyprus, Turkey and Afghanistan.*	*Includes all domestic and regional developments in Latin America, the Caribbean and Canada.*	*Includes all domestic and regional developments in Asia and Pacific nations, extending from Afghanistan through all the Pacific Islands, except Hawaii.*

U.S. Politics & Social Issues	U.S. Foreign Policy & Defense	U.S. Economy & Environment	Science, Technology & Nature	Culture, Leisure & Life Style	
			Pres. Johnson hails yesterday's Ranger 7 mission as proof that the U.S. has regained world "leadership" in the exploration of space.	Don Schollander sets a new world record of 1:57.6 for the 200-meter free-style at the National AAU swimming championships in Los Altos, Calif.	**Aug. 1**
Racial disorders flare in Jersey City, N.J. following rumors of police brutality against an arrested Negro youth. . . . GOP vice presidential candidate William Miller charges that Democratic "political machines" are responsible for the conditions that have caused recent race riots in Northern cities. . . . Southern Regional Council estimates that 500,000 Negroes have been added as registered voters in the past two years bringing to nearly two million the total number of registered Negro voters in the South.	Sen. Hubert Humphrey predicts on the CBS-TV program *Face the Nation* that Goldwater will lose in November because the American people do not want a President with "a nervous finger on the nuclear trigger." Goldwater's alleged nuclear "irresponsibility" has become a major theme of Democratic campaign speeches.	Labor Secy. Willard Wirtz reconvenes the three-man board that settled the 1963 dock strike to study the problem of job security for U.S. longshoremen.		Zaglebie of Sosnowiec, Poland defeats Werder Bremen of West Germany to win the International Soccer League championship at Randalls Island, N.Y.	**Aug. 2**
Rep. John V. Lindsay (R,N.Y.) announces that he cannot support Goldwater for president and will campaign for re-election as an "independent Republican."	GOP candidate Barry Goldwater again criticizes the Johnson administration for allegedly failing to inform the American people of its goals and policies in Vietnam.	The Executive Council of the AFL-CIO, meeting in Chicago, denounces the economic and labor-related planks of the Republican campaign platform as "an insult to the intelligence of American voters."		American novelist and short story writer (Mary) Flannery O'Connor succumbs to bone disease at age 39.	**Aug. 3**
National Urban League leaders, meeting in Louisville, Ky., report that the potential for serious racial disorders exists in each of the 66 cities they represent. They urge immediate employment and community relations programs to head off such violence.	Congress passes a compromise bill (HR 10939) appropriating $46.75 billion for the Defense Dept. in fiscal 1965.	AFL-CIO, meeting in Chicago, adopts a statement of support for the 1964 Civil Rights Act and pledges a major effort to secure equal opportunity in employment.			**Aug. 4**
FBI experts identify three bodies found yesterday in an earthen dam near Philadelphia, Miss. as those of missing civil rights workers Michael Schwerner, Andrew Goodman and James Chaney. Unofficial reports indicate that the three were shot to death. . . . *The New York Times* reports that segregationist white citizens councils are being formed in a number of Northern and Western cities.	Pres. Johnson asks Congress to give him advance authorization for military actions he may need to order in Southeast Asia.				**Aug. 5**
N.Y. Gov. Nelson Rockefeller tells a meeting of state Republican leaders that he will support Goldwater as the party's standard bearer.	Senate and House committees begin joint hearings on Pres. Johnson's request for congressional authorization to take all necessary military actions in Southeast Asia. Defense Secy. McNamara and State Secy. Rusk urge quick approval of the resolution.	The Senate passes and sends to the President a bill (S 1642) to provide more protection to small-scale securities investors.			**Aug. 6**
A New York pathologist reports that an autopsy on slain civil rights worker James Chaney, a Negro, indicates that he had been severely beaten before being shot to death. Mississippi authorities have denied that any of the three murdered workers were beaten.	The House and Senate overwhelmingly approve an administration-drafted resolution giving Pres. Johnson advance approval for any military actions he may order in the Southeast Asian crisis. The measure, known as the Gulf of Tonkin Resolution, specifically authorizes the President to take "all necessary" steps "to prevent further aggression." Only two votes, those of Sens. Wayne Morse (D, Ore.) and Ernest Gruening (D, Alaska) are cast against bill.				**Aug. 7**
F	**G**	**H**	**I**	**J**	
Includes elections, federal-state relations, civil rights and liberties, crime, the judiciary, education, health care, poverty, urban affairs and population.	*Includes formation and debate of U.S. foreign and defense policies, veterans' affairs and defense spending. (Relations with specific foreign countries are usually found under the region concerned.)*	*Includes business, labor, agriculture, taxation, transportation, consumer affairs, monetary and fiscal policy, natural resources, and pollution.*	*Includes worldwide scientific, medical and technological developments, natural phenomena, U.S. weather, natural disasters, and accidents.*	*Includes the arts, religion, scholarship, communications media, sports, entertainment, fashions, fads and social life.*	

	World Affairs	Europe	Africa & the Middle East	The Americas	Asia & the Pacific
Aug. 8		Greek Premier George Papandreou urges Cyprus Pres. Makarios to halt the attacks on Turkish Cypriote villages which have led to the current Turkish air raids. . . . The U.N. Security Council convenes an emergency meeting on the Cyprus crisis.			A North Vietnamese note to the International Control Commission describes the U.S.'s Aug. 5 reprisal raid as an act of aggression against North Vietnam.
Aug. 9		U.N. Security Council approves a U.S.-sponsored resolution calling for an immediate cease-fire on Cyprus.			Over 100,000 Communist Chinese attend a Peking rally to protest the U.S.'s Aug. 5 attack on North Vietnam.
Aug. 10		Turkey and Cyprus agree to a U.N. cease-fire proposal ending the recent air and ground attacks in northwestern Cyprus.			
Aug. 11				Chile breaks diplomatic relations with Cuba in compliance with the OAS's July 26 resolution. Chile had been one of the four states to oppose the OAS action.	
Aug. 12			The U.S. Defense Dept. discloses that it will provide four planes, three helicopters and about 100 support personnel to help the Congolese government in its battle against leftist provincial rebels. . . . Northern Rhodesian sources report that as many as 500 fanatical members of the Lumpa religious cult have been killed in recent suicide charges against armed government troops. Alice (the Prophetess) Lenshina, founder of the cult, is said to have persuaded her followers that they are invulnerable to bullets.		An estimated 2,000 Viet Cong filter into the jungle, escaping a major U.S.-directed operation aimed at trapping the guerrilla force in their temporary base 29 miles north of Saigon.
Aug. 13		*The New York Times* reports that Cypriote officials have informed Greek Premier Papandreou of their indignation over Greece's failure to intervene militarily during the recent Turkish air attacks against Cyprus. . . . Gen. George Grivas is appointed commander of Cyprus's military forces.	Iraq, UAR, Jordan, Kuwait, and Syria sign an agreement in Cairo providing for the creation of an Arab common market.		
Aug. 14					

A	B	C	D	E
Includes developments that affect more than one world region, international organizations and important meetings of major world leaders.	Includes all domestic and regional developments in Europe, including the Soviet Union, Turkey, Cyprus and Malta.	Includes all domestic and regional developments in Africa and the Middle East, including Iraq and Iran and excluding Cyprus, Turkey and Afghanistan.	Includes all domestic and regional developments in Latin America, the Caribbean and Canada.	Includes all domestic and regional developments in Asia and Pacific nations, extending from Afghanistan through all the Pacific Islands, except Hawaii.

U.S. Politics & Social Issues	U.S. Foreign Policy & Defense	U.S. Economy & Environment	Science, Technology & Nature	Culture, Leisure & Life Style	
		The House passes, 226-184, an amended version of Pres. Johnson's $947.5 million anti-poverty bill (HR 11377).			Aug. 8
Most Rev. Richard Gerow, bishop of the Natchez-Jackson diocese, announces that the first grade of all Roman Catholic elementary schools in Miss. will be desegregated when school begins in September.		A presidential emergency board urges the nation's railroads to promptly negotiate a job-protection agreement with six unions representing 150,000 shop workers.			Aug. 9
Supreme Court Justice Hugo Black denies a motion by Lester Maddox asking for a delay in the enforcement of the 1964 Civil Rights Act against his Atlanta, Ga. restaurant.	Pres. Johnson signs the Gulf of Tonkin Resolution. . . . Goldwater charges that the administration's missile-oriented defense planning and its alleged failure to develop new weapons may lead to a 90% reduction in the U.S.'s deliverable nuclear capacity by the mid-1970s.			Pope Paul VI issues his first encyclical letter. The 12,000-word document entitled *Ecclesiam Suam* (His Church) pledges papal participation in the quest for "peaceful relations among nations." The letter also expresses the Pope's respect for the moral and spiritual values of Judaism, Islam and monotheistic religions of Africa and Asia.	Aug. 10
		The administration's $947.5 million anti-poverty bill, (HR 11377) which the House amended and passed Aug. 8, is approved by the Senate and sent to the President. The House amendments require program fund recipients to sign loyalty oaths and permit state governors to veto any federally financed anti-poverty projects within their states.		*A Hard Day's Night*, a musical satire film starring the popular English singing group, the Beatles, opens in New York.	Aug. 11
Sen. Barry Goldwater attends a GOP unity conference in Hershey, Pa. with prominent Republican leaders, including William Scranton and other former opponents of Goldwater's nomination. Most declare support for the national ticket. . . . Pres. Johnson tells an American Bar Association meeting in New York that race violence, whether in Northern cities or Southern states, must "be stopped and punished."	Sen. Goldwater asserts that Pres. Johnson implicitly sanctioned possible use of nuclear weapons when he authorized the exercise of all necessary force against North Vietnam in retaliation for the Gulf of Tonkin incident.			British mystery novelist Ian Fleming, creator of fictional secret agent James Bond, dies in Canterbury, England at age 56.	Aug. 12
Lester Maddox announces he has decided to close his Atlanta restaurant rather than serve Negroes. . . . At least 40 persons are under arrest following three nights of rioting in Negro sections of Paterson and Elizabeth, N.J.					Aug. 13
Miss. public schools are integrated for the first time with the registration of 17 Negro first-graders in two previously all-white Biloxi schools.			Indonesia announces that the first Indonesian-made rocket was launched yesterday to an altitude of 37 miles from a Java site.		Aug. 14

F	G	H	I	J
Includes elections, federal-state relations, civil rights and liberties, crime, the judiciary, education, health care, poverty, urban affairs and population.	*Includes formation and debate of U.S. foreign and defense policies, veterans' affairs and defense spending. (Relations with specific foreign countries are usually found under the region concerned.)*	*Includes business, labor, agriculture, taxation, transportation, consumer affairs, monetary and fiscal policy, natural resources, and pollution.*	*Includes worldwide scientific, medical and technological developments, natural phenomena, U.S. weather, natural disasters, and accidents.*	*Includes the arts, religion, scholarship, communications media, sports, entertainment, fashions, fads and social life.*

	World Affairs	Europe	Africa & the Middle East	The Americas	Asia & the Pacific
Aug. 15	U.S., Britain and the USSR observe the first anniversary of the nuclear test-ban treaty by issuing a joint declaration pledging continued effort to reach negotiated settlements of major world problems. . . . Soviet Premier Khrushchev says in a *London Sunday Times* interview that he would be willing to attend a nuclear disarmament summit conference in 1965.		Congo Republic (Brazzaville) Pres. Alphonse Massamba-Debat charges Congo (Leopoldville) Pres. Tshombe with plotting to overthrow his government. Tshombe has previously accused the Brazzaville regime of actively aiding anti-Tshombe rebels.	Argentine Pres. Arturo Illia assures members of the American Jewish Committee in Buenos Aires that his government will use its full powers to combat a revival of anti-Semitism in Argentina.	
Aug. 16		Soviet Premier Khrushchev denounces Turkey's Aug. 7-9 air attacks on Cyprus as part of a U.S.-British "imperialist plot." The USSR yesterday pledged to "defend" Cyprus "from a foreign invasion."			Premier Nguyen Khanh is elected president of South Vietnam under a new junta-written constitution greatly increasing his personal power. Maj. Gen. Duong Van Minh is ousted from his largely ceremonial post as chief of state.
Aug. 17					An Indonesian force of 40-100 men lands in Malaya in the first reported Indonesian action against the mainland section of the Malaysian Federation.
Aug. 18					
Aug. 19		The Cyprus government announces the lifting of its month-long economic blockade of Turkish Cypriote villages. Turkey simultaneously announces that troops mobilized during the Aug. 7-9 attacks on Cyprus will be returned to their regular NATO units.			Riots and demonstrations erupt in Saigon, Hue and elsewhere to protest the allegedly "anti-democratic" constitution adopted by the Khanh government on Aug. 16.
Aug. 20	The Ethiopian delegation to the Geneva disarmament talks calls for a U.N. conference to enact a worldwide ban on the use of nuclear weapons.				
Aug. 21		Longtime Italian CP leader Palmiro Togliatti dies at age 71 while vacationing in Yalta. Togliatti recently gained considerable world attention as a prominent supporter and expositor of Khrushchev's positions in the Sino-Soviet dispute.	The Congolese government begins deporting thousands of Mali, Burundi and Congo Republic (Brazzaville) citizens on the ground that their governments are supporting the revolt in the Congo's eastern provinces.	Exiled Argentine Peronist leaders announce in Madrid that Juan Peron "has confirmed his irrevocable decision to return to the fatherland this year as a determining factor toward the unity and pacification of all Argentines."	European sources report that Belgian, Dutch and Danish leaders have assured the touring Henry Cabot Lodge of their support for U.S. policy in South Vietnam, but none have offered substantial aid for the war there.
Aug. 22			Libyan Premier Mahmud Muntasser discloses that the U.S. has tentatively agreed to give up its large Wheelus Air Force base in Libya.		

A	B	C	D	E
Includes developments that affect more than one world region, international organizations and important meetings of major world leaders.	Includes all domestic and regional developments in Europe, including the Soviet Union, Turkey, Cyprus and Malta.	Includes all domestic and regional developments in Africa and the Middle East, including Iraq and Iran and excluding Cyprus, Turkey and Afghanistan.	Includes all domestic and regional developments in Latin America, the Caribbean and Canada.	Includes all domestic and regional developments in Asia and Pacific nations, extending from Afghanistan through all the Pacific Islands, except Hawaii.

U.S. Politics & Social Issues	U.S. Foreign Policy & Defense	U.S. Economy & Environment	Science, Technology & Nature	Culture, Leisure & Life Style	
Pres. Johnson tells a Washington news conference that "peace and preparedness and prosperity" will be the major issues of the upcoming national elections.	Pres. Johnson, speaking at a press conference, denounces as "a disservice to our national security" Sen. Goldwater's Aug. 12 assertion that he had authorized possible use of nuclear weapons against North Vietnam. Johnson adds, "we had carefully, explicitly and publicly ruled out use of nuclear weapons.". . . About 200 students clash with N.Y.C. policemen during a protest against what the students call U.S. "military aggression" in Vietnam. Forty demonstrators are arrested.			Mexican painter Gerardo Murillo, inventor of the "Atlcolor" technique, dies in Mexico City at age 89.	Aug. 15
			The tobacco industry-funded Council for Tobacco Research-U.S.A. reports that it has found little evidence that cigarette smoking causes cancer or cardiovascular disease.	Barry Watson of England swims the 22-mile English Channel in a record nine hours 35 minutes.	Aug. 16
Three Negroes attend the previously all-white Greensburg, La. high school. It is the first desegregation of a public school in rural Louisiana.	Defense Secy. McNamara, appearing before the Democratic national platform committee, denies Sen. Goldwater's recent claims that administration policies will lead to a drastic reduction in the U.S.'s deliverable nuclear capacity. . . . Henry Cabot Lodge arrives in Paris to begin an extended European tour reportedly aimed at mustering allied support for U.S. policy in South Vietnam.				Aug. 17
		Pres. Johnson appoints an emergency inquiry commission to forestall a threatened railroad strike by 11 non-operating unions.	Soviet scientists report the successful launch earlier in the day of the 38th, 39th, and 40th unmanned satellites in the Cosmos series. No details are given.		Aug. 18
A St. Augustine, Fla. motel owner who refused to admit Negro guests is fined $400 by a federal judge for violating the public accommodations section of the Civil Rights Act. It is the first penalty levied under the new law.	Pres. Johnson signs a compromise fiscal 1965 defense appropriation bill (HR 10939) totaling $46.75 billion, about $700 million less than the administration requested.	Pres. Johnson signs a law establishing a National Study Commission on Technology, Automation & Economic Progress.	The U.S.'s third synchronous communications satellite, Syncom 3, is successfully orbited from Cape Kennedy.		Aug. 19
Pres. Johnson signs a bill to provide free legal counsel to indigent defendants in federal criminal cases.	Congress passes a bill (HR 11369) appropriating $1.57 billion in fiscal 1965 for construction at U.S. military bases.	The administration's anti-poverty bill is signed into law by Pres. Johnson. . . . Congress passes a compromise bill (HR 11202) appropriating $5.13 billion for the Agriculture Dept. in fiscal 1965.			Aug. 20
					Aug. 21
	A CIA working paper containing a pessimistic assessment of the war in South Vietnam and recommending a "negotiated settlement. . .based upon neutralization" is made public in Washington after a copy was reportedly leaked to the Chicago Tribune . Administration officials stress that the study does not reflect or represent U.S. policy.	The Bureau of Labor Statistics reports that the unemployment rate in July fell to 4.9%, a 53-month low. The jobless rate for Negro teenagers, however, is estimated at between 21% and 25%.		Auto racer Bill Horstemeyer dies of injuries after his car crashes into a wall during the 100-mile Tony Bettenhauser memorial race in Springfield, Ill.	Aug. 22

F	G	H	I	J
Includes elections, federal-state relations, civil rights and liberties, crime, the judiciary, education, health care, poverty, urban affairs and population.	Includes formation and debate of U.S. foreign and defense policies, veterans' affairs and defense spending. (Relations with specific foreign countries are usually found under the region concerned.)	Includes business, labor, agriculture, taxation, transportation, consumer affairs, monetary and fiscal policy, natural resources, and pollution.	Includes worldwide scientific, medical and technological developments, natural phenomena, U.S. weather, natural disasters, and accidents.	Includes the arts, religion, scholarship, communications media, sports, entertainment, fashions, fads and social life.

	World Affairs	Europe	Africa & the Middle East	The Americas	Asia & the Pacific
Aug. 23			South African sources report that Congolese government representatives are supporting white mercenary soldiers in Johannesburg.		Indian CP leaders announce plans for immediate nationwide demonstrations to protest food shortages and high prices.
Aug. 24					Widespread anti-government rioting in South Vietnam continues into its fifth day. . . . U.S. military sources in Saigon report that U.S. combat deaths in Vietnam have climbed to 187.
Aug. 25	U Thant presents a $104.7 million U.N. budget for 1965 to the General Assembly.	Cyprus Pres. Makarios denounces U.N.-sponsored mediation talks on Cyprus currently underway in Geneva. The Geneva discussions are reportedly centering on a U.S. plan calling for the union of Cyprus with Greece in exchange for a large Turkish military base on the island.			Pres. Khanh, responding to growing political disorders, announces repeal of the controversial Aug. 16 constitution and promises a new constitution to return South Vietnam to civilian rule.
Aug. 26					
Aug. 27	The Soviet government declares it will pay nothing toward the cost of U.N. peace-keeping operations under current conditions. The USSR is already over two years behind in its assessed obligations to the financially troubled U.N. . . . The U.S. delegation to the Geneva arms talks denies Soviet charges that Pres. Johnson's plan for an inspected freeze on the production of nuclear weapons systems would lead to the creation of a Western espionage network in the USSR.				South Vietnamese leader Nguyen Khanh announces the formation of an interim ruling triumvirate, which he characterizes as a first step in the fulfillment of his pledge to organize a predominantly civilian government. The triumvirate includes Khanh, Maj. Gen. Duong Van Minh, and Lt. Gen. Tran Thien Khiem.
Aug. 28		Over 10,000 anti-American Turks demonstrate in Ankara in protest against the allegedly anti-Turkish bias of U.S. proposals for settling the Cyprus question.	Recently released Congolese leftist leader Antoine Gizenga announces formation of a new oppositionist political party, the United Lumumbist Party.		Laotian neutralist Premier Souvanna Phouma and Pathet Lao chief Souphanouvong meet in Paris to begin a series of French-sponsored talks aimed at solving the Laotian crisis.
Aug. 29		Turkey, bowing to U.S., British and U.N. appeals, agrees to delay its plans for the rotation of part of its 650-man garrison on Cyprus. Cypriote Pres. Makarios had threatened to use force to prevent the arrival of Turkish replacements.			Anti-government demonstrations continue in South Vietnam despite recently announced constitutional changes designed to placate student and Buddhist dissidents.
Aug. 30	U.N. Statistical Office estimates that world population totaled 3.135 billion as of mid-1962, an increase of 2.1% over the previous year. It is the largest annual percentage increase ever recorded.		Congolese government troops, reportedly assisted by white mercenaries, recapture rebel-held Albertville, capital of North Katanga Province.		
	A	**B**	**C**	**D**	**E**
	Includes developments that affect more than one world region, international organizations and important meetings of major world leaders.	Includes all domestic and regional developments in Europe, including the Soviet Union, Turkey, Cyprus and Malta.	Includes all domestic and regional developments in Africa and the Middle East, including Iraq and Iran and excluding Cyprus, Turkey and Afghanistan.	Includes all domestic and regional developments in Latin America, the Caribbean and Canada.	Includes all domestic and regional developments in Asia and Pacific nations, extending from Afghanistan through all the Pacific Islands, except Hawaii.

U.S. Politics & Social Issues	U.S. Foreign Policy & Defense	U.S. Economy & Environment	Science, Technology & Nature	Culture, Leisure & Life Style	
The Democratic Convention credentials committee rules that members of the all-white Alabama delegation will be seated only if they sign a pledge to support the party's national ticket. The Alabamians, many of whom have publicly declared for Goldwater, reject the offer by a 33-3 vote.				Ken Venturi wins the American Golf Classic at Akron., O. . . . Lorenzo Bandini of Italy, driving a Ferrari, wins the Grand Prix of Austria.	Aug. 23
Sen. John Pastore (R.I.) opens the Democratic National Convention in Atlantic City, N.J. with a keynote address hailing the Johnson administration's "nine miracle months" of domestic accomplishments and its "responsible" leadership in foreign affairs.	The AEC announces the detonation of an underground low-yield nuclear device near Mercury, Nevada. It is the 14th U.S. test reported this year--all described as part of the Plowshare program on the peaceful uses of atomic energy.		Hurricane Cleo hits Haiti killing an estimated 124 people.	The full Roman Catholic mass is celebrated in English for the first time in the U.S. at the opening of the 25th Liturgical Conference in St. Louis, Mo. The singing of Protestant hymns, another innovation, opens and closes the service.	Aug. 24
The Democratic Convention adopts a national platform reviewing the achievements of the Kennedy-Johnson years and pledging strong support for civil rights, opposition to all forms of extremism and maintenance of exclusive presidential control over use of nuclear weapons. . . . The Democratic Credentials Committee bars racial discrimination in the future selection of convention delegates as part of a compromise settlement on the seating of two rival Mississippi delegations--the integrated Freedom Democrats and the all-white regular delegation.			Explorer 20, a small scientific satellite designed to measure electron density in the ionosphere, is launched into near polar orbit from Point Arguello, Calif. . . . The Democratic national platform asserts that the U.S. "must never again settle for second" in the exploration of space.		Aug. 25
Pres. Lyndon B. Johnson is nominated by acclamation by the Democratic National Convention in Atlantic City as the party's presidential candidate. Johnson subsequently announces Minn. Sen. Hubert Humphrey as his choice for a running mate.	Sen. Goldwater advocates U.S. military action in Vietnam "to interdict" Viet Cong supply lines and to force Communist China to recognize that "we can go further."	A bill (HR 9586) permitting private ownership of nuclear reactor fuels is signed by Pres. Johnson.			Aug. 26
In his acceptance speech to the final session of the Democratic National Convention, Pres. Johnson asks the voters "for a mandate" to begin work on building "a great society."				Pal Benko, 36, of New York wins the U.S. Open chess championship in Boston. . . . Grace (Gracie) Allen, radio and TV comedienne, who with her husband George Burns, made up the Burns & Allen comedy team, dies in Hollywood at age 58.	Aug. 27
Pres. Johnson in a statement to the Democratic National Committee predicts that the number of pro-civil rights Republicans backing him will easily exceed the number of normally Democratic "backlash" voters switching to Goldwater.			NASA scientists launch the U.S.'s most advanced meteorological satellite, Nimbus A. The Nimbus A, which did not achieve its intended circular orbit, is expected to provide weather data for 70% of the earth's surface.		Aug. 28
				Maria Itkina of the USSR sets a world record of 53 seconds for the women's 400-meter run in the Soviet national championships at Kiev.	Aug. 29
Nearly 250 persons are reported injured and over 300 arrested following three nights of racial rioting in the predominantly Negro area of North Philadelphia.		Pres. Johnson signs a bill (HR 11579) appropriating $4.43 billion for public works projects and the AEC in fiscal 1965.			Aug. 30

F	G	H	I	J
Includes elections, federal-state relations, civil rights and liberties, crime, the judiciary, education, health care, poverty, urban affairs and population.	Includes formation and debate of U.S. foreign and defense policies, veterans' affairs and defense spending. (Relations with specific foreign countries are usually found under the region concerned.)	Includes business, labor, agriculture, taxation, transportation, consumer affairs, monetary and fiscal policy, natural resources, and pollution.	Includes worldwide scientific, medical and technological developments, natural phenomena, U.S. weather, natural disasters, and accidents.	Includes the arts, religion, scholarship, communications media, sports, entertainment, fashions, fads and social life.

	World Affairs	Europe	Africa & the Middle East	The Americas	Asia & the Pacific
Aug. 31		Cypriote Pres. Makarios, concluding a three-day visit to the UAR, tells newsmen in Cairo that Cyprus "does not want to have any foreign bases"--"Greek bases, Turkish bases, British bases, NATO bases, any bases.". . . In an address on the eve of the 25th anniversary of the invasion of Poland, West German Chancellor Ludwig Erhard lays the burden of guilt for W.W. II on Germany's Nazi regime and declares that the "new Germany" must do "everything humanly possible to make war impossible for all time."			
Sept. 1			Communist China officially denies that it has actively intervened in the Congo, but reiterates its moral support for the rebel cause.		
Sept. 2	*Pravda* charges that Communist China has recently published maps claiming Soviet and other Asiatic areas as Chinese territory.	Cyprus Foreign Min. Spyros Kyprianou charges in Nicosia that Turkey's Aug. 7-9 air raids against Cyprus had the tacit approval of the U.S. and Britain. . . . The Socialist International marks its 100th anniversary at a meeting in Brussels.			About 100 Indonesian guerrilla paratroopers are dropped into Malaya south of Kuala Lumpur.
Sept. 3	Communist China accuses the USSR of "creating constant border incidents" along Sinkiang's Ili region.				
Sept. 4		Dean Acheson, U.S. representative to the Cyprus conciliation talks in Geneva, reports in Washington that the talks have produced no long-run solution, but have greatly eased Greek-Turkish tensions.		Christian Democratic Sen. Eduardo Frei Montalva is elected to a six-year term as president of Chile, defeating Salvador Allende Gossens of the Marxist Popular Action Front by a 3-2 margin in national balloting.	South Vietnamese Premier Khanh announces that his government will turn "all powers" over to a civilian government within two months. Despite the conciliatory announcements, increased police activity, and expressions of support from the U.S., anti-government demonstrations continue.
Sept. 5				Chilean Pres.-elect Eduardo Frei Montalva pledges his government to a policy of continued cooperation with the U.S.	Canadian External Affairs Secy. Paul Martin discloses in Tokyo that Canada is increasing its non-diplomatic contacts with Communist China on "a modest and reciprocal basis."
Sept. 6				Chilean Pres.-elect Eduardo Frei Montalva tells newsmen that the OAS must avoid preoccupation with political tensions if it is to make progress in solving common economic and social problems.	
Sept. 7	Finance and economy ministers from 102 nations gather in Tokyo to attend concurrent annual meetings of the International Monetary Fund (IMF) and the International Bank for Reconstruction & Development (World Bank).	Three British firms announce that they have agreed to capitalize and construct a huge Soviet textile plant in Siberia.			

A	B	C	D	E
Includes developments that affect more than one world region, international organizations and important meetings of major world leaders.	Includes all domestic and regional developments in Europe, including the Soviet Union, Turkey, Cyprus and Malta.	Includes all domestic and regional developments in Africa and the Middle East, including Iraq and Iran and excluding Cyprus, Turkey and Afghanistan.	Includes all domestic and regional developments in Latin America, the Caribbean and Canada.	Includes all domestic and regional developments in Asia and Pacific nations, extending from Afghanistan through all the Pacific Islands, except Hawaii.

U.S. Politics & Social Issues	U.S. Foreign Policy & Defense	U.S. Economy & Environment	Science, Technology & Nature	Culture, Leisure & Life Style	
Census Bureau estimates U.S. population at 191,334,000 as of July 1.		Pres. Johnson signs a bill (HR 10222) expanding the pilot food stamp program into a nationwide, permanent program.	Over 3,000 scientists and industrial observers from 71 countries gather in Geneva to attend the U.N.'s third International Conference on Peaceful Uses of Atomic Energy.		Aug. 31
New York Democrats nominate Robert Kennedy to oppose Sen. Kenneth Keating (R) in his bid for Senate re-election. . . . The AFL-CIO's 166-man general board endorses the Johnson-Humphrey ticket.		The AEC reports that Eskimos living in northern Alaska near the Soviet Arctic nuclear test site of Novaya Zemlya have absorbed dangerous concentrations of radioactive cesium-137 from fallout.			Sept. 1
Justice Dept. files suit in Mobile, Ala. charging Selma, Ala. officials with obstructing enforcement of the public accommodations sections of the 1964 Civil Rights Act.	Sgt. Alvin York, 76, a one-time conscientious objector who became one of the best known American heroes of W.W.I dies in Nashville, Tenn.	Pres. Johnson signs into law an administration-backed Housing Act of 1964 (S 3049) authorizing $1.13 billion for housing and urban renewal through September 1965.	NASA administrator James Webb discloses that plans for sending two probes to the vicinity of Mars in 1966 have been canceled because of budget constraints.		Sept. 2
In a major campaign speech in Prescott, Ariz., GOP nominee Goldwater assails the Johnson administration for contributing to the growth of big federal government, street disorders and lawlessness, appeasement of communism and a decline in U.S. military strength. . . . Twenty-six prominent U.S. business and financial leaders, most of them Republican, announce formation of a National Independent Committee for Pres. Johnson & Sen. Humphrey.	In a Prescott, Ariz. speech, Barry Goldwater pledges, if elected, "to end the draft altogether and as soon as possible."	An administration-backed bill (S 4) to establish a National Wilderness Preservation System, encompassing 9.1 million acres of federally owned land, is signed into law by Pres. Johnson. . . . A compromise bill (HR 11202) appropriating $5.137 billion for the Agriculture Dept. in fiscal 1965 is signed by Pres. Johnson.		Pres. Johnson signs a bill (HR 9586) authorizing $150,000 for the creation of a 25-member National Council on the Arts to encourage development of the arts in the U.S.	Sept. 3
An all-white Madison Co., Ga. jury acquits two white men on charges of the July 11 murder of Negro educator Lemuel Augustus Penn.			A 1,073-pound satellite, dubbed Ogo 1 and described as the most advanced scientific satellite yet constructed, is successfully launched from Cape Kennedy. The craft carries 20 experiments contributed by scientists from seven government laboratories and nine universities.		Sept. 4
Elizabeth Gurley Flynn, chairman of the U.S. CP since 1961, dies while visiting Moscow at age 74.	GOP vice presidential nominee William Miller criticizes Hubert Humphrey for his association with Americans for Democratic Action, a group Miller claims favors recognition of Communist China and opposes all U.S. internal security measures.				Sept. 5
NAACP national director Roy Wilkins warns that a Goldwater victory in November could lead to the creation of a police state.		Sen. Harry Byrd (D, Va.) releases a study indicating that the number of civilian workers employed by the federal government has increased over the past 10 years by 2% to a current total of roughly 2,500,000.			Sept. 6
Democratic vice presidential candidate Hubert Humphrey tells a Labor Day audience in Youngstown, Ohio that the much-discussed white "backlash" vote against the Civil Rights Act will not be a "significant factor" in the November elections.					Sept. 7
F	G	H	I	J	
Includes elections, federal-state relations, civil rights and liberties, crime, the judiciary, education, health care, poverty, urban affairs and population.	Includes formation and debate of U.S. foreign and defense policies, veterans' affairs and defense spending. (Relations with specific foreign countries are usually found under the region concerned.)	Includes business, labor, agriculture, taxation, transportation, consumer affairs, monetary and fiscal policy, natural resources, and pollution.	Includes worldwide scientific, medical and technological developments, natural phenomena, U.S. weather, natural disasters, and accidents.	Includes the arts, religion, scholarship, communications media, sports, entertainment, fashions, fads and social life.	

	World Affairs	Europe	Africa & the Middle East	The Americas	Asia & the Pacific
Sept. 8		East Germany announces that its elderly citizens will be permitted to visit relatives in West Berlin and West Germany.		Uruguay breaks diplomatic relations with Cuba in compliance with the July 26 OAS directive. The action leaves Mexico as the only Latin American nation maintaining relations with the Castro government.	The U.S. agrees to a 600,000 ton increase in India's quarterly wheat allotment to help that country alleviate its continuing food shortage crisis.
Sept. 9		Prof. Heinz Barwich, one of East Germany's most prominent nuclear physicists, defects to the U.S. while attending an Atoms for Peace conference in Geneva.			
Sept. 10			The Organization of African Unity, meeting in Addis Ababa, approves the formation of a 10-nation mediation commission to help end the continuing military and political strife in the Congo. . . . Britain and Southern Rhodesia sign an agreement in London under which Southern Rhodesia would receive its independence if both whites and the predominant but largely voteless Africans approve.		
Sept. 11	The Board of Governors of the World Bank, meeting in Tokyo, vote to bar loans to Indonesia, UAR and Ceylon because they allegedly expropriated foreign investments without adequate compensation.	The U.N. Security Council meets to hear Turkish charges that the Cyprus government has not fulfilled its pledge to lift the economic blockade of Turkish Cypriote villages. Turkey has threatened to intervene to bring relief supplies to the beleaguered communities.	Leaders of the 13 Arab League nations, meeting in Alexandria, agree on a headwaters dam construction plan designed to prevent Israel from diverting Jordan River waters to the Negev Desert.		U.S. Amb.-to-U.N. Adlai Stevenson criticizes Cambodia for allegedly refusing to cooperate with U.N. efforts to ease tensions along the Cambodian-South Vietnamese border.
Sept. 12					Thirteen persons are reported dead in Singapore following a week of racial clashes between Malays and Chinese.
Sept. 13		A German-born U.S. soldier, Hans Puhl, scales the Berlin Wall to help a wounded East German refugee escape into West Berlin. It is the first such direct intervention in an escape by U.S. personnel since the wall was built.	An Israeli government statement warns that it will not tolerate an Arab League attempt to block the headwaters of the Jordan River.		A threatened coup by dissident South Vietnamese army officers collapses in the face of a display of force by loyal troops under the command of Air Commodore Nguyen Cao Ky. Coup leaders reportedly opposed Premier Khanh's announced plans for a restoration of civilian government.
Sept. 14		Turkey agrees at the request of U.N. Secy. Gen. U Thant to delay its plan to ship food and clothing to the allegedly blockaded Turkish Cypriote community of Kokkina.	UAR Pres. Nasser and Saudi Arabian P.M. Faisal announce an agreement to end their nations' intervention in the Yemeni civil war.		
Sept. 15		Hungary and the Vatican sign an accord in Budapest restoring the church's right to form a Roman Catholic hierarchy in Hungary. . . . *Pravda* reports that the USSR's grain yield so far in 1964 has already exceeded the entire 1963 harvest.			The South Vietnamese National Liberation Front calls for stepped-up Viet Cong military efforts to take advantage of Saigon's unsettled political situation.

A	B	C	D	E
Includes developments that affect more than one world region, international organizations and important meetings of major world leaders.	Includes all domestic and regional developments in Europe, including the Soviet Union, Turkey, Cyprus and Malta.	Includes all domestic and regional developments in Africa and the Middle East, including Iraq and Iran and excluding Cyprus, Turkey and Afghanistan.	Includes all domestic and regional developments in Latin America, the Caribbean and Canada.	Includes all domestic and regional developments in Asia and Pacific nations, extending from Afghanistan through all the Pacific Islands, except Hawaii.

U.S. Politics & Social Issues	U.S. Foreign Policy & Defense	U.S. Economy & Environment	Science, Technology & Nature	Culture, Leisure & Life Style	
N.Y. senatorial candidate Robert Kennedy joins his opponent Kenneth Keating in voicing opposition to the long-distance busing of students to achieve racial balance. . . . Seven whites and 1,400 Negroes attend newly-reopened public schools in Prince Edward County, Va. The county schools had been closed since 1959 to avoid a desegregation order.	Senate Foreign Relations Committee Chmn. J. William Fulbright (D, Ark.) charges that Sen. Goldwater's foreign policy views are calculated to revive the Cold War and could lead "sooner or later to the disaster of nuclear war.". . . U.S. Amb.-to-South Vietnam Maxwell Taylor, in Washington for consultations, gives Pres. Johnson, and later the press, a cautiously optimistic assessment of the military and political situation in Vietnam.	AP reports that 531 persons died in U.S. traffic accidents during the 78-hour Labor Day weekend.			Sept. 8
Pres. Johnson orders a full FBI probe into possible outside influences in the recent racial disorders in several Northern cities.		Chrysler Corp. and the United Auto Workers agree in Detroit to a new three-year contract providing a 53-57 cents hourly wage hike.		American League club owners agree to the sale of the New York Yankees to the Columbia Broadcasting System (CBS).	Sept. 9
Sen. Goldwater asserts at a Minneapolis rally that there is a connection between welfare state programs and increasing lawlessness and disrespect for property. . . . The Senate votes 75-3 to reopen its inquiry into the business dealings of former Senate employee Bobby Baker. The action follows new allegations that Baker and Matthew McCloskey, a former Democratic National Committee officer, had been party to an illegal $25,000 contribution to the 1960 Democratic campaign.			Hurricane Dora sweeps across Florida and Georgia causing extensive property damage and at least two deaths.		Sept. 10
In a Chicago speech Republican nominee Goldwater assails the current Supreme Court for repeatedly departing from "the constitutional tradition of limited government.". . . Republican National Committee Chmn. Dean Burch and Democratic National Committee Chmn. John Bailey sign a fair campaign practices code in Washington.	In Sept. 10 testimony released today by a House Foreign Affairs subcommittee, U.S. Amb. Maxwell Taylor predicts that if the Viet Cong win in South Vietnam, all of Southeast Asia will "very shortly thereafter go neutralist, possibly communist."	Pres. Johnson signs a bill (S 1365) establishing the Fire Island National Seashore.			Sept. 11
Martin Luther King, visiting in West Berlin, warns that the election of Barry Goldwater would prompt "violence and riots, the like of which we have never seen before."		Striking East St. Louis, Ill. school teachers end a four-day walkout after winning a 10% salary increase. . . . Pres. Johnson signs a bill (S 27) creating a Canyonlands National Park in Utah.			Sept. 12
				Roy Emerson of Australia defeats Fred Stolle to win the U.S. amateur tennis championship at Forest Hills (N.Y.). . . . Rex Cawley sets a world 400-meter hurdles record of 49.1 seconds at the U.S. Olympic tryouts in Los Angeles. . . . Tony Lema wins the World Series of Golf in Akron, O.	Sept. 13
An estimated 170,000 N.Y.C. public school students boycott classes in a white parents' group-sponsored protest against a pupil-transfer integration plan.	Sen. Wayne Morse renews his criticism of U.S. Southeast Asian policies, charging the administration with withholding "the facts about the war" in Vietnam and characterizing South Vietnamese Premier Khanh as a "military tyrant-dictator, kept in power by the U.S."		The 13th Pugwash Conference on peaceful uses of atomic energy opens in Carlsbad, Czechoslovakia. . . . NASA announces that the first manned flight of the two-man Gemini space capsule has been postponed from December 1964 until at least February of 1965.	Pope Paul VI opens the third session of the Roman Catholic Church's 21st Ecumenical Council, Vatican II, in St. Peter's Basilica. Women auditors attending the session are the first ever to participate in a conciliar assembly.	Sept. 14
Two Negroes unseat white incumbents on the previously all-white Tuskegee (Ala.) City Council. . . . Sen. Goldwater, in a St. Petersburg, Fla. campaign speech, denounces recent Supreme Court decisions which have freed "obviously guilty" defendants because of technical violations of their constitutional rights.			Dr. Alfred Blalock, 65, a physician who in 1944 co-developed a heart operation to save the lives of "blue babies," dies of cancer in Baltimore, Md.		Sept. 15
F	G	H	I	J	
Includes elections, federal-state relations, civil rights and liberties, crime, the judiciary, education, health care, poverty, urban affairs and population.	*Includes formation and debate of U.S. foreign and defense policies, veterans' affairs and defense spending. (Relations with specific foreign countries are usually found under the region concerned.)*	*Includes business, labor, agriculture, taxation, transportation, consumer affairs, monetary and fiscal policy, natural resources, and pollution.*	*Includes worldwide scientific, medical and technological developments, natural phenomena, U.S. weather, natural disasters, and accidents.*	*Includes the arts, religion, scholarship, communications media, sports, entertainment, fashions, fads and social life.*	

	World Affairs	Europe	Africa & the Middle East	The Americas	Asia & the Pacific
Sept. 16		The French government announces an $18.5 billion budget for 1965.	Yemeni sources report a cease-fire has been achieved in the wake of a Sept. 14 Saudi Arabian-UAR agreement to seek a negotiated settlement of Yemen's civil strife.	Cuban Premier Castro announces that planned purchases of machinery and consumer goods from non-communist countries are being curtailed. The action reportedly reflects a critical Cuban revenue shortage caused by the recent decline in world sugar prices.	
Sept. 17	The 17-nation U.N. disarmament conference in Geneva adjourns after agreeing to reconvene in early 1965. Soviet and U.S. delegates exchange charges over who is to blame for the lack of progress in the talks.	Cyprus grants Turkey permission to send emergency relief to Turkish Cypriotes in the village of Kokkina.			A Norwegian resolution deploring Indonesia's Sept. 1-2 air drop of guerrillas into Malaysia is passed by the Security Council, but nullified by the USSR's 102nd U.N. veto.
Sept. 18					
Sept. 19					U.S. Defense Secy. McNamara reports that U.S. destroyers attacked and presumably sunk two small unidentified vessels in the Gulf of Tonkin after they "indicated hostile intent" toward the U.S. ships. North Vietnam condemns the U.S. report as another "myth" created to provide a pretext for future attacks on North Vietnam.
Sept. 20		Swedish Premier Tage Erlander's Social Democratic Party retains a narrow parliamentary majority in national elections.	Dr. Paul Carlson, a U.S. medical missionary in the Congo, is reported to have been "arrested" for "spying" by Congolese rebels near Stanleyville.		
Sept. 21		Malta becomes an independent country within the British Commonwealth.		French Pres. de Gaulle arrives in Venezuela to begin a three-week, 10-nation tour of South America.	Saigon military sources report that South Vietnamese units yesterday clashed with more than 200 North Vietnamese after they crossed the border into South Vietnam.
Sept. 22		Danish Premier Jens Otto Krag's Social Democrats remain the largest party in parliament following national elections.	The Organization of African Unity's newly formed Congo Conciliation Commission urges the U.S. and other foreign powers to end their military assistance to the Congo. The recommendation is assailed by leaders of the central Congolese government.		
Sept. 23		West Germany approves a one-year agreement with East Germany to allow West Berliners to visit relatives in East Berlin during two-week periods at Christmas, Easter, Pentecost, All-Saints Day and at times of family crises.	Charles Helou is inaugurated as the fourth president of Lebanon.		
Sept. 24					Laotian neutralist Premier Souvanna Phouma charges at a Paris news conference that 24 North Vietnamese battalions, about 12,000 men, are currently fighting in Laos in support of the Pathet Lao.

A	B	C	D	E
Includes developments that affect more than one world region, international organizations and important meetings of major world leaders.	Includes all domestic and regional developments in Europe, including the Soviet Union, Turkey, Cyprus and Malta.	Includes all domestic and regional developments in Africa and the Middle East, including Iraq and Iran and excluding Cyprus, Turkey and Afghanistan.	Includes all domestic and regional developments in Latin America, the Caribbean and Canada.	Includes all domestic and regional developments in Asia and Pacific nations, extending from Afghanistan through all the Pacific Islands, except Hawaii.

U.S. Politics & Social Issues	U.S. Foreign Policy & Defense	U.S. Economy & Environment	Science, Technology & Nature	Culture, Leisure & Life Style	
Sen. Strom Thurmond (S.C.) announces that he is switching his affiliation from the Democratic to the Republican Party. In a statement televised across the South, Thurmond charges that the Democrats have "repudiated" the U.S. Constitution.	Pres. Johnson tells a Seattle audience that his administration has taken every fail-safe precaution "to ensure that neither a madman nor a malfunction could trigger nuclear war."		Dr. Rebecca Lancefield of the Rockefeller Institute wins the American Heart Association's 1964 Research Achievement Award for her work on streptococcal infections.		Sept. 16
A three-judge federal court in Birmingham, Ala. rules that a small Birmingham restaurant is exempt from the public accommodations section of the 1964 Civil Rights Act because it is in no meaningful way involved in interstate commerce.	Pres. Johnson discloses in a Sacramento, Calif. speech that the U.S. has developed two new weapons systems capable of intercepting and destroying armed satellites. Observers regard the disclosure as a response to Goldwater's charge that the administration has neglected new weapon technology.	Pres. Johnson outlines his administration's conservation goals in a Portland, Ore. speech.			Sept. 17
		Ford Motor Co. and the UAW agree on a new three-year contract 55 minutes before the strike deadline.	An 80-ft. mock-up model of the U.S.'s three-man Apollo lunar spacecraft is orbited for the first time by means of a Saturn I rocket launched from Cape Kennedy.	Irish playwright Sean O'Casey dies in Torquay, England at age 84.	Sept. 18
		Sen. Goldwater, campaigning in Buffalo, N.D. assails inconsistencies in the administration's farm policies and reiterates his pledge to eliminate federal support programs.	Pres. Johnson signs an appropriations bill (HR 10309) allocating: $35 million for water pollution control, $28 million for community health activities, $20 million for air pollution control, and $140 million for the National Cancer Institute.	Pres. Johnson signs a general appropriations bill (HR 10309) which allocates $13 million for educational TV facilities.	Sept. 19
					Sept. 20
Goldwater attacks Pres. Johnson for not facing "the issues" and for letting others speak for him, including "socialistic radicals like his running mate Hubert Horatio (Humphrey)."				The U.S.'s *Constellation* defeats England's *Sovereign*, four races to none, in the 19th America's Cup 12-meter yacht races off Newport, R.I. . . . Saul Bellow's novel *Herzog* is published in New York.	Sept. 21
	A federal jury in Brooklyn, N.Y. indicts nine persons on charges of conspiring to arrange U.S. student trips to Cuba in violation of a State Dept. ban.	The Senate confirms Peace Corps director Sargent Shriver as head of the new Office of Economic Opportunity.		*Fiddler on the Roof* opens at the Imperial Theater in New York. . . . Emile Griffith retains the world welterweight boxing championship in a 15-round decision over Englishman Brian Curvis in London.	Sept. 22
Dynamite explosions damage two Negro-owned homes in McComb, Miss. The incidents bring to 16 the number of reported house bombings in the McComb area since April.					Sept. 23
The Senate approves by a 44-38 vote a "sense of Congress" resolution urging federal district courts to give state legislatures at least six months to comply with the Supreme Court's June 15 decision requiring both houses of a state legislature to be apportioned on a population basis. . . . Ex-Birmingham Police Commissioner Eugene (Bull) Connor wins a $40,000 libel judgment against *The New York Times* in connection with two April 1960 articles on the Birmingham racial situation.		The SEC announces new regulations for stock specialists on the New York and American Stock Exchanges.			Sept. 24

F	G	H	I	J
Includes elections, federal-state relations, civil rights and liberties, crime, the judiciary, education, health care, poverty, urban affairs and population.	Includes formation and debate of U.S. foreign and defense policies, veterans' affairs and defense spending. (Relations with specific foreign countries are usually found under the region concerned.)	Includes business, labor, agriculture, taxation, transportation, consumer affairs, monetary and fiscal policy, natural resources, and pollution.	Includes worldwide scientific, medical and technological developments, natural phenomena, U.S. weather, natural disasters, and accidents.	Includes the arts, religion, scholarship, communications media, sports, entertainment, fashions, fads and social life.

	World Affairs	Europe	Africa & the Middle East	The Americas	Asia & the Pacific
Sept. 25		British P.M. Alec Douglas-Home dissolves Parliament in advance of national elections scheduled for Oct. 15. . . . The U.N. Security Council unanimously approves a resolution extending the U.N. peace keeping force in Cyprus for another three months.		Visiting French Pres. de Gaulle tells an Ecuadorian audience that France and South America are naturally linked by their common Latin and Christian culture. Increased cultural and technical cooperation between France and Latin America has emerged as the principal theme of de Gaulle's current tour.	
Sept. 26					The Japan Newspaper Association announces the negotiation of a journalist exchange agreement with Communist China. . . . South Vietnamese Premier Khanh announces formation of a 17-member civilian High National Council to help draft a new civilian constitution.
Sept. 27		The seven-nation European Free Trade Association issues an annual report detailing the economic gains achieved during the trade zone's four years of operations. The study notes that the combined GNP of EFTA members rose 3.7% in 1963, "double the increase of the previous year."			Demonstrations and disorders against the South Vietnamese interim government of Premier Khanh continue on a wide scale despite his repeated pledge to restore civilian control before the end of October.
Sept. 28					
Sept. 29	U.S. Secy. of State Dean Rusk says that American intelligence indicates that Communist China is on the verge of detonating its first nuclear device.	Greece and Bulgaria announce they have agreed to abandon permanently all territorial claims against each other.			U.S. Asst. State Secy. William Bundy, speaking in Tokyo, warns that expansion of the Vietnam War may "be forced upon us by the increased external pressures of the Communists, including a rising scale of infiltration."
Sept. 30	Newsmen in Europe, Latin America and Communist-bloc countries report that the Warren Commission's conclusions have done little to diminish popularly held views that Pres. Kennedy was the victim of a conspiracy.	A Soviet agreement to provide Cyprus with an unspecified amount of military and economic aid is signed in Moscow.			
Oct. 1					
Oct. 2		A plan to complete the Common Market's envisioned uniform external tariff barrier and its internal customs union by Jan. 1, 1967, three years ahead of schedule, is presented to the six member states by EEC Executive Commission Pres. Walter Hallstein.			

A	B	C	D	E
Includes developments that affect more than one world region, international organizations and important meetings of major world leaders.	Includes all domestic and regional developments in Europe, including the Soviet Union, Turkey, Cyprus and Malta.	Includes all domestic and regional developments in Africa and the Middle East, including Iraq and Iran and excluding Cyprus, Turkey and Afghanistan.	Includes all domestic and regional developments in Latin America, the Caribbean and Canada.	Includes all domestic and regional developments in Asia and Pacific nations, extending from Afghanistan through all the Pacific Islands, except Hawaii.

U.S. Politics & Social Issues	U.S. Foreign Policy & Defense	U.S. Economy & Environment	Science, Technology & Nature	Culture, Leisure & Life Style	
		Over 250,000 United Auto Workers go on strike against 89 plants of the General Motors Corp.			Sept. 25
In a report to Pres. Johnson, the FBI concludes that recent urban race disorders have been, on the whole, unplanned, uninstigated, and spontaneous. No evidence of significant communist involvement was uncovered.				Vincente Saldivar of Mexico scores a 12th round TKO over Cuban exile Ultiminio (Sugar) Ramos to win the world flyweight boxing championship in Mexico City.	Sept. 26
The seven-member Warren Commission makes public its report on the assassination of Pres. John Kennedy. The report, based on previous FBI, state and local investigations and on the testimony of 552 witnesses, concludes that Lee Harvey Oswald acted alone, and that neither he nor his murderer Jack Ruby was "part of any conspiracy, domestic or foreign.". . . The report also outlines recommendations for improving the protection of the President.	Sen. Goldwater indicates that, if elected, he would appoint Richard Nixon as Secretary of State.				Sept. 27
In a Portland, Me. speech, Pres. Johnson appeals for bipartisan support from Democrats and "forward-looking" Republicans. . . . Copies of the 250,000-word Warren Commission report on the Kennedy assassination are made available to the public.				The Australian team of Roy Emerson and Fred Stolle defeats the U.S. team of Chuck McKinley and Dennis Ralston to win the tennis Davis Cup championship in Cleveland, Ohio. . . . Harpo (Arthur) Marx, of the Marx Brothers comedy team, dies in Hollywood at age 70.	Sept. 28
	In a Cincinnati speech Goldwater accuses the Johnson administration of being "soft on communism."				Sept. 29
The Senate Permanent Investigations Subcommittee's final report on the Billie Sol Estes case clears Agriculture Dept. officials of deliberate favoritism, but adds that federal bureaucratic inertia contributed to the scandal.	Congress passes a bill (HR 9124) revising and expanding the Reserve Officers Training Corps (ROTC) programs in U.S. high schools and colleges.	Congress passes a bill (HR 10053) extending for one year federal subsidies on construction of U.S. merchant ships.			Sept. 30
Martin Luther King, addressing the eighth annual convention of the Southern Christian Leadership Conference, urges Negroes to support systematic political action to eliminate the social and economic evils which demonstrations alone can only dramatize and highlight.		Pres. Johnson appoints a Taft-Hartley fact-finding board to halt a strike of Atlantic and Gulf Coast dock workers.	A group of 22 scientists, convened by the U.N. Education, Scientific & Cultural Organization (UNESCO), issues a unanimous statement declaring there to be no scientific foundation whatever for any racist theory.		Oct. 1
Five Philadelphia, Miss. law enforcement officials are indicted on charges of illegally detaining and beating Negroes in October 1962 and on Jan. 26, 1964. The charges are not related to the murder of three civil rights workers near Philadelphia earlier this summer.	The U.S. drops prosecution of accused Soviet spies Aleksandr Sokolov and his wife after it becomes clear that their trial defense would expose U.S. counter-espionage agents.				Oct. 2
F	G	H	I	J	
Includes elections, federal-state relations, civil rights and liberties, crime, the judiciary, education, health care, poverty, urban affairs and population.	Includes formation and debate of U.S. foreign and defense policies, veterans' affairs and defense spending. (Relations with specific foreign countries are usually found under the region concerned.)	Includes business, labor, agriculture, taxation, transportation, consumer affairs, monetary and fiscal policy, natural resources, and pollution.	Includes worldwide scientific, medical and technological developments, natural phenomena, U.S. weather, natural disasters, and accidents.	Includes the arts, religion, scholarship, communications media, sports, entertainment, fashions, fads and social life.	

	World Affairs	Europe	Africa & the Middle East	The Americas	Asia & the Pacific
Oct. 3			Officials in charge of preparations for an October 5 world conference of unaligned nations in Cairo vote to bar attendance by Congo Premier Moise Tshombe.		
Oct. 4					South Vietnamese government troops mass in Saigon to head off possible violent demonstrations by anti-government elements and labor unionists.
Oct. 5	Leaders of 57 neutralist and unaligned nations meet in Cairo for a week-long conference on world problems. . . . The U.N. Food & Agriculture Organization reports that the world's total agricultural output (not counting Communist China) increased 1%-2% over the past year, while total population grew at least 2%.	Fifty-seven East Germans escape to West Berlin before Communist guards discover and destroy their secret tunnel under the Berlin Wall.		British Queen Elizabeth arrives in Canada for a week-long goodwill visit.	Britain announces agreement on arrangements to grant partial home rule to the Solomon Islands.
Oct. 6		First Secy. Walter Ulbricht announces that 10,000 East German political prisoners will be freed under an official amnesty by the end of 1964.	Congo Premier Moise Tshombe is placed under virtual house arrest in Cairo after attempting to attend the world neutralist conference, from which he had been formally barred.	The Nicaraguan Congress approves a motion repudiating a 1914 U.S.-Nicaraguan pact granting the U.S. perpetual rights to build a canal through Nicaragua.	Cambodian Prince Sihanouk, concluding an eight-day state visit to Peking, announces that Communist China has pledged significant economic and military aid to Cambodia. . . . Philippine Pres. Diosdado Macapagal concludes two days of Washington talks on Asian problems with Pres. Johnson. Macapagal reportedly urged Johnson to authorize U.S. attacks on North Vietnamese bases used to support the Viet Cong.
Oct. 7	Indian P.M. Lal Bahadur Shastri suggests that the Cairo conference of unaligned nations send a special mission to persuade Communist China "to desist from developing nuclear weapons."	U.S., France and Britain protest the staging of an East German military parade in East Berlin.	Congolese government troops, assisted by South African white mercenaries, recapture the rebel-held Lake Tanganyika port of Uvira. Thirty European hostages held by the rebels are found unharmed.		
Oct. 8	The U.S. publicly informs U.N. Secy. Gen. U Thant that it will insist, under Article 19 of the U.N. Charter, that the USSR be stripped of its voting right (because of unpaid assessments) at the forthcoming regular meeting of the General Assembly.				
Oct. 9	Soviet U.N. delegate Nikolai Fedorenko declares that his government will not pay "a single cent" of its "alleged arrears" to the U.N.	The Institute of German Industry reports a 15-17% increase in West German exports over the last year.	Congo Premier Moise Tshombe leaves Cairo after angrily condemning the allegedly anti-Congo policies of UAR Pres. Nasser.		South Vietnamese Premier Khanh renews threats to bomb North Vietnam in order to halt infiltration of soldiers and supplies to the Viet Cong.
Oct. 10				In a speech to Uruguayan government officials, visiting French Pres. de Gaulle warns of the dangers to smaller nations of becoming trapped in the struggle between the U.S. and the USSR.	U.S. military sources in Saigon disclose that South Vietnamese pilots recently killed 30 civilians in Bien Hoa Province in an accidental bombing.
	A	**B**	**C**	**D**	**E**
	Includes developments that affect more than one world region, international organizations and important meetings of major world leaders.	*Includes all domestic and regional developments in Europe, including the Soviet Union, Turkey, Cyprus and Malta.*	*Includes all domestic and regional developments in Africa and the Middle East, including Iraq and Iran and excluding Cyprus, Turkey and Afghanistan.*	*Includes all domestic and regional developments in Latin America, the Caribbean and Canada.*	*Includes all domestic and regional developments in Asia and Pacific nations, extending from Afghanistan through all the Pacific Islands, except Hawaii.*

U.S. Politics & Social Issues	U.S. Foreign Policy & Defense	U.S. Economy & Environment	Science, Technology & Nature	Culture, Leisure & Life Style	
The second and final session of the 88th Congress adjourns. Democrats hail the session as one of great achievements, citing the Civil Rights Act, tax reduction, anti-poverty program, aid-to-education, and the National Wilderness System bill. Pending legislation not enacted includes: aged health care, increased Social Security benefits, and an Appalachian aid program.		The adjourned second session of the 88th Congress appropriated a total of $105.96 billion, about $4 billion less than the total requested by the administration.	Explorer 21, a scientific satellite equipped to measure magnetic fields and solar wind in inter-planetary space, is successfully launched from Cape Kennedy.		Oct. 3
			Hurricane Hilda ravages Louisiana coastal areas killing at least 32 persons.	The St. Louis Cardinals win the National League pennant, finishing the season one game ahead of the Philadelphia Phillies and Cincinnati Red Legs. The New York Yankees clinched their 29th (fifth consecutive) American League pennant yesterday, edging out the Chicago White Sox by one game. . . . Graham Hill, driving a BRM, wins the U.S. Grand Prix at Watkins Glen, N.Y.	Oct. 4
	A Republican task force report charges that the administration's "overextended" stress on presidential control of nuclear weapons has undermined our NATO allies' faith in the U.S. commitment to defend Western Europe in the event of surprise attack.	General Motors Corp. and the United Auto Workers agree on a new three-year contract, but the 10-day strike continues due to still unsettled local plant issues.			Oct. 5
During a campaign stop in a Philadelphia suburb, Sen. Goldwater charges that "minority groups are running this country and Americans are getting sick and tired of it."		Pres. Johnson, in a campaign speech at North Carolina State College, ridicules Barry Goldwater's proposal for a quick termination of federal farm support programs.	A new test for detecting hidden cancers through chemical analysis of enzymes is outlined by Dr. Myron Arlen at the clinical congress of the American College of Physicians in Chicago.		Oct. 6
Over 175,000 people, the largest crowd in Iowa history, turn out to greet Pres. Johnson on his arrival in Des Moines to begin a six-day, 10-state campaign swing. . . . Democratic vice presidential candidate Hubert Humphrey accuses Goldwater of not realizing that his game "of nuclear 'chicken' will eventually result in the annihilation of both players."	Pres. Johnson signs a $3.25 billion foreign aid appropriations bill (HR 11812) for fiscal 1965. The total reflects an unusually small congressional cut of 7.5% from the administration's original foreign aid request. . . . Fail Safe, a motion picture about accidental nuclear war, premiers in New York.		Dr. Seymour Rinzler, in a paper to the annual American Public Health Association meeting in New York, reports a sharply lower incidence of coronary heart disease among middle-aged men on diets low in animal fats and dairy products.		Oct. 7
GOP candidate Goldwater tells a Lubbock, Tex. crowd that Pres. Johnson is "backing socialism" whether he knows it or not.	Secy. of State Dean Rusk denies Sen. Goldwater's recent charge that the administration is postponing decisions on Vietnam until after the election.				Oct. 8
		The Northwestern National Life Insurance Co. issues a study indicating that graduate study in non-technical fields is (from an economic viewpoint) a waste of time and money for most students.			Oct. 9
				The 1964 Summer Olympic Games open in Tokyo. . . . TV, radio and vaudeville comedian Eddie Cantor dies in Hollywood at age 72.	Oct. 10

F	G	H	I	J
Includes elections, federal-state relations, civil rights and liberties, crime, the judiciary, education, health care, poverty, urban affairs and population.	Includes formation and debate of U.S. foreign and defense policies, veterans' affairs and defense spending. (Relations with specific foreign countries are usually found under the region concerned.)	Includes business, labor, agriculture, taxation, transportation, consumer affairs, monetary and fiscal policy, natural resources, and pollution.	Includes worldwide scientific, medical and technological developments, natural phenomena, U.S. weather, natural disasters, and accidents.	Includes the arts, religion, scholarship, communications media, sports, entertainment, fashions, fads and social life.

	World Affairs	Europe	Africa & the Middle East	The Americas	Asia & the Pacific
Oct. 11	World neutralist leaders conclude their six-day conference in Cairo after adopting resolutions asking an end to foreign intervention in Cuba, Southeast Asia, Cyprus and the Congo.				
Oct. 12				Leftist Venezuelan terrorists release kidnapped U.S. Lt. Col. Michael Smolen after holding him for three days in an apparent effort to draw attention to their guerrilla movement.	
Oct. 13		The Labor Party's proposal for nationalization of the entire steel industry and its opposition to maintaining a British nuclear deterrent independent of the U.S. have emerged as the central issues in the final days of campaigning for the Oct. 15 British parliamentary elections. . . . West German government presents Parliament with a record 1965 budget of $16 billion. Defense expenditures are estimated at $5.075 billion, down $75 million from 1964.		Ex-Cuban Pres. Manuel Urrutia announces in New York the formation of a Democratic Revolutionary Alliance of Cuban refugees to coordinate anti-Castro efforts.	
Oct. 14	The Nobel Peace Prize for 1964 is awarded in Oslo to Dr. Martin Luther King, U.S. Negro civil rights leader and advocate of non-violence.			A federal-provincial conference of attorney generals in Ottawa unanimously approves a method to amend Canada's Constitution without formal consent by the British Parliament.	
Oct. 15	A Soviet government statement announces that Nikita S. Khrushchev has been removed from his official posts as CP first secretary and as chairman of the USSR Council of Ministers (premier). Leonid Brezhnev is elected as the party's new first secretary and Aleksei Kosygin succeeds Khrushchev as premier. The new Soviet leaders pledge to continue Khrushchev's foreign policies.	Nikita S. Khrushchev, 70, is ousted as Soviet leader after 10 years of rule. The official announcement cites the former premier's "advanced age," but most observers attribute the ouster to Khrushchev's increasingly mercurial leadership style, his frequent and inconsistent reforms of Soviet farm policy, and his failure to prevent the Sino-Soviet ideological dispute from undermining Soviet-bloc unity. . . . The British Labor Party wins a narrow four-seat victory over the Conservative government of P.M. Alec Douglas-Home in national parliamentary elections.			
Oct. 16	Communist China detonates its first nuclear device in the atmosphere above the Taklamakan Desert in Sinkiang Province. U.S. sources estimate the force of the explosion at 20 kilotons. An official Chinese statement says the test was necessary to break the U.S.-USSR nuclear monopoly and thus pave the way for genuine nuclear disarmament.	Labor Party leader Harold Wilson, 48, is sworn in as British prime minister, ending 13 years of Conservative Party rule. Wilson names Patrick Gordon Walker as foreign secretary.	UAR and Iraq issue a joint communique announcing that steps will be taken toward "political unification" of the two countries within two years.		

A	B	C	D	E
Includes developments that affect more than one world region, international organizations and important meetings of major world leaders.	Includes all domestic and regional developments in Europe, including the Soviet Union, Turkey, Cyprus and Malta.	Includes all domestic and regional developments in Africa and the Middle East, including Iraq and Iran and excluding Cyprus, Turkey and Afghanistan.	Includes all domestic and regional developments in Latin America, the Caribbean and Canada.	Includes all domestic and regional developments in Asia and Pacific nations, extending from Afghanistan through all the Pacific Islands, except Hawaii.

U.S. Politics & Social Issues	U.S. Foreign Policy & Defense	U.S. Economy & Environment	Science, Technology & Nature	Culture, Leisure & Life Style	
The House Intergovernmental Relations Subcommittee unanimously reports that it has found no evidence to implicate Pres. Johnson in the illegal grain storage or other fraudulent dealings of convicted Texas financier Billie Sol Estes. . . . Martin Luther King, speaking in Brooklyn, N.Y., urges all registered Negroes to vote against Sen. Goldwater. . . . FBI Director J. Edgar Hoover announces that 11 whites have been arrested in connection with a recent series of house bombings in the McComb, Miss. area.	Sen. Goldwater's task force on defense issues a report reiterating claims that the Johnson administration has neglected nuclear weapons development since the signing of the nuclear test-ban treaty. An AEC spokesman subsequently tells newsmen that the U.S. has conducted 28 announced weapons-related underground tests since mid-1963.			Five persons are killed in a crash during the 1,000 Kilometers of Paris auto race.	**Oct. 11**
Sen. Goldwater says in an NBC-TV interview that his presidential campaign has been seriously hurt by the "outright lie that I am trigger-happy."			A Soviet spacecraft with a three-man crew is launched into orbit from the Soviet space center at Baikonur, Kazakhstan. It is the first time that a capsule carrying more than one man has been sent into space.		**Oct. 12**
Senate Rules Committee Chmn. Everett Jordan (D, N.C.), disregarding GOP protests, announces that further investigation into the Bobby Baker case will be postponed until after the November elections.		The New York City Health Dept. opens the first of several planned tobacco withdrawal clinics.	The three-man Soviet spacecraft, known as Voskhod I, returns safely to earth after completing 16 orbits. Western scientists attribute the unexpectedly short duration of the mission to undisclosed technical problems. The Soviet press describes the mission as an unqualified success.		**Oct. 13**
Martin Luther King is named winner of the 1964 Nobel Peace Prize. He is the 12th American and second American Negro to be so honored. . . . The White House announces the resignation of special presidential assistant Walter Jenkins following disclosure of his Oct. 7 Washington, D.C. arrest on sexually related morals charges. . . . Goldwater denounces the Senate's postponement of the Bobby Baker investigation as a "cover-up."	In a New York campaign speech, Pres. Johnson defends a flexible, non-monolithic foreign policy approach to communist states--one which recognizes that "Russia is a different kind of danger from Yugoslavia."				**Oct. 14**
			Konrad F. Bloch of Harvard and Feodor Lynen of the University of Munich are named co-winners of the 1964 Nobel Prize for Medicine for their research into the regulation of cholesterol and fatty acid metabolism.	The St. Louis Cardinals defeat the New York Yankees, 7-5, in the seventh and deciding game of baseball's 1964 World Series. . . . American sprinter Bob Hayes equals a world record of 10 seconds flat in winning the 100-meter dash at the Tokyo Olympics. . . . Popular song writer Cole Porter dies in Santa Monica, Calif. at age 71.	**Oct. 15**
Sen. Goldwater, in his first major campaign speech on civil rights, declares that "forced integration is just as wrong as forced segregation," adding that busing students to end *de facto* segregation is "morally" unacceptable.	Pres. Johnson issues a statement deploring the Communist Chinese nuclear test, but adding that the "military significance" of the blast "should not be overestimated" in view of China's lack of an effective delivery system.			Gary Anderson of the U.S. wins a gold medal in the Olympic free rifle competition in Tokyo.	**Oct. 16**

F	G	H	I	J
Includes elections, federal-state relations, civil rights and liberties, crime, the judiciary, education, health care, poverty, urban affairs and population.	*Includes formation and debate of U.S. foreign and defense policies, veterans' affairs and defense spending. (Relations with specific foreign countries are usually found under the region concerned.)*	*Includes business, labor, agriculture, taxation, transportation, consumer affairs, monetary and fiscal policy, natural resources, and pollution.*	*Includes worldwide scientific, medical and technological developments, natural phenomena, U.S. weather, natural disasters, and accidents.*	*Includes the arts, religion, scholarship, communications media, sports, entertainment, fashions, fads and social life.*

	World Affairs	Europe	Africa & the Middle East	The Americas	Asia & the Pacific
Oct. 17	An official *Pravda* editorial asserts that the USSR's new "collective" leadership under First Secy. Brezhnev and Premier Kosygin will continue to pursue "peaceful co-existence" and will renew efforts to reconstruct the ideological and political unity of the world communist movement.	A *Pravda* editorial contrasts the stability promised by the new "collective rule" of the Brezhnev-Kosygin regime with the "subjectivism," "hare-brained scheming" and "bragging" of Khrushchev's last years.	The United Republic of Tanganyika and Zanzibar is renamed Tanzania.		
Oct. 18	Press reports indicate that Khrushchev's ouster has provoked a varied reaction among world communist leaders, ranging from outright approval by Communist China and Albania to demands for a full explanation by party spokesmen in Eastern and Western Europe.		Algerian Premier Ben Bella announces the virtual suppression of the Socialist Forces Front's recently renewed revolt against his rule.		
Oct. 19		Soviet First Secy. Leonid Brezhnev stresses collective leadership, peaceful co-existence and Soviet-bloc unity in an address to a Red Square rally marking the return of the USSR's three recently orbited cosmonauts.			Indian P.M. Lal Bahadur Shastri denounces China's Oct. 16 nuclear test as an attempt "to build a mighty war machine and thus create fear in the minds of us all."
Oct. 20	Communist China discloses that Premier Chou En-lai has asked world leaders to join in a summit meeting to ban all nuclear weapons.	West Germany informs its EEC partners that it is not prepared to reduce grain prices to levels specified in a Common Market plan for the creation of a uniform European agricultural system.			South Vietnam's High National Council, a newly created legislative body, makes public a new constitution providing for a civilian government to replace Premier Nguyen Khanh's interim regime.
Oct. 21		The French government warns that it will withdraw from the EEC unless West Germany permits the completion of a uniform European agricultural market.			Cambodia charges that South Vietnamese planes yesterday attacked the Cambodian border town of Anlong, killing eight civilians.
Oct. 22	U.N. Secy. Gen. U Thant suggests at a news conference that the U.S., Communist China, USSR, France and Britain meet in 1965 to discuss the banning of nuclear weapons. Thant notes that recent appeals for such a meeting have been advanced by Communist Chinese leaders and former U.S. Republican leader Alfred Landon.	U.N. authorities in Cyprus announce that Turkish Cypriotes have agreed to give U.N. troops control of the strategic Nicosia-Kyrenia road in exchange for rotation of about one-half of the Turkish army's garrison on the island.			
Oct. 23	U.S. administration officials indicate disinterest in recent Communist Chinese and U.N. proposals for nuclear ban talks, noting that acceptance of the bids would amount to rewarding China for its development of atomic weapons.		Southern Rhodesia is renamed Rhodesia.		

A	B	C	D	E
Includes developments that affect more than one world region, international organizations and important meetings of major world leaders.	*Includes all domestic and regional developments in Europe, including the Soviet Union, Turkey, Cyprus and Malta.*	*Includes all domestic and regional developments in Africa and the Middle East, including Iraq and Iran and excluding Cyprus, Turkey and Afghanistan.*	*Includes all domestic and regional developments in Latin America, the Caribbean and Canada.*	*Includes all domestic and regional developments in Asia and Pacific nations, extending from Afghanistan through all the Pacific Islands, except Hawaii.*

U.S. Politics & Social Issues	U.S. Foreign Policy & Defense	U.S. Economy & Environment	Science, Technology & Nature	Culture, Leisure & Life Style	
				Dallas Long of the U.S. wins a gold medal in the shot put with an Olympic record toss of 66 ft. 8 1/2 in.	Oct. 17
	Pres. Johnson, in a televised address, tells the American people that he has been "officially informed" that the USSR's new leaders plan "no changes in basic foreign policy" and that efforts to negotiate East-West problems will continue.		NASA announces the selection of a third group of American astronauts for future space programs.	Don Schollander wins his third Olympic gold medal as a member of the U.S.'s victorious 800-meter free-style relay swim team. Schollander set individual Olympic and world records in winning the 100-meter and 400-meter free-style events earlier in the games. . . . Pope Paul VI proclaims 22 new African saints. The saints, known as the Blessed Martyrs of Uganda, were a group of converts who were converted and killed 1885-1887.	Oct. 18
GOP vice presidential candidate William Miller charges in San Diego, Calif. that U.S. national security had been endangered by the presence of Walter Jenkins in the administration.			New Soviet leader Leonid Brezhnev, addressing a Red Square rally, hails the USSR's continuing lead in the exploration of space.		Oct. 19
Herbert Clark Hoover, 31st President of the U.S. (1929-1933), dies in New York of abdominal cancer at age 90. Pres Johnson declares a 30-day national mourning period.	Ex-Kansas Gov. Alfred Landon, the GOP's 1936 presidential candidate, proposes in a Columbus, Ohio speech that the U.S. meet with Communist China and other nuclear powers for a serious attempt to ban atomic weapons. Landon reaffirms his long-time support for recognition and U.N. admission of Communist China.	The Dow Jones average of industrial stock prices closes at a new record 881.71.			Oct. 20
Pres. Johnson, campaigning in Kansas City, Mo., predicts that "a stronger Republican Party" will be built by "moderate leaders" after the November elections. . . . White House reveals that all presidential aides have been required to resubmit security clearance applications in the wake of the Walter Jenkins disclosures.	Sen. Goldwater assails the Johnson administration for making unrealistic distinctions between "good" and "bad" communists and for accepting the sincerity of the USSR's "peaceful co-existence" doctrine. . . . Rep. Harris McDowell (D, Del.) tells reporters that photo data from orbiting reconnaissance satellites gave the administration advance warning of China's Oct. 16 atomic test.				Oct. 21
The FBI reports to Pres. Johnson that a full investigation has uncovered no evidence that Walter Jenkins ever "compromised the security or interests" of the U.S.	The AEC detonates a low-yield, underground nuclear device near Baxterville, Miss. in a test of U.S. techniques for long-distance detection of underground nuclear blasts. It is the first atomic test conducted east of the Mississippi.			The Swedish Academy names French author-philosopher Jean-Paul Sartre as the winner of the 1964 Nobel Prize for literature.	Oct. 22
Mississippi Circuit Judge W. H. Watkins gives suspended sentences to nine white men convicted in connection with the recent bombings of Negro homes and churches in the McComb, Miss. area. Watkins says he decided to suspend penalties because the defendants had been "unduly provoked" by civil rights workers.				Joe Frazier of the U.S. wins the gold medal in the heavyweight division of the Olympic boxing competition in Tokyo.	Oct. 23

F	G	H	I	J
Includes elections, federal-state relations, civil rights and liberties, crime, the judiciary, education, health care, poverty, urban affairs and population.	Includes formation and debate of U.S. foreign and defense policies, veterans' affairs and defense spending. (Relations with specific foreign countries are usually found under the region concerned.)	Includes business, labor, agriculture, taxation, transportation, consumer affairs, monetary and fiscal policy, natural resources, and pollution.	Includes worldwide scientific, medical and technological developments, natural phenomena, U.S. weather, natural disasters, and accidents.	Includes the arts, religion, scholarship, communications media, sports, entertainment, fashions, fads and social life.

	World Affairs	Europe	Africa & the Middle East	The Americas	Asia & the Pacific
Oct. 24	U Thant predicts that the likelihood of another world war will increase if the U.N. fails to resolve its financial and organizational disputes.	*Tass* announces that CP First Secy. Brezhnev and Premier Kosygin have just returned from discussions in Poland with Polish party chief Wladyslaw Gomulka. Observers view the meeting as perhaps the first phase of a Soviet government effort to ease disquiet over the Kremlin shake-up among long-time Eastern European supporters of Khrushchev.	The British protectorate of Northern Rhodesia becomes the independent Republic of Zambia. . . . Rhodesian P.M. Ian Smith rejects a proposal by British P.M. Wilson for a London conference on revising Rhodesia's white supremacy constitution.		The South Vietnamese High National Council elects Phanh Khac Suu as chief of state under the newly proclaimed constitution. Suu is expected to appoint a new premier to replace Gen. Khanh in the near future.
Oct. 25			British P.M. Wilson warns Rhodesian P.M. Smith that a unilateral Rhodesian declaration of independence under its present constitution will be viewed as an act of "rebellion.". . . Congo Premier Tshombe charges in Leopoldville that the UAR, Mali and Algeria are supporting plots to assassinate central Congolese government leaders.		Japanese Premier Hayato Ikeda announces his resignation because of failing health.
Oct. 26		A British Labor government white paper announces the imposition of a 15% surcharge on imports to protect the pound sterling and to bolster Britain's sagging economy. The action draws criticism from Britain's partners in the European Free Trade Association. . . . Britain informs France that it wishes to restudy the expensive joint Anglo-French project for construction of the supersonic airliner, the Concorde.	At least 10 persons are dead following four days of anti-government rioting in the Sudanese capital of Khartoum. The disorders against Pres. Ibrahim Abboud's government are reported to stem from Sudanese Negroes' resistance to the Arab-dominated central government and political opposition to the continuation of military rule.		
Oct. 27	British Foreign Secy. Patrick Gordon Walker announces Britain's readiness to consider seriously any U.N. proposals for halting the spread of nuclear weapons.	Moscow sources report that the new Soviet leaders are planning to meet shortly with Hungarian CP First Secy. Janos Kadar, who has openly expressed his misgivings over Khrushchev's abrupt removal. . . . An Italian CP delegation arrives in Moscow to get a first-hand account of the reasons for Khrushchev's ouster.			Cambodian Prince Sihanouk issues a statement warning that Cambodia will break relations with the U.S. if American-supported South Vietnamese attacks on Cambodian territory continue. . . . A Malaysian security spokesman tells newsmen that guerrillas from Indonesia who had invaded Malayan territory in August and September have been almost entirely killed or captured.
Oct. 28				Anti-government student riots erupt in La Paz, Bolivia for the fifth straight day. At least three students have been killed in clashes with police.	U.S. and South Vietnamese leaders in Saigon admit that increased Viet Cong activity from Cambodian bases has precipitated at least five recent U.S.-Vietnamese attacks on Cambodian targets.
Oct. 29		The AP reports from Moscow that former Soviet Premier Khrushchev is living on a modest pension in a four-room apartment near the Kremlin.	Congolese rebel leader Christophe Gbenye warns Belgian King Baudouin that he can "no longer guarantee the security of Belgian subjects" under his control in view of Belgium's military support of the central Congolese government.	Bolivia severs relations with Czechoslovakia after accusing the Czech embassy in La Paz of actively encouraging the current anti-government street protests.	
Oct. 30	French Pres. de Gaulle informs Communist Chinese Premier Chou En-lai that France is prepared to join with the other nuclear powers in "serious negotiations" on an atomic weapons ban.				South Vietnamese chief of state Phan Khac Suu appoints ex-Saigon Mayor Tran Van Huong to succeed Nguyen Khanh as premier.
Oct. 31		Austrian Foreign Min Bruno Kreisky ends three days of diplomatic talks in Budapest, Hungary. He is the first Western foreign minister to visit Hungary since World War II.	Sudan's six-year-old military junta, pressed by growing popular disorders, transfers governing authority to a 24-member civilian cabinet. Former junta chief Ibrahim Abboud is appointed to the newly created position of chief of state. . . . The Algerian government confirms that ex-National Assembly Pres. Ferhat Abbas has been imprisoned for anti-government activity.	An Alliance for Progress review report submitted to Pres. Johnson asserts that 1964 was a year of exceptional economic growth for Venezuela, Mexico and Central America.	Communist China publicly reiterates a pledge to aid Cambodia in its dispute with South Vietnam and the U.S.
	A	B	C	D	E
	Includes developments that affect more than one world region, international organizations and important meetings of major world leaders.	*Includes all domestic and regional developments in Europe, including the Soviet Union, Turkey, Cyprus and Malta.*	*Includes all domestic and regional developments in Africa and the Middle East, including Iraq and Iran and excluding Cyprus, Turkey and Afghanistan.*	*Includes all domestic and regional developments in Latin America, the Caribbean and Canada.*	*Includes all domestic and regional developments in Asia and Pacific nations, extending from Afghanistan through all the Pacific Islands, except Hawaii.*

U.S. Politics & Social Issues	U.S. Foreign Policy & Defense	U.S. Economy & Environment	Science, Technology & Nature	Culture, Leisure & Life Style	
In a paid political TV broadcast, Pres. Johnson cites Social Security-financed health care for the elderly as his top legislative priority for 1965. . . . *Editor & Publisher* reports that a majority of large circulation daily papers have editorially endorsed Pres. Johnson's candidacy. Many of the papers cited have consistently supported the GOP in past elections.				The USSR, with 96 medals (30 gold), and the U.S., with 90 medals (36 gold), capture unofficial team honors at the Summer Olympic Games in Tokyo. The U.S. dominated track and field, and swimming, while the Soviets scored well in wrestling, weight lifting, gymnastics and boxing.	Oct. 24
		The UAW calls off its strike against General Motors following settlement of most local plant disputes.			Oct. 25
			Maj. Gen. Samuel Phillips is named director of the U.S. Apollo moon program.		Oct. 26
Sen. Goldwater, campaigning in Cleveland, attacks the 1964 Civil Rights Act as an example of government's increasing interference in the "private affairs of men."				Russia's Bolshoi Opera gives its first performance outside the USSR in Milan, Italy. . . . Art Arfons, driving his jet-powered Green Monster, sets a world land speed record of 536.71 mph. on the Bonneville Salt Flats, Utah.	Oct. 27
					Oct. 28
	Sen. Goldwater, speaking in Pittsburgh, accuses the State Dept. of suppressing and harassing departmental critics of administration foreign policy.		Prof. Charles Townes of the U.S. and Profs. Nikolai Basov and Aleksandr Prochorov of the USSR are named co-winners of the 1964 Nobel Physics Prize for their development of maser and laser principles of producing high intensity radiation beams.		Oct. 29
		The Bureau of Labor Statistics reports that the weekly take-home pay of factory workers with three dependents averaged a record $92.98 in September.			Oct. 30
	U.S. Alliance for Progress coordinator Thomas Mann reports to Pres. Johnson that the Alliance made significant progress in 1964, compared with previous years.		Capt. Theodore Freeman, 34, a member of the third group of American astronauts (chosen Oct. 18) is killed in the crash of a T-38 jet trainer outside of Houston, Tex.		Oct. 31

F	G	H	I	J
Includes elections, federal-state relations, civil rights and liberties, crime, the judiciary, education, health care, poverty, urban affairs and population.	*Includes formation and debate of U.S. foreign and defense policies, veterans' affairs and defense spending. (Relations with specific foreign countries are usually found under the region concerned.)*	*Includes business, labor, agriculture, taxation, transportation, consumer affairs, monetary and fiscal policy, natural resources, and pollution.*	*Includes worldwide scientific, medical and technological developments, natural phenomena, U.S. weather, natural disasters, and accidents.*	*Includes the arts, religion, scholarship, communications media, sports, entertainment, fashions, fads and social life.*

	World Affairs	Europe	Africa & the Middle East	The Americas	Asia & the Pacific
Nov. 1		Mrs. Olga Ivinskaya, an assistant to the late Boris Pasternak, is reported to have been released from a Soviet prison after serving four years for accepting royalties on an unauthorized foreign edition of *Dr. Zhivago*.			Viet Cong guerrillas launch a dawn attack on a U.S. air base at Bien Hoa, 12 miles north of Saigon, killing five Americans, wounding 76 and destroying 10 B-57s.
Nov. 2			Saudi Arabian King Saud is dethroned by his half brother Crown Prince Faisal. The ailing Saud had served as little more than a figure-head monarch since March.	Leftist and student opposition to the Bolivian government of Pres. Victor Paz Estenssoro continues despite increased police efforts to suppress the demonstrations.	
Nov. 3	Lyndon Johnson is elected to a full four-year term as President of the U.S.	The British Labor government's plan to nationalize the steel industry is presented to the opening session of the new Parliament. . . . The delegation sent to Moscow by the Italian CP to seek an explanation of Khrushchev's ouster returns to Rome, saying that it had not been satisfied by the reasons it had received.		In his inauguration speech new Chilean Pres. Eduardo Frei Montalva promises major social and economic reforms "within liberty and law.". . . Terrorists of the pro-Castro Armed Forces for National Liberation are credited with the bombing of seven U.S.-owned oil facilities in Venezuela.	Cambodian officials formally accept a shipment of Soviet arms at the Pnom-penh airport.
Nov. 4	World leaders, many of whom had expressed concern over the candidacy of conservative Sen. Barry Goldwater, voice satisfaction and relief at the news of Pres. Johnson's landslide victory.			Bolivian military chiefs led by Gen. Alfredo Obando Candia overthrow the government of Pres. Victor Paz Estenssoro. The action follows two weeks of escalating disorders by leftist students.	New South Vietnamese Premier Tran Van Huong appoints a civilian cabinet made up of non-partisan civil servants independent of South Vietnam's major political, military and religious factions.
Nov. 5		The USSR, in a statement issued in East Germany, says that it "cannot guarantee the safety" of recently inaugurated direct commercial air line flights between the U.S. and West Berlin.	Christophe Gbenye, leader of the Stanleyville-based rebel Congolese People's Republic, declares that U.S. and Belgian civilians behind rebel lines will be considered prisoners of war if the U.S. and Belgium do not halt their support of the Congolese government's anti-rebel campaign. Sixty Americans, 500 Belgians and 500 other whites are reportedly being held hostage by Congo rebels.	Gen. Rene Barrientos, a leader of yesterday's coup against Pres. Victor Paz Estenssoro, is sworn in as the new president of Bolivia.	Premier Tran Van Huong's non-partisan cabinet appointments draw criticism from almost every faction in South Vietnamese politics. Nguyen Xuan Chu resigns as chairman of the High National Council, charging that Huong's cabinet can never "win the confidence of the population."
Nov. 6	Delegations representing every communist nation except Albania arrive in Moscow to attend tomorrow's celebration of the 47th anniversary of the Bolshevik Revolution. Extensive discussions between the delegates and the USSR's new leaders are expected.	The West German government publishes a plan for resumption of negotiations on the political unification of Western Europe. Serious talks on the issue have been stymied in recent years because of French Pres. de Gaulle's opposition to any supranational political institutions that would diminish the sovereignty of individual European states. . . . Soviet CP First Secy. Brezhnev indicates in a Moscow speech that Soviet leaders intend to reverse Khrushchev's policies of full farm collectivization and increase emphasis on private farming and private ownership of livestock.	Three African nationalist leaders are hanged in Pretoria, South Africa after being convicted of anti-government sabotage. . . . Iraq's rebellious Kurdish tribesmen are reported to have proclaimed creation of a Kurdistan state in northern Iraq under the leadership of Mullah Mustafa al-Barzini. Political negotiations between the Iraqi government and Kurdish representatives recently collapsed in Baghdad.	New Bolivian Pres. Rene Barrientos promises free elections "within six months or a year."	

A	B	C	D	E
Includes developments that affect more than one world region, international organizations and important meetings of major world leaders.	Includes all domestic and regional developments in Europe, including the Soviet Union, Turkey, Cyprus and Malta.	Includes all domestic and regional developments in Africa and the Middle East, including Iraq and Iran and excluding Cyprus, Turkey and Afghanistan.	Includes all domestic and regional developments in Latin America, the Caribbean and Canada.	Includes all domestic and regional developments in Asia and Pacific nations, extending from Afghanistan through all the Pacific Islands, except Hawaii.

U.S. Politics & Social Issues	U.S. Foreign Policy & Defense	U.S. Economy & Environment	Science, Technology & Nature	Culture, Leisure & Life Style	
	Pres. Johnson appoints a special panel to study ways of halting the spread of nuclear weapons.			Jack Nicklaus of the U.S. wins the Australian Open golf championship in Sydney, Australia.	Nov. 1
Gallup and Harris polls, taken in the final days of the campaign, forecast a 64%-36% victory for the Johnson-Humphrey ticket tomorrow.					Nov. 2
Pres. Lyndon Johnson captures 61% of the presidential vote in scoring a landslide victory over Republican challenger Sen. Barry Goldwater. Johnson receives 486 electoral votes to Goldwater's 52, losing only five Southern states (Ala., Ga., La., Miss. and S.C.) plus Goldwater's home state of Arizona. . . . Democrats win 28 Senate seats, Republicans seven, resulting in a new Senate party alignment of 68-32, a net increase of two for the Democratic majority. House results give the Democrats 295 seats, Republicans 140--a Democratic gain of 38 seats.			U.S. TV network computers, analyzing votes from selected precincts, predict final presidential election results with unprecedented accuracy.		Nov. 3
Analysts of yesterday's presidential election indicate that 90% of the Negro vote went to the Democrats. Northern white reaction or "backlash" against the Democrats' civil rights stand appears to have been much smaller than anticipated. . . . Significant victories in yesterday's voting: Robert Kennedy (D) wins a N.Y. Senate seat; Michigan Gov. George Romney (R) scores an impressive re-election victory.	Sen. Barry Goldwater cites media distortion of his foreign policy views as a factor in his crushing election defeat.				Nov. 4
		The AEC conducts an underground nuclear test designed to determine the possible industrial uses of nuclear explosions in breaking up underground rock formations for ore, oil and gas recovery.	The U.S. and USSR sign an accord to exchange weather data obtained from satellites, aircraft and weather balloons. The USSR plans to launch its first meteorological satellite sometime in 1965. . . . A Mars-bound U.S. Mariner 3 inter-planetary probe is declared unsuccessful after its on-board solar energy panels failed to deploy.		Nov. 5
FBI agents and local police arrest two residents of Meadville, Miss. for the murder of two Negroes, whose maimed bodies were found July 12-13 near Tallulah, La.			An Explorer 23 satellite, equipped to gather data on the resistance of various materials to penetration by meteoroids, is successfully launched from the U.S. rocket site at Wallops Island, Va.		Nov. 6

F	G	H	I	J
Includes elections, federal-state relations, civil rights and liberties, crime, the judiciary, education, health care, poverty, urban affairs and population.	Includes formation and debate of U.S. foreign and defense policies, veterans' affairs and defense spending. (Relations with specific foreign countries are usually found under the region concerned.)	Includes business, labor, agriculture, taxation, transportation, consumer affairs, monetary and fiscal policy, natural resources, and pollution.	Includes worldwide scientific, medical and technological developments, natural phenomena, U.S. weather, natural disasters, and accidents.	Includes the arts, religion, scholarship, communications media, sports, entertainment, fashions, fads and social life.

	World Affairs	Europe	Africa & the Middle East	The Americas	Asia & the Pacific
Nov. 7	An official editorial in the *Peking People's Daily* denounces ousted Soviet Premier Khrushchev as a traitor to communism. Chou En-lai is currently in Moscow for discussions with the new Soviet leaders.	Several new missile and rocket weapons are displayed for the first time in the USSR's annual Nov. 7 military parade through Red Square. . . . The French National Assembly approves a $4.1 billion defense budget for 1965.		Havana newspapers estimate the value of Cuban-Soviet trade over the past five years at $2.7 billion.	
Nov. 8		West Berlin sources report that a record 377,000 West Berliners visited East Berlin Oct. 30-Nov.7 (All Saints Day/week) under the new Berlin pass accord.	Yemeni Pres. Abdullah al-Salal announces a formal cease-fire in the two-year-old civil war between his republican forces and royalist followers of the ousted Imam Mohamad al-Badr. . . . The Tunisian government announces that Habib Bourguiba has been overwhelmingly re-elected to a second seven-year term as president.	Cuban Premier Castro warns in a *New York Times* interview that Cuban forces are prepared to shoot down U.S. reconnaissance planes if U-2 missions are continued.	Twelve delegates to a national meeting of India's ruling Congress Party call for Indian development of nuclear weapons. The appeal is denounced by Congress Party leader P.M. Lal Bahadur Shastri.
Nov. 9		British P.M. Harold Wilson's new Labor government survives (by six votes) a vote of confidence on its proposal for renationalization of the steel industry.			The Japanese Diet formally elects Eisaku Sato of the governing Liberal-Democratic Party to succeed the resigned Hayato Ikeda as prime minister.
Nov. 10					U.S. sources in Saigon report that a record 20 Americans died in Vietnam combat during October. South Vietnamese deaths for October are listed at 775.
Nov. 11	U.S. Amb.-to-U.N. Stevenson says the U.S. is prepared to consider any reasonable compromise to settle the Soviet U.N. debt question.	West Germany's Christian Democratic Party, responding to strong French pressure, votes to delay the Bonn government's formal commitment to the proposed NATO multi-lateral nuclear force. . . . British Chancellor of the Exchequer James Callaghan submits to Parliament an emergency anti-inflation budget providing for general tax increases to curb purchasing power.	Tunisian Pres. Habib Bourguiba announces a major cabinet reorganization.		
Nov. 12		Antonin Novotny is elected to a second five-year term as president of Czechoslovakia.			
Nov. 13	U.S. Amb.-to-U.N. Stevenson says the U.S. would not object to a plan by which the USSR could pay its U.N. arrears without earmarking the funds for the peace keeping operations to which the Soviets have objected. . . . Chou En-lai and other Communist Chinese leaders conclude five days of talks in Moscow with Soviet CP First Secy. Brezhnev and Premier Kosygin. No major breakthroughs in the Sino-Soviet ideological dispute are reported.				Laotian neutralist sources report that a counter-offensive by government troops has forced the Pathet Lao to retreat from recently gained strongholds in the Plaine des Jarres region.
Nov. 14		The USSR warns that it will take "appropriate measures" to protect its security if the U.S. and West Germany cooperate in the creation of a multi-lateral nuclear force under NATO.	For the second day Syrian and Israeli ground and air forces clash along the frontier north of the Sea of Galilee. Four Israelis and seven Syrians are reported killed.		For the third day Japanese leftists demonstrate in Tokyo and elsewhere against the arrival of the U.S. nuclear submarine *Seadragon* at the Sasebo Naval Base.
Nov. 15		The six Common Market states reach agreement in Brussels on a unified negotiating position for the Kennedy Round of tariff-cutting talks due to open in Geneva tomorrow.	Gen. Ibrahim Abboud resigns as Sudanese chief of state in the face of continuing demands that the last vestiges of the former military government be removed from Sudan's new civilian government.		Communist China reports shooting down an unmanned U.S. reconnaissance rocket plane over its territory. The U.S. has acknowledged using the so-called "drones" over North Vietnam, but offers no comment on the Chinese claim.
	A	**B**	**C**	**D**	**E**
	Includes developments that affect more than one world region, international organizations and important meetings of major world leaders.	*Includes all domestic and regional developments in Europe, including the Soviet Union, Turkey, Cyprus and Malta.*	*Includes all domestic and regional developments in Africa and the Middle East, including Iraq and Iran and excluding Cyprus, Turkey and Afghanistan.*	*Includes all domestic and regional developments in Latin America, the Caribbean and Canada.*	*Includes all domestic and regional developments in Asia and Pacific nations, extending from Afghanistan through all the Pacific Islands, except Hawaii.*

U.S. Politics & Social Issues	U.S. Foreign Policy & Defense	U.S. Economy & Environment	Science, Technology & Nature	Culture, Leisure & Life Style	
					Nov. 7
					Nov. 8
	The U.S. reaches agreement with Yugoslavia on the exchange of Fulbright scholars and professors beginning in 1965. It is the U.S.'s first such agreement with a communist country.	Over 1,200 Oklahoma school teachers take a one-day "professional holiday" to protest low salaries.		Dean Chance of the Los Angeles Angels is named winner of the 1964 Cy Young Award as major league baseball's best pitcher.	Nov. 9
Richard Nixon tells reporters that the Republican Party should be led by those in the political "center," adding "I'm perhaps at dead center."				Songwriter and actor Jimmie Dodd, best known as the "chief Mouseketeer" of TV's *Mickey Mouse Club*, dies in Honolulu at age 54.	Nov. 10
				The British comedy *Luv*, directed by Mike Nichols, opens on Broadway.	Nov. 11
On Target, the monthly newsletter of the ultra-conservative Minutemen, asserts that Pres. Johnson's landslide victory proves that the U.S. cannot be saved from communism by "traditional political processes."		National Agricultural Advisory Commission issues a report recommending continued acreage retirement and new quota controls for tobacco and milk.		Ann Sidney of England is named winner of the 1964 Miss World beauty pageant in London.	Nov. 12
					Nov. 13
Defeated GOP presidential candidate Barry Goldwater calls for a "realignment" of the Democratic and Republican parties along clear liberal-conservative lines.				Gordie Howe of the Detroit Red Wings scores his 627th goal, a National Hockey League record, in a game against the Montreal Canadiens.	Nov. 14
			Torrential rains and severe flooding ravage the central highlands of Vietnam, killing as many as 6,000 persons.		Nov. 15

F	G	H	I	J
Includes elections, federal-state relations, civil rights and liberties, crime, the judiciary, education, health care, poverty, urban affairs and population.	Includes formation and debate of U.S. foreign and defense policies, veterans' affairs and defense spending. (Relations with specific foreign countries are usually found under the region concerned.)	Includes business, labor, agriculture, taxation, transportation, consumer affairs, monetary and fiscal policy, natural resources, and pollution.	Includes worldwide scientific, medical and technological developments, natural phenomena, U.S. weather, natural disasters, and accidents.	Includes the arts, religion, scholarship, communications media, sports, entertainment, fashions, fads and social life.

	World Affairs	Europe	Africa & the Middle East	The Americas	Asia & the Pacific
Nov. 16	The world conference of the General Agreement on Tariffs and Trade (GATT) opens in Geneva. The talks, known as the Kennedy Round, are aimed at producing reciprocal cuts of 50% on the greatest possible number of industrial products involved in world trade. . . . The U.S. announces it will withhold any contribution to U.N. technical assistance programs until the general question of unpaid assessments is settled.		The U.N. Security Council meets in emergency session to hear charges arising from the Nov. 13-14 clashes between Syria and Israel.		
Nov. 17		Major changes in the composition of the Soviet CP Presidium and in the regional and district organization of the party are announced in Moscow. Among those listed as dismissed from the CP's Central Committee is Aleksei Adzhubei, Khrushchev's son-in-law and recently fired editor of *Izvestia* .	The U.S. warns Congolese rebel leaders in Stanleyville that they will be held directly responsible for the safety of Americans in regions under their control. . . . British P.M. Wilson announces the suspension of all arms shipments to South Africa to protest apartheid.	Brazil and the U.S. exchange documents to ratify an extradition treaty that had been signed Jan. 13, 1961. The accord goes into effect Dec. 17.	
Nov. 18	Secy. Gen. U Thant says in a Finnish TV interview that the controversy over unpaid assessments may further imperil the U.N.'s already critical financial situation.	The British government and the U.S. State Dept. make public captured Nazi documents asserting that Pope Pius XII sympathized with the Axis during W.W. II. The documents were recently discovered in the West German Foreign Ministry archives by Swiss historian Saul Friedlander.			Defense Secy. McNamara discloses that another U.S. F-100 jet has been shot down over Pathet Lao territory in Laos; the American pilot is reported killed. It is the third F-100 downed since the U.S. reconnaissance missions began. . . . A large, joint U.S.-Vietnamese drive against a supposed Viet Cong stronghold near Saigon fails to encounter a significant number of guerrillas.
Nov. 19		Vatican officials deny that Pope Pius XII ever expressed pro-Axis sentiments.			
Nov. 20	Soviet C.P. First Secy. Brezhnev, speaking in Tashkent, explicitly reaffirms the new Soviet leadership's commitment to peaceful co-existence. An editorial in the *Peking People's Daily* condemns the USSR's continuing adherence to the "revisionist" deviations of the Khrushchev era. Observers view the editorial as sign that the Sino-Soviet dispute, moderated since mid-October, has resumed in full force. . . . In his annual report U.N. Secy. Gen. Thant proposes that representatives of non-member states be allowed to attend U.N. meetings as observers.	*The New York Times* reports that Rumanian Communist leaders have indicated a desire to play a more independent role in the context of the Sino-Soviet dispute.	U.S. Air Force transports carry several hundred Belgian paratroopers to the British island of Ascension off the coast of West Africa in what is believed to be a preparatory step toward intervention against Congolese rebels. Rebel leaders have allegedly threatened to kill the more than 1,000 whites under their control.		
Nov. 21			Khartoum sources report an intensification of the African secessionist rebellion in southern Sudan despite efforts of the new civilian government to suppress it. Secessionists charge that the new government is as Arab-dominated as the ousted military junta.		U.S. reports that another American reconnaissance jet, the second this week, has been downed by Pathet Lao ground fire.
Nov. 22	Communist China announces that it has no interest in participating in the 17-nation Geneva disarmament conference.				Widespread opposition to South Vietnamese Premier Huong's "non-political" government prompts serious anti-government rioting in Saigon and elsewhere.

A	B	C	D	E
Includes developments that affect more than one world region, international organizations and important meetings of major world leaders.	*Includes all domestic and regional developments in Europe, including the Soviet Union, Turkey, Cyprus and Malta.*	*Includes all domestic and regional developments in Africa and the Middle East, including Iraq and Iran and excluding Cyprus, Turkey and Afghanistan.*	*Includes all domestic and regional developments in Latin America, the Caribbean and Canada.*	*Includes all domestic and regional developments in Asia and Pacific nations, extending from Afghanistan through all the Pacific Islands, except Hawaii.*

U.S. Politics & Social Issues	U.S. Foreign Policy & Defense	U.S. Economy & Environment	Science, Technology & Nature	Culture, Leisure & Life Style	
The New Jersey Supreme Court issues a ruling forbidding prosecutors, police and defense lawyers from giving potentially prejudicial statements to newsmen. . . . Gov. Nelson Rockefeller denounces Goldwater's Nov. 14 suggestion for an ideological realignment of U.S. parties as a threat to the whole two-party system. Henry Cabot Lodge levelled similar criticism at the plan yesterday.					Nov. 16
Miss. Judge Stokes Robertson issues a permanent injunction barring the Mississippi Freedom Democratic Party from using the word "Democratic.". . . Minn. Atty. Gen. Walter Mondale (D) is named to the Senate seat to be vacated by V.P.-elect Hubert Humphrey.			The Krebiozen Research Foundation of Chicago and four prominent scientific supporters of the alleged anti-cancer drug Krebiozen are indicted by a federal grand jury on various charges of fraud and mislabeling.	Delegates to the Roman Catholic Church's 21st Ecumenical Council approve a papal decree, *De Ecclesia*, clearly reaffirming the Pope's supremacy, but acknowledging the rightful influence of bishops in the governing of the church.	Nov. 17
During a lengthy Washington press conference, FBI Director J. Edgar Hoover denounces Martin Luther King as "the most notorious liar in the country" for his claim that the FBI is inadequately protecting civil rights workers in the South. Hoover also assails the Warren Commission report for its charge that the FBI failed in its advance security work on Pres. Kennedy's Dallas trip.	Defense Secy. McNamara announces that 80 U.S. military installations and 15 foreign bases will be closed in his continuing economy drive.	The Dow Jones industrial stock price average climbs to a new record closing of 891.71.			Nov. 18
Martin Luther King, commenting on J. Edgar Hoover's Nov. 18 accusation against him, says that the FBI Director has "apparently faltered" under the long-carried burdens of his office, adding "I have nothing but sympathy for this man who has served his country so well."			The Communist Youth League *Komsomolskaya Pravda* accuses the Soviet Academy of Agricultural Sciences of trying to build a "cult" around biologist Trofim Lysenko's theories of agricultural genetics.		Nov. 19
		The Dow Jones average of utility stock prices climbs to a record 155.71.		A papal decree, *De Oecumenismo (On Christian Unity)*, is endorsed by the Vatican II Ecumenical Council. The decree encourages Roman Catholics "to converse and collaborate" with followers of other religions and exonerates Jews of guilt in the crucifixion of Christ.	Nov. 20
			Two U.S. scientific satellites, Explorer 24 and 25, are launched into polar orbit from Vandenberg Air Force base by means of a single Scout rocket. The satellites are designed for high altitude atmospheric and radiation studies.	The third session of the Roman Catholic Church's 21st Ecumenical Council, Vatican II, is officially closed in Rome by Pope Paul VI. A fourth and final session will be held sometime next year.	Nov. 21
		A general walkout on the nation's railroads is averted as three shop-craft unions agree to Labor Secy. Willard Wirtz's plea to delay their scheduled strike pending further wage dispute negotiations in Washington.		The Thoroughbred Racing Association names Kelso as horse of the year for the fifth straight year. Kelso has won 36 of 56 starts in his six-year track career.	Nov. 22

F	G	H	I	J
Includes elections, federal-state relations, civil rights and liberties, crime, the judiciary, education, health care, poverty, urban affairs and population.	Includes formation and debate of U.S. foreign and defense policies, veterans' affairs and defense spending. (Relations with specific foreign countries are usually found under the region concerned.)	Includes business, labor, agriculture, taxation, transportation, consumer affairs, monetary and fiscal policy, natural resources, and pollution.	Includes worldwide scientific, medical and technological developments, natural phenomena, U.S. weather, natural disasters, and accidents.	Includes the arts, religion, scholarship, communications media, sports, entertainment, fashions, fads and social life.

	World Affairs	Europe	Africa & the Middle East	The Americas	Asia & the Pacific
Nov. 23		Britain's Labor government raises the bank interest rate from 5% to 7% in an effort to attract foreign capital and halt inflationary speculation in sterling.	Israeli and Syrian forces clash near the Sea of Galilee. Each side blames the other for starting the fighting.	About 2,500 Panamanian students demonstrate in front of the Legislative Palace in Panama City, demanding a tougher line against the U.S. in the current canal-related negotiations.	South Vietnamese Buddhist leaders publicly declare their opposition to the Huong government. The action follows a step-up in police efforts to suppress anti-government demonstrations.
Nov. 24		In a telegram to American Jewish leaders, West German Foreign Min. Gerhard Schroder explains and defends the Erhard government's tentative decision not to extend the 20-year statute of limitations on Nazi murder prosecutions due to expire in mid-1965. . . . The Union of Soviet Writers charges that geneticist Trofim Lysenko has been responsible for "colossal harm" to Soviet agriculture.	Nearly 600 Belgian paratroopers, dropped from U.S. planes, join up with mercenary-led Congolese ground troops to recapture the rebel stronghold of Stanleyville. Early reports indicate that two American and 30 Belgian hostages were executed by the retreating rebels. . . . but that over 500 other whites were found unharmed. . . . The U.S. and Belgium characterize their intervention as a Congo-authorized humanitarian mission aimed only at liberating innocent civilians.	The Panamanian National Assembly adopts a resolution strongly supporting Pres. Marco Robles' efforts to negotiate an abrogation of the 1903 Panama Canal treaty with the U.S. . . . Chile resumes diplomatic relations with the USSR for the first time since 1947.	
Nov. 25		The central banks of 11 nations pledge $3 billion in credit to Britain in an effort to maintain the pound sterling at its official exchange value of $2.80.	Demonstrations are staged throughout Africa and in several communist-bloc capitals in protest against the U.S.-Belgian intervention in the Congo. . . . Lt. Gen. Odd Bull of the U.N. Mideast Truce Supervision Organization reports to the Security Council that Syria was responsible for beginning the Nov. 23 clash with Israeli troops near the Sea of Galilee.		
Nov. 26				Brazilian Pres. Humberto Castelo Branco issues a decree ousting Mauro Borges as governor of Goias State on charges of promoting communist subversion.	The South Vietnamese government declares martial law in Saigon to cope with continuing anti-government riots spearheaded by Buddhists. . . . The USSR publicly reaffirms its pledge to give North Vietnam all "necessary assistance" to combat U.S. "air attacks" on North Vietnamese territory.
Nov. 27			The Organization of African Unity's nine-nation Congo Conciliation Commission meets in emergency session in Nairobi, Kenya. Delegates indicate indignation over the U.S.-Belgian intervention as well as strong sympathy for the Congolese rebel cause.		
Nov. 28		The Cypriote Parliament votes to replace separate Greek and Turkish Cypriote municipal councils in major towns with a single council appointed by the Greek-dominated Cypriote government. Turkish Cypriote representatives have boycotted Parliament since December 1963. . . . The formation of a right-wing National Democratic Party of Germany is announced in Hanover, West Germany.	The U.S. and Belgium announce the completion of their rescue operations in the Congo. Over 1,300 whites were rescued during the five-day mission; 80 others were found murdered, and 800-900 whites and Asians are reportedly still in rebel hands. . . . Morocco, Libya, Algeria and Tunisia reach agreement in Tangier on preliminary steps toward the formation of a North African common market.		Over 700,000 persons reportedly attend a rally in Peking to protest U.S.-Belgian actions in the Congo.
Nov. 29					

A	B	C	D	E
Includes developments that affect more than one world region, international organizations and important meetings of major world leaders.	Includes all domestic and regional developments in Europe, including the Soviet Union, Turkey, Cyprus and Malta.	Includes all domestic and regional developments in Africa and the Middle East, including Iraq and Iran and excluding Cyprus, Turkey and Afghanistan.	Includes all domestic and regional developments in Latin America, the Caribbean and Canada.	Includes all domestic and regional developments in Asia and Pacific nations, extending from Afghanistan through all the Pacific Islands, except Hawaii.

U.S. Politics & Social Issues	U.S. Foreign Policy & Defense	U.S. Economy & Environment	Science, Technology & Nature	Culture, Leisure & Life Style	
The Supreme Court declines to review (and thus upholds) a N.Y.S. court ruling that public school students' use of the words "under God" in the pledge of allegiance does not violate First Amendment religious freedom guarantees. . . . Supreme Court rules that the First Amendment severely limits the imposition of libel or criminal penalties for criticizing public officials.	In a *Life* magazine interview released in Saigon, U.S. chief of Vietnamese operations Gen. William Westmoreland says: "It is absolutely inconceivable to me that the Vietcong could ever militarily defeat the armed forces of South Vietnam."	The Mid-America Interpool Network, the largest U.S. electric power pool, is formed in Chicago.			Nov. 23
		Office of Economic Opportunity director Sargent Shriver describes to newsmen the initial Job Corps, VISTA, and Neighborhood Youth Corps projects to be undertaken under the administration's anti-poverty program.		Notre Dame quarterback John Huarte is named winner of the 1964 Heisman Trophy as the year's outstanding collegiate football player. . . . USSR wins the 16th Chess Olympiad in Tel Aviv. . . . St. Louis Cardinals third-baseman Ken Boyer is named the National League's most valuable player. Brooks Robinson of the Baltimore Orioles wins in the American League.	Nov. 24
Who Killed Kennedy?, a book by Thomas Buchanan which argues that Kennedy's death was the result of a conspiracy, is published in New York. . . . Motorola, Inc. announces it will contest an Illinois Fair Employment Practices Commission decision barring the company from giving its current intelligence test to job applicants. The Commission ruled the test "unfair to culturally deprived and disadvantaged groups."		The *Detroit Free Press* and *Detroit News* resume publication after settlement of a 134-day strike.			Nov. 25
Univ. of Wisconsin demographer Karl Taeuber reports that racial segregation in the U.S. has been increasing slightly but steadily over the past 25 years. Taeuber's full study will be published in the January issue of the *American Journal of Sociology*.					Nov. 26
Treasury Secy. Douglas Dillon announces the hiring of 75 new Secret Service agents as a "first step" in a $3 billion program to increase total Secret Service strength by 50%.		FCC announces it is beginning an investigation into charges that payola and related practices are continuing in the U.S. broadcasting industry.	The U.N. Scientific Committee on Radiation reports that world radioactive fallout declined by about 33% in 1964 due to the nuclear test-ban.		Nov. 27
			An unmanned U.S. interplanetary probe, dubbed Mariner 4, is successfully launched from Cape Kennedy. It is hoped that the probe will relay close-up TV pictures of Mars when it passes in the vicinity of the planet in mid-July 1965.	The Baseball Writers Association names Philadelphia Phillies third-baseman Richie Allen as the National League Rookie of the Year. Minnesota Twins outfielder Tony Oliva won rookie honors in the American League.	Nov. 28
				Newly approved liturgical reforms, including the change from Latin to English in most of the mass, become effective in all Roman Catholic churches in the U.S.	Nov. 29
F	G	H	I	J	
Includes elections, federal-state relations, civil rights and liberties, crime, the judiciary, education, health care, poverty, urban affairs and population.	*Includes formation and debate of U.S. foreign and defense policies, veterans' affairs and defense spending. (Relations with specific foreign countries are usually found under the region concerned.)*	*Includes business, labor, agriculture, taxation, transportation, consumer affairs, monetary and fiscal policy, natural resources, and pollution.*	*Includes worldwide scientific, medical and technological developments, natural phenomena, U.S. weather, natural disasters, and accidents.*	*Includes the arts, religion, scholarship, communications media, sports, entertainment, fashions, fads and social life.*	

	World Affairs	Europe	Africa & the Middle East	The Americas	Asia & the Pacific
Nov. 30					
Dec. 1	The 19th regular session of the U.N. General Assembly opens after delegates agreed to an "understanding" that all votes taken will be by acclamation. The move is designed to avert a paralyzing confrontation over U.S. demands that the USSR be deprived of its Assembly vote because of unpaid assessments. . . . The 64-member nations of the General Agreement on Tariffs & Trade issue a declaration pledging to open themselves "to the fullest possible extent" to imports from lesser developed countries.	West Germany tentatively agrees to reduce its grain prices to uniform levels required under Common Market plans for completion of a Europe-wide agricultural system. The action averts a major EEC crisis created by France's threat to withdraw from the Common Market unless West Germany agreed to the price reduction plan.	Fourteen African states ask for an emergency Security Council session to investigate U.S.' and Belgium's "illegal" intervention into African affairs. . . . Alex Quaison-Sackey of Ghana is "acclaimed" president of the General Assembly, becoming the first black African to hold that post.	In his inaugural address Mexican Pres. Gustavo Diaz Ordaz pledges a broad program of rural and agrarian reform.	
Dec. 2		West Germany warns East Germany that it will withdraw its recent offer of trade concessions if East Germany continues to force unfair currency exchanges on Western visitors.	Congo Premier Tshombe ends two days of talks in Paris after apparently failing to persuade Pres. de Gaulle to issue a strong statement of support for his Leopoldville government.	Ex-Argentine dictator Juan Peron, seeking to return to his native land from exile in Madrid, arrives by plane in Rio de Janeiro. Brazilian authorities order Peron returned to Spain within 24 hours.	
Dec. 3	U.S. Amb.-to-U.N. Stevenson asks U Thant to take charge personally of the negotiations concerning the USSR's unpaid U.N. assessments.			Juan Peron is flown back to Spain under orders of the Brazilian government.	Malaysian P.M. Abdul Rahman tells parliament that the Indonesia-Malaysia dispute has changed from a state of confrontation to a state of war.
Dec. 4	Japanese Foreign Min. Etsusaburo Shiina condemns Communist China's Oct. 16 nuclear test in an address to the U.N. General Assembly.		Congolese Premier Tshombe announces that government troops aided by mercenaries have rescued 600 more whites from rebel-held territory in the northern Congo since the termination of the U.S.-Belgian operation Nov. 28. U.S. and Belgium reported rescuing some 1,800 whites during their four-day intervention.	Bolivia's new military junta announces that national elections will be held May 30, 1965.	South Vietnamese armed forces leaders, meeting in Dalat, proclaim their full support for Premier Huong's beleaguered civilian regime. . . . Over 1,000 rock-throwing Indonesian students attack the U.S. Cultural Center in Jakarta, protesting U.S. policies in the Congo.
Dec. 5					
Dec. 6		An editorial in the Soviet CP newspaper *Pravda* says that the party's future role in Soviet affairs will be confined to "political guidance." The editorial is viewed as rejection of Khrushchev's policy of direct party control over government agencies. . . . Antonio Segni, 73, resigns as president of Italy because of failing health.	Cairo sources report that the USSR has agreed to finance and supply an Algerian-UAR aid airlift to the Congolese rebels.		

A	B	C	D	E
Includes developments that affect more than one world region, international organizations and important meetings of major world leaders.	*Includes all domestic and regional developments in Europe, including the Soviet Union, Turkey, Cyprus and Malta.*	*Includes all domestic and regional developments in Africa and the Middle East, including Iraq and Iran and excluding Cyprus, Turkey and Afghanistan.*	*Includes all domestic and regional developments in Latin America, the Caribbean and Canada.*	*Includes all domestic and regional developments in Asia and Pacific nations, extending from Afghanistan through all the Pacific Islands, except Hawaii.*

U.S. Politics & Social Issues	U.S. Foreign Policy & Defense	U.S. Economy & Environment	Science, Technology & Nature	Culture, Leisure & Life Style	
Presidential Press Secy. George Reedy denies reports that Pres. Johnson is anxious to replace J. Edgar Hoover as director of the FBI.		The SEC adopts its first rule governing over-the-counter stock trading. The rule requires large broker-dealers to identify themselves to the SEC.	The U.S. reports that the USSR earlier in the day launched an interplanetary probe, Zond 2, on a course toward Mars similar to that of the U.S.'s Mariner 4 launched Nov. 28.	World Buddhist leaders gather in Sarnath, India for a six-day conference devoted to the problems of Buddhists in Tibet and Vietnam. . . . Willie Pastrano of Miami retains the world light heavyweight boxing championship with an 11th round TKO over Britain's Terry Downes in Manchester, England.	Nov. 30
Martin Luther King confers in Washington with J. Edgar Hoover on their differences concerning the FBI's civil rights activities in the South. No statement is issued. . . . John Birch Society leader Robert Welch asserts in the society's magazine *American Opinion* that the civil rights movement is "a most important and integral part of the long-range communist plan for gradual take-over of the United States."	U.S. Amb.-to-South Vietnam Maxwell Taylor confers in Washington with Pres. Johnson and top administration officials. Following the meeting the White House issues a statement reaffirming "the basic United States policy of providing all possible and useful assistance" to South Vietnam.		Soviet scientists disclose a power failure aboard the Mars-bound Zond 2 interplanetary probe launched yesterday. According to Western sources, the flight marks the sixth unsuccessful Russian shot toward Mars.		Dec. 1
The American Medical Association's House of Delegates, meeting in Miami Beach, adopts a resolution reaffirming the group's opposition to enactment of an elderly health care program financed through Social Security.	A federal grand jury in New York convicts John Butenko of Orange, N.J. and Igor Ivanov, a Soviet trade agency employee, of conspiring to give command systems secrets of the U.S. Strategic Air Command to the USSR.	Pres. Johnson tells the U.S. Business Council in Washington that inflation, the balance of payments deficit and high teenage unemployment are the major economic problems confronting the nation.		An estimated million Indians turn out to greet Pope Paul VI on his arrival in Bombay to attend the 38th International Eucharistic Congress. It is the easternmost journey ever made by a Roman Catholic pope.	Dec. 2
Over 800 students at the Univ. California's Berkeley campus are arrested during a sit-down demonstration to protest a school administration threat to expel student leader Mario Savio. Savio has gained prominence as leader of the Free Speech Movement, a protest group which formed in September to challenge a university rule barring political activity on the campus. . . . The Senate Rules Committee resumes hearings into the business dealings of ex-Senate Democratic secretary Robert (Bobby) Baker.					Dec. 3
FBI agents in Mississippi arrest two law enforcement officers and 19 other whites, most of them Ku Klux Klan members, in connection with the June 21 murder of civil rights workers Michael Schwerner, Andrew Goodman and James Chaney near Philadelphia, Miss. All are charged with conspiracy and nine with directly participating in the slaying.		The Labor Dept. reports that the U.S. jobless rate fell from 5.2% in September and October to 5% in November. Teenage unemployment remains about 15%.	A study published in the *Journal of the American Medical Association* concludes that "the heaviest cigarette smokers experience a hazard (of death) three times that of non-smokers."		Dec. 4
The Republican Governors Association, meeting in Denver, calls for a major revamping of national GOP leadership to promote "a policy of inclusion, rather than exclusion." The action is seen as a demand for the ouster of national chairman Dean Burch and other pro-Goldwater conservatives currently in control of the party.	Pres. Johnson awards the Medal of Honor to Army Capt. Roger Donlon for "conspicuous gallantry" during a July 6 South Vietnamese battle. It is the first time the medal has been presented since the Korean War. . . . Defense Secy. McNamara predicts that the fiscal 1966 defense budget will be $50 billion "or under."	The Labor Dept. announces that it has contracted with the Institute of Computer Technology for the development of programs with state employment services for the training of workers in electronic data processing.			Dec. 5
Martin Luther King, in London enroute to Oslo to accept the Nobel Peace Prize, critcizes black nationalist "extremists" noting that "the doctrine of black supremacy is as great a danger as the doctrine of white supremacy."					Dec. 6

F	G	H	I	J
Includes elections, federal-state relations, civil rights and liberties, crime, the judiciary, education, health care, poverty, urban affairs and population.	*Includes formation and debate of U.S. foreign and defense policies, veterans' affairs and defense spending. (Relations with specific foreign countries are usually found under the region concerned.)*	*Includes business, labor, agriculture, taxation, transportation, consumer affairs, monetary and fiscal policy, natural resources, and pollution.*	*Includes worldwide scientific, medical and technological developments, natural phenomena, U.S. weather, natural disasters, and accidents.*	*Includes the arts, religion, scholarship, communications media, sports, entertainment, fashions, fads and social life.*

	World Affairs	Europe	Africa & the Middle East	The Americas	Asia & the Pacific
Dec. 7	In an address to the U.N. General Assembly, Soviet Foreign Min. Gromyko condemns U.S. plans for a multilateral nuclear NATO force as a threat to peace in Europe and denounces recent U.S. actions in Southeast Asia, Cuba and the Congo as aggressive "imperialism."	*The New York Times* reports that French Pres. de Gaulle has informed U.S. officials that France will renounce the Franco-West German cooperation treaty if West Germany decides to participate in the proposed multi-lateral nuclear force.	African leaders, appearing before the General Assembly, reiterate appeals for strong U.N. action against Portuguese colonialism and South African apartheid. . . . At least 41 persons are believed killed following two days of fighting between Sudanese black Africans and Arabs in the capital city of Khartoum. . . . An official Algerian news source confirms that Algerian planes have begun transporting "food and medicine" to Congolese rebels.	British Guianaian Premier Cheddi Jagan's East Indian-dominated People's Progressive Party is defeated in national elections by a coalition of opposition parties headed by Forbes Burnham, a Negro. Jagan charges vote fraud. . . . U.S. resumes diplomatic relations and aid programs with Bolivia. Ties were broken Nov. 10 following the military coup in Bolivia.	
Dec. 8		West German Foreign Min. Gerhard Schroder is reported to have urged the U.S., France and Britain to press the USSR to join in serious negotiations on German reunification. . . . Greek Foreign Min. Stavros Costopoulos demands in a General Assembly address that Cyprus be given full self-determination, including the right to decide on union with Greece.			Gen. Phoumi Nosavan, rightwing Laotian vice premier, tells the U.N. General Assembly that his government has "irrefutable evidence" of North Vietnamese intervention in Laos. . . . U.S. and Cambodian representatives open talks in New Delhi in an effort to improve the deteriorating relations between the two countries.
Dec. 9		P.M. Harold Wilson tells a Washington news conference that Britain is opposed to any plan involving the elimination of the U.S.'s final veto over the use of NATO nuclear weapons.	U.N. Security Council opens debate Dec. 9 on a complaint by 21 Afro-Asian nations that the U.S.-Belgian air rescue of white hostages in the Congo constituted an unwarranted interference in African affairs. Foreign Min. Charles-David Gonoa of the Congo Republic (Brazzaville) charges that the operation resulted in "the massacre of scores of thousands of innocent blacks on the pretext of saving an insignificant number of whites."		The Viet Cong capture the government district headquarters of Anlao after a three-day battle with South Vietnamese army and paramilitary forces. U.S. military personnel cite the loss of Anlao as a typical example of the government's tendency to overextend its forces into territory it cannot hold.
Dec. 10	U.S. civil rights leader Martin Luther King accepts the Nobel Peace Prize in Oslo on "behalf of all men who love peace and brotherhood."		Mercenaries employed by the central Congolese government rescue 59 whites from a rebel-held village 60 miles from Stanleyville. Six whites were found slain.		South Vietnamese Buddhist leaders announce the launching of a new anti-government campaign aimed at forcing Premier Tran Van Huong's resignation.
Dec. 11	A small mortar bomb explodes in the East River about 200 yards from the U.N. building moments after Cuban Industry Min. Ernesto (Che) Guevara begins addressing the General Assembly.	Soveit Premier Kosygin announces that a $110.6 billion 1965 budget, designed to stimulate production of quality consumer goods, has been approved by the Supreme Soviet. The budget calls for military expenditures of $14.208 billion, $555 million less than 1964.	South Africa announces that a new amendment strengthening the nation's residential apartheid law will go into effect Jan. 1, 1965. The measure gives seven million Africans living in white areas the status of "temporary dwellers.". . . Belgian Foreign Min. Paul-Henri Spaak defends his nation's November intervention in the Congo in a speech to the U.N. Security Council.	Cuban Industry Min. Ernesto Guevara charges before the U.N. General Assembly that "the U.S. and its Central American allies (are) readying armed attacks on Cuba. U.S. Amb. Stevenson denies the allegation, saying that the U.S. has "taken every step necessary to ensure that raids against Cuba are not launched, manned or equipped from United States territory. . . . The Alliance for Progress concludes a week-long annual review conference in Lima, Peru. Most delegates reported greater progress in the last 12 months than in the two previous years of the program.	South Vietnam announces that the U.S. has agreed to increase its military and economic support of the war against the Viet Cong. Washington officials stress that the increased aid has no connection with any plans to expand the fighting to North Vietnam.
Dec. 12	The Soviet CP publicly proposes that the 26 ruling Communist Parties meet in Moscow March 1, 1965 to prepare for a full-scale world communist conference sometime later in the year. Communist Chinese leaders are reportedly opposed to the meeting.				Peking officials estimate Communist China's 1964 grain harvest at 190 million metric tons, the biggest crop since 1957. The successful harvest is attributed to good weather and increased use of chemical fertilizer.

A	B	C	D	E
Includes developments that affect more than one world region, international organizations and important meetings of major world leaders.	*Includes all domestic and regional developments in Europe, including the Soviet Union, Turkey, Cyprus and Malta.*	*Includes all domestic and regional developments in Africa and the Middle East, including Iraq and Iran and excluding Cyprus, Turkey and Afghanistan.*	*Includes all domestic and regional developments in Latin America, the Caribbean and Canada.*	*Includes all domestic and regional developments in Asia and Pacific nations, extending from Afghanistan through all the Pacific Islands, except Hawaii.*

U.S. Politics & Social Issues	U.S. Foreign Policy & Defense	U.S. Economy & Environment	Science, Technology & Nature	Culture, Leisure & Life Style	
The Supreme Court rules that a Florida law barring racially mixed unmarried couples from living together is an unconstitutional violation of the 14th Amendment.		The Treasury Dept. reports that the U.S. withdrew a total of $525 million from the International Monetary Fund during 1964. . . . The Supreme Court unanimously upholds the practice of weighted voting at labor union conventions.			Dec. 7
U.S. Office of Education reports that U.S. college enrollment increased from 4,800,924 in September 1963 to 5,320,924 in September 1964.					Dec. 8
Martin Luther King, speaking to newsmen in Oslo, Norway, calls for a "grand alliance" of American intellectuals, liberals, labor and religious leaders to fight the final battles in the civil rights struggle. King says that all his Nobel Peace Prize money will go to the rights movement in the South.	Ex-Secy. of State Dean Acheson, speaking at Amherst College, calls for the abandoning of a moralistic approach to U.S. foreign policy in favor of "a strategic approach" based on a calculated assessment of how certain actions will contribute to U.S. policy objectives. . . . White House Press Secy. George Reedy denies reports that the U.S. and USSR have agreed to a policy of mutual defense spending cuts.	Ex-Pres. Eisenhower, speaking in New York, warns against federal deficit financing and the trend "toward federal domination over almost every phase of our economy."			Dec. 9
The *Congressional Quarterly* publishes official results of the Nov. 3 election showing that the Johnson-Humphrey ticket received a record 43,121,085 votes, or a record 61% of the record 70,640,289 votes cast. . . . Pres. Johnson announces that V.P.-elect Humphrey will be charged with coordinating all federal civil rights programs.					Dec. 10
			NASA scientists successfully orbit a dummy model of the Surveyor moon exploration vehicle by means of an Atlas-Centaur rocket launched from Cape Kennedy.		Dec. 11
U.S. Commissioner Esther Carter in Meridian, Miss. dismisses charges against 20 men arrested in connection with the murder of three civil rights workers near Philadelphia, Miss. on the ground that insufficient evidence had been presented to her to warrant holding the men for federal grand jury action. The ruling is denounced by the Justice Dept. and civil rights leaders.	Plans to eliminate the unit structure of the Army Reserve and to merge the Reserve with an enlarged Army National Guard are announced by Defense Secy. McNamara. The Reserve Officers Association denounces the proposal.	The Federal Power Commission issues a study recommending an expansion of power interconnections, greater coordination of power systems, and increased reliance on large generating units. The study predicts that U.S. power requirements by 1980 will be two-and-a-half times greater than at present and that 13% of the 1980 capacity will be in nuclear plants.			Dec. 12

F	G	H	I	J
Includes elections, federal-state relations, civil rights and liberties, crime, the judiciary, education, health care, poverty, urban affairs and population.	*Includes formation and debate of U.S. foreign and defense policies, veterans' affairs and defense spending. (Relations with specific foreign countries are usually found under the region concerned.)*	*Includes business, labor, agriculture, taxation, transportation, consumer affairs, monetary and fiscal policy, natural resources, and pollution.*	*Includes worldwide scientific, medical and technological developments, natural phenomena, U.S. weather, natural disasters, and accidents.*	*Includes the arts, religion, scholarship, communications media, sports, entertainment, fashions, fads and social life.*

	World Affairs	Europe	Africa & the Middle East	The Americas	Asia & the Pacific
Dec. 13		The Yugoslav CP Congress, meeting in Belgrade, adopts a resolution stressing foreign policies of non-alignment, co-existence, autonomy of Communist Parties and condemnation of Communist China.		Cuban Industry Min. Ernesto (Che) Guevara predicts in a U.S. TV interview that violent revolution will eventually erupt "in every country of Latin America."	
Dec. 14			Israeli P.M. Levi Eshkol and his cabinet resign as a result of an internal dispute within the Mapai Party over ex-P.M. Ben-Gurion's demand for a re-opening of the investigation into the still-secret 1954 security mishap involving ex-Defense Min. Pinhas Lavon. . . . Congolese army commander Joseph Mobutu charges that the rebel movement is being kept alive by aid from the USSR, Algeria and the UAR. . . . U.S. Amb.-to-U.N. Stevenson, responding to African condemnations of the U.S.'s Nov. 24-28 Congo rescue mission, warns that the "antidote to white racism is not black racism."	Forbes Burnham, Negro leader of the People's National Congress, is sworn in as prime minister of British Guiana.	
Dec. 15		West Germany and the five other Common Market members reach final agreement on uniform "target" prices for grain purchases throughout the EEC. The accord ends a year-long deadlock that had brought a French threat to withdraw from the EEC unless the grain matter was settled to France's satisfaction. . . . NATO Council convenes in Paris for a ministerial-level meeting devoted to the U.S. proposal for establishment of a joint Western multilateral force of nuclear-armed naval vessels.	Nigerian Foreign Min. Jaja Wachuku defends the U.S.-Belgian "rescue" operation in the Congo in a speech to the U.N. Security Council.	The Canadian House of Commons approves P.M. Lester Pearson's plan for a new national flag of distinctive Canadian design: a red maple leaf on a white center with a vertical red stripe at each end.	
Dec. 16	New York newspapers report that the USSR has privately indicated a willingness to accept some kind of compromise plan for settlement of its U.N. peace keeping debt. No official confirmation is offered, but talks on the problem are known to be continuing.	French Pres. de Gaulle hails the EEC's uniform grain price accord as a major step toward the economic unification of Europe. . . . British P.M. Wilson announces that Soviet Premier Kosygin has accepted an invitation to visit Britain some time during 1965.		The Spanish government announces that ex-Argentine dictator Juan Peron has been allowed to return to a life of exile in Spain on the condition that he abandon all political activity while in the country.	Albanian Foreign Min. Behar Shtylla charges before the U.N. General Assembly that India is preparing a large-scale attack on Communist China with the aid "of certain powers."
Dec. 17		Britain's seven European Free Trade Association partners protest the new British 15% surcharge on industrial imports as a virtual nullification of the tariff concessions established by the EFTA. . . . The British observer to the EEC warns that the basis for the Western political and military cooperation will be undermined unless the Common Market abandons policies of exclusion and works toward political unity with Britain and the rest of Western Europe.			U.S.-Cambodian differences remain unresolved at the conclusion of nine days of conciliation talks in New Delhi.
Dec. 18	*Tass* reports that the Soviet Presidium has ratified amendments to the U.N. Charter that would increase Security Council membership from 11 to 15. USSR is the 44th nation to approve the change; 77 are needed. . . . The General Agreement on Tariffs and Trade (GATT) Council, meeting in Geneva, rules that Britain's 15% surcharge on industrial imports violates its obligations under the GATT treaty.	U.N. Security Council votes another three month extension for the Cyprus peace keeping force.		Pres. Johnson announces that the U.S. is prepared to negotiate with Panama on a new treaty to replace the 1903 accord governing the Panama Canal. Johnson simultaneously discloses that plans are being developed for the building of a new sea-level canal. . . . The OAS approves a resolution making Canada eligible for membership if it wishes to join.	

A	B	C	D	E
Includes developments that affect more than one world region, international organizations and important meetings of major world leaders.	Includes all domestic and regional developments in Europe, including the Soviet Union, Turkey, Cyprus and Malta.	Includes all domestic and regional developments in Africa and the Middle East, including Iraq and Iran and excluding Cyprus, Turkey and Afghanistan.	Includes all domestic and regional developments in Latin America, the Caribbean and Canada.	Includes all domestic and regional developments in Asia and Pacific nations, extending from Afghanistan through all the Pacific Islands, except Hawaii.

U.S. Politics & Social Issues	U.S. Foreign Policy & Defense	U.S. Economy & Environment	Science, Technology & Nature	Culture, Leisure & Life Style	
					Dec. 13
The Supreme Court upholds the constitutionality of the public accommodations section of the 1964 Civil Rights Act. The decision reverses a federal district court ruling that a small Birmingham, Ala. restaurant was not genuinely involved in interstate commerce and thus exempt from the Act.		Three shop craft unions, responding to administration appeals, agree to postpone until 1965 a threatened strike against the nation's railroads.			**Dec. 14**
			A NASA-trained Italian crew, using a U.S. Scout rocket, launches an Italian-built scientific satellite, San Marcos 1, from Wallops Island, Va. It is the first launch conducted by a foreign team under the NASA international cooperation program.		**Dec. 15**
		Commerce Secy. Luther Hodges announces his resignation. Pres. Johnson names John T. Connor as his successor. . . . Negotiators for the International Longshoremen's Association (AFL-CIO) agree to a four-year work contract. It is the first long-term settlement in the union's history.			**Dec. 16**
					Dec. 17
	U.S. AEC acknowledges that it has warned manufacturers not to export any equipment that may be used for the testing and development of hydrogen weapons. The ban is reportedly aimed principally at France which is believed to be preparing for atmospheric hydrogen bomb tests in 1966. . . . The U.S. Strategic Air Command confirms that several Nationalist Chinese are being given U-2 reconnaissance pilot training in the U.S. The announcement comes hours after the crash of a Chinese-piloted U-2 near Tucson, Ariz.	Pres. Johnson reports that total U.S. personal income reached a record annual rate of $502 billion in November, exceeding the $500 billion mark for the first time.			**Dec. 18**

F	G	H	I	J
Includes elections, federal-state relations, civil rights and liberties, crime, the judiciary, education, health care, poverty, urban affairs and population.	Includes formation and debate of U.S. foreign and defense policies, veterans' affairs and defense spending. (Relations with specific foreign countries are usually found under the region concerned.)	Includes business, labor, agriculture, taxation, transportation, consumer affairs, monetary and fiscal policy, natural resources, and pollution.	Includes worldwide scientific, medical and technological developments, natural phenomena, U.S. weather, natural disasters, and accidents.	Includes the arts, religion, scholarship, communications media, sports, entertainment, fashions, fads and social life.

	World Affairs	Europe	Africa & the Middle East	The Americas	Asia & the Pacific
Dec. 19		The Berlin Wall opens to allow West Berliners to visit relatives in the Communist sector during the two-week Christmas season. . . . Soviet news sources indicate that several regional CP officials, dismissed by Khrushchev in recent years, have been reinstated.	UAR jets shoot down a U.S. oil company plane after it allegedly ignored warnings to land.		A group of South Vietnamese military officers, led by Air Commodore Nguyen Cao Ky and Brig. Gen. Nguyen Van Thieu, force the dissolution of the government's High National Council and arrest a number of prominent critics of Premier Huong's government. The soldiers say their coup-like intervention was necessary to end the government's paralysis in the face of growing political dissent.
Dec. 20		Washington sources report that Pres. Johnson has ordered a relaxation in the U.S. campaign for creation of a multilateral nuclear fleet (MLF) in view of the differences generated within NATO by the proposal.			U.S. Amb.-to-South Vietnam Maxwell Taylor denounces the military's intervention in South Vietnam's government affairs and warns that continuation of such unconstitutional interference may force the U.S. to reconsider its alliance with South Vietnam in the war against the Vietcong.
Dec. 21		French officials hail a reported easing of U.S. pressure for a multilateral nuclear fleet as a vindication of France's long opposition to the plan. Johnson administration spokesmen, however, stress that the proposal has not been abandoned. . . . The British House of Commons approves a resolution abolishing the death penalty for murder.	The U.N. Security Council votes 8-3 to ask Syria and Israel to cooperate to prevent further clashes in the Sea of Galilee area. The USSR, charging that Israel was solely responsible for past fighting, vetoes the resolution. . . . South African Foreign Min. Hilgard Muller defends his country's apartheid policies in a speech to the U.N. General Assembly.		
Dec. 22			U.S. State Dept. issues a statement criticizing the UAR's Dec. 19 downing of a U.S.-owned plane as a wholly unwarranted action. . . . The Israeli Knesset votes to return Levi Eshkol and his coalition cabinet to office.	Three anti-Castro Cuban exiles are arrested in New York for the Dec. 11 firing of a bazooka shell which exploded in the East River short of U.N. headquarters.	
Dec. 23	The USSR is reported to have offered to pay an undisclosed portion of its U.N. arrears in exchange for a Western pledge to drop permanently the question of the Soviet Union's voting right in the General Assembly. The U.S. is believed to have rejected the proposal.	The Soviet press agency Tass denounces the West German government's decision not to extend the statute of limitations on Nazi murder prosecutions when it expires in May, 1965.	In a Port Said speech, UAR Pres. Nasser denounces U.S. foreign policy, adding that UAR policies will not become hostage to American threats to withhold foreign aid. . . .		
Dec. 24			Congo Pres. Tshombe charges in a letter to Secy. Gen. U Thant that UAR and Algerian officers are leading rebel Congolese units.		A terrorist bomb explodes outside a U.S. officers' billet in Saigon, killing two Americans and injuring 98 others.
Dec. 25			Sources in Yemen continue to report sporadic fighting between republican and royalist forces despite a six-week-old cease-fire agreement.		Armed sentries are posted around all U.S. housing in Saigon as a precaution against further terrorist attacks.
Dec. 26					Right-wing Laotian leader Phoumi Nosavan is reported to have informed South Vietnamese officials that Laotian air force planes have begun heavy bombing of the Ho Chi Minh Trail, a major supply route from North Vietnam (through Laos) to Viet Cong bases in South Vietnam.
Dec. 27			Yemen's entire 25-member cabinet is reported to have resigned in protest against the allegedly corrupt rule of Pres. Abdullah al-Salal and against the continued presence of 40,000 Egyptian troops in Yemen.		

A	B	C	D	E
Includes developments that affect more than one world region, international organizations and important meetings of major world leaders.	Includes all domestic and regional developments in Europe, including the Soviet Union, Turkey, Cyprus and Malta.	Includes all domestic and regional developments in Africa and the Middle East, including Iraq and Iran and excluding Cyprus, Turkey and Afghanistan.	Includes all domestic and regional developments in Latin America, the Caribbean and Canada.	Includes all domestic and regional developments in Asia and Pacific nations, extending from Afghanistan through all the Pacific Islands, except Hawaii.

U.S. Politics & Social Issues	U.S. Foreign Policy & Defense	U.S. Economy & Environment	Science, Technology & Nature	Culture, Leisure & Life Style	
					Dec. 19
The White House releases a report indicating that the number of Negroes employed by the federal government has increased from 6.8% to 19.5% over June 1963 in the various pay categories.					Dec. 20
	The F-111, formerly called the TFX, is successfully test flown outside Fort Worth, Tex.		A small Explorer 26 satellite, equipped to provide data on how high-energy particles are trapped and eventually lost in the Van Allen radiation belt, is successfully orbited from Cape Kennedy.	UPI poll of sportswriters picks swimmer Don Schollander as U.S. sportsman of the year.	Dec. 21
	Defense Secy. McNamara reveals that Pres. Johnson has approved preliminary development of the world's largest jet plane, a military transport called the CX, capable of carrying 500-700 persons.			Pope Paul VI, in a special Christmas message, condemns racism, militarism and nationalism as "obstacles in the way of human brotherhood."	Dec. 22
					Dec. 23
					Dec. 24
					Dec. 25
	The U.S. is reported to have suspended non-essential aid programs to South Vietnam in reprisal for the military's Dec. 19 ouster of the High National Council.			The Buffalo Bills defeat the San Diego Chargers to win the American Football League championship.	Dec. 26
The President's Commission on Equal Opportunity in the Armed Forces urges "drastic action" to end off-base discrimination against U.S. Negro troops serving abroad.				The Cleveland Browns defeat the Baltimore Colts, 27-0, to win the National Football League championship.	Dec. 27

F	G	H	I	J
Includes elections, federal-state relations, civil rights and liberties, crime, the judiciary, education, health care, poverty, urban affairs and population.	Includes formation and debate of U.S. foreign and defense policies, veterans' affairs and defense spending. (Relations with specific foreign countries are usually found under the region concerned.)	Includes business, labor, agriculture, taxation, transportation, consumer affairs, monetary and fiscal policy, natural resources, and pollution.	Includes worldwide scientific, medical and technological developments, natural phenomena, U.S. weather, natural disasters, and accidents.	Includes the arts, religion, scholarship, communications media, sports, entertainment, fashions, fads and social life.

	World Affairs	Europe	Africa & the Middle East	The Americas	Asia & the Pacific
Dec. 28		The Italian National Assembly elects Foreign Min. Giuseppe Saragat, a Democratic Socialist, to a seven-year term as Italian president.			
Dec. 29					
Dec. 30	U.N. General Assembly begins a three-week recess without having taken any action on the unpaid peace keeping assessments of the USSR.		U.N. Security Council approves a resolution urging an immediate cease-fire in the Congo and the withdrawal of all foreign personnel and privately hired mercenaries. The resolution also endorses the Organization of African Unity Congo conciliation efforts. . . . Nigerian P.M. Abubakar Tafawa Balewa's conservative National Nigerian Alliance wins an apparent majority in legislative elections. Opposition parties boycotted the balloting.		
Dec. 31		In a New Year's broadcast French Pres. de Gaulle reaffirms his determination to maintain France's undiluted sovereignty in "the political, economic, financial and defense fields."		Members of the Progressive People's Party, headed by Cheddi Jagan, boycott the British Guianaian national assembly to protest the allegedly fraudulent elections which turned them out of power.	

A	B	C	D	E
Includes developments that affect more than one world region, international organizations and important meetings of major world leaders.	Includes all domestic and regional developments in Europe, including the Soviet Union, Turkey, Cyprus and Malta.	Includes all domestic and regional developments in Africa and the Middle East, including Iraq and Iran and excluding Cyprus, Turkey and Afghanistan.	Includes all domestic and regional developments in Latin America, the Caribbean and Canada.	Includes all domestic and regional developments in Asia and Pacific nations, extending from Afghanistan through all the Pacific Islands, except Hawaii.

U.S. Politics & Social Issues	U.S. Foreign Policy & Defense	U.S. Economy & Environment	Science, Technology & Nature	Culture, Leisure & Life Style	
	Washington sources report that administration officials are delaying action on a proposed food grant to the UAR in reprisal for Pres. Nasser's increasingly "anti-American" stand.			New York Film Critics vote *My Fair Lady* as the best U.S. film of 1964. . . . Soviet broadcasters name Lidiya Skoblikova as Soviet athlete of the year.	Dec. 28
The New York Times reports that Barry Goldwater is strongly supporting retention of Dean Burch and other conservatives in GOP leadership positions.					Dec. 29
		Bureau of Labor Statistics reports that the average weekly take-home pay of the U.S. factory worker with three dependents rose to a record $93.61 in November.			Dec. 30
					Dec. 31

F	G	H	I	J
Includes elections, federal-state relations, civil rights and liberties, crime, the judiciary, education, health care, poverty, urban affairs and population.	Includes formation and debate of U.S. foreign and defense policies, veterans' affairs and defense spending. (Relations with specific foreign countries are usually found under the region concerned.)	Includes business, labor, agriculture, taxation, transportation, consumer affairs, monetary and fiscal policy, natural resources, and pollution.	Includes worldwide scientific, medical and technological developments, natural phenomena, U.S. weather, natural disasters, and accidents.	Includes the arts, religion, scholarship, communications media, sports, entertainment, fashions, fads and social life.

127289

10-25-91

ROCK SPRINGS PUBLIC LIBRARY
Sweetwater County Branch
Rock Springs, Wyoming